Microsoft®

Office 2010 for Medical Professionals

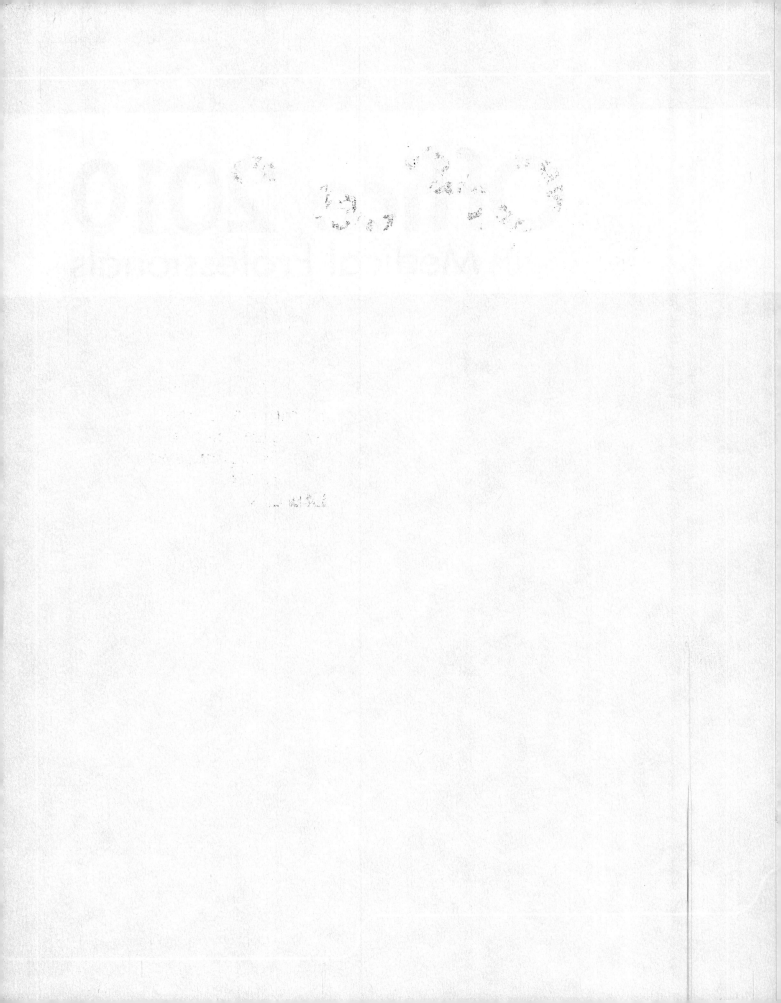

Microsoft®

Office 2010

for Medical Professionals

Beskeen/Duffy/Friedrichsen/Reding

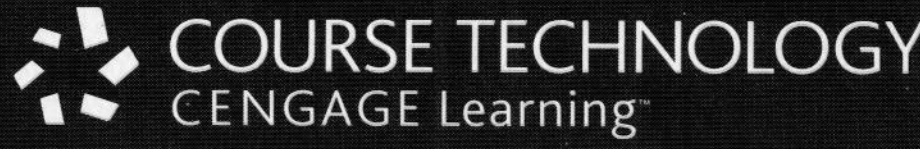

Australia • Brazil • Japan • Korea • Mexico • Singapore • Spain • United Kingdom • United States

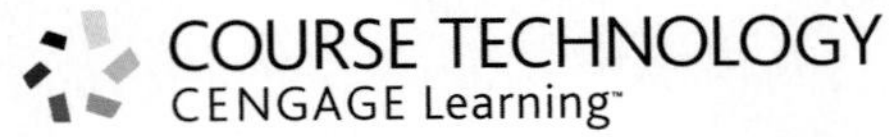

Microsoft® Office 2010 for Medical Professionals

Beskeen/Duffy/Friedrichsen/Reding

Vice President, Publisher: Nicole Jones Pinard

Executive Editor: Marjorie Hunt

Associate Acquisitions Editor: Amanda Lyons

Senior Product Manager: Christina Kling Garrett

Associate Product Manager: Kim Klasner

Editorial Assistant: Brandelynn Perry

Director of Marketing: Cheryl Costantini

Senior Marketing Manager: Ryan DeGrote

Marketing Coordinator: Kristen Panciocco

Contributing Authors: Rachel Biheller Bunin and Carol Cram

Developmental Editors: Rachel Biheller Bunin, Pam Conrad, Lisa Ruffolo, Karen Stevens

Content Project Manager: Heather Hopkins

Copy Editor: Mark Goodin

Proofreader: Vicki Zimmer

Indexer: BIM Indexing and Proofreading Services

QA Manuscript Reviewers: Serge Palladino, Susan Pedicini, Jeff Schwartz, Ashlee Welz Smith, Marianne Snow

Print Buyer: Fola Orekoya

Cover Designer: GEX Publishing Services

Composition: GEX Publishing Services

For product information and technology assistance, contact us at
Cengage Learning Customer & Sales Support, 1-800-354-9706

For permission to use material from this text or product, submit all requests online at **www.cengage.com/permissions**
Further permissions questions can be emailed to
permissionrequest@cengage.com

Library of Congress Control Number: 2010943253

ISBN-13: 978-1-111-82099-2
ISBN-10: 1-111-82099-6

Course Technology
20 Channel Center Street
Boston, MA 02210
USA

Cengage Learning is a leading provider of customized learning solutions with office locations around the globe, including Singapore, the United Kingdom, Australia, Mexico, Brazil, and Japan. Locate your local office at:
international.cengage.com/region

Cengage Learning products are represented in Canada by Nelson Education, Ltd.

To learn more about Course Technology, visit **www.cengage.com/coursetechnology**

To learn more about Cengage Learning, visit **www.cengage.com**

Purchase any of our products at your local college store or at our preferred online store **www.cengagebrain.com**

Printed in the United States of America
1 2 3 4 5 6 7 8 9 19 18 17 16 15 14 13 12 11

Brief Contents

PowerPoint 2010

Web Apps

Contents

Office 2010

Word 2010

Excel 2010

Access 2010

Web Apps

Preface

Welcome to *Microsoft Office 2010 for Medical Professionals*. This book is designed to meet the needs of students who are training for careers in the medical field. What makes this book unique is that every lesson and exercise features a real-world example related to the medical profession. As they learn Office skills, students work with documents they are likely to encounter in a typical medical practice, clinic, or hospital.

If this is your first experience with this book, you'll see it has a unique design: each skill is presented on two facing pages, with steps on the left and screens on the right. The layout makes it easy to learn a skill without having to read a lot of text and flip pages to see an illustration.

See the illustration on the right to learn more about the pedagogical and design elements of a typical lesson.

About This Book

- **Coverage.** Provides skills training on Windows 7 and Microsoft Office 2010 core applications for students who are preparing for careers in the medical field. An Appendix covers cloud computing concepts and using Microsoft Office Web Apps.
- **Maps to SAM 2010.** This book is designed to work with SAM (Skills Assessment Manager) 2010. **SAM Assessment** contains performance-based, hands-on SAM exams for each unit of this book, and **SAM Training** provides hands-on training for skills covered in the book. (SAM sold separately.) See page xx for more information on SAM.

Each two-page spread focuses on a single skill.

Introduction briefly explains why the lesson skill is important.

A case scenario motivates the the steps and puts learning in context.

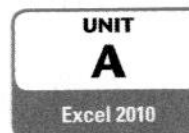

Editing Cell Entries

You can change, or **edit**, the contents of an active cell at any time. To do so, double-click the cell, click in the formula bar, or just start typing. Excel switches to Edit mode when you are making cell entries. Different pointers, shown in Table A-3, guide you through the editing process. You noticed some errors in the worksheet and want to make corrections. The first error is in cell A11, which contains a misspelled name.

STEPS

1. **Click cell A11, then click to the right of P in the formula bar**
   As soon as you click in the formula bar, a blinking vertical line called the **insertion point** appears on the formula bar at the location where new text will be inserted. See Figure A-9. The mouse pointer changes to I when you point anywhere in the formula bar.
2. **Press [Delete], then click the Enter button ✓ on the formula bar**
   Clicking the Enter button accepts the edit, and the spelling of the employee's first name is corrected. You can also press [Enter] or [Tab] to accept an edit. Pressing [Enter] to accept an edit moves the cell pointer down one cell, and pressing [Tab] to accept an edit moves the cell pointer one cell to the right.
3. **Click cell C12, then press [F2]**
   Excel switches to Edit mode, and the insertion point blinks in the cell. Pressing [F2] activates the cell for editing directly in the cell instead of the formula bar. Whether you edit in the cell or the formula bar is simply a matter of preference; the results in the worksheet are the same.
4. **Press [Backspace], type 8, then press [Enter]**
   The value in the cell changes from 35 to 38, and cell C13 becomes the active cell. Did you notice that the calculations in cells C21 and F12 also changed? That's because those cells contain formulas that include cell C12 in their calculations. If you make a mistake when editing, you can click the Cancel button ✗ on the formula bar *before* pressing [Enter] to confirm the cell entry. The Enter and Cancel buttons appear only when you're in Edit mode. If you notice the mistake *after* you have confirmed the cell entry, click the Undo button on the Quick Access toolbar.
5. **Click cell A15, then double-click the word Juan in the formula bar**
   Double-clicking a word in a cell selects it.
6. **Type Javier, then press [Enter]**
   When text is selected, typing deletes it and replaces it with the new text.
7. **Double-click cell D18, press [Delete], type 4, then click ✓**
   Double-clicking a cell activates it for editing directly in the cell. Compare your screen to Figure A-10.
8. **Save your work**
   Your changes to the workbook are saved.

QUICK TIP On some keyboards, you might need to press an [F Lock] key to enable the function keys.

QUICK TIP The Undo button allows you to reverse up to 100 previous actions, one at a time.

QUICK TIP You can use the keyboard to select all cell contents by clicking to the right of the cell contents in the cell or formula bar, pressing and holding [Shift], then pressing [Home].

Recovering unsaved changes to a workbook file

You can use Excel's AutoRecover feature to automatically save (Autosave) your work as often as you want. This means that if you suddenly lose power or if Excel closes unexpectedly while you're working, you can recover all or some of the changes you made since you last saved it. (Of course, this is no substitute for regularly saving your work: this is just added insurance.) To customize the AutoRecover settings, click the File tab, click Options, then click Save. AutoRecover lets you decide how often and into which location it should Autosave files. When you restart Excel after losing power, a Document Recovery pane opens and provides access to the saved and Autosaved versions of the files that were open when Excel closed. You can also click the File tab, click Recent on the navigation bar, then click Recover Unsaved Workbooks to open Autosaved workbooks using the Open dialog box.

Excel 10 Getting Started with Excel 2010

Tips and troubleshooting advice, right where you need it–next to the step itself.

Clues to Use boxes provide useful information related to the lesson skill.

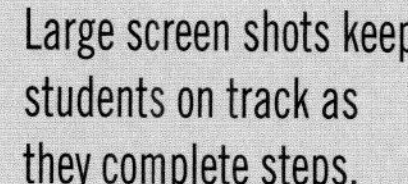

Large screen shots keep
students on track as
they complete steps.

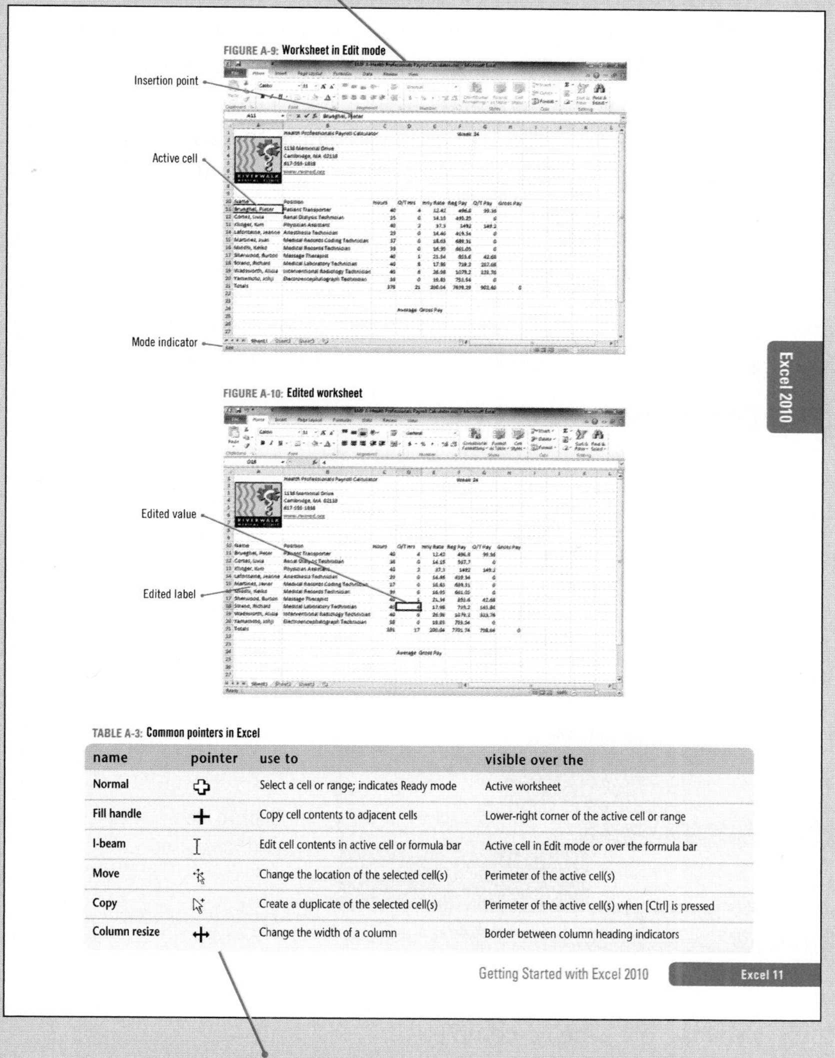

FIGURE A-9: Worksheet in Edit mode

FIGURE A-10: Edited worksheet

TABLE A-3: Common pointers in Excel

name	pointer	use to	visible over the
Normal	✚	Select a cell or range; indicates Ready mode	Active worksheet
Fill handle	+	Copy cell contents to adjacent cells	Lower-right corner of the active cell or range
I-beam	I	Edit cell contents in active cell or formula bar	Active cell in Edit mode or over the formula bar
Move	✥	Change the location of the selected cell(s)	Perimeter of the active cell(s)
Copy	↖⁺	Create a duplicate of the selected cell(s)	Perimeter of the active cell(s) when [Ctrl] is pressed
Column resize	✛	Change the width of a column	Border between column heading indicators

Getting Started with Excel 2010 Excel 11

Excel 2010

Tables provide helpful summaries of key terms, buttons, or keyboard shortcuts.

Assignments

The lessons use Riverwalk Medical Clinic, a fictional outpatient medical facility, as the case study. The assignments on the light yellow pages at the end of each unit increase in difficulty. Assignments include:

- **Concepts Review** consist of multiple choice, matching, and screen identification questions.
- **Skills Reviews** are hands-on, step-by-step exercises that review the skills covered in each lesson in the unit.
- **Independent Challenges** are case projects requiring critical thinking and application of the unit skills. The Independent Challenges increase in difficulty, with the first one in each unit being the easiest. Independent Challenges 2 and 3 become increasingly open-ended, requiring more independent problem solving.
- **Real Life Independent Challenges** are practical exercises in which students create documents to help them with their every day lives.
- **Advanced Challenge Exercises** set within the Independent Challenges provide optional steps for more advanced students.
- **Visual Workshops** are practical, self-graded capstone projects that require independent problem solving.

About SAM

SAM is the premier proficiency-based assessment and training environment for Microsoft Office. Web-based software along with an inviting user interface provide maximum teaching and learning flexibility. SAM builds students' skills and confidence with a variety of real-life simulations, and SAM Projects' assignments prepare students for today's workplace.

The SAM system includes Assessment and Training featuring page references and remediation for this book as well as Course Technology's Microsoft Office textbooks. With SAM, instructors can enjoy the flexibility of creating assignments based on content from their favorite Microsoft Office books or based on specific course objectives. Instructors appreciate the scheduling and reporting options that have made SAM the market-leading online testing and training software for over a decade. Over 2,000 performance-based questions and matching Training simulations, as well as tens of thousands of objective-based questions from many Course Technology texts, provide instructors with a variety of choices across multiple applications from the introductory level through the comprehensive level. The inclusion of hands-on Projects guarantee that student knowledge will skyrocket from the practice of solving real-world situations using Microsoft Office software. (SAM sold separately).

SAM Assessment

- Content for these hands-on, performance-based tasks includes Word, Excel, Access, PowerPoint, Internet Explorer, Outlook, and Windows. Includes tens of thousands of objective-based questions from many Course Technology texts.

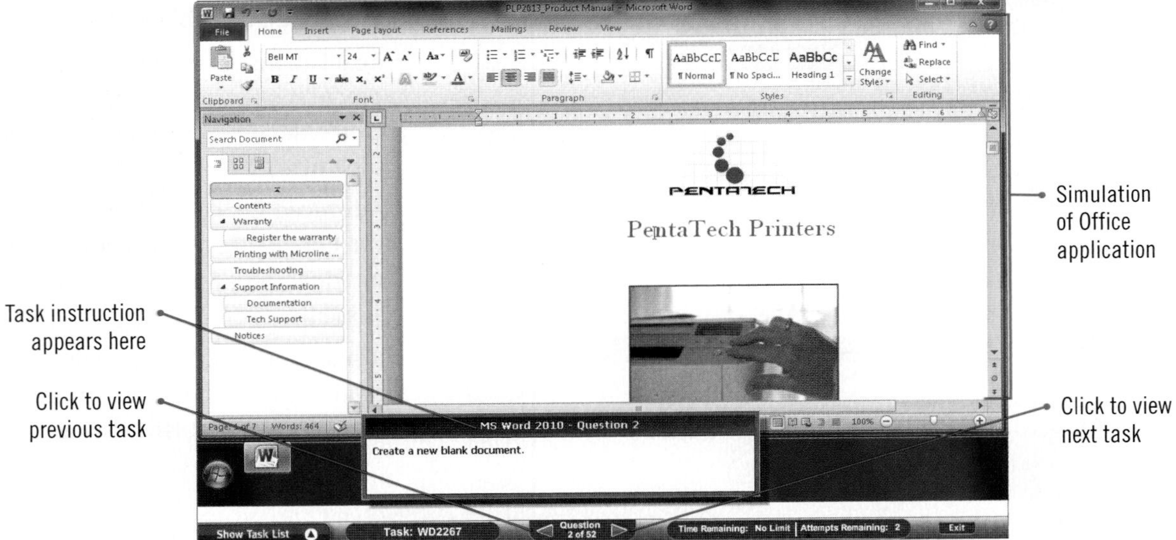

SAM Training

- Observe mode allows the student to watch and listen to a task as it is being completed.
- Practice mode allows the student to follow guided arrows and hear audio prompts to help visual learners know how to complete a task.
- Apply mode allows the student to prove what they've learned by completing a task using helpful instructions.

SAM Projects

- Live-in-the-application assignments in Word, Excel, Access and PowerPoint that help students be sure they know how to effectively communicate, solve a problem or make a decision. (*Note*:There are no SAM Projects that are based on the content in this book.)

Instructor Resources

The Instructor Resources CD is Course Technology's way of putting the resources and information needed to teach and learn effectively into your hands. With an integrated array of teaching and learning tools that offer you and your students a broad range of technology-based instructional options, we believe this CD represents the highest quality and most cutting edge resources available to instructors today. The resources available with this book are:

- **Instructor's Manual**—Available as an electronic file, the Instructor's Manual includes detailed lecture topics with teaching tips for each unit.

- **Sample Syllabus**—Prepare and customize your course easily using this sample course outline.

- **PowerPoint Presentations**—Each unit has a corresponding PowerPoint presentation that you can use in lecture, distribute to your students, or customize to suit your course.

- **Figure Files**—The figures in the text are provided on the Instructor Resources CD to help you illustrate key topics or concepts. You can create traditional overhead transparencies by printing the figure files. Or you can create electronic slide shows by using the figures in a presentation program such as PowerPoint.

- **Solutions to Exercises**—Solutions to Exercises contains every file students are asked to create or modify in the lessons and end-of-unit material. Also provided in this section, there is a document outlining the solutions for the end-of-unit Concepts Review, Skills Review, and Independent Challenges. An Annotated Solution File and Grading Rubric accompany each file and can be used together for quick and easy grading.

- **Data Files for Students**—To complete most of the units in this book, your students will need Data Files. You can post the Data Files on a file server for students to copy. The Data Files are available on the Instructor Resources CD-ROM, the Review Pack, and can also be downloaded from cengagebrain.com. For more information on how to download the Data Files, see the inside back cover.

Instruct students to use the Data Files List included on the Review Pack and the Instructor Resources CD. This list gives instructions on copying and organizing files.

- **ExamView**—ExamView is a powerful testing software package that allows you to create and administer printed, computer (LAN-based), and Internet exams. ExamView includes hundreds of questions that correspond to the topics covered in this text, enabling students to generate detailed study guides that include page references for further review. The computer-based and Internet testing components allow students to take exams at their computers, and also saves you time by grading each exam automatically.

Acknowledgements

Instructor Advisory Board

We thank our Instructor Advisory Board who gave us their opinions and guided our decisions as we updated our texts for Microsoft Office 2010. They are as follows:

Terri Helfand, Chaffey Community College

Barbara Comfort, J. Sargeant Reynolds Community College

Brenda Nielsen, Mesa Community College

Sharon Cotman, Thomas Nelson Community College

Marian Meyer, Central New Mexico Community College

Audrey Styer, Morton College

Richard Alexander, Heald College

Xiaodong Qiao, Heald College

Author Acknowledgements

Elizabeth Eisner Reding Creating a book of this magnitude is a team effort. I would like to thank my husband, Michael, as well as Christina Kling Garrett, the project manager, and my development editor, Karen Stevens, for her suggestions and corrections. I would also like to thank the production and editorial staff for all their hard work that made this project a reality.

David W. Beskeen Being a part of the extremely talented and experienced Office Illustrated team makes working on this book that much more enjoyable—many thanks to Rachel Biheller Bunin, Christina Kling Garrett, the production group, the testers, and the rest of the Cengage team!

Jennifer Duffy Many talented people at Course Technology worked tirelessly to shape this book—thank you all. I am especially grateful to Pam Conrad, editor extraordinaire, whose dedication, wisdom, and precision are evident on every page.

Lisa Friedrichsen The Access portion is dedicated to my students, and all who are using this book to teach and learn Access. Thank you. Also, thank you to all of the professionals who helped me create this book.

Read This Before You Begin

Frequently Asked Questions

What are Data Files?

A Data File is a partially completed Word document, Excel workbook, Access database, PowerPoint presentation or another type of file that you use to complete the steps in the units and exercises to create the final document that you submit to your instructor. Each unit opener page lists the Data Files that you need for that unit.

Where are the Data Files?

Your instructor will provide the Data Files to you or direct you to a location on a network drive from which you can download them. For information on how to download the Data Files from cengagebrain.com, see the inside back cover.

What software was used to write and test this book?

This book was written and tested using a typical installation of Microsoft Office 2010 Professional Plus on a computer with a typical installation of Microsoft Windows 7 Ultimate.

The browser used for any Web-dependent steps is Internet Explorer 8.

Do I need to be connected to the Internet to complete the steps and exercises in this book?

Some of the exercises in this book require that your computer be connected to the Internet. If you are not connected to the Internet, see your instructor for information on how to complete the exercises.

What do I do if my screen is different from the figures shown in this book?

This book was written and tested on computers with monitors set at a resolution of 1024 × 768. If your screen shows more or less information than the figures in the book, your monitor is probably set at a higher or lower resolution. If you don't see something on your screen, you might have to scroll down or up to see the object identified in the figures.

The Ribbon—the blue area at the top of the screen—in Microsoft Office 2010 adapts to different resolutions. If your monitor is set at a lower resolution than 1024 × 768, you might not see all of the buttons shown in the figures. The groups of buttons will always appear, but the entire group might be condensed into a single button that you need to click to access the buttons described in the instructions.

CENGAGEbrain.com

Buy. Rent. Access.

Access Student Data Files and other study tools on **cengagebrain.com**.

For detailed instructions visit **www.cengage.com/ct/studentdownload**.

Store your Data Files on a USB drive for maximum efficiency in organizing and working with the files.

Macintosh users should use a program to expand WinZip or PKZip archives. Ask your instructor or lab coordinator for assistance.

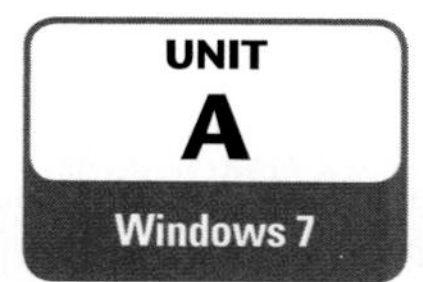

Getting Started with Windows 7

The Windows 7 operating system lets you use your computer. Windows 7 shares many features with other Windows programs, so once you learn how to work with Windows 7, you will find it easier to use the programs that run on your computer. In this unit, you learn to start Windows 7 and work with windows and other screen objects. You work with icons that represent programs and files, and you move and resize windows. As you use your computer, you will often have more than one window on your screen, so it's important that you learn how to manage them. As you complete this unit, you create a simple drawing in a program called Paint to help you learn how to use buttons, menus, and dialog boxes. After finding assistance in the Windows 7 Help and Support system, you end your Windows 7 session. Tony Sanchez, R.N., the office manager for the Riverwalk Medical Clinic, just hired you to work as an administrative assistant for Dr. Carla Zimmerman. You need to develop basic Windows skills to keep track of patient appointments, records, and prescriptions.

OBJECTIVES

- Start Windows 7
- Learn the Windows 7 desktop
- Point and click
- Start a Windows 7 program
- Work with windows
- Work with multiple windows
- Use command buttons, menus, and dialog boxes
- Get help
- Exit Windows 7

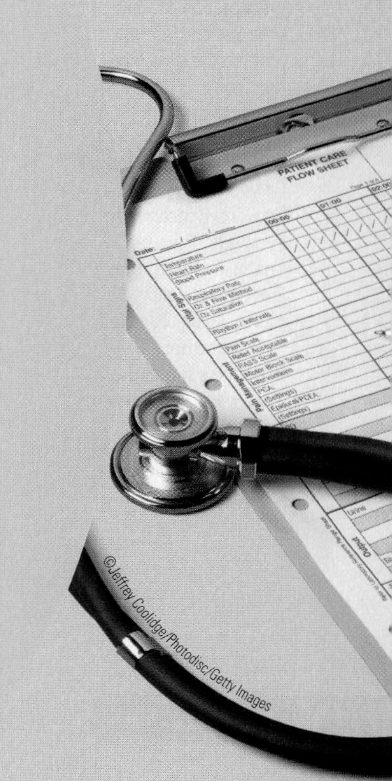

©Jeffrey Coolidge/Photodisc/Getty Images

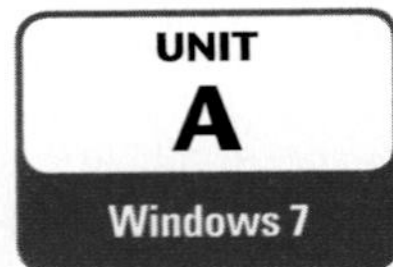

Starting Windows 7

Windows 7 is an **operating system**, which is a program that lets you run your computer. A **program** is a set of instructions written for a computer. When you turn on your computer, the Windows 7 operating system starts automatically. If your computer did not have an operating system, you wouldn't see anything on the screen when you turn it on. For each user, the operating system can reserve a special area called a **user account** where each user can keep his or her own files. A medical office might assign a user account to each doctor as well as each staff member or nurse. If your computer is set up for more than one user, you might need to **log in**, or select your user account name when the computer starts. If you are the only user on your computer, you won't have to select an account. You might also need to enter a **password**, a special sequence of numbers and letters each user can create. A password allows you to enter and use the files in your user account area. Users cannot see each others' account areas without their passwords, so passwords help keep your computer information secure. After you log in, you see a welcome message, and then the Windows 7 desktop. You will learn about the desktop in the next lesson. Because Dr. Carla Zimmerman needs you to get started right away with the patient record system, Tony Sanchez asks you to start learning about the Windows 7 operating system.

STEPS

1. **Push your computer's power button, which might look like or , then if the monitor is not turned on, press its power button to turn it on**

   On a desktop computer, the power button is probably on the front panel. On a laptop computer it's most likely at the top of the keys on your keyboard. After a few moments, a Starting Windows message appears. Then you might see a screen that lets you choose a user account, as shown in Figure A-1.

2. **Click a user name if necessary**

   The name you click represents your user account that lets you use the computer. The user account may have your name assigned to it, or it might have a general name, like Student, or Lab User. A password screen may appear. If necessary, ask your instructor or technical support person which user account and password you should use.

3. **Type your password if necessary, using uppercase and lowercase letters as necessary, as shown in Figure A-2**

   Passwords are **case sensitive**, which means that if you type any letter using capital letters when lowercase letters are needed, Windows will not allow you to access your account. For example, if your password is "book", typing "Book" or "BOOK" will not let you enter your account. As you type your password, its characters appear as a series of dots on the screen. This makes it more difficult for anyone watching you to see your password, giving you additional security.

4. **Click the Go button**

   You see a welcome message, and then the Windows 7 desktop, shown in Figure A-3.

TROUBLE
If you do not see a screen that lets you choose a user account, go to Step 3.

TROUBLE
If you clicked the wrong user in Step 2, change to the correct user by clicking the Switch User button on the password screen.

TROUBLE
If you type your password incorrectly, you see "The user name or password is incorrect." Click OK to try again. To help you remember, Windows shows the Password Hint that you entered when you created your password.

FIGURE A-1: Selecting a user name

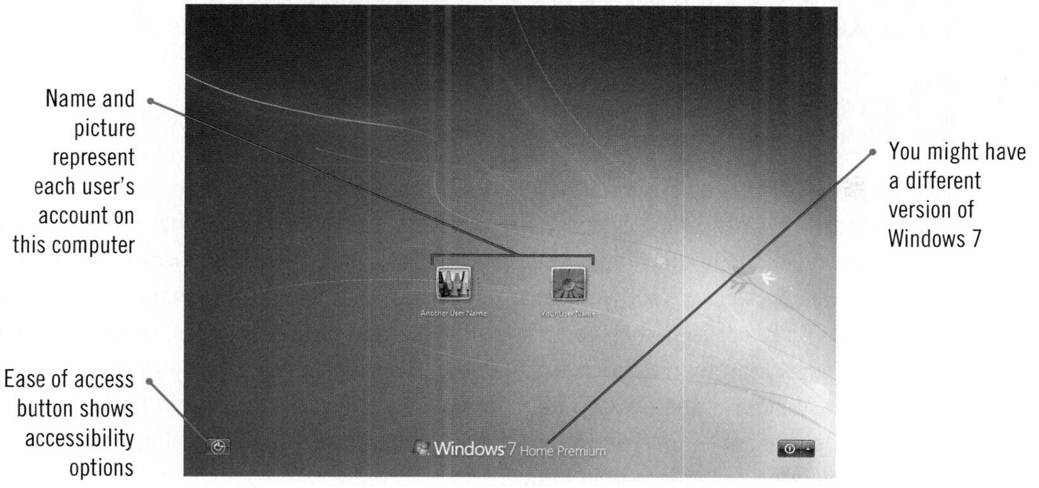

FIGURE A-2: Password screen

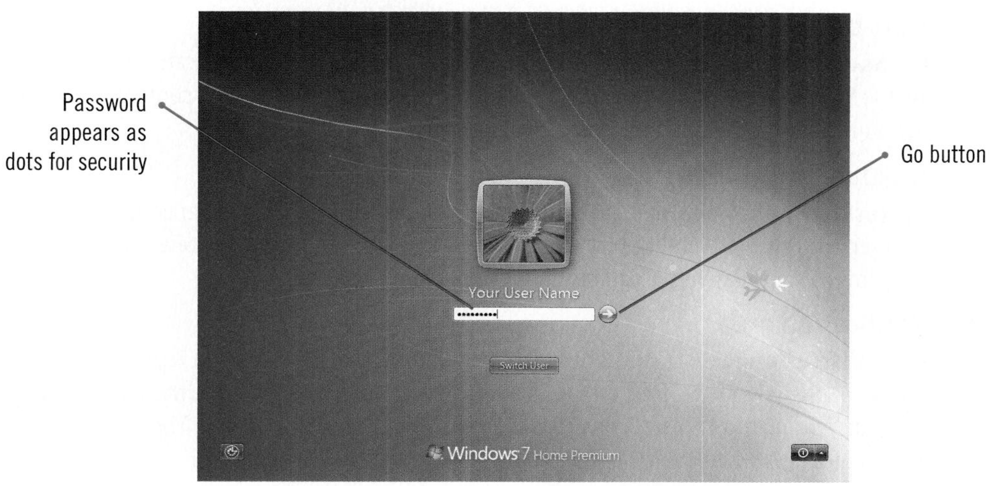

FIGURE A-3: Windows 7 desktop

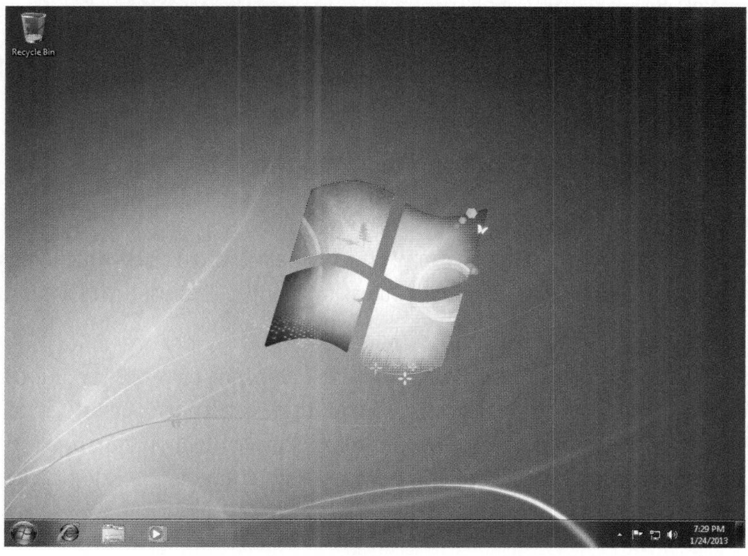

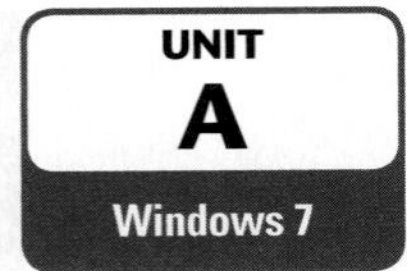

Learning the Windows 7 Desktop

After Windows 7 starts up, you see the Windows 7 desktop. The **desktop** consists of a shaded or picture background with small graphics called icons. **Icons** are small images that represent items such as the Recycle Bin on your computer. You can rearrange, add, and delete desktop icons. Like an actual desktop, the Windows 7 desktop acts as your work area. You can use the desktop to manage the files and folders on your computer. A **file** is a collection of stored information, such as a letter, video, or program. A **folder** is a container that helps you organize your files, just like a cardboard folder on your desk. If you're using a new installation of Windows, the desktop might show only a Recycle Bin icon in the upper-left corner and the **taskbar**, the horizontal bar at the bottom of your screen. Tony asks you to explore the Windows 7 desktop to begin learning how to communicate with your computer.

DETAILS

Windows 7 computers show these desktop elements. Refer to Figure A-4.

- **Start button**
  The **Start button** is your launching point when you want to communicate with your computer. You can use the Start button to start programs, to open windows that show you the contents of your computer, and to end your Windows session and turn off your computer.

QUICK TIP

If your taskbar is a different color than the one in Figure A-4, your computer might have different settings. This won't affect your work in this chapter.

- **Taskbar**
  The **taskbar** is the horizontal bar at the bottom of the desktop. The taskbar contains the Start button as well as other buttons representing programs, folders, and files. You can use these buttons to immediately open programs or view files and programs that are on your computer.

- **Notification area**
  The **notification area** at the right side of the taskbar contains icons that represent informational messages and programs you might find useful. It also contains information about the current date and time. Some programs automatically place icons here so they are easily available to you. The notification area also displays pop-up messages when something on your computer needs your attention.

- **Recycle Bin**
  Like the wastepaper basket in your office, the **Recycle Bin** is where you place the files and folders that you don't need anymore and want to delete. All objects you place in the Recycle Bin stay there until you empty it. If you put an object there by mistake, you can easily retrieve it, as long as you haven't emptied the bin.

- **Desktop background**
  The **desktop background** is the shaded area behind your desktop objects. You can change the desktop background to show different colors or even pictures.

You might see the following on your desktop:

- **Icons and shortcuts**
  On the desktop background, you can place icons called **shortcuts**, which you can double-click to access programs, files, folders, and devices that you use frequently. That way, they are immediately available to you.

- **Gadgets**
  Gadgets are optional programs that present helpful or entertaining information on your desktop. They include items such as clocks, current news headlines, calendars, picture albums, and weather reports. Some gadgets come with Windows 7 and you can easily place them on your desktop. You can download additional gadgets from the Internet. Figure A-5 shows a desktop that has a desktop background picture and shortcuts to programs, folders, and devices, as well as four gadgets.

FIGURE A-4: Windows 7 desktop after a new Windows installation

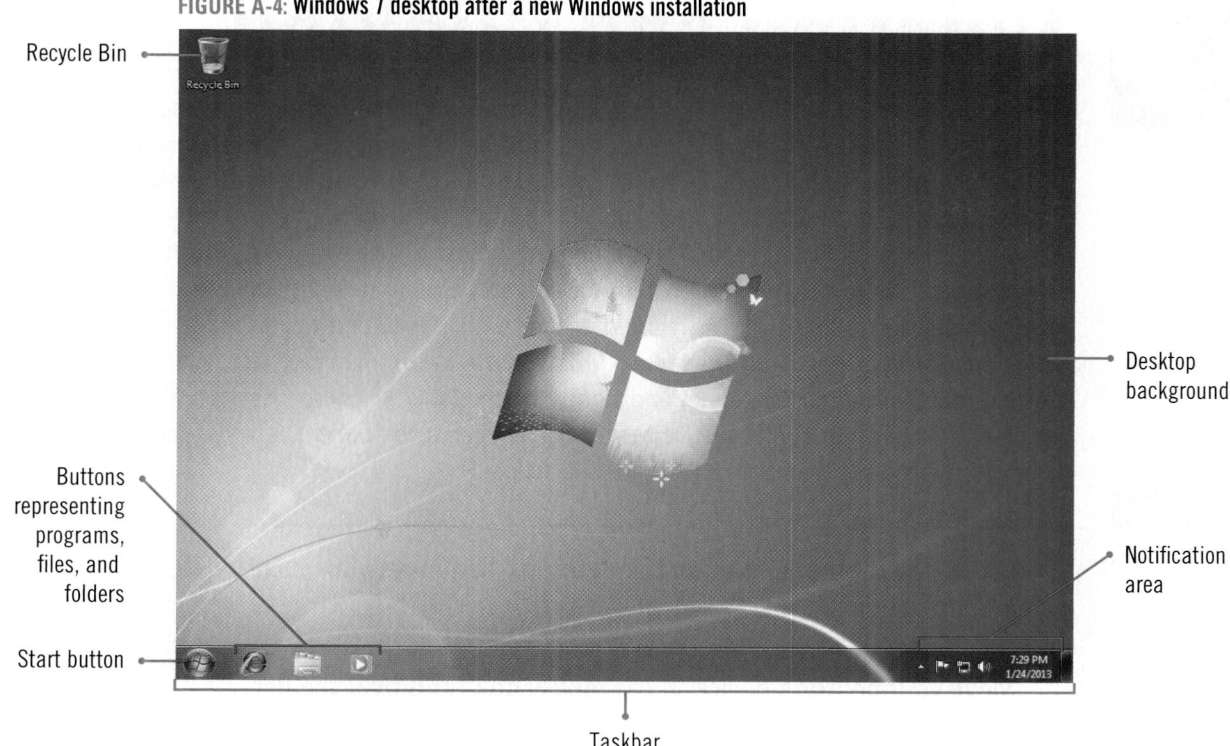

FIGURE A-5: Windows 7 desktop with shortcuts, gadgets, and a picture background

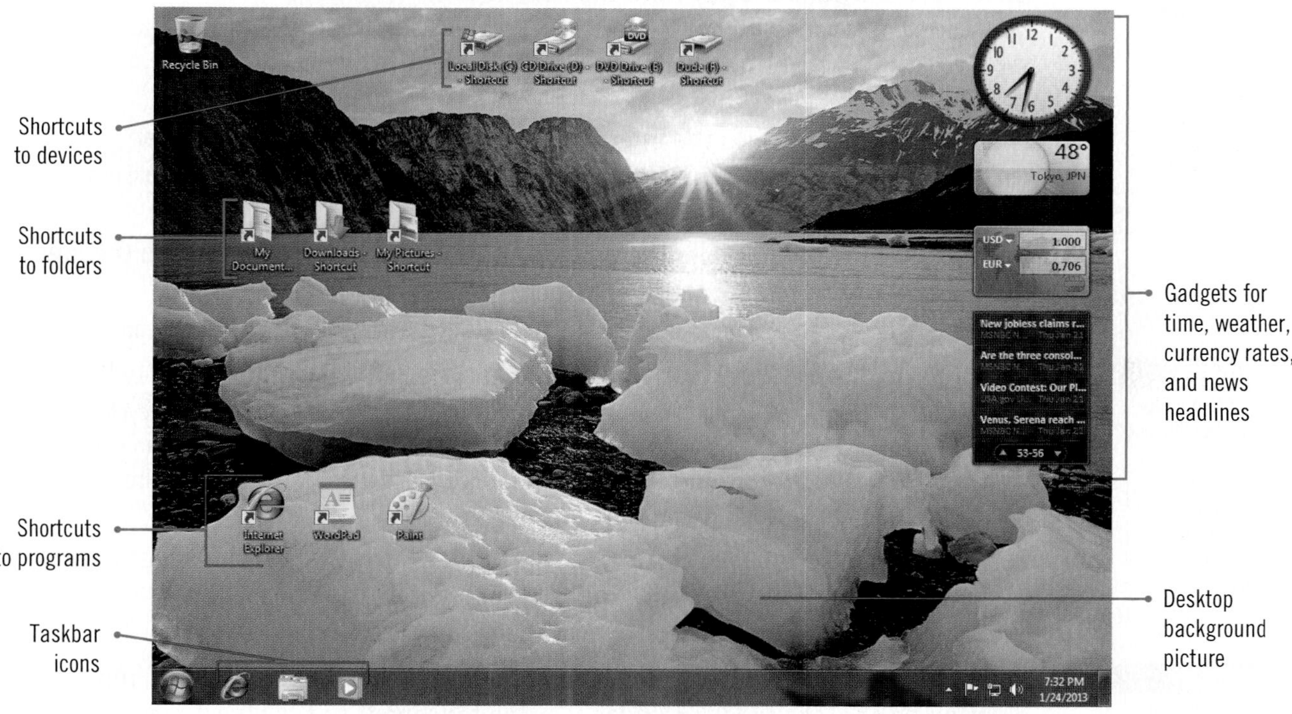

What if my desktop looks different from these figures?

If you are using a computer that has been used by others, a different version of Windows 7, or a computer in a school lab, your desktop might be a different color, it might have a different design on it, or it might have different shortcuts and gadgets. Your Recycle Bin might be in a different desktop location. Don't be concerned with these differences. They will not interfere with your work in these units.

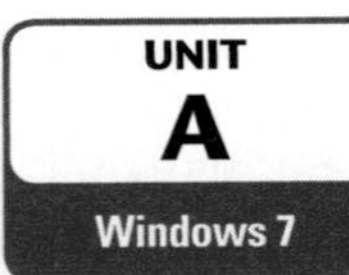

Pointing and Clicking

After you start Windows 7 and see the desktop, you can communicate with Windows using a pointing device. A **pointing device** controls the movement of the mouse pointer on your computer screen. The **mouse pointer** is a small arrow or other symbol that moves on the screen. The mouse pointer's shape changes depending on where you point and on the options available to you when you point. Your pointing device could be a mouse, trackball, touchpad, pointing stick, on-screen touch pointer, or a tablet. Figure A-6 shows some common pointing devices. A pointing device might be attached to your computer with a wire, connect wirelessly using an electronic signal, or it might be built into your computer. There are five basic **pointing device actions** you use to communicate with your computer: pointing, clicking, double-clicking, dragging, and right-clicking. Table A-1 describes each action. As you prepare to work as an administrative assistant maintaining the patient records, you communicate with your computer using the basic pointing device actions.

STEPS

1. **Locate the mouse pointer on the desktop, then move your pointing device left, right, up, and down**
   The mouse pointer moves in the same direction as your pointing device.
2. **Move your pointing device so the mouse pointer is over the Recycle Bin**
   You are pointing to the Recycle Bin. The pointer shape is the **Select pointer** . The Recycle Bin icon becomes **highlighted**, looking as though it is framed in a box with a lighter color background and a border.

> **QUICK TIP**
> Use the tip of the pointer when pointing to an object.

3. **While pointing to the Recycle Bin, press and quickly release the left mouse button once, then move the pointer away from the Recycle Bin**
   Click a desktop icon once to **select** it, and then the interior of the border around it changes color. When you select an icon, you signal Windows 7 that you want to perform an action. You can also use pointing to identify screen items.
4. **Point to (but do not click) the Internet Explorer button on the taskbar**
   The button border appears and an informational message called a **ScreenTip** identifies the program the button represents.
5. **Move the mouse pointer over the time and date in the notification area in the lower-right corner of the screen, read the ScreenTip, then click once**
   A pop-up window appears, containing a calendar and a clock displaying the current date and time.

> **TROUBLE**
> You need to double-click quickly, with a fast click-click, without moving the mouse. If a window didn't open, try again with a faster click-click.

6. **Place the tip of the mouse pointer over the Recycle Bin, then quickly click twice**
   You **double-clicked** the Recycle Bin. A window opens, showing the contents of the Recycle Bin, shown in Figure A-7. The area near the top of the screen is the **Address bar**, which shows the name of the item you have opened. If your Recycle Bin contains any discarded items, they appear in the white area below the Address bar. You can use single clicking to close a window.
7. **Place the tip of the mouse pointer over the Close button in the upper-right corner of the Recycle Bin window, notice the Close ScreenTip, then click once**
   The Recycle Bin window closes. You can use dragging to move icons on the desktop.

> **QUICK TIP**
> You'll use dragging in other Windows 7 programs to move folders, files, and other objects to new locations.

8. **Point to the Recycle Bin icon, press and hold down the left mouse button, move the pointing device (or drag your finger over the touchpad) so the object moves right about an inch, as shown in Figure A-8, then release the mouse button**
   You dragged the Recycle Bin icon to a new location.
9. **Repeat Step 8 to drag the Recycle Bin back to its original location**

FIGURE A-6: **Pointing devices**

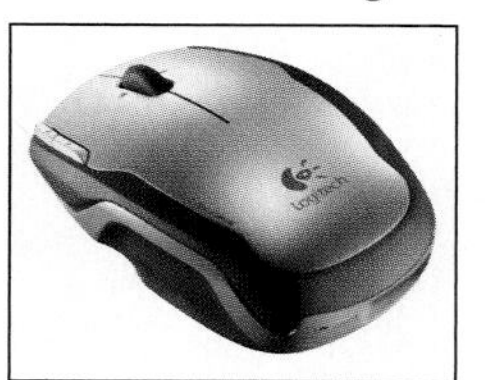

Mouse

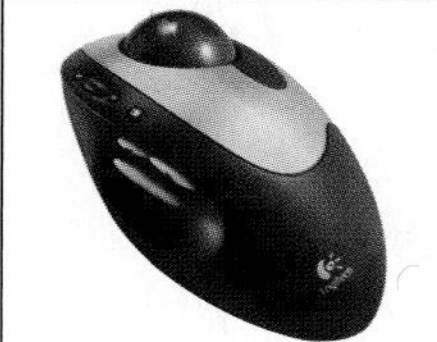

Trackball

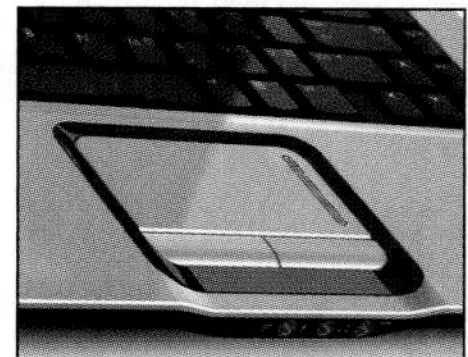

Touchpad

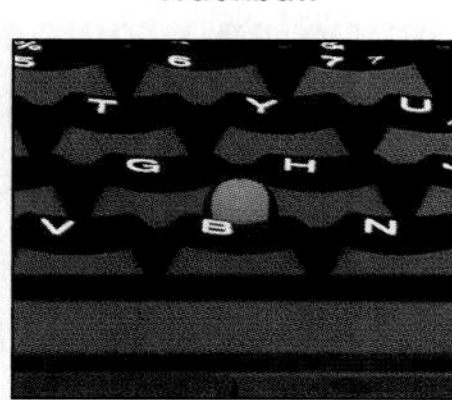

Pointing stick

FIGURE A-7: **Recycle Bin window**

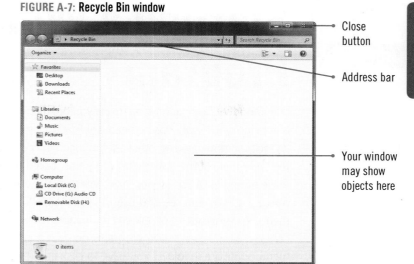

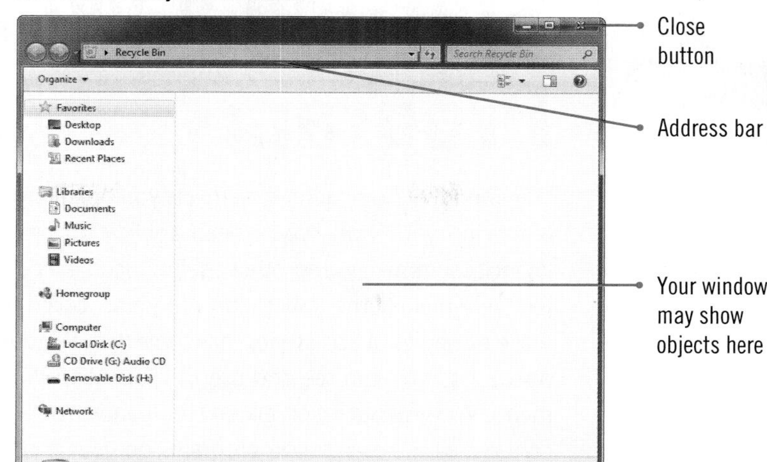

FIGURE A-8: **Dragging the Recycle Bin icon**

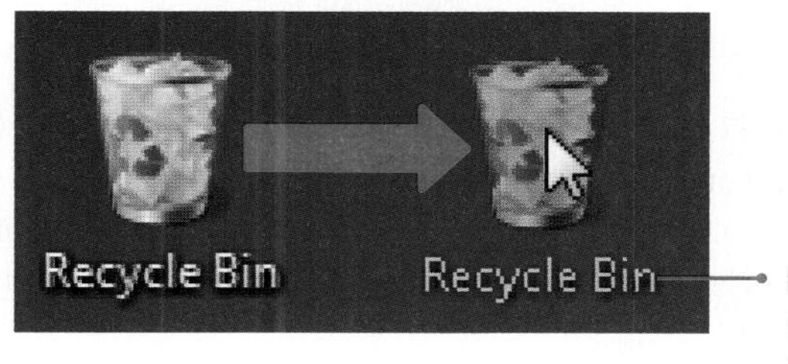

TABLE A-1: **Five pointing device actions**

action	how to	use for
Pointing	Move the pointing device to position the tip of the pointer over an object, option, or item	Highlighting objects or options, or displaying informational boxes called ScreenTips
Clicking	Quickly press and release the left mouse button once	Selecting objects or commands, opening menus or items on the taskbar
Double-clicking	Quickly press and release the left mouse button twice	Opening programs, folders, or files represented by desktop icons
Dragging	Point to an object, press and hold down the left mouse button, move the object to a new location, then release the mouse button	Moving objects, such as icons on the desktop
Right-clicking	Point to an object, then press and release the right mouse button	Displaying a shortcut menu containing options specific to the object

Using right-clicking

For some actions, you click items using the right mouse button, known as right-clicking. You can **right-click** almost any icon on your desktop to open a shortcut menu. A **shortcut menu** lists common commands for an object. A **command** is an instruction to perform a task, such as emptying the Recycle Bin. The shortcut menu commands depend on the object you right-click. Figure A-9 shows the shortcut menu that appears if you right-click the Recycle Bin. Then you click (with the left mouse button) a shortcut menu command to issue that command.

FIGURE A-9: **Right-click to show shortcut menu**

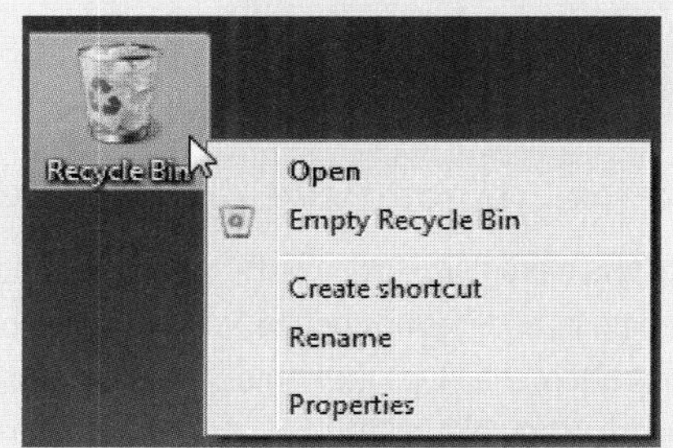

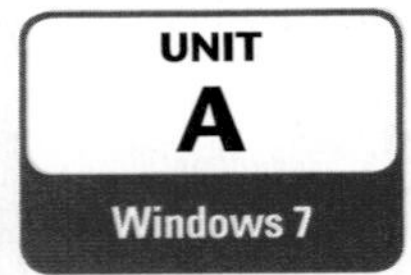

Starting a Windows 7 Program

The Windows 7 operating system lets you operate your computer and see the programs and files it contains. But to do your work, you'll need application programs. **Application programs** let you create letters, financial summaries, and other useful documents as well as view Web pages on the Internet and send and receive e-mail. Some application programs, called **accessories**, come with Windows 7. (See Table A-2 for some examples of accessories that come with Windows 7.) To use an application program, you must start (or open) it so you can see and use its tools. With Windows 7 you start application programs using the Start menu. A **menu** is a list of related commands. You use the Start menu to open the All Programs menu, which contains all the application programs on your computer. You can see some programs on the All Programs menu; some are in folders you have to click first. To start a program, you click its name on the All Programs menu. Tony asks you to explore the Paint accessory program to design flyers that will hang on the doors of the pediatric evaluation rooms.

STEPS

1. **Click the Start button on the taskbar in the lower-left corner of screen**

   The Start menu opens, showing frequently used programs on the left side. The gray area on the right contains links to folders and other locations you are likely to use frequently. It also lets you get help and shut down your computer. See Figure A-10. Not all the programs available on your computer are shown.

2. **Point to All Programs**

   This menu shows programs installed on your computer. Your program list will differ, depending on what you (or your lab) have installed on your machine. Some program names are immediately available, and others are inside folders.

3. **Click the Accessories folder**

   A list of Windows accessory programs appears, as shown in Figure A-11. The program names are indented to the right from the Accessories folder, meaning that they are inside that folder.

4. **Move the pointer over Paint and click once**

   The Paint program window opens on your screen, as shown in Figure A-12. When Windows opens an application program, it starts the program from your computer's hard disk, where it's permanently stored. Then it places the program in your computer's memory so you can use it.

5. **If your Paint window fills the screen completely, click the Restore Down button in the upper-right corner of the window**

   If your Paint window doesn't look like Figure A-12, point to the lower-right corner of the window until the pointer becomes , then drag until it matches the figure.

Searching for programs and files using the Start menu

If you need to find a program, folder, or file on your computer quickly, the Search programs and files box on the Start menu can help. Click the Start button, then type the name of the item you want to find in the Search programs and files box. As you type, Windows 7 lists all programs, documents, e-mail messages, and files that contain the text you typed in a box above the Search programs and files box. The items appear as links, which means you only have to click the hand pointer on the item you want, and Windows 7 opens it.

FIGURE A-10: Start menu

FIGURE A-11: Accessories folder on All Programs menu

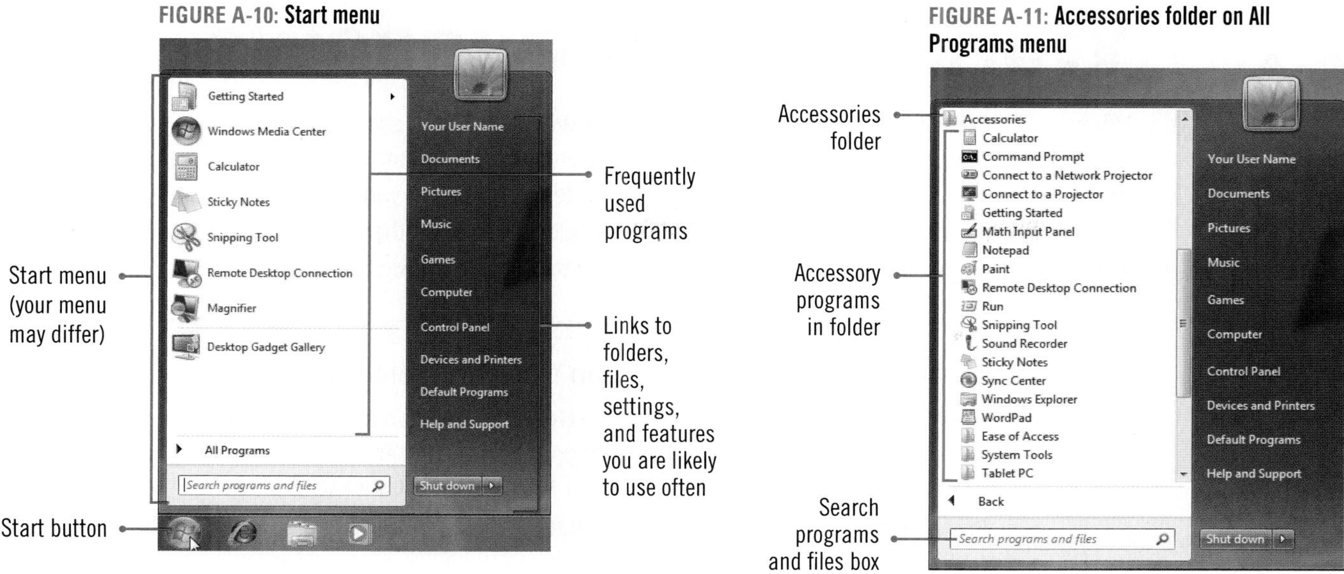

FIGURE A-12: Paint program window

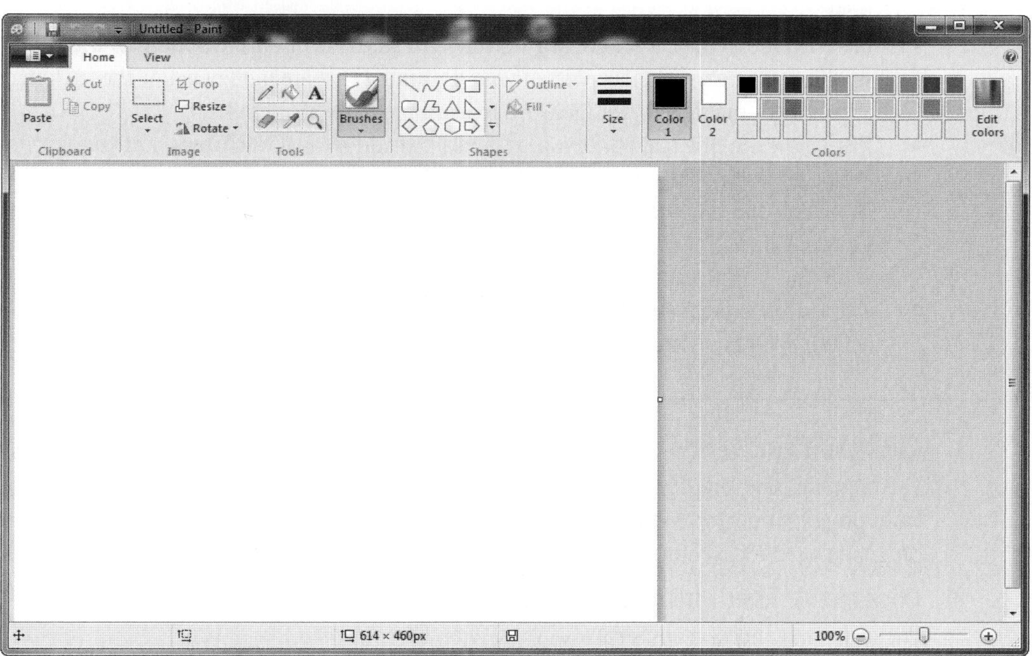

TABLE A-2: Some Windows 7 Accessory programs

accessory program name	use to
Math Input Panel	Interpret math expressions handwritten on a tablet and create a formula suitable for printing or inserting in another program
Notepad	Create text files with basic text formatting
Paint	Create and edit drawings using lines, shapes, and colors
Snipping Tool	Capture an image of any screen area that you can save to use in a document
Sticky Notes	Create short text notes that you can use to set reminders or create to-do lists for yourself
Windows Explorer	View and organize the files and folders on your computer
WordPad	Type letters or other text documents with formatting

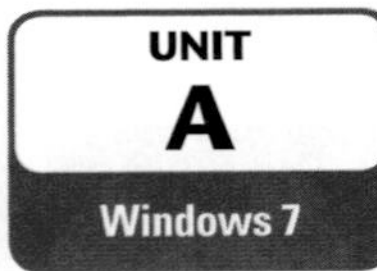

Working with Windows

When you start an application program, its **program window** opens, showing you the tools you need to use the program. A new, blank file also opens. In the Paint program, you create a drawing that you can save as a file and print. All windows in the Windows 7 operating system have similar window elements. Once you can use a window in one program, you can then work with windows in many other programs. As you develop the flyers for the pediatric exam rooms, you work with the open Paint window using Windows 7 elements.

DETAILS

Many windows have the following common elements. Refer to Figure A-13:

- At the top of every open window, you see a **title bar**, a transparent or solid-colored strip that contains the name of the program and document you opened. This document has not been saved, so it has the temporary name "Untitled." On the right side of the title bar, you see three icons.

  The **Minimize button** temporarily hides the window, making it a button on the taskbar. The program is still running, but its window is hidden until you click its taskbar button to display it again. The **Maximize button** enlarges the window to fill the entire computer screen. If a window is already maximized, the Maximize button changes to the **Restore Down button**. Restoring a window reduces it to the last nonmaximized size. The **Close button** closes the program. To use it later, you need to start it again.
- Many windows have a **scroll bar** on the right side and/or on the bottom of the window. You click the scroll bar elements to show parts of your document that are hidden below the bottom edge or off to the right side of the screen. See Table A-3 to learn the parts of a scroll bar.
- Just below the title bar, at the top of the Paint window, is the **Ribbon**, a strip that contains tabs. **Tabs** are pages that contain buttons that you click to perform actions. The Paint window has two tabs, the Home tab and the View tab. Tabs are divided into **groups** of command buttons. The Home tab has five groups: Clipboard, Image, Tools, Shapes, and Colors. Some programs have **menus**, words you click to show lists of commands, and **toolbars**, containing program buttons.
- The **Quick Access toolbar**, in the upper-left corner of the window, lets you quickly perform common actions such as saving a file.

QUICK TIP
If your Ribbon looks different from Figure A-13, your window is a little narrower. A narrow window collapses some buttons so you can only see group names. In that case, you might need to click a group name to see buttons.

STEPS

1. **Click the Paint window Minimize button**
   The program is now represented only by its button on the taskbar. See Figure A-14. The taskbar button for the Paint program now has a gradient background with blue and white shading. Taskbar buttons for closed programs have a solid blue background.
2. **Click the taskbar button representing the Paint program**
   The program window reappears.
3. **Drag the Paint scroll box down, notice the lower edge of the Paint canvas that appears, then click the Paint Up scroll arrow until you see the top edge of the canvas**
   In the Ribbon, the Home tab is in front of the View tab.
4. **Point to the View tab with the tip of the mouse pointer, then click the View tab once**
   The View tab moves in front of the Home tab and shows commands for viewing your drawings. The View tab has three groups: Zoom, Show or hide, and Display.
5. **Click the Home tab**
6. **Click the Paint window Maximize button**
   The window fills the screen and the Maximize button becomes the Restore Down button.
7. **Click the Paint window's Restore Down button**
   The Paint window returns to its previous size on the screen.

TROUBLE
If your screen resolution is set higher than 1024 × 768, you might not see a scroll box. You can continue with the lesson.

QUICK TIP
To quickly restore down the selected window, press and hold down the Windows key and then press the down arrow key.

FIGURE A-13: **Paint program window elements**

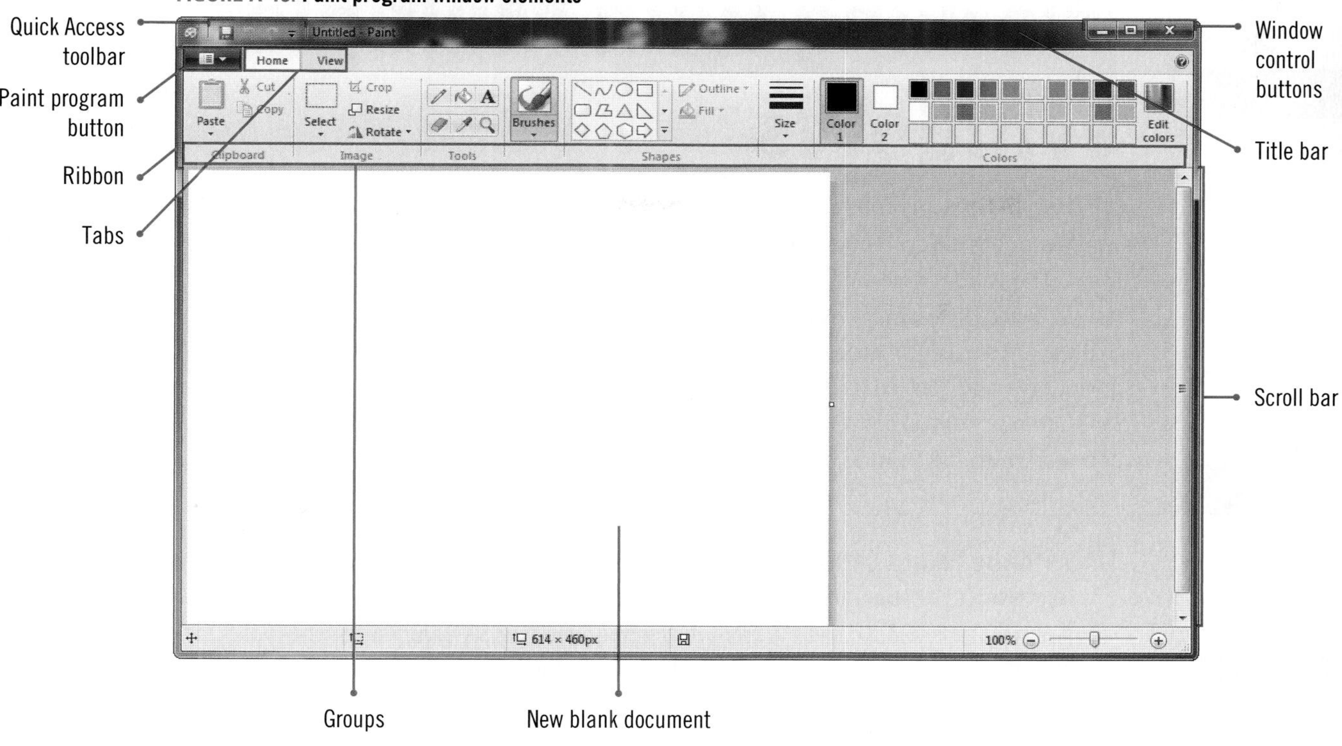

FIGURE A-14: **Taskbar showing Paint program button**

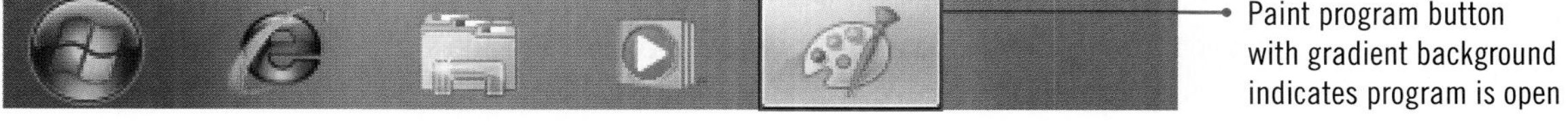

TABLE A-3: **Parts of a scroll bar**

name	looks like	use for
Scroll box	(Size may vary)	Drag to scroll quickly through a long document
Scroll arrows		Click to scroll up or down in small amounts
Shaded area	(Above and below scroll box)	Click to move up or down by one screen

Using the Quick Access toolbar

On the left side of the title bar, the Quick Access toolbar lets you perform common tasks with just one click. The Save button saves the changes you have made to a document. The Undo button lets you reverse (undo) the last action you performed. The Redo button reinstates the change you just undid. Use the Customize Quick Access Toolbar button to add other frequently used buttons to the toolbar, move the toolbar below the Ribbon, or hide the Ribbon.

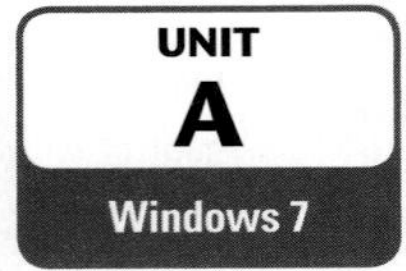

Working with Multiple Windows

Windows 7 lets you work with more than one program at a time. If you open two or more programs, a window opens for each one. You can work with each open program window, going back and forth between them. The window in front is called the **active window**. Any other open window behind the active window is called an **inactive window**. For ease in working with multiple windows, you can move, arrange, make them smaller or larger, minimize, or restore them so they're not in the way. To resize a window, drag a window's edge, called its **border**. You can also use the taskbar to switch between windows. See Table A-4 for a summary of taskbar actions. Keeping the Paint program open, you open the WordPad program and work with the Paint and WordPad program windows.

STEPS

QUICK TIP
To click an inactive window to make it active, click its title bar, window edge, or a blank area. To move a window, you must drag its title bar.

QUICK TIP
To instantly minimize all inactive windows, point to the active window's title bar, and quickly "shake" the window back and forth. This feature is called Aero Shake.

TROUBLE
Point to any edge of a window until you see the ⇔ or ⇕ pointer and drag to make it larger or smaller in one direction only.

1. **With the Paint window open, click the Start button, point to All Programs, click the Accessories folder, then click WordPad**

   The WordPad window opens in front of the Paint window. See Figure A-15. The WordPad window is in front, indicating that it is the active window. The Paint window is the inactive window. On the taskbar, the gradient backgrounds on the WordPad and Paint program buttons on the taskbar tell you that both programs are open. You want to move the WordPad window out of the way so you can see both windows at once.

2. **Point to a blank part of the WordPad window title bar, then drag the WordPad window so you can see more of the Paint window**

3. **Click once on the Paint window's title bar**

   The Paint window is now the active window and appears in front of the WordPad window. You can make any window active by clicking it. You can use the taskbar to do the same thing. You can also move among open program windows by pressing and holding down the [Alt] key on your keyboard and pressing the [Tab] key. A small window opens in the middle of the screen, showing miniature versions of each open program window. Each time you press [Tab], you select the next open program window. When you release [Tab] and [Alt], the selected program window becomes active.

4. **On the taskbar, click the WordPad window button**

   The WordPad window is now active. When you open multiple windows on the desktop, you may need to resize windows so they don't get in the way of other open windows. You can use dragging to resize a window.

5. **Point to the lower-right corner of the WordPad window until the pointer becomes ⤡, then drag up and to the left about an inch to make the window smaller**

   Windows 7 has a special feature that lets you automatically resize a window so it fills half the screen.

6. **Point to the WordPad window title bar, drag the window to the left side of the screen until the mouse pointer reaches the screen edge and the left half of the screen turns a transparent blue color, then release the mouse button**

   The WordPad window "snaps" to fill the left side of the screen.

7. **Point to the Paint window title bar, then drag the window to the right side of the screen until it snaps to fill the right half of the screen**

   The Paint window fills the right side of the screen. The Snap feature makes it easy to arrange windows side by side to view the contents of both at the same time.

8. **Click the WordPad window Close button then click the Maximize button in the Paint window's title bar**

   The WordPad program closes, so you can no longer use its tools unless you open it again. The Paint program window remains open and fills the screen.

FIGURE A-15: **WordPad window in front of Paint window**

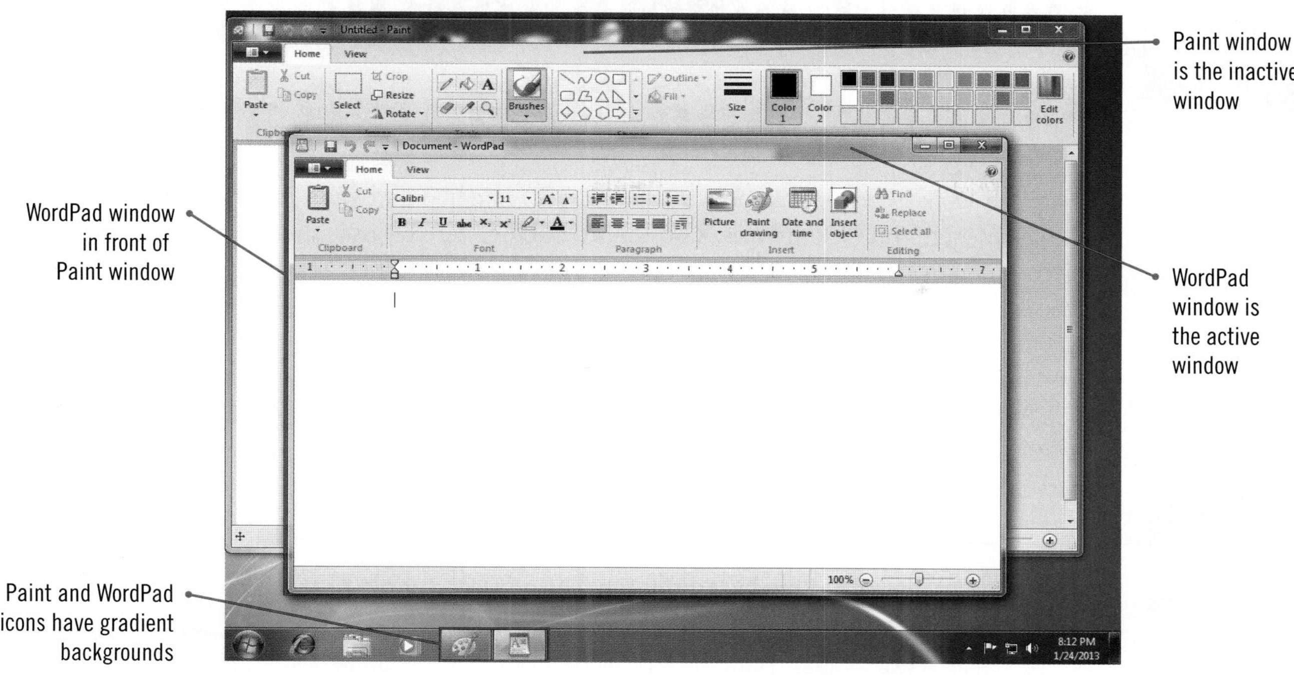

TABLE A-4: **Using the Windows taskbar**

to	do this
Add buttons to taskbar	Drag a program name from the Start menu over the taskbar, until a ScreenTip reads Pin to Taskbar
Change order of taskbar buttons	Drag any icon to a new taskbar location
See a list of recent documents opened in a taskbar program	Right-click taskbar program button
Close a document using the taskbar	Point to taskbar button, point to document name in jump list, then click Close button
Minimize all open windows	Click Show desktop button to the right of taskbar date and time
Redisplay all minimized windows	Click Show desktop button to the right of taskbar date and time
Make all windows transparent (Aero only)	Point to Show desktop button to the right of taskbar date and time
See preview of documents in taskbar (Aero only)	Point to taskbar button for open program

Switching windows with Windows Aero

Windows Aero is a set of special effects for Windows 7. If your windows have transparent "glass" backgrounds like those shown in the figures in this book, your Aero feature is turned on. Your windows show subtle animations when you minimize, maximize, and move windows. When you arrange windows using Aero, your windows can appear in a three-dimensional stack that you can quickly view without having to click the taskbar. To achieve this effect, called **Aero Flip 3D**, press and hold [Ctrl][⊞], then press [Tab]. Press [Tab] repeatedly to move through the stack, then press [Enter] to enlarge the document in the front of the stack. In addition, when you point to a taskbar button, Aero shows you small previews of the document, photo, or video—a feature called **Aero Peek**. Aero is turned on automatically when you start Windows, if you have an appropriate video card and enough computer memory to run Aero. If it is not on, to turn on the Aero feature, right-click the desktop, left-click Personalize, then select one of the Aero Themes.

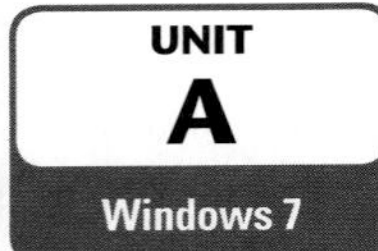

Using Command Buttons, Menus, and Dialog Boxes

When you work in an open program window, you communicate with the program using command buttons, menus, and dialog boxes. **Command buttons** let you issue instructions to modify program objects. Command buttons are sometimes organized on a Ribbon into tabs, and then into groups like those in the Paint window. Some command buttons have text on them, and others only have icons that represent what they do. Other command buttons reveal **menus**, lists of commands you can choose. And some command buttons open up a **dialog box**, a window with controls that lets you tell Windows what you want. Table A-5 lists the common types of controls you find in dialog boxes. You use command buttons, menus, and dialog boxes to create a simple geometric image with the Paint program that will decorate the doors of the pediatric exam rooms.

STEPS

QUICK TIP
If you need to move the oval, use the keyboard arrow keys to move it left, right, up, or down.

TROUBLE
Don't be concerned if your object isn't exactly like the one in the figure.

TROUBLE
If you prefer not to print your document, click Cancel.

1. **In the Shapes group on the Home tab, click the Rectangle button**
2. **In the Colors group, click the Gold color button , move the pointer over the white drawing area, called the canvas, then drag to draw a rectangle a similar size to the one in Figure A-16**
3. **In the Shapes group, click the Oval button , click the Green color button in the Colors group, then drag a small oval above the rectangle, using Figure A-16 as a guide**
4. **Click the Fill with color icon in the Tools group, click the Light turquoise color button in the Colors group, click inside the oval, click the Purple color button, then click inside the rectangle, and compare your drawing to Figure A-16**
5. **In the Image group, click the Select list arrow, then click Select all, as shown in Figure A-17**
   The entire drawing is selected, marked by the dotted line surrounding the white drawing area.
6. **In the Image group, click the Rotate or flip button, then click Rotate right 90°**
7. **Click the Paint menu button just below the title bar, then click Print**
   The Print dialog box opens, as shown in Figure A-18. This dialog box lets you choose a printer, specify which part of your document or drawing you want to print, and choose how many copies you want to print. The **default**, or automatically selected, number of copies is 1, which is what you want.
8. **Click Print**
   The drawing prints on your printer. You decide to close the program without saving your drawing.
9. **Click , click Exit, then click Don't Save**

TABLE A-5: Common dialog box controls

element	example	description
Text box	132	A box in which you type text or numbers
Spin box	1	A box with up and down arrows; click arrows or type to increase or decrease value
Option button		A small circle you click to select the option
Check box		Turns on an option when checked or off when unchecked
List box	Select Printer Add Printer Dell Laser Printer 3000cn PCL6 Fax	A box that lets you select an option from a list of options
Command button	Save	A button that completes or cancels the selected settings

FIGURE A-16: **Rectangle and oval shapes with fill**

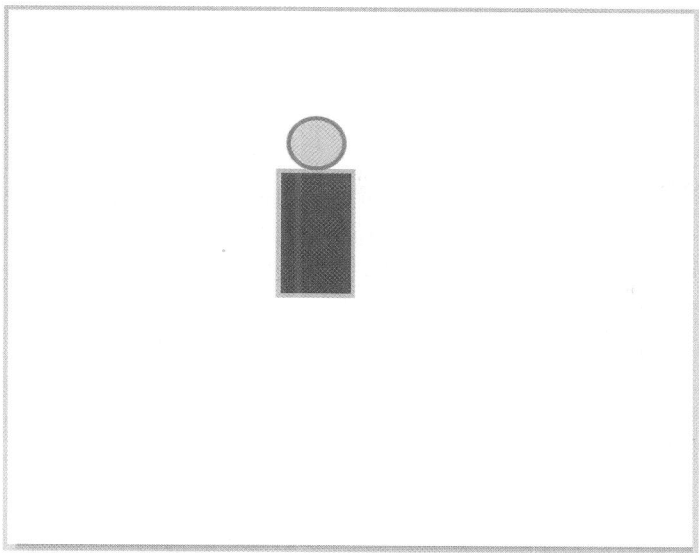

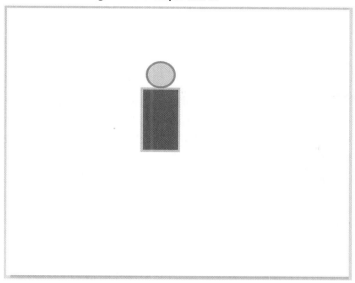

FIGURE A-17: **Select list arrow**

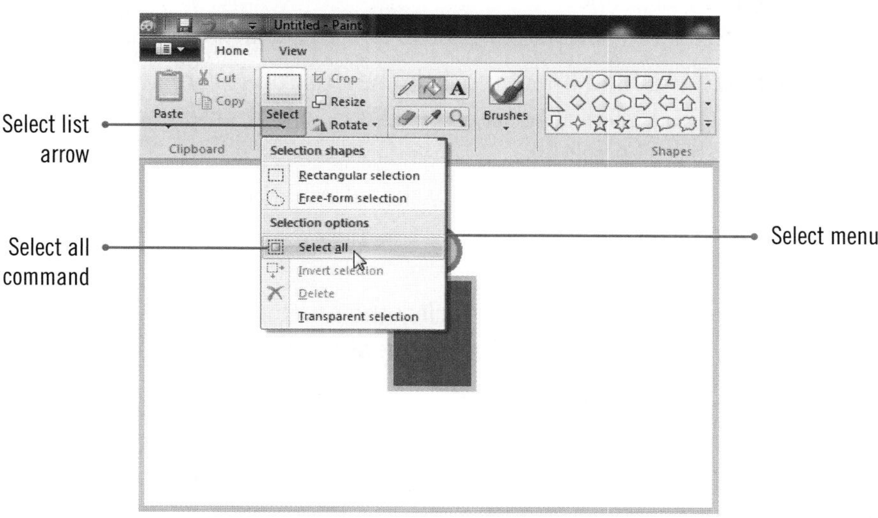

FIGURE A-18: **Print dialog box**

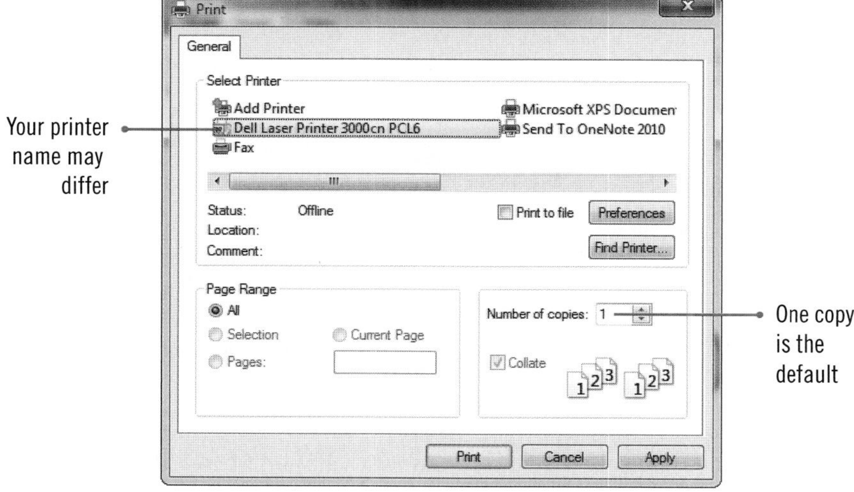

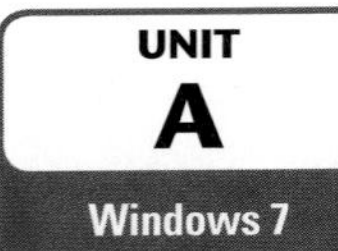

Getting Help

As you use Windows 7, you might feel ready to learn more about it, or you might have a problem and need some advice. You can open the Windows 7 Help and Support to find information you need. You can browse Help and Support topics by clicking a category, such as "Learn about Windows Basics." Within this category, you see more specific categories. Each category has topics in blue or purple text called **links** that you can click to learn more. You can also search Help and Support by typing one or more descriptive words called **keywords**, such as "taskbar," to ask Windows to find topics related to your keywords. The Help toolbar contains icons that give you more Help options. Table A-6 describes the Help toolbar icons. You use Windows 7 help to learn more about Windows and the WordPad accessory.

STEPS

TROUBLE
If your computer is not connected to the Internet, you will see an alert at the top of the Help window. You can continue with the steps in this lesson.

QUICK TIP
If you are using a mouse with a scroll wheel, you can use the scroll wheel to scroll up and down. If you are using a touchpad, the right side of your touchpad might let you scroll.

QUICK TIP
Search text is not case sensitive. Typing wordpad, Wordpad, or WordPad finds the same results.

1. **Click the Start button, then on the right side of the Start menu, click Help and Support**
   The Windows Help and Support window opens, as shown in Figure A-19. A search box appears near the top of the window. Three topics appear as blue or purple text, meaning that they are links. Below them, you see descriptive text and a link to a Web site that contains more information about Windows.
2. **Under Not sure where to start?, position the hand pointer over Learn about Windows Basics, then click once**
   Several categories of Windows Basics topics appear, with links under each one.
3. **Under Desktop fundamentals, click The desktop (overview)**
   Help and Support information about the desktop appears, divided into several categories. Some of the text appears as a blue or purple link.
4. **Drag the scroll box down to view the information, then drag the scroll box back to the top of the scroll bar**
   You decide to learn more about the taskbar.
5. **Under The desktop (overview), click the blue or purple text The taskbar (overview), then scroll down and read the information about the taskbar**
6. **Click in the Search Help text box, type wordpad, then click the Search Help button**
   A list of links related to the WordPad accessory program appears. See Figure A-20.
7. **Click Using WordPad, scroll down if necessary, then click Create, open, and save documents**
8. **Scroll down and view the information, clicking any other links that interest you**
9. **Click the Close button in the upper-right corner of the Windows Help and Support window**
   The Windows Help and Support window closes.

TABLE A-6: Help toolbar icons

help toolbar icon	name	action
	Help and Support home	Displays the Help and Support Home page
	Print	Prints the currently-displayed help topic
	Browse Help	Displays a list of Help topics organized by subject
Ask	Ask	Describes other ways to get help
Options	Options	Lets you print, browse, search, set Help text size, and adjust settings

FIGURE A-19: **Windows Help and Support window**

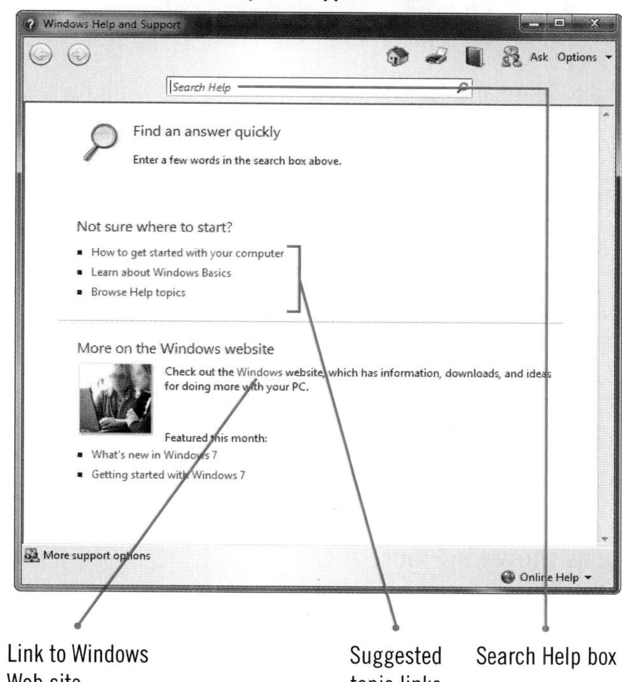

FIGURE A-20: **Results of a search on WordPad**

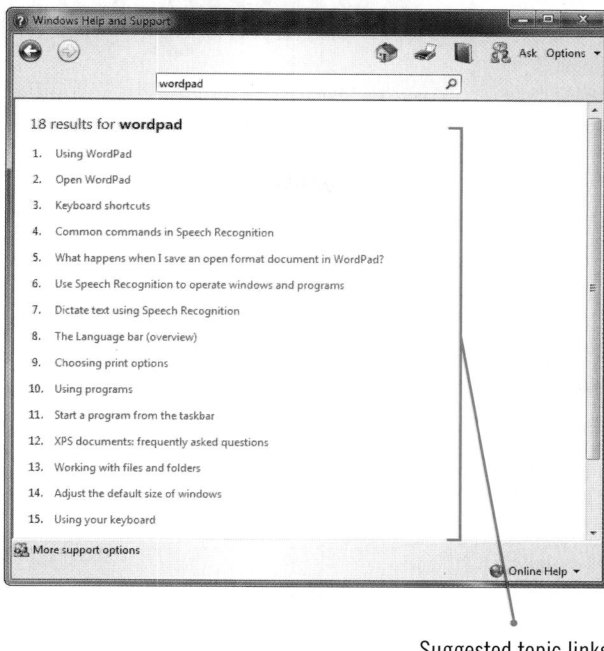

Finding other ways to get help

As you use Windows 7, you might want more help than you can find by clicking links or searching. You will find many other methods in the Windows Help and Support Home window. Click the Windows website link to locate blogs (Web logs, which are personal commentaries), downloads, Windows 7 video tours, and other current Windows 7 resources. Click the Ask button in the Help and Support window toolbar to learn about **Windows Remote Assistance**, which lets you connect with another computer, perhaps that of a trusted friend or instructor, so they can operate your computer using an Internet connection. The same window lets you open Microsoft Answers. **Microsoft Answers** is a website the lets you search **forums** (electronic gathering places where anyone can add questions and answers on computer issues), Microsoft help files, and even on-screen video demonstrations about selected topics.

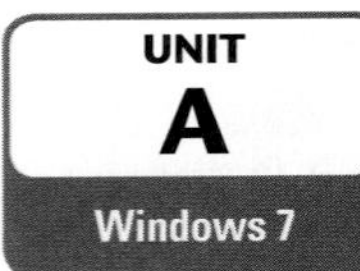

Exiting Windows 7

When you finish working on your computer, save and close any open files, close any open programs, close any open windows, and exit (or **shut down**) Windows 7. Table A-7 shows several options for ending your Windows 7 sessions. Whichever option you choose, it's important to shut down your computer in an orderly way. If you turn off or unplug the computer while Windows 7 is running, you could lose data or damage Windows 7 and your computer. If you are working in a computer lab, follow your instructor's directions and your lab's policies for ending your Windows 7 session. Tony is pleased with the progress you made learning Windows 7. You have examined the basic ways you can use Windows 7, so you are ready to end your Windows 7 session.

STEPS

1. **Click the Start button on the taskbar**

   The lower-right corner of the Start menu lets you shut down your computer. It also displays a menu with other options for ending a Windows 7 session.

2. **Point to the Power button list arrow, as shown in Figure A-21**

   The Power button menu lists other shutdown options.

3. **If you are working in a computer lab, follow the instructions provided by your instructor or technical support person for ending your Windows 7 session. If you are working on your own computer, click Shut down or the option you prefer for ending your Windows 7 session**

4. **After you shut down your computer, you may also need to turn off your monitor and other hardware devices, such as a printer, to conserve energy**

TROUBLE

If a previous user has customized your computer, your button and menu commands might be in different locations. For example, the Power button may show "Restart," and "Shut down" may appear on the menu.

Installing updates when you exit Windows

Sometimes, after you shut down your machine, you might find that your machine does not shut down immediately. Instead, Windows might install software updates. If your power button shows this yellow icon, that means that Windows will install updates on your next shutdown. If you see a window indicating that updates are being installed, do not unplug or press the power switch to turn off your machine. Allow the updates to install completely. After the updates are installed, your computer will shut down, as you originally requested.

FIGURE A-21: **Shutting down your computer**

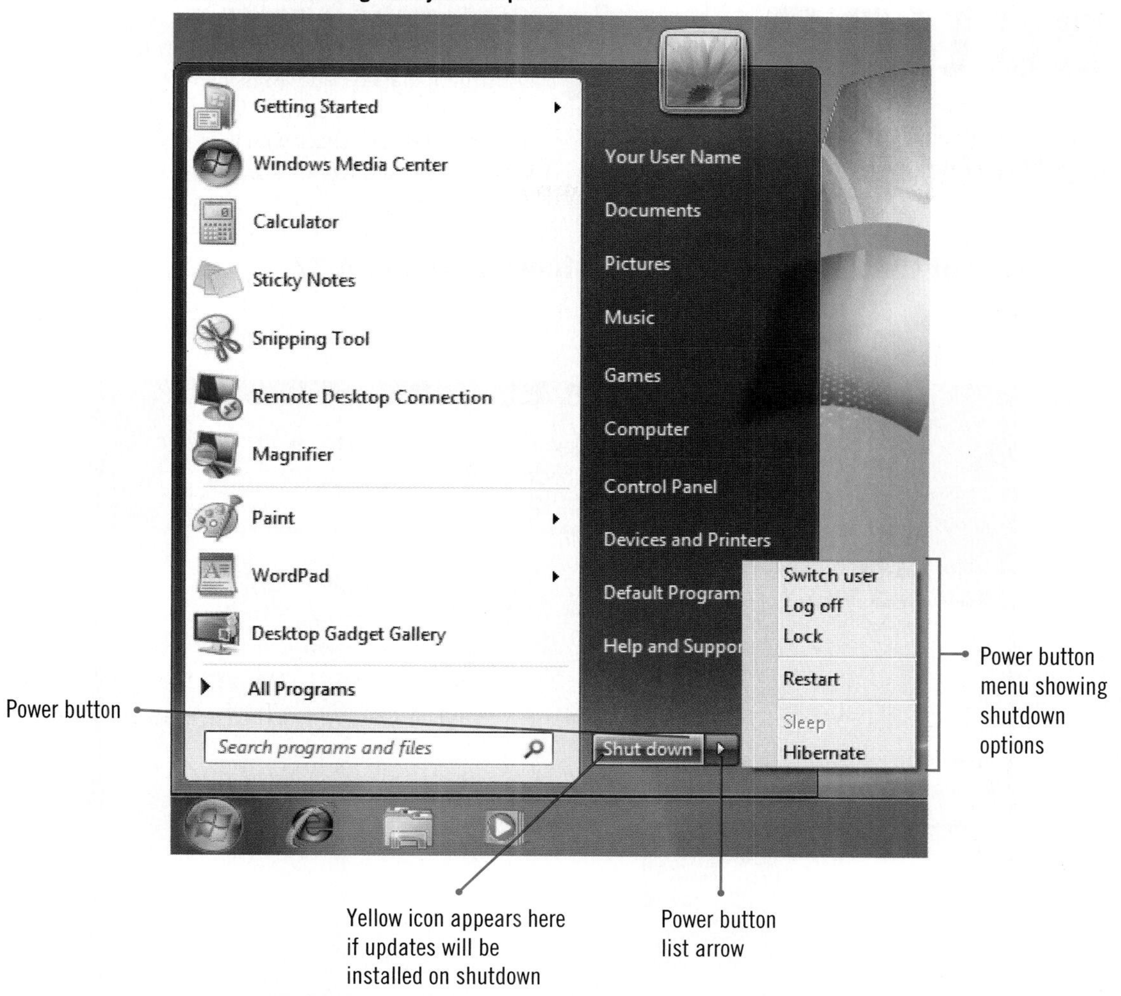

TABLE A-7: **Options for ending a Windows 7 session**

option	description	click
Shut down	Completely turns off your computer	Start button, Shut down
Switch user	Locks your user account and displays the Welcome screen so another user can log on	Start button, Power button list arrow, Switch user
Log off	Closes all windows, programs, and documents, then displays the Log in screen	Start button, Power button list arrow, Log off
Lock	Locks computer so only current user (or administrator) can use it	Start button, Power button list arrow, Lock
Restart	Shuts down your computer, then restarts it	Start button, Power button list arrow, Restart
Sleep	Puts computer in a low-power state while preserving your session in the computer's memory	Start button, Power button list arrow, Sleep
Hibernate	Turns off computer drives and screens but saves image of your work; when you turn on your machine, it starts where you left off	Start button, Power button list arrow, Hibernate

Practice

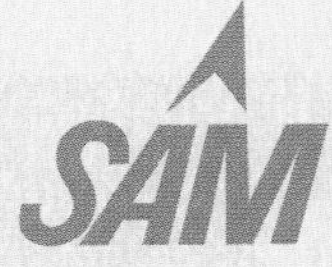

For current SAM information, including versions and content details, visit SAM Central (http://www.cengage.com/samcentral). If you have a SAM user profile, you may have access to hands-on instruction, practice, and assessment of the skills covered in this unit. Since various versions of SAM are supported throughout the life of this text, check with your instructor for the correct instructions and URL/Web site for accessing assignments.

Concepts Review

Label the elements of the Windows 7 window shown in Figure A-22.

FIGURE A-22

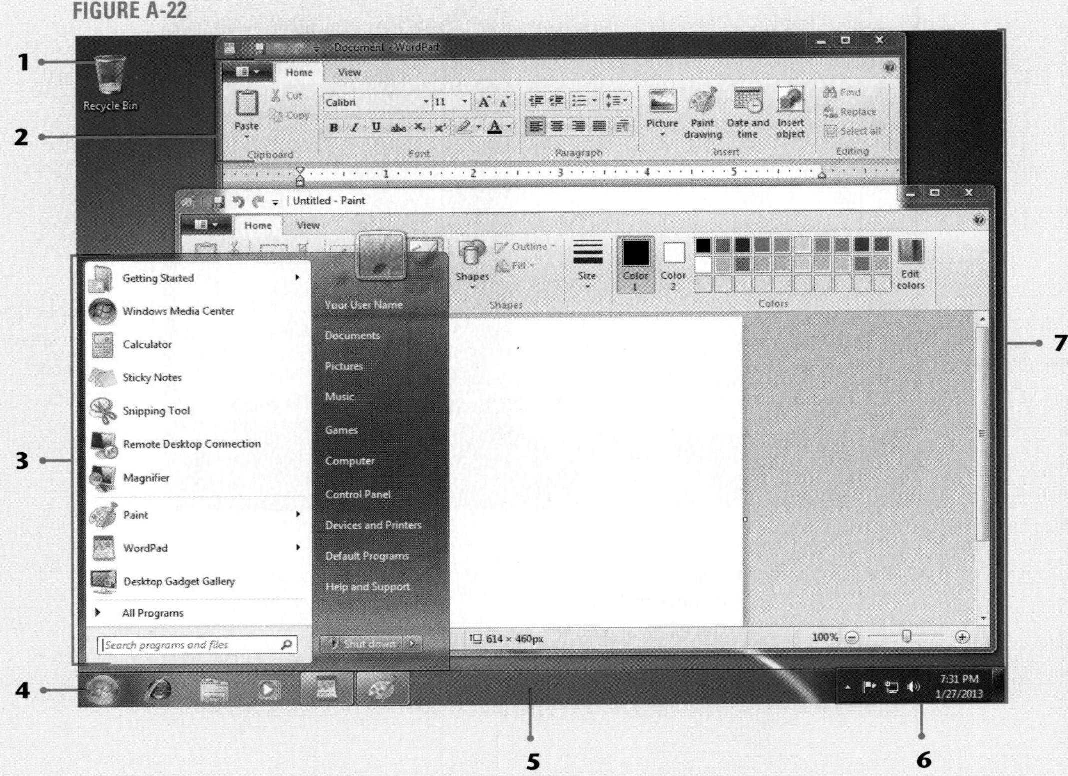

Match each term with the statement that best describes it.

8. **Accessory**
9. **Keyword**
10. **Trackball**
11. **Active window**
12. **Password**
13. **Operating system**
14. **Taskbar**

a. A sequence of numbers and letters users create to keep information secure
b. The window in front of other windows
c. Horizontal strip at bottom of screen that contains buttons
d. A pointing device
e. Application program that comes with Windows 7
f. Descriptive word you use to search Windows Help and Support
g. A program necessary to run your computer

Select the best answer from the list of choices.

15. What part of a window shows the name of the program you opened?

a. Title bar
b. Scroll bar
c. Ribbon
d. Quick Access toolbar

16. You use the Maximize button to:
- **a.** Restore a window to a previous size.
- **b.** Expand a window to fill the entire screen.
- **c.** Temporarily hide a window.
- **d.** Scroll down a window.

17. Which of the following is not an accessory program?
- **a.** Snipping Tool
- **b.** Paint
- **c.** WordPad
- **d.** Windows 7

18. Which button do you click to reduce an open window to a button on the taskbar?
- **a.** Maximize button
- **b.** Restore Down button
- **c.** Minimize button
- **d.** Close button

19. Right-clicking is an action that:
- **a.** Starts a program.
- **b.** Requires a password.
- **c.** Displays a shortcut menu.
- **d.** Opens the taskbar.

20. The Windows 7 feature that shows windows with transparent "glass" backgrounds is:
- **a.** Paint.
- **b.** Aero.
- **c.** Taskbar.
- **d.** Sticky Notes.

21. Windows 7 is a(n):
- **a.** Accessory program.
- **b.** Application program.
- **c.** Operating system.
- **d.** Gadget.

Skills Review

1. Start Windows 7.
- **a.** If your computer and monitor are not running, press your computer's and your monitor's power buttons.
- **b.** If necessary, click the user name that represents your user account.
- **c.** Enter a password if necessary, using correct uppercase and lowercase letters, then click the Go button.

2. Learn the Windows 7 desktop.
- **a.** Examine the Windows 7 desktop to identify the Start button, the taskbar, the notification area, the Recycle Bin, the desktop background, desktop icons, and gadgets, if any.

3. Point and click.
- **a.** On the Windows desktop, select the Recycle Bin.
- **b.** Open the Start menu, then close it.
- **c.** Open the clock and calendar on the right side of the taskbar.
- **d.** Click the desktop to close the calendar.
- **e.** Open the Recycle Bin window, then close it.

4. Start a Windows 7 program.
- **a.** Use the Start button to open the Start menu.
- **b.** Open the All Programs menu.
- **c.** On the All Programs menu, open the Accessories folder.
- **d.** Open the WordPad accessory.

5. Work with Windows.
- **a.** Minimize the WordPad window.
- **b.** Redisplay it using a taskbar button.
- **c.** In the WordPad window, click the WordPad button in the Ribbon, then click the About WordPad command. (*Hint*: The WordPad button is next to the Home tab.)
- **d.** Close the About WordPad window.
- **e.** Maximize the WordPad window, then restore it down.
- **f.** Display the View tab in the WordPad window.

Skills Review (continued)

6. **Work with multiple windows.**
   a. Leaving WordPad open, open Paint.
   b. Make the WordPad window the active window.
   c. Make the Paint window the active window.
   d. Minimize the Paint window.
   e. Drag the WordPad window so it automatically fills the left side of the screen.
   f. Redisplay the Paint window.
   g. Drag the Paint window so it automatically fills the right side of the screen.
   h. Close the WordPad window, maximize the Paint window, then restore down the Paint window.
7. **Use command buttons, menus, and dialog boxes.**
   a. In the Paint window, draw a red triangle, similar to Figure A-23.
   b. Use the Fill with color button to fill the triangle with a gold color.
   c. Draw a green rectangle just below the triangle.
   d. Use the Fill with color button to fill the green triangle with a light turquoise color.
   e. Fill the drawing background with purple and compare your drawing with Figure A-23.
   f. Use the Select list arrow and menu to select the entire drawing, then use the Rotate or flip command to rotate the drawing left 90°.
   g. Close the Paint program without saving the drawing.

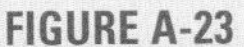
FIGURE A-23

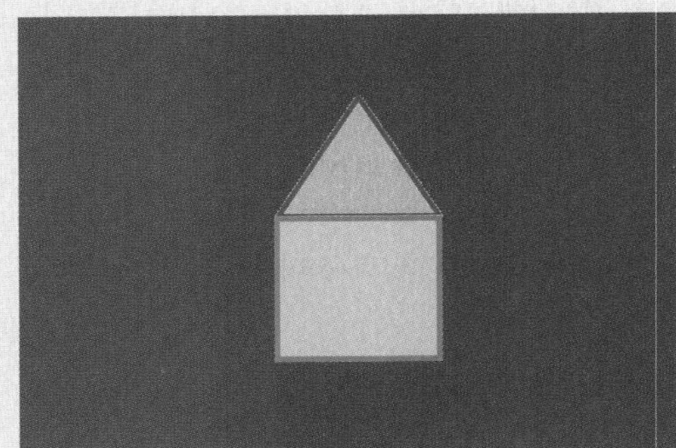

8. **Get help.**
   a. Open the Windows Help and Support window.
   b. Open the "How to get started with your computer" topic.
   c. Open the "First week tasks" topic, click a link called "Create a user account", then read the topic information.
   d. In the Search Help text box, search for help about user accounts.
   e. Find the link that describes what a user account is and click it.
   f. Read the topic, then close the Windows Help and Support window.
9. **Exit Windows 7.**
   a. Shut down your computer using the Shut down command or the command for your work or school setting.
   b. Turn off your monitor.

Independent Challenge 1

You work for River Dell Medical Supply, a distributor of wheelchairs, walkers, and respiration equipment, as well as other home health care supplies. River Dell sells a large number of nylon fabric and hard shell wrist braces for repetitive stress injuries. The company services customers throughout the New York metropolitan area. As part of a community outreach program, the owner, Gabriel Medina, gives seminars on how to avoid repetitive stress injuries to the hands and arms. He knows this can also be a big problem for computer users, so he asks you to research the topic and write some guidelines.

a. Start your computer, log on to Windows 7 if necessary, then open Windows Help and Support.
b. Click the Learn about Windows Basics link.
c. In the Learn about your computer section, read the topic about using your mouse.
d. At the bottom of the topic, read the Tips for using your mouse safely.
e. Using pencil and paper, write a short memo to Gabriel listing, in your own words, the most important tips for avoiding soreness or injury when using a mouse. Close the Windows Help and Support window, then exit Windows.

Independent Challenge 2

You are the new office manager for Dr. Jennifer Sterling, a dermatologist in Chatham, Massachusetts. Dr. Sterling's patients often have to pay a copayment for each visit. As the office manager, you are responsible for tracking payments from patients. Dr. Sterling asks you to investigate how the Windows 7 Calculator accessory can help with this accounting task.

Independent Challenge 2 (continued)

a. Start your computer, log on to Windows 7 if necessary, then open the Windows 7 accessory called Calculator.
b. Drag the Calculator window to place it in the lower-left corner of the desktop just above the taskbar.
c. Minimize the Calculator window, then redisplay it.
d. Click to enter the number **87** on the Calculator.
e. Click the division sign (/) button.
f. Click the number 2.
g. Click the equals sign button (=), and write the result shown in the Calculator window on a piece of paper. See Figure A-24.
h. Click the Help menu in the Calculator window, then click View Help. In the Using Calculator window, determine the three ways of entering calculations in the Calculator. Write the three methods on your handwritten list.
i. Close the Help window.

FIGURE A-24

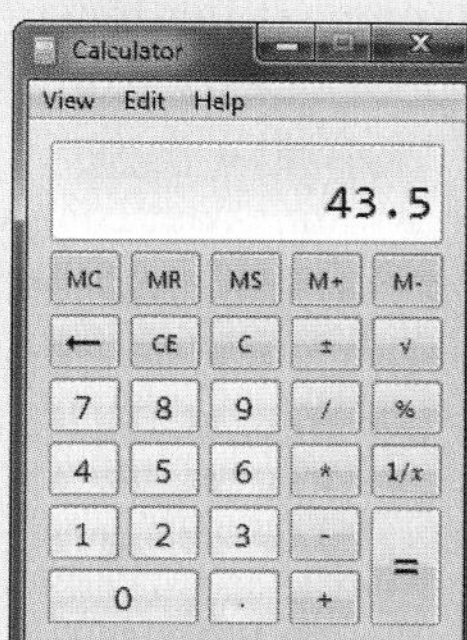

Advanced Challenge Exercise

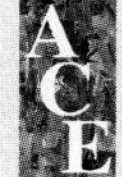

- Open the View menu on the Calculator window, and click Date calculation.
- Click the list arrow under Select the date calculation you want, then click Calculate the difference between two dates.
- Write how a medical practice might use this to calculate the length of time it takes a customer's insurance company to pay a bill.
- Click the View menu, point to Worksheets, then click Fuel economy (mpg).
- Click in the Distance (miles) text box and enter **100**; click in the Fuel used (gallons) text box and type **5**, then use the Calculate button to calculate the mileage.
- Write a short paragraph on how you can use this feature to help calculate your monthly commuting costs.
- Click the View menu and return to the Basic view.
- Try to click the Calculator window's Maximize button. Note the result and add this fact to your document.

j. Close the Calculator, then exit Windows.

Independent Challenge 3

You are the office manager for David's Healthy Foods, a service business in San Diego, CA, that specializes in shipping gluten-free, low-sodium, and other special diet foods to Canada and the United States. It's important to know the temperature in the destination city so that the food won't spoil from extreme temperatures when delivered. David has asked you to find a way to easily monitor temperatures in destination cities. You decide to use a Windows gadget so you can see current temperatures in Celsius on your desktop.

To complete this Independent Challenge, you need an Internet connection. You also need permission to add gadgets to the Windows Desktop. If you are working in a computer lab, check with your instructor or technical support person.

a. Start your computer, log on to Windows 7 if necessary, then click the Start button, open the All Programs menu, then click Desktop Gadget Gallery.
b. Double-click the Weather gadget, then close the Gallery window.
c. Move the pointer over the Weather gadget on the desktop, then notice the small buttons that appear on its right side.
d. Click the Larger size button (the middle button).
e. Click the Options button (the third button down) to open the weather options window.
f. In the Select current location text box, type **Juneau, Alaska**, then click the Search button.
g. Verify that the window shows the current location as "Juneau, Alaska."
h. Click the Celsius option button, then click OK.
i. To close the gadget, point to the gadget, then click the Close button (the top button).
j. Write David a memo outlining how you can use the Windows Weather gadget to help keep food safe, then exit Windows.

Real Life Independent Challenge

As a professional photographer, you often evaluate pictures. You decide to explore a Windows Desktop gadget that will let you display a slide show on your desktop using photos you choose.

To complete this Independent Challenge, you need an Internet connection. You also need permission to add gadgets to the Windows Desktop. If you are working in a computer lab, check with your instructor or technical support person.

a. Start your computer, log on to Windows 7 if necessary, click the Start button, open the All Programs menu, then click Desktop Gadget Gallery.
b. Double-click the Slide Show gadget, then close the Gallery window.
c. Move the pointer over the Slide Show gadget on the desktop, then notice the small buttons that appear on its right side.
d. Click the Larger size button (the second button down).
e. Click the Options button (the third button down) to open the Slide Show options window.
f. Click the Folder list arrow and click the My Pictures folder. If you do not have pictures on your computer, click the Sample Pictures folder.
g. Click the Show each picture list arrow and select a duration.
h. Click the Transition between pictures list arrow and select a transition.
i. If you want the pictures to be in random order, click the Shuffle pictures check box.
j. Click OK.

Advanced Challenge Exercise

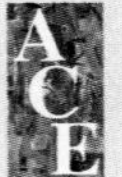

- Place the mouse pointer over the Slide Show window, then right-click.
- Point to Opacity and left-click an opacity level, then move the mouse pointer over the desktop. Adjust the opacity to the level you prefer.
- Drag the gadget to the desktop location you choose.

k. View your slide show, click the Slide Show window's Close button, then exit Windows.

Visual Workshop

As owner of Icons Plus, an icon design business, you decide to customize your desktop and resize your Help window to better suit your needs as you work with Paint. Organize your screen as shown in Figure A-25. Note the position of the Recycle Bin, the location of the Paint window, and the size and location of the Help and Support window. Write a paragraph summarizing how you used clicking and dragging to make your screen look like Figure A-25. Then exit Windows.

FIGURE A-25

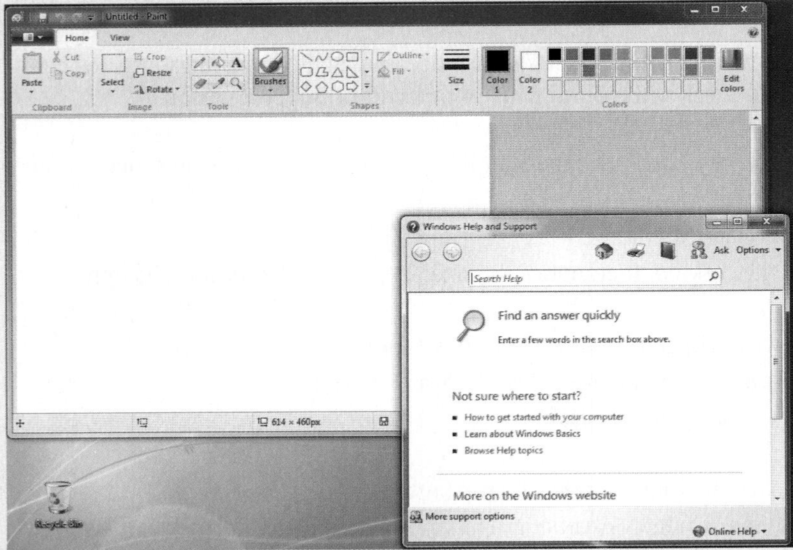

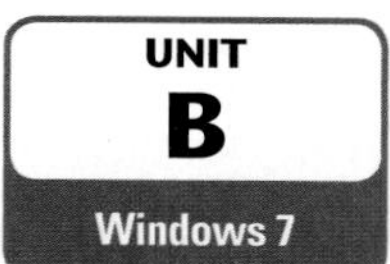

Understanding File Management

No files needed.

To work with the folders and files on your computer, you need to understand how your computer stores them. You should also know how to organize them so you can always find the information you need. These skills are called **file management** skills. When you create a document and save it as a file, it is important that you save the file in a place where you can find it later. To keep your computer files organized, you will need to copy, move, and rename them. When you have files you don't need any more, it's a good idea to move or delete them so your computer has only current files. The Riverwalk Medical Clinic office manager, Tony Sanchez, asks you to learn how to manage your computer files so you can begin creating and organizing documents as you work as an administrative assistant for Dr. Carla Zimmerman.

OBJECTIVES

- Understand folders and files
- Create and save a file
- Explore the files and folders on your computer
- Change file and folder views
- Open, edit, and save files
- Copy files
- Move and rename files
- Search for files, folders, and programs
- Delete and restore files

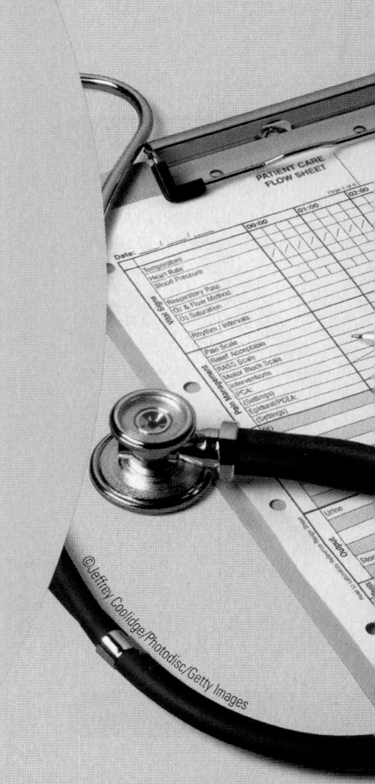

©Jeffrey Coolidge/Photodisc/Getty Images

UNIT B
Windows 7

Understanding Folders and Files

As you work with your computer programs, you create and save files, such as letters, drawings, or budgets. When you save files, you usually save them inside folders, which are storage areas on your computer. You use folders to group related files, as with paper folders in a file cabinet. The files and folders on your computer are organized in a **file hierarchy**, a system that arranges files and folders in different levels, like the branches of a tree. Figure B-1 shows a sample file hierarchy. Tony asks you to look at some important facts about files and folders to help you store your Riverwalk Medical Clinic files.

DETAILS

Use the following guidelines as you organize files using your computer's file hierarchy:

- **Use folders and subfolders to organize files**
  As you work with your computer, you can add folders to your hierarchy and rename them to help you organize your work. You should give folders unique names that help you easily identify them. You can also create **subfolders**, which are folders that are inside of other folders. Windows comes with several existing folders, such as My Documents, My Music, and My Pictures, that you can use as a starting point.

> **QUICK TIP**
> You can also start Windows Explorer by clicking the Windows Explorer button on the taskbar.

- **View files in windows**
  You view your computer contents by opening a **window**, like the one in Figure B-2. A window is divided into sections. The **Navigation pane** on the left side of the window shows the folder structure on your computer. When you click a folder in the Navigation pane, you see its contents in the **File list** on the right side. The **Details pane** at the bottom of the window provides information about selected files in the File list. A window actually opens in an accessory program called **Windows Explorer**, although the program name does not appear on the window. You can open this program from the Start menu, or just double-click a folder to open its window and view its contents.

- **Understand file addresses**
  A window also contains an **Address bar**, an area just below the title bar that shows the location, or address, of the files that appear in the File list. An **address** is a sequence of folder names separated by the ▸ symbol that describes a file's location in the file hierarchy. An address shows the folder with the highest hierarchy level on the left and steps through each hierarchy level toward the right, sometimes called a **path**. For example, the My Documents folder might contain a subfolder named Notes. In this case, the Address bar would show My Documents ▸ Notes. Each location between the ▸ symbols represents a level in the file hierarchy.

> **QUICK TIP**
> Remember that you single-click a folder or subfolder in the Address bar to show its contents. But in the File list, you double-click a subfolder to open it.

- **Navigate upward and downward using the Address bar and File list**
  You can use the Address bar and the File list to move up or down in the hierarchy one or more levels at a time. To **navigate upward** in your computer's hierarchy, you can click a folder or subfolder name in the Address bar. For example, in Figure B-2, you would move up in the hierarchy by clicking once on Users in the Address bar. Then the File list would show the subfolders and files inside the Users folder. To **navigate downward** in the hierarchy, double-click a subfolder in the File list. The path in the Address bar then shows the path to that subfolder.

- **Navigate upward and downward using the Navigation pane**
  You can also use the Navigation pane to navigate among folders. Move the mouse pointer over the Navigation pane, then click the small triangles or to the left of a folder name to show ▷ or hide ◢ the folder's contents under the folder name. Subfolders appear indented under the folders that contain them, showing that they are inside that folder. Figure B-2 shows a folder named Users in the Navigation pane. The subfolders Katharine, Public, and Your User Name are inside the Users folder.

FIGURE B-1: Sample folder and file hierarchy

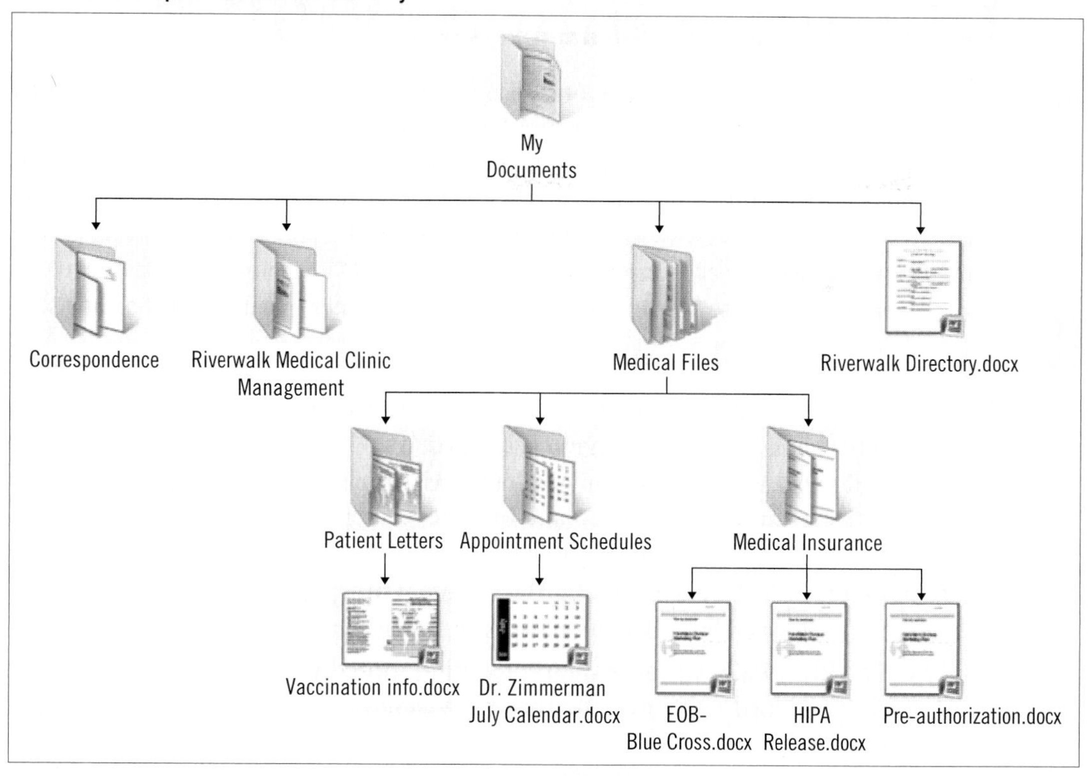

FIGURE B-2: Windows Explorer window

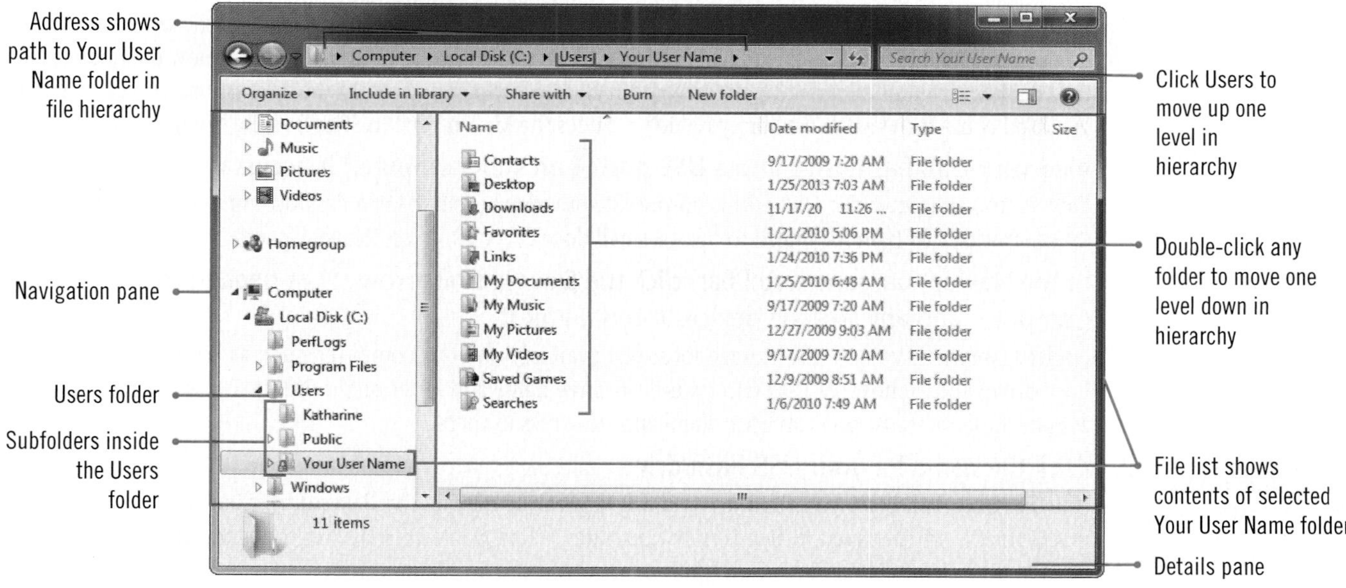

Plan your file organization

As you manage your files, you should plan how you want to organize them. First, identify the types of files with which you work, such as images, music, and reports. Think about the content, such as personal, business, clients, or projects. Then think of a folder organization that will help you find them later. For example, use subfolders in the My Pictures folder to separate family photos from business photos or to group them by year. In the My Documents folder, you might group personal files in one subfolder and business files in another subfolder. Then create additional subfolders to further separate sets of files. You can always move files among folders and rename folders. You should periodically reevaluate your folder structure to make sure that it continues to meet your needs.

UNIT B

Windows 7

Creating and Saving a File

After you start a program and create a new file, the file exists only in your computer's **random access memory (RAM)**, which is a temporary storage location. RAM only contains information when your computer is on. When you turn off your computer, it automatically clears the contents of RAM. So you need to save a new file onto a storage device that permanently stores the file so that you can open, change, and use it later. One important storage device is your computer's hard disk built into your computer. Another popular option is a **USB flash drive**, a small, portable storage device. Dr. Zimmerman asks you to use the WordPad accessory program to create a short summary of the doctor rotation planning meeting and save it.

STEPS

1. **Start Windows if necessary, click the Start button on the taskbar, point to All Programs, click Accessories, then click WordPad**

   The WordPad program opens. Near the top of the screen you see the Ribbon containing command buttons, similar to those you used in Paint in Unit A. The Home tab appears in front. A new, blank document appears in the document window. The blinking insertion point shows you where the next character you type will appear.

2. **Type Meeting Notes, October 11, then press [Enter]**

   WordPad inserts a new blank line and places the insertion point at the beginning of the next line.

> **TROUBLE**
> If you make a typing mistake, press [Backspace] to delete the character to the left of the insertion point.

3. **Type The Riverwalk winter planning meeting, press [Enter], type Zimmerman, press [Enter], type Nordgren, press [Enter], type Quinn, press [Enter], then type your name; see Figure B-3**

4. **Click the WordPad button on the upper-left side of the window below the title bar, then click Save on the WordPad menu**

   The first time you save a file using the Save button, the Save As dialog box opens. Use this dialog box to name the document file and choose a storage location for it. The Save As dialog box has many of the same elements as a Windows Explorer window, including an Address bar, a Navigation pane, and a File list. Below the Address bar, the **toolbar** contains command buttons you can click to perform actions. In the Address bar, you can see that WordPad chose the Documents library (which includes the My Documents folder) as the storage location.

> **TROUBLE**
> If you don't have a USB flash drive, save the document in the My Documents folder instead.

5. **Plug your USB flash drive into a USB port on your computer, if necessary**

   On a laptop computer, the USB port is on the side of your computer. On a desktop computer, the USB port is on the front panel (you may need to open a small door to see it), or on the back panel.

6. **In the Navigation pane scroll bar, click the Down scroll arrow as needed to see Computer and any storage devices listed under it**

   Under Computer, you see the storage locations available on your computer, such as Local Disk (C:) (your hard drive) and Removable Disk (H:) (your USB drive name and letter might differ). These storage locations act like folders because you can open them and store files in them.

7. **Click the name for your USB flash drive**

   The files and folders on your USB drive, if any, appear in the File list. The Address bar shows the location where the file will be saved, which is now Computer > Removable Disk (H:) (or the name of your drive). You need to give your document a meaningful name so you can find it later.

> **TROUBLE**
> If your Save As dialog box or title bar does not show the .rtf file extension, open any Windows Explorer window, click Organize on the toolbar, click Folder and search options, click the View tab, then under Files and Folders, click to remove the check mark from Hide extensions for known file types.

8. **Click in the File name text box to select the default name Document, type Doctor Rotation Meeting, compare your screen to Figure B-4, then click Save**

   The document is saved as a file on your USB flash drive. The filename Doctor Rotation Meeting.rtf appears in the title bar at the top of the window. The ".rtf" at the end of the filename is the file extension. A **file extension** is a three- or four-letter sequence, preceded by a period, that identifies the file as a particular type of document, in this case Rich Text Format, to your computer. The WordPad program creates files using the RTF format. Windows adds the .rtf file extension automatically after you click Save.

9. **Click the Close button on the WordPad window**

   The WordPad program closes. Your meeting minutes are now saved on your USB flash drive.

FIGURE B-3: Saving a document

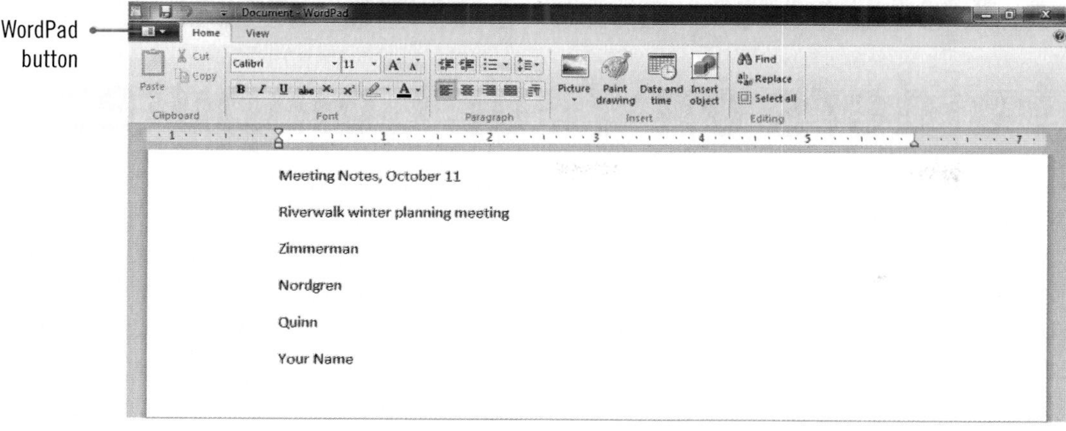

FIGURE B-4: Save As dialog box

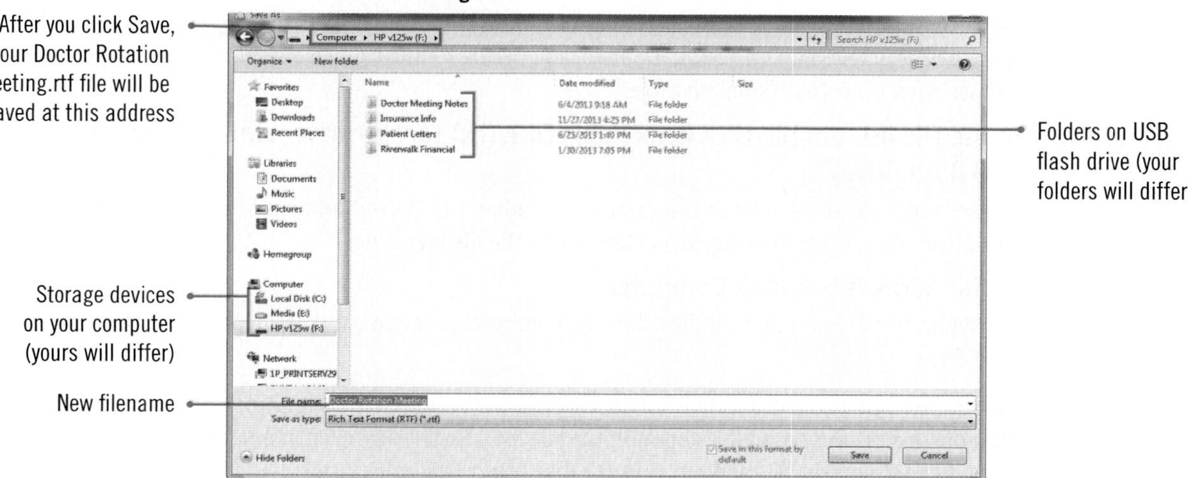

Using Windows 7 libraries

The Navigation pane contains not only files and folders, but also Libraries. A **library** gathers files and folders from different locations on your computer and displays them in one location. For example, you might have pictures in several different folders on your storage devices. You can add these folder locations to your Pictures library. Then when you want to see all your pictures, you open your Pictures library, instead of several different folders. The picture files stay in their original locations, but their names appear in the Pictures library. A library is not a folder that stores files, but rather a way of viewing similar types of documents that you have stored in multiple locations on your computer. Figure B-5 shows the four libraries that come with Windows 7: Documents, Music, Pictures, and Videos. To help you distinguish between library locations and actual folder locations, library names differ from actual folder names. For example, the My Documents folder is on your hard drive, but the library name is Documents. To add a location to a library, click the blue locations link (at the top of the File list) in the library you want to add to, click the Add button, navigate to the folder location you want to add, then click Include folder. If you delete a file or folder from a library, you delete them from their source locations. If you delete a library, you do not delete the files in it. The Documents Library that comes with Windows already has the My Documents folder listed as a save location. So if you save a document to the Documents library, it is automatically saved to your My Documents folder.

FIGURE B-5: Libraries

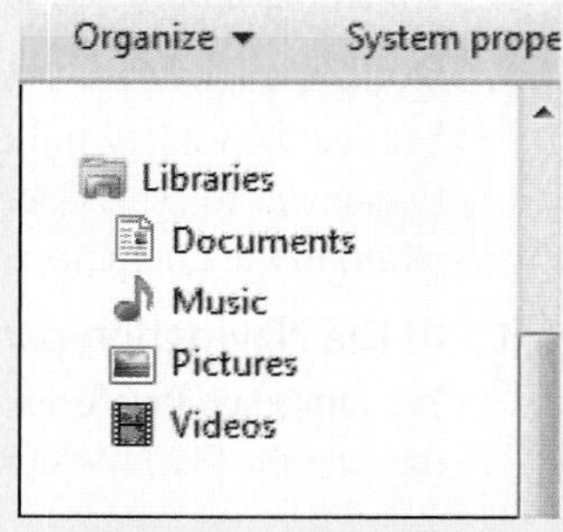

UNIT B
Windows 7

Exploring the Files and Folders on Your Computer

In the last lesson, you navigated to your USB flash drive as you worked in the Save As dialog box. But even if you're not saving a document, you will want to examine your computer and its existing folder and file structure. That way, you'll know where to save files as you work with Windows application programs. In a Windows Explorer window, you can navigate through your computer contents using the File list, the Address bar, and the Navigation pane. As you prepare for your job as an administrative assistant at the Riverwalk Medical Clinic, you look at the files and folders on your computer.

STEPS

TROUBLE
If you don't see the colored bar, click the More Options list arrow on the menu bar, then click Tiles.

TROUBLE
If you do not have a USB flash drive, click the Documents library in the Navigation pane instead.

QUICK TIP
Click the Back button, to the left of the Address bar, to return to the window you last viewed. In the Address bar, click ▸ to the right of a folder name to see a list of the subfolders. If the folder is open, its name appears in bold.

1. **Click the Start button on the taskbar, then click Computer**
   Your computer's storage devices appear in a window, as shown in Figure B-6, including hard drives; devices with removable storage, such as CD and DVD drives or USB flash drives; and portable devices such as personal digital assistants (PDAs). Table B-1 lists examples of different drive types. A colored bar shows you how much space has been taken up on your hard drive. You decide to move down a level in your computer's hierarchy and see what is on your USB flash drive.

2. **In the File list, double-click Removable Disk (H:) (or the drive name and letter for your USB flash drive)**
   You see the contents of your USB flash drive, including the Doctor Rotation Meeting.rtf file you saved in the last lesson. You decide to navigate one level up in the file hierarchy.

3. **In the Address bar, click Computer**
   You return to the Computer window showing your storage devices. You decide to look at the contents of your hard drive.

4. **In the Navigation pane, click Local Disk (C:)**
   The contents of your hard drive appear in the File list. The Users folder contains a subfolder for each user who has a user account on this computer. Recall that you double-click items in the File list to open them. In the Address bar and in the Navigation pane, you only need to single-click.

5. **In the File list, double-click the Users folder**
   You see folders for each user registered on your computer. You might see a folder with your user account name on it. Each user's folder contains that person's documents. User folder names are the log-in names that were entered when your computer was set up. When a user logs in, the computer allows that user access to the folder with the same user name. If you are using a computer with more than one user, you might not have permission to view other users' folders. There is also a Public folder that any user can open.

6. **Double-click the folder with your user name on it**
   Depending on how your computer is set up, this folder might be labeled with your name; however, if you are using a computer in a lab or a public location, your folder might be called Student or Computer User or something similar. You see a list of folders, such as My Documents, My Music, and others. See Figure B-7.

7. **Double-click My Documents**
   You see the folders and documents you can open and work with. In the Address bar, the path to the My Documents folder is Computer ▸ Local Disk (C:) ▸ Users ▸ Your User Name ▸ My Documents. You decide to return to the Computer window.

8. **In the Navigation pane, click Computer**
   You moved up four levels in your hierarchy. You can also move one level up at a time in your file hierarchy by pressing the [Backspace] key on your keyboard. You once again see your computer's storage devices.

FIGURE B-6: Computer window showing storage devices

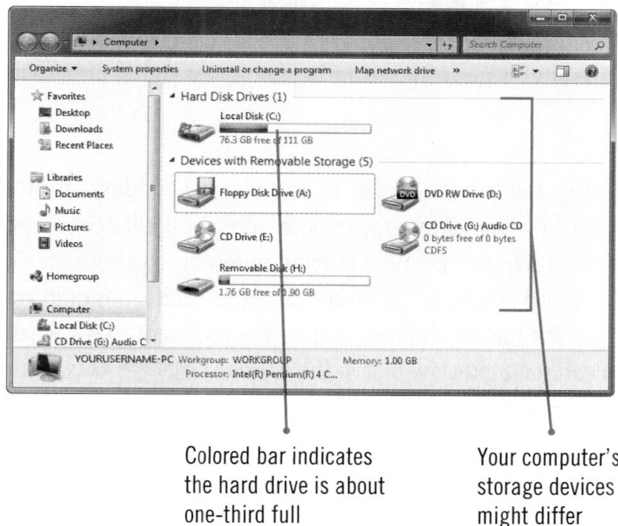

FIGURE B-7: Your User Name folder

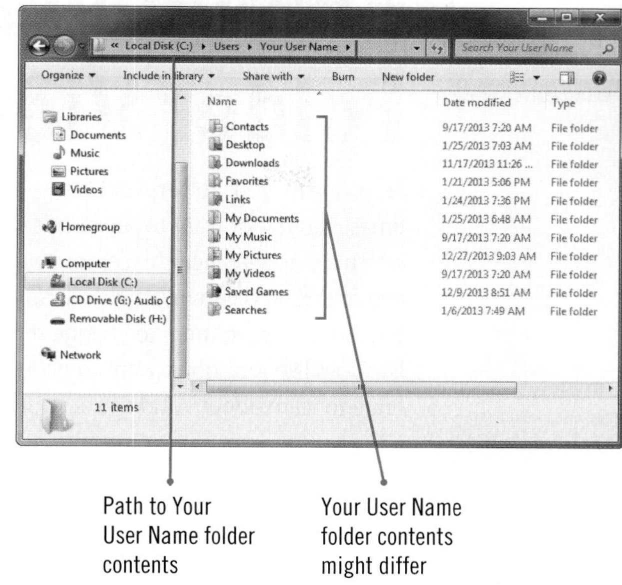

TABLE B-1: Drive names and icons

drive type	drive icon	drive name
hard drive		C:
CD drive		Next available drive letter, such as D:
DVD drive		Next available drive letter, such as E:
USB flash drive		Next available drive letter, such as F, G:, or H:

Sharing information with homegroups and libraries

Windows 7 lets you create a **homegroup**, a named set of computers that can share information. If your computer is in a homegroup with other Windows 7 computers, you can share libraries and printers with those computers. Click Start, then click Control Panel. Under Network and Internet, click Choose homegroup and sharing options. Click to place a check mark next to the libraries and printers you want to share, then click Save changes. To share libraries that you have created on your computer with others in your homegroup, click Start, click your user name, then in the Navigation pane, click the library you want to share, click Share with on the toolbar, then click the sharing option you want, as shown in Figure B-8.

FIGURE B-8: Sharing a library

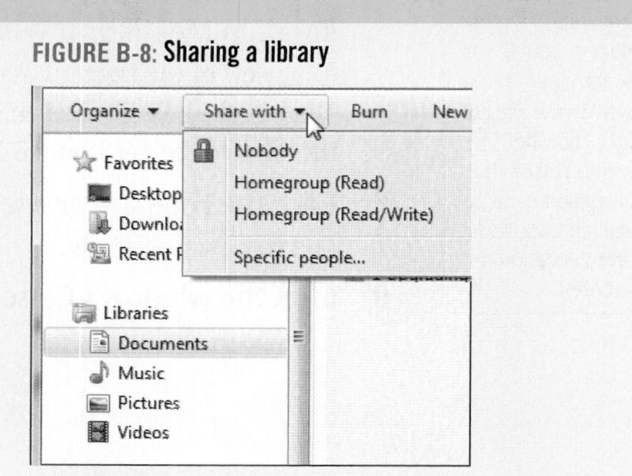

UNIT B

Windows 7

Changing File and Folder Views

As you view your folders and files, you might want to see as many items as possible in a window. At other times, you might want to see details about each item. Windows 7 lets you choose from eight different **views**, which are appearance choices for your folder contents. Each view provides different information about the files and folders in different ways. You can list your folders and files by using several different-sized icons or in lists. You can also **sort** them to change the order in which the folders and files are listed. If you want to see what a file looks like, but don't want to open the file, you can see a preview of it in the window. As you continue to learn about Windows 7, you review picture files in various views.

STEPS

1. **In the Navigation pane, under Libraries, click Pictures, then in the File list, double-click the Sample Pictures folder**

   You opened the Sample Pictures folder, which is inside your Pictures library.

2. **In the toolbar, click the Change your view More options list arrow**

   The list of available views appears in a shortcut menu. See Figure B-9.

3. **Click Large Icons**

   In this view, the pictures appear as large-sized icons in the File list, as shown in Figure B-10. For image files, this view is very helpful. You can click any view name or you can drag a slider control to move through each of the available views.

4. **Click the Change your view More options list arrow again, point to the slider, then drag it you select to Details**

   As you drag, Live Preview shows you how each view looks in your folder. In Details view, you can see filenames, the date that files were created or modified, and other information. In Details view, you can also control the order in which the folders and files appear. In the Name column heading, you see a small triangle Name. This indicates that the sample pictures are in alphabetical order (A, B, C,...).

5. **Click the Name column heading**

   The items now appear in descending (Z, Y, X,...) order. The icon in the column header changes to Name.

6. **Click the Show the preview pane button on the toolbar**

   The Preview pane opens on the right side of the screen. The **Preview pane** is an area on the right side of a window that shows you what a selected file looks like without opening it. It is especially useful for document files so you can see the first few paragraphs of a large document.

7. **Click the name of your USB flash drive in the Navigation pane, then click the Doctor Rotation Meeting.rtf filename in the File list**

   A preview of the Doctor Rotation Meeting file you created earlier in this unit appears in the Preview pane. The WordPad file is not open, but you can still see its contents. The Details pane gives you information about the selected file. See Figure B-11.

8. **Click the Hide the preview pane button**

   The Preview pane closes.

9. **Click the window's Close button**

QUICK TIP

You can also click the Change your view button (not its list arrow) repeatedly to cycle through five of the eight views.

QUICK TIP

Click a column heading a second time to reverse the order.

QUICK TIP

The Navigation pane also contains Favorites, which are links to folders you use frequently. To add a folder to your Favorites list, open the folder in the File list. Right-click the Favorites link in the Navigation pane, then left-click Add current location to Favorites.

FIGURE B-9: More options shortcut menu showing views

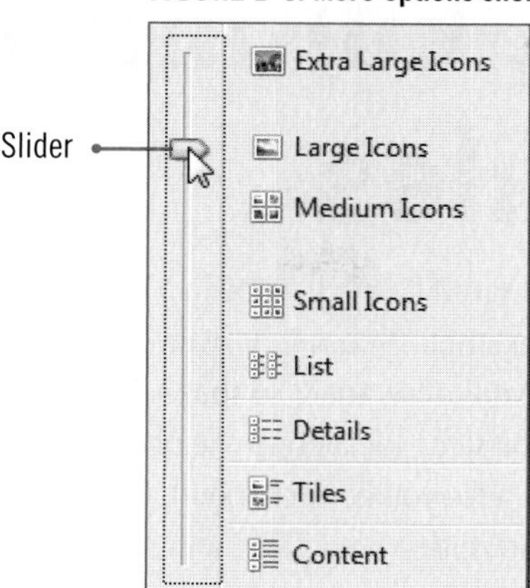

FIGURE B-10: Sample pictures library as large icons

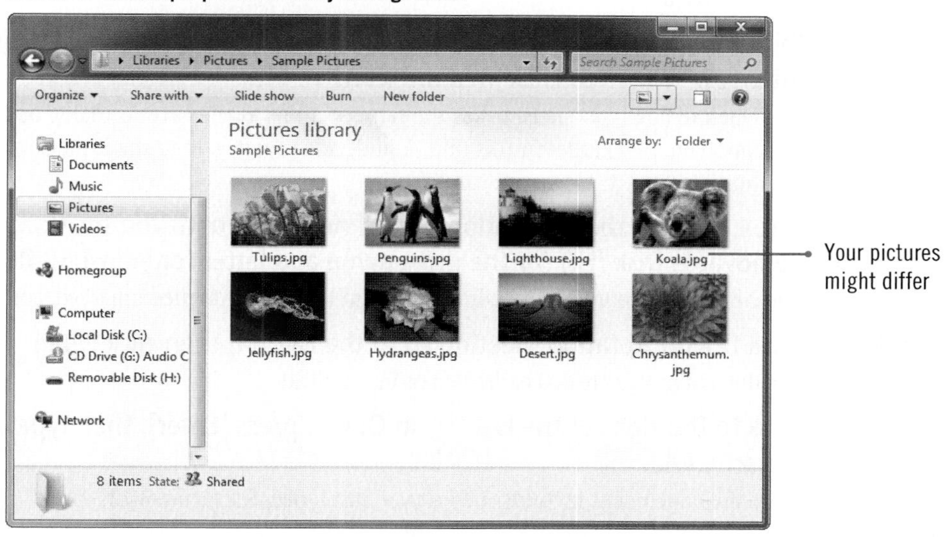

FIGURE B-11: Preview of selected Doctor Rotation Meeting.rtf file

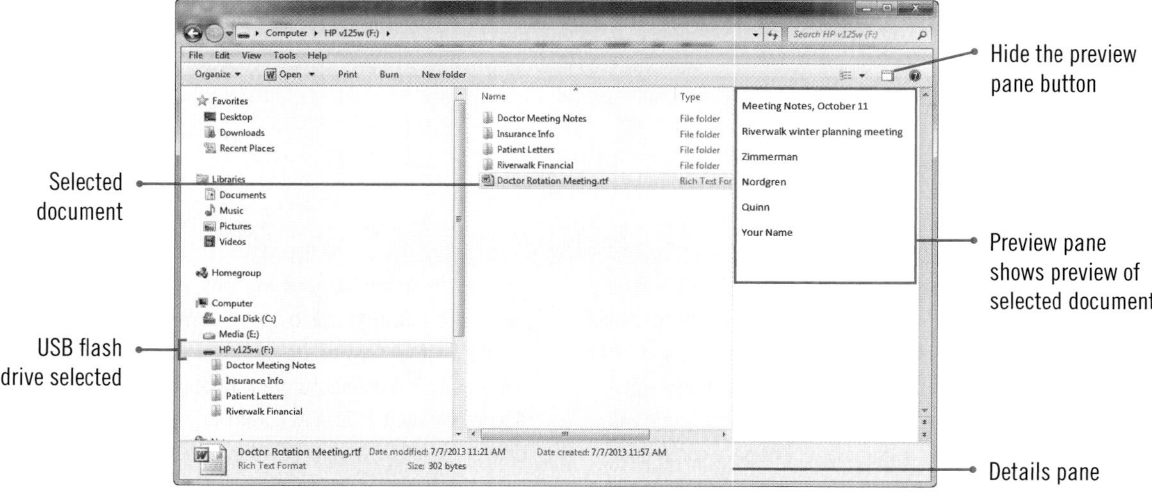

Opening, Editing, and Saving Files

Once you have created a file and saved it with a name in a folder on a storage device, you can easily open it and **edit** (make changes to) it. For example, you might want to add or delete text to a document, or change the color in a drawing. Then you save the file again so that it contains your latest changes. Usually you save a file with the same filename and in the same location as the original, which replaces the existing file with the latest, updated version. When you save a file you have changed, you use the Save command. Dr. Zimmerman asks you to complete the meeting notes.

STEPS

> **TROUBLE**
> If you are not using a USB flash drive, click an appropriate storage location in the Navigation pane.

> **QUICK TIP**
> You can also double-click the filename in the File list to open the file.

> **QUICK TIP**
> Instead of using the WordPad menu and Save command to save a document, you can also click the Save button on the Quick Access toolbar at the top of the WordPad window.

1. **Click the Start button on the taskbar, point to All Programs, click the Accessories folder, then click WordPad**
   If you use WordPad frequently, it's name might appear on the left side of the Start menu. If it does, you can click it there to open it.
2. **Click the WordPad button, click Open, click the Change your view More Options list arrow then click Medium Icons**
   The Open dialog box opens. It has the same sections as the Save As dialog box and the Windows Explorer windows you used earlier in this unit. You decide to navigate to the location where you saved your Doctor Rotation Meeting.rtf file so you can open it.
3. **Scroll down in the Navigation pane if necessary until you see Computer, then click Removable Disk (H:) (or the drive name and letter for your USB flash drive)**
   The contents of your USB flash drive appear in the File list as medium sized icons, as shown in Figure B-12.
4. **Click Doctor Rotation Meeting.rtf in the File list, then click Open**
   The document you created earlier opens in WordPad.
5. **Click to the right of the last "n" in Quinn, press [Enter], then type Tony Sanchez will print the schedule.**
   The edited document includes the text you just typed. See Figure B-13.
6. **Click the WordPad button, then click Save, as shown in Figure B-14**
   WordPad saves the document with your most recent changes, using the filename and location you specified when you saved it for the first time. When you save an existing file, the Save As dialog box does not open.
7. **Click, then click Exit**
   If you click Exit before saving any changes, you will get a message box asking if you want to save any changes to the document before exiting the program. WordPad closes and you see the Windows desktop.

Comparing Save and Save As

The WordPad menu has two save command options—Save and Save As. When you first save a file, the Save As dialog box opens (whether you choose Save or Save As). Here you can select the drive and folder where you want to save the file and enter its filename. If you edit a previously saved file, you can save the file to the same location with the same filename using the Save command. The Save command updates the stored file using the same location and filename without opening the Save As dialog box. In some situations, you might want to save another copy of the existing document using a different filename or in a different storage location. To do this, open the document, use the Save As command, and then navigate to a different location, and/or edit the name of the file.

FIGURE B-12: **Navigating in the Open dialog box**

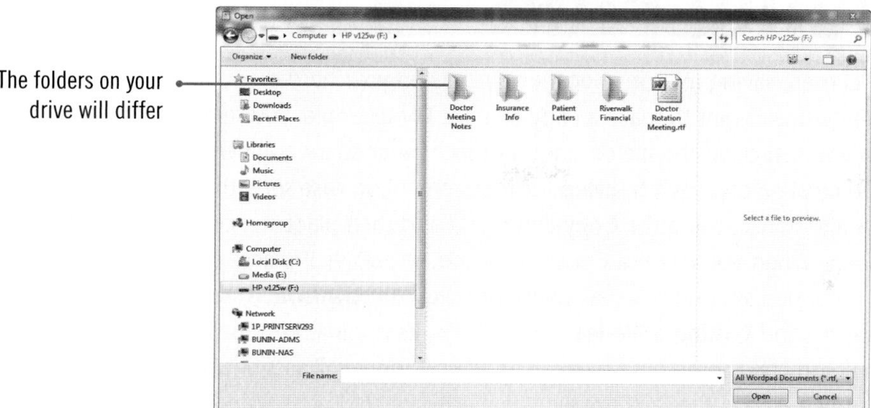

FIGURE B-13: **Edited document**

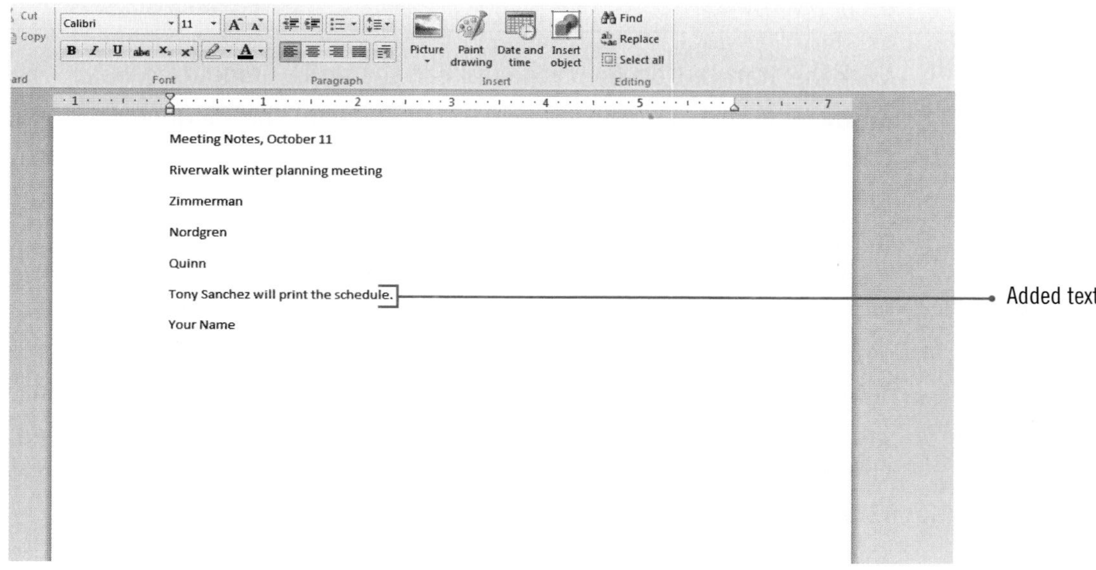

FIGURE B-14: **Saving a revised document**

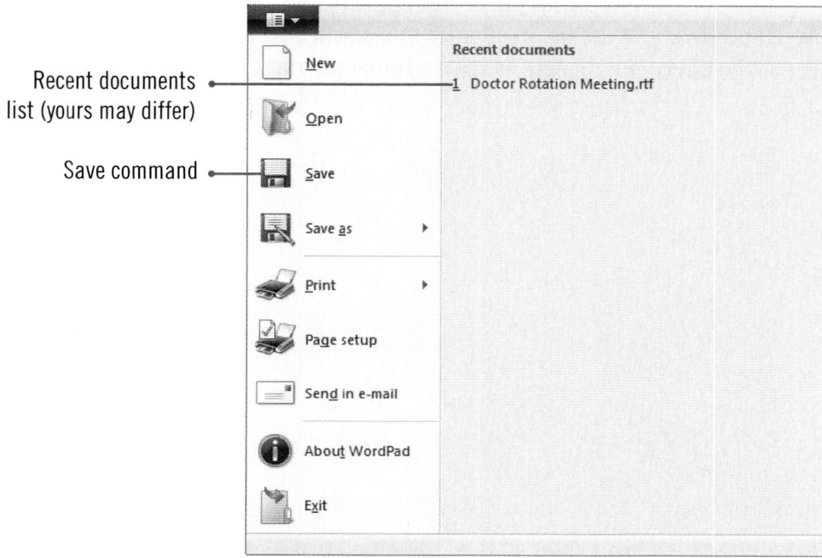

Copying Files

As you have learned, saving a file in a location such as on your hard drive, stores it so you can open it later. But sometimes you will want to make a copy of a file. For example, you might want to put a copy on a USB flash drive so you can open the file on another machine or share a file with a friend or colleague. Or you might want to create a copy as a **backup**, or replacement, in case something happens to your original file. You copy files and folders using the Copy command and then place the copy in another location using the Paste command. When you use the Copy command, Windows 7 places a duplicate copy of the file in an area of your computer's random access memory called the **clipboard**, ready to paste, or place, in a new location. Copying and pasting a file leaves the file in its original location. The copied file remains on the clipboard until you copy something else or end your Windows 7 session. You cannot have two copies of a file with the same name in the same folder. If you attempt to do this, Windows 7 will ask you if you want to replace the first one then gives you a chance to give the second copy a different name. Tony asks you to create a backup copy of the meeting notes document you created and paste it in a new folder you create on your USB flash drive.

STEPS

1. **Click the Start button on the taskbar, then click Computer**
2. **In the folder list, double-click Removable Disk (H:) (or the drive name and letter for your USB flash drive)**
   First you create the new folder.
3. **In the toolbar, click the New folder button**
   A new folder appears in the File list, with its name, New folder, selected inside a black rectangle. Because the folder name is selected, any text you type replaces the selected text as the folder name.
4. **Type Schedule Notes, as shown in Figure B-15, then press [Enter]**
   You named the new folder Schedule Notes. Next, you copy your original Doctor Rotation Meeting.rtf file.
5. **In the File list, click the Doctor Rotation Meeting.rtf document you saved earlier, click the Organize button on the toolbar, then click Copy**
6. **In the File list, double-click the Schedule Notes folder**
   The folder opens. As of now, there are no files or folders in this folder.
7. **Click the Organize button on the toolbar, then click Paste**
   A copy of your Doctor Rotation Meeting.rtf file is pasted into your new Schedule Notes folder. See Figure B-16. You now have two copies of the Doctor Rotation Meeting.rtf file: one on your USB flash drive in the main folder, and a copy of the file in a folder called Schedule Notes on your USB flash drive. The file remains on the clipboard so you can paste it again to other locations if you like.

QUICK TIP
You can also copy a file by right-clicking the file in the File list and then clicking Copy. To use the keyboard, press and hold [Ctrl] and press [C], then release both keys.

QUICK TIP
To paste using the keyboard, press and hold [Ctrl] and press [V], then release both keys.

FIGURE B-15: Creating a folder

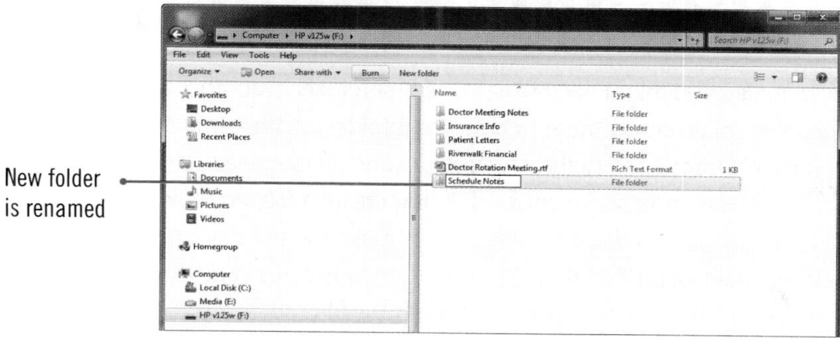

FIGURE B-16: Duplicate file pasted into Schedule Notes folder

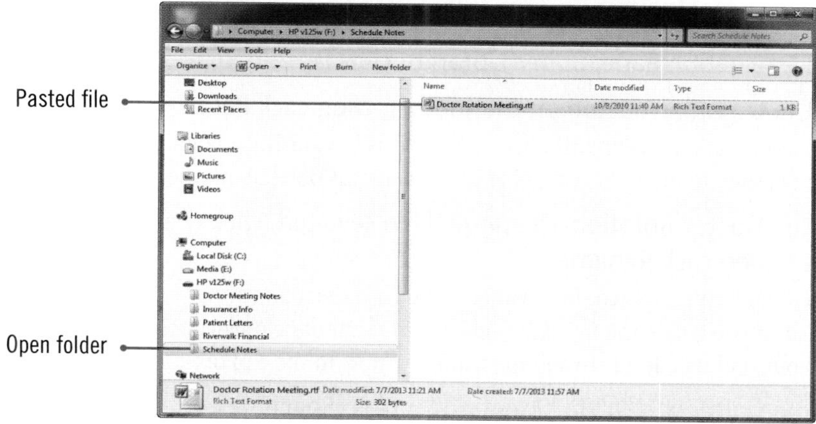

Copying files using Send to

You can also copy and paste a file to an external storage device using the Send to command. In a window, right-click the file you want to copy, point to Send to, then in the shortcut menu, click the name of the device where you want to send a copy of the file. This leaves the original file on your hard drive and creates a copy on the external device, all with just one command. See Table B-2 for a short summary of other shortcut menu commands.

TABLE B-2: Selected Send to menu commands

menu option	use to	menu option	use to
Compressed (zipped) folder	Create a new compressed (smaller) file with a .zip file extension	**Documents**	Copy the file to the Documents library
Desktop (create shortcut)	Create a shortcut (link) for the file on the desktop	**DVD RW Drive (D:)**	Copy the file to your computer's DVD drive
Mail recipient	Create an e-mail with the file attached to it (only if you have an e-mail program on your computer)	**Removable Disk (H:)**	Copy the file to your removable disk (H:) (*Note:* Drive letter will differ for each computer.)

UNIT B
Windows 7

Moving and Renaming Files

As you work with files, you might need to move files or folders to another location. You can move one or more files or folders. You might move them to a different folder on the same drive or a different drive. When you **move** a file, the file is transferred to the new location and no longer exists in its original location. You can move a file using the Cut and Paste commands. After you create a file, you might find that the original name you gave the file isn't adequate so you can rename it to make it more descriptive or accurate. You decide to move your original Doctor Rotation Meeting.rtf document to your Documents library. After you move it, you decide to edit the filename so it better describes the file contents.

STEPS

QUICK TIP
You can also cut a file by right-clicking the file in the File list and then clicking Cut. To use the keyboard, press and hold [Ctrl] and press [X], then release both keys.

QUICK TIP
You can also paste a file by right-clicking an empty area in the File list and then clicking Paste. To use the keyboard, press and hold [Ctrl] and press [V], then release both keys.

1. **In the Address bar, click Removable Disk (H:) (or the drive name and letter for your USB flash drive)**
2. **Click the Doctor Rotation Meeting.rtf document to select it**
3. **Click the Organize button on the toolbar, then click Cut**

   The icon representing the cut file becomes lighter in color, indicating you have cut it, as shown in Figure B-17. You navigate to your Documents library, in preparation for pasting the cut document there.
4. **In the Navigation Pane, under Libraries, click Documents**
5. **Click the Organize button on the toolbar, then click Paste**

   The Doctor Rotation Meeting.rtf document appears in your Documents library. See Figure B-18. The filename could be clearer, to help you remember that it contains notes about the winter from your meeting.
6. **With the Doctor Rotation Meeting.rtf file selected, click the Organize button on the toolbar, then click Rename**

   The filename is highlighted. In a window, the file extension cannot change because it identifies the file to WordPad. If you delete the file extension, the file cannot be opened. You could type a new name to replace the old one, but you decide to add the word "Winter" to the end of the filename instead.
7. **Click the I after the "g" in "Meeting", press [Spacebar], then type -Winter, as shown in Figure B-19, then press [Enter]**

   You changed the name of the document copy in the Documents library. The filename now reads Doctor Rotation Meeting -Winter.rtf.
8. **Close the Documents library window**

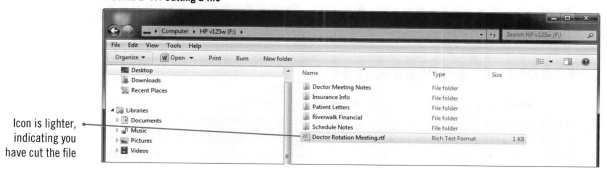

FIGURE B-17: **Cutting a file**

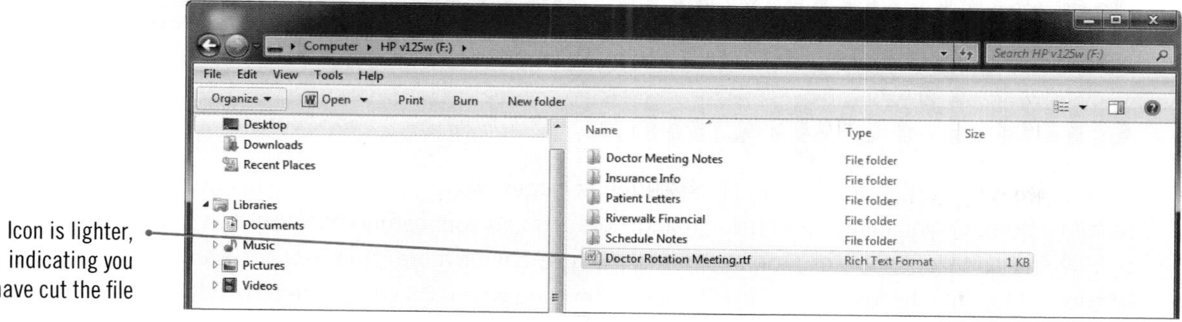

FIGURE B-18: **Pasted file in Documents library**

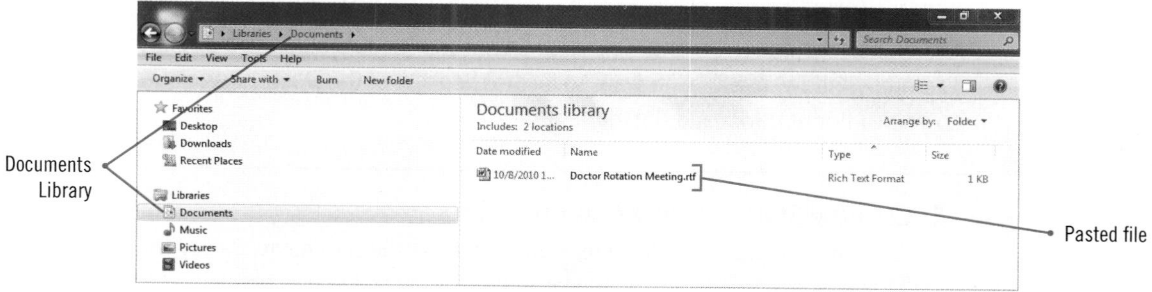

FIGURE B-19: **Renaming a file**

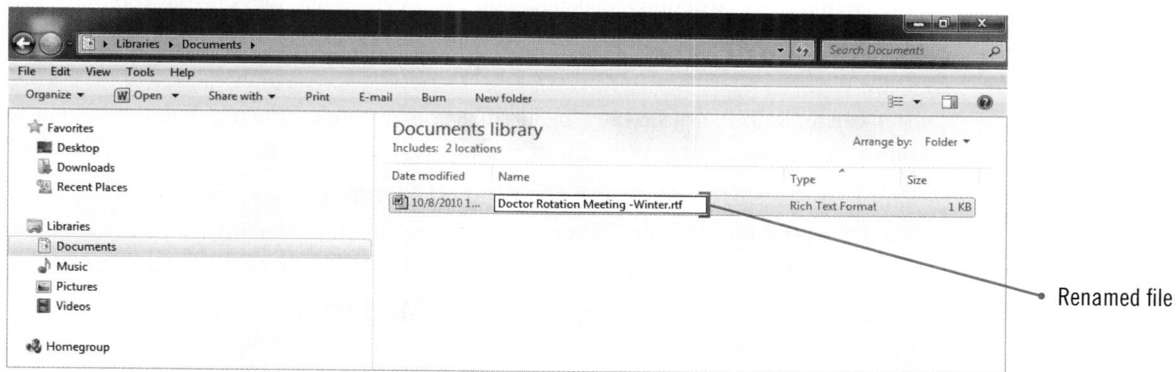

Using drag and drop to copy or move files to new locations

You can also use the mouse to copy a file and place the copy in a new location. **Drag and drop** is a technique in which you use your pointing device to drag a file or folder into a different folder and then drop it, or let go of the mouse button, to place it in that folder. Using drag and drop does not copy your file to the clipboard. If you drag and drop a file to a folder on another drive, Windows *copies* the file. See Figure B-20. However, if you drag and drop a file to a folder on the same drive, Windows 7 *moves* the file into that folder instead. If you want to move a file to another drive, hold down [Shift] while you drag and drop. If you want to copy a file to another folder on the same drive, hold down [Ctrl] while you drag and drop.

FIGURE B-20: **Copying a file using drag and drop**

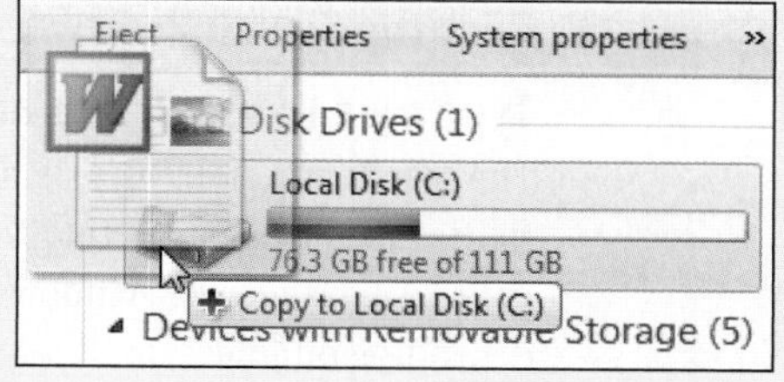

UNIT B Windows 7

Searching for Files, Folders, and Programs

After copying or moving folders and files, you might forget where you stored a particular folder or file, its name, or both. Or you might need help finding a program on your computer. **Windows Search** helps you quickly find any file, folder, or program. You must type one or more letter sequences or words that help Windows 7 identify the item you want. The search text you type is called your **search criteria**. Your search criteria can be a filename, part of a filename, or any other characters you choose. Windows 7 will find files with that information in its name or with that information inside the file. For example, if you type "word," Windows 7 will find the program Microsoft Word, any documents with "word" in its title, or any document with "word" inside the file. To search your entire computer, including its attached drives, you can use the Search box on the Start menu. To search within a particular folder, you can use the Search box in a Windows Explorer window. You want to locate the copy of the Doctor Rotation Meeting -Winter.rtf document so you can print it for each doctor.

STEPS

1. **Click the Start button on the taskbar**

   The Search programs and files box at the bottom of the Start menu already contains the insertion point, ready for you to type search criteria. You begin your search by typing a part of a word that is in the filename.

2. **Type me**

   Even before you finish typing the word "meeting", the Start menu lists all programs, files, and Control Panel items that have the letters "me" in their title or somewhere inside the file or the file properties. See Figure B-21. Your search results will differ, depending on the programs and files on your computer. **File properties** are details that Windows stores about a file. Windows arranges the search results into categories.

3. **Type e**

   The search results narrow to only the files that contain "mee". The search results become more specific every time you add more text to your criteria finding the two versions of your meeting notes file. See Figure B-22.

4. **Point to the Doctor Rotation Meeting.rtf filename under Files**

   The ScreenTip shows the file location. This Doctor Rotation Meeting.rtf file is on the USB flash drive. The filenames are links to the document. You only need to single-click a file to open it.

5. **Under Documents, click Doctor Rotation Meeting -Winter.rtf**

   The file opens in WordPad.

6. **Click the Close button in the program window's title bar**

   You can search in a folder or on a drive using the search box in any Windows Explorer window.

7. **Click , click Computer, in the Navigation pane click Removable Disk (H:) (or the drive name and letter for your USB flash drive)**

8. **Click the Search Removable Disk (H:) text box, to the right of the Address bar**

9. **Type mee to list all files and folders on your USB flash drive that contain "mee"**

   The search criterion, mee, is highlighted in the filenames. The results as shown in Figure B-23 include the folder called Doctor Meeting Notes and the file named Doctor Rotation Meeting.rtf. Because you navigated to your USB flash drive, Windows only lists the document version that is on that drive. Your results may differ depending on folders and files on your USB drive.

10. **Double-click Doctor Rotation Meeting.rtf in the File list to open the document file in WordPad, view the file, close WordPad, then close the Windows Explorer window**

QUICK TIP

Search text is not case sensitive. Typing lowercase "mee", you will still find items that start with "Mee" or "mee".

TROUBLE

Your file might open in another program on your computer that reads RTF files. You can continue with the lesson.

TROUBLE

If you do not have a USB flash drive, click another storage location in the Navigation pane.

FIGURE B-21: Searching on criterion "me"

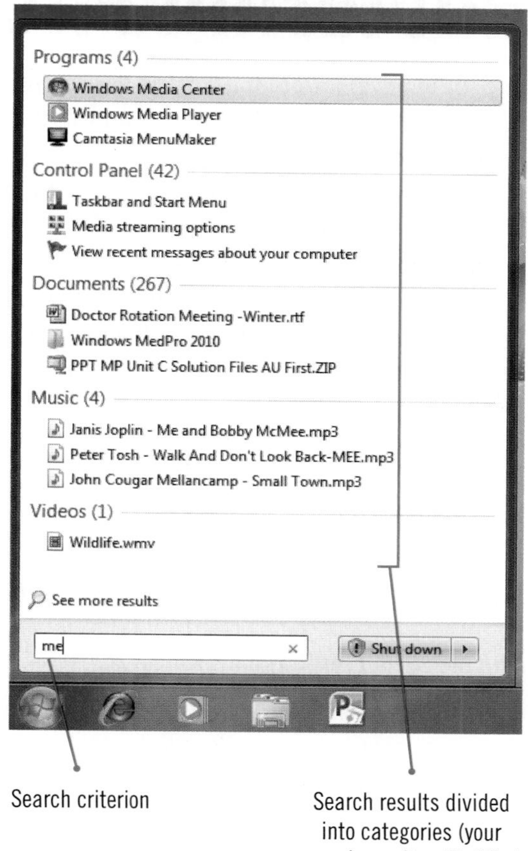

FIGURE B-22: Searching on criterion "mee"

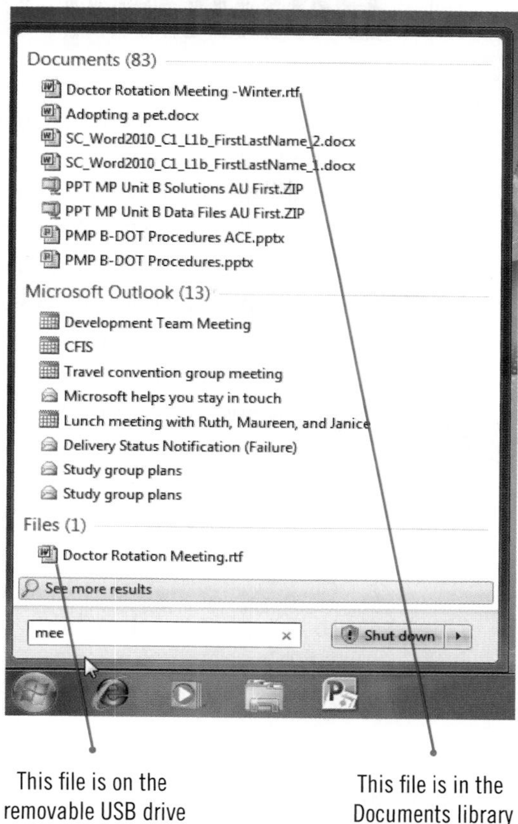

FIGURE B-23: Searching using the Search Computer text box in folder window

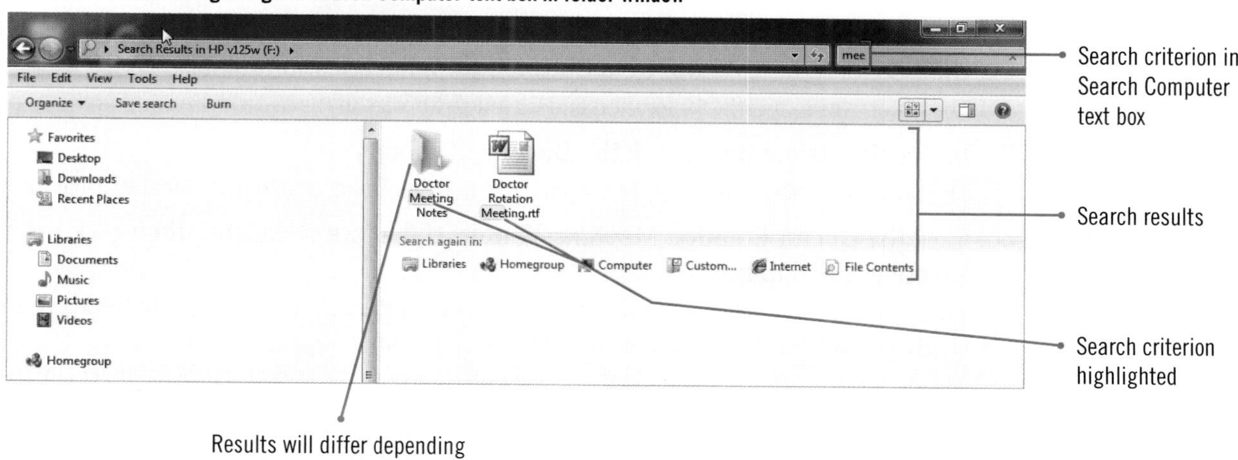

Performing more advanced searches

To locate all files that have the same file extension (such as .rtf), type the file extension as your search criterion. If you want to locate files created by a certain person, use the first name, last name, or first and last name as your search criteria. If you want to locate files created on a certain date, type the date (for example, 12/12/2012) as your search criterion. If you remember the title in a document, type the title as your search criterion. If you have created e-mail contacts in your Contacts folder, you can type the person's name to find his or her e-mail address.

UNIT B

Windows 7

Deleting and Restoring Files

If you no longer need a folder or file, you can delete (or remove) it from the storage device. By regularly deleting files and folders you no longer need and emptying the Recycle Bin, you free up valuable storage space on your computer. This also keeps your computer uncluttered. Windows 7 places folders and files you delete from your hard drive in the Recycle Bin. If you delete a folder, Windows 7 removes the folder as well as all files and subfolders stored in it. If you later discover that you need a deleted file or folder, you can restore it to its original location, but only if you have not yet emptied the Recycle Bin. Emptying the Recycle Bin permanently removes the deleted folders and files from your computer. However, files and folders you delete from a removable drive, such as a USB flash drive, do not go to the Recycle Bin. They are immediately and permanently deleted and cannot be restored. You delete the Doctor Rotation Meeting-Winter.rtf copy saved in the Documents library and then restore it.

STEPS

1. **Click the Start button on the taskbar, then click Documents**

   Your Documents library opens.

2. **Click Doctor Rotation Meeting -Winter.rtf to select it, click the Organize button on the toolbar, then click Delete**

   The Delete File dialog box opens so you can confirm the deletion, as shown in Figure B-24.

3. **Click Yes**

   You deleted the file from the Documents library. Windows moved it into the Recycle Bin.

4. **Click the Minimize button on the window's title bar and examine the Recycle Bin icon**

   The Recycle Bin icon appears to contain crumpled paper. This tells you that the Recycle Bin contains deleted folders and files.

5. **Double-click the Recycle Bin icon on the desktop**

   The Recycle Bin window opens and displays any previously deleted folders and files, including the Doctor Rotation Meeting -Winter.rtf file.

6. **Click the Doctor Rotation Meeting -Winter.rtf file to select it, as shown in Figure B-25, then click the Restore this item button on the Recycle Bin toolbar**

   The file returns to its original location and no longer appears in the Recycle Bin window.

7. **In the Navigation pane, click the Documents library**

   The Documents library window contains the restored file. You decide to permanently delete this file.

8. **Click the Doctor Rotation Meeting -Winter.rtf file, press [Delete], then click Yes in the Delete File dialog box**

   The Doctor Rotation Meeting-Winter.rtf file moves from the Documents library to the Recycle Bin. You decide to permanently delete all documents in the Recycle Bin.

   NOTE: If you are using a computer that belongs to someone else, or that is in a computer lab, make sure you have permission to empty the Recycle Bin before proceeding with the next step.

9. **Minimize the window to display the Windows desktop, double-click the Recycle Bin icon, click the Empty the Recycle Bin button on the toolbar, click Yes in the dialog box, then close all open windows**

QUICK TIP

If the Recycle Bin icon does not contain crumpled paper, then it is empty.

QUICK TIP

To delete a file completely in one action, click the file to select it, press and hold [Shift], then press [Delete]. A message will ask if you want to permanently delete the file. If you click Yes, Windows deletes the file without sending it to the Recycle Bin. Use caution, however, because you cannot restore the file.

FIGURE B-24: Delete File dialog box

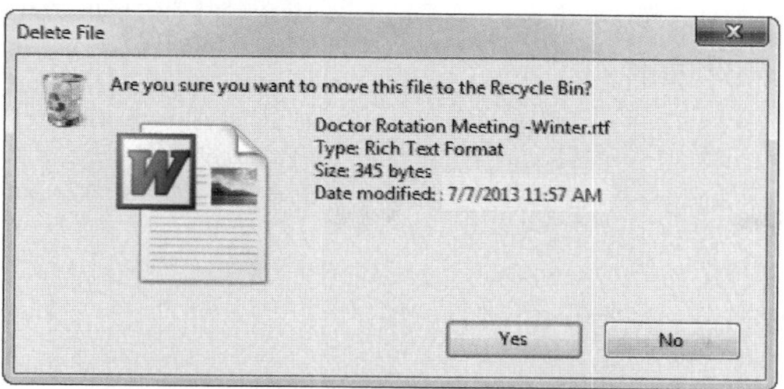

FIGURE B-25: Restoring a file from the Recycle Bin

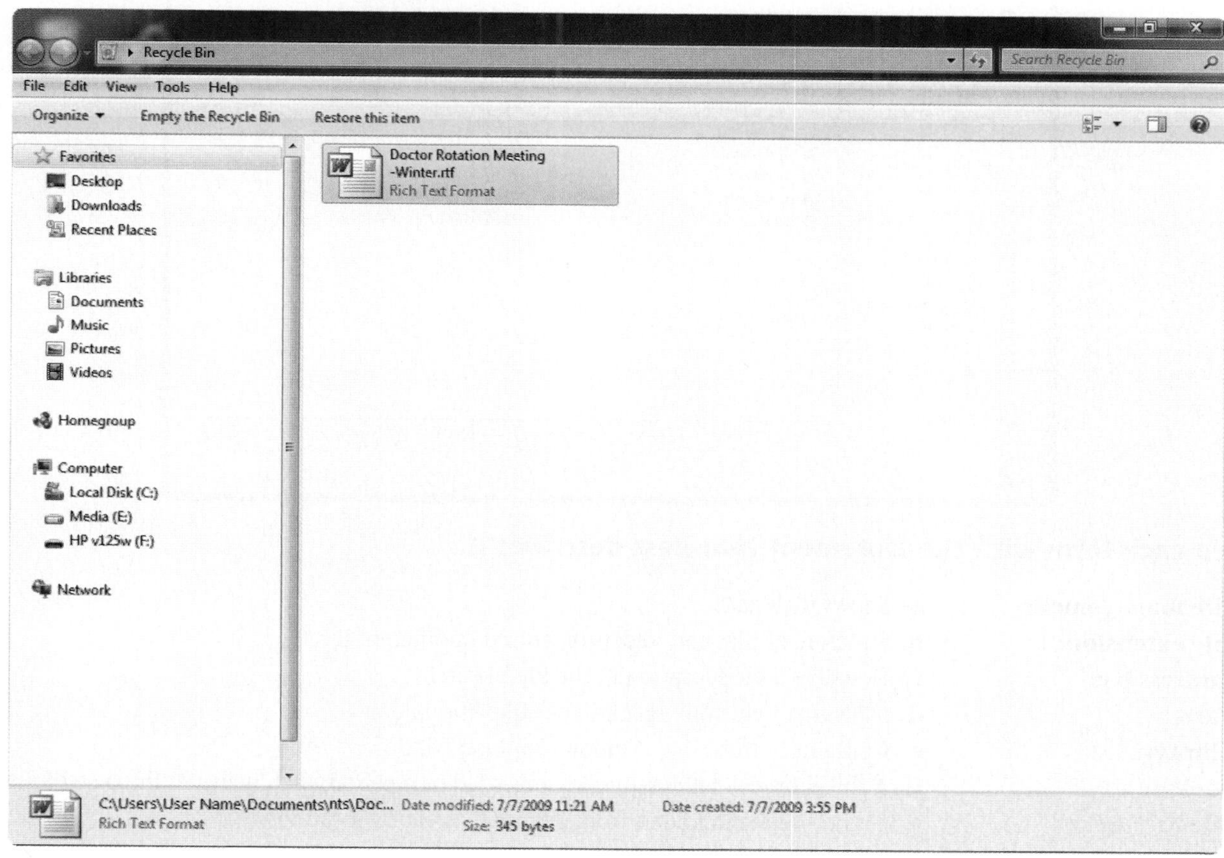

Selecting more than one file

You might want to select a group of files or folders in order to cut, copy, or delete them all at once. To select a group of items that are next to each other in a window, click the first item in the group, press and hold [Shift], then click the last item in the group. Both items you click and all the items between them become selected.

To select files that are not next to each other, click the first file, press and hold [Ctrl], then click the other items you want to select as a group. Then you can copy, cut, or delete the group of files or folders you selected.

Practice

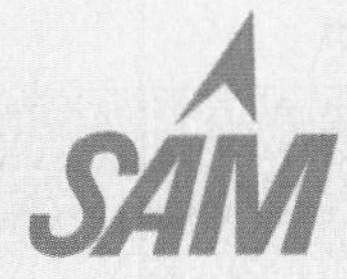

For current SAM information, including versions and content details, visit SAM Central (http://www.cengage.com/samcentral). If you have a SAM user profile, you may have access to hands-on instruction, practice, and assessment of the skills covered in this unit. Since various versions of SAM are supported throughout the life of this text, check with your instructor for the correct instructions and URL/Web site for accessing assignments.

Concepts Review

Label the elements of the Windows 7 window shown in Figure B-26.

FIGURE B-26

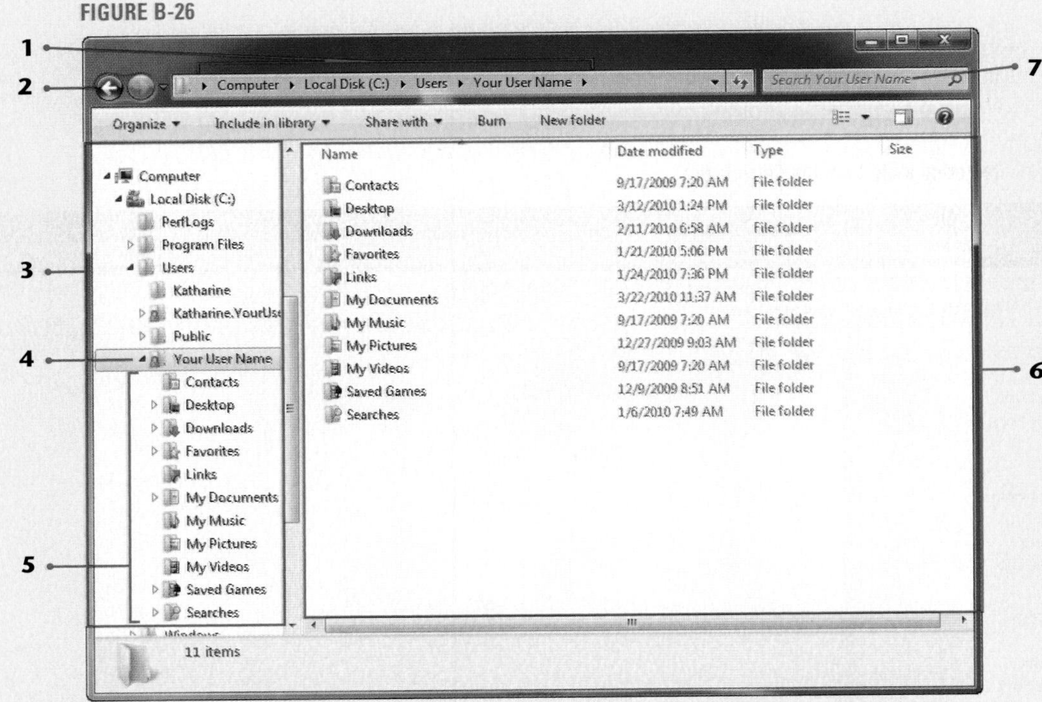

Match each term with the statement that best describes it.

8. File management
9. File extension
10. Address bar
11. Path
12. Library
13. Toolbar
14. File hierarchy

a. Shows file's path
b. Structure of files and folders organized in different levels
c. Describes a file's location in the file hierarchy
d. Skills that help you organize your files and folders
e. Contains buttons in a Windows Explorer window
f. A three- or four-letter sequence, preceded by a period, that identifies the type of file
g. Gathers files and folders from different computer locations

Select the best answer from the list of choices.

15. The way your files appear in the Details pane is determined by the:
a. Path.
b. View.
c. Subfolder.
d. Criterion.

16. When you move a file:
a. It remains in its original location.
b. It is no longer in its original location.
c. It is copied to another location.
d. It is no longer in your file hierarchy.

17. The text you type in the Search programs and files box on the Start menu is called:
a. Search criteria.
b. RAM.
c. Sorting.
d. Clipboard.

18. Which of the following is not a window section?

a. Address bar
b. File list
c. Navigation pane
d. Clipboard

19. Which part of a window lets you see a file's contents without opening the file?

a. File list
b. Preview pane
c. Navigation pane
d. Address bar

20. In a file hierarchy, a folder inside another folder is called a(n):

a. Subfolder.
b. Internal hard disk.
c. Clipboard.
d. Path.

21. After you delete a file from your hard disk, it is automatically placed in the:

a. USB flash drive.
b. Clipboard.
c. Recycle bin.
d. Search box.

22. When you copy a file, it is automatically placed on the:

a. Preview pane.
b. My Documents folder.
c. Hierarchy.
d. Clipboard.

Skills Review

1. Understand folders and files.

a. Assume that you sell books as a home business. How would you organize your folders and files using a file hierarchy? How would you use folders and subfolders? Draw a diagram and write a short paragraph explaining your answer.

2. Create and save a file.

a. Connect your USB flash drive to a USB port on your computer, then open WordPad from the All Programs menu.
b. Type **Marketing Plan: Holistic Healing** as the title, then start a new line.
c. Type your name, then press [Enter] twice.
d. Create the following list:

Brochures
Direct e-mail
Web ads
Travel conventions

e. Save the WordPad file with the filename **Holistic Healing Marketing Plan.rtf** on your USB flash drive.
f. View the filename in the WordPad title bar, then close WordPad.

3. Explore the files and folders on your computer.

a. Open a Windows Explorer window that shows the contents of your computer.
b. Navigate to your USB flash drive using the method of your choice. (If you do not have a USB flash drive, navigate to your Documents library using the Navigation pane.)
c. Use the Address bar to navigate to Computer again.
d. Use the Navigation pane to navigate to your hard drive.
e. Use the File list to open the Users folder, and then open the folder that represents your user name.
f. Open the My Documents folder. (*Hint*: The path is Local Disk (C:) ▸ Users ▸ [Your User Name] ▸ My Documents.)
g. Use the Navigation pane to navigate back to your computer contents.

4. Change file and folder views.

a. Navigate to your USB flash drive using the method of your choice.
b. View its contents as large icons.
c. Use the View slider to view the drive contents in all the other seven views.
d. Use the Change your view button to cycle through the five available views.
e. Open the Preview pane, then click a file and view its preview. Repeat with two more files.
f. Close the Preview pane.

Skills Review (continued)

5. **Open, edit, and save files.**
   a. Open WordPad.
   b. Use the Open dialog box to open the Holistic Healing Marketing Plan.rtf document you created.
   c. After the text "Travel conventions," add a line with the text **Sustainable Farming**.
   d. Save the document and close WordPad.
6. **Copy files.**
   a. In the Windows Explorer window, navigate to your USB flash drive if necessary.
   b. Copy the Holistic Healing Marketing Plan.rtf document.
   c. Create a new folder named **Marketing** on your USB flash drive, then open the folder. (If you don't have a USB flash drive, create the folder in your Documents library.)
   d. Paste the document copy in the new folder.
7. **Move and rename files.**
   a. Navigate to your USB flash drive.
   b. Select the original Holistic Healing Marketing Plan.rtf document, then cut it.
   c. Navigate to your Documents library and paste the file there.
   d. Rename the file **Holistic Healing Marketing Plan - Backup.rtf**.
8. **Search for files, folders, and programs.**
   a. Use the Search programs and files box on the Start menu to enter the search criterion **ma**.
   b. Change your search criterion so it reads **mar**.
   c. Open the backup copy of your Holistic Healing Marketing Plan document from the Start menu, then close WordPad.
   d. In Windows Explorer, navigate to your Documents library, then use the criterion **mar** in the Search Documents box.
   e. Open the backup copy of the Holistic Healing Marketing Plan document from the File list, then close WordPad.
9. **Delete and restore files.**
   a. Navigate to your Documents library if necessary.
   b. Delete the Holistic Healing Marketing Plan - Backup.rtf file.
   c. Open the Recycle Bin, and restore the document to its original location, navigate to your Documents library, then move the Holistic Healing Marketing Plan - Backup file to your USB flash drive.

Independent Challenge 1

To meet the needs of people requiring home health care in your town, you have opened a high quality, affordable, home health-care business named WeCare. Clients hire you to come to their homes and do basic housekeeping, medicine management, shopping, and cooking in their own homes. To promote your new business, you want to develop a newspaper ad and a flyer.

a. Connect your USB flash drive to your computer, if necessary.
b. Create a new folder named **WeCare** on your USB flash drive.
c. In the WeCare folder, create two subfolders named **Advertising** and **Flyers**.
d. Use WordPad to create a short ad for your local newspaper that describes your business:
   - Use the name of the business as the title for your document.
   - Write a short paragraph about the business. Include a fictitious location, street address, and phone number.
   - After the paragraph, type your name.
e. Save the document with the filename **Newspaper Ad** in the Advertising folder, then close the document and exit WordPad.
f. Open a Windows Explorer window, and navigate to the Advertising folder.
g. View the contents in at least three different views, then choose the view option that you prefer.
h. Copy the Newspaper Ad.rtf file, then paste a copy in the Flyers folder.
i. Rename the copy **Newspaper Ad-Backup.rtf**, then close the folder.

Independent Challenge 2

As a freelance editor for several national publishers of medical journals, you depend on your computer to meet critical deadlines. Whenever you encounter a computer problem, you contact a computer consultant who helps you resolve the problem. This consultant asked you to document, or keep records of, your computer's current settings.

a. Connect your USB flash drive to your computer, if necessary.
b. Open the Computer window so that you can view information on your drives and other installed hardware.
c. View the window contents using three different views, then choose the one you prefer.
d. Open WordPad and create a document with the title **My Hardware Documentation** and your name on separate lines.
e. List the names of the hard drive (or drives), devices with removable storage, and any other hardware devices, installed on the computer you are using. Also include the total size and amount of free space on your hard drive(s) and removable storage drive(s). (*Hint*: If you need to check the Computer window for this information, use the taskbar button for the Computer window to view your drives, then use the WordPad taskbar button to return to WordPad.)

Advanced Challenge Exercise

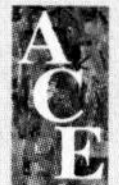

- Navigate your computer's file hierarchy, and determine its various levels.
- On paper, draw a diagram showing your file hierarchy, starting with Computer at the top, and going down at least four levels if available.

f. Save the WordPad document with the filename **My Hardware Documentation** on your USB flash drive.
g. Preview your document, print your WordPad document, then close WordPad.

Independent Challenge 3

You are a physician's assistant at Binghamton Medical, a medical practice that includes seven full-time physicians and three allied health care professionals. You participate in their outreach program by speaking at career days in area high schools. You teach students about career opportunities available in the field of medicine. You want to create a folder structure on your USB flash drive to store the files for each session.

a. Connect your USB flash drive to your computer, then open the window for your USB flash drive.
b. Create a folder named **Career Days**.
c. In the Career Days folder, create a subfolder named **Binghamton High**.

Advanced Challenge Exercise

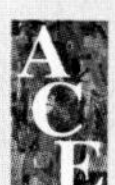

- In the Binghamton High folder, create subfolders named **Class Outline** and **Visual Aids**.
- Rename the Visual Aids folder **Class Handouts**.
- Create a new folder named **Interactive Presentations** in the Class Handouts subfolder.

d. Close the Binghamton High window.
e. Use WordPad to create a document with the title **Career Areas** and your name on separate lines, and the following list of items:
Current Opportunities:
Medical Doctor
Physician's Assistant
Research Scientist
Nurse
Radiology Technician
f. Save the WordPad document with the filename **Careers Listing.rtf** in the Binghamton High folder. (*Hint:* After you switch to your USB flash drive in the Save As dialog box, open the Career Days folder, then open the Binghamton High folder before saving the file.)
g. Close WordPad.

Independent Challenge 3 (continued)

- **h.** Open WordPad and the Careers Listing document again, then add **Hospital Administrator** to the bottom of the list, then save the file and close WordPad.
- **i.** Using pencil and paper, draw a diagram of your new folder structure.
- **j.** Use the Start menu to search your computer using the search criterion **car**. Locate the Careers Listing.rtf document in the list, and use the link to open the file.
- **k.** Close the file.

Real Life Independent Challenge

Think of a hobby or volunteer activity that you do now, or one that you would like to do. You will use your computer to help you manage your plans or ideas for this activity.

- **a.** Using paper and a pencil, sketch a folder structure using at least two subfolders that you could create on your USB flash drive to contain your documents for this activity.
- **b.** Connect your USB flash drive to your computer, then open the window for your USB flash drive.
- **c.** Create the folder structure for your activity, using your sketch as a reference.
- **d.** Think of at least three tasks that you can do to further your work in your chosen activity.
- **e.** Open WordPad and create a document with the title **Next Steps** at the top of the page and your name on the next line.
- **f.** List the three tasks, then save the file in one of the folders you created on your USB flash drive, using the title **To Do.rtf**.
- **g.** Close WordPad, then open a Windows Explorer window for the folder where you stored the document.
- **h.** Create a copy of the file, give the copy a new name, then place a copy of the document in your Documents library.
- **i.** Delete the document copy from your Documents library.
- **j.** Open the Recycle Bin window, and restore the document to the Documents library.

Visual Workshop

You are a technical support specialist at Emergency Services. The company supplies medical staff members to hospital emergency rooms in Los Angeles. You need to respond to your company's employee questions quickly and thoroughly. You decide that it is time to evaluate and reorganize the folder structure on your computer. That way, you'll be able to respond more quickly to staff requests. Create the folder structure shown in Figure B-27 on your USB flash drive. As you work, use WordPad to prepare a simple outline of the steps you follow to create the folder structure. Add your name to the document, and store it in an appropriate location.

FIGURE B-27

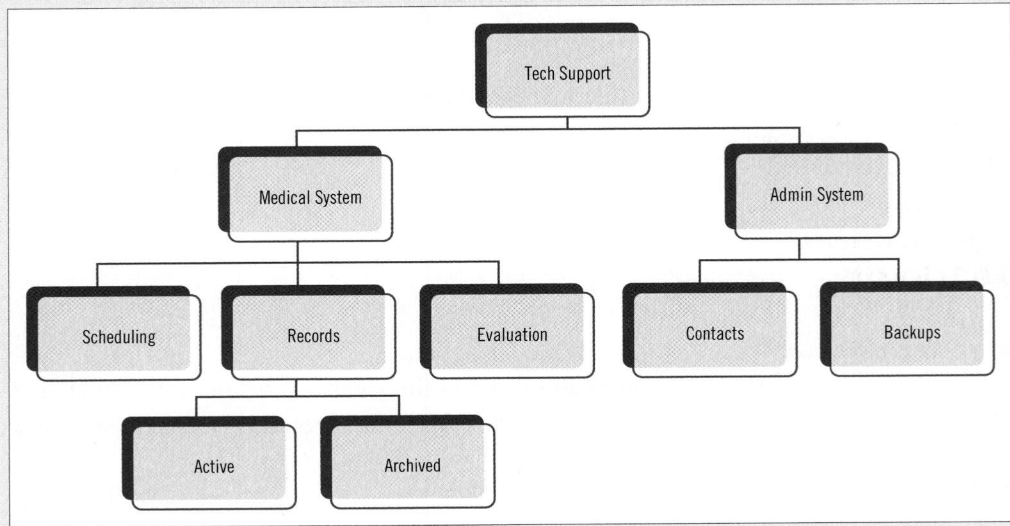

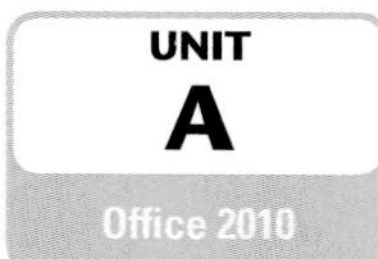

Getting Started with Microsoft Office 2010

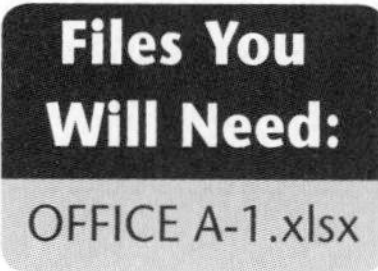

Microsoft Office 2010 is a group of software programs designed to help you create documents, collaborate with coworkers, and track and analyze information. Each program is designed so you can work quickly and efficiently to create professional-looking results. You use different Office programs to accomplish specific tasks, such as writing a letter or producing a sales presentation, yet all the programs have a similar look and feel. Once you become familiar with one program, you'll find it easy to transfer your knowledge to the others. This unit introduces you to the most frequently used programs in Office, as well as common features they all share.

OBJECTIVES

- Understand the Office 2010 suite
- Start and exit an Office program
- View the Office 2010 user interface
- Create and save a file
- Open a file and save it with a new name
- View and print your work
- Get Help and close a file

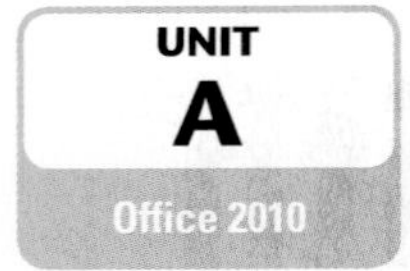

Understanding the Office 2010 Suite

Microsoft Office 2010 features an intuitive, context-sensitive user interface, so you can get up to speed faster and use advanced features with greater ease. The programs in Office are bundled together in a group called a **suite** (although you can also purchase them separately). The Office suite is available in several configurations, but all include Word, Excel, and PowerPoint. Other configurations include Access, Outlook, Publisher, and other programs. Each program in Office is best suited for completing specific types of tasks, though there is some overlap in capabilities.

DETAILS

The Office programs covered in this book include:

- **Microsoft Word 2010**
  When you need to create any kind of text-based document, such as a memo, newsletter, or multipage report, Word is the program to use. You can easily make your documents look great by inserting eye-catching graphics and using formatting tools such as themes, which are available in most Office programs. **Themes** are predesigned combinations of color and formatting attributes you can apply to a document. The Word document shown in Figure A-1 was formatted with the Solstice theme.

- **Microsoft Excel 2010**
  Excel is the perfect solution when you need to work with numeric values and make calculations. It puts the power of formulas, functions, charts, and other analytical tools into the hands of every user, so you can analyze sales projections, calculate loan payments, and present your findings in style. The Excel worksheet shown in Figure A-1 tracks personal expenses. Because Excel automatically recalculates results whenever a value changes, the information is always up to date. A chart illustrates how the monthly expenses are broken down.

- **Microsoft PowerPoint 2010**
  Using PowerPoint, it's easy to create powerful presentations complete with graphics, transitions, and even a soundtrack. Using professionally designed themes and clip art, you can quickly and easily create dynamic slide shows such as the one shown in Figure A-1.

- **Microsoft Access 2010**
  Access helps you keep track of large amounts of quantitative data, such as product inventories or employee records. The form shown in Figure A-1 was created for a grocery store inventory database. Employees use the form to enter data about each item. Using Access enables employees to quickly find specific information such as price and quantity without hunting through store shelves and stockrooms.

Microsoft Office has benefits beyond the power of each program, including:

- **Common user interface: Improving business processes**
  Because the Office suite programs have a similar **interface**, or look and feel, your experience using one program's tools makes it easy to learn those in the other programs. In addition, Office documents are **compatible** with one another, meaning that you can easily incorporate, or **integrate**, an Excel chart into a PowerPoint slide, or an Access table into a Word document.

- **Collaboration: Simplifying how people work together**
  Office recognizes the way people do business today, and supports the emphasis on communication and knowledge sharing within companies and across the globe. All Office programs include the capability to incorporate feedback—called **online collaboration**—across the Internet or a company network.

FIGURE A-1: Microsoft Office 2010 documents

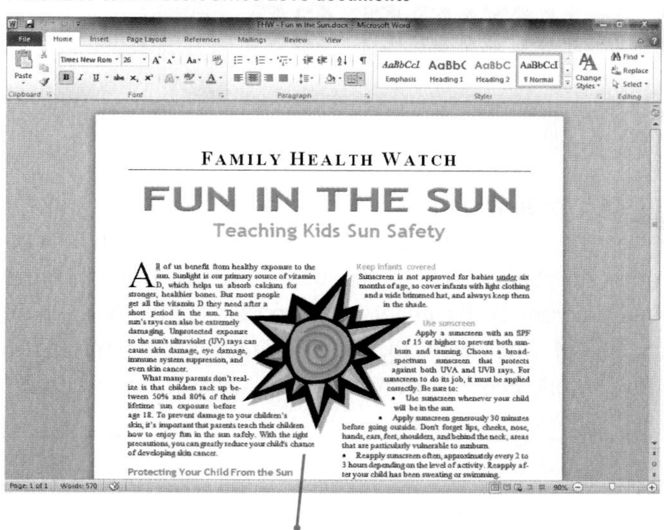

Newsletter created in Word

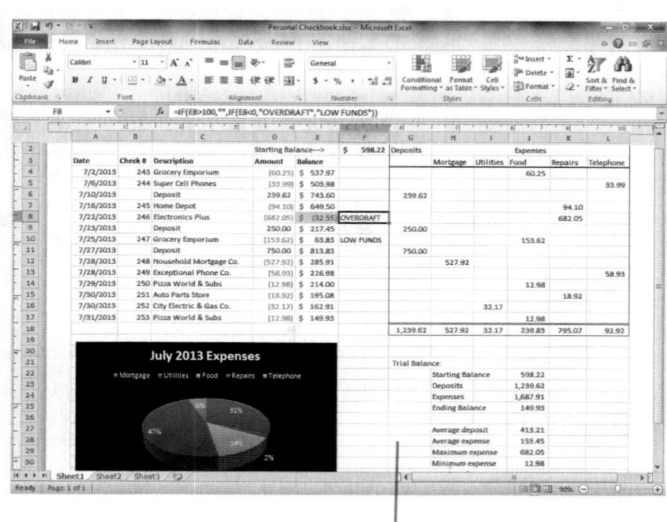

Checkbook register created in Excel

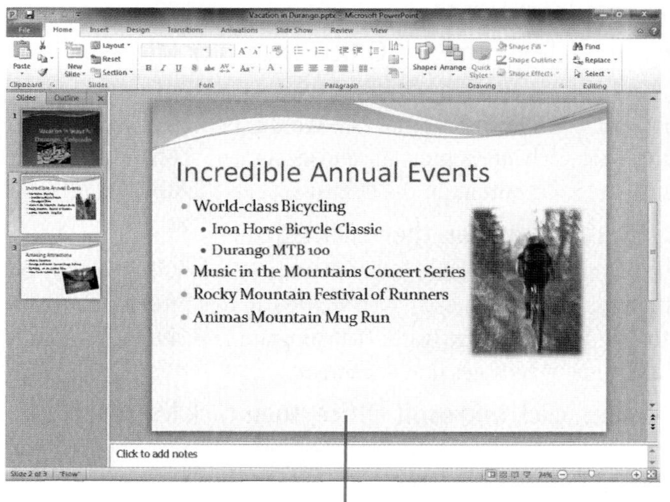

Tourism presentation created in PowerPoint

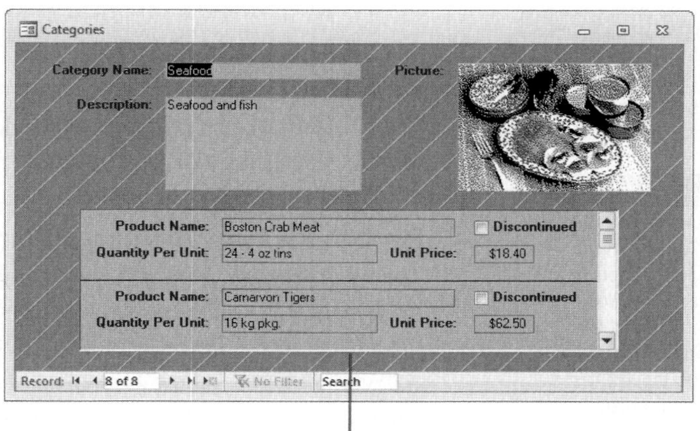

Store inventory form created in Access

Deciding which program to use

Every Office program includes tools that go far beyond what you might expect. For example, although Excel is primarily designed for making calculations, you can use it to create a database. So when you're planning a project, how do you decide which Office program to use? The general rule of thumb is to use the program best suited for your intended task, and make use of supporting tools in the program if you need them. Word is best for creating text-based documents, Excel is best for making mathematical calculations, PowerPoint is best for preparing presentations, and Access is best for managing quantitative data. Although the capabilities of Office are so vast that you *could* create an inventory in Excel or a budget in Word, you'll find greater flexibility and efficiency by using the program designed for the task. And remember, you can always create a file in one program, and then insert it in a document in another program when you need to, such as including sales projections (Excel) in a memo (Word).

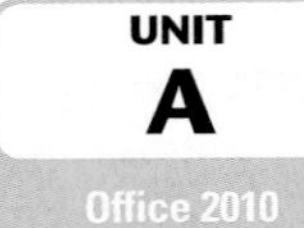

Starting and Exiting an Office Program

The first step in using an Office program is to open, or **launch**, it on your computer. The easiest ways to launch a program are to click the Start button on the Windows taskbar or to double-click an icon on your desktop. You can have multiple programs open on your computer simultaneously, and you can move between open programs by clicking the desired program or document button on the taskbar or by using the [Alt][Tab] keyboard shortcut combination. When working, you'll often want to open multiple programs in Office and switch among them as you work. Begin by launching a few Office programs now.

STEPS

QUICK TIP
You can also launch a program by double-clicking a desktop icon or clicking the program name on the Start menu.

QUICK TIP
It is not necessary to close one program before opening another.

QUICK TIP
As you work in Windows, your computer adapts to your activities. You may notice that after clicking the Start button, the name of the program you want to open appears in the Start menu above All Programs; if so, you can click it to start the program.

TROUBLE
If you don't have Access installed on your computer, proceed to the next lesson.

1. **Click the Start button on the taskbar**
   The Start menu opens. If the taskbar is hidden, you can display it by pointing to the bottom of the screen. Depending on your taskbar property settings, the taskbar may be displayed at all times, or only when you point to that area of the screen. For more information, or to change your taskbar properties, consult your instructor or technical support person.
2. **Click All Programs, scroll down if necessary in the All Programs menu, click Microsoft Office as shown in Figure A-2, then click Microsoft Word 2010**
   Word 2010 starts, and the program window opens on your screen.
3. **Click on the taskbar, click All Programs, click Microsoft Office, then click Microsoft Excel 2010**
   Excel 2010 starts, and the program window opens, as shown in Figure A-3. Word is no longer visible, but it remains open. The taskbar displays a button for each open program and document. Because this Excel document is **active**, or in front and available, the Excel button on the taskbar appears slightly lighter.
4. **Point to the Word program button on the taskbar, then click**
   The Word program window is now in front. When the Aero feature is turned on in Windows 7, pointing to a program button on the taskbar displays a thumbnail version of each open window in that program above the program button. Clicking a program button on the taskbar activates that program and the most recently active document. Clicking a thumbnail of a document activates that document.
5. **Click on the taskbar, click All Programs, click Microsoft Office, then click Microsoft PowerPoint 2010**
   PowerPoint 2010 starts and becomes the active program.
6. **Click the Excel program button on the taskbar**
   Excel is now the active program.
7. **Click on the taskbar, click All Programs, click Microsoft Office, then click Microsoft Access 2010**
   Access 2010 starts and becomes the active program. Now all four Office programs are open at the same time.
8. **Click Exit on the navigation bar in the Access program window, as shown in Figure A-4**
   Access closes, leaving Excel active and Word and PowerPoint open.

Using shortcut keys to move between Office programs

As an alternative to the Windows taskbar, you can use a keyboard shortcut to move among open Office programs. The [Alt][Tab] keyboard combination lets you either switch quickly to the next open program or file or choose one from a gallery. To switch immediately to the next open program or file, press [Alt][Tab]. To choose from all open programs and files, press and hold [Alt], then press and release [Tab] without releasing [Alt]. A gallery opens on screen, displaying the filename and a thumbnail image of each open program and file, as well as of the desktop. Each time you press [Tab] while holding [Alt], the selection cycles to the next open file or location. Release [Alt] when the program, file, or location you want to activate is selected.

FIGURE A-2: Start menu

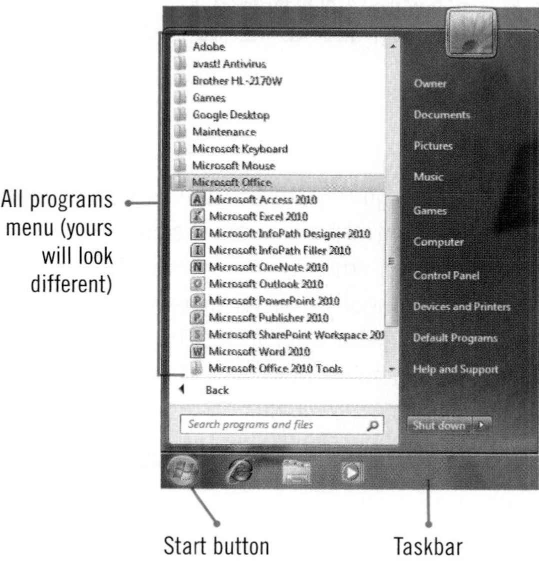

FIGURE A-3: Excel program window and Windows taskbar

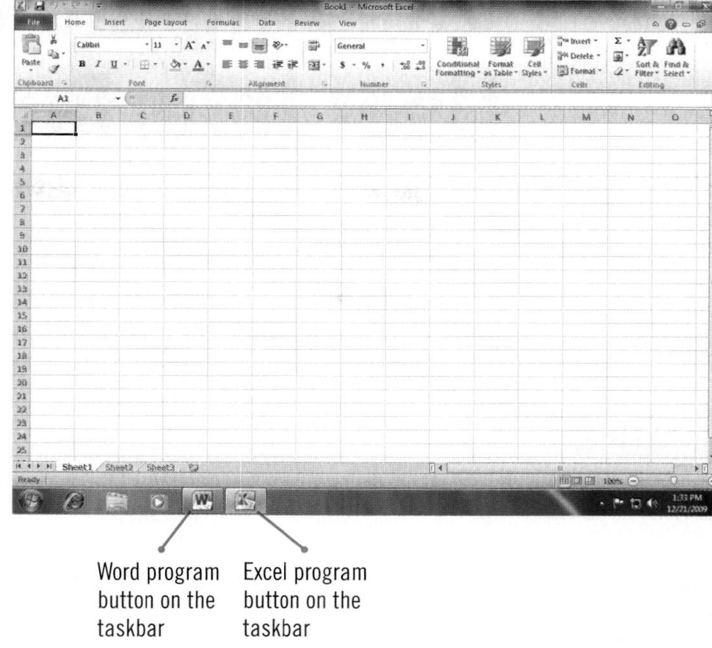

FIGURE A-4: Access program window

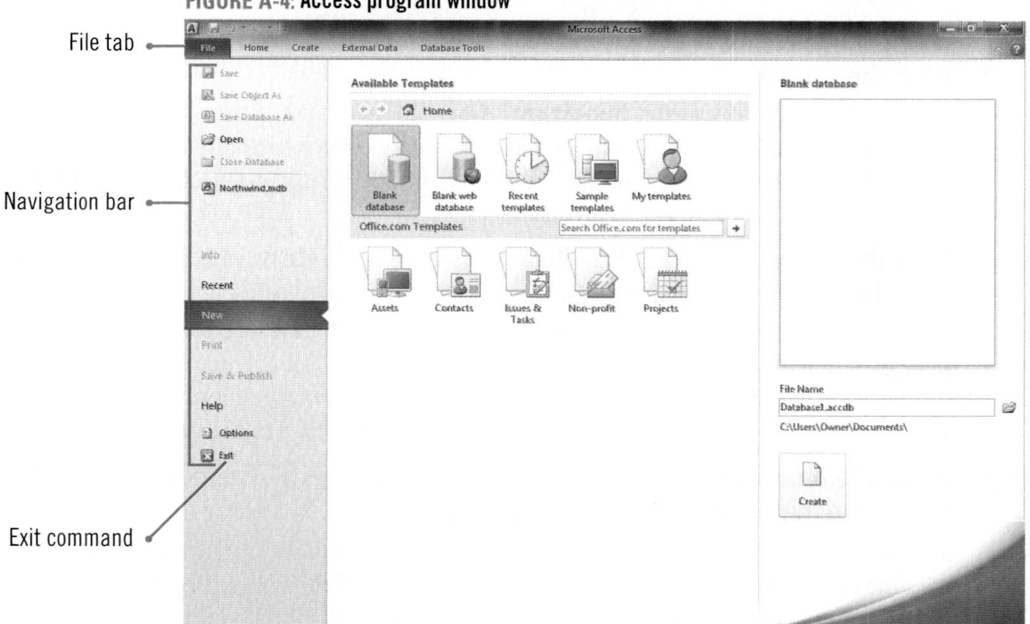

Windows Live and Microsoft Office Web Apps

All Office programs include the capability to incorporate feedback—called online collaboration—across the Internet or a company network. Using **cloud computing** (work done in a virtual environment), you can take advantage of Web programs called Microsoft Office Web Apps, which are simplified versions of the programs found in the Microsoft Office 2010 suite. Because these programs are online, they take up no computer disk space and are accessed using Windows Live SkyDrive, a free service from Microsoft. Using Windows Live SkyDrive, you and your colleagues can create and store documents in a "cloud" and make the documents available to whomever you grant access. To use Windows Live SkyDrive, you need a free Windows Live ID, which you obtain at the Windows Live Web site. You can find more information in the "Working with Windows Live and Office Web Apps" appendix.

Viewing the Office 2010 User Interface

One of the benefits of using Office is that the programs have much in common, making them easy to learn and making it simple to move from one to another. Individual Office programs have always shared many features, but the innovations in the Office 2010 user interface mean even greater similarity among them all. That means you can also use your knowledge of one program to get up to speed in another. A **user interface** is a collective term for all the ways you interact with a software program. The user interface in Office 2010 provides intuitive ways to choose commands, work with files, and navigate in the program window. 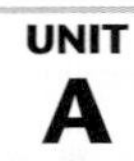 Familiarize yourself with some of the common interface elements in Office by examining the PowerPoint program window.

STEPS

QUICK TIP
In addition to the standard tabs on the Ribbon, **contextual tabs** open when needed to complete a specific task; they appear in an accent color and close when no longer needed. To minimize the display of the buttons and commands on tabs, click the Minimize the Ribbon button on the right end of the Ribbon.

1. **Click the PowerPoint program button on the taskbar**

   PowerPoint becomes the active program. Refer to Figure A-5 to identify common elements of the Office user interface. The **document window** occupies most of the screen. In PowerPoint, a blank slide appears in the document window, so you can build your slide show. At the top of every Office program window is a **title bar** that displays the document name and program name. Below the title bar is the **Ribbon**, which displays commands you're likely to need for the current task. Commands are organized onto **tabs**. The tab names appear at the top of the Ribbon, and the active tab appears in front. The Ribbon in every Office program includes tabs specific to the program, but all Office programs include a File tab and Home tab on the left end of the Ribbon.

2. **Click the File tab**

   The File tab opens, displaying **Backstage view**. The navigation bar on the left side of Backstage view contains commands to perform actions common to most Office programs, such as opening a file, saving a file, and closing the current program. Just above the File tab is the **Quick Access toolbar**, which also includes buttons for common Office commands.

3. **Click the File tab again to close Backstage view and return to the document window, then click the Design tab on the Ribbon**

   To display a different tab, you click the tab on the Ribbon. Each tab contains related commands arranged into **groups** to make features easy to find. On the Design tab, the Themes group displays available design themes in a **gallery**, or visual collection of choices you can browse. Many groups contain a **dialog box launcher**, an icon you can click to open a dialog box or task pane from which to choose related commands.

QUICK TIP
Live Preview is available in many galleries and menus throughout Office.

4. **Move the mouse pointer over the Angles theme in the Themes group as shown in Figure A-6, but do not click the mouse button**

   The Angles theme is temporarily applied to the slide in the document window. However, because you did not click the theme, you did not permanently change the slide. With the **Live Preview** feature, you can point to a choice, see the results right in the document, and then decide if you want to make the change.

QUICK TIP
If you accidentally click a theme, click the Undo button on the Quick Access toolbar.

5. **Move away from the Ribbon and towards the slide**

   If you had clicked the Angles theme, it would be applied to this slide. Instead, the slide remains unchanged.

QUICK TIP
You can also use the Zoom button in the Zoom group on the View tab to enlarge or reduce a document's appearance.

6. **Point to the Zoom slider on the status bar, then drag to the right until the Zoom level reads 166%**

   The slide display is enlarged. Zoom tools are located on the status bar. You can drag the slider or click the Zoom In or Zoom Out buttons to zoom in or out on an area of interest. **Zooming in**, or choosing a higher percentage, makes a document appear bigger on screen, but less of it fits on the screen at once; **zooming out**, or choosing a lower percentage, lets you see more of the document but at a reduced size.

7. **Drag on the status bar to the left until the Zoom level reads 73%**

FIGURE A-5: PowerPoint program window

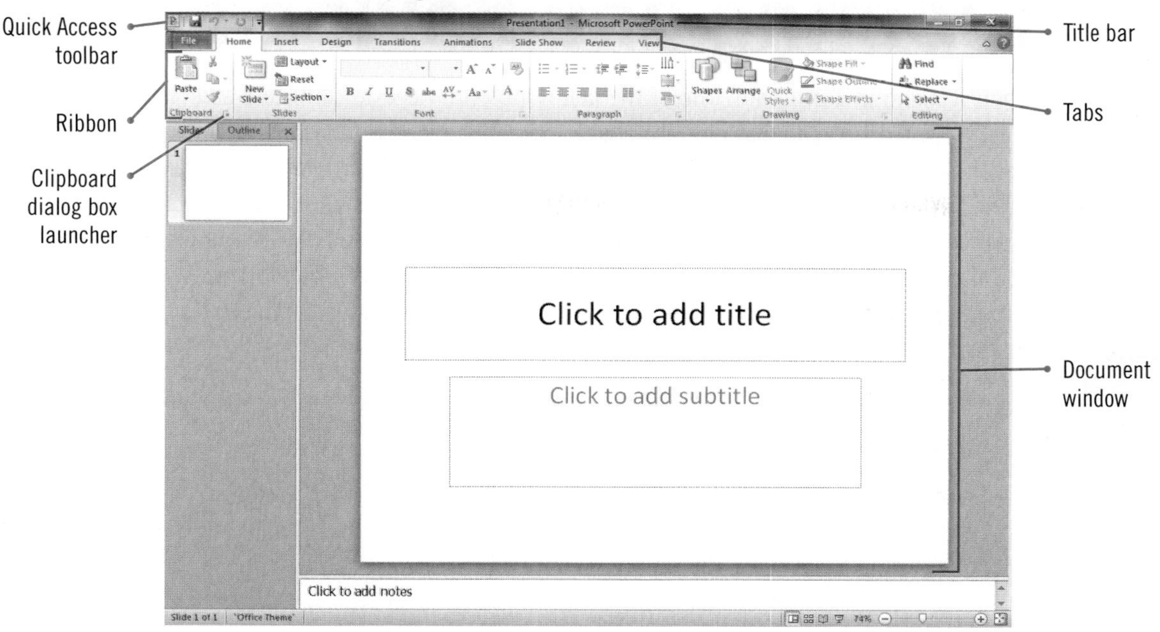

FIGURE A-6: Viewing a theme with Live Preview

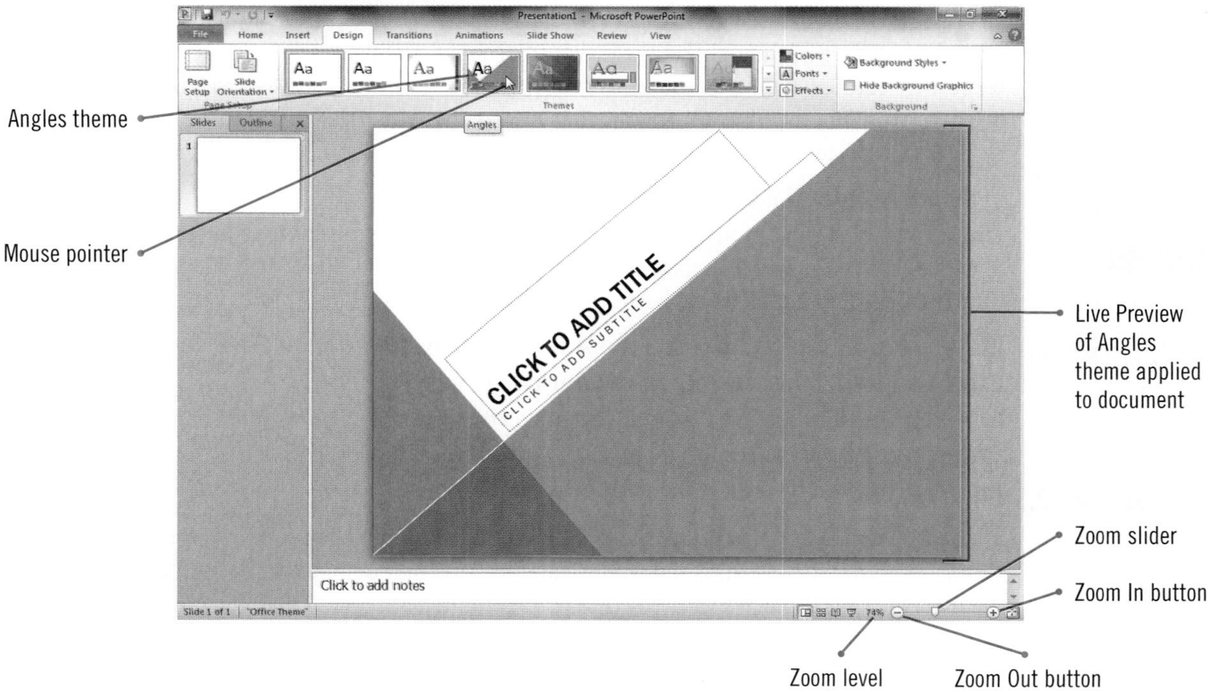

Using Backstage view

Backstage view in each Microsoft Office program offers "one stop shopping" for many commonly performed tasks, such as opening and saving a file, printing and previewing a document, defining document properties, sharing information, and exiting a program. Backstage view opens when you click the File tab in any Office program, and while features such as the Ribbon, Mini toolbar, and Live Preview all help you work *in* your documents, the File tab and Backstage view help you work *with* your documents.

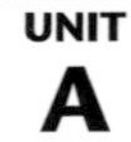

UNIT A
Office 2010

Creating and Saving a File

When working in a program, one of the first things you need to do is to create and save a file. A **file** is a stored collection of data. Saving a file enables you to work on a project now, then put it away and work on it again later. In some Office programs, including Word, Excel, and PowerPoint, a new file is automatically created when you start the program, so all you have to do is enter some data and save it. In Access, you must expressly create a file before you enter any data. You should give your files meaningful names and save them in an appropriate location so that they're easy to find. Use Word to familiarize yourself with the process of creating and saving a document. First you'll type some notes about a possible location for a corporate meeting, then you'll save the information for later use.

STEPS

1. **Click the Word program button on the taskbar**
2. **Type Locations for Corporate Meeting, then press [Enter] twice**
   The text appears in the document window, and the **insertion point** blinks on a new blank line. The insertion point indicates where the next typed text will appear.
3. **Type Las Vegas, NV, press [Enter], type Orlando, FL, press [Enter], type Boston, MA, press [Enter] twice, then type your name**
   Compare your document to Figure A-7.
4. **Click the Save button on the Quick Access toolbar**
   Because this is the first time you are saving this document, the Save As dialog box opens, as shown in Figure A-8. The Save As dialog box includes options for assigning a filename and storage location. Once you save a file for the first time, clicking saves any changes to the file *without* opening the Save As dialog box, because no additional information is needed. The Address bar in the Save As dialog box displays the default location for saving the file, but you can change it to any location. The File name field contains a suggested name for the document based on text in the file, but you can enter a different name.
5. **Type OF A-Potential Corporate Meeting Locations**
   The text you type replaces the highlighted text. (The "OF A-" in the filename indicates that the file is created in Office Unit A. You will see similar designations throughout this book when files are named. For example, a file named in Excel Unit B would begin with "EX B-" .)
6. **In the Save As dialog box, use the Address bar or Navigation Pane to navigate to the drive and folder where you store your Data Files**
   Many students store files on a flash drive, but you can also store files on your computer, a network drive, or any storage device indicated by your instructor or technical support person.
7. **Click Save**
   The Save As dialog box closes, the new file is saved to the location you specified, then the name of the document appears in the title bar, as shown in Figure A-9. (You may or may not see the file extension ".docx" after the filename.) See Table A-1 for a description of the different types of files you create in Office, and the file extensions associated with each.

QUICK TIP
A filename can be up to 255 characters, including a file extension, and can include upper- or lowercase characters and spaces, but not ?, ", /, \, <, >, *, |, or :.

QUICK TIP
Saving a file to the Desktop creates a desktop icon that you can double-click to both launch a program and open a document.

QUICK TIP
To create a new blank file when a file is open, click the File tab, click New on the navigation bar, then click Create near the bottom of the document preview pane.

TABLE A-1: Common filenames and default file extensions

file created in	is called a	and has the default extension
Word	document	.docx
Excel	workbook	.xlsx
PowerPoint	presentation	.pptx
Access	database	.accdb

FIGURE A-7: Document created in Word

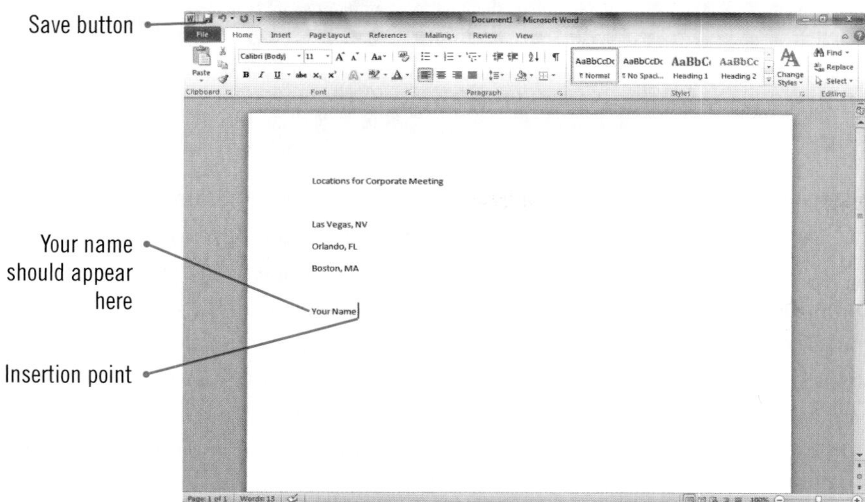

FIGURE A-8: Save As dialog box

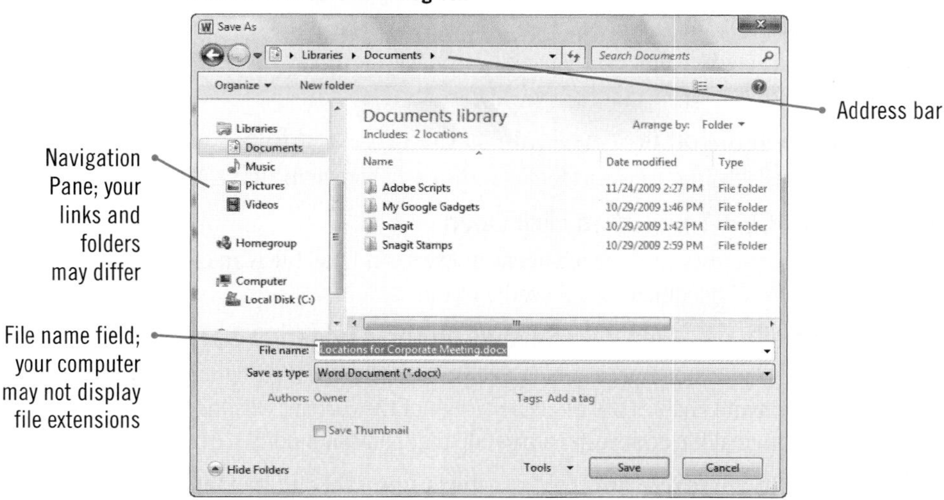

FIGURE A-9: Saved and named Word document

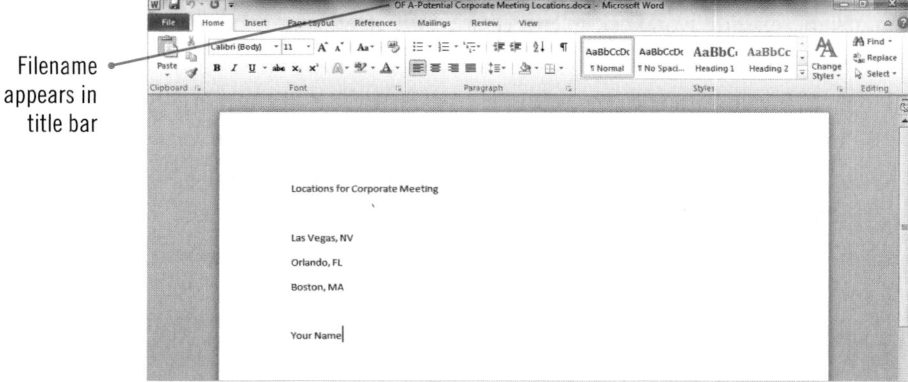

Using the Office Clipboard

You can use the Office Clipboard to cut and copy items from one Office program and paste them into others. The Office Clipboard can store a maximum of 24 items. To access it, open the Office Clipboard task pane by clicking the dialog box launcher in the Clipboard group on the Home tab. Each time you copy a selection, it is saved in the Office Clipboard. Each entry in the Office Clipboard includes an icon that tells you the program it was created in. To paste an entry, click in the document where you want it to appear, then click the item in the Office Clipboard. To delete an item from the Office Clipboard, right-click the item, then click Delete.

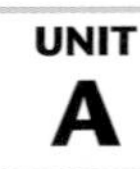

UNIT A
Office 2010

Opening a File and Saving It with a New Name

In many cases as you work in Office, you start with a blank document, but often you need to use an existing file. It might be a file you or a coworker created earlier as a work in progress, or it could be a complete document that you want to use as the basis for another. For example, you might want to create a budget for this year using the budget you created last year; you could type in all the categories and information from scratch, or you could open last year's budget, save it with a new name, and just make changes to update it for the current year. By opening the existing file and saving it with the Save As command, you create a duplicate that you can modify to your heart's content, while the original file remains intact. Use Excel to open an existing workbook file, and save it with a new name so the original remains unchanged.

STEPS

QUICK TIP
Click Recent on the navigation bar to display a list of recent workbooks; click a file in the list to open it.

1. **Click the Excel program button on the taskbar, click the File tab, then click Open on the navigation bar**
   The Open dialog box opens, where you can navigate to any drive or folder accessible to your computer to locate a file.
2. **In the Open dialog box, navigate to the drive and folder where you store your Data Files**
   The files available in the current folder are listed, as shown in Figure A-10. This folder contains one file.

TROUBLE
Click Enable Editing on the Protected View bar near the top of your document window if prompted.

3. **Click OFFICE A-1.xlsx, then click Open**
   The dialog box closes, and the file opens in Excel. An Excel file is an electronic spreadsheet, so it looks different from a Word document or a PowerPoint slide.
4. **Click the File tab, then click Save As on the navigation bar**
   The Save As dialog box opens, and the current filename is highlighted in the File name text box. Using the Save As command enables you to create a copy of the current, existing file with a new name. This action preserves the original file and creates a new file that you can modify.

QUICK TIP
The Save As command works identically in all Office programs, except Access; in Access, this command lets you save a copy of the current database object, such as a table or form, with a new name, but not a copy of the entire database.

5. **Navigate to the drive and folder where you store your Data Files if necessary, type OF A-Budget for Corporate Meeting in the File name text box, as shown in Figure A-11, then click Save**
   A copy of the existing workbook is created with the new name. The original file, Office A-1.xlsx, closes automatically.
6. **Click cell A19, type your name, then press [Enter], as shown in Figure A-12**
   In Excel, you enter data in cells, which are formed by the intersection of a row and a column. Cell A19 is at the intersection of column A and row 19. When you press [Enter], the cell pointer moves to cell A20.
7. **Click the Save button on the Quick Access toolbar**
   Your name appears in the workbook, and your changes to the file are saved.

Working in Compatibility Mode

Not everyone upgrades to the newest version of Office. As a general rule, new software versions are **backward compatible**, meaning that documents saved by an older version can be read by newer software. To open documents created in older Office versions, Office 2010 includes a feature called Compatibility Mode. When you use Office 2010 to open a file created in an earlier version of Office, "Compatibility Mode" appears in the title bar, letting you know the file was created in an earlier but usable version of the program. If you are working with someone who may not be using the newest version of the software, you can avoid possible incompatibility problems by saving your file in another, earlier format. To do this in an Office program, click the File tab, click Save As on the navigation bar, click the Save as type list arrow in the Save As dialog box, then click an option on the list. For example, if you're working in Excel, click Excel 97-2003 Workbook format in the Save as type list to save an Excel file so that it can be opened in Excel 97 or Excel 2003.

FIGURE A-10: Open dialog box

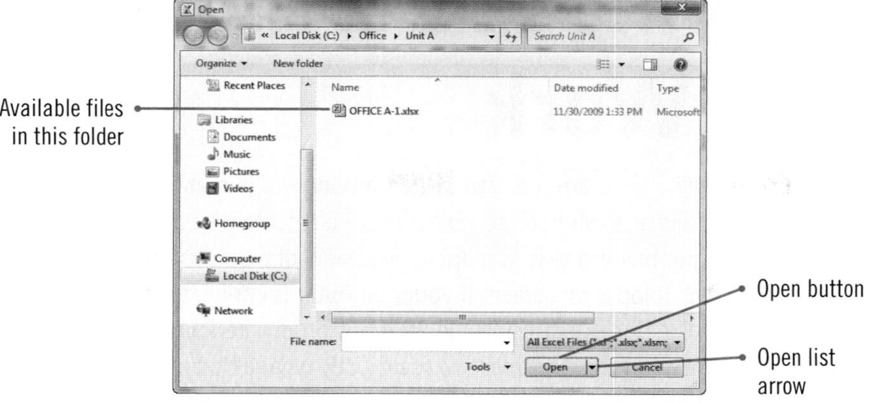

FIGURE A-11: Save As dialog box

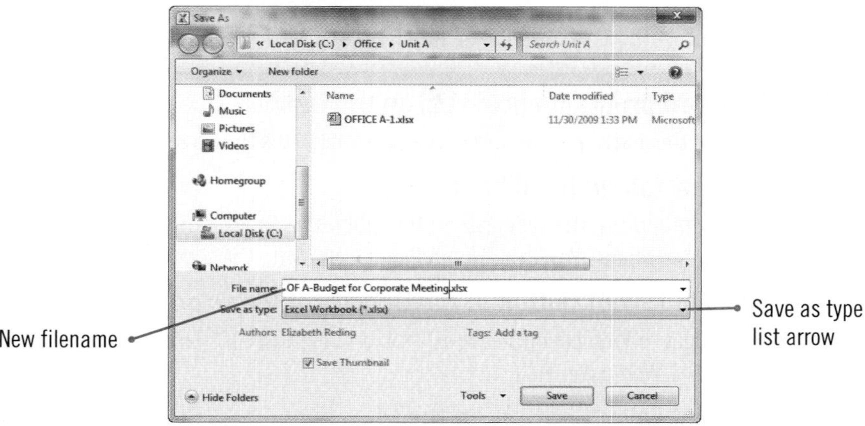

FIGURE A-12: Your name added to the workbook

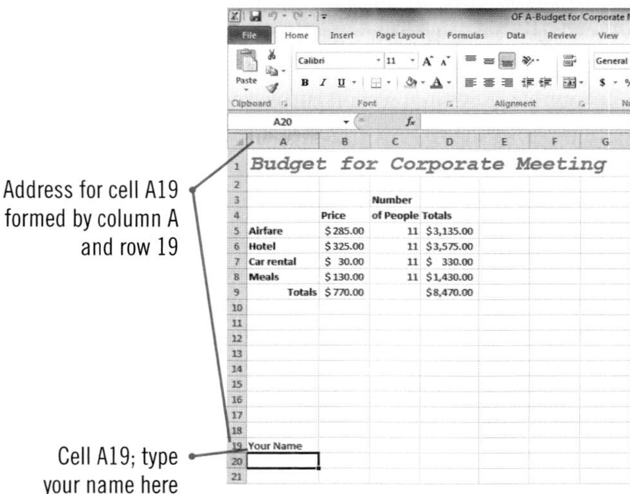

Office 2010

Exploring File Open options

You might have noticed that the Open button on the Open dialog box includes an arrow. In a dialog box, if a button includes an arrow you can click the button to invoke the command, or you can click the arrow to choose from a list of related commands. The Open list arrow includes several related commands, including Open Read-Only and Open as Copy. Clicking Open Read-Only opens a file that you can only save with a new name; you cannot save changes to the original file. Clicking Open as Copy creates a copy of the file already saved and named with the word "Copy" in the title. Like the Save As command, these commands provide additional ways to use copies of existing files while ensuring that original files do not get changed by mistake.

UNIT A Office 2010

Viewing and Printing Your Work

Each Microsoft Office program lets you switch among various **views** of the document window to show more or fewer details or a different combination of elements that make it easier to complete certain tasks, such as formatting or reading text. Changing your view of a document does not affect the file in any way, it affects only the way it looks on screen. If your computer is connected to a printer or a print server, you can easily print any Office document using the Print button on the Print tab in Backstage view. Printing can be as simple as **previewing** the document to see exactly what a document will look like when it is printed and then clicking the Print button. Or, you can customize the print job by printing only selected pages or making other choices. Experiment with changing your view of a Word document, and then preview and print your work.

STEPS

1. **Click the Word program button on the taskbar**
   Word becomes the active program, and the document fills the screen.
2. **Click the View tab on the Ribbon**
   In most Office programs, the View tab on the Ribbon includes groups and commands for changing your view of the current document. You can also change views using the View buttons on the status bar.
3. **Click the Web Layout button in the Document Views group on the View tab**
   The view changes to Web Layout view, as shown in Figure A-13. This view shows how the document will look if you save it as a Web page.
4. **Click the Print Layout button on the View tab**
   You return to Print Layout view, the default view in Word.
5. **Click the File tab, then click Print on the navigation bar**
   The Print tab opens in Backstage view. The preview pane on the right side of the window automatically displays a preview of how your document will look when printed, showing the entire page on screen at once. Compare your screen to Figure A-14. Options in the Settings section enable you to change settings such as margins, orientation, and paper size before printing. To change a setting, click it, and then click the new setting you want. For instance, to change from Letter paper size to Legal, click Letter in the Settings section, then click Legal on the menu that opens. The document preview is updated as you change the settings. You also can use the Settings section to change which pages to print and even the number of pages you print on each sheet of printed paper. If you have multiple printers from which to choose, you can change from one installed printer to another by clicking the current printer in the Printer section, then clicking the name of the installed printer you want to use. The Print section contains the Print button and also enables you to select the number of copies of the document to print.
6. **Click the Print button in the Print section**
   A copy of the document prints, and Backstage view closes.

QUICK TIP

You can add the Quick Print button to the Quick Access toolbar by clicking the Customize Quick Access Toolbar button, then clicking Quick Print. The Quick Print button prints one copy of your document using the default settings.

Customizing the Quick Access toolbar

You can customize the Quick Access toolbar to display your favorite commands. To do so, click the Customize Quick Access Toolbar button in the title bar, then click the command you want to add. If you don't see the command in the list, click More Commands to open the Quick Access Toolbar tab of the current program's Options dialog box. In the Options dialog box, use the Choose commands from list to choose a category, click the desired command in the list on the left, click Add to add it to the Quick Access toolbar, then click OK. To remove a button from the toolbar, click the name in the list on the right in the Options dialog box, then click Remove. To add a command to the Quick Access toolbar on the fly, simply right-click the button on the Ribbon, then click Add to Quick Access Toolbar on the shortcut menu. To move the Quick Access toolbar below the Ribbon, click the Customize Quick Access Toolbar button, and then click Show Below the Ribbon.

FIGURE A-13: Web Layout view

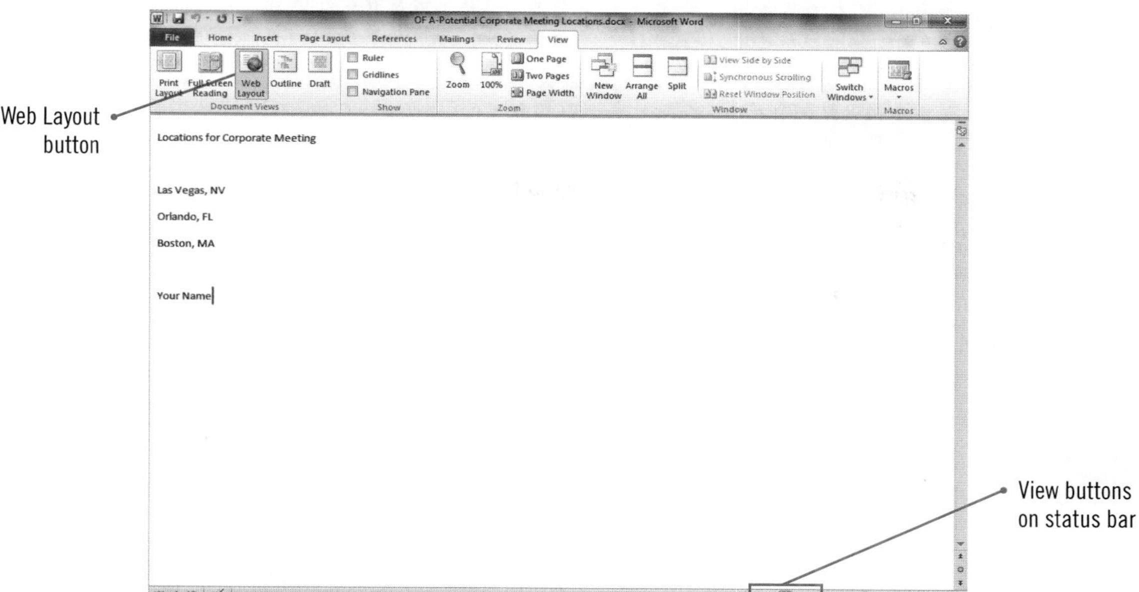

FIGURE A-14: Print tab in Backstage view

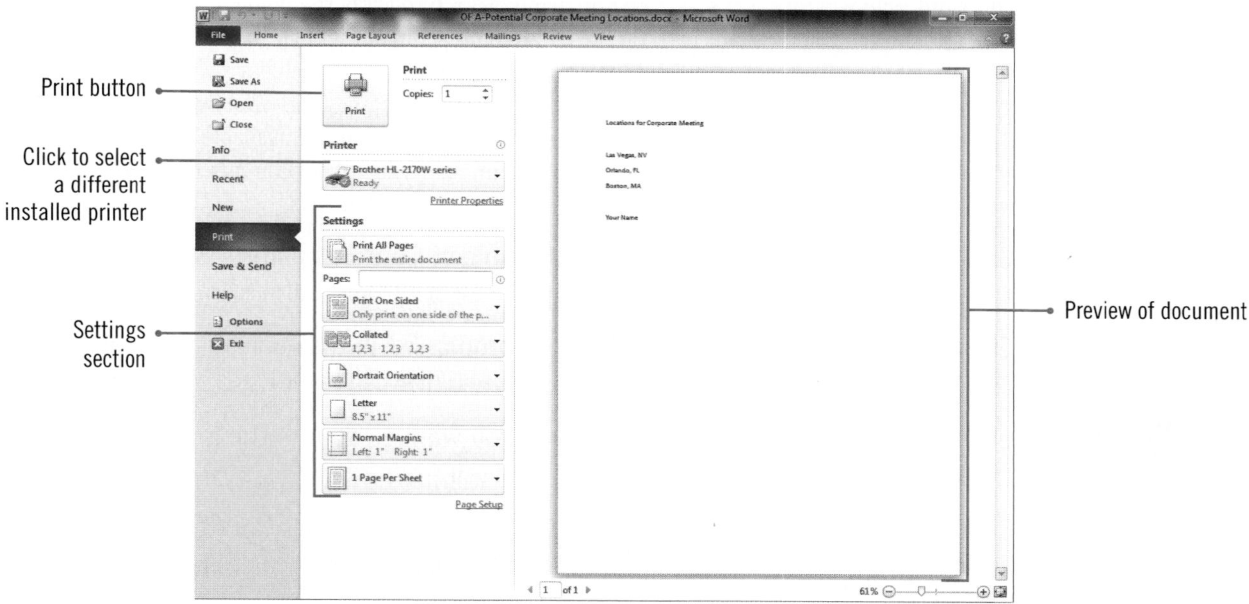

Creating a screen capture

A **screen capture** is a digital image of your screen, as if you took a picture of it with a camera. For instance, you might want to take a screen capture if an error message occurs and you want Technical Support to see exactly what's on the screen. You can create a screen capture using features found in Windows 7 or Office 2010. Windows 7 comes with the Snipping Tool, a separate program designed to capture whole screens or portions of screens. To open the Snipping Tool, click it on the Start menu or click All Programs, click Accessories, then click Snipping Tool. After opening the Snipping Tool, drag the pointer on the screen to select the area of the screen you want to capture. When you release the mouse button, the screen capture opens in the Snipping Tool window, and you can save, copy, or send it in an e-mail. In Word, Excel, and PowerPoint 2010, you can capture screens or portions of screens and insert them in the current document using the Screenshot button on the Insert tab. And finally, you can create a screen capture by pressing [PrtScn]. (Keyboards differ, but you may find the [PrtScn] button in or near your keyboard's function keys.) Pressing this key places a digital image of your screen in the Windows temporary storage area known as the **Clipboard**. Open the document where you want the screen capture to appear, click the Home tab on the Ribbon (if necessary), then click the Paste button on the Home tab. The screen capture is pasted into the document.

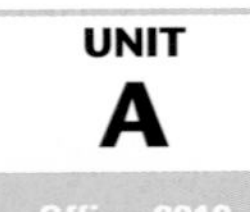

UNIT A

Office 2010

Getting Help and Closing a File

You can get comprehensive help at any time by pressing [F1] in an Office program. You can also get help in the form of a ScreenTip by pointing to almost any icon in the program window. When you're finished working in an Office document, you have a few choices regarding ending your work session. You can close a file or exit a program by using the File tab or by clicking a button on the title bar. Closing a file leaves a program running, while exiting a program closes all the open files in that program as well as the program itself. In all cases, Office reminds you if you try to close a file or exit a program and your document contains unsaved changes. Explore the Help system in Microsoft Office, and then close your documents and exit any open programs.

STEPS

TROUBLE

If the Table of Contents pane doesn't appear on the left in the Help window, click the Show Table of Contents button on the Help toolbar to show it.

QUICK TIP

You can also open the Help window by clicking the Microsoft Office Word Help button to the right of the tabs on the Ribbon.

QUICK TIP

You can print the entire current topic by clicking the Print button on the Help toolbar, then clicking Print in the Print dialog box.

1. **Point to the Zoom button on the View tab of the Ribbon**

   A ScreenTip appears that describes how the Zoom button works and explains where to find other zoom controls.

2. **Press [F1]**

   The Word Help window opens, as shown in Figure A-15, displaying the home page for help in Word on the right and the Table of Contents pane on the left. In both panes of the Help window, each entry is a hyperlink you can click to open a list of related topics. The Help window also includes a toolbar of useful Help commands and a Search field. The connection status at the bottom of the Help window indicates that the connection to Office.com is active. Office.com supplements the help content available on your computer with a wide variety of up-to-date topics, templates, and training. If you are not connected to the Internet, the Help window displays only the help content available on your computer.

3. **Click the Creating documents link in the Table of Contents pane**

   The icon next to Creating documents changes, and a list of subtopics expands beneath the topic.

4. **Click the Create a document link in the subtopics list in the Table of Contents pane**

   The topic opens in the right pane of the Help window, as shown in Figure A-16.

5. **Click Delete a document under "What do you want to do?" in the right pane**

   The link leads to information about deleting a document.

6. **Click the Accessibility link in the Table of Contents pane, click the Accessibility features in Word link, read the information in the right pane, then click the Help window Close button**

7. **Click the File tab, then click Close on the navigation bar; if a dialog box opens asking whether you want to save your changes, click Save**

   The Potential Corporate Meeting Locations document closes, leaving the Word program open.

8. **Click the File tab, then click Exit on the navigation bar**

   Word closes, and the Excel program window is active.

9. **Click the File tab, click Exit on the navigation bar to exit Excel, click the PowerPoint program button on the taskbar if necessary, click the File tab, then click Exit on the navigation bar to exit PowerPoint**

   Excel and PowerPoint both close.

FIGURE A-15: **Word Help window**

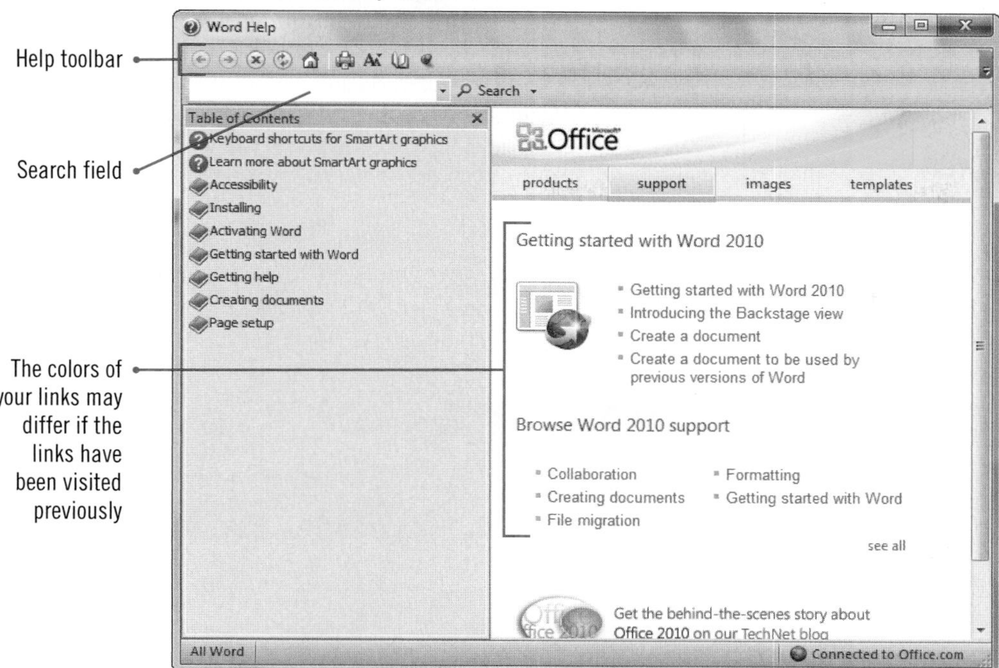

FIGURE A-16: **Create a document Help topic**

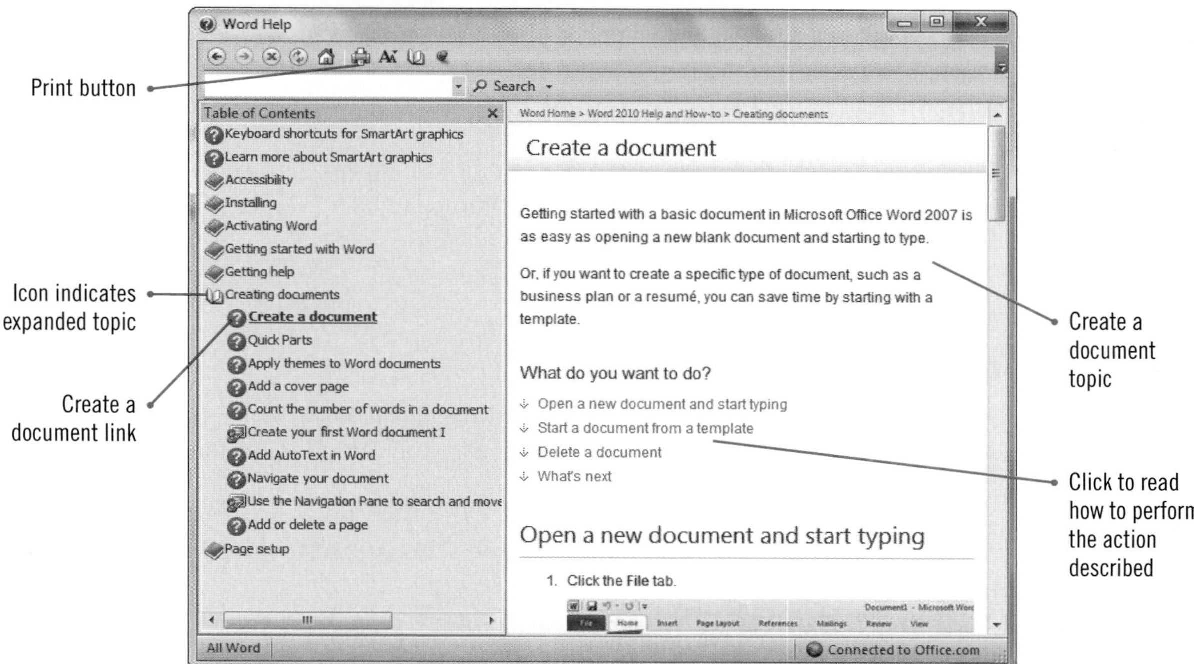

Recovering a document

Each Office program has a built-in recovery feature that allows you to open and save files that were open at the time of an interruption such as a power failure. When you restart the program(s) after an interruption, the Document Recovery task pane opens on the left side of your screen displaying both original and recovered versions of the files that were open. If you're not sure which file to open (original or recovered), it's usually better to open the recovered file because it will contain the latest information. You can, however, open and review all versions of the file that were recovered and save the best one. Each file listed in the Document Recovery task pane displays a list arrow with options that allow you to open the file, save it as is, delete it, or show repairs made to it during recovery.

Practice

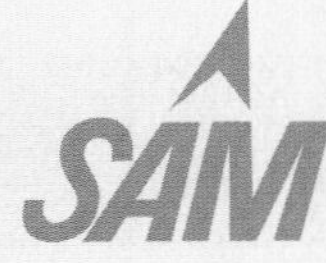

For current SAM information, including versions and content details, visit SAM Central (http://www.cengage.com/samcentral). If you have a SAM user profile, you may have access to hands-on instruction, practice, and assessment of the skills covered in this unit. Since various versions of SAM are supported throughout the life of this text, check with your instructor for the correct instructions and URL/Web site for accessing assignments.

Concepts Review

Label the elements of the program window shown in Figure A-17.

FIGURE A-17

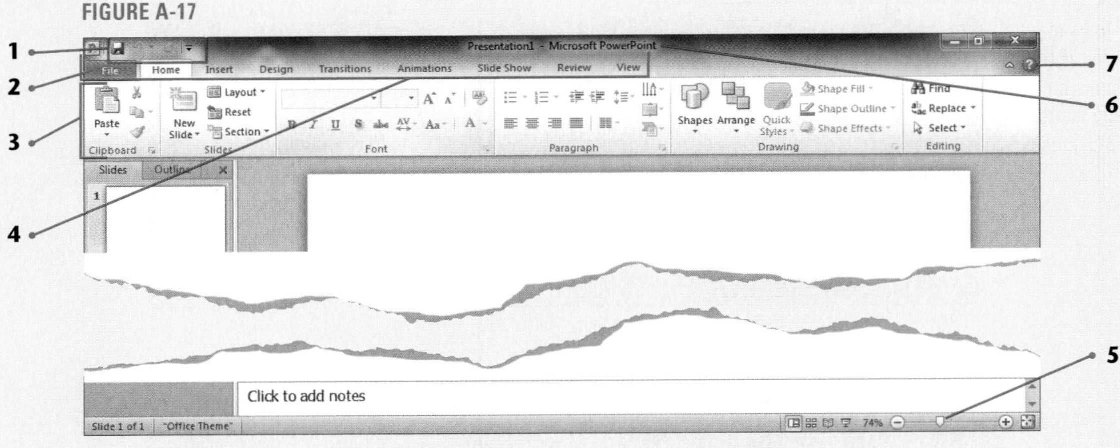

Match each project with the program for which it is best suited.

8. Microsoft Access	**a.** Corporate convention budget with expense projections
9. Microsoft Excel	**b.** Business cover letter for a job application
10. Microsoft Word	**c.** Department store inventory
11. Microsoft PowerPoint	**d.** Presentation for city council meeting

Independent Challenge 1

You just accepted an administrative position with a local independently owned produce vendor that has recently invested in computers and is now considering purchasing Microsoft Office for the company. You are asked to propose ways Office might help the business. You produce your document in Word.

a. Start Word, then save the document as **OF A-Microsoft Office Document** in the drive and folder where you store your Data Files.

b. Type **Microsoft Word**, press [Enter] twice, type **Microsoft Excel**, press [Enter] twice, type **Microsoft PowerPoint**, press [Enter] twice, type **Microsoft Access**, press [Enter] twice, then type your name.

c. Click the line beneath each program name, type at least two tasks suited to that program (each separated by a comma), then press [Enter].

Advanced Challenge Exercise

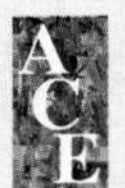

- Press the [PrtScn] button to create a screen capture.
- Click after your name, press [Enter] to move to a blank line below your name, then click the Paste button in the Clipboard group on the Home tab.

d. Save the document, then submit your work to your instructor as directed.

e. Exit Word.

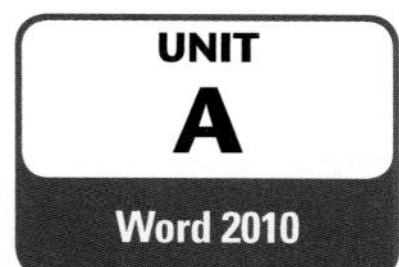

Creating Documents with Word 2010

Files You Will Need:

WMP A-1.docx

Microsoft Word 2010 is a word processing program that makes it easy to create a variety of professional-looking documents, from simple letters and memos to newsletters, research papers, blog posts, business cards, résumés, financial reports, and other documents that include multiple pages of text and sophisticated formatting. In this unit, you will explore the editing and formatting features available in Word and create two documents. You have been hired to work at the Riverwalk Medical Clinic, a large outpatient medical facility staffed by family physicians, specialists, nurses, and other allied health professionals. Shortly after reporting to your new position, the office manager, Tony Sanchez, R.N., asks you to use Word to create a memo to the clinic staff and a fax to the director of the clinic.

OBJECTIVES

- Understand word processing software
- Explore the Word program window
- Start a document
- Save a document
- Select text
- Format text using the Mini toolbar
- Create a document using a template
- View and navigate a document

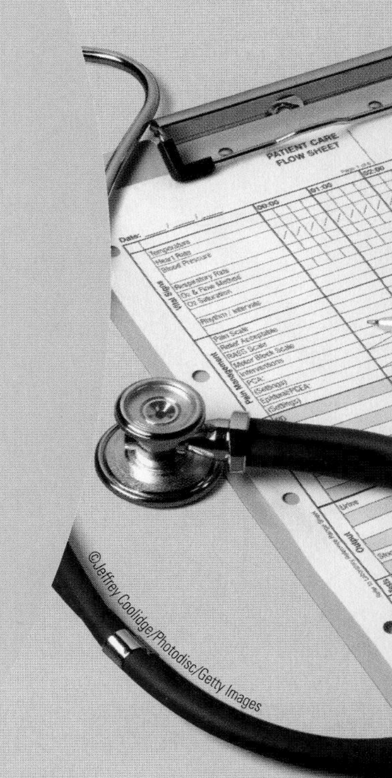

©Jeffrey Coolidge/Photodisc/Getty Images

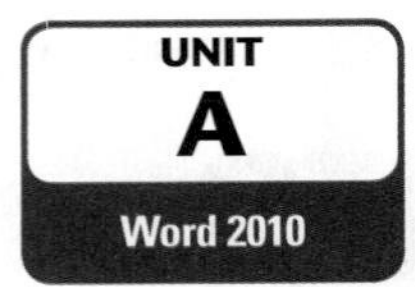

Understanding Word Processing Software

A **word processing program** is a software program that includes tools for entering, editing, and formatting text and graphics. Microsoft Word is a powerful word processing program that allows you to create and enhance a wide range of documents quickly and easily. Figure A-1 shows the first page of a report created using Word and illustrates some of the Word features you can use to enhance your documents. The electronic files you create using Word are called **documents**. One of the benefits of using Word is that document files can be stored on a hard disk, CD, flash drive, or other storage device, making them easy to transport, exchange, and revise. Before beginning your memo to the clinic staff, you explore the editing and formatting features available in Word.

DETAILS

You can use Word to accomplish the following tasks:

- **Type and edit text**
  The Word editing tools make it simple to insert and delete text in a document. You can add text to the middle of an existing paragraph, replace text with other text, undo an editing change, and correct typing, spelling, and grammatical errors with ease.

- **Copy and move text from one location to another**
  Using the more advanced editing features of Word, you can copy or move text from one location and insert it in a different location in a document. You can also copy and move text between documents. This means you don't have to retype text that is already entered in a document.

- **Format text and paragraphs with fonts, colors, and other elements**
  The sophisticated formatting tools in Word allow you to make the text in your documents come alive. You can change the size, style, and color of text, add lines and shading to paragraphs, and enhance lists with bullets and numbers. Creatively formatting text helps to highlight important ideas in your documents.

- **Format and design pages**
  The page-formatting features in Word give you power to design attractive newsletters, create powerful résumés, and produce documents such as research papers, business cards, CD labels, and books. You can change the paper size and orientation of your documents, organize text in columns, and control the layout of text and graphics on each page of a document. For quick results, Word includes preformatted cover pages, pull quotes, and headers and footers, as well as galleries of coordinated text, table, and graphic styles that you can rely on to give documents a polished look. If you are writing a research paper, Word makes it easy to manage reference sources and create footnotes, endnotes, and bibliographies.

- **Enhance documents with tables, charts, diagrams, and graphics**
  Using the powerful graphics tools in Word, you can spice up your documents with pictures, photographs, lines, shapes, and diagrams. You can also illustrate your documents with tables and charts to help convey your message in a visually interesting way.

- **Use Mail Merge to create form letters and mailing labels**
  The Word Mail Merge feature allows you to send personalized form letters to many different people. You can also use Mail Merge to create mailing labels, directories, e-mail messages, and other types of documents.

- **Share documents securely**
  The security features in Word make it quick and easy to remove comments, tracked changes, and unwanted personal information from your files before you share them with others. You can also add a password or a digital signature to a document and convert a file to a format suitable for publishing on the Web.

FIGURE A-1: A report created using Word

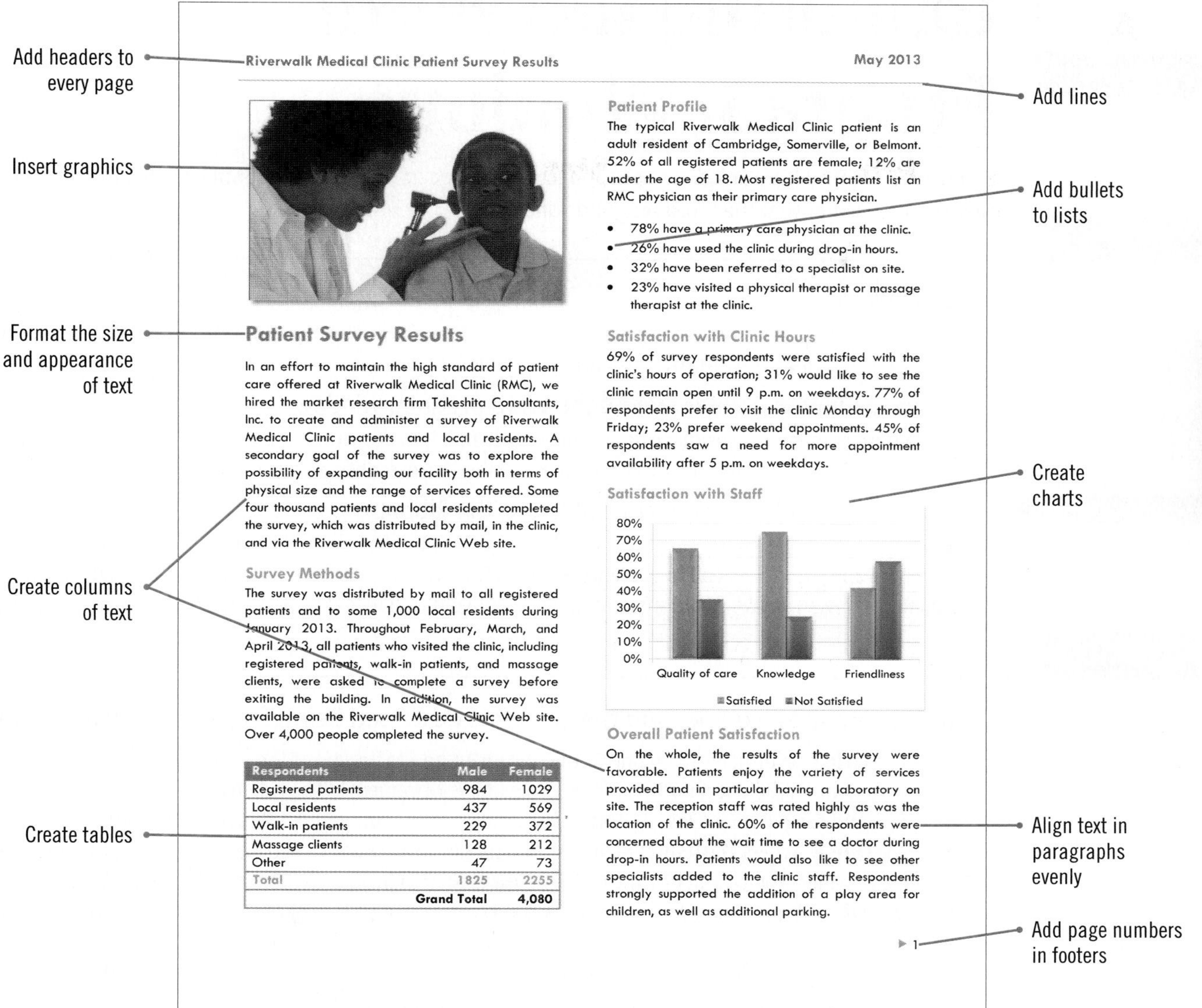

Riverwalk Medical Clinic Patient Survey Results

May 2013

Patient Survey Results

In an effort to maintain the high standard of patient care offered at Riverwalk Medical Clinic (RMC), we hired the market research firm Takeshita Consultants, Inc. to create and administer a survey of Riverwalk Medical Clinic patients and local residents. A secondary goal of the survey was to explore the possibility of expanding our facility both in terms of physical size and the range of services offered. Some four thousand patients and local residents completed the survey, which was distributed by mail, in the clinic, and via the Riverwalk Medical Clinic Web site.

Survey Methods

The survey was distributed by mail to all registered patients and to some 1,000 local residents during January 2013. Throughout February, March, and April 2013, all patients who visited the clinic, including registered patients, walk-in patients, and massage clients, were asked to complete a survey before exiting the building. In addition, the survey was available on the Riverwalk Medical Clinic Web site. Over 4,000 people completed the survey.

Respondents	Male	Female
Registered patients	984	1029
Local residents	437	569
Walk-in patients	229	372
Massage clients	128	212
Other	47	73
Total	1825	2255
	Grand Total	4,080

Patient Profile

The typical Riverwalk Medical Clinic patient is an adult resident of Cambridge, Somerville, or Belmont. 52% of all registered patients are female; 12% are under the age of 18. Most registered patients list an RMC physician as their primary care physician.

- 78% have a primary care physician at the clinic.
- 26% have used the clinic during drop-in hours.
- 32% have been referred to a specialist on site.
- 23% have visited a physical therapist or massage therapist at the clinic.

Satisfaction with Clinic Hours

69% of survey respondents were satisfied with the clinic's hours of operation; 31% would like to see the clinic remain open until 9 p.m. on weekdays. 77% of respondents prefer to visit the clinic Monday through Friday; 23% prefer weekend appointments. 45% of respondents saw a need for more appointment availability after 5 p.m. on weekdays.

Satisfaction with Staff

Overall Patient Satisfaction

On the whole, the results of the survey were favorable. Patients enjoy the variety of services provided and in particular having a laboratory on site. The reception staff was rated highly as was the location of the clinic. 60% of the respondents were concerned about the wait time to see a doctor during drop-in hours. Patients would also like to see other specialists added to the clinic staff. Respondents strongly supported the addition of a play area for children, as well as additional parking.

1

Planning a document

Before you create a new document, it's a good idea to spend time planning it. Identify the message you want to convey, the audience for your document, and the elements, such as tables or charts, you want to include. You should also think about the tone and look of your document—are you writing a business letter, which should be written in a pleasant, but serious tone and have a formal appearance, or are you creating a flyer that must be colorful, eye-catching, and fun to read? The purpose and audience for your document determine the appropriate design. Planning the layout and design of a document involves deciding how to organize the text, selecting the fonts to use, identifying the graphics to include, and selecting the formatting elements that will enhance the message and appeal of the document. For longer documents, such as newsletters, it can be useful to sketch the layout and design of each page before you begin.

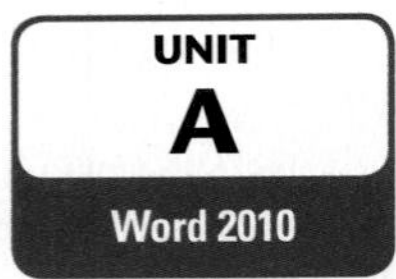
UNIT A
Word 2010

Exploring the Word Program Window

When you start Word, a blank document appears in the document window in Print Layout view. You examine the elements of the Word program window.

STEPS

1. **Start Word**

   The **Word program window** opens, as shown in Figure A-2. The blinking vertical line in the document window is the **insertion point**. It indicates where text appears as you type.

2. **Move the mouse pointer around the Word program window**

   The mouse pointer changes shape depending on where it is in the Word program window. You use pointers to move the insertion point or to select text to edit. Table A-1 describes common pointers in Word.

> **QUICK TIP**
> The buttons visible on your Ribbon may differ.

3. **Place the mouse pointer over a button on the Ribbon**

   When you place the mouse pointer over a button or some other elements of the Word program window, a ScreenTip appears. A **ScreenTip** is a label that identifies the name of the button or feature, briefly describes its function, conveys any keyboard shortcut for the command, and includes a link to associated help topics, if any.

DETAILS

Using Figure A-2 as a guide, find the elements described below in your program window:

- The **title bar** displays the name of the document and the name of the program. Until you give a new document a different name, its temporary name is Document1. The title bar also contains resizing buttons and the program Close button. These buttons are common to all Windows programs.
- The **Quick Access toolbar** contains buttons for saving a document and for undoing, redoing, and repeating a change. You can modify the Quick Access toolbar to include the commands you use frequently.
- The **File tab** provides access to **Backstage view**, where you manage files and the information about them. Backstage view includes commands related to working with documents, such as opening, printing, and saving a document. The File tab also provides access to resources for help using Word and to the Word Options dialog box, which is used to customize the way you use Word.

> **QUICK TIP**
> To display a different tab, you simply click its name on the Ribbon.

- The **Ribbon** contains the Word tabs. Each **tab** on the Ribbon includes buttons for commands related to editing and formatting documents. The commands are organized in **groups**. For example, the Home tab includes the Clipboard, Font, Paragraph, Styles, and Editing groups. The Ribbon also includes the **Microsoft Word Help button**, which you use to access the Word Help system.
- The **document window** displays the current document. You enter text and format your document in the document window.

> **TROUBLE**
> Click the View Ruler button at the top of the vertical scroll bar to display the rulers if they are not already displayed.

- The rulers appear in the document window in Print Layout view. The **horizontal ruler** displays left and right document margins as well as the tab settings and paragraph indents, if any, for the paragraph in which the insertion point is located. The **vertical ruler** displays the top and bottom document margins.
- The **vertical scroll bar** and the **horizontal scroll bar** are used to display different parts of the document in the document window. The scroll bars include **scroll boxes** and **scroll arrows**, which you can use to scroll through a document.
- The **status bar** displays the page number of the current page, the total number of pages and words in the document, and the status of spelling and grammar checking. It also includes the view buttons, the Zoom level button, and the Zoom slider. You can customize the status bar to display other information.
- The **view buttons** on the status bar allow you to display the document in Print Layout, Full Screen Reading, Web Layout, Outline, or Draft view.
- The **Zoom level** button and the **Zoom slider** provide quick ways to enlarge and decrease the size of the document in the document window, making it easy to zoom in on a detail of a document or to view the layout of the document as a whole.

FIGURE A-2: **Elements of the Word program window**

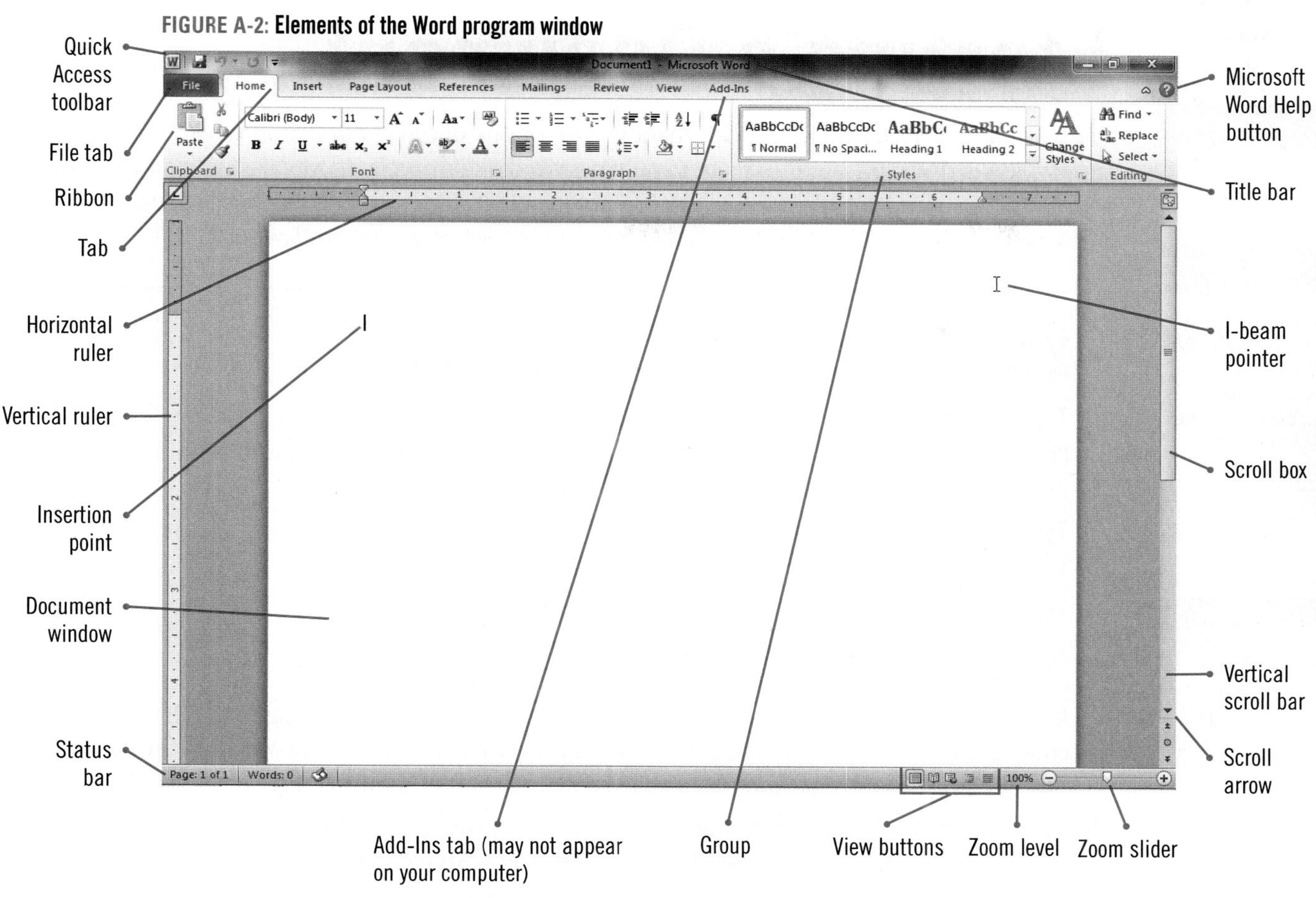

Word 2010

TABLE A-1: **Common mouse pointers in Word**

name	pointer	use to
I-beam pointer	I	Move the insertion point in a document or to select text
Click and Type pointers, including left-align and center-align	I≡ or I	Move the insertion point to a blank area of a document in Print Layout or Web Layout view; double-clicking with a Click and Type pointer automatically applies the paragraph formatting (alignment and indentation) required to position text or a graphic at that location in the document
Selection pointer		Click a button or other element of the Word program window; appears when you point to elements of the Word program window
Right-pointing arrow pointer		Select a line or lines of text; appears when you point to the left edge of a line of text in the document window
Hand pointer		Open a hyperlink; appears when you point to a hyperlink in a task pane or when you press [Ctrl] and point to a hyperlink in a document
Hide white space pointer		Hide the white space in the top and bottom margins of a document in Print Layout view
Show white space pointer		Show the white space in the top and bottom margins of a document in Print Layout view

UNIT A
Word 2010

Starting a Document

You begin a new document by simply typing text in a blank document in the document window. Word includes a **word-wrap** feature so that as you type, Word automatically moves the insertion point to the next line of the document when you reach the right margin. You only press [Enter] when you want to start a new paragraph or insert a blank line. 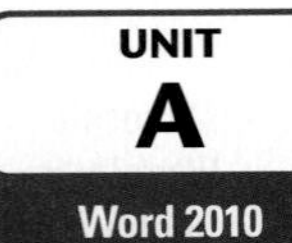 You type a quick memo to the clinic staff.

STEPS

1. **Type** Memorandum, **then press** [Enter] **twice**
   Each time you press [Enter] the insertion point moves to the start of the next line.

2. **Type** TO:, **then press** [Tab] **twice**
   Pressing [Tab] moves the insertion point several spaces to the right. You can use the [Tab] key to align the text in a memo header or to indent the first line of a paragraph.

3. **Type** All Employees, **then press** [Enter]
   The insertion point moves to the start of the next line.

4. **Type:** FROM: [Tab] [Tab] Tony Sanchez [Enter]
   DATE: [Tab] [Tab] July 7, 2013 [Enter]
   RE: [Tab] [Tab] Staff Meeting [Enter] [Enter]
   Red or green wavy lines may appear under the words you typed, indicating a possible spelling or grammar error. Spelling and grammar checking is one of the many automatic features you will encounter as you type. Table A-2 describes several of these automatic features. You can correct any typing errors you make later.

5. **Type** The next clinic staff meeting will be held on the 11th of July at 1 p.m. in the Kogan conference room on the ground floor., **then press** [Spacebar]
   As you type, notice that the insertion point moves automatically to the next line of the document. You also might notice that Word automatically changed "11th" to "11th" in the memo. This feature is called **AutoCorrect**. AutoCorrect automatically makes typographical adjustments and detects and adjusts typing errors, certain misspelled words (such as "taht" for "that"), and incorrect capitalization as you type.

6. **Type** Heading the agenda will be a discussion of our new community health fair, scheduled for September.
   When you type the first few characters of "September," the Word AutoComplete feature displays the complete word in a ScreenTip. **AutoComplete** suggests text to insert quickly into your documents. You can ignore AutoComplete for now. Your memo should resemble Figure A-3.

7. **Press** [Enter], **then type** The event will include free screenings and adult immunizations. A preliminary draft of the program for the health fair is attached. Bring your creative ideas for promoting and planning this exciting new event to the meeting.
   When you press [Enter] and type the new paragraph, notice that Word adds more space between the paragraphs than it does between the lines in each paragraph. This is part of the default style for paragraphs in Word, called the **Normal style**.

8. **Position the I pointer after** new **(but before the space) in the last sentence of the first paragraph, then click**
   Clicking moves the insertion point after "new."

9. **Press** [Backspace] **three times, then type** upcoming
   Pressing [Backspace] removes the character before the insertion point.

10. **Move the insertion point before** clinic **in the first sentence, then press** [Delete] **seven times to remove the word "clinic" and the space after it**
    Pressing [Delete] removes the character after the insertion point. Figure A-4 shows the revised memo.

TROUBLE
If you press the wrong key, press [Backspace] to erase the mistake, then try again.

QUICK TIP
Wavy lines and other automatic feature markers appear on screen but do not print.

TROUBLE
To reverse an AutoCorrect adjustment, immediately click the Undo button on the Quick Access toolbar.

QUICK TIP
If you want uniform spacing between lines and paragraphs, apply the No Spacing style to the document by clicking the No Spacing button in the Styles group on the Home tab before you begin to type. Alternatively, select the text and then click the No Spacing button.

FIGURE A-3: Memo text in the document window

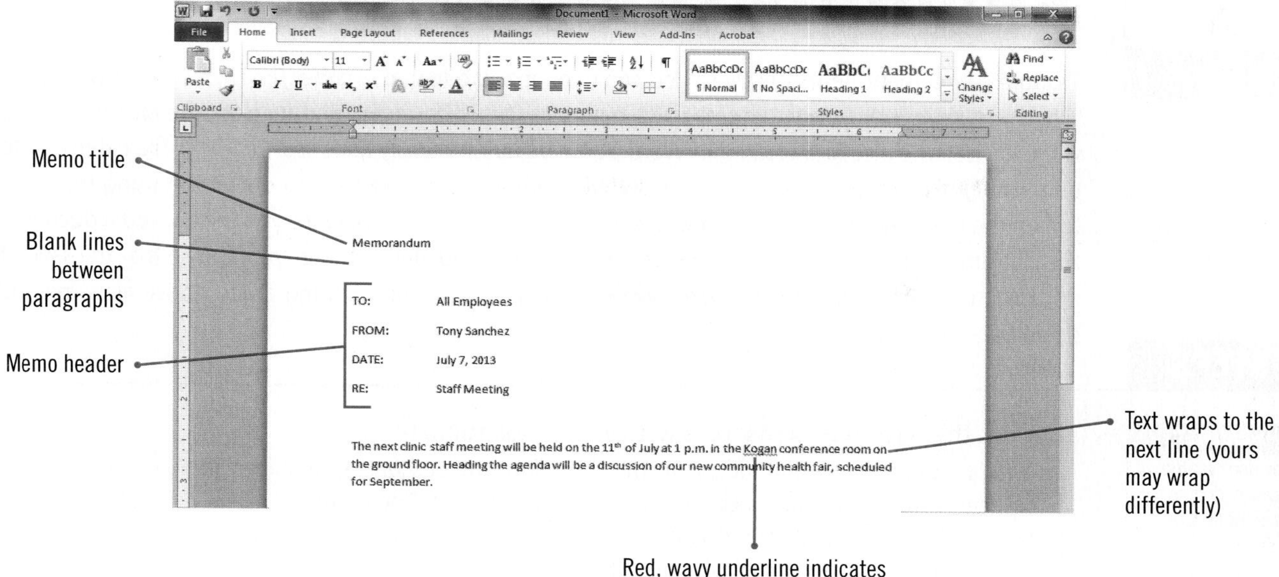

FIGURE A-4: Edited memo text

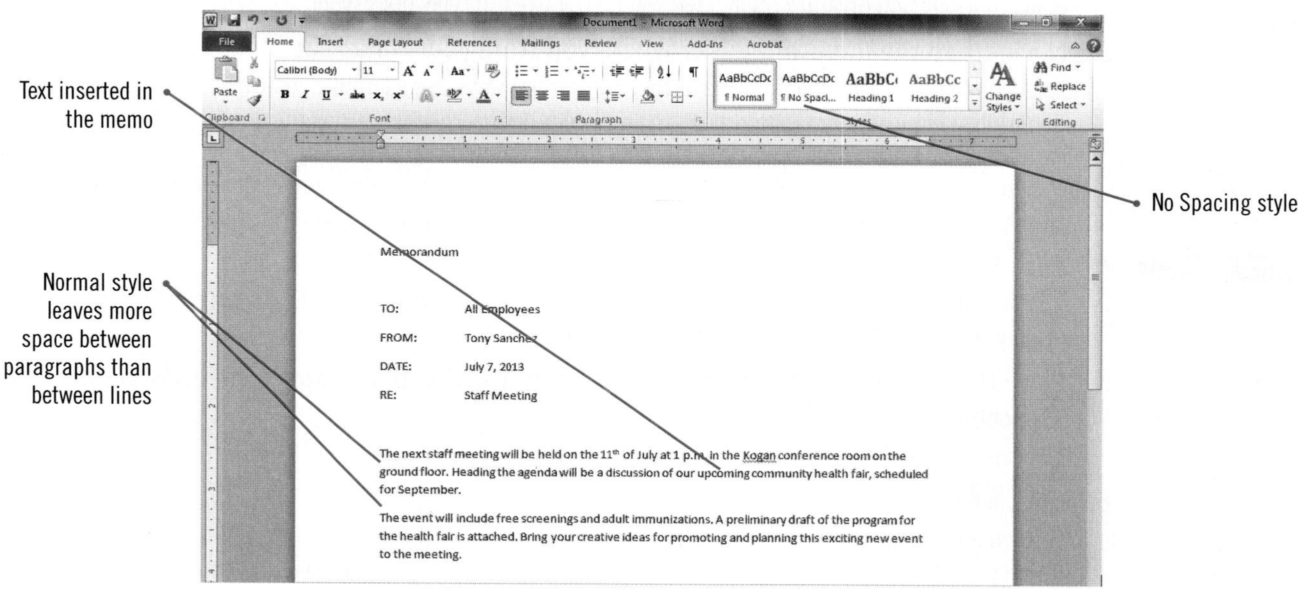

TABLE A-2: Automatic features that appear as you type in Word

feature	what appears	to use
AutoComplete	A ScreenTip suggesting text to insert appears as you type	Press [Enter] to insert the text suggested by the ScreenTip; continue typing to reject the suggestion
AutoCorrect	A small blue box appears when you place the pointer over text corrected by AutoCorrect; an AutoCorrect Options button appears when you point to the blue box	Word automatically corrects typos, minor spelling errors, and capitalization, and adds typographical symbols (such as © and ™) as you type; to reverse an AutoCorrect adjustment, click the AutoCorrect Options list arrow, then click the option that will undo the action
Spelling and Grammar	A red wavy line under a word indicates a possible misspelling; a green wavy line under text indicates a possible grammar error	Right-click red- or green-underlined text to display a shortcut menu of correction options; click a correction option to accept it and remove the wavy underline

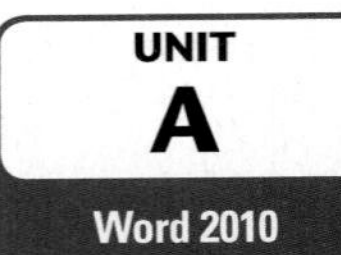

Saving a Document

To store a document permanently so you can open it and edit it at another time, you must save it as a **file**. When you **save** a document you give it a name, called a **filename**, and indicate the location where you want to store the file. Files created in Word 2010 are automatically assigned the .docx file extension to distinguish them from files created in other software programs. You can save a document using the Save button on the Quick Access toolbar or the Save command on the File tab. Once you have saved a document for the first time, you should save it again every few minutes and always before printing so that the saved file is updated to reflect your latest changes. You save your memo using a descriptive filename and the default file extension.

STEPS

TROUBLE

If you don't see the extension .docx as part of the filename, the setting in Windows to display file extensions is not active.

1. **Click the Save button on the Quick Access toolbar**

   The first time you save a document, the Save As dialog box opens, as shown in Figure A-5. The default filename, Memorandum, appears in the File name text box. The default filename is based on the first few words of the document. The default file extension, .docx, appears in the Save as type list box. Table A-3 describes the functions of some of the buttons in the Save As dialog box.

2. **Type WMP A-Staff Memo in the File name text box**

   The new filename replaces the default filename. Giving your documents brief descriptive filenames makes it easier to locate and organize them later. You do not need to type .docx when you type a new filename.

3. **Navigate to the drive and folder where you store your Data Files**

   You can navigate to a different drive or folder in several ways. For example, you can click a drive or folder in the Address bar or the navigation pane to go directly to that location. Click the double arrow in the Address bar to display a list of drives and folders. You can also double-click a drive or folder in the folder window to change the active location. When you are finished navigating to the drive or folder where you store your Data Files, that location appears in the Address bar. Your Save As dialog box should resemble Figure A-6.

QUICK TIP

To save a document so it can be opened in an older version of Word, click the Save as type list arrow, then click Word 97-2003 Document (*.doc).

4. **Click Save**

   The document is saved to the drive and folder you specified in the Save As dialog box, and the title bar displays the new filename, WMP A-Staff Memo.docx.

5. **Place the insertion point before September in the first paragraph, type early, then press [Spacebar]**

   You can continue to work on a document after you have saved it with a new filename.

6. **Click**

   Your change to the memo is saved. After you save a document for the first time, you must continue to save the changes you make to the document. You can also press [Ctrl][S] to save a document.

Windows Live and Microsoft Office Web Apps

All Office programs include the capability to incorporate feedback—called online collaboration—across the Internet or a company network. Using **cloud computing** (work done in a virtual environment), you can take advantage of Web programs called Microsoft Office Web Apps, which are simplified versions of the programs found in the Microsoft Office 2010 suite. Because these programs are online, they take up no computer disk space and are accessed using Windows Live SkyDrive, a free service from Microsoft. Using Windows Live SkyDrive, you and your colleagues can create and store documents in a "cloud" and make the documents available to whomever you grant access. To use Windows Live SkyDrive, you need a free Windows Live ID, which you obtain at the Windows Live Web site. You can find more information in the "Working with Windows Live and Office Web Apps" appendix.

FIGURE A-5: **Save As dialog box**

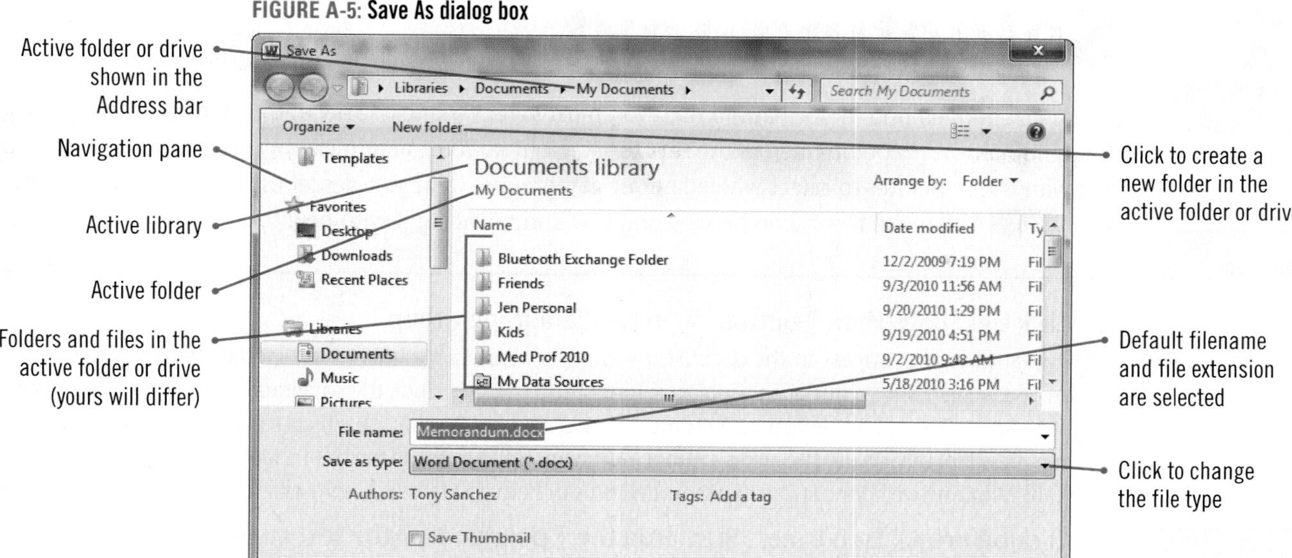

FIGURE A-6: **File to be saved to the Unit A folder**

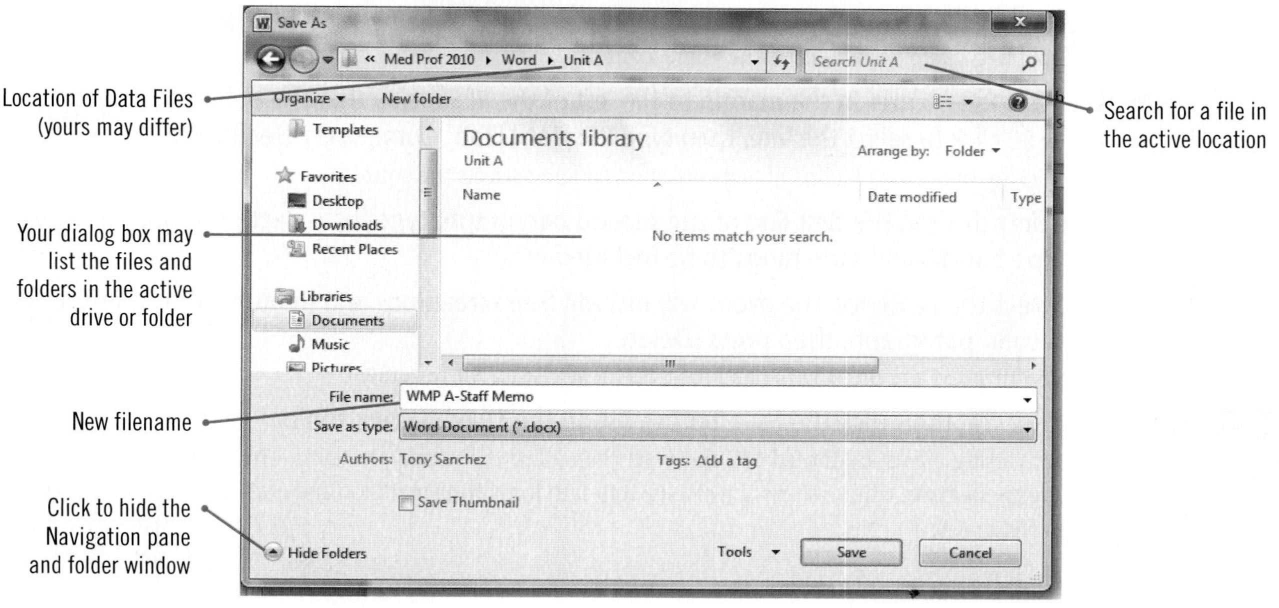

TABLE A-3: **Save As dialog box buttons**

button	use to
Back	Navigate back to the last location shown in the Address bar
Forward	Navigate to the location that was previously shown in the Address bar
Organize ▾	Open a menu of commands related to organizing the selected file or folder, including Cut, Copy, Delete, Rename, and Properties
New folder	Create a new folder in the current folder or drive
Change your view	Change the way folder and file information is shown in the folder window in the Save As dialog box; click the Change your view button to toggle between views, or click the list arrow to open a menu of view options

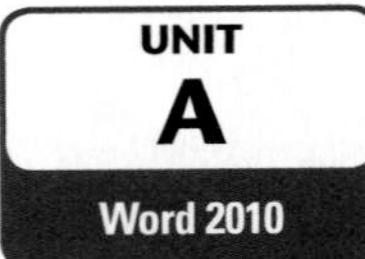

Selecting Text

Before deleting, editing, or formatting text, you must **select** the text. Selecting text involves clicking and dragging the I-beam pointer across the text to highlight it. You can also click in the margin to the left of text with the pointer to select whole lines or paragraphs. Table A-4 describes the many ways to select text. You revise the memo by selecting text and replacing it with new text.

STEPS

1. **Click the Show/Hide ¶ button ¶ in the Paragraph group**
   Formatting marks appear in the document window. **Formatting marks** are special characters that appear on your screen but do not print. Common formatting marks include the paragraph symbol (¶), which shows the end of a paragraph—wherever you press [Enter]; the dot symbol (·), which represents a space—wherever you press [Spacebar]; and the arrow symbol (→), which shows the location of a tab stop—wherever you press [Tab]. Working with formatting marks turned on can help you to select, edit, and format text with precision.

QUICK TIP
You deselect text by clicking anywhere in the document window.

2. **Click before All Employees, then drag the I pointer over the text to select it**
   The words are selected, as shown in Figure A-7. For now, you can ignore the faint toolbar that appears over text when you first select it.

3. **Type Medical Staff**
   The text you type replaces the selected text.

4. **Double-click Tony, type your first name, double-click Sanchez, then type your last name**
   Double-clicking a word selects the entire word.

TROUBLE
If you delete text by mistake, immediately click the Undo button on the Quick Access toolbar to restore the deleted text to the document.

5. **Place the pointer in the margin to the left of the RE: line so that the pointer changes to , click to select the line, then type RE: [Tab] [Tab] Community Health Fair**
   Clicking to the left of a line of text with the pointer selects the entire line.

6. **Select draft in the first line of the second paragraph, type list, select program for, then type booths and screenings to be included in**

7. **Select the sentence The event will include free screenings and immunizations. in the second paragraph, then press [Delete]**
   Selecting text and pressing [Delete] removes the text from the document.

QUICK TIP
Always save before and after editing text.

8. **Click ¶, then click the Save button on the Quick Access toolbar**
   Formatting marks are turned off, and your changes to the memo are saved. The Show/Hide ¶ button is a **toggle button**, which means you can use it to turn formatting marks on and off. The edited memo is shown in Figure A-8.

FIGURE A-7: Text selected in the memo

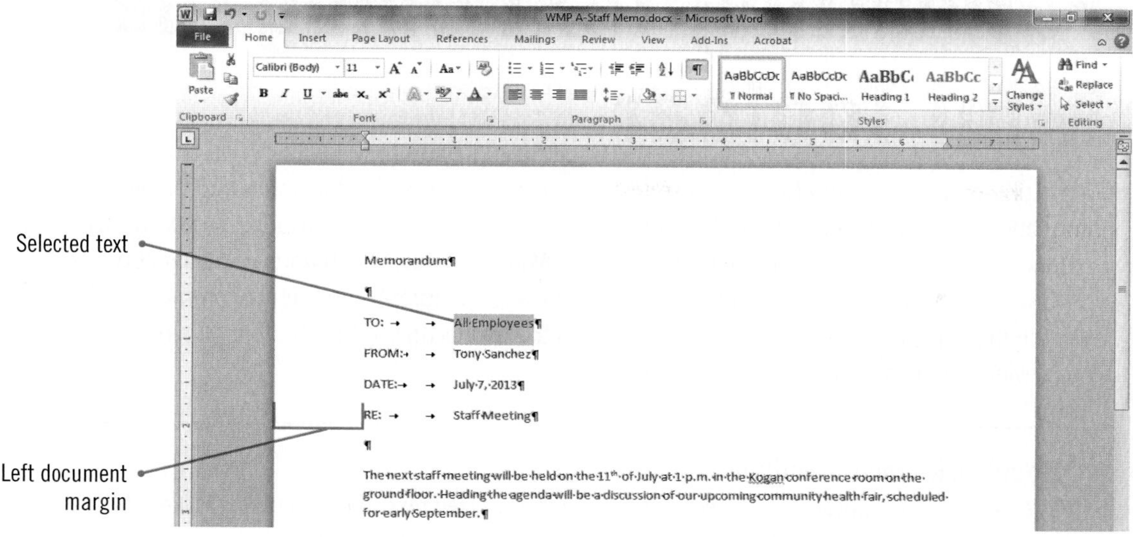

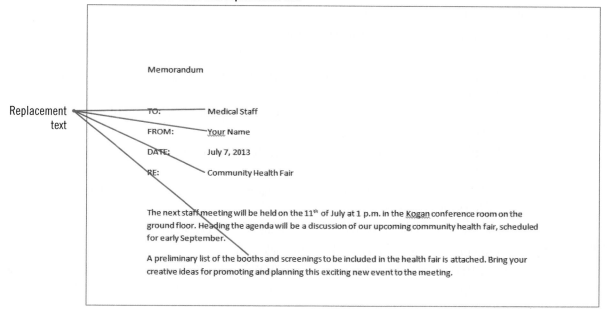

FIGURE A-8: Edited memo with replacement text

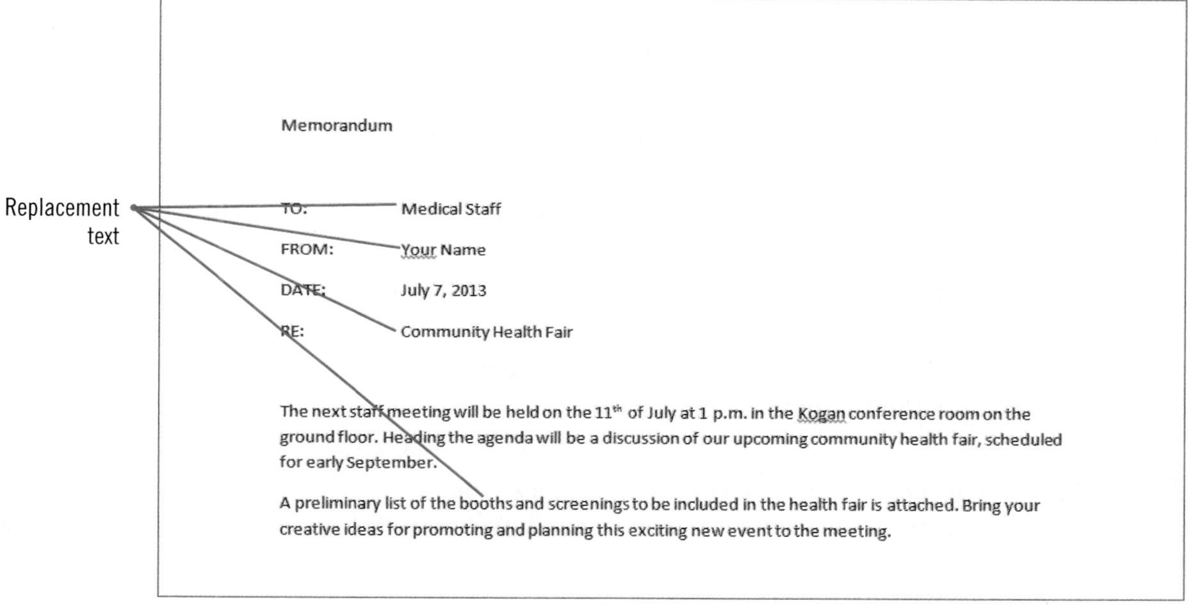

TABLE A-4: Methods for selecting text

to select	use the pointer to
Any amount of text	Drag over the text
A word	Double-click the word
A line of text	Click with the pointer to the left of the line
A sentence	Press and hold [Ctrl], then click the sentence
A paragraph	Triple-click the paragraph or double-click with the pointer to the left of the paragraph
A large block of text	Click at the beginning of the selection, press and hold [Shift], then click at the end of the selection
Multiple nonconsecutive selections	Select the first selection, then press and hold [Ctrl] as you select each additional selection
An entire document	Triple-click with the pointer to the left of any text; press [Ctrl][A]; or click the Select button in the Editing group on the Home tab, and then click Select All

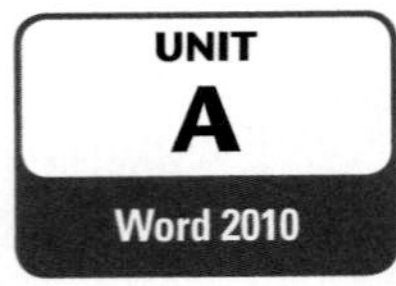

UNIT A
Word 2010

Formatting Text Using the Mini Toolbar

Formatting text is a fast and fun way to spruce up the appearance of a document and highlight important information. You can easily change the font, color, size, style, and other attributes of text by selecting the text and clicking a command on the Home tab. The **Mini toolbar**, which appears faintly above text when you first select it, also includes commonly used text and paragraph formatting commands. You enhance the appearance of the memo by formatting the text using the Mini toolbar. When you are finished, you preview the memo for errors and then print it.

STEPS

TROUBLE
If the Mini toolbar disappears, right-click the selection to display it again.

1. **Double-click Memorandum**
   The Mini toolbar appears in ghosted fashion over the selected text. When you point to the Mini toolbar, it becomes solid, as shown in Figure A-9. You click a formatting option on the Mini toolbar to apply it to the selected text. Table A-5 describes the function of the buttons on the Mini toolbar. The buttons on the Mini toolbar are also available on the Ribbon.

2. **Click the Center button on the Mini toolbar**
   The word "Memorandum" is centered between the left and right document margins.

QUICK TIP
Click the Shrink Font button to decrease the font size.

3. **Click the Grow Font button on the Mini toolbar eight times, then click the Bold button B on the Mini toolbar**
   Each time you click the Grow Font button the selected text is enlarged. Applying **bold** to the text makes it thicker and darker.

4. **Select TO:, click B, select FROM:, click B, select DATE:, click B, select RE:, then click B**
   Bold is applied to the heading text.

5. **Click the blank line between the RE: line and the body text, then click the Bottom Border button in the Paragraph group**
   A single-line border is added between the heading and the body text in the memo.

QUICK TIP
You can customize your Quick Access toolbar to include the Quick Print button, which prints a document using the default print settings.

6. **Save the document, click the File tab, then click Print**
   Information related to printing the document appears on the Print tab in Backstage view. Options for printing the document appear on the left side of the Print tab and a preview of the document as it will look when printed appears on the right side, as shown in Figure A-10. Before you print a document, it's a good habit to examine it closely so you can identify and correct any problems.

7. **Click the Zoom In button five times, then proofread your document carefully for errors**
   The document is enlarged in print preview. If you notice errors in your document, you need to correct them before you print. To do this, press [Esc] or click the Home tab to close Backstage view, correct any mistakes, save your changes, click the File tab, and then click the Print command again to be ready to print the document.

8. **Click the Print button on the Print tab**
   A copy of the memo prints using the default print settings. To change the current printer, change the number of copies to print, select what pages of a document to print, or modify another print setting, you simply change the appropriate setting on the Print tab before clicking the Print button.

9. **Click the File tab, then click Close**
   The document closes, but the Word program window remains open.

FIGURE A-9: Mini toolbar

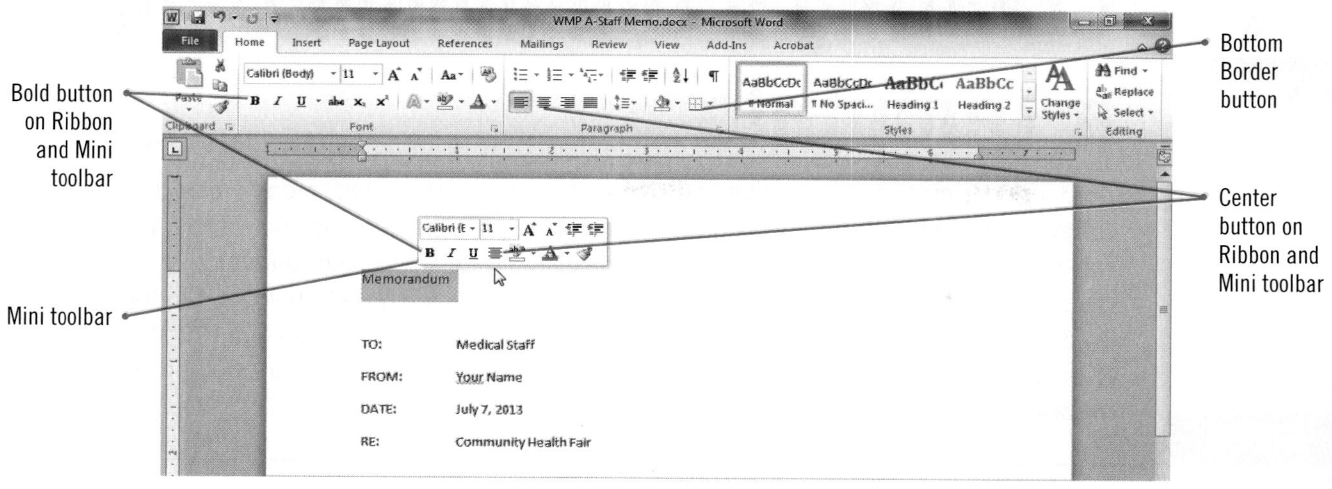

FIGURE A-10: Preview of the completed memo

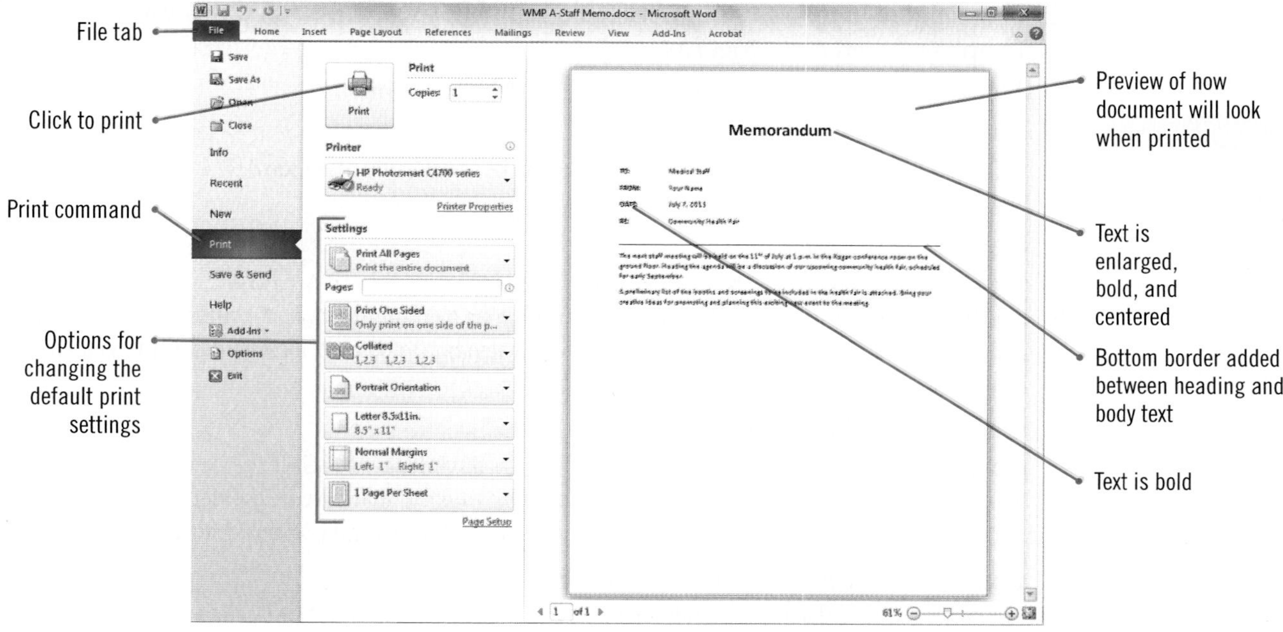

TABLE A-5: Buttons on the Mini toolbar

button	use to	button	use to
Calibri (E ▾	Change the font of text	*I*	Italicize text
11 ▾	Change the font size of text	U	Underline text
A˄	Make text larger	≡	Center text between the margins
A˅	Make text smaller	ab ▾	Apply colored highlighting to text
⇤	Decrease the indent level of a paragraph	A ▾	Change the color of text
⇥	Increase the indent level of a paragraph	🖌	Copy the formats applied to text to other text
B	Apply bold to text		

UNIT
A
Word 2010

Creating a Document Using a Template

Word includes many templates that you can use to create faxes, letters, reports, brochures, and other professionally designed documents quickly. A **template** is a formatted document that contains placeholder text, which you replace with your own text. To create a document that is based on a template, you use the New command on the File tab, and then select a template to use. You can then customize the document and save it with a new filename. You want to fax a draft of the health fair program to Dr. Carla Zimmerman, director of the clinic, who is attending a conference in Morocco. You use a template to create a fax cover sheet.

STEPS

QUICK TIP
To create a new blank document, click Create.

QUICK TIP
Double-clicking a template icon also opens a new document based on the template.

QUICK TIP
You can delete a content control by right-clicking it, and then clicking Remove Content Control on the menu that opens.

1. **Click the File tab, then click New**

   The New tab opens in Backstage view, as shown in Figure A-11.

2. **Click Sample templates in the Available Templates section, scroll down the list of Available Templates, then click Oriel Fax**

   A preview of the Oriel Fax template appears in the preview section.

3. **Click Create**

   The Oriel Fax template opens as a new document in the document window. It contains placeholder text, which you can replace with your own information.

4. **Click [Pick the date]**

   The placeholder text is selected and appears inside a content control. A **content control** is an interactive object that you use to customize a document with your own information. A content control might include placeholder text, a drop-down list of choices, or a calendar. To deselect a content control, you click a blank area of the document.

5. **Click the Pick the date list arrow**

   A calendar opens below the content control. You use the calendar to select the date you want to appear on your document—simply click a date on the calendar to enter that date in the document. You can use the arrows to the left and right of the month and year to scroll the calendar and display a different month.

6. **Click the Today button on the calendar**

   The current date replaces the placeholder text.

7. **Click [TYPE THE RECIPIENT NAME], type Dr. Carla Zimmerman, Guest, click [Type the recipient fax number], then type 1-212-44-555-1510**

   You do not need to drag to select the placeholder text in a content control, you can simply click it. The text you type replaces the placeholder text.

8. **Click [Type the recipient phone number], press [Delete] twice, press [Backspace] seven times, then type HOTEL MARRAKECH, ROOM 1275**

   The recipient phone number content control is removed from the document.

9. **If the text in the From line is not your name, drag to select the text, then type your name**

   When the document is created, Word automatically enters the user name identified in the Word Options dialog box in the From line. This text is not placeholder text, so you have to drag to select it.

10. **Replace the remaining heading placeholder text with the text shown in Figure A-12, delete the CC: content control, click the File tab, click Save As, then save the document as WMP A-Zimmerman Fax to the drive and folder where you store your Data Files**

    The document is saved with the filename WMP A-Zimmerman Fax.

FIGURE A-11: New tab in Backstage view

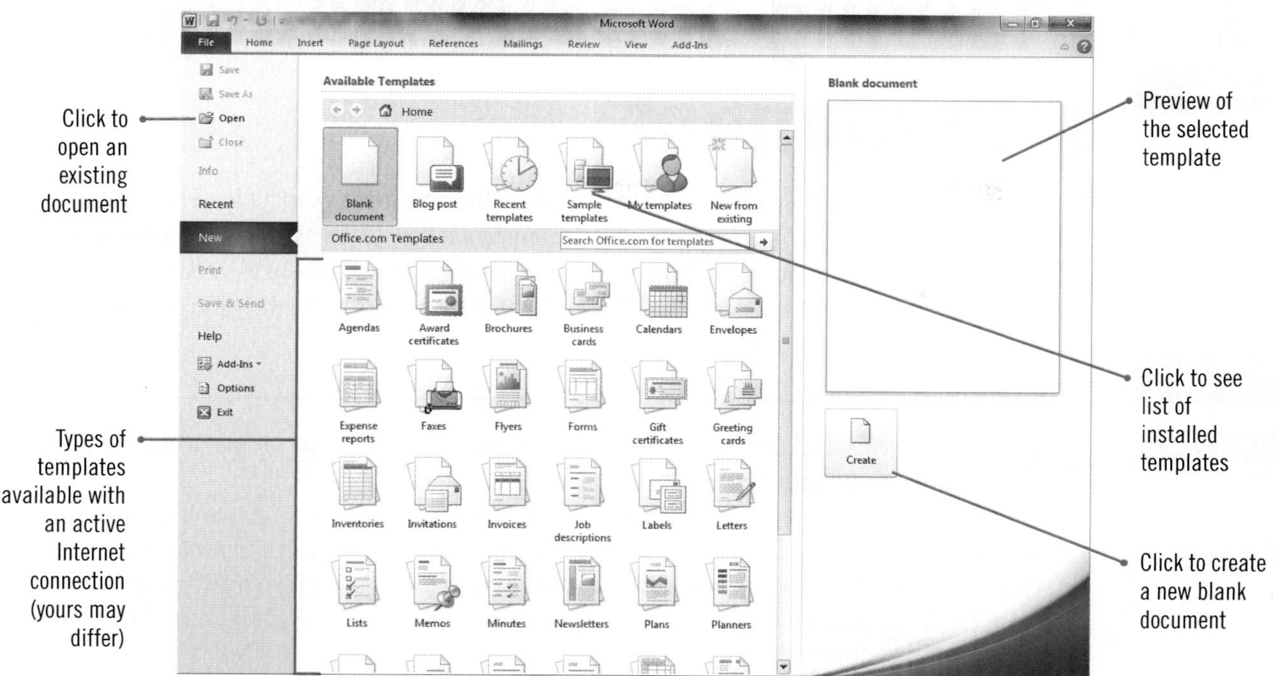

FIGURE A-12: Document created using the Oriel fax template

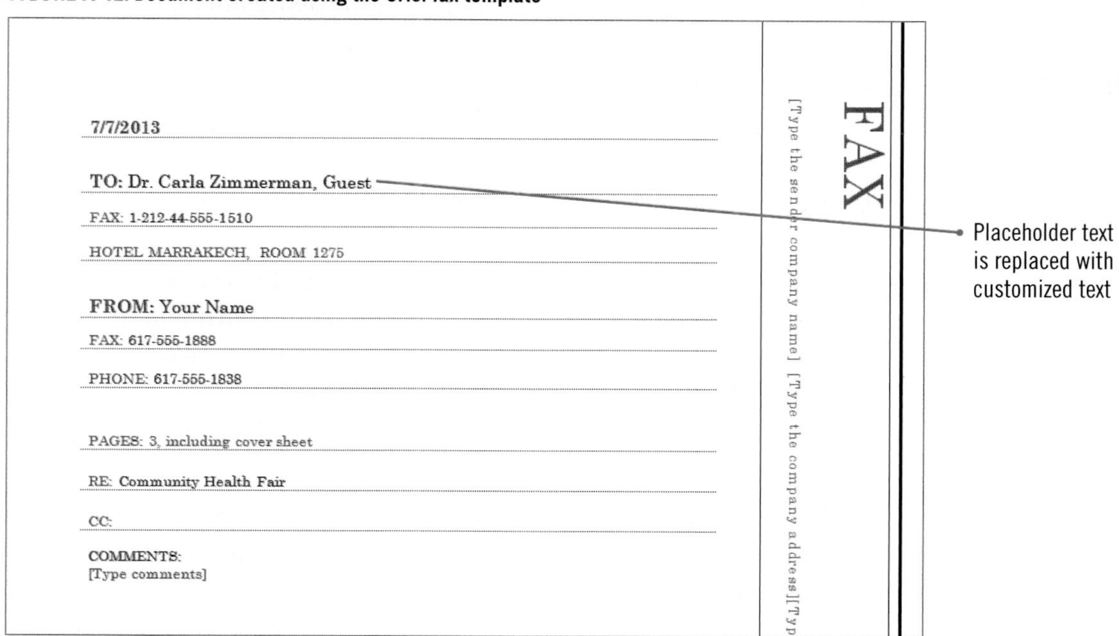

Using the Undo, Redo, and Repeat commands

Word remembers the editing and formatting changes you make so that you can easily reverse or repeat them. You can reverse the last action you took by clicking the Undo button on the Quick Access toolbar, or you can undo a series of actions by clicking the Undo list arrow and selecting the action you want to reverse. When you undo an action using the Undo list arrow, you also undo all the actions above it in the list—that is, all actions that were performed after the action you selected. Similarly, you can keep the change you just reversed by using the Redo button on the Quick Access toolbar. The Redo button appears only immediately after clicking the Undo button to undo a change.

If you want to repeat an action you just completed, you can use the Repeat button on the Quick Access toolbar. For example, if you just typed "thank you," clicking inserts "thank you" at the location of the insertion point. If you just applied bold, clicking applies bold to the currently selected text. You can also repeat the last action you took by pressing [F4].

Word 2010

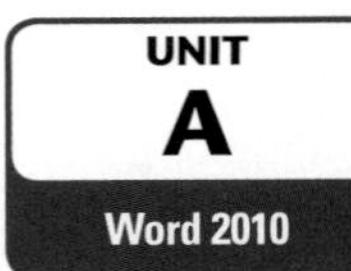

Viewing and Navigating a Document

The Word Zoom feature lets you enlarge a document in the document window to get a close-up view of a detail or reduce the size of the document in the document window for an overview of the layout as a whole. You zoom in and out on a document using the tools in the Zoom group on the View tab and the Zoom level buttons and Zoom slider on the status bar. You find it is helpful to zoom in and out on the document as you finalize the fax cover sheet.

STEPS

QUICK TIP
When the horizontal scroll bar is available, you can use the scroll bar and the scroll box to move the document left and right in the document window.

1. **Click the down scroll arrow at the bottom of the vertical scroll bar until COMMENTS: is near the top of your document window**
   The scroll arrows or scroll bars allow you to **scroll** through a document. You scroll through a document when you want to display different parts of the document in the document window. You can also scroll by clicking the scroll bar above and below the scroll box, or by dragging the scroll box up or down in the scroll bar. In longer documents, you can click the Previous Page button or the Next Page button on the scroll bar to display the document page by page.
2. **Click [Type comments], then type A draft list of the free screenings, adult immunizations, and information booths to be included in the September community health fair is attached. Please edit the list and return it to me.**
3. **Click the Zoom level button 100% on the status bar**
   The Zoom dialog box opens. You use the Zoom dialog box to select a zoom level for displaying the document in the document window.

QUICK TIP
You can also click the Zoom button in the Zoom group on the View tab to open the Zoom dialog box.

4. **Click the Whole page option button, then click OK**
   The entire document is displayed in the document window.
5. **Click the text at the bottom of the page to move the insertion point to the bottom of the page, click the View tab, then click the Page Width button in the Zoom group**
   The document is enlarged to the width of the document window. When you enlarge a document, the area where the insertion point is located appears in the document window.
6. **Click in the Urgent box, type x, then click the One Page button in the Zoom group**
   The entire document is displayed in the document window.
7. **Click Fax to move the insertion point to the upper-right corner of the page, then move the Zoom slider to the right until the Zoom percentage is 100%, as shown in Figure A-13**
   Moving the Zoom slider to the right enlarges the document in the document window. Moving the zoom slider to the left allows you to see more of the page at a reduced size. You can also move the Zoom slider by clicking a point on the Zoom slide, or by clicking the Zoom Out and Zoom In buttons.

TROUBLE
Your company name content control might include the name of a company, such as Microsoft. Right-click it, click Remove Content Control, then select the text and press [Delete].

8. **Click the Zoom In button three times, right-click the vertical placeholder [Type the sender company name], click Remove Content Control, right-click [Type the company address], click Remove Content Control, click [Type the company phone number], then type Riverwalk Medical Clinic, Cambridge, MA**
   The text you type replaces the vertical placeholder text. You do not always need to replace the placeholder text with the type of information suggested in the content control.
9. **Click 130%, click the 100% option button, click OK, then save the document**
   The completed fax cover sheet is shown in Figure A-14.
10. **Submit the document to your instructor, close the file, then exit Word**

FIGURE A-13: Zoom slider

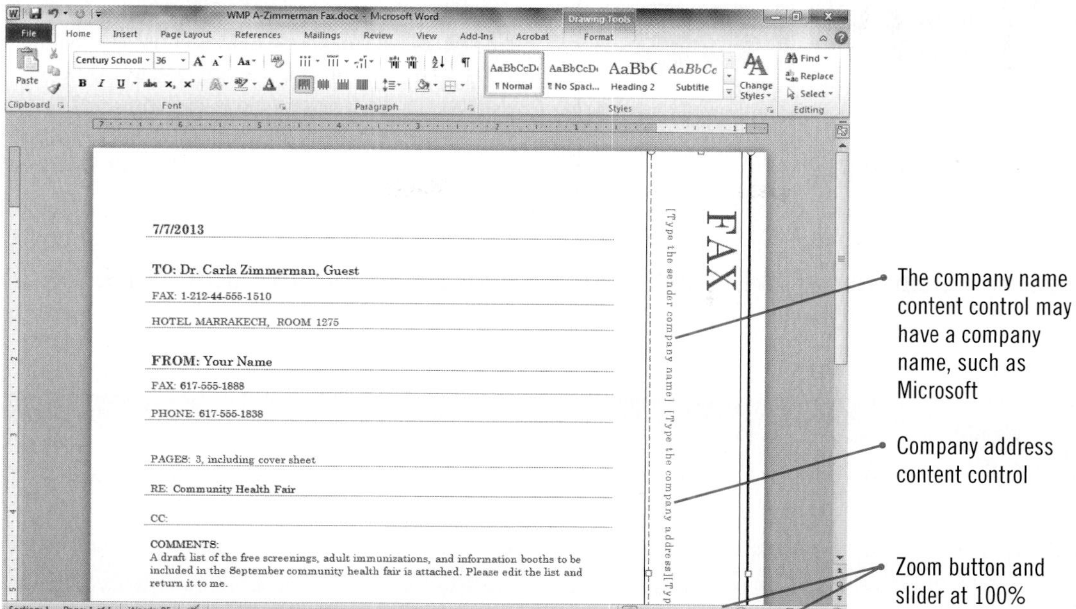

FIGURE A-14: Completed fax cover sheet

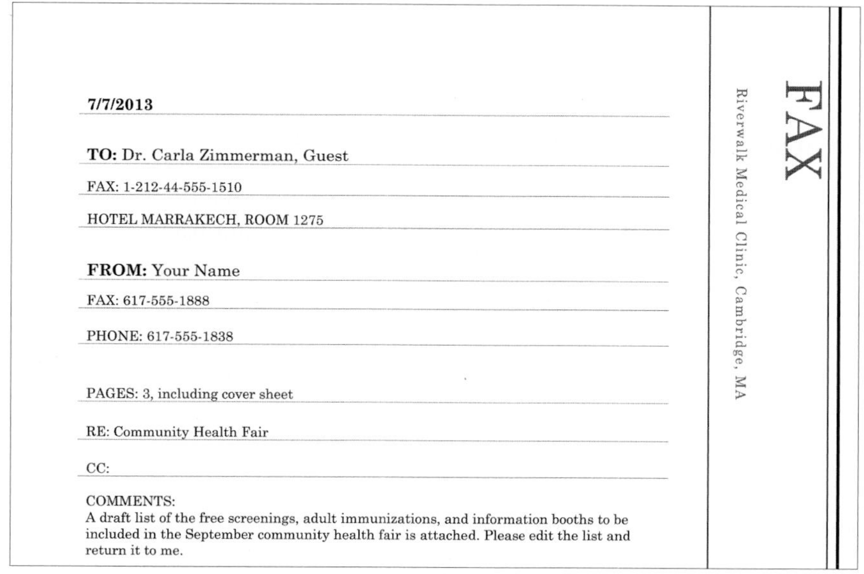

FAX

Riverwalk Medical Clinic, Cambridge, MA

7/7/2013

TO: Dr. Carla Zimmerman, Guest

FAX: 1-212-44-555-1510

HOTEL MARRAKECH, ROOM 1275

FROM: Your Name

FAX: 617-555-1888

PHONE: 617-555-1838

PAGES: 3, including cover sheet

RE: Community Health Fair

CC:

COMMENTS:
A draft list of the free screenings, adult immunizations, and information booths to be included in the September community health fair is attached. Please edit the list and return it to me.

Using Word document views

Document **views** are different ways of displaying a document in the document window. Each Word view provides features that are useful for working on different types of documents. The default view, **Print Layout view**, displays a document as it will look on a printed page. Print Layout view is helpful for formatting text and pages, including adjusting document margins, creating columns of text, inserting graphics, and formatting headers and footers. Also useful is **Draft view**, which shows a simplified layout of a document, without margins, headers and footers, or graphics. When you want to quickly type, edit, and format text, it's often easiest to work in Draft view. Other Word views are helpful for performing specialized tasks. **Full Screen Reading view** displays document text so that it is easy to read and annotate. You can easily highlight content, add comments, and track and review changes in Full Screen Reading view. **Web Layout view** allows you to format Web pages or documents that will be viewed on a computer screen. In Web Layout view, a document appears just as it will when viewed with a Web browser. Finally, **Outline view** is useful for editing and formatting longer documents that include multiple headings. Outline view allows you to reorganize text by moving the headings. You switch between views by clicking the view buttons on the status bar or by using the commands on the View tab. Changing views does not affect how the printed document will appear. It simply changes the way you view the document in the document window.

Practice

Concepts Review

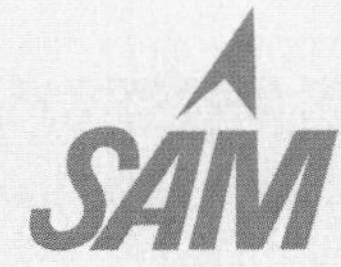

For current SAM information, including versions and content details, visit SAM Central (http://www.cengage.com/samcentral). If you have a SAM user profile, you may have access to hands-on instruction, practice, and assessment of the skills covered in this unit. Since various versions of SAM are supported throughout the life of this text, check with your instructor for the correct instructions and URL/Web site for accessing assignments.

Label the elements of the Word program window shown in Figure A-15.

FIGURE A-15

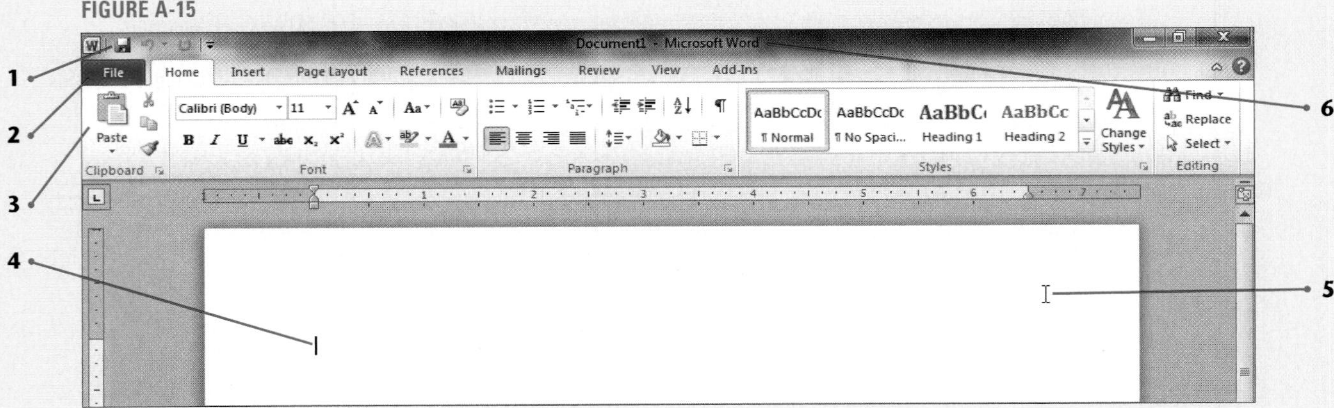

Match each term with the statement that best describes it.

7. Template
8. Formatting marks
9. Status bar
10. Ribbon
11. AutoComplete
12. Horizontal ruler
13. AutoCorrect
14. Zoom slider

a. Provides access to Word commands
b. A formatted document that contains placeholder text
c. Displays tab settings and paragraph indents
d. Enlarges and reduces the document in the document window
e. Suggests text to insert into a document
f. Displays the number of pages in the current document
g. Fixes certain errors as you type
h. Special characters that appear on screen but do not print

Select the best answer from the list of choices.

15. Which tab includes buttons for formatting text?
- **a.** View
- **b.** Page Layout
- **c.** Insert
- **d.** Home

16. Which of the following shows the number of words in the document?
- **a.** The status bar
- **b.** The Mini toolbar
- **c.** The title bar
- **d.** The Ribbon

17. Which element of the Word program window shows the settings for the top and bottom document margins?
- **a.** Vertical scroll bar
- **b.** View tab
- **c.** Vertical ruler
- **d.** Status bar

18. Which of the following is not included in a ScreenTip for a command?
- **a.** Description of the function of the command
- **b.** Link to a help topic on the command
- **c.** Keyboard shortcut for the command
- **d.** Alternative location of the command

19. Which view is best for annotating text with comments and highlighting?

a. Full Screen Reading view
b. Draft view
c. Print Layout view
d. Outline view

20. What is the default file extension for a document created in Word 2010?

a. .dot
b. .doc
c. .dotx
d. .docx

Skills Review

1. Explore the Word program window.

a. Start Word.
b. Identify as many elements of the Word program window as you can without referring to the unit material.
c. Click the File tab, then click the Info, Recent, New, Print, Save & Send, and Help commands.
d. Click each tab on the Ribbon, review the groups and buttons on each tab, then return to the Home tab.
e. Point to each button on the Home tab and read the ScreenTips.
f. Click the view buttons to view the blank document in each view, then return to Print Layout view.
g. Use the Zoom slider to zoom all the way in and all the way out on the document, then return to 100%.

2. Start a document.

a. In a new blank document, type **FAX** at the top of the page, then press [Enter] two times.
b. Type the following, pressing [Tab] as indicated and pressing [Enter] at the end of each line:
To: [Tab] [Tab] **Valley OB/GYN**
From: [Tab] [Tab] **Your Name**
Date: [Tab] [Tab] **Today's date**
Re: [Tab] [Tab] **Changes at PMC Labs**
Pages: [Tab] [Tab] **2**
Fax: [Tab] [Tab] **(802) 555-5478**
c. Press [Enter] again, then type **Effective June 1st, PMC Labs will pick up laboratory specimens at 10:00 a.m. and 4:15 p.m. daily. We trust the addition of the afternoon pick up time will improve the efficiency of our service. All abnormal results will continue to be reported to your office by telephone.**
d. Press [Enter], then type **As always, we welcome your comments and suggestions on how we can better serve you. Our clients are important to us.**
e. Insert this sentence at the beginning of the second paragraph: **The lab will continue to be open until 7:00 p.m. for drop-in service.**
f. Use the [Backspace] key to delete **2** in the Pages: line, then type **1**.
g. Use the [Delete] key to delete **4:15** in the first paragraph, then type **3:30**.

3. Save a document.

a. Click the Save button on the Quick Access toolbar.
b. Save the document as **WMP A-Valley Fax** with the default file extension to the drive and folder where you store your Data Files.
c. After your name, type a comma, press [Spacebar], then type **PMC Labs**.
d. Save the document.

4. Select text.

a. Turn on the display of formatting marks.
b. Select the **Re:** line, then type **Re:** [Tab] [Tab] **New morning pick-up time**.
c. Select **June 1st,** (including the comma) in the first sentence, then type **May 15th,** (including the comma).
d. Select **afternoon** in the second sentence of the first paragraph, then type **morning**.
e. Delete the sentence **Our clients are important to us.**
f. Turn off the display of formatting marks, then save the document.

Skills Review (continued)

5. **Format text using the Mini toolbar.**
   a. Select **FAX**, then click the Grow Font button on the Mini toolbar 11 times.
   b. Apply bold to the word **FAX**, then center it on the page.
   c. Apply a bottom border under the word **FAX**.
   d. Apply bold to the following words in the fax heading: **To:**, **From:**, **Date:**, **Re:**, **Pages:**, and **Fax:**.
   e. Preview the document using the Print command.
   f. Zoom in on the document, then proofread the fax.
   g. Correct any typing errors in your document, then save the document. Compare your document to Figure A-16.
   h. Submit the fax to your instructor, then close the document.

FIGURE A-16

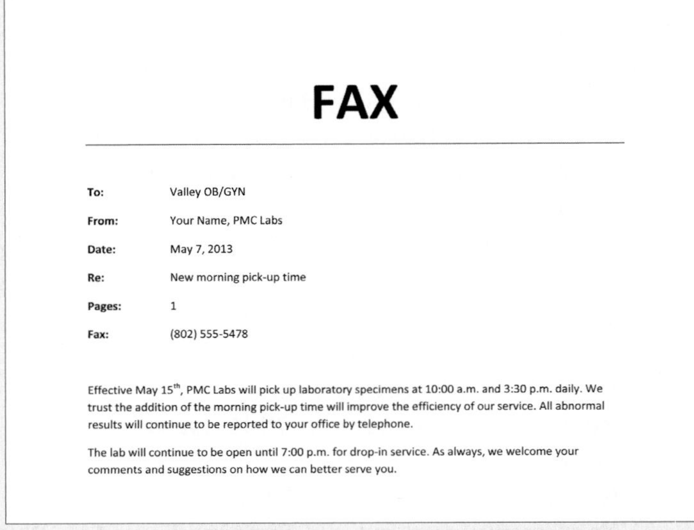

FAX

To: Valley OB/GYN
From: Your Name, PMC Labs
Date: May 7, 2013
Re: New morning pick-up time
Pages: 1
Fax: (802) 555-5478

Effective May 15th, PMC Labs will pick up laboratory specimens at 10:00 a.m. and 3:30 p.m. daily. We trust the addition of the morning pick-up time will improve the efficiency of our service. All abnormal results will continue to be reported to your office by telephone.

The lab will continue to be open until 7:00 p.m. for drop-in service. As always, we welcome your comments and suggestions on how we can better serve you.

6. **Create a document using a template.**
   a. Click the File tab, click New, then click Sample templates.
   b. Create a new document using the Origin Fax template.
   c. Insert today's date using the date content control.
   d. If your name is not on the From line, select the text in the From content control, then type your name.
   e. Click the "Type the sender phone number" placeholder text, press [Delete]; click the "Type the sender fax number" placeholder text, type **555-5748**; click the "Type the sender company name" placeholder text, then type **PMC Labs**.
   f. Type **Staff** to replace the "To:" placeholder text; select "Phone:", type **Re:**; type **New PMC Labs pick-up time** to replace the "Type the recipient phone number" placeholder text; type **555-1176** to replace the "Type the recipient fax number" placeholder text; then type **North Mountain Family Health** to replace the "Type the recipient company name" placeholder text.
   g. Save the document with the filename **WMP A-Lab Fax** to the drive and folder where you store your Data Files.
7. **View and navigate a document.**
   a. Scroll down until Comments is near the top of your document window.
   b. Replace the Comments placeholder text with the following text: **PMC Labs has added a morning pick-up time for laboratory specimens. Effective May 15th, PMC Labs will pick up specimens at 10:00 a.m. and 3:30 p.m.**
   c. Use the Zoom dialog box to view the Whole Page.
   d. Click Comments to move the insertion point to the middle of the page, then use the Zoom slider to set the Zoom percentage at approximately 100%.
   e. Scroll to the bottom of the page, click in the Please Recycle box, type **x** if one is not added automatically when you click the box, then save your changes.
   f. Preview the document, then correct any errors, saving changes if necessary. Compare your document to Figure A-17. Submit the document to your instructor, close the file, then exit Word.

FIGURE A-17

Fax 5/7/2013

From: Your Name
Phone:
Fax: 555-5748
Company Name: PMC Labs

To: Staff
Re: New PMC Labs pick-up time
Fax: 555-1176
Company Name: North Mountain Family Health

Comments:

PMC Labs has added a morning pick-up time for laboratory specimens. Effective May 15th, PMC Labs will pick up specimens at 10:00 a.m. and 3:30 p.m.

Independent Challenge 1

Yesterday you interviewed for a job as marketing director at Oakland Medical Associates. You spoke with several people at the office, including Sharon Price, director of human resources, whose business card is shown in Figure A-18. You need to write a follow-up letter to Ms. Price, thanking her for the interview and expressing your interest in the practice and the position. She also asked you to send her some documents you have created, which you will enclose with the letter.

a. Start Word and save a new blank document as **WMP A-Price Letter** to the drive and folder where you store your Data Files.

b. Begin the letter by clicking the No Spacing button in the Styles group. You use this button to apply the No Spacing style to the document so that your document does not include extra space between paragraphs.

c. Type a personal letterhead for the letter that includes your name, address, telephone number, and e-mail address. If Word formats your e-mail address as a hyperlink, right-click your e-mail address, then click Remove Hyperlink. (*Note*: Format the letterhead after you finish typing the letter.)

d. Three lines below the bottom of the letterhead, type today's date.

e. Four lines below the date, type the inside address, referring to Figure A-18 for the address information. Be sure to include the recipient's title, company name, and full mailing address in the inside address.

f. Two lines below the inside address, type **Dear Ms. Price:** for the salutation.

g. Two lines below the salutation, type the body of the letter according to the following guidelines:
- In the first paragraph, thank her for the interview. Then restate your interest in the position and express your desire to work for the practice. Add any specific details you think will enhance the power of your letter.
- In the second paragraph, note that you are enclosing three samples of your work, and explain something about the samples you are enclosing.
- Type a short final paragraph.

FIGURE A-18

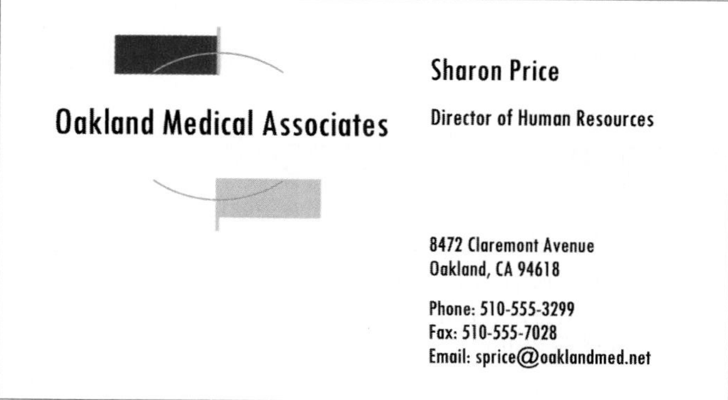

h. Two lines below the last body paragraph, type a closing, then four lines below the closing, type the signature block. Be sure to include your name in the signature block.

i. Two lines below the signature block, type an enclosure notation. (*Hint*: An enclosure notation usually includes the word "Enclosures" or the abbreviation "Enc." followed by the number of enclosures in parentheses.)

j. Format the letterhead with bold, centering, and a bottom border.

k. Save your changes.

l. Preview the letter, submit it to your instructor, then close the document and exit Word.

Independent Challenge 2

Your company has recently installed Word 2010 on its company network. As the training manager, it's your responsibility to teach employees how to use the new software productively. Now that they have begun working with Word 2010, several employees have asked you about sharing documents with colleagues using Windows Live SkyDrive. In response, you wrote a memo to all employees explaining Windows Live SkyDrive, some of its features, and how to register for a Windows Live ID. You now need to format the memo before distributing it.

a. Start Word, open the file **WMP A-1.docx** from the drive and folder where you store your Data Files, then read the memo to get a feel for its contents.

b. Save the file as **WMP A-SkyDrive Memo** to the drive and folder where you store your Data Files.

Independent Challenge 2 (continued)

c. Replace the information in the memo header with the information shown in Figure A-19. Make sure to include your name in the From line and the current date in the Date line.

d. Apply bold to **To:**, **From:**, **Date:**, and **Re:**.

e. Increase the size of **WORD TRAINING MEMORANDUM** to match Figure A-19, center the text on the page, add a border below it, then save your changes.

FIGURE A-19

WORD TRAINING MEMORANDUM

To:	All employees
From:	Your Name, Training Manager
Date:	Today's Date
Re:	Windows Live SkyDrive

Advanced Challenge Exercise

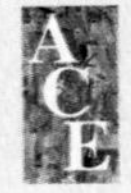

- Using the Font list on the Mini toolbar, apply a different font to **WORD TRAINING MEMORANDUM**. Make sure to select a font that is appropriate for a business memo.
- Using the Font Color button on the Mini toolbar, change the color of **WORD TRAINING MEMORANDUM** to an appropriate color.
- Save a copy of the memo in Word 97-2003 Document (*.doc) format as **WMP A-SkyDrive Memo ACE** to the drive or folder where you store your Data Files. (*Hint*: Use the Save as type list arrow in the Save As dialog box.)

f. Preview the memo, submit it to your instructor, then close the document and exit Word.

Independent Challenge 3

You are a cardiologist and research investigator for numerous trials pertaining to the study of heart disease. The president of the Allied Cardiology Association, Dr. Nathan Cummings, has asked you to be the keynote speaker at an upcoming conference on heart disease, to be held in Glacier National Park. You use one of the Word letter templates to write a letter to Dr. Cummings accepting the invitation and confirming the details. Your letter to Dr. Cummings should reference the following information:

- The conference will be held August 4–6, 2013, at the Many Glacier Hotel in the park.
- You have been asked to speak for an hour on Saturday, August 5, followed by one half hour for questions.
- Dr. Cummings suggested the lecture topic "Hope for the Heart: Advancements in Diagnosis and Treatment."
- Your talk will include a 45-minute slide presentation.
- The Allied Cardiology Association will make your travel arrangements.
- Your preference is to arrive at Glacier Park International Airport in Kalispell on the morning of Friday, August 4, and to depart on Monday, August 7. You would like to rent a car at the airport for the drive to the Many Glacier Hotel.
- You want to fly in and out of the airport closest to your home.

a. Start Word, click the File tab, click New, click Sample templates, and then select an appropriate letter template. Save the document as **WMP A-Cummings Letter** to the drive and folder where you store your Data Files.

b. Replace the placeholders in the letterhead with your personal information. Include your name, address, phone number, and e-mail address. Delete any placeholders that do not apply. (*Hints*: Depending on the template you choose, the letterhead might be located at the top or on the side of the document. You can press [Enter] when typing in a horizontal placeholder to add an additional line of text. You can also change the format of text typed in a placeholder. If your e-mail address appears as a hyperlink, right-click the e-mail address and click Remove Hyperlink.)

c. Use the Pick the date content control to select the current date.

d. Replace the placeholders in the inside address. Be sure to include Dr. Cumming's title and the name of the organization. Make up a street address and zip code.

e. Type **Dear Dr. Cummings:** for the salutation.

f. Use the information listed previously to type the body of the letter:
- In the first paragraph, accept the invitation to speak.
- In the second paragraph, confirm the important conference details, confirm your lecture topic, and provide any relevant details.

Independent Challenge 3 (continued)

- In the third paragraph, state your travel preferences.
- Type a short final paragraph.

g. Type **Sincerely,** for the closing, then include your name in the signature block.

h. Adjust the formatting of the letter as necessary. For example, remove bold formatting or change the font color of text to a more appropriate color.

Advanced Challenge Exercise

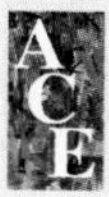

- Zoom in on the title "Hope for the Heart: Advancements in Diagnosis and Treatment", delete any quotation marks, then apply italics to the title.
- Select one word in the letter, such as an adjective, and replace it with another similar word to improve the meaning of the sentence.
- Correct your spelling and grammar errors, if any, by right-clicking any red- or green-underlined text and then choosing from the options on the shortcut menu.
- View the letter in Full Screen Reading view, then click the Close button to return to Print Layout view.

i. Proofread your letter, make corrections as needed, then save your changes.

j. Submit the letter to your instructor, close the document, then exit Word.

Real Life Independent Challenge

This Independent Challenge requires an Internet connection.

The computer keyboard has become as essential an office tool as the pencil. The more adept you become at touch typing—the fastest and most accurate way to type—the more comfortable you will be working with computers and the more saleable your office skills to a potential employer. The Internet is one source of information on touch typing, and many Web sites include free typing tests and online tutorials to help you practice and improve your typing skills. In this independent challenge, you will take an online typing test to check your typing skills. You will then research the fundamentals of touch typing and investigate some of the ergonomic factors important to becoming a productive keyboard typist.

a. Use your favorite search engine to search the Internet for information on typing. Use the keywords **typing** and **typing ergonomics** to conduct your search.

b. Review the Web sites you find. Choose a site that offers a free online typing test, take the test, then print the Web page showing the results of your typing test if requested to do so by your instructor.

c. Start Word and save a new blank document as **WMP A-Touch Typing** to the drive and folder where you store your Data Files.

d. Type your name at the top of the document.

e. Type a brief report on the results of your research. Your report should answer the following questions:

- What are the URLs of the Web sites you visited to research touch typing and keyboard ergonomics? (*Hint*: A URL is a Web page's address. An example of a URL is www.course.com.)
- What are some benefits of using the touch typing method?
- On which keys should the fingers of the left and right hands rest when using the touch typing method?
- What ergonomic factors are important to keep in mind while typing?

f. Save your changes to the document, preview and submit it to your instructor, then close the document and exit Word.

Visual Workshop

Create the letter shown in Figure A-20. Before beginning to type, click the No Spacing button in the Styles group on the Home tab. Add the bottom border to the letterhead after typing the letter. Save the document as **WMP A-Insurance Letter** to the drive and folder where you store your Data Files, submit the letter to your instructor, then close the document and exit Word.

FIGURE A-20

Seattle Memorial Health Care

345 Madison Street, Seattle, WA 98111

Tel: 206-555-7283; www.seattlememorialhealth.com

April 27, 2013

Ms. Jessica Frank
827 Cherry Street
Seattle, WA 98102

Dear Ms. Frank:

Thank you for choosing Seattle Memorial Health Care as your health care provider.

As a result of your recent visit to our emergency facility, our records show your primary care insurance as Northwest Indemnity (#80053 0331), policy #446 38 9876, and group #732556-22-994. At this time, our records show you do not have a secondary care insurance provider.

If the insurance information in this letter is correct, no action is required on your part.

If the insurance information is incomplete or incorrect, please contact us with more accurate billing information by calling a Financial Counselor at (206) 993-5600.

Once we have billed your insurance, we will send you a statement identifying any patient responsibility.

Sincerely,

Your Name
Patient Business Services
Seattle Memorial Health Care

UNIT B

Word 2010

Editing Documents

Files You Will Need:

WMP B-1.docx
WMP B-2.docx
WMP B-3.docx
WMP B-4.docx
WMP B-5.docx
WMP B-6.docx
WMP B-7.docx

The sophisticated editing features in Word make it easy to revise and polish your documents. In this unit, you learn how to revise an existing file by opening it, copying and moving text, and then saving the document as a new file. You also learn how to perfect your documents using proofing tools and how to quickly prepare a document for distribution to the public. You have been asked to edit and finalize a press release for a new lecture series sponsored by the Riverwalk Medical Clinic. The press release should provide information about the series so that newspapers, radio stations, and other media outlets can announce it to the public. Press releases from the Riverwalk Medical Clinic are disseminated by fax and by e-mail. Before distributing the file electronically to your lists of press contacts, you add several hyperlinks and then strip the file of private information.

OBJECTIVES

- Cut and paste text
- Copy and paste text
- Use the Office Clipboard
- Find and replace text
- Check spelling and grammar
- Research information
- Add hyperlinks
- Work with document properties

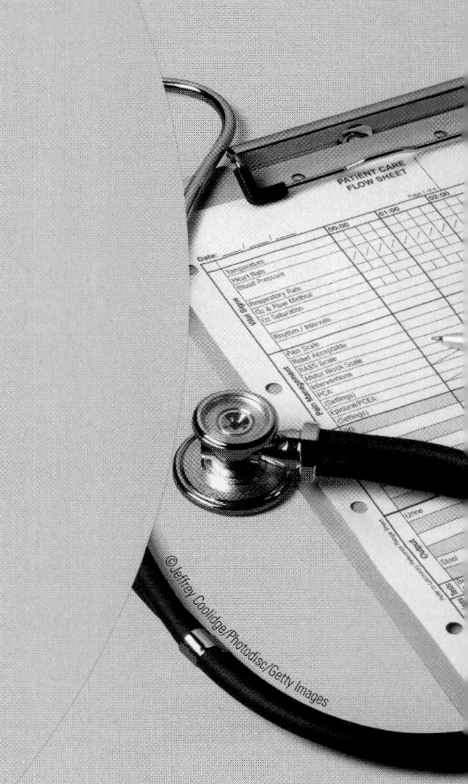

UNIT B

Word 2010

Cutting and Pasting Text

The editing features in Word allow you to move text from one location to another in a document. Moving text is often called **cut and paste**. When you **cut** text, it is removed from the document and placed on the **Clipboard**, a temporary storage area for text and graphics that you cut or copy from a document. You can then **paste**, or insert, text that is stored on the Clipboard in the document at the location of the insertion point. You cut and paste text using the Cut and Paste buttons in the Clipboard group on the Home tab. You can also move selected text by dragging it to a new location using the mouse. This operation is called **drag and drop**. You open the press release that was drafted by a colleague, save it with a new filename, and then reorganize the information in the press release using the cut-and-paste and drag-and-drop methods.

STEPS

1. **Start Word, click the File tab, click Open, navigate to the drive and folder where you store your Data Files, click WMP B-1.docx, then click Open**

   The document opens. Once you have opened a file, you can edit it and use the Save or the Save As command to save your changes. You use the **Save** command when you want to save the changes you make to a file, overwriting the file that is stored on a disk. You use the **Save As** command when you want to leave the original file intact and create a duplicate file with a different filename, file extension, or location.

2. **Click the File tab, click Save As, type WMP B-Lecture PR in the File name text box, then click Save**

   You can now make changes to the press release file without affecting the original file.

3. **Replace Owen Spade with your name, scroll down until the headline "Dr. Timothy Yalobush to Speak..." is at the top of your document window, then click the Show/Hide ¶ button ¶ in the Paragraph group on the Home tab to display formatting marks**

4. **Select lead and other heavy metals, (including the comma and the space after it) in the fourth body paragraph, then click the Cut button in the Clipboard group**

   The text is removed from the document and placed on the Clipboard. Word uses two different clipboards: the **system Clipboard** (the Clipboard), which holds just one item, and the **Office Clipboard**, which holds up to 24 items. The last item you cut or copy is always added to both clipboards. You'll learn more about the Office Clipboard in a later lesson.

5. **Place the insertion point before pesticides (but after the space) in the second line of the fourth paragraph, then click the Paste button in the Clipboard group**

   The text is pasted at the location of the insertion point, as shown in Figure B-1. The Paste Options button appears below text when you first paste it in a document. You'll learn more about the Paste Options button in the next lesson. For now, you can ignore it.

6. **Press and hold [Ctrl], click the sentence Ticket prices include lunch. in the third paragraph, then release [Ctrl]**

   The entire sentence is selected.

7. **Press and hold the mouse button over the selected text until the pointer changes to**

   The pointer's vertical line is the insertion point. You drag the pointer to position the insertion point where you want the text to be inserted when you release the mouse button.

8. **Drag the pointer's vertical line to the end of the fifth paragraph (between the period and the paragraph mark) as shown in Figure B-2, then release the mouse button**

   The selected text is moved to the location of the insertion point. It is convenient to move text using the drag-and-drop method when the locations of origin and destination are both visible on the screen. Text is not placed on the Clipboard when you drag and drop it.

9. **Deselect the text, then click the Save button on the Quick Access toolbar**

TROUBLE

If you make a mistake, click the Undo button on the Quick Access toolbar, then try again.

FIGURE B-1: **Moved text with Paste Options button**

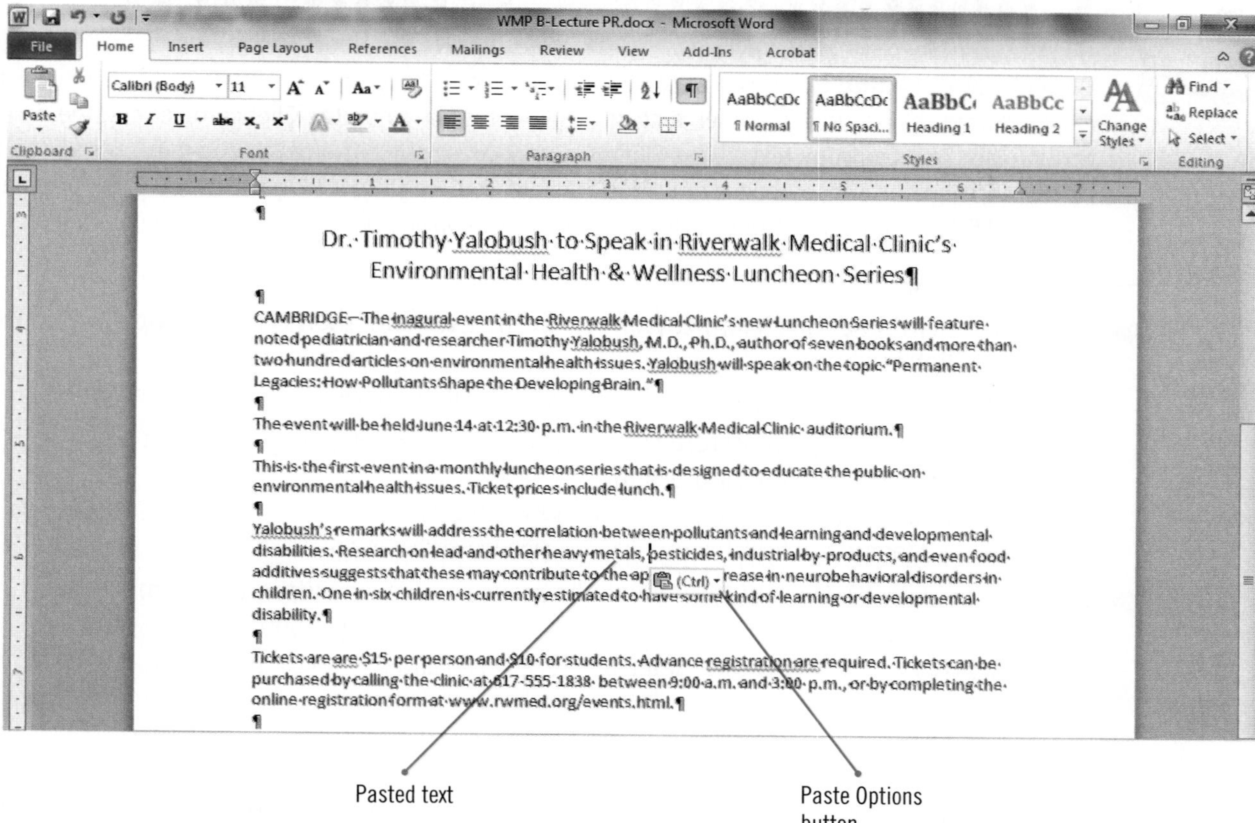

FIGURE B-2: **Dragging and dropping text in a new location**

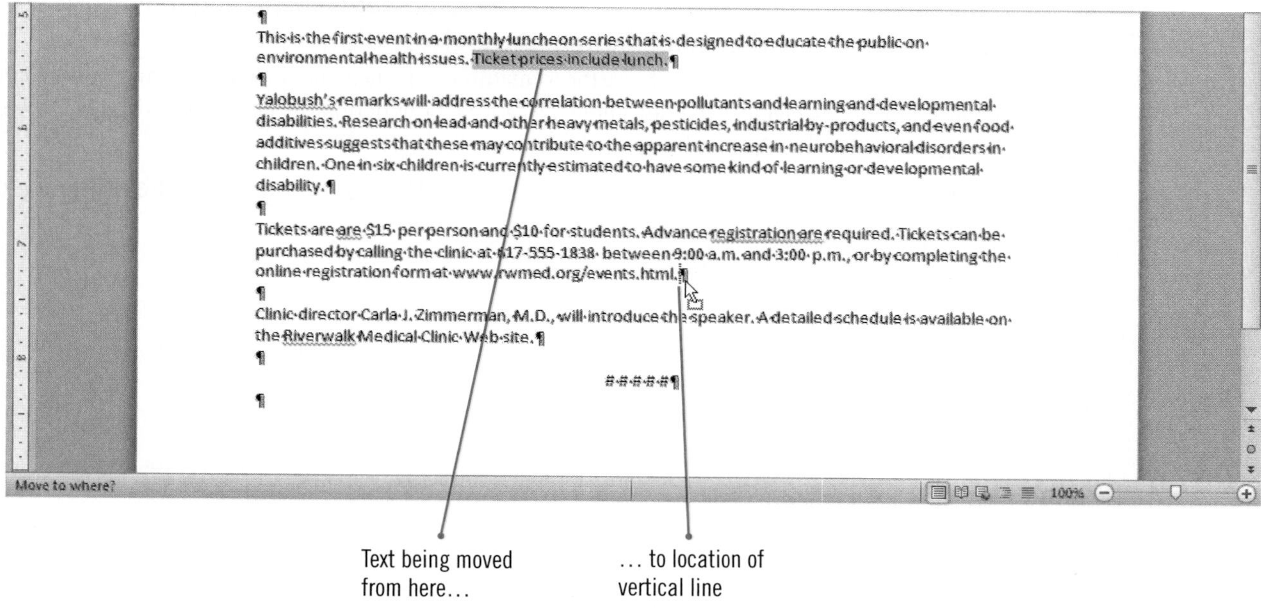

Using keyboard shortcuts

A **shortcut key** is a function key, such as [F1], or a combination of keys, such as [Ctrl][S], that you press to perform a command. For example, instead of using the Cut, Copy, and Paste commands on the Ribbon or the Mini toolbar, you can use the **keyboard shortcuts** [Ctrl][X] to cut text, [Ctrl][C] to copy text, and [Ctrl][V] to paste text. You can also press [Ctrl][S] to save changes to a document instead of clicking the Save button on the Quick Access toolbar or clicking Save on the File tab. Becoming skilled at using keyboard shortcuts can help you quickly accomplish many of the tasks you perform in Word. If a keyboard shortcut is available for a command, then it is listed in the ScreenTip for that command.

UNIT B

Word 2010

Copying and Pasting Text

Copying and pasting text is similar to cutting and pasting text, except that the text you **copy** is not removed from the document. Rather, a copy of the text is placed on the Clipboard, leaving the original text in place. You can copy text to the Clipboard using the Copy button in the Clipboard group on the Home tab, or you can copy text by pressing [Ctrl] as you drag the selected text from one location to another. You continue to edit the press release by copying text from one location to another.

STEPS

QUICK TIP
You can also cut or copy text by right-clicking the selected text, and then clicking the Cut or Copy command on the menu that opens.

1. **Select Environmental Health & Wellness in the headline, then click the Copy button in the Clipboard group**
A copy of the selected text is placed on the Clipboard, leaving the original text you copied in place.

2. **Place the insertion point before Luncheon in the first body paragraph, then click the Paste button in the Clipboard group**
"Environmental Health & Wellness" is inserted before "Luncheon," as shown in Figure B-3. Notice that the pasted text is formatted differently than the paragraph in which it was inserted.

QUICK TIP
If you don't like the result of a paste option, try another option or click the Undo button, and then paste the text again.

3. **Click the Paste Options button, move the mouse over each button on the menu that opens to read its ScreenTip, then click the Keep Text Only (T) button**
The formatting of "Environmental Health & Wellness" is changed to match the rest of the paragraph. The buttons on the Paste Options menu allow you to change the formatting of pasted text. You can choose to keep the original formatting (Keep Source Formatting), match the destination formatting (Merge Formatting), or paste the text unformatted (Keep Text Only).

4. **Select www.rwmed.org in the fifth paragraph, press and hold [Ctrl], then press and hold the mouse button until the pointer changes to**

5. **Drag the pointer's vertical line to the end of the last paragraph, placing it between site and the period, release the mouse button, then release [Ctrl]**
The text is copied to the last paragraph. Since the formatting of the text you copied is the same as the formatting of the destination paragraph, you can ignore the Paste Options button. Text is not copied to the Clipboard when you copy it using the drag-and-drop method.

6. **Place the insertion point before www.rwmed.org in the last paragraph, type at followed by a space, then save the document**
Compare your document with Figure B-4.

Splitting the document window to copy and move items in a long document

If you want to copy or move items between parts of a long document, it can be useful to split the document window into two panes. This allows you to display the item you want to copy or move in one pane and the destination for the item in the other pane. To split a window, click the Split button in the Window group on the View tab, drag the horizontal split bar that appears to the location you want to split the window, and then click. Once the document window is split into two panes, you can drag the split bar to resize the panes and use the scroll bars in each pane to display different parts of the document. To copy or move an item from one pane to another, you can use the Cut, Copy, and Paste commands, or you can drag the item between the panes. When you are finished editing the document, double-click the split bar to restore the window to a single pane, or click the Remove Split button in the Window group on the View tab.

FIGURE B-3: Text pasted in document

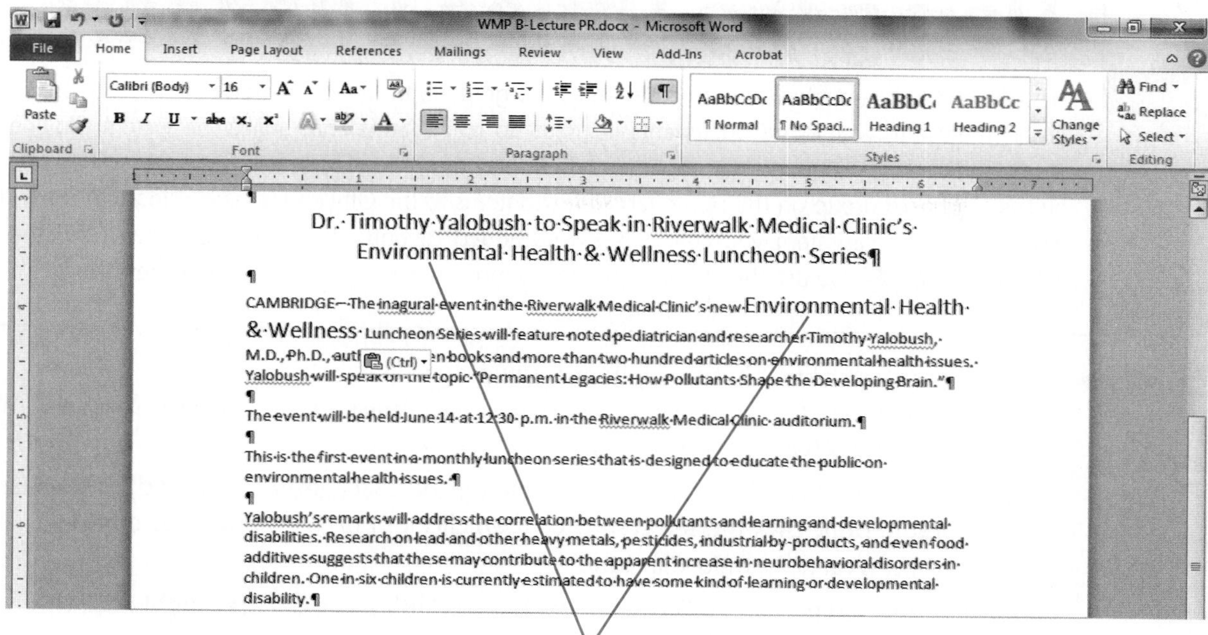

Formatting of the pasted text matches the headline text

FIGURE B-4: Copied text in document

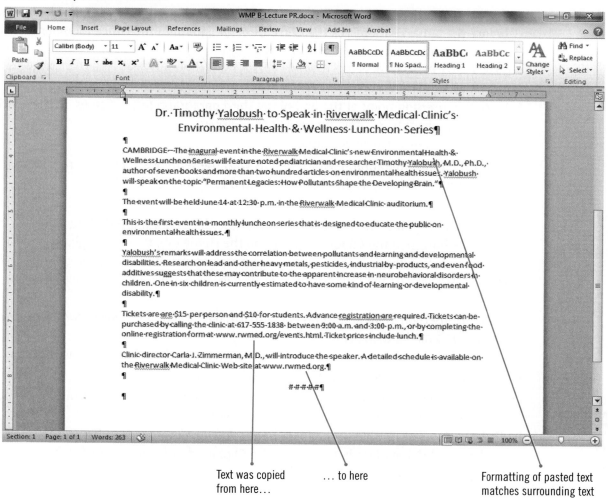

Text was copied from here…

… to here

Formatting of pasted text matches surrounding text

Word 2010

UNIT B

Word 2010

Using the Office Clipboard

The Office Clipboard allows you to collect text and graphics from files created in any Office program and insert them into your Word documents. It holds up to 24 items and, unlike the system Clipboard, the items on the Office Clipboard can be viewed. To display the Office Clipboard, you simply click the launcher in the Clipboard group on the Home tab. You add items to the Office Clipboard using the Cut and Copy commands. The last item you collect is always added to both the system Clipboard and the Office Clipboard. You use the Office Clipboard to move several sentences in your press release.

STEPS

QUICK TIP

You can set the Office Clipboard to open automatically when you cut or copy two items consecutively by clicking Options in the Clipboard task pane, and then selecting Show Office Clipboard Automatically.

1. **Click the launcher in the Clipboard group**

   The Office Clipboard opens in the Clipboard task pane. It contains the Environmental Health & Wellness item you copied in the last lesson.

2. **Select the sentence Clinic director… (including the space after the period) in the last paragraph, right-click the selected text, then click Cut on the menu that opens**

   The sentence is cut to the Office Clipboard.

3. **Select the sentence A detailed schedule is… (including the ¶ mark), right-click the selected text, then click Cut**

   The Office Clipboard displays the items you cut or copied, as shown in Figure B-5. The icon next to each item indicates the items are from a Word document. The last item collected is displayed at the top of the Clipboard task pane. As new items are collected, the existing items move down the task pane.

4. **Place the insertion point at the end of the second paragraph (after "auditorium." but before the ¶ mark), then click the Clinic Director… item on the Office Clipboard**

   Clicking an item on the Office Clipboard pastes the item in the document at the location of the insertion point. Items remain on the Office Clipboard until you delete them or close all open Office programs. Also, if you add a 25th item to the Office Clipboard, the first item you collected is deleted.

5. **Place the insertion point at the end of the third paragraph (after "issues."), then click the A detailed schedule is… item on the Office Clipboard**

   The sentence is pasted into the document.

6. **Select the fourth paragraph, which begins with the sentence Yalobush's remarks… (including the ¶ mark), right-click the selected text, then click Cut**

   The paragraph is cut to the Office Clipboard.

7. **Place the insertion point at the beginning of the third paragraph (before "This…"), click the Paste button in the Clipboard group on the Home tab, then press [Enter]**

   The sentences from the "Yalobush's remarks…" paragraph are pasted at the beginning of the "This is the first…" paragraph. You can paste the last item collected using either the Paste command or the Office Clipboard.

8. **Place the insertion point at the end of the fourth paragraph (after "www.rwmed.org" and before the ¶ mark), then press [Delete] twice**

   Two ¶ symbols and the corresponding blank lines between the fourth and fifth paragraphs are deleted.

9. **Click the Show/Hide ¶ button in the Paragraph group**

   Compare your press release with Figure B-6. Note that many Word users prefer to work with formatting marks on at all times. Experiment to see which method you prefer.

QUICK TIP

To delete an individual item from the Office Clipboard, click the list arrow next to the item, then click Delete.

10. **Click the Clear All button on the Clipboard task pane to remove the items from the Office Clipboard, click the Close button on the Clipboard task pane, press [Ctrl][Home], then save the document**

    Pressing [Ctrl][Home] moves the insertion point to the top of the document.

FIGURE B-5: **Office Clipboard in Clipboard task pane**

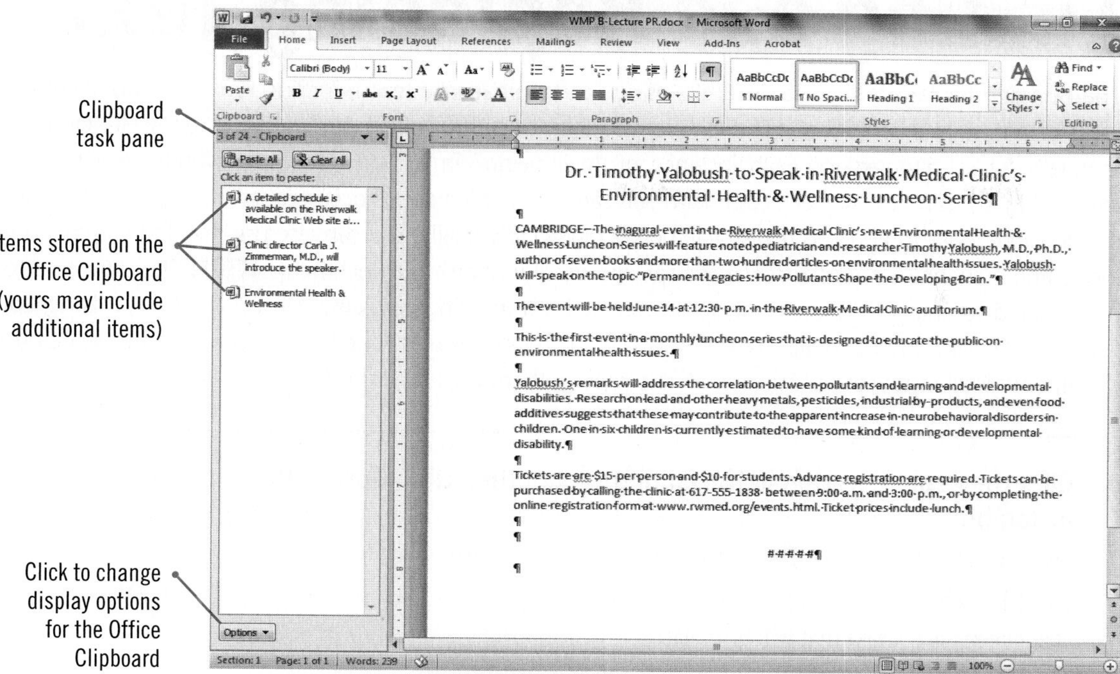

FIGURE B-6: **Revised press release**

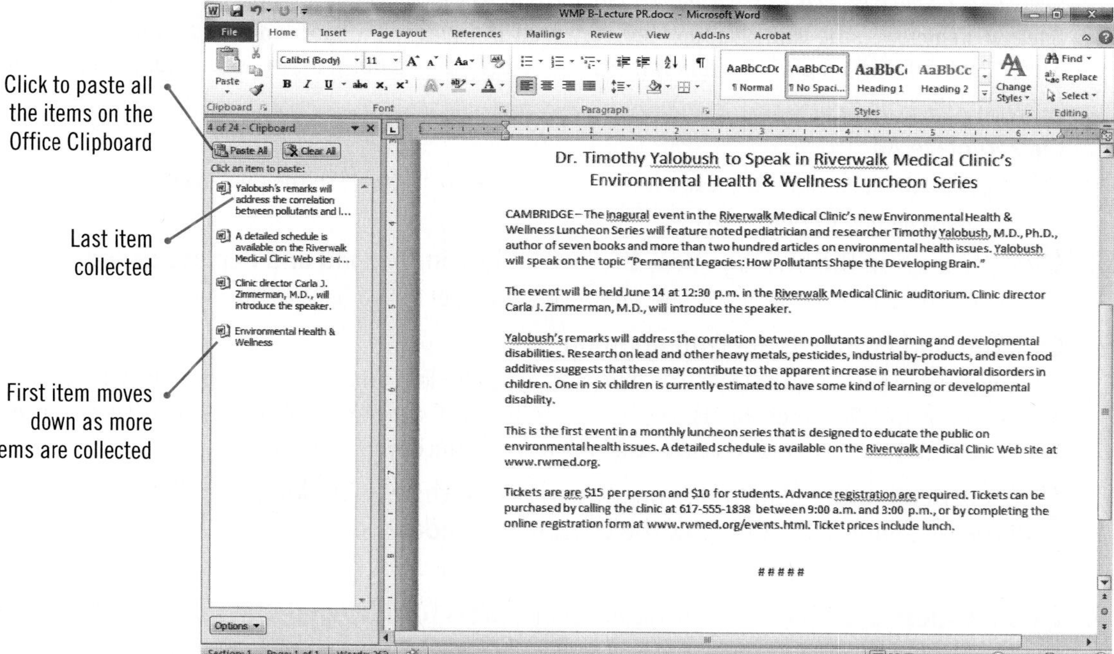

Copying and moving items between documents

You can also use the system and Office Clipboards to copy and move items between documents. To do this, open both documents and the Clipboard task pane in the program window. With multiple documents open, copy or cut an item from one document and then switch to the other document and paste the item. To switch between open documents, point to the Word icon on the taskbar, and then click the document you want to appear in the document window. You can also display more than one document at the same time by clicking the Arrange All button or the View Side by Side button in the Window group on the View tab.

UNIT B

Word 2010

Finding and Replacing Text

The Find and Replace feature in Word allows you to automatically search for and replace all instances of a word or phrase in a document. For example, you might need to substitute "wellness" for "well-being." To manually locate and replace each instance of "well-being" in a long document would be very time-consuming. By using the Replace command you can find and replace all occurrences of specific text at once, or you can choose to find and review each occurrence individually. You can also use the Find command to locate and highlight every occurrence of a specific word or phrase in a document. The clinic director has decided to change the name of the lecture series from "Environmental Health & Wellness Luncheon Series" to "Environmental Health & Wellness Lecture Series." You use the Replace command to search the document for all instances of "Luncheon" and replace them with "Lecture."

STEPS

TROUBLE

If any of the Search Options check boxes are selected in your Find and Replace dialog box, deselect them. If Format appears under the Find what or Replace with text box, click in the text box, then click the No Formatting button.

1. **Click the Replace button in the Editing group, then click More in the Find and Replace dialog box**

   The Find and Replace dialog box opens and expands, as shown in Figure B-7.

2. **Type Luncheon in the Find what text box**

   "Luncheon" is the text that will be replaced.

3. **Press [Tab], then type Lecture in the Replace with text box**

   "Lecture" is the text that will replace "Luncheon."

4. **Click the Match case check box in the Search Options section to select it**

   Selecting the Match case check box tells Word to find only exact matches for the uppercase and lowercase characters you entered in the Find what text box. You want to replace all instances of "Luncheon" in the proper name "Environmental Health & Wellness Luncheon Series." You do not want to replace "luncheon" when it refers to a lunchtime event.

QUICK TIP

To find, review, and replace each occurrence individually, click Find Next.

5. **Click Replace All**

   Clicking Replace All changes all occurrences of "Luncheon" to "Lecture" in the press release. A message box reports two replacements were made.

6. **Click OK to close the message box, then click Close in the Find and Replace dialog box**

   Word replaced "Luncheon" with "Lecture" in two locations, but did not replace "luncheon."

QUICK TIP

Alternately, you can also use the Find tab in the Find and Replace dialog box to find text in a document.

7. **Click the Find button in the Editing group**

   Clicking the Find button opens the Navigation pane, which is used to browse a longer document by headings, by pages, or by specific text or objects. The Find command allows you to quickly locate all instances of text in a document. You use it to verify that Word did not replace "luncheon."

8. **Type luncheon in the Search document text box in the Navigation pane, then scroll up until the headline is at the top of the document window**

   The word "luncheon" is highlighted and selected in the document, as shown in Figure B-8.

9. **Click the Close button in the Navigation pane, press [Ctrl][Home], then save the document**

   The highlighting is removed from the text when you close the Navigation pane.

FIGURE B-7: Find and Replace dialog box

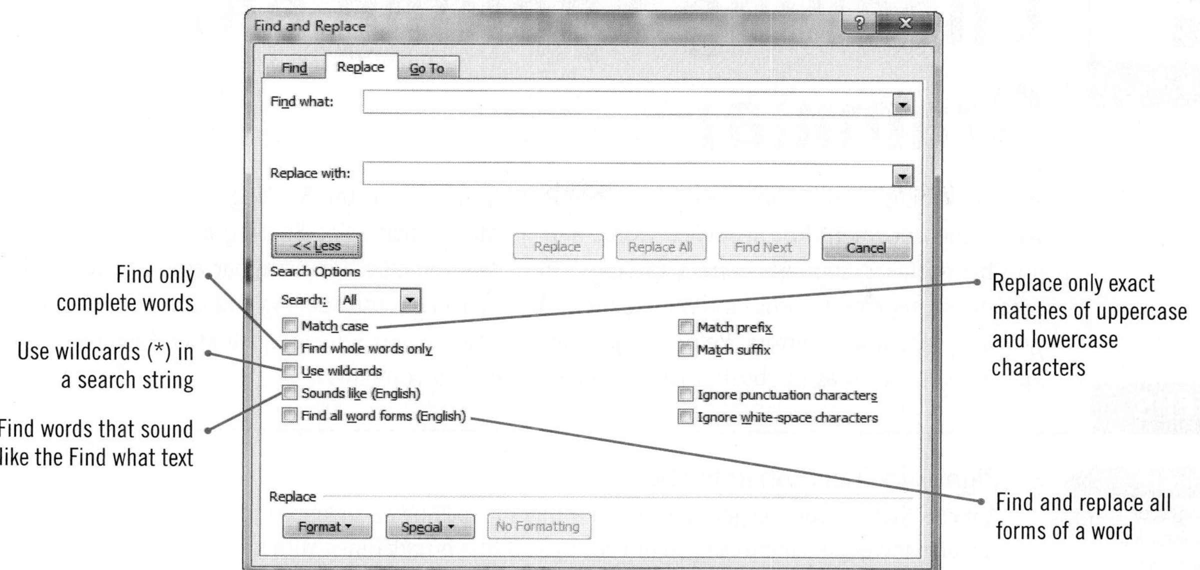

FIGURE B-8: Found text highlighted in document

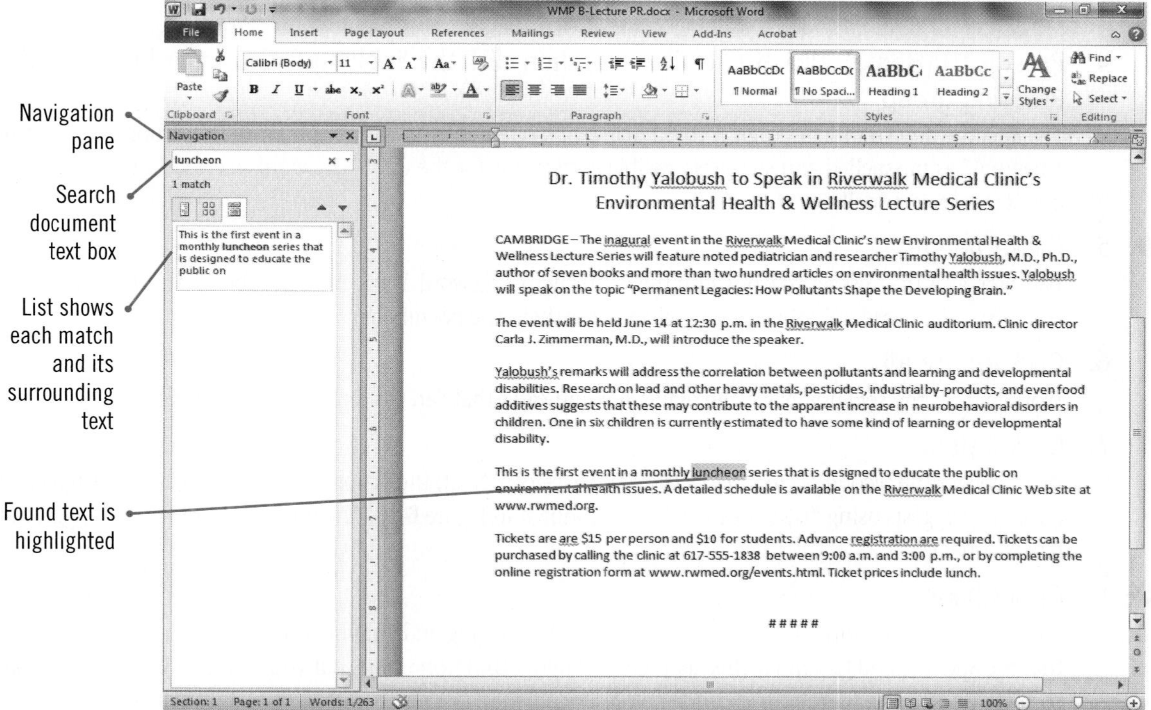

Navigating a document using the Go To command

Rather than scrolling to move to a different place in a longer document, you can use the Go To command to quickly move the insertion point to a specific location. To move to a specific page, section, line, table, graphic, or other item in a document, you use the Go To tab in the Find and Replace dialog box. To open the Find and Replace dialog box with the Go To tab active, click the Page number button on the status bar. On the Go To tab in the Find and Replace dialog box, select the type of item you want to find in the Go to what list box, enter the relevant information about that item, and then click Go To or Next to move the insertion point to the item.

UNIT B

Word 2010

Checking Spelling and Grammar

When you finish typing and revising a document, you can use the Spelling and Grammar command to search the document for misspelled words and grammar errors. The Spelling and Grammar checker flags possible mistakes, suggests correct spellings, and offers remedies for grammar errors such as subject–verb agreement, repeated words, and punctuation. You use the Spelling and Grammar checker to search your press release for errors. Before beginning the search, you set the Spelling and Grammar checker to ignore words, such as Yalobush, that you know are spelled correctly.

STEPS

TROUBLE

If Word flags your name as misspelled, right-click it, then click Ignore All. If "Yalobush" or "Riverwalk" are not flagged as misspelled, skip to Step 4.

QUICK TIP

To change the language used by the Word proofing tools, click the Language button in the Language group on the Review tab, click Set Proofing Language, then click the language you prefer on the menu that opens.

TROUBLE

You might need to correct other spelling and grammar errors.

QUICK TIP

If Word does not offer a valid correction, correct the error yourself.

1. **Right-click Yalobush in the headline**

   A menu that includes suggestions for correcting the spelling of "Yalobush" opens. You can correct individual spelling and grammar errors by right-clicking text that is underlined with a red or green wavy line and selecting a correction. Although "Yalobush" is not in the Word dictionary, it is spelled correctly in the document.

2. **Click Ignore All**

   Clicking Ignore All tells Word not to flag "Yalobush" as misspelled.

3. **Right-click Riverwalk at the top of the document, then click Ignore All**

   The red, wavy underline is removed from all instances of "Riverwalk."

4. **Press [Ctrl][Home], click the Review tab, then click the Spelling & Grammar button in the Proofing group**

   The Spelling and Grammar: English (U.S.) dialog box opens, as shown in Figure B-9. The dialog box identifies "inagural" as misspelled and suggests possible corrections for the error. The word selected in the Suggestions box is the correct spelling.

5. **Click Change**

   Word replaces the misspelled word with the correctly spelled word. Next, the dialog box identifies "Yalobush's" as a misspelled word. "Yalobush's" is spelled correctly in the document.

6. **Click Ignore All**

   Word ignores the spelling. Next, the dialog box indicates that "are" is repeated in a sentence.

7. **Click Delete**

   Word deletes the second occurrence of the repeated word. Next, the dialog box flags a subject–verb agreement error and suggests using "is" instead of "are," as shown in Figure B-10. The phrase selected in the Suggestions box is correct.

8. **Click Change**

   Word replaces "are" with "is" in the sentence, and the Spelling and Grammar dialog box closes. Keep in mind that the Spelling and Grammar checker identifies many common errors, but you cannot rely on it to find and correct all spelling and grammar errors in your documents. Always proofread your documents carefully.

9. **Click OK to complete the spelling and grammar check, press [Ctrl][Home], then save the document**

FIGURE B-9: **Spelling and Grammar: English (U.S.) dialog box**

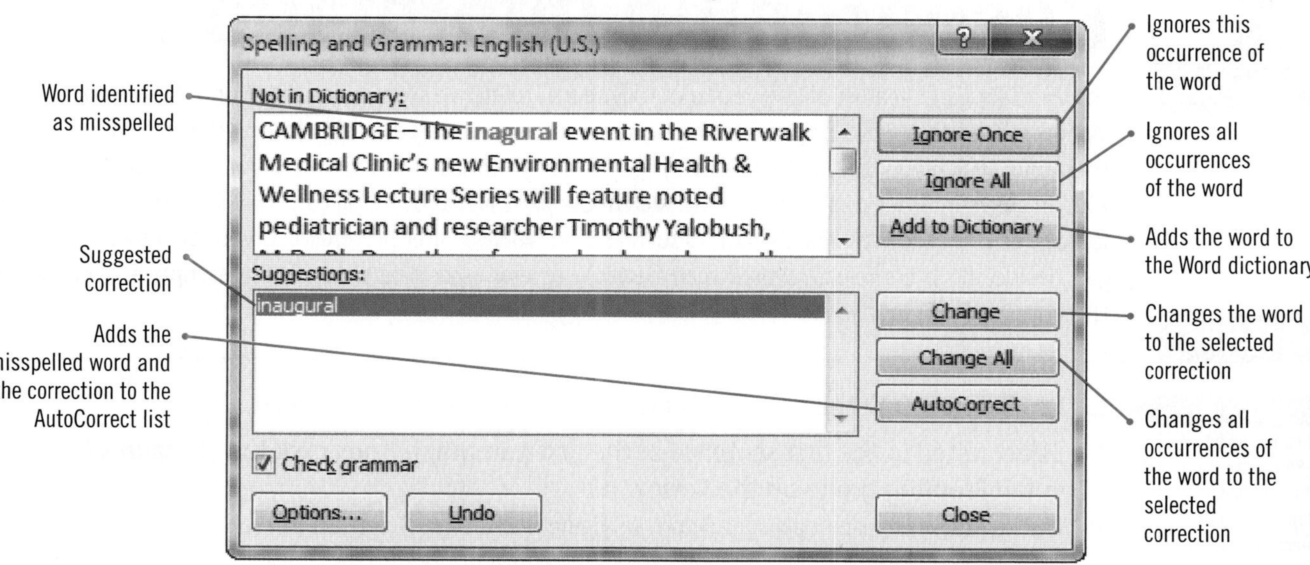

FIGURE B-10: **Grammar error identified in Spelling and Grammar dialog box**

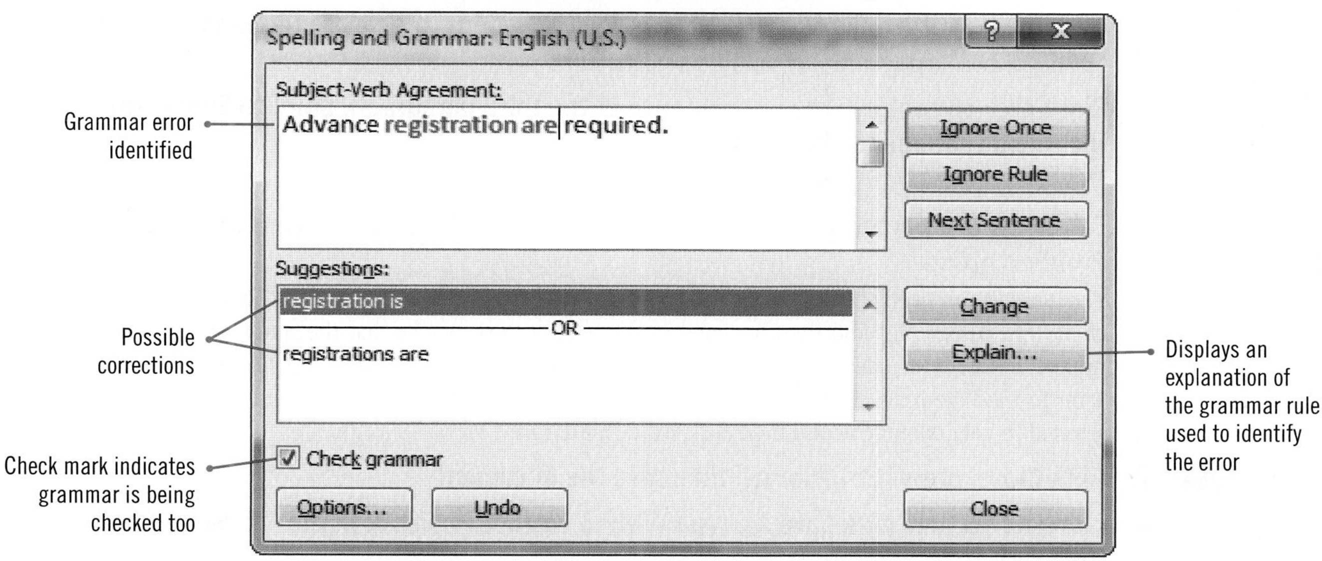

Inserting text with AutoCorrect

As you type, AutoCorrect automatically corrects many commonly misspelled words. By creating your own AutoCorrect entries, you can set Word to insert text that you type often, such as your name or contact information, or to correct words you misspell frequently. For example, you could create an AutoCorrect entry so that the name "Ronald T. Dawson" is automatically inserted whenever you type "rtd" followed by a space. You create AutoCorrect entries and customize other AutoCorrect and AutoFormat options using the AutoCorrect dialog box. To open the AutoCorrect dialog box, click the File tab, click Options, click Proofing in the Word Options dialog box that opens, and then click AutoCorrect Options. On the AutoCorrect tab in the AutoCorrect dialog box, type the text you want to be corrected automatically in the Replace text box (such as "rtd"), type the text you want to be inserted in its place automatically in the With text box (such as "Ronald T. Dawson"), and then click Add. The AutoCorrect entry is added to the list. Click OK to close the AutoCorrect dialog box, and then click OK to close the Word Options dialog box. Word inserts an AutoCorrect entry in a document when you press [Spacebar] or a punctuation mark after typing the text you want Word to correct. For example, Word inserts "Ronald T. Dawson" when you type "rtd" followed by a space.

If you want to remove an AutoCorrect entry you created, simply open the AutoCorrect dialog box, select the AutoCorrect entry you want to remove in the list, click Delete, click OK, and then click OK to close the Word Options dialog box.

UNIT B Word 2010

Researching Information

The Word Research feature allows you to quickly search reference sources and the World Wide Web for information related to a word or phrase. Among the reference sources available in the Research task pane is a Thesaurus, which you can use to look up synonyms for awkward or repetitive words. When you are working with an active Internet connection, the Research task pane also provides access to dictionary and translation sources, as well as to Web search engines such as Bing. After proofreading your document for errors, you decide the press release would read better if several adjectives were more descriptive. You use the Thesaurus to find synonyms.

STEPS

QUICK TIP You can also click the Research button in the Proofing group to open the Research task pane.

QUICK TIP To look up synonyms for a different word, type the word in the Search for text box, then click the green Start searching button.

QUICK TIP To add or remove available reference sources, click Research options in the Research task pane.

1. **Scroll down until the headline is displayed at the top of your screen**
2. **Select noted in the first sentence of the first paragraph, then click the Thesaurus button in the Proofing group on the Review tab**

   The Research task pane opens, as shown in Figure B-11. "Noted" appears in the Search for text box, and possible synonyms for "noted" are listed under the Thesaurus: English (U.S.) heading in the task pane.
3. **Point to distinguished in the list of synonyms**

   A box containing a list arrow appears around the word.
4. **Click the list arrow, click Insert on the menu that opens, then close the Research task pane**

   "Distinguished" replaces "noted" in the press release.
5. **Right-click currently in the last sentence of the third paragraph, point to Synonyms on the menu that opens, then click now**

   "Now" replaces "currently" in the press release.
6. **Select the five paragraphs of body text, then click the Word Count button in the Proofing group**

   The Word Count dialog box opens, as shown in Figure B-12. The dialog box lists the number of pages, words, characters, paragraphs, and lines included in the selected text. Notice that the status bar also displays the number of words included in the selected text and the total number of words in the entire document. If you want to view the page, character, paragraph, and line count for the entire document, make sure nothing is selected in your document, and then click Word Count in the Proofing group.
7. **Click Close, press [Ctrl][Home], then save the document**
8. **Click the File tab, click Save As, type WMP B-Lecture PR Public in the File name text box, then click Save**

   The WMP B-Lecture PR file closes, and the WMP B-Lecture PR Public file is displayed in the document window. You will modify this file to prepare it for electronic release to the public.

Publishing a blog directly from Word

A **blog**, which is short for weblog, is an informal journal that is created by an individual or a group and available to the public on the Internet. A blog usually conveys the ideas, comments, and opinions of the blogger and is written using a strong personal voice. The person who creates and maintains a blog, the **blogger**, typically updates the blog daily. If you have or want to start a blog, you can configure Word to link to your blog site so that you can write, format, and publish blog entries directly from Word.

To create a new blog post, click the File tab, click New, then double-click Blog post to open a predesigned blog post document that you can customize with your own text, formatting, and images. You can also publish an existing document as a blog post by opening the document, clicking the File tab, clicking Save & Send, clicking Publish as Blog Post, and then clicking the Publish as Blog Post button. In either case, Word prompts you to log onto your personal blog account. To blog directly from Word, you must first obtain a blog account with a blog service provider. Resources, such as the Word Help system and online forums, provide detailed information on obtaining and registering your personal blog account with Word.

FIGURE B-11: Research task pane

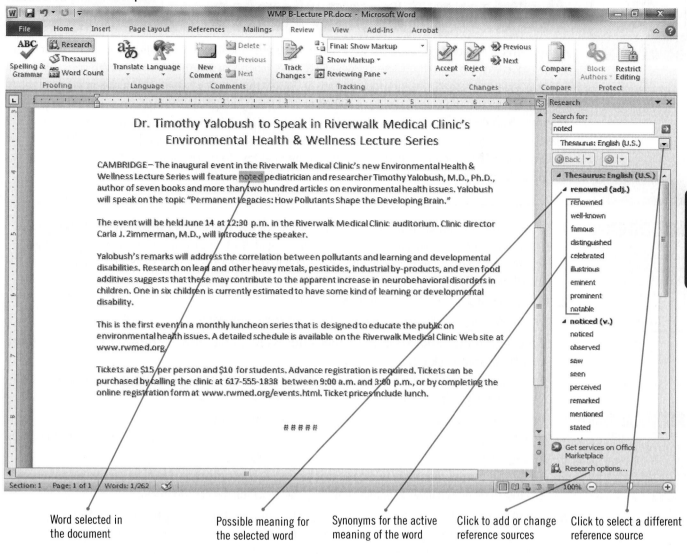

Word selected in the document

Possible meaning for the selected word

Synonyms for the active meaning of the word

Click to add or change reference sources

Click to select a different reference source

Word 2010

FIGURE B-12: Word Count dialog box

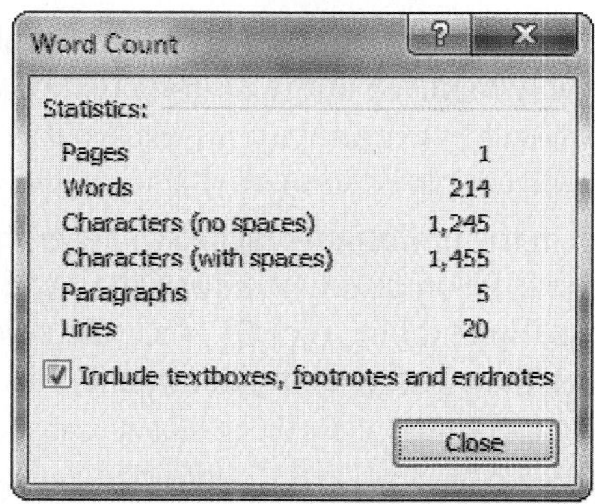

UNIT
B
Word 2010

Adding Hyperlinks

A **hyperlink** is text or a graphic that, when clicked, "jumps" the viewer to a different location or program. When a document is viewed on screen, hyperlinks allow readers to link (or jump) to a Web page, an e-mail address, a file, or a specific location in a document. When you create a hyperlink in a document, you select the text or graphic you want to use as a hyperlink and then you specify the location you want to jump to when the hyperlink is clicked. You create a hyperlink using the Hyperlink button in the Links group on the Insert tab. Text that is formatted as a hyperlink appears as colored, underlined text. Your press contacts will receive the press release by e-mail or Internet fax. To make it easier for these people to access additional information about the series, you add several hyperlinks to the press release.

STEPS

QUICK TIP
By default, Word automatically creates a hyperlink to an e-mail address or URL when you type the address or URL in a document.

1. **Select your name, click the Insert tab, then click the Hyperlink button in the Links group**
   The Insert Hyperlink dialog box opens, as shown in Figure B-13. You use this dialog box to specify the location of the Web page, file, e-mail address, or position in the current document you want to jump to when the hyperlink—in this case, your name—is clicked.
2. **Click E-mail Address in the Link to section**
   The Insert Hyperlink dialog box changes so you can create a hyperlink to your e-mail address.
3. **Type your e-mail address in the E-mail address text box, type Lecture Series in the Subject text box, then click OK**
   As you type, Word automatically adds mailto: in front of your e-mail address. After you close the dialog box, the hyperlink text—your name—is formatted in blue and underlined.

QUICK TIP
To remove a hyperlink, right-click it, then click Remove Hyperlink. Removing a hyperlink removes the link, but the text remains.

4. **Press and hold [Ctrl], then click the your name hyperlink**
   An e-mail message addressed to you with the subject "Lecture Series" opens in the default e-mail program. People can use this hyperlink to send you an e-mail message.
5. **Close the e-mail message window, not saving it if prompted**
   The hyperlink text changes to purple, indicating the hyperlink has been followed.
6. **Scroll down, select environmental health in the fourth paragraph, click the Hyperlink button, click Existing File or Web Page in the Link to section, type www.cdc.gov/environmental in the Address text box, then click OK**
   As you type the Web address, Word automatically adds "http://" in front of "www." The text "environmental health" is formatted as a hyperlink to the Centers for Disease Control and Prevention's Environmental Health home page at www.cdc.gov/environmental. When clicked, the hyperlink will open the Web page in the default browser window.
7. **Select detailed schedule in the last sentence of the fourth paragraph, click the Hyperlink button, type www.rwmed.org in the Address text box, then click OK**
   The text "detailed schedule" is formatted as a hyperlink to the clinic Web site. If you point to a hyperlink in Word, the link to location appears in a ScreenTip. You can edit ScreenTip text to make it more descriptive.

QUICK TIP
You can also edit the hyperlink destination or the hyperlink text.

8. **Right-click health in the environmental health hyperlink, click Edit Hyperlink, click ScreenTip in the Edit Hyperlink dialog box, type Information and links related to environmental health issues in the ScreenTip text box, click OK, click OK, save your changes, then point to the environmental health hyperlink in the document**
   The ScreenTip you created appears above the environmental health hyperlink, as shown in Figure B-14.

TROUBLE
If you are not working with an active Internet connection, skip this step.

9. **Press [Ctrl], click the environmental health hyperlink, click the Word icon on the taskbar, press [Ctrl], click the detailed schedule hyperlink, verify that the links opened in separate tabs in your browser, close the tabs, then click the Word icon on the taskbar to return to the press release document in Word**
   Before distributing a document, it's important to test each hyperlink to verify it works as you intended.

FIGURE B-13: **Insert Hyperlink dialog box**

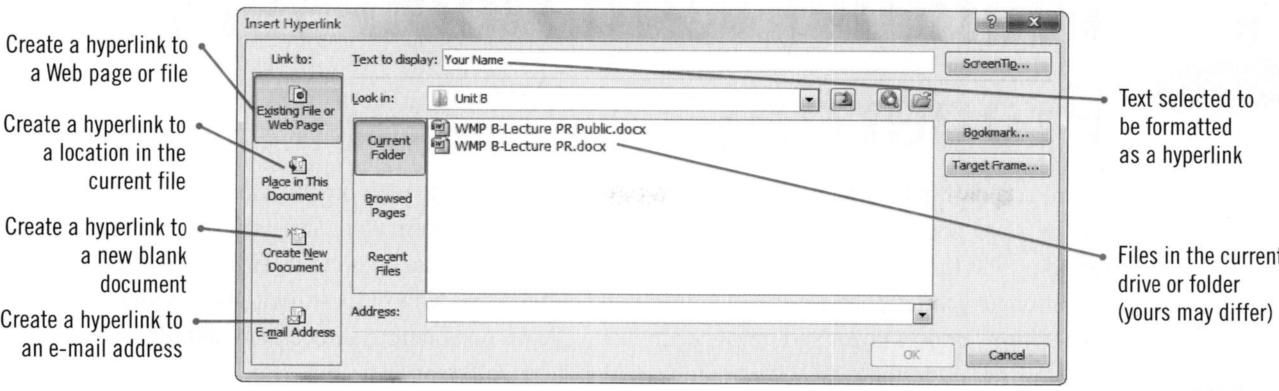

Word 2010

FIGURE B-14: **Hyperlinks in the document**

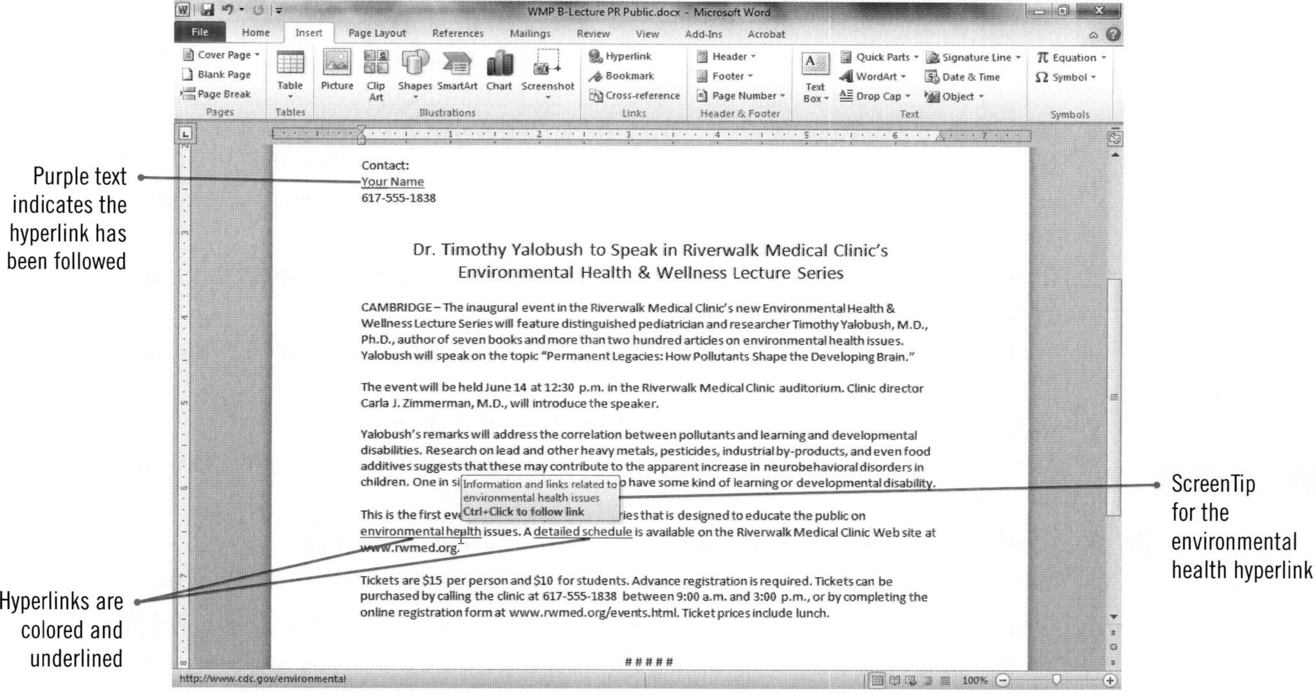

E-mailing and faxing documents directly from Word

Word includes several options for distributing and sharing documents over the Internet directly from within Word, including e-mailing and faxing documents. When you e-mail a document from within Word, the document is sent as an attachment to an e-mail message using your default e-mail program. To e-mail a file, open the file in Word, click the File tab, click Save & Send, and then select one of the options under Send Using E-mail on the Save & Send tab. You can choose to attach the document as a Word file, a .pdf file, or an .xps file, or to send it as an Internet fax. When you click an option, a message window opens that includes the filename of the current file as the message subject and the file as an attachment. Type the e-mail address(es) of the recipient(s) in the To and Cc text boxes, any message you want in the message window, and then click Send on the message window toolbar to send the message. The default e-mail program sends a copy of the document to each recipient. Note that faxing a document directly from Word requires registration with a third-party Internet fax service. Fax services generally charge a monthly or per page fee for sending and receiving faxes.

UNIT B

Word 2010

Working with Document Properties

Before you distribute a document electronically to people outside your organization, it's wise to make sure the file does not include embedded private or confidential information. The Info tab in Backstage view includes tools for stripping a document of sensitive information, for securing its authenticity, and for guarding it from unwanted changes once it is distributed to the public. One of these tools, the Document Inspector, detects and removes unwanted private or confidential information from a document. Before sending the press release to the public, you remove all identifying information from the file.

STEPS

QUICK TIP
To create or modify document properties for a file, type in the Document Properties panel text boxes.

1. **Press [Ctrl][Home], then click the File tab**
   Backstage view opens with the Info tab displayed. The Information pane, in the middle of the tab, includes options related to stripping the file of private information. See Table B-1. The preview pane, on the right side of the tab, displays basic information about the document. Notice that the file contains document properties. You might want to remove these before you distribute the press release to the public.

2. **Click the Properties button in the preview pane, then click Show Document Panel**
   The Document Properties panel opens above the document window, as shown in Figure B-15. It shows the standard document properties for the press release. **Document properties** are user-defined details about a file that describe its contents and origin, including the name of the author, the title of the document, and keywords that you can assign to help organize and search your files. You decide to remove this information from the file before you distribute it electronically.

3. **Click the File tab, click the Check for Issues button, then click Inspect Document, clicking Yes if prompted to save changes**
   The Document Inspector dialog box opens. You use this dialog box to indicate which private or identifying information you want to search for and remove from the document.

4. **Make sure all the check boxes are selected, then click Inspect**
   After a moment, the Document Inspector dialog box changes to indicate that the file contains document properties.

QUICK TIP
A document property, such as author name, might appear automatically in a content control in a document. Stripping a file of document properties does not remove this information from a content control.

5. **Click Remove All next to Document Properties, then click Close**
   The standard document property information is removed from the press release document.

6. **Click the Properties button in the preview pane, then click Show Document Panel**
   The Document Properties panel opens and shows that the document properties have been removed from the file.

7. **Click the Close button in the Document Properties panel, save the document, submit it to your instructor, close the file, then exit Word**
   The completed press release is shown in Figure B-16.

TABLE B-1: Options on the Info tab

option	use to
Protect Document	Mark a document as final so that it is read-only and cannot be edited; encrypt a document so that a password is required to open it; restrict what kinds of changes can be made to a document and by whom; and add a digital signature to a document to verify its integrity
Check for Issues	Detect and remove unwanted information from a document, including document properties and comments; check for content that people with disabilities might find difficult to read; and check the document for features that are not supported by previous versions of Microsoft Word
Manage versions	Browse through and delete draft versions of unsaved files

FIGURE B-15: Document Properties panel

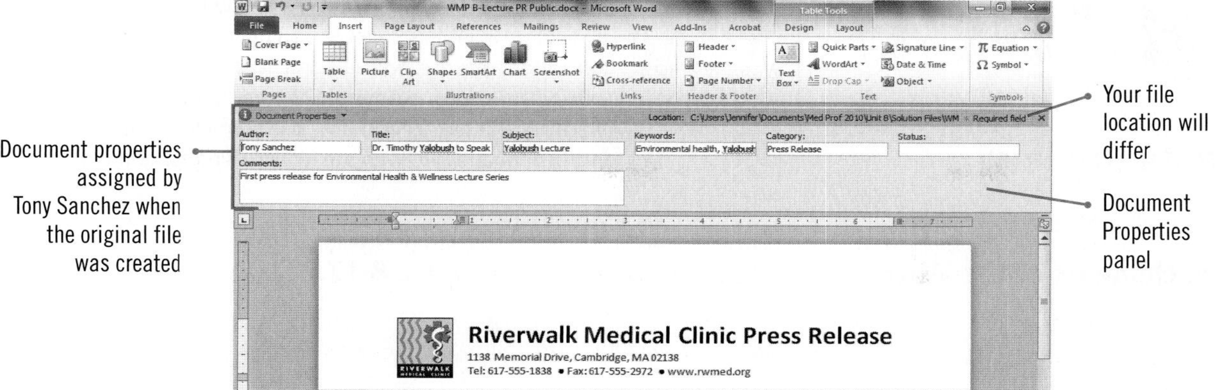

FIGURE B-16: Completed press release for electronic distribution

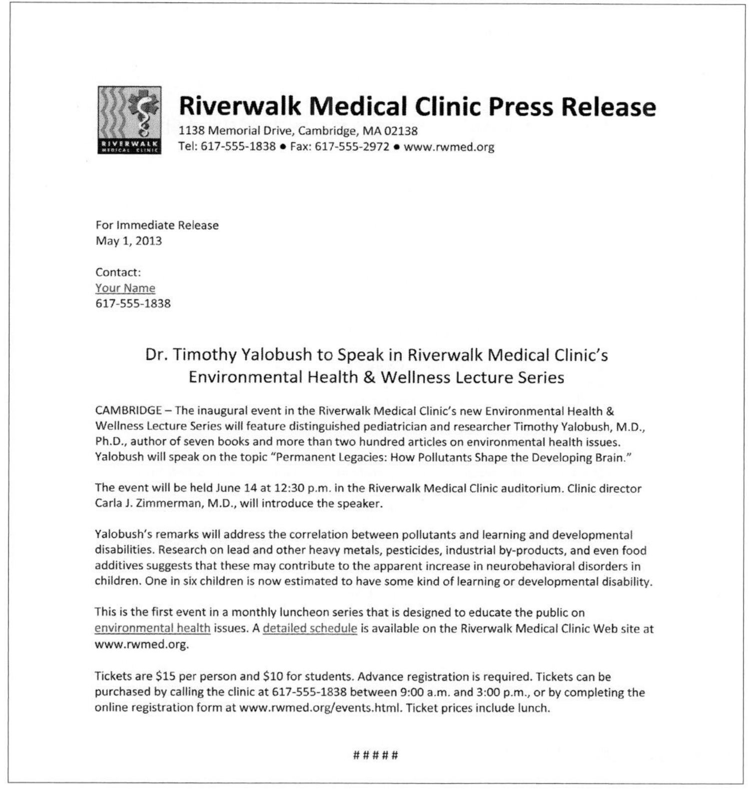

Riverwalk Medical Clinic Press Release
1138 Memorial Drive, Cambridge, MA 02138
Tel: 617-555-1838 • Fax: 617-555-2972 • www.rwmed.org

For Immediate Release
May 1, 2013

Contact:
Your Name
617-555-1838

Dr. Timothy Yalobush to Speak in Riverwalk Medical Clinic's
Environmental Health & Wellness Lecture Series

CAMBRIDGE – The inaugural event in the Riverwalk Medical Clinic's new Environmental Health & Wellness Lecture Series will feature distinguished pediatrician and researcher Timothy Yalobush, M.D., Ph.D., author of seven books and more than two hundred articles on environmental health issues. Yalobush will speak on the topic "Permanent Legacies: How Pollutants Shape the Developing Brain."

The event will be held June 14 at 12:30 p.m. in the Riverwalk Medical Clinic auditorium. Clinic director Carla J. Zimmerman, M.D., will introduce the speaker.

Yalobush's remarks will address the correlation between pollutants and learning and developmental disabilities. Research on lead and other heavy metals, pesticides, industrial by-products, and even food additives suggests that these may contribute to the apparent increase in neurobehavioral disorders in children. One in six children is now estimated to have some kind of learning or developmental disability.

This is the first event in a monthly luncheon series that is designed to educate the public on environmental health issues. A detailed schedule is available on the Riverwalk Medical Clinic Web site at www.rwmed.org.

Tickets are $15 per person and $10 for students. Advance registration is required. Tickets can be purchased by calling the clinic at 617-555-1838 between 9:00 a.m. and 3:00 p.m., or by completing the online registration form at www.rwmed.org/events.html. Ticket prices include lunch.

#####

Viewing and modifying advanced document properties

The Document Properties panel includes summary information about the document that you enter to suit your needs. To view more detailed document properties, including those entered automatically by Word when the document is created, click the Document Properties button in the Document Properties panel, and then click Advanced Properties to open the Properties dialog box. You can also click the Properties button on the Info tab and then click Advanced Properties to open the Properties dialog box. The General, Statistics, and Contents tabs of the Properties dialog box display information about the file that is automatically created and updated by Word. The General tab shows the file type, location, size, and date and time the file was created and last modified; the Statistics tab displays information about revisions to the document along with the number of pages, words, lines, paragraphs, and characters in the file; and the Contents tab shows the title of the document.

You can define other document properties using the Properties dialog box Summary and Custom tabs. The Summary tab shows information similar to the information shown in the Document Properties panel. The Custom tab allows you to create new document properties, such as client, project, or date completed. To create a custom property, select a property name in the Name list box on the Custom tab, use the Type list arrow to select the type of data you want for the property, type the identifying detail (such as a project name) in the Value text box, and then click Add. When you are finished viewing or modifying the document properties, click OK to close the Properties dialog box, then click the Close button on the Document Properties panel.

Practice

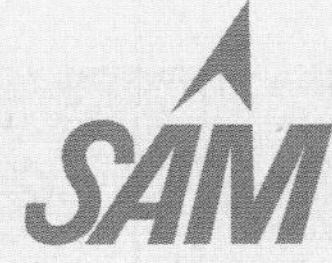

For current SAM information, including versions and content details, visit SAM Central (http://www.cengage.com/samcentral). If you have a SAM user profile, you may have access to hands-on instruction, practice, and assessment of the skills covered in this unit. Since various versions of SAM are supported throughout the life of this text, check with your instructor for the correct instructions and URL/Web site for accessing assignments.

Concepts Review

Label the elements of the Word program window shown in Figure B-17.

FIGURE B-17

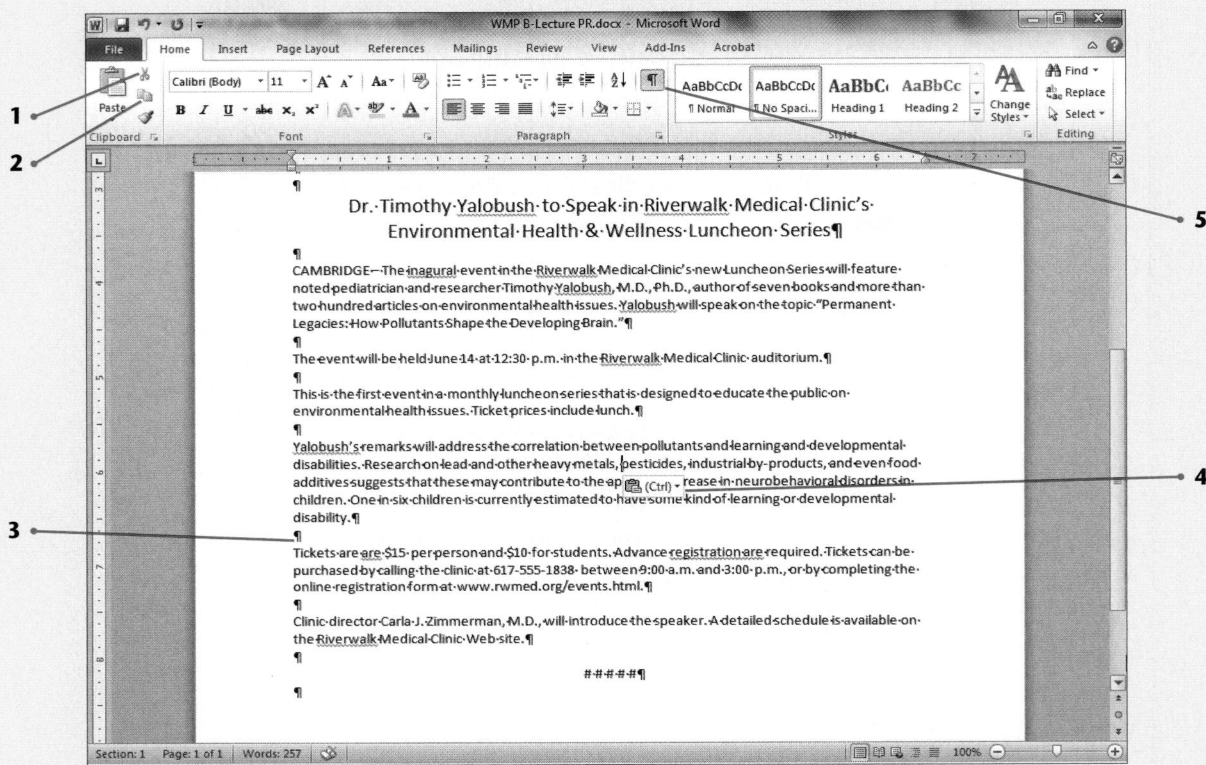

Match each term with the statement that best describes it.

6. **Paste**
7. **Shortcut key**
8. **System Clipboard**
9. **Document properties**
10. **Office Clipboard**
11. **Cut**
12. **Thesaurus**
13. **Hyperlink**
14. **Blog**

a. Command used to insert text stored on the Clipboard into a document
b. Temporary storage area for up to 24 items collected from Office files
c. Temporary storage area for only the last item cut or copied from a document
d. A function key or a combination of keys that perform a command when pressed
e. Text or a graphic that jumps the reader to a different location or program when clicked
f. An informal journal that is available to the public on the Internet
g. User-defined details about a file that describe its contents and origin
h. Feature used to suggest synonyms for words
i. Command used to remove text from a document and place it on the Clipboard

Select the best answer from the list of choices.

15. Which of the following statements is *not* true?

a. You can view the contents of the Office Clipboard.
b. The Office Clipboard can hold more than one item.
c. The last item cut or copied from a document is stored on the system Clipboard.
d. When you move text by dragging it, a copy of the text you move is stored on the system Clipboard.

16. What is the keyboard shortcut for the Paste command?

a. [Ctrl][P]
b. [Ctrl][X]
c. [Ctrl][V]
d. [Ctrl][C]

17. Which command is used to display a document in two panes in the document window?

a. Split
b. New Window
c. Arrange All
d. Two Pages

18. To locate and highlight all instances of a word in a document, which command do you use?

a. Find
b. Search
c. Select
d. Replace

19. A hyperlink *cannot* be linked to which of the following?

a. ScreenTip
b. Document
c. Web page
d. E-mail address

20. Which of the following is an example of a document property?

a. Permission
b. URL
c. Language
d. Keyword

Skills Review

1. Cut and paste text.

a. Start Word, click the File tab, then open the file WMP B-2.docx from the drive and folder where you store your Data Files.
b. Save the document with the filename **WMP B-PHF 2013 PR**.
c. Select **Your Name** and replace it with your name.
d. Display paragraph and other formatting marks in your document if they are not already displayed.
e. Use the Cut and Paste buttons to switch the order of the two sentences in the fourth paragraph (which begins The famous children's entertainer...).
f. Use the drag-and-drop method to switch the order of the second and third paragraphs.
g. Adjust the spacing if necessary so that there is one blank line between paragraphs, then save your changes.

2. Copy and paste text.

a. Use the Copy and Paste buttons to copy **PHF 2011** from the headline and paste it before the word **map** in the third paragraph.
b. Change the formatting of the pasted text to match the formatting of the third paragraph, then insert a space between **2011** and **map** if necessary.
c. Use the drag-and-drop method to copy **PHF** from the third paragraph and paste it before the word **stage** in the second sentence of the fourth paragraph, then save your changes.

3. Use the Office Clipboard.

a. Use the launcher in the Clipboard group to open the Clipboard task pane.
b. Scroll so that the first body paragraph is displayed at the top of the document window.
c. Select the fifth paragraph (which begins Health fair maps...) and cut it to the Office Clipboard.
d. Select the third paragraph (which begins Portsmouth is easily accessible...) and cut it to the Office Clipboard.
e. Use the Office Clipboard to paste the Health fair maps... item as the new fourth paragraph.
f. Use the Office Clipboard to paste the Portsmouth is easily accessible... item as the new fifth paragraph.
g. Adjust the spacing if necessary so there is one blank line between each of the six body paragraphs.
h. Turn off the display of formatting marks, clear and close the Office Clipboard, then save your changes.

Skills Review (continued)

4. **Find and replace text.**
   a. Using the Replace command, replace all instances of **2011** with **2013**.
   b. Replace all instances of **eighth** with **tenth**.
   c. Replace all instances of the abbreviation **st** with **street**, taking care to replace whole words only when you perform the replace. (*Hint*: Deselect Match case if it is selected.)
   d. Use the Find tab in the Find and Replace dialog box to find all instances of **st** in the document and to make sure no errors occurred when you replaced st with street. (*Hint*: Deselect the Find whole words only check box.)
   e. Save your changes to the press release.
5. **Check spelling and grammar and research information.**
   a. Switch to the Review tab.
   b. Move the insertion point to the top of the document, then use the Spelling and Grammar command to search for and correct any spelling and grammar errors in the press release.
   c. Use the Thesaurus to replace **famous** in the third paragraph with a different suitable word.
   d. Check the word count of the press release body text.
   e. Proofread your press release, correct any errors, then save your changes.
6. **Add hyperlinks.**
   a. Save the document as **WMP B-PHF 2013 PR Public**, then switch to the Insert tab.
   b. Select your name, then open the Insert Hyperlink dialog box.
   c. Create a hyperlink to your e-mail address with the subject **PHF 2013**.
   d. Test the your name hyperlink, then close the message window that opens. (*Hint*: Press [Ctrl], then click the hyperlink.)
   e. Select **NIH** in the last paragraph of the press release, then create a hyperlink to the Web page with the URL **www.nih.gov**.
   f. Right-click the NIH hyperlink, then edit the hyperlink ScreenTip to become **Information on the National Institutes of Health**.
   g. Point to the NIH hyperlink to view the new ScreenTip, then save your changes.
   h. If you are working with an active Internet connection, press [Ctrl], click the NIH hyperlink, view the NIH home page in the browser window, then close the browser window.
7. **Work with document properties.**
   a. Click the File tab, click the Properties button in the preview pane, then open the Document Properties panel to view the document properties for the press release.
   b. Click the File tab to return to Backstage view with the Info tab displayed, then use the Check for Issues command to run the Document Inspector.
   c. Remove the document property data, click the Home tab, close the Document Properties panel, then save your changes. The finished press release is shown in Figure B-18.
   d. Save the document, submit it to your instructor, close the file, then exit Word.

FIGURE B-18

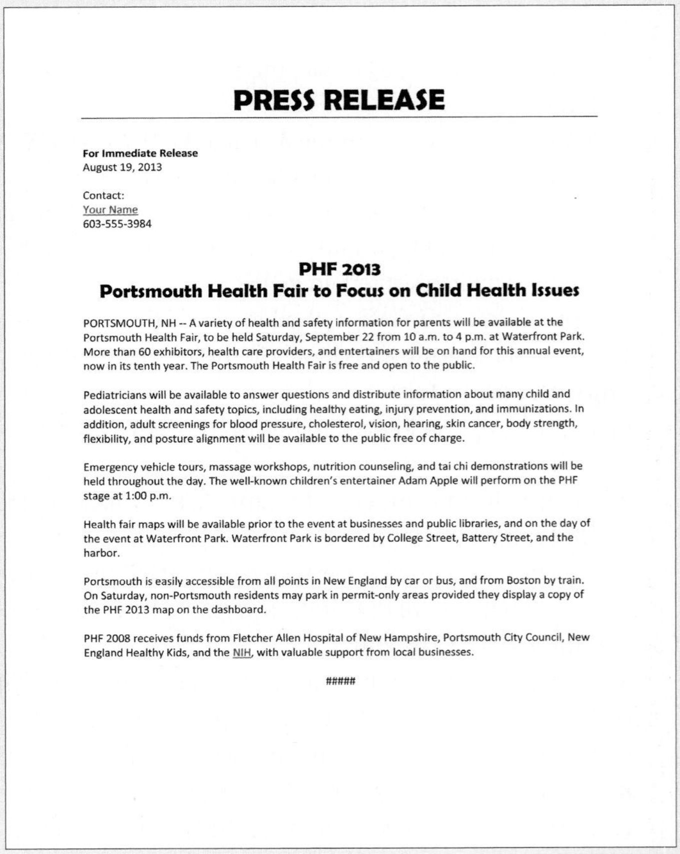

PRESS RELEASE

For Immediate Release
August 19, 2013

Contact:
Your Name
603-555-3984

PHF 2013
Portsmouth Health Fair to Focus on Child Health Issues

PORTSMOUTH, NH -- A variety of health and safety information for parents will be available at the Portsmouth Health Fair, to be held Saturday, September 22 from 10 a.m. to 4 p.m. at Waterfront Park. More than 60 exhibitors, health care providers, and entertainers will be on hand for this annual event, now in its tenth year. The Portsmouth Health Fair is free and open to the public.

Pediatricians will be available to answer questions and distribute information about many child and adolescent health and safety topics, including healthy eating, injury prevention, and immunizations. In addition, adult screenings for blood pressure, cholesterol, vision, hearing, skin cancer, body strength, flexibility, and posture alignment will be available to the public free of charge.

Emergency vehicle tours, massage workshops, nutrition counseling, and tai chi demonstrations will be held throughout the day. The well-known children's entertainer Adam Apple will perform on the PHF stage at 1:00 p.m.

Health fair maps will be available prior to the event at businesses and public libraries, and on the day of the event at Waterfront Park. Waterfront Park is bordered by College Street, Battery Street, and the harbor.

Portsmouth is easily accessible from all points in New England by car or bus, and from Boston by train. On Saturday, non-Portsmouth residents may park in permit-only areas provided they display a copy of the PHF 2013 map on the dashboard.

PHF 2008 receives funds from Fletcher Allen Hospital of New Hampshire, Portsmouth City Council, New England Healthy Kids, and the NIH, with valuable support from local businesses.

#####

Independent Challenge 1

Dr. Callahan, a physician in your office, is leaving her practice at Buffalo General Hospital for a practice at another hospital in Buffalo. She asks you to draft a letter to her patients informing them of the move. You'll create a change of address letter for Dr. Callahan by modifying a letter you wrote for another doctor.

a. Start Word, open the file WMP B-3.docx from the drive and folder where you store your Data Files, then save it as **WMP B-Change of Address Letter**.
b. Replace the doctor's name and address, the date, the inside address, and the salutation with the text shown in Figure B-19.

FIGURE B-19

Beatrice Callahan, M.D.
878 Elmwood Avenue, Buffalo, NY 14642; Tel: 585-555-8374

April 14, 2013

Mr. Merrill Frank
263 Montgomery Street
Buffalo, NY 14632

Dear Mr. Frank:

c. Use the Replace command to replace all instances of **Saint Mary's** with **Buffalo General**.
d. In the second body paragraph, replace the text **1478 Portland Street** with **878 Elmwood Avenue**.
e. Use the Find command to locate the word **superb**, then use the Thesaurus to replace the word with a synonym.
f. Create an AutoCorrect entry that inserts **Lake Memorial Hospital of the University of Buffalo** whenever you type **lmh**.
g. Select each instance of Highland Hospital, type **lmh** followed by a space, then delete the extra space before the period.
h. Move the last sentence of the first body paragraph so that it becomes the first sentence of the third body paragraph, adjusting the space as needed.
i. Replace Kate Champlain with **Beatrice Callahan** in the signature block, then replace the typists initials yi with your initials.
j. Use the Spelling and Grammar command to check for and correct spelling and grammar errors.
k. Delete the AutoCorrect entry you created for lmh. (*Hint*: Open the AutoCorrect dialog box, select the AutoCorrect entry you created, then click [Delete].)

Advanced Challenge Exercise

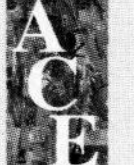

- Open the Document Properties panel, add your name as the author, change the title to **Beatrice Callahan, M.D.**, add the keywords **address change**, then add the comment **Change of address letter**.
- Open the Properties dialog box, review the properties on the Summary tab, then review the paragraph, line, word, and character count on the Statistics tab.
- On the Custom tab, add a property named **Office** with the value **Address Change**, then close the dialog box and the Document Properties panel.

l. Proofread the letter, correct any errors, save your changes, submit a copy to your instructor, close the document, then exit Word.

Independent Challenge 2

An advertisement for job openings in San Francisco caught your eye and you have decided to apply. The ad, shown in Figure B-20, was printed in last weekend's edition of your local newspaper. Instead of writing a cover letter from scratch, you revise a draft of a cover letter you wrote several years ago for a summer internship position.

a. Read the ad shown in Figure B-20 and decide for which position to apply. Choose the position that most closely matches your qualifications.

b. Start Word, open WMP B-4.docx from the drive and folder where you store your Data Files, then save it as **WMP B-Cover Letter**.

c. Replace the name, address, telephone number, and e-mail address in the letterhead with your own information.

d. Remove the hyperlink from the e-mail address.

e. Replace the date with today's date, then replace the inside address and the salutation with the information shown in Figure B-20.

f. Read the draft cover letter to get a feel for its contents.

g. Rework the text in the body of the letter to address your qualifications for the job you have chosen to apply for in the following ways:

- Delete the third paragraph.
- Adjust the first sentence of the first paragraph as follows: specify the job you are applying for, including the position code, and indicate where you saw the position advertised.
- Move the first sentence in the last paragraph, which briefly states your qualifications and interest in the position, to the end of the first paragraph, then rework the sentence to describe your current qualifications.
- Adjust the second paragraph as follows: describe your work experience and skills. Be sure to relate your experience and qualifications to the position requirements listed in the advertisement. Add a third paragraph if your qualifications are extensive.
- Adjust the final paragraph as follows: politely request an interview for the position and provide your phone number and e-mail address.

h. Include your name in the signature block.

i. When you are finished revising the letter, check it for spelling and grammar errors, and correct any mistakes. Make sure to remove any hyperlinks.

j. Save your changes to the letter, submit the file to your instructor, close the document, then exit Word.

FIGURE B-20

Bay Area Health

The Neighborhood Health Center

Bay Area Comprehensive Community Health Center (BACCHC), offering quality health care to the San Francisco community for over thirty years, is seeking candidates for the following positions:

Registered Nurses
Openings in Adult Medicine and Pediatrics. Must have two years of nursing experience. Current RN license and CPR required. **Position B12C6**

Laboratory Technician
Perform a variety of routine laboratory tests and procedures. Certification as MLT (ASCP) required, plus two years work experience. **Position C14B5**

Correspondence Coordinator
Process all correspondence mail in our medical records department. Must have knowledge of HIPAA regulations. Fluency with Microsoft Word required. **Position C13D4**

Medical Assistant
Maintain patient flow, assist physicians using sterile techniques, and educate patients on health issues. Must enjoy interacting with patients and be proficient with Microsoft Word. MA certification preferred. CPR required. **Position B16F5**

Positions offer competitive compensation, outstanding benefits, and career growth opportunities.

Send resume and cover letter referencing position code to:

Katherine Winn
Director of Human Resources
Bay Area Comprehensive Community Health Center
3826 Sacramento Street
San Francisco, CA 94118
Fax to 415-555-2939 or Email to hr@lcchc.com

Independent Challenge 3

As director of public education at Haven Community Hospital, you drafted a memo to the nursing staff asking them to help you finalize the schedule for the Healthy Living seminar series, which is presented by the nursing staff. Today, you'll examine the draft and make revisions before distributing it as an e-mail attachment.

a. Start Word, open the file WMP B-5.docx from the drive and folder where you store your Data Files, then save it as **WMP B-Healthy Living Memo**.

b. Replace Your Name with your name in the From line, then scroll down until the first body paragraph is at the top of the screen.

Advanced Challenge Exercise

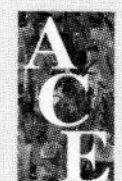

- Use the Split command on the View tab to split the window under the first body paragraph, then scroll until the last paragraph of the memo is displayed in the bottom pane.
- Use the Cut and Paste buttons to move the sentence **If you are planning to lead...** from the first body paragraph to become the first sentence in the last paragraph of the memo.
- Double-click the split bar to restore the window to a single pane.

c. Use the [Delete] key to merge the first two paragraphs into one paragraph.

d. Use the Office Clipboard to reorganize the list of brown bag lunch topics so that the topics are listed in alphabetical order, then clear and close the Office Clipboard.

e. Use the drag-and-drop method to reorganize the list of Saturday morning lectures so that the lectures are listed in alphabetical order.

f. Select the phrase "Web site" in the first paragraph, then create a hyperlink to the URL **www.course.com** with the ScreenTip **2014 Healthy Living Series Schedule**.

g. Select "e-mail me" in the last paragraph, then create a hyperlink to your e-mail address with the subject **Final Healthy Living Series Schedule**.

h. Use the Spelling and Grammar command to check for and correct spelling and grammar errors. Be sure to read each choice and to make decisions based on the content of the memo.

i. Use the Document Inspector to strip the document of document property information, ignore any other content that is flagged by the Document Inspector, then close the Document Inspector.

j. Proofread the memo, correct any errors, save your changes, submit a copy to your instructor, close the document, then exit Word.

Real Life Independent Challenge

This Independent Challenge requires an Internet connection.

Reference sources—dictionaries, thesauri, style and grammar guides, and guides to business etiquette and procedure—are essential for day-to-day use in the workplace. Much of this reference information is available on the World Wide Web. In this independent challenge, you will locate general and medical reference sources on the Web and use some of them to look up medical terms. Your goal is to familiarize yourself with online reference sources so you can use them later in your work.

a. Start Word, open the file WMP B-6.docx from the drive and folder where you store your Data Files, then save it as **WMP B-Web Reference Sources**. This document contains the questions you will answer about the Web reference sources you find. You will type your answers to the questions in the document.

b. Replace the placeholder text at the top of the Web Reference Sources document with your name and the date.

c. Use your favorite search engine to search the Web for grammar and style guides, dictionaries, and thesauri. Use the keywords **grammar**, **usage**, **medical dictionary**, **glossary**, and **thesaurus** to conduct your search.

d. Complete the Web Reference Sources document, then proofread it and correct any mistakes.

e. Save the document, submit a copy to your instructor, close the document, then exit Word.

Visual Workshop

Open WMP B-7.docx from the drive and folder where you store your Data Files, then save the document as **WMP B-Termination Letter**. Replace the placeholders for the date, letterhead, inside address, salutation, and closing with the information shown in Figure B-21, then use the Office Clipboard to reorganize the sentences to match Figure B-21. Correct spelling and grammar errors, remove the document property information from the file, then submit a copy to your instructor.

FIGURE B-21

Your Name, M.D.
682 East 8th Avenue, Portland, ME 04105; Tel: 207-555-1728

12/9/2013

Mr. James Bush
44 Harbor Street
Portland, ME 04123

Dear Mr. Bush:

As a result of a change in our insurance affiliations, I am no longer able to provide medical care to you as your dermatologist. Consequently, you should identify another physician to assume your care.

If you have not received a referral to another provider or if you wish to contact a provider who has not previously cared for you, contact your primary care physician. You may also contact the Cumberland County Medical Society at 207-555-2983.

I will remain available to treat you for a limited time, not to exceed thirty (30) days from the date of this letter. Please try to transfer your care as soon as possible within this period. In the event you have an emergency prior to your transfer of care to another provider, you may contact me through my office.

Copies of your medical record will be sent to the new provider you have selected, upon receipt of your written authorization. A copy of a release form is enclosed for you to complete and return to this office, allowing the record to be transferred.

Sincerely,

Your Name, M.D.

Enc.
Certified Mail, Return Receipt Request
Mailed on December 9, 2013

UNIT C

Word 2010

Formatting Text and Paragraphs

Files You Will Need:

WMP C-1.docx

WMP C-2.docx

WMP C-3.docx

WMP C-4.docx

WMP C-5.docx

WMP C-6.docx

Formatting can enhance the appearance of a document, create visual impact, and help illustrate a document's structure. The formatting of a document can also set a tone, allowing readers to know at a glance if the document is business-like, informal, or fun. In this unit you learn how to format text using fonts and a variety of paragraph-formatting effects, such as borders, shading, and bullets. You also learn how to illustrate a document with clip art. You have finished drafting the text for an information sheet on the flu to distribute to patients. Now, you need to format the information sheet so it is attractive and highlights the significant information.

OBJECTIVES

- Format with fonts
- Copy formats using the Format Painter
- Change line and paragraph spacing
- Align paragraphs
- Work with tabs
- Work with indents
- Add bullets and numbering
- Add borders and shading
- Insert clip art

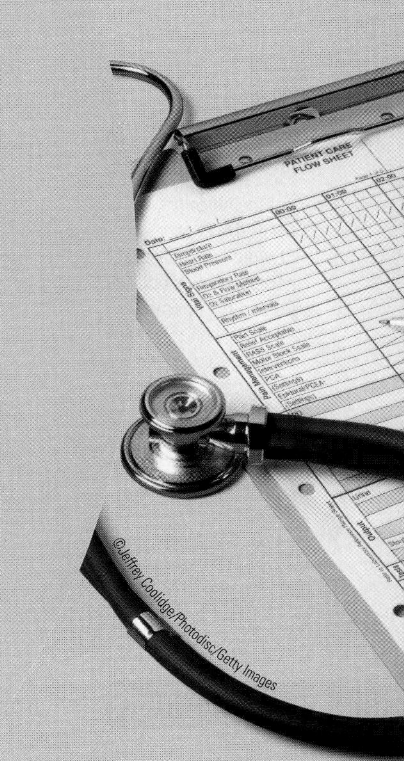

©Jeffrey Coolidge/Photodisc/Getty Images

UNIT
C
Word 2010

Formatting with Fonts

Formatting text with fonts is a quick and powerful way to enhance the appearance of a document. A **font** is a complete set of characters with the same typeface or design. Arial, Times New Roman, Courier, Tahoma, and Calibri are some of the more common fonts, but there are hundreds of others, each with a specific design and feel. Another way to change the appearance of text is to increase or decrease its **font size**. Font size is measured in points. A **point** is 1/72 of an inch. You change the font and font size of the body text, title, and headings in the information sheet. You select fonts and font sizes that enhance the tone of the document and help to structure the information visually for readers.

STEPS

1. **Start Word, open the file WMP C-1.docx from the drive and folder where you store your Data Files, then save it as WMP C-Flu Info Sheet**

   Notice that the name of the font used in the document, Calibri, is displayed in the Font list box in the Font group. The word "(Body)" in the Font list box indicates Calibri is the font used for body text in the current theme, the default theme. A **theme** is a related set of fonts, colors, styles, and effects that is applied to an entire document to give it a cohesive appearance. The font size, 11, appears in the Font Size list box in the Font group.

> **QUICK TIP**
> There are two types of fonts: serif fonts have a small stroke, called a serif, at the ends of characters; sans serif fonts do not have a serif. Garamond is a serif font. Trebuchet MS is a sans serif font.

2. **Scroll the document to get a feel for its contents, press [Ctrl][Home], press [Ctrl][A] to select the entire document, then click the Font list arrow in the Font group**

   The Font list, which shows the fonts available on your computer, opens as shown in Figure C-1. The font names are formatted in the font. Font names can appear in more than one location on the font list.

3. **Drag the pointer slowly down the font names in the Font list, drag the scroll box to scroll down the Font list, then click Garamond**

   Dragging the pointer down the font list allows you to preview how the selected text will look in the highlighted font. Clicking a font name applies the font. The font of the flyer changes to Garamond.

> **QUICK TIP**
> You can also type a font size in the Font Size text box.

4. **Click the Font Size list arrow in the Font group, drag the pointer slowly up and down the Font Size list, then click 12**

   Dragging the pointer over the font sizes allows you to preview how the selected text will look in the highlighted font size. Clicking 12 increases the font size of the selected text to 12 points.

5. **Select the title Riverwalk Medical Clinic Influenza Information Sheet, click the Font list arrow, scroll to and click Trebuchet MS, click the Font Size list arrow, click 22, then click the Bold button in the Font group**

   The title is formatted in 22-point Trebuchet MS bold.

> **QUICK TIP**
> To use a different set of theme colors, click the Page Layout tab, click the Theme Colors button in the Themes group, then select a different color set.

6. **Click the Font Color list arrow in the Font group**

   A gallery of colors opens. It includes the set of theme colors in a range of tints and shades as well as a set of standard colors. You can point to a color in the gallery to preview it applied to the selected text.

7. **Click Purple, Accent 4, Darker 25% as shown in Figure C-2, then deselect the text**

   The color of the title text changes to purple. The active color on the Font Color button also changes to purple.

8. **Select the heading Flu Vaccine, then, using the Mini toolbar, click the Font list arrow, click Trebuchet MS, click the Font Size list arrow, click 14, click , click , then deselect the text**

   The heading is formatted in 14-point Trebuchet MS bold with a purple color. Notice that when you use the buttons on the Mini toolbar to format text, you cannot preview the formatting options in the document.

9. **Press [Ctrl][Home], then click the Save button on the Quick Access toolbar**

   Compare your document to Figure C-3.

FIGURE C-1: **Font list**

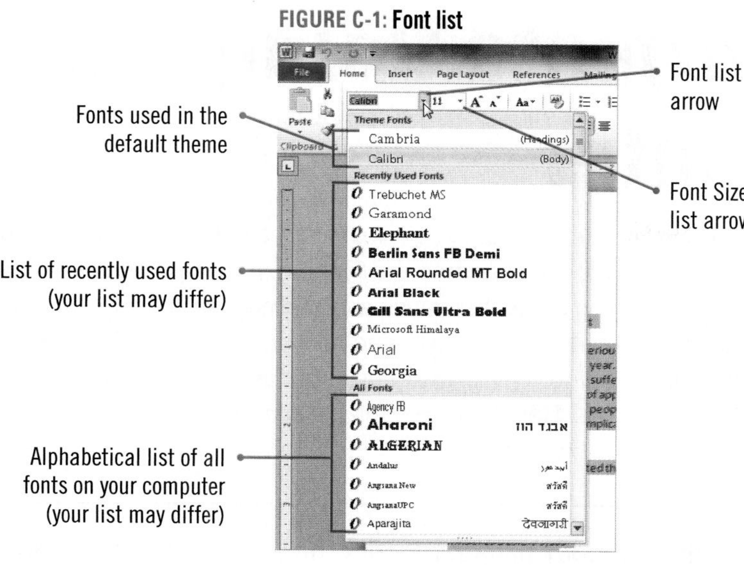

FIGURE C-2: **Font Color Palette**

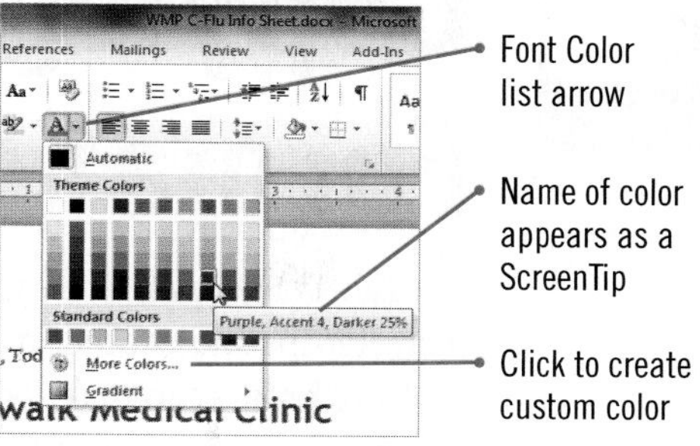

FIGURE C-3: **Document formatted with fonts**

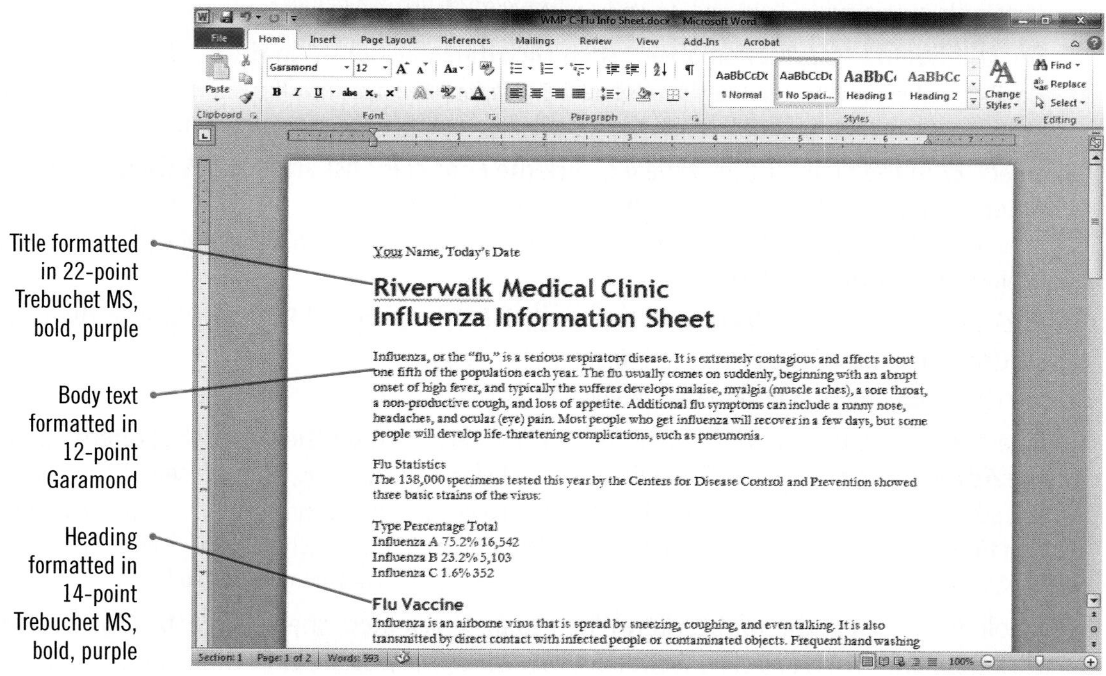

Adding a drop cap

A fun way to illustrate a document with fonts is to add a drop cap to a paragraph. A **drop cap** is a large initial capital letter, often used to set off the first paragraph of an article. To create a drop cap, place the insertion point in the paragraph you want to format, click the Insert tab, and then click the Drop Cap button in the Text group to open a menu of Drop cap options. Preview and select one of the options on the menu, or click Drop Cap Options to open the Drop Cap dialog box, shown in Figure C-4. In the Drop Cap dialog box, select the position, font, number of lines to drop, and the distance you want the drop cap to be from the paragraph text, and then click OK. The drop cap is added to the paragraph as a graphic object.

Once a drop cap is inserted in a paragraph, you can modify it by selecting it and then changing the settings in the Drop Cap dialog box. For even more interesting effects, you can enhance a drop cap with font color, font styles, or font effects. You can also fill the graphic object with shading or add a border around it. To enhance a drop cap, first select it, and then experiment with the formatting options available in the Font dialog box and in the Borders and Shading dialog box.

FIGURE C-4: **Drop Cap dialog box**

Drop Cap
Position
None | Dropped | In margin
Options
Font: Garamond
Lines to drop: 3
Distance from text: 0"
OK | Cancel

UNIT C
Word 2010

Copying Formats Using the Format Painter

You can dramatically change the appearance of text by applying different font styles, font effects, and character-spacing effects. For example, you can use the buttons in the Font group to make text darker by applying **bold** or to make text slanted by applying **italic**. When you are satisfied with the formatting of certain text, you can quickly apply the same formats to other text using the Format Painter. The **Format Painter** is a powerful Word feature that allows you to copy all the format settings applied to selected text to other text that you want to format the same way. You spice up the appearance of the text in the document by applying different font styles and effects.

STEPS

1. **Select extremely contagious in the first body paragraph, click the Bold button B on the Mini toolbar, select the entire paragraph, then click the Italic button I**
   "Extremely contagious" is bold, and the entire paragraph is formatted in italic.

2. **Select Influenza Information Sheet, then click the launcher in the Font group**
   The Font dialog box opens, as shown in Figure C-5. You can use options on the Font tab to change the font, font style, size, and color of text, and to add an underline and apply font effects to text.

3. **Select 22 in the Size list box, type 42, click the Font color list arrow, click Olive Green, Accent 3, Darker 25%, then click the Text Effects button**
   The Format Text Effects dialog box opens. You use this dialog box to apply text effects, such as shadows, outlines, and reflections, to text.

4. **Click Shadow, click the Presets list arrow, click Offset Diagonal Bottom Right in the Outer section, click Close, click OK, then deselect the text**
   The text is larger, green, and has a shadow effect.

5. **Select Influenza Information Sheet, right-click, click Font on the menu that opens, click the Advanced tab, click the Scale list arrow, click 80%, click OK, then deselect the text**
   You use the Advanced tab in the Font dialog box to change the scale, or width, of the selected characters, to alter the spacing between characters, or to raise or lower the characters. Decreasing the scale of the characters makes them narrower and gives the text a tall, thin appearance, as shown in Figure C-6.

6. **Scroll down, select the subheading When to Be Vaccinated, then, using the Mini toolbar, click the Font list arrow, click Trebuchet MS, click B, click I, click the Font Color list arrow A, click Olive Green, Accent 3, Darker 25%, then deselect the text**
   The subheading is formatted in Trebuchet MS, bold, italic, and green.

7. **Select When to Be Vaccinated, then click the Format Painter button in the Clipboard group**
   The pointer changes to .

8. **Scroll down, select Who Should Be Vaccinated with the pointer, then deselect the text**
   The subheading is formatted in Trebuchet MS, bold, italic, and green, as shown in Figure C-7.

9. **Scroll up as needed, select Flu Vaccine, then double-click**
   Double-clicking the Format Painter button allows the Format Painter to remain active until you turn it off. By keeping the Format Painter active, you can apply formatting to multiple items.

10. **Scroll down, select the headings Prevention, Treatment, and Medications with the pointer, click to turn off the Format Painter, then save your changes**
    The headings are formatted in 14-point Trebuchet MS bold with a purple font color.

QUICK TIP
To change the case of selected text from lowercase to uppercase—and visa versa—click the Change Case button in the Font group, and then select the case style you want to use.

TROUBLE
Move the pointer over the document text to see the pointer.

QUICK TIP
You can also press [Esc] to turn off the Format Painter.

FIGURE C-5: Font tab in Font dialog box

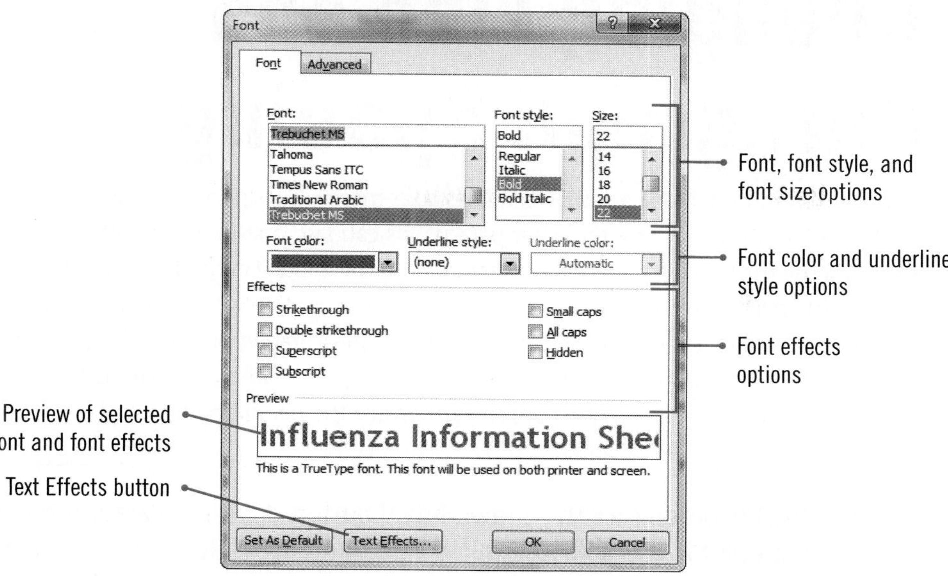

FIGURE C-6: Font and character spacing effects applied to text

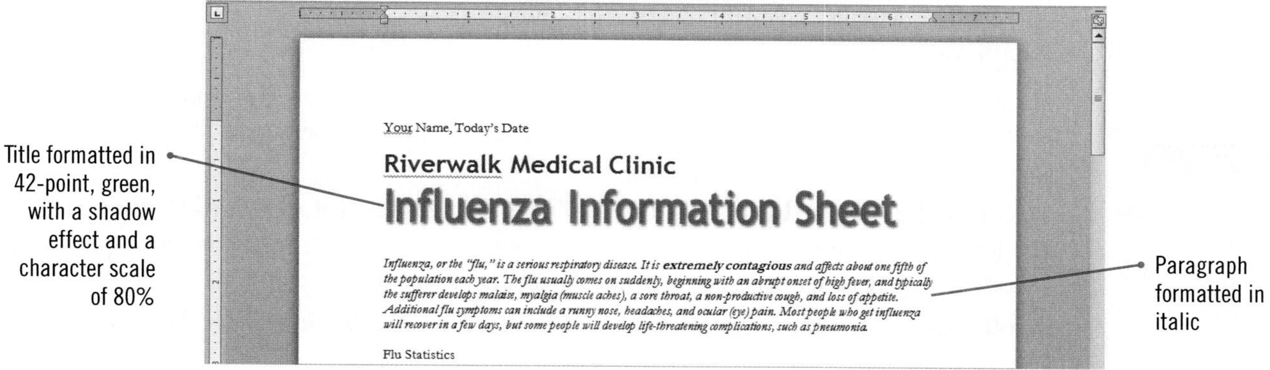

FIGURE C-7: Formats copied and applied using the Format Painter

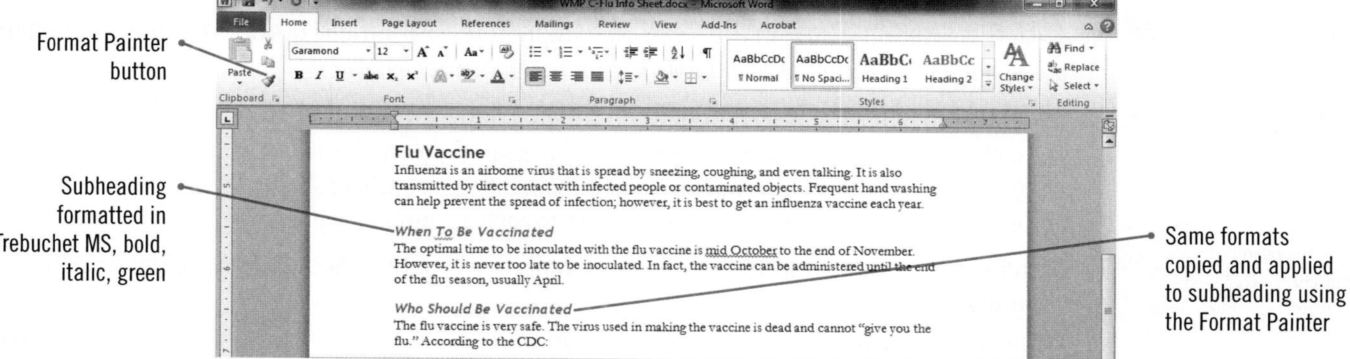

Underlining text

Another creative way to call attention to text and to jazz up the appearance of a document is to apply an underline style to words you want to highlight. The Underline list arrow in the Font group displays straight, dotted, wavy, dashed, and mixed underline styles, along with a gallery of colors from which to choose. To apply an underline to text, simply select it, click the Underline list arrow, and then select an underline style from the list. For a wider variety of underline styles, click More Underlines in the list, and then select an underline style in the Font dialog box. You can change the color of an underline at any time by selecting the underlined text, clicking the Underline list arrow, pointing to Underline Color, and then choosing from the options in the color gallery. If you want to remove an underline from text, select the underlined text, and then click the Underline button.

Word 2010

UNIT C
Word 2010

Changing Line and Paragraph Spacing

Increasing the amount of space between lines adds more white space to a document and can make it easier to read. Adding space before and after paragraphs can also open up a document and improve its appearance. You use the Line and Paragraph Spacing list arrow in the Paragraph group on the Home tab to quickly change line spacing. To change paragraph spacing, you use the Spacing options in the Paragraph group on the Page Layout tab. Line and paragraph spacing are measured in points. You increase the line spacing of several paragraphs and add extra space under each heading to give the flyer a more open feel. You work with formatting marks turned on, so you can see the paragraph marks (¶).

STEPS

1. **Press [Ctrl][Home], click the Show/Hide ¶ button ¶ in the Paragraph group, place the insertion point in the italicized paragraph under the title, then click the Line and Paragraph Spacing list arrow in the Paragraph group on the Home tab**
   The Line Spacing list opens. This list includes options for increasing the space between lines. The check mark on the Line Spacing list indicates the current line spacing.
2. **Click 1.15**
   The space between the lines in the paragraph increases to 1.15 lines. Notice that you do not need to select an entire paragraph to change its paragraph formatting; simply place the insertion point in the paragraph you want to format.
3. **Select the four-line list that begins with "Type Percentage Total", click , then click 1.5**
   The line spacing between the selected paragraphs changes to 1.5. To change the paragraph-formatting features of more than one paragraph, you must select the paragraphs.
4. **Scroll down, place the insertion point in the heading Flu Vaccine, then click the Page Layout tab**
   The paragraph spacing settings for the active paragraph are shown in the Before and After text boxes in the Paragraph group on the Page Layout tab.
5. **Click the After up arrow in the Spacing section in the Paragraph group so that 6 pt appears**
   Six points of space are added after the Flu Vaccine heading paragraph.
6. **Scroll down, place the insertion point in the heading Prevention, then press [F4]**
   Pressing [F4] repeats the last action you took. In this case, six points of space are added after the Prevention heading. Note that using [F4] is not the same as using the Format painter. Pressing [F4] repeats only the last action. You can use the Format Painter at any time to apply multiple format settings.
7. **Scroll down, select Treatment, press and hold [Ctrl], select Medications, release [Ctrl], then press [F4]**
   When you press [Ctrl] as you select items, you can select and format multiple items at once. Six points of space are added after each heading.
8. **Press [Ctrl][Home], place the insertion point in Influenza Information Sheet, click the Before up arrow in the Spacing section in the Paragraph group twice so that 12 pt appears**
   The second line of the title has 12 points of space before it. Compare your document with Figure C-8.
9. **Click the Home tab, click ¶, then save your changes**

QUICK TIP
Word recognizes any string of text that ends with a paragraph mark as a paragraph, including titles, headings, and single lines in a list.

QUICK TIP
You can also type a number in the Before and After text boxes.

TROUBLE
If your [F4] key does not work, use the After up arrow to apply 6 pts of space to the headings listed in Steps 6 and 7, then continue with Step 8.

QUICK TIP
Adjusting the space between paragraphs is a more precise way to add white space to a document than inserting blank lines.

FIGURE C-8: **Line and paragraph spacing applied to document**

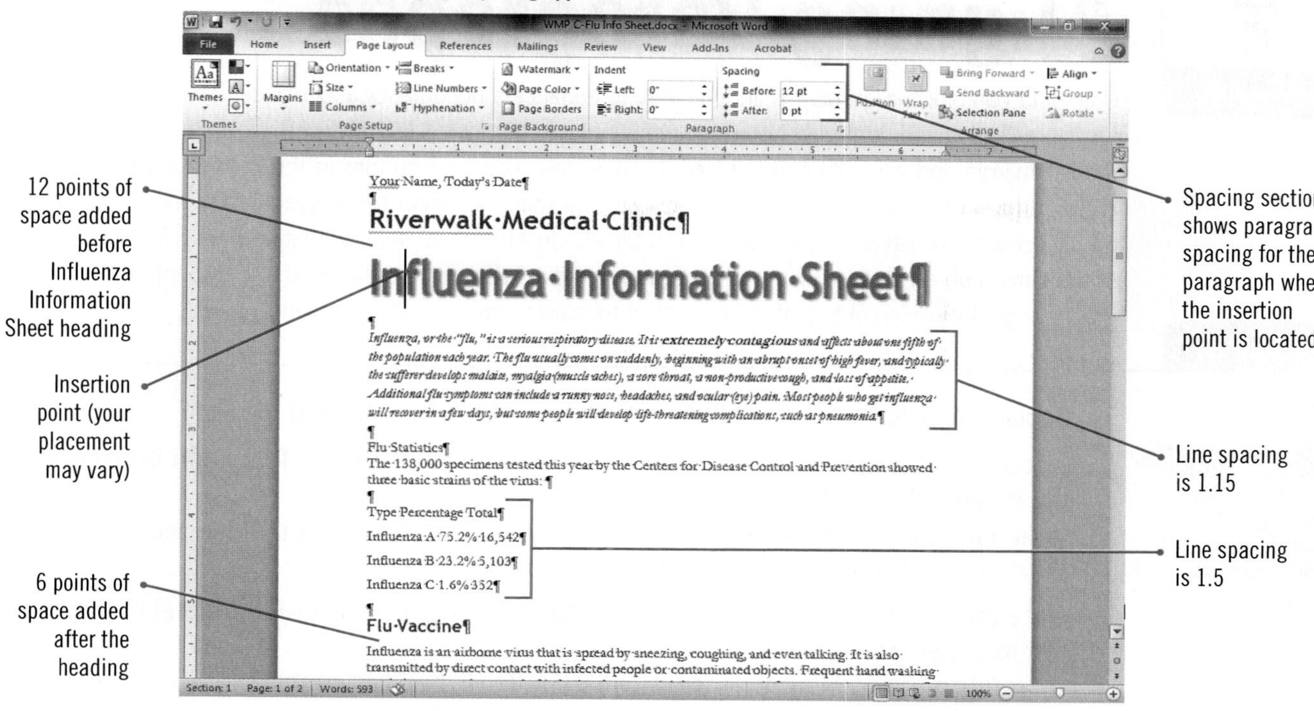

Word 2010

Formatting with Quick Styles

You can also apply multiple format settings to text in one step by applying a style. A **style** is a set of formats, such as font, font size, and paragraph alignment, that are named and stored together. Formatting a document with styles is a quick and easy way to give it a professional appearance. To make it even easier, Word includes sets of styles, called **Quick Styles**, that are designed to be used together in a document to make it attractive and readable. A Quick Style set includes styles for a title, several heading levels, body text, quotes, and lists. The styles in a Quick Style set use common fonts, colors, and formats so that using the styles together in a document gives the document a cohesive look.

To view the active set of Quick Styles, click the More button in the Styles group on the Home tab to expand the Quick Styles gallery, shown in Figure C-9. As you move the pointer over each style in the gallery, a preview of the style is applied to the selected text. To apply a style to the selected text, you simply click the style in the Quick Styles gallery. To remove a style from selected text, you click the Clear Formatting button in the Font group or in the Quick Styles gallery.

If you want to change the active set of Quick Styles to a Quick Style set with a different design, click the Change Styles button in the Styles group, point to Style Set, and then select the Quick Style set that best suits your document's content, tone, and audience.

When you change the Quick Style set, a complete set of new fonts and colors is applied to the entire document. You can also change the color scheme or font used in the active Quick Style set by clicking the Change Styles button, pointing to Colors or to Fonts, and then selecting from the available color schemes or font options.

FIGURE C-9: **Quick Styles gallery**

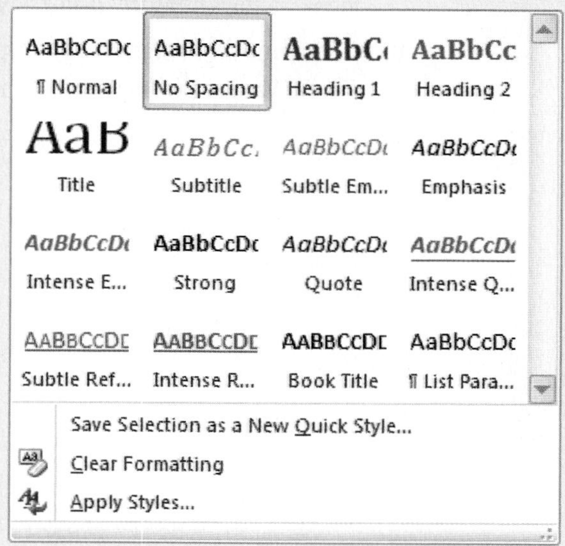

UNIT C

Word 2010

Aligning Paragraphs

Changing paragraph alignment is another way to enhance a document's appearance. Paragraphs are aligned relative to the left and right margins in a document. By default, text is **left-aligned**, which means it is flush with the left margin and has a ragged right edge. Using the alignment buttons in the Paragraph group, you can **right-align** a paragraph—make it flush with the right margin—or **center** a paragraph so that it is positioned evenly between the left and right margins. You can also **justify** a paragraph so that both the left and right edges of the paragraph are flush with the left and right margins. You change the alignment of several paragraphs at the beginning of the information sheet to make it more visually interesting.

STEPS

TROUBLE

Click the View Ruler button at the top of the vertical scroll bar to display the rulers if they are not already displayed.

QUICK TIP

Click the Align Text Left button in the Paragraph group to left-align a paragraph.

1. **Replace Your Name, Today's Date with your name, a comma, and the date**
2. **Select your name, the comma, and the date, then click the Align Text Right button in the Paragraph group**

   The text is aligned with the right margin. In Page Layout view, the place where the white and shaded sections of the horizontal ruler meet shows the left and right margins.
3. **Place the insertion point between your name and the comma, press [Delete] to delete the comma, then press [Enter]**

   The new paragraph containing the date is also right-aligned. Pressing [Enter] in the middle of a paragraph creates a new paragraph with the same text and paragraph formatting as the original paragraph.
4. **Select the two-line title, then click the Center button in the Paragraph group**

   The two paragraphs that make up the title are centered between the left and right margins.
5. **Scroll down as needed, place the insertion point in the Flu Vaccine heading, then click**

   The Flu Vaccine heading is centered.
6. **Place the insertion point in the italicized paragraph under the title, then click the Justify button in the Paragraph group**

   The paragraph is aligned with both the left and right margins, as shown in Figure C-10. When you justify a paragraph, Word adjusts the spacing between words so that each line in the paragraph is flush with the left and the right margins.
7. **Place the insertion point in Flu Vaccine, then click the launcher in the Paragraph group**

   The Paragraph dialog box opens, as shown in Figure C-11. The Indents and Spacing tab shows the paragraph format settings for the paragraph where the insertion point is located. You can check or change paragraph format settings using this dialog box.
8. **Click the Alignment list arrow, click Left, click OK, then save your changes**

   The Flu Vaccine heading is left-aligned.

FIGURE C-10: **Modified paragraph alignment**

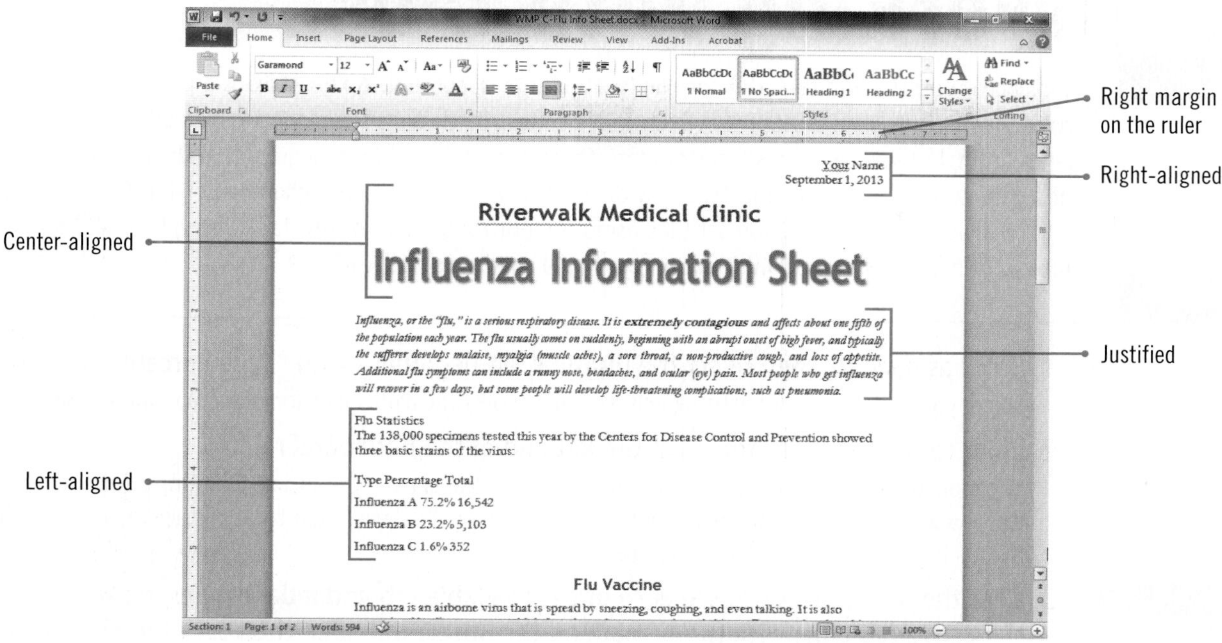

FIGURE C-11: **Indents and Spacing tab in Paragraph dialog box**

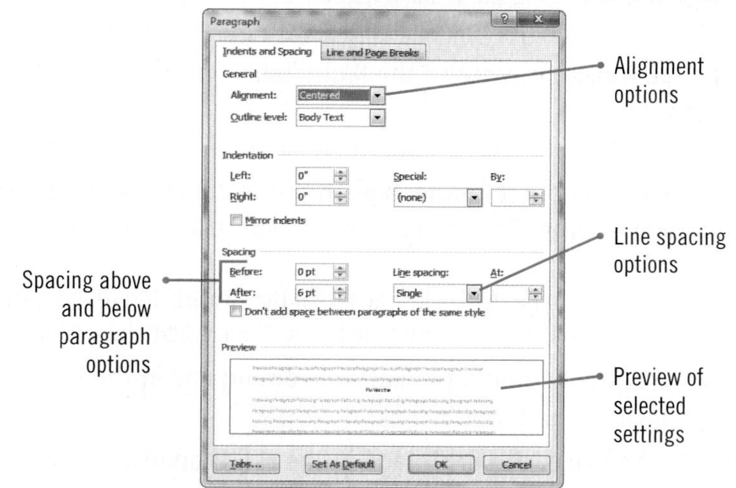

Formatting a document using themes

Changing the theme applied to a document is another powerful and efficient way to tailor a document's look and feel, particularly when a document is formatted with a Quick Style set. By default, all documents created in Word are formatted with the default Office theme—which uses Calibri as the font for the body text—but you can change the theme at any time to fit the content, tone, and purpose of a document. When you change the theme for a document, a complete set of new theme colors, fonts, and effects is applied to the whole document.

To preview how various themes look when applied to the current document, click the Themes button in the Themes group on the Page Layout tab, and then move the pointer over each theme in the gallery and notice how the document changes. When you click the theme you like, all document content that uses theme colors, all text that is formatted with a style, including default body text, and all table styles and graphic effects change to the colors, fonts, and effects used by the theme. In addition, the gallery of colors changes to display the set of theme colors, and the active Quick Style set changes to employ the theme colors and fonts. Note that changing the theme does not affect the formatting of text to which font formatting has already been applied, nor does it change any standard or custom colors used in the document.

If you want to tweak the document design further, you can modify it by applying a different set of theme colors, heading and body text fonts, or graphic effects. To do this, simply click the Theme Colors, Theme Fonts, or Theme Effects button in the Themes group, move the pointer over each option in the gallery to preview it in the document, and then click the option you like best.

UNIT C

Word 2010

Working with Tabs

Tabs allow you to align text at a specific location in a document. A **tab stop** is a point on the horizontal ruler that indicates the location at which to align text. By default, tab stops are located every ½" from the left margin, but you can also set custom tab stops. Using tabs, you can align text to the left, right, or center of a tab stop, or you can align text at a decimal point or insert a bar character. Table C-1 describes the different types of tab stops. You set tabs using the horizontal ruler or the Tabs dialog box. You use tabs to format the statistical information on the flu so it is easy to read.

STEPS

1. **Scroll as needed, then select the four-line list beginning with "Type Percentage Total"**
   Before you set tab stops for existing text, you must select the paragraphs for which you want to set tabs.

2. **Point to the tab indicator at the left end of the horizontal ruler**
   The icon that appears in the tab indicator indicates the active type of tab; pointing to the tab indicator displays a ScreenTip with the name of the active tab type. By default, left tab is the active tab type. Clicking the tab indicator scrolls through the types of tabs and indents.

QUICK TIP
To remove a tab stop, drag it up or down off the ruler.

3. **Click the tab indicator to see each of the available tab and indent types, make Left Tab the active tab type, click the 1" mark on the horizontal ruler, then click the 3½" mark on the horizontal ruler**
   A left tab stop is inserted at the 1" mark and the 3½" on the horizontal ruler. Clicking the horizontal ruler inserts a tab stop of the active type for the selected paragraph or paragraphs.

4. **Click the tab indicator twice so the Right Tab icon is active, then click the 5" mark on the horizontal ruler**
   A right tab stop is inserted at the 5" mark on the horizontal ruler, as shown in Figure C-12.

5. **Place the insertion point before Type in the first line in the list, press [Tab], place the insertion point before Percentage, press [Tab], place the insertion point before Total, then press [Tab]**
   Inserting a tab before "Type" left-aligns the text at the 1" mark, inserting a tab before "Percentage" left-aligns the text at the 3½" mark, and inserting a tab before "Total" right-aligns "Total" at the 5" mark.

6. **Insert a tab at the beginning of each remaining line in the list**
   The paragraphs left-align at the 1" mark.

QUICK TIP
Place the insertion point in a paragraph to see the tab stops for that paragraph on the horizontal ruler.

7. **Insert a tab before each percentage in the list, then insert a tab before each total number in the list**
   The percentages left-align at the 3½" mark. The total numbers right-align at the 5" mark.

8. **Select the four lines of tabbed text, drag the right tab stop to the 5½" mark on the horizontal ruler, then deselect the text**
   Dragging the tab stop moves it to a new location. The total numbers right-align at the 5½" mark.

QUICK TIP
Double-click a tab stop on the ruler to open the Tabs dialog box.

9. **Select the last three lines of tabbed text, click the launcher in the Paragraph group, then click the Tabs button at the bottom of the Paragraph dialog box**
   The Tabs dialog box opens, as shown in Figure C-13. You can use the Tabs dialog box to set tab stops, change the position or alignment of existing tab stops, clear tab stops, and apply tab leaders to tabs. **Tab leaders** are lines that appear in front of tabbed text.

10. **Click 3.5" in the Tab stop position list box, click the 2 option button in the Leader section, click Set, click 5.5" in the Tab stop position list box, click the 2 option button in the Leader section, click Set, click OK, deselect the text, then save your changes**
    A dotted tab leader is added before each 3.5" and 5.5" tab stop in the last three lines of tabbed text, as shown in Figure C-14.

FIGURE C-12: Left and right tab stops on the horizontal ruler

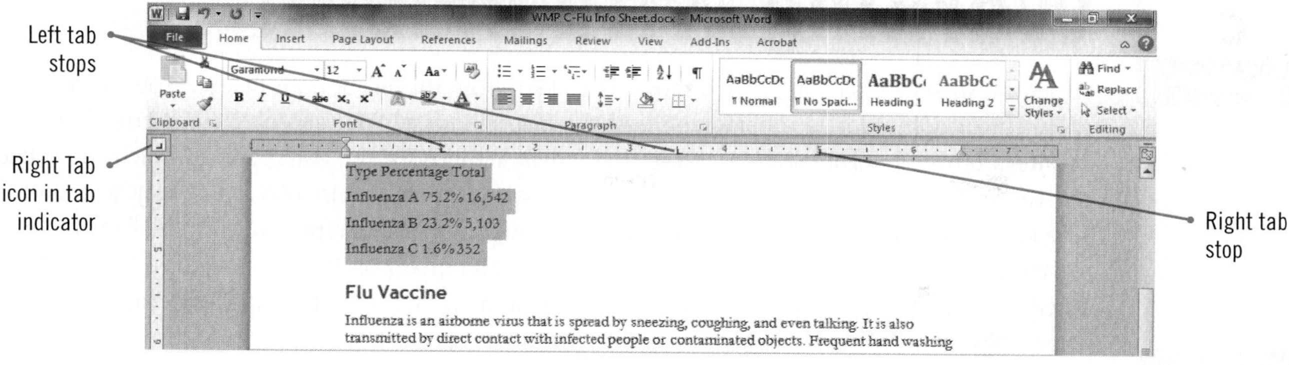

FIGURE C-13: Tabs dialog box

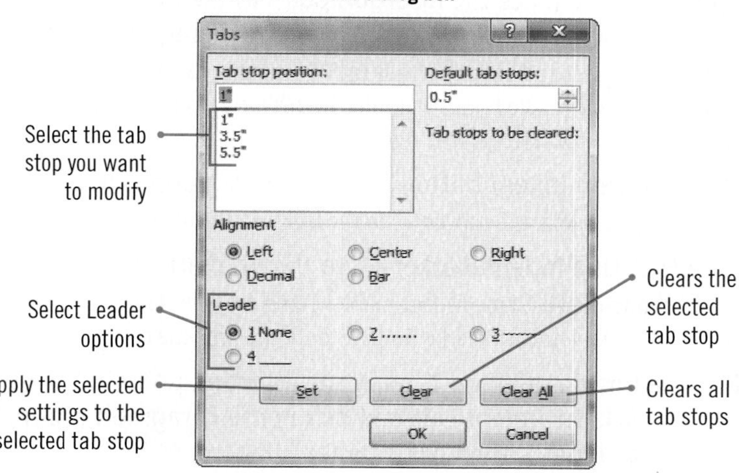

FIGURE C-14: Tab leaders

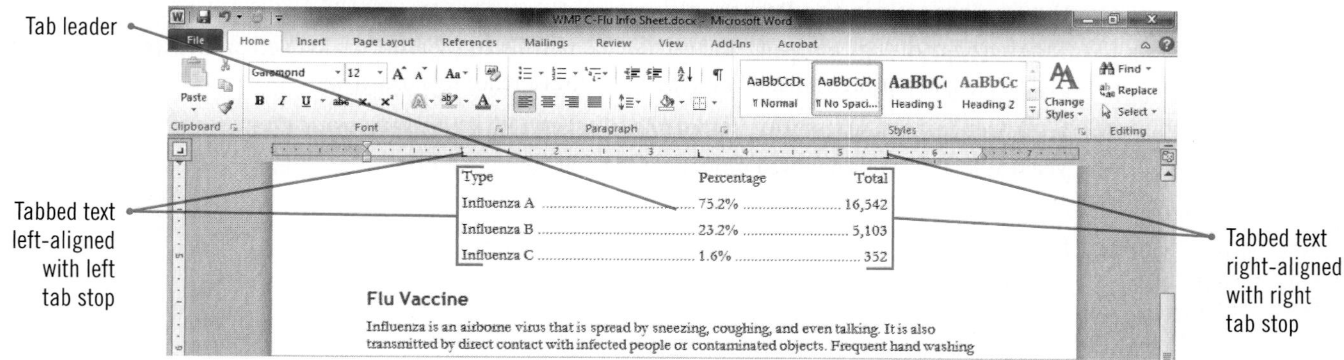

TABLE C-1: Types of tabs

tab	use to
Left tab	Set the start position of text so that text runs to the right of the tab stop as you type
Center tab	Set the center align position of text so that text stays centered on the tab stop as you type
Right tab	Set the right or end position of text so that text moves to the left of the tab stop as you type
Decimal tab	Set the position of the decimal point so that numbers align around the decimal point as you type
Bar tab	Insert a vertical bar at the tab position

UNIT C

Word 2010

Working with Indents

When you **indent** a paragraph, you move its edge in from the left or right margin. You can indent the entire left or right edge of a paragraph, just the first line, or all lines except the first line. The **indent markers** on the horizontal ruler indicate the indent settings for the paragraph in which the insertion point is located. Dragging an indent marker to a new location on the ruler is one way to change the indentation of a paragraph; changing the indent settings in the Paragraph group on the Page Layout tab is another; and using the indent buttons in the Paragraph group on the Home tab is a third. Table C-2 describes different types of indents and some of the methods for creating each. You indent several paragraphs in the information sheet.

STEPS

QUICK TIP

Press [Tab] at the beginning of a paragraph to indent the first line ½".

TROUBLE

Take care to drag only the First Line Indent marker. If you make a mistake, click the Undo button on the Quick Access toolbar, then try again.

1. **Press [Ctrl][Home], place the insertion point in the italicized paragraph under the title, then click the Increase Indent button in the Paragraph group on the Home tab**

   The entire paragraph is indented ½" from the left margin, as shown in Figure C-15. The indent marker also moves to the ½" mark on the horizontal ruler. Each time you click the Increase Indent button, the left edge of a paragraph moves another ½" to the right.

2. **Click the Decrease Indent button in the Paragraph group**

   The left edge of the paragraph moves ½" to the left, and the indent marker moves back to the left margin.

3. **Drag the First Line Indent marker to the ¼" mark on the horizontal ruler**

   Figure C-16 shows the First Line Indent marker being dragged. The first line of the paragraph is indented ¼". Dragging the First Line Indent marker indents only the first line of a paragraph.

4. **Scroll to the bottom of page 1, place the insertion point in the quotation, click the Page Layout tab, click the Indent Left text box in the Paragraph group, type .5, click the Indent Right text box, type .5, then press [Enter]**

   The left and right edges of the paragraph are indented ½" from the margins, as shown in Figure C-17.

5. **Press [Ctrl][Home], place the insertion point in the italicized paragraph, then click the launcher in the Paragraph group**

   The Paragraph dialog box opens. You can use the Indents and Spacing tab to check or change the alignment, indentation, and paragraph and line spacing settings applied to a paragraph.

6. **Click the Special list arrow, click (none), click OK, then save your changes**

   The first line indent is removed from the paragraph.

Clearing formatting

If you are unhappy with the way text is formatted, you can use the Clear Formatting command to return the text to the default format settings. The default format includes font and paragraph formatting: text is formatted in 11-point Calibri, and paragraphs are left-aligned with 1.15 point line spacing, 10 points of space below, and no indents. To clear formatting from text and return it to the default format, select the text you want to clear, and then click the Clear Formatting button in the Font group on the Home tab. If you prefer to return the text to the default font and remove all paragraph formatting, making the text 11-point Calibri, left-aligned, single spaced, with no paragraph spacing or indents, select the text and then simply click the No Spacing button in the Styles group on the Home tab.

FIGURE C-15: Indented paragraph

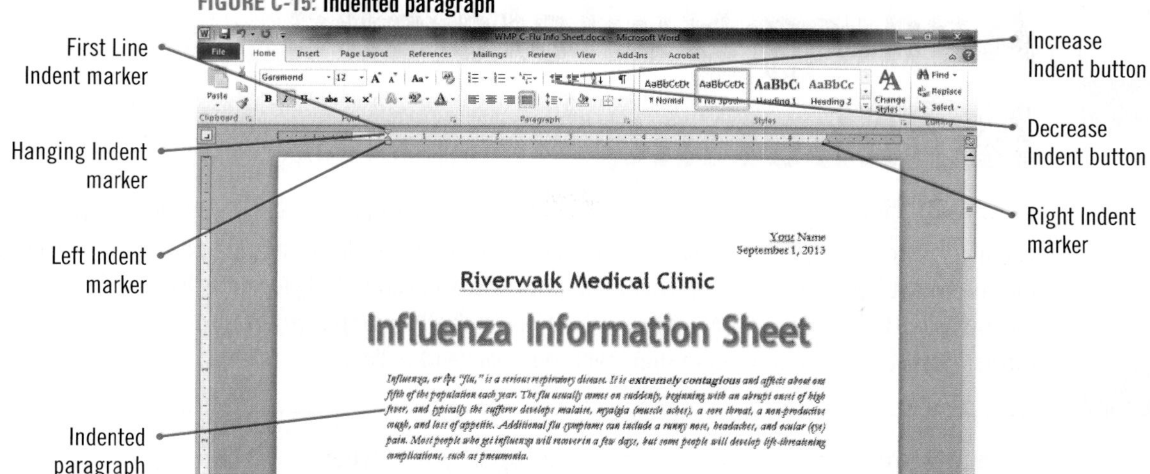

FIGURE C-16: Dragging the First Line Indent marker

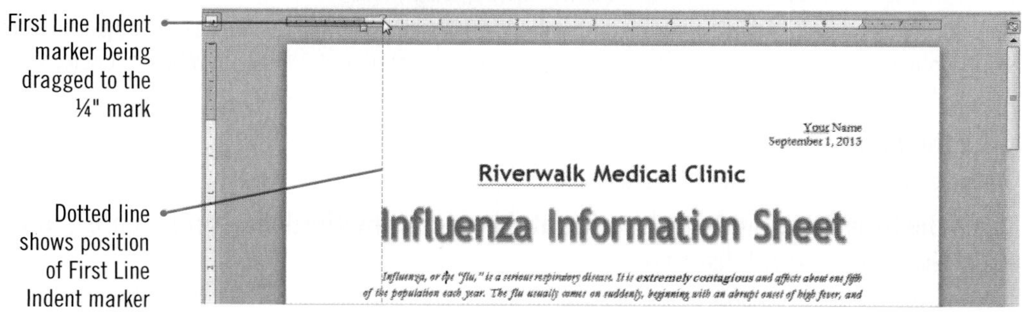

FIGURE C-17: Paragraph indented from the left and right

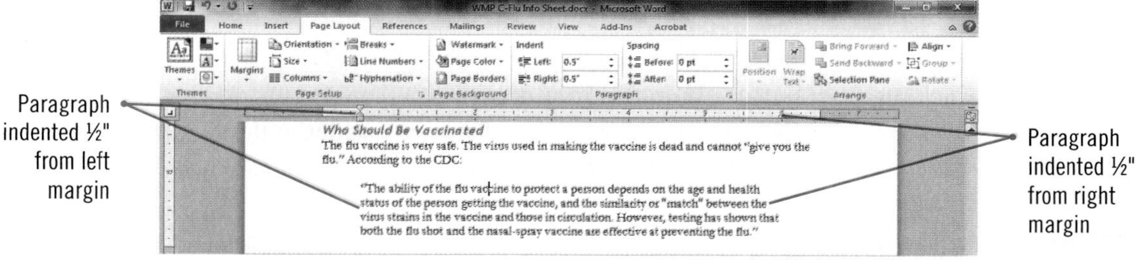

TABLE C-2: Types of indents

indent type: description	to create
Left indent: The left edge of a paragraph is moved in from the left margin	Drag the Left Indent marker on the ruler to the right to the position where you want the left edge of the paragraph to align
Right indent: The right edge of a paragraph is moved in from the right margin	Drag the Right Indent marker on the ruler to the left to the position where you want the right edge of the paragraph to align
First line indent: The first line of a paragraph is indented more than the subsequent lines	Drag the First Line Indent marker on the ruler to the right to the position where you want the first line of the paragraph to begin; or activate the First Line Indent marker in the tab indicator, and then click the ruler at the position where you want the first line of the paragraph to begin
Hanging indent: The subsequent lines of a paragraph are indented more than the first line	Drag the Hanging Indent marker on the ruler to the right to the position where you want the hanging indent to begin; or activate the Hanging Indent marker in the tab indicator, and then click the ruler at the position where you want the second and remaining lines of the paragraph to begin
Negative indent (or Outdent): The left edge of a paragraph is moved to the left of the left margin	Drag the Left Indent marker on the ruler to the left to the position where you want the negative indent to begin

UNIT C

Word 2010

Adding Bullets and Numbering

Formatting a list with bullets or numbering can help to organize the ideas in a document. A **bullet** is a character, often a small circle, that appears before the items in a list to add emphasis. Formatting a list as a numbered list helps illustrate sequences and priorities. You can quickly format a list with bullets or numbering by using the Bullets and Numbering buttons in the Paragraph group on the Home tab. You format the lists in the information sheet with numbers and bullets.

STEPS

1. **Scroll until the top of page 2 is at the top of your screen**

2. **Select the four-line list above the Prevention heading, click the Home tab, then click the Numbering list arrow in the Paragraph group**

   The Numbering Library opens, as shown in Figure C-18. You use this list to choose or change the numbering style applied to a list. You can drag the pointer over the numbering styles to preview how the selected text will look if the numbering style is applied.

3. **Click the numbering style shown in Figure C-18**

   The paragraphs are formatted as a numbered list.

4. **Place the insertion point after vaccine at the end of the third line, press [Enter], then type An active neurological disorder**

   Pressing [Enter] in the middle of the numbered list creates a new numbered paragraph and automatically renumbers the remainder of the list. Similarly, if you delete a paragraph from a numbered list, Word automatically renumbers the remaining paragraphs.

5. **Click 1 in the list**

   Clicking a number in a list selects all the numbers, as shown in Figure C-19.

6. **Click the Bold button in the Font group**

   The numbers are all formatted in bold. Notice that the formatting of the items in the list does not change when you change the formatting of the numbers. You can also use this technique to change the formatting of bullets in a bulleted list.

7. **Select the list of rules under the Prevention heading, then click the Bullets button in the Paragraph group**

   The five paragraphs are formatted as a bulleted list using the most recently used bullet style.

8. **Click a bullet in the list to select all the bullets, click the Bullets list arrow in the Paragraph group, click the check mark bullet style, click the document to deselect the text, then save your changes**

   The bullet character changes to a check mark, as shown in Figure C-20.

QUICK TIP
To change the style, font, number format, and alignment of the numbers in a list, right-click the list, point to Numbering, then click Define New Number Format.

QUICK TIP
To remove a bullet or number, select the paragraph(s), then click or .

QUICK TIP
To use a symbol or a picture for a bullet character, click Define New Bullet in the Bullet list, and then select from the options in the Define New Bullet dialog box.

Creating multilevel lists

You can create lists with hierarchical structures by applying a multilevel list style to a list. To create a **multilevel list**, also called an outline, begin by applying a multilevel list style using the Multilevel List list arrow in the Paragraph group on the Home tab, then type your outline, pressing [Enter] after each item. To demote items to a lower level of importance in the outline, place the insertion point in the item, then click the Increase Indent button in the Paragraph group on the Home tab. Each time you indent a paragraph, the item is demoted to a lower level in the outline. Similarly, you can use the Decrease Indent button to promote an item to a higher level in the outline. You can also create a hierarchical structure in any bulleted or numbered list by using and to demote and promote items in the list. To change the multilevel list style applied to a list, select the list, click , and then select a new style.

FIGURE C-18: **Numbering list**

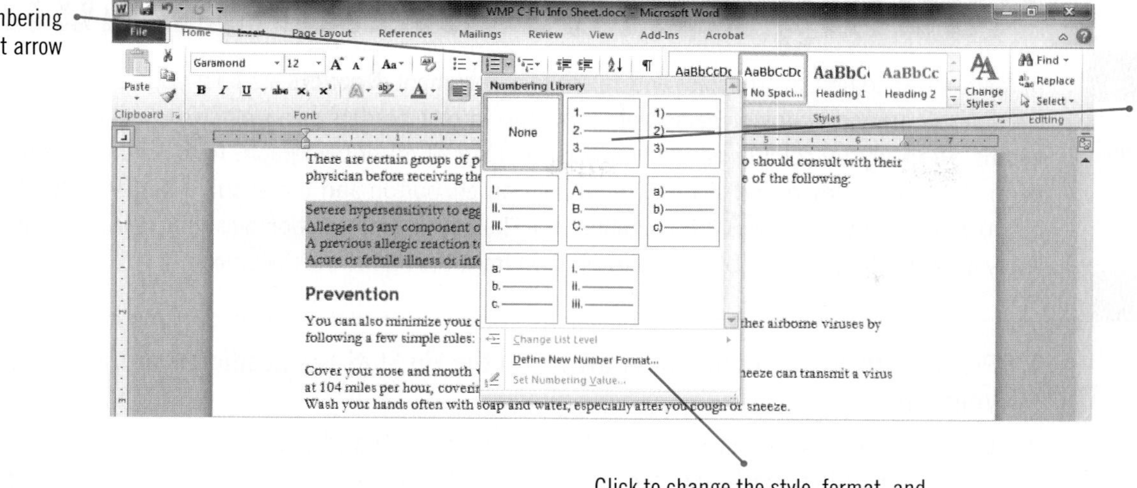

FIGURE C-19: **Numbered list**

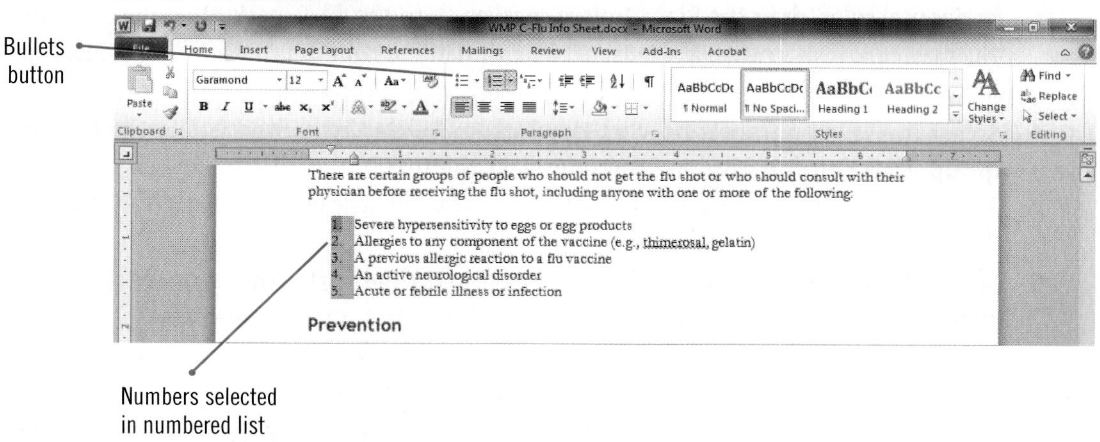

FIGURE C-20: **Check mark bullets applied to the list**

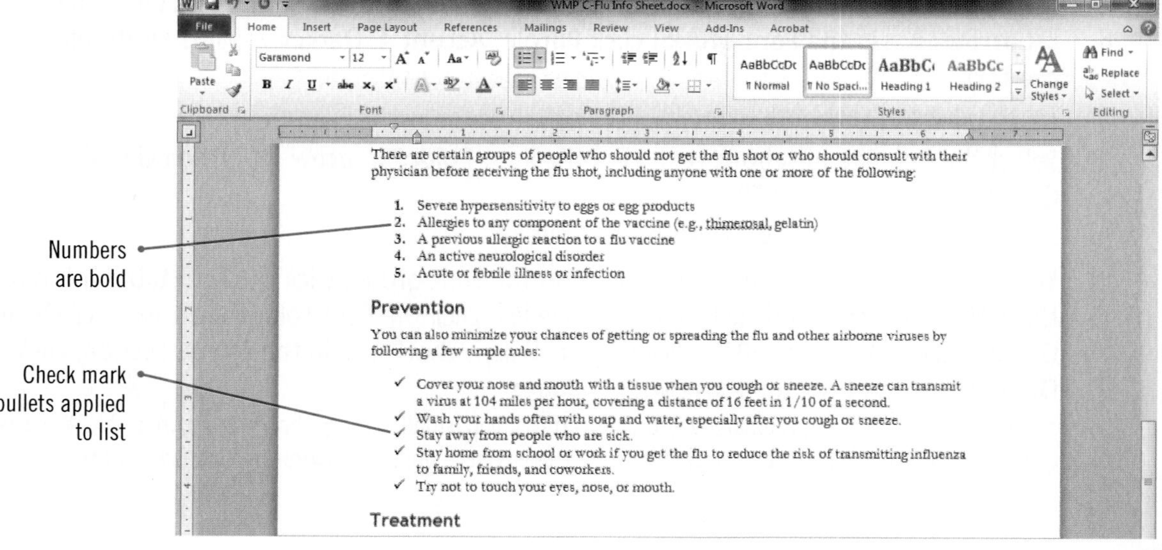

Word 2010

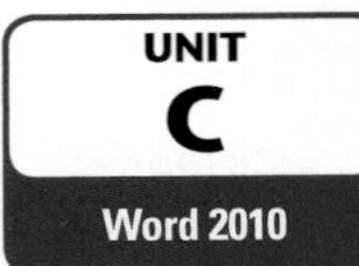

Adding Borders and Shading

Borders and shading can add color and splash to a document. **Borders** are lines you add above, below, to the side, or around words or paragraphs. You can format borders using different line styles, colors, and widths. **Shading** is a color or pattern you apply behind words or paragraphs to make them stand out on a page. You apply borders and shading using the Borders button and the Shading button in the Paragraph group on the Home tab. You enhance the Flu Statistics information by adding shading to it. You also apply a border around the tabbed text to set it off from the rest of the document.

STEPS

1. **Press [Ctrl][Home], then scroll down until the Flu Statistics heading is at the top of your screen**
2. **Click and drag to select Flu Statistics, the paragraph and blank line below it, and the four paragraphs of tabbed text; click the Shading list arrow in the Paragraph group on the Home tab, click Purple, Accent 4, Lighter 60%, then deselect the text**
   Light purple shading is applied to the seven paragraphs. Notice that the shading is applied to the entire width of the paragraphs, despite the tab settings.
3. **Select the seven shaded paragraphs, drag the Left Indent marker to the ¾" mark on the horizontal ruler, drag the Right Indent marker to the 5¾" mark, then deselect the text**
   The shading for the paragraphs is indented from the left and right, which makes it look more attractive, as shown in Figure C-21.
4. **Select the seven paragraphs, click the Bottom Border list arrow in the Paragraph group, click Outside Borders, then deselect the text**
   A black outside border is added around the selected text. The style of the border added is the most recently used border style, in this case the default, a thin black line.
5. **Select the seven paragraphs, click the Outside Borders list arrow, click No Border, click the No Border list arrow, then click Borders and Shading**
   The Borders and Shading dialog box opens, as shown in Figure C-22. You use the Borders tab to change the border style, color, and width, and to add boxes and lines to words or paragraphs.
6. **Click the Box box in the Setting section, scroll down the Style list, click the double-line style, click the Color list arrow, click Purple, Accent 4, Darker 25%, click the Width list arrow, click 1½ pt, click OK, then deselect the text**
   A 1½-point dark purple double-line border is added around the tabbed text.
7. **Select the seven paragraphs, click the Bold button in the Font group, click the Font Color list arrow in the Font group, click Purple, Accent 4, Darker 25%, then deselect the text**
   The text changes to bold dark purple.
8. **Select the first line of tabbed text, click the Font Color list arrow, then click Olive Green, Accent 3, Darker 50%**
   The text in the first line of tabbed text changes to green.
9. **Select Flu Statistics, click the launcher in the Font group, click the Font tab if it is not the active tab, scroll and click 14 in the Size list, click the Font color list arrow, click Olive Green, Accent 3, Darker 50%, click the Small caps check box in the Effects section, click OK, deselect the text, then save your changes**
   The Flu Statistics heading is enlarged and changed to green, small caps, as shown in Figure C-23. When you change text to small caps, the lowercase letters are changed to uppercase letters in a smaller font size.

FIGURE C-21: **Shading applied to the tabbed text**

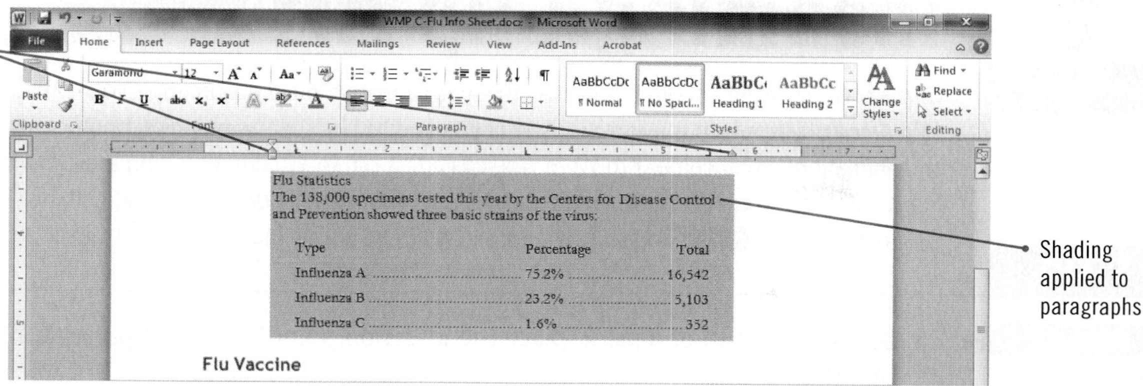

FIGURE C-22: **Borders tab in Borders and Shading dialog box**

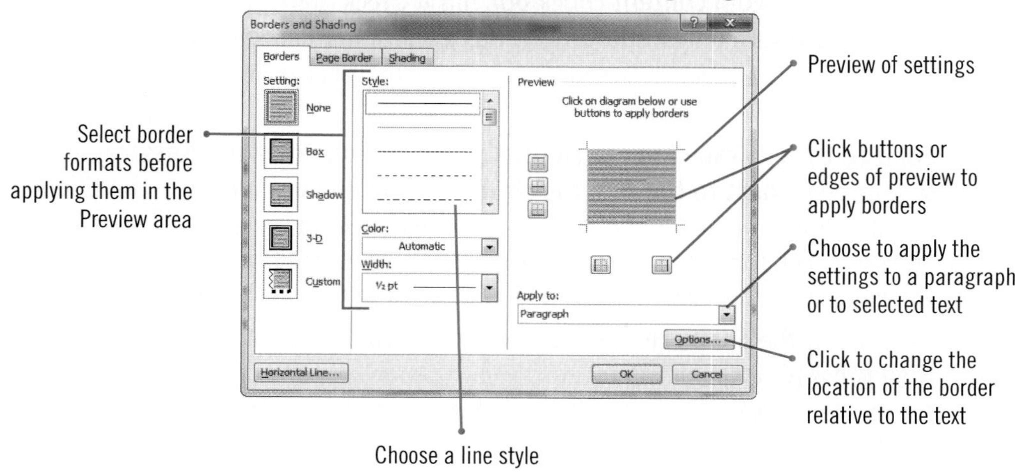

FIGURE C-23: **Borders and shading applied to the document**

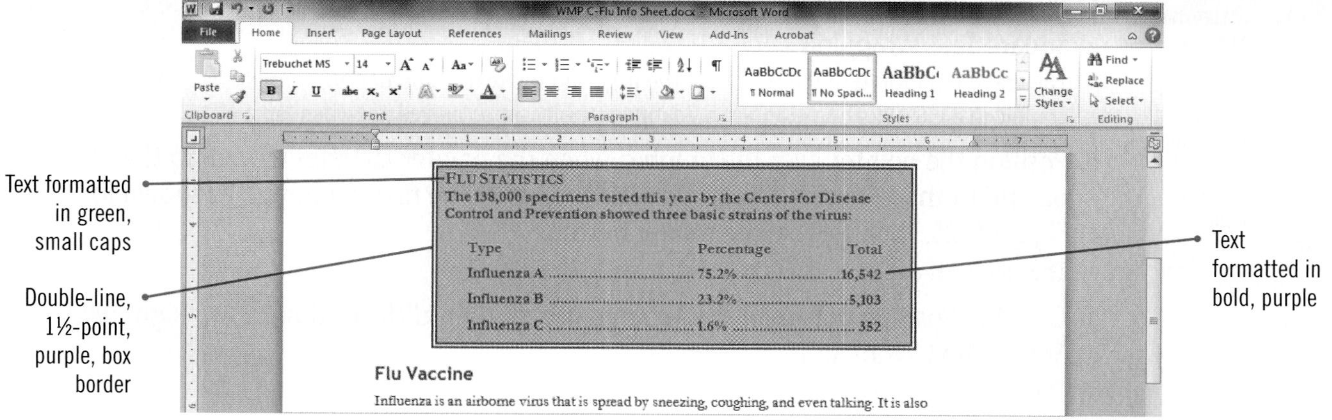

Highlighting text in a document

The Highlight tool allows you to mark and find important text in a document. **Highlighting** is transparent color that is applied to text using the Highlight pointer. To highlight text, click the Text Highlight Color list arrow in the Font group on the Home tab, select a color, then use the I-beam part of the pointer to select the text you want to highlight. Click to turn off the Highlight pointer. To remove highlighting, select the highlighted text, click, then click No Color. Highlighting prints, but it is used most effectively when a document is viewed on screen.

UNIT C
Word 2010

Inserting Clip Art

Clip art is a collection of graphic images that you can insert into a document. Clip art images are stored in the **Clip Organizer**, which is a library of the **clips**—media files such as graphics, photographs, sounds, movies, and animations—that come with Word. You can add a clip to a document using the Clip Art command on the Insert tab. Once you insert a clip art image, you can wrap text around it, resize it, enhance it, and move it to a different location. You illustrate the second page of the document with a clip art image.

STEPS

QUICK TIP
You must be working with an active Internet connection to complete this lesson.

1. **Scroll to the top of page 2, place the insertion point in the first paragraph, click the Insert tab, then click the Clip Art button in the Illustrations group**
   The Clip Art task pane opens. You can use this task pane to search for clips related to a keyword.
2. **Select the text in the Search for text box if necessary, type sneezing, make sure the Include Office.com content check box has a check mark, click the Results should be list arrow, make sure only Photographs has a check mark, then click Go**
   Clips that have the keyword "sneezing" associated with them appear in the Clip Art task pane, as shown in Figure C-24.

TROUBLE
Select a different clip if the clip shown in Figure C-24 is not available to you.

3. **Point to the clip called out in Figure C-24 (scrolling down if necessary), click the list arrow that appears next to the clip, click Insert on the menu, then close the Clip Art task pane**
   The clip is inserted at the location of the insertion point. When a graphic is selected, the active tab changes to the Picture Tools Format tab. This tab contains commands used to adjust, enhance, arrange, and size graphics. The white circles that appear on the square edges of the graphic are the **sizing handles**.
4. **Type 2.5 in the Shape Height text box in the Size group on the Picture Tools Format tab, then press [Enter]**
   The size of the graphic is reduced. When you decreased the height of the graphic, the width decreased proportionally. You can also resize a graphic proportionally by dragging a corner sizing handle. Now that the graphic is smaller, you can see that it was inserted at the location of the insertion point. Until you apply text wrapping to a graphic, it is part of the line of text in which it was inserted (an **inline graphic**). To move a graphic independently of text, you must make it a **floating graphic**.

QUICK TIP
To position a graphic using precise measurements, click the Position button, click More Layout Options, then adjust the settings on the Position tab in the Layout dialog box.

5. **Click the Position button in the Arrange group, then click Position in Middle Center with Square Text Wrapping**
   The graphic is moved to the middle of the page and the text wraps around it. Applying text wrapping to the graphic made it a floating graphic. A floating graphic can be moved anywhere on a page.
6. **Position the pointer over the graphic, when the pointer changes to drag the graphic up and to the left so its top aligns with the top of the first paragraph as shown in Figure C-25, then release the mouse button**
   The graphic is moved to the upper-left corner of the page.
7. **Click the Position button in the Arrange group, then click Position in Top Right with Square Text Wrapping**
   The graphic is moved to the upper-right corner of the page.
8. **Click the More button in the Picture Styles group, point to each picture style to see a preview of the style applied to the graphic, then click Drop Shadow Rectangle**
   A drop shadow effect is applied to the graphic.

TROUBLE
If your document is longer than two pages, reduce the size of the clip art graphic by dragging the lower-left corner sizing handle up and to the right.

9. **Click the View tab, then click the Two Pages button**
   The completed document is shown in Figure C-26.
10. **Save your changes, submit the document to your instructor, then close the document and exit Word**

FIGURE C-24: Clip Art task pane

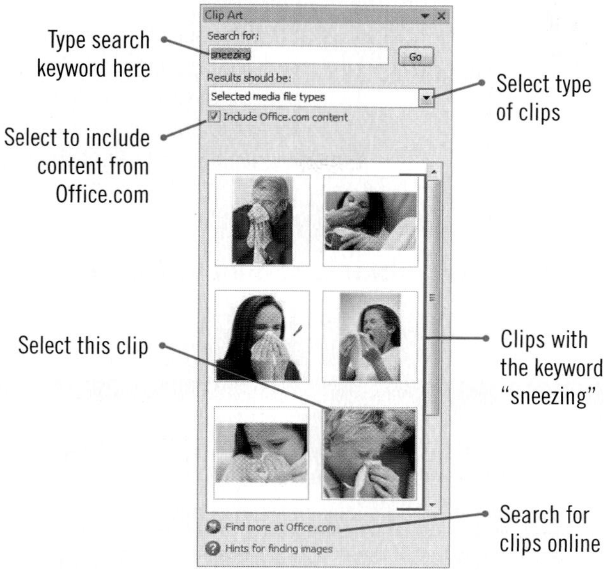

FIGURE C-25: Graphic being moved to a new location

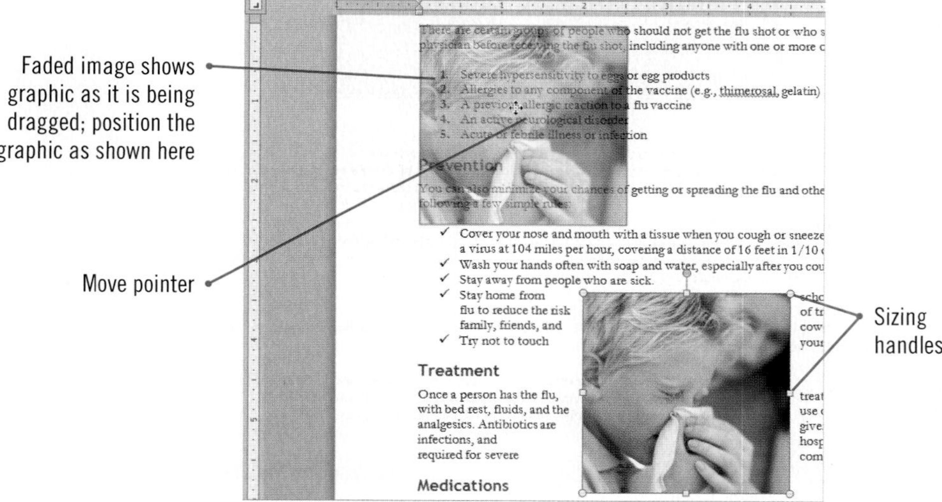

FIGURE C-26: Completed document

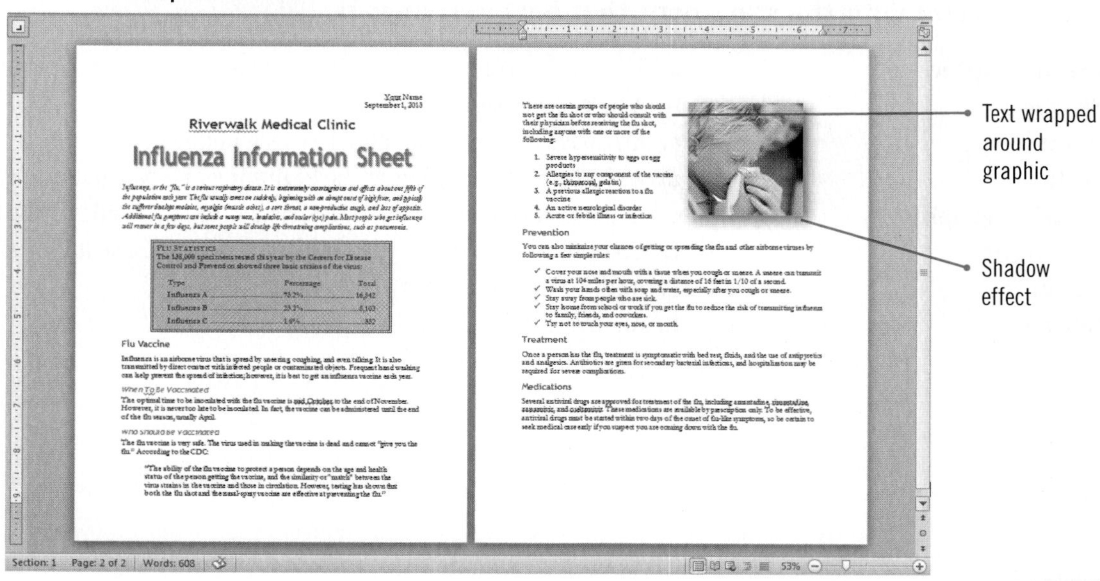

Practice

Concepts Review

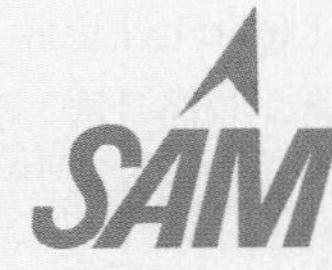

For current SAM information, including versions and content details, visit SAM Central (http://www.cengage.com/samcentral). If you have a SAM user profile, you may have access to hands-on instruction, practice, and assessment of the skills covered in this unit. Since various versions of SAM are supported throughout the life of this text, check with your instructor for the correct instructions and URL/Web site for accessing assignments.

Label each element of the Word program window shown in Figure C-27.

FIGURE C-27

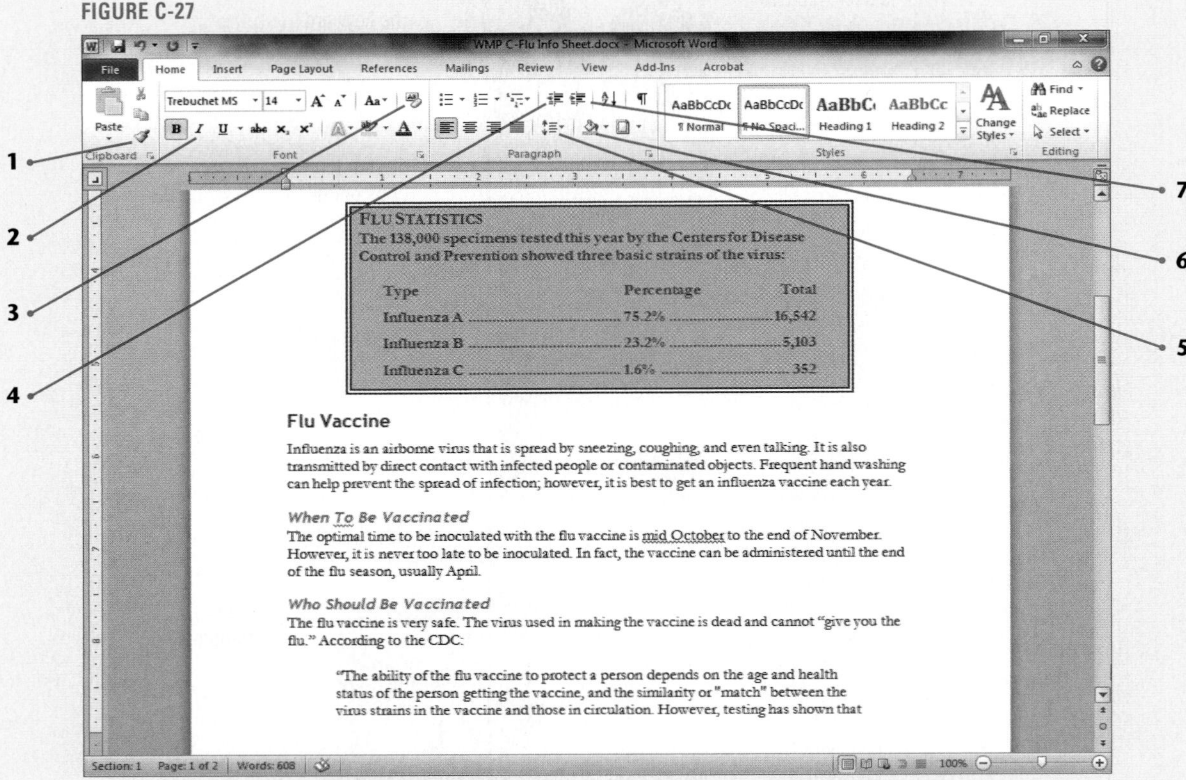

Match each term with the statement that best describes it.

8. Inline graphic	**a.** Transparent color that is applied to text to mark it in a document
9. Shading	**b.** A unit of measurement equal to 1/72 of an inch
10. Point	**c.** An image that text wrapping has been applied to
11. Style	**d.** A character that appears at the beginning of a paragraph to add emphasis
12. Floating graphic	**e.** A line that can be applied above, below, or to the sides of a paragraph
13. Highlight	**f.** Color or pattern that is applied behind text to make it look attractive
14. Bullet	**g.** A set of format settings
15. Border	**h.** An image that is inserted as part of a line of text

Select the best answer from the list of choices.

16. What is Calibri?

a. A character format
b. A style
c. A font
d. A text effect

17. Which type of indent results in subsequent lines of a paragraph being indented more than the first line?

a. Right indent
b. First line indent
c. Negative indent
d. Hanging indent

18. What is the most precise way to increase the amount of white space between two paragraphs?

a. Indent the paragraphs
b. Change the font size
c. Change the before paragraph spacing for the second paragraph
d. Change the line spacing of the paragraphs

19. Which button is used to align a paragraph with both the left and right margins?

a.
b.
c.
d.

20. Which dialog box is used to change the scale of characters?

a. Tabs
b. Font
c. Paragraph
d. Borders and Shading

Skills Review

1. Format with fonts.

a. Start Word, open the file WMP C-2.docx from the drive and folder where you store your Data Files, save it as **WMP C-Scheduling Guidelines**, then scroll through the document to get a feel for its contents.
b. Press [Ctrl][A], then format the text in 12-point Californian FB. Choose a different serif font if Californian FB is not available to you.
c. Press [Ctrl][Home], format the report title **Saint Joan Family Health** in 36-point Berlin Sans FB Demi. Choose a different sans serif font if Berlin Sans FB Demi is not available to you.
d. Change the font color of the report title to Red, Accent 2.
e. Format the subtitle **Guidelines for Scheduling and Processing Patients** in 18-point Berlin Sans FB Demi, then press [Enter] before Processing in the subtitle.
f. Format the heading **Our policy** in 14-point Berlin Sans FB Demi with the Red, Accent 2 font color.
g. Press [Ctrl][Home], then save your changes to the report.

2. Copy formats using the Format Painter.

a. Use the Format Painter to copy the format of the Our policy heading to the following headings: **Five-step approach…, Determining the time…, Processing new patients**.
b. Show formatting marks, then format the paragraph under the Our policy heading in italic.
c. Format **Appointment Time**, the first line in the six-line list under the Determining the time… heading, in bold, small caps, with Red, Accent 2, Darker 50% font color.
d. Change the font color of the five lines under Appointment Time to Red, Accent 2, Darker 50%.
e. Scroll to the top of the report, change the character scale of Saint Joan Family Health to 80%, then save your changes.

3. Change line and paragraph spacing.

a. Change the line spacing of the three-line list under the first body paragraph to 1.5 lines.
b. Add 12 points of space after the title Saint Joan Family Health.
c. Add 12 points of space after the Our policy heading, then add 12 points of space after each additional heading in the report (Five-step approach…, Determining the time…, Processing new patients).

Skills Review (continued)

- **d.** Add 6 points of space after each paragraph in the list under the Five-step approach... heading, except the last paragraph.
- **e.** Change the line spacing of the six-line list under the Determining the time... heading that begins with Appointment Time to 1.15.
- **f.** Add 6 points of space after each paragraph under the Processing new patients... heading.
- **g.** Press [Ctrl][Home], then save your changes to the report.

4. Align paragraphs.

- **a.** Press [Ctrl][A] to select the entire document, then justify all the paragraphs.
- **b.** Center the report title and its subtitle.
- **c.** Press [Ctrl][End], type your name, press [Enter], type the current date, then right-align your name and the date.
- **d.** Save your changes to the report.

5. Work with tabs.

- **a.** Scroll up and select the six-line list of appointment time information under the Determining the time... heading.
- **b.** Set left tab stops at the 1¾" mark and the 3¾" mark.
- **c.** Insert a tab at the beginning of each line in the list.
- **d.** In the first line, insert a tab before Time. In the second line, insert a tab before 45 minutes. In the remaining lines, insert a tab before each number.
- **e.** Select all the lines, then drag the first tab stop to the 2" mark on the horizontal ruler.
- **f.** Select the last five lines, then insert dotted line tab leaders before the 3¾" tab stop.
- **g.** Press [Ctrl][Home], then save your changes to the report.

6. Work with indents.

- **a.** Indent the paragraph under the Our policy heading ½" from the left and ½" from the right.
- **b.** Indent the first line of each of the three body paragraphs under the Determining the time... heading ½".
- **c.** Press [Ctrl][Home], then save your changes to the report.

7. Add bullets and numbering.

- **a.** Apply bullets to the three-line list under the first body paragraph. Change the bullet style to small black circles if that is not the current bullet symbol.
- **b.** Change the font color of the bullets to Red, Accent 2.
- **c.** Scroll down until the Five-step approach... heading is at the top of your screen.
- **d.** Format the five-paragraph list under the Five-step approach... heading as a numbered list.
- **e.** Format the numbers in 12-point Berlin Sans FB Demi, then change the font color to Red, Accent 2.
- **f.** Scroll down until the Processing new patients... heading is at the top of your screen, then format the paragraphs under the heading as a bulleted list using check marks as the bullet style.
- **g.** Change the font color of the bullets to Red, Accent 2, press [Ctrl][Home], then save your changes to the report.

8. Add borders and shading.

- **a.** Add a 1-point Orange, Accent 6, Darker 25% border below the Our policy heading.
- **b.** Use the Format Painter or the F4 key to add the same border to the other headings in the report (Five-step approach..., Determining the time..., Processing new patients).
- **c.** Under the Determining the time... heading, select the six lines of tabbed text, which are formatted in red, then apply Orange, Accent 6, Lighter 40% shading to the paragraphs.
- **d.** Select the six lines of tabbed text again if necessary, then add a 1½-point Orange, Accent 6, Darker 25% single line box border around the paragraphs.
- **e.** Indent the shading and border around the paragraphs 1¾" from the left and 1¾" from the right.
- **f.** Turn off the display of formatting marks, then save your changes.

9. Insert clip art.

- **a.** Press [Ctrl][Home], then open the Clip Art task pane.
- **b.** Click the Results should be in list arrow, make sure All media types has a check mark, then search for clips related to the keyword **appointment**.

Skills Review (continued)

c. Insert the clip shown in Figure C-28, then close the Clip Art task pane. (*Note*: An active Internet connection is needed to select the clip shown in the figure. Select a different clip if this one is not available to you. It is best to select a clip that is similar in shape to the clip shown in Figure C-28.)
d. Select the graphic if necessary, then drag the upper-right sizing handle down and to the left so that the graphic is about 1" wide.
e. Use the Position command to position the clip art in the top left with square text wrapping.
f. Use the Shape Width text box in the Size group on the Format tab to change the width of the graphic to 1.3".
g. Apply Simple Frame, Black picture style to the graphic.
h. Save your changes to the document, submit it to your instructor, close the file, and then exit Word.

Word 2010

FIGURE C-28

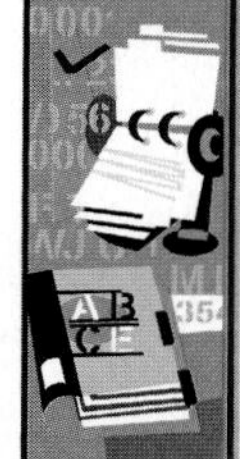

Saint Joan Family Health

Guidelines for Scheduling and Processing Patients

A well-managed schedule of appointments is an important factor in delivering quality health care to patients, and is critical to the smooth and efficient running of Saint Joan Family Health. With that in mind, there are several factors to consider when scheduling patients for appointments:

- The specialty and personal preferences of each physician.
- The type of appointment required by the patient's condition.
- The urgency with which the patient needs to see a physician.

Our policy

Our patients have entrusted us with their health care. Many physicians charge patients who fail to keep appointments. At Saint Joan Family Health, we extend equal consideration to patients who take time out of their busy work day to allow us to participate in their health care. We respect that patients make every effort to arrive on time for appointments, and we endeavor to be available to them when they arrive.

Five-step approach to scheduling appointments

1. When a patient calls to schedule an appointment, assess the reason for the appointment and determine the urgency and how much time will be needed.
2. Ask the patient when he or she is not available for the appointment. This demonstrates a willingness to accommodate the patient's needs.
3. Offer the patient at least two choices of available times, if possible. Always state the day of the week, the date, and the time. This enables the patient to choose between alternatives and demonstrates the importance of the patient's input.
4. Repeat the agreed upon time to the patient. If the patient is present at the time of the booking, write down the day, date, and time of the appointment on an appointment reminder card and give it to the patient.
5. Close with an expression of anticipation of the next visit, such as "We'll see you at 10:00 a.m. on March 1st." This provides further verification of the date.

Determining the time required for an appointment

The time allotted for an appointment is particular to each physician's specialty and the patient's condition. Physicians are as frustrated as patients if appointments do not run smoothly, or if not enough time has been allowed to adequately address the patient's needs. The following table offers general guidelines for determining the amount of time to book for each type of appointment:

APPOINTMENT	TIME
New patient	45 minutes
Complete physical	30 minutes
Counseling	30 minutes
Sick visit	15 minutes
Other	15 minutes

In addition, it is important to schedule into each day several "emergency" booking slots that can be used to accommodate patients who need same day appointments. This is particularly critical during flu season. Be sure to analyze the appointment schedule regularly to ensure that it is meeting the needs of patients and physicians.

When a patient telephones to book an appointment, it is important to obtain his/her full name (ask for correct spelling), current home and work phone numbers (for contact purposes), and the reason for the visit. Patients sometimes object to providing this personal information. When this happens, you can explain to the patient that you require this information to schedule an adequate amount of time for the appointment, and so that any paperwork or special equipment that might be required will be ready when he/she arrives. Also, reassure the patient that all information he/she provides to Saint Joan Family Health remains confidential.

Processing new patients

- ✓ Gather as much information as you can from the new patient over the telephone when he/she calls to book an appointment.
- ✓ Ask the patient to complete a patient information form as soon as he/she arrives at the office, and check the form for completeness.
- ✓ Photocopy the patient's insurance card(s).
- ✓ Ask the patient to read and sign a copy of our privacy notice.
- ✓ Enter the information from the patient information form into our database.

Your Name
Today's Date

Independent Challenge 1

You work for Prairie Orthopedic Associates. Your boss has given you the text for a Notice of Patient Rights and Responsibilities and has asked you to format it on letterhead. It's important that the Notice has a clean, striking design, and reflects the practice's professionalism.

a. Start Word, open the file WMP C-3.docx from the drive and folder where you store your Data Files, save it as **WMP C-Notice of Rights**, then read the document to get a feel for its contents. Figure C-29 shows how you will format the letterhead.

FIGURE C-29

Prairie Orthopedic Associates

1900 East Prairie SE, Suite 108, Grand Rapids, MI 49503; Tel: 616-555-2921; Fax: 616-555-2231

Karl Rattan, M.D. Margaret Canton, M.D. Elise McDonald, M.D. Edward Kaplan, M.D. Mary Shipman, M.D.

b. Select the entire document, change the style to No Spacing, then change the font to 11-point Californian FB.

c. In the first paragraph, format **Prairie Orthopedic Associates** in 36-point Californian FB, then change the character spacing to 80%.

d. Change the font size of the next two paragraphs—the address and the physician information—to 9 point, then bold the paragraph that lists the physicians.

e. Center the three-line letterhead.

f. Add 6 points of space after the address line paragraph, then add a ½-point black border below the address line paragraph.

g. With the insertion point in the address line, open the Borders and Shading dialog box, click Options to open the Border and Shading Options dialog box, change the Bottom setting to 5 pt, then click OK twice to adjust the location of the border relative to the line of text.

h. Format the title **Patient Rights and Responsibilities** in 16-point Trebuchet MS, bold, then center the title.

i. Format the following headings (including the colons) in 12-point Trebuchet MS, bold: **Your Rights as a Patient**, **Your Responsibilities as a Patient**, **Advance Directives**, **Financial Concerns**, **Income Guidelines**, and **Acknowledgement of Receipt.....**

j. Format the lists under Your Rights as a Patient and Your Responsibilities as a Patient as bulleted lists, using a bullet style of your choice.

k. Apply bold italic to **Living Wills and Durable Powers of Attorney for Healthcare** under the Advance Directives heading.

l. Center the Income Guidelines heading, select the 9-line list under the heading, then set a left tab stop at the 1¾" mark and right tab stops at the 3½" and 4¾" marks. Insert tabs before every line in the list, then insert tabs before every $.

m. Select the text in the first line of tabbed text, then apply an underline. Select the remaining eight lines of tabbed text, then add dotted line tab leaders to the 3½" and 4¾" tab stops.

n. Type your name as the patient name, then type the current date.

o. Examine the document carefully for formatting errors, and make any necessary adjustments.

p. Save the document, submit it to your instructor, then close the file and exit Word.

Independent Challenge 2

Your employer, Learn and Be Healthy, is a nonprofit organization devoted to educating the public on health issues. Your boss has written the text for a flyer about Peripheral Artery Disease, and asks you to format it so that it is eye catching and attractive.

FIGURE C-30

LEARN AND BE HEALTHY

Peripheral Artery Disease

What is peripheral artery disease?

Peripheral artery disease (PAD) is a circulation disorder that is caused by fatty buildups (atherosclerosis) in the inner walls of arteries. These fatty buildups block normal blood flow. PAD is a type of peripheral vascular disease (PVD), which refers to diseases of blood vessels outside the heart and brain.

- **a.** Open the file WMP C-4.docx from the drive and folder where you store your Data Files, save it as **WMP C-PAD Flyer**, then read the document. Figure C-30 shows how you will format the first several paragraphs of the flyer.
- **b.** Select the entire document, change the style to No Spacing, then change the font to 10.5-point Arial Narrow. (*Hint*: Select the font size, they type 10.5.)
- **c.** Center the first line, **Learn and Be Healthy**, and apply shading to the paragraph. Choose a dark custom shading color of your choice for the shading color. (*Hint*: Click More Colors, then select a color from the Standard or Custom tab.) Format the text in 26-point Arial Narrow, bold, with a white font color. Expand the character spacing by 8 points. (*Hint*: Use the Advanced tab in the Font dialog box, set the Spacing to Expanded, and then type 8 in the By text box.)
- **d.** Format the second line, **Peripheral Artery Disease**, in 36-point Arial Black. Change the character scale to 90%, then center the line.
- **e.** Format each question heading in 12-point Arial, bold. Change the font color to the same custom color used for shading the title. (*Note*: The color now appears in the Recent Colors section of the Font Color gallery.) Add a single-line ½-point black border under each heading.
- **f.** Format each subheading (**PAD may require...** and **Lifestyle changes...**) in 10.5-point Arial, bold. Add 3 points of spacing before each subheading. (*Hint*: Select 0 in the Before text box, type 3, then press Enter.)
- **g.** Indent each body paragraph and subheading ¼", except for the last two lines in the document.
- **h.** Format the three lines under the **PAD may require...** subheading as a bulleted list. Use a bullet symbol of your choice, and format the bullets in the custom font color.
- **i.** Format the six lines under the **Lifestyle changes...** subheading as a bulleted list. If necessary, use the Format Painter to copy the bullet style you just applied to the six-line list.
- **j.** Format the **For more information** heading in 14-point Arial, bold, with the custom font color, then center the heading.
- **k.** Format the last line in 11-point Arial Narrow, and center the line. In the contact information, replace Your Name with your name, then apply bold to your name.

Advanced Challenge Exercise

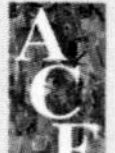

- Change the font color of the Peripheral Artery Disease heading to a dark gray, and add a shadow effect.
- Add a shadow effect to each question heading.
- Add a 2¼-point dotted black border above the For more information heading.

- **l.** Examine the document carefully for formatting errors, and make any necessary adjustments.
- **m.** Save the flyer, submit it to your instructor, then close the file and exit Word.

Independent Challenge 3

One of your responsibilities as patient care coordinator at Metropolitan Healthcare is to facilitate patient-staff interactions to achieve excellent care for patients at the facility. You have drafted a memo to Metropolitan Healthcare staff to outline several ways they can encourage patients to be involved in their own healthcare. You need to format the memo so it is professional looking and easy to read.

a. Start Word, open the file WMP C-5.docx from the drive and folder where you store your Data Files, then save it as **WMP C-Metropolitan Healthcare Memo**.

b. Select the heading **Metropolitan Healthcare Memorandum**, apply the Quick Style Title to it, then center the heading. (*Hint*: Open the Quick Style gallery, then click the Title style.)

c. In the memo header, replace Today's Date and Your Name with the current date and your name.

d. Select the four-line memo header, set a left tab stop at the ¾" mark, then insert tabs before the date, the recipient's name, your name, and the subject of the memo.

e. Apply the Quick Style Strong to **Date:**, **To:**, **From:**, and **Re:**.

f. Apply the Quick Style Heading 2 to the headings **Encourage questions**, **Offer an interpreter**, **Identify yourself**, and **Ensure medication safety**.

g. Under the Offer an interpreter heading, apply the Quick Style Intense Emphasis to the words **Interpreters' hours:** and **Languages:**.

h. On the second page of the document, format the list under the Ensure medication safety heading as a multilevel list. Figure C-31 shows the hierarchical structure of the outline. (*Hint*: Apply a multilevel list style, then use the Increase Indent and Decrease Indent buttons to change the level of importance of each item.)

i. Change the outline numbering style to the bullet numbering style shown in Figure C-31 if a different style is used in your outline.

FIGURE C-31

- ❖ Information patients need to share with healthcare providers
  - ➢ Details about everything they take
    - ▪ Prescription medications
    - ▪ Non-prescription medications
      - • Aspirin
      - • Antacids
      - • Laxatives
      - • Etc.
    - ▪ Vitamins
    - ▪ Herbs or other supplements
      - • St. John's Wort
      - • Ginko biloba
      - • Etc.
  - ➢ Information about allergic reactions to medications
    - ▪ Rashes
    - ▪ Difficulty breathing
    - ▪ Etc.
  - ➢ Details of illnesses or medical conditions
    - ▪ High blood pressure
    - ▪ Glaucoma
    - ▪ Diabetes
    - ▪ Thyroid disease
    - ▪ Etc.
- ❖ Information healthcare providers need to share with patients
  - ➢ What each prescribed medication is and what it is used for
    - ▪ Name of medication
    - ▪ Purpose of medication
    - ▪ Dosage
    - ▪ Side effects
    - ▪ Drug interactions
  - ➢ Written directions for the dosage and purpose
    - ▪ "Take once a day for high blood pressure"

Advanced Challenge Exercise

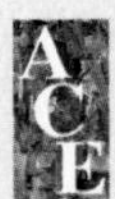

- Zoom out on the memo so that two pages are displayed in the document window, then, using the Change Styles button, change the style set to Modern.
- Using the Change Case button, change the title Metropolitan Healthcare Memorandum so that only the initial letter of each word is capitalized.
- Using the Themes button on the Page Layout tab, change the theme applied to the document to a different appropriate theme.
- Using the Theme Fonts button, change the fonts to a font set of your choice. Choose fonts that allow the document to fit on two pages.
- Using the Theme Colors button, change the colors to a color palette of your choice.
- Apply different styles and adjust other formatting elements as necessary to make the memo attractive, eye catching, and readable. The finished memo should fit on two pages.

j. Save the document, submit it to your instructor, then close the file and exit Word.

Real Life Independent Challenge

The fonts you choose for a document can have a major effect on the document's tone. Not all fonts are appropriate for use in a business or medical document, and some fonts, especially those with a definite theme, are appropriate only for specific purposes. In this Independent Challenge, you will use font formatting and other formatting features to design a letterhead and a fax coversheet for yourself or your place of work. The letterhead and coversheet should not only look professional and attract interest, but also say something about the character of your place of work or your personality. Figure C-32 shows an example of a letterhead for a chiropractor.

- **a.** Start Word, and save a new blank document as **WMP C-Personal Letterhead** to the drive and folder where you store your Data Files.
- **b.** Type your name or the name of your place of work, your address, your phone number, your fax number, and your Web site or e-mail address.
- **c.** Format your name or the name of your place of work in a font that expresses your personality or says something about the nature of your place of work. Use fonts, font colors, font effects, borders, shading, paragraph formatting, and other formatting features to design a letterhead that is appealing and professional.
- **d.** Save your changes, submit the document to your instructor, then close the file.
- **e.** Open a new blank document, and save it as **WMP C-Personal Fax Coversheet**. Type FAX, your name or the name of your place of work, your address, your phone number, your fax number, and your Web site or e-mail address at the top of the document.
- **f.** Type a fax header that includes the following: Date; To; From; Re; Number of pages, including cover sheet; and Comments.
- **g.** Format the information in the fax coversheet using fonts, font effects, borders, shading, paragraph formatting, and other formatting features. Since a fax coversheet is designed to be faxed, all fonts and other formatting elements should be black.
- **h.** Save your changes, submit the document to your instructor, close the file, then exit Word.

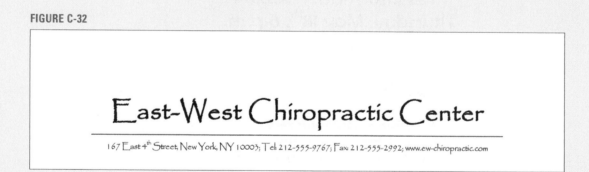

FIGURE C-32

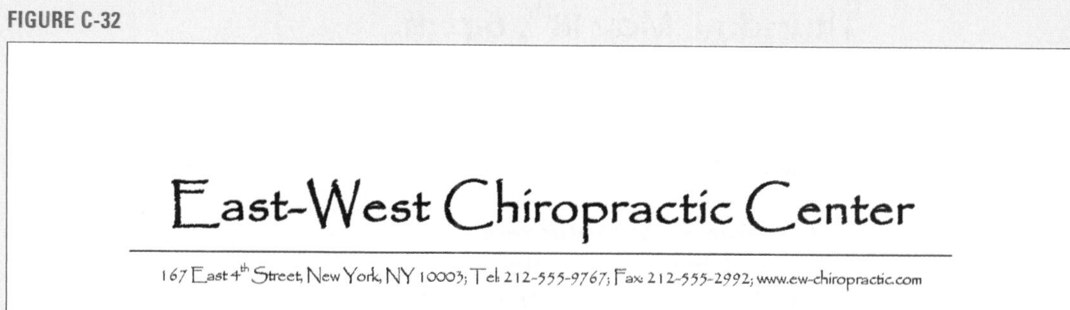

Visual Workshop

Open the file WMP C-6.docx from the drive and folder where you store your Data Files. Create the flyer shown in Figure C-33. (*Hints*: Use Berlin Sans FB or a similar font, and a font color of your choice. Align the text in the box using a right and then a left tab stop. Use paragraph spacing to adjust the spacing between paragraphs, if necessary, so that all the text fits on one page.) Save the flyer as **WMP C-Simple Steps**, then submit a copy to your instructor.

FIGURE C-33

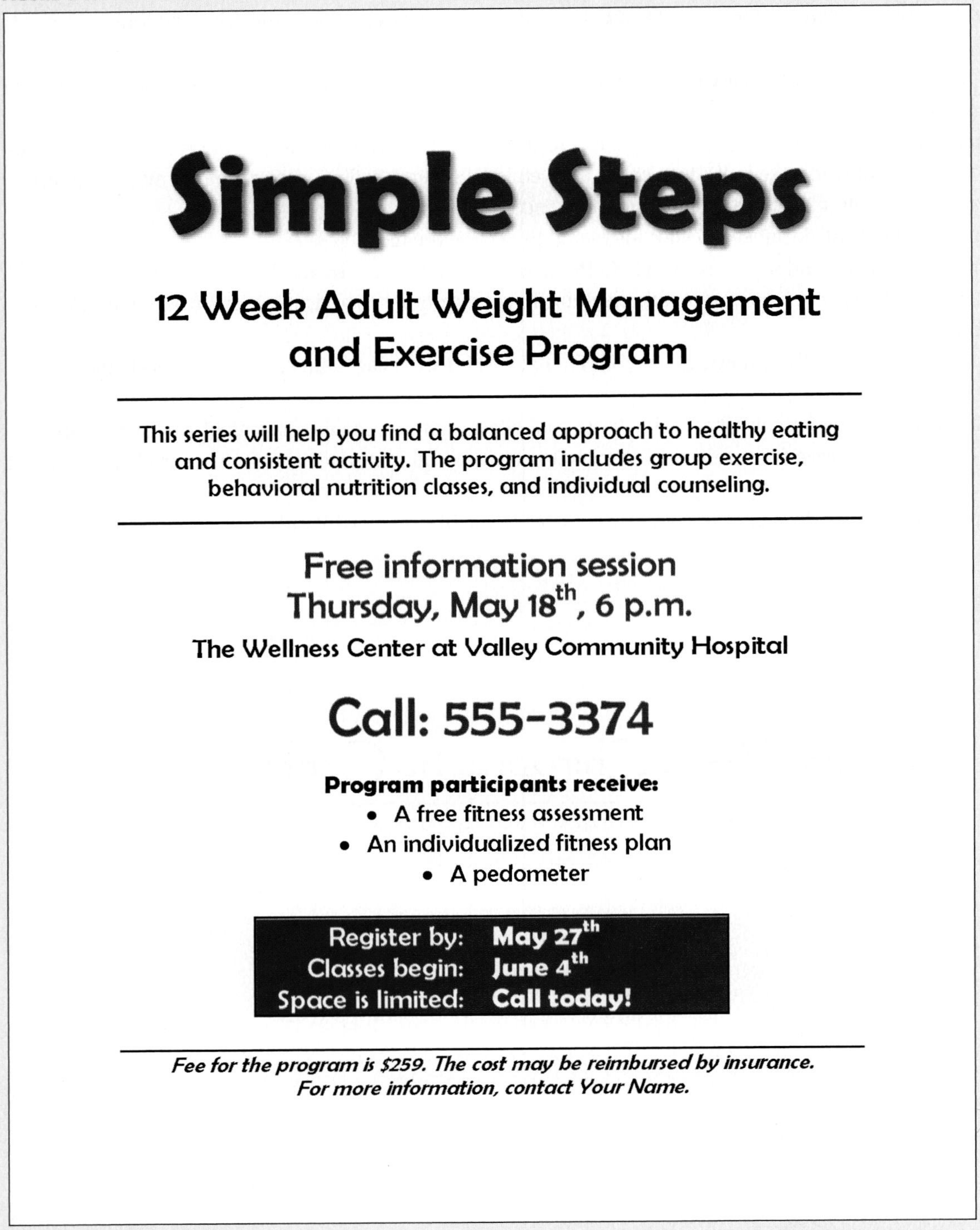

Simple Steps

12 Week Adult Weight Management and Exercise Program

This series will help you find a balanced approach to healthy eating and consistent activity. The program includes group exercise, behavioral nutrition classes, and individual counseling.

Free information session
Thursday, May 18th, 6 p.m.

The Wellness Center at Valley Community Hospital

Call: 555-3374

Program participants receive:

- A free fitness assessment
- An individualized fitness plan
- A pedometer

Register by:	**May 27th**
Classes begin:	**June 4th**
Space is limited:	**Call today!**

Fee for the program is $259. The cost may be reimbursed by insurance.
For more information, contact Your Name.

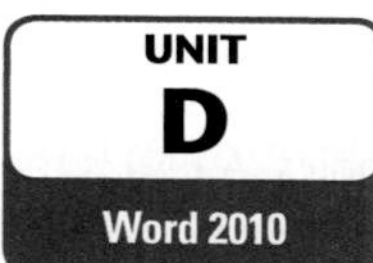

Creating and Formatting Tables

Files You Will Need:

WMP D-1.docx

WMP D-2.docx

Tables are commonly used to display information for quick reference and analysis. In this unit, you learn how to create and modify a table in Word, how to sort table data and perform calculations, and how to format a table with borders and shading. You also learn how to use a table to structure the layout of a page. You are preparing a summary budget for an advertising campaign aimed at the greater Cambridge market. The goals of the ad campaign are to educate the community about the services provided by the Riverwalk Medical Clinic and to attract new patients. You decide to format the budget information as a table so that it is easy to read and analyze.

OBJECTIVES

- Insert a table
- Insert and delete rows and columns
- Modify rows and columns
- Sort table data
- Split and merge cells
- Perform calculations in tables
- Apply a table style
- Create a custom format for a table

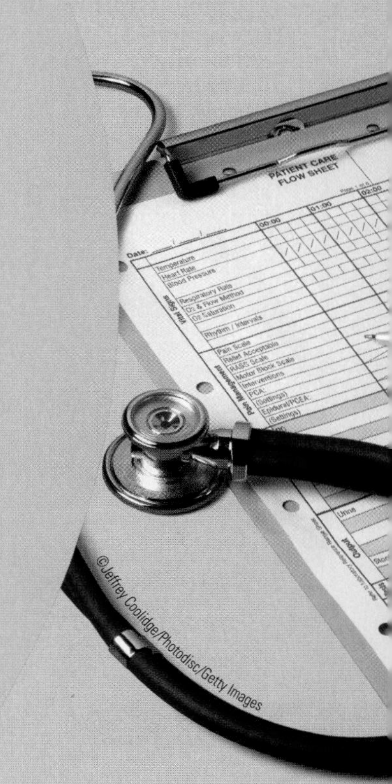

UNIT D

Word 2010

Inserting a Table

A **table** is a grid made up of rows and columns of cells that you can fill with text and graphics. A **cell** is the box formed by the intersection of a column and a row. The lines that divide the columns and rows and help you see the grid-like structure of a table are called **borders**. You can create a table in a document by using the Table command in the Tables group on the Insert tab. Once you have created a table, you can add text and graphics to it. You begin by inserting a blank table and adding text to it.

STEPS

QUICK TIP
Click the View Ruler button at the top of the vertical scroll bar to display the rulers if they are not already displayed.

1. **Start Word, click the View tab, then click the Page Width button in the Zoom group**
2. **Click the Insert tab, then click the Table button in the Tables group**
   The Table menu opens. It includes a grid for selecting the number of columns and rows you want the table to contain, as well as several commands for inserting a table. Table D-1 describes these commands. As you move the pointer across the grid, a preview of the table with the specified number of columns and rows appears in the document at the location of the insertion point.
3. **Point to the second box in the fourth row to select 2×4 Table, then click**
   A table with two columns and four rows is inserted in the document, as shown in Figure D-1. Black borders surround the table cells. The insertion point is in the first cell in the first row.

TROUBLE
Don't be concerned if the paragraph spacing under the text in your table is different from that shown in the figures.

4. **Type Location, then press [Tab]**
   Pressing [Tab] moves the insertion point to the next cell in the row.
5. **Type Cost, press [Tab], then type The Boston Globe**
   Pressing [Tab] at the end of a row moves the insertion point to the first cell in the next row.
6. **Press [Tab], type 5,075, press [Tab], then type the following text in the table, pressing [Tab] to move from cell to cell**
   WickedLocal.com 1,080
   Cambridge River Festival 600
7. **Press [Tab]**
   Pressing [Tab] at the end of the last cell of a table creates a new row at the bottom of the table, as shown in Figure D-2. The insertion point is located in the first cell in the new row.

TROUBLE
If you pressed [Tab] after the last row, click the Undo button on the Quick Access toolbar to remove the new blank row.

8. **Type the following, pressing [Tab] to move from cell to cell and to create new rows**
   Boston Herald 1,760
   Boston.com 1,250
   Mass mailing 1,440
   Cambridge Chronicle 1,860
9. **Click the Save button on the Quick Access toolbar, then save the document as WMP D-Clinic Ad Budget to the drive and folder where you store your Data Files**
   The table is shown in Figure D-3.

TABLE D-1: Table menu commands

command	use to
Insert Table	Create a table with any number of columns and rows and select an AutoFit behavior
Draw Table	Create a complex table by drawing the table columns and rows
Convert Text to Table	Convert text that is separated by tabs, commas, or another separator character into a table
Excel Spreadsheet	Insert a blank Excel worksheet into the document as an embedded object
Quick Tables	Insert a preformatted table template and replace the placeholder data with your own data

FIGURE D-1: Blank table

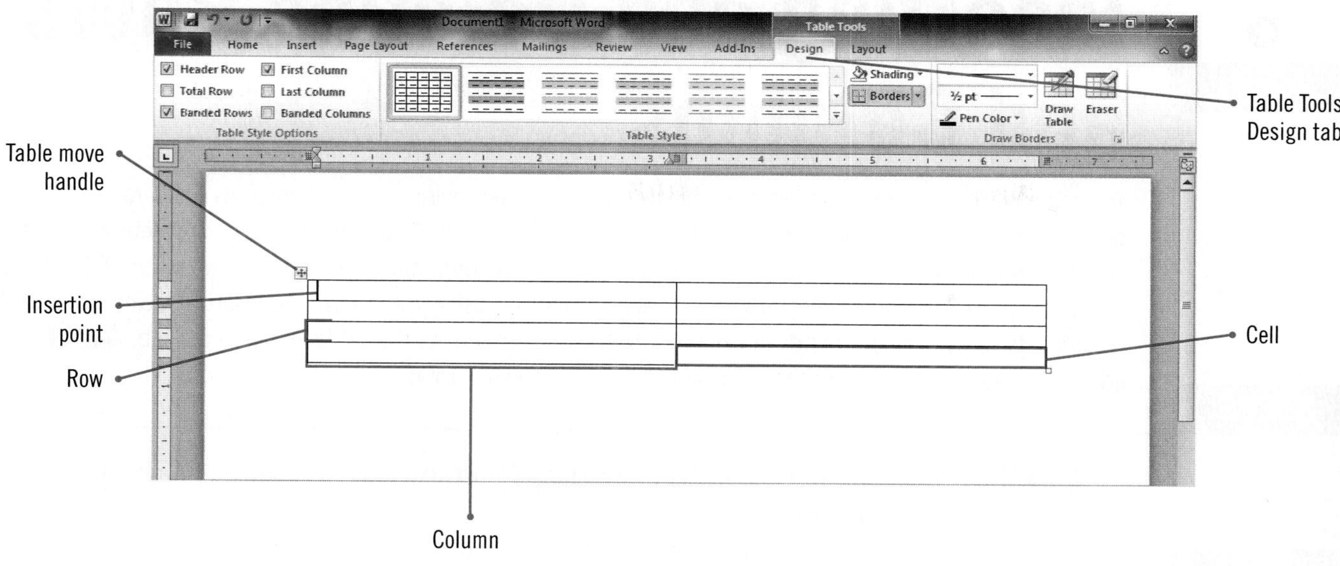

FIGURE D-2: New row in table

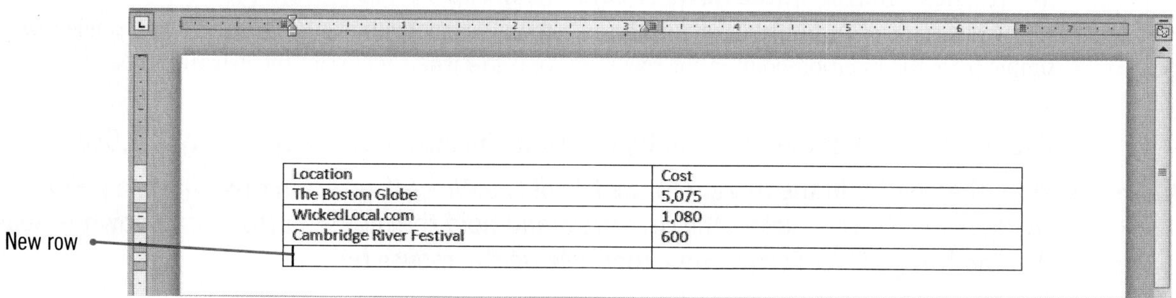

Location	Cost
The Boston Globe	5,075
WickedLocal.com	1,080
Cambridge River Festival	600

FIGURE D-3: Text in the table

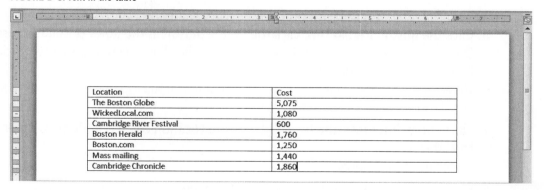

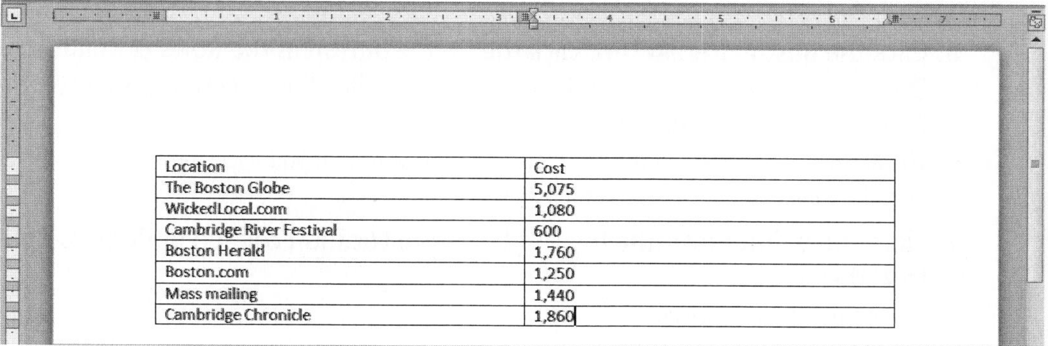

Location	Cost
The Boston Globe	5,075
WickedLocal.com	1,080
Cambridge River Festival	600
Boston Herald	1,760
Boston.com	1,250
Mass mailing	1,440
Cambridge Chronicle	1,860

Converting text to a table and a table to text

Another way to create a table is to convert text that is separated by a tab, a comma, or another separator character into a table. For example, to create a two-column table of last and first names, you could type the names as a list with a comma separating the last and first name in each line, and then convert the text to a table. The separator character—a comma in this example—indicates where you want to divide the table into columns, and a paragraph mark indicates where you want to begin a new row. To convert text to a table, select the text, click the Table button in the Tables group on the Insert tab, and then click Convert Text to Table. In the Convert Text to Table dialog box, select from the options for structuring and formatting the table, and then click OK to create the table.

Conversely, you can convert a table to text that is separated by tabs, commas, or some other character by selecting the table, clicking the Table Tools Layout tab, and then clicking the Convert to Text button in the Data group.

UNIT D
Word 2010

Inserting and Deleting Rows and Columns

You can easily modify the structure of a table by adding and removing rows and columns. First, you must click or select an existing row or column in the table to indicate where you want to insert or delete a row or a column. You can select any element of a table using the Select command in the Table group on the Table Tools Layout tab, but it is often easier to select rows and columns using the mouse. To insert or delete rows and columns, you use the commands in the Rows & Columns group on the Table Tools Layout tab. You add new rows and columns to the table, and delete unnecessary rows.

STEPS

1. **Click the Home tab, then click the Show/Hide ¶ button ¶ in the Paragraph group to display formatting marks**
   An end of cell mark appears at the end of each cell and an end of row mark appears at the end of each row.

> **QUICK TIP**
> You can also insert a row by right-clicking a row, pointing to Insert, then clicking Insert Rows Above or Insert Rows Below.

2. **Click the Table Tools Layout tab, click the first cell of the Boston.com row, then click the Insert Above button in the Rows & Columns group**
   A new row is inserted directly above the Boston.com row, as shown in Figure D-4. To insert a single row, you simply place the insertion point in the row above or below where you want the new row to be inserted, and then insert the row.
3. **Click the first cell of the new row, type Boston Phoenix, press [Tab], then type 2,850**

> **QUICK TIP**
> If the end of row mark is not selected, you have selected only the text in the row, not the row itself.

4. **Place the pointer in the margin to the left of the WickedLocal.com row until the pointer changes to ↗, click to select the row, press and hold the mouse button, drag down to select the Cambridge River Festival row, then release the mouse button**
   The two rows are selected, including the end of row marks.
5. **Click the Insert Below button in the Rows & Columns group**
   Two new rows are added below the selected rows. To insert multiple rows, you select the number of rows you want to insert before inserting the rows.
6. **Click the Boston Herald row, click the Delete button in the Rows & Columns group, click Delete Rows, select the two blank rows, right-click the selected rows, then click Delete Rows on the menu that opens**
   The Boston Herald row and the two blank rows are deleted. If you select a row and press [Delete], you delete only the contents of the row, not the row itself.
7. **Place the pointer over the top border of the Location column until the pointer changes to ↓, then click**
   The entire column is selected.

> **QUICK TIP**
> To select a cell, place the ↗ pointer near the left border of the cell, then click.

8. **Click the Insert Left button in the Rows & Columns group, then type Type**
   A new column is inserted to the left of the Location column, as shown in Figure D-5.
9. **Click in the Location column, click the Insert Right button in the Rows & Columns group, then type Details in the first cell of the new column**
   A new column is added to the right of the Location column.
10. **Press [↓] to move the insertion point to the next cell in the Details column, click the Home tab, click ¶ to turn off the display of formatting marks, enter the text shown in Figure D-6 in each cell in the Details and Type columns, then save your changes**
    You can use the arrow keys to move the insertion point from cell to cell. Notice that text wraps to the next line in the cell as you type. Compare your table to Figure D-6.

FIGURE D-4: **Inserted row**

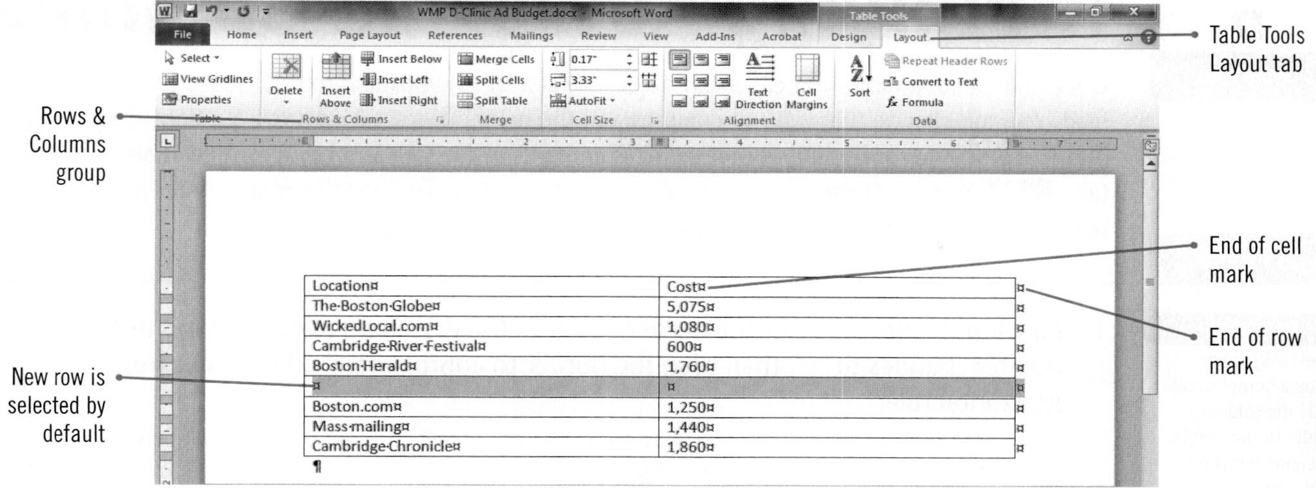

Location	Cost
The Boston Globe	5,075
WickedLocal.com	1,080
Cambridge River Festival	600
Boston Herald	1,760
Boston.com	1,250
Mass mailing	1,440
Cambridge Chronicle	1,860

FIGURE D-5: **Inserted column**

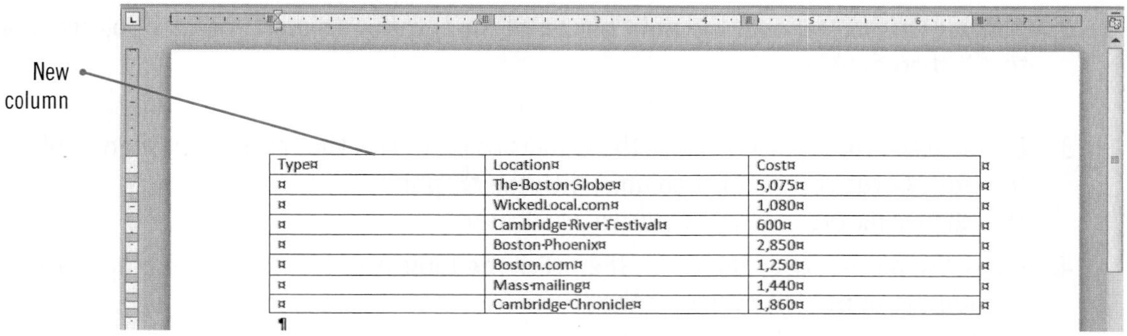

Type	Location	Cost
	The Boston Globe	5,075
	WickedLocal.com	1,080
	Cambridge River Festival	600
	Boston Phoenix	2,850
	Boston.com	1,250
	Mass mailing	1,440
	Cambridge Chronicle	1,860

FIGURE D-6: **Text in Type and Details columns**

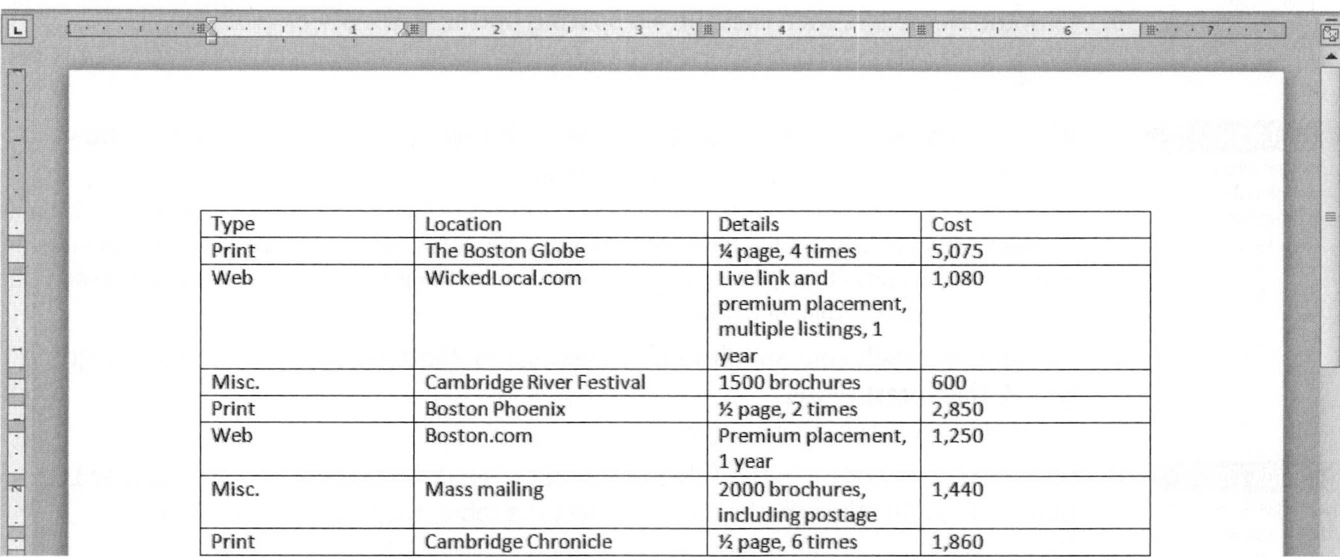

Type	Location	Details	Cost
Print	The Boston Globe	¼ page, 4 times	5,075
Web	WickedLocal.com	Live link and premium placement, multiple listings, 1 year	1,080
Misc.	Cambridge River Festival	1500 brochures	600
Print	Boston Phoenix	½ page, 2 times	2,850
Web	Boston.com	Premium placement, 1 year	1,250
Misc.	Mass mailing	2000 brochures, including postage	1,440
Print	Cambridge Chronicle	½ page, 6 times	1,860

Copying and moving rows and columns

You can copy and move rows and columns within a table in the same manner you copy and move text. Select the row or column you want to move, then use the Copy or Cut button to place the selection on the Clipboard. Place the insertion point in the location where you want to insert the row or column, then click the Paste button to paste the selection. Rows are inserted above the row containing the insertion point; columns are inserted to the left of the column containing the insertion point. You can also copy or move columns and rows by selecting them and using the pointer to drag them to a new location in the table.

UNIT D

Word 2010

Modifying Rows and Columns

Once you create a table, you can easily adjust the size of columns and rows to make the table easier to read. You can change the width of columns and the height of rows by dragging a border, by using the AutoFit command, or by setting precise measurements in the Cell Size group on the Table Tools Layout tab. You adjust the size of the columns and rows to make the table more attractive and easier to read. You also center the text vertically in each table cell.

STEPS

QUICK TIP
Press [Alt] as you drag a border to display the column width or row height measurements on the ruler.

1. **Position the pointer over the border between the first and second columns until the pointer changes to ↔, then drag the border to approximately the ½" mark on the horizontal ruler**

   The dotted line that appears as you drag represents the border. Dragging the column border changes the width of the first and second columns: the first column is narrower and the second column is wider. When dragging a border to change the width of an entire column, make sure no cells are selected in the column. You can also drag a row border to change the height of the row above it.

2. **Position the pointer over the right border of the Location column until the pointer changes to ↔, then double-click**

   Double-clicking a column border automatically resizes the column to fit the text.

3. **Double-click the right border of the Details column with the ↔ pointer, then double-click the right border of the Cost column with the ↔ pointer**

   The widths of the Details and Cost columns are adjusted.

4. **Move the pointer over the table, then click the table move handle that appears outside the upper-left corner of the table**

   Clicking the table move handle selects the entire table. You can also use the Select button in the Table group on the Table Tools Layout tab to select an entire table.

5. **Click the Home tab, then click the No Spacing button in the Styles group**

   Changing the style to No Spacing removes the paragraph spacing below the text in each table cell, if your table includes extra paragraph spacing.

QUICK TIP
Quickly resize a table by dragging the table resize handle to a new location.

6. **With the table still selected, click the Table Tools Layout tab, click the Distribute Rows button in the Cell Size group, then click in the table to deselect it**

   All the rows in the table become the same height, as shown in Figure D-7. You can also use the Distribute Columns button to make all the columns the same width, or you can use the AutoFit button to make the width of the columns fit the text, to adjust the width of the columns so the table is justified between the margins, or to set fixed column widths.

7. **Click in the Details column, click the Table Column Width text box in the Cell Size group, type 4, then press [Enter]**

   The width of the Details column changes to 4".

QUICK TIP
Quickly center a table on a page by selecting the table and clicking the Center button in the Paragraph group on the Home tab.

8. **Click the Select button in the Table group, click Select Table, click the Align Center Left button in the Alignment group, deselect the table, then save your changes**

   The text is centered vertically in each table cell, as shown in Figure D-8. You can use the alignment buttons in the Alignment group to change the vertical and horizontal alignment of the text in selected cells or in the entire table.

FIGURE D-7: Resized columns and rows

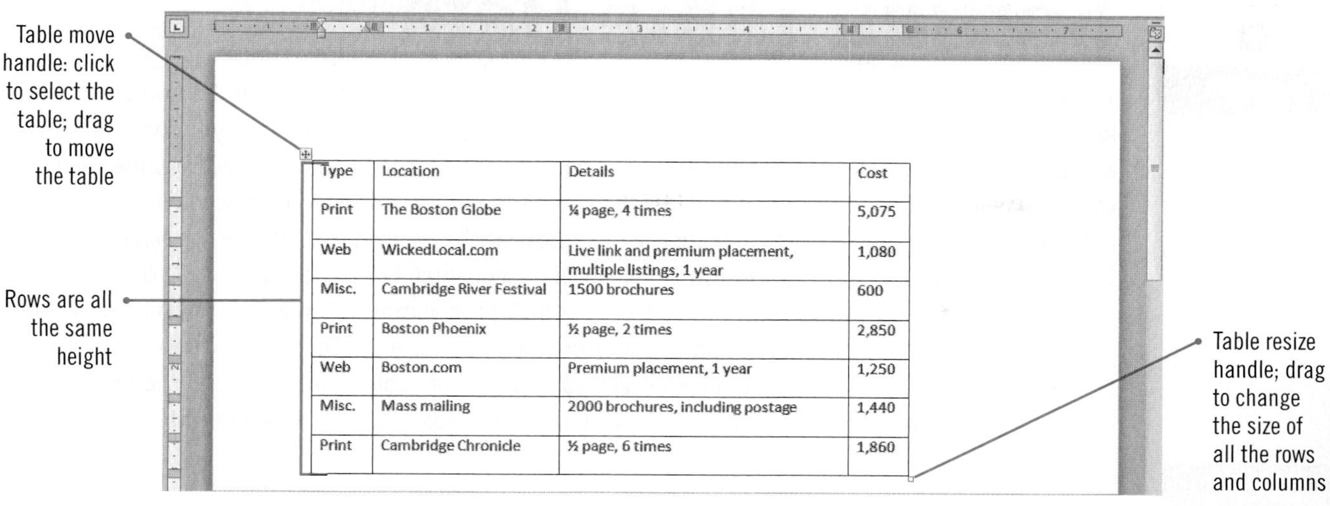

Table move handle: click to select the table; drag to move the table
Rows are all the same height
Table resize handle; drag to change the size of all the rows and columns
Type
Location
Details
Cost
Print
The Boston Globe
¼ page, 4 times
5,075
Web
WickedLocal.com
Live link and premium placement, multiple listings, 1 year
1,080
Misc.
Cambridge River Festival
1500 brochures
600
Print
Boston Phoenix
½ page, 2 times
2,850
Web
Boston.com
Premium placement, 1 year
1,250
Misc.
Mass mailing
2000 brochures, including postage
1,440
Print
Cambridge Chronicle
½ page, 6 times
1,860

FIGURE D-8: Text centered vertically in cells

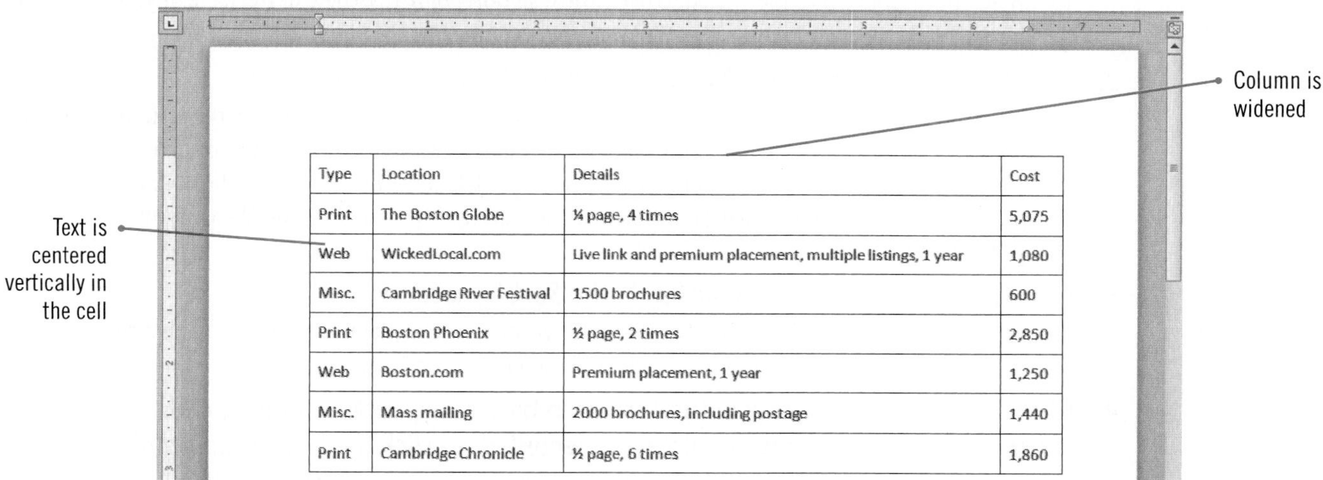

Column is widened
Text is centered vertically in the cell
Type
Location
Details
Cost
Print
The Boston Globe
¼ page, 4 times
5,075
Web
WickedLocal.com
Live link and premium placement, multiple listings, 1 year
1,080
Misc.
Cambridge River Festival
1500 brochures
600
Print
Boston Phoenix
½ page, 2 times
2,850
Web
Boston.com
Premium placement, 1 year
1,250
Misc.
Mass mailing
2000 brochures, including postage
1,440
Print
Cambridge Chronicle
½ page, 6 times
1,860

Setting advanced table properties

When you want to wrap text around a table, indent a table, or set other advanced table properties, you click the Properties command in the Table group on the Table Tools Layout tab to open the Table Properties dialog box, shown in Figure D-9. By using the Table tab in this dialog box, you can set a precise width for the table, change the horizontal alignment of the table between the margins, indent the table, and set text wrapping options for the table. You can also click Options on the Table tab to open the Table Options dialog box, which you use to customize the table's default cell margins and the spacing between table cells. Alternatively, click Borders and Shading on the Table tab to open the Borders and Shading dialog box, which you can use to create a custom format for the table.

The Column, Row, and Cell tabs in the Table Properties dialog box allow you to set an exact width for columns, to specify an exact height for rows, and to indicate an exact size for individual cells. The Alt Text tab is used to add alternative text for a table that will appear on a Web page.

FIGURE D-9: Table Properties dialog box

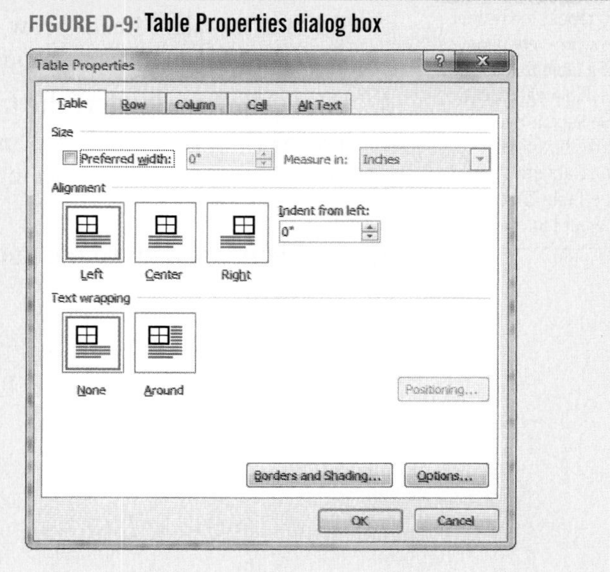

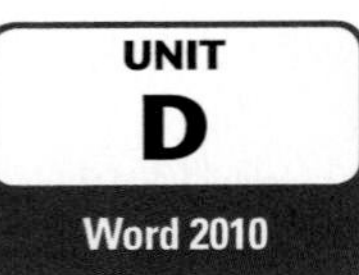

Sorting Table Data

Tables are often easier to interpret and analyze when the data is **sorted**, which means the rows are organized in alphabetical or sequential order based on the data in one or more columns. When you sort a table, Word arranges all the table data according to the criteria you set. You set sort criteria by specifying the column (or columns) by which you want to sort and indicating the sort order—ascending or descending—you want to use. **Ascending order** lists data alphabetically or sequentially (from A to Z, 0 to 9, or earliest to latest). **Descending order** lists data in reverse alphabetical or sequential order (from Z to A, 9 to 0, or latest to earliest). You can sort using the data in one column or multiple columns. When you sort by multiple columns you must select primary, secondary, and tertiary sort criteria. You use the Sort command in the Data group on the Table Tools Layout tab to sort a table. You sort the table so that all ads of the same type are listed together. You also add secondary sort criteria so that the ads within each type are listed in descending order by cost.

STEPS

1. **Place the insertion point anywhere in the table**
   To sort an entire table, you simply need to place the insertion point anywhere in the table. If you want to sort specific rows only, then you must select the rows you want to sort.

2. **Click the Sort button in the Data group on the Table Tools Layout tab**
   The Sort dialog box opens, as shown in Figure D-10. You use this dialog box to specify the column or columns by which you want to sort, the type of information you are sorting (text, numbers, or dates), and the sort order (ascending or descending). Column 1 is selected by default in the Sort by list box. Since you want to sort your table first by the information in the first column—the type of ad (Print, Web, or Misc.)—you don't change the Sort by criteria.

3. **Click the Descending option button in the Sort by section**
   The ad type information will be sorted in descending—or reverse alphabetical—order, so that the "Web" ads will be listed first, followed by the "Print" ads, and then the "Misc." ads.

4. **Click the Then by list arrow in the first Then by section, click Column 4, click the Type list arrow, click Number if it is not already selected, then click the Descending option button**
   Within the Web, Print, and Misc. groups, the rows will be sorted by the cost of the ad, which is the information contained in the fourth column. The rows will appear in descending order within each group, with the most expensive ad listed first.

5. **Click the Header row option button in the My list has section to select it**
   The table includes a **header row**, which is the first row of a table that contains the column headings. You select the Header row option button when you do not want the header row included in the sort.

6. **Click OK, then deselect the table**
   The rows in the table are sorted first by the information in the Type column and second by the information in the Cost column, as shown in Figure D-11. The first row of the table, which is the header row, is not included in the sort.

7. **Save your changes to the document**

QUICK TIP

To repeat the header row on every page of a table that spans multiple pages, click the Repeat Header Rows button in the Data group on the Table Tools Layout tab.

FIGURE D-10: **Sort dialog box**

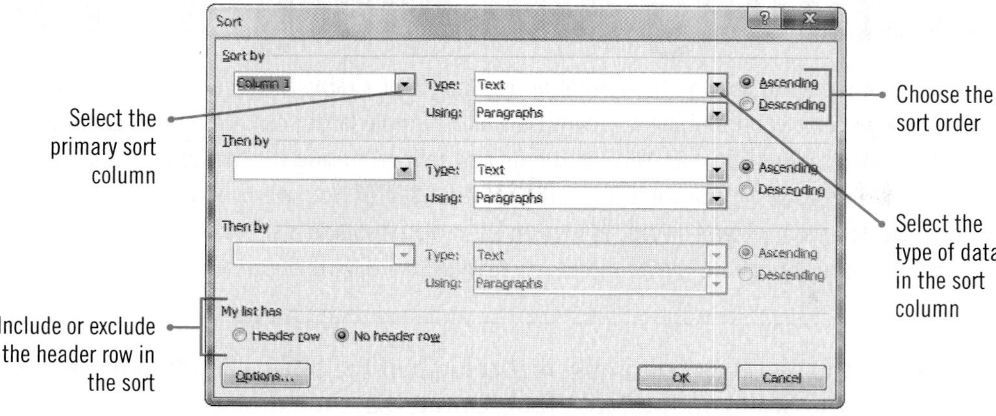

FIGURE D-11: **Sorted table**

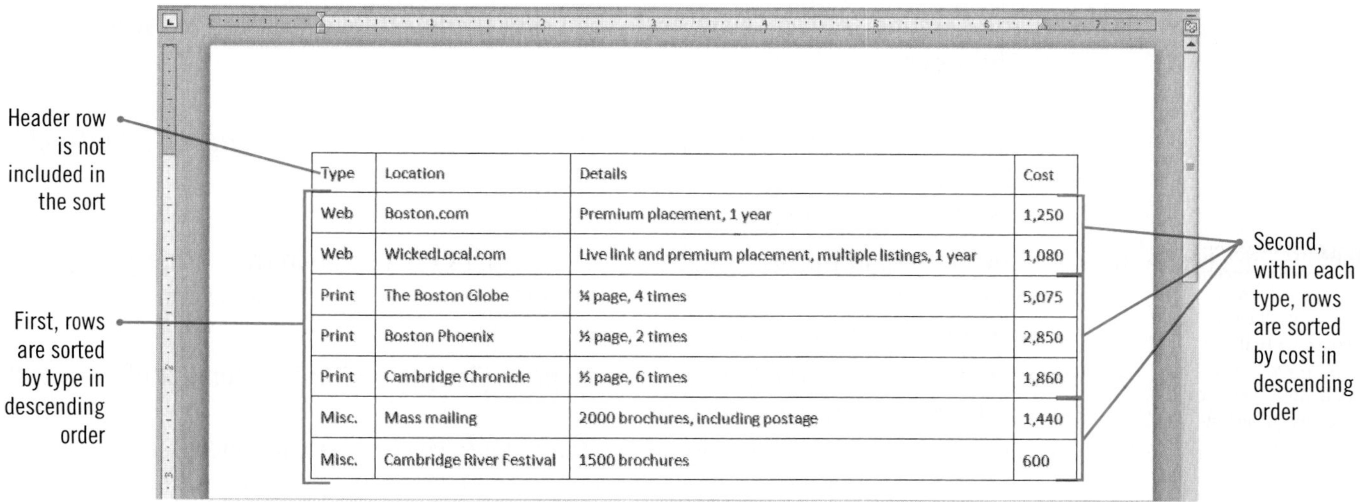

Type	Location	Details	Cost
Web	Boston.com	Premium placement, 1 year	1,250
Web	WickedLocal.com	Live link and premium placement, multiple listings, 1 year	1,080
Print	The Boston Globe	¼ page, 4 times	5,075
Print	Boston Phoenix	½ page, 2 times	2,850
Print	Cambridge Chronicle	½ page, 6 times	1,860
Misc.	Mass mailing	2000 brochures, including postage	1,440
Misc.	Cambridge River Festival	1500 brochures	600

Sorting lists and paragraphs

In addition to sorting table data, you can use the Sort command to alphabetize text or sort numerical data. When you want to sort data that is not formatted as a table, such as lists and paragraphs, you use the Sort command in the Paragraph group on the Home tab. To sort lists and paragraphs, select the items you want included in the sort, then click the Sort button. In the Sort Text dialog box, use the Sort by list arrow to select the sort by criteria (paragraphs or fields), use the Type list arrow to select the type of data (text, numbers, or dates), and then click the Ascending or Descending option button to choose a sort order.

When sorting text information in a document, the term "fields" refers to text or numbers that are separated by a character, such as a tab or a comma. For example, you might want to sort a list of names alphabetically. If the names you want to sort are listed in "Last name, First name" order, then last name and first name are each considered a field. You can choose to sort the list in alphabetical order by last name or by first name. Use the Options button in the Sort Text dialog box to specify the character that separates the fields in your lists or paragraphs, along with other sort options.

UNIT D
Word 2010

Splitting and Merging Cells

A convenient way to change the format and structure of a table is to merge and split the table cells. When you **merge** cells, you combine adjacent cells into a single larger cell. When you **split** a cell, you divide an existing cell into multiple cells. You can merge and split cells using the Merge Cells and Split Cells commands in the Merge group on the Table Tools Layout tab. You merge cells in the first column to create a single cell for each ad type—Web, Print, and Misc. You also add a new row to the bottom of the table, and split the cells in the row to create three new rows with a different structure.

STEPS

TROUBLE

If you click below the table to deselect it, the active tab changes to the Home tab. If necessary, click in the table, then click the Table Tools Layout tab to continue with the steps in this lesson.

1. **Select the two Web cells in the first column of the table, click the Merge Cells button in the Merge group on the Table Tools Layout tab, then deselect the text**
   The two Web cells merge to become a single cell. When you merge cells, Word converts the text in each cell into a separate paragraph in the merged cell.
2. **Select the first Web in the cell, then press [Delete]**
3. **Select the three Print cells in the first column, click the Merge Cells button, type Print, select the two Misc. cells, click the Merge Cells button, then type Misc.**
   The three Print cells merge to become one cell and the two Misc. cells merge to become one cell.
4. **Click the Cambridge River Festival cell, then click the Insert Below button in the Rows & Columns group**
   A row is added to the bottom of the table.
5. **Select the first three cells in the new last row of the table, click the Merge Cells button, then deselect the cell**
   The three cells in the row merge to become a single cell.

QUICK TIP

To split a table in two, click the row you want to be the first row in the second table, then click the Split Table button in the Merge group.

6. **Click the first cell in the last row, then click the Split Cells button in the Merge group**
   The Split Cells dialog box opens, as shown in Figure D-12. You use this dialog box to split the selected cell or cells into a specific number of columns and rows.
7. **Type 1 in the Number of columns text box, press [Tab], type 3 in the Number of rows text box, click OK, then deselect the cells**
   The single cell is divided into three rows of equal height. When you split a cell into multiple rows, the width of the original column does not change. When you split a cell into multiple columns, the height of the original row does not change. If the cell you split contains text, all the text appears in the upper-left cell.
8. **Click the last cell in the Cost column, click the Split Cells button, repeat Step 7, then save your changes**
   The cell is split into three rows, as shown in Figure D-13. The last three rows of the table now have only two columns.

FIGURE D-12: **Split Cells dialog box**

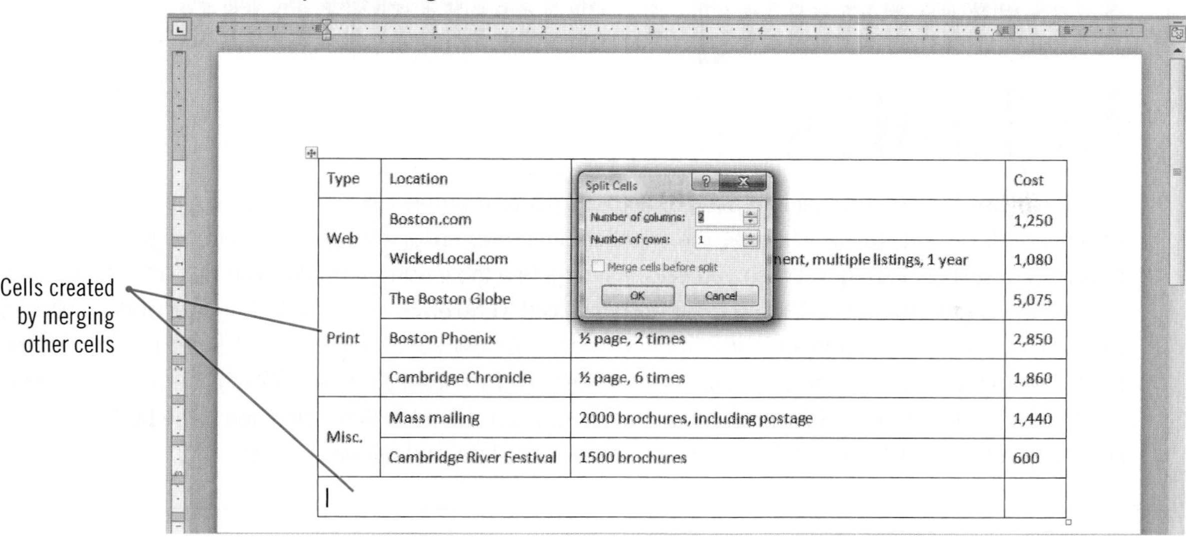

FIGURE D-13: **Cells split into three rows**

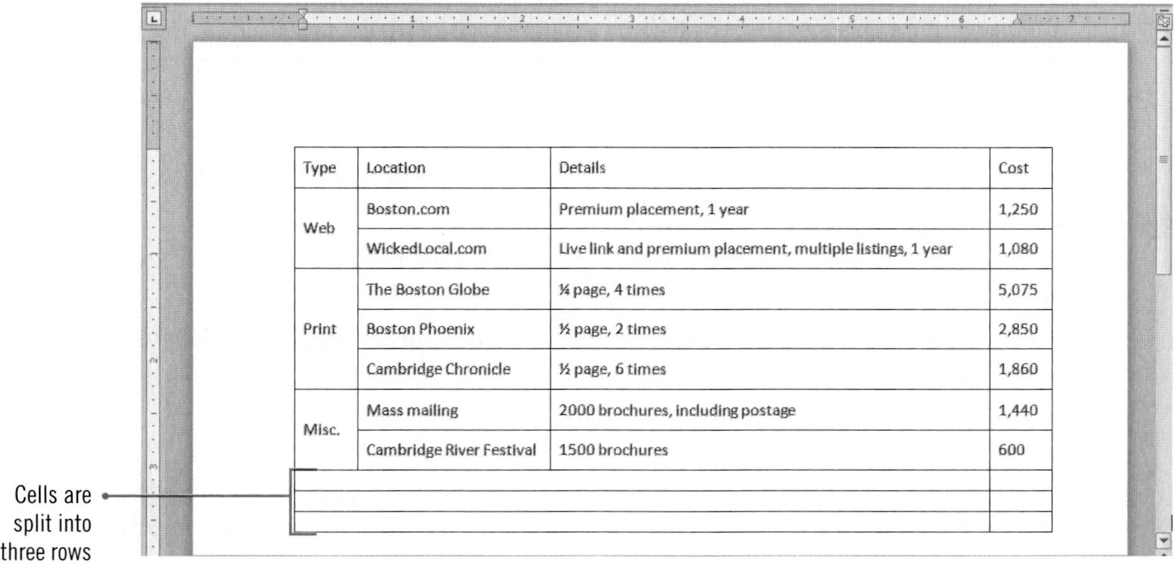

Changing cell margins

By default, table cells have .08" left and right cell margins with no spacing between the cells, but you can adjust these settings for a table using the Cell Margins button in the Alignment group on the Table Tools Layout tab. First, place the insertion point in the table, and then click the Cell Margins button to open the Table Options dialog box. Enter new settings for the top, bottom, left, and right cell margins in the text boxes in the Default cell margins section of the dialog box, or select the Allow spacing between cells check box and then enter a setting in the Cell spacing section to increase the spacing between table cells. You can also deselect the Automatically resize to fit contents check box in the Options section of the dialog box to turn off the setting that causes table cells to widen to fit the text as you type. Any settings you change in the Table Options dialog box are applied to the entire table.

UNIT D
Word 2010

Performing Calculations in Tables

If your table includes numerical information, you can perform simple calculations in the table. The Formula command allows you to quickly total the numbers in a column or row, and to perform other standard calculations, such as averages. When you calculate data in a table using formulas, you use cell references to refer to the cells in the table. Each cell has a unique **cell reference** composed of a letter and a number; the letter represents its column and the number represents its row. For example, the cell in the third row of the fourth column is cell D3. Figure D-14 shows the cell references in a simple table. You use the Formula command to calculate the total cost of the ad campaign. You also add information about the budgeted cost, and create a formula to calculate the difference between the total and budgeted costs.

STEPS

QUICK TIP
If a column or row contains blank cells, you must type a zero in any blank cell before using the SUM function.

1. **Click the first blank cell in column 1, type Total Cost, press [Tab], then click the Formula button in the Data group on the Table Tools Layout tab**

   The Formula dialog box opens, as shown in Figure D-15. The SUM function appears in the Formula text box followed by the reference for the cells to include in the calculation, (ABOVE). The formula =SUM(ABOVE) indicates that Word will sum the numbers in the cells above the active cell.

2. **Click OK**

   Word totals the numbers in the cells above the active cell and inserts the sum as a field. You can use the SUM function to quickly total the numbers in a column or a row. If the cell you select is at the bottom of a column of numbers, Word totals the column. If the cell is at the right end of a row of numbers, Word totals the row.

3. **Select 600 in the cell above the total, then type 750**

   If you change a number that is part of a calculation, you must recalculate the field result.

QUICK TIP
To change a field result to regular text, click the field to select it, then press [Ctrl][Shift][F9].

4. **Press [↓], right-click the cell, then click Update Field**

   The information in the cell is updated. When the insertion point is in a cell that contains a formula, you can also press [F9] to update the field result.

5. **Press [Tab], type Budgeted, press [Tab], type 13,850, press [Tab], type Difference, then press [Tab]**

   The insertion point is in the last cell of the table.

6. **Click the Formula button**

   The Formula dialog box opens. Word proposes to sum the numbers above the active cell, but you want to insert a formula that calculates the difference between the total and budgeted costs. You can type simple custom formulas using a plus sign (+) for addition, a minus sign (–) for subtraction, an asterisk (*) for multiplication, and a slash (/) for division.

QUICK TIP
Cell references are determined by the number of columns in each row, not by the number of columns in the table. Therefore, rows 9 and 10 have only two columns.

7. **Select =SUM(ABOVE) in the Formula text box, then type =B9–B10**

   You must type an equal sign (=) to indicate that the text following it is a formula. You want to subtract the budgeted cost in the second column of row 10 from the total cost in the second column of row 9; therefore, you type a formula to subtract the value in cell B10 from the value in cell B9.

8. **Click OK, then save your changes**

   The difference appears in the cell, as shown in Figure D-16.

FIGURE D-14: **Cell references in a table**

	A	B	C	D
1	A1	B1	C1	D1
2	A2	B2	C2	D2
3	A3	B3	C3	D3

Column D (fourth column)

Row 3

Cell reference indicates the cell's column and row

FIGURE D-15: **Formula dialog box**

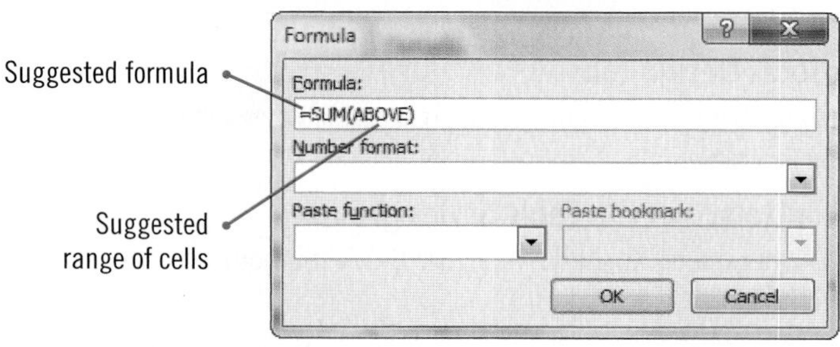

FIGURE D-16: **Difference calculated in table**

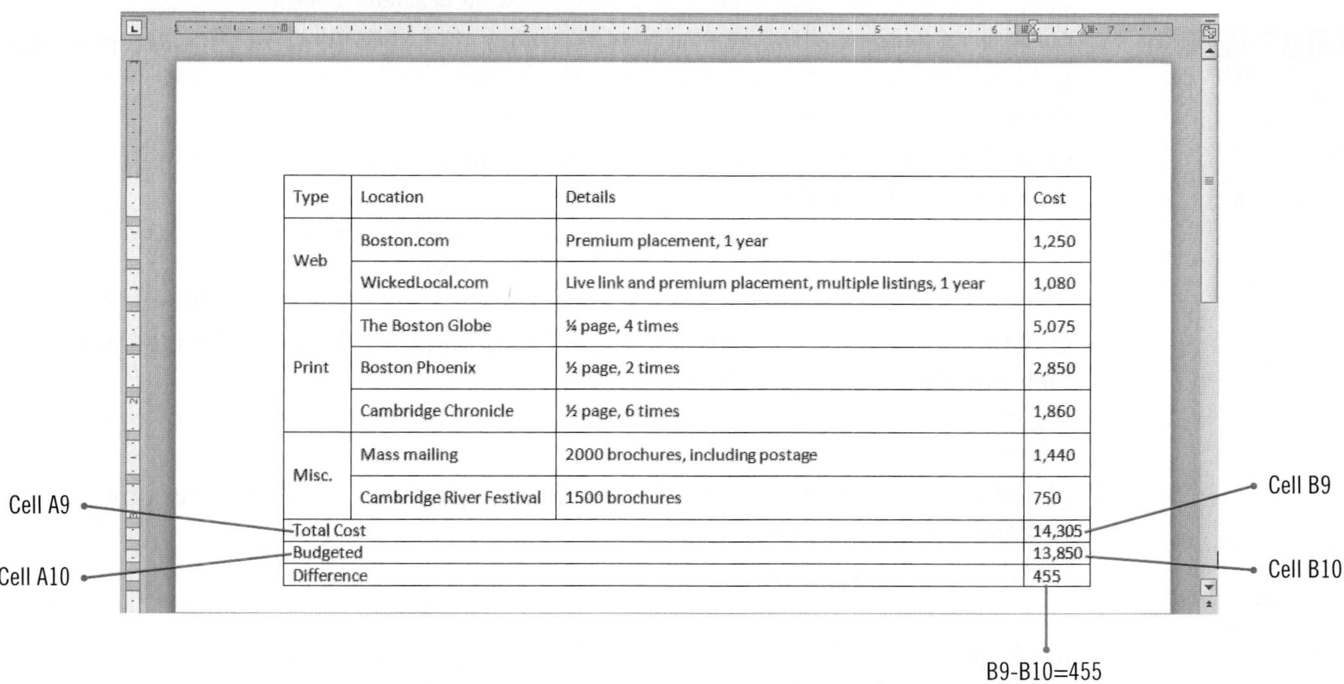

Type	Location	Details	Cost
Web	Boston.com	Premium placement, 1 year	1,250
	WickedLocal.com	Live link and premium placement, multiple listings, 1 year	1,080
Print	The Boston Globe	¼ page, 4 times	5,075
	Boston Phoenix	½ page, 2 times	2,850
	Cambridge Chronicle	½ page, 6 times	1,860
Misc.	Mass mailing	2000 brochures, including postage	1,440
	Cambridge River Festival	1500 brochures	750
Total Cost			14,305
Budgeted			13,850
Difference			455

Working with formulas

In addition to the SUM function, Word includes formulas for averaging, counting, and rounding data, to name a few. To use a Word formula, delete any text in the Formula text box, type =, click the Paste function list arrow in the Formula dialog box, select a function, and then insert the cell references of the cells you want to include in the calculation in parentheses after the name of the function. When entering formulas, you must separate cell references by a comma. For example, if you want to average the values in cells A1, B3, and C4, enter the formula =AVERAGE(A1,B3,C4). You must separate cell ranges by a colon. For example, to total the values in cells A1 through A9, enter the formula =SUM(A1:A9). To display the result of a calculation in a particular number format, such as a decimal percentage (0.00%), click the Number format list arrow in the Formula dialog box and select a number format. Word inserts the result of a calculation as a field in the selected cell.

Word 2010

UNIT D
Word 2010

Applying a Table Style

Adding shading and other design elements to a table can help give it a polished appearance and make the data easier to read. Word includes predefined, built-in table styles that you can apply to a table to format it quickly. Table styles include borders, shading, fonts, alignment, colors, and other formatting effects. You can apply a table style to a table using the buttons in the Table Styles group on the Table Tools Design tab. You want to enhance the appearance of the table with shading, borders, and other formats, so you apply a table style to the table. After applying a style, you change the theme colors to a more pleasing palette.

STEPS

1. **Click the Table Tools Design tab**
   The Table Tools Design tab includes buttons for applying table styles and for adding, removing, and customizing borders and shading in a table.

2. **Click the More button in the Table Styles group**
   The gallery of table styles opens, as shown in Figure D-17. You point to a table style in the gallery to preview the style applied to the table.

3. **Move the pointer over several styles in the gallery, then click the Light Grid – Accent 4 style**
   The Light Grid – Accent 4 style is applied to the table, as shown in Figure D-18. Because of the structure of the table, this style neither enhances the table nor helps make the data more readable.

4. **Click the More button in the Table Styles group, then click the Light List – Accent 4 style**
   This style works better with the structure of the table, and makes the table data easier to read. Notice that the alignment of the text in the table changed back to top left when you applied a table style.

5. **In the Table Style Options group, click the First Column check box to clear it, then click the Banded Columns check box to select it**
   The bold formatting is removed from the first column, and column borders are added to the table. When the banded columns or banded rows setting is active, borders are added between the columns or rows, or the odd columns or rows are formatted differently from the even columns or rows to make the table data easier to read.

6. **Click the Page Layout tab, click the Theme Colors list arrow in the Themes group, then click Paper in the gallery that opens**
   The color palette for the document changes to the colors used in the Paper theme, and the table color changes to lavender.

7. **Click the Table Tools Design tab, click the More button in the Table Styles group, then click the Light List – Accent 6 style**
   The table color changes to blue-gray.

8. **Click the Table Tools Layout tab, click the table move handle to select the table, click the Align Center Left button in the Alignment group, select the Type column, click the Align Center button in the Alignment group, select the Cost column, then click the Align Center Right button in the Alignment group**
   First, the data in the table is left-aligned and centered vertically, then the data in the Type column is centered, and finally the data in the Cost column is right-aligned.

9. **Select the last three rows of the table, click the Bold button on the Mini toolbar, then click the Align Center Right button in the Alignment group on the Table Tools Layout tab**
   The text in the last three rows is right-aligned and bold is applied.

10. **Select the first row of the table, click the Center button on the Mini toolbar, click the Font Size list arrow on the Mini toolbar, click 14, deselect the row, then save your changes**
    The text in the header row is centered and enlarged, as shown in Figure D-19. You can also use the alignment buttons in the Paragraph group on the Home tab to change the alignment of text in a table.

TROUBLE
If your gallery of table styles does not match the figure, use the ScreenTips to help you locate the correct style.

QUICK TIP
Click Clear in the gallery of table styles to remove all borders, shading, and other style elements from the table.

TROUBLE
When you select the Type column, the first column in the last three rows is also selected.

FIGURE D-17: **Gallery of table styles**

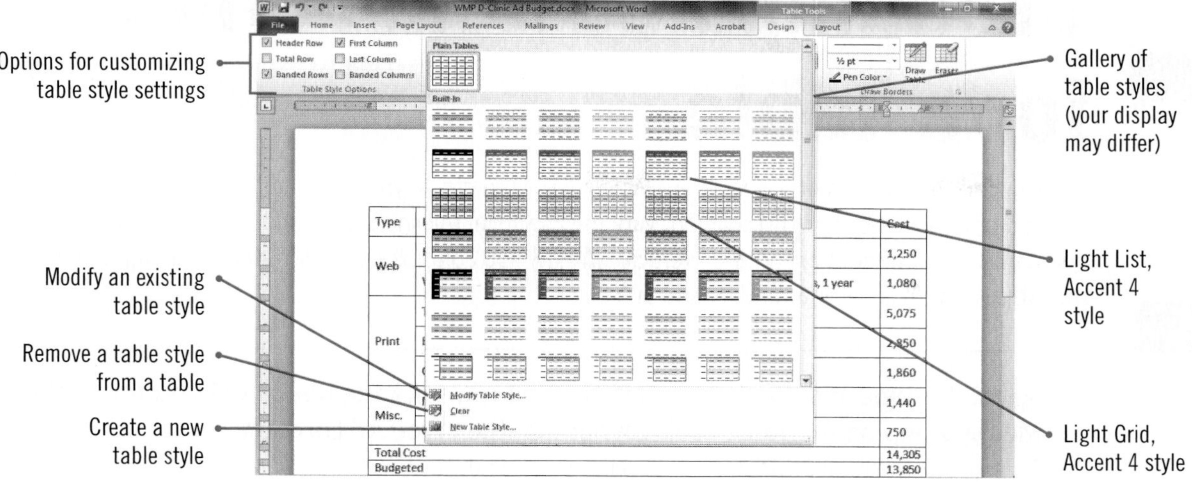

FIGURE D-18: **Light Grid, Accent 4 style applied to table**

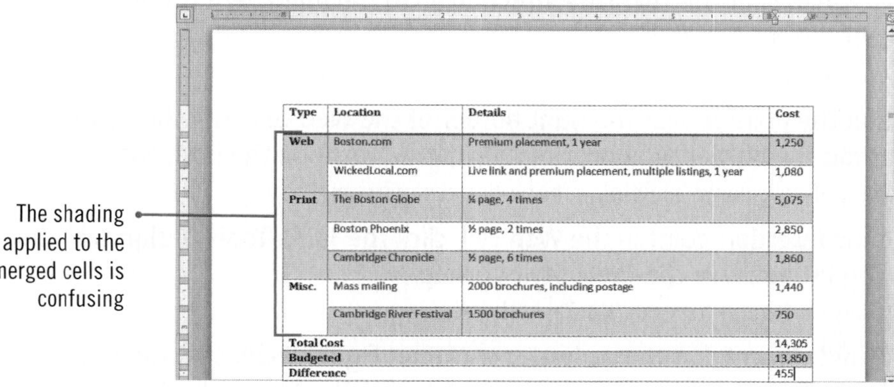

Type	Location	Details	Cost
Web	Boston.com	Premium placement, 1 year	1,250
	WickedLocal.com	Live link and premium placement, multiple listings, 1 year	1,080
Print	The Boston Globe	¼ page, 4 times	5,075
	Boston Phoenix	½ page, 2 times	2,850
	Cambridge Chronicle	½ page, 6 times	1,860
Misc.	Mass mailing	2000 brochures, including postage	1,440
	Cambridge River Festival	1500 brochures	750
Total Cost			14,305
Budgeted			13,850
Difference			455

FIGURE D-19: **Light List, Accent 6 style (Paper theme) applied to table**

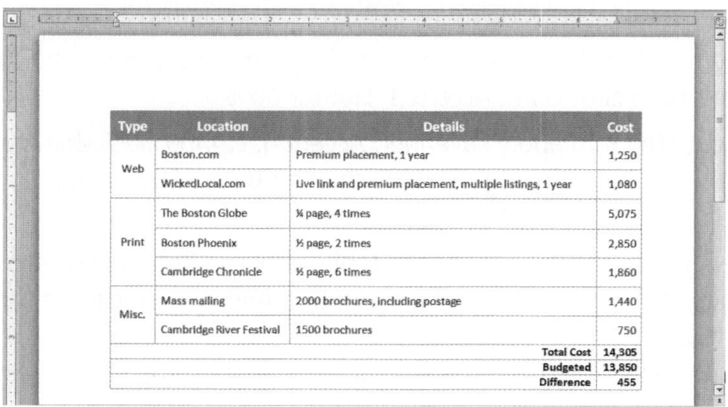

Type	Location	Details	Cost
Web	Boston.com	Premium placement, 1 year	1,250
	WickedLocal.com	Live link and premium placement, multiple listings, 1 year	1,080
Print	The Boston Globe	¼ page, 4 times	5,075
	Boston Phoenix	½ page, 2 times	2,850
	Cambridge Chronicle	½ page, 6 times	1,860
Misc.	Mass mailing	2000 brochures, including postage	1,440
	Cambridge River Festival	1500 brochures	750
		Total Cost	14,305
		Budgeted	13,850
		Difference	455

Using tables to lay out a page

Tables are often used to display information for quick reference and analysis, but you can also use tables to structure the layout of a page. You can insert any kind of information in the cell of a table—including graphics, bulleted lists, charts, and other tables (called **nested tables**). For example, you might use a table to lay out a résumé, a newsletter, or a Web page. When you use a table to lay out a page, you generally remove the table borders to hide the table structure from the reader. After you remove borders, it can be helpful to display the table gridlines onscreen while you work. **Gridlines** are blue dotted lines that show the boundaries of cells, but do not print. If your document will be viewed online—for example, if you are planning to e-mail your résumé to potential employers—you should turn off the display of gridlines before you distribute the document so that it looks the same online as it looks when printed. To turn gridlines off or on, click the View Gridlines button in the Table group on the Table Tools Layout tab.

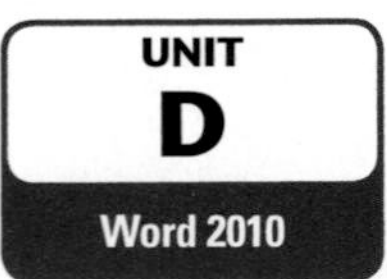

Creating a Custom Format for a Table

You can also use the formatting tools available in Word to create your own table designs. For example, you can add or remove borders and shading; vary the line style, thickness, and color of borders; and change the orientation of text from horizontal to vertical. You adjust the text direction, shading, and borders in the table to make it easier to understand at a glance.

STEPS

1. **Select the Type and Location cells in the first row, click the Merge Cells button in the Merge group on the Table Tools Layout tab, then type Ad Location**

   The two cells are combined into a single cell containing the text "Ad Location."

2. **Select the Web, Print, and Misc. cells in the first column, click the Bold button B on the Mini toolbar, click the Text Direction button in the Alignment group twice, then deselect the cells**

   The text is rotated 270 degrees.

3. **Position the pointer over the right border of the Web cell until the pointer changes to +||+, then drag the border to approximately the ¼" mark on the horizontal ruler**

   The width of the column containing the vertical text narrows.

QUICK TIP
In cells with vertical text, the I-beam pointer is rotated 90 degrees, and the buttons in the Alignment group change to vertical alignment.

4. **Place the insertion point in the Web cell, click the Table Tools Design tab, then click the Shading list arrow in the Table Styles group**

   The gallery of shading colors for the Paper theme opens.

5. **Click Gold, Accent 3 in the gallery as shown in Figure D-20, click the Print cell, click the Shading list arrow, click Lavender, Accent 4, click the Misc. cell, click the Shading list arrow, then click Blue-Gray, Accent 6**

   Shading is applied to each cell.

6. **Drag to select the six white cells in the Web rows (rows 2 and 3), click the Shading list arrow, then click Gold, Accent 3, Lighter 60%**

7. **Repeat Step 6 to apply Lavender, Accent 4, Lighter 60% shading to the Print rows and Blue-Gray, Accent 6, Lighter 60% shading to the Misc. rows**

   Shading is applied to all the cells in rows 1–8.

TROUBLE
If gridlines appear, click the Borders list arrow, then click View Gridlines to turn off the display.

8. **Select the last three rows of the table, click the Borders list arrow in the Table Styles group, click No Border on the menu that opens, then click in the table to deselect the rows**

   The top, bottom, left, and right borders are removed from each cell in the selected rows.

QUICK TIP
On the Borders menu, click the button that corresponds to the border you want to add or remove.

9. **Click the Pen Color list arrow in the Draw Borders group, click Blue-Gray, Accent 6, select the Total Cost row, click the Borders list arrow, click Top Border, click the 13,850 cell, click the Borders list arrow, then click Bottom Border**

   The active pen color for borders is Blue-Gray, Accent 6. You use the buttons in the Draw Borders group to change the active pen color, line weight, and line style settings before adding a border to a table. A top border is added to each cell in the Total Cost row, and a bottom border is added below 13,850. The completed table is shown in Figure D-21.

10. **Press [Ctrl][Home], press [Enter], type your name, save your changes, submit the document to your instructor, close the document, then exit Word**

    Press [Enter] at the beginning of a table to move the table down one line in a document.

FIGURE D-20: **Gallery of shading colors from the Origin theme**

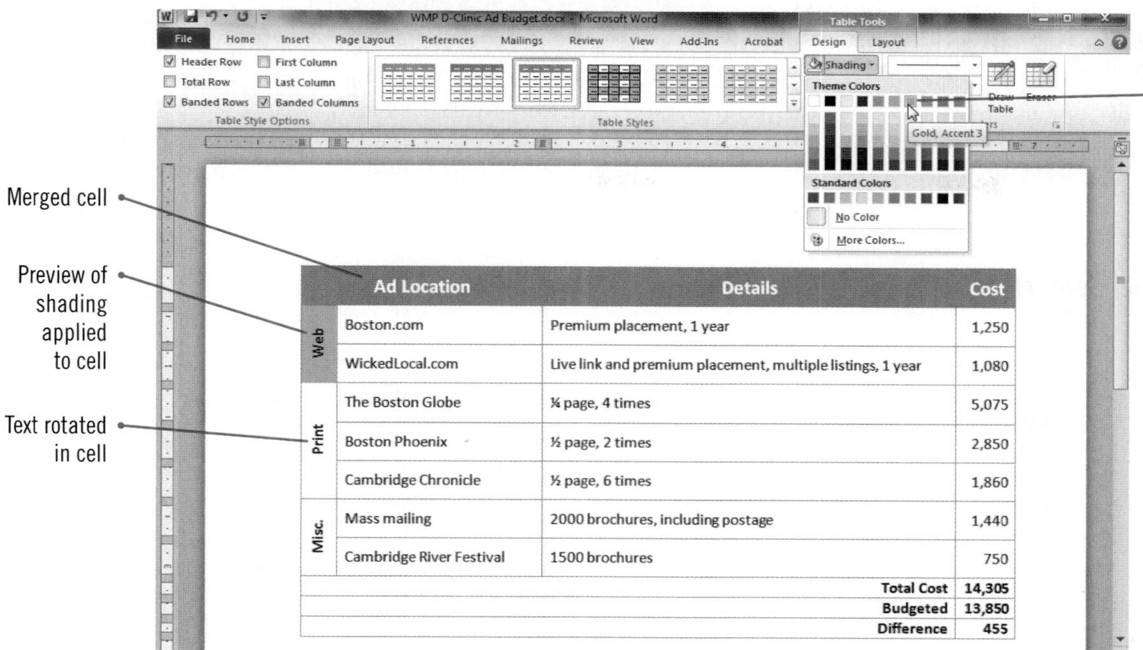

	Ad Location	Details	Cost
Web	Boston.com	Premium placement, 1 year	1,250
	WickedLocal.com	Live link and premium placement, multiple listings, 1 year	1,080
Print	The Boston Globe	¼ page, 4 times	5,075
	Boston Phoenix	½ page, 2 times	2,850
	Cambridge Chronicle	½ page, 6 times	1,860
Misc.	Mass mailing	2000 brochures, including postage	1,440
	Cambridge River Festival	1500 brochures	750
		Total Cost	14,305
		Budgeted	13,850
		Difference	455

Gold, Accent 3; use ScreenTips as needed to identify colors

FIGURE D-21: **Completed table**

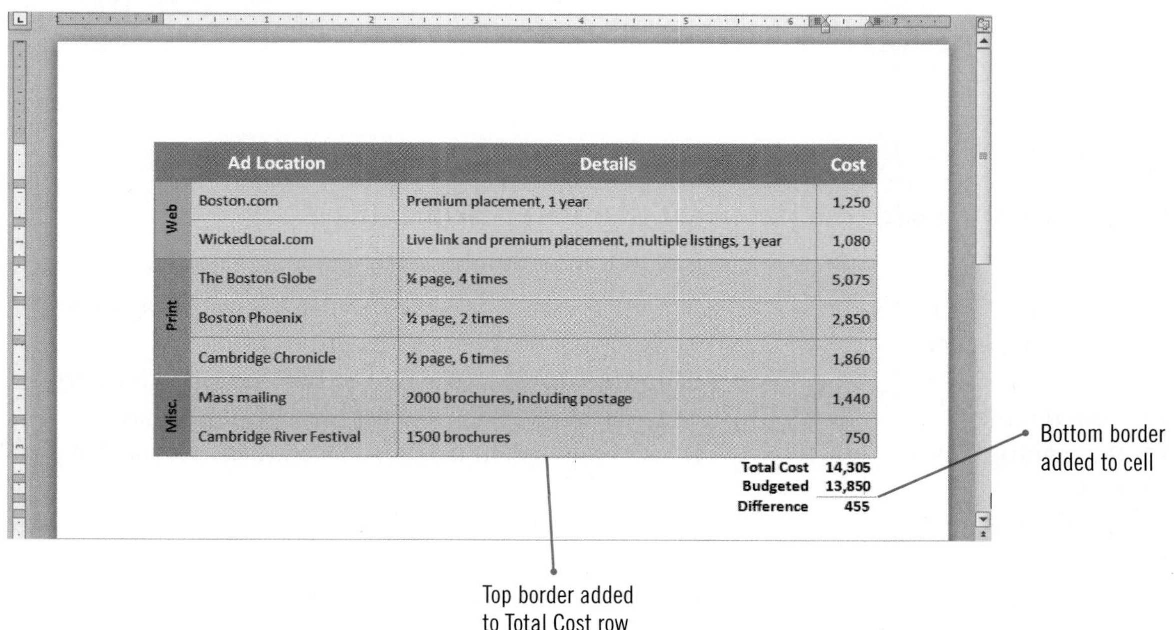

Drawing a table

The Word Draw Table feature allows you to draw table cells exactly where you want them. To draw a table, click the Table button on the Insert tab, and then click Draw Table. If a table is already started, you can click the Draw Table button in the Draw Borders group on the Table Tools Design tab to turn on the Draw pointer, and then click and drag to draw a cell. Using the same method, you can draw borders within the cell to create columns and rows, or draw additional cells attached to the first cell. Click the Draw Table button to turn off the draw feature. The borders you draw are added using the active line style, line weight, and pen color settings.

If you want to remove a border from a table, click the Eraser button in the Draw Borders group to activate the Eraser pointer, and then click the border you want to remove. Click the Eraser button to turn off the erase feature. You can use the Draw pointer and the Eraser pointer to change the structure of any table, not just the tables you draw from scratch.

Practice

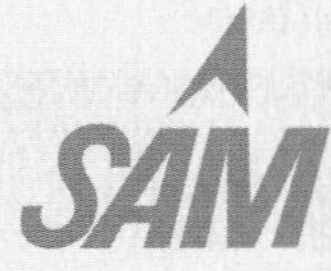

For current SAM information, including versions and content details, visit SAM Central (http://www.cengage.com/samcentral). If you have a SAM user profile, you may have access to hands-on instruction, practice, and assessment of the skills covered in this unit. Since various versions of SAM are supported throughout the life of this text, check with your instructor for the correct instructions and URL/Web site for accessing assignments.

Concepts Review

Label each element shown in Figure D-22.

FIGURE D-22

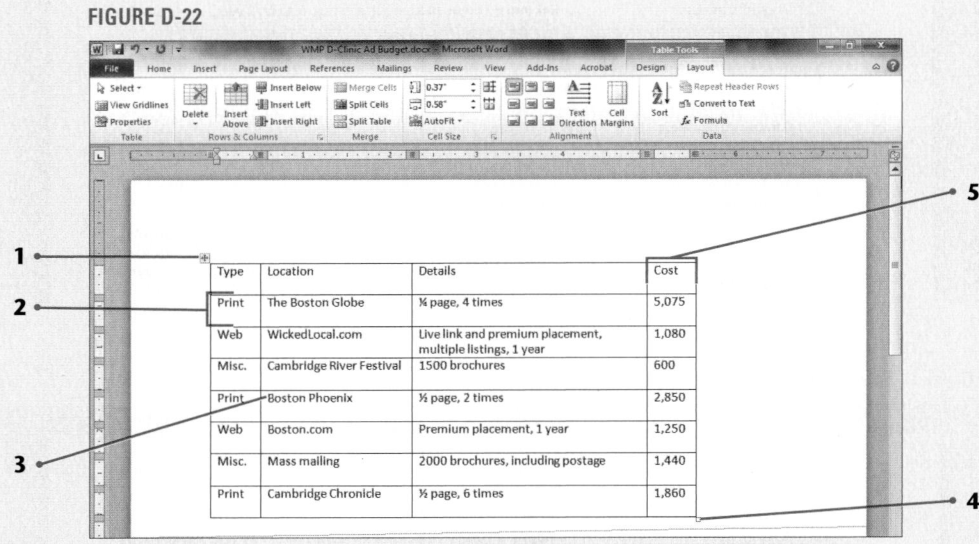

Match each term with the statement that best describes it.

6. Split
7. Borders
8. Ascending order
9. Merge
10. Nested table
11. Descending order
12. Cell
13. Header row
14. Cell reference
15. Gridlines

a. Sort order that organizes text from A to Z
b. The box formed by the intersection of a column and a row
c. An object inserted in a table cell
d. The first row of a table that contains the column headings
e. To combine two or more adjacent cells into one larger cell
f. Lines that separate columns and rows in a table and that print
g. To divide an existing cell into multiple cells
h. Lines that show columns and rows in a table but that do not print
i. A cell address composed of a column letter and a row number
j. Sort order that organizes text from Z to A

Select the best answer from the list of choices.

16. Which button do you use to change the alignment of text in a cell?

a.
b.
c.
d.

17. Which of the following is the cell reference for the third cell in the second column?

a. 3B
b. B3
c. C2
d. 2C

18. What happens when you double-click a column border?

a. The column width is adjusted to fit the text.
b. The columns in the table are distributed evenly.
c. A new column is added to the left.
d. A new column is added to the right.

19. Which of the following is *not* a valid way to add a new row to the bottom of a table?

a. Click in the bottom row, open the Properties dialog box, then insert a row using the options on the Row tab.
b. Place the insertion point in the last cell of the last row, then press [Tab].
c. Right-click the bottom row, point to Insert, then click Insert Rows Below.
d. Click in the bottom row, then click the Insert Below button in the Rows & Columns group on the Table Tools Layout tab.

20. Which of the following is *not* a correct formula for adding the values in cells A1, A2, and A3?

a. =A1+A2+A3
b. =SUM(A1~A3)
c. =SUM(A1,A2,A3)
d. =SUM(A1:A3)

Skills Review

1. Insert a table.

a. Start Word, then save the new blank document as **WMP D-Flu Mortality** to the drive and folder where you store your Data Files.
b. Type your name, press [Enter] twice, type **Influenza Mortality in Selected Major Cities**, then press [Enter].
c. Insert a table that contains four columns and four rows.
d. Type the text shown in Figure D-23, pressing [Tab] to add rows as necessary. (*Note*: Do not format text or the table at this time.)
e. Save your changes.

FIGURE D-23

City	>=65	25-64	<25
Boston	272	115	8
San Diego	129	68	3
Philadelphia	523	198	27
Detroit	217	143	17
Miami	186	98	9
Phoenix	138	57	6

2. Insert and delete rows and columns.

a. Insert a row above the Philadelphia row, then type the following text in the new row:
Houston 315 112 13
b. Delete the Boston row.
c. Insert a column to the right of the <25 column, type **Date Reported** in the header row, then enter a June 2013 date in each cell in the column using the format MM/DD/YY (for example, 06/27/13).
d. Move the Date Reported column to the right of the City column, then save your changes.

3. Modify rows and columns.

a. Double-click the border between the first and second columns to resize the columns.
b. Drag the border between the second and third columns to the $1\frac{3}{4}$" mark on the horizontal ruler.
c. Double-click the right border of the >=65, 25-64, and <25 columns.
d. Select the >=65, 25-64, and <25 columns, then distribute the columns evenly.
e. Select the table, apply the No Spacing style, select rows 2–7, set the row height to exactly .3", then save your changes.

4. Sort table data.

Perform three separate sorts as follows:

a. Sort the table data, excluding the header row, in descending order by the information in the >=65 column, then click OK.
b. Sort the table data, excluding the header row, in ascending order by date reported, then click OK.
c. Sort the table data, excluding the header row, by city name in alphabetical order, click OK, then save your changes.

5. Split and merge cells.

a. Insert a row above the header row, then merge the first cell in the new row with the City cell.
b. Merge the second cell in the new row with the Date Reported cell.
c. Merge the three remaining blank cells in the first row into a single cell, then type **Mortality by Age** in the merged cell.
d. Add a new row to the bottom of the table.
e. Merge the first two cells in the new row, then type **Average Mortality by Age** in the merged cell.
f. Select the first seven cells in the first column (from City to San Diego), open the Split Cells dialog box, clear the Merge cells before split check box, then split the cells into two columns.
g. Type **State** as the heading for the new column, then enter the following text in the remaining cells in the column: **MI, TX, FL, PA, AZ, CA.**
h. Double-click the right border of the first column to resize the column, then save your changes.

Skills Review (continued)

6. Perform calculations in tables.

a. Place the insertion point in the last cell in the >=65 column.

b. Open the Formula dialog box, delete the text in the Formula text box, type **=average(above)**, then click OK.

c. Repeat Step b to insert the average number of cases in each age category in the last cell in the 25-64 and <25 columns.

d. Change the value of the >=65 mortality rate for Phoenix to **182**.

e. Recalculate the average for the number of cases reported for the >=65 category. (*Hint*: Right-click the cell and select Update Field, or use [F9].)

f. Double-click the right border of the first column to resize the column, then double-click the right border of the >=65, 25-64, and <25 columns to resize the columns.

g. Select the last three columns in the table, distribute the columns evenly, then save your changes.

7. Apply a table style.

a. Click the Table Tools Design tab, preview table styles applied to the table, and then apply an appropriate style. Was the style you chose effective?

b. Apply the Light Shading style to the table, then remove the style from First Column and Banded Rows.

c. Apply bold to the >=65, 25-64, and <25 column headings, and to the bottom row of the table.

d. Center the table between the margins, center the table title **Influenza Mortality in Selected Major Cities**, increase the font size of the title to 14 points, apply bold, then save your changes.

8. Create a custom format for a table.

a. Select the entire table, then use the Align Center button in the Alignment group on the Table Tools Layout tab to center the text in every cell vertically and horizontally.

b. Center right-align the dates in column 3 and the numbers in columns 4–6.

c. Center left-align the city names and state abbreviations in columns 1 and 2, but not the column headings.

d. Center right-align the text in the bottom row. Make sure the text in the header row is still centered.

e. Change the theme colors to Executive.

f. Select all the cells in the header row, including the >=65, 25-64, and <25 column headings, change the shading color to Dark Green, Accent 5, then change the font color to white.

g. Apply Dark Green, Accent 5, Lighter 60% shading to the cells containing the city names and state abbreviations, and Dark Green Accent 5, Lighter 80% shading to the cells containing the dates.

h. To the cells containing the >=65, 25-64, and <25 data (excluding the Average Mortality data), apply Indigo, Accent 1, Lighter 60% shading; Orange, Accent 3, Lighter 60% shading; and Red, Accent 2, Lighter 60% shading, respectively.

i. Apply Dark Green Accent 5, Lighter 80% shading to the last row of the table.

j. Add a $\frac{1}{2}$-point white bottom border to the Mortality by Age cell in the header row. (*Hint*: Change the Line Weight to $\frac{1}{2}$ pt, change the Pen Color to White, then add the bottom border.)

k. Add a $1\frac{1}{2}$-point black border around the outside of the table. (*Hint*: Select the table, open the Borders and Shading dialog box, then add the outside border.)

l. Add a $\frac{1}{2}$-point black top border to the Detroit row and to the last row of the table. (*Hint*: Do not remove any borders.)

m. Compare your table to Figure D-24, make any necessary adjustments, save your changes, submit a copy to your instructor, close the file, then exit Word.

FIGURE D-24

Influenza Mortality in Selected Major Cities

City	State	Date Reported	Mortality by Age		
			>=65	25-64	<25
Detroit	MI	06/14/13	217	143	17
Houston	TX	06/07/13	315	112	13
Miami	FL	06/22/13	186	98	9
Philadelphia	PA	06/25/13	523	198	27
Phoenix	AZ	06/28/13	182	57	6
San Diego	CA	06/11/13	129	68	3
Average Mortality by Age			**258.67**	**112.67**	**12.5**

Independent Challenge 1

You are the office manager for a dental office. In preparation for a meeting about next year's budget, you create a table showing quarterly expenditures for the fiscal year 2013.

a. Start Word, then save the new blank document as **WMP D-2013 Expenditures** to the drive and folder where you store your Data Files.

b. Type the table heading **Quarterly Expenditures, Fiscal Year 2013** at the top of the document, then press [Enter] twice.

c. Insert a table with five columns and four rows, then enter the data shown in Figure D-25 into the table, adding rows as necessary. (*Note*: Do not format text or the table at this time.)

d. Resize the columns to fit the text.

e. Sort the table rows in alphabetical order by Item.

f. Add a new row to the bottom of the table, type **Total** in the first cell, then enter a formula in each remaining cell in the new row to calculate the sum of the cells above it.

FIGURE D-25

Item	Q1	Q2	Q3	Q4
Impression Products	1283	1627	1374	1723
Instruments	920	847	862	798
Anesthetics	1023	948	926	897
Cements and Liners	834	812	912	1029
Finishing and Polishing	463	394	472	289
Pins and Posts	730	695	463	586

g. Add a new column to the right side of the table, type **Total** in the first cell, then enter a formula in each remaining cell in the new column to calculate the sum of the cells to the left of it. (*Hint*: Make sure the formula you insert in each cell sums the cells to the left, not the cells above. In the last cell in the last column, you can sum the cells to the left or the cells above; either way the total should be the same.)

h. Apply a table style to the table. Select a style that enhances the information contained in the table, and adjust the Table Style Options to suit the content.

i. Center the text in the header row, left-align the remaining text in the first column, then right-align the numerical data in the table.

j. Enhance the table with fonts, font colors, shading, and borders to make the table attractive and easy to read at a glance.

k. Increase the font size of the table heading to 18 points, then center the table heading and the table on the page.

l. Press [Ctrl][End], press [Enter], type your name, save your changes, submit the file to your instructor, close the file, then exit Word.

Word 2010

Independent Challenge 2

You are a medical assistant in a busy family practice office. One of your responsibilities at the office is to create a list of scheduled appointments for the day. You find it easiest to format this information as a table.

a. Start Word, open the file WMP D-1.docx, then save it as **WMP D-April 14 Appointments** to the drive and folder where you store your Data Files.

b. Center the table heading, then increase the font size to 18 points.

c. Turn on formatting marks, select the tabbed text in the document, then convert the text to a table.

d. Add a row above the first row in the table, then enter the following column headings in the new header row: **Last Name**, **First Name**, **DOB**, **Phone**, **Physician**, **Time**.

e. Apply an appropriate table style to the table. Add or remove the style from various elements of the table using the options in the Table Style Options group, as necessary.

f. Adjust the column widths so that the table is attractive and readable.

g. Make the height of each row at least .25".

h. Center left-align the text in each cell in the first column, then Center Align the text in each cell in the DOB and Phone columns.

i. Center right-align the text in each cell in the Time column, including the column heads.

j. Center the column headings, then center the entire table on the page.

k. Sort the table by last name and then by first name in alphabetical order.

Independent Challenge 2 (continued)

Advanced Challenge Exercise

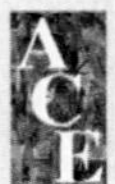

- Sort the entire table by physician in alphabetical order.
- Change the shading color of the Boxer, Dixon, and Wilson rows, each to a different color.
- Sort the table by Time and then by Physician, in ascending order. Move the Time column to become the first column in the table, then adjust the column width to fit the text. Move the rows for the appointments from 9:30 to 12:30 to the beginning of the table.

l. Enhance the table with borders, shading, fonts, and other formats, if necessary, to make it attractive and readable.
m. Type your name at the bottom of the document or in the footer, save your changes, submit a copy of the table to your instructor, close the document, then exit Word.

Independent Challenge 3

You work in a pediatrician's office. Your boss has given you data on appropriate Ibuprofen and Acetaminophen doses for children and has asked you to format the information for parents. You'll use tables to lay out the information so it is easily understandable.

a. Start Word, open the file WMP D-2.docx from the drive and folder where you store your Data Files, then save it as **WMP D-Dosages**. Read the document to get a feel for its contents.
b. Merge the cell in the first row of the table, then merge the cells in the Acetaminophen Doses row.
c. Insert a new row under the first row. Type **One dose lasts 6-8 hours** in the new cell.
d. Insert a new row under the Acetaminophen Doses row. Type **One dose lasts 4-6 hours** in the new row.
e. Change all the text in the table to 10-point Arial, then center all the text horizontally and vertically in the cells. (*Hint*: Use the Center Align button.)
f. Make the height of each row at least .25".
g. Select the third row of the table, copy it, then paste the row below the One dose lasts 4-6 hours row.
h. Split the table above the Acetaminophen Doses row, then press [Enter].
i. Refer to Figure D-26 and follow the steps below as you format the Ibuprofen and Acetaminophen tables. (*Hint*: Turn on gridlines to help you see the structure of the table as you format it.)
j. Format the header row in 14-point Arial, bold, then remove all the borders.
k. Format the second row in 12-point Arial, then remove all the borders.
l. In each column, merge the cells in rows 3 and 4. Remove the left border from the first cell in the new row 3. In the remaining cells in the row, apply bold to the text, then add a top border.
m. Apply bold to the text in the fourth row, then apply Orange, Accent 6 shading to the cells.
n. In the fifth row, merge the cells in columns 2-6, then apply bold to the text in the merged cell.
o. In columns 2-5, merge all adjoining blank cells, then remove the borders between the blank cells. (*Hint*: You might need to reapply borders to some adjacent cells after you remove the borders between the blank cells.)

FIGURE D-26

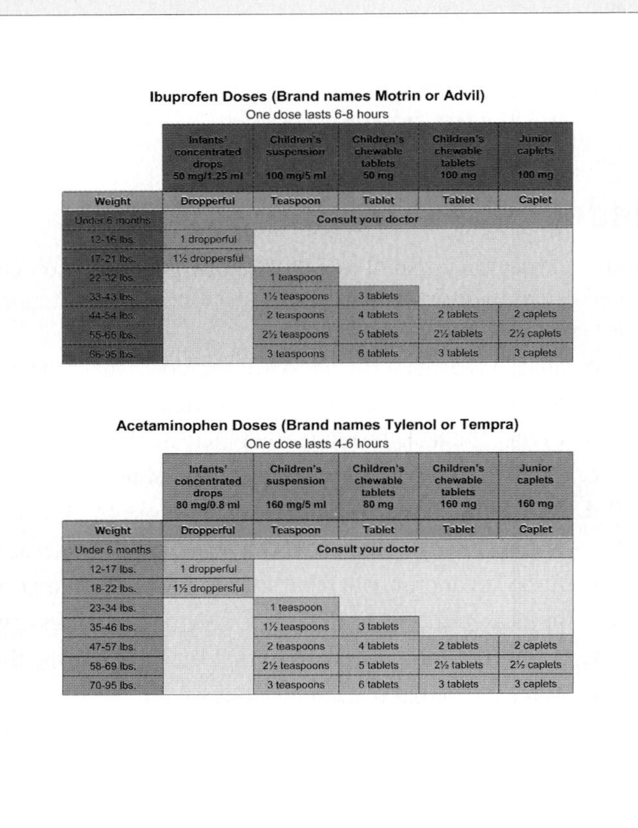

Ibuprofen Doses (Brand names Motrin or Advil)

One dose lasts 6-8 hours

	Infants' concentrated drops 50 mg/1.25 ml	Children's suspension 100 mg/5 ml	Children's chewable tablets 50 mg	Children's chewable tablets 100 mg	Junior caplets 100 mg
Weight	**Dropperful**	**Teaspoon**	**Tablet**	**Tablet**	**Caplet**
Under 6 months	**Consult your doctor**				
12-16 lbs.	1 dropperful				
17-21 lbs.	1½ droppersful				
22-32 lbs.		1 teaspoon			
33-43 lbs.		1½ teaspoons	3 tablets		
44-54 lbs.		2 teaspoons	4 tablets	2 tablets	2 caplets
55-65 lbs.		2½ teaspoons	5 tablets	2½ tablets	2½ caplets
66-95 lbs.		3 teaspoons	6 tablets	3 tablets	3 caplets

Acetaminophen Doses (Brand names Tylenol or Tempra)

One dose lasts 4-6 hours

	Infants' concentrated drops 80 mg/0.8 ml	Children's suspension 160 mg/5 ml	Children's chewable tablets 80 mg	Children's chewable tablets 160 mg	Junior caplets 160 mg
Weight	**Dropperful**	**Teaspoon**	**Tablet**	**Tablet**	**Caplet**
Under 6 months	**Consult your doctor**				
12-17 lbs.	1 dropperful				
18-22 lbs.	1½ droppersful				
23-34 lbs.		1 teaspoon			
35-46 lbs.		1½ teaspoons	3 tablets		
47-57 lbs.		2 teaspoons	4 tablets	2 tablets	2 caplets
58-69 lbs.		2½ teaspoons	5 tablets	2½ tablets	2½ caplets
70-95 lbs.		3 teaspoons	6 tablets	3 tablets	3 caplets

Independent Challenge 3 (continued)

p. Repeat Steps j-o to format the Acetaminophen table.

q. In the Ibuprofen table, apply Blue, Accent 1 shading to the cells in row 3, columns 2-6, and to the cells in column 1, rows 5-12.

r. Apply Blue, Accent 1, Lighter 80% shading to the blank cells in columns 2-5.

s. Apply Blue, Accent 1, Lighter 40% shading to the remaining table cells in columns 2-5.

t. Repeat Steps q-s to apply shading to the Acetaminophen table, using shades of Olive Green, Accent 3 shading.

Advanced Challenge Exercise

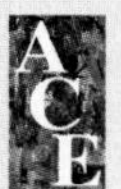

- In both tables, change the font color of the third row to white, then change the font color of the cells in column 1, rows 5-12 to white.
- Change the theme colors to a palette of your choice.
- Adjust the shading in each table so that the table is attractive and the dosage information is presented as clearly as possible.

u. Examine the document for errors, then make any necessary adjustments.

v. Press [Ctrl][End], press [Enter], type your name, save your changes to the document, preview it, submit the file to your instructor, close the file, then exit Word.

Real Life Independent Challenge

This Independent Challenge requires an Internet connection.

A well-written and well-formatted résumé gives you an advantage when it comes to getting a job interview. In a winning résumé, the content and format support your career objective and effectively present your background and qualifications. One simple way to create a résumé is to lay out the page using a table. In this exercise you research guidelines for writing and formatting résumés. You then create your own résumé using a table for its layout.

a. Use your favorite search engine to search the Web for information on writing and formatting résumés. Use the keywords **resume advice**.

b. Print helpful advice on writing and formatting résumés from at least two Web sites.

c. Think about the information you want to include in your résumé. The header should include your name, address, telephone number, and e-mail address. The body should include your career objective and information on your education, work experience, and skills. You may want to add additional information.

d. Sketch a layout for your résumé using a table as the underlying grid. Include the table rows and columns in your sketch.

e. Start Word, open a new blank document, then save it as **WMP D-My Resume** to the drive and folder where you store your Data Files.

f. Set appropriate margins, then insert a table to serve as the underlying grid for your résumé. Split and merge cells, and adjust the size of the table columns as necessary.

g. Type your résumé in the table cells. Take care to use a professional tone and keep your language to the point.

h. Format your résumé with fonts, bullets, and other formatting features. Adjust the spacing between sections by resizing the table columns and rows.

i. When you are satisfied with the content and format of your résumé, remove the borders from the table, then hide the gridlines if they are visible. You may want to add some borders back to the table to help structure the résumé for readers.

j. Check your résumé for spelling and grammar errors.

k. Save your changes, preview your résumé, submit a copy to your instructor, close the file, then exit Word.

Visual Workshop

Create the calendar shown in Figure D-27 using a table to lay out the entire page. (*Hint*: The font is Century Gothic.) Type your name in the last table cell, save the calendar with the file name **WMP D-October 2013** to the drive and folder where you store your Data Files, then print a copy.

FIGURE D-27

Atlantic Community Hospital

Community Education Calendar

October 2013						
Sunday	Monday	Tuesday	Wednesday	Thursday	Friday	Saturday
		1 Diabetes Mgmt. Education 1:30 p.m.	2	3	4 Yoga 9:00 a.m.	5 Women's AA 9:00 a.m. AA 8:00 p.m.
6 OA 6:30 p.m.	7	8 Diabetes Mgmt. Education 1:30 p.m.	9	10 Nursing Mother's Support Group 10:00 a.m.	11 Yoga 9:00 a.m.	12 Women's AA 9:00 a.m. AA 8:00 p.m.
13 OA 6:30 p.m.	14 Cancer Support Group 7:00 p.m.	15 Diabetes Mgmt. Education 1:30 p.m.	16	17	18 Yoga 9:00 a.m.	19 Women's AA 9:00 a.m. AA 8:00 p.m.
20 OA 6:30 p.m.	21	22 Diabetes Mgmt. Education 1:30 p.m.	23 Stroke Support Group 1:30 p.m.	24 Nursing Mother's Support Group 10:00 a.m.	25 Yoga 9:00 a.m.	26 Women's AA 9:00 a.m. AA 8:00 p.m.
27 OA 6:30 p.m.	28 Cancer Support Group 7:00 p.m.	29 Diabetes Mgmt. Education 1:30 p.m.	30	31		Your Name
All groups meet in Conference Room 1. For more information, call 555-4745						

UNIT
E
Word 2010

Formatting Documents

Files You Will Need:

WMP E-1.docx
WMP E-2.docx
WMP E-3.docx
WMP E-4.docx
WMP E-5.docx
WMP E-6.docx
WMP E-7.docx

The page-formatting features of Word allow you to lay out and design documents of all types, including reports, brochures, newsletters, and research documents. In this unit, you learn how to change the document margins, add page numbers, insert headers and footers, and format text in columns. You also learn how to work with the Word reference features to add footnotes, insert citations, and create a bibliography. You have written and formatted the text for an informational report for Riverwalk Medical Clinic patients about staying healthy while traveling. You are now ready to format the pages. You plan to organize the text in columns, to illustrate the report with a table, and to add footnotes and a bibliography.

OBJECTIVES

- Set document margins
- Create sections and columns
- Insert page breaks
- Insert page numbers
- Add headers and footers
- Insert a table
- Add footnotes and endnotes
- Insert citations
- Manage sources and create a bibliography

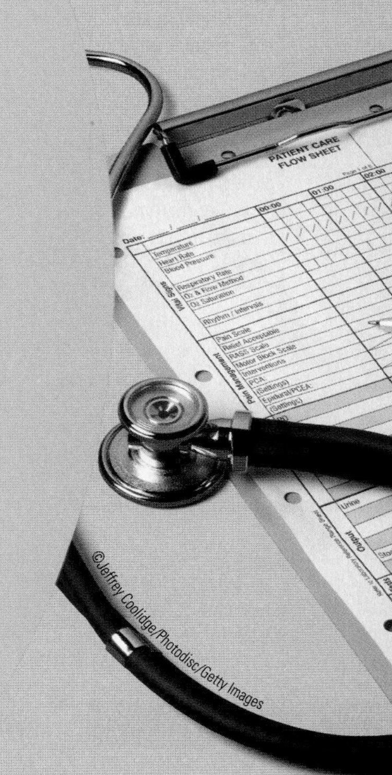

©Jeffrey Coolidge/Photodisc/Getty Images

UNIT
E
Word 2010

Setting Document Margins

Changing a document's margins is one way to change the appearance of a document and control the amount of text that fits on a page. The **margins** of a document are the blank areas between the edge of the text and the edge of the page. When you create a document in Word, the default margins are 1" at the top, bottom, left, and right sides of the page. You can adjust the size of a document's margins using the Margins command on the Page Layout tab or using the rulers. The report should be a four-page document when finished. You begin by reducing the size of the document margins so that more text fits on each page.

STEPS

TROUBLE

Click the View Ruler button at the top of the vertical scroll bar to display the rulers if they are not already displayed.

1. **Start Word, open the file WMP E-1.docx from the drive and folder where you store your Data Files, then save it as WMP E-Healthy Traveler**

   The report opens in Print Layout view.

2. **Scroll through the report to get a feel for its contents, then press [Ctrl][Home]**

   The report is currently five pages long. Notice that the status bar indicates the page where the insertion point is located and the total number of pages in the document.

3. **Click the Page Layout tab, then click the Margins button in the Page Setup group**

   The Margins menu opens. You can select predefined margin settings from this menu, or you can click Custom Margins to create different margin settings.

QUICK TIP

You can also click the launcher in the Page Setup group to open the Page Setup dialog box.

4. **Click Custom Margins**

   The Page Setup dialog box opens with the Margins tab displayed, as shown in Figure E-1. You can use the Margins tab to change the top, bottom, left, or right document margin, to change the orientation of the pages from portrait to landscape, and to alter other page layout settings. **Portrait orientation** means a page is taller than it is wide; **landscape orientation** means a page is wider than it is tall. This report uses portrait orientation. You can also use the Orientation button in the Page Setup group on the Page Layout tab to change the orientation of a document.

5. **Click the Top down arrow three times until 0.7" appears, then click the Bottom down arrow until 0.7" appears**

   The top and bottom margins of the report will be .7". Notice that the margins in the Preview section of the dialog box change as you adjust the margin settings.

QUICK TIP

The minimum allowable margin settings depend on your printer and the size of the paper you are using. Word displays a warning message if you set margins that are too narrow for your printer.

6. **Press [Tab], type .7 in the Left text box, press [Tab], then type .7 in the Right text box**

   The left and right margins of the report will also be .7". You can change the margin settings by using the arrows or by typing a value in the appropriate text box.

7. **Click OK**

   The document margins change to .7", as shown in Figure E-2. The location of each margin (right, left, top, and bottom) is shown on the horizontal and vertical rulers at the intersection of the white and shaded areas. You can also change a margin setting by using the pointer to drag the intersection to a new location on the ruler.

8. **Click the View tab, then click the Two Pages button in the Zoom group**

   The first two pages of the document appear in the document window.

9. **Scroll down to view all five pages of the report, press [Ctrl][Home], click the Page Width button in the Zoom group, then save your changes**

FIGURE E-1: **Margins tab in Page Setup dialog box**

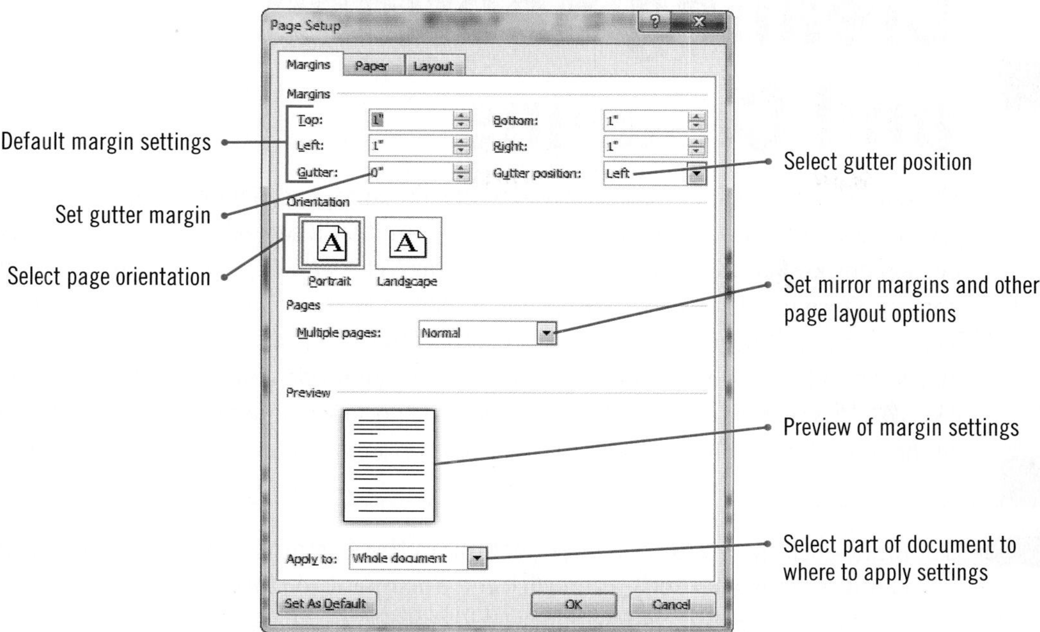

FIGURE E-2: **Report with smaller margins**

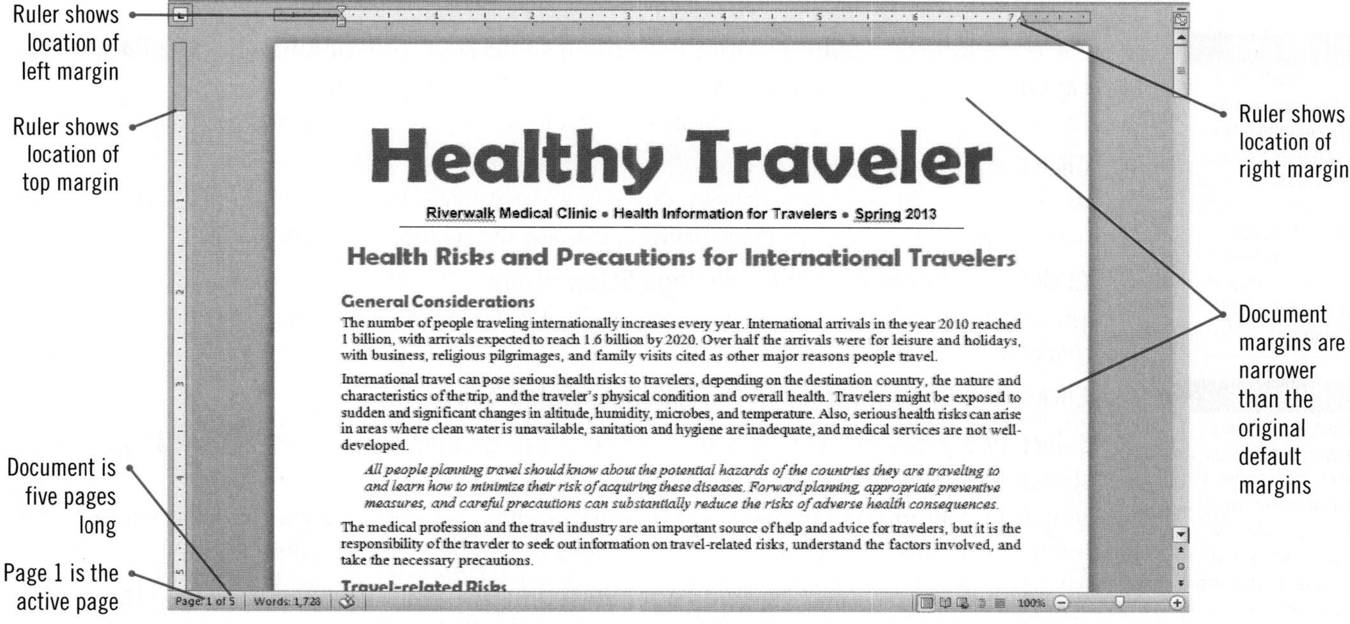

Changing orientation, margin settings, and paper size

By default, the documents you create in Word use an 8½" × 11" paper size in portrait orientation with the default margin settings. You can change the orientation, margin settings, and paper size to common settings using the Orientation, Margins, and Size buttons in the Page Setup group on the Page Layout tab. You can also adjust these settings and others in the Page Setup dialog box. For example, to change the layout of multiple pages, use the Multiple pages list arrow on the Margins tab to create pages that use mirror margins, that include two pages per sheet of paper, or that are formatted using a book fold. **Mirror margins** are used in a document with facing pages, such as a magazine, where the margins on the left page of the document are a mirror image of the margins on the right page. Documents with mirror margins have inside and outside margins, rather than right and left margins. Another type of margin is a gutter margin, which is used in documents that are bound, such as books. A **gutter** adds extra space to the left, top, or inside margin to allow for the binding. Add a gutter to a document by adjusting the setting in the Gutter position text box on the Margins tab. To change the size of the paper used, use the Paper size list arrow on the Paper tab to select a standard paper size, or enter custom measurements in the Width and Height text boxes.

UNIT
E
Word 2010

Creating Sections and Columns

Dividing a document into sections allows you to format each section of the document with different page layout settings. A **section** is a portion of a document that is separated from the rest of the document by section breaks. **Section breaks** are formatting marks that you insert in a document to show the end of a section. Once you have divided a document into sections, you can format each section with different column, margin, page orientation, header and footer, and other page layout settings. By default, a document is formatted as a single section, but you can divide a document into as many sections as you like. You insert a section break to divide the document into two sections, and then format the text in the second section in two columns. First, you customize the status bar to display section information.

STEPS

QUICK TIP
Use the Customize Status Bar menu to turn on and off the display of information in the status bar.

QUICK TIP
When you insert a section break at the beginning of a paragraph, Word inserts the break at the end of the previous paragraph. A section break stores the formatting information for the preceding section.

QUICK TIP
When you delete a section break, you delete the section formatting of the text before the break. That text becomes part of the following section, and it assumes the formatting of that section.

1. **Right-click the status bar, click Section on the Customize Status Bar menu that opens (if it is not already checked), then click the document to close the menu**
   The status bar indicates the insertion point is located in section 1 of the document.
2. **Click the Home tab, then click the Show/Hide ¶ button ¶ in the Paragraph group**
   Turning on formatting marks allows you to see the section breaks you insert in a document.
3. **Place the insertion point before the heading General Considerations, click the Page Layout tab, then click the Breaks button in the Page Setup group**
   The Breaks menu opens. You use this menu to insert different types of section breaks. See Table E-1.
4. **Click Continuous**
   Word inserts a continuous section break, shown as a dotted double line, above the heading. The document now has two sections. Notice that the status bar indicates the insertion point is in section 2.
5. **Click the Columns button in the Page Setup group**
   The columns menu opens. You use this menu to format text using preset column formats or to create custom columns.
6. **Click More Columns to open the Columns dialog box**
7. **Select Two in the Presets section, click the Spacing down arrow twice until 0.3" appears as shown in Figure E-3, then click OK**
   Section 2 is formatted in two columns of equal width with .3" of spacing between, as shown in Figure E-4. Formatting text in columns is another way to increase the amount of text that fits on a page.
8. **Click the View tab, click the Two Pages button in the Zoom group, scroll down to examine all four pages of the document, press [Ctrl][Home], then save the document**
   The text in section 2—all the text below the continuous section break—is formatted in two columns. Text in columns flows automatically from the bottom of one column to the top of the next column.

TABLE E-1: Types of section breaks

section	function
Next page	Begins a new section and moves the text following the break to the top of the next page
Continuous	Begins a new section on the same page
Even page	Begins a new section and moves the text following the break to the top of the next even-numbered page
Odd page	Begins a new section and moves the text following the break to the top of the next odd-numbered page

FIGURE E-3: Columns dialog box

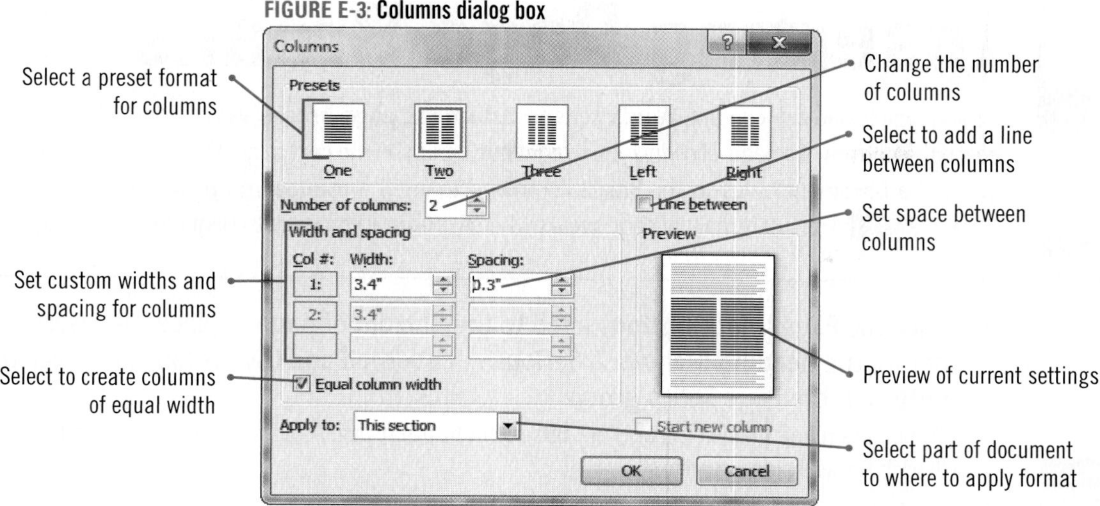

FIGURE E-4: Continuous section break and columns

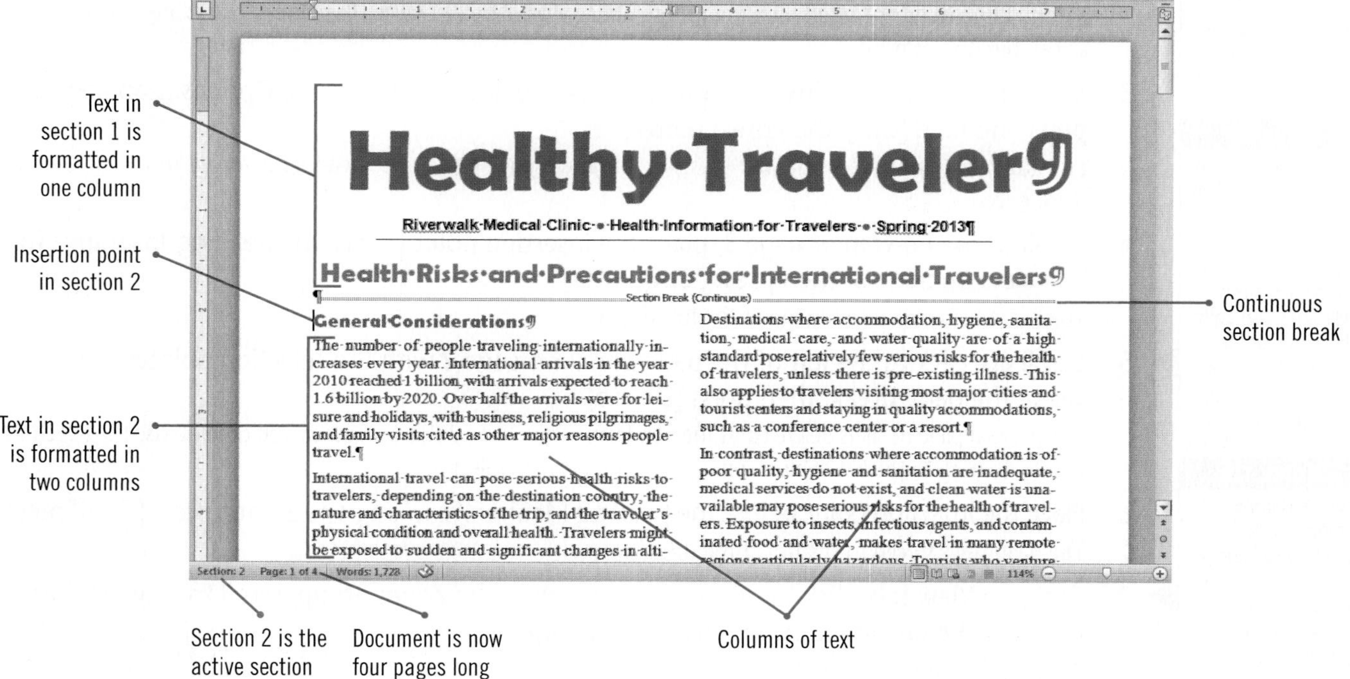

Changing page layout settings for a section

Dividing a document into sections allows you to vary the layout of a document. In addition to applying different column settings to sections, you can apply different margins, page orientation, paper size, vertical alignment, header and footer, page numbering, footnotes, endnotes, and other page layout settings. For example, if you are formatting a report that includes a table with many columns, you might want to change the table's page orientation to landscape so that it is easier to read. To do this, you would insert a section break before and after the table to create a section that contains only the table, and then you would change the page orientation of the section that contains the table to landscape. If the table does not fill the page, you could also change the vertical alignment of the table so that it is centered vertically on the page. To do this, use the Vertical alignment list arrow on the Layout tab of the Page Setup dialog box.

To check or change the page layout settings for an individual section, place the insertion point in the section, then open the Page Setup dialog box. Select any options you want to change, click the Apply to list arrow, click This section, then click OK. When you select This section in the Apply to list box, the settings are applied to the current section only. If you select Whole document in the Apply to list box, the settings are applied to all the sections in the document. Use the Apply to list arrow in the Columns dialog box or the Footnote and Endnote dialog box to change those settings for a section.

UNIT
E
Word 2010

Inserting Page Breaks

As you type text in a document, Word inserts an **automatic page break** (also called a soft page break) when you reach the bottom of a page, allowing you to continue typing on the next page. You can also force text onto the next page of a document by using the Breaks command to insert a **manual page break** (also called a hard page break). You insert manual page breaks where you know you want to begin each new page of the report.

STEPS

1. **Click the Page Width button, scroll to the bottom of page 1, place the insertion point before the heading Malaria: A Serious..., click the Page Layout tab, then click the Breaks button in the Page Setup group**

   The Breaks menu opens. You also use this menu to insert page, column, and text-wrapping breaks. Table E-2 describes these types of breaks.

2. **Click Page**

   Word inserts a manual page break before "Malaria: A Serious Health Risk for Travelers" and moves all the text following the page break to the beginning of the next page, as shown in Figure E-5. The page break appears as a dotted line in Print Layout view when formatting marks are displayed. Page break marks are visible on the screen but do not print.

3. **Scroll down, place the insertion point before the heading Preventive Options... on page 2, press and hold [Ctrl], then press [Enter]**

   Pressing [Ctrl][Enter] is a fast way to insert a manual page break. The heading is forced to the top of the third page.

4. **Scroll to the bottom of page 3, place the insertion point before the heading Insurance for Travelers on page 3, then press [Ctrl][Enter]**

   The heading is forced to the top of the fourth page.

5. **Scroll up, click to the left of the page break on page 2 with the selection pointer to select the page break, then press [Delete]**

   The manual page break is deleted and the text from pages 2 and 3 flows together. You can also use the selection pointer to click to the left of a section or a column break to select it.

6. **Place the insertion point before the heading Medical Kit.... on page 2, then press [Ctrl][Enter]**

   The heading is forced to the top of the third page.

7. **Click the View tab, click the Two Pages button in the Zoom group, scroll to view all four pages of the document, then save your changes**

   Pages 3 and 4 are shown in Figure E-6.

QUICK TIP

To control the flow of text between columns, insert a column break to force the text after the break to the top of the next column.

QUICK TIP

You can also double-click a page break to select it, and then press [Delete] to delete it. You know the page break is selected when both the words and the paragraph mark at the end of the page break are selected.

QUICK TIP

You can balance columns of unequal length on a page by inserting a continuous section break at the end of the last column on the page.

Controlling automatic pagination

Another way to control the flow of text between pages (or between columns) is to apply pagination settings to specify where Word positions automatic page breaks. For example, you might want to make sure an article appears on the same page as its heading, or you might want to prevent a page from breaking in the middle of the last paragraph of a report. To manipulate automatic pagination, simply select the paragraphs(s) or line(s) you want to control, click the launcher in the Paragraph group on the Home or Page Layout tab, click the Line and Page Breaks tab in the Paragraph dialog box, select one or more of the following settings in the Pagination section, and then click OK. Pagination settings include the following:

- Keep with next setting—apply to any paragraph you want to appear together with the next paragraph on a single page in order to prevent the page from breaking between the paragraphs.
- Keep lines together setting—apply to selected paragraph or lines to prevent a page from breaking in the middle of a paragraph or between certain lines.
- Page break before setting—apply to specify that a selected paragraph follows an automatic page break.
- Widow/Orphan control setting—turned on by default in the Pagination section of the dialog box. This setting ensures that at least two lines of a paragraph appear at the top and bottom of every page. In other words, it prevents a page from beginning with just the last line of a paragraph (a **widow**), and prevents a page from ending with only the first line of a new paragraph (an **orphan**).

FIGURE E-5: **Manual page break in document**

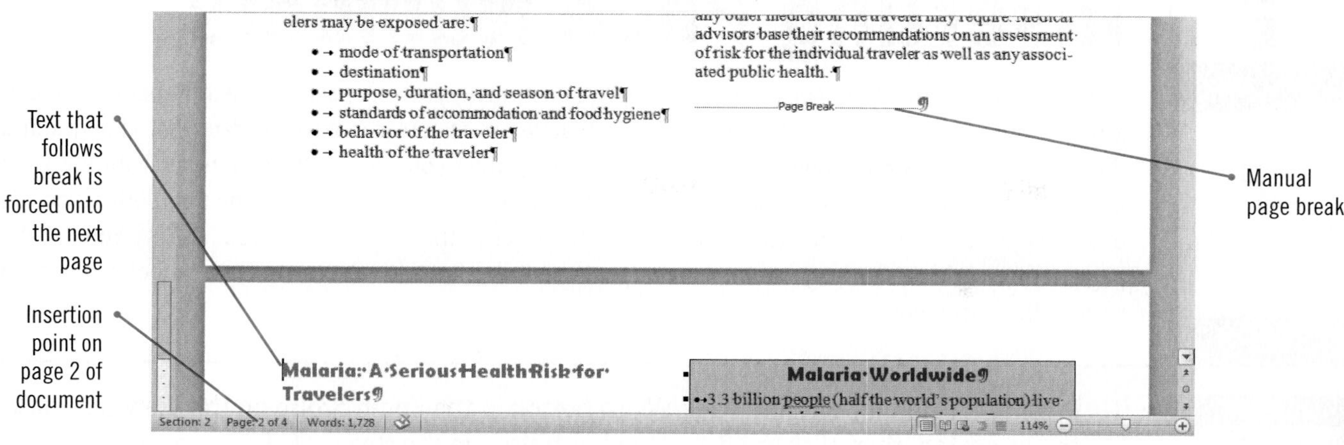
elers may be exposed are:
mode of transportation
destination
purpose, duration, and season of travel
standards of accommodation and food hygiene
behavior of the traveler
health of the traveler
advisors base their recommendations on an assessment of risk for the individual traveler as well as any associated public health.
Page Break
Malaria: A Serious Health Risk for Travelers
Malaria Worldwide
3.3 billion people (half the world's population) live
Text that follows break is forced onto the next page
Insertion point on page 2 of document
Manual page break
Section: 2 Page: 2 of 4 Words: 1,728
114%

Word 2010

FIGURE E-6: **Pages 3 and 4**

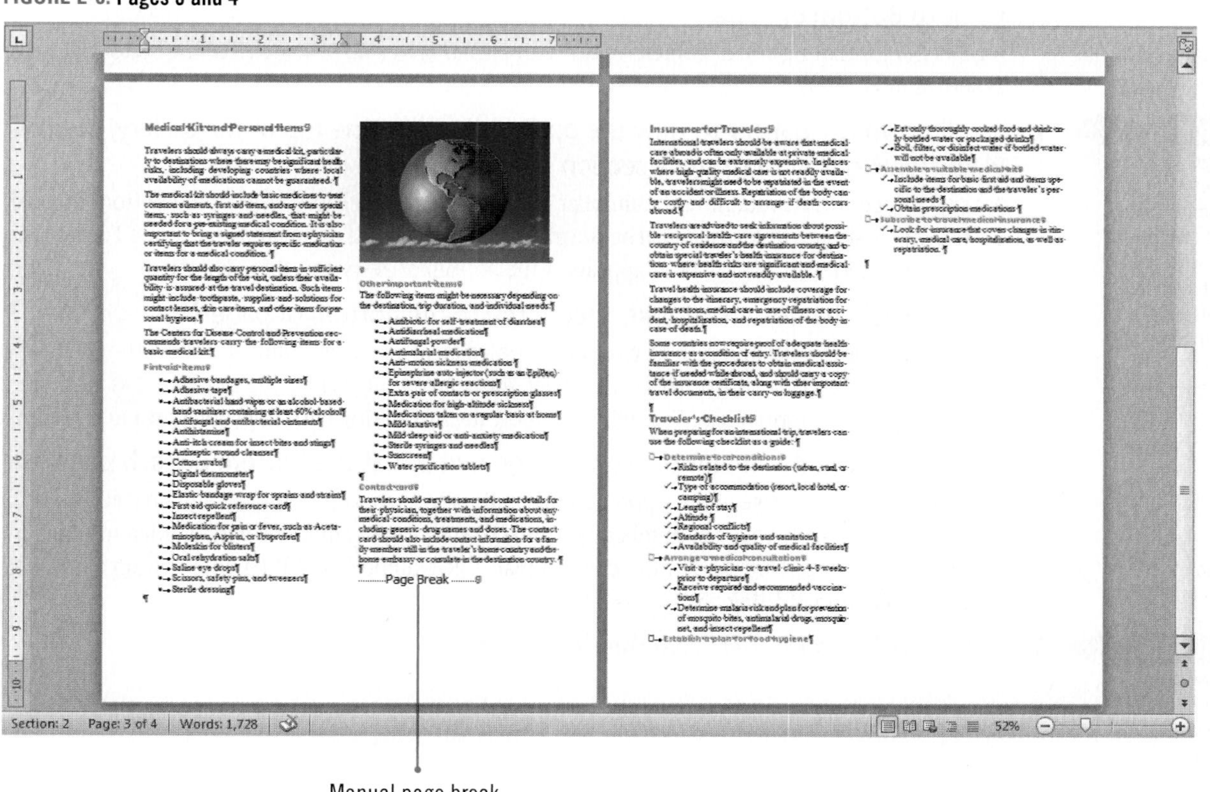
Medical Kit and Personal Items
Other important items
Contact card
Page Break
Insurance for Travelers
Traveler's Checklist
Section: 2 Page: 3 of 4 Words: 1,728
52%
Manual page break

TABLE E-2: **Types of breaks**

break	function
Page	Forces the text following the break to begin at the top of the next page
Column	Forces the text following the break to begin at the top of the next column
Text Wrapping	Forces the text following the break to begin at the beginning of the next line

UNIT E
Word 2010

Inserting Page Numbers

If you want to number the pages of a multiple-page document, you can insert a page number field to add a page number to each page. A **field** is a code that serves as a placeholder for data that changes in a document, such as a page number or the current date. When you use the Page Number button on the Insert tab to add page numbers to a document, you insert the page number field at the top, bottom, or side of any page, and Word automatically numbers all the pages in the document for you. You insert a page number field so that page numbers will appear centered between the margins at the bottom of each page in the document.

STEPS

QUICK TIP
Point to Current Position to insert a page number field at the location of the insertion point.

1. **Press [Ctrl][Home], click the Page Width button in the Zoom group on the View tab, click the Insert tab, then click the Page Number button in the Header & Footer group**
   The Page Number menu opens. You use this menu to select the position for the page numbers. If you choose to add a page number field to the top, bottom, or side of a document, a page number will appear on every page in the document. If you choose to insert it in the document at the location of the insertion point, the field will appear on that page only.

2. **Point to Bottom of Page**
   A gallery of formatting and alignment options for page numbers to be inserted at the bottom of a page opens, as shown in Figure E-7.

QUICK TIP
To change the location or formatting of page numbers, click the Page Number button, point to a page number location, then select a format from the gallery.

3. **Scroll down the gallery to view the options, scroll to the top of the gallery, then click Plain Number 2 in the Simple section**
   A page number field containing the number 1 is centered in the Footer area at the bottom of page 1 of the document, as shown in Figure E-8. The document text is gray, or dimmed, because the Footer area is open. Text that is inserted in a Footer area appears at the bottom of every page in a document.

4. **Double-click the document text, then scroll to the bottom of page 1**
   Double-clicking the document text closes the Footer area. The page number is now dimmed because it is located in the Footer area, which is no longer the active area. When the document is printed, the page numbers appear as normal text. You will learn more about working with the Footer area in the next lesson.

5. **Scroll down the document to see the page number at the bottom of each page**
   Word numbered each page of the report automatically, and each page number is centered at the bottom of the page. If you want to change the numbering format or start page numbering with a different number, you can simply click the Page Number button, click Format Page Numbers, and then choose from the options in the Page Number Format dialog box.

QUICK TIP
To remove page numbers from a document, click the Page Number button, then click Remove Page Numbers.

6. **Press [Ctrl][Home], then save the document**

Moving around in a long document

Rather than scrolling to move to a different place in a long document, you can use the Browse by Object feature to move the insertion point to a specific location quickly. Browse by Object allows you to browse to the next or previous page, section, line, table, graphic, or other item of the same type in a document. To do this, first click the Select Browse Object button below the vertical scroll bar to open a palette of object types. On this palette, click the button for the type of item you want to browse through, and then click the Next or Previous buttons to scroll through the items of that type in the document.

FIGURE E-7: Page Number gallery

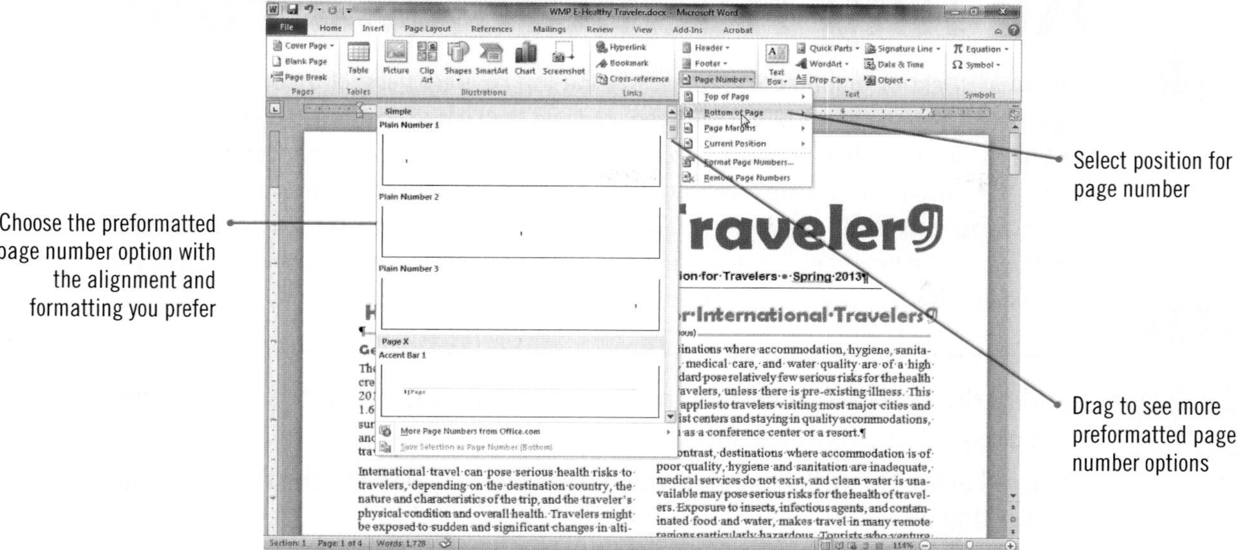

FIGURE E-8: Page number in document

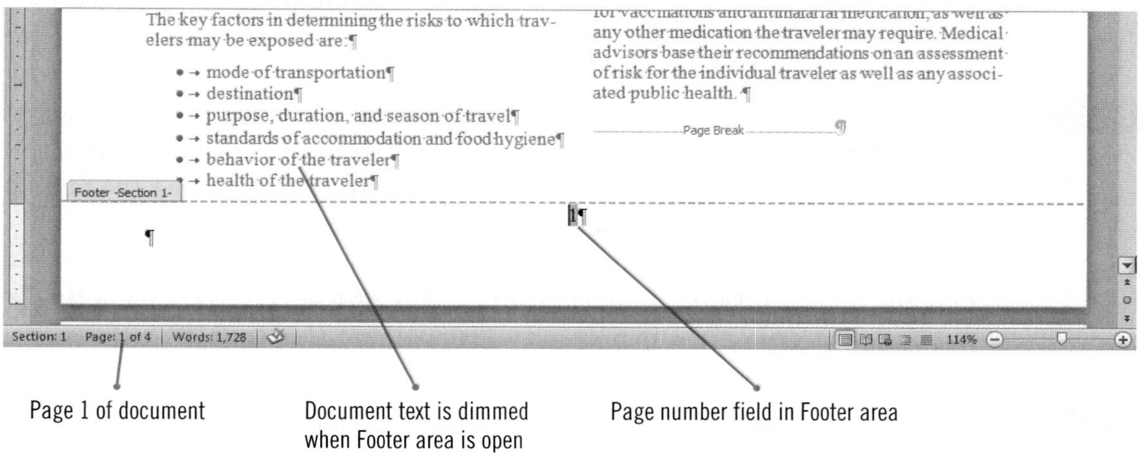

Inserting Quick Parts

The Word Quick Parts feature makes it easy to insert reusable pieces of content into a document quickly. The **Quick Parts** items you can insert include fields, such as for the current date or the total number of pages in a document; document property information, such as the author and title of a document; and building blocks, which are customized content that you create, format, and save for future use.

To insert a Quick Part into a document at the location of the insertion point, click the Quick Parts button in the Text group on the Insert tab (or, if headers and footers are open, click the Quick Parts button in the Insert group on the Header & Footer Tools Design tab), and then select the type of Quick Part you want to insert. To insert a field into a document, click Field on the Quick Parts menu that opens, click the name of the field you want to insert in the Field dialog box, and then click OK. Field information is updated automatically each time the document is opened or saved.

To insert a document property, point to Document Property on the Quick Parts menu, and then click the property you want to insert. The property is added to the document as a content control and contains the document property information you entered in the Document panel. If you did not assign a document property, the content control contains a placeholder, which you can replace with your own text. Once you replace the placeholder text—or edit the document property information that appears in the content control—this text replaces the document property information in the Document panel.

To insert a building block, click Building Blocks Organizer on the Quick Parts menu, select the building block you want, and then click Insert. You will learn more about working with building blocks in later lessons.

UNIT E

Word 2010

Adding Headers and Footers

A **header** is text or graphics that appears at the top of every page of a document. A **footer** is text or graphics that appears at the bottom of every page. In longer documents, headers and footers often contain the title of the publication or chapter, the name of the author, or a page number. You can add headers and footers to a document by double-clicking the top or bottom margin of a document to open the Header and Footer areas, and then inserting text and graphics into them. You can also use the Header or Footer command on the Insert tab to insert predesigned headers and footers that you can modify to include your information. You create a header that includes the name of the report.

STEPS

QUICK TIP
Unless you set different headers and footers for different sections, the information you insert in any Header or Footer area appears on every page in the document.

QUICK TIP
You can also use the Insert Alignment Tab button in the Position group to left-, center-, and right-align text in the Header and Footer areas.

QUICK TIP
To change the distance between the header and footer and the edge of the page, change the Header from Top and Footer from Bottom settings in the Position group.

QUICK TIP
To remove headers or footers from a document, click the Header or Footer button, and then click Remove Header or Remove Footer.

1. **Click the Insert tab, then click the Header button in the Header & Footer group**
   A gallery of built-in header designs opens.
2. **Scroll down the gallery to view the header designs, scroll to the top of the gallery, then click Blank**
   The Header and Footer areas open, and the document text is dimmed. When the document text is dimmed, it cannot be edited. The Header & Footer Tools Design tab also opens and is the active tab, as shown in Figure E-9. This tab is available whenever the Header and Footer areas are open.
3. **Type Healthy Traveler: Travel and Health Information from Riverwalk Medical Clinic in the content control in the Header area**
   This text will appear at the top of every page in the document.
4. **Select the header text, click the Home tab, click the Font list arrow in the Font group, click Berlin Sans FB Demi, click the Font Color list arrow, click Olive Green, Accent 3, Darker 25%, click the Center button in the Paragraph group, click the Bottom Border button, then click in the Header area to deselect the text**
   The text is formatted in olive green Berlin Sans FB Demi and centered in the Header area with a bottom border.
5. **Click the Header & Footer Tools Design tab, then click the Go to Footer button in the Navigation group**
   The insertion point moves to the Footer area, where a page number field is centered in the Footer area.
6. **Select the page number field in the footer, use the Mini toolbar to change the formatting to Berlin Sans FB Demi and Olive Green, Accent 3, Darker 25%, then click in the Footer area to deselect the text and field**
   The footer text is formatted in olive green Berlin Sans FB Demi.
7. **Click the Close Header and Footer button in the Close group, then scroll down until the bottom of page 1 and the top of page 2 appear in the document window**
   The Header and Footer areas close, and the header and footer text is dimmed, as shown in Figure E-10.
8. **Press [Ctrl][Home]**
   The report already includes the name of the document at the top of the first page, making the header information redundant. You can modify headers and footers so that the header and footer text does not appear on the first page of a document or a section.
9. **Position the pointer over the header text at the top of page 1, then double-click**
   The Header and Footer areas open. The Options group on the Header & Footer Tools Design tab includes options for creating a different header and footer for the first page of a document or a section, and for creating different headers and footers for odd- and even-numbered pages.
10. **Click the Different First Page check box to select it, click the Close Header and Footer button, scroll to see the header and footer on pages 2, 3, and 4, then save the document**
    The header and footer text is removed from the Header and Footer areas on the first page.

FIGURE E-9: Header area

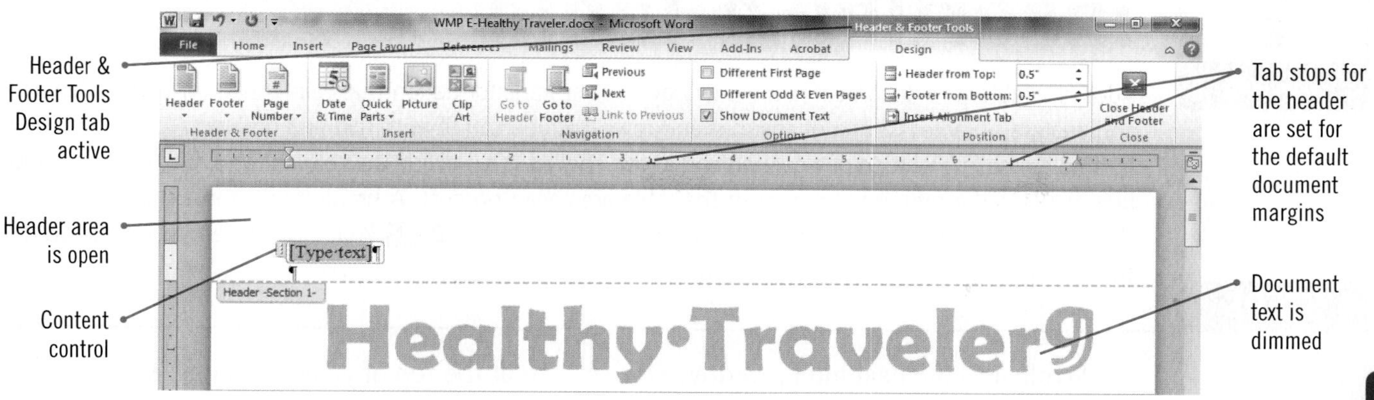

Word 2010

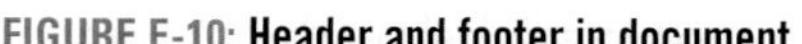

FIGURE E-10: Header and footer in document

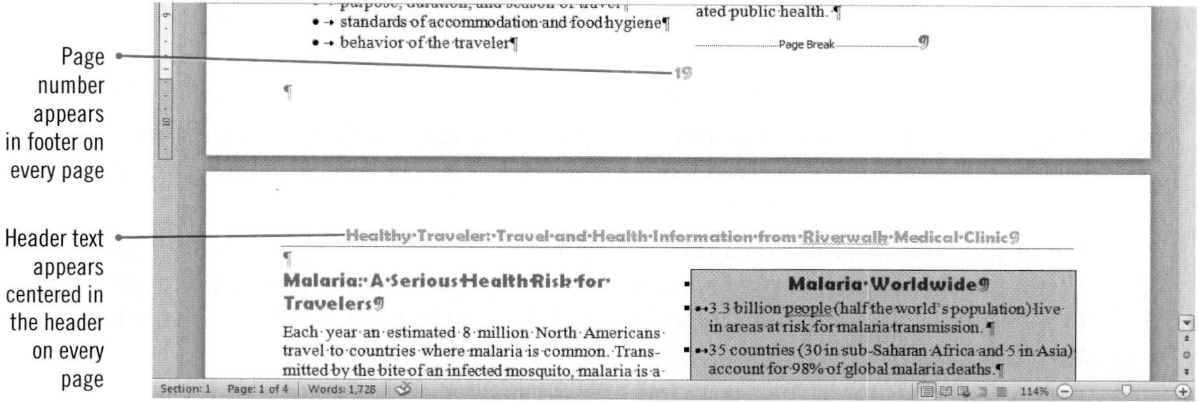

Adding a custom header or footer to the gallery

When you design a header that you want to use again in other documents, you can add it to the Header gallery by saving it as a building block. **Building blocks** are reusable pieces of formatted content or document parts, including headers and footers, page numbers, and text boxes, that are stored in galleries. Building blocks include predesigned content that comes with Word, as well as content that you create and save for future use. For example, you might create a custom header that contains your company name and logo and is formatted using the fonts, border, and colors you use in all company documents.

To add a custom header to the Header gallery, select all the text in the header, including the last paragraph mark, click the Header button, and then click Save Selection to Header Gallery. In the Create New Building Block dialog box that opens, type a unique name for the header in the Name text box, click the Gallery list arrow and select the appropriate gallery, verify that the Category is General, and then type a brief description of the new header design in the Description text box. This description appears in a ScreenTip when you point to the custom header in the gallery. When you are finished, click OK. The new header appears in the Header gallery under the General category.

To remove a custom header from the Header gallery, right-click it, click Organize and Delete, make sure the appropriate building block is selected in the Building Blocks Organizer that opens, click Delete, click Yes, and then click Close. You can follow the same process to add or remove a custom footer to the Footer gallery.

UNIT E

Word 2010

Inserting a Table

Adding a table to a document is a useful way to illustrate information that is intended for quick reference and analysis. A table is a grid of columns and rows that you can fill with text and graphics. A cell is the box formed by the intersection of a column and a row. The lines that divide the columns and rows of a table and help you see the grid-like structure of the table are called borders. A simple way to insert a table into a document is to use the Insert Table command on the Insert tab. You add a table to page 2 showing the preventive options for serious travel health diseases.

STEPS

1. **Scroll until the heading Preventive Options... is at the top of your document window**
2. **Select the heading Preventive Options... and the two paragraph marks below it, click the Page Layout tab, click the Columns button in the Page Setup group, click One, click the heading to deselect the text, then scroll down to see the bottom half of page 2**
   A continuous section break is inserted before the heading and after the second paragraph mark, creating a new section, section 3, as shown in Figure E-11. The document now includes four sections, with the heading Preventive Options... in Section 3. Section 3 is formatted as a single column.
3. **Place the insertion point before the first paragraph mark below the heading, click the Insert tab, click the Table button in the Tables group, then click Insert Table**
   The Insert Table dialog box opens. You use this dialog box to create a blank table.

QUICK TIP
To delete a table, click in the table, click the Table Tools Layout tab, click the Delete button in the Rows & Columns group, then click Delete Table.

4. **Type 5 in the Number of columns text box, press [Tab], type 6 in the Number of rows text box, make sure the Fixed column width option button is selected, then click OK**
   A blank table with five columns and six rows is inserted in the document. The insertion point is in the upper-left cell of the table, and the Table Tools Design tab becomes the active tab.
5. **Click the Home tab, click the Show/Hide ¶ button in the Paragraph group, type Disease in the first cell in the first row, press [Tab], type Vaccine, press [Tab], type Prophylaxis Drug, press [Tab], type Eat and Drink Safely, press [Tab], type Avoid Insects, then press [Tab]**
   Pressing [Tab] moves the insertion point to the next cell in the row or to the first cell in the next row.

QUICK TIP
You can also click in a cell to move the insertion point to it.

6. **Type Malaria, press [Tab][Tab], click the Bullets list arrow in the Paragraph group, click the check mark style, press [Tab][Tab], then click the Bullets button**
   The active bullet style changes to a check mark. A check mark is added to a cell when you click the Bullets button.

TROUBLE
If you pressed [Tab] after the last row, click the Undo button on the Quick Access toolbar to remove the blank row.

7. **Type the text shown in Figure E-12 in the table cells**
   Don't be concerned if the text wraps to the next line in a cell as you type because you will adjust the width of the columns later.
8. **Click the Table Tools Layout tab, click the AutoFit button in the Cell Size group, click AutoFit Contents, click the AutoFit button again, then click AutoFit Window**
   The width of the table columns is adjusted to fit the text and then the window.

QUICK TIP
You can also format table text using the buttons on the Mini toolbar or the Home tab.

9. **Click the Select button in the Table group, click Select Table, click the Align Center button in the Alignment group, click Disease in the table, click the Select button, click Select Column, click the Align Center Left button, then click in the table to deselect the column**
   The text in the table is centered in each cell, and then the text in the first column is left-aligned.
10. **Click the Table Tools Design tab, click the More button in the Table Styles group to expand the Table Styles gallery, click the Light List – Accent 3 style, then save your changes**
    The Light List - Accent 3 table style is applied to the table, as shown in Figure E-13. A table style includes format settings for the text, borders, and shading in a table.

FIGURE E-11: New section

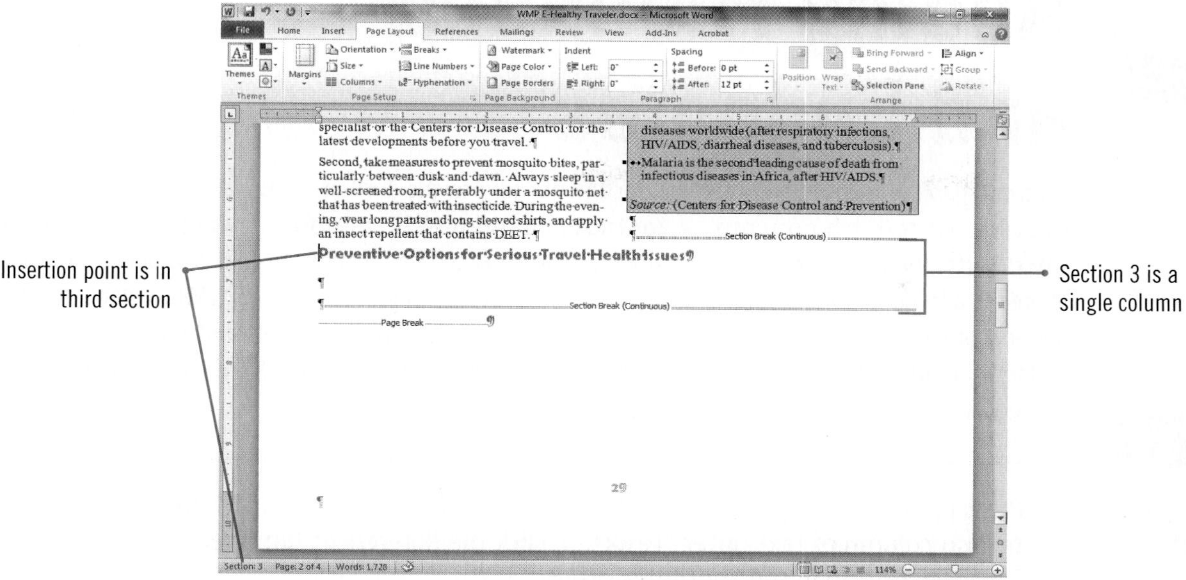

FIGURE E-12: Text in table

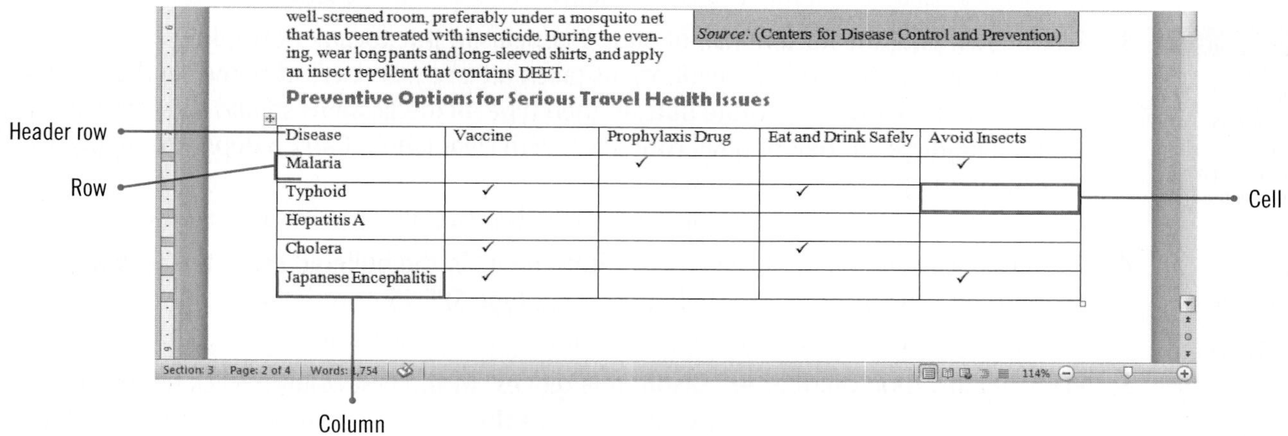

Disease	Vaccine	Prophylaxis Drug	Eat and Drink Safely	Avoid Insects
Malaria		✓		✓
Typhoid	✓		✓	
Hepatitis A	✓			
Cholera	✓		✓	
Japanese Encephalitis	✓			✓

FIGURE E-13: Completed table

Preventive Options for Serious Travel Health Issues

Disease	Vaccine	Prophylaxis Drug	Eat and Drink Safely	Avoid Insects
Malaria		✓		✓
Typhoid	✓		✓	
Hepatitis A	✓			
Cholera	✓		✓	
Japanese Encephalitis	✓			✓

Section: 3 Page: 2 of 4 Words: 1,754 114%

Word 2010

UNIT
E
Word 2010

Adding Footnotes and Endnotes

Footnotes and endnotes are used in documents to provide further information, explanatory text, or references for text in a document. A **footnote** or **endnote** is an explanatory note that consists of two linked parts: the note reference mark that appears next to text to indicate that additional information is offered in a footnote or endnote, and the corresponding footnote or endnote text. Word places footnotes at the end of each page and endnotes at the end of the document. You insert and manage footnotes and endnotes using the tools in the Footnotes group on the References tab. You add several footnotes to the report.

STEPS

TROUBLE
Scroll up as needed to see the note reference mark; then scroll down to see the footnote.

1. **Press [Ctrl][Home], place the insertion point at the end of the first body paragraph in the second column of text (after "resort."), click the References tab, then click the Insert Footnote button in the Footnotes group**

   A note reference mark, in this case a superscript 1, appears after "resort.", and the insertion point moves below a separator line at the bottom of the page. A note reference mark can be a number, a symbol, a character, or a combination of characters.

2. **Type Behavior is a critical factor, regardless of the quality of accommodations. For example, going outdoors in a malaria-endemic area could result in becoming infected with malaria.**

   The footnote text appears below the separator line at the bottom of page 1, as shown in Figure E-14.

QUICK TIP
To change the number format of the note reference mark or to use a symbol instead of a character, click the launcher in the Footnotes group, select from the options in the Footnote and Endnote dialog box, then click Apply.

3. **Scroll down until the bottom half of page 3 appears in the document window, place the insertion point at the end of "Medications taken on a regular basis at home" in the second column, click the Insert Footnote button, then type All medications should be stored in carry-on luggage, in their original containers with clear labels. Carry a duplicate supply in checked luggage.**

   The footnote text for the second footnote appears at the bottom of the second column on page 3.

4. **Place the insertion point at the end of "Sunscreen" in the bulleted list in the second column, click the Insert Footnote button, then type SPF 15 or greater.**

   The footnote text for the third footnote appears under the second footnote text at the bottom of page 3.

5. **Place the insertion point after "Disposable gloves" in the first column, click the Insert Footnote button, type At least two pairs., place the insertion point after "Scissors, safety pins, and tweezers" in the first column, click the Insert Footnote button, then type Pack these items in checked luggage.**

   Notice that when you inserted new footnotes between existing footnotes, Word automatically renumbered the footnotes. The new footnotes appear at the bottom of the first column on page 3, as shown in Figure E-15.

6. **Press [Ctrl][Home], then click the Next Footnote button in the Footnotes group**

   The insertion point moves to the first reference mark in the document.

QUICK TIP
To convert all footnotes to endnotes, click the launcher in the Footnotes group, click Convert, click OK, then click Close.

7. **Click the Next Footnote button, press [Delete] to select the number 2 reference mark, then press [Delete] again**

   The second reference mark and associated footnote are deleted from the document and the footnotes are renumbered automatically. You must select a reference mark to delete a footnote; you can not simply delete the footnote text itself.

8. **Press [Ctrl][Home], then save your changes**

FIGURE E-14: Footnote in the document

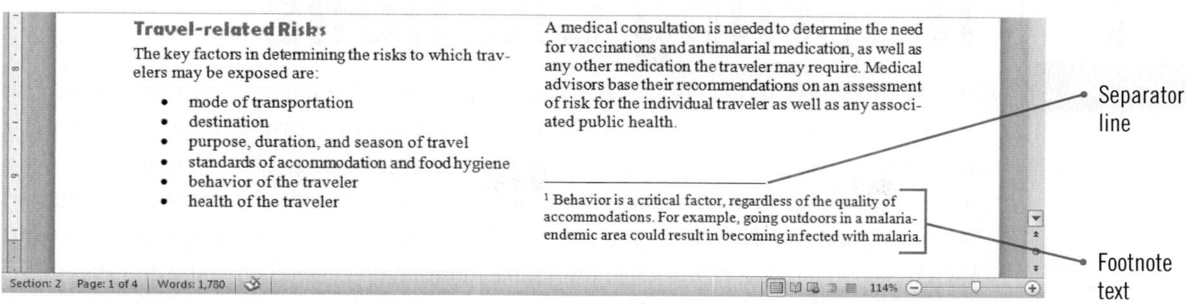

Travel-related Risks
The key factors in determining the risks to which travelers may be exposed are:
mode of transportation
destination
purpose, duration, and season of travel
standards of accommodation and food hygiene
behavior of the traveler
health of the traveler
A medical consultation is needed to determine the need for vaccinations and antimalarial medication, as well as any other medication the traveler may require. Medical advisors base their recommendations on an assessment of risk for the individual traveler as well as any associated public health.
1 Behavior is a critical factor, regardless of the quality of accommodations. For example, going outdoors in a malaria-endemic area could result in becoming infected with malaria.
Section: 2 Page: 1 of 4 Words: 1,780
114%
Separator line
Footnote text

FIGURE E-15: Renumbered footnotes in the document

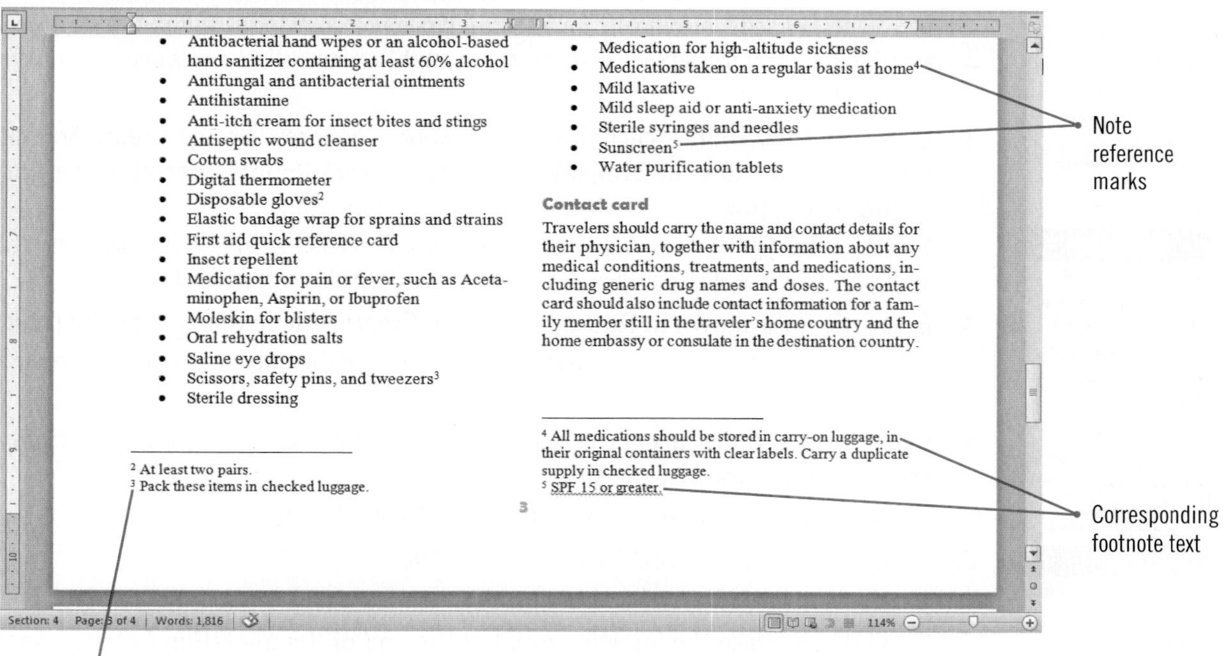

Antibacterial hand wipes or an alcohol-based hand sanitizer containing at least 60% alcohol
Antifungal and antibacterial ointments
Antihistamine
Anti-itch cream for insect bites and stings
Antiseptic wound cleanser
Cotton swabs
Digital thermometer
Disposable gloves2
Elastic bandage wrap for sprains and strains
First aid quick reference card
Insect repellent
Medication for pain or fever, such as Acetaminophen, Aspirin, or Ibuprofen
Moleskin for blisters
Oral rehydration salts
Saline eye drops
Scissors, safety pins, and tweezers3
Sterile dressing
2 At least two pairs.
3 Pack these items in checked luggage.
Medication for high-altitude sickness
Medications taken on a regular basis at home4
Mild laxative
Mild sleep aid or anti-anxiety medication
Sterile syringes and needles
Sunscreen5
Water purification tablets
Contact card
Travelers should carry the name and contact details for their physician, together with information about any medical conditions, treatments, and medications, including generic drug names and doses. The contact card should also include contact information for a family member still in the traveler's home country and the home embassy or consulate in the destination country.
4 All medications should be stored in carry-on luggage, in their original containers with clear labels. Carry a duplicate supply in checked luggage.
5 SPF 15 or greater.
3
Section: 4 Page: 3 of 4 Words: 1,816
114%
Note reference marks
Corresponding footnote text
Notes are renumbered when a new note is added

UNIT
E
Word 2010

Inserting Citations

The Word References feature allows you to keep track of the reference sources you consult when writing research papers, reports, and other documents, and makes it easy to insert a citation in a document. A **citation** is a parenthetical reference in the document text that gives credit to the source for a quotation or other information used in a document. Citations usually include the name of the author and, for print sources, a page number. When you insert a citation you can use an existing source or create a new source. Each time you create a new source, the source information is saved on your computer so that it is available for use in any document. The report already includes two citations. You add several more citations to the report.

STEPS

1. **Place the insertion point after "people travel" but before the period at the end of the first paragraph in the first column of text, click the Style list arrow in the Citations & Bibliography group, then click APA Fifth Edition**

   You will format the sources and citations in the report using the style recommended by the American Psychological Association (APA).

2. **Click the Insert Citation button in the Citations & Bibliography group**

   A list of the sources already used in the document opens. You can choose to cite one of these sources, create a new source, or add a placeholder for a source. When you add a new citation to a document, the source is added to the list of master sources that is stored on the computer. The new source is also associated with the document.

3. **Click Add New Source, click the Type of Source list arrow in the Create Source dialog box, scroll down to view the available source types, click Report, then click the Corporate Author check box**

   You select the type of source and enter the source information in the Create Source dialog box. The fields available in the dialog box change, depending on the type of source selected.

4. **Enter the data shown in Figure E-16 in the Create Source dialog box, then click OK**

   The citation (World Tourism Organization, 2012) appears at the end of the paragraph. Because the source is a print publication, it needs to include a page number.

5. **Click the citation to select it, click the Citation Options list arrow on the right side of the citation, then click Edit Citation**

   The Edit Citation dialog box opens, as shown in Figure E-17.

6. **Type 19 in the Pages text box, then click OK**

   The page number 19 is added to the citation.

7. **Scroll down, place the insertion point at the end of the quotation (after ...consequences.), click the Insert Citation button, click Add New Source, enter the information shown in Figure E-18, then click OK**

   A citation for the Web publication from where the quotation was taken is added to the report. No page number is used in this citation because the source is a Web site.

8. **Scroll to the bottom of page 2, click under the table, type Source:, italicize Source:, click after Source:, click the Insert Citation button, then click Johnson, Margaret in the list of sources**

   The citation (Johnson) appears under the table.

9. **Click the citation, click the Citation Options list arrow, click Edit Citation, type 55 in the Pages text box, click OK, then save your changes**

   The page number 55 is added to the citation.

QUICK TIP
When you create a new source for a document, it appears automatically in the bibliography when you generate it.

QUICK TIP
Only sources that you associate with a document stay with the document when you move it to another computer. The master list of sources remains on the computer where it was created.

QUICK TIP
You can also choose to add or remove the author, year, or title from a citation.

FIGURE E-16: Adding a Report source

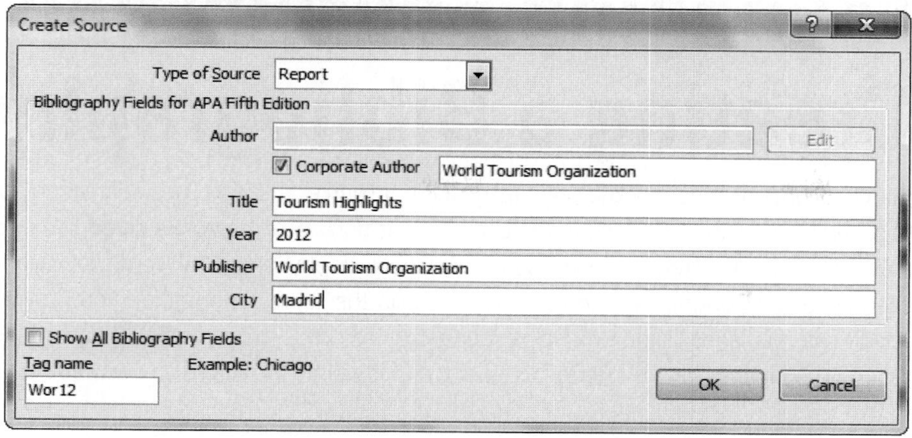

Word 2010

FIGURE E-17: Edit Citation dialog box

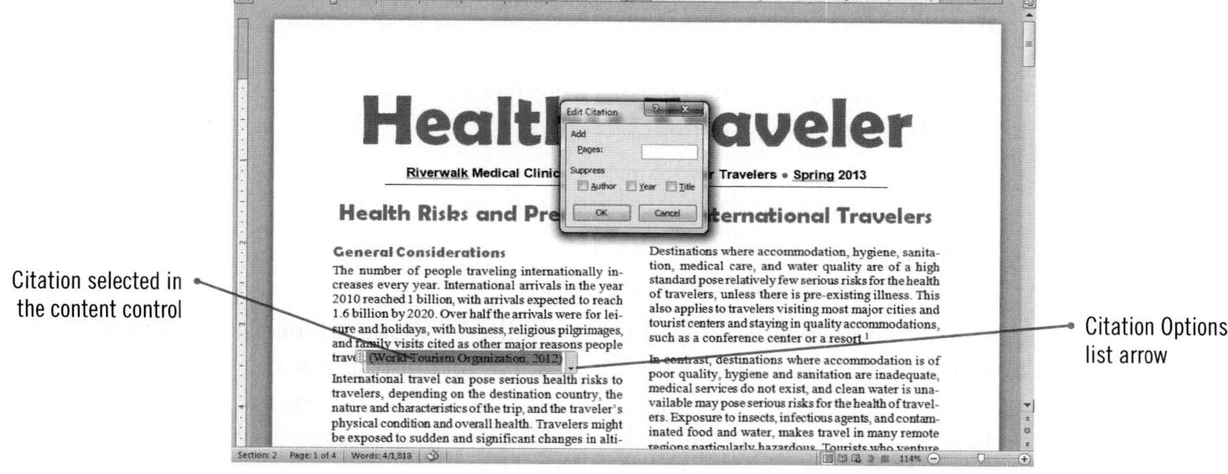

FIGURE E-18: Adding a Web publication source

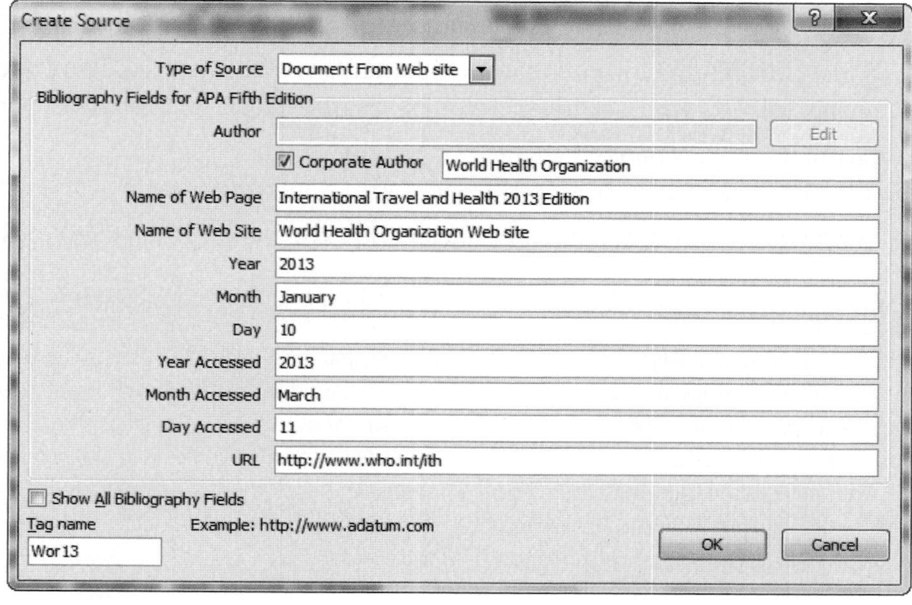

UNIT
E
Word 2010

Managing Sources and Creating a Bibliography

Many documents require a **bibliography**, a list of sources that you used in creating the document. The list of sources can include only the works cited in your document (a **works cited** list) or both the works cited and the works consulted (a bibliography). The Bibliography feature in Word allows you to generate a works cited list or a bibliography automatically based on the source information you provide for the document. The Source Manager dialog box helps you to organize your sources. You add a bibliography to the report. The bibliography is inserted as a field, and it can be formatted any way you choose.

STEPS

QUICK TIP
You must copy sources from the Master List to the Current List for the sources to be available when you open the document on another computer.

1. **Press [Ctrl][End] to move the insertion point to the end of the document, then click the Manage Sources button in the Citations & Bibliography group**

   The Source Manager dialog box opens, as shown in Figure E-19. The Master List shows the sources available on your computer. The Current List shows the sources available in the current document. A check mark next to a source indicates the source is cited in the document. You use the tools in the Source Manager dialog box to add, edit, and delete sources from the lists, and to copy sources between the Master List and the Current List. The sources that appear in the Current List are the sources that will appear in the bibliography.

2. **Click the Baker, Mary source in the Current List**

   A preview of the citation and bibliographical entry for the source in MLA style appears in the Preview box. You do not want this source to be included in your bibliography for the report.

3. **Click Delete**

   The source is removed from the Current List.

4. **Click Close, click the Bibliography button in the Citations & Bibliography group, click Bibliography, then scroll up to see the heading Bibliography at the top of the field**

   A Bibliography field is added at the location of the insertion point. The bibliography includes all the sources associated with the document, formatted in the MLA style for bibliographies. The text in the Bibliography field is formatted with the default styles. You want to format the text to match the rest of the report.

TROUBLE
Don't be concerned if the list of sources becomes gray when you select the heading Bibliography. This simply indicates the Bibliography field is active. Text that is selected is highlighted in blue.

5. **Select Bibliography; apply the following formats: Berlin Sans FB Demi, bold, and the Blue, Accent 1 font color; drag down the list of sources to select the entire list and change the font size to 11; then click outside the bibliography to deselect it**

   The format of the bibliography text now matches the rest of the report.

6. **Press [Ctrl][End], type your name, click the View tab, then click Two Pages**

   Completed pages 3 and 4 of the report are shown in the document window, as shown in Figure E-20.

7. **Scroll up to view pages 1 and 2**

   Completed pages 1 and 2 are shown in Figure E-21.

8. **Save your changes, submit your document, close the file, then exit Word**

Working with Web sources

Publications found on the Web can be challenging to document. Many Web sites can be accessed under multiple domains, and URLs change frequently or are so long that they cannot be typed easily. In addition, electronic publications are often updated frequently, making each visit to a Web site potentially unique. For these reasons, it's best to rely on the author, title, and publication information for a Web publication when citing it as a source in a research document. If possible, you can include a URL as supplementary information only, along with the date the Web site was last updated and the date you accessed the site. Whatever format you use for citing Web publications, it's important to be consistent throughout your document. Since Web sites are often removed, it's also a good idea to download or print any Web source you use so that it can be verified later.

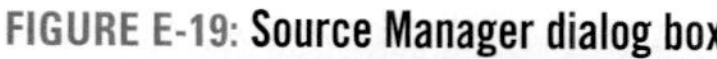
FIGURE E-19: Source Manager dialog box

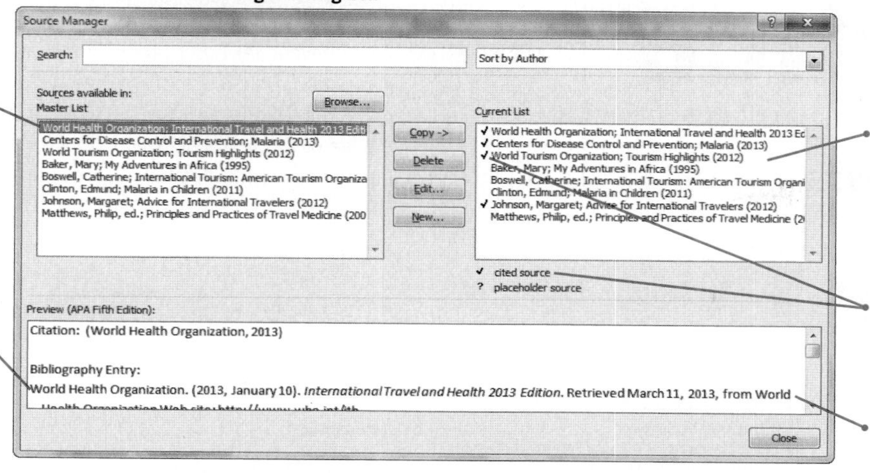

FIGURE E-20: Completed pages 3 and 4

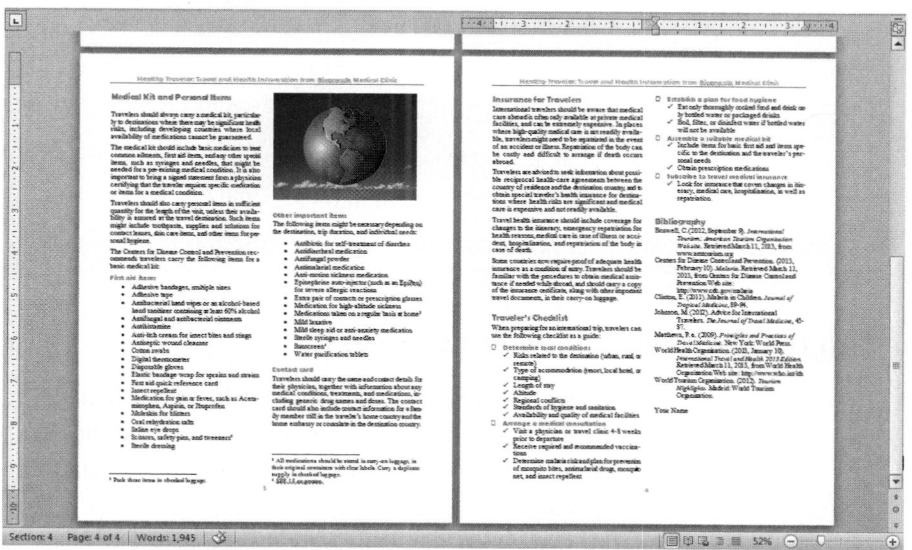

FIGURE E-21: Completed pages 1 and 2

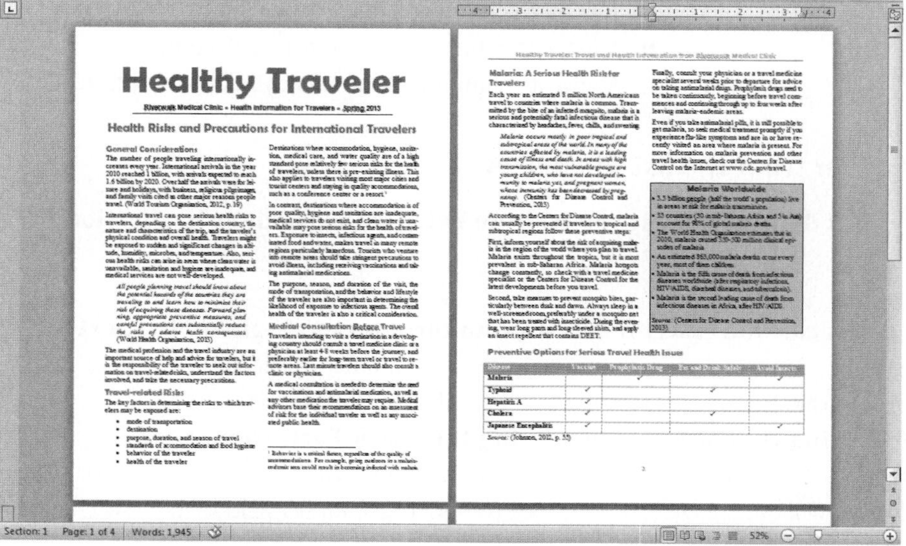

Practice

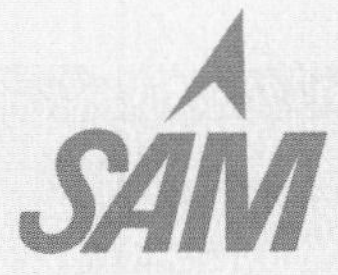
SAM

For current SAM information, including versions and content details, visit SAM Central (http://www.cengage.com/samcentral). If you have a SAM user profile, you may have access to hands-on instruction, practice, and assessment of the skills covered in this unit. Since various versions of SAM are supported throughout the life of this text, check with your instructor for the correct instructions and URL/Web site for accessing assignments.

Concepts Review

Label each element shown in Figure E-22.

FIGURE E-22

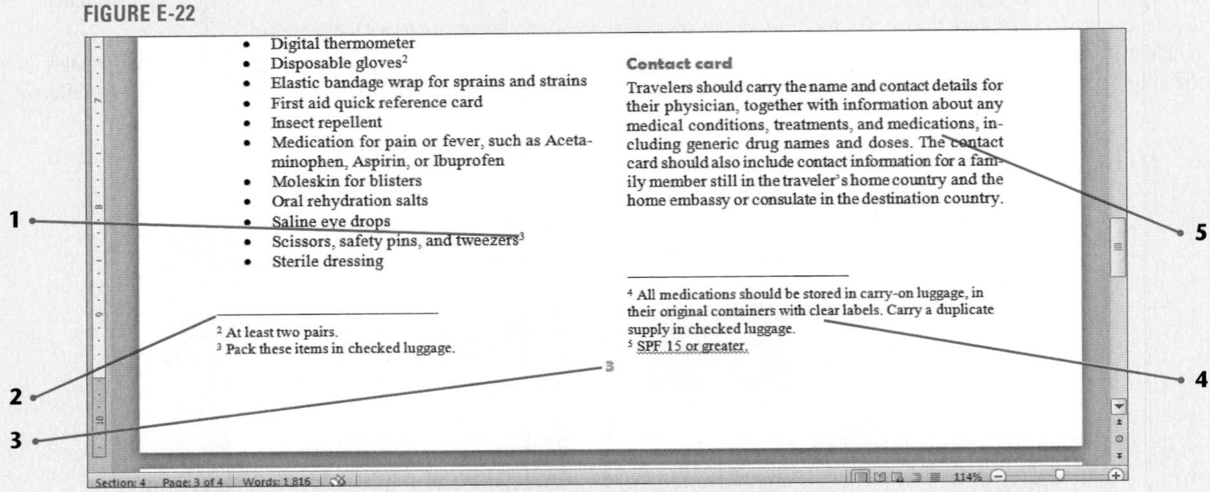

Digital thermometer
Disposable gloves2
Elastic bandage wrap for sprains and strains
First aid quick reference card
Insect repellent
Medication for pain or fever, such as Acetaminophen, Aspirin, or Ibuprofen
Moleskin for blisters
Oral rehydration salts
Saline eye drops
Scissors, safety pins, and tweezers3
Sterile dressing
2 At least two pairs.
3 Pack these items in checked luggage.
Contact card
Travelers should carry the name and contact details for their physician, together with information about any medical conditions, treatments, and medications, including generic drug names and doses. The contact card should also include contact information for a family member still in the traveler's home country and the home embassy or consulate in the destination country.
4 All medications should be stored in carry-on luggage, in their original containers with clear labels. Carry a duplicate supply in checked luggage.
5 SPF 15 or greater.
1
2
3
4
5
Section: 4
Page: 3 of 4
Words: 1,816
114%

Match each term with the statement that best describes it.

6. **Table**
7. **Manual page break**
8. **Section break**
9. **Footer**
10. **Header**
11. **Citation**
12. **Field**
13. **Margin**
14. **Bibliography**

- **a.** A parenthetical reference in the document text that gives credit to a source
- **b.** The blank area between the edge of the text and the edge of the page
- **c.** A formatting mark that divides a document into parts that can be formatted differently
- **d.** Text or graphics that appear at the bottom of every page in a document
- **e.** A placeholder for information that changes
- **f.** A formatting mark that forces the text following the mark to begin at the top of the next page
- **g.** Text or graphics that appear at the top of every page in a document
- **h.** A list of the sources used to create a document
- **i.** A grid of columns and rows that you can fill with text and graphics

Select the best answer from the list of choices.

15. Which type of break do you insert if you want to balance the columns in a section?

- **a.** Manual page break
- **b.** Text wrapping break
- **c.** Column break
- **d.** Continuous section break

16. Which type of break can you insert if you want to force text to begin on the next page?

- **a.** Text wrapping break
- **b.** Next page section break
- **c.** Automatic page break
- **d.** Continuous section break

17. Which of the following cannot be inserted using the Quick Parts command?

- **a.** Document property
- **b.** AutoText building block
- **c.** Page break
- **d.** Page number field

18. Which of the following do documents with mirror margins always have?

a. Inside and outside margins
b. Different first page headers and footers
c. Gutters
d. Landscape orientation

19. What name describes formatted pieces of content that are stored in galleries?

a. Field
b. Header
c. Property
d. Building Block

20. Which appears at the end of a document?

a. Citation
b. Endnote
c. Footnote
d. Page break

Skills Review

1. Set document margins.

a. Start Word, open the file WMP E-2.docx from the drive and folder where you store your Data Files, then save it as **WMP E-Elmwood Fitness**.

b. Change the top and bottom margin settings to Moderate: 1" top and bottom, and .75" left and right.

c. Save your changes to the document.

2. Create sections and columns.

a. Turn on the display of formatting marks, then customize the status bar to display sections if they are not displayed already.

b. Insert a continuous section break before the **Welcome to the Elmwood Fitness Center** heading.

c. Format the text in section 2 in two columns, then save your changes to the document.

3. Insert page breaks.

a. Scroll to page 3, then insert a manual page break before the heading **Facilities and Services**.

b. Scroll down and insert a manual page break before the heading **Membership**, then press [Ctrl][Home].

c. On page 1, select the heading **Welcome to the Elmwood Fitness Center** and the paragraph mark below it, use the Columns button to format the selected text as one column, then center the heading on the page.

d. Follow the direction in Step c to format the heading **Facilities and Services** and the paragraph mark below it on page 3, and the heading **Membership** and the paragraph mark below it on page 4, as one column, with centered text, then save your changes to the document.

4. Insert page numbers.

a. Insert page numbers in the document at the bottom of the page. Select the Plain Number 2 page number style from the gallery.

b. Close the Footer area, scroll through the document to view the page number on each page, then save your changes to the document.

5. Add headers and footers.

a. Double-click the margin at the top of a page to open the Header and Footer areas.

b. With the insertion point in the Header area, click the Quick Parts button in the Insert Group on the Header & Footer Tools Design tab, point to Document Property, then click Author.

c. Replace the text in the Author content control with your name, press [End] to move the insertion point out of the content control, then press [Spacebar]. (*Note*: If your name does not appear in the header, right-click the Author content control, click Remove Content Control, then type your name in the header.)

d. Click the Insert Alignment Tab button in the Position group, select the Right option button and keep the alignment relative to the margin, then click OK in the dialog box to move the insertion point to the right margin.

e. Use the Insert Date and Time command in the Insert group to insert the current date using a format of your choice as static text. (*Hint*: Be sure the Update automatically check box is not checked.)

f. Apply italic to the text in the header.

g. Move the insertion point to the Footer area.

h. Double-click the page number to select it, then format the page number in bold and italic.

Skills Review (continued)

- **i.** Move the insertion point to the header on page 1 if it is not already there, use the Header & Footer Tools Design tab to create a different header and footer for the first page of the document, type your name in the First Page Header area, then apply italic to your name.
- **j.** Close headers and footers, scroll to view the header and footer on each page, then save your changes to the document.

6. Insert a table.

- **a.** On page 4, double-click the word Table to select it at the end of the Membership Rates section, press [Delete], open the Insert Table dialog box, then create a table with two columns and five rows.
- **b.** Apply the purple Light List - Accent 4 table style to the table.
- **c.** Press [Tab] to leave the first cell in the header row blank, then type **Rate**.
- **d.** Press [Tab], then type the following text in the table, pressing [Tab] to move from cell to cell.

Enrollment/Individual	$100
Enrollment/Couple	$150
Monthly membership/Individual	$35
Monthly membership/Couple	$60

- **e.** With the insertion point in the table, right-click the table, use the AutoFit command to select the AutoFit to Contents option, and then select the AutoFit to Window option. (*Note*: In this case AutoFit to Window fits the table to the width of the column of text.)
- **f.** Save your changes to the document.

7. Add footnotes and endnotes.

- **a.** Press [Ctrl[Home], scroll down, place the insertion point at the end of the first body paragraph, insert a footnote, then type **People who are active live longer and feel better.**
- **b.** Place the insertion point at the end of the first paragraph under the Benefits of Exercise heading, insert a footnote, then type **There are 1,440 minutes in every day. Schedule 30 of them for physical activity.**
- **c.** Place the insertion point at the end of the first paragraph under the Tips for Staying Motivated heading, insert a footnote, type **Always consult your physician before beginning an exercise program.**, then save your changes.

8. Insert citations.

- **a.** Place the insertion point at the end of the second paragraph under the Benefits of Exercise heading (after "down from 52% in 2010" but before the period), then change the style for citations and bibliography to APA Fifth Edition.
- **b.** Insert a citation, add a new source, enter the source information shown in the Create Source dialog box in Figure E-23, then click OK.

FIGURE E-23

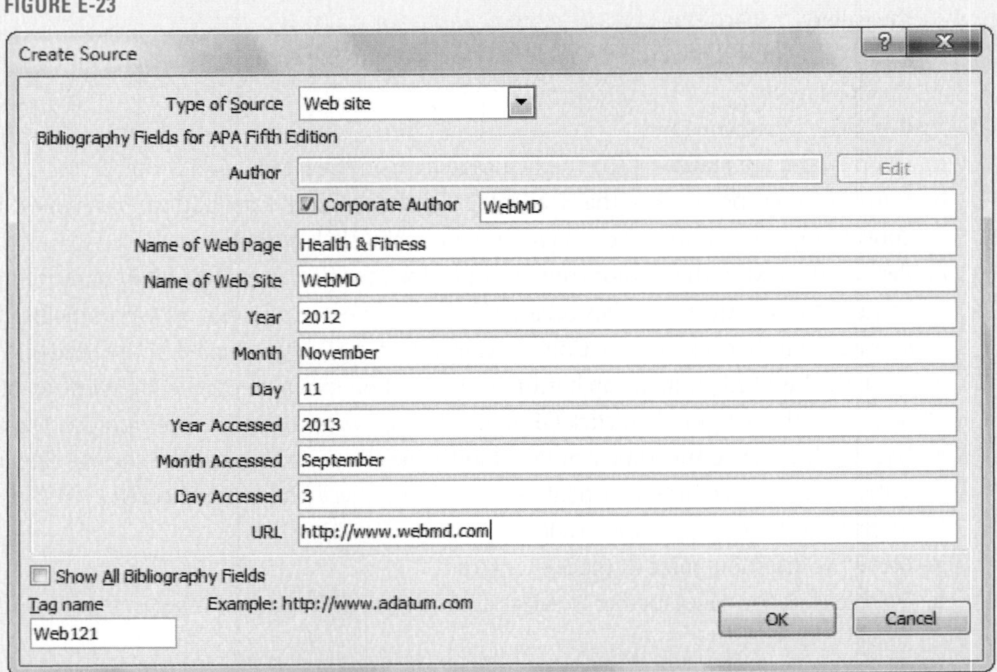

c. Place the insertion point at the end of the italicized quotation in the second column of text, insert a citation, then select Jason, Laura from the list of sources.

d. Edit the citation to include the page number **25**.

e. Scroll to page 2, place the insertion point at the end of the "Be a morning exerciser" paragraph but before the ending period, insert a citation for WebMD, then save your changes.

9. Manage sources and create a bibliography.

a. Press [Ctrl][End], then open the Source Manager dialog box.

b. Select the source Health, National Institute of in the Current List, click Edit, click the Corporate Author check box, edit the entry so it reads **National Institutes of Health**, click OK, click Yes if prompted, then click Close.

c. Insert a bibliography.

d. Select Bibliography, then change the font to 14-point Tahoma with a black font color. Pages 1 and 4 of the formatted document are shown in Figure E-24.

e. Save your changes to the document, submit it to your instructor, then close the document and exit Word.

FIGURE E-24

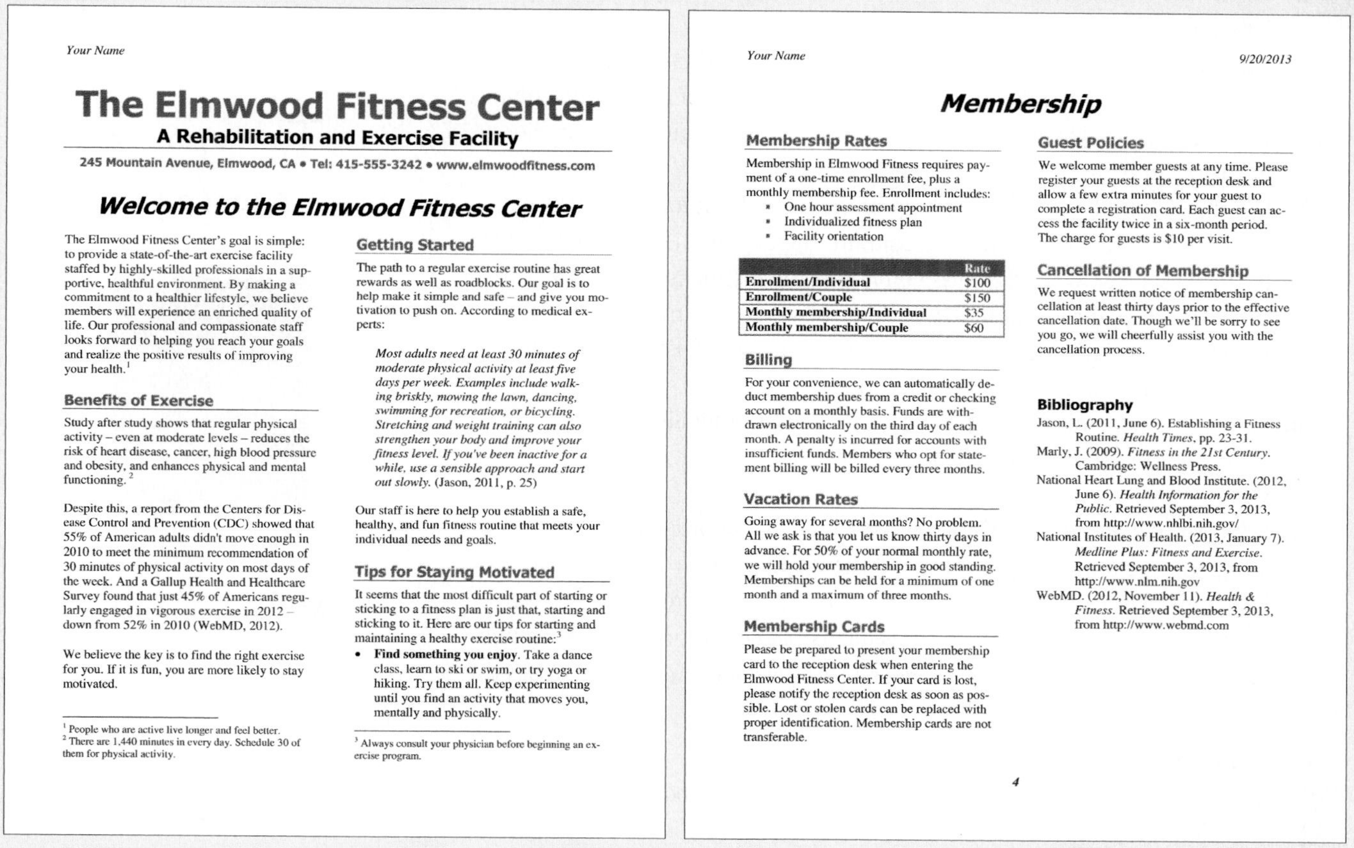

Your Name

The Elmwood Fitness Center

A Rehabilitation and Exercise Facility

245 Mountain Avenue, Elmwood, CA • Tel: 415-555-3242 • www.elmwoodfitness.com

Welcome to the Elmwood Fitness Center

The Elmwood Fitness Center's goal is simple: to provide a state-of-the-art exercise facility staffed by highly-skilled professionals in a supportive, healthful environment. By making a commitment to a healthier lifestyle, we believe members will experience an enriched quality of life. Our professional and compassionate staff looks forward to helping you reach your goals and realize the positive results of improving your health.[1]

Benefits of Exercise

Study after study shows that regular physical activity – even at moderate levels – reduces the risk of heart disease, cancer, high blood pressure and obesity, and enhances physical and mental functioning.[2]

Despite this, a report from the Centers for Disease Control and Prevention (CDC) showed that 55% of American adults didn't move enough in 2010 to meet the minimum recommendation of 30 minutes of physical activity on most days of the week. And a Gallup Health and Healthcare Survey found that just 45% of Americans regularly engaged in vigorous exercise in 2012 – down from 52% in 2010 (WebMD, 2012).

We believe the key is to find the right exercise for you. If it is fun, you are more likely to stay motivated.

[1] People who are active live longer and feel better.
[2] There are 1,440 minutes in every day. Schedule 30 of them for physical activity.

Getting Started

The path to a regular exercise routine has great rewards as well as roadblocks. Our goal is to help make it simple and safe – and give you motivation to push on. According to medical experts:

> *Most adults need at least 30 minutes of moderate physical activity at least five days per week. Examples include walking briskly, mowing the lawn, dancing, swimming for recreation, or bicycling. Stretching and weight training can also strengthen your body and improve your fitness level. If you've been inactive for a while, use a sensible approach and start out slowly.* (Jason, 2011, p. 25)

Our staff is here to help you establish a safe, healthy, and fun fitness routine that meets your individual needs and goals.

Tips for Staying Motivated

It seems that the most difficult part of starting or sticking to a fitness plan is just that, starting and sticking to it. Here are our tips for starting and maintaining a healthy exercise routine:[3]

- **Find something you enjoy**. Take a dance class, learn to ski or swim, or try yoga or hiking. Try them all. Keep experimenting until you find an activity that moves you, mentally and physically.

[3] Always consult your physician before beginning an exercise program.

Your Name *9/20/2013*

Membership

Membership Rates

Membership in Elmwood Fitness requires payment of a one-time enrollment fee, plus a monthly membership fee. Enrollment includes:

- One hour assessment appointment
- Individualized fitness plan
- Facility orientation

	Rate
Enrollment/Individual	$100
Enrollment/Couple	$150
Monthly membership/Individual	$35
Monthly membership/Couple	$60

Billing

For your convenience, we can automatically deduct membership dues from a credit or checking account on a monthly basis. Funds are withdrawn electronically on the third day of each month. A penalty is incurred for accounts with insufficient funds. Members who opt for statement billing will be billed every three months.

Vacation Rates

Going away for several months? No problem. All we ask is that you let us know thirty days in advance. For 50% of your normal monthly rate, we will hold your membership in good standing. Memberships can be held for a minimum of one month and a maximum of three months.

Membership Cards

Please be prepared to present your membership card to the reception desk when entering the Elmwood Fitness Center. If your card is lost, please notify the reception desk as soon as possible. Lost or stolen cards can be replaced with proper identification. Membership cards are not transferable.

Guest Policies

We welcome member guests at any time. Please register your guests at the reception desk and allow a few extra minutes for your guest to complete a registration card. Each guest can access the facility twice in a six-month period. The charge for guests is $10 per visit.

Cancellation of Membership

We request written notice of membership cancellation at least thirty days prior to the effective cancellation date. Though we'll be sorry to see you go, we will cheerfully assist you with the cancellation process.

Bibliography

Jason, L. (2011, June 6). Establishing a Fitness Routine. *Health Times*, pp. 23-31.

Marly, J. (2009). *Fitness in the 21st Century*. Cambridge: Wellness Press.

National Heart Lung and Blood Institute. (2012, June 6). *Health Information for the Public*. Retrieved September 3, 2013, from http://www.nhlbi.nih.gov/

National Institutes of Health. (2013, January 7). *Medline Plus: Fitness and Exercise*. Retrieved September 3, 2013, from http://www.nlm.nih.gov

WebMD. (2012, November 11). *Health & Fitness*. Retrieved September 3, 2013, from http://www.webmd.com

4

Independent Challenge 1

You are the owner of the Muscular Therapy Center, which offers a variety of massage services to clients. You have begun work on the text for a brochure advertising your business and are now ready to lay out the pages and prepare the final copy. The brochure will be printed on both sides of an 8½" × 11" sheet of paper, and folded in thirds.

a. Start Word, open the file WMP E-3.docx from the drive and folder where you store your Data Files, then save it as **WMP E-Massage Brochure**. Read the document to get a feel for its contents.
b. Change the page orientation to landscape, and change all four margins to .5".
c. Format the document in three columns of equal width.
d. On page 2, insert a next page section break before the heading **Welcome to the Muscular Therapy Center**.
e. On page 1, insert column breaks before the headings **Menu of Massage Services** and **Shiatsu Massage**.
f. Change the column spacing in section 1 (which is the first page) to .4", then add lines between the columns on the first page.
g. Double-click the bottom margin to open the footer area, create a different header and footer for the first page, then type **A variety of choices to meet your needs.** in the First Page Footer - Section 1- area.
h. Center the text in the footer area, format it in 14-point Papyrus, all caps, bold, with an Olive Green, Accent 3, Darker 50% font color, then close headers and footers.
i. On page 2, insert a column break before Your Name, then press [Enter] 21 times to move the contact information to the bottom of the second column.
j. Replace Your Name with your name, then center the contact information in the column.
k. Insert a column break at the bottom of the second column. Type the text shown in Figure E-25 in the third column, then apply the No Spacing style to the text. Refer to the figure as you follow the instructions for formatting the text in the third column. (*Hint*: Remove any hyperlinks that appear.)
l. Format Therapeutic Massage in 28-point Papyrus, bold. Format Muscular Therapy Center in 20-point Papyrus bold.
m. Format the remaining text in 14-point Papyrus. Center all the text in the third column, then change the font color to Olive Green, Accent 3, Darker 50%.
n. Insert the clip art graphic shown in Figure E-25 or another appropriate clip art graphic. Do not wrap text around the graphic. Apply the Soft Edge Rectangle picture style to the graphic. (*Hint*: Use the search term massage.)
o. Resize the graphic and add or remove blank paragraphs in the third column of your brochure so that the spacing between elements roughly matches the spacing shown in Figure E-25.

FIGURE E-25

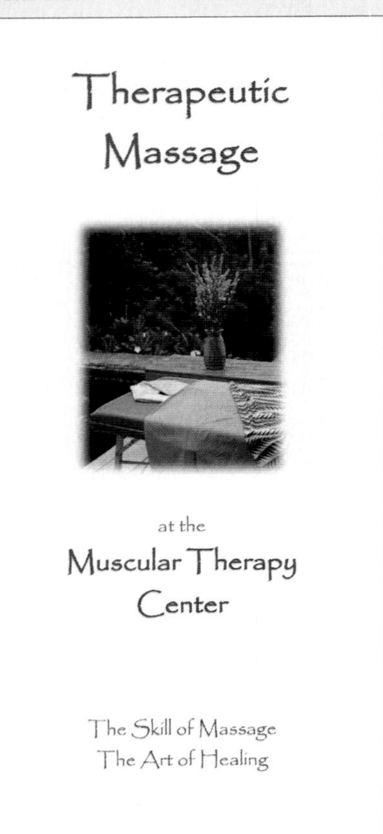

Therapeutic
Massage
at the
Muscular Therapy
Center
The Skill of Massage
The Art of Healing

Advanced Challenge Exercise

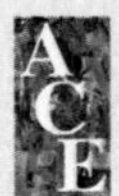

- Insert a different appropriate clip art graphic at the bottom of the first column on page 2.
- Apply text wrapping to the graphic, then resize the graphic and position it so it enhances the design of the brochure.
- Apply a suitable picture style or picture effect to the graphic.

p. Save your changes, then submit a copy to your instructor. If possible, you can print the brochure with the two pages back to back so that the brochure can be folded in thirds.
q. Close the document and exit Word.

Independent Challenge 2

You work in the Campus Safety Department at Pacific State University Hospital. You have written the text for an informational flyer about parking regulations on the hospital campus, and now you need to format the flyer so it is attractive and readable.

a. Start Word, open the file WMP E-4.docx from the drive and folder where you store your Data Files, then save it as **WMP E-Parking FAQ**. Read the document to get a feel for its contents.

b. Change all four margins to .7".

c. Insert a continuous section break before **1. May I drive a car to work at the hospital?** (*Hint*: Place the insertion point before May.)

d. Scroll down and insert a next page section break before **Sample Parking Permit**.

e. Format the text in section 2 in three columns of equal width with .3" of space between the columns.

f. Hyphenate the document using the automatic hyphenation feature. (*Hint*: Use the Hyphenation button in the Page Setup group on the Page Layout tab.)

g. Add a 3-point dotted-line bottom border to the blank paragraph under Pacific State University Hospital (PSUH). (*Hint*: Place the insertion point before the paragraph mark under Pacific State University Hospital...)

h. Open the Header area, and insert your name in the header. Right-align your name, and format it in 10-point Arial.

i. Add the following text to the footer, inserting symbols between words as indicated: **Parking and Shuttle Service Office • 54 Buckley Street • PSUH • 942-555-2227**. (*Hint*: Click the Symbol command in the Symbols group on the Insert tab to insert a symbol.)

j. Format the footer text in 9-point Arial Black, and center it in the footer.

k. Apply a 3-point dotted-line border above the footer text. Make sure to apply the border to the paragraph.

l. Add a continuous section break at the end of section 2 to balance the columns in section 2.

m. Add the clip art graphic shown in Figure E-26 (or another appropriate clip art graphic) to the upper-right corner of the document, above the border. Make sure the graphic does not obscure the border. (*Hint*: Apply text wrapping to the graphic before positioning it.)

n. Place the insertion point on page 2 (which is section 4). Change the page orientation of section 4 to landscape.

o. Change the vertical alignment of section 4 to center. (*Hint*: Use the Vertical Alignment list arrow on the Layout tab in the Page Setup dialog box.)

p. Apply an appropriate table style to the table, such as the style shown in Figure E-27. (*Hint*: Check and uncheck the options in the Table Style Options group on the Table Tools Design tab to customize the style so it enhances the table data.)

q. Save your changes, submit your work, close the document, then exit Word.

FIGURE E-26

Frequently Asked Questions

Parking & Shuttle Service Office

Pacific State University Hospital (PSUH)

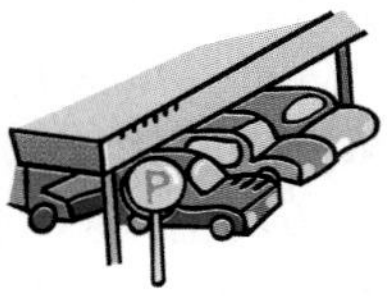

FIGURE E-27

Sample Parking Permit

Pacific State University Hospital **Office of Parking and Shuttle Service** 2013-14 Parking Permit	
License number:	VA 498 359
Make:	Subaru
Model:	Forester
Year:	2011
Color:	Blue
Permit Issue Date:	September 8, 2013
Permit Expiration Date:	September 7, 2014
Restrictions: ***Parking is permitted in the Pacific State University Hospital Greene Street lot 24 hours a day, 7 days a week. Shuttle service is available from the Greene Street lot to the hospital and other campus locations from 6 a.m. to 11 p.m. Monday through Friday. Parking is also permitted in any on-campus lot from 4:30 p.m. Friday to midnight Sunday.***	

Independent Challenge 3

A book publisher would like to publish an article you wrote on stormwater pollution in Australia as a chapter in a forthcoming book called *Environmental Issues for the New Millennium*. The publisher has requested that you format your article like a book chapter before submitting it for publication, and has provided you with a style sheet. According to the style sheet, the citations and bibliography should be formatted in Chicago style. You have already created the sources for the chapter, but you need to insert the citations.

a. Start Word, open the file WMP E-5.docx from the drive and folder where you store your Data Files, then save it as **WMP E-Chapter 7**.

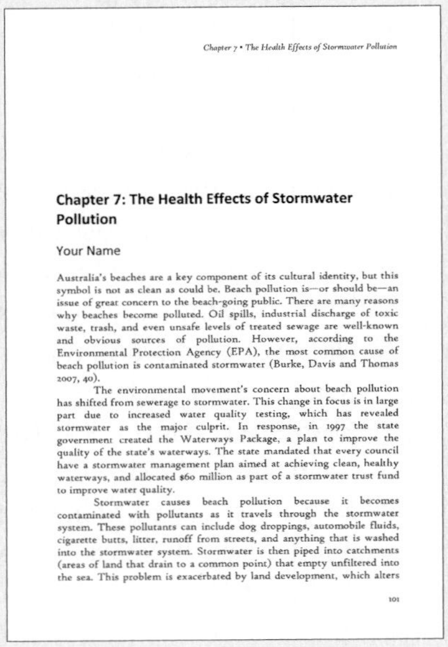

b. Change the font of the entire document to 11-point High Tower Text. If this font is not available to you, select a different font suitable for the pages of a book. Change the alignment to justified.

c. Change the paper size to 6" × 9".

d. Create mirror margins. (*Hint*: Use the Multiple pages list arrow.) Change the top and bottom margins to .8", change the inside margin to .4", change the outside margin to .6", and create a .3" gutter to allow room for the book's binding.

e. Change the Zoom level to Page Width, open the Header and Footer areas, then apply the setting to create different headers and footers for odd- and even-numbered pages.

f. In the odd-page header, type **Chapter 7**, insert a small square symbol, then type **The Health Effects of Stormwater Pollution**.

g. Format the header text in 9-point High Tower Text italic, then right-align the text.

h. In the even-page header, type your name.

i. Format the header text in 9-point High Tower Text italic. The even-page header should be left-aligned.

j. Insert a left-aligned page number field in the even-page footer area, format it in 10-point High Tower Text, insert a right-aligned page number field in the odd-page footer area, then format it in 10-point High Tower Text.

k. Format the page numbers so that the first page of your chapter, which is Chapter 7 in the book, begins on page 101. (*Hint*: Select a page number field, click the Page Number button, then click Format Page Numbers.)

l. Go to the beginning of the document, press [Enter] 10 times, type **Chapter 7: The Health Effects of Stormwater Pollution**, press [Enter] twice, type your name, then press [Enter] twice.

m. Format the chapter title in 16-point Calibri bold, format your name in 14-point Calibri, then left-align the title text and your name.

n. Click the References tab, make sure the citations and bibliography style is set to Chicago Fifteenth Edition, place the insertion point at the end of the first body paragraph on page 1 but before the ending period, insert a citation for Alice Burke, et. al., then add the page number 40 to the citation, as shown in Figure E-28.

o. Add the citations listed in Table E-3 to the document using the sources already associated with the document.

FIGURE E-28

Chapter 7 ▪ The Health Effects of Stormwater Pollution

Chapter 7: The Health Effects of Stormwater Pollution

Your Name

Australia's beaches are a key component of its cultural identity, but this symbol is not as clean as could be. Beach pollution is—or should be—an issue of great concern to the beach-going public. There are many reasons why beaches become polluted. Oil spills, industrial discharge of toxic waste, trash, and even unsafe levels of treated sewage are well-known and obvious sources of pollution. However, according to the Environmental Protection Agency (EPA), the most common cause of beach pollution is contaminated stormwater (Burke, Davis and Thomas 2007, 40).

The environmental movement's concern about beach pollution has shifted from sewerage to stormwater. This change in focus is in large part due to increased water quality testing, which has revealed stormwater as the major culprit. In response, in 1997 the state government created the Waterways Package, a plan to improve the quality of the state's waterways. The state mandated that every council have a stormwater management plan aimed at achieving clean, healthy waterways, and allocated $60 million as part of a stormwater trust fund to improve water quality.

Stormwater causes beach pollution because it becomes contaminated with pollutants as it travels through the stormwater system. These pollutants can include dog droppings, automobile fluids, cigarette butts, litter, runoff from streets, and anything that is washed into the stormwater system. Stormwater is then piped into catchments (areas of land that drain to a common point) that empty unfiltered into the sea. This problem is exacerbated by land development, which alters

101

TABLE E-3

page	location for citation	source	page number
2	End of the first complete paragraph (after ...WCSMP, but before the period)	City of Weston	3
3	End of the first complete paragraph (after ...pollution, but before the colon)	Jensen	135
4	End of second paragraph (after ...health effects, but before the period)	City of Weston	5
4	End of fourth bulleted list item (after 1 month.)	Seawatch	None
5	End of third paragraph (after ...problem arises, but before the period)	Burke, et. al.	55
6	End of first sentence (after ...stormwater system, but before the period)	City of Weston	7
6	End of first paragraph under Conclusion (after ...include, but before the colon)	Jensen	142

Independent Challenge 3 (continued)

p. Press [Ctrl][End], insert a Works Cited list, format the Works Cited heading in 11-point High Tower Text, black font color, bold, then format the list of works cited in High Tower Text.

Advanced Challenge Exercise

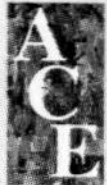

- Scroll to page 4 in the document, place the insertion point at the end of the paragraph above the Potential health effects... heading, press [Enter] twice, type **Table 1: Total annual pollutant loads per year in the Fairy Creek Catchment**, format the text as bold, then press [Enter] twice.
- Insert a table with four columns and four rows.
- Type the text shown in Figure E-29 in the table. Do not be concerned when the text wraps to the next line in a cell.
- Apply the Light List table style. Make sure the text in the header row is bold, then remove any bold formatting from the text in the remaining rows.
- Use AutoFit to make the table fit the contents, then use AutoFit to make the table fit the window.

FIGURE E-29

Area	Nitrogen	Phosphorus	Suspended solids
Fairy Creek	9.3 tonnes	1.2 tonnes	756.4 tonnes
Durras Arm	6.2 tonnes	.9 tonnes	348.2 tonnes
Cabbage Tree Creek	9.8 tonnes	2.3 tonnes	485.7 tonnes

q. Save your changes, submit your work, then close the document and exit Word.

Real Life Independent Challenge

One of the most common opportunities to use the page layout features of Word is when formatting a research paper. The format recommended by the *Publication Manual of the American Psychological Association*, a style guide that includes information on preparing, writing, and formatting research papers, is the standard format used by many programs for medical professionals. In this independent challenge, you will research the APA guidelines for formatting a research paper and use the guidelines you find to format the pages of a sample research report.

a. Use your favorite search engine to search the Web for information on the APA guidelines for formatting a research report. Use the keywords **APA Style** and **research paper format** to conduct your search.

b. Look for information on the proper formatting for the following aspects of a research paper: paper size, margins, line spacing, paragraph indentation, page numbers, short title, title page, abstract, and first page of the body of the report. Also find information on proper formatting for citations and a references page. Print the information you find.

c. Start Word, open the file WMP E-6.docx from the drive and folder where you store your Data Files, then save it as **WMP E-APA Research Paper**. Using the information you learned, format this document as a research report.

d. Adjust the margins, set the line spacing, and add a short title and page numbers to the document header in the format recommended by the APA. Use **Advances in the Treatment of Type 1 Diabetes** as the title for your sample report, use your name as the author name, and make up information about your affiliation (for example, your school or class), if necessary. You do not need to include a running head. Make sure to format the title page exactly as the APA style dictates.

e. Format the remaining text as the abstract and body of the research report.

f. Create three sources, insert three citations in the document—a book, a journal article, and a Web site—and create a references page, following APA style. If necessary, edit the format of the citations and references page to conform to APA format. (*Note*: For this practice document, you are allowed to make up sources. Never make up sources for real research papers.)

g. Save the document, submit a copy to your instructor, close the document, then exit Word.

Visual Workshop

Open the file WMP E-7.docx from the drive and folder where you store your Data Files, then modify it to create the article shown in Figure E-30. (*Hint*: Change all four margins to .6". Add the footnotes as shown in the figure. To locate the clip art image, search using the keyword **hiker**, and be sure only the Illustrations check box in the Results should be in list box in the Clip Art task pane has a check mark. Select a different clip if the clip shown in the figure is not available to you.) Save the document with the filename **WMP E-Lyme Disease**, then print a copy.

FIGURE E-30

TRAVELER'S HEALTH WATCH

On the Lookout for Lyme Disease

By Your Name

Lyme disease, an inflammatory disease transmitted by the bite of a deer tick, has become a serious public health risk in certain areas of the United States and Canada. Campers, hikers, fishermen, outdoor enthusiasts, and other travelers or residents in endemic areas who have frequent or prolonged exposure to tick habitats are at increased risk for Lyme disease.

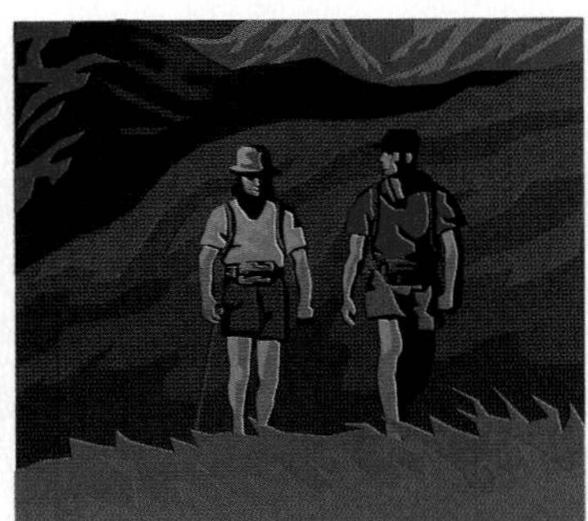

How ticks spread the disease

The bacterium that causes Lyme disease is spread by the bite of infected *Ixodes* ticks, commonly known as deer ticks. Ticks can attach to any part of the human body, but are most often found in hairy areas such as the scalp, groin, and armpit. In most cases the tick must be attached for at least 48 hours before the bacteria can be transmitted. During the spring and summer months, when people dress lightly and spend more time outdoors, the young (nymphal) ticks are most often responsible for spreading the disease. These ticks are tiny (about the size of the head of a pin) and rarely noticed, making it difficult for people to find and remove an infected tick.

Tick habitat and geographic distribution

The risk of exposure to infected ticks in greatest in woods and in thick brush or long grass, but ticks can also be carried by animals into lawns and gardens and into houses by pets. In the United States, most infections occur in the:

- Northeast, from Maryland to Massachusetts.
- North central states, mostly in Wisconsin and Minnesota.
- West coast, particularly California.

Symptoms and signs

Early Lyme disease is characterized initially by *erythema migrans*, the bull's eye rash that often occurs on the skin around a tick bite. The rash usually appears within three days to one month after being bitten. Other flulike symptoms of early Lyme disease include fatigue, headache, chills and fever, muscle and joint pain, and swollen lymph nodes.[1]

Treatment and prognosis

Lyme disease can usually be cured by antibiotics if treatment begins in the early stages of infection. Most people who are treated in the later stages also respond well to antibiotics, although some may have persistent or recurring symptoms.

Protection from tick bites

Here are some precautions to decrease the chances of being bitten by a tick:

- Avoid tick-infested areas, particularly in May, June, and July.[2]
- Wear light-colored clothing, including long pants, socks, and long-sleeved shirts.
- Tuck pant legs into socks or boots and shirt into pants so ticks cannot crawl under clothing.
- Spray insect repellent containing a 20-30% concentration of DEET on clothes and exposed skin other than the face.
- Walk in the center of trails to avoid contact with overgrown brush and grass.
- Wash and dry clothing at a high temperature, inspect body surfaces carefully, and remove attached ticks with tweezers. ■

[1] If left untreated, Lyme disease can result in chronic arthritis and nerve and heart dysfunction.

[2] Ticks are especially common near deer trails.

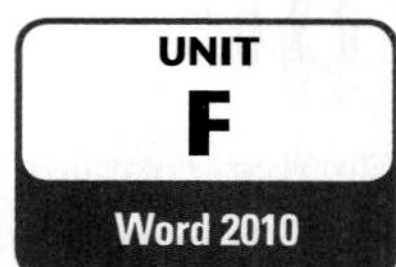

Merging Word Documents

Files You Will Need:

WMP F-1.docx
WMP F-2.mdb
WMP F-3.docx
WMP F-4.mdb

A mail merge operation combines a standard document, such as a form letter, with customized data, such as a set of names and addresses, to create a set of personalized documents. You can perform a mail merge to create letters, labels, and other documents used in mass mailings, or to create standard documents that typically include customized information, such as business cards. In this unit, you learn how to use both the Mail Merge task pane and the commands on the Mailings tab to perform a mail merge. You need to send a letter to patients who recently had a routine mammogram screening, informing them that their mammogram showed no evidence of cancer. You also need to send a reminder card to patients who need to schedule an appointment for a routine mammogram. You use mail merge to create a personalized form letter about the mammogram, and mailing labels for the reminder cards.

OBJECTIVES

- Understand mail merge
- Create a main document
- Design a data source
- Enter and edit records
- Add merge fields
- Merge data
- Create labels
- Sort and filter records

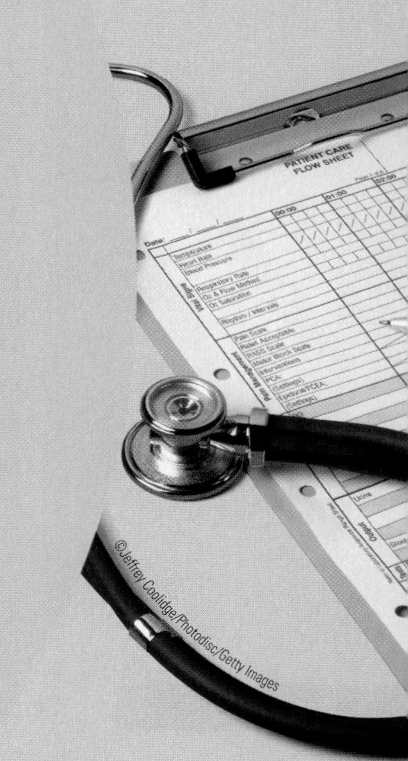

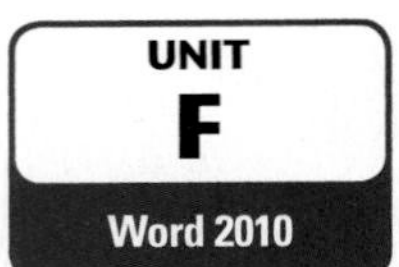

Understanding Mail Merge

When you perform a **mail merge**, you merge a standard Word document with a file that contains customized information for many individuals or items. The standard document is called the **main document**. The file with the unique data for individual people or items is called the **data source**. Merging the main document with a data source results in a **merged document** that contains customized versions of the main document, as shown in Figure F-1. The Mail Merge task pane steps you through the process of setting up and performing a mail merge. You can also perform a mail merge using the commands on the Mailings tab. You decide to use the Mail Merge task pane to create your form letters and the commands on the Mailings tab to create your mailing labels. Before beginning, you explore the steps involved in performing a mail merge.

DETAILS

- **Create the main document**
  The main document contains the text—often called **boilerplate text**—that appears in every version of the merged document. The main document also includes the merge fields, which indicate where the customized information is inserted when you perform the merge. You insert the merge fields in the main document after you have created or selected the data source. You can create a main document using either the current document, a template, or an existing document.

- **Create a data source or select an existing data source**
  The data source is a file that contains the unique information for each individual or item, such as a person's name. It provides the information that varies in every version of the merged document. A data source is composed of data fields and data records. A **data field** is a category of information, such as last name, first name, street address, city, or postal code. A **data record** is a complete set of related information for an individual or an item, such as one person's name and address. It is easiest to think of a data source file as a table: the header row contains the names of the data fields (the **field names**), and each row in the table is an individual data record. You can create a new data source, or you can use an existing data source, such as a data source created in Word, an Outlook contact list, an Access database, or an Excel worksheet.

- **Identify the fields to include in the data source and enter the records**
  When you create a new data source, you must first identify the fields to include, such as first name, last name, and street address if you are creating a data source that will include addresses. It is also important to think of and include all the fields you will need (not just the obvious ones) before you begin to enter data. For example, if you are creating a data source that includes names and addresses, you might need to include fields for a person's middle name, title, apartment number, department name, or country, even if some records in the data source will not include that information. Once you have identified the fields and set up your data source, you are ready to enter the data for each record.

- **Add merge fields to the main document**
  A **merge field** is a placeholder that you insert in the main document to indicate where the data from each record should be inserted when you perform the merge. For example, you insert a zip code merge field in the location where you want to insert a zip code. The merge fields in a main document must correspond with the field names in the associated data source. Merge fields must be inserted, not typed, in the main document. The Mail Merge task pane and the Mailings tab provide access to the dialog boxes you use to insert merge fields.

- **Merge the data from the data source into the main document**
  Once you have established your data source and inserted the merge fields in the main document, you are ready to perform the merge. You can merge to a new file, which contains a customized version of the main document for each record in the data source, or you can merge directly to a printer or e-mail message.

FIGURE F-1: Mail merge process

Exam Date	Title	First Name	Last Name	Address Line 1	City	State	Zip Code	Country
10/2/13	Ms.	Sarah	Bass	62 Cloud St.	Somerville	MA	02144	US
10/3/13	Ms.	Claudia	Beck	23 Plum St.	Boston	MA	02483	US
9/30/13	Ms.	Anne	Gans	456 Elm St.	Arlington	MA	02474	US
10/2/13	Ms.	Jane	Miller	48 East Ave.	Vancouver	BC	V6F 1AH	CANADA
10/1/13	Ms.	Laura	Bright	56 Pearl St.	Cambridge	MA	02139	US

Data record

Field name

Data source document

Main document

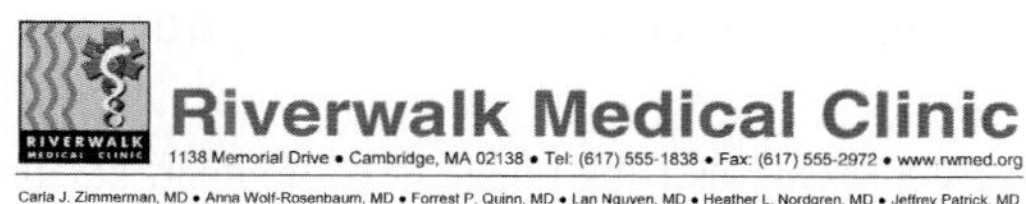

October 12, 2013

«AddressBlock»

«GreetingLine»

We are happy to inform you that your «Exam_Date» mammogram showed no evidence of cancer.

Routine screening mammography is the most sensitive way to detect the early signs of cancer, and significantly reduces breast cancer mortality. However, not all breast cancers are detected by the mammogram. Some can be felt before they can be seen. Thus, to complete the screening procedure and detect all breast cancers as early as possible, you must be examined by your physician annually and perform proper breast self examinations monthly. The enclosed brochure details the proper method of breast self-examination.

If you develop any lumps or other significant breast problems, contact your physician immediately. Do not wait for your next routine check up.

All of your X-ray films will be stored at the Riverwalk Medical Clinic, and made available upon your written request.

Sincerely,

Lan Nguyen, M.D.

LN/yn
Enclosure

Merged document

Riverwalk Medical Clinic
1138 Memorial Drive • Cambridge, MA 02138 • Tel: (617) 555-1838 • Fax: (617) 555-2972 • www.rwmed.org
Carla J. Zimmerman, MD • Anna Wolf-Rosenbaum, MD • Forrest P. Quinn, MD • Lan Nguyen, MD • Heather L. Nordgren, MD • Jeffrey Patrick, MD

October 12, 2013

Ms. Sarah Bass
62 Cloud St.
Somerville, MA 02144

Dear Ms. Bass:

We are happy to inform you that your 10/2/13 mammogram showed no evidence of cancer.

Routine screening mammography is the most sensitive way to detect the early signs of cancer, and significantly reduces breast cancer mortality. However, not all breast cancers are detected by the mammogram. Some can be felt before they can be seen. Thus, to complete the screening procedure and detect all breast cancers as early as possible, you must be examined by your physician annually and perform proper breast self examinations monthly. The enclosed brochure details the proper method of breast self-examination.

If you develop any lumps or other significant breast problems, contact your physician immediately. Do not wait for your next routine check up.

All of your X-ray films will be stored at the Riverwalk Medical Clinic, and made available upon your written request.

Sincerely,

Lan Nguyen, M.D.

LN/yn
Enclosure

Boilerplate text

Merge fields

Customized information

UNIT F

Word 2010

Creating a Main Document

The first step in performing a mail merge is to create the main document—the file that contains the boilerplate text. You can create a main document from scratch, save an existing document as a main document, or use a mail merge template to create a main document. The Mail Merge task pane walks you through the process of selecting the type of main document to create. You use an existing form letter for your main document. You begin by opening the Mail Merge task pane.

STEPS

TROUBLE

A document, blank or otherwise, must be open in the program window for the commands on the Mailings tab to be available.

QUICK TIP

If you choose "Use the current document" and the current document is blank, you can create a main document from scratch. Either type the boilerplate text at this step, or wait until the task pane prompts you to do so.

1. **Start Word, click the Mailings tab, click the Start Mail Merge button in the Start Mail Merge group, then click Step by Step Mail Merge Wizard**

   The Mail Merge task pane opens, as shown in Figure F-2, and displays information for the first step in the mail merge process: Select document type (the type of merge document to create).

2. **Make sure the Letters option button is selected, then click Next: Starting document to continue with the next step**

   The task pane displays the options for the second step: Select starting document (the main document). You can use the current document, start with a mail merge template, or use an existing file.

3. **Select the Start from existing document option button, make sure (More files...) is selected in the Start from existing list box, then click Open**

   The Open dialog box opens.

4. **Navigate to the location where you store your Data Files, select the file WMP F-1.docx, then click Open**

   The letter that opens contains the boilerplate text for the main document. Notice the filename in the title bar is Document1. When you create a main document that is based on an existing document, Word gives the main document a default temporary filename.

5. **Click the Save button on the Quick Access toolbar, then save the main document with the filename WMP F-Mammogram Results Letter Main to the drive and folder where you store your Data Files**

   It's a good idea to include "main" in the filename so that you can easily recognize the file as a main document.

6. **Click the Zoom level button on the status bar, click the 100% option button, click OK, select October 9, 2013 in the letter, type today's date, scroll down, select Lan Nguyen, type your name, press [Ctrl][Home], then save your changes**

   The edited main document is shown in Figure F-3.

7. **Click Next: Select recipients to continue with the next step**

   You continue with Step 3 of 6 in the next lesson.

Using mail merge template

If you are creating letters or faxes, you can use a mail merge template to start your main document. Each template includes boilerplate text (which you can customize), and merge fields (which you can match to the field names in your data source). To create a main document that is based on a mail merge template, click the Start from a template option button in the Step 2 of 6 Mail Merge task pane, and then click Select template. In the Select Template dialog box, select a template from the Letters or Faxes tab that includes the word "Merge" in its name, and then click OK to create the document. Once you have created the main document, you can customize it with your own information: edit the boilerplate text; change the document format; or add, remove, or modify the merge fields.

Before performing the merge, make sure to match the names of the merge fields used in the template with the field names used in your data source. To match the field names, click the Match Fields button in the Write & Insert Fields group on the Mailings tab, and then use the list arrows in the Match Fields dialog box to select the field name in your data source that corresponds to each address field component in the main document.

FIGURE F-2: **Step 1 of 6 Mail Merge task pane**

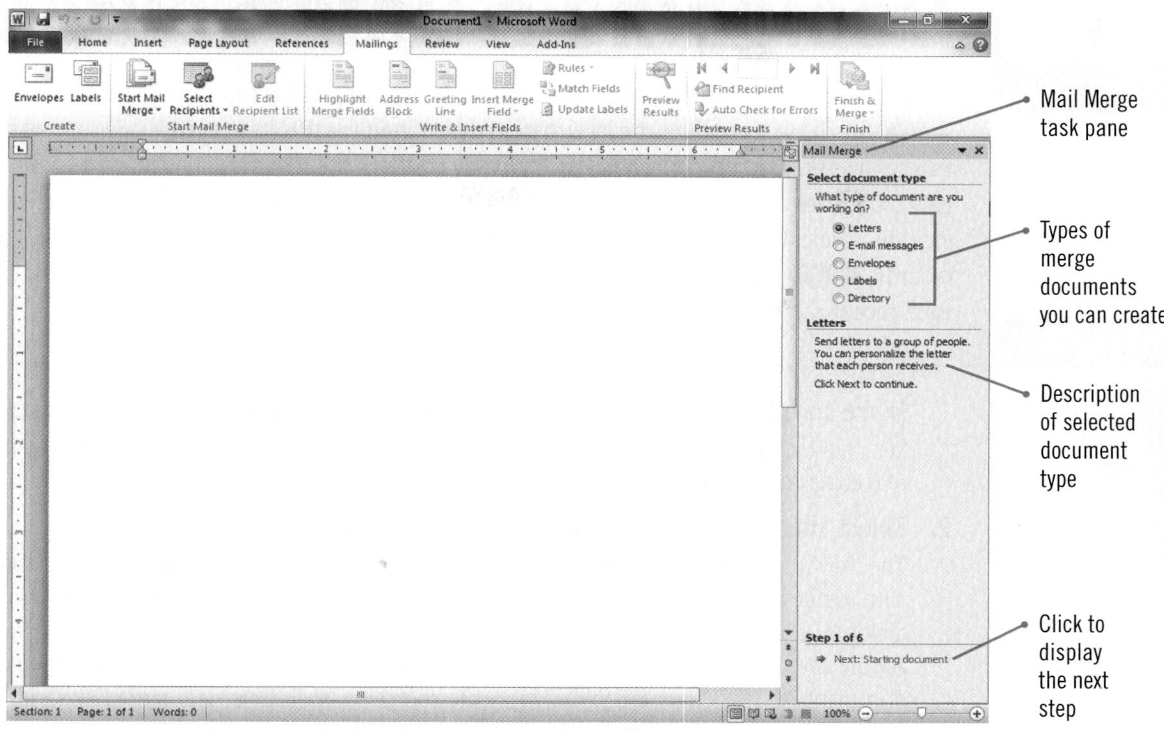

FIGURE F-3: **Main document with Step 2 of 6 Mail Merge task pane**

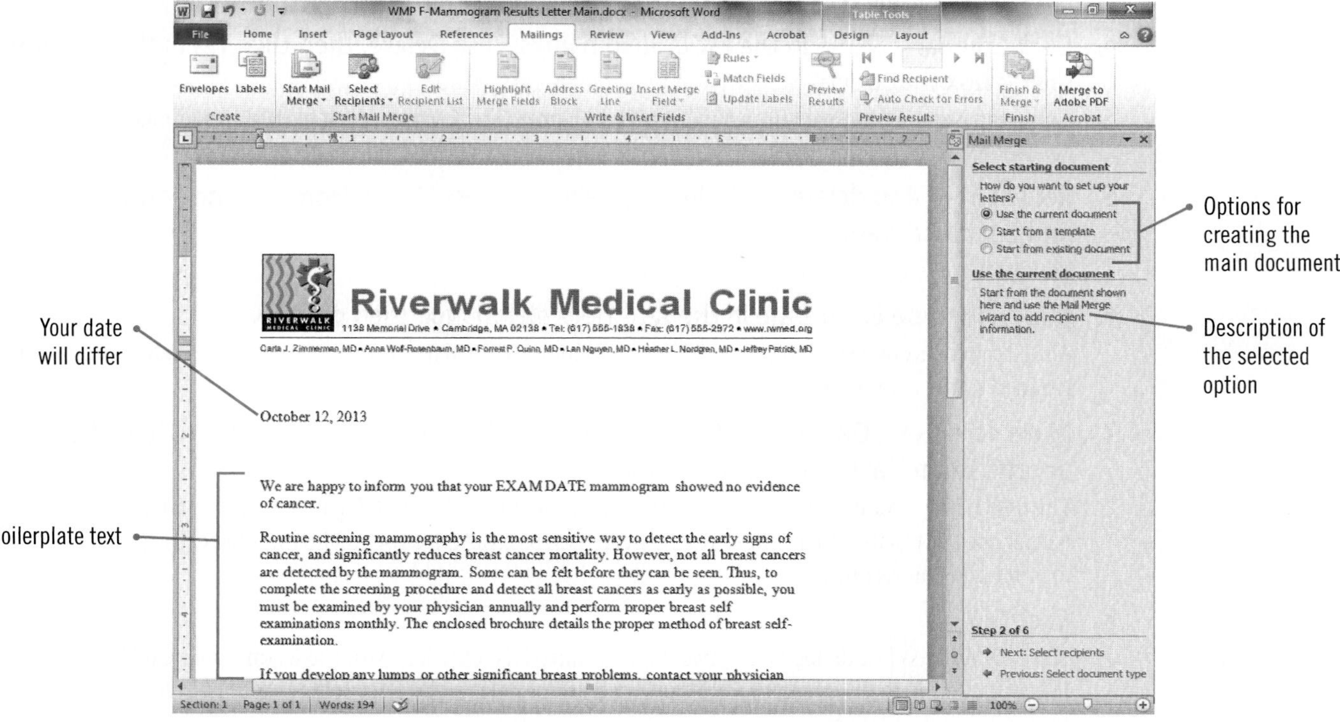

Word 2010

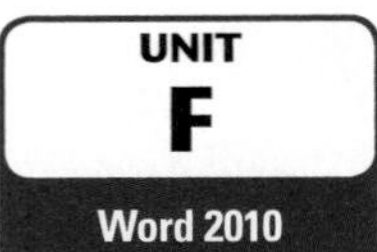

Designing a Data Source

Once you have identified the main document, the next step in the mail merge process is to identify the data source, the file that contains the information that is used to customize each version of the merge document. You can use an existing data source that already contains the records you want to include in your merge, or you can create a new data source. When you create a new data source you must determine the fields to include—the categories of information, such as a first name, last name, city, or zip code—and then add the records. You create a new data source that includes fields for the name, address, and exam date for each recent mammogram patient.

STEPS

1. **Make sure Step 3 of 6 is displayed at the bottom of the Mail Merge task pane**
   Step 3 of 6 involves selecting a data source to use for the merge. You can use an existing data source, use a list of contacts created in Microsoft Outlook, or create a new data source.
2. **Select the Type a new list option button, then click Create**
   The New Address List dialog box opens, as shown in Figure F-4. You use this dialog box both to design your data source and to enter records. The column headings in the Type recipient information... section of the dialog box are fields that are commonly used in form letters, but you can customize your data source by adding and removing columns (fields) from this table. A data source can be merged with more than one main document, so it's important to design a data source to be flexible. The more fields you include in a data source, the more flexible it is. For example, if you include separate fields for a person's title, first name, middle name, and last name, you can use the same data source to create an envelope addressed to "Mr. John Montgomery Smith" and a form letter with the greeting "Dear John."
3. **Click Customize Columns**
   The Customize Address List dialog box opens. You use this dialog box to add, delete, rename, and reorder the fields in the data source.
4. **Click Company Name in the list of field names, click Delete, then click Yes in the warning dialog box that opens**
   Company Name is removed from the list of field names. The Company Name field is no longer a part of the data source.
5. **Repeat Step 4 to delete the following fields: Address Line 2, Home Phone, Work Phone, and E-mail Address**
   The fields are removed from the data source.
6. **Click Add, type Exam Date in the Add Field dialog box, then click OK**
   A field called "Exam Date," which you will use to indicate the date of the patient's most recent mammogram, is added to the data source.
7. **Make sure Exam Date is selected in the list of field names, then click Move Up eight times or until Exam Date is at the top of the list**
   The field name "Exam Date" is moved to the top of the list, as shown in Figure F-5. Although the order of field names does not matter in a data source, it's convenient to arrange the field names logically to make it easier to enter and edit records.
8. **Click OK**
   The New Address List dialog box shows the customized list of fields, with the Exam Date field first in the list. The next step is to enter each record you want to include in the data source. You add records to the data source in the next lesson.

FIGURE F-4: **New Address List dialog box**

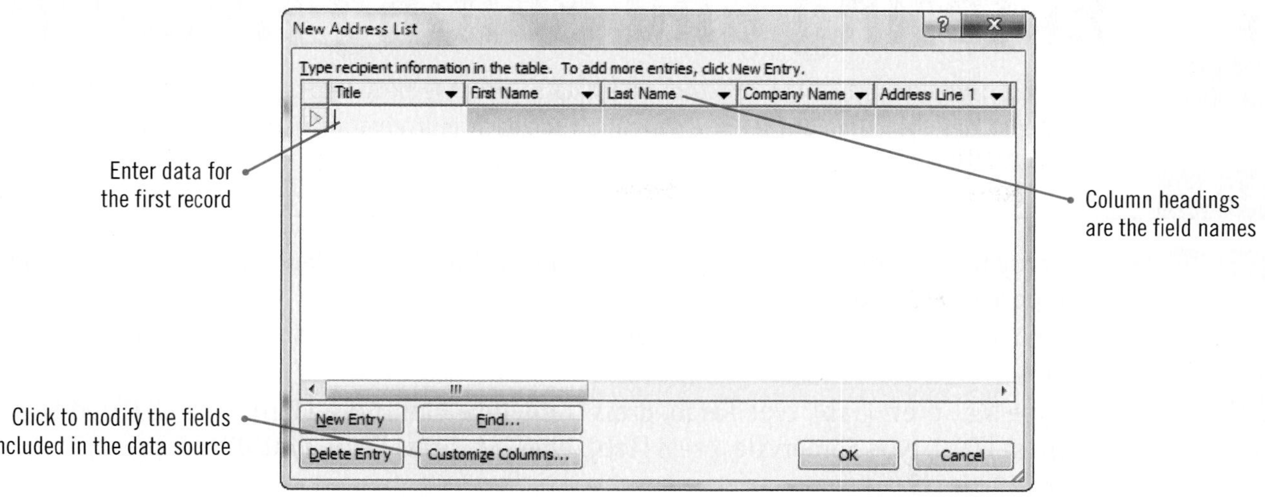

FIGURE F-5: **Customize Address List dialog box**

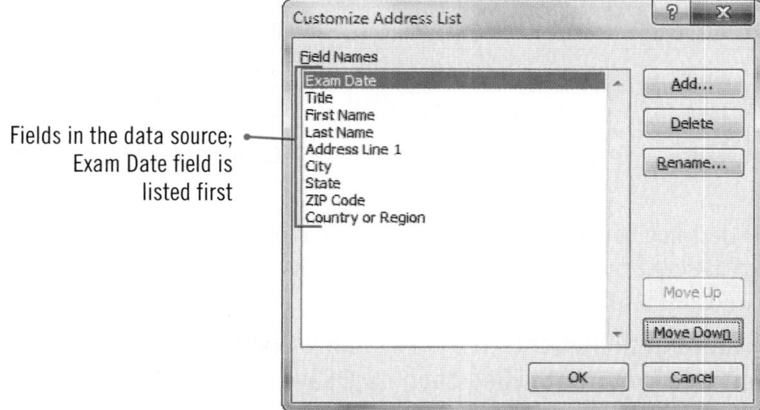

Merging with an Outlook data source

If you maintain lists of contacts in Microsoft Outlook, you can use one of your Outlook contact lists as a data source for a merge. To merge with an Outlook data source, click the Select from Outlook contacts option button in the Step 3 of 6 Mail Merge task pane, then click Choose Contacts Folder to open the Choose Profile dialog box. In this dialog box, use the Profile Name list arrow to select the profile you want to use, then click OK to open the Select Contacts dialog box. In this dialog box, select the contact list you want to use as the data source, and then click OK. All the contacts included in the selected folder appear in the Mail Merge Recipients dialog box. Here you can refine the list of recipients to include in the merge by sorting and filtering the records. When you are satisfied, click OK in the Mail Merge Recipients dialog box.

UNIT F
Word 2010

Entering and Editing Records

Once you have established the structure of a data source, the next step is to enter the records. Each record includes the complete set of information for each individual or item you include in the data source. You create a record for each recent mammogram patient.

STEPS

QUICK TIP
Be careful not to add spaces or extra punctuation after an entry in a field, or these will appear when the data is merged.

1. **Verify the insertion point is in the Exam Date text box in the New Address List dialog box, type 10/2/13, then press [Tab]**
   "10/2/13" appears in the Exam Date field, and the insertion point moves to the next column in the table, the Title field.

2. **Type Ms., press [Tab], type Sarah, press [Tab], type Bass, press [Tab], type 62 Cloud St., press [Tab], type Somerville, press [Tab], type MA, press [Tab], type 02144, press [Tab], then type US**
   Data is entered in all the fields for the first record. You used each field for this record, but it's okay to leave a field blank if you do not need it for a record.

3. **Click New Entry**
   The record for Sarah Bass is added to the data source, and the dialog box displays empty fields for the next record, as shown in Figure F-6.

QUICK TIP
You can also press [Tab] at the end of the last field to start a new record.

4. **Enter the following four records, pressing [Tab] to move from field to field, and clicking New Entry at the end of each record except the last:**

Exam Date	Title	First Name	Last Name	Address Line 1	City	State	ZIP Code	Country
10/3/13	Ms.	Claudia	Beck	23 Plum St.	Boston	MA	02483	US
9/30/13	Ms.	Anne	Gans	456 Elm St.	Arlington	MA	02474	US
10/2/13	Ms.	Jane	Miller	48 East Ave.	Vancouver	BC	V6F 1AH	CANADA
10/1/13	Ms.	Laura	Bright	56 Pearl St.	Cambridge	MA	02139	US

5. **Click OK**
   The Save Address List dialog box opens. Data sources are saved by default in the My Data Sources folder so that you can easily locate them to use in other merge operations. Data sources you create in Word are saved in Microsoft Office Address Lists (*.mdb) format.

TROUBLE
If a check mark appears in the blank record under Laura Bright, click the check mark to eliminate the record from the merge.

6. **Type WMP F-Mammogram Patients in the File name text box, navigate to the drive and folder where you store your Data Files, then click Save**
   The data source is saved, and the Mail Merge Recipients dialog box opens, as shown in Figure F-7. The dialog box shows the records in the data source in table format. You can use the dialog box to sort and filter records, and to select the recipients to include in the mail merge. You will learn more about sorting and filtering in a later lesson. The check marks in the second column indicate the records that will be included in the merge.

7. **Click WMP F-Mammogram Patients.mdb in the Data Source list box at the bottom of the dialog box, then click Edit**
   The Edit Data Source dialog box opens, as shown in Figure F-8. You use this dialog box to edit a data source, including adding and removing fields, editing field names, adding and removing records, and editing existing records.

8. **Click Ms. in the Title field of the Anne Gans record to select it, type Dr., click OK, then click Yes**
   The data in the Title field for Anne Gans changes from "Ms." to "Dr.", and the Edit Data Source dialog box closes.

QUICK TIP
If you want to add new records or modify existing records, click Edit recipient list in the task pane.

9. **Click OK in the Mail Merge Recipients dialog box**
   The dialog box closes. The file type and filename of the data source attached to the main document now appear under Use an existing list in the Mail Merge task pane.

FIGURE F-6: **Record in New Address List dialog box**

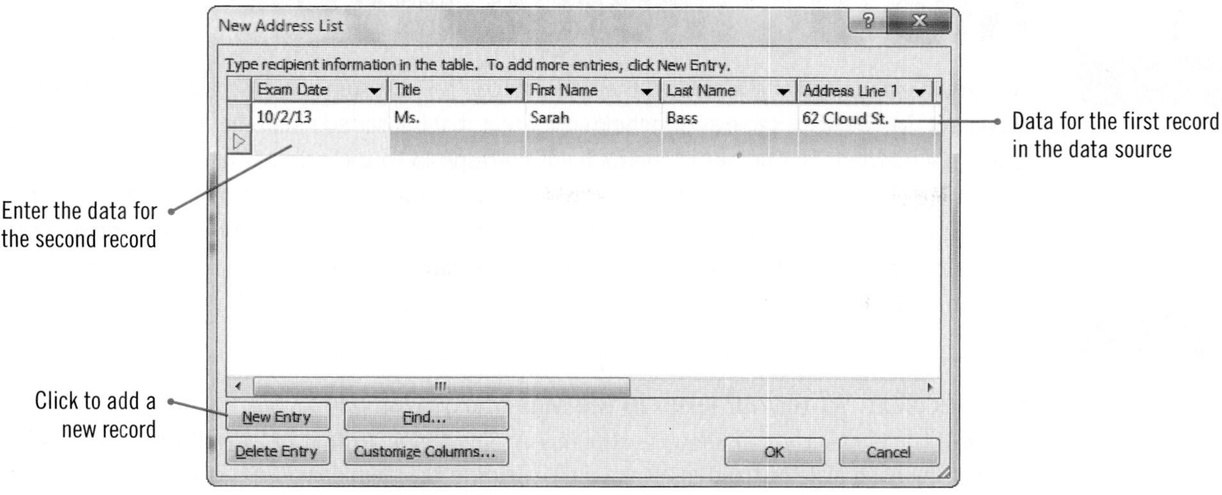

FIGURE F-7: **Mail Merge Recipients dialog box**

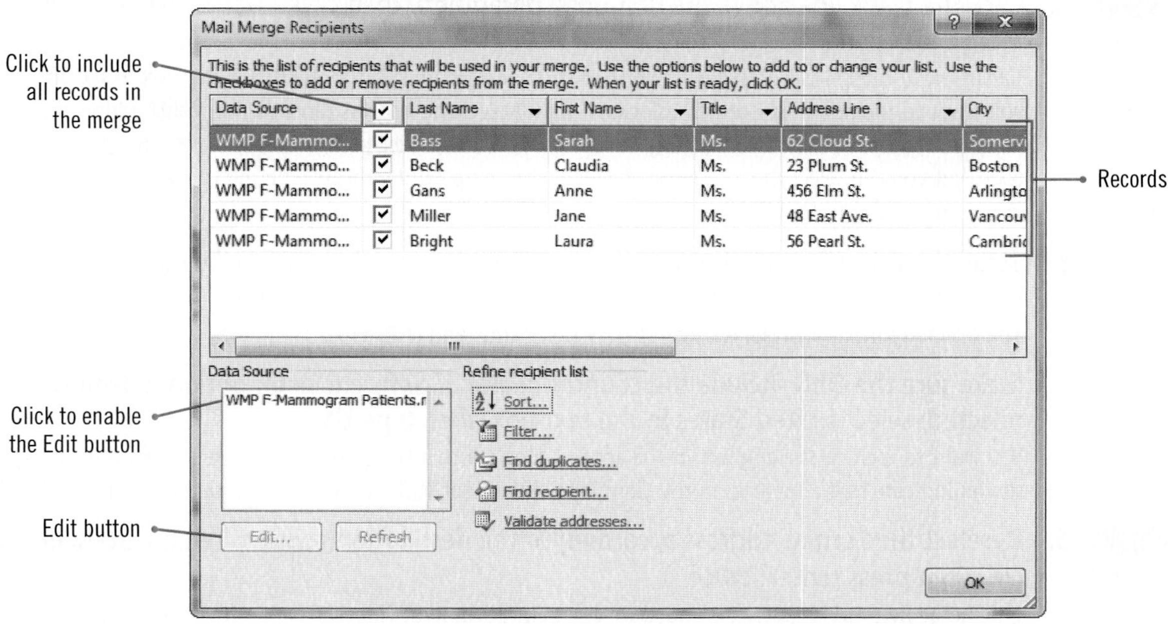

FIGURE F-8: **Edit Data Source dialog box**

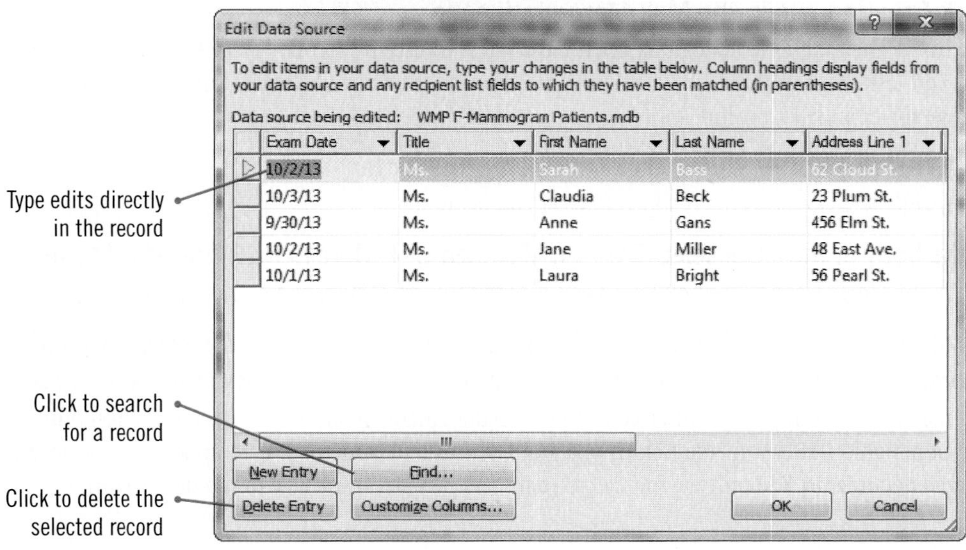

UNIT F

Word 2010

Adding Merge Fields

After you have created and identified the data source, the next step is to insert the merge fields in the main document. Merge fields serve as placeholders for text that is inserted when the main document and the data source are merged. The names of merge fields correspond to the field names in the data source. You can insert merge fields using the Mail Merge task pane or the Address Block, Greeting Line, and Insert Merge Field buttons in the Write & Insert Fields group on the Mailings tab. You cannot type merge fields into the main document. You use the Mail Merge task pane to insert merge fields for the inside address and greeting of the letter. You also insert a merge field for the exam date in the body of the letter.

STEPS

1. **Click Next: Write your letter in the Mail Merge task pane**
   The Mail Merge task pane shows the options for Step 4 of 6: Write your letter. During this step, you write or edit the boilerplate text and insert the merge fields in the main document. Since your form letter is already written, you are ready to add the merge fields to it.

> **QUICK TIP**
> You can also click the Address Block button in the Write & Insert Fields group on the Mailings tab to insert an address block.

2. **Click the blank line above the first body paragraph, then click Address block in the Mail Merge task pane**
   The Insert Address Block dialog box opens, as shown in Figure F-9. You use this dialog box to specify the fields you want to include in an address block. In this merge, the address block is the inside address of the form letter. An address block automatically includes fields for the recipient's name, street, city, state, and postal code, but you can select the format for the recipient's name and indicate whether to include a company name or country in the address.

3. **Scroll the list of formats for a recipient's name to get a feel for the kinds of formats you can use, then click Mr. Joshua Randall Jr. if it is not already selected**
   The selected format uses the recipient's title, first name, and last name.

4. **Make sure the Only include the country/region if different than: option button is selected, select United States in the text box, then type US**
   You want to include the country in the address block only if the country is different than the United States, so you indicate that all entries in the Country field, except "US," should be included in the printed address.

> **QUICK TIP**
> You cannot simply type chevrons around a field name. You must insert merge fields using the Mail Merge task pane or the buttons in the Write & Insert Fields group on the Mailings tab.

5. **Deselect the Format address according to the destination country/region check box, click OK, then press [Enter] twice**
   The merge field AddressBlock is added to the main document. Chevrons (<< and >>) surround a merge field to distinguish it from the boilerplate text.

6. **Click Greeting line in the Mail Merge task pane**
   The Insert Greeting Line dialog box opens. You want to use the format "Dear Mr. Randall:" (the recipient's title and last name, followed by a colon) for a greeting. The default format uses a comma, so you have to change the comma to a colon.

7. **Click the , list arrow, click :, click OK, then press [Enter]**
   The merge field GreetingLine is added to the main document.

> **QUICK TIP**
> You can also click the Insert Merge Field button or list arrow in the Write & Insert Fields group on the Mailings tab to insert a merge field.

8. **In the body of the letter select EXAM DATE, then click More items in the Mail Merge task pane**
   The Insert Merge Field dialog box opens and displays the list of field names included in the data source.

9. **Make sure Exam Date is selected, click Insert, click Close, press [Spacebar] to add a space between the merge field and "mammogram" if there is no space, then save your changes**
   The merge field Exam_Date is inserted in the main document, as shown in Figure F-10. You must type spaces and punctuation after a merge field if you want spaces and punctuation to appear in that location in the merged documents. You preview the merged data and perform the merge in the next lesson.

FIGURE F-9: **Insert Address Block dialog box**

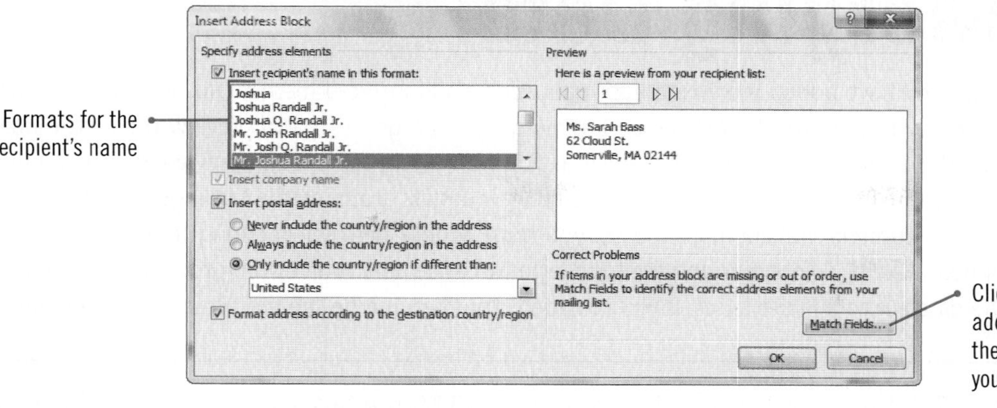

FIGURE F-10: **Merge fields in the main document**

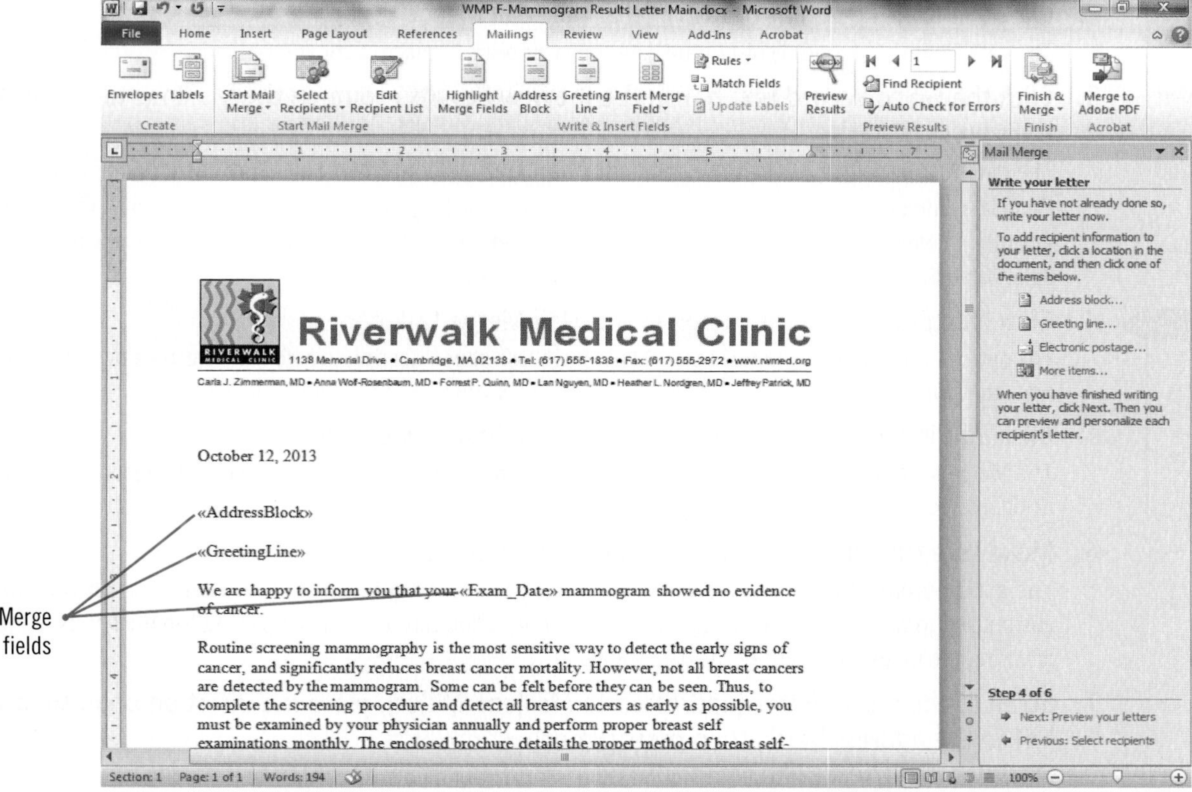

Matching fields

The merge fields you insert in a main document must correspond with the field names in the associated data source. If you are using the Address Block merge field, you must make sure that the default address field names correspond with the field names used in your data source. If the default address field names do not match the field names in your data source, click Match Fields in the Insert Address Block dialog box, then use the list arrows in the Match Fields dialog box to select the field name in the data source that corresponds to each default address field name. You can also click the Match Fields button in the Write & Insert Fields group on the Mailings tab to open the Match Fields dialog box.

UNIT F

Word 2010

Merging Data

Once you have added records to your data source and inserted merge fields in the main document, you are ready to perform the merge. Before merging, it's a good idea to preview the merged data to make sure the printed documents will appear as you want them to. You can preview the merge using the task pane or the Preview Results button in the Preview Results group on the Mailings tab. When you merge the main document with the data source, you must choose between merging to a new file or directly to a printer. Before merging the form letter with the data source, you preview the merge to make sure the data appears in the letter as you intended. You then merge the two files to a new document.

STEPS

QUICK TIP
To adjust the main document, click the Preview Results button in the Preview Results group on the Mailings tab, then make any necessary changes. Click the Preview Results button again to preview the merged data.

1. **Click Next: Preview your letters in the Mail Merge task pane, then scroll down as necessary to see the exam date in the document**

   The data from the first record in the data source appears in place of the merge fields in the main document, as shown in Figure F-11. Always preview a document to verify that the merge fields, punctuation, page breaks, and spacing all appear as you intend before you perform the merge.

2. **Click the Next Recipient button in the Mail Merge task pane**

   The data from the second record in the data source appears in place of the merge fields.

3. **Click the Go to Record text box in the Preview Results group on the Mailings tab, type 4, then press [Enter]**

   The data for the fourth record appears in the document window. The non-U.S. country name, in this case Canada, is included in the address block, just as you specified. You can also use the First Record, Previous Record, Next Record, and Last Record buttons in the Preview Results group to preview the merged data. Table F-1 describes other commands on the Mailings tab.

QUICK TIP
If your data source contains many records, you can merge directly to a printer to avoid creating a large file.

4. **Click Next: Complete the merge in the Mail Merge task pane**

   The options for Step 6 of 6 appear in the Mail Merge task pane. Merging to a new file creates a document with one letter for each record in the data source. This allows you to edit the individual letters.

5. **Click Edit individual letters to merge the data to a new document**

   The Merge to New Document dialog box opens. You can use this dialog box to specify the records to include in the merge.

6. **Make sure the All option button is selected, then click OK**

   The main document and the data source are merged to a new document called Letters1, which contains a customized form letter for each record in the data source. You can now further personalize the letters without affecting the main document or the data source.

7. **Scroll to the fourth letter (addressed to Ms. Jane Miller), place the insertion point before V6F in the address block, then press [Enter]**

   The postal code is now consistent with the proper format for a Canadian address.

8. **Click the Save button on the Quick Access toolbar to open the Save As dialog box, then save the merged document as WMP F-Mammogram Results Letter Merge to the drive and folder where you store your Data Files**

   You may decide not to save a merged file if your data source is large. Once you have created the main document and the data source, you can create the letters by performing the merge again.

TROUBLE
Print only one letter if you are required to submit a printed document to your instructor.

9. **Submit the document to your instructor, then close all open Word files, saving changes if prompted**

FIGURE F-11: Preview of merged data

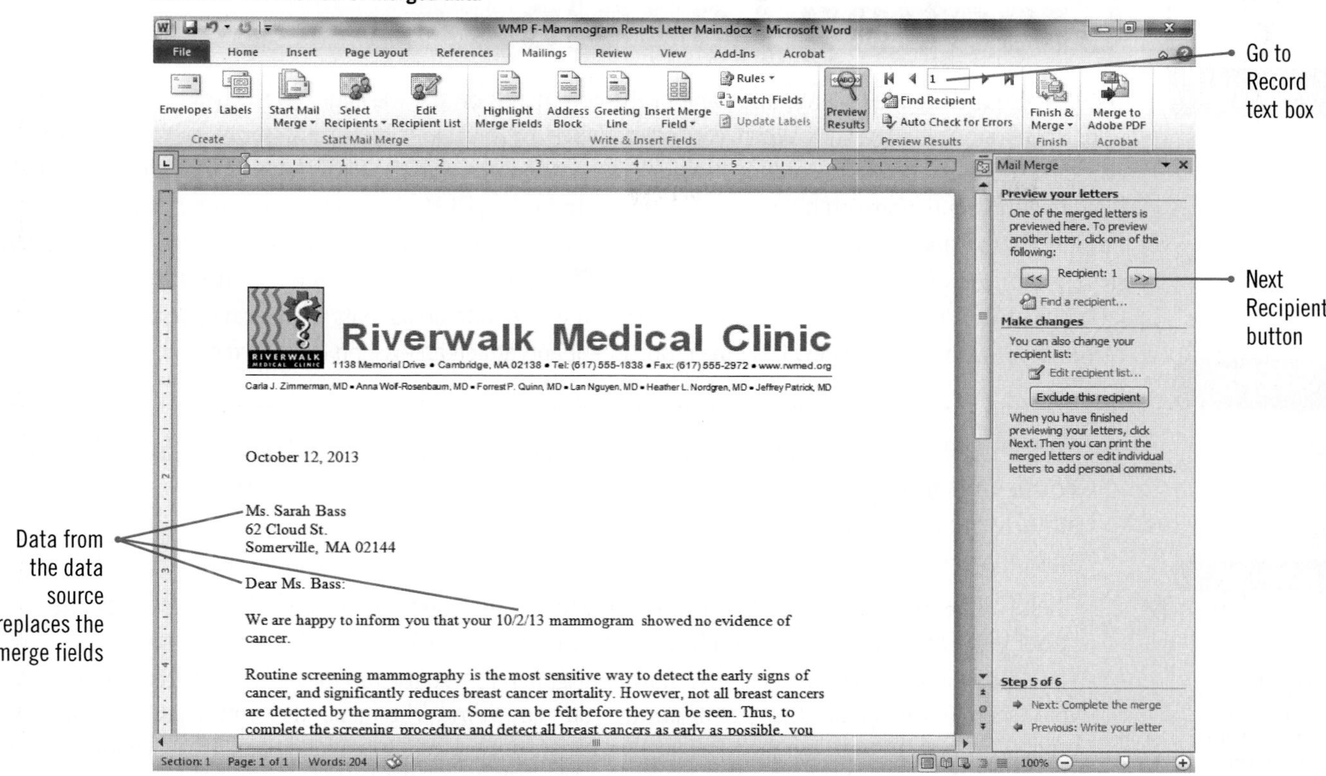

TABLE F-1: Commands on the Mailings tab

command	use to
Envelopes	Create and print an individual envelope
Labels	Create and print an individual label
Start Mail Merge	Select the type of mail merge document to create and start the mail merge process
Select Recipients	Attach an existing data source to a main document or create a new data source
Edit Recipient List	Edit, sort, and filter the associated data source
Highlight Merge Fields	Highlight the merge fields in the main document
Address Block	Insert an Address Block merge field in the main document
Greeting Line	Insert a Greeting Line merge field in the main document
Insert Merge Field	Insert a merge field from the data source in the main document
Rules	Set rules to control how Word merges the data in the data source with the main document
Match Fields	Match the names of address or greeting fields used in a main document with the field names used in the data source
Update Labels	Update all the labels in a label main document to match the content and formatting of the first label
Preview Results	Switch between viewing the main document with merge fields or with merged data
Find Recipient	Search for a specific record in the merged document
Auto Check for Errors	Check for and report errors in the merge
Finish & Merge	Specify whether to merge to a new document or directly to a printer or e-mail, and then complete the merge

UNIT
F
Word 2010

Creating Labels

You can also use the Mail Merge task pane or the commands on the Mailings tab to create mailing labels or print envelopes for a mailing. When you create labels or envelopes, you must select a standard label or envelope size to use as the main document, select a data source, and then insert the merge fields in the main document before performing the merge. In addition to mailing labels, you can use mail merge to create labels for CDs, videos, and other items, and to create documents that are based on standard or custom label sizes, such as business cards, name tags, and postcards. You decide to use the commands on the Mailings tab to create mailing labels for the reminder card you will send to all patients who need to schedule a routine mammogram. You create a new label main document and attach an existing data source.

STEPS

1. **Click the File tab, click New, make sure Blank document is selected, click Create, click the Zoom level button on the status bar, click the 100% option button if the view is not already set to 100%, click OK, then click the Mailings tab**

   A blank document must be open for the commands on the Mailings tab to be available.

QUICK TIP

To create an envelope mail merge, click Envelopes on the Start Mail Merge list to open the Envelope Options dialog box, and then select the envelope size and other options.

2. **Click the Start Mail Merge button in the Start Mail Merge group, click Labels, click the Label vendors list arrow, then click Microsoft if Microsoft is not already displayed**

   The Label Options dialog box opens, as shown in Figure F-12. You use this dialog box to select a label size for your labels and to specify the type of printer you plan to use. The name Microsoft appears in the Label vendors list box. You can use the Label vendors list arrow to select other brand name label vendors, such as Avery or Office Depot. Many standard-sized labels for mailings, CD/DVD faces, business cards, postcards, and other types of labels are listed in the Product number list box. The type, height, width, and page size for the selected product are displayed in the Label information section.

TROUBLE

If your labels do not match Figure F-13, click the Undo button on the Quick Access toolbar, then repeat Step 3, making sure to click the second instance of 30 Per Page.

3. **Click the second instance of 30 Per Page in the Product number list, click OK, click the Table Tools Layout tab, click View Gridlines in the Table group to turn on the display of gridlines if they are not displayed, then click the Mailings tab**

   A table with gridlines appears in the main document, as shown in Figure F-13. Each table cell is the size of a label for the label product you selected.

4. **Save the label main document with the filename WMP F-Mammogram Reminder Labels Main to the drive and folder where you store your Data Files**

   Next, you need to select a data source for the labels.

5. **Click the Select Recipients button in the Start Mail Merge group, then click Use Existing List**

   The Select Data Source dialog box opens.

QUICK TIP

To create or change the return address for an envelope mail merge, click the File tab, click Options, click Advanced in the left pane of the Word Options dialog box, then scroll down the right pane and enter the return address in the Mailing address text box in the General section.

6. **Navigate to the drive and folder where you store your Data Files, open the file WMP F-2.mdb, then save your changes**

   The data source file is attached to the label main document and <<Next Record>> appears in every cell in the table except the first cell, which is blank. In the next lesson you sort and filter the records before performing the mail merge.

FIGURE F-12: Label Options dialog box

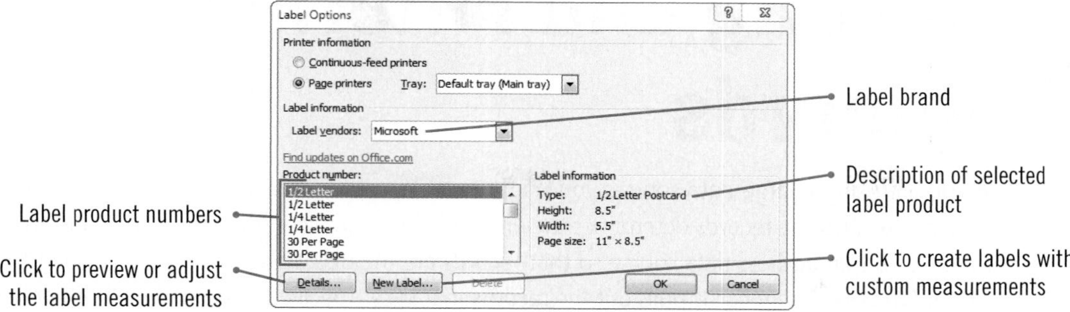

FIGURE F-13: Label main document

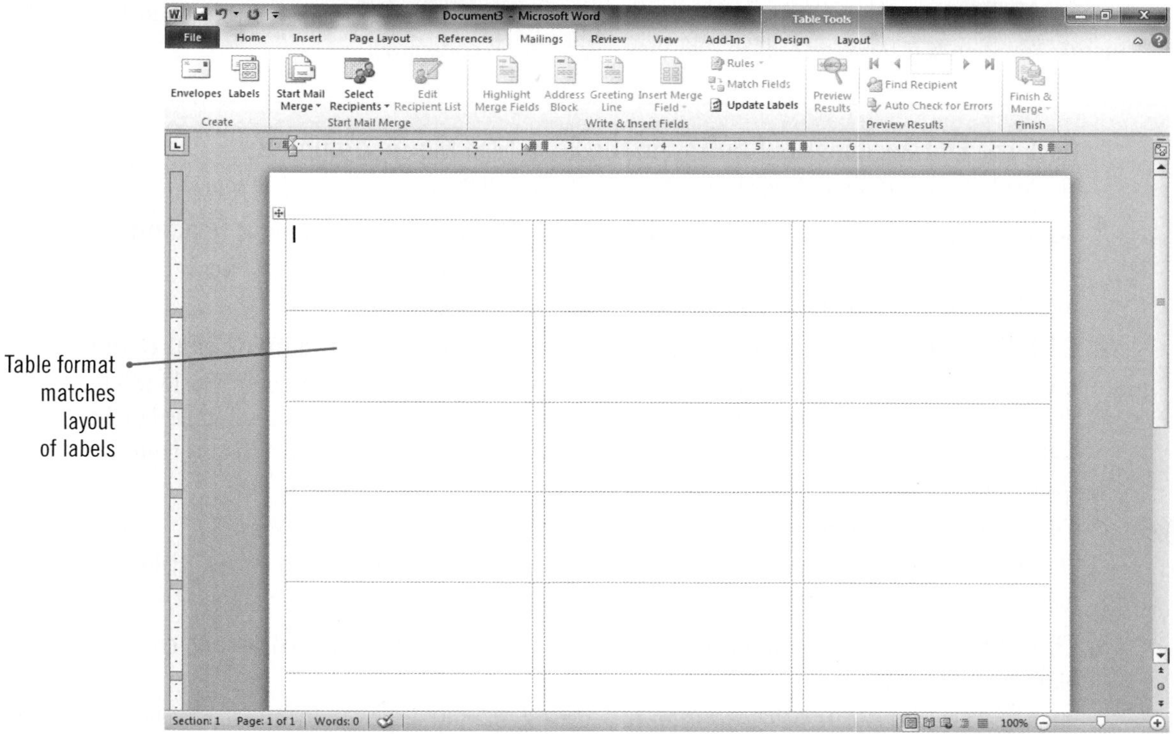

Printing individual envelopes and labels

The Mail Merge feature enables you to easily print envelopes and labels for mass mailings, but you can also quickly format and print individual envelopes and labels using the Envelopes or Labels commands in the Create group on the Mailings tab. Simply click the Envelopes button or Labels button to open the Envelopes and Labels dialog box. On the Envelopes tab, shown in Figure F-14, type the recipient's address in the Delivery address box and the return address in the Return address box. Click Options to open the Envelope Options dialog box, which you can use to select the envelope size, change the font and font size of the delivery and return addresses, and change the printing options. When you are ready to print the envelope, click Print in the Envelopes and Labels dialog box. The procedure for printing an individual label is similar to printing an individual envelope: enter the recipient's address in the Address box on the Labels tab, click Options to select a label product number, click OK, and then click Print.

FIGURE F-14: Envelopes and Labels dialog box

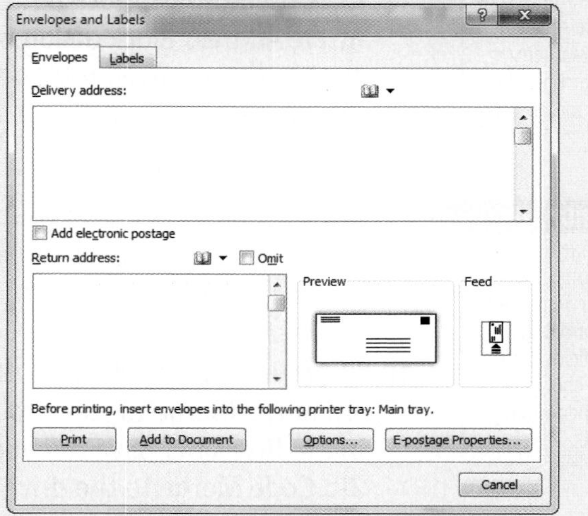

UNIT F

Word 2010

Sorting and Filtering Records

If you are using a large data source, you might want to sort and/or filter the records before performing a merge. **Sorting** the records determines the order in which the records are merged. For example, you might want to sort an address data source so that records are merged alphabetically by last name or in zip code order. **Filtering** the records pulls out the records that meet specific criteria and includes only those records in the merge. For instance, you might want to filter a data source to send a mailing only to people who live in the state of New York. You can use the Mail Merge Recipients dialog box both to sort and to filter a data source. You apply a filter to the data source so that only United States addresses are included in the merge. You then sort those records so that they merge in zip code order.

STEPS

1. **Click the Edit Recipient List button in the Start Mail Merge group**
   The Mail Merge Recipients dialog box opens and displays all the records in the data source.
2. **Scroll right to display the Country field, then click the Country column heading**
   The records are sorted in ascending alphabetical order by country, with Canadian records listed first. If you want to reverse the sort order, you can click the column heading again.
3. **Click the Country column heading list arrow, then click US on the menu that opens**
   A filter is applied to the data source so that only the records with "US" in the Country field will be merged. The grayish-blue arrow in the Country column heading indicates that a filter has been applied to the column. You can filter a data source by as many criteria as you like. To remove a filter, click a column heading list arrow, then click (All).
4. **Click Sort in the Refine recipient list section of the dialog box**
   The Filter and Sort dialog box opens with the Sort Records tab displayed. You can use this dialog box to apply more advanced sort and filter options to the data source.
5. **Click the Sort by list arrow, click ZIP Code, click the first Then by list arrow, click Last Name, then click OK**
   The Mail Merge Recipients dialog box (shown in Figure F-15) now displays only the records with a US address sorted first in zip code order, and then alphabetically by last name.
6. **Click OK**
   The sort and filter criteria you set are saved for the current merge.
7. **Click the Address Block button in the Write & Insert Fields group, then click OK in the Insert Address Block dialog box**
   The Address Block merge field is added to the first label.
8. **Click the Update Labels button in the Write & Insert Fields group**
   The merge field is copied from the first label to every label in the main document.
9. **Click the Preview Results button in the Preview Results group**
   A preview of the merged label data appears in the main document, as shown in Figure F-16. Only U.S. addresses are included, and the labels are organized in zip code order, with recipients with the same zip code listed in alphabetical order.
10. **Click the Finish & Merge button in the Finish group, click Edit Individual Documents, click OK in the Merge to New Document dialog box, replace Ms. Julia Packer with your name in the first label, save the document as WMP F-Mammogram Reminder Labels US Only Zip Code Merge to the drive and folder where you store your Data Files, submit the labels to your instructor, save and close all open files, then exit Word**

QUICK TIP
Use the options on the Filter tab to apply more than one filter to the data source.

QUICK TIP
Sorting and filtering a data source does not alter the records in a data source; it simply reorganizes the records for the current merge only.

QUICK TIP
To change the font or paragraph formatting of merged data, format the merge fields, including the chevrons, before performing a merge.

FIGURE F-15: **US records sorted in zip code order**

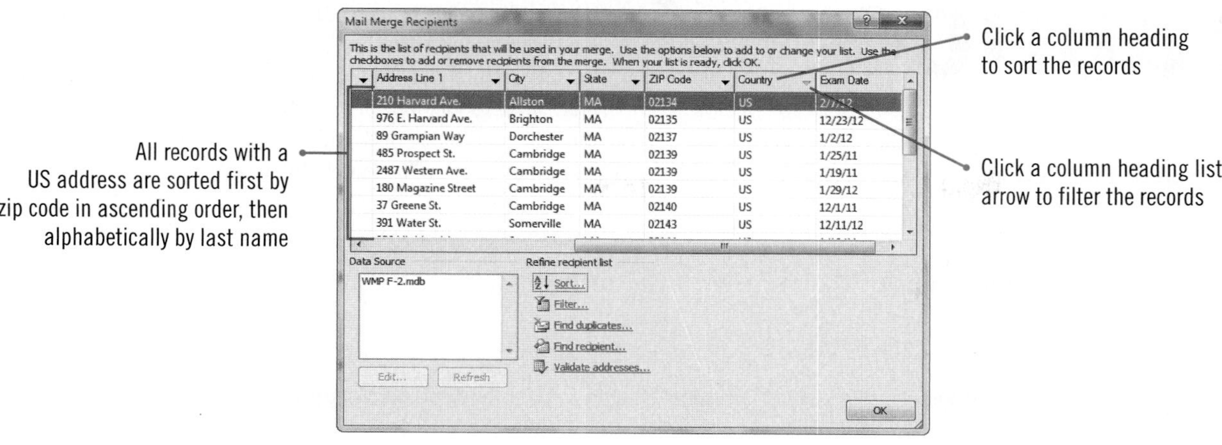
All records with a US address are sorted first by zip code in ascending order, then alphabetically by last name
Click a column heading to sort the records
Click a column heading list arrow to filter the records

FIGURE F-16: **Merged labels**

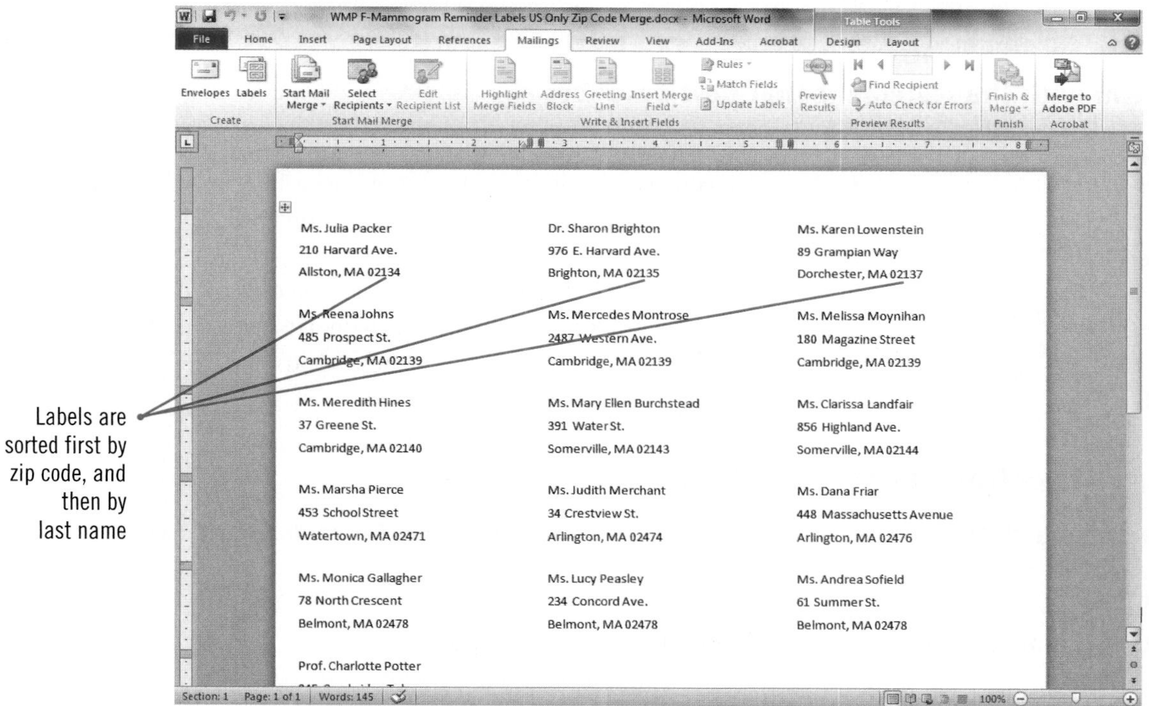
Labels are sorted first by zip code, and then by last name

Word 2010

Inserting individual merge fields

You must include proper punctuation, spacing, and blank lines between the merge fields in a main document if you want punctuation, spaces, and blank lines to appear between the data in the merge documents. For example, to create an address line with a city, state, and zip code, you insert the City merge field, type a comma and a space, insert the State merge field, type a space, and then insert the ZIP Code merge field: <<City>>, <<State>> <<ZIP Code>>.

You can insert an individual merge field by clicking the Insert Merge Field list arrow in the Write & Insert Fields group and then selecting the field name from the menu that opens. Alternatively, you can click the Insert Merge Field button to open the Insert Merge Field dialog box, which you can use to insert several merge fields at once by clicking a field name in the dialog box, clicking Insert, clicking another field name, clicking Insert, and so on. When you have finished inserting the merge fields, click Close to close the dialog box. You can then add spaces, punctuation, and lines between the merge fields you inserted in the main document.

Practice

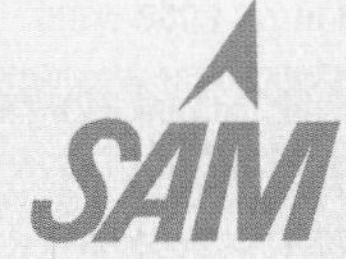

For current SAM information, including versions and content details, visit SAM Central (http://www.cengage.com/samcentral). If you have a SAM user profile, you may have access to hands-on instruction, practice, and assessment of the skills covered in this unit. Since various versions of SAM are supported throughout the life of this text, check with your instructor for the correct instructions and URL/Web site for accessing assignments.

Concepts Review

Describe the function of each button shown in Figure F-17.

FIGURE F-17

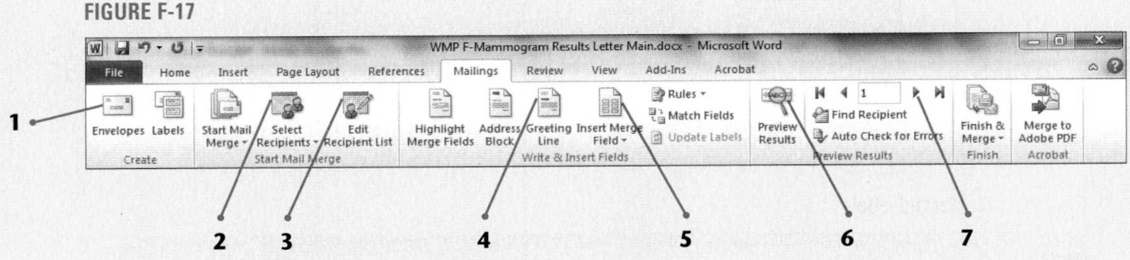

Match each term with the statement that best describes it.

8. Data record
9. Main document
10. Data field
11. Data source
12. Sort
13. Boilerplate text
14. Filter
15. Merge field

a. To organize records in a sequence
b. A file that contains customized information for each item or individual
c. A complete set of information for one item or individual
d. A category of information in a data source
e. A placeholder for merged data in the main document
f. The standard text that appears in every version of a merged document
g. A file that contains boilerplate text and merge fields
h. To pull out records that meet certain criteria

Select the best answer from the list of choices.

16. In a mail merge, which type of file contains the information that varies for each individual or item?
- **a.** Data source
- **b.** Main document
- **c.** Sorted document
- **d.** Filtered document

17. To change the font of merged data, which element should you format?
- **a.** Boilerplate text
- **b.** Field name
- **c.** Data record
- **d.** Merge field

18. Which command is used to synchronize the field names in a data source with the merge fields in a document?
- **a.** Rules
- **b.** Update Labels
- **c.** Match Fields
- **d.** Highlight Merge Fields

19. Which action do you perform on a data source in order to merge only certain records?
- **a.** Filter records
- **b.** Delete records
- **c.** Edit records
- **d.** Sort records

20. Which action do you perform on a data source to reorganize the order of the records for a merge?
- **a.** Edit records
- **b.** Sort records
- **c.** Filter records
- **d.** Delete records

Skills Review

1. **Create a main document.**
   a. Start Word, change the style of the document to No Spacing, then open the Mail Merge task pane.
   b. Use the Mail Merge task pane to create a letter main document, click Next, then select the current (blank) document.
   c. At the top of the blank document, type **New England Health and Life**, press [Enter], then type **1375 Harbor Street, Portsmouth, NH 03828; Tel: 603-555-8457; www.nehealthandlife.net**.
   d. Press [Enter] five times, type today's date, press [Enter] five times, then type **We are writing to confirm your choice of a Primary Care Physician in STATE. According to our records, you selected PCP as your Primary Care Physician.**
   e. Press [Enter] twice, then type **It's important that you contact your Primary Care Physician to coordinate all your medical care. If you need to see a specialist, your Primary Care Physician will refer you to one who is affiliated with his or her hospital or medical group.**
   f. Press [Enter] twice, then type **If the physician listed above is not the one you selected, please call Member Services at 1-800-555-1328.**
   g. Press [Enter] twice, type **Sincerely,** press [Enter] four times, type your name, press [Enter], then type **Member Services**.
   h. Center the first two lines of text, change the font used for New England Health and Life to 20 point Gill Sans Ultra Bold, then remove the hyperlink in the second line of text. (*Hint*: Right-click the hyperlink.)
   i. Save the main document as **WMP F-Subscriber PCP Letter Main** to the drive and folder where you store your Data Files.
2. **Design a data source.**
   a. Click Next, select the Type a new list option button in the Step 3 of 6 Mail Merge task pane, then click Create.
   b. Click Customize Columns in the New Address List dialog box, then remove these fields from the data source: Company Name, Address Line 2, Country or Region, Home Phone, Work Phone, and E-mail Address.
   c. Add an **ID** field and a **PCP** field to the data source. Be sure these fields follow the ZIP Code field.
   d. Rename the Address Line 1 field **Street**, then click OK to close the Customize Address List dialog box.
3. **Enter and edit records.**
   a. Add the records shown in Table F-2 to the data source.

TABLE F-2

Title	First Name	Last Name	Street	City	State	ZIP Code	ID	PCP
Mr.	Rich	Sargent	34 Mill St.	Exeter	NH	03833	MT3948	Susan Trifilo, M.D.
Mr.	Eric	Jenkins	289 Sugar Hill Rd.	Franconia	NH	03632	CZ2846	Richard Pattavina, M.D.
Ms.	Mary	Curtis	742 Main St.	Derby	VT	04634	MT1928	Edwin Marsh, M.D.
Mr.	Alex	Field	987 Ocean Rd.	Portsmouth	NH	03828	CF8725	Rebecca Keller, M.D.
Ms.	Eva	Juarez	73 Bay Rd.	Durham	NH	03814	MK2991	Anna Doherty, M.D.
Ms.	Molly	Reed	67 Apple St.	Northfield	MA	01360	CG8231	Bruce Dewey, M.D.
Ms.	Jenna	Suzuki	287 Mountain Rd.	Dublin	NH	03436	MT1878	Lisa Giaimo, M.D.

   b. Save the data source as **WMP F-Subscriber Data** to the drive and folder where you store your Data Files.
   c. Change the PCP for record 2 (Eric Jenkins) from Richard Pattanvina, M.D. to **Diana Ray, M.D.**
   d. Click OK to close the Mail Merge Recipients dialog box.
4. **Add merge fields.**
   a. Click Next, then in the blank line above the first body paragraph, insert an Address Block merge field.
   b. In the Insert Address Block dialog box, click Match Fields.
   c. Click the list arrow next to Address 1 in the Match Fields dialog box, click Street, then click OK. (*Hint*: If a warning box opens, click Yes, then click OK to close the dialog box.)
   d. Press [Enter] twice, type **Member ID:**, insert a space, then insert the ID merge field.
   e. Press [Enter] twice, insert a Greeting Line merge field using the default greeting line format, then press [Enter].
   f. In the first body paragraph, replace STATE with the State merge field and PCP with the PCP merge field. (*Note*: Make sure to insert a space before or after each merge field as needed.) Save your changes to the main document.

Skills Review (continued)

5. **Merge data.**
   a. Click Next to preview the merged data, then use the Next Record button to scroll through each letter, examining it carefully for errors.
   b. Click the Preview Results button on the Mailings tab, make any necessary adjustments to the main document, save your changes, then click the Preview Results button to return to the preview of the document.
   c. Click Next, click Edit individual letters, then merge all the records to a new file.
   d. Save the merged document as **WMP F-Subscriber PCP Letter Merge** to the drive and folder where you store your Data Files. The last letter is shown in Figure F-18. Submit the file or a copy of the last letter per your instructor's directions, then save and close all open files.
6. **Create labels.**
   a. Open a new blank document, click the Start Mail Merge button on the Mailings tab, then create a Labels main document.
   b. In the Label Options dialog box, select Avery US Letter 5160 Easy Peel Address labels, then click OK.
   c. Click the Select Recipients button, then open the WMP F-Subscriber Data.mdb file you created.
   d. Save the label main document as **WMP F-Subscriber Labels Main** to the drive and folder where you store your Data Files.
7. **Sort and filter records.**
   a. Click the Edit Recipient List button, filter the records so that only the records with NH in the State field are included in the merge, sort the records in zip code order, then click OK.
   b. Insert an Address Block merge field using the default settings, click the Preview Results button, then notice that the street address is missing. (*Note*: When you preview results, you see only one record at a time.)
   c. Click the Preview Results button, then click the Match Fields button to open the Match Fields dialog box.
   d. Click the list arrow next to Address 1, click Street, then click OK. (*Hint*: If a warning box opens, click Yes, then click OK to close the dialog box.)
   e. Click the Preview Results button to preview the merged data, and notice that the address block now includes the street address.
   f. Click the Update Labels button, examine the merged data for errors, then correct any mistakes.
   g. Merge all the records to an individual document, shown in Figure F-19, then save the merged file as **WMP F-Subscriber Labels NH Only Merge** to the drive and folder where you store your Data Files.
   h. In the first label, change Ms. Jenna Suzuki to your name, submit the document to your instructor, save and close all open Word files, then exit Word.

FIGURE F-18

New England Health and Life

1375 Harbor Street, Portsmouth, NH 03828; Tel: 603-555-8457; www.nehealthandlife.net

September 1, 2013

Ms. Jenna Suzuki
287 Mountain Rd.
Dublin, NH 03436

Member ID: MT1878

Dear Ms. Suzuki,

We are writing to confirm your choice of a Primary Care Physician in NH. According to our records, you selected Lisa Giaimo, M.D. , as your Primary Care Physician.

It's important that you contact your Primary Care Physician to coordinate all your medical care. If you need to see a specialist, your Primary Care Physician will refer you to one who is affiliated with his or her hospital or medical group.

If the physician listed above is not the one you selected, please call Member Services at 1-800-555-1328.

Sincerely,

Your Name
Member Services

FIGURE F-19

Ms. Jenna Suzuki 287 Mountain Rd. Dublin, NH 03436	Mr. Eric Jenkins 289 Sugar Hill Rd. Franconia, NH 03632	Ms. Eva Juarez 73 Bay Rd. Durham, NH 03814
Mr. Alex Field 987 Ocean Rd. Portsmouth, NH 03828	Mr. Rich Sargent 34 Mill St. Exeter, NH 03833	

Independent Challenge 1

You work for Rocky Mountain Eye Care. Your office has designed a maintenance program for gas permeable (GP) contact lenses, and you want to send a letter introducing the program to all patients who wear GP lenses. You'll use Mail Merge to create the letter. If you are performing the ACE steps and are able to print envelopes on your printer, you will also use Word to print an envelope for one letter.

a. Start Word, then using either the Mailings tab or the Mail Merge task pane, create a letter main document using the file WMP F-3.docx from the drive and folder where you store your Data Files.

b. Replace Your Name with your name in the signature block, then save the main document as **WMP F-GP Letter Main**.

c. Use the file WMP F-4.mdb from the drive and folder where you store your Data Files as the data source.

d. Sort the data source by last name in alphabetical order, then filter the data so that only records with GP as the lens are included in the merge.

e. Insert an Address Block and a Greeting Line merge field in the main document, then preview the merged letters.

f. Merge all the records to a new document, then save it as **WMP F-GP Letter Merge**.

Advanced Challenge Exercise

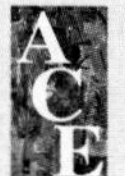

- If you can print envelopes, select the inside address in the first merge letter, then click the Envelopes button in the Create group on the Mailings tab.
- On the Envelopes tab, verify that the Omit check box is not selected, then type your name in the Return address text box along with the address **Rocky Mountain Eye Care, 60 Crandall Street, Boulder, CO 80306.**
- Click Options. On the Envelope Options tab, make sure the Envelope size is set to Size 10, then change the font of the Delivery address and the Return address to Times New Roman.
- On the Printing Options tab, select the appropriate Feed method for your printer, then click OK.
- Click Add to Document, click No if a message box opens asking if you want to save the new return address as the default return address, then print the envelope and submit it to your instructor.

g. Submit the file or a copy of the first merge letter per your instructor's directions, close all open Word files, saving changes, and then exit Word.

Independent Challenge 2

One of your responsibilities at Northwest Family Health, a growing family health clinic, is to create business cards for the staff. You use mail merge to create the cards so that you can easily produce standard business cards for future employees.

a. Start Word, then use the Mailings tab or the Mail Merge task pane to create labels using the current blank document.

b. Select Microsoft North American Size, which is described as Horizontal Card, 2" high × 3.5" wide. (*Hint*: Select the second instance of North American Size in the Product number list box.)

c. Create a new data source that includes the fields and records shown in Table F-3:

TABLE F-3

Title	First Name	Last Name	Phone	Fax	E-mail	Hire Date
Medical Director	Ruth	Harrington	(503) 555-3982	(503) 555-6654	rharrington@nwfh.com	1/12/10
Nurse Practitioner	Diego	Banks	(503) 555-2323	(503) 555-4956	dbanks@nwfh.com	3/18/11

d. Add six more records to the data source, including records for a Medical Assistant, an Immunization Coordinator, three Physicians, and an Administrative Assistant. Include your name in the record for the Administrative Assistant. (*Hint*: Be careful not to add a blank row at the bottom of the data source.)

e. Save the data source with the filename **WMP F-NWFH Employee Data** to the drive and folder where you store your Data Files, then sort the data by Title.

Independent Challenge 2 (continued)

f. In the first table cell, create the Northwest Family Health business card. Figure F-20 shows a sample business card, but you should create your own design. Include the clinic name, a street address, and the Web site address **www.nwfh.com**. Also include First Name, Last Name, Title, Phone, Fax, and E-mail merge fields. (*Hint*: If your design includes a graphic, insert the graphic before inserting the merge fields. Insert each merge field individually, adjusting the spacing between merge fields as necessary.)

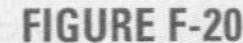
FIGURE F-20

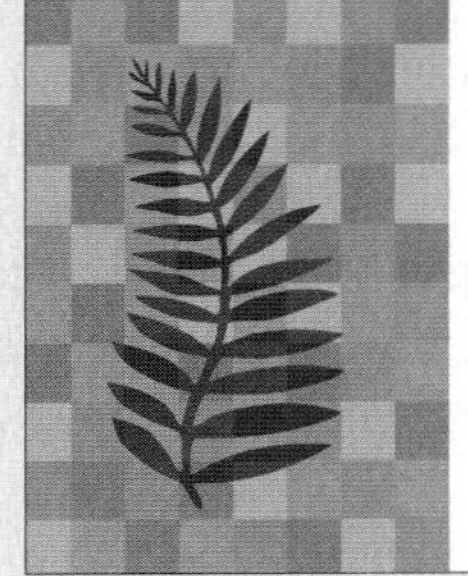

g. Format the business card with fonts, colors, and other formatting features. (*Hint*: Make sure to select the entire merge field, including the chevrons, before formatting.)

h. Update all the labels, preview the data, make any necessary adjustments, then merge all the records to a new document.

i. Save the merge document as **WMP F-NWFH Business Cards Merge** to the drive and folder where you store your Data Files, submit a copy to your instructor, then close the file.

j. Save the main document as **WMP F-NWFH Business Cards Main** to the drive and folder where you store your Data Files, close the file, then exit Word.

Independent Challenge 3

You need to create a class list for a fitness and nutrition class you teach for children who are overweight. You want the class list to include contact information for the children, as well as their age and Body Mass Index (BMI) at the time they registered for the class. You decide to use mail merge to create the class list. If you are completing the ACE steps, you will also use mail merge to create mailing labels.

a. Start Word, then use the Mailings tab or the Mail Merge task pane to create a directory using the current blank document.

b. Create a new data source that includes the following fields: First Name, Last Name, Age, BMI, Parent First Name, Parent Last Name, Address, City, State, ZIP Code, and Home Phone.

c. Enter the records shown in Table F-4 in the data source.

TABLE F-4

First Name	Last Name	Age	BMI	Parent First Name	Parent Last Name	Address	City	State	ZIP Code	Home Phone
Sophie	Wright	8	25.31	Kerry	Wright	58 Main St.	Camillus	NY	13031	555-2345
Will	Jacob	7	20.02	Bob	Jacob	32 North Way	Camillus	NY	13031	555-9827
Jackson	Rule	8	22.52	Sylvia	Rule	289 Sylvan Way	Marcellus	NY	13032	555-9724
Abby	Herman	7	21.89	Sarah	Thomas	438 Lariat St.	Marcellus	NY	13032	555-8347

d. Add five additional records to the data source using the following last names and BMIs:
O'Keefe, 24.03
George, 26.12
Goleman, 21.17
Siebert, 21.63
Choy, 23.45
Make up the remaining information for these five records.

e. Save the data source as **WMP F-Kids Fitness Class Data** to the drive and folder where you store your Data Files, then sort the records by last name.

f. Insert a table that includes six columns and one row in the main document.

g. In the first table cell, insert the First Name and Last Name merge fields, separated by a space.

h. In the second cell, insert the Age merge field.

i. In the third cell, insert the BMI merge field.

Independent Challenge 3 (continued)

- **j.** In the fourth cell, insert the Address and City merge fields, separated by a comma and a space.
- **k.** In the fifth cell, insert the Home Phone merge field.
- **l.** In the sixth cell, insert the Parent First Name and Parent Last Name merge fields, separated by a space.
- **m.** Preview the merged data and make any necessary adjustments. (*Hint*: Only one record is displayed at a time when you preview the data.)
- **n.** Merge all the records to a new document, then save the document as **WMP F-Kids Fitness Class List Merge** to the drive and folder where you store your Data Files.
- **o.** Press [Ctrl][Home], press [Enter], type **Fitness and Nutrition for Children** at the top of the document, press [Enter], type **Instructor:** followed by your name, then center the two lines.
- **p.** Insert a new row at the top of the table, then type the following column headings in the new row: **Name**, **Age**, **BMI**, **Address**, **Phone**, **Parent Name**.
- **q.** Format the class list to make it attractive and readable, save your changes, submit a copy to your instructor, then close the file.
- **r.** Close the main document without saving changes.

Advanced Challenge Exercise

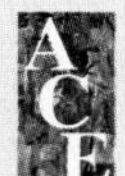

- Open a new blank document, then use mail merge to create mailing labels using Avery US Letter 5162 Easy Peel Address labels.
- Use the WMP F-Kids Fitness Class Data data source you created, and sort the records first in zip code order, and then alphabetically by parent last name.
- In the first table cell, create your own address block using the Parent First Name, Parent Last Name, Address, City, State, and Zip Code merge fields. Be sure to include proper spacing and punctuation.
- Update all the labels, preview the merged data, merge all the records to a new document, then type your name centered in the document header.
- Save the document as **WMP F-Kids Fitness Class Labels Merge ACE** to the drive and folder where you store your Data Files, submit a copy to your instructor, close the file, then close the main document without saving changes.

- **s.** Exit Word.

Real Life Independent Challenge

Mail merge can be used not only for mailings, but to create CD/DVD labels, labels for file folders, phone directories, business cards, and many other types of documents. In this independent challenge, you design and create a data source that you can use at work or in your personal life, and then you merge the data source with a main document that you create. Your data source might include contact information for your friends and associates, inventory for your business, details for an event such as a wedding (guests invited, responses, gifts received), data on one of your collections (such as music or photos), or some other type of information.

- **a.** Determine the content of your data source, list the fields you want to include, and then determine the logical order of the fields. Be sure to select your fields carefully so that your data source is flexible and can be merged with many types of documents. Generally it is better to include more fields, even if you don't enter data in them for each record.
- **b.** Start Word, start a mail merge for the type of document you want to create (such as a directory or a label), then create a new data source.
- **c.** Customize the columns in the data source to include the fields and organization you determined in Step a.
- **d.** Add at least five records to the data source, then save it as **WMP F-Your Name Data** to the location where you store your Data Files.
- **e.** Write and format the main document, insert the merge fields, preview the merge, make any necessary adjustments, then merge the files to a document.
- **f.** Adjust the formatting of the merge document as necessary, add your name to the header, save the merge document as **WMP F-Your Name Merge** to the drive and folder where you store your Data Files, submit a copy to your instructor, close the file, close the main document without saving changes, then exit Word.

Visual Workshop

Using mail merge, create the postcards shown in Figure F-21. Use Avery US Letter 3263 Postcard labels for the main document, and create a data source that contains at least four records, including your name. Save the data source as **WMP F-Patient Data**, save the merge document as **WMP F-Patient Reminder Card Merge**, and save the main document as **WMP F-Patient Reminder Card Main**, all to the drive and folder where you store your Data Files. (*Hints*: Notice that the postcard label main document is formatted as a table. To lay out the postcard, insert a nested table with two columns and one row in the upper-left postcard; add the text, graphic, and merge field to the nested table; and then remove the outside borders on the nested table. The clip art graphic uses the keyword "eye chart," and the fonts are Berlin Sans FB Demi and Calibri.) Submit a copy of the postcards to your instructor.

FIGURE F-21

Elizabeth B. Sloan, M.D. 974 West 96th Street, Suite 100 New York, NY 10025 Telephone: 212-555-8634 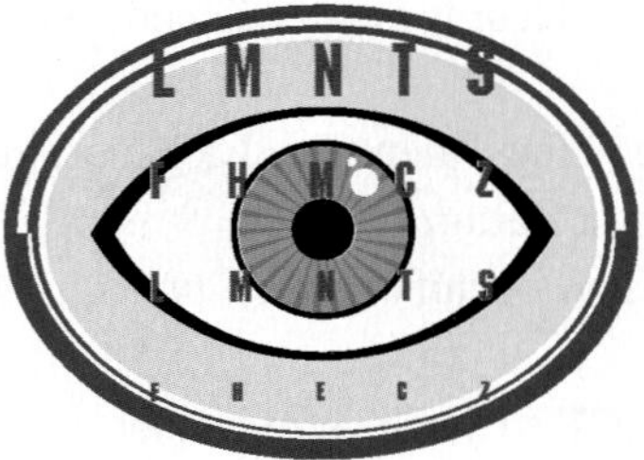 **Our records indicate it is time for your annual eye exam. Please call our office to schedule an appointment.**	Mr. Liam Geery 983 Broadway Apt. 74 New York, NY 10025
Elizabeth B. Sloan, M.D. 974 West 96th Street, Suite 100 New York, NY 10025 Telephone: 212-555-8634 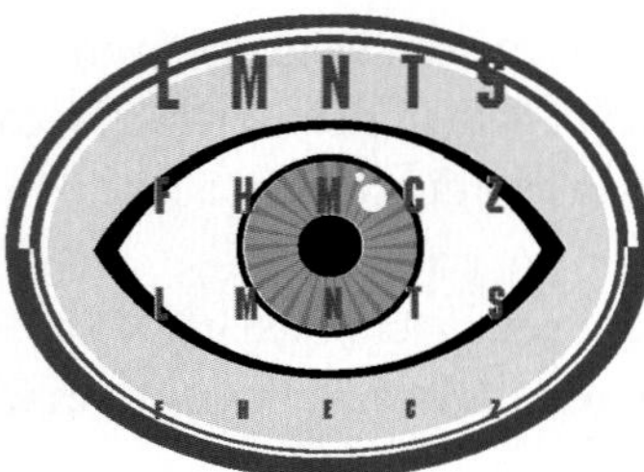 **Our records indicate it is time for your annual eye exam. Please call our office to schedule an appointment.**	Mr. Zeke Platte 234 W. 110th St. Apt. 112 New York, NY 10027

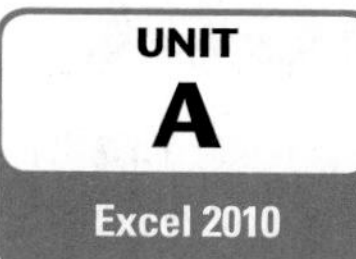

Getting Started with Excel 2010

Files You Will Need:

EMP A-1.xlsx
EMP A-2.xlsx
EMP A-3.xlsx
EMP A-4.xlsx
EMP A-5.xlsx

In this unit, you will learn how spreadsheet software helps you analyze data and make business decisions, even if you aren't a math pro. You'll become familiar with the different elements of a spreadsheet and learn your way around the Excel program window. You will also work in an Excel worksheet and make simple calculations. You have been hired as an assistant at Riverwalk Medical Clinic (RMC), a large outpatient medical facility staffed by family physicians, specialists, nurses, and other allied health professionals. You report to Tony Sanchez, R.N., the office manager. As Tony's assistant, you create worksheets to analyze data from various departments so you can help him make sound decisions on company expansion and investments, as well as day-to-day operations.

OBJECTIVES

- Understand spreadsheet software
- Tour the Excel 2010 window
- Understand formulas
- Enter labels and values and use the Sum button
- Edit cell entries
- Enter and edit a simple formula
- Switch worksheet views
- Choose print options

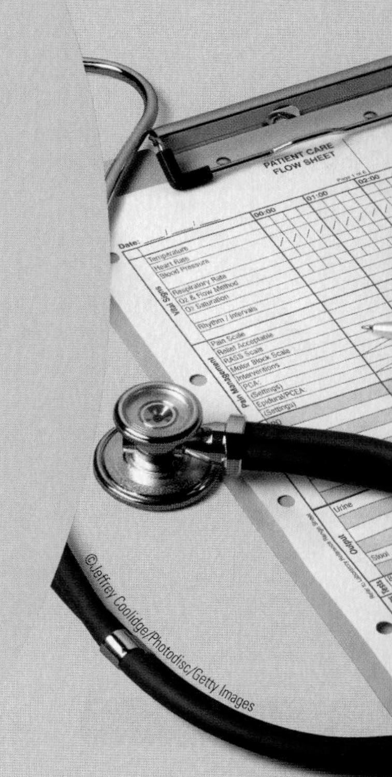

©Jeffrey Coolidge/Photodisc/Getty Images

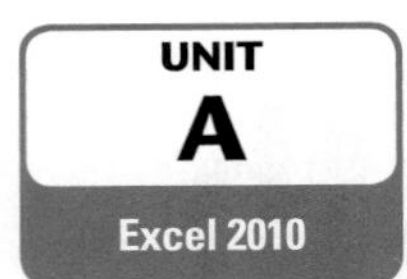

Understanding Spreadsheet Software

Microsoft Excel is the electronic spreadsheet program within the Microsoft Office suite. An **electronic spreadsheet** is an application you use to perform numeric calculations and to analyze and present numeric data. One advantage of spreadsheet programs over pencil and paper is that your calculations are updated automatically, so you can change entries without having to manually recalculate. Table A-1 shows some of the common business tasks people accomplish using Excel. In Excel, the electronic spreadsheet in which you work is called a **worksheet**, and it is contained in a file called a **workbook**, which has the file extension .xlsx. At Riverwalk Medical Clinic, you use Excel extensively to track finances and manage corporate data.

DETAILS

When you use Excel, you have the ability to:

- **Enter data quickly and accurately**
  With Excel, you can enter information faster and more accurately than with pencil and paper. Figure A-1 shows a payroll worksheet created using pencil and paper. Figure A-2 shows the same worksheet created using Excel. Equations were added to calculate the hours and pay. You can use Excel to recreate this information for each week by copying the worksheet's structure and the information that doesn't change from week to week, then entering unique data and formulas for each week. You can also quickly create charts and other elements to help visualize how the payroll is distributed.

- **Recalculate data easily**
  Fixing typing errors or updating data is easy in Excel. In the payroll example, if you receive updated hours for an employee, you just enter the new hours and Excel recalculates the pay.

- **Perform what-if analysis**
  The ability to change data and quickly view the recalculated results gives you the power to make informed business decisions. For instance, if you're considering raising the hourly rate for a medical records technician from $16.95 to $18.00, you can enter the new value in the worksheet and immediately see the impact on the overall payroll as well as on the individual employee. Any time you use a worksheet to ask the question "What if?" you are performing **what-if analysis**. Excel also includes a Scenario Manager where you can name and save different what-if versions of your worksheet.

- **Change the appearance of information**
  Excel provides powerful features for making information visually appealing and easier to understand. You can format text and numbers in different fonts, colors, and styles to make it stand out.

- **Create charts**
  Excel makes it easy to create charts based on worksheet information. Charts are updated automatically in Excel whenever data changes. The worksheet in Figure A-2 includes a 3-D pie chart.

- **Share information**
  It's easy for everyone at RMC to collaborate in Excel using the company intranet, the Internet, or a network storage device. For example, you can complete the weekly payroll that your boss, Tony Sanchez, began to create. You can also take advantage of collaboration tools, such as shared workbooks, so that multiple people can edit a workbook simultaneously.

- **Build on previous work**
  Instead of creating a new worksheet for every project, it's easy to modify an existing Excel worksheet. When you are ready to create next week's payroll, you can open the file for last week's payroll, save it with a new filename, and modify the information as necessary. You can also use predesigned, formatted files called **templates** to create new worksheets quickly. Excel comes with many templates that you can customize.

FIGURE A-1: Traditional paper worksheet

Riverwalk Medical Clinic
Health Professionals Payroll Calculator

Name	Position	Hours	O/T Hours	Hrly Rate	Reg Pay	O/T Pay	Gross Pay
Brueghel, Pieter	Patient Transporter	40	4	12.42	423.60	84.72	596.16
Cortez, Livia	Renal Dialysis Technician	35	0	14.15	495.25	-	495.25
Klinger, Kim	Physician Assistant	40	2	37.30	1,492.00	149.20	1,641.20
Lafontaine, Jeanne	Anesthesia Technician	29	0	14.46	419.34	-	419.34
Martinez, Juan	Medical Records Coding Technician	37	0	18.63	689.31	-	689.31
Mioshi, Keiko	Medical Records Technician	39	0	16.95	661.05	-	661.05
Sherwood, Burton	Massage Therapist	40	1	21.34	853.60	42.68	853.60
Strano, Richard	Medical Laboratory Technician	40	8	17.98	719.20	287.68	1,006.88
Wadsworth, Alicia	Interventional Radiology Technician	40	5	26.98	1,079.20	269.80	1,349.00
Yamamoto, Johji	Electroencephalograph Technician	38	0	19.83	753.54	-	753.54

FIGURE A-2: Excel worksheet

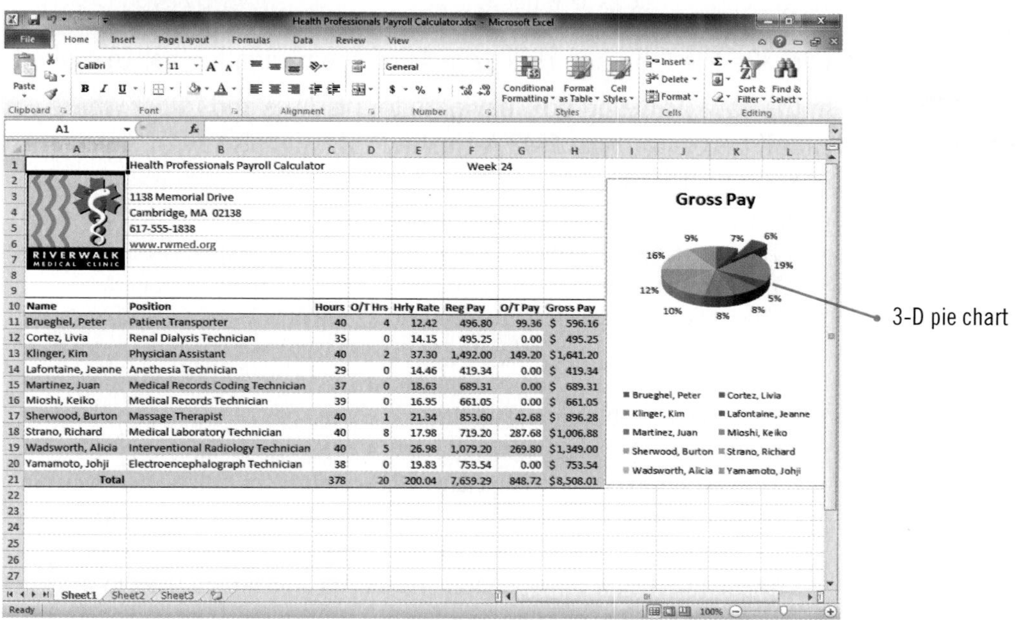

TABLE A-1: Business tasks you can accomplish using Excel

you can use spreadsheets to:	by:
Perform calculations	Adding formulas and functions to worksheet data; for example, adding a list of sales results or calculating a car payment
Represent values graphically	Creating charts based on worksheet data; for example, creating a chart that displays expenses
Generate reports	Creating workbooks that combine information from multiple worksheets, such as summarized sales information from multiple stores
Organize data	Sorting data in ascending or descending order; for example, alphabetizing a list of products or customer names, or prioritizing orders by date
Analyze data	Creating data summaries and short lists using PivotTables or AutoFilters; for example, making a list of the top 10 customers based on spending habits
Create what-if data scenarios	Using variable values to investigate and sample different outcomes; for example, changing the interest rate or payment schedule on a loan

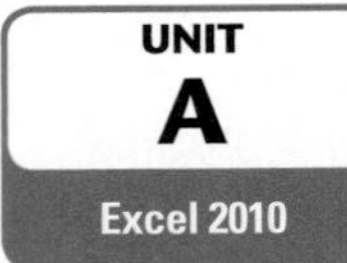

UNIT A

Excel 2010

Touring the Excel 2010 Window

To start Excel, Microsoft Windows must be running. Similar to starting any program in Office, you can use the Start button on the Windows taskbar, or you may have a shortcut on your desktop you prefer to use. If you need additional assistance, ask your instructor or technical support person. You decide to start Excel and familiarize yourself with the worksheet window.

STEPS

QUICK TIP

For more information on starting a program or opening and saving a file, see the unit "Getting Started with Microsoft Office 2010."

TROUBLE

If you don't see the extension .xlsx on the filenames in the Save As dialog box, don't worry; Windows can be set up to display or not to display the file extensions.

1. **Start Excel, click the File tab, then click Open on the navigation bar to open the Open dialog box**
2. **In the Open dialog box, navigate to the drive and folder where you store your Data Files, click EMP A-1.xlsx, then click Open**

   The file opens in the Excel window.
3. **Click the File tab, then click Save As on the navigation bar to open the Save As dialog box**
4. **In the Save As dialog box, navigate to the drive and folder where you store your Data Files if necessary, type EMP A-Health Professionals Payroll Calculator in the File name text box, then click Save**

   Using Figure A-3 as a guide, identify the following items:
   - The **Name box** displays the active cell address. "A1" appears in the Name box.
   - The **formula bar** allows you to enter or edit data in the worksheet.
   - The worksheet window contains a grid of columns and rows. Columns are labeled alphabetically and rows are labeled numerically. The worksheet window can contain a total of 1,048,576 rows and 16,384 columns. The intersection of a column and a row is called a **cell**. Cells can contain text, numbers, formulas, or a combination of all three. Every cell has its own unique location or **cell address**, which is identified by the coordinates of the intersecting column and row.
   - The **cell pointer** is a dark rectangle that outlines the cell in which you are working. This cell is called the **active cell**. In Figure A-3, the cell pointer outlines cell A1, so A1 is the active cell. The column and row headings for the active cell are highlighted, making it easier to locate.
   - **Sheet tabs** below the worksheet grid let you switch from sheet to sheet in a workbook. By default, a workbook file contains three worksheets—but you can use just one, or have as many as 255, in a workbook. The Insert Worksheet button to the right of Sheet 3 allows you to add worksheets to a workbook. **Sheet tab scrolling buttons** let you navigate to additional sheet tabs when available.
   - You can use the **scroll bars** to move around in a worksheet that is too large to fit on the screen at once.
   - The **status bar** is located at the bottom of the Excel window. It provides a brief description of the active command or task in progress. The **mode indicator** in the lower-left corner of the status bar provides additional information about certain tasks.
5. **Click cell D4**

   Cell D4 becomes the active cell. To activate a different cell, you can click the cell or press the arrow keys on your keyboard to move to it.
6. **Click cell C11, press and hold the mouse button, drag ✣ to cell C20, then release the mouse button**

   You selected a group of cells and they are now highlighted, as shown in Figure A-4. A selection of two or more cells such as C11:C20 is called a **range**; you select a range when you want to perform an action on a group of cells at once, such as moving them or formatting them. When you select a range, the status bar displays the average, count (or number of items selected), and sum of the selected cells as a quick reference.

FIGURE A-3: Open workbook

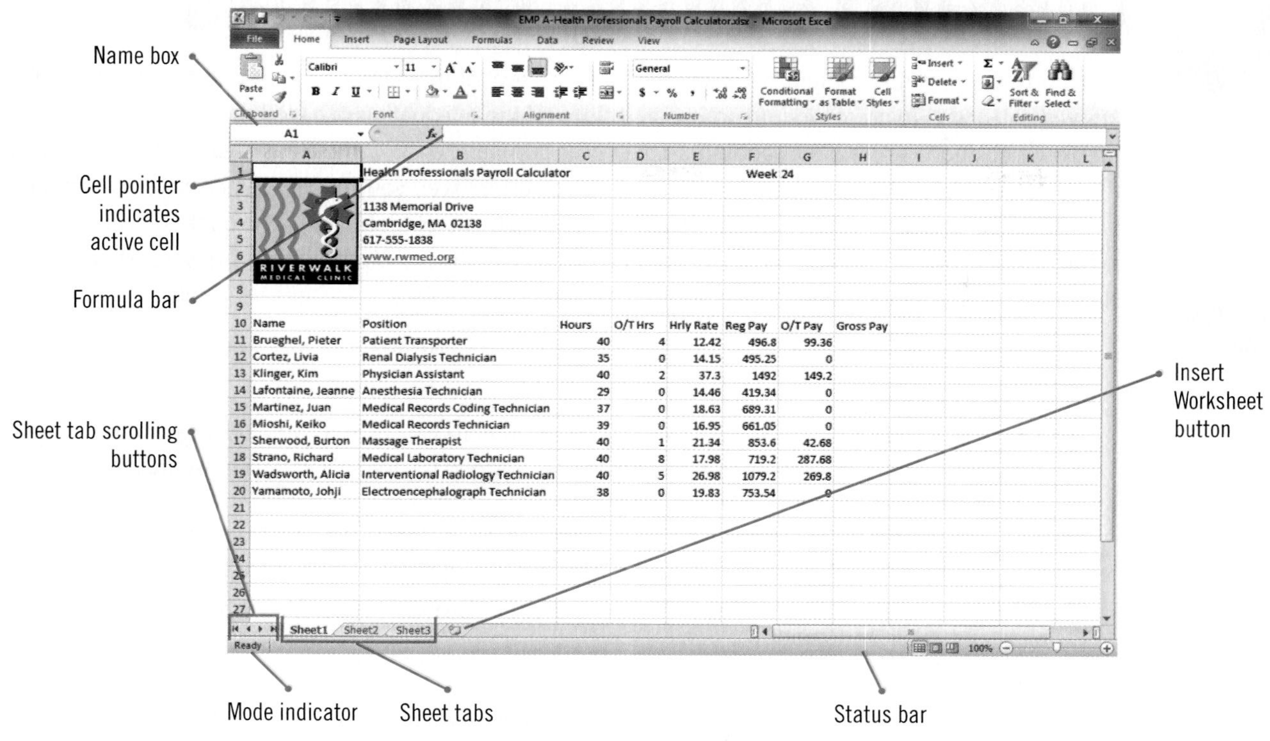

FIGURE A-4: Selected range

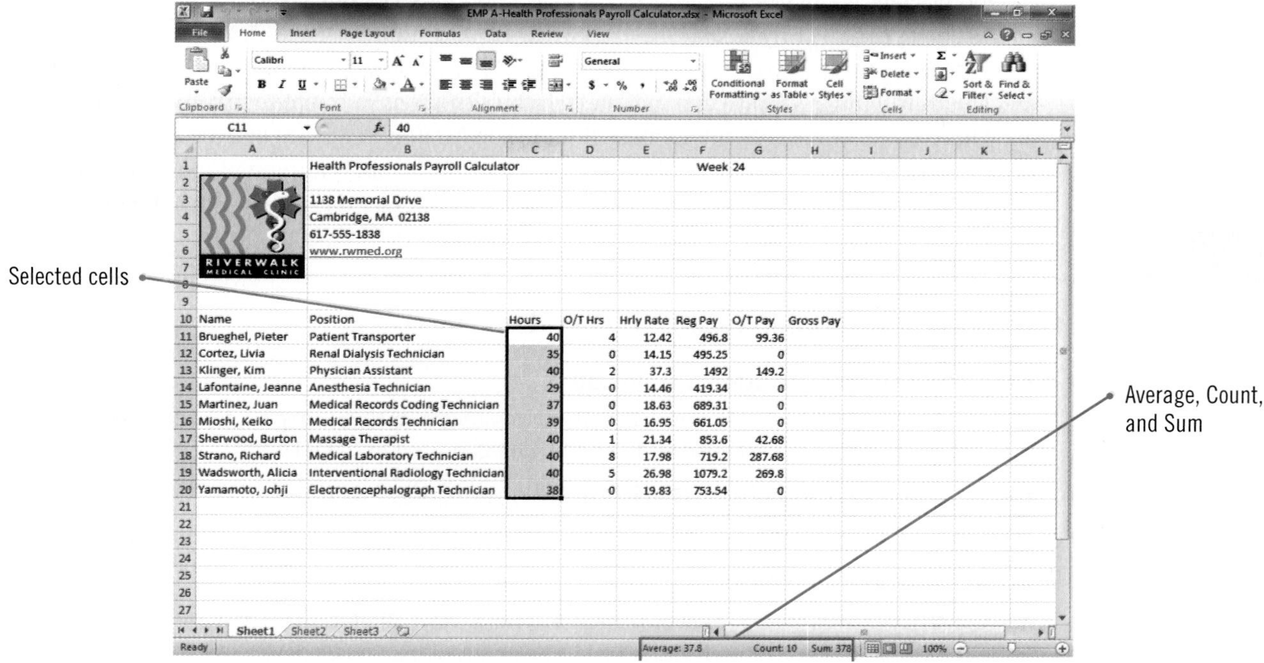

Windows Live and Microsoft Office Web Apps

All Office programs include the capability to incorporate feedback—called online collaboration—across the Internet or a company network. Using **cloud computing** (work done in a virtual environment), you can take advantage of Web programs called Microsoft Office Web Apps, which are simplified versions of the programs found in the Microsoft Office 2010 suite. Because these programs are online, they take up no computer disk space and are accessed using Windows Live SkyDrive, a free service from Microsoft. Using Windows Live SkyDrive, you and your colleagues can create and store documents in a "cloud" and make the documents available to whomever you grant access. To use Windows Live SkyDrive, you need a free Windows Live ID, which you obtain at the Windows Live Web site. You can find more information in the "Working with Windows Live and Office Web Apps" appendix.

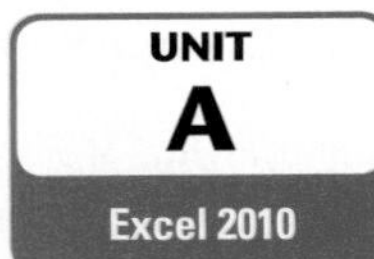

Understanding Formulas

Excel is a truly powerful program because users at every level of mathematical expertise can make calculations with accuracy. To do so, you use formulas. A **formula** is an equation in a worksheet. You use formulas to make calculations as simple as adding a column of numbers, or as complex as creating profit-and-loss projections for a global corporation. To tap into the power of Excel, you should understand how formulas work. Managers at RMC use the Health Professionals Payroll Calculator workbook to keep track of employee hours prior to submitting them to the Payroll Department. You'll be using this workbook regularly, so you need to understand the formulas it contains and how Excel calculates the results.

STEPS

1. **Click cell F11**

   The active cell contains a formula, which appears on the formula bar. All Excel formulas begin with the equal sign (=). If you want a cell to show the result of adding 4 plus 2, the formula in the cell would look like this: =4+2. If you want a cell to show the result of multiplying two values in your worksheet, such as the values in cells C11 and E11, the formula would look like this: =C11*E11, as shown in Figure A-5. While you're entering a formula in a cell, the cell references and arithmetic operators appear on the formula bar. See Table A-2 for a list of commonly used arithmetic operators. When you're finished entering the formula, you can either click the Enter button on the formula bar or press [Enter].

2. **Click cell G11**

   An example of a more complex formula is the calculation of overtime pay. At RMC, overtime pay is calculated at twice the regular hourly rate times the number of overtime hours. The formula used to calculate overtime pay for the employee in row 11 is:

   O/T Hrs times (2 times Hrly Rate)

   In the worksheet cell, you would enter: =D11*(2*E11), as shown in Figure A-6. The use of parentheses creates groups within the formula and indicates which calculations to complete first—an important consideration in complex formulas. In this formula, first the hourly rate is multiplied by 2, because that calculation is within the parentheses. Next, that value is multiplied by the number of overtime hours. Because overtime is calculated at twice the hourly rate, managers are aware that they need to closely watch this expense.

DETAILS

In creating calculations in Excel, it is important to:

- **Know where the formulas should be**

  An Excel formula is created in the cell where the formula's results should appear. This means that the formula calculating Gross Pay for the employee in row 11 will be entered in cell H11.

- **Know exactly what cells and arithmetic operations are needed**

  Don't guess; make sure you know exactly what cells are involved before creating a formula.

- **Create formulas with care**

  Make sure you know exactly what you want a formula to accomplish before it is created. An inaccurate formula may have far-reaching effects if the formula or its results are referenced by other formulas.

- **Use cell references rather than values**

  The beauty of Excel is that whenever you change a value in a cell, any formula containing a reference to that cell is automatically updated. For this reason, it's important that you use cell references in formulas, rather than actual values, whenever possible.

- **Determine what calculations will be needed**

  Sometimes it's difficult to predict what data will be needed within a worksheet, but you should try to anticipate what statistical information may be required. For example, if there are columns of numbers, chances are good that both column and row totals should be present.

FIGURE A-5: Viewing a formula

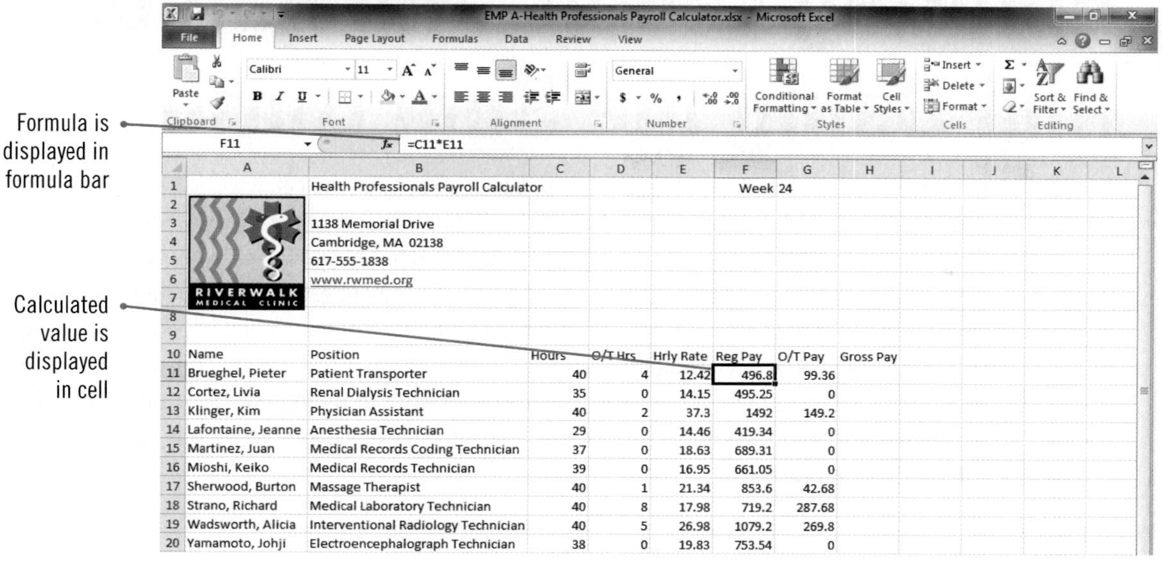

FIGURE A-6: Formula with multiple operators

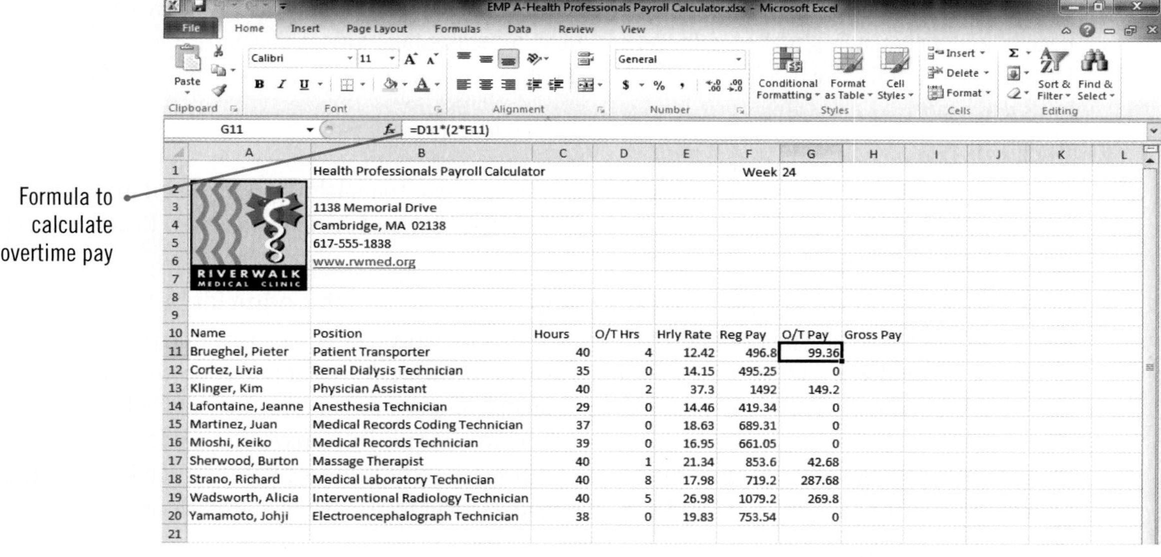

Excel 2010

TABLE A-2: Excel arithmetic operators

operator	purpose	example
+	Addition	=A5+A7
-	Subtraction or negation	=A5-10
*	Multiplication	=A5*A7
/	Division	=A5/A7
%	Percent	=35%
^ (caret)	Exponent	=6^2 (same as 6^2)

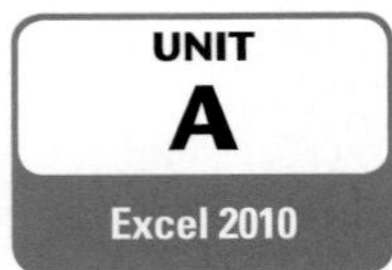

Entering Labels and Values and Using the Sum Button

To enter content in a cell, you can type on the formula bar or directly in the cell itself. When entering content in a worksheet, you should start by entering all the labels first. **Labels** are entries that contain text and numerical information not used in calculations, such as "2013 Revenue" or "Travel Expenses." Labels help you identify data in worksheet rows and columns, making your worksheet easier to understand. **Values** are numbers, formulas, and functions that can be used in calculations. To enter a calculation, you type an equal sign (=) plus the formula for the calculation; some examples of an Excel calculation are "=2+2" and "=C5+C6." Functions are Excel's built-in formulas; you learn more about them in the next unit. You want to enter some information in the Health Professionals Payroll Calculator workbook, and use a very simple function to total a range of cells.

STEPS

1. **Click cell A21, then click in the formula bar**
   Notice that the **mode indicator** on the status bar now reads "Edit", indicating you are in Edit mode. You are in Edit mode any time you are entering or changing the contents of a cell.

QUICK TIP
If you change your mind and want to cancel an entry in the formula bar, click the Cancel button on the formula bar.

2. **Type Totals, then click the Enter button on the formula bar**
   Clicking the Enter button accepts the entry. The new text is left-aligned in the cell. Labels are left-aligned by default, and values are right-aligned by default. Excel recognizes an entry as a value if it is a number or it begins with one of these symbols: +, -, =, @, #, or $. When a cell contains both text and numbers, Excel recognizes it as a label.
3. **Click cell C21**
   You want this cell to total the hours worked by all the employees. You might think you need to create a formula that looks like this: =C11+C12+C13+C14+C15+C16+C17+C18+C19+C20. However, there's an easier way to achieve this result.
4. **Click the Sum button in the Editing group on the Home tab on the Ribbon**
   The SUM function is inserted in the cell, and a suggested range appears in parentheses, as shown in Figure A-7. A **function** is a built-in formula; it includes the **arguments** (the information necessary to calculate an answer) as well as cell references and other unique information. Clicking the Sum button sums the adjacent range (that is, the cells next to the active cell) above or to the left, though you can adjust the range if necessary by selecting a different range before accepting the cell entry. Using the SUM function is quicker than entering a formula, and using the range C11:C20 is more efficient than entering individual cell references.

QUICK TIP
You can create formulas in a cell even before you enter the values to be calculated; the results will be recalculated as soon as the data is entered.

5. **Click on the formula bar**
   Excel calculates the total contained in cells C11:C20 and displays the result, 378, in cell C21.The cell actually contains the formula =SUM(C11:C20), and the result is displayed.
6. **Click cell D19, type 6, then press [Enter]**
   The number 6 replaces the cell's contents, the cell pointer moves to cell D20, and the value in cell G19 changes.

QUICK TIP
If making horizontal entries, you can also press [Tab] to complete a cell entry and move the cell pointer to the right.

7. **Click cell D24, type Average Gross Pay, then press [Enter]**
   The new label is entered in cell D24. The contents appear to spill into the empty cells to the right.
8. **Click cell C21, position the pointer on the lower-right corner of the cell (the fill handle) so that the pointer changes to +, drag the + to cell H21, then release the mouse button**
   Dragging the fill handle across a range of cells copies the contents of the first cell into the other cells in the range. In the range C21:H21, each filled cell now contains a function that sums the range of cells above, as shown in Figure A-8.
9. **Save your work**

FIGURE A-7: Creating a formula using the Sum button

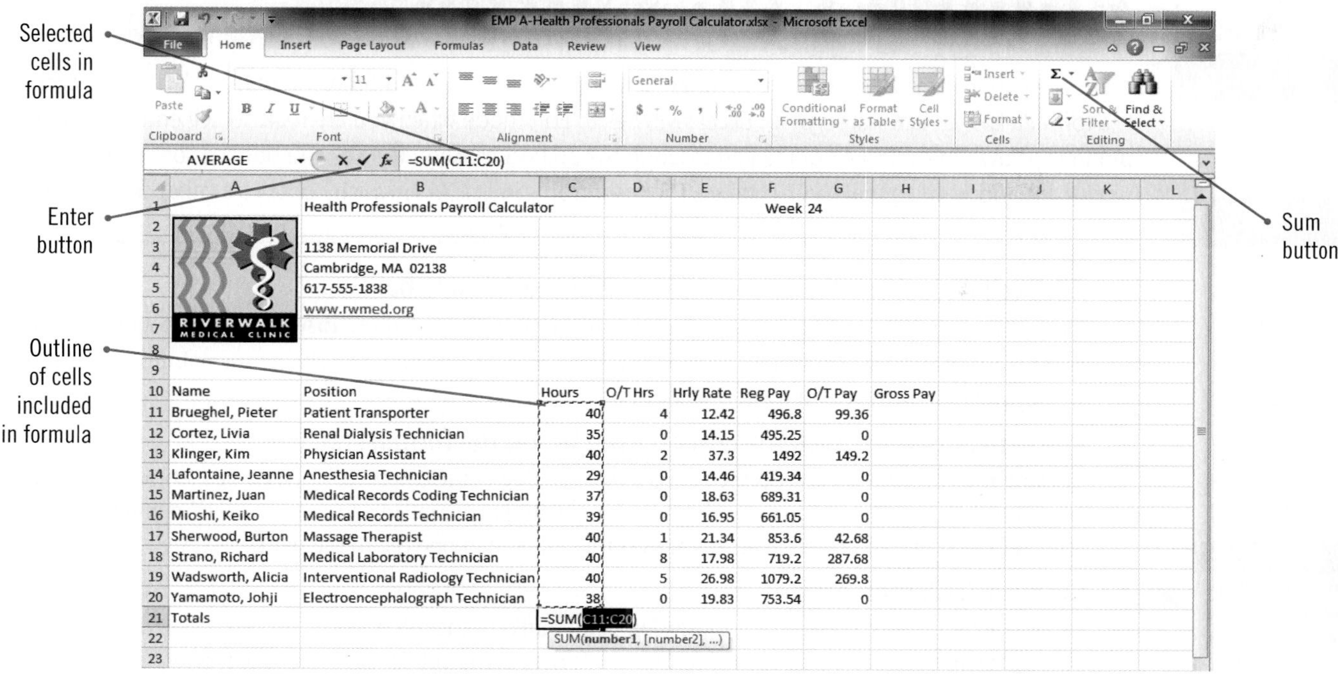

FIGURE A-8: Results of copied SUM functions

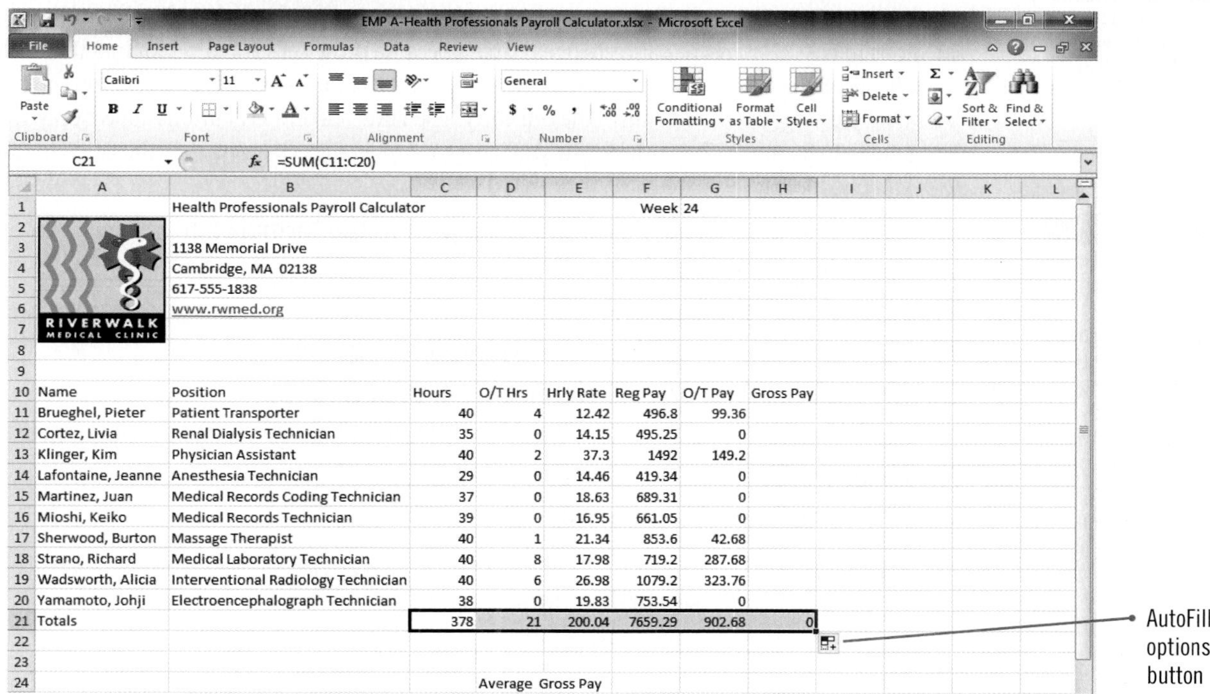

Excel 2010

Navigating a worksheet

With over a million cells available in a worksheet, it is important to know how to move around, or **navigate**, in a worksheet. You can use the arrow keys on the keyboard [↑],[↓], [→], or [←] to move one cell at a time, or press [Page Up] or [Page Down] to move one screen at a time. To move one screen to the left press [Alt][Page Up]; to move one screen to the right press [Alt][Page Down]. You can also use the mouse pointer to click the desired cell. If the desired cell is not visible in the worksheet window, use the scroll bars or use the Go To command by clicking the Find & Select button in the Editing group on the Home tab on the Ribbon. To quickly jump to the first cell in a worksheet press [Ctrl][Home]; to jump to the last cell, press [Ctrl][End].

UNIT A

Excel 2010

Editing Cell Entries

You can change, or **edit**, the contents of an active cell at any time. To do so, double-click the cell, click in the formula bar, or just start typing. Excel switches to Edit mode when you are making cell entries. Different pointers, shown in Table A-3, guide you through the editing process. You noticed some errors in the worksheet and want to make corrections. The first error is in cell A11, which contains a misspelled name.

STEPS

1. **Click cell A11, then click to the right of P in the formula bar**

   As soon as you click in the formula bar, a blinking vertical line called the **insertion point** appears on the formula bar at the location where new text will be inserted. See Figure A-9. The mouse pointer changes to I when you point anywhere in the formula bar.

2. **Press [Delete], then click the Enter button ✓ on the formula bar**

   Clicking the Enter button accepts the edit, and the spelling of the employee's first name is corrected. You can also press [Enter] or [Tab] to accept an edit. Pressing [Enter] to accept an edit moves the cell pointer down one cell, and pressing [Tab] to accept an edit moves the cell pointer one cell to the right.

3. **Click cell C12, then press [F2]**

   Excel switches to Edit mode, and the insertion point blinks in the cell. Pressing [F2] activates the cell for editing directly in the cell instead of the formula bar. Whether you edit in the cell or the formula bar is simply a matter of preference; the results in the worksheet are the same.

4. **Press [Backspace], type 8, then press [Enter]**

   The value in the cell changes from 35 to 38, and cell C13 becomes the active cell. Did you notice that the calculations in cells C21 and F12 also changed? That's because those cells contain formulas that include cell C12 in their calculations. If you make a mistake when editing, you can click the Cancel button ✗ on the formula bar *before* pressing [Enter] to confirm the cell entry. The Enter and Cancel buttons appear only when you're in Edit mode. If you notice the mistake *after* you have confirmed the cell entry, click the Undo button on the Quick Access toolbar.

5. **Click cell A15, then double-click the word Juan in the formula bar**

   Double-clicking a word in a cell selects it.

6. **Type Javier, then press [Enter]**

   When text is selected, typing deletes it and replaces it with the new text.

7. **Double-click cell D18, press [Delete], type 4, then click ✓**

   Double-clicking a cell activates it for editing directly in the cell. Compare your screen to Figure A-10.

8. **Save your work**

   Your changes to the workbook are saved.

QUICK TIP

On some keyboards, you might need to press an [F Lock] key to enable the function keys.

QUICK TIP

The Undo button allows you to reverse up to 100 previous actions, one at a time.

QUICK TIP

You can use the keyboard to select all cell contents by clicking to the right of the cell contents in the cell or formula bar, pressing and holding [Shift], then pressing [Home].

Recovering unsaved changes to a workbook file

You can use Excel's AutoRecover feature to automatically save (Autosave) your work as often as you want. This means that if you suddenly lose power or if Excel closes unexpectedly while you're working, you can recover all or some of the changes you made since you last saved it. (Of course, this is no substitute for regularly saving your work: this is just added insurance.) To customize the AutoRecover settings, click the File tab, click Options, then click Save. AutoRecover lets you decide how often and into which location it should Autosave files. When you restart Excel after losing power, a Document Recovery pane opens and provides access to the saved and Autosaved versions of the files that were open when Excel closed. You can also click the File tab, click Recent on the navigation bar, then click Recover Unsaved Workbooks to open Autosaved workbooks using the Open dialog box.

FIGURE A-9: **Worksheet in Edit mode**

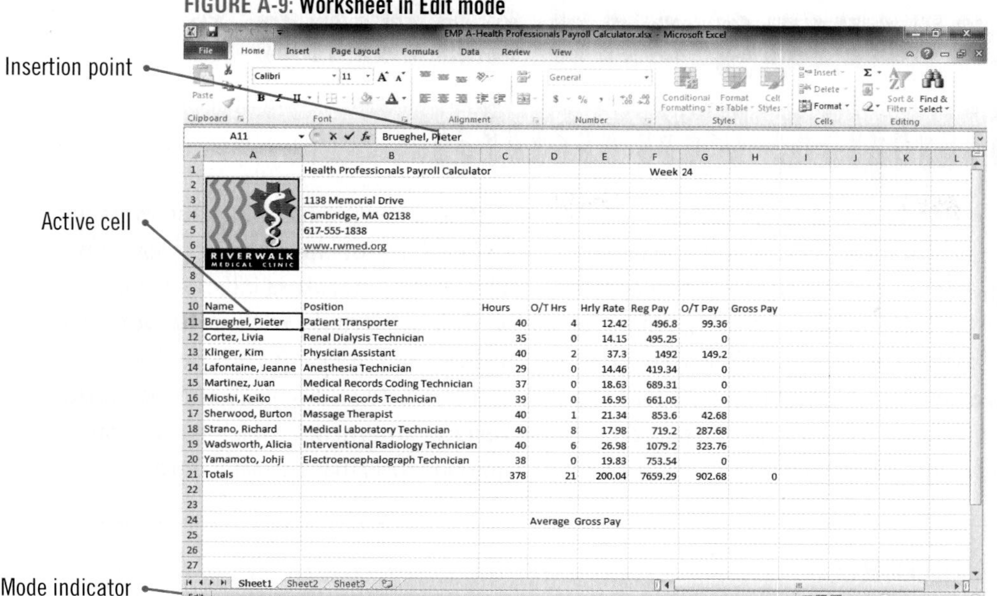

FIGURE A-10: **Edited worksheet**

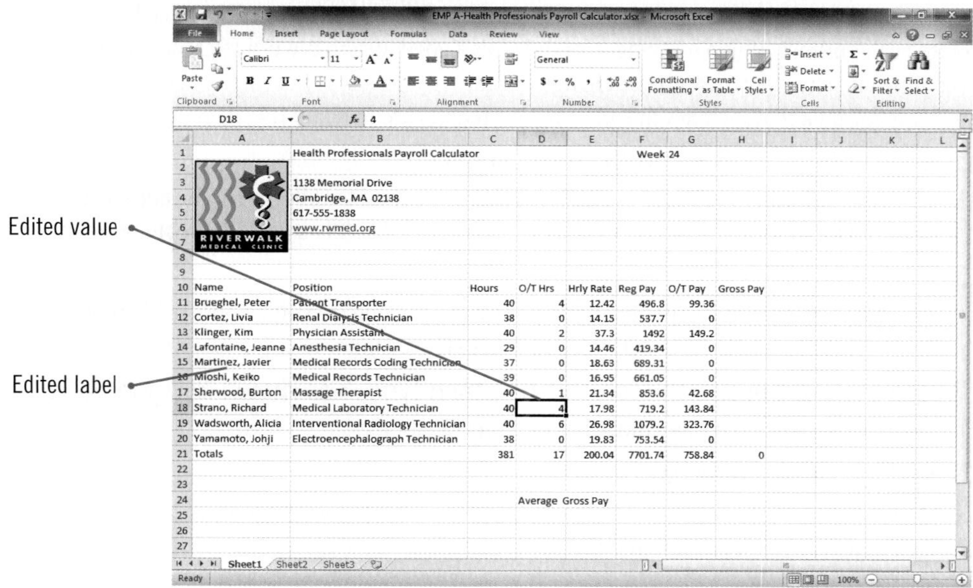

TABLE A-3: **Common pointers in Excel**

name	pointer	use to	visible over the
Normal	✥	Select a cell or range; indicates Ready mode	Active worksheet
Fill handle	+	Copy cell contents to adjacent cells	Lower-right corner of the active cell or range
I-beam	I	Edit cell contents in active cell or formula bar	Active cell in Edit mode or over the formula bar
Move	✥	Change the location of the selected cell(s)	Perimeter of the active cell(s)
Copy	↖+	Create a duplicate of the selected cell(s)	Perimeter of the active cell(s) when [Ctrl] is pressed
Column resize	↔	Change the width of a column	Border between column heading indicators

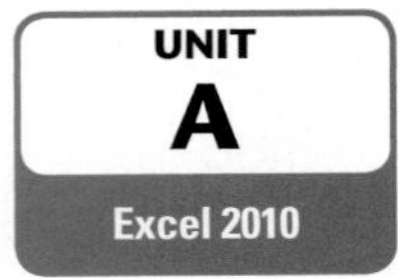

Entering and Editing a Simple Formula

You use formulas in Excel to perform calculations such as adding, multiplying, and averaging. Formulas in an Excel worksheet start with the equal sign (=), also called the **formula prefix**, followed by cell addresses, range names, values, and calculation operators. **Calculation operators** indicate what type of calculation you want to perform on the cells, ranges, or values. They can include **arithmetic operators**, which perform mathematical calculations (see Table A-2 in the "Understanding Formulas" lesson); **comparison operators**, which compare values for the purpose of true/false results; **text concatenation operators**, which join strings of text in different cells; and **reference operators**, which enable you to use ranges in calculations. You want to create a formula in the worksheet that calculates gross pay for each employee.

STEPS

1. **Click cell H11**

   This is the first cell where you want to insert the formula. To calculate gross pay, you need to add regular pay and overtime pay. For employee Peter Brueghel, regular pay appears in cell F11 and overtime pay appears in cell G11.

2. **Type =, click cell F11, type +, then click cell G11**

   Compare your formula bar to Figure A-11. The blue and green cell references in cell H11 correspond to the colored cell outlines. When entering a formula, it's a good idea to use cell references instead of values whenever you can. That way, if you later change a value in a cell (if, for example, Peter's regular pay changes to 500), any formula that includes this information reflects accurate, up-to-date results.

> **QUICK TIP**
> You can reference a cell in a formula either by typing the cell reference or clicking the cell in the worksheet; when you click a cell to add a reference, the Mode indicator changes to "Point."

3. **Click the Enter button ✓ on the formula bar**

   The result of the formula =F11+G11, 596.16, appears in cell H11. This same value appears in cell H21 because cell H21 contains a formula that totals the values in cells H11:H20, and there are no other values now.

4. **Click cell G11**

   The formula in this cell calculates overtime pay by multiplying overtime hours (D11) times twice the regular hourly rate (2*E11). You want to edit this formula to reflect a new overtime pay rate.

5. **Click to the right of 2 in the formula bar, then type .5 as shown in Figure A-12**

   The formula that calculates overtime pay has been edited.

6. **Click ✓ on the formula bar**

   Compare your screen to Figure A-13. Notice that the calculated values in cells G21, H11, and H21 have all changed to reflect your edits to cell G11.

7. **Save your work**

Understanding named ranges

It can be difficult to remember the cell locations of critical information in a worksheet, but using cell names can make this task much easier. You can name a single cell or a range of contiguous, or touching, cells. For example, you might name a cell that contains data on average gross pay "AVG_GP" instead of trying to remember the cell address C18. A named range must begin with a letter or an underscore. It cannot contain any spaces or be the same as a built-in name, such as a function or another object (for example a different named range) in the workbook. To name a range, select the cell(s) you want to name, click the Name box in the formula bar, type the name you want to use, then press [Enter]. You can also name a range by clicking the Formulas tab, then clicking the Define Name button in the Defined Names group. Type the new range name in the Name text box in the New Name dialog box, verify the selected range, then click OK. When you use a named range in a formula, the named range appears instead of the cell address. You can also create a named range using the contents of a cell already in the range. Select the range containing the text you want to use as a name, then click the Create from Selection button in the Defined Names group. The Create Names from Selection dialog box opens. Choose the location of the name you want to use, then click OK.

FIGURE A-11: **Simple formula in a worksheet**

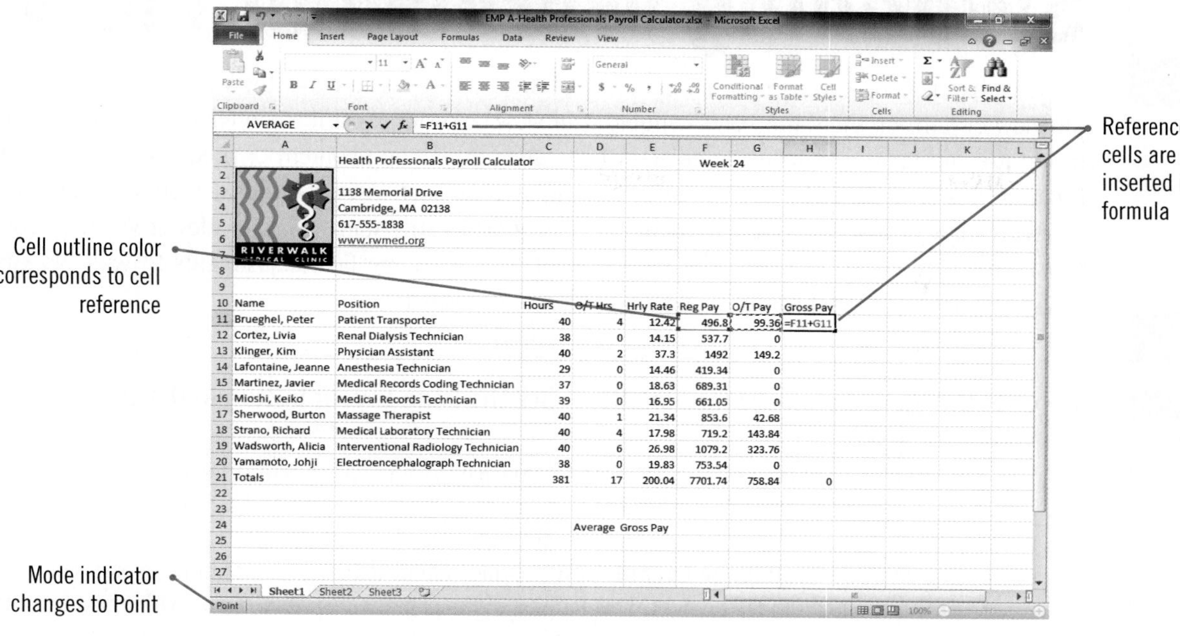

FIGURE A-12: **Edited formula in a worksheet**

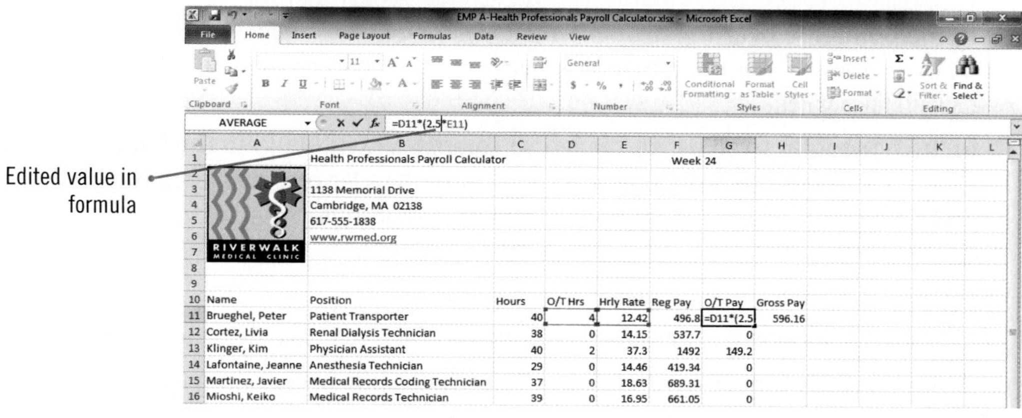

FIGURE A-13: **Edited formula with changes**

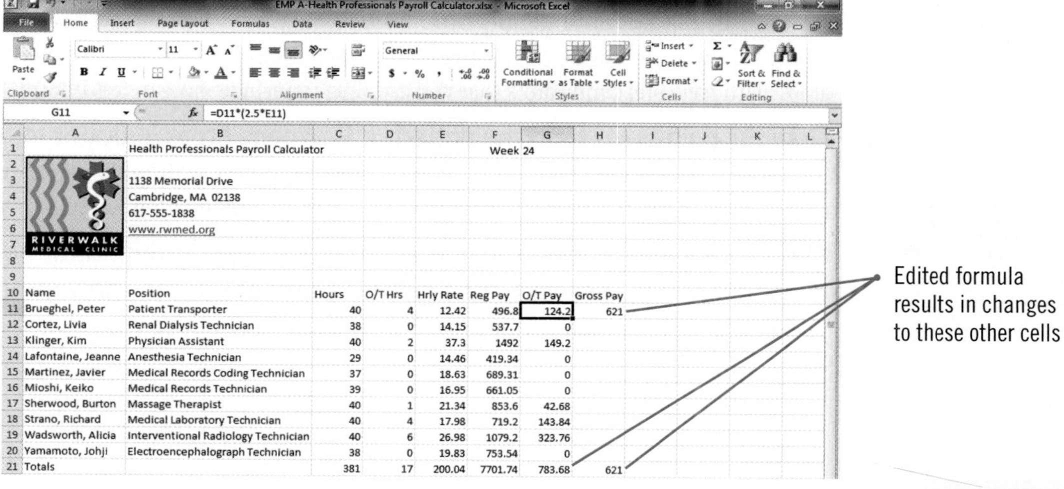

Excel 2010

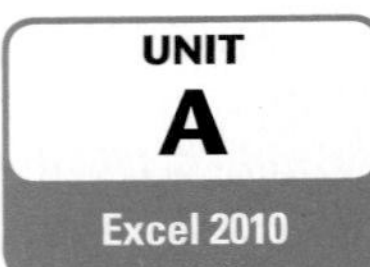
UNIT A
Excel 2010

Switching Worksheet Views

You can change your view of the worksheet window at any time, using either the View tab on the Ribbon or the View buttons on the status bar. Changing your view does not affect the contents of a worksheet; it just makes it easier for you to focus on different tasks, such as entering content or preparing a worksheet for printing. The View tab includes a variety of viewing options, such as View buttons, zoom controls, and the ability to show or hide worksheet elements such as gridlines. The status bar offers fewer View options but can be more convenient to use. You want to make some final adjustments to your worksheet, including adding a header so the document looks more polished.

STEPS

> **QUICK TIP**
> Although a worksheet can contain more than a million rows and thousands of columns, the current document contains only as many pages as necessary for the current project.

1. **Click the View tab on the Ribbon, then click the Page Layout button in the Workbook Views group**

   The view switches from the default view, Normal, to Page Layout view. **Normal view** shows the worksheet without including certain details like headers and footers, or tools like rulers and a page number indicator; it's great for creating and editing a worksheet, but may not be detailed enough when you want to put the finishing touches on a document. **Page Layout view** provides a more accurate view of how a worksheet will look when printed, as shown in Figure A-14. The margins of the page are displayed, along with a text box for the header. A footer text box appears at the bottom of the page, but your screen may not be large enough to view it without scrolling. Above and to the left of the page are rulers. Part of an additional page appears to the right of this page. If the next page did not contain any data, it would appear dimmed. A page number indicator on the status bar tells you the current page and the total number of pages in this worksheet.

2. **Drag the pointer over the header *without clicking***

   The header is made up of three text boxes: left, center, and right. Each text box is highlighted blue as you pass over it with the pointer.

> **QUICK TIP**
> You can change header and footer information using the Header & Footer Tools Design tab that opens on the Ribbon when a header or footer is active. For example, you can insert the date by clicking the Current Date button in the Header & Footer Elements group, or insert the time by clicking the Current Time button.

3. **Drag the horizontal scroll bar to the left so column A is visible, click the left header text box, type Riverwalk Medical Clinic, click the center header text box, type Health Prof Payroll Calculator, click the right header text box, then type Week 24**

   The new text appears in the text boxes, as shown in Figure A-15.

4. **Select the range B1:G1, then press [Delete]**

   The duplicate information you just entered in the header is deleted from cells in the worksheet.

5. **Click the View tab if necessary, click the Ruler check box in the Show group, then click the Gridlines check box in the Show group**

   The rulers and the gridlines are hidden. By default, gridlines in a worksheet do not print, so hiding them gives you a more accurate image of your final document.

6. **Click the Page Break Preview button on the status bar, then click OK in the Welcome to Page Break Preview dialog box, if necessary**

   Your view changes to **Page Break Preview**, which displays a reduced view of each page of your worksheet, along with page break indicators that you can drag to include more or less information on a page.

7. **Drag the pointer ↔ from the dotted vertical page break indicator to the right of column I**

   See Figure A-16. When you're working on a large worksheet with multiple pages, sometimes you need to adjust where pages break; in this worksheet, however, the information will all fit comfortably on one page.

> **QUICK TIP**
> Once you view a worksheet in Page Break Preview, the page break indicators appear as dotted lines after you switch back to Normal view or Page Layout view.

8. **Click the Page Layout button in the Workbook Views group, click the Ruler check box in the Show group, then click the Gridlines check box in the Show group**

   The rulers and gridlines are no longer hidden. You can show or hide View tab items in any view.

9. **Save your work**

FIGURE A-14: **Page Layout view**

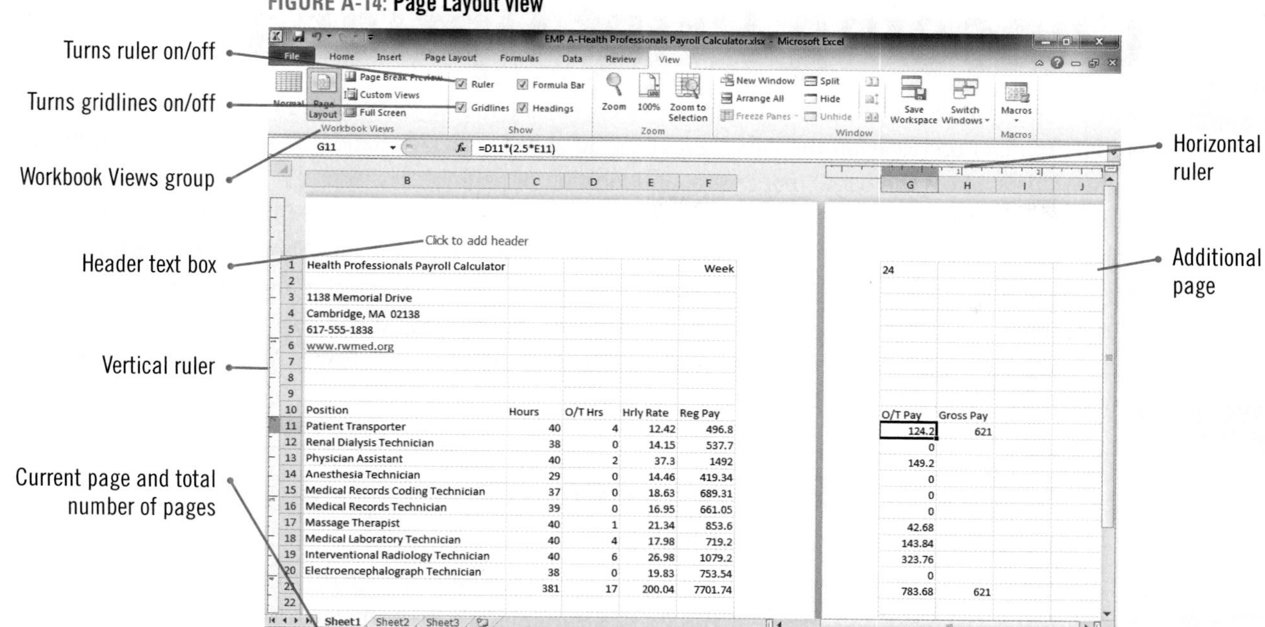

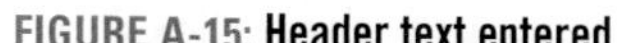

FIGURE A-15: **Header text entered**

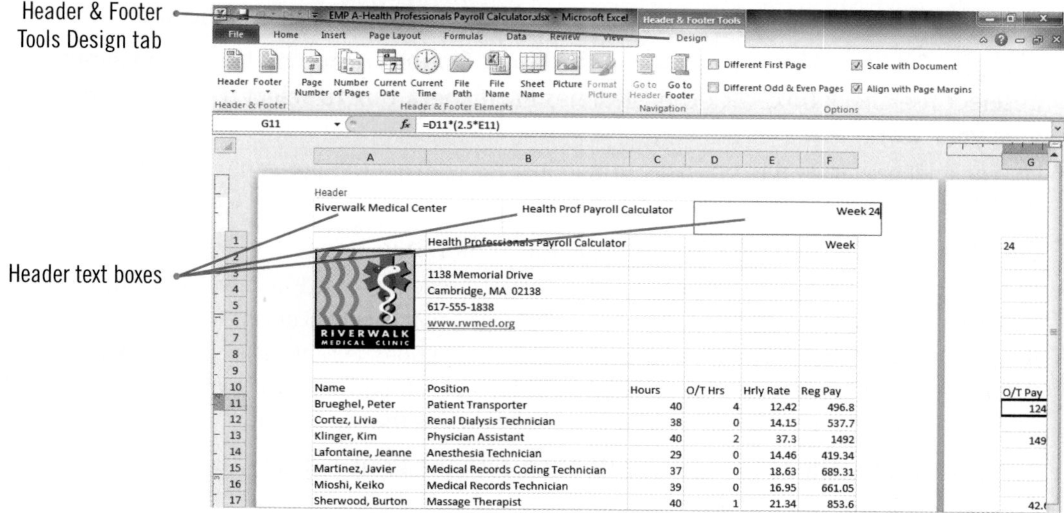

FIGURE A-16: **Page Break Preview**

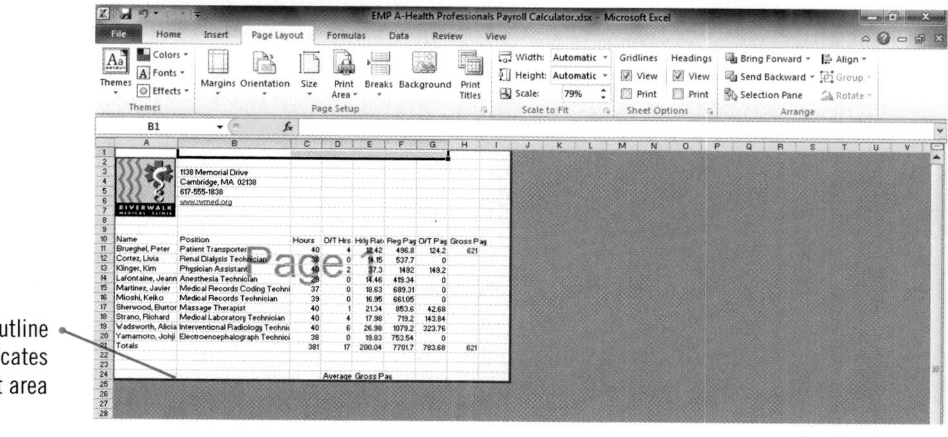

UNIT A

Excel 2010

Choosing Print Options

Before printing a document, you may want to review it using the Page Layout tab to fine-tune your printed output. You can use tools on the Page Layout tab to adjust print orientation (the direction in which the content prints across the page), paper size, and location of page breaks. You can also use the Scale to Fit options on the Page Layout tab to fit a large amount of data on a single page without making changes to individual margins, and to turn gridlines and column/row headings on and off. When you are ready to print, you can set print options such as the number of copies to print and the correct printer, and you can preview your document in Backstage view using the File tab. You can also adjust page layout settings from within Backstage view and immediately see the results in the document preview. You are ready to prepare your worksheet for printing.

STEPS

1. **Click cell A24, type your name, then press [Enter]**
2. **Click the Page Layout tab on the Ribbon**
   Compare your screen to Figure A-17. The dotted line indicates the default **print area**, the area to be printed.
3. **Click the Orientation button in the Page Setup group, then click Landscape**
   The paper orientation changes to **landscape**, so the contents will print across the length of the page instead of across the width.
4. **Click the Orientation button in the Page Setup group, then click Portrait**
   The orientation returns to **portrait**, so the contents will print across the width of the page.
5. **Click the Gridlines View check box in the Sheet Options group on the Page Layout tab to deselect the check box, click the Gridlines Print check box to select it if necessary, then save your work**
   Printing gridlines makes the data easier to read, but the gridlines will not print unless the Gridlines Print check box is checked.
6. **Click the File tab, then click Print on the navigation bar**
   The Print tab in Backstage view displays a preview of your worksheet exactly as it will look when it is printed. To the left of the worksheet preview, you can also change a number of document settings and print options. To open the Page Setup dialog box and adjust page layout options, click the Page Setup link in the Settings section. Compare your preview screen to Figure A-18. You can print from this view by clicking the Print button, or return to the worksheet without printing by clicking the File tab again.
7. **Compare your settings to Figure A-18, then click the Print button**
   One copy of the worksheet prints.
8. **Submit your work to your instructor as directed, then exit Excel**

QUICK TIP
You can use the Zoom slider on the status bar at any time to enlarge your view of specific areas of your worksheet.

QUICK TIP
To change the active printer, click the current printer in the Printer section in Backstage view, then choose a different printer.

QUICK TIP
If the Quick Print button appears on the Quick Access Toolbar, you can print your worksheet using the default settings by clicking it.

Printing worksheet formulas

Sometimes you need to keep a record of all the formulas in a worksheet. You might want to do this to see exactly how you came up with a complex calculation, so you can explain it to others. To prepare a worksheet to show formulas rather than results when printed, open the workbook containing the formulas you want to print. Click the Formulas tab, then click the Show Formulas button in the Formula Auditing group to select it. When the Show Formulas button is selected, formulas rather than resulting values are displayed in the worksheet on screen and when printed.

FIGURE A-17: Worksheet with portrait orientation

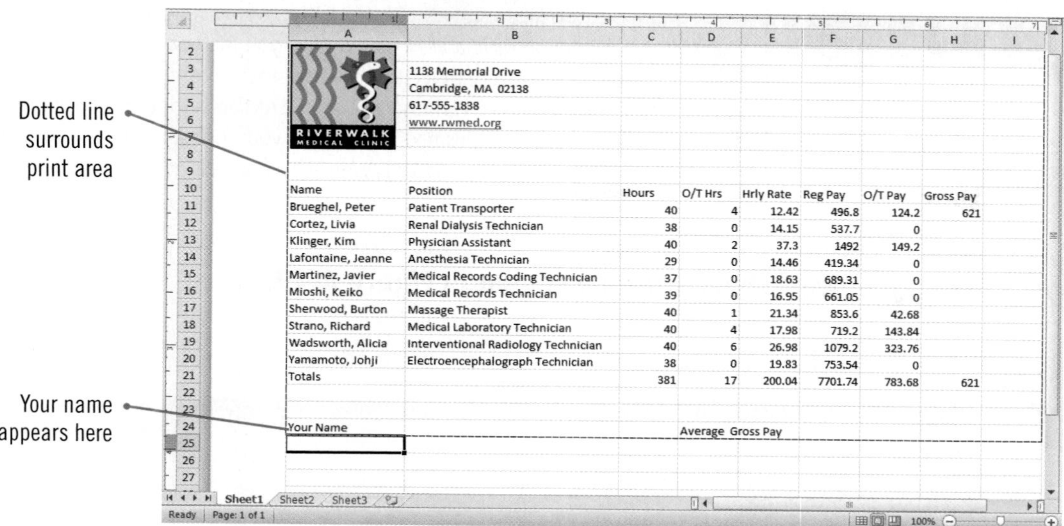

FIGURE A-18: Worksheet in Backstage view

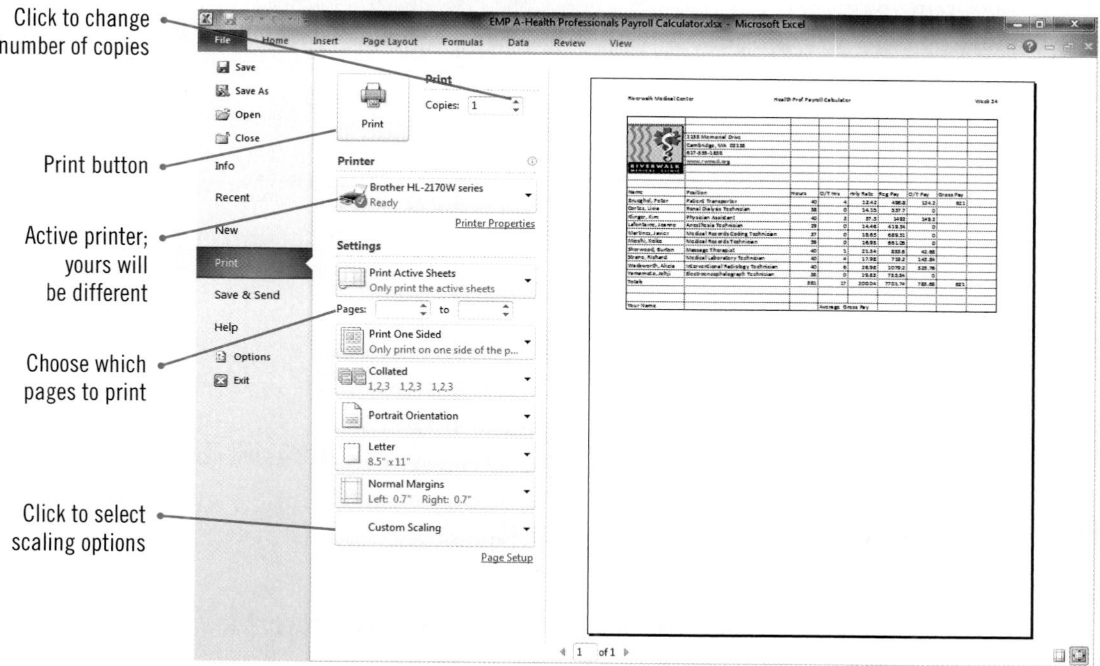

Scaling to fit

If you have a large amount of data that you want to fit to a single sheet of paper, but you don't want to spend a lot of time trying to adjust the margins and other settings, you have several options. You can easily print your work on a single sheet by clicking the No Scaling list arrow in the Settings section on the Print tab in Backstage view, then clicking Fit Sheet on One Page. Another method for fitting worksheet content onto one page is to click the Page Layout tab, then change the Width and Height settings in the Scale to Fit group each to 1 Page. You can also use the Fit to option in the Page Setup dialog box to fit a worksheet on one page. To open the Page Setup dialog box, click the dialog box launcher in the Scale to Fit group on the Page Layout tab, or click the Page Setup link on the Print tab in Backstage view. Make sure the Page tab is selected in the Page Setup dialog box, then click the Fit to option button.

Practice

Concepts Review

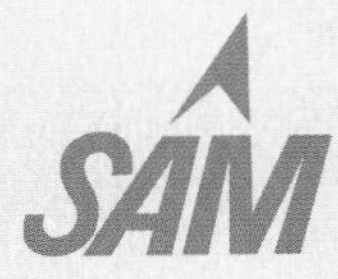

For current SAM information, including versions and content details, visit SAM Central (http://www.cengage.com/samcentral). If you have a SAM user profile, you may have access to hands-on instruction, practice, and assessment of the skills covered in this unit. Since various versions of SAM are supported throughout the life of this text, check with your instructor for the correct instructions and URL/Web site for accessing assignments.

Label the elements of the Excel worksheet window shown in Figure A-19.

FIGURE A-19

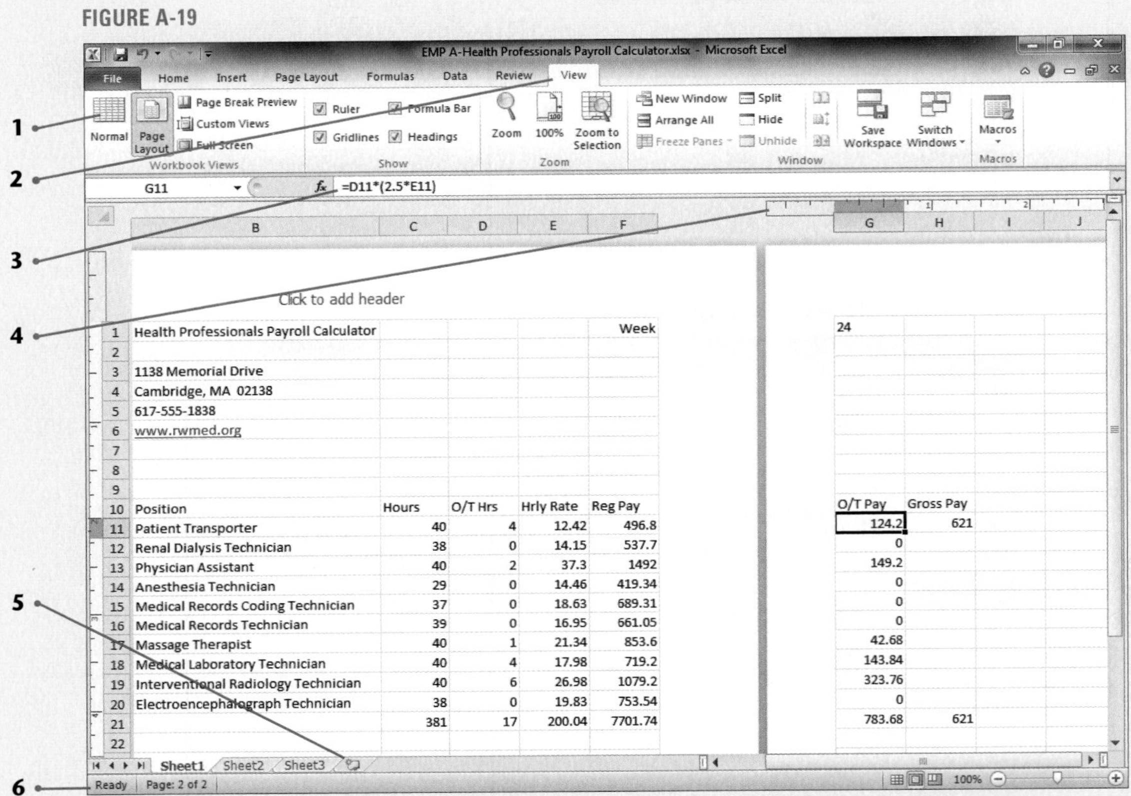

Match each term with the statement that best describes it.

7. **Formula prefix**
8. **Normal view**
9. **Name box**
10. **Cell**
11. **Orientation**
12. **Workbook**

- **a.** Default view in Excel
- **b.** Direction in which contents of page will print
- **c.** Equal sign preceding a formula
- **d.** File consisting of one or more worksheets
- **e.** Intersection of a column and a row
- **f.** Part of the Excel program window that displays the active cell address

Select the best answer from the list of choices.

13. The maximum number of worksheets you can include in a workbook is:

a. 3.
b. 250.
c. 255.
d. Unlimited.

14. Using a cell address in a formula is known as:

a. Formularizing.
b. Prefixing.
c. Cell referencing.
d. Cell mathematics.

15. Which feature could be used to print a very long worksheet on a single sheet of paper?

a. Show Formulas
b. Scale to fit
c. Page Break Preview
d. Named Ranges

16. A selection of multiple cells is called a:

a. Group.
b. Range.
c. Reference.
d. Package.

17. Which worksheet view shows how your worksheet will look when printed?

a. Page Layout
b. Data
c. Review
d. View

18. Which key can you press to switch to Edit mode?

a. [F1]
b. [F2]
c. [F4]
d. [F6]

19. Which view shows you a reduced view of each page of your worksheet?

a. Normal
b. Page Layout
c. Thumbnail
d. Page Break Preview

20. In which area can you see a preview of your worksheet?

a. Page Setup
b. Backstage view
c. Printer Setup
d. View tab

21. In which view can you see the header and footer areas of a worksheet?

a. Normal view
b. Page Layout view
c. Page Break Preview
d. Header/Footer view

Skills Review

1. Understand spreadsheet software.

a. What is the difference between a workbook and a worksheet?
b. Identify five common business uses for electronic spreadsheets.
c. What is what-if analysis?

2. Tour the Excel 2010 window.

a. Start Excel.
b. Open the file EMP A-2.xlsx from the drive and folder where you store your Data Files, then save it as **EMP A-Weather Statistics**.
c. Locate the formula bar, the Sheet tabs, the mode indicator, and the cell pointer.

3. Understand formulas.

a. What is the average high temperature of the listed cities? (*Hint*: Select the range B5:G5 and use the status bar.)
b. What formula would you create to calculate the difference in altitude between Denver and Phoenix? Enter your answer (as an equation) in cell D13.

4. Enter labels and values and use the Sum button.

a. Click cell H8, then use the Sum button to calculate the total snowfall.
b. Click cell H7, then use the Sum button to calculate the total rainfall.
c. Save your changes to the file.

Skills Review (continued)

5. **Edit cell entries.**
   a. Use [F2] to correct the spelling of SanteFe in cell G3 (the correct spelling is Santa Fe).
   b. Click cell A17, then type your name.
   c. Save your changes.
6. **Enter and edit a simple formula.**
   a. Change the value 41 in cell C8 to **52**.
   b. Change the value 37 in cell D6 to **35.4**.
   c. Select cell J4, then use the fill handle to copy the formula in cell J4 to cells J5:J8.
   d. Save your changes.
7. **Switch worksheet views.**
   a. Click the View tab on the Ribbon, then switch to Page Layout view.
   b. Add the header **Average Annual Weather Statistics** to the center header text box.
   c. Add your name to the right header box.
   d. Add the multi-line header **Potential Medical Research Locations** to the left header box.
   e. Delete the contents of the range A1:H1 and cell A17.
   f. Save your changes.
8. **Choose print options.**
   a. Use the Page Layout tab to change the orientation to Portrait.
   b. Turn off gridlines by deselecting both the Gridlines View and Gridlines Print check boxes (if necessary) in the Sheet Options group.
   c. Scale the worksheet so all the information fits on one page. (*Hint*: Click the Width list arrow in the Scale to Fit group, click 1 page, click the Height list arrow in the Scale to Fit group, then click 1 page.) Compare your screen to Figure A-20.
   d. Preview the worksheet in Backstage view, then print the worksheet.
   e. Save your changes, submit your work to your instructor as directed, then close the workbook and exit Excel.

FIGURE A-20

Independent Challenge 1

The Human Resources division of Allied Cardiology Associates has just notified you that they have hired two new physicians who will be relocating to your area. They would like you to create a workbook that contains real estate properties for their consideration. You've started a worksheet for this project that contains labels but no data.

a. Open the file EMP A-3.xlsx from where you store your Data Files, then save it as **EMP A-Property Listings**.
b. Enter the data shown in Table A-4 in columns A, C, D, and E (the property address information should spill into column B).

TABLE A-4

Property Address	Price	Bedrooms	Bathrooms
1507 Pinon Lane	425000	4	2.5
32 Zanzibar Way	325000	3	4
60 Pottery Lane	475500	2	2
902 Excelsior Drive	300000	4	3

Independent Challenge 1 (continued)

c. Use Page Layout view to create a header with the following components: the title **Property Listings** in the center and your name on the right.

d. Create formulas for totals in cells C6:E6.

e. Save your changes, then compare your worksheet to Figure A-21.

f. Submit your work to your instructor as directed.

g. Close the worksheet and exit Excel.

FIGURE A-21

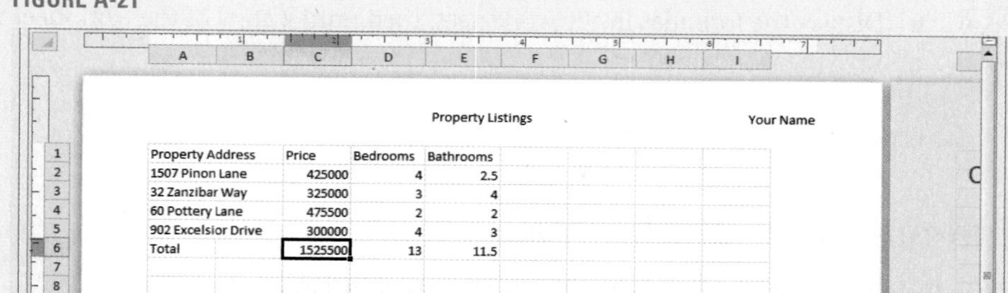

Independent Challenge 2

You are the General Manager for Top Flight Medical Supplies, Inc., a small wholesaler of medical supplies. Although the company is just 5 years old, it is expanding rapidly, and you are continually looking for ways to save time. You recently began using Excel to manage and maintain data on inventory and sales, which has greatly helped you to track information accurately and efficiently.

a. Start Excel.

b. Save a new workbook as **EMP A-Top Flight Medical Supplies** in the drive and folder where you store your Data Files.

c. Switch to an appropriate view, then add a header that contains your name in the left header text box and the title **Top Flight Medical Supplies** in the center header text box.

d. Using Figure A-22 as a guide, create labels for at least seven medical supply manufacturers and sales for the three months in Quarter 2. Include other labels as appropriate. The manufacturers should be in column A and the months should be in columns C, D, and E. A Total row should be beneath the data, and a Total column should be in column F.

FIGURE A-22

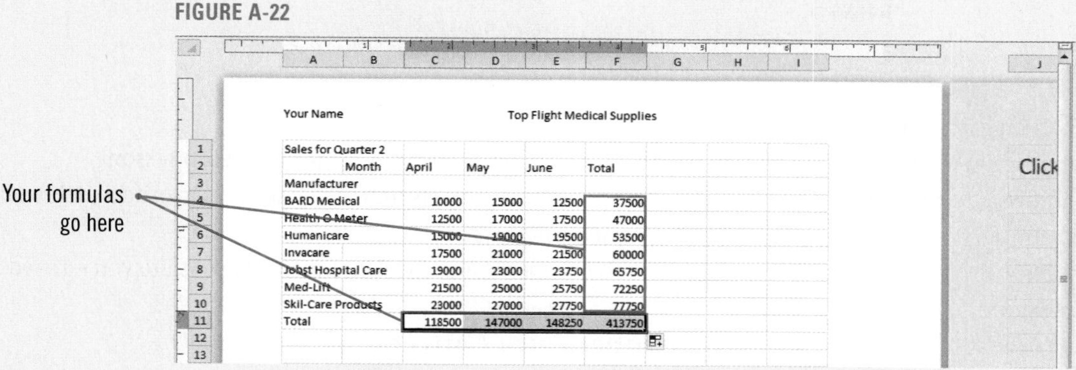

Your formulas go here
Your Name
Top Flight Medical Supplies
Sales for Quarter 2
Month April May June Total
Manufacturer
BARD Medical 10000 15000 12500 37500
Health-O-Meter 12500 17000 17500 47000
Humanicare 15000 19000 19500 53500
Invacare 17500 21000 21500 60000
Jobst Hospital Care 19000 23000 23750 65750
Med-Lift 21500 25000 25750 72250
Skil-Care Products 23000 27000 27750 77750
Total 118500 147000 148250 413750
Click

e. Enter values of your choice for the monthly sales for each manufacturer.

f. Add formulas in the Total column to calculate total quarterly sales for each manufacturer. Add formulas at the bottom of each column of values to calculate the total for that column. Remember that you can use the Sum button and the fill handle to save time.

g. Save your changes, preview the worksheet in Backstage view, then submit your work to your instructor as directed.

Independent Challenge 2 (continued)

Advanced Challenge Exercise

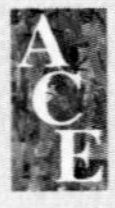

- Create a label two rows beneath the data in column A that says **15% increase**.
- Create a formula in each of the cells C13, D13, and E13 that calculates monthly sales plus a 15% increase.
- Display the formulas in the worksheet, then print a copy of the worksheet with formulas displayed.
- Save the workbook.

h. Close the workbook and exit Excel.

Independent Challenge 3

This Independent Challenge requires an Internet connection.

Some of the research staff at Great Plains Hospital prefer to use Celsius, rather than Fahrenheit temperatures, so you thought it would be helpful to create a worksheet that can be used to convert Fahrenheit temperatures. This will help employees who are unfamiliar with this type of temperature measurement.

a. Start Excel, then save a blank workbook as **EMP A-Temperature Conversions** in the drive and folder where you store your Data Files.

b. Create column headings using Figure A-23 as a guide. (*Hint*: You can widen column B by clicking cell B1, clicking the Format button in the Cells group on the Home tab, then clicking AutoFit Column Width.)

FIGURE A-23

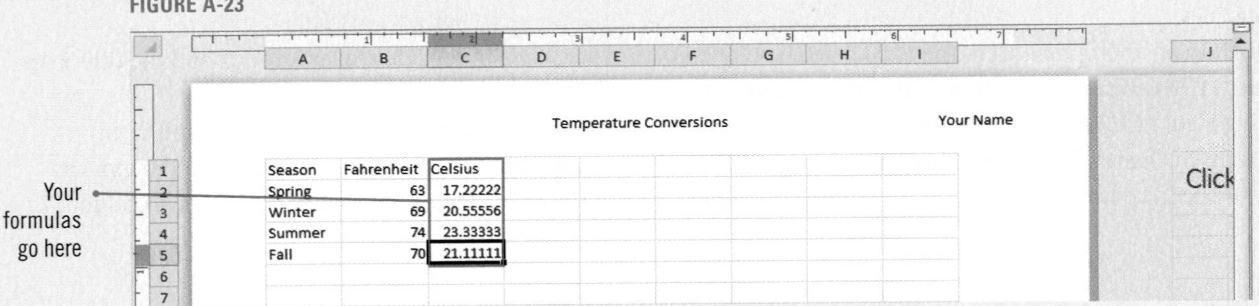

c. Create row labels for each of the seasons.

d. In the appropriate cells, enter what you determine to be a reasonable indoor temperature for each season.

e. Use your Web browser to find out the conversion rate for Fahrenheit to Celsius. (*Hint*: Use your favorite search engine to search on a term such as **temperature conversion formula**.)

f. In the appropriate cells, create a formula that calculates the conversion of the Fahrenheit temperature you entered into a Celsius temperature.

g. In Page Layout View, add your name and the title **Temperature Conversions** to the header.

h. Save your work, then submit your work to your instructor as directed.

i. Close the file, then exit Excel.

Real Life Independent Challenge

You've recently started working as a bookkeeper at the Candandaigua Clinic. You've set up a sample Excel worksheet to keep track of the many start-up expenses.

a. Start Excel, open the file EMP A-4.xlsx from the drive and folder where you store your Data Files, then save it as **EMP A-Candandaigua Clinic Checkbook**.

b. Type check numbers (using your choice of a starting number) in cells A5 through A9.

c. Create sample data for the date, item, and amount in cells B5 through D9.

d. Save your work.

Advanced Challenge Exercise

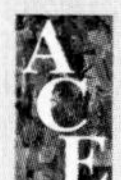

- Use Help to find out about creating a series of numbers.
- Delete the contents of cells A5:A9.
- Create a series of numbers in cells A5:A9.
- In cell C15, type a brief description of how you created the series.
- Save the workbook.

e. Create formulas in cells E5:E9 that calculate a running balance. (*Hint*: For the first check, the running balance equals the starting balance minus a check; for the subsequent checks, the running balance equals the previous balance value minus each check value.)

f. Create a formula in cell D10 that totals the amount of the checks.

g. Enter your name in cell C12, then compare your screen to Figure A-24.

h. Save your changes to the file, submit your work to your instructor, then exit Excel.

FIGURE A-24

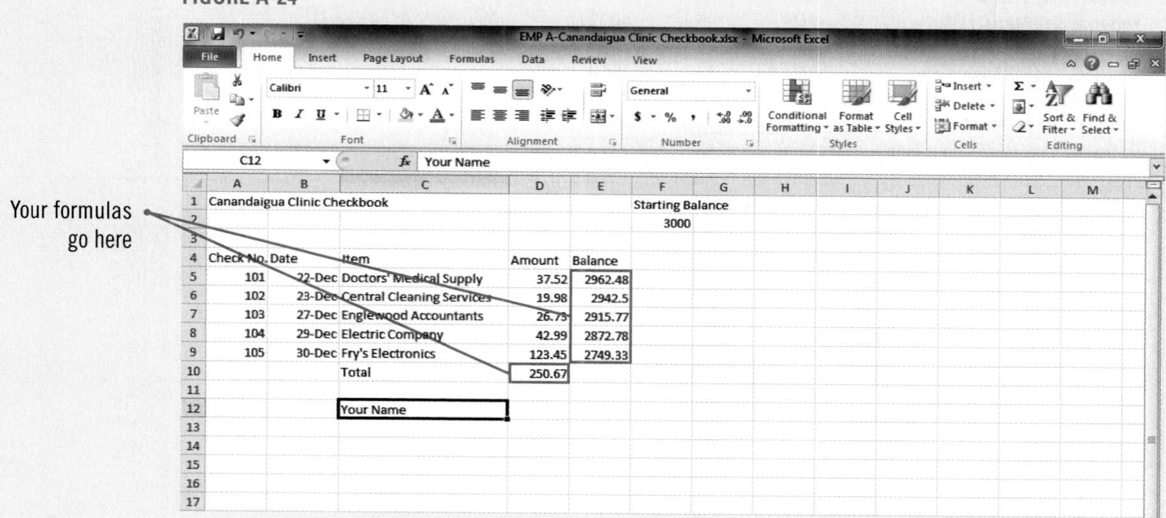

Visual Workshop

Open the file EMP A-5.xlsx from the drive and folder where you store your Data Files, then save it as **EMP A-Gold Coast Clinic Inventory Items**. Using the skills you learned in this unit, modify your worksheet so it matches Figure A-25. Enter formulas in cells D4 through D13 and in cells B14 and C14. Use the Sum button and fill handle to make entering your formulas easier. Add your name in the left header text box, print one copy of the worksheet with the formulas displayed, then turn off the formula display.

FIGURE A-25

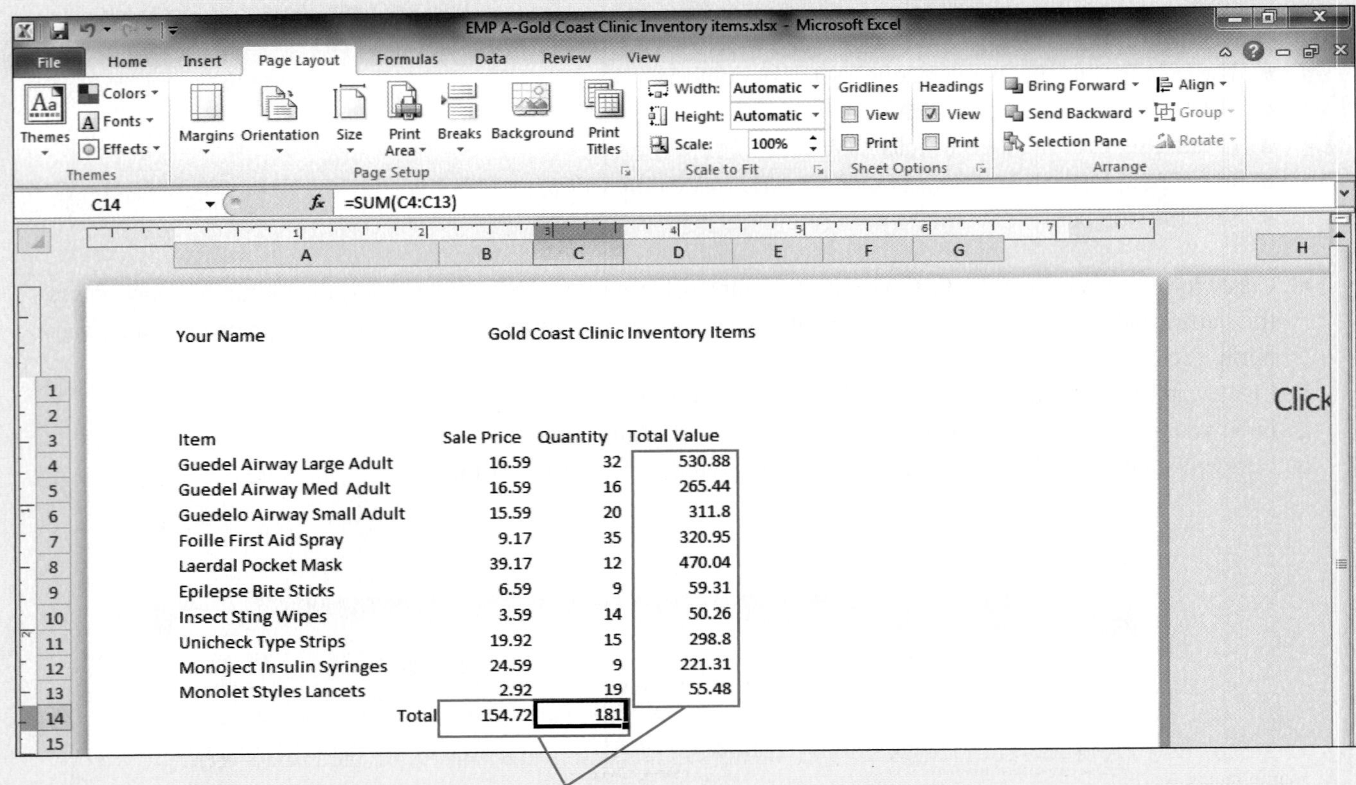

UNIT
B
Excel 2010

Working with Formulas and Functions

Files You Will Need:

EMP B-1.xlsx
EMP B-2.xlsx
EMP B-3.xlsx
EMP B-4.xlsx

Using your knowledge of Excel basics, you can develop your worksheets to include more complex formulas and functions. To work more efficiently, you can copy and move existing formulas into other cells instead of manually retyping the same information. When copying or moving, you can also control how cell references are handled so that your formulas always reference the intended cells. Tony Sanchez, R.N., office manager at Riverwalk Medical Clinic, needs to analyze departmental insurance reimbursements for the current year. He has asked you to prepare a worksheet that summarizes this reimbursement data and includes some statistical analysis. He would also like you to perform some what-if analysis, to see what quarterly revenues would look like with various projected increases.

OBJECTIVES

Create a complex formula
Insert a function
Type a function
Copy and move cell entries
Understand relative and absolute cell references
Copy formulas with relative cell references
Copy formulas with absolute cell references
Round a value with a function

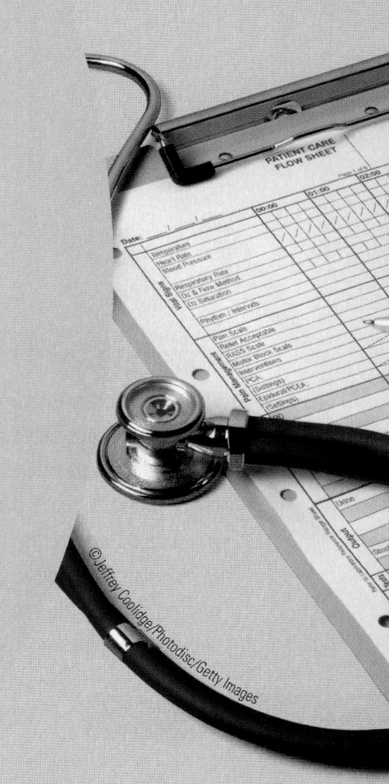

UNIT B

Excel 2010

Creating a Complex Formula

A **complex formula** is one that uses more than one arithmetic operator. You might, for example, need to create a formula that uses addition and multiplication. In formulas containing more than one arithmetic operator, Excel uses the standard **order of precedence** rules to determine which operation to perform first. You can change the order of precedence in a formula by using parentheses around the part you want to calculate first. For example, the formula =4+2*5 equals 14, because the order of precedence dictates that multiplication is performed before addition. However, the formula =(4+2)*5 equals 30, because the parentheses cause 4+2 to be calculated first. You want to create a formula that calculates a 20% increase in insurance reimbursements.

STEPS

1. **Start Excel, open the file EMP B-1.xlsx from the drive and folder where you store your Data Files, then save it as EMP B-Insurance Reimbursement Analysis**
2. **Click cell B19, type =, click cell B17, then type +**

   In this first part of the formula, you are using a reference to the total insurance reimbursements for Quarter 1.
3. **Click cell B17, then type *.2**

   The second part of this formula adds a 20% increase (B17*.2) to the original value of the cell (the total insurance reimbursements for Quarter 1). Compare your worksheet to Figure B-1.
4. **Click the Enter button ✓ on the formula bar**

   The result, 410122.344, appears in cell B19.
5. **Press [Tab], type =, click cell C17, type +, click cell C17, type *.2, then click ✓**

   The result, 434969.712, appears in cell C19.
6. **Drag the fill handle from cell C19 to cell E19**

   The calculated values appear in the selected range, as shown in Figure B-2. Dragging the fill handle on a cell copies the cell's contents or continues a series of data (such as Quarter 1, Quarter 2, etc.) into adjacent cells. This option is called **Auto Fill**.
7. **Save your work**

QUICK TIP

When the mode indicator on the status bar says "Point," cells you click are added to the formula.

QUICK TIP

You can also copy the formulas by selecting the range C14:E14, clicking the Fill button in the Editing group on the Home tab, then clicking Right.

Reviewing the order of precedence

When you work with formulas that contain more than one operator, the order of precedence is very important because it affects the final value. If a formula contains two or more operators, such as 4+.55/4000*25, Excel performs the calculations in a particular sequence based on the following rules: Operations inside parentheses are calculated before any other operations. Reference operators (such as ranges) are calculated first. Exponents are calculated next, then any multiplication and division—progressing from left to right. Finally, addition and subtraction are calculated from left to right. In the example 4+.55/4000*25, Excel performs the arithmetic operations by first dividing 4000 into .55, then multiplying the result by 25, then adding 4. You can change the order of calculations by using parentheses. For example, in the formula (4+.55)/4000*25, Excel would first add 4 and .55, then divide that amount by 4000, then finally multiply by 25.

FIGURE B-1: Formula containing multiple arithmetic operators

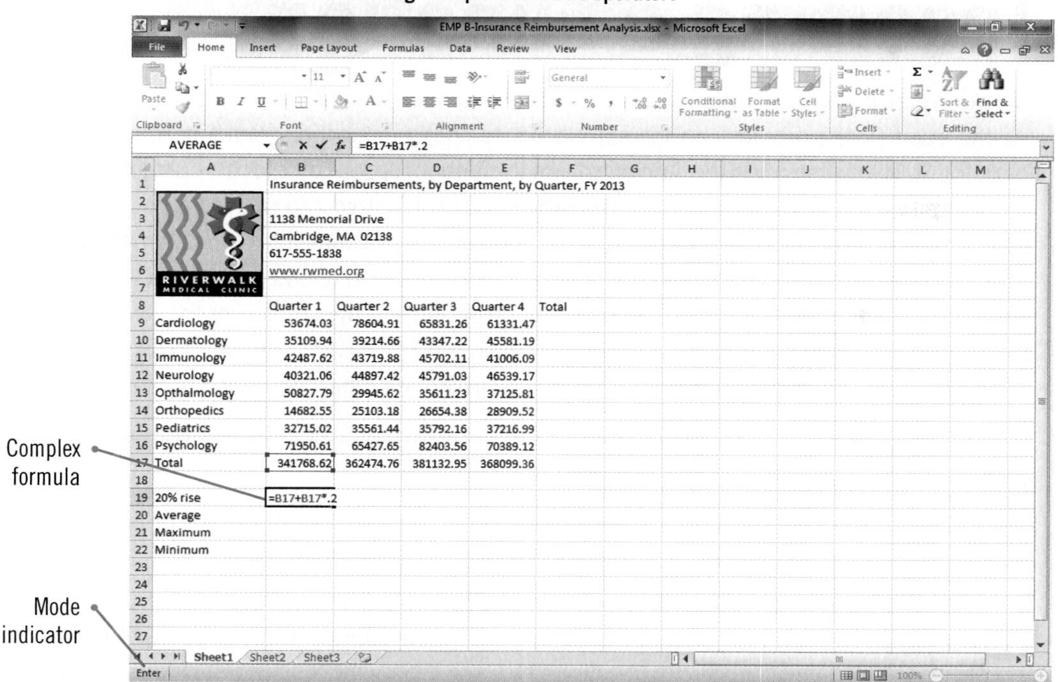

FIGURE B-2: Complex formulas in worksheet

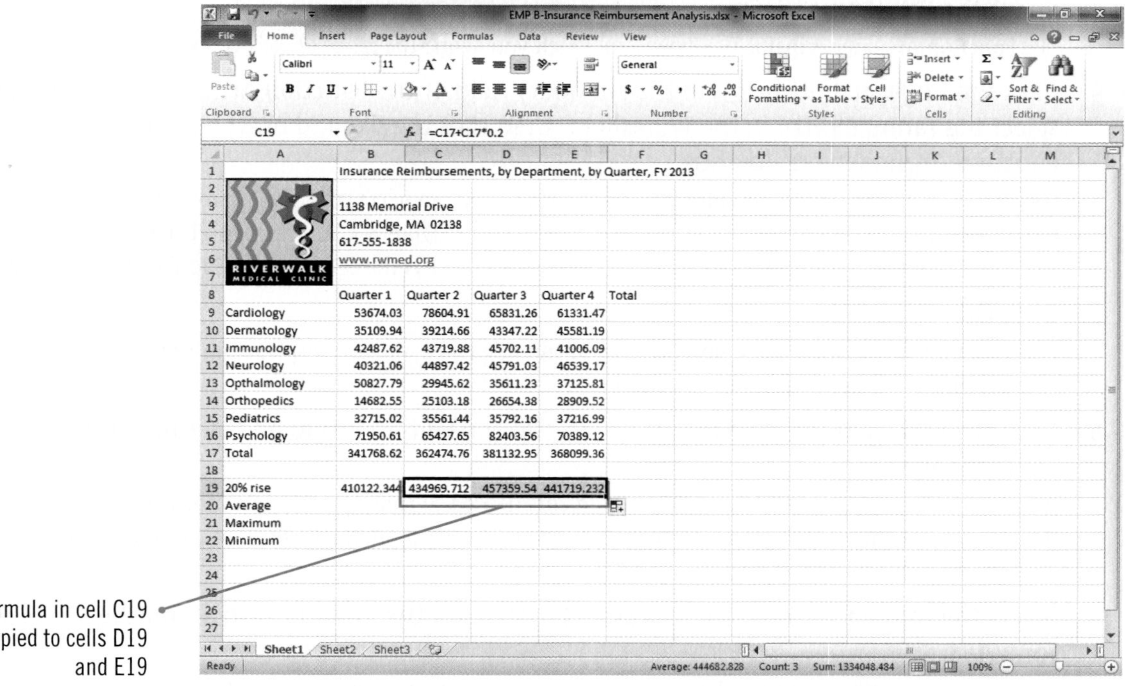

Excel 2010

UNIT B

Excel 2010

Inserting a Function

Functions are predefined worksheet formulas that enable you to perform complex calculations easily. You can use the Insert Function button on the formula bar to choose a function from a dialog box. You can quickly insert the SUM function using the Sum button on the Ribbon, or you can click the Sum list arrow to enter other frequently used functions, such as AVERAGE. Functions are organized into categories, such as Financial, Date & Time, and Statistical, based on their purposes. You can insert a function on its own or as part of another formula. For example, you have used the SUM function on its own to add a range of cells. You could also use the SUM function within a formula that adds a range of cells and then multiplies the total by a decimal. If you use a function alone, it always begins with an equal sign (=) as the formula prefix. You need to calculate the average reimbursements for the first quarter of the year, and decide to use a function to do so.

STEPS

1. **Click cell B20**

   This is the cell where you want to enter the calculation that averages reimbursements per department for the first quarter. You want to use the Insert Function dialog box to enter this function.

2. **Click the Insert Function button on the formula bar**

   An equal sign (=) is inserted in the active cell and in the formula bar, and the Insert Function dialog box opens, as shown in Figure B-3. In this dialog box, you specify the function you want to use by clicking it in the Select a function list. The Select a function list initially displays recently used functions. If you don't see the function you want, you can click the Or select a category list arrow to choose the desired category. If you're not sure which category to choose, you can type the function name or a description in the Search for a function field. The AVERAGE function is a statistical function, but you don't need to open the Statistical category because this function already appears in the Most Recently Used category.

3. **Click AVERAGE in the Select a function list if necessary, read the information that appears under the list, then click OK**

   The Function Arguments dialog box opens, in which you define the range of cells you want to average.

4. **Click the Collapse button in the Number1 field of the Function Arguments dialog box, select the range B9:B16 in the worksheet, then click the Expand button in the Function Arguments dialog box**

   Clicking the Collapse button minimizes the dialog box so you can select cells in the worksheet. When you click the Expand button, the dialog box is restored, as shown in Figure B-4. You can also begin dragging in the worksheet to automatically minimize the dialog box; after you select the desired range, the dialog box is restored.

5. **Click OK**

   The Function Arguments dialog box closes, and the calculated value is displayed in cell B20. The average reimbursement per department for Quarter 1 is 42721.0775.

6. **Click cell C20, click the Sum list arrow Σ in the Editing group on the Home tab, then click Average**

   A ScreenTip beneath cell C20 displays the arguments needed to complete the function. The text "number1" is shown in boldface type, telling you that the next step is to supply the first cell in the group you want to average. You want to average a range of cells.

7. **Select the range C9:C16 in the worksheet, then click the Enter button on the formula bar**

   The average reimbursements per department for the second quarter appears in cell C20.

8. **Drag the fill handle from cell C20 to cell E20**

   The formula in cell C20 is copied to the rest of the selected range, as shown in Figure B-5.

9. **Save your work**

QUICK TIP
When using the Insert Function button or the Sum list arrow, it is not necessary to type the equal sign (=); Excel adds it as necessary.

QUICK TIP
To learn about a function, click it in the Select a function list. The arguments and format required for the function appear below the list.

QUICK TIP
When selecting a range, remember to select all the cells between and including the two references in the range.

FIGURE B-3: Insert Function dialog box

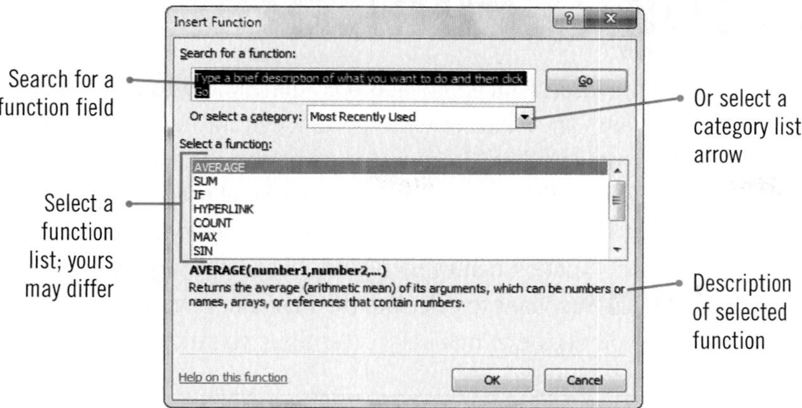

FIGURE B-4: Expanded Function Arguments dialog box

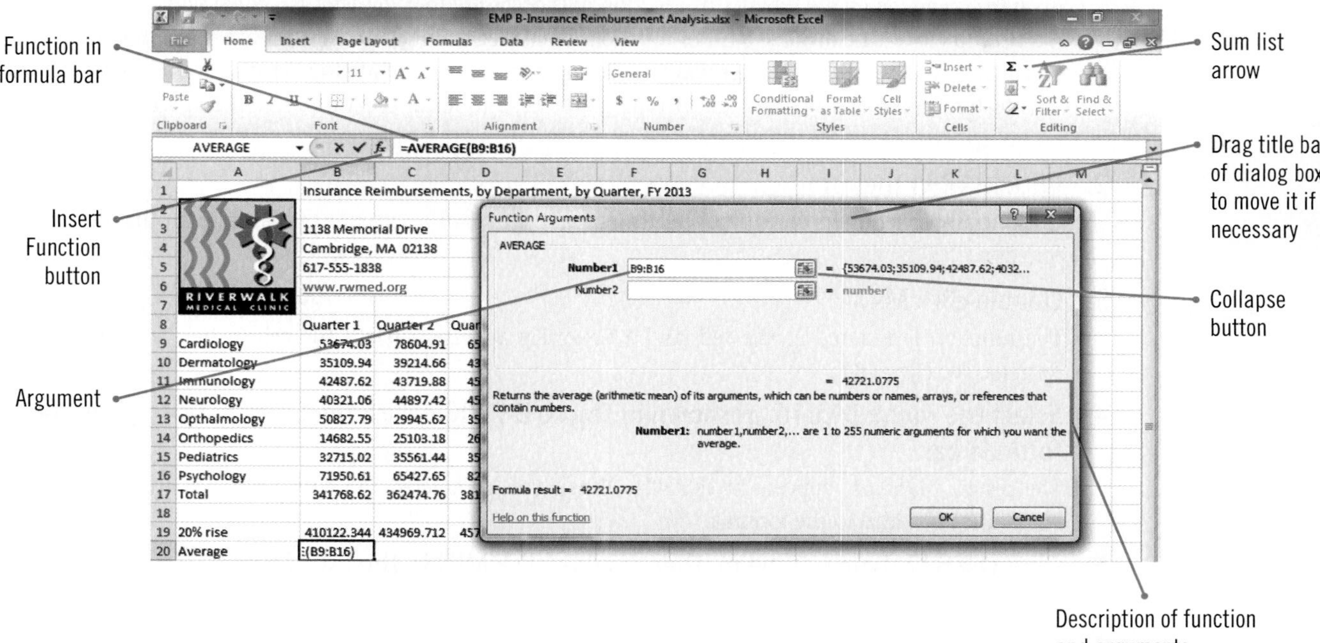

FIGURE B-5: Average functions used in worksheet

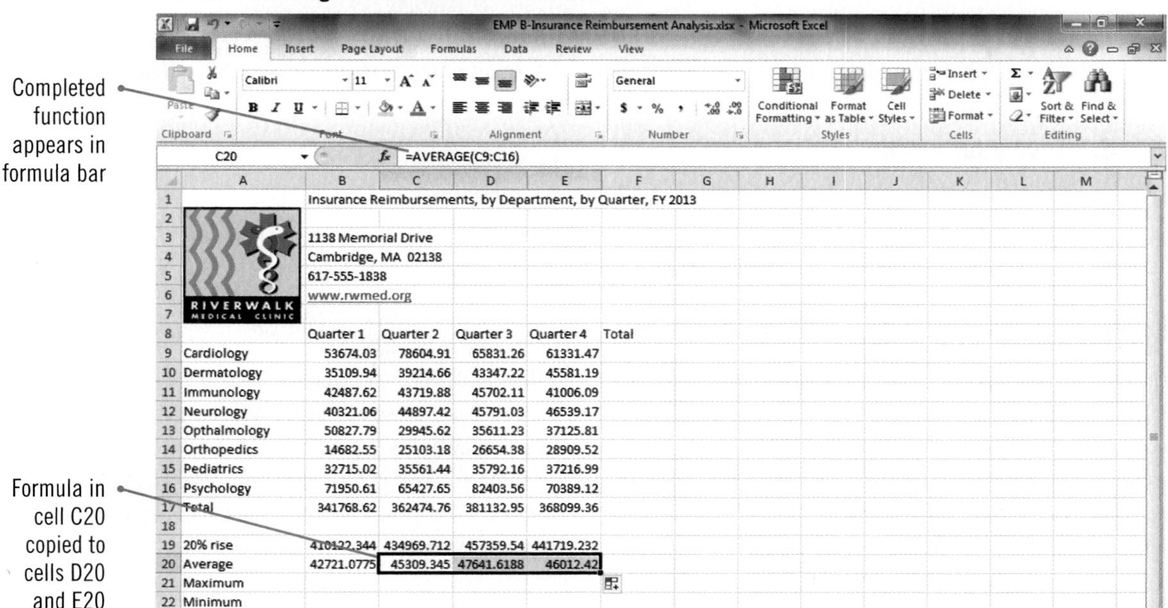

	A	B	C	D	E	F
8		Quarter 1	Quarter 2	Quarter 3	Quarter 4	Total
9	Cardiology	53674.03	78604.91	65831.26	61331.47	
10	Dermatology	35109.94	39214.66	43347.22	45581.19	
11	Immunology	42487.62	43719.88	45702.11	41006.09	
12	Neurology	40321.06	44897.42	45791.03	46539.17	
13	Opthalmology	50827.79	29945.62	35611.23	37125.81	
14	Orthopedics	14682.55	25103.18	26654.38	28909.52	
15	Pediatrics	32715.02	35561.44	35792.16	37216.99	
16	Psychology	71950.61	65427.65	82403.56	70389.12	
17	Total	341768.62	362474.76	381132.95	368099.36	
18						
19	20% rise	410122.344	434969.712	457359.54	441719.232	
20	Average	42721.0775	45309.345	47641.6188	46012.42	
21	Maximum					
22	Minimum					

Excel 2010

UNIT B

Excel 2010

Typing a Function

In addition to using the Insert Function dialog box, the Sum button, or the Sum list arrow on the Ribbon to enter a function, you can manually type the function into a cell and then complete the arguments needed. This method requires that you know the name and initial characters of the function, but it can be faster than opening several dialog boxes. Experienced Excel users often prefer this method, but it is only an alternative, not better or more correct than any other method. Excel's Formula AutoComplete feature makes it easier to enter function names by typing, because it suggests functions depending on the first letters you type. You want to calculate the maximum and minimum quarterly reimbursements in your worksheet, and you decide to manually enter these statistical functions.

STEPS

1. **Click cell B21, type =, then type m**

   Because you are manually typing this function, it is necessary to begin with the equal sign (=). The Formula AutoComplete feature displays a list of function names beginning with "M" beneath cell B21. Once you type an equal sign in a cell, each letter you type acts as a trigger to activate the Formula AutoComplete feature. This feature minimizes the amount of typing you need to do to enter a function and reduces typing and syntax errors.

2. **Click MAX in the list**

   Clicking any function in the Formula AutoComplete list opens a ScreenTip next to the list that describes the function.

3. **Double-click MAX**

   The function is inserted in the cell, and a ScreenTip appears beneath the cell to help you complete the formula. See Figure B-6.

4. **Select the range B9:B16, as shown in Figure B-7, then click the Enter button ✓ on the formula bar**

   The result, 71950.61, appears in cell B21. When you completed the entry, the closing parenthesis was automatically added to the formula.

5. **Click cell B22, type =, type m, then double-click MIN in the list of function names**

   The MIN function appears in the cell.

6. **Select the range B9:B16, then press [Enter]**

   The result, 14682.55, appears in cell B22.

7. **Select the range B21:B22, then drag the fill handle from cell B22 to cell E22**

   The maximum and minimum values for all of the quarters appear in the selected range, as shown in Figure B-8.

8. **Save your work**

Using the COUNT and COUNTA functions

When you select a range, a count of cells in the range that are not blank appears in the status bar. For example, if you select the range A1:A5 and only cells A1 and A2 contain data, the status bar displays "Count: 2." To count nonblank cells more precisely, or to incorporate these calculations in a worksheet, you can use the COUNT and COUNTA functions. The COUNT function returns the number of cells in a range that contain numeric data, including numbers, dates, and formulas. The COUNTA function returns the number of cells in a range that contain any data at all, including numeric data, labels, and even a blank space. For example, the formula =COUNT(A1:A5) returns the number of cells in the range that contain numeric data, and the formula =COUNTA(A1:A5) returns the number of cells in the range that are not empty.

FIGURE B-6: **MAX function in progress**

18					
19	20% rise	410122.344	434969.712	457359.54	441719.232
20	Average	42721.0775	45309.345	47641.6188	46012.42
21	Maximum	=MAX(			
22	Minimum	MAX(**number1**, [number2], ...)			
23					

FIGURE B-7: **Completing the MAX function**

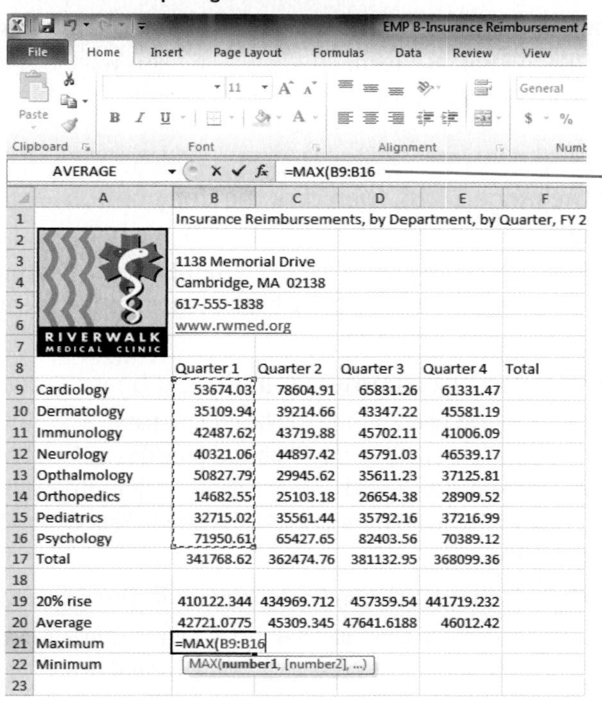

	A	B	C	D	E	F
1		Insurance Reimbursements, by Department, by Quarter, FY 2				
2						
3		1138 Memorial Drive				
4		Cambridge, MA 02138				
5		617-555-1838				
6	RIVERWALK	www.rwmed.org				
7	MEDICAL CLINIC					
8		Quarter 1	Quarter 2	Quarter 3	Quarter 4	Total
9	Cardiology	53674.03	78604.91	65831.26	61331.47	
10	Dermatology	35109.94	39214.66	43347.22	45581.19	
11	Immunology	42487.62	43719.88	45702.11	41006.09	
12	Neurology	40321.06	44897.42	45791.03	46539.17	
13	Opthalmology	50827.79	29945.62	35611.23	37125.81	
14	Orthopedics	14682.55	25103.18	26654.38	28909.52	
15	Pediatrics	32715.02	35561.44	35792.16	37216.99	
16	Psychology	71950.61	65427.65	82403.56	70389.12	
17	Total	341768.62	362474.76	381132.95	368099.36	
18						
19	20% rise	410122.344	434969.712	457359.54	441719.232	
20	Average	42721.0775	45309.345	47641.6188	46012.42	
21	Maximum	=MAX(B9:B16				
22	Minimum	MAX(**number1**, [number2], ...)				
23						

Closing parenthesis will automatically be added when you accept the entry

FIGURE B-8: **Completed MAX and MIN functions**

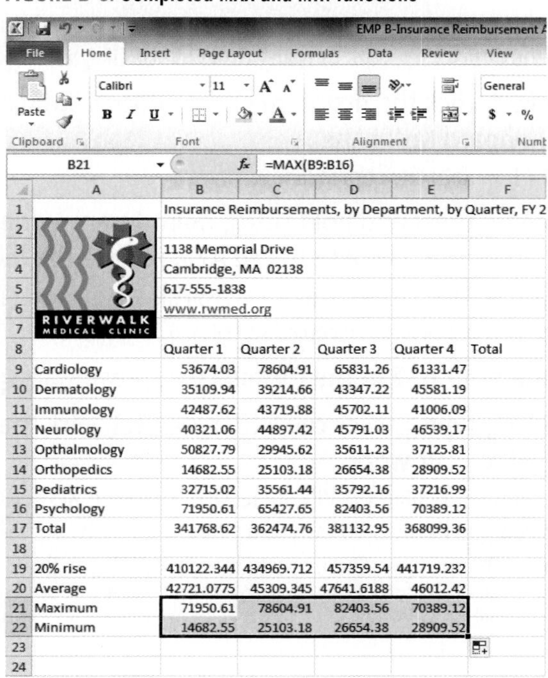

	A	B	C	D	E	F
1		Insurance Reimbursements, by Department, by Quarter, FY 2				
2						
3		1138 Memorial Drive				
4		Cambridge, MA 02138				
5		617-555-1838				
6	RIVERWALK	www.rwmed.org				
7	MEDICAL CLINIC					
8		Quarter 1	Quarter 2	Quarter 3	Quarter 4	Total
9	Cardiology	53674.03	78604.91	65831.26	61331.47	
10	Dermatology	35109.94	39214.66	43347.22	45581.19	
11	Immunology	42487.62	43719.88	45702.11	41006.09	
12	Neurology	40321.06	44897.42	45791.03	46539.17	
13	Opthalmology	50827.79	29945.62	35611.23	37125.81	
14	Orthopedics	14682.55	25103.18	26654.38	28909.52	
15	Pediatrics	32715.02	35561.44	35792.16	37216.99	
16	Psychology	71950.61	65427.65	82403.56	70389.12	
17	Total	341768.62	362474.76	381132.95	368099.36	
18						
19	20% rise	410122.344	434969.712	457359.54	441719.232	
20	Average	42721.0775	45309.345	47641.6188	46012.42	
21	Maximum	71950.61	78604.91	82403.56	70389.12	
22	Minimum	14682.55	25103.18	26654.38	28909.52	
23						
24						

UNIT B Excel 2010

Copying and Moving Cell Entries

There are three ways you can copy or move cells and ranges (or the contents within them) from one location to another: the Cut, Copy, and Paste buttons on the Home tab on the Ribbon; the fill handle in the lower-right corner of the active cell or range; or the drag-and-drop feature. When you copy cells, the original data remains in the original location; when you cut or move cells, the original data is deleted from its original location. You can also cut, copy, and paste cells or ranges from one worksheet to another. In addition to the 20% rise in insurance reimbursements, you also want to show a 30% rise. Rather than retype this information, you copy and move the labels in these cells.

STEPS

QUICK TIP
To cut or copy selected cell contents, activate the cell, then select the characters within the cell that you want to cut or copy.

1. **Select the range B8:E8, then click the Copy button in the Clipboard group on the Home tab**
   The selected range (B8:E8) is copied to the **Clipboard**, a temporary Windows storage area that holds the selections you copy or cut. A moving border surrounds the selected range until you press [Esc] or copy an additional item to the Clipboard.
2. **Click the dialog box launcher in the Clipboard group**
   The Office Clipboard opens in the Clipboard task pane, as shown in Figure B-9. When you copy or cut an item, it is cut or copied both to the Clipboard provided by Windows and to the Office Clipboard. Unlike the Windows Clipboard, which holds just one item at a time, the Office Clipboard contains up to 24 of the most recently cut or copied items from any Office program. Your Clipboard task pane may contain more items than shown in the figure.

QUICK TIP
Once the Office Clipboard contains 24 items, the oldest existing item is automatically deleted each time you add an item.

3. **Click cell B25, then click the Paste button in the Clipboard group**
   A copy of the contents of range B8:E8 is pasted into the range B25:E25. When pasting an item from the Office Clipboard or Clipboard into a worksheet, you only need to specify the upper-left cell of the range where you want to paste the selection. Notice that the information you copied remains in the original range B8:E8; if you had cut instead of copied, the information would have been deleted from its original location once it was pasted.
4. **Press [Delete]**
   The selected cells are empty. You have decided to paste the cells in a different row. You can repeatedly paste an item from the Office Clipboard as many times as you like, as long as the item remains in the Office Clipboard.

QUICK TIP
You can also close the Office Clipboard pane by clicking the dialog box launcher in the Clipboard group.

5. **Click cell B24, click the first item in the Office Clipboard, then click the Close button on the Clipboard task pane**
   Cells B24:E24 contain the copied labels.
6. **Click cell A19, press and hold [Ctrl], point to any edge of the cell until the pointer changes to , drag cell A19 to cell A25, release the mouse button, then release [Ctrl]**
   The copy pointer continues to appear as you drag, as shown in Figure B-10. When you release the mouse button, the contents of cell A19 are copied to cell A25.
7. **Click to the right of 2 in the formula bar, press [Backspace], type 3, then press [Enter]**
8. **Click cell B25, type =, click cell B17, type *1.3, click the Enter button on the formula bar, then save your work**
   This new formula calculates a 30% increase of the expenses for Quarter 1, though using a different method from what you previously used. Anything you multiply by 1.3 returns an amount that is 130% of the original amount, or a 30% increase. Compare your screen to Figure B-11.

FIGURE B-9: Copied data in Office Clipboard

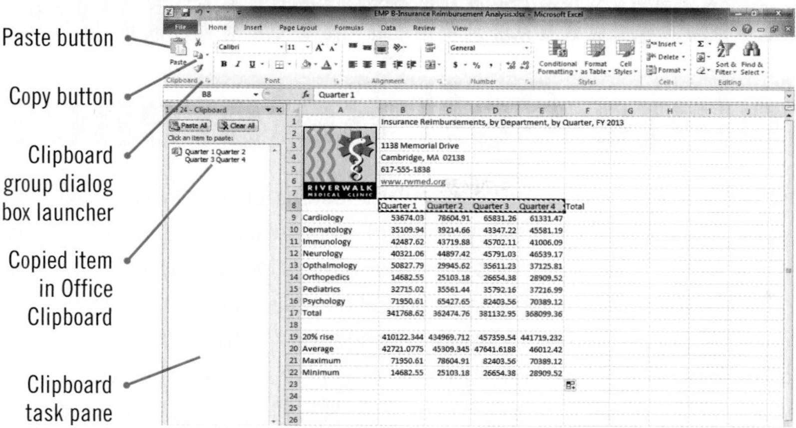

FIGURE B-10: Copying cell contents with drag-and-drop

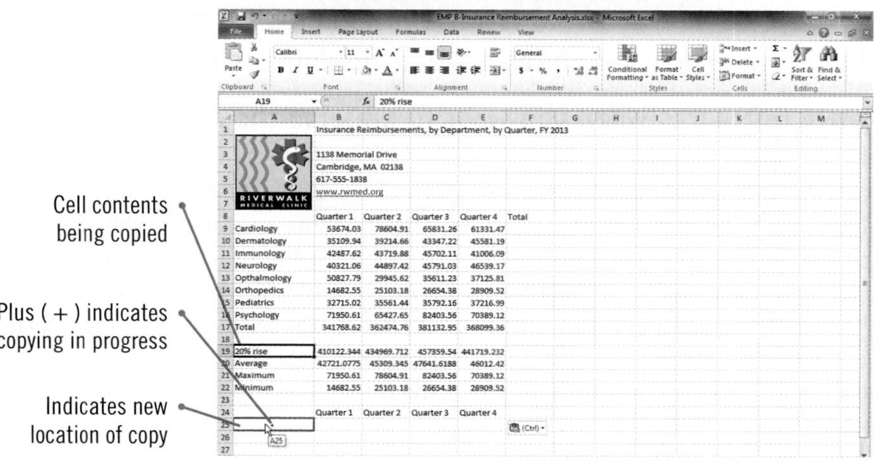

FIGURE B-11: Formula entered to calculate a 30% increase

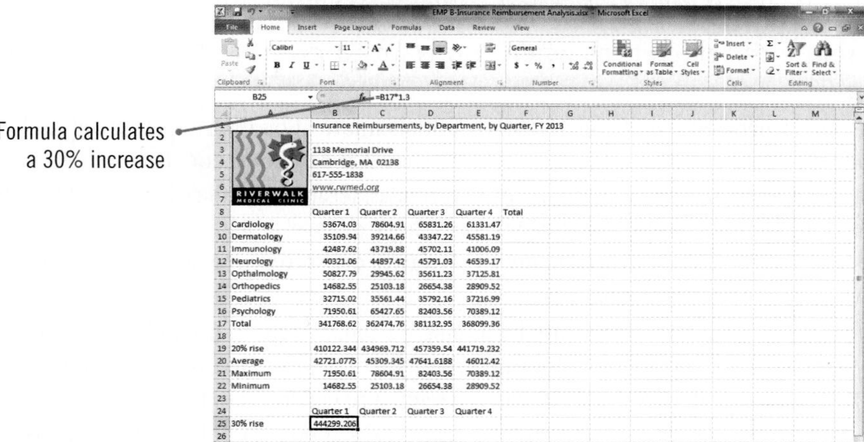

Excel 2010

Inserting and deleting selected cells

As you add formulas to your workbook, you may need to insert or delete cells. When you do this, Excel automatically adjusts cell references to reflect their new locations. To insert cells, click the Insert list arrow in the Cells group on the Home tab, then click Insert Cells. The Insert dialog box opens, asking if you want to insert a cell and move the current active cell down or to the right of the new one. To delete one or more selected cells, click the Delete list arrow in the Cells group, click Delete Cells, and in the Delete dialog box, indicate which way you want to move the adjacent cells. When using this option, be careful not to disturb row or column alignment that may be necessary to maintain the accuracy of cell references in the worksheet. Click the Insert button or Delete button in the Cells group to insert or delete a single cell.

UNIT B

Excel 2010

Understanding Relative and Absolute Cell References

As you work in Excel, you may want to reuse formulas in different parts of a worksheet to reduce the amount of data you have to retype. For example, you might want to include a what-if analysis in one part of a worksheet showing a set of sales projections if reimbursements increase by 10%. To include another analysis in another part of the worksheet showing projections if reimbursements increase by 50%, you can copy the formulas from one section to another and simply change the "1" to a "5". But when you copy formulas, it is important to make sure that they refer to the correct cells. To do this, you need to understand the difference between relative and absolute cell references. You plan to reuse formulas in different parts of your worksheets, so you want to understand relative and absolute cell references.

DETAILS

Consider the following when using relative and absolute cell references:

- **Use relative references when you want to preserve the relationship to the formula location**

  When you create a formula that references another cell, Excel normally does not "record" the exact cell address for the cell being referenced in the formula. Instead, it looks at the relationship that cell has to the cell containing the formula. For example, in Figure B-12, cell F5 contains the formula: =SUM(B5:E5). When Excel retrieves values to calculate the formula in cell F5, it actually looks for "the four cells to the left of the formula," which in this case is cells B5:E5. This way, if you copy the cell to a new location, such as cell F6, the results will reflect the new formula location, and will automatically retrieve the values in cells B6, C6, D6, and E6. These are **relative cell references**, because Excel is recording the input cells *in relation to* or *relative to* the formula cell.

  In most cases, you want to use relative cell references when copying or moving, so this is the Excel default. In Figure B-12, the formulas in F5:F12 and in B13:F13 contain relative cell references. They total the "four cells to the left of" or the "eight cells above" the formulas.

- **Use absolute cell references when you want to preserve the exact cell address in a formula**

  There are times when you want Excel to retrieve formula information from a specific cell, and you don't want the cell address in the formula to change when you copy it to a new location. For example, you might have a price in a specific cell that you want to use in all formulas, regardless of their location. If you use relative cell referencing, the formula results would be incorrect, because Excel would use a different cell every time you copy the formula. Therefore you need to use an **absolute cell reference**, which is a reference that does not change when you copy the formula.

  You create an absolute cell reference by placing a $ (dollar sign) in front of both the column letter and the row number of the cell address. You can either type the dollar sign when typing the cell address in a formula (for example, "=C12*B16"), or you can select a cell address on the formula bar and then press [F4] and the dollar signs are added automatically. Figure B-13 shows formulas containing both absolute and relative references. The formulas in cells B19 to E26 use absolute cell references to refer to a potential sales increase of 50%, shown in cell B16.

FIGURE B-12: **Formulas containing relative references**

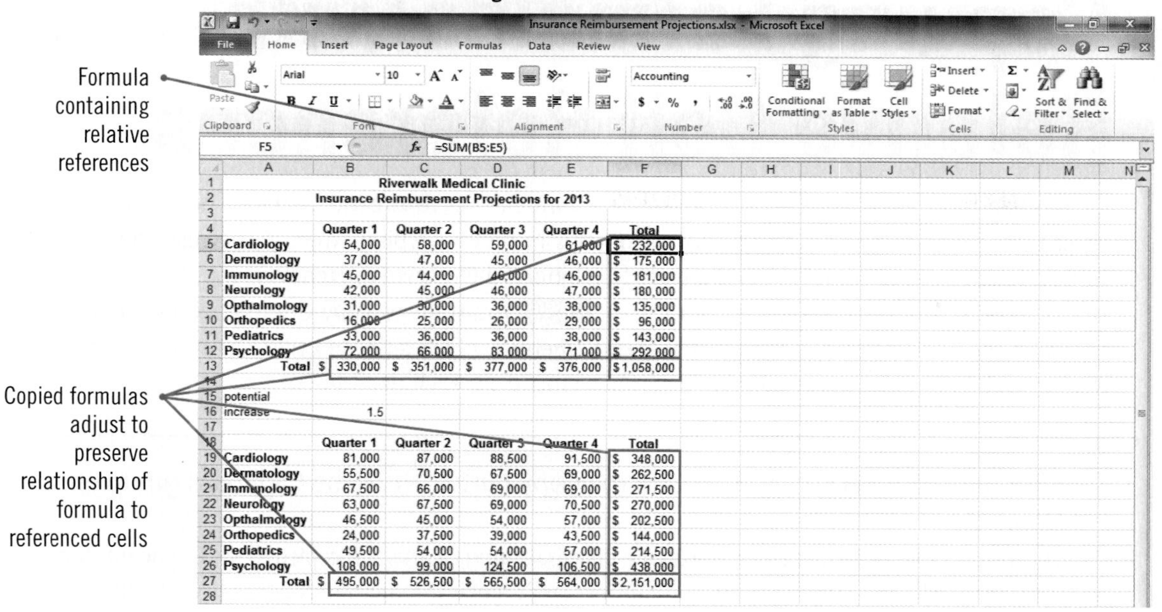

FIGURE B-13: **Formulas containing absolute and relative references**

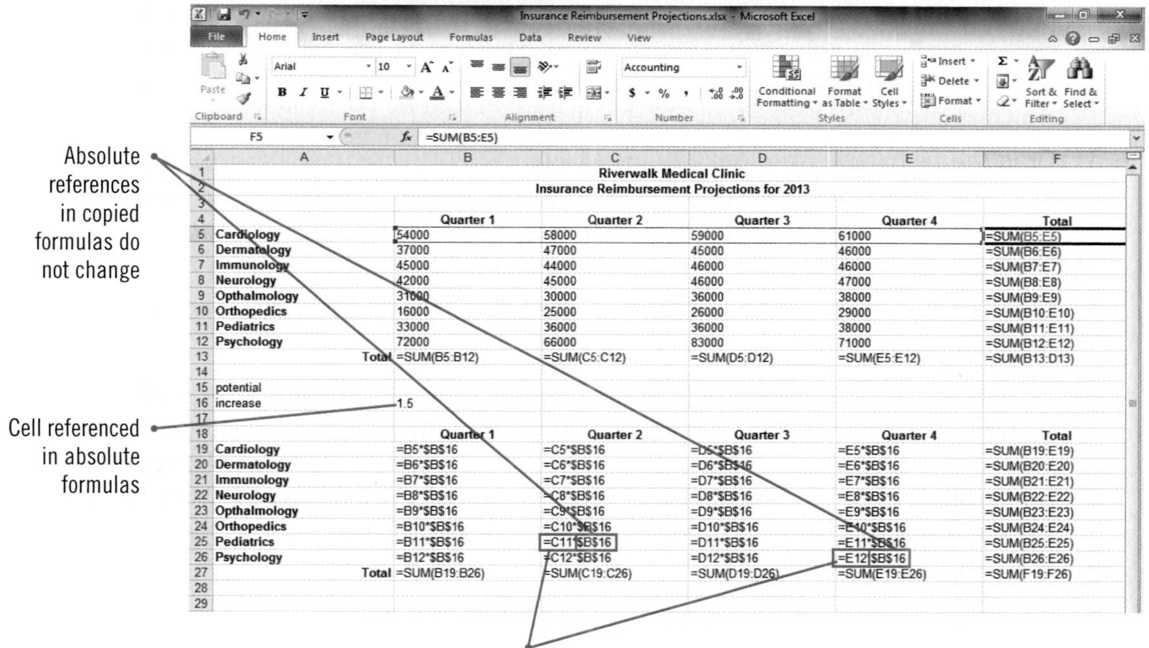

Using a mixed reference

Sometimes when you copy a formula, you want to change the row reference, but keep the column reference the same. This type of cell referencing combines elements of both absolute and relative referencing and is called a **mixed reference**. For example, when copied, a formula containing the mixed reference C$14 would change the column letter relative to its new location, but not the row number. In the mixed reference $C14, the column letter would not change, but the row number would be updated relative to its location. Like an absolute reference, a mixed reference can be created by pressing the [F4] function key with the cell reference selected. With each press of the [F4] key, you cycle through all the possible combinations of relative, absolute, and mixed references (C14, C$14, $C14, and C14).

UNIT B Excel 2010

Copying Formulas with Relative Cell References

Copying and moving a cell allows you to reuse a formula you've already created. Copying cells is usually faster than retyping the formulas in them and helps to prevent typing errors. If the cells you are copying contain relative cell references and you want to maintain the relative referencing, you don't need to make any changes to the cells before copying them. You want to copy the formula in cell B25, which calculates the 30% increase in insurance reimbursements for Quarter 1, to cells C25 through E25. You also want to create formulas to calculate total reimbursements for each department.

STEPS

1. **Click cell B25 if necessary, then click the Copy button in the Clipboard group on the Home tab**
   The formula for calculating the 30% expense increase during Quarter 1 is copied to the Clipboard. Notice that the formula =B17*1.3 appears in the formula bar, and a moving border surrounds the active cell.

2. **Click cell C25, then click the Paste button *(not the list arrow)* in the Clipboard group**
   The formula from cell B25 is copied into cell C25, where the new result of 471217.188 appears. Notice in the formula bar that the cell references have changed, so that cell C17 is referenced in the formula. This formula contains a relative cell reference, which tells Excel to substitute new cell references within the copied formulas as necessary. This maintains the same relationship between the new cell containing the formula and the cell references within the formula. In this case, Excel adjusted the formula so that cell C17—the cell reference eight rows above C25—replaced cell B17, the cell reference nine rows above B25.

3. **Drag the fill handle from cell C25 to cell E25**
   A formula similar to the one in cell C25 now appears in cells D25 and E25. After you use the fill handle to copy cell contents, the **Auto Fill Options button** appears, as seen in Figure B-14. You can use the Auto Fill Options button to fill the cells with only specific elements of the copied cell if you wish.

4. **Click cell F9, click the Sum button in the Editing group, then click the Enter button on the formula bar**

5. **Click in the Clipboard group, select the range F10:F11, then click the Paste button**
   See Figure B-15. After you click the Paste button, the **Paste Options button** appears, which you can use to paste only specific elements of the copied selection if you wish. The formula for calculating total expenses for tours in Britain appears in the formula bar. You would like totals to appear in cells F12:F16. The Fill button in the Editing group can be used to copy the formula into the remaining cells.

6. **Select the range F11:F16**

7. **Click the Fill button in the Editing group, then click Down**
   The formulas containing relative references are copied to each cell. Compare your worksheet to Figure B-16.

8. **Save your work**

QUICK TIP

To paste only specific components of a copied cell or range, click the Paste list arrow in the Clipboard group, then click Paste Special. You can selectively copy formulas, values, or other choices using options in the Paste Special dialog box.

Using Paste Preview

You can selectively copy formulas, values, or other choices using the Paste list arrow, and you can see how the pasted contents will look using the Paste Preview feature. When you click the Paste list arrow, a gallery of paste option icons opens. When you point to an icon, a preview of how the content will be pasted using that option is shown in the worksheet. Options include pasting values only, pasting values with number formatting, pasting formulas only, pasting formatting only, pasting transposed data so that column data appears in rows and row data appears in columns, and pasting with no borders (to remove any borders around pasted cells).

FIGURE B-14: Formula copied using the fill handle

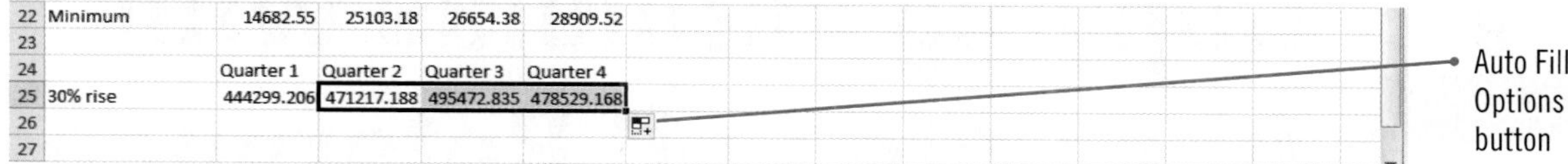

FIGURE B-15: Formulas pasted in the range F10:F11

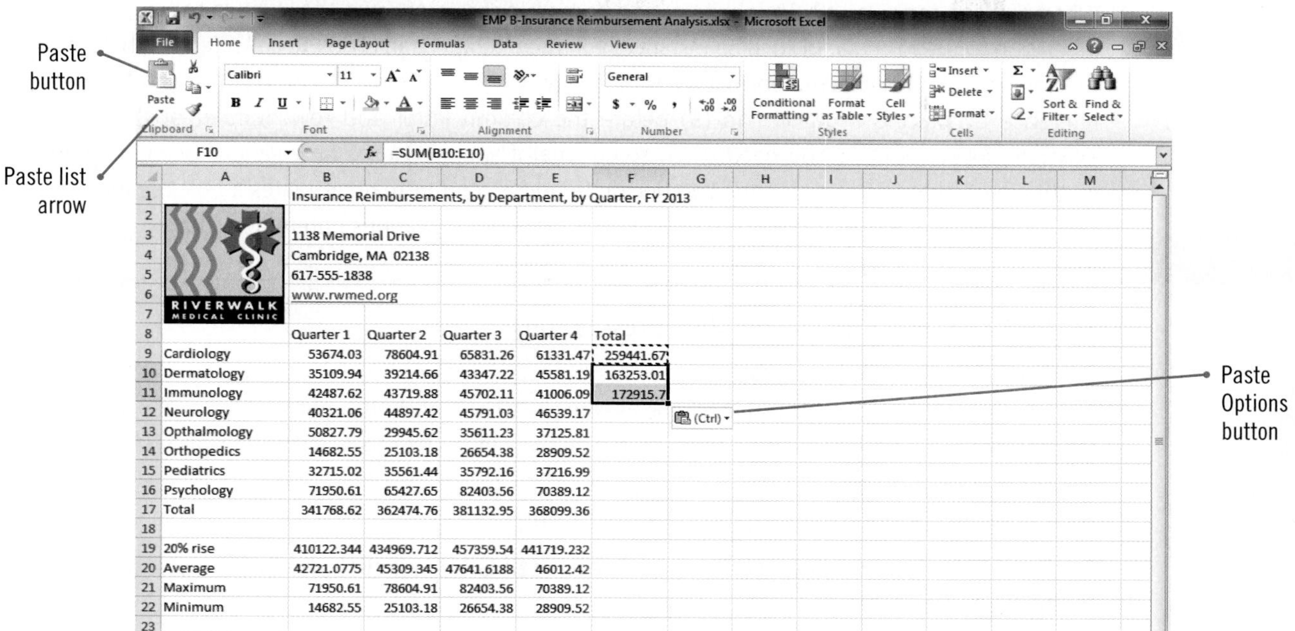

FIGURE B-16: Cells copied using Fill Down

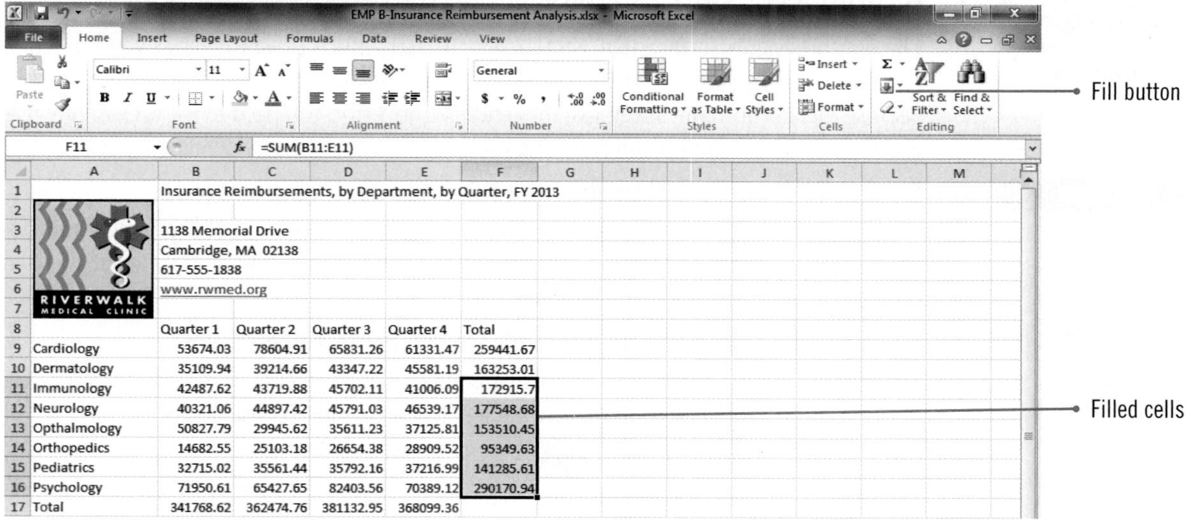

Excel 2010

Using Auto Fill Options

When you use the fill handle to copy cells, the Auto Fill Options button appears. Auto Fill options differ depending on what you are copying. If you had selected cells containing a series (such as "Monday" and "Tuesday") and then used the fill handle, you would see options for continuing the series (such as "Wednesday" and "Thursday") or for simply pasting the copied cells. Clicking the Auto Fill Options button opens a list that lets you choose from the following options: Copy Cells, Fill Series (if applicable), Fill Formatting Only, or Fill Without Formatting. Choosing Copy Cells means that the cell's contents and its formatting will be copied. The Fill Formatting Only option copies only the formatting attributes, but not cell contents. The Fill Without Formatting option copies the cell contents, but no formatting attributes. Copy Cells is the default option when using the fill handle to copy a cell, so if you want to copy the cell's contents and its formatting, you can ignore the Auto Fill Options button.

UNIT B

Excel 2010

Copying Formulas with Absolute Cell References

When copying formulas, you might want one or more cell references in the formula to remain unchanged in relation to the formula. In such an instance, you need to apply an absolute cell reference before copying the formula to preserve the specific cell address when the formula is copied. You create an absolute reference by placing a dollar sign ($) before the column letter and row number of the address (for example, A1). You need to do some what-if analysis to see how various percentage increases might affect total reimbursements. You decide to add a column that calculates a possible increase in the total reimbursements, and then change the percentage to see various potential results.

STEPS

1. **Click cell G6, type Change, then press [Enter]**
2. **Type 1.1, then press [Enter]**

   You store the increase factor that will be used in the what-if analysis in this cell (G7). The value 1.1 can be used to calculate a 10% increase; anything you multiply by 1.1 returns an amount that is 110% of the original amount.
3. **Click cell H8, type What if?, then press [Enter]**
4. **In cell H9, type =, click cell F9, type *, click cell G7, then click the Enter button ✓ on the formula bar**

   The result, 285385.8, appears in cell H9. This value represents the total annual insurance reimbursements for the cardiology department if there is a 10% increase. You want to perform a what-if analysis for all the departments.
5. **Drag the fill handle from cell H9 to cell H16**

   The resulting values in the range H9:H16 are all zeros, which is *not* the result you wanted. Because you used relative cell addressing in cell H9, the copied formula adjusted so that the formula in cell H10 is =F10*G8. Because there is no value in cell G8, the result is 0, an error. You need to use an absolute reference in the formula to keep the formula from adjusting itself. That way, it will always reference cell G7.
6. **Click cell H9, press [F2] to change to Edit mode, then press [F4]**

   When you press [F2], the range finder outlines the arguments of the equation in blue and green. The insertion point appears next to the G7 cell reference in cell H9. When you press [F4], dollar signs are inserted in the G7 cell reference, making it an absolute reference. See Figure B-17.
7. **Click ✓, then drag the fill handle from cell H9 to cell H16**

   Because the formula correctly contains an absolute cell reference, the correct values for a 10% increase appear in cells H9:H16. You now want to see what a 20% increase in expenses looks like.
8. **Click cell G7, type 1.2, then click ✓**

   The values in the range H9:H16 change to reflect the 20% increase. Compare your worksheet to Figure B-18.
9. **Save your work**

QUICK TIP

Before you copy or move a formula, always check to see if you need to use an absolute cell reference.

QUICK TIP

When changing a cell reference to an absolute reference, make sure the reference is selected or the insertion point is next to it in the cell before pressing [F4].

FIGURE B-17: Absolute reference created in formula

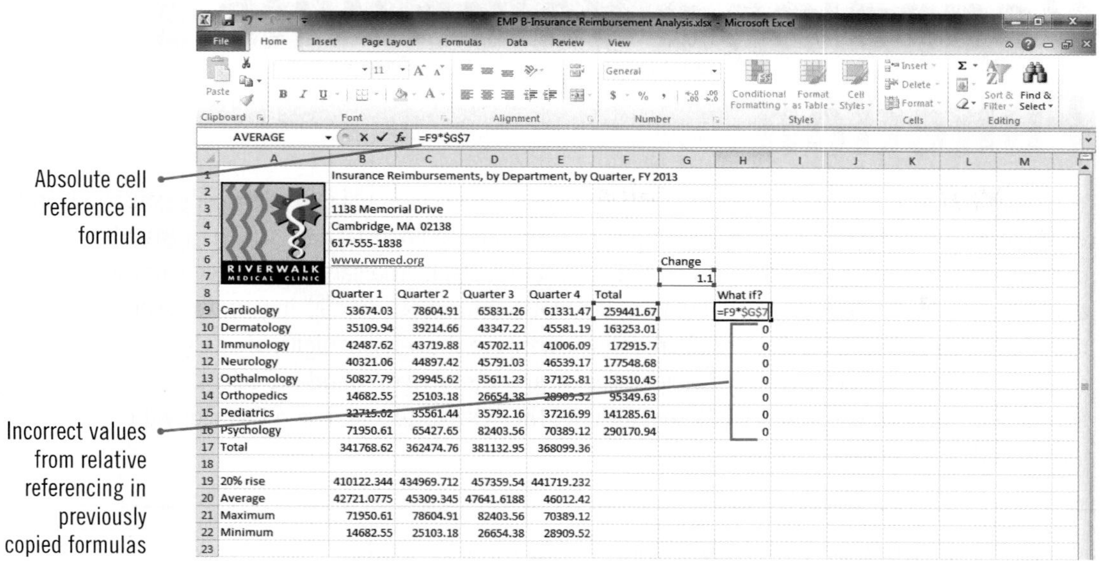

FIGURE B-18: What-if analysis with modified change factor

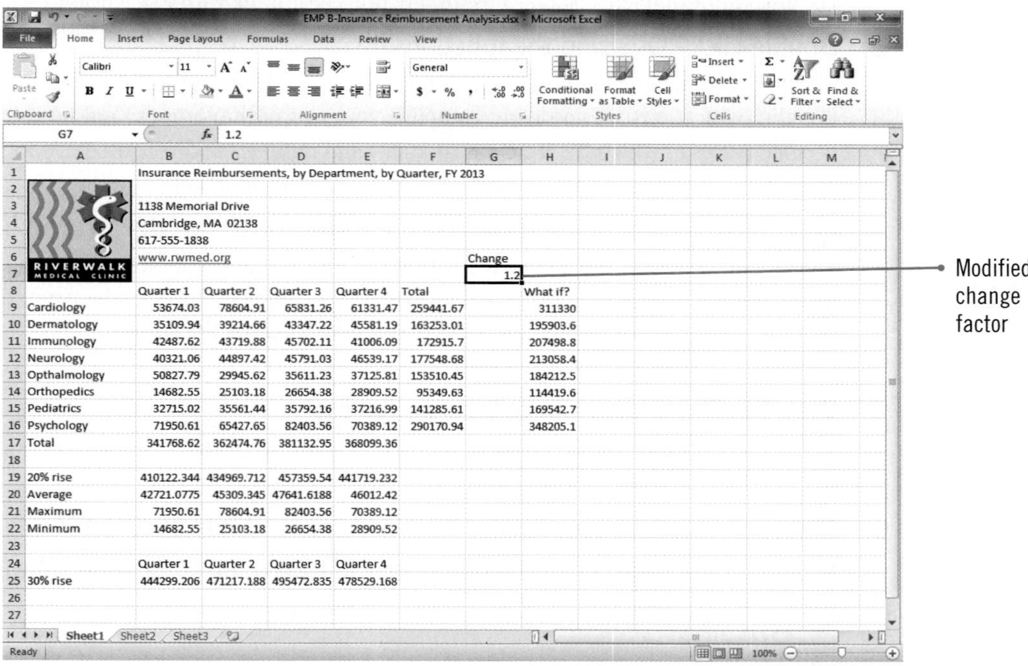

Using the fill handle for sequential text or values

Often, you need to fill cells with sequential text: months of the year, days of the week, years, or text plus a number (Quarter 1, Quarter 2,...). For example, you might want to create a worksheet that calculates data for every month of the year. Using the fill handle, you can quickly and easily create labels for the months of the year just by typing "January" in a cell. Drag the fill handle from the cell containing "January" until you have all the monthly labels you need. You can also easily fill cells with a date sequence by dragging the fill handle on a single cell containing a date. You can fill cells with a number sequence (such as 1, 2, 3,...) by dragging the fill handle on a selection of two or more cells that contain the sequence. To create a number sequence using the value in a single cell, press and hold [Ctrl] as you drag the fill handle of the cell. As you drag the fill handle, Excel automatically extends the existing sequence into the additional cells. (The content of the last filled cell appears in the ScreenTip.) To examine all the fill series options for the current selection, click the Fill button in the Editing group on the Home tab, then click Series to open the Series dialog box.

UNIT B Excel 2010

Rounding a Value with a Function

The more you explore features and tools in Excel, the more ways you'll find to simplify your work and convey information more efficiently. For example, cells containing financial data are often easier to read if they contain fewer decimal places than those that appear by default. You can round a value or formula result to a specific number of decimal places by using the ROUND function. In your worksheet, you'd like to round the cells showing the 20% rise in reimbursements to show fewer digits; after all, it's not important to show cents in the projections, only whole dollars. You want Excel to round the calculated value to the nearest integer. You decide to edit cell B19 so it includes the ROUND function, and then copy the edited formula into the other formulas in this row.

STEPS

1. **Click cell B19, then click to the right of = in the formula bar**
   You want to position the function at the beginning of the formula, before any values or arguments.

2. **Type RO**
   Formula AutoComplete displays a list of functions beginning with RO beneath the formula bar.

3. **Double-click ROUND in the functions list**
   The new function and an opening parenthesis are added to the formula, as shown in Figure B-19. A few additional modifications are needed to complete your edit of the formula. You need to indicate the number of decimal places to which the function should round numbers and you also need to add a closing parenthesis around the set of arguments that comes after the ROUND function.

4. **Press [END], type ,0), then click the Enter button ✓ on the formula bar**
   The comma separates the arguments within the formula, and 0 indicates that you don't want any decimal places to appear in the calculated value. When you complete the edit, the parentheses at either end of the formula briefly become bold, indicating that the formula has the correct number of open and closed parentheses and is balanced.

5. **Drag the fill handle from cell B19 to cell E19**
   The formula in cell B19 is copied to the range C19:E19. All the values are rounded to display no decimal places. Compare your worksheet to Figure B-20.

6. **Click cell A27, type your name, then click ✓ on the formula bar**

7. **Save your work, preview the worksheet in Backstage view, then submit your work to your Instructor as directed**

8. **Exit Excel**

QUICK TIP
In the Insert Function dialog box, the ROUND function is in the Math & Trig category.

TROUBLE
If you have too many or too few parentheses, the extraneous parenthesis is displayed in green, or a warning dialog box opens with a suggested solution to the error.

FIGURE B-19: **ROUND function added to an existing formula**

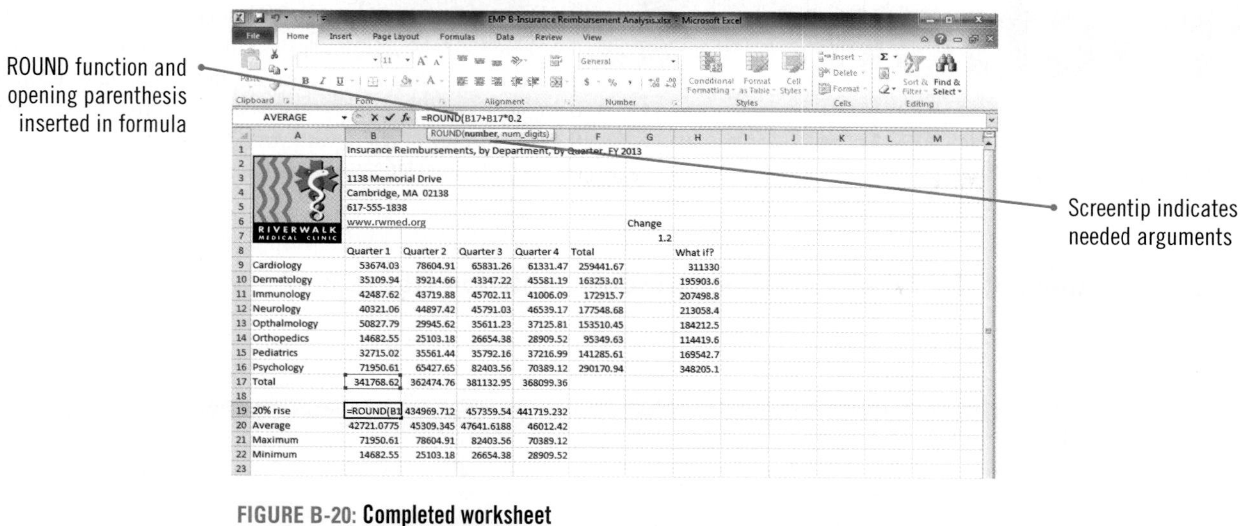

FIGURE B-20: **Completed worksheet**

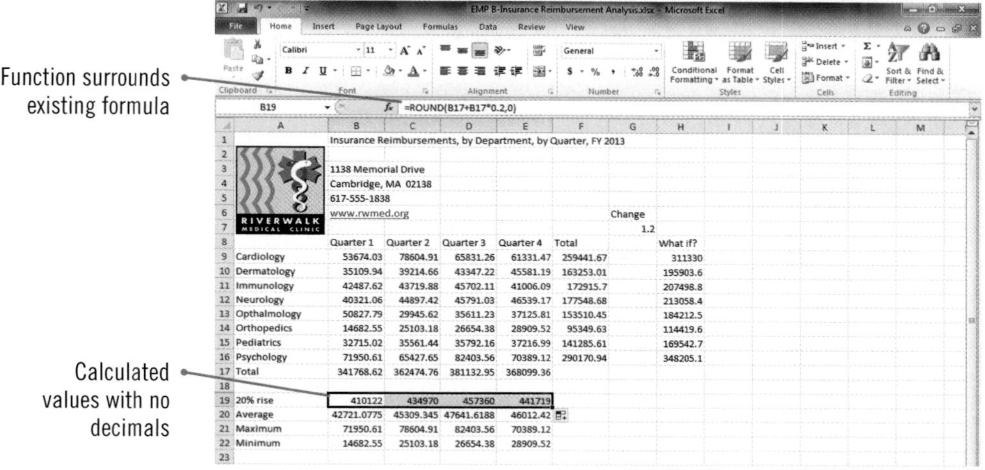

Creating a new workbook using a template

Excel **templates** are predesigned workbook files intended to save time when you create common documents such as balance sheets, budgets, or time cards. Templates contain labels, values, formulas, and formatting, so all you have to do is customize them with your own information. Excel comes with many templates, and you can also create your own or find additional templates on the Web. Unlike a typical workbook, which has the file extension .xlsx, a template has the extension .xltx. To create a workbook using a template, click the File tab, then click New on the navigation bar. The Available Templates pane in Backstage view lists templates installed on your computer and templates available through Office.com. The Blank Workbook template is selected by default and is used to create a blank workbook with no content or special formatting. A preview of the selected template appears to the right of the Available Templates pane. To select a template, click a category in the Available Templates pane, select the template you want in the category, then click Create (if you've selected an installed template) or Download (if you've selected an Office.com template). Figure B-21 shows a template selected in the Budgets category of Office.com templates. (Your list of templates may differ.) When you click Create or Download, a new workbook is created based on the template; when you save the new file in the default format, it has the regular .xlsx extension. To save a workbook of your own as a template, open the Save As dialog box, click the Save as type list arrow, then change the file type to Excel Template.

FIGURE B-21: **Budget template selected in Backstage view**

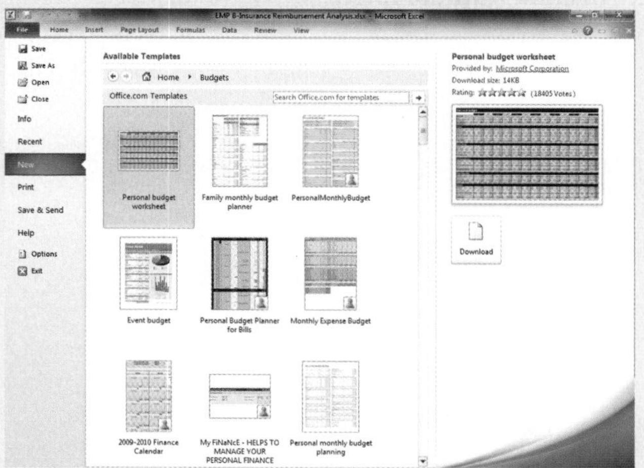

Practice

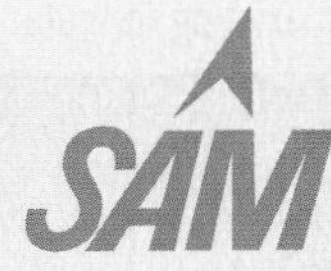

For current SAM information, including versions and content details, visit SAM Central (http://www.cengage.com/samcentral). If you have a SAM user profile, you may have access to hands-on instruction, practice, and assessment of the skills covered in this unit. Since various versions of SAM are supported throughout the life of this text, check with your instructor for the correct instructions and URL/Web site for accessing assignments.

Concepts Review

Label each element of the Excel worksheet window shown in Figure B-22.

FIGURE B-22

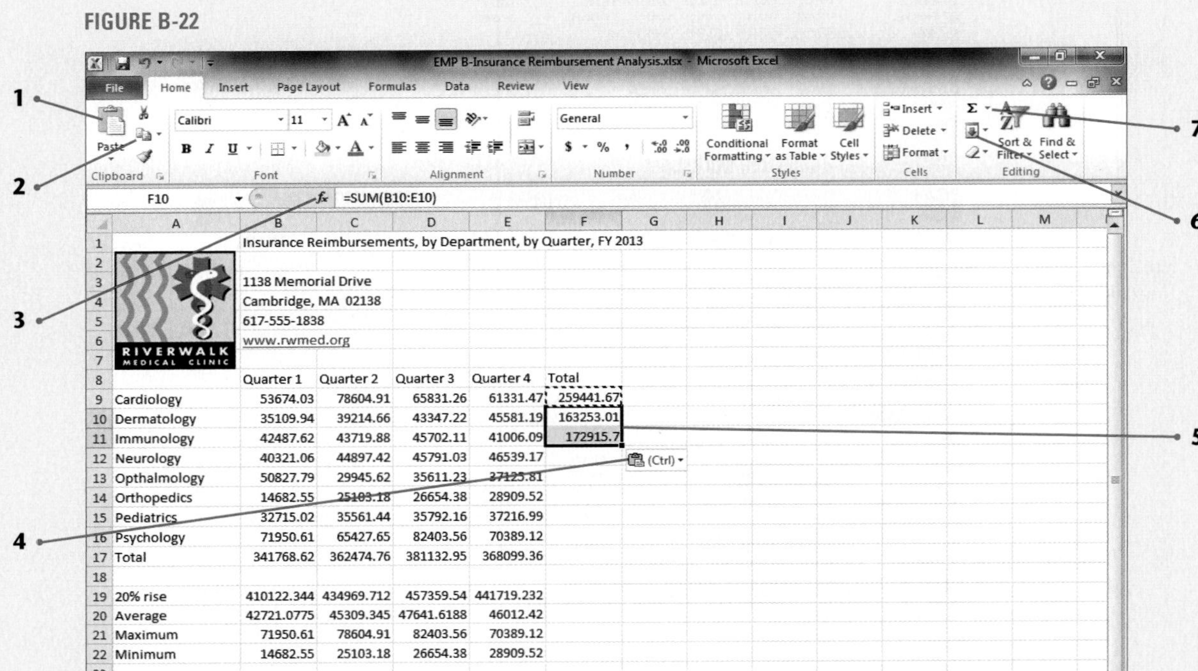

Match each term or button with the statement that best describes it.

8. Fill handle	**a.** Clears the contents of selected cells
9. Dialog box launcher	**b.** Item on the Ribbon that opens a dialog box or task pane
10. Drag-and-drop method	**c.** Lets you move or copy data from one cell to another without using the Clipboard
11. [Delete]	**d.** Displays an alphabetical list of functions from which you can choose
12. Formula AutoComplete	**e.** Lets you copy cell contents or continue a series of data into a range of selected cells

Select the best answer from the list of choices.

13. Which key do you press to copy while dragging and dropping selected cells?

a. [Alt]
b. [Ctrl]
c. [F2]
d. [Tab]

14. What type of cell reference is C$19?

a. Relative
b. Absolute
c. Mixed
d. Certain

15. What type of cell reference changes when it is copied?

a. Circular
b. Absolute
c. Relative
d. Specified

16. Which key do you press to convert a relative cell reference to an absolute cell reference?

a. [F2]
b. [F4]
c. [F5]
d. [F6]

17. You can use any of the following features to enter a function *except*:

a. Insert Function button.
b. Formula AutoComplete.
c. Sum list arrow.
d. Clipboard.

Skills Review

1. Create a complex formula.

a. Open the file EMP B-2.xlsx from the drive and folder where you store your Data Files, then save it as **EMP B-Medical Supply Company Inventory**.

b. In cell B11, create a complex formula that calculates a 30% decrease in the total number of cases of O_2 Masks.

c. Use the fill handle to copy this formula into cell C11 through cell E11.

d. Save your work.

2. Insert a function.

a. Use the Sum list arrow to create a formula in cell B13 that averages the number of cases of O_2 Masks in each storage area.

b. Use the Insert Function button to create a formula in cell B14 that calculates the maximum number of cases of O_2 Masks in a storage area.

c. Use the Sum list arrow to create a formula in cell B15 that calculates the minimum number of cases of O_2 Masks in a storage area.

d. Save your work.

3. Type a function.

a. In cell C13, type a formula that includes a function to average the number of cases of O_2 Tubes in each storage area. (*Hint*: Use Formula AutoComplete to enter the function.)

b. In cell C14, type a formula that includes a function to calculate the maximum number of cases of O_2 Tubes in a storage area.

c. In cell C15, type a formula that includes a function to calculate the minimum number of cases of O_2 Tubes in a storage area.

d. Save your work.

Skills Review (continued)

4. **Copy and move cell entries.**
   a. Select the range B3:F3.
   b. Copy the selection to the Clipboard.
   c. Open the Clipboard task pane, then paste the selection into cell B17.
   d. Close the Clipboard task pane, then select the range A4:A9.
   e. Use the drag-and-drop method to copy the selection to cell A18. (*Hint*: The results should fill the range A18:A23.)
   f. Save your work.
5. **Understand relative and absolute cell references.**
   a. Write a brief description of the difference between relative and absolute references.
   b. List at least three situations in which you think a business might use an absolute reference in its calculations. Examples can include calculations for different types of worksheets, such as time cards, invoices, and budgets.
6. **Copy formulas with relative cell references.**
   a. Calculate the total in cell F4.
   b. Use the Fill button to copy the formula in cell F4 down to cells F5:F8.
   c. Select the range C13:C15.
   d. Use the fill handle to copy these cells to the range D13:F15.
   e. Save your work.
7. **Copy formulas with absolute cell references.**
   a. In cell H1, enter the value **1.575**.
   b. In cell H4, create a formula that multiplies F4 and an absolute reference to cell H1.
   c. Use the fill handle to copy the formula in cell H4 to cells H5 and H6.
   d. Use the Copy and Paste buttons to copy the formula in cell H4 to cells H7 and H8.
   e. Change the amount in cell H1 to **2.3**.
   f. Save your work.
8. **Round a value with a function.**
   a. Click cell H4.
   b. Edit this formula to include the ROUND function showing one decimal place.
   c. Use the fill handle to copy the formula in cell H4 to the range H5:H8.
   d. Enter your name in cell A25, then compare your work to Figure B-23.
   e. Save your work, preview the worksheet in Backstage view, then submit your work to your instructor as directed.
   f. Close the workbook, then exit Excel.

FIGURE B-23

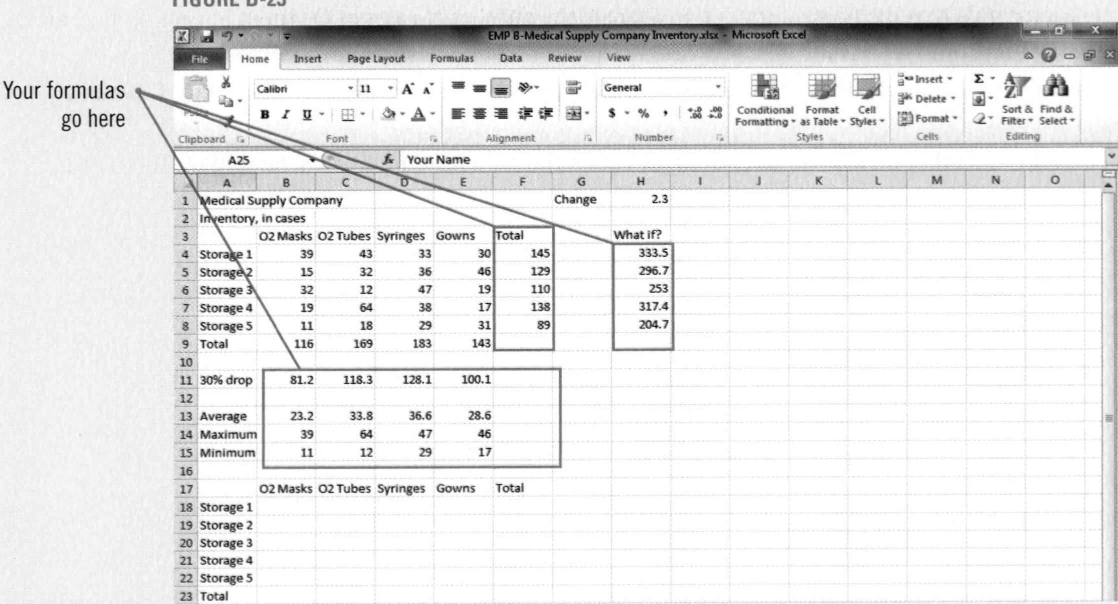

Independent Challenge 1

You keep the accounts for a local charity that wants to start a small clinic in an area that currently doesn't offer its residents any medical services. Before you begin, you need to evaluate what you think your monthly expenses will be. You've started a workbook, but need to complete the entries and add formulas.

a. Open the file EMP B-3.xlsx from the drive and folder where you store your Data Files, then save it as **EMP B-Estimated Clinic Expenses.**
b. Make up your own expense data, and enter it in cells B4:B10. (Monthly expenses are already included in the worksheet.)
c. Create a formula in cell C4 that calculates the annual rent.
d. Copy the formula in cell C4 to the range C5:C10.
e. Move the label in cell A15 to cell A14.
f. Create formulas in cells B11 and C11 that total the monthly and annual expenses.
g. Create a formula in cell C13 that calculates annual reimbursements.
h. Create a formula in cell B14 that determines whether the clinic will make a profit or loss, then copy the formula into cell C14.
i. Copy the labels in cells B3:C3 to cells E3:F3.
j. Type **Projection Increase** in cell G1, then type **.2** in cell I1.
k. Create a formula in cell E4 that calculates an increase in the monthly rent by the amount in cell I1. You will be copying this formula to other cells, so you'll need to use an absolute reference.
l. Create a formula in cell F4 that calculates the increased annual rent expense based on the calculation in cell E4.
m. Copy the formulas in cells E4:F4 into cells E5:F10 to calculate the remaining monthly and annual expenses.
n. Create a formula in cell E11 that calculates the total monthly expenses, then copy that formula to cell F11.
o. Copy the contents of cells B13:C13 into cells E13:F13.
p. Create formulas in cells E14 and F14 that calculate profit/loss based on the projected increase in monthly and annual reimbursements.
q. Change the projected increase to **.15**, then compare your work to the sample in Figure B-24.
r. Enter your name in a cell in the worksheet.
s. Save your work, preview the worksheet in Backstage view, submit your work to your instructor as directed, close the workbook, and exit Excel.

FIGURE B-24

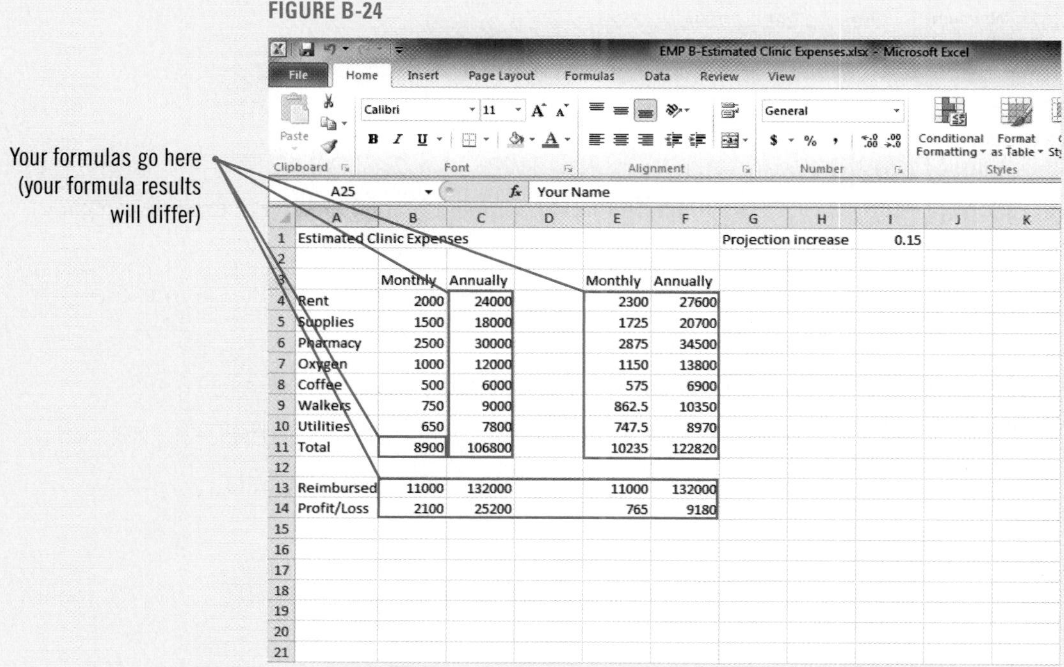

Independent Challenge 2

The Flight Nurse Training Academy is a small, growing flight nurse training center that has hired you to organize its accounting records using Excel. The owners want you to track the company's expenses. Before you were hired, one of the bookkeepers began entering last year's expenses in a workbook, but the analysis was never completed.

a. Start Excel, open the file EMP B-4.xlsx from the drive and folder where you store your Data Files, then save it as **EMP B-Flight Nurse Training Academy**. The worksheet includes labels for functions such as the average, maximum, and minimum amounts of each of the expenses in the worksheet.

b. Think about what information would be important for the bookkeeping staff to know.

c. Using the SUM function, create formulas for each expense in the Total column and each quarter in the Total row.

d. Create formulas for each expense and each quarter in the Average, Maximum, and Minimum columns and rows using the method of your choice.

e. Save your work, then compare your worksheet to the sample shown in Figure B-25.

FIGURE B-25

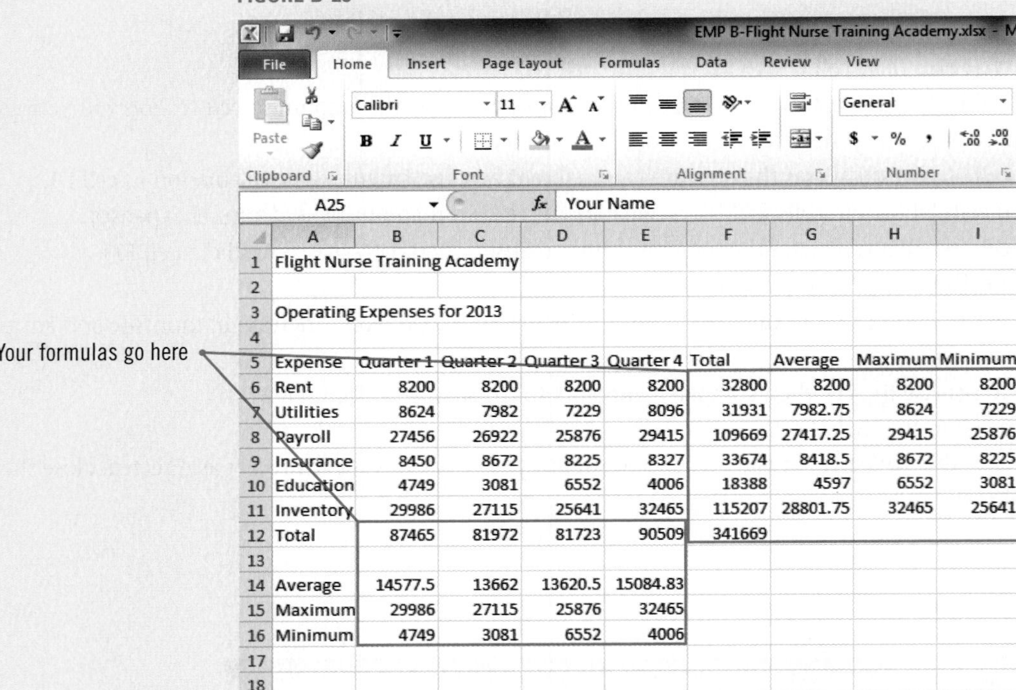

	A	B	C	D	E	F	G	H	I
1	Flight Nurse Training Academy								
2									
3	Operating Expenses for 2013								
4									
5	Expense	Quarter 1	Quarter 2	Quarter 3	Quarter 4	Total	Average	Maximum	Minimum
6	Rent	8200	8200	8200	8200	32800	8200	8200	8200
7	Utilities	8624	7982	7229	8096	31931	7982.75	8624	7229
8	Payroll	27456	26922	25876	29415	109669	27417.25	29415	25876
9	Insurance	8450	8672	8225	8327	33674	8418.5	8672	8225
10	Education	4749	3081	6552	4006	18388	4597	6552	3081
11	Inventory	29986	27115	25641	32465	115207	28801.75	32465	25641
12	Total	87465	81972	81723	90509	341669			
13									
14	Average	14577.5	13662	13620.5	15084.83				
15	Maximum	29986	27115	25876	32465				
16	Minimum	4749	3081	6552	4006				
17									
18									

Advanced Challenge Exercise

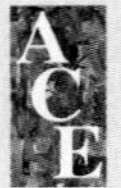

- Create the label **Expense categories** in cell B19.
- In cell A19, create a formula using the COUNT function that determines the total number of expense categories listed per quarter.
- Save the workbook.

f. Enter your name in cell A25.

g. Preview the worksheet, then submit your work to your instructor as directed.

h. Close the workbook and exit Excel.

Independent Challenge 3

As the accounting manager of an independently-managed laboratory within a hospital, it is your responsibility to calculate accrued sales tax payments on a monthly basis and then submit the payments to the state government. You've decided to use an Excel workbook to make these calculations.

a. Start Excel, then save a new, blank workbook to the drive and folder where you store your Data Files as **EMP B-Sales Tax Calculations**.
b. Decide on the layout for all columns and rows. The worksheet will contain data for four labs, which you can name by department, or another method of your choice. For each lab, you will calculate total sales tax based on the local sales tax rate. You'll also calculate total tax owed by all four labs.
c. Make up sales data for all four labs.
d. Enter the rate to be used to calculate the sales tax, using your own local rate.
e. Create formulas to calculate the sales tax owed for each lab. If you don't know the local tax rate, use **6.65%**.
f. Create a formula to total all the owed sales tax, and reference the cell containing the total tax two rows down with descriptive text preceding it.

FIGURE B-26

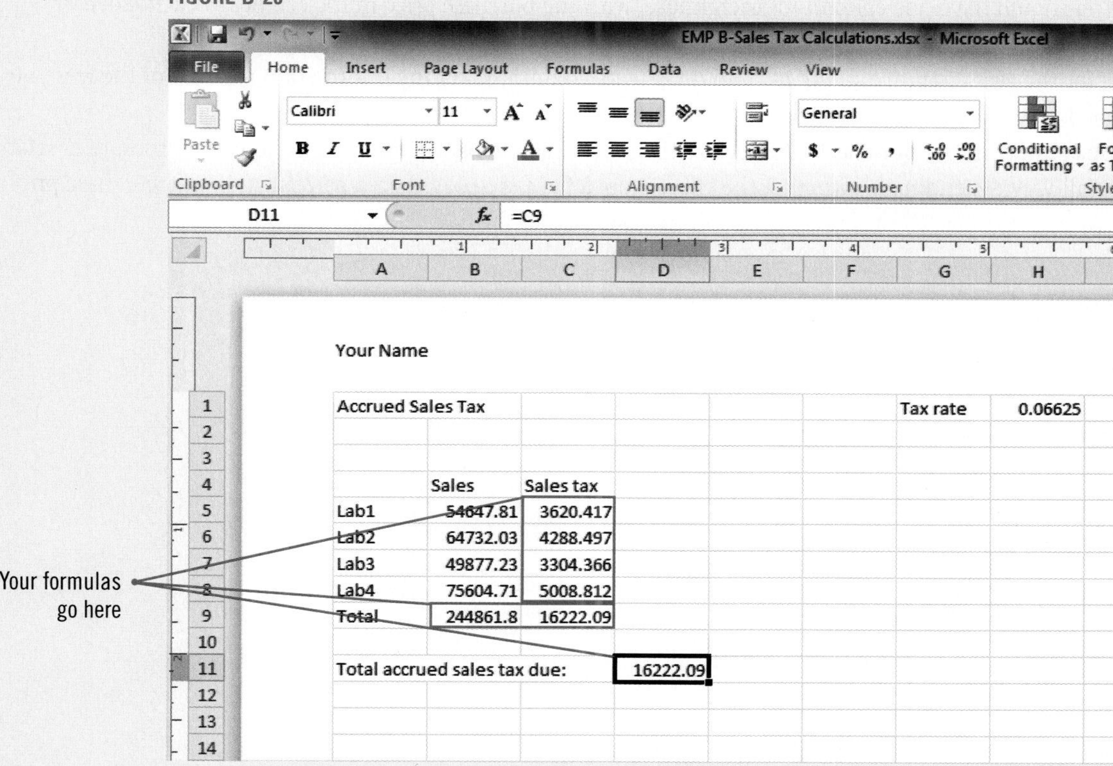

Advanced Challenge Exercise

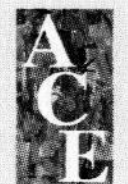

- Use the ROUND function to eliminate any decimal places in the sales tax figures for each lab and the total due.
- Save the workbook.

g. Add your name to the header.
h. Save your work, preview the worksheet, compare your work to the sample shown in Figure B-26, and submit your work to your instructor as directed.
i. Close the workbook and exit Excel.

Real Life Independent Challenge

The doctors for whom you work are thinking of buying a residence and converting it into a private practice, and have asked you to help them with the process. As you begin the round of open houses and realtors' listings, you notice that there are many fees associated with buying a home. Some fees are based on a percentage of the purchase price, and others are a flat fee; overall, they seem to represent a substantial amount above the purchase prices you see listed. You've seen five houses so far that interest you; one is easily affordable, and the remaining four are all nice, but increasingly more expensive. Although the practice will be financing the house, the bottom line is still important to you, so you decide to create an Excel workbook to figure out the real cost of buying each one.

a. Find out the typical cost or percentage rate of at least three fees that are usually charged when buying a house and taking out a mortgage. (*Hint*: If you have access to the Internet you can research the topic of home buying on the Web, or you can ask friends about standard rates or percentages for items such as title insurance, credit reports, and inspection fees.)

b. Start Excel, then save a new, blank workbook to the drive and folder where you store your Data Files as **EMP B-Home Purchase Costs**.

c. Create labels and enter data for at least three houses. If you enter this information across the columns in your worksheet, you should have one column for each house, with the purchase price in the cell below each label. Be sure to enter a different purchase price for each house.

d. Create labels for the Fees column and for an Amount or Rate column. Enter the information for each of the fees you have researched.

e. In each house column, enter formulas that calculate the fee for each item. The formulas (and use of absolute or relative referencing) will vary depending on whether the charges are a flat fee or based on a percentage of the purchase price.

Real Life Independent Challenge (continued)

f. Total the fees for each house, then create formulas that add the total fees to the purchase price. A sample of what your workbook might look like is shown in Figure B-27.

g. Enter a title for the worksheet in the header.

h. Enter your name in the header, save your work, preview the worksheet, then submit your work to your instructor as directed.

i. Close the file and exit Excel.

FIGURE B-27

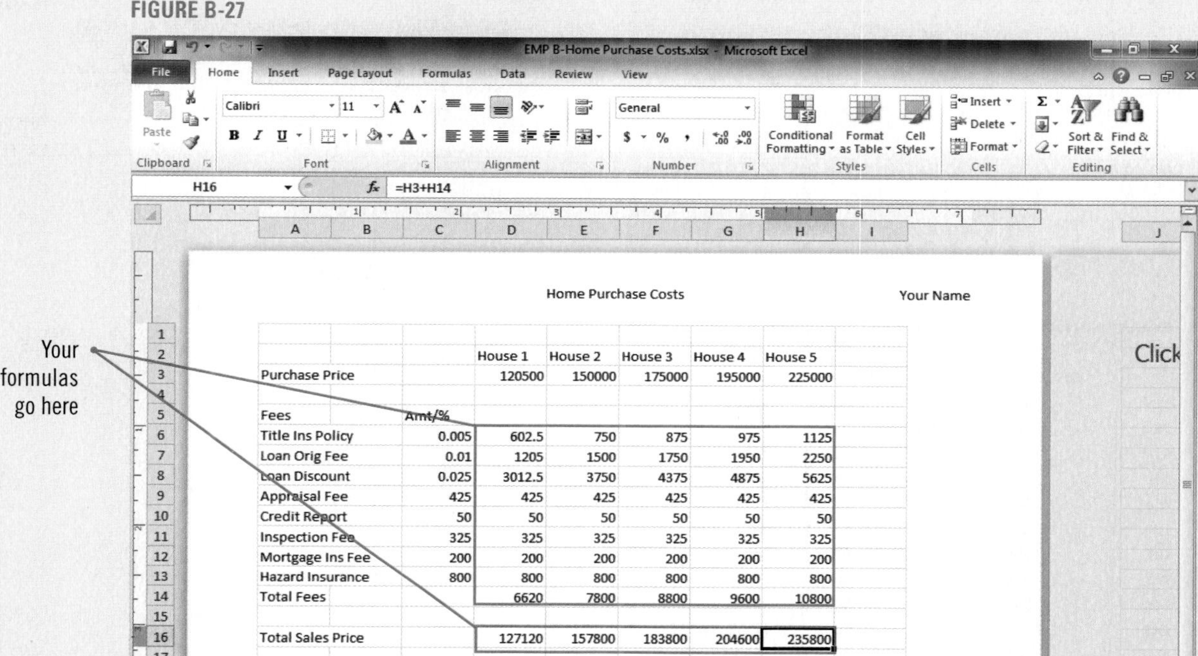

		House 1	House 2	House 3	House 4	House 5
Purchase Price		120500	150000	175000	195000	225000
Fees	Amt/%					
Title Ins Policy	0.005	602.5	750	875	975	1125
Loan Orig Fee	0.01	1205	1500	1750	1950	2250
Loan Discount	0.025	3012.5	3750	4375	4875	5625
Appraisal Fee	425	425	425	425	425	425
Credit Report	50	50	50	50	50	50
Inspection Fee	325	325	325	325	325	325
Mortgage Ins Fee	200	200	200	200	200	200
Hazard Insurance	800	800	800	800	800	800
Total Fees		6620	7800	8800	9600	10800
Total Sales Price		127120	157800	183800	204600	235800

Visual Workshop

Create the worksheet shown in Figure B-28 using the skills you learned in this unit. Save the workbook as **EMP B-Health Insurance Cost Analysis** to the drive and folder where you store your Data Files. Enter your name in the header as shown, hide the gridlines, preview the worksheet, and then submit your work to your instructor as directed.

FIGURE B-28

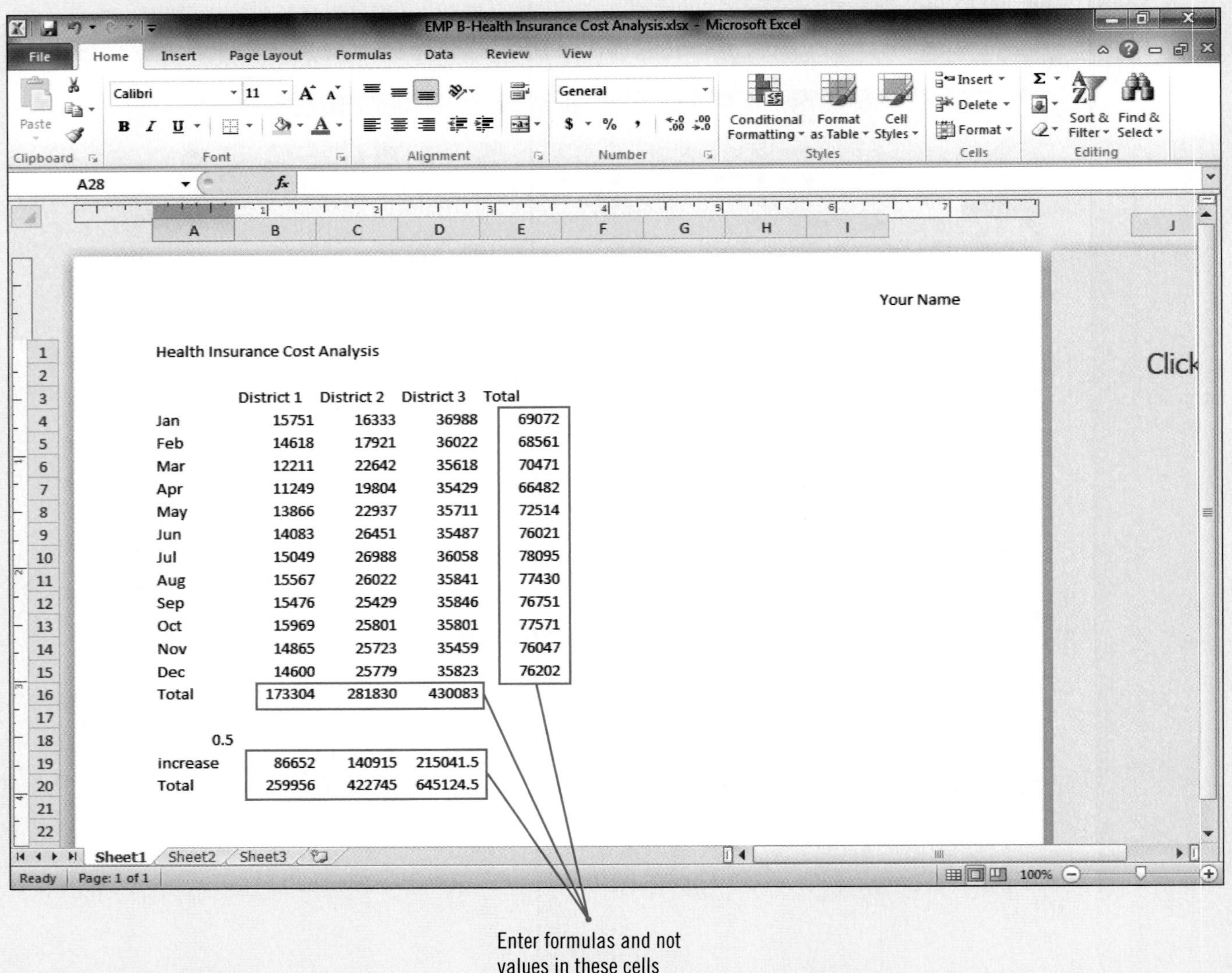

Your Name

Health Insurance Cost Analysis

	District 1	District 2	District 3	Total
Jan	15751	16333	36988	69072
Feb	14618	17921	36022	68561
Mar	12211	22642	35618	70471
Apr	11249	19804	35429	66482
May	13866	22937	35711	72514
Jun	14083	26451	35487	76021
Jul	15049	26988	36058	78095
Aug	15567	26022	35841	77430
Sep	15476	25429	35846	76751
Oct	15969	25801	35801	77571
Nov	14865	25723	35459	76047
Dec	14600	25779	35823	76202
Total	173304	281830	430083	
0.5				
increase	86652	140915	215041.5	
Total	259956	422745	645124.5	

UNIT C

Excel 2010

Formatting a Worksheet

Files You Will Need:

EMP C-1.xlsx
EMP C-2.xlsx
EMP C-3.xlsx
EMP C-4.xlsx
EMP C-5.xlsx

You can use formatting features to make a worksheet more attractive or easier to read, and to emphasize key data. You can apply different formatting attributes such as colors, font styles, and font sizes to the cell contents; you can adjust column width and row height; and you can insert or delete columns and rows. You can also apply conditional formatting so that cells meeting certain conditions are formatted differently from other cells. This makes it easy to emphasize selected information, such as sales that exceed or fall below a certain threshold. The administrators at RMC have requested data on expenses incurred during the first quarter of this year. Tony Sanchez has created a worksheet listing this information. He asks you to format the worksheet to make it easier to read and to call attention to important data.

OBJECTIVES

- Format values
- Change font and font size
- Change font styles and alignment
- Adjust column width
- Insert and delete rows and columns
- Apply colors, patterns, and borders
- Apply conditional formatting
- Rename and move a worksheet
- Check spelling

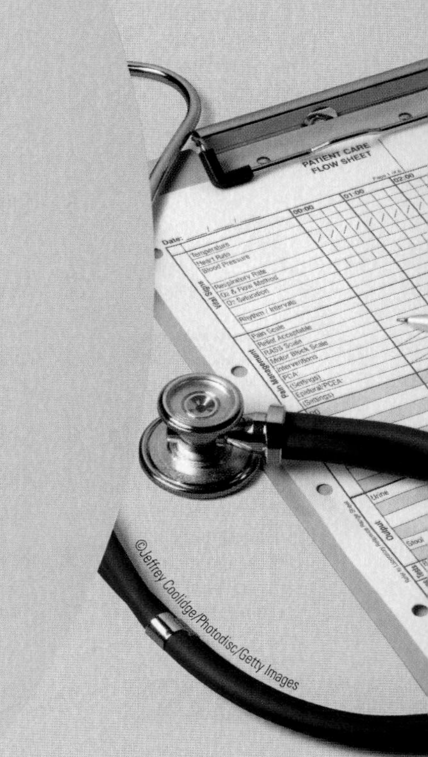

©Jeffrey Coolidge/Photodisc/Getty Images

UNIT C

Excel 2010

Formatting Values

The **format** of a cell determines how the labels and values look—for example, whether the contents appear boldfaced, italicized, or with dollar signs and commas. Formatting changes only the appearance of a value or label; it does not alter the actual data in any way. To format a cell or range, first you select it, then you apply the formatting using the Ribbon, Mini toolbar, or a keyboard shortcut. You can apply formatting before or after you enter data in a cell or range. Tony has provided you with a worksheet that lists individual emergency room expenses, and you're ready to improve its appearance and readability. You decide to start by formatting some of the values so they are displayed as currency, percentages, and dates.

STEPS

1. **Start Excel, open the file EMP C-1.xlsx from the drive and folder where you store your Data Files, then save it as EMP C-RMC Emergency Room Expenses**

   This worksheet is difficult to interpret because all the information is crowded and looks the same. In column A, the contents appear cut off because there is too much data to fit given the current column width. You decide not to widen the column yet, because the other changes you plan to make might affect column width and row height. The first thing you want to do is format the data showing the cost of each ad.

2. **Select the range D11:D39, then click the Accounting Number Format button $ in the Number group on the Home tab**

   The default **Accounting number format** adds dollar signs and two decimal places to the data, as shown in Figure C-1. Formatting this data in Accounting format makes it clear that its values are monetary values. Excel automatically resizes the column to display the new formatting. The Accounting and Currency number formats are both used for monetary values, but the Accounting format aligns currency symbols and decimal points of numbers in a column.

3. **Select the range F11:H39, then click the Comma Style button , in the Number group**

   The values in columns F, G, and H display the Comma Style format, which does not include a dollar sign but can be useful for some types of accounting data.

4. **Select the range J11:J39, click the Number Format list arrow, click Percentage, then click the Increase Decimal button in the Number group three times**

   The Number Format list arrow lets you choose from popular number formats and shows an example of what the selected cell or cells would look like in each format (when multiple cells are selected, the example is based on the first cell in the range). Each time you click the Increase Decimal button, you add one decimal place; clicking the button twice would add two decimal places.

5. **Click the Decrease Decimal button in the Number group twice**

   Two decimal places are removed from the percentage values in column J. The data in the % of Total column is now formatted with a percent sign (%) and three decimal places.

6. **Select the range B11:B38, then click the dialog box launcher in the Number group**

   The Format Cells dialog box opens with the Date category already selected on the Number tab.

7. **Select the first 14-Mar-01 format in the Type list box as shown in Figure C-2, then click OK**

   The dates in column B appear in the 14-Mar-01 format. The second 14-Mar-01 format in the list displays all days in two digits (it adds a leading zero if the day is only a single-digit number), while the one you chose displays single-digit days without a leading zero.

8. **Select the range C11:C38, right-click the range, click Format Cells on the shortcut menu, click 14-Mar in the Type list box in the Format Cells dialog box, then click OK**

   Compare your worksheet to Figure C-3.

9. **Press [Ctrl][Home], then save your work**

QUICK TIP

You can use a different type of currency, such as Euros or British pounds, by clicking the Accounting Number Format list arrow, then clicking a different currency format.

QUICK TIP

Select any range of contiguous cells by clicking the upper-left cell of the range, pressing and holding [Shift], then clicking the lower-right cell of the range. Add a row to the selected range by continuing to hold down [Shift] and pressing ↓; add a column by pressing →.

QUICK TIP

Make sure you examine formatted data to confirm that you have applied the appropriate formatting; for example, dates should not have a currency format, and monetary values should not have a date format.

FIGURE C-1: Accounting number format applied to range

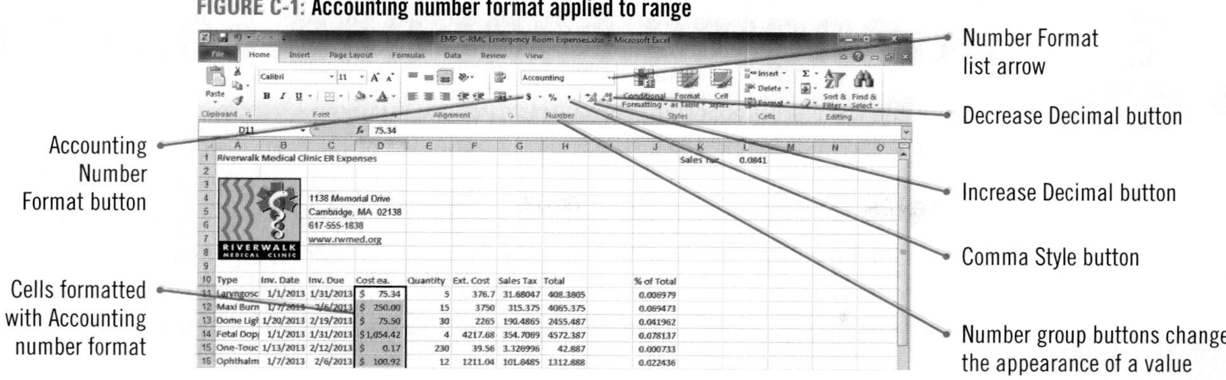

FIGURE C-2: Format Cells dialog box

Sample of selected type

Number categories

This format looks similar to the one below it but displays single digit months and days with a preceding zero

Date format types

FIGURE C-3: Worksheet with formatted values

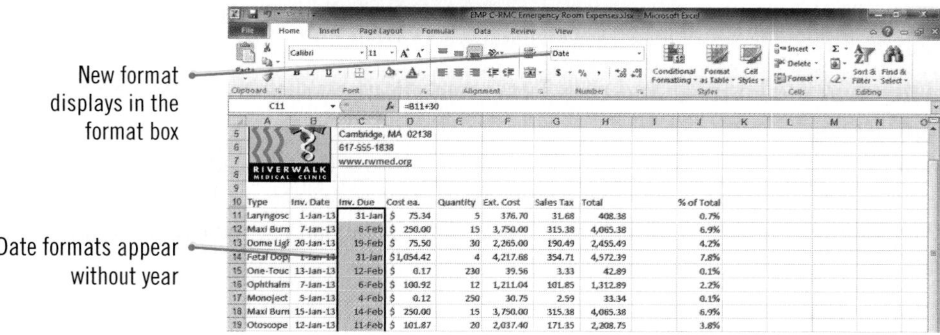

Formatting as a table

Excel includes 60 predefined **table styles** to make it easy to format selected worksheet cells as a table. You can apply table styles to any range of cells that you want to format quickly, or even to an entire worksheet, but they're especially useful for those ranges with labels in the left column and top row, and totals in the bottom row or right column. To apply a table style, select the data to be formatted or click anywhere within the intended range (Excel can automatically detect a range of cells filled with data), click the Format as Table button in the Styles group on the Home tab, then click a style in the gallery, as shown in Figure C-4. Table styles are organized in three categories: Light, Medium, and Dark. Once you click a style, Excel asks you to confirm the range selection, then applies the style. Once you have formatted a range as a table, you can use Live Preview to preview the table in other styles by pointing to any style in the Table Styles gallery.

FIGURE C-4: Table Styles gallery

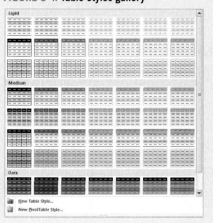

Excel 2010

UNIT C

Excel 2010

Changing Font and Font Size

A **font** is the name for a collection of characters (letters, numbers, symbols, and punctuation marks) with a similar, specific design. The **font size** is the physical size of the text, measured in units called points. A **point** is equal to 1/72 of an inch. The default font and font size in Excel is 11-point Calibri. Table C-1 shows several fonts in different font sizes. You can change the font and font size of any cell or range using the Font and Font Size list arrows. The Font and Font Size list arrows appear on the Home tab on the Ribbon and on the Mini toolbar, which opens when you right-click a cell or range. You want to change the font and font size of the labels and the worksheet title so that they stand out more from the data.

STEPS

QUICK TIP
To quickly move to a font in the Font list, type the first few characters of its name.

1. **Click cell A1, click the Font list arrow in the Font group on the Home tab, scroll down in the Font list to see an alphabetical listing of the fonts available on your computer, then click Times New Roman, as shown in Figure C-5**

   The font in cell A1 changes to Times New Roman. Notice that the font names on the list are displayed in the font they represent.

QUICK TIP
When you point to an option in the Font or Font Size list, Live Preview shows the selected cells with the option temporarily applied.

2. **Click the Font Size list arrow in the Font group, then click 20**

   The worksheet title appears in 20-point Times New Roman, and the Font and Font Size list boxes on the Home tab display the new font and font size information.

3. **Click the Increase Font Size button A in the Font group twice**

   The font size of the title increases to 24 point.

4. **Select the range A10:J10, right-click, then click the Font list arrow in the Font group on the Mini toolbar**

   The Mini toolbar includes the most commonly used formatting tools, so it's great for making quick formatting changes.

QUICK TIP
You can format an entire row by clicking the row indicator button to select the row before formatting (or select an entire column by clicking the column indicator button before formatting).

5. **Scroll down in the Font list and click Times New Roman, click the Font Size list arrow on the Mini toolbar, then click 14**

   The Mini toolbar closes when you move the pointer away from the selection. Compare your worksheet to Figure C-6. Notice that some of the column labels are now too wide to appear fully in the column. Excel does not automatically adjust column widths to accommodate cell formatting; you have to adjust column widths manually. You'll learn to do this in a later lesson.

6. **Save your work**

TABLE C-1: Examples of fonts and font sizes

font	12 point	24 point
Calibri	Excel	Excel
Playbill	Excel	Excel
Comic Sans MS	Excel	Excel
Times New Roman	Excel	Excel

FIGURE C-5: Font list in the Format Cells dialog box

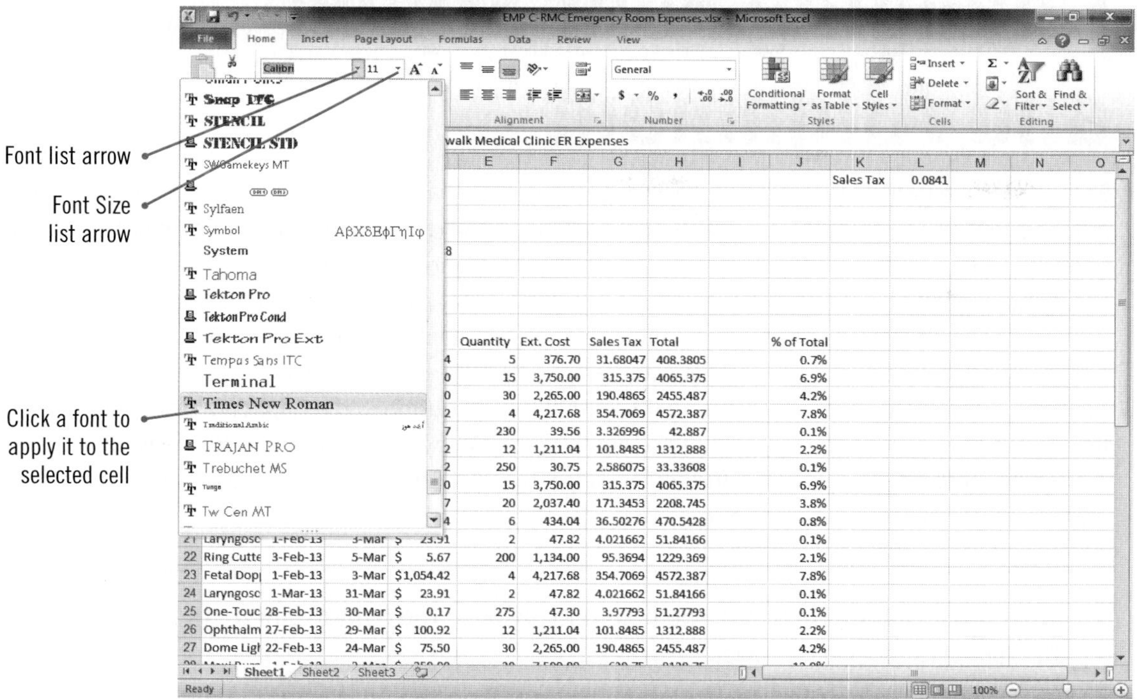

FIGURE C-6: Worksheet with formatted title and column labels

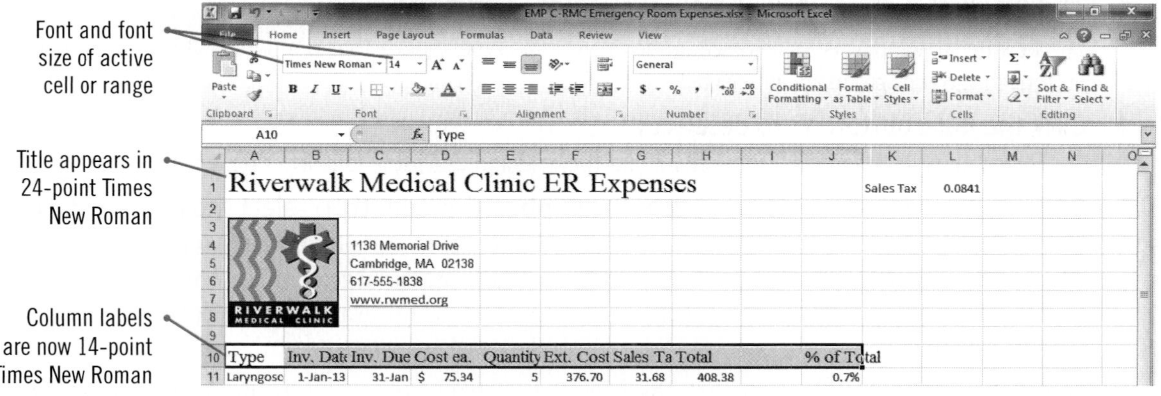

Excel 2010

Inserting and adjusting clip art and other images

You can illustrate your worksheets using clip art and other images. A **clip** is an individual media file, such as a graphic, sound, animation, or a movie. **Clip art** refers to images such as a corporate logo, a picture, or a photo. Microsoft Office comes with many clips available for your use. (The RMC files in this unit display the hospital's logo.) To add a clip to a worksheet, click the Clip Art button in the Illustrations group on the Insert tab. The Clip Art task pane opens. Here you can search for clips by typing one or more keywords (words related to your subject) in the Search for text box, then click Go. Clips that relate to your keywords appear in the Clip Art task pane, as shown in Figure C-7. (If you have a standard Office installation and an active Internet connection, click the Include Office.com content check box to see clips available through Office.com in addition to those on your computer.) When you click the image you want in the Clip Art task pane, the image is inserted at the location of the active cell. To add your own images to a worksheet, click the Insert tab on the Ribbon, then click the Picture button. Navigate to the file you want, then click Insert. To resize an image, drag any corner sizing handle. To move an image, point inside the clip until the pointer changes to ✥, then drag it to a new location.

FIGURE C-7: Results of Clip Art search

Click to begin search

Type keyword(s) here

UNIT C
Excel 2010

Changing Font Styles and Alignment

Font styles are formats such as bold, italic, and underlining that you can apply to affect the way text and numbers look in a worksheet. You can also change the **alignment** of labels and values in cells to position them in relation to the cells' edges—such as left-aligned, right-aligned, or centered. You can apply font styles and alignment options using the Home tab, the Format Cells dialog box, or the Mini toolbar. See Table C-2 for a description of common font style and alignment buttons that are available on the Home tab and the Mini toolbar. Once you have formatted a cell the way you want it, you can "paint" or copy the cell's formats into other cells by using the Format Painter button in the Clipboard group on the Home tab. This is similar to using copy and paste, but instead of copying cell contents, it copies only the cell's formatting. You want to further enhance the worksheet's appearance by adding bold and underline formatting and centering some of the labels.

STEPS

QUICK TIP
You can use the following keyboard shortcuts to format a selected cell or range: [Ctrl][B] to bold, [Ctrl][I] to italicize, and [Ctrl][U] to underline.

QUICK TIP
Overuse of any font style and random formatting can make a workbook difficult to read. Be consistent and add the same formatting to similar items throughout a worksheet or in related worksheets.

QUICK TIP
To clear all formatting from a selected range, click the Clear button in the Editing group on the Home tab, then click Clear Formats.

1. **Press [Ctrl][Home], then click the Bold button B in the Font group on the Home tab**
   The title in cell A1 appears in bold.
2. **Click cell A10, then click the Underline button U in the Font group**
   The column label is now underlined, though this may be difficult to see with the cell selected.
3. **Click the Italic button I in the Font group, then click B**
   The heading now appears in boldface, underlined, italic type. Notice that the Bold, Italic, and Underline buttons in the Font group are all selected.
4. **Click the Italic button I to deselect it**
   The italic font style is removed from cell A3, but the bold and underline font styles remain.
5. **Click the Format Painter button in the Clipboard group, then select the range B10:J10**
   The formatting in cell A10 is copied to the rest of the column labels. To paint the formats on more than one selection, double-click the Format Painter button to keep it activated until you turn it off. You can turn off the Format Painter by pressing [Esc] or by clicking . You decide the title would look better if it were centered over the data columns.
6. **Select the range A1:H1, then click the Merge & Center button in the Alignment group**
   The Merge & Center button creates one cell out of the eight cells across the row, then centers the text in that newly created, merged cell. The title "Riverwalk Medical Clinic ER Expenses" is centered across the eight columns you selected. To split a merged cell into its original components, select the merged cell, then click the Merge & Center button to deselect it. The merged and centered text might look awkward now, but you'll be changing the column widths shortly.
7. **Select the range A10:J10, right-click, then click the Center button on the Mini toolbar**
   Compare your screen to Figure C-8. Although they may be difficult to read, notice that all the headings are centered within their cells.
8. **Save your work**

FIGURE C-8: Worksheet with font styles and alignment applied

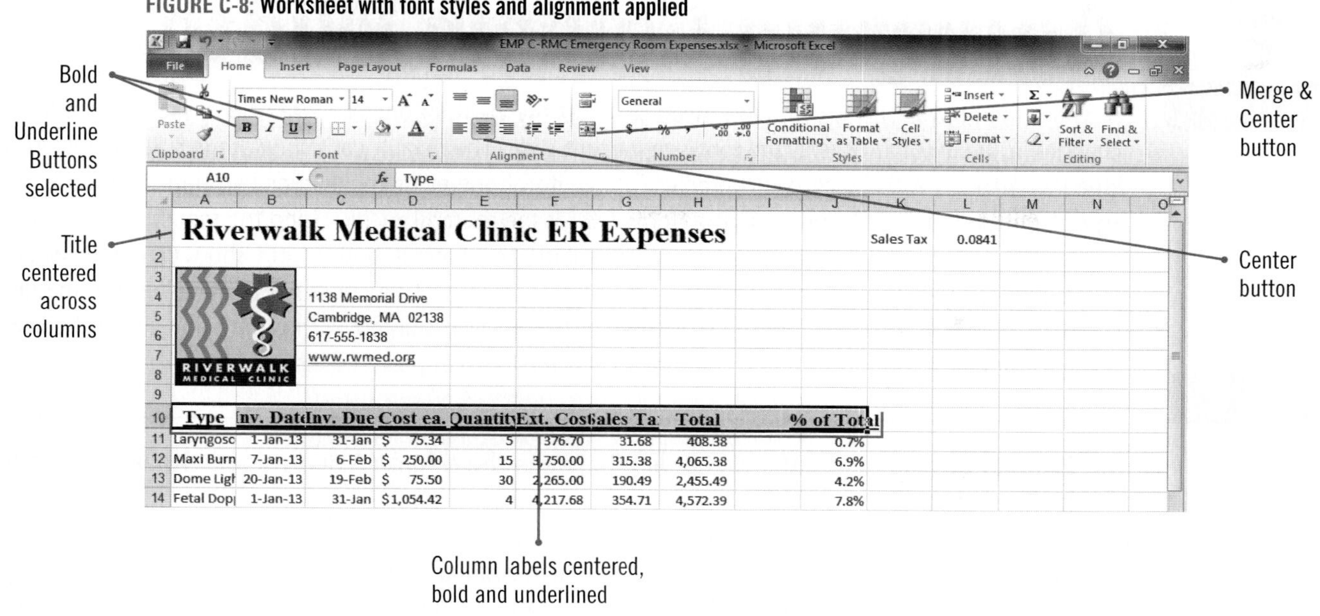

Excel 2010

TABLE C-2: Common font style and alignment buttons

button	description	button	description
B	Bolds text		Aligns text at the left edge of the cell
I	Italicizes text		Centers text horizontally within the cell
U	Underlines text		Aligns text at the right edge of the cell
	Centers text across columns, and combines two or more selected, adjacent cells into one cell		

Rotating and indenting cell entries

In addition to applying fonts and font styles, you can rotate or indent data within a cell to further change its appearance. You can rotate text within a cell by altering its alignment. To change alignment, select the cells you want to modify, then click the dialog box launcher in the Alignment group to open the Alignment tab of the Format Cells dialog box. Click a position in the Orientation box or type a number in the Degrees text box to rotate text from its default horizontal orientation, then click OK. You can indent cell contents using the Increase Indent button in the Alignment group, which moves cell contents to the right one space, or the Decrease Indent button, which moves cell contents to the left one space.

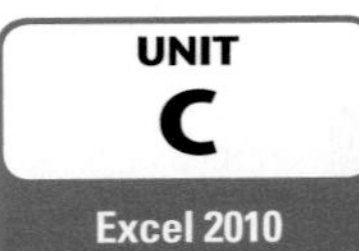

Adjusting Column Width

As you format a worksheet, you might need to adjust the width of one or more columns to accommodate changes in the amount of text, the font size, or font style. The default column width is 8.43 characters, a little less than 1". With Excel, you can adjust the width of one or more columns by using the mouse, the Format button in the Cells group on the Home tab, or the shortcut menu. Using the mouse, you can drag or double-click the right edge of a column heading. The Format button and shortcut menu include commands for making more precise width adjustments. Table C-3 describes common column formatting commands. You have noticed that some of the labels in columns A through J don't fit in the cells. You want to adjust the widths of the columns so that the labels appear in their entirety.

STEPS

1. **Position the mouse pointer on the line between the column A and column B headings until it changes to ✛**

   See Figure C-9. The **column heading** is the box at the top of each column containing a letter. Before you can adjust column width using the mouse, you need to position the pointer on the right edge of the column heading for the column you want to adjust. The cell entry "Monoject Syringes" is the widest in the column.

> **QUICK TIP**
> If "#######" appears after you adjust a column of values, the column is too narrow to display the values completely; increase the column width until the values appear.

2. **Click and drag the ✛ to the right until the column displays the "Monoject Syringes" cell entries fully (approximately 16.43 characters, 1.31", or 120 pixels)**

   As you change the column width, a ScreenTip is displayed listing the column width. In Normal view, the ScreenTip lists the width in characters and pixels; in Page Layout view, the ScreenTip lists the width in inches and pixels.

3. **Position the pointer on the line between columns B and C until it changes to ✛, then double-click**

   Double-clicking the right edge of a column heading activates the **AutoFit** feature, which automatically resizes the column to accommodate the widest entry in the column. Column B automatically widens to fit the widest entry, which is the column label "Inv. Date".

4. **Use AutoFit to resize columns D and J, and resize column C so it has a width of 10 characters**

5. **Select the range E12:H12**

   You can change the width of multiple columns at once, by first selecting either the column headings or at least one cell in each column.

> **QUICK TIP**
> If an entire column rather than a column cell is selected, you can change the width of the column by right-clicking the column heading, then clicking Column Width on the shortcut menu.

6. **Click the Format button in the Cells group, then click Column Width**

   The Column Width dialog box opens. Column width measurement is based on the number of characters that will fit in the column when formatted in the Normal font and font size (in this case, 11 pt Calibri).

7. **Drag the dialog box by its title bar if its placement obscures your view of the worksheet, type 11 in the Column width text box, then click OK**

   The widths of columns E, F, G, and H change to reflect the new setting. See Figure C-10.

8. **Save your work**

TABLE C-3: Common column formatting commands

command	description	available using
Column Width	Sets the width to a specific number of characters	Format button; shortcut menu
AutoFit Column Width	Fits to the widest entry in a column	Format button; mouse
Hide & Unhide	Hides or displays hidden column(s)	Format button; shortcut menu
Default Width	Resets column to worksheet's default column width	Format button

FIGURE C-9: Preparing to change the column width

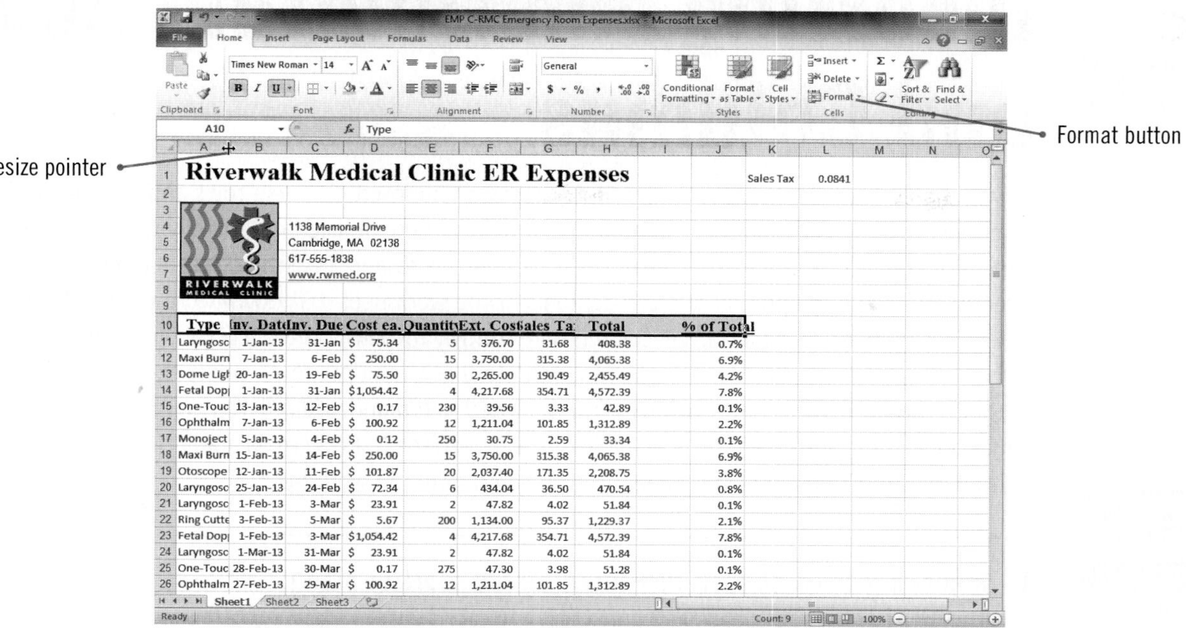

FIGURE C-10: Worksheet with column widths adjusted

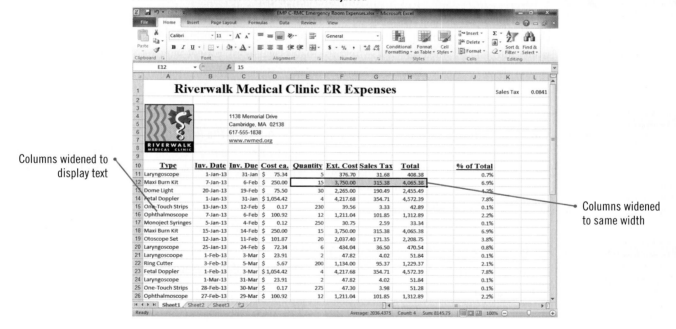

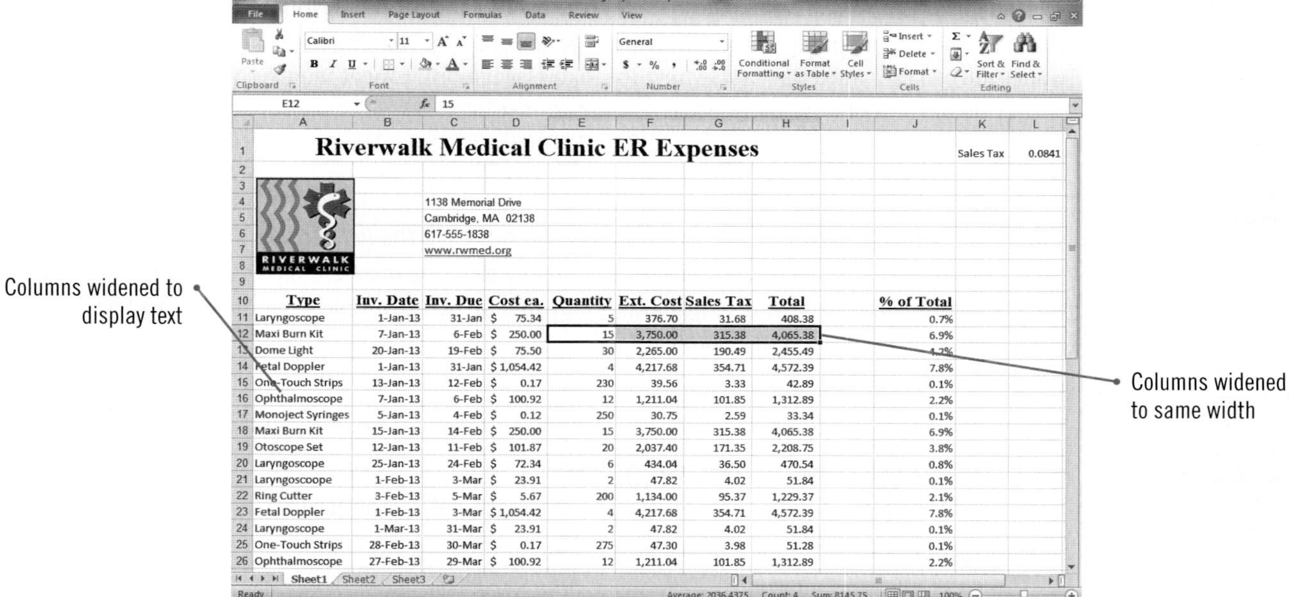

Changing row height

Changing row height is as easy as changing column width. Row height is calculated in points, the same units of measure used for fonts. The row height must exceed the size of the font you are using. Normally, you don't need to adjust row heights manually, because row heights adjust automatically to accommodate font size changes. If you format something in a row to be a larger point size, Excel adjusts the row to fit the largest point size in the row. However, you have just as many options for changing row height as you do column width. Using the mouse, you can place the ‡ pointer on the line dividing a row heading from the heading below, and then drag to the desired height; double-clicking the line AutoFits the row height where necessary. You can also select one or more rows, then use the Row Height command on the shortcut menu, or click the Format button on the Home tab and click the Row Height or AutoFit Row Height command.

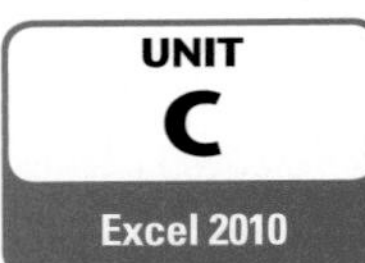

Inserting and Deleting Rows and Columns

As you modify a worksheet, you might find it necessary to insert or delete rows and columns to keep your worksheet current. For example, you might need to insert rows to accommodate new inventory products or remove a column of yearly totals that are no longer necessary. When you insert a new row, the row is inserted above the cell pointer and the contents of the worksheet shift down from the newly inserted row. When you insert a new column, the column is inserted to the left of the cell pointer and the contents of the worksheet shift to the right of the new column. To insert multiple rows, select the same number of row headings as you want to insert before using the Insert command. You want to improve the overall appearance of the worksheet by inserting a row between the last row of data and the totals. Also, you have learned that row 34 and column J need to be deleted from the worksheet.

STEPS

QUICK TIP
To insert a single row or column, right-click the row heading immediately below where you want the new row, or right-click the column heading to the right of where you want the new column, then click Insert on the shortcut menu.

QUICK TIP
If you inadvertently click the Delete list arrow instead of the button itself, click Delete Sheet Rows in the menu that opens.

QUICK TIP
After inserting or deleting rows or columns in a worksheet, be sure to proof formulas that contain relative cell references.

1. **Right-click cell A39, then click Insert on the shortcut menu**
   The Insert dialog box opens. See Figure C-11. You can choose to insert a column or a row; insert a single cell and shift the cells in the active column to the right; or insert a single cell and shift the cells in the active row down. An additional row between the last row of data and the totals will visually separate the totals.
2. **Click the Entire row option button, then click OK**
   A blank row appears between the Otoscope Set data and the totals, and the formula result in cell E40 has not changed. The Insert Options button appears beside cell A40. Pointing to the button displays a list arrow, which you can click and then choose from the following options: Format Same As Above (the default setting, already selected), Format Same As Below, or Clear Formatting.
3. **Click the row 34 heading**
   All of row 34 is selected, as shown in Figure C-12.
4. **Click the Delete button in the Cells group; *do not click the list arrow***
   Excel deletes row 34, and all rows below it shift up one row. You must use the Delete button or the Delete command on the shortcut menu to delete a row or column; pressing [Delete] on the keyboard removes only the *contents* of a selected row or column.
5. **Click the column J heading**
   The percentage information is calculated elsewhere and is no longer necessary in this worksheet.
6. **Click the Delete button in the Cells group**
   Excel deletes column J. The remaining columns to the right shift left one column.
7. **Save your work**

Hiding and unhiding columns and rows

When you don't want data in a column or row to be visible, but you don't want to delete it, you can hide the column or row. To hide a selected column, click the Format button in the Cells group on the Home tab, point to Hide & Unhide, then click Hide Columns. A hidden column is indicated by a dark black vertical line in its original position. This black line disappears when you click elsewhere in the worksheet. You can display a hidden column by selecting the columns on either side of the hidden column, clicking the Format button in the Cells group, pointing to Hide & Unhide, and then clicking Unhide Columns. (To hide or unhide one or more rows, substitute Hide Rows and Unhide Rows for the Hide Columns and Unhide Columns commands.)

FIGURE C-11: Insert dialog box

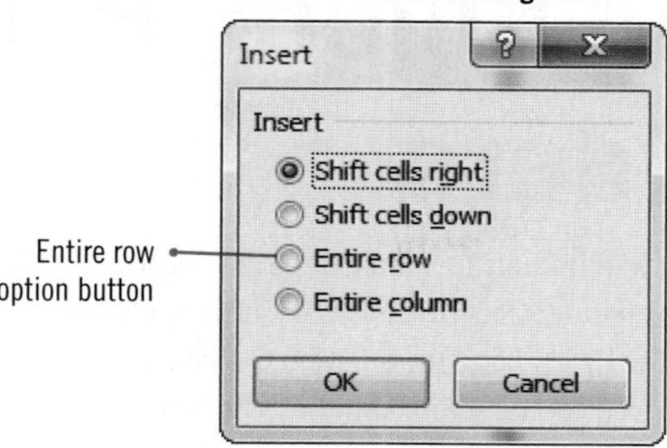

FIGURE C-12: Worksheet with row 34 selected

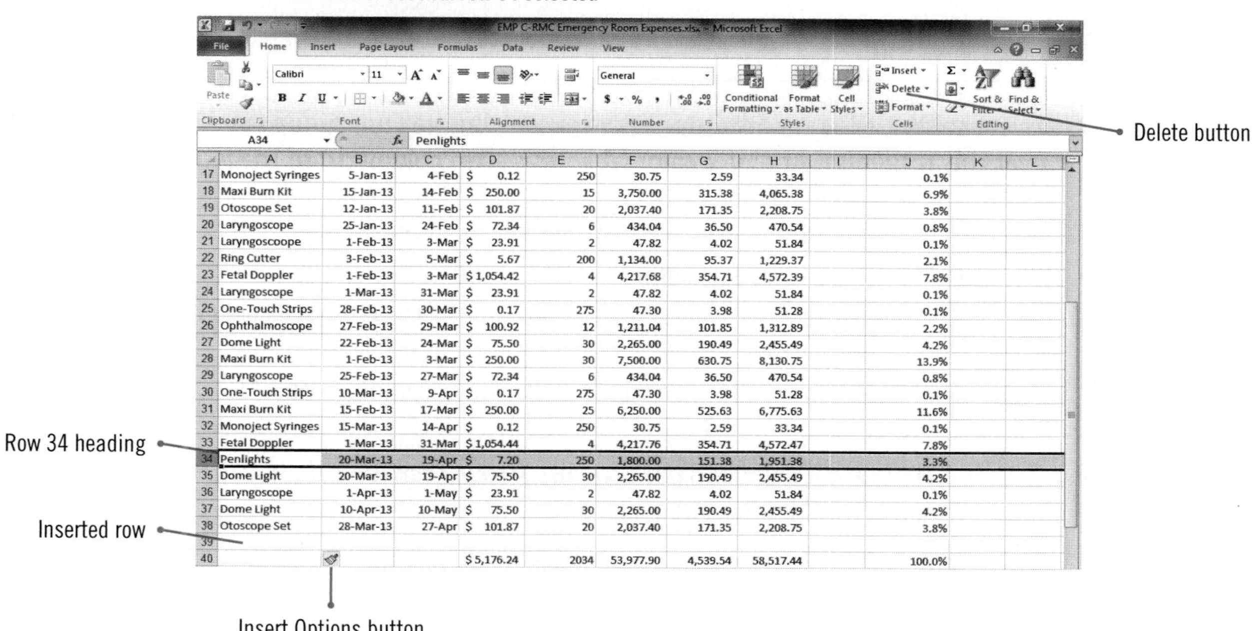

	A	B	C	D	E	F	G	H	I	J	K	L
17	Monoject Syringes	5-Jan-13	4-Feb	$ 0.12	250	30.75	2.59	33.34		0.1%		
18	Maxi Burn Kit	15-Jan-13	14-Feb	$ 250.00	15	3,750.00	315.38	4,065.38		6.9%		
19	Otoscope Set	12-Jan-13	11-Feb	$ 101.87	20	2,037.40	171.35	2,208.75		3.8%		
20	Laryngoscope	25-Jan-13	24-Feb	$ 72.34	6	434.04	36.50	470.54		0.8%		
21	Laryngoscoope	1-Feb-13	3-Mar	$ 23.91	2	47.82	4.02	51.84		0.1%		
22	Ring Cutter	3-Feb-13	5-Mar	$ 5.67	200	1,134.00	95.37	1,229.37		2.1%		
23	Fetal Doppler	1-Feb-13	3-Mar	$ 1,054.42	4	4,217.68	354.71	4,572.39		7.8%		
24	Laryngoscope	1-Mar-13	31-Mar	$ 23.91	2	47.82	4.02	51.84		0.1%		
25	One-Touch Strips	28-Feb-13	30-Mar	$ 0.17	275	47.30	3.98	51.28		0.1%		
26	Ophthalmoscope	27-Feb-13	29-Mar	$ 100.92	12	1,211.04	101.85	1,312.89		2.2%		
27	Dome Light	22-Feb-13	24-Mar	$ 75.50	30	2,265.00	190.49	2,455.49		4.2%		
28	Maxi Burn Kit	1-Feb-13	3-Mar	$ 250.00	30	7,500.00	630.75	8,130.75		13.9%		
29	Laryngoscope	25-Feb-13	27-Mar	$ 72.34	6	434.04	36.50	470.54		0.8%		
30	One-Touch Strips	10-Mar-13	9-Apr	$ 0.17	275	47.30	3.98	51.28		0.1%		
31	Maxi Burn Kit	15-Feb-13	17-Mar	$ 250.00	25	6,250.00	525.63	6,775.63		11.6%		
32	Monoject Syringes	15-Mar-13	14-Apr	$ 0.12	250	30.75	2.59	33.34		0.1%		
33	Fetal Doppler	1-Mar-13	31-Mar	$ 1,054.44	4	4,217.76	354.71	4,572.47		7.8%		
34	Penlights	20-Mar-13	19-Apr	$ 7.20	250	1,800.00	151.38	1,951.38		3.3%		
35	Dome Light	20-Mar-13	19-Apr	$ 75.50	30	2,265.00	190.49	2,455.49		4.2%		
36	Laryngoscope	1-Apr-13	1-May	$ 23.91	2	47.82	4.02	51.84		0.1%		
37	Dome Light	10-Apr-13	10-May	$ 75.50	30	2,265.00	190.49	2,455.49		4.2%		
38	Otoscope Set	28-Mar-13	27-Apr	$ 101.87	20	2,037.40	171.35	2,208.75		3.8%		
39												
40				$ 5,176.24	2034	53,977.90	4,539.54	58,517.44		100.0%		

Adding and editing comments

Much of your work in Excel may be in collaboration with teammates with whom you share worksheets. You can share ideas with other worksheet users by adding comments within selected cells. To include a comment in a worksheet, click the cell where you want to place the comment, click the Review tab on the Ribbon, then click the New Comment button in the Comments group. You can type your comments in the resizable text box that opens containing the computer user's name. A small, red triangle appears in the upper-right corner of a cell containing a comment. If comments are not already displayed in a workbook, other users can point to the triangle to display the comment. To see all worksheet comments, as shown in Figure C-13, click the Show All Comments button in the Comments group. To edit a comment, click the cell containing the comment, then click the Edit Comment button in the Comments group. To delete a comment, click the cell containing the comment, then click the Delete button in the Comments group.

FIGURE C-13: Comments displayed in a worksheet

19	Otoscope Set	12-Jan-13	11-Feb	$ 101.87	20	2,037.40
20	Laryngoscope	25-Jan-13	24-Feb	$ 72.34	6	434.04
21	Laryngoscope	1-Feb-13	3-Mar	$ 23.91	2	47.82
22	Ring Cutter	3-Feb-13	5-Mar	$ 5.67		
23	Fetal Doppler	1-Feb-13	3-Mar	$ 1,054.42		
24	Laryngoscope	1-Mar-13	31-Mar	$ 23.91		
25	One-Touch Strips	28-Feb-13	30-Mar	$ 0.17		
26	Ophthalmoscope	27-Feb-13	29-Mar	$ 100.92	12	1,211.04
27	Dome Light	22-Feb-13	24-Mar	$ 75.50	30	2,265.00
28	Maxi Burn Kit	1-Feb-13	3-Mar	$ 250.00	30	7,500.00
29	Laryngoscope	25-Feb-13	27-Mar	$ 72.34		
30	One-Touch Strips	10-Mar-13	9-Apr	$ 0.17		
31	Maxi Burn Kit	15-Feb-13	17-Mar	$ 250.00		
32	Monoject Syringes	15-Mar-13	14-Apr	$ 0.12		

Tony Sanchez:
These items are very costly. How can we economize?

Tony Sanchez:
We've gotten a great price on these!

UNIT C

Excel 2010

Applying Colors, Patterns, and Borders

You can use colors, patterns, and borders to enhance the overall appearance of a worksheet and make it easier to read. You can add these enhancements by using the Borders, Font Color, and Fill Color buttons in the Font group on the Home tab of the Ribbon and on the Mini toolbar, or by using the Fill tab and the Border tab in the Format Cells dialog box. You can open the Format Cells dialog box by clicking the dialog box launcher in the Font, Alignment, or Number group on the Home tab, or by right-clicking a selection, then clicking Format Cells on the shortcut menu. You can apply a color to the background of a cell or a range or to cell contents (such as letters and numbers), and you can apply a pattern to a cell or range. You can apply borders to all the cells in a worksheet or only to selected cells to call attention to selected information. To save time, you can also apply **cell styles**, predesigned combinations of formats. You want to add a pattern, a border, and color to the title of the worksheet to give the worksheet a more professional appearance.

STEPS

1. **Select cell A1, click the Fill Color list arrow in the Font group, then hover the pointer over the Turquoise, Accent 2 color (first row, sixth column from the left)**

   See Figure C-14. Live Preview shows you how the color will look *before* you apply it. (Remember that cell A1 spans columns A through H because the Merge & Center command was applied.)

2. **Click the Turquoise, Accent 2 color**

   The color is applied to the background (or fill) of this cell. When you change fill or font color, the color on the Fill Color or Font Color button changes to the last color you selected.

3. **Right-click cell A1, then click Format Cells on the shortcut menu**

   The Format Cells dialog box opens.

4. **Click the Fill tab, click the Pattern Style list arrow, click the 6.25% Gray style (first row, sixth column from the left), then click OK**

5. **Click the Borders list arrow in the Font group, then click Thick Bottom Border**

   Unlike underlining, which is a text-formatting tool, borders extend to the width of the cell, and can appear at the bottom of the cell, at the top, on either side, or on any combination of the four sides. It can be difficult to see a border when the cell is selected.

6. **Select the range A10:H10, click the Font Color list arrow in the Font group, then click the Blue, Accent 1 color (first Theme color row, fifth column from the left) on the palette**

   The new color is applied to the labels in the selected range.

7. **Select the range J1:K1, click the Cell Styles button in the Styles group, then click the Neutral cell style (first row, fourth column from the left) in the gallery**

   The font and color change in the range, as shown in Figure C-15.

8. **Save your work**

> **QUICK TIP**
> Use fill colors and patterns sparingly. Too many colors can be distracting or make it hard to see which information is important.

> **QUICK TIP**
> You can also create custom cell borders. Click the Borders list arrow in the Font group, click More Borders, then click the individual border buttons to apply the borders you want to the selected cell(s).

FIGURE C-14: Live Preview of fill color

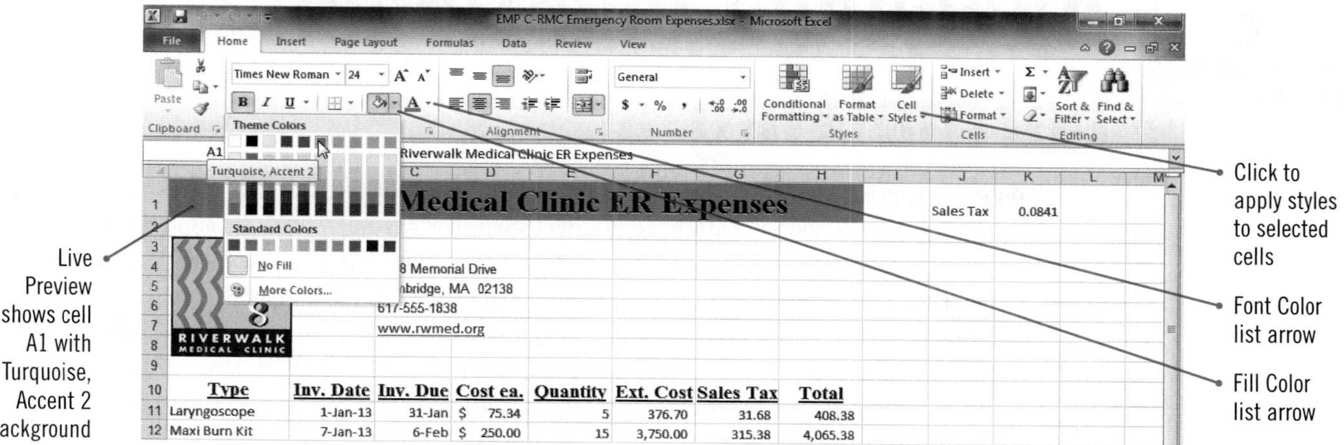

FIGURE C-15: Worksheet with color, patterns, border, and style applied

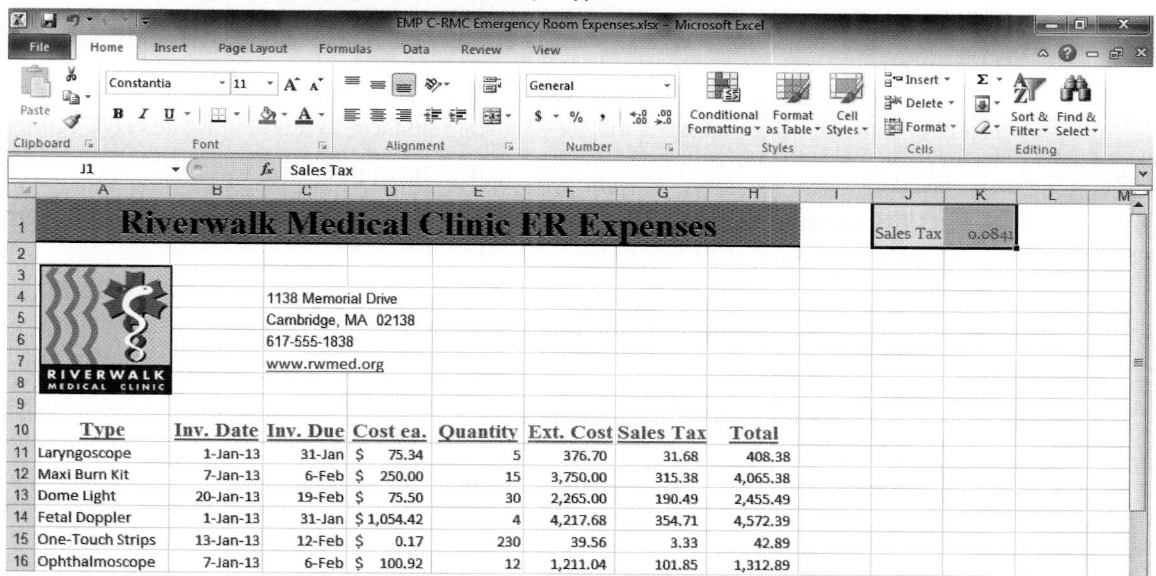

Excel 2010

Working with themes and cell styles

Using themes and cell styles makes it easier to ensure that your worksheets are consistent. A **theme** is a predefined set of formats that gives your Excel worksheet a professional look. Formatting choices included in a theme are colors, fonts, and line and fill effects. To apply a theme, click the Themes button in the Themes group on the Page Layout tab to open the Themes gallery, as shown in Figure C-16, then click a theme in the gallery. **Cell styles** are sets of cell formats based on themes, so they are automatically updated if you change a theme. For example, if you apply the 20% - Accent1 cell style to cell A1 in a worksheet that has no theme applied, the fill color changes to light blue and the font changes to Constantia. If you change the theme of the worksheet to Metro, cell A1's fill color changes to light green and the font changes to Corbel, because these are the new theme's associated formats.

FIGURE C-16: Themes gallery

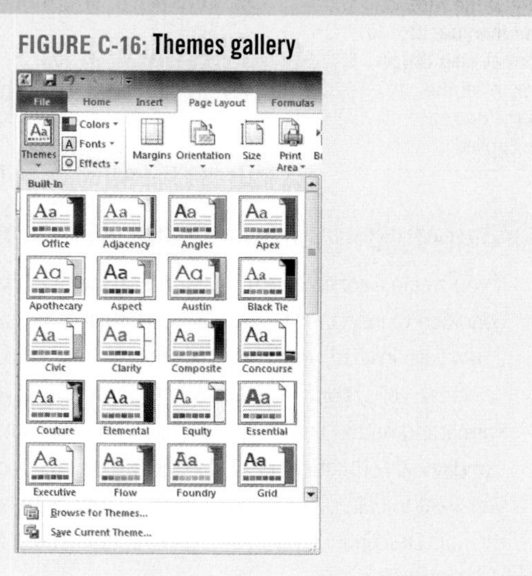

UNIT C

Excel 2010

Applying Conditional Formatting

So far, you've used formatting to change the appearance of different types of data, but you can also use formatting to highlight important aspects of the data itself. For example, you can apply formatting that changes the font color to red for any cells where ER costs exceed $4000 and to green where ER costs are below $2000. This is called **conditional formatting** because Excel automatically applies different formats to data if the data meets conditions you specify. The formatting is updated if you change data in the worksheet. You can also copy conditional formats the same way you copy other formats. Tony is concerned about emergency room costs exceeding the yearly budget. You decide to use conditional formatting to highlight certain trends and patterns in the data so that it's easy to spot the highest expenditures.

STEPS

1. **Select the range H11:H37, click the Conditional Formatting button in the Styles group on the Home tab, point to Data Bars, then point to the Light Blue Data Bar (second row, second from left)**

   Data bars are colored horizontal bars that visually illustrate differences between values in a range of cells. Live Preview shows how this formatting will appear in the worksheet, as shown in Figure C-17.

2. **Point to the Green Data Bar (first row, second from left), then click it**

3. **Select the range F11:F37, click the Conditional Formatting button in the Styles group, then point to Highlight Cells Rules**

   The Highlight Cells Rules submenu displays choices for creating different formatting conditions. For example, you can create a rule for values that are greater than or less than a certain amount, or between two amounts.

4. **Click Between on the submenu**

   The Between dialog box opens, displaying input boxes you can use to define the condition and a default format (Light Red Fill with Dark Red Text) selected for cells that meet that condition. Depending on the condition you select in the Highlight Cells Rules submenu (such as "Greater Than" or "Less Than"), this dialog box displays different input boxes. You define the condition using the input boxes and then assign the formatting you want to use for cells that meet that condition. Values used in input boxes for a condition can be constants, formulas, cell references, or dates.

5. **Type 2000 in the first text box, type 4000 in the second text box, click the with list arrow, click Light Red Fill, compare your settings to Figure C-18, then click OK**

   All cells with values between 2000 and 4000 in column F appear with a light red fill.

6. **Click cell F14, type 3975.55, then press [Enter]**

   When the value in cell F14 changes, the formatting also changes because the new value meets the condition you set. Compare your results to Figure C-19.

7. **Press [Ctrl][Home] to select cell A1, then save your work**

QUICK TIP

You can apply an Icon Set to a selected range by clicking the Conditional Formatting button in the Styles group, then pointing to Icon Sets; icons appear within the cells to illustrate differences in values.

QUICK TIP

To define custom formatting for data that meets the condition, click Custom Format at the bottom of the with list, and then use the Format Cells dialog box to set the formatting to be applied.

Managing conditional formatting rules

If you create a conditional formatting rule and then want to change the condition to reflect a different value or format, you don't need to create a new rule; instead, you can modify the rule using the Rules Manager. Select the cell(s) containing conditional formatting, click the Conditional Formatting button in the Styles group, then click Manage Rules. The Conditional Formatting Rules Manager dialog box opens. Select the rule you want to edit, click Edit Rule, and then modify the settings in the Edit the Rule Description area in the Edit Formatting Rule dialog box. To change the formatting for a rule, click the Format button in the Edit the Rule Description area, select the formatting styles you want the text to have, then click OK three times to close the Format Cells dialog box, the Edit Formatting Rule dialog box, and then the Conditional Formatting Rules Manager dialog box. The rule is modified, and the new conditional formatting is applied to the selected cells. To delete a rule, select the rule in the Conditional Formatting Rules Manager dialog box, then click the Delete Rule button.

FIGURE C-17: **Previewing data bars in a range**

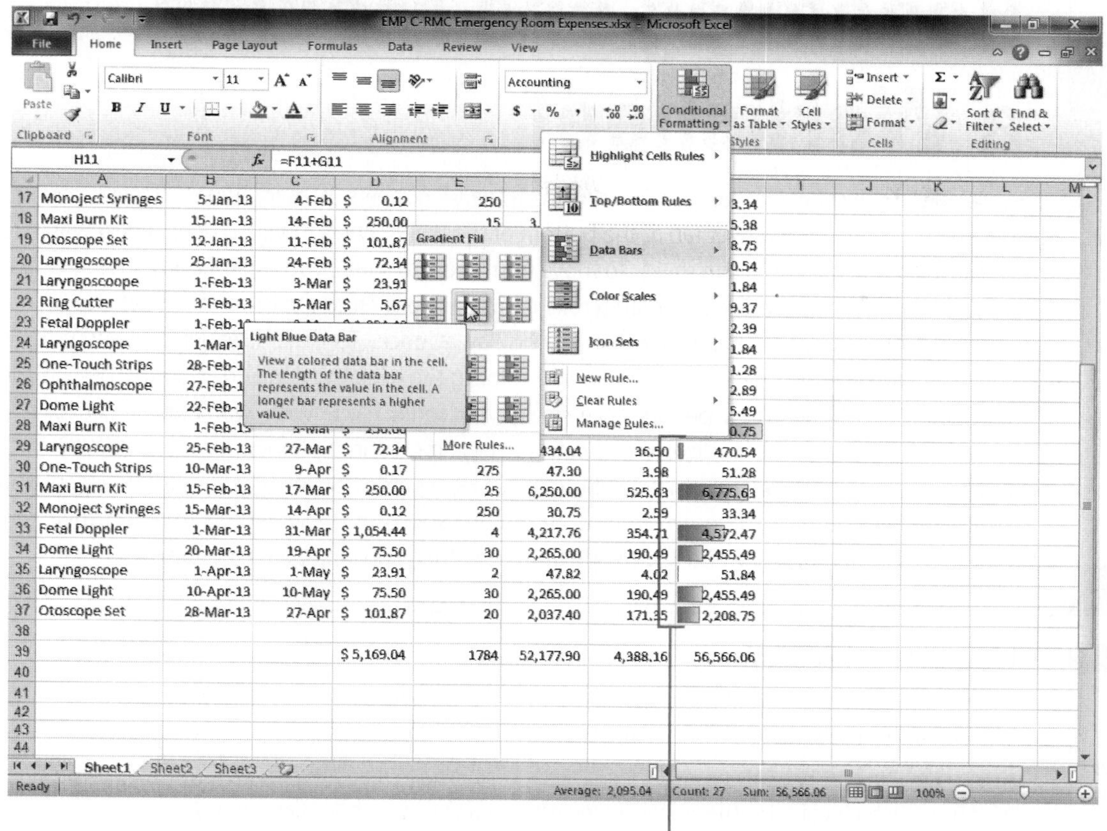

Live Preview shows data bars displayed in selected range

FIGURE C-18: **Between dialog box**

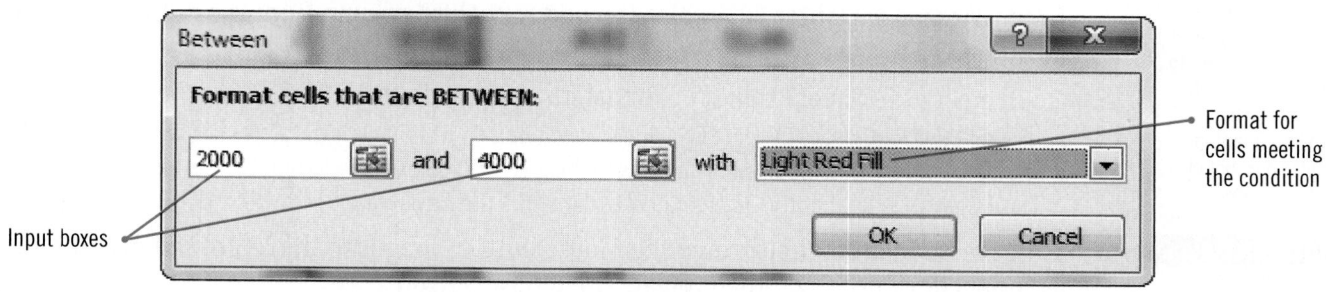

FIGURE C-19: **Worksheet with conditional formatting**

10	Type	Inv. Date	Inv. Due	Cost ea.	Quantity	Ext. Cost	Sales Tax	Total
11	Laryngoscope	1-Jan-13	31-Jan	$ 75.34	5	376.70	31.68	408.38
12	Maxi Burn Kit	7-Jan-13	6-Feb	$ 250.00	15	3,750.00	315.38	4,065.38
13	Dome Light	20-Jan-13	19-Feb	$ 75.50	30	2,265.00	190.49	2,455.49
14	Fetal Doppler	1-Jan-13	31-Jan	$ 1,054.42	4	3,975.55	334.34	4,309.89
15	One-Touch Strips	13-Jan-13	12-Feb	$ 0.17	230	39.56	3.33	42.89
16	Ophthalmoscope	7-Jan-13	6-Feb	$ 100.92	12	1,211.04	101.85	1,312.89
17	Monoject Syringes	5-Jan-13	4-Feb	$ 0.12	250	30.75	2.59	33.34
18	Maxi Burn Kit	15-Jan-13	14-Feb	$ 250.00	15	3,750.00	315.38	4,065.38
19	Otoscope Set	12-Jan-13	11-Feb	$ 101.87	20	2,037.40	171.35	2,208.75
20	Laryngoscope	25-Jan-13	24-Feb	$ 72.34	6	434.04	36.50	470.54
21	Laryngoscoope	1-Feb-13	3-Mar	$ 23.91	2	47.82	4.02	51.84
22	Ring Cutter	3-Feb-13	5-Mar	$ 5.67	200	1,134.00	95.37	1,229.37
23	Fetal Doppler	1-Feb-13	3-Mar	$ 1,054.42	4	4,217.68	354.71	4,572.39
24	Laryngoscope	1-Mar-13	31-Mar	$ 23.91	2	47.82	4.02	51.84
25	One-Touch Strips	28-Feb-13	30-Mar	$ 0.17	275	47.30	3.98	51.28
26	Ophthalmoscope	27-Feb-13	29-Mar	$ 100.92	12	1,211.04	101.85	1,312.89

Sheet1 Sheet2 Sheet3

Ready

Excel 2010

UNIT C
Excel 2010

Renaming and Moving a Worksheet

By default, an Excel workbook initially contains three worksheets, named Sheet1, Sheet2, and Sheet3. Each sheet name appears on a sheet tab at the bottom of the worksheet. When you open a new workbook, the first worksheet, Sheet1, is the active sheet. To move from sheet to sheet, you can click any sheet tab at the bottom of the worksheet window. The sheet tab scrolling buttons, located to the left of the sheet tabs, are useful when a workbook contains too many sheet tabs to display at once. To make it easier to identify the sheets in a workbook, you can rename each sheet and add color to the tabs. You can also organize them in a logical way. For instance, to better track performance goals, you could name each workbook sheet for an individual salesperson, and you could move the sheets so they appear in alphabetical order. In the current worksheet, Sheet1 contains information about actual ER expenses. Sheet2 contains an ER expense budget, and Sheet3 contains no data. You want to rename the two sheets in the workbook to reflect their contents, add color to a sheet tab to easily distinguish one from the other, and change their order.

STEPS

QUICK TIP
You can also rename a sheet by right-clicking the tab, clicking Rename on the shortcut menu, typing the new name, then pressing [Enter].

QUICK TIP
To delete a sheet, click its tab, click the Delete list arrow in the Cells group, then click Delete Sheet. To insert a worksheet, click the Insert Worksheet button to the right of the sheet tabs.

QUICK TIP
If you have more sheet tabs than are visible, you can move between sheets by using the tab scrolling buttons to the left of the sheet tabs: the First Worksheet button ; the Last Worksheet button ; the Previous Worksheet button ; and the Next Worksheet button .

1. **Click the Sheet2 tab**
   Sheet2 becomes active, appearing in front of the Sheet1 tab; this is the worksheet that contains the budgeted emergency room expenses. See Figure C-20.
2. **Click the Sheet1 tab**
   Sheet1, which contains the actual emergency room expenses, becomes active again.
3. **Double-click the Sheet2 tab, type Budget, then press [Enter]**
   The new name for Sheet2 automatically replaces the default name on the tab. Worksheet names can have up to 31 characters, including spaces and punctuation.
4. **Right-click the Budget tab, point to Tab Color on the shortcut menu, then click the Bright Green, Accent 4, Lighter 80% color (second row, third column from the right) as shown in Figure C-21**
5. **Double-click the Sheet1 tab, type Actual, then press [Enter]**
   Notice that the color of the Budget tab changes depending on whether it is the active tab; when the Actual tab is active, the color of the Budget tab changes to the green tab color you selected. You decide to rearrange the order of the sheets, so that the Budget tab is to the left of the Actual tab.
6. **Click the Budget tab, hold down the mouse button, drag it to the left of the Actual tab, as shown in Figure C-22, then release the mouse button**
   As you drag, the pointer changes to , the sheet relocation pointer, and a small, black triangle just above the tabs shows the position the moved sheet will be in when you release the mouse button. The first sheet in the workbook is now the Budget sheet. See Figure C-23.
7. **Click the Actual sheet tab, click the Page Layout button on the status bar to open Page Layout view, enter your name in the left header text box, then click anywhere in the worksheet to deselect the header**
8. **Click the Page Layout tab on the Ribbon, click the Orientation button in the Page Setup group, then click Landscape**
9. **Press [Ctrl][Home], then save your work**

FIGURE C-20: Sheet tabs in workbook

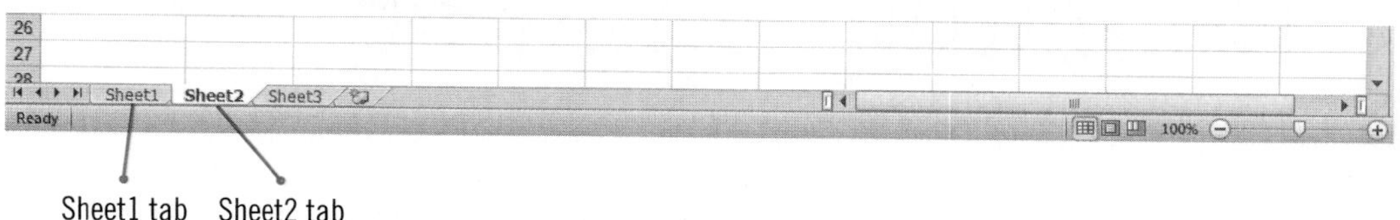

FIGURE C-21: Tab Color palette

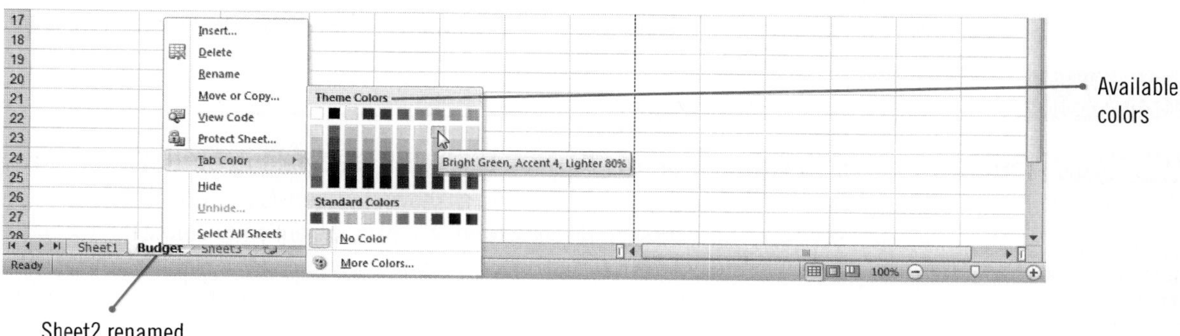

FIGURE C-22: Moving the Budget sheet

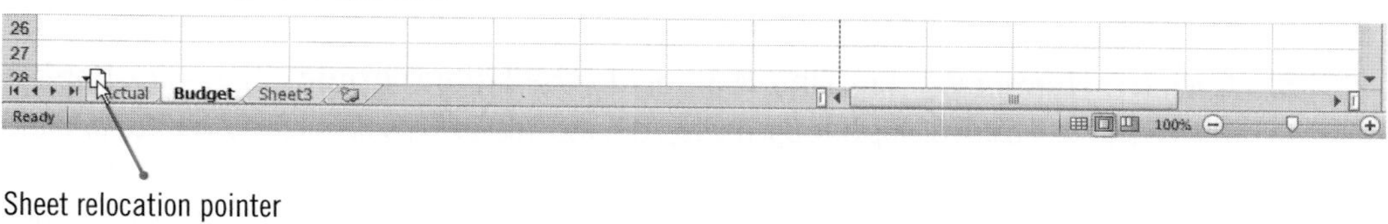

FIGURE C-23: Reordered sheets

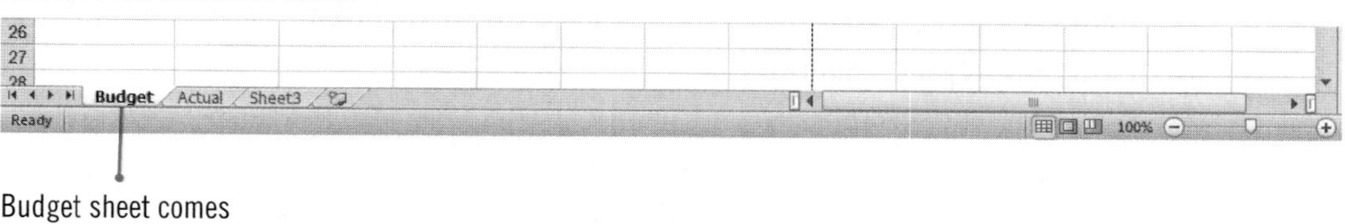

Copying worksheets

There are times when you may want to copy a worksheet. For example, a workbook might contain a sheet with Quarter 1 expenses, and you want to use that sheet as the basis for a sheet containing Quarter 2 expenses. To copy a sheet within the same workbook, press and hold [Ctrl], drag the sheet tab to the desired tab location, release the mouse button, then release [Ctrl]. A duplicate sheet appears with the same name as the copied sheet followed by "(2)" indicating it is a copy. You can then rename the sheet to a more meaningful name. To copy a sheet to a different workbook, both the source and destination workbooks must be open. Select the sheet to copy or move, right-click the sheet tab, then click Move or Copy in the shortcut menu. Complete the information in the Move or Copy dialog box. Be sure to click the Create a copy check box if you are copying rather than moving the worksheet. Carefully check your calculation results whenever you move or copy a worksheet.

UNIT
C
Excel 2010

Checking Spelling

Excel includes a spell checker to help you ensure that the words in your worksheet are spelled correctly. The spell checker scans your worksheet, displays words it doesn't find in its built-in dictionary, and suggests replacements when they are available. To check all of the sheets in a multiple-sheet workbook, you need to display each sheet individually and run the spell checker for each one. Because the built-in dictionary cannot possibly include all the words that anyone needs, you can add words to the dictionary, such as your company name, an acronym, or an unusual technical term. Once you add a word or term, the spell checker no longer considers that word misspelled. Any words you've added to the dictionary using Word, Access, or PowerPoint are also available in Excel. Before you distribute this workbook to Tony and the administrators, you check its spelling.

STEPS

QUICK TIP
The Spelling dialog box lists the name of the language currently being used in its title bar.

1. **Click the Review tab on the Ribbon, then click the Spelling button in the Proofing group**
   The Spelling: English (U.S.) dialog box opens, as shown in Figure C-24, with "Riverwalk" selected as the first misspelled word in the worksheet. For any word, you have the option to Ignore this case of the flagged word, Ignore All cases of the flagged word, Change the word to the selected suggestion, Change All instances of the flagged word to the selected suggestion, or add the flagged word to the dictionary using Add to Dictionary.
2. **Click Ignore All, then click Ignore All for the next two cases (Monoject and Otoscope)**
   Next, the spell checker finds the word "Laryngoscoope" and suggests "Laryngoscope" as an alternative.
3. **Verify that the word Laryngoscope is selected in the Suggestions list, then click Change**
   When no more incorrect words are found, Excel displays a message indicating that the spell check is complete.
4. **Click OK**
5. **Click the Home tab, click Find & Select in the Editing group, then click Replace**
   The Find and Replace dialog box opens. You can use this dialog box to replace a word or phrase. It might be a misspelling of a proper name that the spell checker didn't recognize as misspelled, or it could simply be a term that you want to change throughout the worksheet. Tony has just told you that each instance of "Maxi" in the worksheet should be changed to "ACE".
6. **Type Maxi in the Find what text box, press [Tab], then type ACE in the Replace with text box**
   Compare your dialog box to Figure C-25.
7. **Click Replace All, click OK to close the Microsoft Excel dialog box, then click Close to close the Find and Replace dialog box**
   Excel has made four replacements.
8. **Click the File tab, click Print on the navigation bar, click the No Scaling setting in the Settings section on the Print tab, then click Fit Sheet on One Page**
9. **Click the File tab to return to your worksheet, save your work, submit it to your instructor as directed, close the workbook, then exit Excel**
   The completed worksheet is shown in Figure C-26.

E-mailing a workbook

You can send an entire workbook from within Excel using your installed e-mail program, such as Microsoft Outlook. To send a workbook as an e-mail message attachment, open the workbook, click the File tab, then click Save & Send on the navigation bar. With the Send Using E-mail option selected in the Save & Send section in Backstage view, click Send as Attachment in the right pane. An e-mail message opens in your default e-mail program with the workbook automatically attached; the filename appears in the Attached field. Complete the To and optional Cc fields, include a message if you wish, then click Send.

FIGURE C-24: Spelling: English (U.S.) dialog box

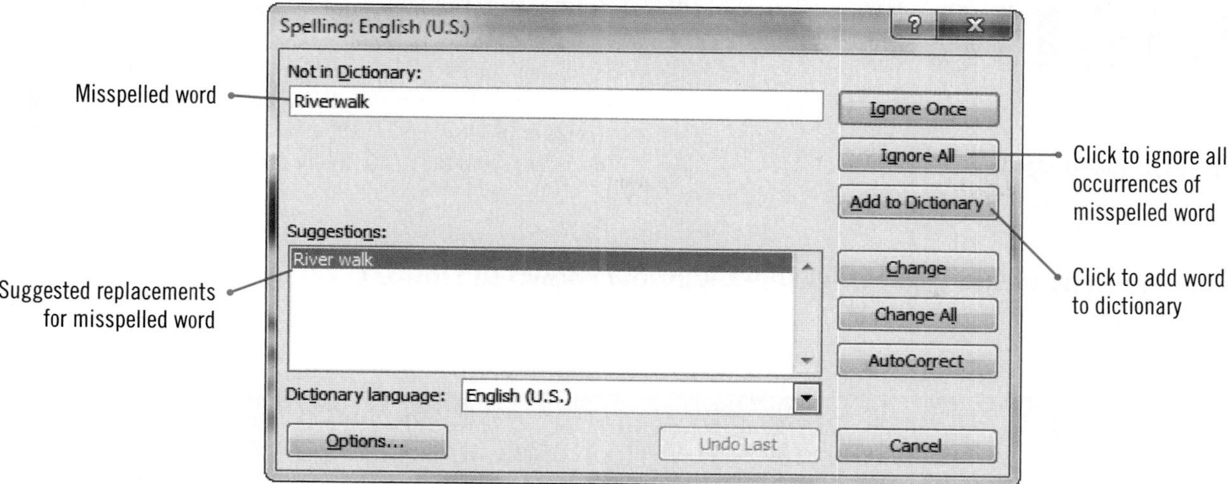

FIGURE C-25: Find and Replace dialog box

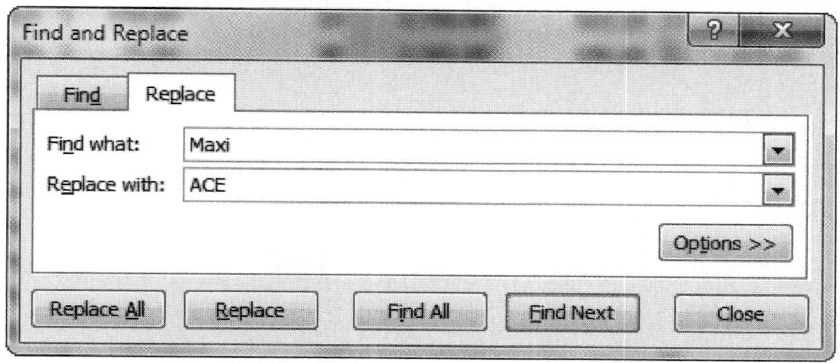

FIGURE C-26: Completed worksheet

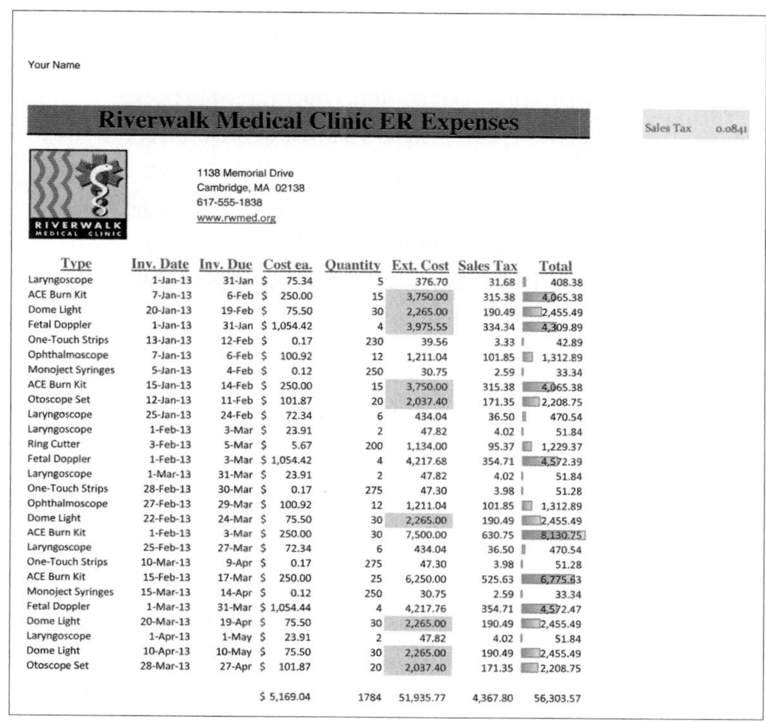

Your Name

Riverwalk Medical Clinic ER Expenses

Sales Tax 0.0841

RIVERWALK MEDICAL CLINIC

1138 Memorial Drive
Cambridge, MA 02138
617-555-1838
www.rwmed.org

Type	Inv. Date	Inv. Due	Cost ea.	Quantity	Ext. Cost	Sales Tax	Total
Laryngoscope	1-Jan-13	31-Jan	$ 75.34	5	376.70	31.68	408.38
ACE Burn Kit	7-Jan-13	6-Feb	$ 250.00	15	3,750.00	315.38	4,065.38
Dome Light	20-Jan-13	19-Feb	$ 75.50	30	2,265.00	190.49	2,455.49
Fetal Doppler	1-Jan-13	31-Jan	$ 1,054.42	4	3,975.55	334.34	4,309.89
One-Touch Strips	13-Jan-13	12-Feb	$ 0.17	230	39.56	3.33	42.89
Ophthalmoscope	7-Jan-13	6-Feb	$ 100.92	12	1,211.04	101.85	1,312.89
Monoject Syringes	5-Jan-13	4-Feb	$ 0.12	250	30.75	2.59	33.34
ACE Burn Kit	15-Jan-13	14-Feb	$ 250.00	15	3,750.00	315.38	4,065.38
Otoscope Set	12-Jan-13	11-Feb	$ 101.87	20	2,037.40	171.35	2,208.75
Laryngoscope	25-Jan-13	24-Feb	$ 72.34	6	434.04	36.50	470.54
Laryngoscope	1-Feb-13	3-Mar	$ 23.91	2	47.82	4.02	51.84
Ring Cutter	3-Feb-13	5-Mar	$ 5.67	200	1,134.00	95.37	1,229.37
Fetal Doppler	1-Feb-13	3-Mar	$ 1,054.42	4	4,217.68	354.71	4,572.39
Laryngoscope	1-Mar-13	31-Mar	$ 23.91	2	47.82	4.02	51.84
One-Touch Strips	28-Feb-13	30-Mar	$ 0.17	275	47.30	3.98	51.28
Ophthalmoscope	27-Feb-13	29-Mar	$ 100.92	12	1,211.04	101.85	1,312.89
Dome Light	22-Feb-13	24-Mar	$ 75.50	30	2,265.00	190.49	2,455.49
ACE Burn Kit	1-Feb-13	3-Mar	$ 250.00	30	7,500.00	630.75	8,130.75
Laryngoscope	25-Feb-13	27-Mar	$ 72.34	6	434.04	36.50	470.54
One-Touch Strips	10-Mar-13	9-Apr	$ 0.17	275	47.30	3.98	51.28
ACE Burn Kit	15-Feb-13	17-Mar	$ 250.00	25	6,250.00	525.63	6,775.63
Monoject Syringes	15-Mar-13	14-Apr	$ 0.12	250	30.75	2.59	33.34
Fetal Doppler	1-Mar-13	31-Mar	$ 1,054.44	4	4,217.76	354.71	4,572.47
Dome Light	20-Mar-13	19-Apr	$ 75.50	30	2,265.00	190.49	2,455.49
Laryngoscope	1-Apr-13	1-May	$ 23.91	2	47.82	4.02	51.84
Dome Light	10-Apr-13	10-May	$ 75.50	30	2,265.00	190.49	2,455.49
Otoscope Set	28-Mar-13	27-Apr	$ 101.87	20	2,037.40	171.35	2,208.75
			$ 5,169.04	1784	51,935.77	4,367.80	56,303.57

Practice

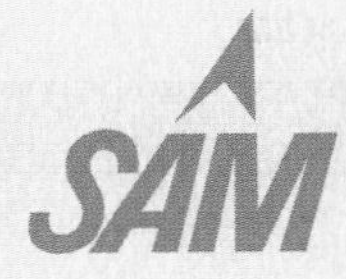

For current SAM information, including versions and content details, visit SAM Central (http://www.cengage.com/samcentral). If you have a SAM user profile, you may have access to hands-on instruction, practice, and assessment of the skills covered in this unit. Since various versions of SAM are supported throughout the life of this text, check with your instructor for the correct instructions and URL/Web site for accessing assignments.

Concepts Review

Label each element of the Excel worksheet window shown in Figure C-27.

FIGURE C-27

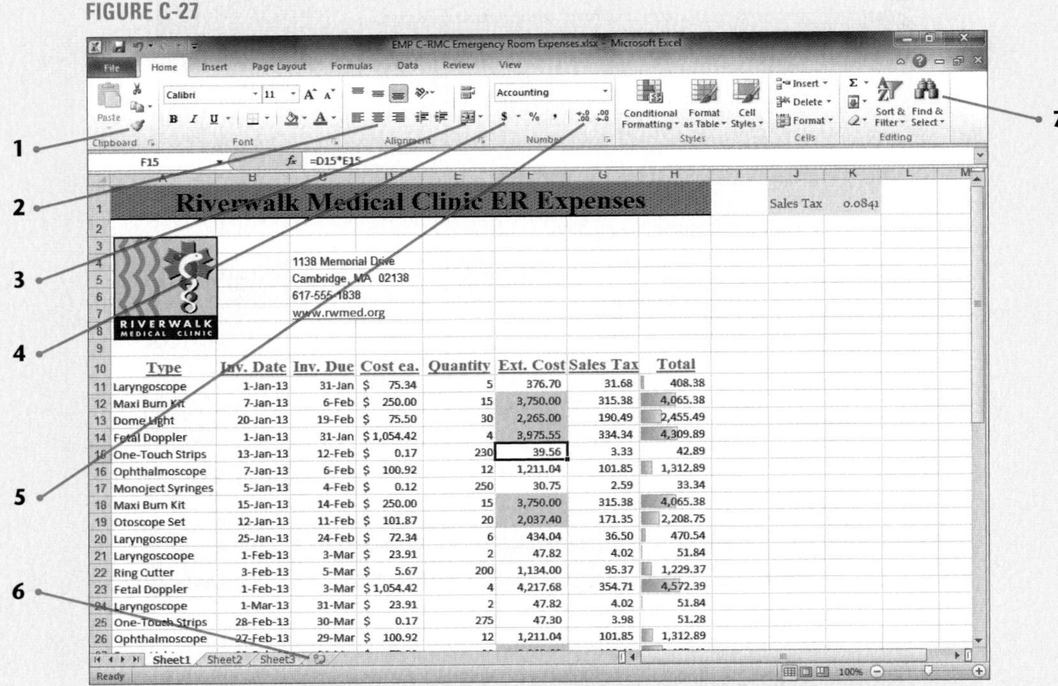

Match each command or button with the statement that best describes it.

8. **Conditional formatting**
9.
10. **Spelling button**
11. **[Ctrl][Home]**
12.
13. **$**

a. Centers cell contents over multiple cells
b. Adds dollar signs and two decimal places to selected data
c. Changes formatting of a cell that meets a certain rule
d. Displays background color options for a cell
e. Moves cell pointer to cell A1
f. Checks for apparent misspellings in a worksheet

Select the best answer from the list of choices.

14. Which of the following is an example of Accounting number format?

a. 5555
b. $5,555.55
c. 55.55%
d. 5,555.55

15. What feature is used to delete a conditional formatting rule?

a. Rules Reminder
b. Conditional Formatting Rules Manager
c. Condition Manager
d. Format Manager

16. Which button removes the italic font style from selected cells?

a. *I*
b. **B**
c. ✓
d. *I*

17. What is the name of the feature used to resize a column to accommodate its widest entry?

a. AutoFormat
b. AutoFit
c. AutoResize
d. AutoRefit

18. Which button increases the number of decimal places in selected cells?

a.
b.
c.
d.

19. Which button copies multiple formats from selected cells to other cells?

a.
b.
c.
d.

Skills Review

1. Format values.

a. Start Excel, open the file EMP C-2.xlsx from the drive and folder where you store your Data Files, then save it as **EMP C-Health Insurance Premiums**.
b. Enter a formula in cell B10 that totals the number of employees.
c. Create a formula in cell C5 that calculates the monthly insurance premium for the accounting department. (*Hint*: Make sure you use the correct type of cell reference in the formula. To calculate the department's monthly premium, multiply the number of employees by the monthly premium in cell B14.)
d. Copy the formula in cell C5 to the range C6:C10.
e. Format the range C5:C10 using Accounting number format.
f. Change the format of the range C5:C9 to the Comma Style.
g. Reduce the number of decimals in cell B14 to 0 using a button in the Number group on the Home tab.
h. Save your work.

2. Change font and font sizes.

a. Select the range of cells containing the column labels (in row 4).
b. Change the font of the selection to Times New Roman.
c. Increase the font size of the selection to 12 points.
d. Increase the font size of the label in cell A1 to 14 points.
e. Save your changes.

3. Change font styles and alignment.

a. Apply the bold and italic font styles to the worksheet title in cell A1.
b. Use the Merge & Center button to center the Health Insurance Premiums label over columns A through C.
c. Apply the italic font style to the Health Insurance Premiums label.
d. Add the bold font style to the labels in row 4.
e. Use the Format Painter to copy the format in cell A4 to the range A5:A10.
f. Apply the format in cell C10 to cell B14.

Skills Review (continued)

- **g.** Change the alignment of cell A10 to Align Right using a button in the Alignment group.
- **h.** Select the range of cells containing the column labels, then center them.
- **i.** Remove the italic font style from the Health Insurance Premiums label, then increase the font size to 14.
- **j.** Move the Health Insurance Premiums label to cell A3, then add the bold and underline font styles.
- **k.** Save your changes.

4. Adjust column width.

- **a.** Resize column C to a width of 10.71 characters.
- **b.** Use the AutoFit feature to resize columns A and B.
- **c.** Clear the contents of cell A13 (do not delete the cell).
- **d.** Change the text in cell A14 to **Monthly Insurance Premium**, then change the width of the column to 25 characters.
- **e.** Save your changes.

5. Insert and delete rows and columns.

- **a.** Insert a new row between rows 5 and 6.
- **b.** Add a new department, **Charity**, in the newly inserted row. Enter **6** as the number of employees in the department.
- **c.** Copy the formula in cell C7 to C6.
- **d.** Add the following comment to cell A6: **New Department**. Display the comment, then drag to move it out of the way, if necessary.
- **e.** Add a new column between the Department and Employees columns with the title **Family Coverage**, then resize the column using AutoFit.
- **f.** Delete the Legal row from the worksheet.
- **g.** Move the value in cell C14 to cell B14.
- **h.** Save your changes.

6. Apply colors, patterns, and borders.

- **a.** Add Outside Borders around the range A4:D10.
- **b.** Add a Bottom Double Border to cells C9 and D9 (above the calculated employee and premium totals).
- **c.** Apply the Aqua, Accent 5, Lighter 80% fill color to the labels in the Department column (do not include the Total label).
- **d.** Apply the Orange, Accent 6, Lighter 60% fill color to the range A4:D4.
- **e.** Change the color of the font in the range A4:D4 to Red, Accent 2, Darker 25%.
- **f.** Add a 12.5% Gray pattern style to cell A1.
- **g.** Format the range A14:B14 with a fill color of Dark Blue, Text 2, Lighter 40%, change the font color to White, Background 1, then apply the bold font style.
- **h.** Save your changes.

7. Apply conditional formatting.

- **a.** Select the range D5:D9, then create a conditional format that changes cell contents to green fill with dark green text if the value is between 150 and 275.
- **b.** Select the range C5:C9, then create a conditional format that changes cell contents to red text if the number of employees exceeds 10.
- **c.** Apply a blue gradient-filled data bar to the range C5:C9. (*Hint*: Click Blue Data Bar in the Gradient Fill section.)
- **d.** Use the Rules Manager to modify the conditional format in cells C5:C9 to display values greater than 10 in bold dark red text.
- **e.** Merge and center the title (cell A1) over columns A through D.
- **f.** Save your changes.

8. Rename and move a worksheet.

- **a.** Name the Sheet1 tab **Insurance Data**.
- **b.** Name the Sheet3 tab **Employee Data**.
- **c.** Change the Insurance Data tab color to Red, Accent 2, Lighter 40%.
- **d.** Change the Employee Data tab color to Aqua, Accent 5, Lighter 40%.
- **e.** Move the Employee Data sheet so it comes after (to the right of) the Insurance Data sheet.
- **f.** Make the Insurance Data sheet active, enter your name in cell A20, then save your work.

Skills Review (continued)

9. Check spelling.

   a. Move the cell pointer to cell A1.

   b. Use the Find & Select feature to replace the Accounting label in cell A5 with **Accounting/Legal**.

   c. Check the spelling in the worksheet using the spell checker, and correct any spelling errors if necessary.

   d. Save your changes, then compare your Insurance Data sheet to Figure C-28.

   e. Preview the Insurance Data sheet in Backstage view, submit your work to your instructor as directed, then close the workbook and exit Excel.

FIGURE C-28

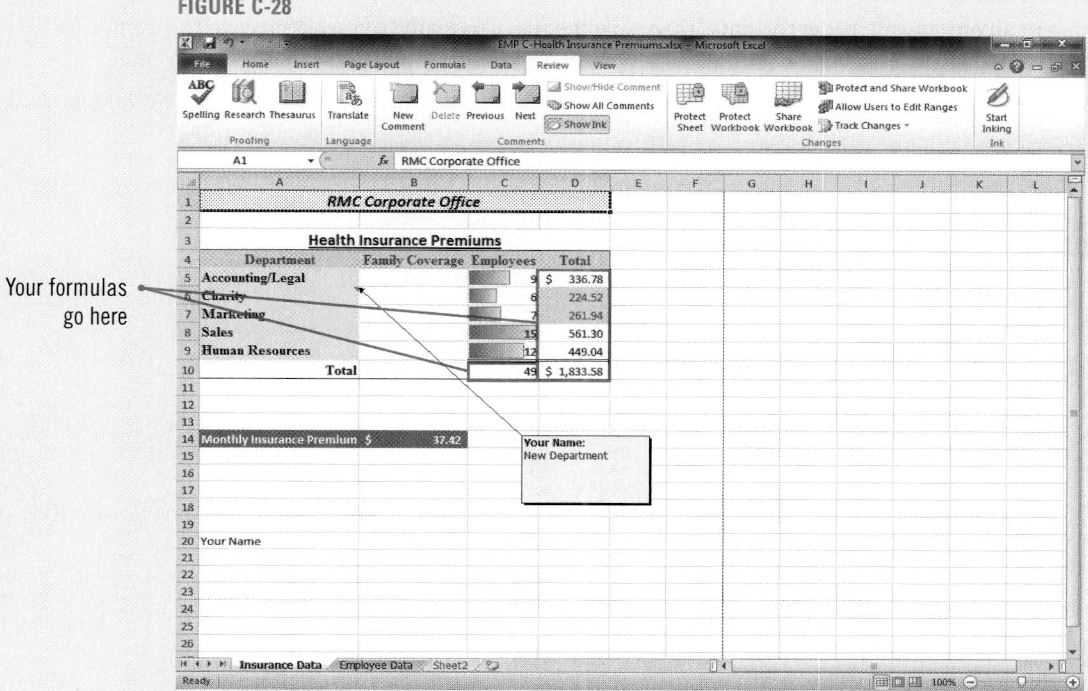

Independent Challenge 1

You run a wholesale medical supply distribution business, and one of your newest clients is Montebello, a small assisted living facility. Now that you've converted the facility's inventory records to Excel, the manager would like you to work on an analysis of the Montebello inventory. Although more items will be added later, the worksheet has enough items for you to begin your modifications.

   a. Start Excel, open the file EMP C-3.xlsx from the drive and folder where you store your Data Files, then save it as **EMP C-Medical Supply Inventory**.

   b. Create a formula in cell E4 that calculates the value of the items in stock based on the price paid per item in cell B4. Format the cell in the Comma Style.

   c. In cell F4, calculate the sale price of the items in stock using an absolute reference to the markup value shown in cell H1.

   d. Copy the formulas created above into the range E5:F14; first convert any necessary cell references to absolute so that the formulas work correctly.

   e. Apply bold to the column labels, and italicize the inventory items in column A.

   f. Make sure all columns are wide enough to display the data and labels.

   g. Format the values in the Sale Price column as Accounting number format with two decimal places.

   h. Format the values in the Price Paid column as Comma Style with two decimal places.

Excel 2010

Independent Challenge 1 (continued)

i. Add a row under Thera-Band Assists for **Nail files**, price paid **$0.31**, sold individually (**each**), with **24** on hand. Copy the appropriate formulas to cells E5:F5.

j. Verify that all the data in the worksheet is visible and formulas are correct. Adjust any items as needed, and check the spelling of the entire worksheet.

k. Use conditional formatting to apply yellow fill with dark yellow text to items with a quantity of 25 or less on hand.

l. Use an icon set of your choosing in the range D4:D15 to illustrate the relative differences between values in the range.

m. Add an outside border around the data in the Item column (do not include the Item column label).

n. Delete the row containing the Pins entry.

o. Enter your name in an empty cell below the data, then save the file. Compare your worksheet to the sample in Figure C-29.

p. Preview the worksheet in Backstage view, submit your work to your instructor as directed, close the workbook, then exit Excel.

FIGURE C-29

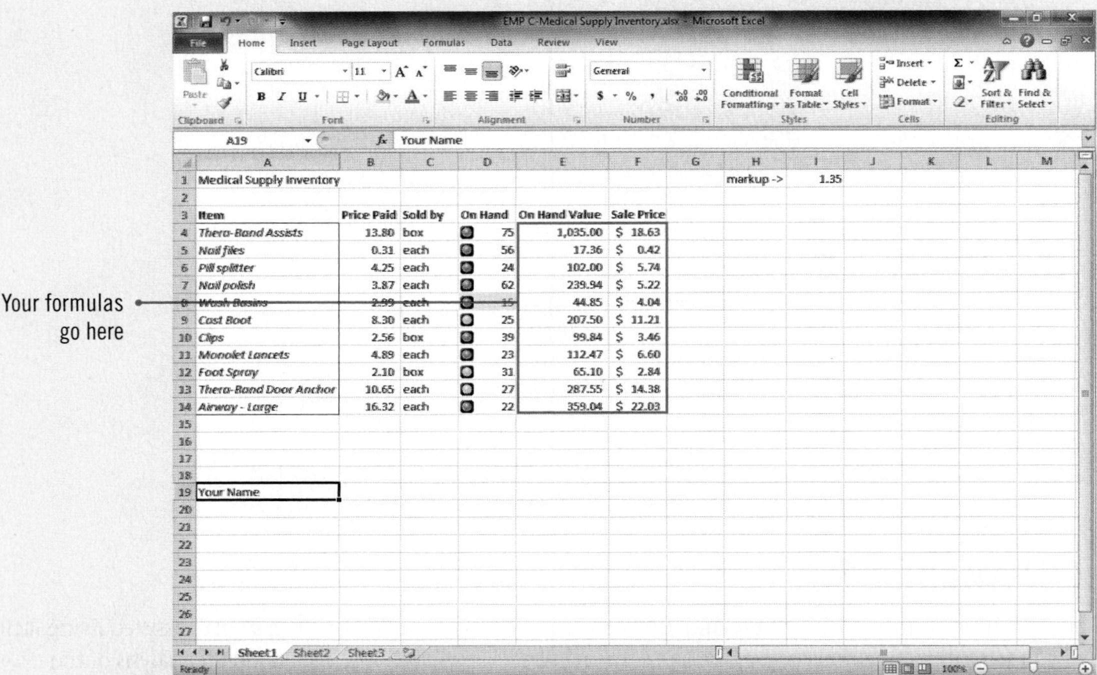

Independent Challenge 2

You are an administrative assistant with the Houston Association of Medical Clinics, and you are in charge of maintaining the membership list. You're currently planning a mailing campaign to members in certain regions of the city. You also want to create renewal letters for members whose membership expires soon. You decide to format the list to enhance the appearance of the worksheet and make your upcoming tasks easier to plan.

a. Start Excel, open the file EMP C-4.xlsx from the drive and folder where you store your Data Files, then save it as **EMP C-Houston Association of Medical Clinics**.

b. Remove any blank columns.

c. Create a conditional format in the Zip Code column so that entries greater than 77249 appear in light red fill with dark red text.

d. Make all columns wide enough to fit their data and labels.

e. Use formatting enhancements, such as fonts, font sizes, font styles, and fill colors, to make the worksheet more attractive.

f. Center the column labels.

Independent Challenge 2 (continued)

g. Use conditional formatting so that entries for Year of Membership Expiration that are between 2014 and 2017 appear in green fill with bold black text. (*Hint*: Create a custom format for cells that meet the condition.)

h. Adjust any items as necessary, then check the spelling.

i. Change the name of the Sheet1 tab to one that reflects the sheet's contents, then add a tab color of your choice.

j. Enter your name in an empty cell, then save your work.

k. Preview the worksheet in Backstage view, make any final changes you think necessary, then submit your work to your instructor as directed. Compare your work to the sample shown in Figure C-30.

l. Close the workbook, then exit Excel.

FIGURE C-30

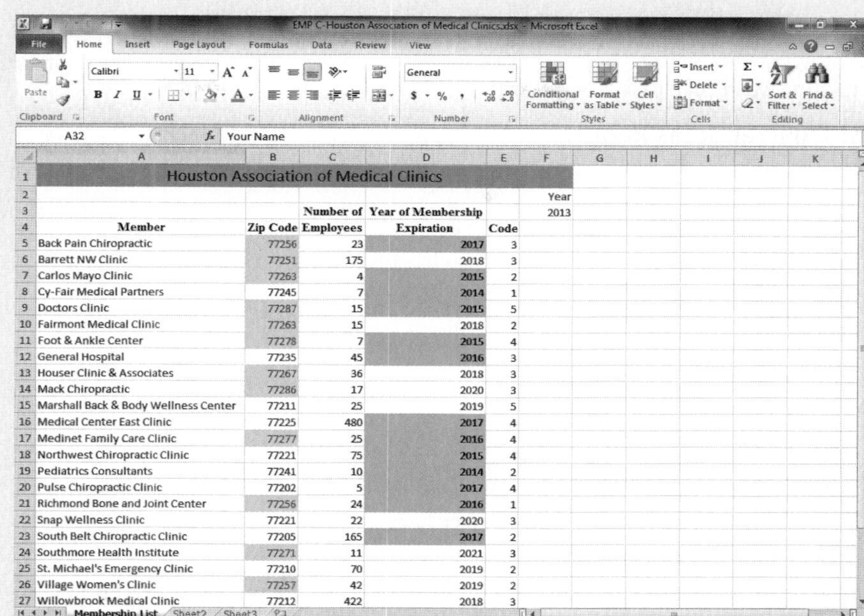

Member	Zip Code	Number of Employees	Year of Membership Expiration	Code
Back Pain Chiropractic	77256	23	2017	3
Barrett NW Clinic	77251	175	2018	3
Carlos Mayo Clinic	77263	4	2015	2
Cy-Fair Medical Partners	77245	7	2014	1
Doctors Clinic	77287	15	2015	5
Fairmont Medical Clinic	77263	15	2018	2
Foot & Ankle Center	77278	7	2015	4
General Hospital	77235	45	2016	3
Houser Clinic & Associates	77267	36	2018	3
Mack Chiropractic	77286	17	2020	3
Marshall Back & Body Wellness Center	77211	25	2019	5
Medical Center East Clinic	77225	480	2017	4
Medinet Family Care Clinic	77277	25	2016	4
Northwest Chiropractic Clinic	77221	75	2015	4
Pediatrics Consultants	77241	10	2014	2
Pulse Chiropractic Clinic	77202	5	2017	4
Richmond Bone and Joint Center	77256	24	2016	1
Snap Wellness Clinic	77221	22	2020	3
South Belt Chiropractic Clinic	77205	165	2017	2
Southmore Health Institute	77271	11	2021	3
St. Michael's Emergency Clinic	77210	70	2019	2
Village Women's Clinic	77257	42	2019	2
Willowbrook Medical Clinic	77212	422	2018	3

Independent Challenge 3

Emergent Health Care Systems is a Chicago-based healthcare provider that offers clinic and urgent-care services. As the finance manager for the company, one of your responsibilities is to analyze the monthly reports from the five district sales offices. Your boss, Joanne Bennington, has asked you to prepare a quarterly sales report for an upcoming meeting. Because several top executives will be attending this meeting, Joanne reminds you that the report must look professional. In particular, she asks you to emphasize the company's surge in profits during the last month and to highlight the fact that the Northeastern district continues to outpace the other districts.

a. Plan a worksheet that shows the company's revenue during the first quarter. Make sure you include the following:
   - The number of patients seen (clients seen) and the associated revenues (revenue) for each of the five district sales offices. The five sales districts are Northeastern, Midwestern, Southeastern, Southern, and Western.
   - Calculations that show month-by-month totals for January, February, and March, and a 3-month cumulative total.
   - Calculations that show each district's share of sales (percent of Total Revenue).
   - Labels that reflect the month-by-month data as well as the cumulative data.
   - Formatting enhancements and data bars that emphasize the recent month's sales surge.

b. Ask yourself the following questions about the organization and formatting of the worksheet: What worksheet title and labels do you need, and where should they appear? How can you calculate the totals? What formulas can you copy to save time and keystrokes? Do any of these formulas need to use an absolute reference? How do you show dollar amounts? What information should be shown in bold? Do you need to use more than one font? Should you use more than one point size?

c. Start Excel, then save a new, blank workbook as **EMP C-Emergent Health Care Systems** to the drive and folder where you store your Data Files.

Independent Challenge 3 (continued)

d. Build the worksheet with your own number of clients seen and revenue data. Enter the titles and labels first, then enter the numbers and formulas. You can use the information in Table C-4 to get started.

TABLE C-4

Emergent Health Care Systems										
1st Quarter Sales Report										
		January		February		March		Total		
	Facilities	Clients Seen	Revenue	Clients Seen	Revenue	Clients Seen	Revenue	Clients Seen	Revenue	Total % Revenue
Northeastern										
Midwestern										
Southeastern										
Southern										
Western										

e. Add a row beneath the data containing the totals for each column.

f. Adjust the column widths as necessary.

g. Change the height of row 1 to 33 points.

h. Format labels and values to enhance the look of the worksheet, and change the font styles and alignment if necessary.

i. Resize columns and adjust the formatting as necessary.

j. Add data bars for the monthly Clients Seen columns.

k. Add a column that calculates a 25% increase in total revenue. Use an absolute cell reference in this calculation. (*Hint*: Make sure the current formatting is applied to the new information.)

Advanced Challenge Exercise

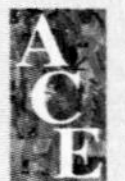

- Delete the contents of cells J4:K4 if necessary, then merge and center cell I4 over column I:K.
- Insert a clip art image related to healthcare in an appropriate location, adjusting its size and position as necessary.
- Save your work.

l. Enter your name in an empty cell.

m. Check the spelling in the workbook, change to a landscape orientation, save your work, then compare your work to Figure C-31.

n. Preview the worksheet in Backstage view, then submit your work to your instructor as directed.

o. Close the workbook file, then exit Excel.

FIGURE C-31

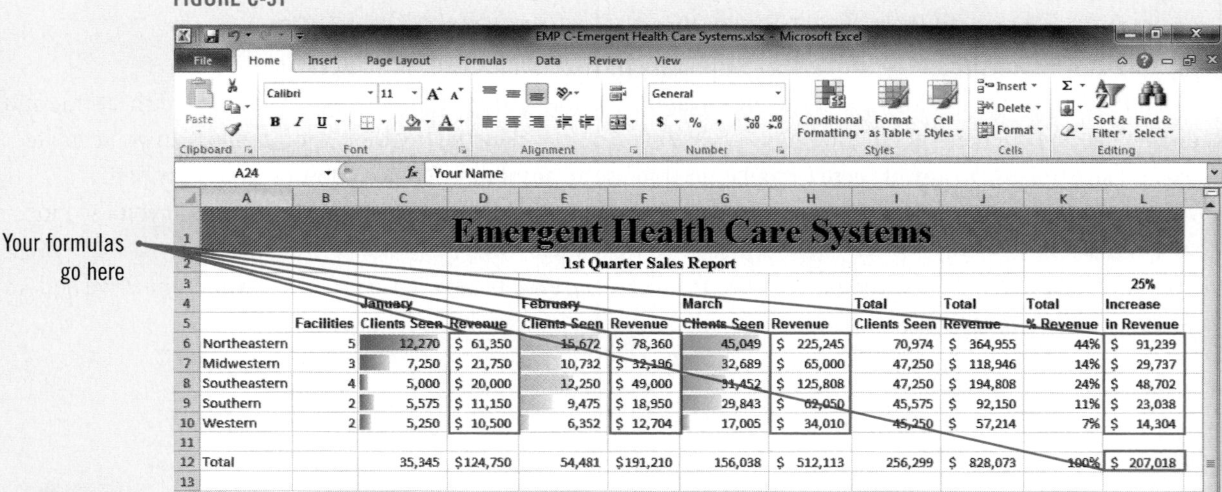

Real Life Independent Challenge

This project requires an Internet connection.

You have been notified that your research grant to study the spread of airborne diseases has been approved. You plan to visit seven different countries over the course of 2 months, and you have budgeted an identical spending allowance in each country. You want to create a worksheet that calculates the amount of native currency you will have in each country based on the budgeted amount. You want the workbook to reflect the currency information for each country.

- **a.** Start Excel, then save a new, blank workbook as **EMP C-Research Grant Travel Budget** to the drive and folder where you store your Data Files.
- **b.** Add a title at the top of the worksheet.
- **c.** Think of seven countries you would like to visit, then enter column and row labels for your worksheet. (*Hint*: You may wish to include row labels for each country, plus column labels for the country, the $1 equivalent in native currency, the total amount of native currency you'll have in each country, and the name of each country's monetary unit.)
- **d.** Decide how much money you want to bring to each country (for example, $1,000), and enter that in the worksheet.
- **e.** Use your favorite search engine to find your own information sources on currency conversions for the countries you plan to visit.
- **f.** Enter the cash equivalent to $1 in U.S. dollars for each country on your list.
- **g.** Create an equation that calculates the amount of native currency you will have in each country, using an absolute cell reference in the formula.
- **h.** Format the entries in the column containing the native currency $1 equivalent as Number number format with three decimal places, and format the column containing the total native currency budget with two decimal places, using the correct currency number format for each country. (*Hint*: Use the Number tab in the Format cells dialog box; choose the appropriate currency number format from the Symbol list.)
- **i.** Create a conditional format that changes the font style and color of the calculated amount in the $1,000 US column to light red fill with dark red text if the amount exceeds **1000** units of the local currency.
- **j.** Merge and center the worksheet title over the column headings.
- **k.** Add any formatting you want to the column headings, and resize the columns as necessary.
- **l.** Add a background color to the title.

Advanced Challenge Exercise

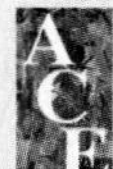

- Modify the conditional format in the $1,000 US column so that entries between 1500 and 3999 are displayed in red, boldface type; and entries above 4000 appear in blue, boldface type with a light red background.
- Delete all the unused sheets in the workbook.
- Save your work as **EMP C-Research Grant Travel Budget ACE** to the drive and folder where you store your Data Files.
- If you have access to an e-mail account, e-mail this workbook to your instructor as an attachment.

- **m.** Enter your name in the header of the worksheet.
- **n.** Spell check the worksheet, save your changes, compare your work to Figure C-32, then preview the worksheet in Backstage view, and submit your work to your instructor as directed.
- **o.** Close the workbook and exit Excel.

FIGURE C-32

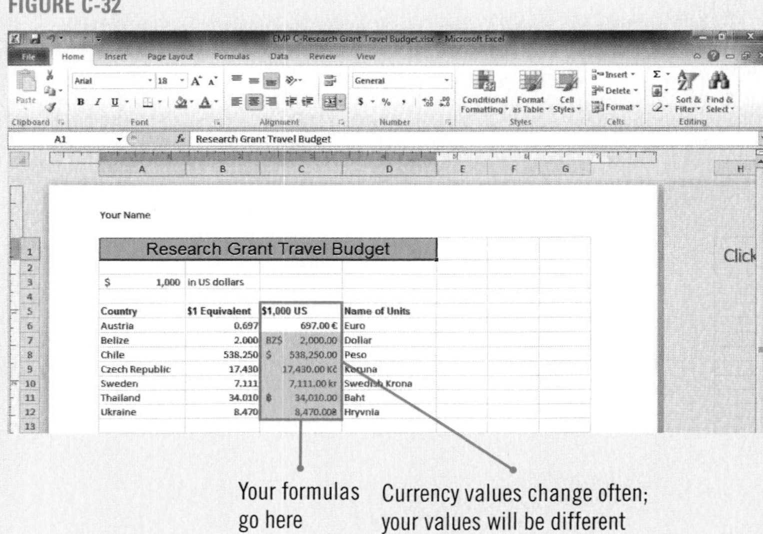

Visual Workshop

Open the file EMP C-5.xlsx from the drive and folder where you store your Data Files, then save it as **EMP C-Tacoma General Hospital Administrative Staff**. Use the skills you learned in this unit to format the worksheet so it looks like the one shown in Figure C-33. Create a conditional format in the Level column so that entries greater than 3 appear in red text. Create an additional conditional format in the Review Cycle column so that any value equal to 3 appears in green bold text. Replace the Accounting department label with **Paralegal**. (*Hint*: The only additional font used in this exercise is 16-point Times New Roman in row 1.) Enter your name in cell A25, check the spelling in the worksheet, save your changes, then submit your work to your instructor as directed.

FIGURE C-33

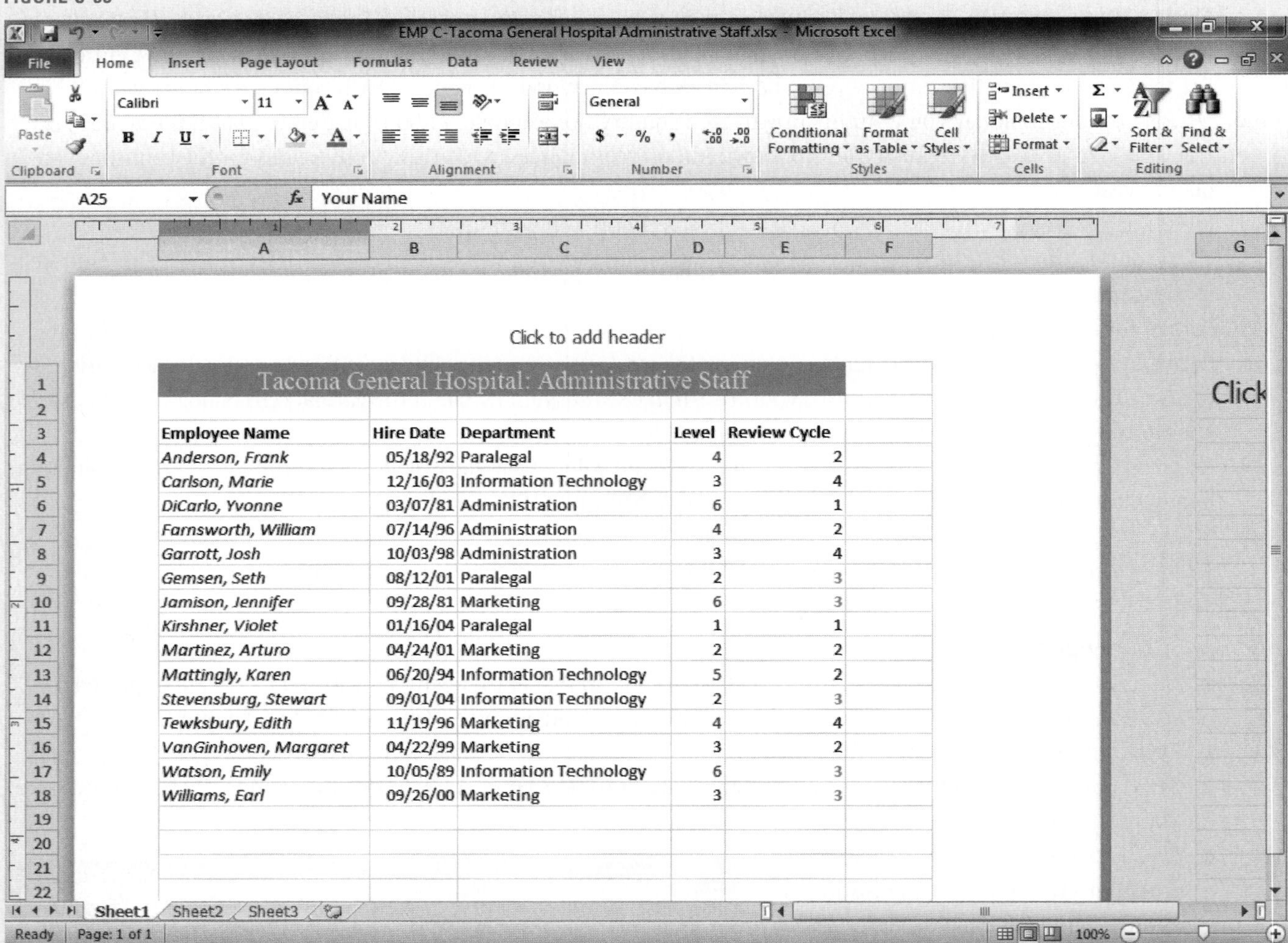

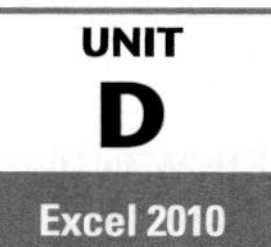

Working with Charts

Files You Will Need:

EMP D-1.xlsx
EMP D-2.xlsx
EMP D-3.xlsx
EMP D-4.xlsx
EMP D-5.xlsx
EMP D-6.xlsx

Worksheets provide an effective layout for calculating and organizing data, but the grid layout is not always the best format for presenting your work to others. To display information so it's easier to interpret, you can create a chart. **Charts**, sometimes called graphs, present information in a graphic format, making it easier to see patterns, trends, and relationships. In this unit, you learn how to create a chart, how to edit the chart and change the chart type, how to add text annotations and arrows, and how to preview and print the chart. At the upcoming annual meeting, Tony Sanchez wants to emphasize a growth trend at Riverwalk Medical Clinic. He asks you to create a chart showing the increase in insurance reimbursements over the past four quarters.

OBJECTIVES

Plan a chart
Create a chart
Move and resize a chart
Change the chart design
Change the chart layout
Format a chart
Annotate and draw on a chart
Create a pie chart

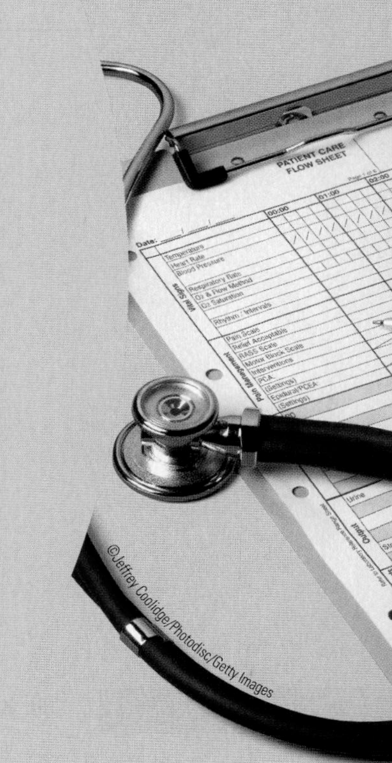

©Jeffrey Coolidge/Photodisc/Getty Images

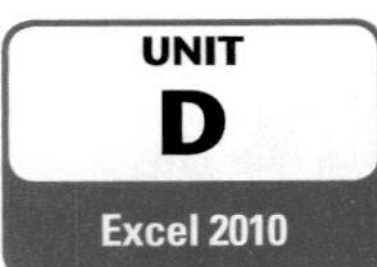

Planning a Chart

Before creating a chart, you need to plan the information you want your chart to show and how you want it to look. Planning ahead helps you decide what type of chart to create and how to organize the data. Understanding the parts of a chart makes it easier to format and to change specific elements so that the chart best illustrates your data. In preparation for creating the chart for Tony's presentation, you identify your goals for the chart and plan its layout.

DETAILS

Use the following guidelines to plan the chart:

- **Determine the purpose of the chart, and identify the data relationships you want to communicate graphically**

  You want to create a chart that shows quarterly insurance reimbursements throughout Riverwalk Medical Clinic. This worksheet data is shown in Figure D-1. In the first quarter, the Opthalmology department settled a dispute with a large insurance carrier, which resulted in greatly increased reimbursements starting in the third quarter. You also want the chart to illustrate whether the quarterly reimbursements for each department increased or decreased from quarter to quarter.

- **Determine the results you want to see, and decide which chart type is most appropriate**

  Different chart types display data in distinctive ways. For example, a pie chart compares parts to the whole, so it's useful for showing what proportion of a budget amount was spent on print ads relative to what was spent on direct mail or radio commercials. A line chart, in contrast, is best for showing trends over time. To choose the best chart type for your data, you should first decide how you want your data displayed and interpreted. Table D-1 describes several different types of charts you can create in Excel and their corresponding buttons on the Insert tab on the Ribbon. Because you want to compare RMC reimbursements in multiple departments over a period of four quarters, you decide to use a column chart.

- **Identify the worksheet data you want the chart to illustrate**

  Sometimes you use all the data in a worksheet to create a chart, while at other times you may need to select a range within the sheet. The worksheet from which you are creating your chart contains expense data for each of the past four quarters and the totals for the past year. You will need to use all the quarterly data contained in the worksheet except the quarterly totals.

- **Understand the elements of a chart**

  The chart shown in Figure D-2 contains basic elements of a chart. In the figure, RMC departments are on the horizontal axis (also called the **x-axis**) and expense dollar amounts are on the vertical axis (also called the **y-axis**). The horizontal axis is also called the **category axis** because it often contains the names of data groups, such as locations, months, or years. The vertical axis is also called the **value axis** because it often contains numerical values that help you interpret the size of chart elements. (3-D charts also contain a **z-axis**, for comparing data across both categories and values.) The area inside the horizontal and vertical axes is the **plot area**. The **tick marks**, on the vertical axis, and **gridlines** (extending across the plot area) create a scale of measure for each value. Each value in a cell you select for your chart is a **data point**. In any chart, a **data marker** visually represents each data point, which in this case is a column. A collection of related data points is a **data series**. In this chart, there are four data series (Quarter 1, Quarter 2, Quarter 3, and Quarter 4). Each is made up of column data markers of a different color, so a **legend** is included to make it easy to identify them.

FIGURE D-1: Worksheet containing reimbursement data

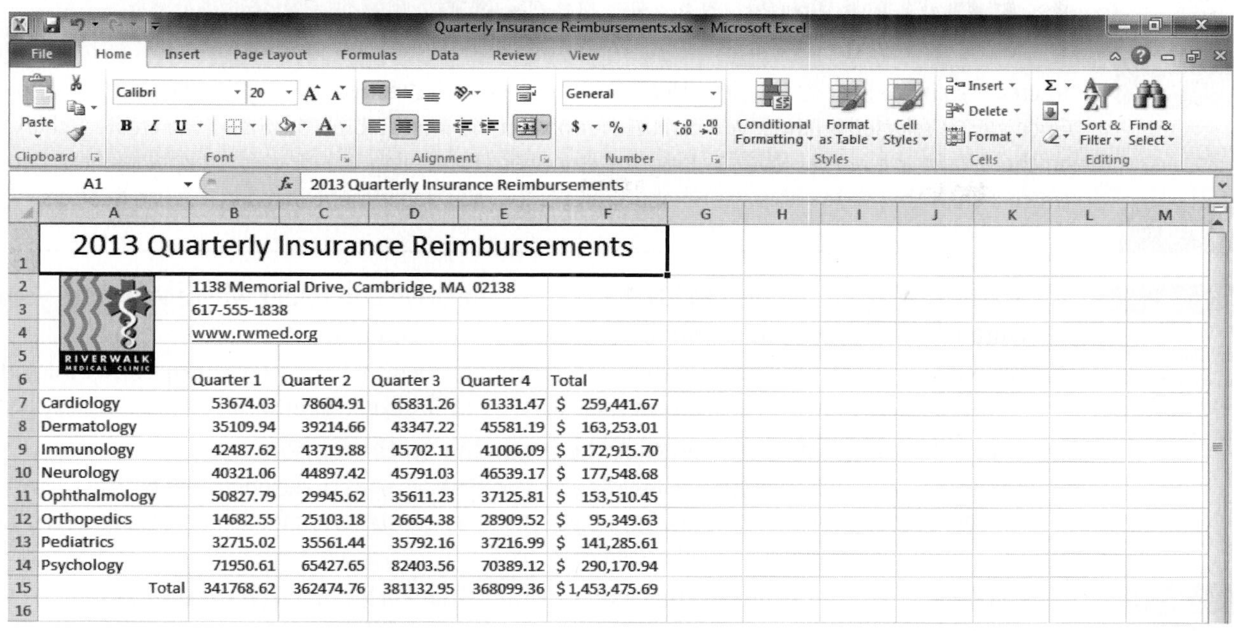

	A	B	C	D	E	F
1	2013 Quarterly Insurance Reimbursements					
2		1138 Memorial Drive, Cambridge, MA 02138				
3		617-555-1838				
4		www.rwmed.org				
5	RIVERWALK MEDICAL CLINIC					
6		Quarter 1	Quarter 2	Quarter 3	Quarter 4	Total
7	Cardiology	53674.03	78604.91	65831.26	61331.47	$ 259,441.67
8	Dermatology	35109.94	39214.66	43347.22	45581.19	$ 163,253.01
9	Immunology	42487.62	43719.88	45702.11	41006.09	$ 172,915.70
10	Neurology	40321.06	44897.42	45791.03	46539.17	$ 177,548.68
11	Ophthalmology	50827.79	29945.62	35611.23	37125.81	$ 153,510.45
12	Orthopedics	14682.55	25103.18	26654.38	28909.52	$ 95,349.63
13	Pediatrics	32715.02	35561.44	35792.16	37216.99	$ 141,285.61
14	Psychology	71950.61	65427.65	82403.56	70389.12	$ 290,170.94
15	Total	341768.62	362474.76	381132.95	368099.36	$1,453,475.69
16						

FIGURE D-2: Chart elements

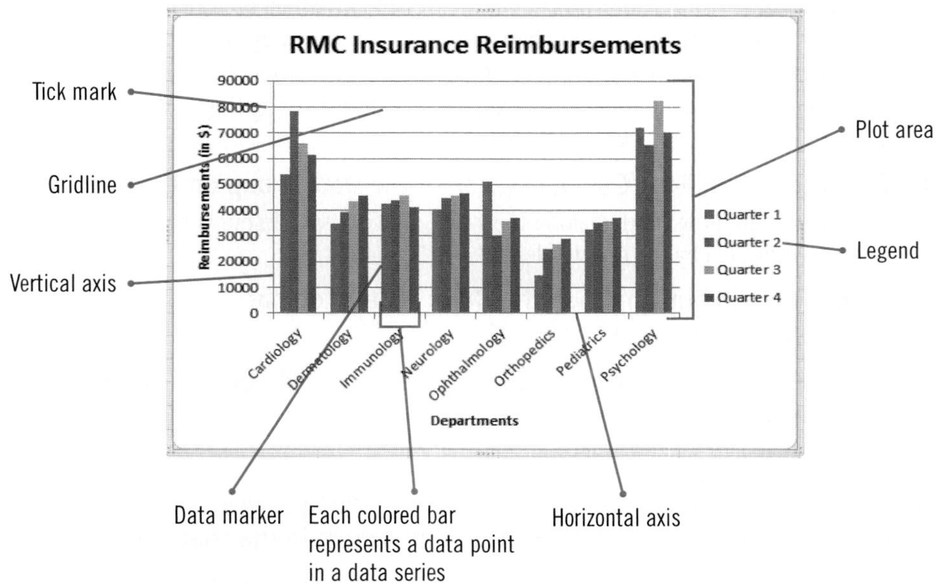

TABLE D-1: Common chart types

type	button	description
Column		Compares data using columns; the Excel default; sometimes referred to as a bar chart in other spreadsheet programs
Line		Compares trends over even time intervals; looks similar to an area chart, but does not emphasize total
Pie		Compares sizes of pieces as part of a whole; used for a single series of numbers
Bar		Compares data using horizontal bars; sometimes referred to as a horizontal bar chart in other spreadsheet programs
Area		Shows how individual volume changes over time in relation to total volume
Scatter		Compares trends over uneven time or measurement intervals; used in scientific and engineering disciplines for trend spotting and extrapolation

UNIT D

Excel 2010

Creating a Chart

To create a chart in Excel, you first select the range in a worksheet containing the data you want to chart. Once you've selected a range, you can use buttons on the Insert tab on the Ribbon to create a chart based on the data in the range. Using the worksheet containing the quarterly reimbursement data, you create a chart that shows how the reimbursements for each department varied across the quarters.

STEPS

QUICK TIP
When charting data for a particular time period, make sure all series are for the same time period.

1. **Start Excel, open the file EMP D-1.xlsx from the drive and folder where you store your Data Files, then save it as EMP D-Quarterly Insurance Reimbursements**

   You want the chart to include the quarterly insurance reimbursement figures, as well as quarter and department labels. You don't include the Total column and row because the figures in these cells would skew the chart.

2. **Select the range A6:E14, then click the Insert tab on the Ribbon**

   The Insert tab contains groups for inserting various types of objects, including charts. The Charts group includes buttons for each major chart type, plus an Other Charts button for additional chart types, such as stock charts for charting stock market data.

QUICK TIP
To base a chart on data in nonadjacent ranges, press and hold [Ctrl] while selecting each range, then use the Insert tab to create the chart.

3. **Click the Column button in the Charts group, then click Clustered Column under 2-D Column in the Column chart gallery, as shown in Figure D-3**

   The chart is inserted in the center of the worksheet, and three contextual Chart Tools tabs appear on the Ribbon: Design, Layout, and Format. On the Design tab, which is currently in front, you can quickly change the chart type, chart layout, and chart style, and you can swap how the columns and rows of data in the worksheet are represented in the chart. Currently, the departments are charted along the horizontal x-axis, with the quarterly reimbursement dollar amounts charted along the y-axis. This lets you easily compare the quarterly reimbursements for each department.

4. **Click the Switch Row/Column button in the Data group on the Chart Tools Design tab**

   The quarters are now charted along the x-axis. The expense amounts per department are charted along the y-axis, as indicated by the updated legend. See Figure D-4.

5. **Click the Undo button on the Quick Access toolbar**

   The chart returns to its original design.

6. **Click the Chart Tools Layout tab, click the Chart Title button in the Labels group, then click Above Chart**

   A title placeholder appears above the chart.

QUICK TIP
You can also triple-click to select the chart title text.

7. **Click anywhere in the Chart Title text box, press [Ctrl][A] to select the text, type Quarterly Insurance Reimbursements, then click anywhere in the chart to deselect the title**

   Adding a title helps identify the chart. The border around the chart and the chart's **sizing handles**, the small series of dots at the corners and sides of the chart's border, indicate that the chart is selected. See Figure D-5. Your chart might be in a different location on the worksheet and may look slightly different; you will move and resize it in the next lesson. Any time a chart is selected, as it is now, a blue border surrounds the worksheet data range on which the chart is based, a purple border surrounds the cells containing the category axis labels, and a green border surrounds the cells containing the data series labels. This chart is known as an **embedded chart** because it is inserted directly in the current worksheet and doesn't exist in a separate file. Embedding a chart in the current sheet is the default selection when creating a chart, but you can also embed a chart on a different sheet in the workbook, or on a newly created chart sheet. A **chart sheet** is a sheet in a workbook that contains only a chart that is linked to the workbook data.

8. **Save your work**

FIGURE D-3: Column chart gallery

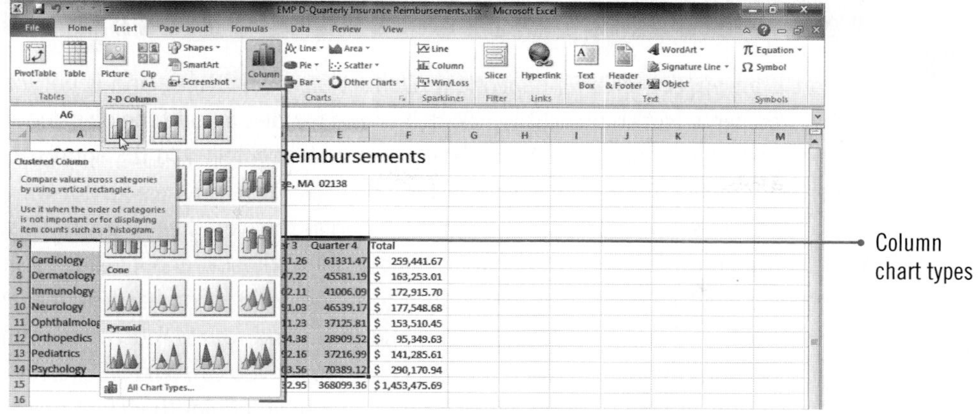

FIGURE D-4: Clustered Column chart with different presentation of data

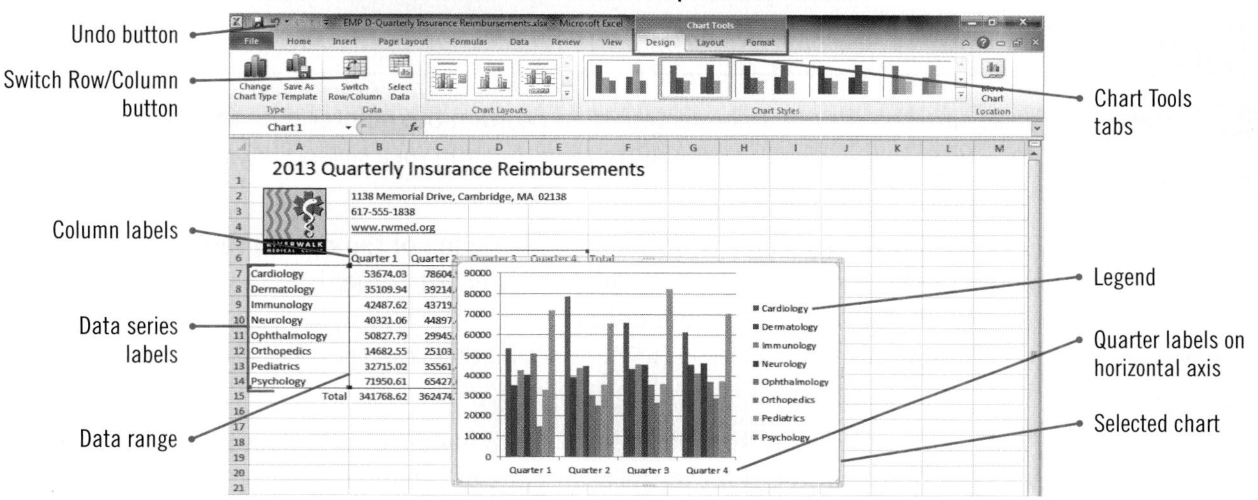

FIGURE D-5: Chart with rows and columns restored and title added

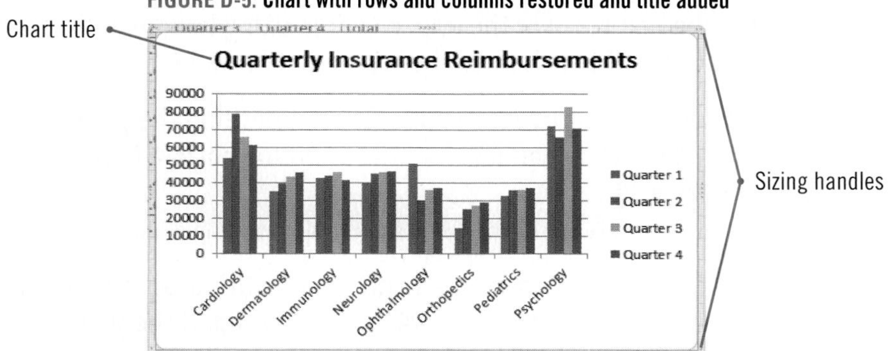

Creating sparklines

You can quickly create a miniature chart called a **sparkline** that serves as a visual indicator of data trends. To do this, select a range of data, click the Insert tab, then click the Line, Column, or Win/Loss button in the Sparklines group. In the Create Sparklines dialog box that opens, enter the cell in which you want the sparkline to appear, then click OK. Figure D-6 shows four sparklines created in four different cells. Any changes to data in the range are reflected in the sparkline. To delete a selected sparkline from a cell, click the Clear button in the Group group on the Sparkline Tools Design tab.

FIGURE D-6: Sparklines in cells

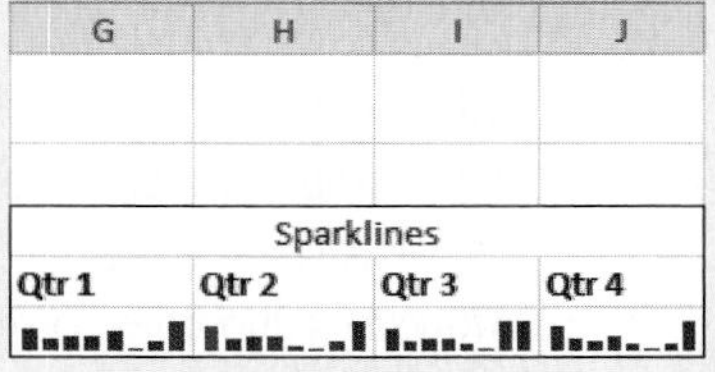

UNIT
D
Excel 2010

Moving and Resizing a Chart

A chart is an **object**, or an independent element on a worksheet, and is not located in a specific cell or range. You can select an object by clicking it; sizing handles around the object indicate it is selected. (When a chart is selected in Excel, the Name box, which normally tells you the address of the active cell, tells you the chart number.) You can move a selected chart anywhere on a worksheet without affecting formulas or data in the worksheet. However, any data changed in the worksheet is automatically updated in the chart. You can even move a chart to a different sheet in the workbook, and it will still reflect the original data. You can resize a chart to improve its appearance by dragging its sizing handles. A chart contains chart objects, such as a title and legend, which you can also move and resize. You can reposition chart objects to predefined locations using commands on the Layout tab, or you can freely move any chart object by dragging it or by cutting and pasting it to a new location. When you point to a chart object, the name of the object appears as a ScreenTip. You want to resize the chart, position it below the worksheet data, and move the legend.

STEPS

QUICK TIP
To delete a selected chart, press [Delete].

TROUBLE
If you do not drag a blank area on the chart, you might inadvertently move a chart element instead of the whole chart; if this happens, undo the action and try again.

QUICK TIP
To resize a selected chart to an exact specification, click the Chart Tools Format tab, then enter the desired height and width in the Size group.

QUICK TIP
You can move a legend to the right, top, left, or bottom of a chart by clicking the Legend button in the Labels group on the Chart Tools Layout tab, then clicking a location option.

1. **Make sure the chart is still selected, then position the pointer over the chart**
   The pointer shape ⁺⇖ indicates that you can move the chart. For a table of commonly used object pointers, refer to Table D-2.

2. **Position ⁺⇖ on a blank area near the upper-left edge of the chart, press and hold the left mouse button, drag the chart until its upper-left corner is at the upper-left corner of cell A18, then release the mouse button**
   As you drag the chart, you can see an outline representing the chart's perimeter. The chart appears in the new location.

3. **Position the pointer on the right-middle sizing handle until it changes to ⇔, then drag the right border of the chart to the right edge of column F**
   The chart is widened. See Figure D-7.

4. **Position the pointer over the upper-middle sizing handle until it changes to ⇕, then drag the top border of the chart to the top edge of row 17**

5. **Scroll down if necessary so row 32 is visible, position the pointer over the lower-middle sizing handle until it changes to ⇕, then drag the bottom border of the chart to the bottom border of row 30**
   You can move any object on a chart. You want to align the top of the legend with the top of the plot area.

6. **Click the legend to select it, press and hold [Shift], drag the legend up using ⁺⇖ so the dotted outline is approximately 1⁄4" above the top of the plot area, then release [Shift]**
   When you click the legend, sizing handles appear around it and "Legend" appears as a ScreenTip when the pointer hovers over the object. As you drag, a dotted outline of the legend border appears. Pressing and holding the [Shift] key holds the horizontal position of the legend as you move it vertically. Although the sizing handles on objects within a chart look different from the sizing handles that surround a chart, they function the same way.

7. **Click cell A14, type Psychiatry, click the Enter button ✓ on the formula bar, use AutoFit to resize column A, then press [Ctrl][Home]**
   The axis label changes to reflect the updated cell contents, as shown in Figure D-8. Changing any data in the worksheet modifies corresponding text or values in the chart. Because the chart is no longer selected, the Chart Tools tabs no longer appear on the Ribbon.

8. **Save your work**

FIGURE D-7: Moved and resized chart

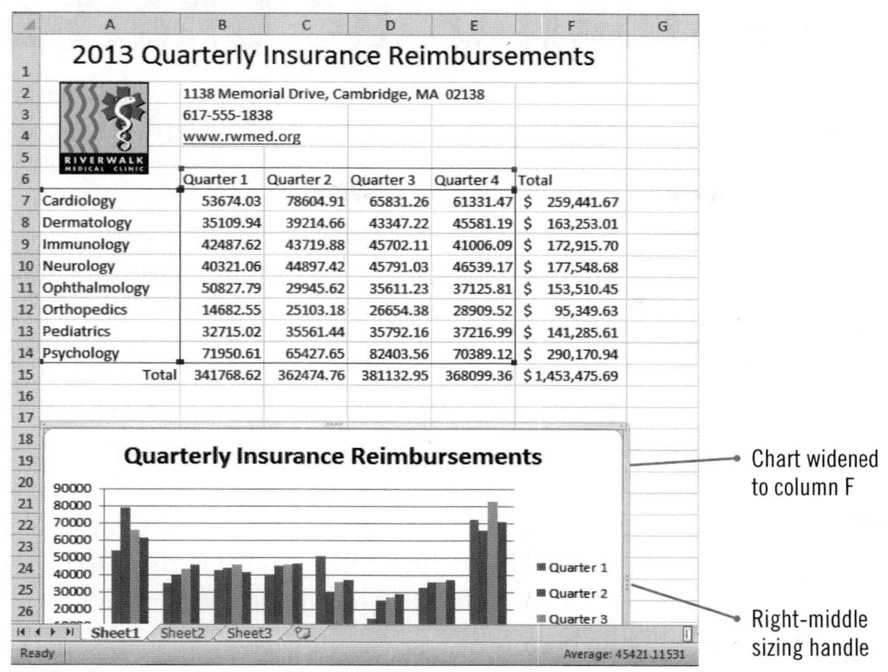

FIGURE D-8: Worksheet with modified legend and label

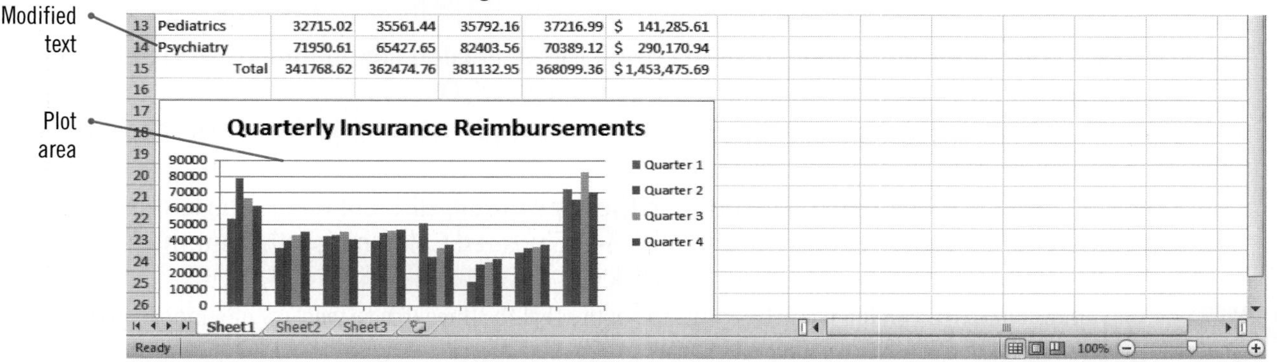

TABLE D-2: Common object pointers

name	pointer	use	name	pointer	use
Diagonal resizing	or	Change chart shape from corners	**I-beam**		Edit object text
Draw		Draw an object	**Move**		Move object
Horizontal resizing		Change object width	**Vertical resizing**		Change object height

Moving an embedded chart to a sheet

Suppose you have created an embedded chart that you decide would look better on a chart sheet or in a different worksheet. You can make this change without recreating the entire chart. To do so, first select the chart, click the Chart Tools Design tab, then click the Move Chart button in the Location group. The Move Chart dialog box opens. To move the chart to its own chart sheet, click the New sheet option button, type a name for the new sheet if desired, then click OK. If the chart is already on its own sheet, click the Object in option button, select the worksheet to where you want to move it, then click OK.

UNIT D
Excel 2010

Changing the Chart Design

Once you've created a chart, it's easy to modify the design using the Chart Tools Design tab. You can change the chart type, modify the data range and column/row configuration, apply a different chart style, and change the layout of objects in the chart. The layouts in the Chart Layouts group on the Chart Tools Design tab offer preconfigured arrangements of objects in your chart, such as its legend, title, or gridlines; choosing one of these layouts is an alternative to manually changing how objects are arranged in a chart. You look over your worksheet and realize the data for Pediatrics and Psychiatry in Quarter 2 is incorrect. After you correct this data, you want to see how the corrected data looks using different chart layouts and types.

STEPS

1. **Click cell C13, type 39462.01, press [Enter], type 62947.18, then press [Enter]**
   In the chart, the Quarter 2 data markers for Pediatrics and Psychiatry reflect the adjusted reimbursements. See Figure D-9.
2. **Select the chart by clicking a blank area within the chart border, click the Chart Tools Design tab on the Ribbon, then click Layout 3 in the Chart Layouts group**
   The legend moves to the bottom of the chart. You prefer the original layout.
3. **Click the Undo button on the Quick Access toolbar, then click the Change Chart Type button in the Type group**
   The Change Chart Type dialog box opens, as shown in Figure D-10. The left pane of the dialog box lists the available categories, and the right pane shows the individual chart types. An orange border surrounds the currently selected chart type.
4. **Click Bar in the left pane of the Change Chart Type dialog box, confirm that the Clustered Bar chart type is selected in the right pane, then click OK**
   The column chart changes to a clustered bar chart. See Figure D-11. You look at the bar chart, then decide to see how the data looks in a three-dimensional column chart.
5. **Click the Change Chart Type button in the Type group, click Column in the left pane of the Change Chart Type dialog box, click 3-D Clustered Column (fourth from the left in the first row) in the right pane, then click OK**
   A three-dimensional column chart appears. You notice that the three-dimensional column format gives you a sense of volume, but it is more crowded than the two-dimensional column format.
6. **Click the Change Chart Type button in the Type group, click Clustered Column (first from the left in the first row) in the right pane of the Change Chart Type dialog box, then click OK**
7. **Click the Style 3 chart style in the Chart Styles group**
   The columns change to shades of blue. You prefer the previous chart style's color scheme.
8. **Click on the Quick Access toolbar, then save your work**

QUICK TIP
You can see more layout choices by clicking the More button in the Chart Layouts group.

QUICK TIP
If you plan to print a chart on a black-and-white printer, you may wish to apply a black-and-white chart style to your chart so you can see how the output will look as you work.

Creating a combination chart

A **combination chart** is two charts in one; a column chart with a line chart, for example. This type of chart (which cannot be used with all data) is helpful when charting dissimilar but related data. For example, you can create a combination chart based on home price and home size data, showing home prices in a column chart, and related home sizes in a line chart. In such a combination chart, a **secondary axis** (such as a vertical axis on the right side of the chart) would supply the scale for the home sizes. To create a combination chart, you can apply a chart type to a data series in an existing chart. Select the chart data series that you want plotted on a secondary axis, then click Format Selection in the Current Selection group on the Chart Tools Layout tab or Format tab to open the Format Data Series dialog box. In the dialog box, click Series Options if necessary, click the Secondary Axis option button under Plot Series On, then click Close. Click the Chart Tools Layout tab if necessary, click the Axes button in the Axes group, then click the type of secondary axis you want and where you want it to appear. To finish, click the Change Chart Type button in the Type group on the Design tab, then select a chart type for the data series.

FIGURE D-9: Worksheet with modified data

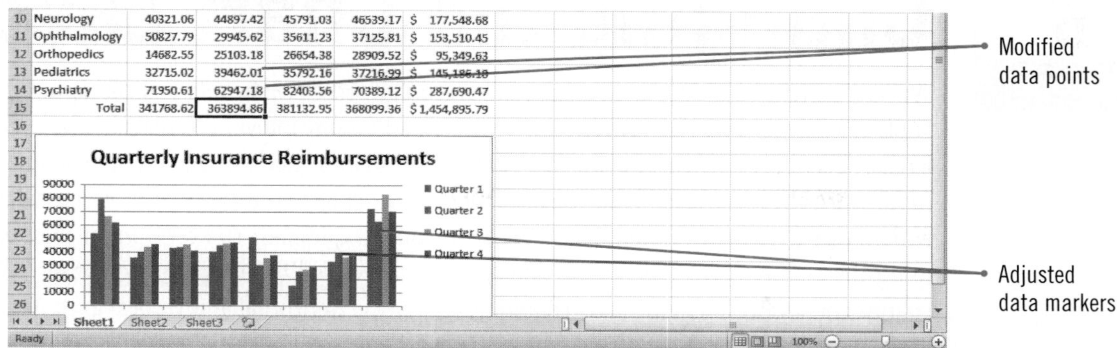

FIGURE D-10: Change Chart Type dialog box

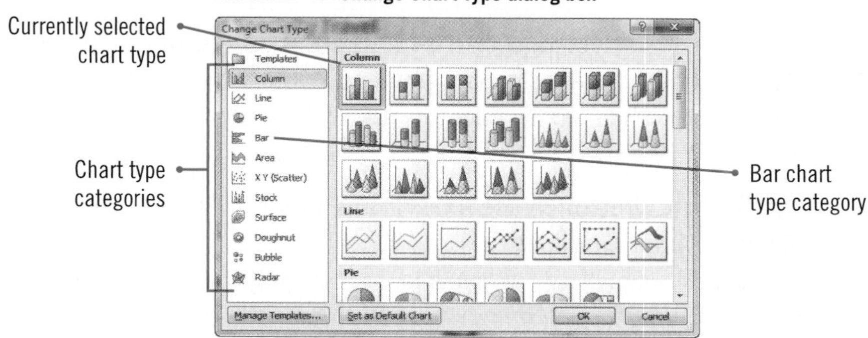

FIGURE D-11: Column chart changed to bar chart

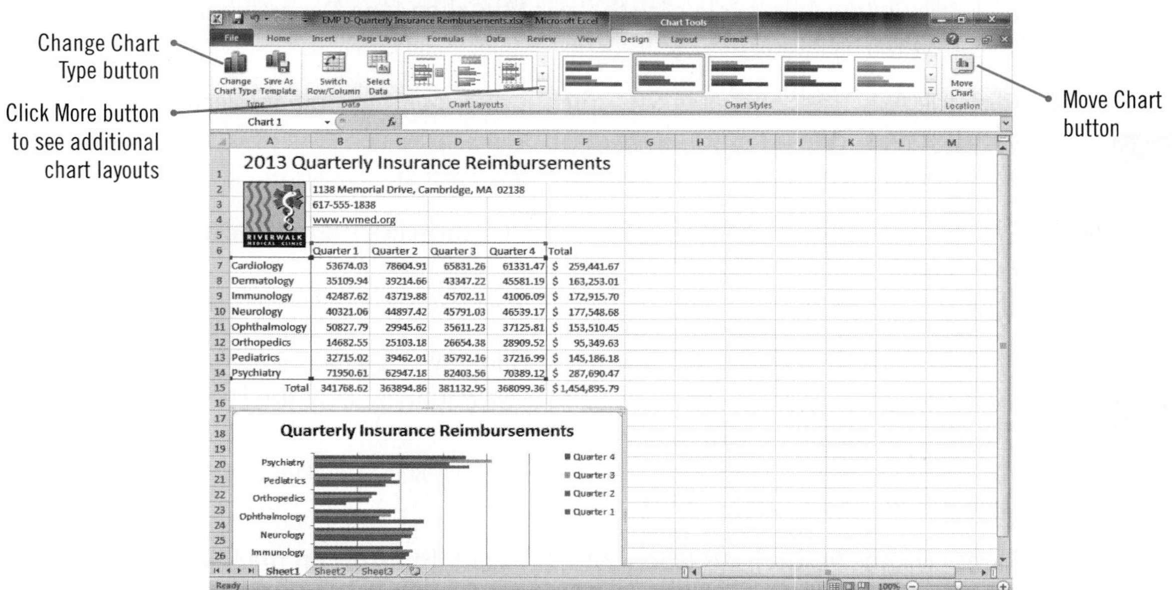

Working with a 3-D chart

Excel includes two kinds of 3-D chart types. In a true 3-D chart, a third axis, called the **z-axis**, lets you compare data points across both categories and values. The z-axis runs along the depth of the chart, so it appears to advance from the back of the chart. To create a true 3-D chart, look for chart types that begin with "3-D," such as 3-D Column. Charts that are formatted in 3-D, but are not true 3-D, contain only two axes but their graphics give the illusion of three-dimensionality. To create a chart that is only formatted in 3-D, look for chart types that end with "in 3-D." In any 3-D chart, data series can sometimes obscure other columns or bars in the same chart, but you can rotate the chart to obtain a better view. Right-click the chart, then click 3-D Rotation. The Format Chart Area dialog box opens with the 3-D Rotation category active. The 3-D Rotation options let you change the orientation and perspective of the chart area, plot area, walls, and floor. The 3-D Format category lets you apply three-dimensional effects to selected chart objects. (Not all 3-D Rotation and 3-D Format options are available on all charts.)

UNIT D
Excel 2010

Changing the Chart Layout

While the Chart Tools Design tab contains preconfigured chart layouts you can apply to a chart, the Chart Tools Layout tab makes it easy to add, remove, and modify individual chart objects such as a chart title or legend. Using buttons on this tab, you can also add shapes, pictures, and additional text to a chart, add and modify labels, change the display of axes, modify the fill behind the plot area, create titles for the horizontal and vertical axes, and eliminate or change the look of gridlines. You can format the text in a chart object using the Home tab or the Mini toolbar, just as you would the text in a worksheet. You want to change the layout of the chart by creating titles for the horizontal and vertical axes. To improve the chart's appearance, you'll add a drop shadow to the chart title.

STEPS

1. **With the chart still selected, click the Chart Tools Layout tab on the Ribbon, click the Gridlines button in the Axes group, point to Primary Horizontal Gridlines, then click None**
   The gridlines that extend from the value axis tick marks across the chart's plot area are removed from the chart, as shown in Figure D-12.

2. **Click the Gridlines button in the Axes group, point to Primary Horizontal Gridlines, then click Major & Minor Gridlines**
   Both major and minor gridlines now appear in the chart. **Major gridlines** represent the values at the value axis tick marks, and **minor gridlines** represent the values between the tick marks.

> **QUICK TIP**
> You can move any title to a new position by clicking one of its edges, then dragging it.

3. **Click the Axis Titles button in the Labels group, point to Primary Horizontal Axis Title, click Title Below Axis, triple-click the axis title, then type Departments**
   Descriptive text on the category axis helps readers understand the chart.

4. **Click the Axis Titles button in the Labels group, point to Primary Vertical Axis Title, then click Rotated Title**
   A placeholder for the vertical axis title is added to the left of the vertical axis.

> **QUICK TIP**
> You can also edit text in a chart or axis title by positioning the pointer over the selected title until it changes to I, clicking the title, then editing the text.

5. **Scroll down so the entire chart is displayed, triple-click the vertical axis title, then type Revenue (in $)**
   The text "Expenses (in $)" appears to the left of the vertical axis, as shown in Figure D-13.

6. **Right-click the horizontal axis labels ("Cardiology", "Dermatology", etc.), click the Font list arrow on the Mini toolbar, click Times New Roman, click the Font Size list arrow on the Mini toolbar, then click 8**
   The font of the horizontal axis labels changes to Times New Roman, and the font size decreases, making more of the plot area visible.

7. **Right-click the vertical axis labels, click the Font list arrow on the Mini toolbar, click Times New Roman, click the Font Size list arrow on the Mini toolbar, then click 8**

> **QUICK TIP**
> You can also apply a border to a selected chart object by clicking the Shape Outline list arrow on the Chart Tools Format tab, and then selecting from the available options.

8. **Right-click the chart title ("Quarterly Insurance Reimbursements"), click Format Chart Title on the shortcut menu, click Border Color in the left pane of the Format Chart Title dialog box, then click the Solid line option button in the right pane**
   A solid border will appear around the chart title with the default blue color.

> **QUICK TIP**
> You can also apply a shadow to a selected chart object by clicking the Shape Effects button on the Chart Tools Format tab, pointing to Shadow, and then clicking a shadow effect.

9. **Click Shadow in the left pane of the Format Chart Title dialog box, click the Presets list arrow, click Offset Diagonal Bottom Right in the Outer group (first row, first from the left), click Close, then save your work**
   A blue border with a drop shadow surrounds the title. Compare your work to Figure D-14.

FIGURE D-12: Gridlines removed from chart

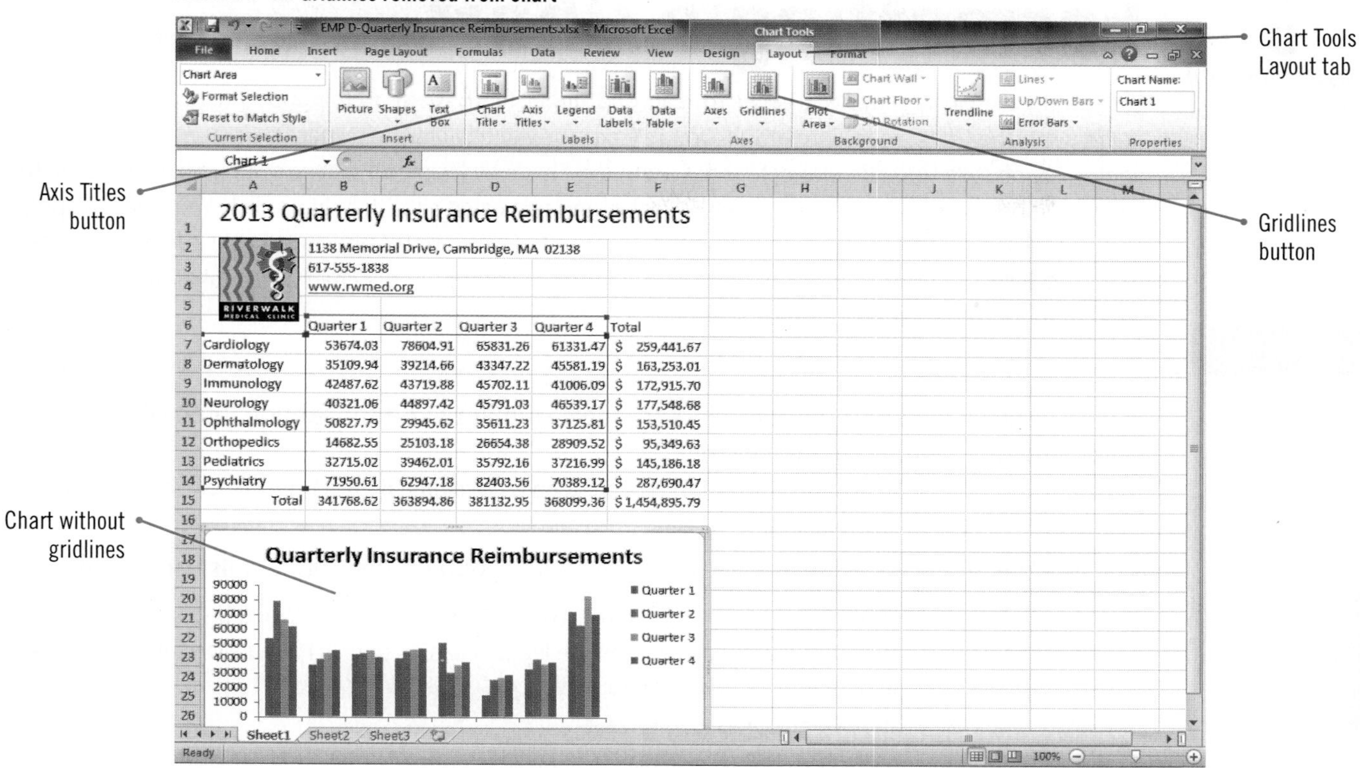

	Quarter 1	Quarter 2	Quarter 3	Quarter 4	Total
Cardiology	53674.03	78604.91	65831.26	61331.47	$ 259,441.67
Dermatology	35109.94	39214.66	43347.22	45581.19	$ 163,253.01
Immunology	42487.62	43719.88	45702.11	41006.09	$ 172,915.70
Neurology	40321.06	44897.42	45791.03	46539.17	$ 177,548.68
Ophthalmology	50827.79	29945.62	35611.23	37125.81	$ 153,510.45
Orthopedics	14682.55	25103.18	26654.38	28909.52	$ 95,349.63
Pediatrics	32715.02	39462.01	35792.16	37216.99	$ 145,186.18
Psychiatry	71950.61	62947.18	82403.56	70389.12	$ 287,690.47
Total	341768.62	363894.86	381132.95	368099.36	$ 1,454,895.79

FIGURE D-13: Axis titles added to chart

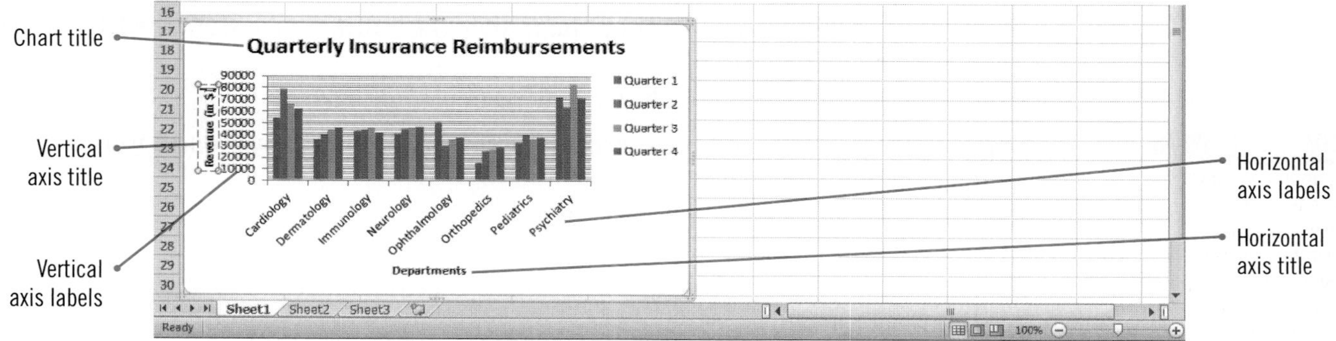

FIGURE D-14: Enhanced chart

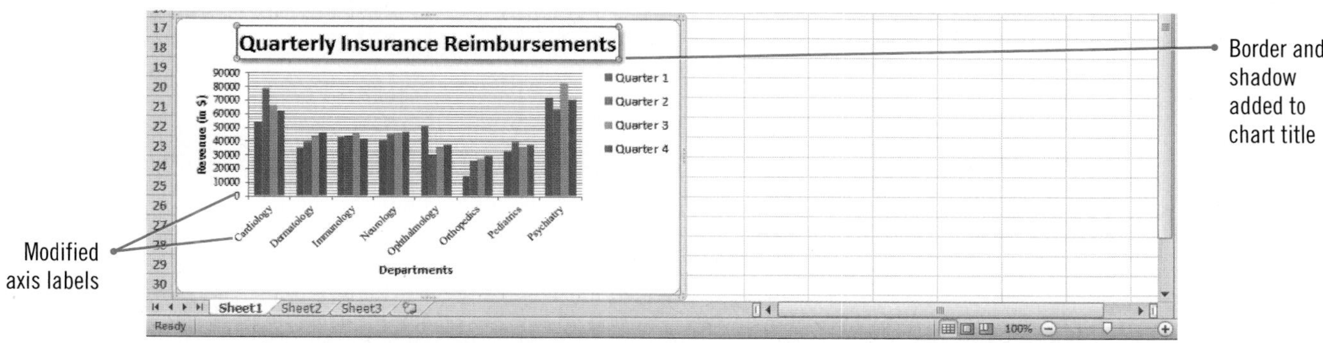

Adding data labels to a chart

There are times when your audience might benefit by seeing data labels on a chart. These labels appear next to the data markers in the chart and can indicate the series name, category name, and/or the value of one or more data points. Once your chart is selected, you can add this information to your chart by clicking the Data Labels button in the Labels group on the Chart Tools Layout tab, and then clicking a display option for the data labels. Once you have added the data labels, you can format them or delete individual data labels. To delete a data label, select it and then press [Delete].

Formatting a Chart

Formatting a chart can make it easier to read and understand. Many formatting enhancements can be made using the Chart Tools Format tab. You can change the fill color for a specific data series, or you can apply a shape style to a title or a data series using the Shape Styles group. Shape styles make it possible to apply multiple formats, such as an outline, fill color, and text color, all with a single click. You can also apply different fill colors, outlines, and effects to chart objects using arrows and buttons in the Shape Styles group. You want to use a different color for one data series in the chart and apply a shape style to another to enhance the look of the chart.

STEPS

1. **With the chart selected, click the Chart Tools Format tab on the Ribbon, then click any column in the Quarter 4 data series**
   The Chart Tools Format tab opens, and handles appear on each column in the Quarter 4 data series, indicating that the entire series is selected.
2. **Click the Shape Fill list arrow in the Shape Styles group on the Chart Tools Format tab**
3. **Click Orange, Accent 6 (first row, 10th from the left) as shown in Figure D-15**
   All the columns for the series become orange, and the legend changes to match the new color. You can also change the color of selected objects by applying a shape style.
4. **Click any column in the Quarter 3 data series**
   Handles appear on each column in the Quarter 3 data series.
5. **Click the More button on the Shape Styles gallery, then hover the pointer over the Moderate Effect – Olive Green, Accent 3 shape style (fifth row, fourth from the left) in the gallery, as shown in Figure D-16**
   Live Preview shows the data series in the chart with the shape style applied.
6. **Click the Subtle Effect – Olive Green, Accent 3 shape style (fourth row, fourth from the left) in the gallery**
   The style for the data series changes, as shown in Figure D-17.
7. **Save your work**

QUICK TIP

To apply a WordArt style to a text object (such as the chart title), select the object, then click a style in the WordArt Styles group on the Chart Tools Format tab.

Changing alignment and angle in axis labels and titles

The buttons on the Chart Tools Layout tab provide a few options for positioning axis labels and titles, but you can customize their position and rotation to exact specifications using the Format Axis dialog box or Format Axis Title dialog box. With a chart selected, right-click the axis text you want to modify, then click Format Axis or Format Axis Title on the shortcut menu. In the dialog box that opens, click Alignment, then select the appropriate Text layout option. You can also create a custom angle by clicking the Custom angle up and down arrows. When you have made the desired changes, click Close.

FIGURE D-15: New shape fill applied to data series

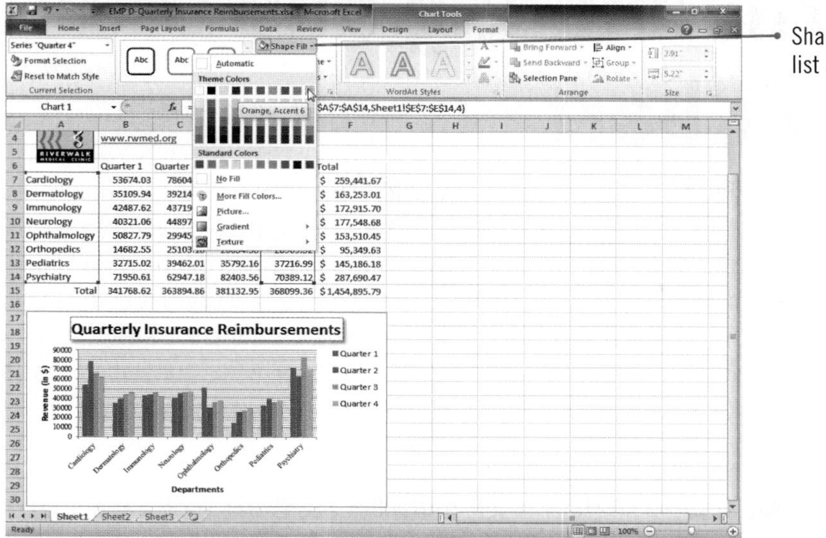

FIGURE D-16: Live Preview of new style applied to data series

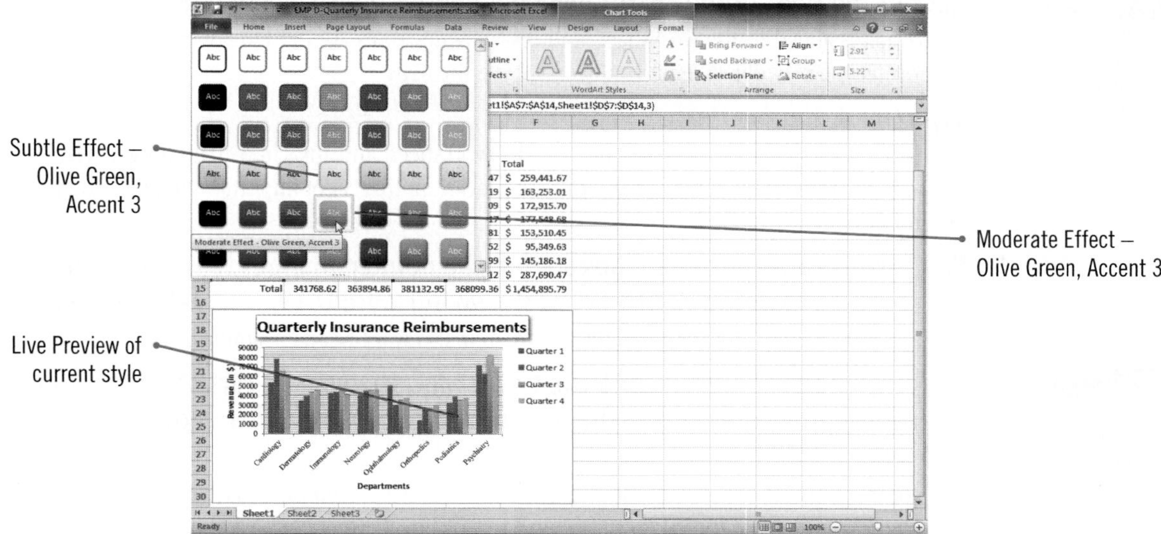

FIGURE D-17: Style of data series changed

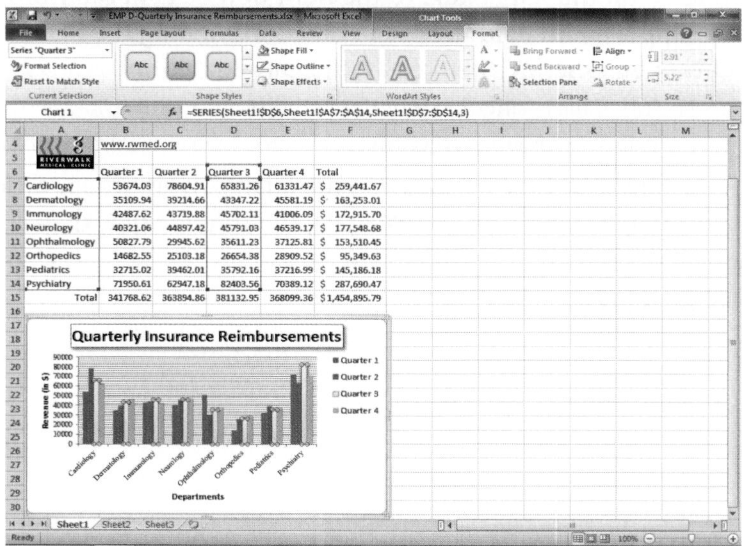

Excel 2010

Annotating and Drawing on a Chart

You can use text annotations and graphics to point out critical information in a chart. **Text annotations** are labels that further describe your data. You can also draw lines and arrows that point to the exact locations you want to emphasize. Shapes such as arrows and boxes can be added from the Illustrations group on the Insert tab or from the Insert group on the Chart Tools Layout group on the Ribbon. These groups are also used to insert pictures and clip art into worksheets and charts. You want to call attention to the Orthopedics revenue increases, so you decide to add a text annotation and an arrow to this information in the chart.

STEPS

1. **Make sure the chart is selected, click the Chart Tools Layout tab, click the Text Box button in the Insert group, then move the pointer over the worksheet**
   The pointer changes to ↓, indicating that you will insert a text box where you next click.
2. **Click to the right of the chart (anywhere *outside* the chart boundary)**
   A text box is added to the worksheet, and the Drawing Tools Format tab appears on the Ribbon so that you can format the new object. First you need to type the text.
3. **Type Great improvement**
   The text appears in a selected text box on the worksheet, and the chart is no longer selected, as shown in Figure D-18. Your text box may be in a different location; this is not important, because you'll move the annotation in the next step.
4. **Point to an edge of the text box so that the pointer changes to ✥, drag the text box into the chart beneath the chart title, as shown in Figure D-19, then release the mouse button**
   The text box is a text annotation for the chart. You also want to add a simple arrow shape in the chart.
5. **Click the chart to select it, click the Chart Tools Layout tab, click the Shapes button in the Insert group, click the Arrow shape in the Lines category, then move the pointer over the text box on the chart**
   The pointer changes to +, and the status bar displays "Click and drag to insert an AutoShape." When + is over the text box, red handles appear around the text in the text box. A red handle can act as an anchor for the arrow.
6. **Position + on the red handle to the right of the "t" in the word "improvement" (in the text box), press and hold the left mouse button, drag the line to the Quarter 1 column for the Orthopedics series, then release the mouse button**
   An arrow points to the Quarter 1 expense for Orthopedics, and the Drawing Tools Format tab displays options for working with the new arrow object. You can resize, format, or delete it just like any other object in a chart.
7. **Click the Shape Outline list arrow in the Shape Styles group, click the Automatic color, click the Shape Outline list arrow again, point to Weight, then click 1½ pt**
   Compare your finished chart to Figure D-20.
8. **Save your work**

QUICK TIP
You can also insert a text box by clicking the Text Box button in the Text group in the Insert tab, then clicking in the worksheet.

QUICK TIP
To annotate a chart using a callout, click the Shapes button in either the Illustrations group on the Insert tab or the Insert group on the Chart Tools Layout tab, then click a shape in the Callouts category of the Shapes gallery.

FIGURE D-18: **Text box added**

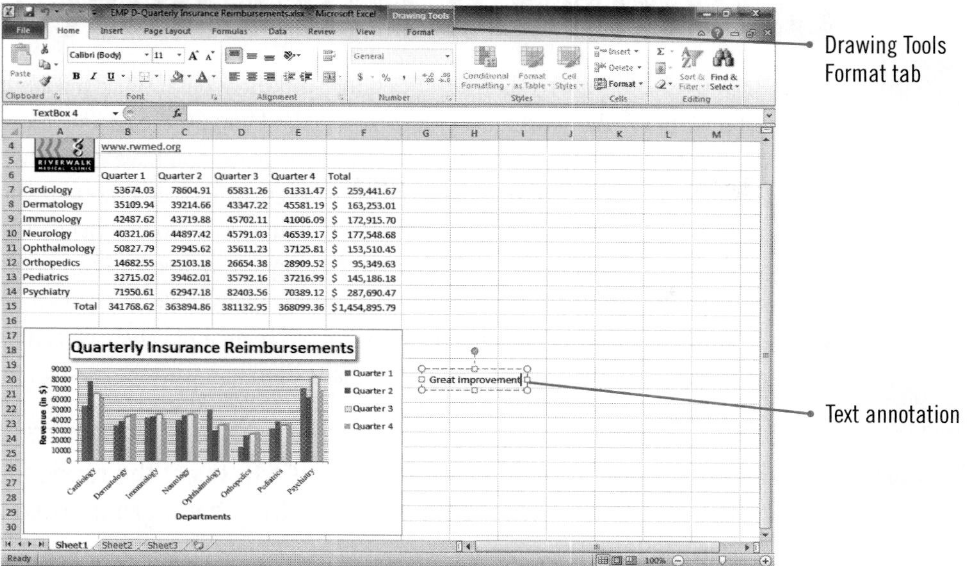

FIGURE D-19: **Text annotation on the chart**

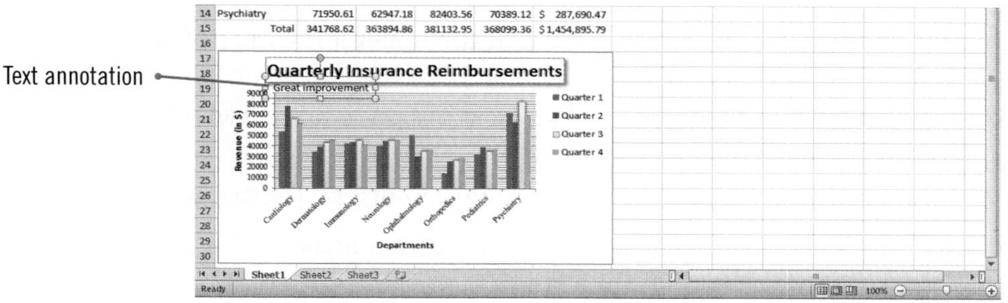

FIGURE D-20: **Arrow shape added to chart**

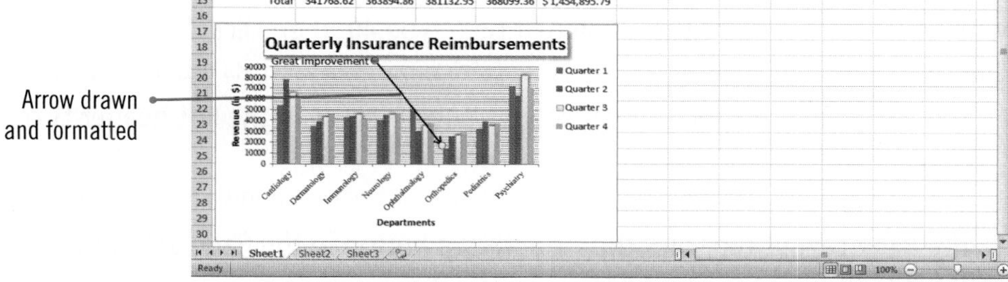

Excel 2010

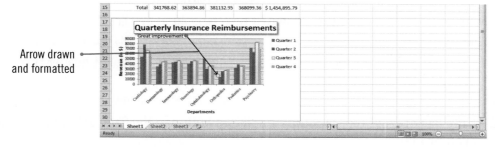

Adding SmartArt graphics

In addition to charts, annotations, and drawn objects, you can create a variety of diagrams using SmartArt graphics. **SmartArt graphics** are available in List, Process, Cycle, Hierarchy, Relationship, Matrix, and Pyramid categories. To insert SmartArt, click the SmartArt button in the Illustrations group on the Insert tab to open the Choose a SmartArt Graphic dialog box. Click a SmartArt category in the left pane, then click the layout for the graphic in the center pane. The right pane shows a sample of the selected SmartArt layout, as shown in Figure D-21. The SmartArt graphic appears in the worksheet as an embedded object with sizing handles. Click the Text Pane button on the SmartArt Tools Design tab to open a text pane next to the graphic; you can enter text into the graphic using the text pane or by typing directly in the shapes in the diagram.

FIGURE D-21: **Choose a SmartArt Graphic dialog box**

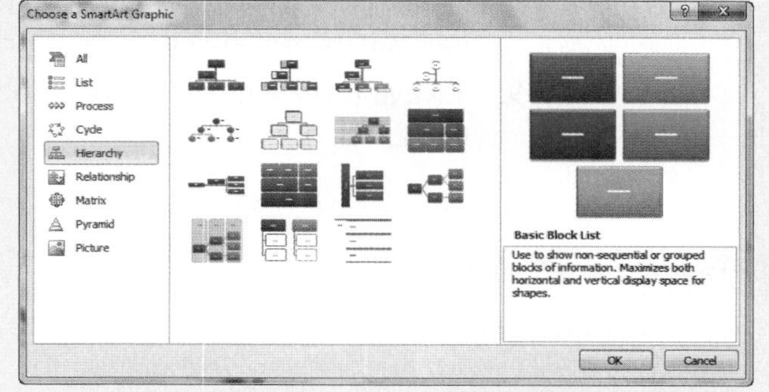

UNIT D
Excel 2010

Creating a Pie Chart

You can create multiple charts based on the same worksheet data. While a column chart may illustrate certain important aspects of your worksheet data, you may find you want to create an additional chart to emphasize a different point. Depending on the type of chart you create, you have additional options for calling attention to trends and patterns. For example, if you create a pie chart, you can emphasize one data point by **exploding**, or pulling that slice away from, the pie chart. When you're ready to print a chart, you can preview it just as you do a worksheet to check the output before committing it to paper. You can print a chart by itself or as part of the worksheet. At an upcoming meeting, Tony plans to discuss the total reimbursement revenue and which departments need improvement. You want to create a pie chart he can use to illustrate total revenue. Finally, you want to fit the worksheet and the charts onto one worksheet page.

STEPS

QUICK TIP
The Exploded pie in 3-D button creates a pie chart in which all slices are exploded.

1. **Select the range A7:A14, press and hold [Ctrl], select the range F7:F14, release [Ctrl], click the Insert tab, click the Pie button in the Charts group, then click Pie in 3-D in the Pie chart gallery**

   The new chart appears in the center of the worksheet. You can move the chart and quickly format it using a chart layout.

2. **Drag the chart so its upper-left corner is at the upper-left corner of cell G1, then click Layout 2 in the Chart Layouts group**

   The chart is repositioned on the page, and its layout changes so that a chart title is added and the legend appears just below the chart title.

TROUBLE
If the Format Data Series command appears on the shortcut menu instead of Format Data Point, double-click the slice you want to explode to make sure it is selected by itself, then right-click it again.

3. **Select the chart title text, then type Reimbursements, by Department**

4. **Click the slice for the Orthopedics data point, click it again so it is the only slice selected, right-click it, then click Format Data Point**

   The Format Data Point dialog box opens, as shown in Figure D-22.You can use the Point Explosion slider to control the distance a pie slice moves away from the pie, or you can type a value in the Point Explosion text box.

5. **Double-click 0 in the Point Explosion text box, type 40, then click Close**

   Compare your chart to Figure D-23. You decide to preview the chart and data before you print.

6. **Click cell A1, switch to Page Layout view, type your name in the left header text box, then click cell A1**

   You decide the chart and data would fit better on the page if they were printed in landscape orientation.

7. **Click the Page Layout tab, click the Orientation button in the Page Setup group, then click Landscape**

8. **Click the File tab, click Print on the navigation bar, click the No Scaling setting in the Settings section on the Print tab, then click Fit Sheet on One Page**

   The data and chart are positioned horizontally on a single page, as shown in Figure D-24. The printer you have selected may affect the appearance of your preview screen.

9. **Save and close the workbook, submit your work to your instructor as directed, then exit Excel**

Previewing a chart

To print or preview just a chart, select the chart (or make the chart sheet active), click the File tab, then click Print on the navigation bar. To reposition a chart by changing the page's margins, click the Show Margins button in the lower-right corner of the Print tab to display the margins in the preview. You can drag the margin lines to the exact settings you want; as the margins change, the size and placement of the chart on the page changes too.

FIGURE D-22: **Format Data Point dialog box**

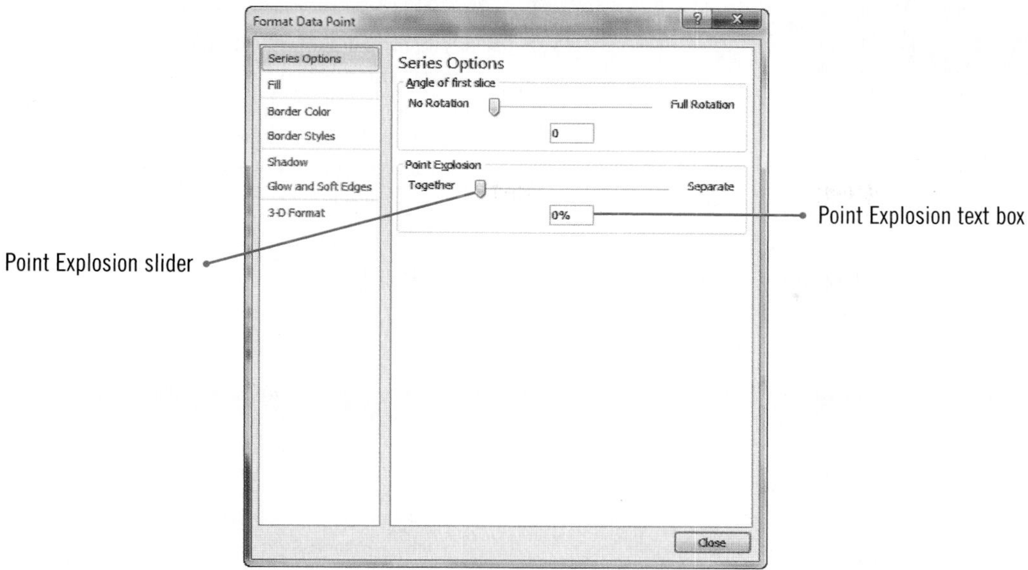

FIGURE D-23: **Exploded pie slice**

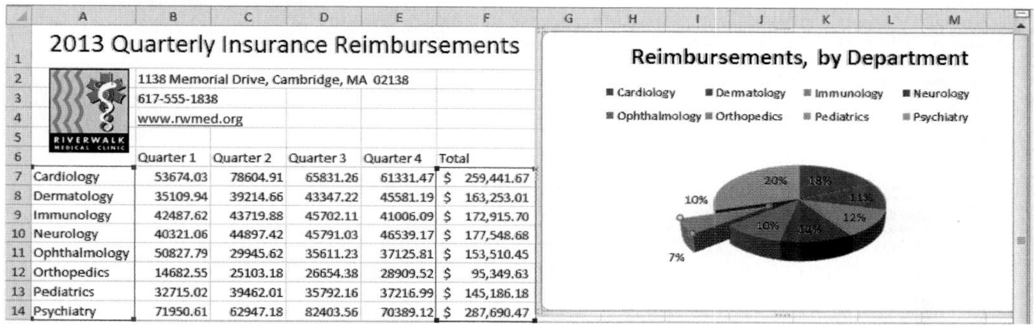

	A	B	C	D	E	F
1	2013 Quarterly Insurance Reimbursements					
2		1138 Memorial Drive, Cambridge, MA 02138				
3		617-555-1838				
4		www.rwmed.org				
5						
6		Quarter 1	Quarter 2	Quarter 3	Quarter 4	Total
7	Cardiology	53674.03	78604.91	65831.26	61331.47	$ 259,441.67
8	Dermatology	35109.94	39214.66	43347.22	45581.19	$ 163,253.01
9	Immunology	42487.62	43719.88	45702.11	41006.09	$ 172,915.70
10	Neurology	40321.06	44897.42	45791.03	46539.17	$ 177,548.68
11	Ophthalmology	50827.79	29945.62	35611.23	37125.81	$ 153,510.45
12	Orthopedics	14682.55	25103.18	26654.38	28909.52	$ 95,349.63
13	Pediatrics	32715.02	39462.01	35792.16	37216.99	$ 145,186.18
14	Psychiatry	71950.61	62947.18	82403.56	70389.12	$ 287,690.47

FIGURE D-24: **Preview of worksheet with charts in Backstage view**

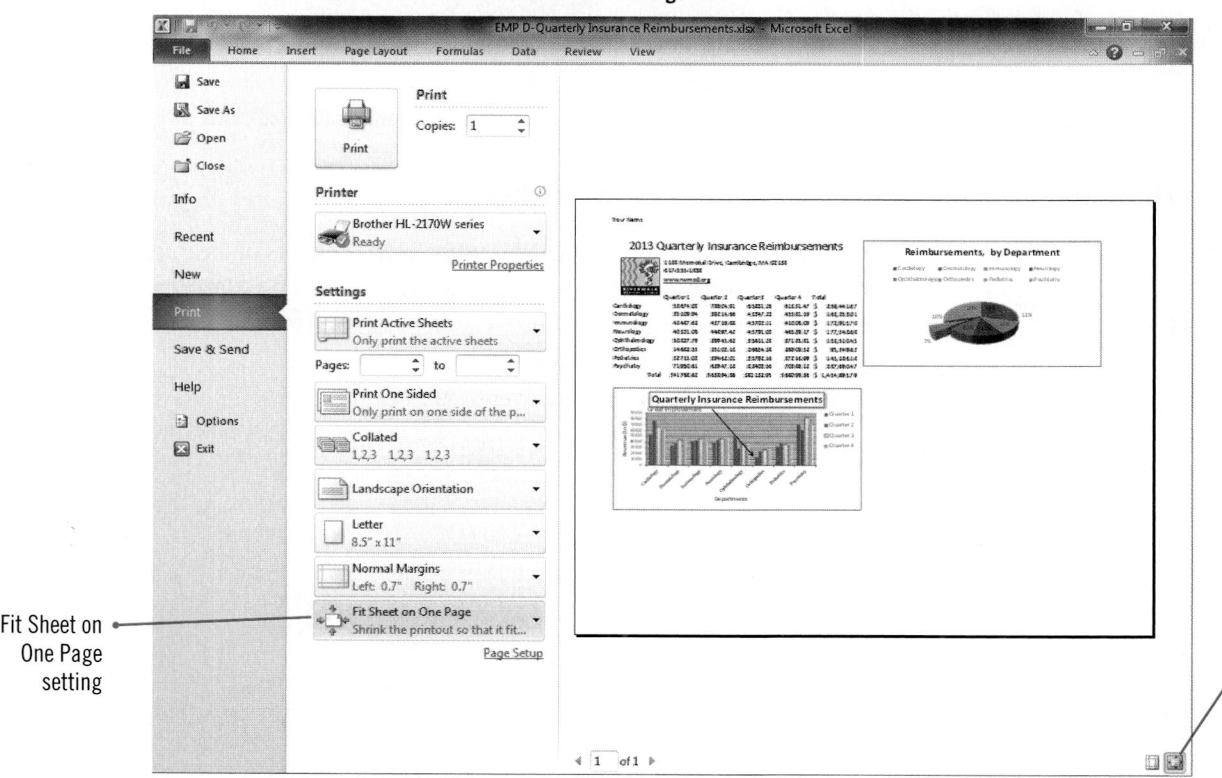

Practice

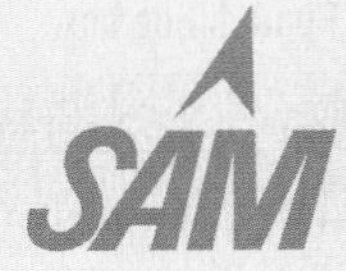

For current SAM information, including versions and content details, visit SAM Central (http://www.cengage.com/samcentral). If you have a SAM user profile, you may have access to hands-on instruction, practice, and assessment of the skills covered in this unit. Since various versions of SAM are supported throughout the life of this text, check with your instructor for the correct instructions and URL/Web site for accessing assignments.

Concepts Review

Label each element of the Excel chart shown in Figure D-25.

FIGURE D-25

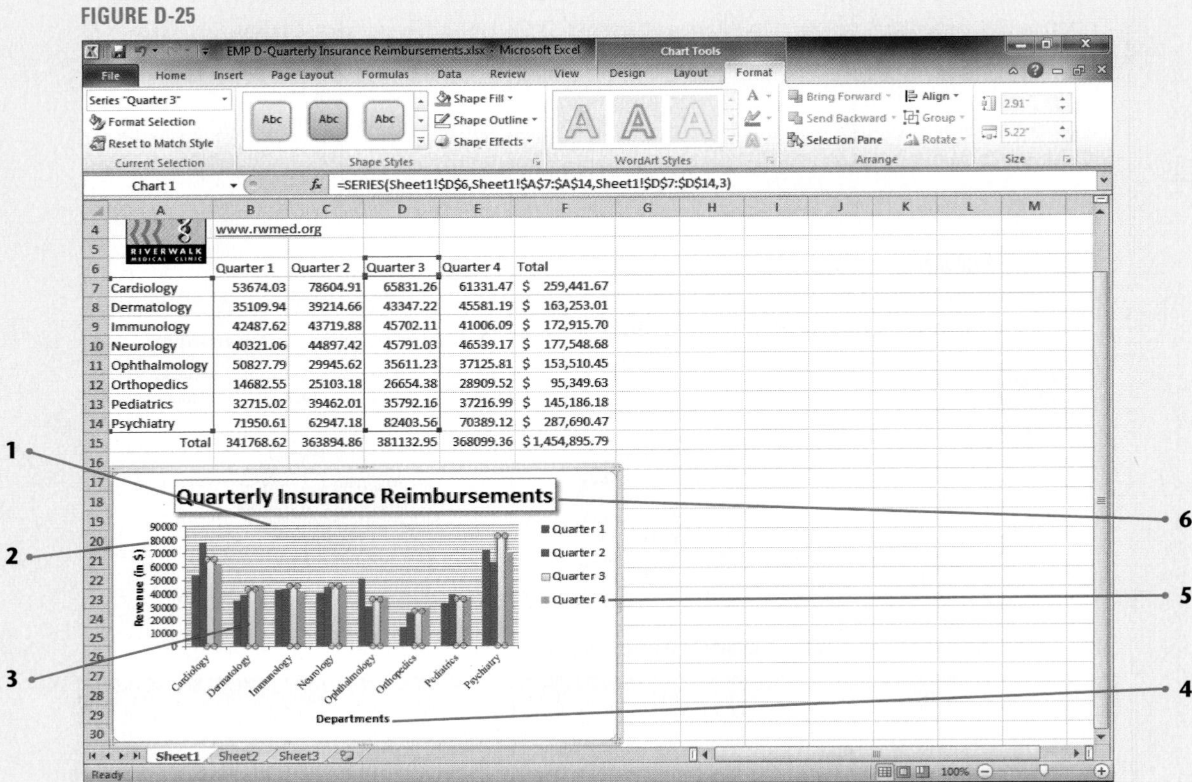

Match each chart type with the statement that best describes it.

7. **Column**
8. **Line**
9. **Combination**
10. **Pie**
11. **Area**

a. Displays a column and line chart using different scales of measurement
b. Compares trends over even time intervals
c. Compares data using columns
d. Compares data as parts of a whole
e. Shows how volume changes over time

Select the best answer from the list of choices.

12. Which pointer do you use to resize a chart?

a. +

b. I

c. ⇕

d. ✥

13. The object in a chart that identifies the colors used for each data series is a(n):

a. Data marker.

b. Data point.

c. Organizer.

d. Legend.

14. Which tab appears only when a chart is selected?

a. Insert

b. Chart Tools Format

c. Review

d. Page Layout

15. How do you move an embedded chart to a chart sheet?

a. Click a button on the Chart Tools Design tab.

b. Drag the chart to the sheet tab.

c. Delete the chart, switch to a different sheet, then create a new chart.

d. Use the Copy and Paste buttons on the Ribbon.

16. Which tab on the Ribbon do you use to create a chart?

a. Design

b. Insert

c. Page Layout

d. Format

17. A collection of related data points in a chart is called a:

a. Data series.

b. Data tick.

c. Cell address.

d. Value title.

Skills Review

1. Plan a chart.

a. Start Excel, open the Data File EMP D-2.xlsx from the drive and folder where you store your Data Files, then save it as **EMP D-Departmental Software Usage**.

b. Describe the type of chart you would use to plot this data.

c. What chart type would you use to compare the number of Excel users in each department?

2. Create a chart.

a. In the worksheet, select the range containing all the data and headings.

b. Click the Insert tab.

c. Create a Clustered Column chart, then add the chart title **Software Usage, by Department** above the chart.

d. Save your work.

3. Move and resize a chart.

a. Make sure the chart is still selected.

b. Move the chart beneath the worksheet data.

c. Widen the chart so it extends to the right edge of column H.

d. Use the Chart Tools Layout tab to move the legend below the charted data. (*Hint*: Click the Legend button, then click Show Legend at Bottom.)

e. Resize the chart so its bottom edge is at the top of row 25.

f. Save your work.

4. Change the chart design.

a. Change the value in cell B3 to **15**. Observe the change in the chart.

b. Select the chart.

c. Use the Chart Layouts group on the Chart Tools Design tab to apply the Layout 7 layout to the chart, then undo the change.

d. Use the Change Chart Type button on the Chart Tools Design tab to change the chart to a Clustered Bar chart.

e. Change the chart to a 3-D Clustered Column chart, then change it back to a Clustered Column chart.

f. Save your work.

Skills Review (continued)

5. **Change the chart layout.**
   a. Use the Chart Tools Layout tab to turn off the major horizontal gridlines in the chart.
   b. Change the font used in the horizontal and vertical axes labels to Times New Roman.
   c. Turn on the major gridlines for both the horizontal and vertical axes.
   d. Change the chart title's font to Times New Roman if necessary, with a font size of 20.
   e. Insert **Departments** as the horizontal axis title.
   f. Insert **Number of Users** as the vertical axis title.
   g. Change the font size of the horizontal and vertical axis titles to 10 and the font to Times New Roman, if necessary.
   h. Change "Personnel" in the worksheet column heading to **Human Resources**, then AutoFit column E.
   i. Change the font size of the legend to 14.
   j. Add a solid line border in the default color and an Offset Diagonal Bottom Right shadow to the chart title.
   k. Save your work.
6. **Format a chart.**
   a. Make sure the chart is selected, then select the Chart Tools Format tab, if necessary.
   b. Change the shape fill of the Excel data series to Dark Blue, Text 2.
   c. Change the shape style of the Excel data series to Subtle Effect Orange, Accent 6.
   d. Save your work.
7. **Annotate and draw on a chart.**
   a. Make sure the chart is selected, then create the text annotation **Needs more users**.
   b. Position the text annotation so the word "Needs" is just below the word "Software" in the chart title.
   c. Select the chart, then use the Chart Tools Layout tab to create a 1½ pt weight arrow that points from the bottom center of the text box to the Excel users in the Neurology department.
   d. Deselect the chart.
   e. Save your work.
8. **Create a pie chart.**
   a. Select the range A1:F2, then create a Pie in 3-D chart.
   b. Drag the 3-D pie chart beneath the existing chart.
   c. Change the chart title to **Excel Users**.
   d. Apply the Style 42 chart style to the chart.
   e. Explode the Human Resources slice from the pie chart at **25%**, then make cell A1 active.
   f. In Page Layout view, enter your name in the left section of the worksheet header.
   g. Preview the worksheet and charts in Backstage view, make sure all the contents fit on one page, then submit your work to your instructor as directed. When printed, the worksheet should look like Figure D-26.
   h. Save your work, close the workbook, then exit Excel.

FIGURE D-26

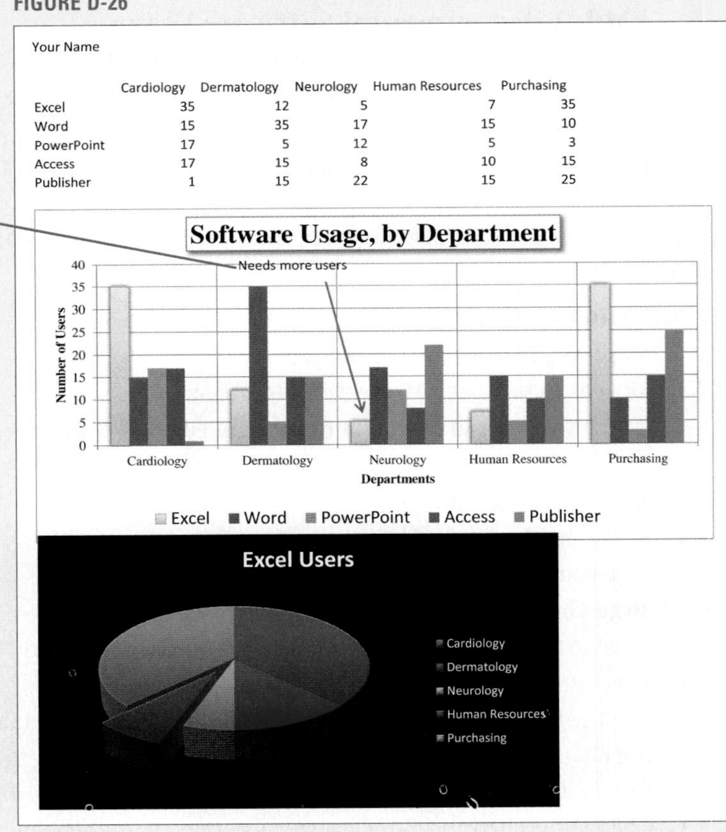

Your Name

	Cardiology	Dermatology	Neurology	Human Resources	Purchasing
Excel	35	12	5	7	35
Word	15	35	17	15	10
PowerPoint	17	5	12	5	3
Access	17	15	8	10	15
Publisher	1	15	22	15	25

The position of your annotation may vary.

Independent Challenge 1

You are the operations manager for the Springfield Medical Research Group in Massachusetts. Each year the group applies to various state and federal agencies for matching funds. For this year's funding proposal, you need to create charts to document the number of grants in previous years.

- **a.** Start Excel, open the file EMP D-3.xlsx from the drive and folder where you store your Data Files, then save it as **EMP D-Springfield Medical Research Group**.
- **b.** Take some time to plan your charts. Which type of chart or charts might best illustrate the information you need to display? What kind of chart enhancements do you want to use? Will a 3-D effect make your chart easier to understand?
- **c.** Create a Clustered Column chart for the data.
- **d.** Change at least one of the colors used in a data series.
- **e.** Make the appropriate modifications to the chart to make it visually attractive and easier to read and understand. Include a legend to the right of the chart, and add chart titles and horizontal and vertical axis titles using the text shown in Table D-3.

TABLE D-3

title	text
Chart title	Number of Research Grants
Vertical axis title	Numbers of Grants
Horizontal axis title	Departments

- **f.** Create at least two additional charts for the same data to show how different chart types display the same data. Reposition each new chart so that all charts are visible in the worksheet. One of the additional charts should be a pie chart; the other is up to you.
- **g.** Modify each new chart as necessary to improve its appearance and effectiveness. A sample worksheet containing three charts based on the worksheet data is shown in Figure D-27.
- **h.** Change the data in cell E3 from 2 to 5.
- **i.** Enter your name in the worksheet header.
- **j.** Save your work. Before printing, preview the worksheet in Backstage view, then adjust any settings as necessary so that all the worksheet data and charts print on a single page.
- **k.** Submit your work to your instructor as directed.
- **l.** Close the workbook, then exit Excel.

FIGURE D-27

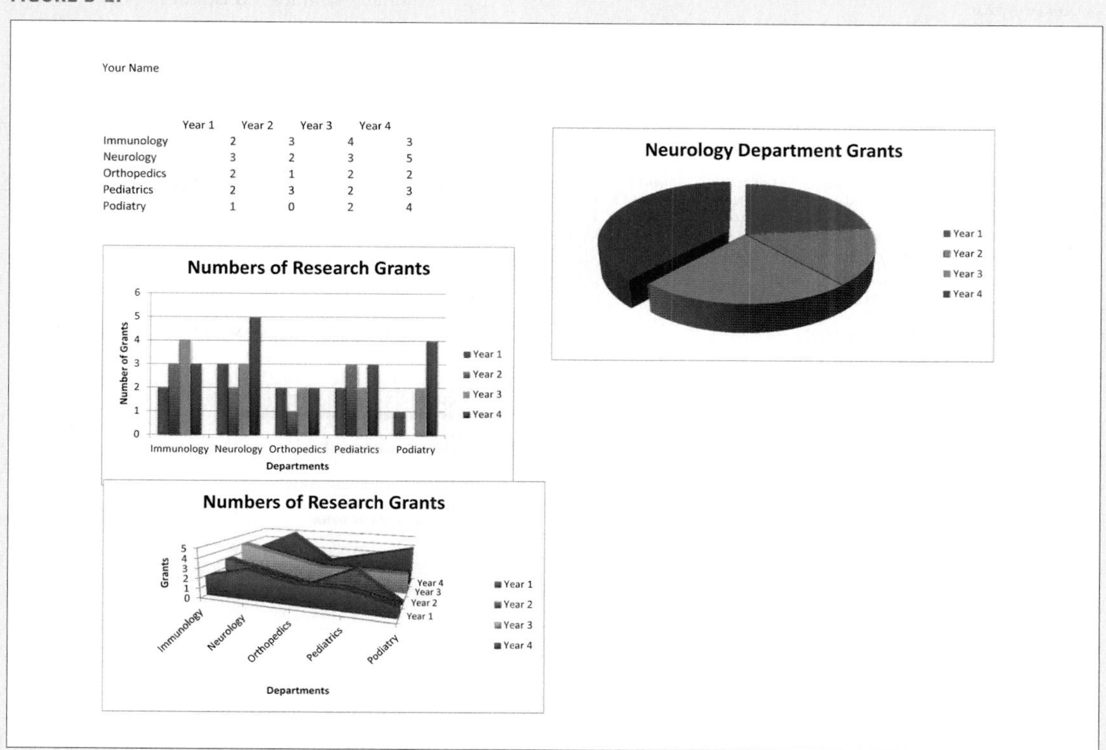

Independent Challenge 2

You work at Pinnacle Medical Consultants, a locally owned medical consortium. One of your responsibilities is to manage the company's revenues and expenses using Excel. Another is to convince the current staff that Excel can help them make daily operating decisions more easily and efficiently. To do this, you've decided to create charts using the previous year's operating expenses including rent, utilities, and payroll. The manager will use these charts at the next monthly meeting.

a. Start Excel, open the Data File EMP D-4.xlsx from the drive and folder where you store your Data Files, then save it as **EMP D-Pinnacle Medical Consultants.**

b. Decide which data in the worksheet should be charted. What chart types are best suited for the information you need to show? What kinds of chart enhancements are necessary?

c. Create a 3-D Clustered Column chart in the worksheet showing the expense data for all four quarters. (*Hint*: The expense categories should appear on the x-axis. Do not include the totals.)

d. Change the vertical axis labels (Expenses data) so that no decimals are displayed. (*Hint*: Right-click the axis labels you want to modify, click Format Axis, click the Number category in the Format Axis dialog box, change the number of decimal places, then click Close.)

e. Using the worksheet data, create two charts on this worksheet: one that analyzes expenses and one that analyzes revenues. (*Hint*: Move each chart to a new location on the worksheet, then deselect it before creating the next one.)

f. In one chart of the expense data, add data labels, then add chart titles as you see fit.

g. Make any necessary formatting changes to make the charts look more attractive, then enter your name in a worksheet cell.

h. Save your work.

i. Preview each chart in Backstage view, and adjust any items as needed. Fit the worksheet to a single page, then submit your work to your instructor as directed. A sample of a printed worksheet is shown in Figure D-28.

j. Close the workbook, then exit Excel.

FIGURE D-28

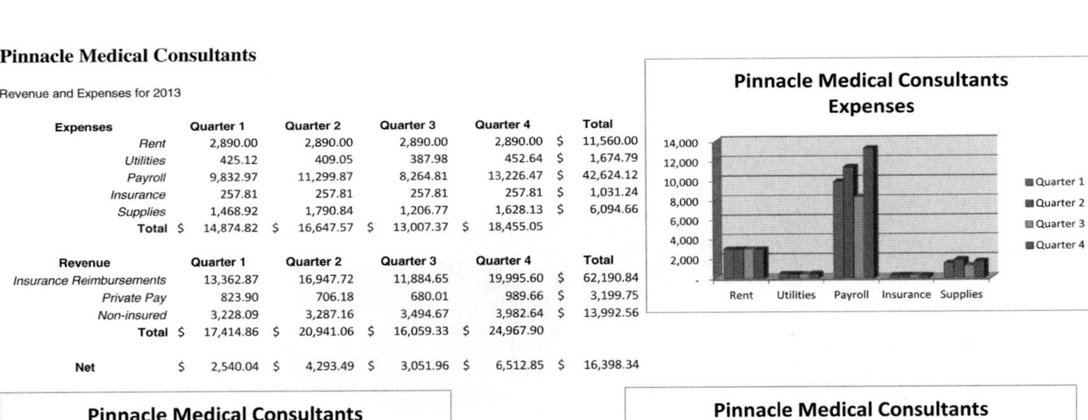

Pinnacle Medical Consultants

Revenue and Expenses for 2013

Expenses	Quarter 1	Quarter 2	Quarter 3	Quarter 4	Total
Rent	2,890.00	2,890.00	2,890.00	2,890.00	$ 11,560.00
Utilities	425.12	409.05	387.98	452.64	$ 1,674.79
Payroll	9,832.97	11,299.87	8,264.81	13,226.47	$ 42,624.12
Insurance	257.81	257.81	257.81	257.81	$ 1,031.24
Supplies	1,468.92	1,790.84	1,206.77	1,628.13	$ 6,094.66
Total	$ 14,874.82	$ 16,647.57	$ 13,007.37	$ 18,455.05	

Revenue	Quarter 1	Quarter 2	Quarter 3	Quarter 4	Total
Insurance Reimbursements	13,362.87	16,947.72	11,884.65	19,995.60	$ 62,190.84
Private Pay	823.90	706.18	680.01	989.66	$ 3,199.75
Non-insured	3,228.09	3,287.16	3,494.67	3,982.64	$ 13,992.56
Total	$ 17,414.86	$ 20,941.06	$ 16,059.33	$ 24,967.90	
Net	$ 2,540.04	$ 4,293.49	$ 3,051.96	$ 6,512.85	$ 16,398.34

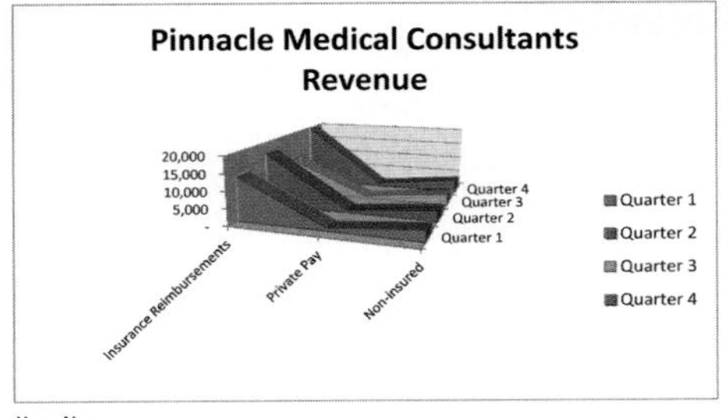

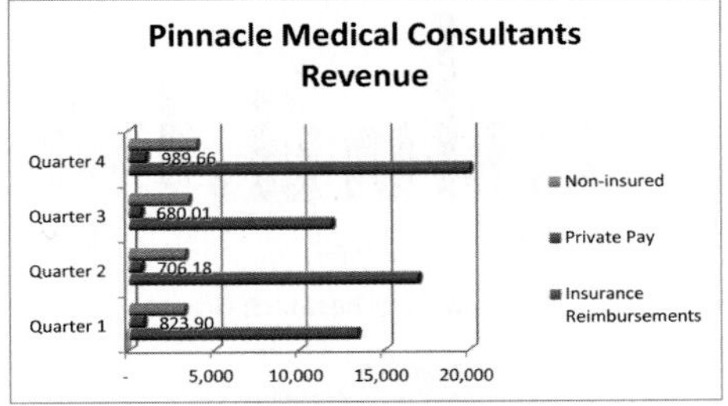

Your Name

Independent Challenge 3

You are reviewing expenses for the Bethesda Medical Hospital's operating room. The board of directors wants to examine the expenses incurred recently and has asked you to prepare charts that can be used in this evaluation. In particular, you want to see how dollar amounts compare among the different expenses, and you also want to see how expenses compare with each other proportionally to the total budget.

a. Start Excel, open the Data File EMP D-5.xlsx from the drive and folder where you store your Data Files, then save it as **EMP D-OR Expenses.**

b. Identify three types of charts that seem best suited to illustrate the data in the range A16:B24. What kinds of chart enhancements are necessary?

c. Create at least two different types of charts that show the distribution of operating room expenses. (*Hint*: Move each chart to a new location on the same worksheet.) One of the charts should be a 3-D pie chart.

d. In at least one of the charts, add annotated text and arrows highlighting important data, such as the largest expense.

e. Change the color of at least one data series in at least one of the charts.

f. Add chart titles and category and value axis titles where appropriate. Format the titles with a font of your choice. Apply a shadow to the chart title in at least one chart.

g. Add your name to a section of the header, then save your work.

h. Preview the worksheet in Backstage view. Adjust any items as needed. Be sure the charts are all visible on one page. Compare your work to the sample in Figure D-29.

Excel 2010

FIGURE D-29

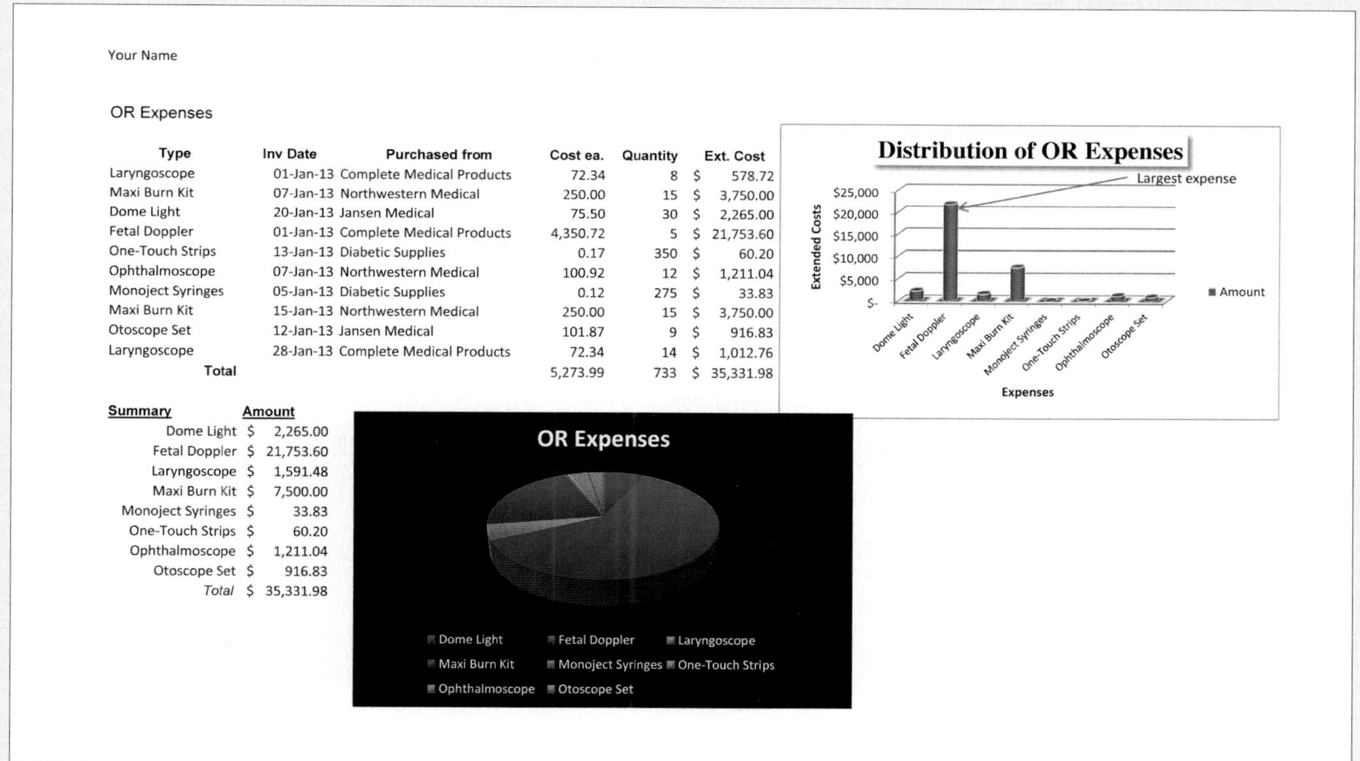
Your Name

OR Expenses

Type	Inv Date	Purchased from	Cost ea.	Quantity	Ext. Cost
Laryngoscope	01-Jan-13	Complete Medical Products	72.34	8	$ 578.72
Maxi Burn Kit	07-Jan-13	Northwestern Medical	250.00	15	$ 3,750.00
Dome Light	20-Jan-13	Jansen Medical	75.50	30	$ 2,265.00
Fetal Doppler	01-Jan-13	Complete Medical Products	4,350.72	5	$ 21,753.60
One-Touch Strips	13-Jan-13	Diabetic Supplies	0.17	350	$ 60.20
Ophthalmoscope	07-Jan-13	Northwestern Medical	100.92	12	$ 1,211.04
Monoject Syringes	05-Jan-13	Diabetic Supplies	0.12	275	$ 33.83
Maxi Burn Kit	15-Jan-13	Northwestern Medical	250.00	15	$ 3,750.00
Otoscope Set	12-Jan-13	Jansen Medical	101.87	9	$ 916.83
Laryngoscope	28-Jan-13	Complete Medical Products	72.34	14	$ 1,012.76
Total			5,273.99	733	$ 35,331.98

Summary	Amount
Dome Light	$ 2,265.00
Fetal Doppler	$ 21,753.60
Laryngoscope	$ 1,591.48
Maxi Burn Kit	$ 7,500.00
Monoject Syringes	$ 33.83
One-Touch Strips	$ 60.20
Ophthalmoscope	$ 1,211.04
Otoscope Set	$ 916.83
Total	$ 35,331.98

Independent Challenge 3 (continued)

Advanced Challenge Exercise

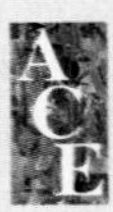

- Explode a slice from the 3-D pie chart.
- Add a data label to the exploded pie slice.
- Change the number format of the data label in the pie chart so no decimals are displayed.
- Save your work, then preview it in Backstage view.

i. Submit your work to your instructor as directed, close the workbook, then exit Excel.

Real Life Independent Challenge

This project requires an Internet connection.

You are so indispensable in your role as financial manager at the Good Health Clinic that the company wants to move you and your family to its new location, which you get to choose. You have a good idea where you'd like to live, and you decide to use the Web to find out more about houses that are currently available.

a. Start Excel, then save a new, blank workbook as **EMP D-My Dream House** to the drive and folder where you save your Data Files.

b. Decide on where you would like to live, and use your favorite search engine to find information sources on homes for sale in that area. (*Hint*: Try using realtor.com or other realtor-sponsored sites.)

c. Determine a price range and features within the home. Find data for at least five homes that meet your location and price requirements, and enter them in the worksheet. See Table D-4 below for a suggested data layout.

TABLE D-4

suggested data layout					
Location					
Price range					
	House 1	House 2	House 3	House 4	House 5
Asking price					
Bedrooms					
Bathrooms					
Year built					
Size (in sq. ft.)					

Real Life Independent Challenge (continued)

d. Format the data so it looks attractive and professional.

e. Create any type of column chart using only the House and Asking Price data. Place it on the same worksheet as the data. Include a descriptive title.

f. Change the colors in the chart using the chart style of your choice.

g. Enter your name in a section of the header.

h. Save the workbook. Preview the worksheet in Backstage view and make adjustments if necessary to fit all of the information on one page. See Figure D-30 for an example of what your worksheet might look like.

i. Submit your work to your instructor as directed.

Advanced Challenge Exercise

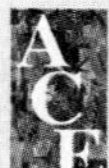

- Change the chart type to a Clustered Column chart.
- Change the data used for the chart to include the size data in cells A9:F9.
- Create a combination chart that plots the asking price on one axis and the size of the home on the other axis. (*Hint*: Use Help to get tips on how to chart with a secondary axis.)

j. Close the workbook, then exit Excel.

FIGURE D-30

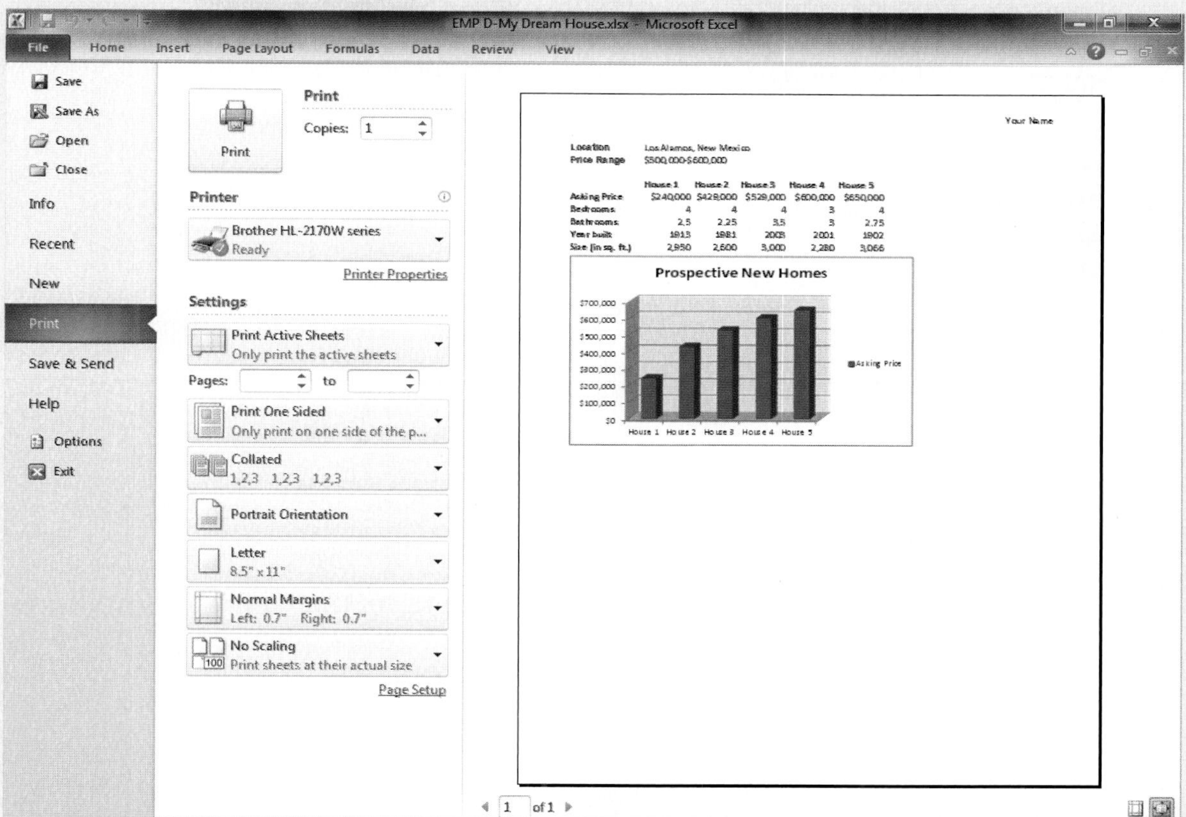

Visual Workshop

Open the Data File EMP D-6.xlsx from the drive and folder where you store your Data Files, then save it as **EMP D-Projected Diagnostics Laboratory Revenue**. Format the worksheet data so it looks like Figure D-31, then create and modify two charts to match the ones shown in the figure. You will need to make formatting, layout, and design changes once you create the charts. (Hint: The shadow used in the 3-D pie chart title is made using the Outer Offset Diagonal Bottom Right shadow.) Enter your name in the left text box of the header, then save and preview the worksheet. Submit your work to your instructor as directed, then close the workbook and exit Excel.

FIGURE D-31

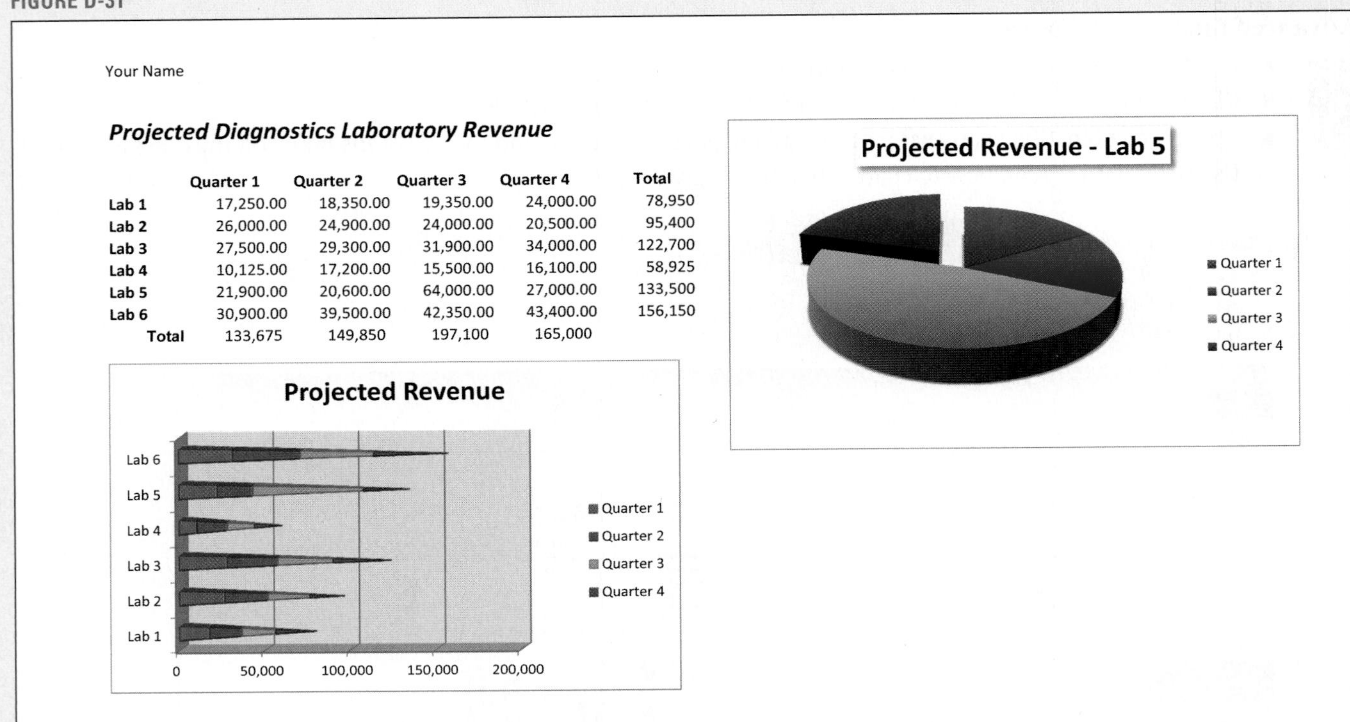

Your Name

Projected Diagnostics Laboratory Revenue

	Quarter 1	Quarter 2	Quarter 3	Quarter 4	Total
Lab 1	17,250.00	18,350.00	19,350.00	24,000.00	78,950
Lab 2	26,000.00	24,900.00	24,000.00	20,500.00	95,400
Lab 3	27,500.00	29,300.00	31,900.00	34,000.00	122,700
Lab 4	10,125.00	17,200.00	15,500.00	16,100.00	58,925
Lab 5	21,900.00	20,600.00	64,000.00	27,000.00	133,500
Lab 6	30,900.00	39,500.00	42,350.00	43,400.00	156,150
Total	133,675	149,850	197,100	165,000	

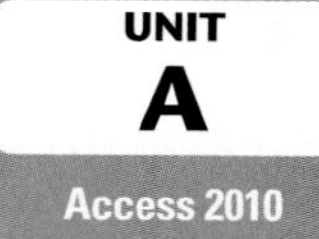

Getting Started with Access 2010

Files You Will Need:

AMP A-A1.accdb
AMP A-A2.accdb
AMP A-A3.accdb
AMP A-A4.accdb

In this unit, you will learn the purpose, advantages, and terminology of Microsoft Access 2010, the relational database program in the Microsoft Office 2010 suite of software. You will create and relate tables, the basic building blocks of an Access relational database. You'll also navigate, enter, update, preview, and print data. Tony Sanchez, R.N. and office manager for Riverwalk Medical Clinic, a large family practice clinic, has hired you to use Access to help enter, store, maintain, and analyze patient information. His ultimate goal is to use Access to create an electronic medical record to maintain patient information in one easy-to-use location.

OBJECTIVES

- Understand relational databases
- Explore a database
- Create a database
- Create a table
- Create primary keys
- Relate two tables
- Enter data
- Edit data

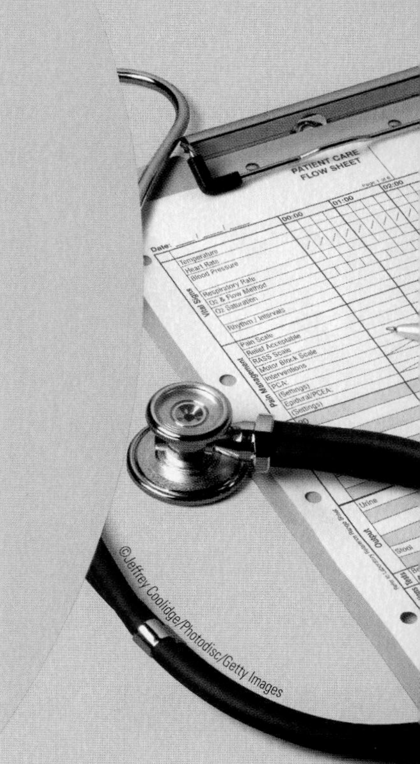

©Jeffrey Coolidge/Photodisc/Getty Images

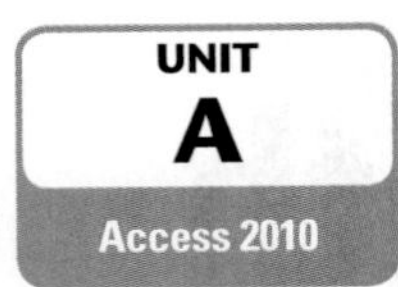

Understanding Relational Databases

Microsoft Access 2010 is relational database software that runs on the Windows operating system. You use **relational database software** to manage data that is organized into lists, such as information about patients, medical procedures, medical diagnosis codes, medicines, employees, doctors, or insurance. Many small clinics and medical companies track some of this information in a spreadsheet program such as Microsoft Excel. Although Excel offers some list management features, Access provides many more tools and advantages for managing large lists of data. The advantages are mainly due to the "relational" nature of the lists that Access manages. Table A-1 compares the two programs. You and Tony Sanchez review the advantages of database software over spreadsheets for managing lists of information.

DETAILS

The advantages of using Access for database management include:

- **Duplicate data is minimized**
  Figures A-1 and A-2 compare how you might store sales data in a single Excel spreadsheet list versus three related Access tables. With Access, you do not have to reenter information such as a patient's name and date of birth or doctor name every time the patient visits the clinic, because lists can be linked, or "related," in relational database software.
- **Information is more accurate, reliable, and consistent because duplicate data is minimized**
  The relational nature of data stored in an Access database allows you to minimize duplicate data entry, which creates more accurate, reliable, and consistent information. For example, patient data in a Patients table is entered only once, not every time a patient seeks medical help at the clinic.
- **Data entry is faster and easier using Access forms**
  Data entry forms (screen layouts) make data entry faster, easier, and more accurate than entering data in a spreadsheet.
- **Information can be viewed and sorted in many ways using Access queries, forms, and reports**
  In Access, you can save queries (questions about the data such as a list of patients with a particular diagnosis or a list of patients who have seen a given doctor during a given time period), data entry forms, and reports, allowing you to use them over and over without performing extra work to recreate a particular view of the data.
- **Information is more secure using Access passwords and security features**
  Access databases can be encrypted and password protected.
- **Several users can share and edit information at the same time**
  Unlike spreadsheets or word-processing documents, more than one person can enter, update, and analyze data in an Access database at the same time.

FIGURE A-1: Using a spreadsheet to organize patient data

Patient information is duplicated each time that patient visits the clinic

	A	B	C	D	E	F	G
1	PtLastName	PtFirstName	DOB	DateofService	DiagDescription	DrLastName	DrFirstName
2	Clark	Beth	8/6/75	5/9/11	Pain in limb	Zimmerman	Carla
3	Clark	Beth	8/6/75	6/8/11	Sunburn	Zimmerman	Carla
4	Clark	Kelsey	4/4/89	8/4/11	Pain in limb	Nguyen	Lan
5	Clark	Kelsey	4/4/89	5/4/11	Knee meniscus injury,	Nguyen	Lan
6	Color	Arnold	1/6/72	5/16/11	Sinusitis, acute, NOS	Rosenbaum	Anna
7	Creek	Lynn	7/8/71	4/12/11	Hypertension, benign	Rosenbaum	Anna
8	Czerski	Sven	7/16/61	6/2/11	Drug withdrawal	Rosenbaum	Anna
9	Czerski	Sven	7/16/61	7/12/11	Psychosis, unspec.	Rosenbaum	Anna
10	Czerski	Sven	7/16/61	5/2/11	Plantar fasciitis	Rosenbaum	Anna
11	Daniels	Hector	9/8/57	5/10/11	Hemorrhoids, NOS	Quinn	Forrest
12	Dao	Chin	8/1/49	5/21/11	Bronchitis, acute	Patrick	Jeffery
13	Dao	Chin	8/1/49	5/21/11	Hypoglycemia, diabetes I	Patrick	Jeffery
14	Darci	Daniel	1/5/83	6/8/11	Sprain/strain: neck,	Zimmerman	Carla
15	Darci	Daniel	1/5/83	5/7/11	Hypoglycemia, diabetes I	Zimmerman	Carla

Doctor information is duplicated for each patient visit

FIGURE A-2: Using a relational database to organize patient data

Patients table

Patient ID	PtLastName	PtFirstName	DOB
1	Clark	Beth	08/06/1975
2	Clark	Kelsey	04/04/1989
3	Color	Arnold	01/06/1972
4	Creek	Lynn	07/08/1971

Visits table

Patient ID	DrCode	DateOfService	Diagnosis
1	CJZ	05/09/11	Pain in limb
2	LN	05/04/11	Knee meniscus injury
3	AWR	05/16/11	Sinusitis, acute

Doctors table

DrCode	DrFirstName	DrMiddleName	DrLastName	DrDegree
CJZ	Carla	J	Zimmerman	MD
LN	Lan		Nguyen	MD
AWR	Anna	Wolf	Rosenbaum	MD

TABLE A-1: Comparing Excel to Access

feature	Excel	Access
Layout	Provides a natural tabular layout for easy data entry	Provides a natural tabular layout as well as the ability to create customized data entry screens called forms
Storage	Restricted to a file's limitations	Virtually unlimited when coupled with the ability to use Microsoft SQL Server to store data
Linked tables	Manages single lists of information—no relational database capabilities	Relates lists of information to reduce data redundancy and create a relational database
Reporting	Limited	Provides the ability to create an unlimited number of reports
Security	Limited to file security options such as marking the file "read-only" or protecting a range of cells	When used with SQL Server, provides extensive security down to the user and data level
Multiuser capabilities	Not allowed	Allows multiple users to simultaneously enter and update data
Data entry	Provides limited data entry screens	Provides the ability to create an unlimited number of data entry forms

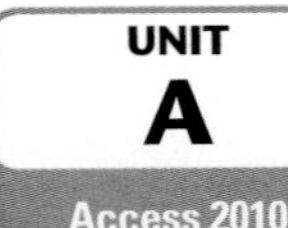

Exploring a Database

You can start Access from the Start menu, from an Access shortcut icon, from a pinned program on the taskbar, or by double-clicking an Access database file on your computer. When you start the Access program from the Start menu, Access displays a window that allows you to open an existing database or create a new one from a template or as a blank database. Tony Sanchez has developed an Access database to start building an electronic medical record for each patient. He asks you to familiarize yourself with the database.

STEPS

1. **Start Access from the Start menu**
   Access starts, as shown in Figure A-3. This window helps you open an existing database, create a new database from a template, or create a new blank database. At this point, if you click the Home, Create, External Data, or Database Tools tabs, no options would be available because Access is running, but no database is open.

TROUBLE
If a yellow Security Warning bar appears below the Ribbon, click Enable Content.

2. **Click the Open button, navigate to the drive and folder where you store your Data Files, click the AMP A-A1.accdb database file, click Open, click the File tab, click Save Database As, type AMP A-Riverwalk in the File name box, click Save, then click Enable Content if prompted**
   The AMP A-Riverwalk.accdb database opens and contains six tables of data named Diagnosis, Doctors, Insurance, Patients, ProcedureCodes, and Visits. It also contains four queries, two forms, and one report. Each of these items (table, query, form, and report) is a different type of **object** in an Access database and is displayed in the **Navigation Pane**. The purpose of each object is defined in Table A-2. To learn about an Access database, you explore its objects.

TROUBLE
If the Navigation Pane is not open, click the Shutter Bar Open/Close button « to open it and view the database objects.

3. **In the Navigation Pane, double-click the Doctors table to open it, double-click the Insurance table to open it, then double-click the Patients table to open it**
   The Doctors, Insurance, and Patients tables open to display the data they store. A **table** is the fundamental building block of a relational database because it stores all of the data.

4. **In the Navigation Pane, double-click the InsuranceCharges query to open it, select any occurrence of Cross in "Blue Cross", type Shield, then click any other row**
   A **query** selects a subset of data from one or more tables. In this case, the InsuranceCharges query selects data from the Patients, Visits, and Insurance tables. Editing data in one object changes it in every other object of the database, which demonstrates the power and productivity of a relational database.

5. **Double-click the ElectronicMedicalRecord form to open it, type Sharon to replace Mildred in the First Name box, then click the Close button at the bottom of the form to close the form**
   An Access **form** is a data entry screen. Users prefer forms for data entry rather than tables and queries because the information can be presented in an easy-to-use layout. Changes to data are automatically saved as you move around the database.

6. **Double-click the Patients report to open it**
   An Access **report** is a professional printout. A report is for printing purposes only, not data entry. As shown in Figure A-4, changing Mildred's name to Sharon in the form automatically updated the report as well.

7. **Click the File tab, then click Exit**
   Exiting Access closes the database on which you are working. If you made any changes to the database that should be saved, Access would remind you to do so before closing.

FIGURE A-3: **Opening Microsoft Access 2010 window**

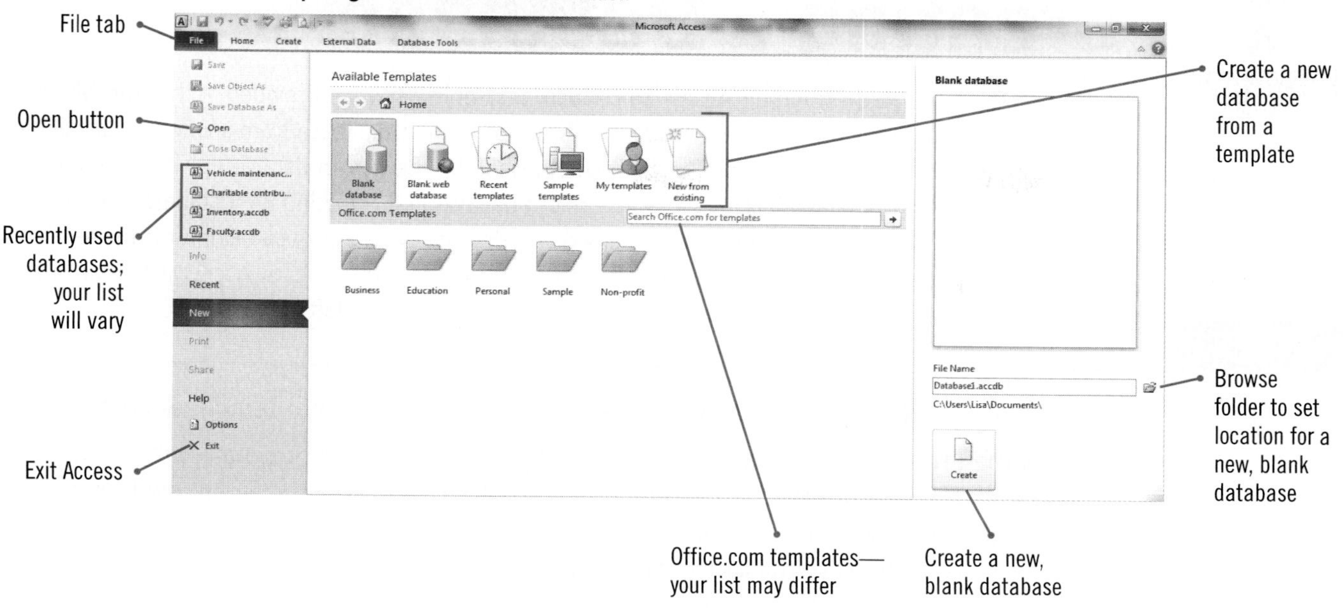

FIGURE A-4: **Objects in the AMP A-Riverwalk database**

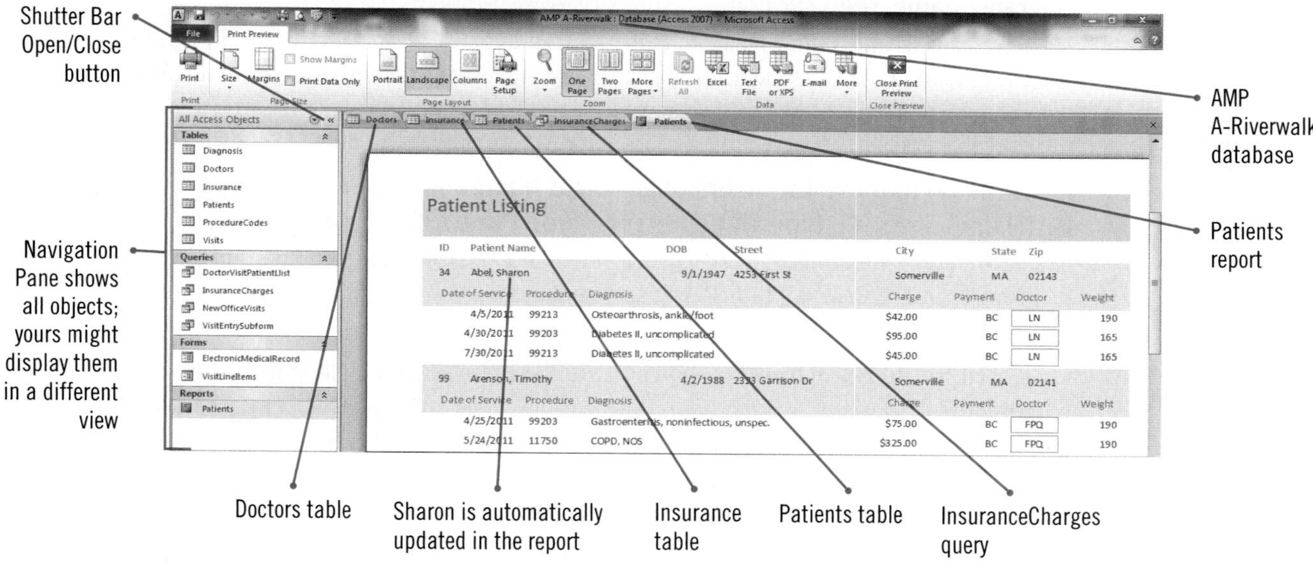

TABLE A-2: **Access objects and their purpose**

object	Navigation Pane icon	purpose
Table		Contains all of the raw data within the database in a spreadsheet-like view; tables are linked with a common field to create a relational database, which minimizes redundant data
Query		Allows you to select a subset of fields or records from one or more tables; queries are created when you have a question about the data
Form		Provides an easy-to-use data entry screen
Report		Provides a professional printout of data that can contain enhancements such as headers, footers, graphics, and calculations on groups of records

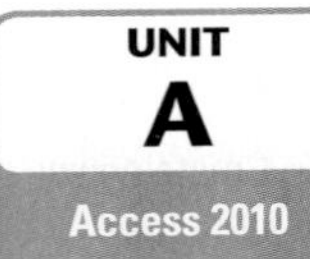
UNIT A
Access 2010

Creating a Database

You can create a database using an Access **template**, a sample database provided within the Microsoft Access program, or you can start with a blank database to create a database from scratch. Your decision depends on whether Access has a template that closely resembles the type of data you plan to manage. If it does, building your own database from a template might be faster than creating the database from scratch. Regardless of which method you use, you can always modify the database later, tailoring it to meet your specific needs. Tony Sanchez reasons that the best way for you to learn Access is to start a new database from scratch, so he asks you to create a database that will track staff information.

STEPS

1. **Start Access, then click the Blank database button in the Available Templates area**
2. **Click the Browse folder button to the right of the File Name box, navigate to the drive and folder where you store your Data Files, type AMP A-Staff in the File name box, click OK, then click the Create button**

   A new, blank database file with a single table named Table1 is created, as shown in Figure A-5. While you might be tempted to start entering data into the table, a better way to build a table is to first define the columns, or **fields**, of data that the table will store. **Table Design View** provides the most options for defining fields.
3. **Click the View button on the Fields tab to switch to Design View, type Employees as the table name, then click OK**

   The table name changes from Table1 to Employees, and you are positioned in Table Design View, a window you use to name and define the fields of a table. Access created a field named ID with an AutoNumber data type. The **data type** is a significant characteristic of a field because it determines what type of data the field can store, such as text, dates, or numbers. See Table A-3 for more information about data types.
4. **Press the [↓] to move to the first blank Field Name cell, type FirstName, press [↓], type LastName, press [↓], type Title, press [↓], type DateOfBirth, then press [↓]**

   Be sure to separate first and last names in all tables so that you can easily sort, find, and filter on either part of the name later. The DateOfBirth field will only contain dates, so you should change its data type from Text (the default data type) to Date/Time.
5. **Click Text in the DateOfBirth row, click the list arrow, then click Date/Time**

   With these five fields properly defined for the new Employees table, as shown in Figure A-6, you're ready to enter data. You switch back to Datasheet View to enter or edit data. **Datasheet View** is a spreadsheet-like view of the data in a table. A **datasheet** is a grid that displays fields as columns and records as rows. The new **field names** you just defined are listed at the top of each column.
6. **Click the View button to switch to Datasheet View, click Yes when prompted to save the table, press [Tab] to move to the FirstName field, type your first name, press [Tab] to move to the LastName field, type your last name, press [Tab] to move to the Title field, type RN, press [Tab], type 1/32/80, then press [Tab]**

   Because 1/32/80 is not a valid date, Access does not allow you to make that entry and displays an error message, as shown in Figure A-7. This shows that setting the best data type for each field before entering data helps prevent data entry errors.
7. **Edit the DateOfBirth entry for the first record to 1/31/80, press [Tab], enter two more sample records containing reasonable data, right-click the Employees table tab, then click Close to close the Employees table**

TROUBLE

Tab through the ID field rather than typing a value. The ID value automatically increments to the next number.

FIGURE A-5: **Creating a database with a new table**

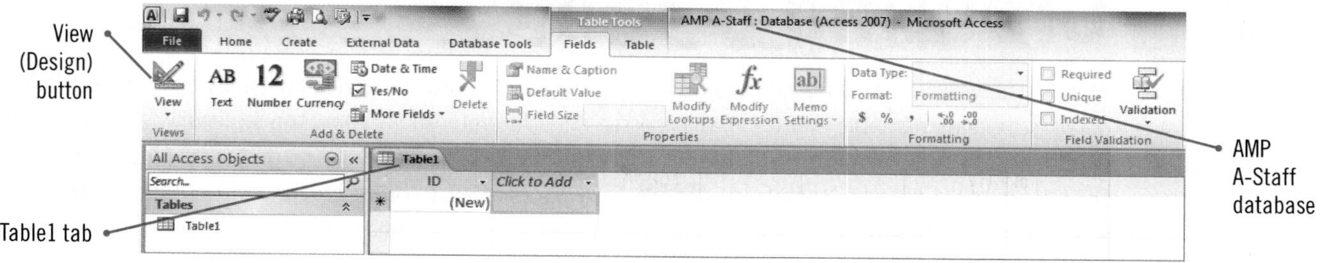

FIGURE A-6: **Defining field names and data types for the Employees table in Table Design View**

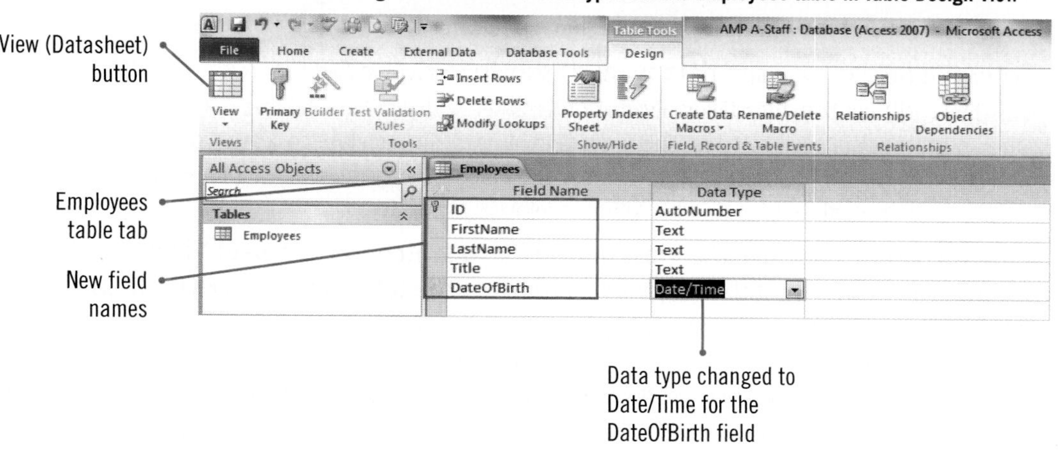

FIGURE A-7: **Entering your first record in the Employees table**

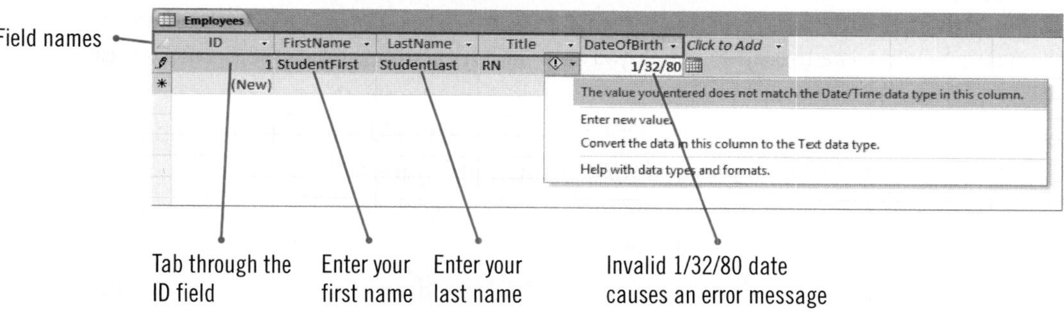

TABLE A-3: **Data types**

data type	description of data
Text	Text or numbers not used in calculations such as a name, zip code, or phone number
Memo	Lengthy text greater than 255 characters, such as comments or notes
Number	Numeric data that can be used in calculations, such as quantities
Date/Time	Dates and times
Currency	Monetary values
AutoNumber	Sequential integers controlled by Access
Yes/No	Only two values: Yes or No
Attachment	External files such as .jpg images, spreadsheets, and documents
Hyperlink	Web and e-mail addresses

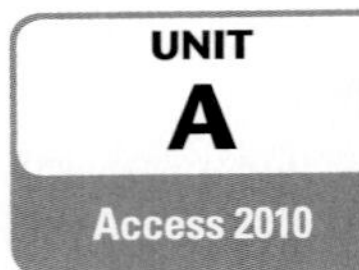

Creating a Table

After creating your database and first table, you need to create new, related tables to build a relational database. Creating a table consists of these essential tasks: determining how the table will participate in the relational database, naming the table, meaningful naming of each field in the table, and selecting an appropriate data type for each field. Tony Sanchez asks you to create another table to store staff evaluations. The new table will be related to the Employees table so each evaluation is linked to the correct employee.

STEPS

1. **Click the Create tab on the Ribbon, then click the Table Design button in the Tables group**

   Design View is a view in which you create and manipulate the structure of an object.

2. **Enter the field names and data types as shown in Figure A-8**

   This table will contain four fields. EvaluationID is set with an AutoNumber data type so each record is automatically numbered by Access. The Notes field has a Memo data type so a large comment can be recorded. EvaluationDate is a Date/Time field to identify the date of the evaluation. EmployeeID has a Number data type and will be used to link this table to the Employees table later.

3. **Click the Home tab, click the View button to switch to Datasheet View, click Yes when prompted to save the table, type Evaluations as the table name, click OK, then click No when prompted to create a primary key**

   A **primary key field** contains unique data for each record. You'll identify a primary key field for the Evaluations table later. For now, you'll enter the first record in the Evaluations table in Datasheet View. A **record** is a row of data in a table. Refer to Table A-4 for a summary of important database terminology.

4. **Press [Tab] to move to the Notes field, type Punctual, courteous and accurate, press [Tab], type 1/22/13 in the EvaluationDate field, press [Tab], then type 1 in the EmployeeID field**

   You entered 1 in the EmployeeID field to connect this comment with the employee in the Employees table that has an ID field value of 1. Knowing which EmployeeID value to enter for each comment is difficult. After you properly relate the tables (a task you have not yet performed), Access can make it easier to associate employees and evaluations.

5. **Point to the column separator line between each field name, then double-click the ✛ to widen each column to see all data as shown in Figure A-9**

   You also resize columns in Access by dragging the ✛ when pointing to a **column separator line**, the thin black line that separates each field name.

6. **Right-click the Evaluations table tab, click Close, then click Yes to save changes to the layout of the table**

Creating a table in Datasheet View

In Access 2010, you can create a new table in *Datasheet View* using commands on the Fields tab of the Ribbon. Entering data in Datasheet View *before* finishing field design activities can introduce a wide variety of data entry errors, such as entering textual data in what should be defined as a Number or Date/Time field. If you design your tables using *Table Design View*, you avoid the temptation of entering data before you finish defining fields, which helps minimize many types of common data entry errors.

FIGURE A-8: Creating the Evaluations table

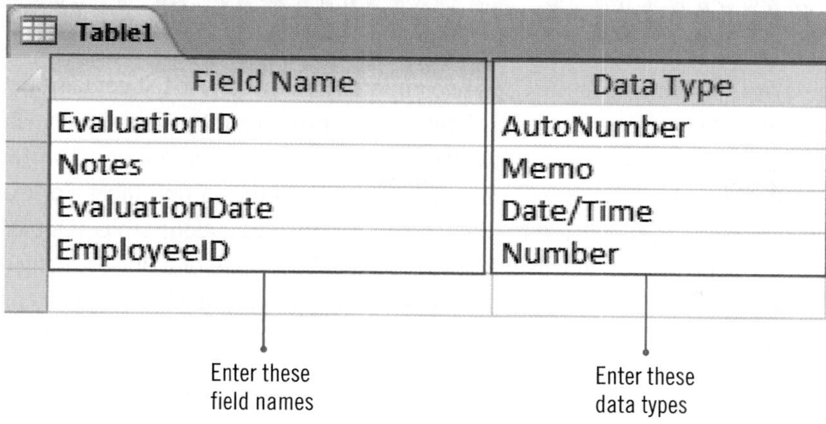

FIGURE A-9: Entering the first record in the Evaluations table

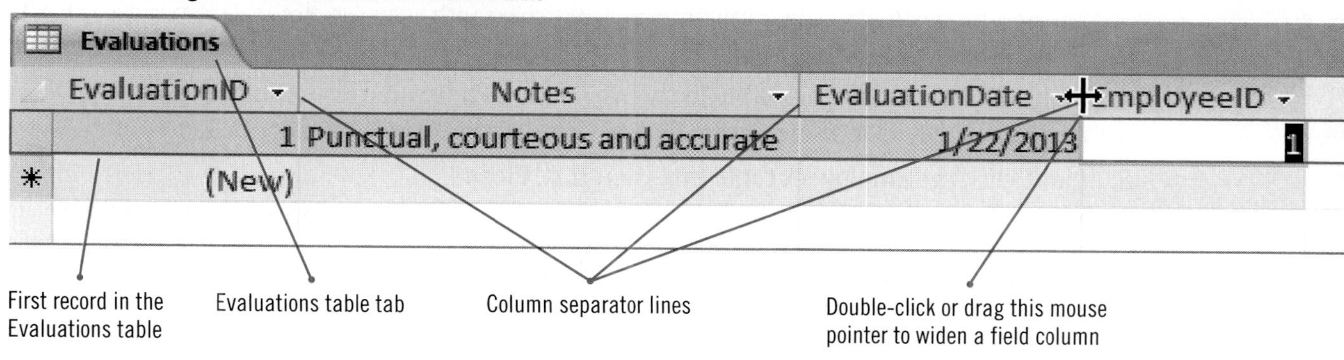

TABLE A-4: Important database terminology

term	description
Field	A specific piece or category of data such as a first name, last name, city, state, or phone number
Record	A group of related fields that describes a person, place, thing, or transaction such as a patient, prescription, physician, or diagnosis
Key field	A field that contains unique information for each record, such as a patient number for a patient
Table	A collection of records for a single subject such as Patients, Doctors, or Insurance
Relational database	Multiple tables that are linked together to address a business process such as creating an electronic medical record at Riverwalk Medical Clinic
Objects	The parts of an Access database that help you view, edit, manage, and analyze the data: **tables**, **queries**, **forms**, **reports**, **macros**, and **modules**

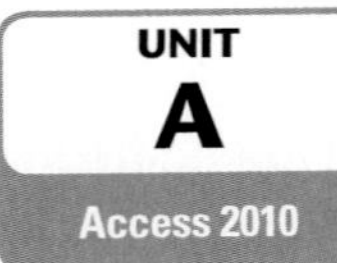

Creating Primary Keys

The primary key field of a table serves two important purposes. First, it contains data that uniquely identifies each record. No two records can have the exact same entry in the field designated as the primary key field. Secondly, the primary key field helps relate one table to another in a **one-to-many relationship**, where one record from one table is related to many records in the second table. For example, one record in the Employees table can be related to many records in the Evaluations table. (One employee may have many evaluations.) The primary key field is always on the "one" side of a one-to-many relationship between two tables. Tony Sanchez asks you to check that a primary key field has been appropriately identified for each table in the new staff database.

STEPS

1. **Right-click the Evaluations table in the Navigation Pane, then click Design View**
   Table Design View for the Evaluations table opens. The field with the AutoNumber data type is generally the best candidate for the primary key field in a table because it automatically contains a unique number for each record.

TROUBLE
Make sure the Design tab is selected on the Ribbon.

2. **Click the EvaluationID field if it is not already selected, then click the Primary Key button in the Tools group on the Design tab**
   The EvaluationID field is now set as the primary key field for the Evaluations table, as shown in Figure A-10.

QUICK TIP
You can also click the Save button on the Quick Access toolbar to save a table.

3. **Right-click the Evaluations table tab, click Close, then click Yes to save the table**
   Any time you must save design changes to an Access object such as a table, Access displays a dialog box to remind you to save the object.
4. **Right-click the Employees table in the Navigation Pane, then click Design View**
   Access has already set ID as the primary key field for the Employees table, as shown in Figure A-11.
5. **Right-click the Employees table tab, then click Close**
   You were not prompted to save the Employees table because you made no design changes. Now that you're sure that each table in the AMP-A-Staff database has an appropriate primary key field, you're ready to link the tables. The primary key field plays a critical role in this relationship.

Cloud computing

Using **cloud computing** (work done in a virtual environment), you can take advantage of Windows Live SkyDrive, a free service from Microsoft. Using Windows Live SkyDrive, you and your colleagues can store files in a "cloud" and retrieve them anytime you are connected to the Internet. That way, you can access files containing data whenever you need them. To use Windows Live SkyDrive, you need a free Windows Live ID, which you obtain at the Windows Live Web site. You can find more information and projects in the "Working with Windows Live and Microsoft Office Web Apps" appendix.

FIGURE A-10: **Creating a primary key field for the Evaluations table**

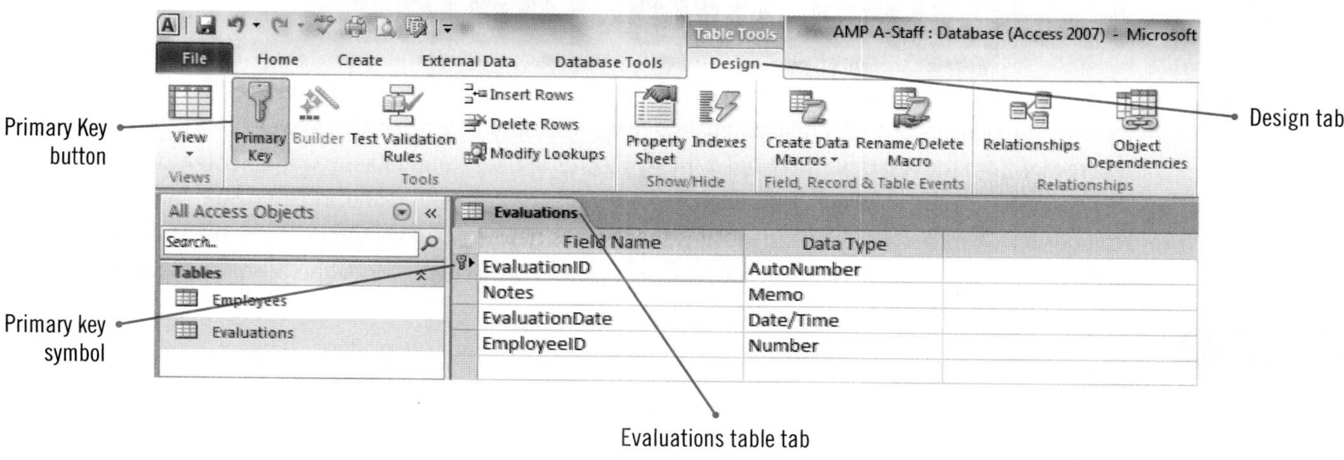

FIGURE A-11: **Confirming the primary key field for the Employees table**

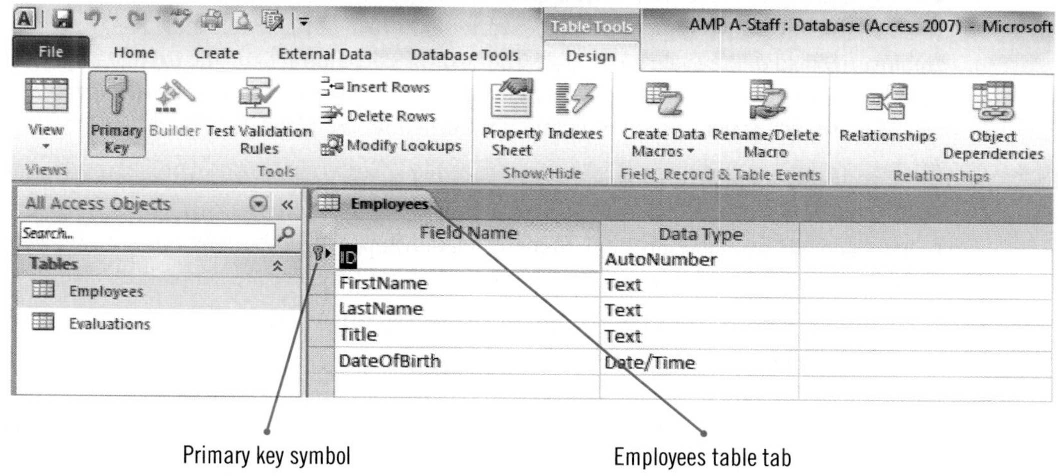

Learning about field properties

Properties are the characteristics that define the field. Two properties are required for every field: Field Name and Data Type. Many other properties, such as Field Size, Format, Caption, and Default Value, are defined in the Field Properties pane in the lower half of a table's Design View. As you add more property entries, you are generally restricting the amount or type of data that can be entered in the field, which increases data entry accuracy. For example, you might change the Field Size property for a State field to 2 to eliminate an incorrect entry such as FLL. Field properties change depending on the data type of the selected field. For example, date fields do not have a Field Size property because Access controls the size of fields with a Date/Time data type.

Access 2010

UNIT
A
Access 2010

Relating Two Tables

After you create tables and set primary key fields, you must link the tables together in one-to-many relationships to enjoy the benefits of a relational database. A **one-to-many relationship** between two tables means that one record from the first table is related to many records in the second table. You use a common field to make this connection. The common field is always the primary key field in the table on the "one" side of the relationship. Tony Sanchez explains that he has new evaluations to enter into the staff database. To easily identify which employee is related to each evaluation record, you define a one-to-many relationship between the Employees and Evaluations tables.

STEPS

1. **Click the Database Tools tab on the Ribbon, then click the Relationships button**

2. **In the Show Table dialog box, double-click Employees, double-click Evaluations, then click Close**

   Each table is represented by a small **field list** window that displays the table's field names. A key symbol identifies the primary key field. To relate the two tables in a one-to-many relationship, you connect them using the common field, which is always the primary key field on the "one" side of the relationship.

3. **Drag ID in the Employees field list to the EmployeeID field in the Evaluations field list**

   The Edit Relationships dialog box opens as shown in Figure A-12. **Referential integrity**, a set of Access rules that governs data entry, helps ensure data accuracy.

4. **Click the Enforce Referential Integrity check box, then click Create**

   The **one-to-many line** shows the link between the ID field of the Employees table (the "one" side) and the EmployeeID field of the Evaluations table (the "many" side, indicated by the **infinity symbol**), as shown in Figure A-13. The linking field on the "many" side is called the **foreign key field**. Now that these tables are related, it is much easier to enter evaluations for the correct employee.

5. **Click the Close button on the Design tab, click Yes to save changes, then double-click the Employees table in the Navigation Pane to open it in Datasheet View**

   When you relate two tables in a one-to-many relationship, expand buttons appear to the left of each record in the table on the "one" side of the relationship. In this case, this is the Employees table.

6. **Click the expand button ⊞ to the left of the first record**

   A **subdatasheet** shows the related comment records for each customer. In other words, the subdatasheet shows the records on the "many" side of a one-to-many relationship. The expand button ⊞ also changed to the collapse button ⊟ for the first employee. Now the task of entering evaluations for the right employee is much more straightforward.

7. **Enter two more evaluations for your second and third employees as shown in Figure A-14**

   Interestingly, the EmployeeID field in the Evaluations table (the foreign key field) is not displayed in the subdatasheet. Behind the scenes, Access is entering the correct EmployeeID value in the Evaluations table, which is the glue that ties each evaluation to the right employee.

8. **Close the Employees table**

TROUBLE
If the Show Table dialog box doesn't appear, click the Show Table button on the Design tab.

QUICK TIP
Drag a table's title bar to move the field list.

TROUBLE
If you need to delete an incorrect relationship, right-click a relationship line, then click Delete.

QUICK TIP
To print the Relationships window, click the Relationship Report button on the Design tab, then click Print.

Enforcing referential integrity

Referential integrity is a set of rules that helps reduce invalid entries and orphan records. An **orphan record** is a record in the "many" table that doesn't have a matching entry in the linking field of the "one" table. With referential integrity enforced on a one-to-many relationship, you cannot enter a value in a foreign key field of the "many" table that does not have a match in the linking field of the "one" table. Referential integrity also prevents you from deleting a record in the "one" table if a matching entry exists in the foreign key field of the "many" table. You should enforce referential integrity on all one-to-many relationships if possible. If you are working with a database that already contains orphan records, you cannot enforce referential integrity on that relationship.

FIGURE A-12: **Edit Relationships dialog box**

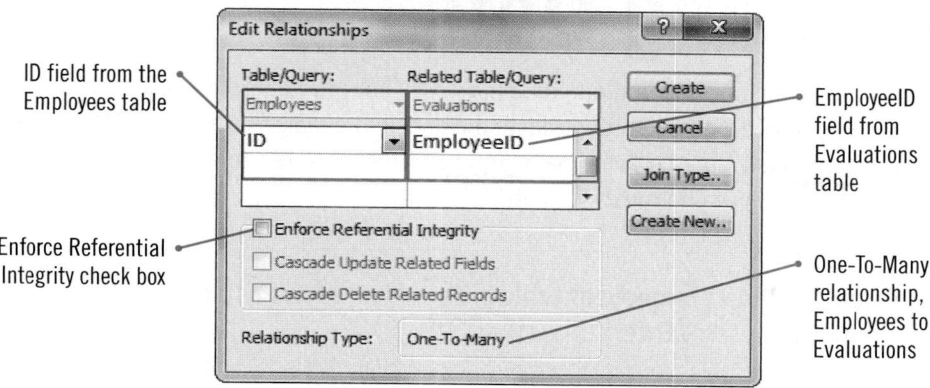

FIGURE A-13: **Linking the Employees and Evaluations tables**

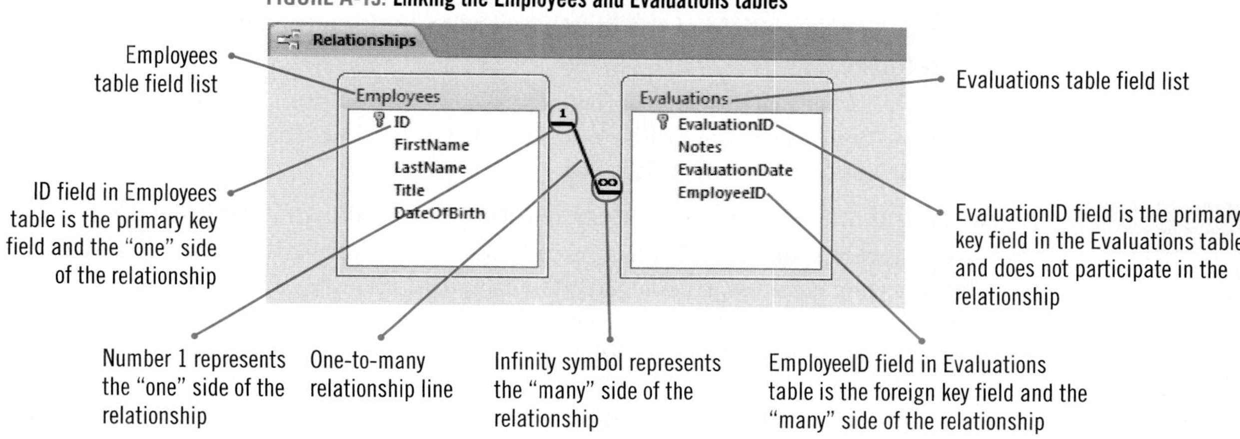

FIGURE A-14: **Entering evaluations using the subdatasheet**

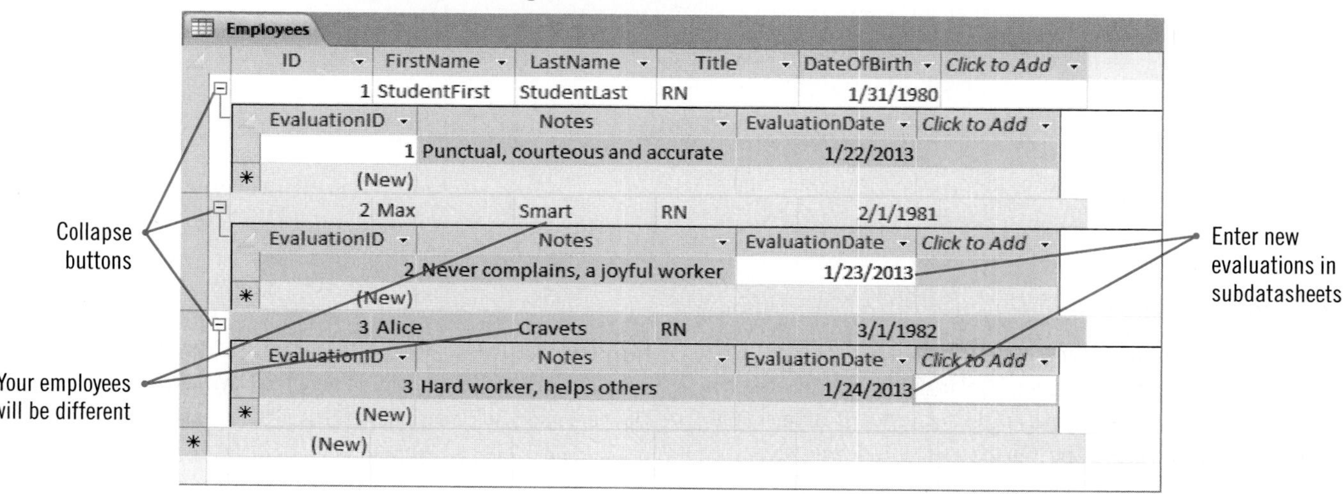

Access 2010

UNIT A
Access 2010

Entering Data

Your skill in navigating and entering data is a key to your success with a relational database. You use either mouse or keystroke techniques to navigate the data in the table's datasheet. Even though you have already successfully entered some data, Tony Sanchez asks you to master this essential skill by entering several more employees in the staff database.

STEPS

1. **Double-click the Employees table in the Navigation Pane to open it, press [Tab] three times, then press [Enter] three times**

   The Employees table reopens. The Evaluations subdatasheets are collapsed. Both the [Tab] and [Enter] keys move the focus to the next field. The **focus** refers to which data you would edit if you started typing. The record that has the focus is highlighted in light blue. The field name that has the focus is highlighted in light orange. When you navigate to the last field of the record, pressing [Tab] or [Enter] advances the focus to the first field of the next record. You can also use the Next record and Previous record **navigation buttons** on the navigation bar in the lower-left corner of the datasheet to navigate the records. The **Current record** text box on the navigation bar tells you the number of the current record as well as the total number of records in the datasheet.

2. **Click the FirstName field of the fourth record to position the insertion point to enter a new record**

   You can also use the New (blank) record button on the navigation bar to move to a new record. You enter new records at the end of the datasheet. You learn how to sort and reorder records later. A complete list of navigation keystrokes is shown in Table A-5.

> **QUICK TIP**
> Access databases are multiuser with one important limitation: two users cannot edit the same *record* at the same time. In that case, a message explains that the second user must wait until the first user moves to a different record.

3. **At the end of the datasheet, enter the three records shown in Figure A-15**

   The **edit record symbol** shown in Figure A-16 appears to the left of the record you are currently editing. When you move to a different record, Access saves the data. Therefore, Access never prompts you to save *data* because it performs that task automatically. Saving data automatically allows Access databases to be **multiuser** databases, which means that more than one person can enter and edit data in the same database at the same time.

   Your ID values might differ from those in Figure A-16. Because the ID field is an **AutoNumber** field, Access automatically enters the next consecutive number into the field as it creates the record. If you delete a record or are interrupted when entering a record, Access discards the value in the AutoNumber field and does not reuse it. AutoNumber values do not represent the number of records in your table. Instead, they provide a unique value per record, similar to check numbers. Each check number is unique, and does not represent the number of checks you have written.

Changing from Navigation mode to Edit mode

If you navigate to another area of the datasheet by clicking with the mouse pointer instead of pressing [Tab] or [Enter], you change from **Navigation mode** to Edit mode. In **Edit mode**, Access assumes that you are trying to make changes to the current field value, so keystrokes such as [Ctrl][End], [Ctrl][Home], [←], and [→] move the insertion point within the field. To return to Navigation mode, press [Tab] or [Enter] (thus moving the focus to the next field), or press [↑] or [↓] (thus moving the focus to a different record).

FIGURE A-15: Three records to add to the Employees table

ID	FirstName	LastName	Title	DateOfBirth
[Tab]	Rebecca	Haines	RN	4/1/1973
[Tab]	Christopher	Finn	RN	5/5/1970
[Tab]	Amber	Oulette	ARNP	8/1/1979

FIGURE A-16: New records in the Employees table

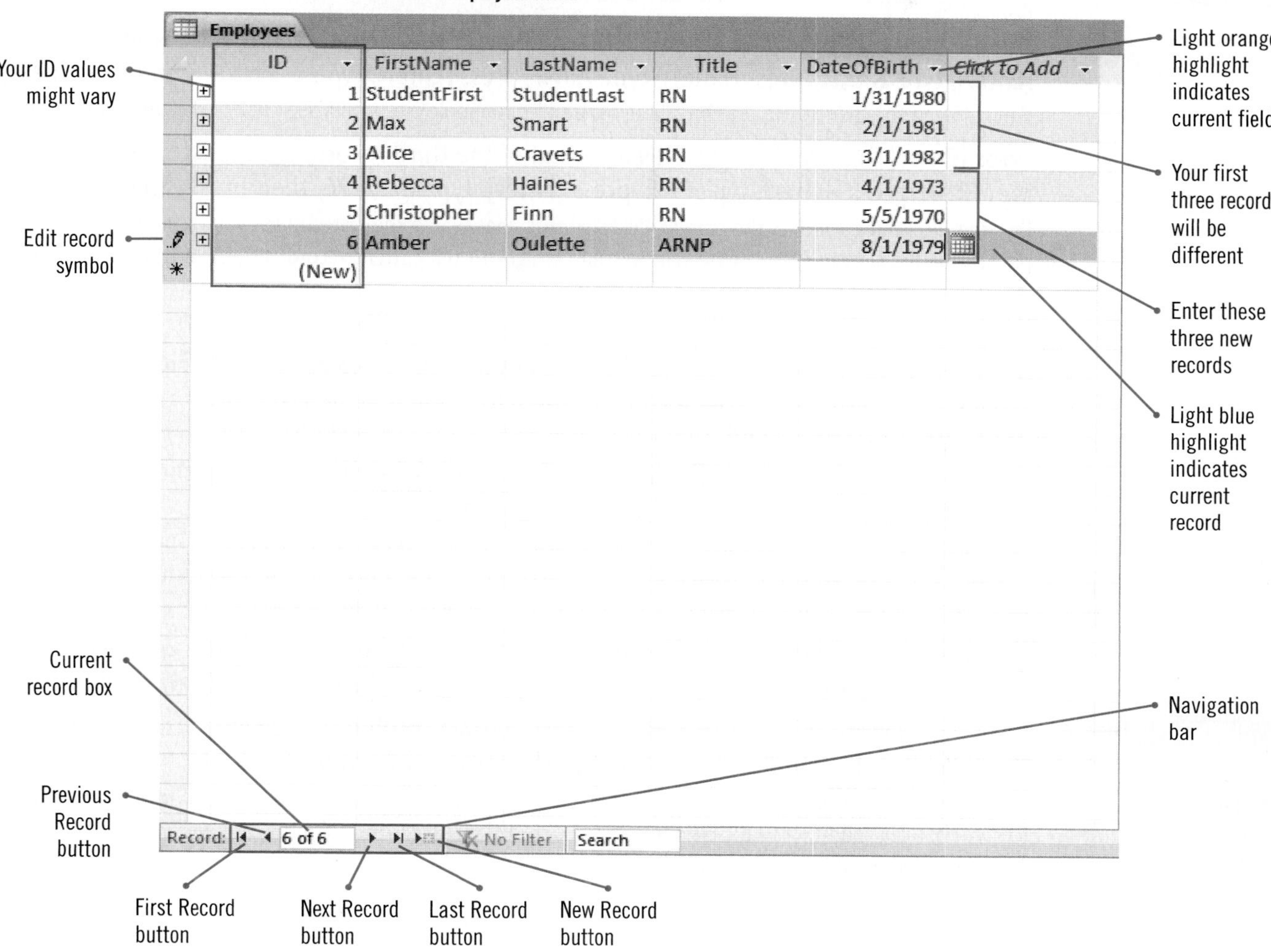

Access 2010

TABLE A-5: Navigation mode keyboard shortcuts

shortcut key	moves to the
[Tab], [Enter], or [→]	Next field of the current record
[Shift][Tab] or [←]	Previous field of the current record
[Home]	First field of the current record
[End]	Last field of the current record
[Ctrl][Home] or [F5]	First field of the first record
[Ctrl][End]	Last field of the last record
[↑]	Current field of the previous record
[↓]	Current field of the next record

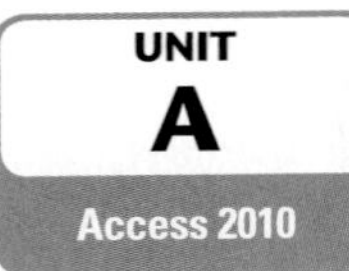

Editing Data

Updating information in a database is another critical data management task. To change the contents of an existing record, navigate to the field you want to change and type the new information. You can delete unwanted data by clicking the field and using [Backspace] or [Delete] to delete text to the left or right of the insertion point. Other data entry keystrokes are summarized in Table A-6. Tony Sanchez asks you to update two records in the Employees table.

STEPS

1. **Double-click the first name in the FirstName field of the second record, type Francis, press [Enter], type Krupp, press [Enter], type ARNP, press [Enter], type 2/15/81, then press [Enter]**
   You changed the name, title, and birthdate of the second employee. You'll also change the third employee.
2. **Press [Enter] to move to the FirstName field of the third record, type Jessica, press [Enter], type Toye, press [Enter], type PAC, press [Enter], type 8/27/76, then press [Esc]**
   Pressing [Esc] once removes the current field's editing changes, so the DateOfBirth value changes back to the previous entry. Pressing [Esc] twice removes all changes to the current record. When you move to another record, Access saves your edits, so you can no longer use [Esc] to remove editing changes to the current record. You can, however, click the Undo button on the Quick Access toolbar to undo changes to a previous record.
3. **Click the Calendar Picker icon, then click August 28, 1976 as shown in Figure A-17**
   When you are working in the DateOfBirth field, which has a Date/Time data type, you can enter a date from the keyboard or use the **Calendar Picker**, a pop-up calendar to find and select a date.
4. **Click the record selector for the last record (the one for Amber Oulette), click the Delete button in the Records group on the Home tab, then click Yes**
   A message warns that you cannot undo a record deletion. The Undo button is dimmed, indicating that you cannot use it. The Employees table now has five records, as shown in Figure A-18. Keep in mind that your ID values might differ from those in the figure because they are controlled by Access.
5. **Click the File tab, click Print, click Print Preview to review the printout of the Employees table before printing, click the Print button, click OK, then click the Close Print Preview button**
6. **Click the File tab, click Exit to close the AMP A-Staff.accdb database and Access 2010, then click Yes if prompted to save design changes to the Employees table**
   Remember you are not prompted to save Access data; data is automatically saved. You are, however, prompted to save changes you make to the structure of the object such as resizing columns in Datasheet View as well as any modification you make in Design View.

QUICK TIP
The ScreenTip for the Undo button displays the action you can undo.

Resizing and moving datasheet columns

You can resize the width of a field in a datasheet by dragging the column separator to the left or right. The pointer changes to ↔ as you make the field wider or narrower. Release the mouse button when you have resized the field. To adjust the column width to accommodate the widest entry in the field, double-click the column separator. To move a column, click the field name to select the entire column, then drag the field name left or right.

FIGURE A-17: **Editing employee records**

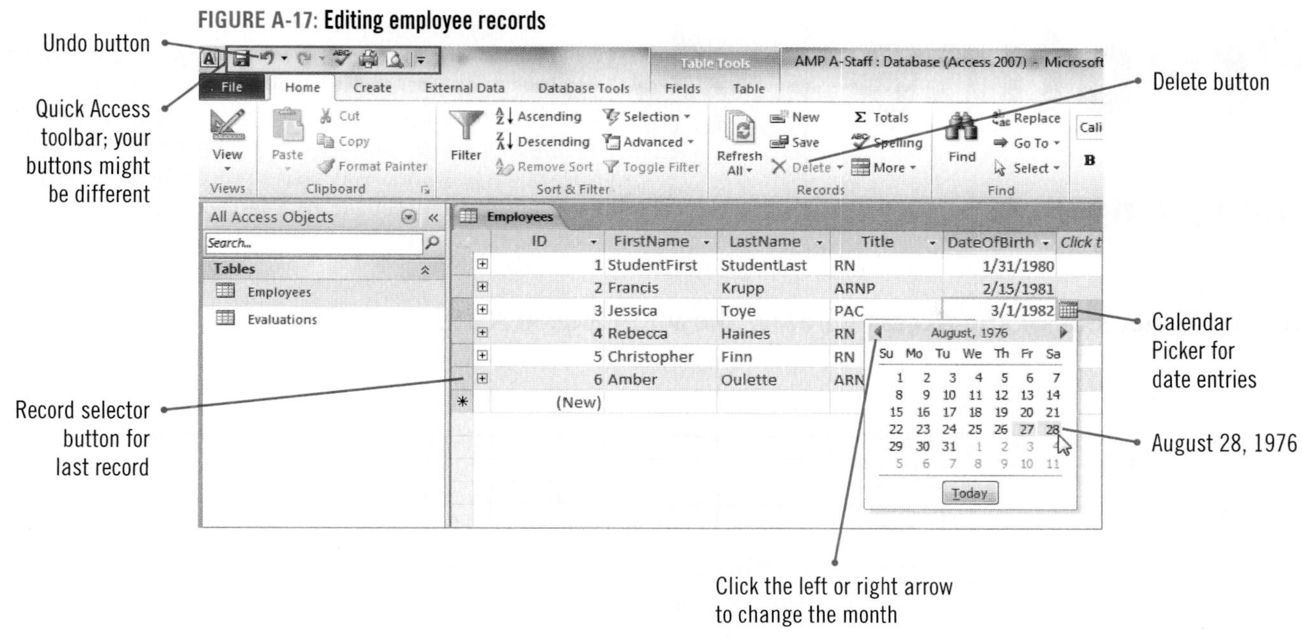

FIGURE A-18: **Final Employees datasheet**

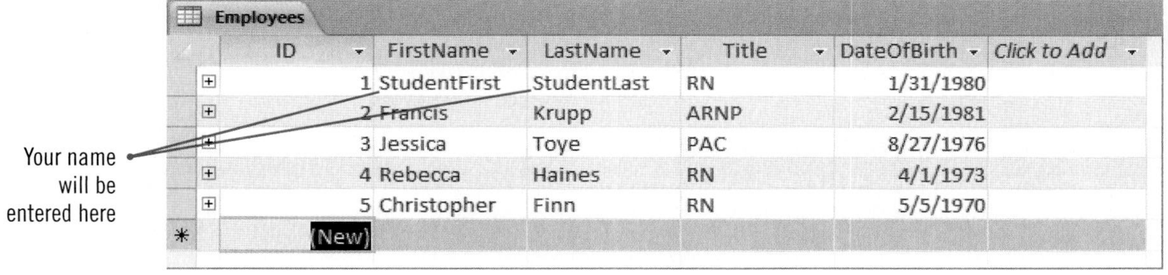

TABLE A-6: **Edit mode keyboard shortcuts**

editing keystroke	action
[Backspace]	Deletes one character to the left of the insertion point
[Delete]	Deletes one character to the right of the insertion point
[F2]	Switches between Edit and Navigation mode
[Esc]	Undoes the change to the current field
[Esc][Esc]	Undoes all changes to the current record
[F7]	Starts the spell-check feature
[Ctrl][']	Inserts the value from the same field in the previous record into the current field
[Ctrl][;]	Inserts the current date in a Date field

Practice

Concepts Review

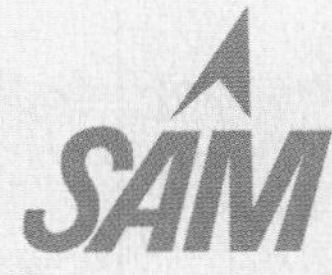

For current SAM information, including versions and content details, visit SAM Central (http://www.cengage.com/samcentral). If you have a SAM user profile, you may have access to hands-on instruction, practice, and assessment of the skills covered in this unit. Since various versions of SAM are supported throughout the life of this text, check with your instructor for the correct instructions and URL/Web site for accessing assignments.

Label each element of the Access window shown in Figure A-19.

FIGURE A-19

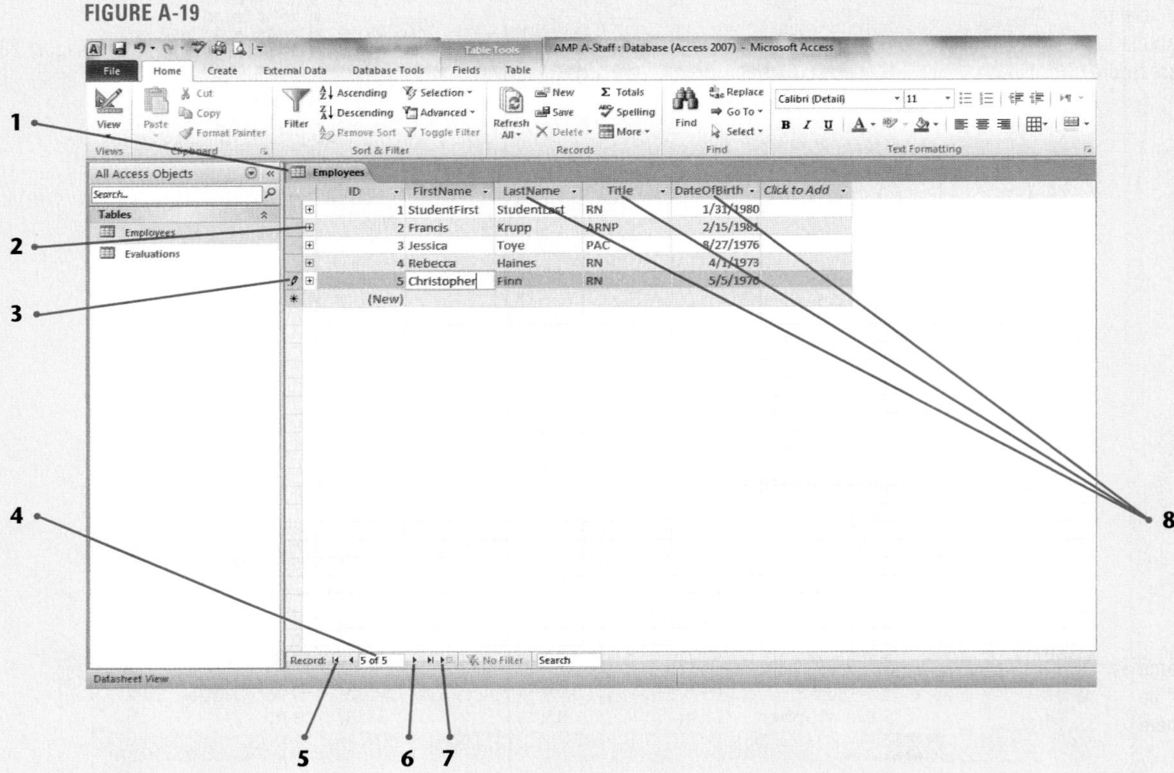

Match each term with the statement that best describes it.

9. **Table**
10. **Query**
11. **Field**
12. **Record**
13. **Datasheet**
14. **Form**
15. **Report**

- **a.** A subset of data from one or more tables
- **b.** A collection of records for a single subject, such as all the customer records
- **c.** A professional printout of database information
- **d.** A spreadsheet-like grid that displays fields as columns and records as rows
- **e.** A group of related fields for one item, such as all of the information for one customer
- **f.** A category of information in a table, such as a company name, city, or state
- **g.** An easy-to-use data entry screen

Select the best answer from the list of choices.

16. Which of the following is *not* a typical benefit of relational databases?

a. More accurate data
b. Faster information retrieval
c. More common than spreadsheets
d. Minimized duplicate data entry

17. Which of the following is *not* an advantage of managing data with relational database software, such as Access, versus spreadsheet software, such as Excel?

a. Allows multiple users to enter data simultaneously
b. Provides data entry forms
c. Reduces duplicate data entry
d. Uses a single table to store all data

18. The object that creates a professional printout of data that includes headers, footers, and graphics is the:

a. Query.
b. Report.
c. Table.
d. Form.

19. The object that contains all of the database data is the:

a. Report.
b. Page.
c. Form.
d. Table.

20. When you create a new database, which object is created first?

a. Query
b. Module
c. Table
d. Form

Skills Review

1. Understand relational databases.

a. Identify five advantages of managing database information in Access versus using a spreadsheet.
b. Create a sentence to explain how the terms *field, record, table,* and *relational database* relate to one another.

2. Explore a database.

a. Start Access.
b. Open the AMP A-A2.accdb database from the drive and folder where you store your Data Files, save it as **AMP A-Diabetes**, then enable content if prompted.
c. Open each of the five tables to study the data they contain. On a sheet of paper, complete Figure A-20. Include a row to describe each of the five tables.

FIGURE A-20

table name	number of fields	number of records

d. Double-click the ConsultsByEmployee query in the Navigation Pane to open it. Change any occurrence of Sonya Able to your name. Move to another record to save your changes.
e. Double-click the EmployeeEntry form in the Navigation Pane to open it. Use the navigation buttons to navigate through the 16 employees to observe each employee's data.
f. Double-click the PatientEntry form in the Navigation Pane to open it. Use the navigation buttons to navigate through several patient records.
g. Double-click the PatientListing report in the Navigation Pane to open it. Scroll to the bottom of the report to observe the grand total calculation.
h. Close the AMP A-Diabetes database, and then close Access 2010.

Skills Review (continued)

3. Create a database.

a. Start Access, use the Browse folder button to navigate to the drive and folder where you store your Data Files, type **AMP A-Personnel** as the File Name, click OK, then click Create to create a new database named AMP A-Personnel.accdb.

b. Switch to Table Design View, name the table **Nurses**, then enter the fields and data types shown in Figure A-21.

c. Save the table, switch to Datasheet View, and enter two records. Tab through the ID field, an AutoNumber field, use your name in the first record and your professor's name in the second, enter **RN** in the degree field for both records, and enter a recent date in the DateOfHire field.

d. Widen each column in the Nurses table so that all data is visible, then save and close the Nurses table.

FIGURE A-21

field name	data type
ID	AutoNumber
NFirst	Text
NLast	Text
Degree	Text
DateOfHire	Date/Time

4. Create a table.

a. Click the Create tab on the Ribbon, click the Table Design button, then create a new table with the two fields and data types shown in Figure A-22.

b. Save the table with the name **Degrees**. Click No when asked if you want Access to create the primary key field.

c. Switch to Datasheet View and enter the two records shown in Figure A-23 into the Degrees table.

d. Widen both columns as needed to view all data.

FIGURE A-22

field name	data type
DegreeAbbrev	Text
DegreeDescrip	Text

FIGURE A-23

DegreeAbbrev	DegreeDescrip
RN	Registered Nurse
LPN	Licensed Practical Nurse

5. Create primary keys.

a. In Table Design View of the Degrees table, set DegreeAbbrev as the primary key field.

b. Save the Degrees table and open it in Datasheet View.

c. Enter one more record, using **ARNP** for the DegreeAbbrev value and **Advanced Registered Nurse Practitioner** for the DegreeDescrip value.

d. Widen the DegreeDescrip column as necessary, then close and save the Degrees table.

6. Relate two tables.

a. From the Database Tools tab, open the Relationships window.

b. Add the Degrees then the Nurses table to the Relationships window.

c. Drag the DegreeAbbrev field from the Degrees table to the Degree field of the Nurses table.

d. In the Edit Relationships dialog box, click the Enforce Referential Integrity check box, then click Create. Your Relationships window should look similar to Figure A-24. If you connect the wrong fields by mistake, right-click the line connecting the two fields, click Delete, then try again.

e. Close the Relationships window, and save changes when prompted.

FIGURE A-24

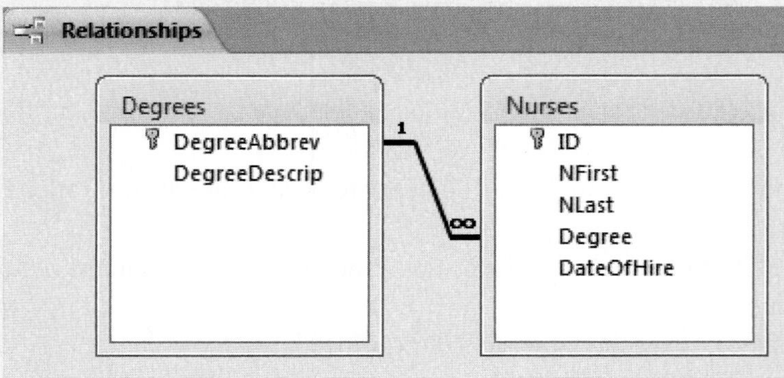

Skills Review (continued)

7. Enter data.

a. Open the Degrees table and enter the additional records shown in Figure A-25.

b. Close and reopen the Degrees table. Notice that Access automatically sorts the records by the values in the primary key field, the DegreeAbbrev field.

FIGURE A-25

DegreeAbbrev field	DegreeDescrip field
BSN	Bachelor of Science in Nursing
CNA	Certified Nurse's Assistant

8. Edit data.

a. Click the Expand button for the RN record to see the two related records from the Nurses table.

b. Enter two more nurse records in the RN subdatasheet using any fictitious but realistic data, and one new nurse record in the LPN subdatasheet using any fictitious but realistic data, as shown in Figure A-26. Do not worry about what ID value is given to each new employee. That value is automatically assigned by Access.

FIGURE A-26

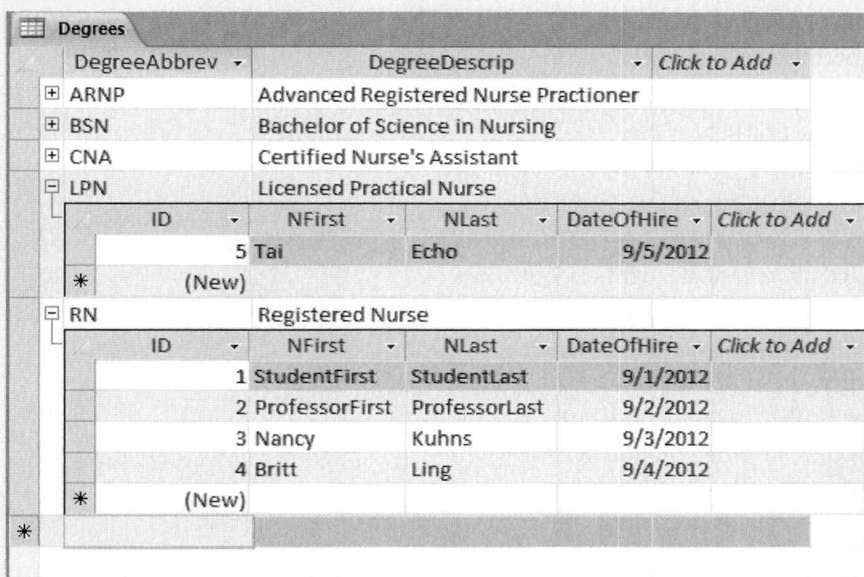

c. If required by your instructor, print the Degrees datasheet and the Nurses datasheet.

d. Click the File tab, then click Exit to close all open objects as well as the AMP A-Personnel.accdb database and Access 2010. If prompted to save any design changes, click Yes.

Independent Challenge 1

Review the following four examples of database tables:

- Medications
- Diagnosis Codes
- Telephone Directory
- College Course Offerings

In a Word document, complete the following tasks.

a. For each example, build a Word table with three to six columns. In the first row, identify field names that you would expect to find in the table.

b. In the second and third rows of each table, enter two possible records. The first table, Medications, is completed in Figure A-27 as an example to follow.

FIGURE A-27

drug type	generic name	brand name
Depressant	Sleep medication	Ambien
Stimulant	Amphetamine	Ritalin

Independent Challenge 2

You are working with a medical school's intern placement program, and started an Access database to track intern evaluations.

a. Start Access, open the AMP A-A3.accdb database from the drive and folder where you store your Data Files, save it as **AMP A-InternMgmt**, then enable content if prompted.

b. Open the InternName table, note the number of fields and records, and add your name as a new record.

c. Switch to Design View to note the primary key field of the table (InternNo) then close the table.

d. In Table Design View, build the new table shown in Figure A-28 named **Evaluations**. Be sure to enter the field names and data types exactly as shown.

FIGURE A-28

Evaluations

Field Name	Data Type	
EvalNo	AutoNumber	
Prompt	Number	1-5 scale, 5 being the highest
Professional	Number	
Knowledgeable	Number	
Respectful	Number	
EvaluatorLastName	Text	
EvaluatorFirstName	Text	
EvaluationDate	Date/Time	
InternNo	Number	foreign key field

e. Set EvalNo as the primary key field, and close the Evaluations table.

f. Open the Relationships window, click the Show Table button to add the field lists for both tables to the Relationships window, and drag the title bars of the field lists to position them as shown in Figure A-29.

g. Create the one-to-many relationship and enforce referential integrity as shown in Figure A-29. If you create the relationship incorrectly, right-click the line linking the fields, click Delete, and try again.

h. If required by your instructor, click the Relationship Report button, then click Print to print a copy of the Relationships for AMP A-InternMgmt report.

i. Close the report, click Yes when prompted to save changes to the report, then click OK to accept the report name.

j. Close the AMP A-InternMgmt.accdb database, then exit Access 2010.

FIGURE A-29

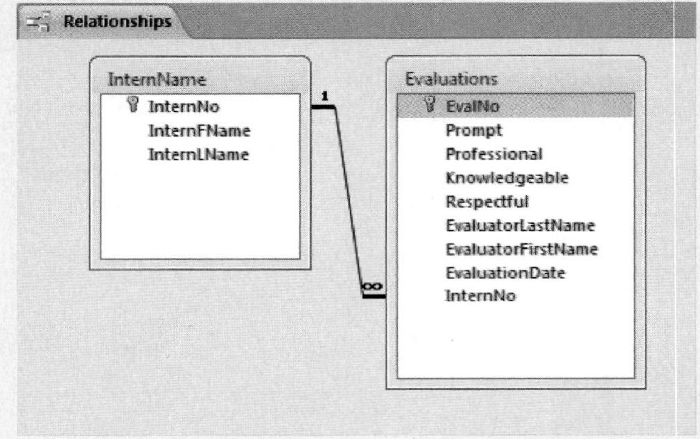

Independent Challenge 3

You are working for a pediatric clinic that has several locations. Each location has several physicians assigned to that location. You have created an Access database to help keep track of which physicians work at each location.

a. Start Access, open the AMP A-A4.accdb database from the drive and folder where you store your Data Files, save it as **AMP A-Pediatrics**, then enable content if prompted.

b. Add a record to the Doctors table, using your first and last names and a unique entry for the DrCode field.

c. In Table Design View, build the new table shown in Figure A-30 named **Locations**. Be sure to enter the field names and data types exactly as shown.

d. Set LocationID as the primary key field, and open the table in Datasheet View.

e. Enter two sample records in the Locations table using fictitious but realistic data. Note the value of the LocationID field for both records (probably 1 and 2).

f. Open the Doctors table in Table Design View, then add a new field named **LocationID** with a Number data type. This field will serve as the foreign key field to connect the Locations and Doctors tables in a one-to-many relationship. Save the Doctors table.

FIGURE A-30

Locations

Field Name	Data Type
LocationID	AutoNumber
Street	Text
City	Text
State	Text
Zip	Text
Telephone	Text

Independent Challenge 3 (continued)

g. Open the Doctors table in Datasheet View, and give each record a LocationID value that matches a LocationID value in the Locations table (probably 1 and 2, but these values *must* match one of the existing values in the LocationID field for the Locations table).

h. Close the Doctors and Locations tables.

i. Open the Relationships window, click the Show Table button to add the field lists for both tables to the Relationships window, and drag the title bars of the field lists to position them as shown in Figure A-31.

j. Create the one-to-many relationship between the Locations and Doctors tables using the common LocationID field, and enforce referential integrity as shown in Figure A-31. If you create the relationship incorrectly or cannot enforce referential integrity, right-click the link line, click Delete, and try again.

FIGURE A-31

Relationships

Locations: LocationID, Street, City, State, Zip, Telephone

Doctors: DrLName, DrFName, DrCode, LocationID

1 — ∞

Advanced Challenge Exercise

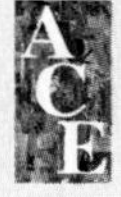

- Click the Relationship Report button on the Design tab, then click Print to print a copy of the Relationships for AMP A-Pediatrics report.
- Close and save changes to the report, then click OK to accept the report name.

k. Close the AMP A-Pediatrics.accdb database, and exit Access 2010.

Real Life Independent Challenge

This Independent Challenge requires an Internet connection.

One of the most challenging aspects of preparing for a career in the medical profession is the vast amount of medical terminology you are required to memorize. In this exercise, you start building a database of medical roots, prefixes, and suffixes to help prepare for tests, board examinations, and day-to-day work in the medical field.

a. Using your favorite search engine, look up the keywords *medical terminology list* to find lists of common medical terms.

b. Review several links, then print one page of medical terminology that you would like to save in an Access database. Be sure to include the Wikipedia list of medical roots, prefixes, and suffixes in your research.

c. Start Access, click the Blank Database button, click the Browse folder button, navigate to the drive and folder where you store your Data Files, type **AMP A-MedicalTerms** in the File name box, click OK, then click Create.

d. In Table Design View, build the new table shown in Figure A-32 and name it **Terminology**. Be sure to enter the field names and data types exactly as shown.

e. Set **TermID** as the primary key field, and open the table in Datasheet View.

f. Enter the two records shown in Figure A-33, then widen each column to view all data.

g. If requested by your instructor, print the Terminology datasheet.

h. Close the AMP A-MedicalTerms.accdb database, and exit Access 2010.

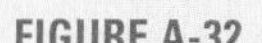

FIGURE A-32

Terminology

Field Name	Data Type
TermID	AutoNumber
PrefixOrSuffix	Text
Meaning	Text
Origin	Text
Example	Text

FIGURE A-33

Terminology

TermID	PrefixOrSuffix	Meaning	Origin	Example
1	a- an-	Denotes an absence of	Ancient Greek	Apathy, Analgia
2	ab-	away from	Latin	abduction
(New)				

Access 2010

Visual Workshop

Start Access, then create a database named **AMP A-Prescriptions.accdb** in the drive and folder where you store your data files. Create a table named ScriptAbbreviations with three Text fields, shown in Figure A-34. Specify the Abbreviation field to be the primary key field. Then enter the 14 records shown in the figure with common prescription abbreviation codes.

FIGURE A-34

ScriptAbbreviations

Abbreviation	Latin	Meaning
ac	ante cibum	before meals
bid	bis in die	twice a day
gt	gutta	drop
hs	hora somni	at bedtime
od	oculus dexter	right eye
os	oculus sinister	left eye
pc	post cibum	after meals
po	per os	by mouth
prn	pro re nata	as needed
q 3 h	quaque 3 hora	every 3 hours
qd	quaque die	every day
qid	quater in die	4 times a day
Sig	signa	write
tid	ter in die	3 times a day
*		

UNIT
B
Access 2010

Building and Using Queries

Files You Will Need:

AMP B-B1.accdb
AMP B-B2.accdb
AMP B-B3.accdb
AMP B-B4.accdb
AMP B-B5.accdb
AMP B-B6.accdb

You build queries in an Access database to ask "questions" about data, such as which doctors saw new patients in the month of July or what types of charges were sent to a particular insurance company. Queries present the answer in a datasheet, which you can sort, filter, and format. Because queries are stored in the database, they can be used multiple times. Each time a query is opened, it displays a current view of the latest updates to the database. Tony Sanchez, R.N., and office manager for Riverwalk Medical Clinic, asks several questions about the patient database. You'll develop queries to provide Tony with up-to-date answers.

OBJECTIVES

- Use the Query Wizard
- Work with data in a query
- Use Query Design View
- Sort and find data
- Filter data
- Apply AND criteria
- Apply OR criteria
- Format a datasheet

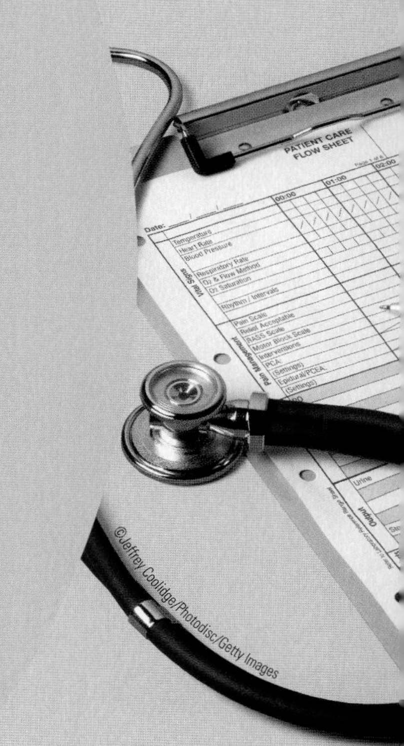

UNIT
B
Access 2010

Using the Query Wizard

A **query** allows you to select a subset of fields and records from one or more tables and then present the selected data as a single datasheet. A major benefit of working with data through a query is that you can focus on only the information you need to answer your question, rather than navigating the fields and records from many large tables. You can enter, edit, and navigate data in a query datasheet just like a table datasheet. However, keep in mind that Access data is physically stored only in tables, even though you can view and edit it through other Access objects such as queries and forms. Because a query doesn't physically store the data, a query datasheet is sometimes called a **logical view** of the data. Technically, a query is a set of **SQL (Structured Query Language)** instructions, but because you can use Access query tools such as Query Design View, you are not required to know SQL to build or use Access queries. You use the Simple Query Wizard to build a query that displays a few fields from the Patients and Visits tables in one datasheet.

STEPS

TROUBLE
If a Microsoft Access Security Notice dialog box opens, click the Open button.

1. **Start Access, click the Open button, navigate to the drive and folder where you store your Data Files, click the AMP B-B1.accdb database file, click Open, click the File tab, click Save Database As, type AMP B-Riverwalk in the File name box, click Save, then enable content if prompted**

   Access provides several tools to create a new query. One way is to use the **Simple Query Wizard**, which prompts you for information it needs to create a new query.

2. **Click the Create tab on the Ribbon, click the Query Wizard button in the Queries group, then click OK to start the Simple Query Wizard**

   The first Simple Query Wizard dialog box opens, prompting you to select the fields you want to view in the new query.

3. **Click the Tables/Queries list arrow, click Table: Patients, double-click PtLastName, then double-click PtFirstName**

   So far, you've selected two fields from the Patients table to display the last and then first name of the patient in this query. You also want to add the Diagnosis and DateofService fields from the Visits table.

TROUBLE
Click the Remove Single Field button < if you need to remove a field from the Selected Fields list.

4. **Click the Tables/Queries list arrow, click Table: Visits, double-click Diagnosis, then double-click DateofService**

   You've selected two fields from the Patients table and two from the Visits table for your new query, as shown in Figure B-1.

5. **Click Next, click Next to select Detail, select Patients Query in the title text box, type PatientDiagnosis as the name of the query, then click Finish**

   The PatientDiagnosis datasheet opens, displaying two fields from the Patients table and two from the Visits table. There are 66 total records as shown in Figure B-2. The query sometimes lists more than one diagnosis and date of service per patient due to the one-to-many relationship between the Patients and Visits tables established in the Relationships window.

FIGURE B-1: **Selecting fields using the Simple Query Wizard**

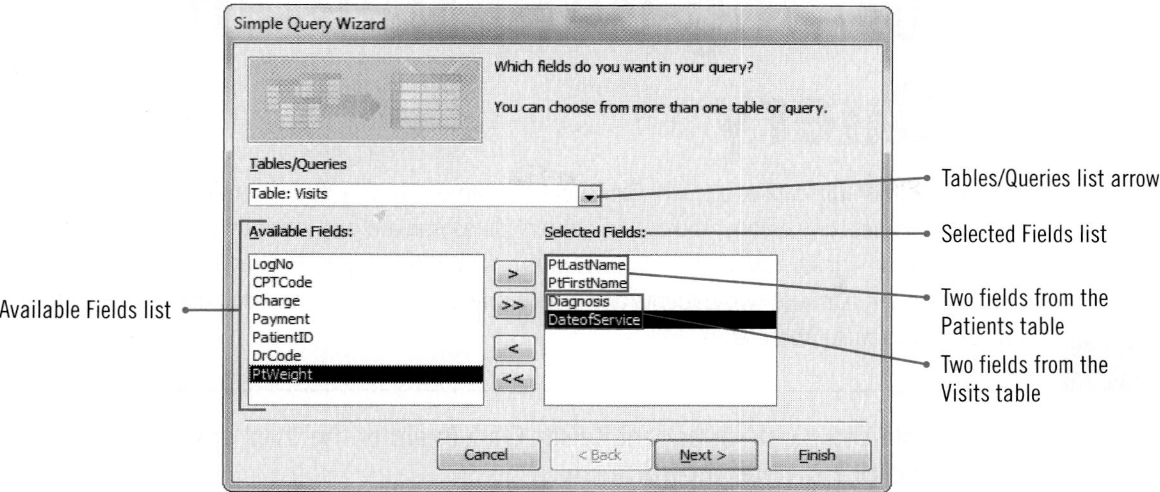

FIGURE B-2: **PatientDiagnosis datasheet**

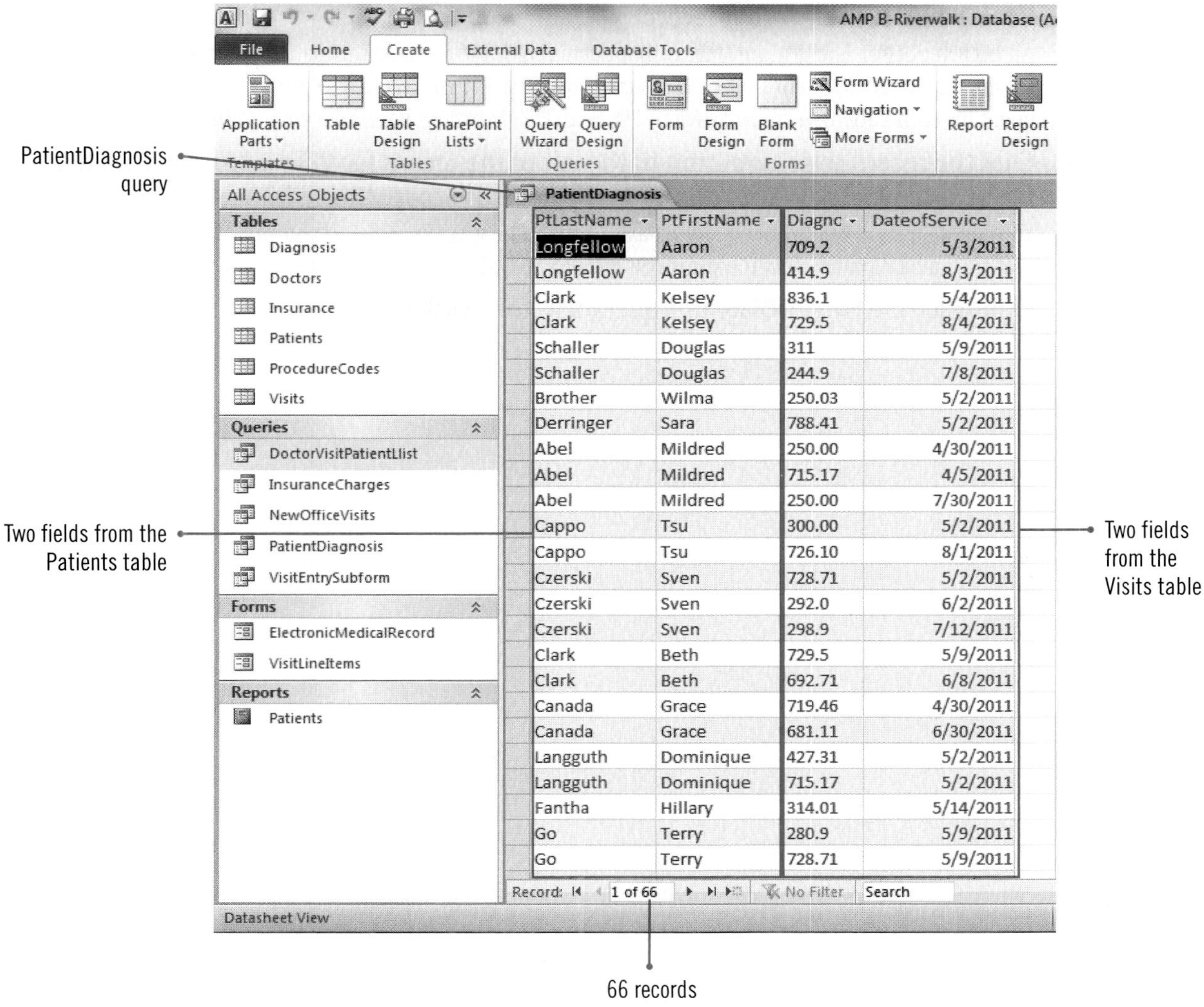

AMP B-Riverwalk : Database (A

File | Home | Create | External Data | Database Tools

Application Parts | Table | Table Design | SharePoint Lists | Query Wizard | Query Design | Form | Form Design | Blank Form | Form Wizard | Navigation | More Forms | Report | Report Design

Templates | Tables | Queries | Forms

PatientDiagnosis query

All Access Objects

Tables
- Diagnosis
- Doctors
- Insurance
- Patients
- ProcedureCodes
- Visits

Queries
- DoctorVisitPatientList
- InsuranceCharges
- NewOfficeVisits
- PatientDiagnosis
- VisitEntrySubform

Forms
- ElectronicMedicalRecord
- VisitLineItems

Reports
- Patients

PatientDiagnosis

PtLastName	PtFirstName	Diagnc	DateofService
Longfellow	Aaron	709.2	5/3/2011
Longfellow	Aaron	414.9	8/3/2011
Clark	Kelsey	836.1	5/4/2011
Clark	Kelsey	729.5	8/4/2011
Schaller	Douglas	311	5/9/2011
Schaller	Douglas	244.9	7/8/2011
Brother	Wilma	250.03	5/2/2011
Derringer	Sara	788.41	5/2/2011
Abel	Mildred	250.00	4/30/2011
Abel	Mildred	715.17	4/5/2011
Abel	Mildred	250.00	7/30/2011
Cappo	Tsu	300.00	5/2/2011
Cappo	Tsu	726.10	8/1/2011
Czerski	Sven	728.71	5/2/2011
Czerski	Sven	292.0	6/2/2011
Czerski	Sven	298.9	7/12/2011
Clark	Beth	729.5	5/9/2011
Clark	Beth	692.71	6/8/2011
Canada	Grace	719.46	4/30/2011
Canada	Grace	681.11	6/30/2011
Langguth	Dominique	427.31	5/2/2011
Langguth	Dominique	715.17	5/2/2011
Fantha	Hillary	314.01	5/14/2011
Go	Terry	280.9	5/9/2011
Go	Terry	728.71	5/9/2011

Record: 1 of 66 No Filter Search

Datasheet View

Two fields from the Patients table

Two fields from the Visits table

66 records

Access 2010

UNIT B

Access 2010

Working with Data in a Query

You enter and edit data in a query datasheet the same way you do in a table datasheet. Because all data is stored in tables, any edits you make in a query datasheet are permanently stored in the underlying tables, and are automatically updated in all views of the data in other queries, forms, and reports. You want to change the name of two patients and delete one patient record. You can use the PatientDiagnosis query datasheet to make these edits.

STEPS

1. **Double-click Clark for patient Kelsey Clark in either the third or fourth record, type Bretz, then click any other record**

   Both occurrences of Kelsey Clark are updated to Kelsey Bretz because this patient's name is stored only once in the Patients table, but is related to two records in the Visits table. The patient's name is selected from the Patients table and displayed in the PatientDiagnosis query for each patient visit.

2. **Double-click Abel for patient Mildred Abel in the ninth, tenth, or eleventh record, type Rubio, then click any other record**

   All occurrences of Abel are automatically updated to Rubio because this patient is entered only once in the Patients table. This patient's name is selected from the Patients table and displayed in the PatientDiagnosis query for each patient visit, as shown in Figure B-3. This patient had three visits to the clinic.

3. **Click the record selector button to the left of the record for Wilma Brother, click the Home tab, click the Delete button in the Records group, then click Yes**

   You can delete records from a query datasheet the same way you delete them from a table datasheet. Notice that the navigation bar now indicates you have 65 records in the datasheet, as shown in Figure B-4.

4. **Right-click the PatientDiagnosis query tab, then click Close**

FIGURE B-3: **Working with data in a query datasheet**

PatientDiagnosis

PtLastName	PtFirstName	Diagnc	DateofService
Longfellow	Aaron	709.2	5/3/2011
Longfellow	Aaron	414.9	8/3/2011
Bretz	Kelsey	836.1	5/4/2011
Bretz	Kelsey	729.5	8/4/2011
Schaller	Douglas	311	5/9/2011
Schaller	Douglas	244.9	7/8/2011
Brother	Wilma	250.03	5/2/2011
Derringer	Sara	788.41	5/2/2011
Rubio	Mildred	250.00	4/30/2011
Rubio	Mildred	715.17	4/5/2011
Rubio	Mildred	250.00	7/30/2011
Cappo	Tsu	300.00	5/2/2011
Cappo	Tsu	726.10	8/1/2011

Update Kelsey Clark to Kelsey Bretz

Record selector button for Wilma Brother record

Change Abel to Rubio

FIGURE B-4: **Final PatientDiagnosis datasheet**

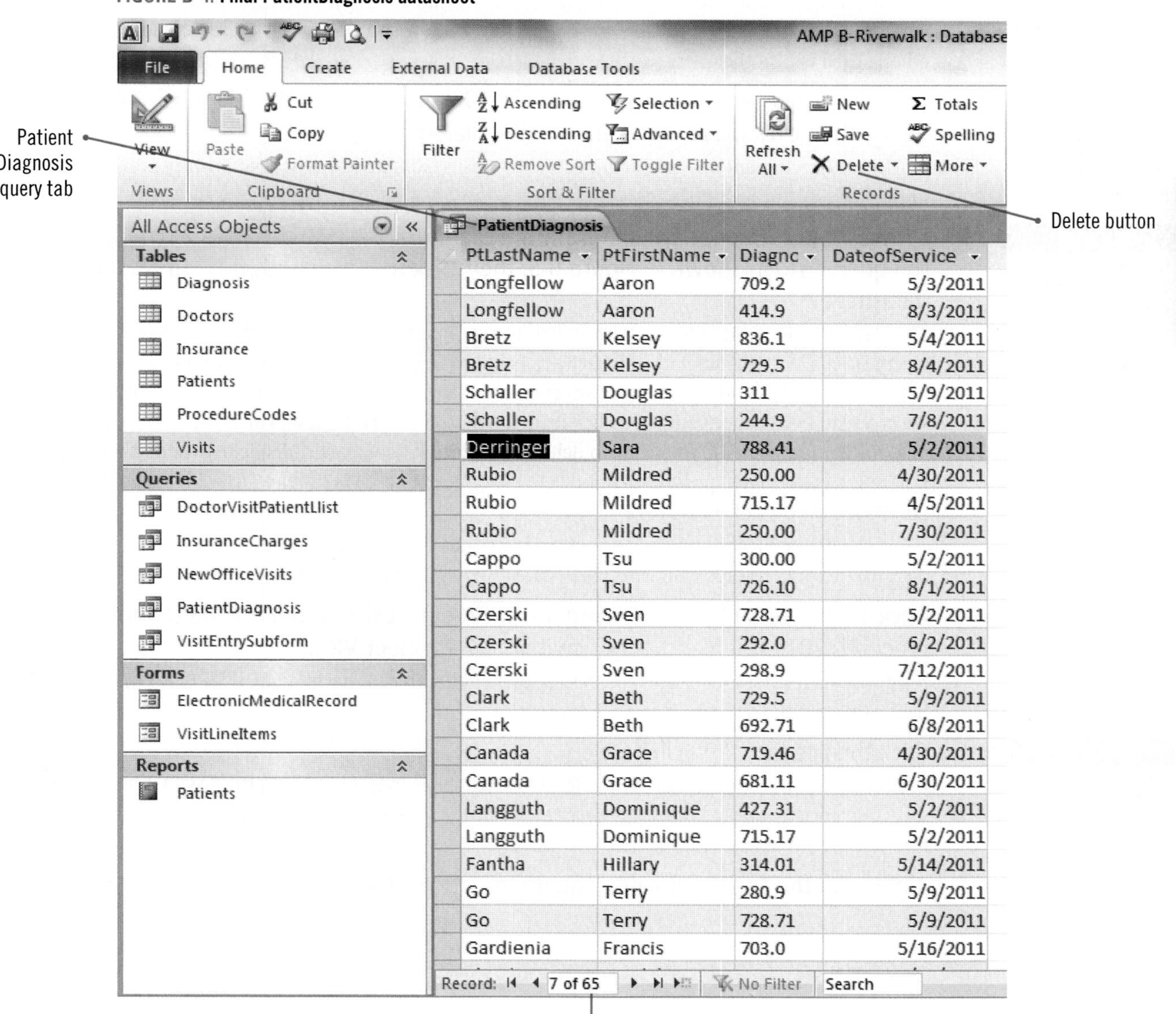

PtLastName	PtFirstName	Diagnc	DateofService
Longfellow	Aaron	709.2	5/3/2011
Longfellow	Aaron	414.9	8/3/2011
Bretz	Kelsey	836.1	5/4/2011
Bretz	Kelsey	729.5	8/4/2011
Schaller	Douglas	311	5/9/2011
Schaller	Douglas	244.9	7/8/2011
Derringer	Sara	788.41	5/2/2011
Rubio	Mildred	250.00	4/30/2011
Rubio	Mildred	715.17	4/5/2011
Rubio	Mildred	250.00	7/30/2011
Cappo	Tsu	300.00	5/2/2011
Cappo	Tsu	726.10	8/1/2011
Czerski	Sven	728.71	5/2/2011
Czerski	Sven	292.0	6/2/2011
Czerski	Sven	298.9	7/12/2011
Clark	Beth	729.5	5/9/2011
Clark	Beth	692.71	6/8/2011
Canada	Grace	719.46	4/30/2011
Canada	Grace	681.11	6/30/2011
Langguth	Dominique	427.31	5/2/2011
Langguth	Dominique	715.17	5/2/2011
Fantha	Hillary	314.01	5/14/2011
Go	Terry	280.9	5/9/2011
Go	Terry	728.71	5/9/2011
Gardienia	Francis	703.0	5/16/2011

UNIT B
Access 2010

Using Query Design View

You use **Query Design View** to add, delete, or move the fields in an existing query, to specify sort orders, or to add **criteria** to limit the number of records shown in the resulting datasheet. You can also use Query Design View to create a new query from scratch. Query Design View presents the fields you can use for that query in small windows called field lists. If you use the fields of two or more related tables in the query, the relationship between two tables is displayed with a **join line** (also called a **link line**) identifying which fields are used to establish the relationship. Tony Sanchez asks you to add a diagnosis description to the PatientDiagnosis query and to limit the records to a specific date of service. You use Query Design View to modify the existing PatientDiagnosis query to meet his request.

STEPS

1. **Open the PatientDiagnosis query, then click the View button on the Home tab to switch to Query Design View**

   Query Design View displays the tables used in the query in the upper pane of the window. The link line shows that the Patients and Visits tables are related using the common PatientID field. The lower pane of the window, called the **query design grid** (or query grid for short), displays the field names, sort orders, and criteria used within the query.

> **TROUBLE**
> When you create a query using the Simple Query Wizard, link lines between tables do not show the one and many symbols.

2. **Click the Show Table button, double-click Diagnosis to add the Diagnosis table to the query, then click Close in the Show Table dialog box**

   The Diagnosis table automatically connects to the Visits table based on the relationships previously established in the Relationships window.

> **QUICK TIP**
> Drag the split bar in Query Design View to resize the upper and lower portions of the window.

3. **Drag the DiagDescription field from the Diagnosis table to the DateofService column in the query grid as shown in Figure B-5, then click the View button to display the datasheet**

   The DateofService field automatically shifted to the right to accommodate the new DiagDescription field in Query Design View. When you double-click a field in a field list, Access inserts it in the next available position in the query design grid. You can also select a field, and then drag it to a specific column of the query grid. To select a field in the query grid, you click its field selector. The **field selector** is the thin gray bar above each field in the query grid. If you want to delete a field from a query, click its field selector, then press [Delete]. Deleting a field from a query does not delete it from the underlying table; the field is only deleted from the query's logical view of the data.

   In Datasheet View, the DiagDescription field adds a description for each DiagnosisCode. To limit the datasheet to only records with a 5/2/2011 date of service, you return to Design View and enter criteria.

4. **Click to switch back to Design View, click the Criteria cell for the DateofService field, type 5/2/2011, then click to switch to Datasheet View**

   Now only six records are selected, because only six of the records have a date of 5/2/2011 in the DateofService field, as shown in Figure B-6.

> **QUICK TIP**
> You can also click the Save button on the Quick Access toolbar to save the current object.

5. **Click the File tab, then click Save**

   In Access, the **Save command** on the File tab saves the current object, and the **Save Object As command** saves the current object with a new name. Recall that Access saves *data* automatically as you move from record to record or close the object.

6. **Right-click the PatientDiagnosis query tab, then click Close**

FIGURE B-5: PatientDiagnosis query in Design View

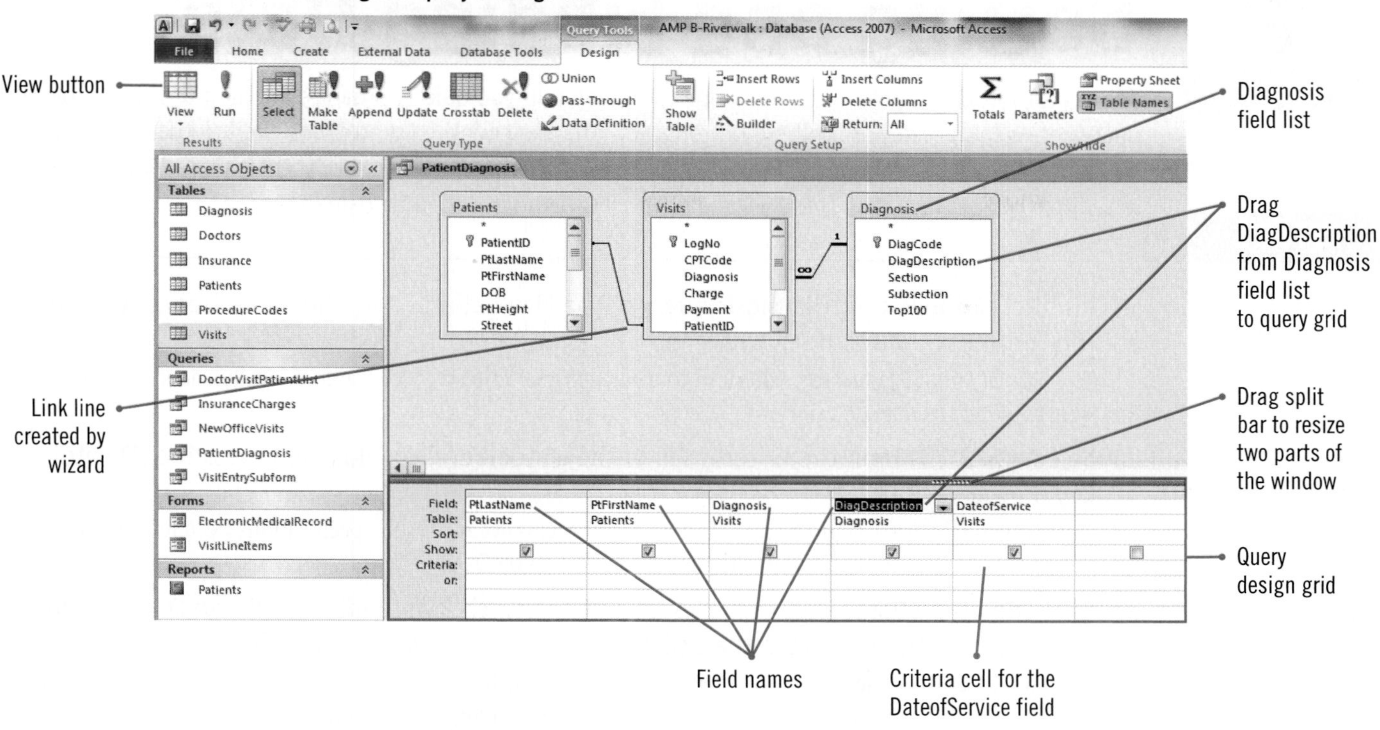

Access 2010

FIGURE B-6: PatientDiagnosis datasheet with DiagDescription field and DateofService criterion

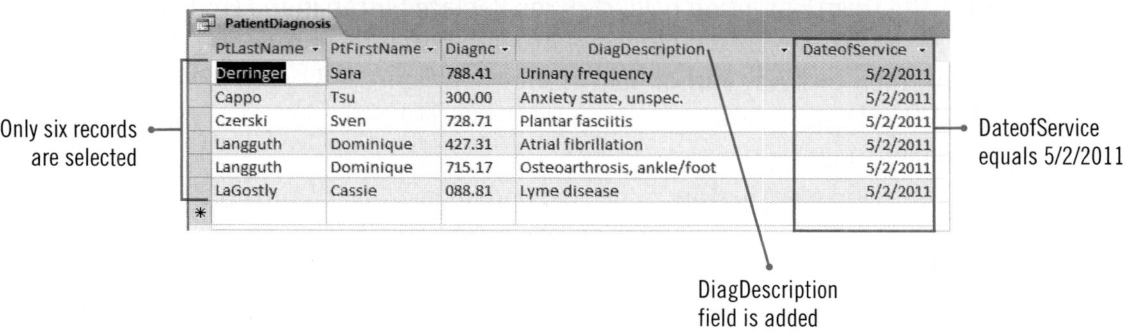

PtLastName	PtFirstName	Diagnc	DiagDescription	DateofService
Derringer	Sara	788.41	Urinary frequency	5/2/2011
Cappo	Tsu	300.00	Anxiety state, unspec.	5/2/2011
Czerski	Sven	728.71	Plantar fasciitis	5/2/2011
Langguth	Dominique	427.31	Atrial fibrillation	5/2/2011
Langguth	Dominique	715.17	Osteoarthrosis, ankle/foot	5/2/2011
LaGostly	Cassie	088.81	Lyme disease	5/2/2011

Adding or deleting a table in a query

To add a new table to Query Design View, click the Show Table button on the Design tab, then add the desired table(s). To delete an unneeded table from Query Design View, click its title bar, then press [Delete].

UNIT B

Access 2010

Sorting and Finding Data

The Access sort and find features are handy tools that help you quickly organize and find data in a table or query datasheet. Besides using these buttons, you can also click the list arrow on the field name in a datasheet, and then click a sorting option. Tony Sanchez asks you to modify the PatientDiagnosis query to redisplay all the records sorted by the patient's last name and then by date of service.

STEPS

1. **Right-click the PatientDiagnosis query in the Navigation Pane, then click Design View on the shortcut menu to open the query in Design View**

   To redisplay all of the records, you need to delete existing criteria. Access automatically added the # (pound signs) around the date criterion.

2. **Select #5/2/2011# in the Criteria cell of the DateofService field, then press the [Delete] key on the keyboard**

   Currently, the PatientDiagnosis query is not sorted. Access evaluates sort specifications from left to right. You want to sort this query first by the PtLastName field then by DateofService.

3. **Click the PtLastName Sort cell, click the list arrow, click Ascending, click the DateofService Sort cell, click the list arrow, then click Ascending as shown in Figure B-7**

   The records are now set to be sorted in ascending order, first by PtLastName, then by the values in the DateofService field. Because sort orders always work left to right, you sometimes need to rearrange the fields before applying a sort order that uses more than one field. To move a field in the query design grid, click its field selector, then drag it left or right.

4. **Click the View button in the Results group to display the query datasheet**

   The records are now sorted in ascending order by the PtLastName field. If two records have the same PtLastName value, they are further sorted by DateofService. You can also sort directly in the datasheet using the Ascending and Descending buttons on the Home tab, but to specify multiple sort orders on nonconsecutive fields, it's best to use Query Design View.

   Your next task is to replace all occurrences of "unspec." with "unspecified" in the DiagDescription field.

5. **Click the DiagDescription field, click the Replace button in the Find group, type unspec. in the Find What box, click in the Replace With box, type unspecified, click the Match list arrow, then click Any Part of field as shown in Figure B-8**

   The Find and Replace dialog box can be used to find or replace any series of characters in the current field or the entire datasheet.

6. **Click the Find Next button in the Find and Replace dialog box, click Replace as many times as necessary to replace all occurrences, click OK when prompted that Access cannot find the text specified, then click Cancel in the Find and Replace dialog box**

   Access replaced all occurrences of "unspec." with "unspecified" in the Category field, as shown in Figure B-9. Although you may be tempted to click the Replace All button to make all of the replacements very quickly, if you are unfamiliar with the data, it's best to review each replacement by using the Replace button.

7. **Right-click the PatientDiagnosis query tab, click Close, then click Yes when prompted to save changes**

TROUBLE

If your find-and-replace effort did not work correctly, click the Undo button and repeat Steps 5 and 6.

FIGURE B-7: **Setting sort orders for the PatientDiagnosis query**

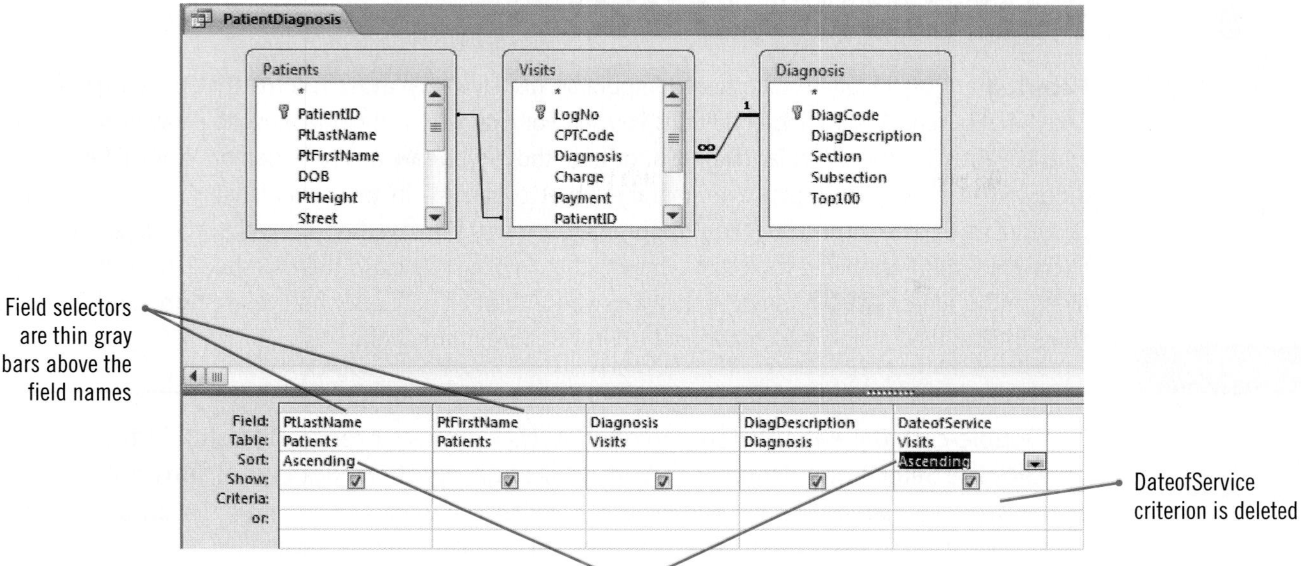

FIGURE B-8: **Find and Replace dialog box**

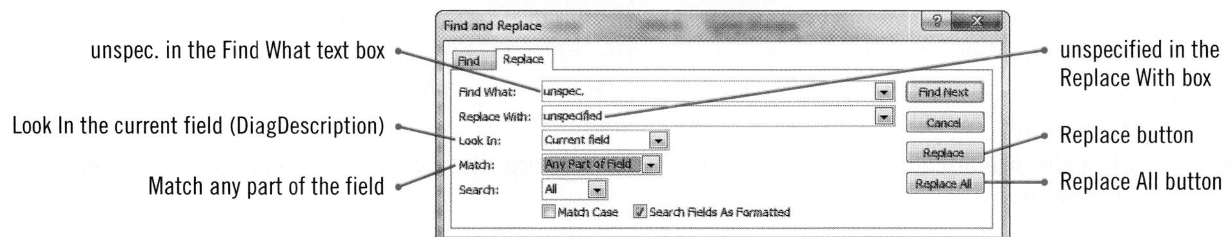

FIGURE B-9: **Final PatientDiagnosis datasheet with new sort orders**

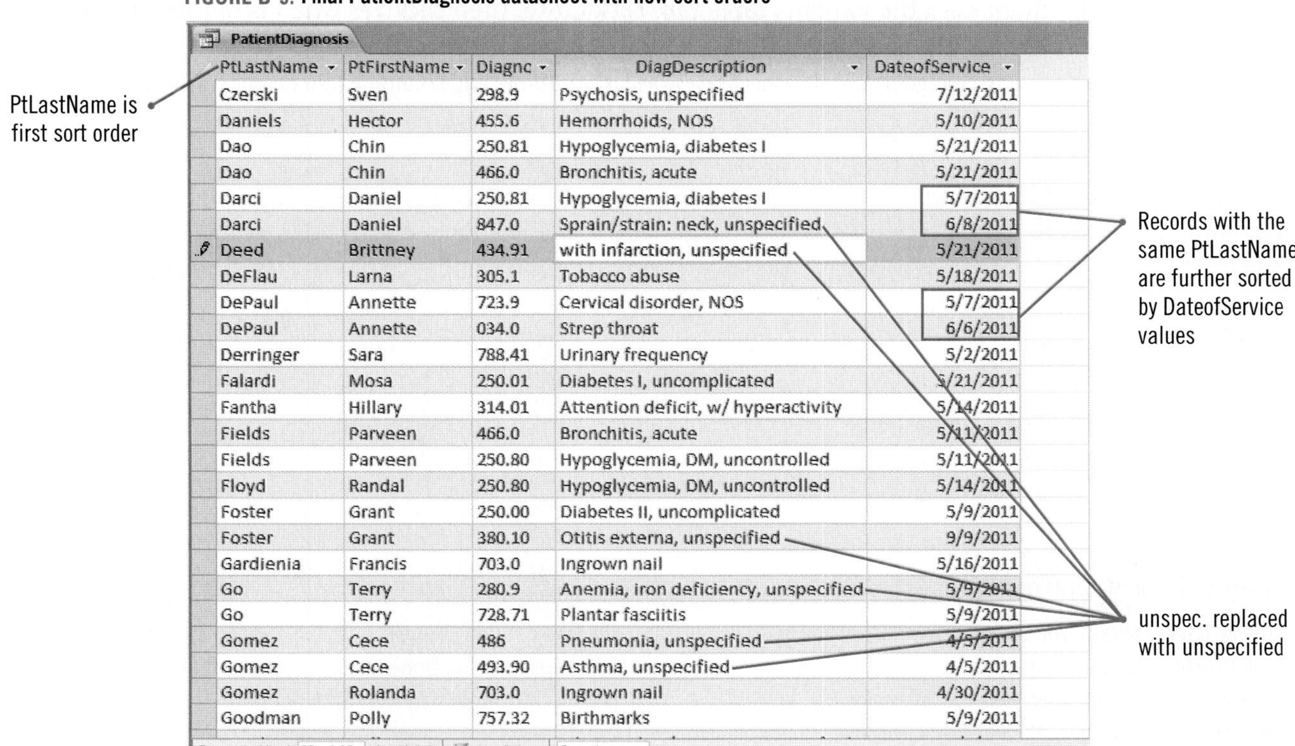

PtLastName	PtFirstName	Diagnc	DiagDescription	DateofService
Czerski	Sven	298.9	Psychosis, unspecified	7/12/2011
Daniels	Hector	455.6	Hemorrhoids, NOS	5/10/2011
Dao	Chin	250.81	Hypoglycemia, diabetes I	5/21/2011
Dao	Chin	466.0	Bronchitis, acute	5/21/2011
Darci	Daniel	250.81	Hypoglycemia, diabetes I	5/7/2011
Darci	Daniel	847.0	Sprain/strain: neck, unspecified	6/8/2011
Deed	Brittney	434.91	with infarction, unspecified	5/21/2011
DeFlau	Larna	305.1	Tobacco abuse	5/18/2011
DePaul	Annette	723.9	Cervical disorder, NOS	5/7/2011
DePaul	Annette	034.0	Strep throat	6/6/2011
Derringer	Sara	788.41	Urinary frequency	5/2/2011
Falardi	Mosa	250.01	Diabetes I, uncomplicated	5/21/2011
Fantha	Hillary	314.01	Attention deficit, w/ hyperactivity	5/14/2011
Fields	Parveen	466.0	Bronchitis, acute	5/11/2011
Fields	Parveen	250.80	Hypoglycemia, DM, uncontrolled	5/11/2011
Floyd	Randal	250.80	Hypoglycemia, DM, uncontrolled	5/14/2011
Foster	Grant	250.00	Diabetes II, uncomplicated	5/9/2011
Foster	Grant	380.10	Otitis externa, unspecified	9/9/2011
Gardienia	Francis	703.0	Ingrown nail	5/16/2011
Go	Terry	280.9	Anemia, iron deficiency, unspecified	5/9/2011
Go	Terry	728.71	Plantar fasciitis	5/9/2011
Gomez	Cece	486	Pneumonia, unspecified	4/5/2011
Gomez	Cece	493.90	Asthma, unspecified	4/5/2011
Gomez	Rolanda	703.0	Ingrown nail	4/30/2011
Goodman	Polly	757.32	Birthmarks	5/9/2011

Access 2010

UNIT
B
Access 2010

Filtering Data

Filtering a table or query datasheet temporarily displays only those records that match given criteria. Recall that criteria are limiting conditions you set. For example, you might want to show only the patients who have received a particular diagnosis, or only those who saw a certain doctor. While filters provide a quick and easy way to display a temporary subset of records in the current datasheet, they are not as powerful or flexible as queries. Most importantly, a query is a saved object within the database, whereas filters are temporary because Access removes them when you close the datasheet. Table B-1 compares filters and queries. Tony Sanchez asks you to find all patients who live in Boston and Cambridge. You can filter the Patients table datasheet to provide this information.

STEPS

1. **Double-click the Patients table to open it, click any occurrence of Boston in the City field, click the Selection button in the Sort & Filter group, then click Equals "Boston"**

   Ten records are selected as shown in Figure B-10. A filter icon appears to the right of the City field. Filtering by the selected field value, called **Filter By Selection**, is a fast and easy way to filter the records for an exact match. To add Cambridge to the filter, you can use the Filter arrow for the City field.

2. **Click the Filter button for the City field, click the Cambridge check box as shown in Figure B-11, then click OK**

   Twenty-one records are selected, those with a City value of Boston or Cambridge. To filter for comparative data (for example, where DateofService is *equal to* or *greater than* 7/1/2011), you must use the **Filter By Form** feature. An asterisk (*) in the day position of the date criterion (7/*/2011) works as a wildcard, selecting any date in the month of July (the seventh month) in the year 2011. The Filter By Form feature as well as the Clear All Filters options are found on the Advanced button.

3. **Click the Advanced button in the Sort & Filter group, then click Clear All Filters to display all records**

   All filters are cleared and all 39 patient records are displayed. Note that filter icon next to the City field is removed as well.

4. **Right-click the Patients table tab, click Close, then click Yes when prompted to save the changes**

   Saving changes to the datasheet saves the last sort order and column width changes. Filters are not saved.

QUICK TIP

Be sure to remove existing filters before applying a new filter, or the new filter will apply to the current subset of records instead of the entire datasheet.

Using wildcard characters

To search for a pattern, you can use a **wildcard** character to represent any character in the condition entry. Use a question mark (?) to search for any single character, and an asterisk (*) to search for any number of characters. Wildcard characters are often used with the **Like operator**. For example, the criterion Like "12/*/13" would find all dates in December of 2013, and the criterion Like "F*" would find all entries that start with the letter F.

FIGURE B-10: Filtering the Tours table

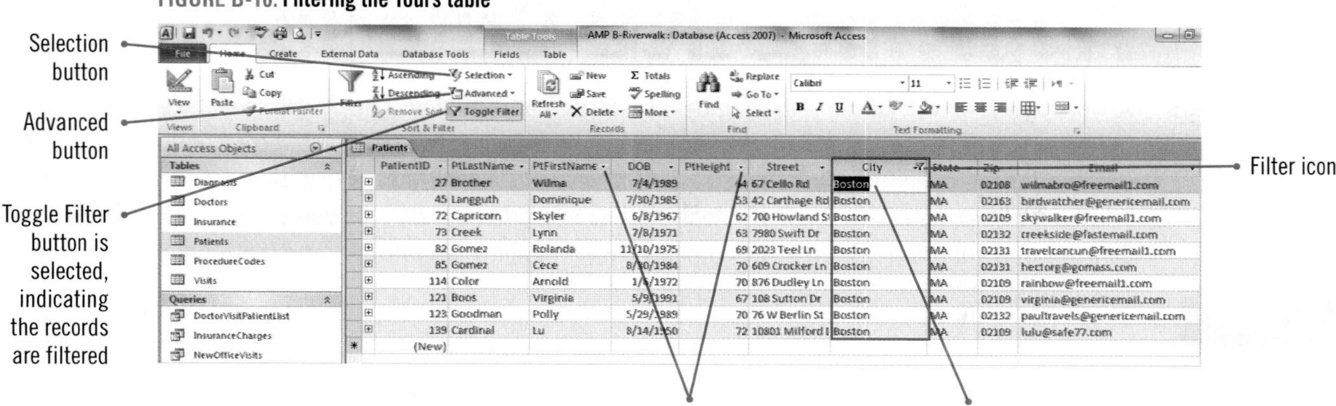

FIGURE B-11: Using the Sort and Filter options

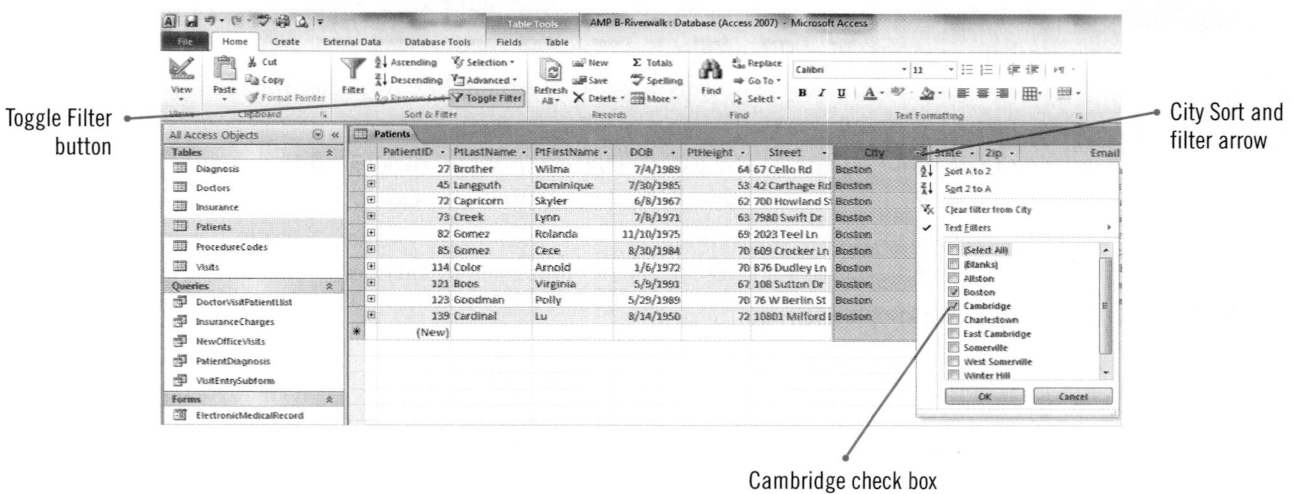

Access 2010

TABLE B-1: Filters vs. queries

characteristics	filters	queries
Are saved as an object in the database	No	Yes
Can be used to select a subset of records in a datasheet	Yes	Yes
Can be used to select a subset of fields in a datasheet	No	Yes
Resulting datasheet used to enter and edit data	Yes	Yes
Resulting datasheet used to sort, filter, and find records	Yes	Yes
Commonly used as the source of data for a form or report	No	Yes
Can calculate sums, averages, counts, and other types of summary statistics across records	No	Yes
Can be used to create calculated fields	No	Yes

UNIT B
Access 2010

Applying AND Criteria

As you have seen, you can limit the number of records that appear on a query datasheet by entering criteria in Query Design View. Criteria are tests, or limiting conditions, for which the record must be true to be selected for the query datasheet. To create **AND criteria**, which means that all criteria must be true to select the record, enter two or more criteria on the same Criteria row of the query design grid. Tony Sanchez asks you to provide a list of all patient visits for Dr. Quinn in the month of April. You use Query Design View and AND criteria to meet his request.

STEPS

1. **Click the Create tab on the Ribbon, click the Query Design button in the Queries group, double-click Doctors, double-click Visits, double-click Patients, then click Close in the Show Table dialog box**
   You want the doctor's name, the date of the visit, and the patient's name in this query.
2. **Double-click DrLastName from the Doctors table, drag the lower edge of the Visits field list down to display all of the fields, double-click DateofService, double-click PtFirstName from the Patients table, then double-click PtLastName from the Patients table**
   First add criteria to select only those records for Dr. Quinn.
3. **Click the first Criteria cell for the DrLastName field, type Quinn, then click the View button to display the results**
   Querying for only Dr. Quinn's patients selects seven records. Next, you add criteria to select only those records with a date of service in April 2011.
4. **Click the View button to switch to Design View, click the first Criteria cell for the DateofService field, then type 4/*/2011 as shown in Figure B-12**
   Criteria added to the same line of the query design grid are AND criteria. When entered on the same line, each criterion must be true for the record to appear in the resulting datasheet.
5. **Click to display the query results**
   Querying for both Quinn and 4/*/2011 selects four records as shown in Figure B-13. Every time you add AND criteria, you *narrow* the number of records that are selected because the record must be true for *all* criteria. Access assists you with **criteria syntax**, rules that specify how to enter criteria. Access automatically adds "quotation marks" around text criteria in Text fields ("Quinn") and the Like operator if you use the * wildcard character in criteria. The criteria in Number, Currency, and Yes/No fields are not surrounded by any characters. See Table B-2 for more information about comparison operators such as > (greater than).
6. **Click the Save button on the Quick Access toolbar, type QuinnApril as the query name, click OK, then close the query**
   The query is saved with the new name, QuinnApril, as a new object in the AMP B-Riverwalk database.

QUICK TIP
Text criteria are not case sensitive, so Quinn equals QUINN equals quinn.

TROUBLE
If your datasheet doesn't match Figure B-13, return to Query Design View and compare your criteria to that of Figure B-12.

Searching for blank fields

Is Null and Is Not Null are two other types of common criteria. The **Is Null** criterion finds all records where no entry has been made in the field. **Is Not Null** finds all records where there is any entry in the field, even if the entry is 0. Primary key fields cannot have a null entry.

FIGURE B-12: Query Design View with AND criteria

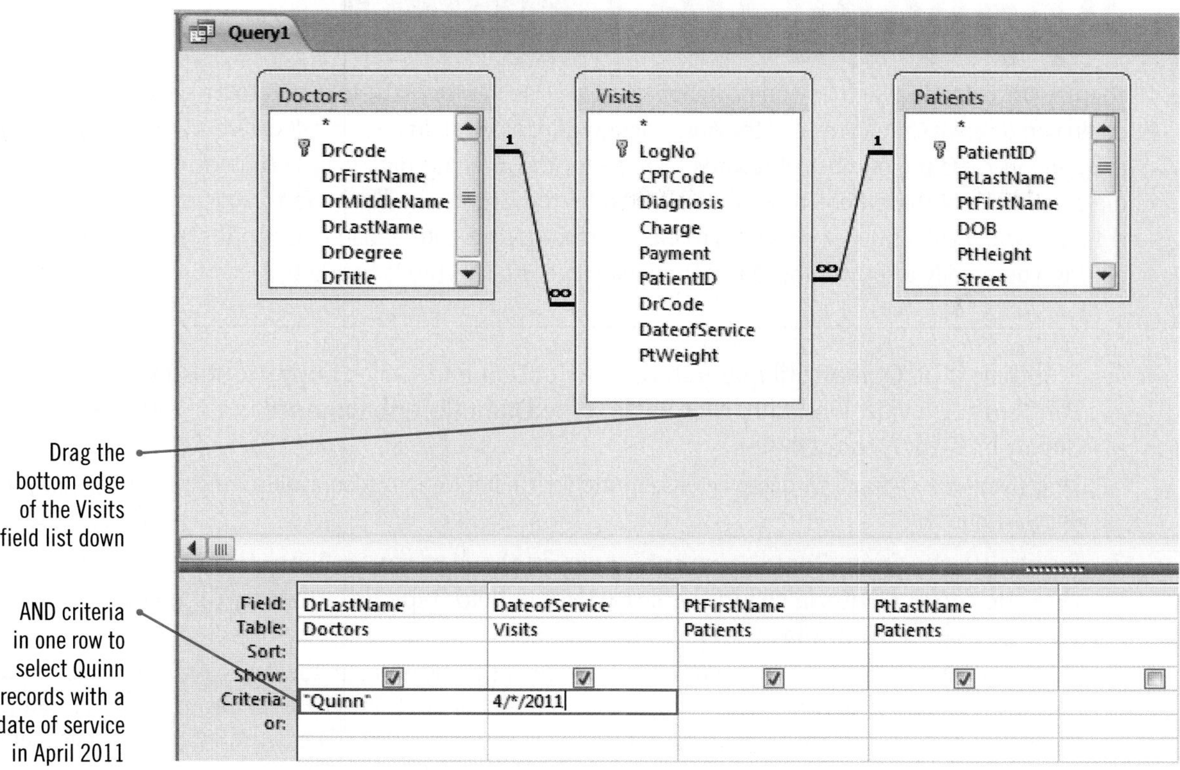

FIGURE B-13: Final datasheet of QuinnApril query

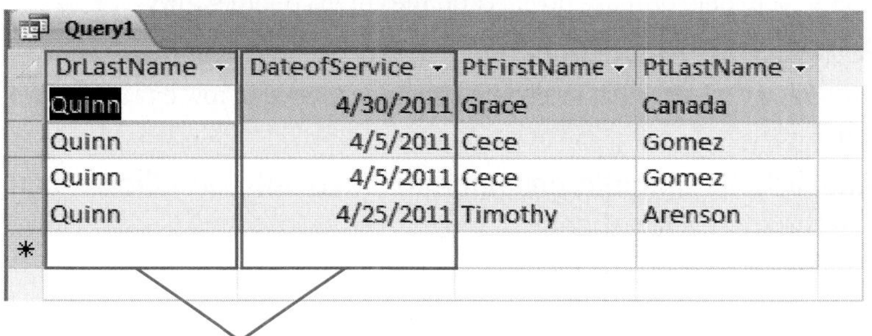

TABLE B-2: Comparison operators

operator	description	expression	meaning
>	Greater than	>500	Numbers greater than 500
>=	Greater than or equal to	>=500	Numbers greater than or equal to 500
<	Less than	<"Braveheart"	Names from A to Braveheart, but not Braveheart
<=	Less than or equal to	<="Bridgewater"	Names from A through Bridgewater, inclusive
<>	Not equal to	<>"Fontanelle"	Any name except for Fontanelle

Access 2010

UNIT
B
Access 2010

Applying OR Criteria

You use **OR criteria** when any one criterion must be true in order for the record to be selected. Enter OR criteria on *different* Criteria rows of the query design grid. As you add rows of OR criteria to the query design grid, you *increase* the number of records selected for the resulting datasheet because the record needs to match *only one* of the Criteria rows to be selected for the datasheet. Tony Sanchez asks you to add criteria to the previous query. He wants to include records for Dr. Rosenbaum during the month of April. To do this, you modify a copy of the QuinnApril query and use OR criteria to add the records.

STEPS

1. **Right-click the QuinnApril query in the Navigation Pane, click Copy, right-click a blank spot in the Navigation Pane, click Paste, type QuinnRosenbaumApril in the Paste As dialog box, then click OK**

   By copying the QuinnApril query before starting your modifications, you avoid changing the QuinnApril query by mistake.

2. **Right-click the QuinnRosenbaumApril query in the Navigation Pane, click Design View, click the second Criteria cell in the DrLastName field, type Rosenbaum, then click the View button to display the query datasheet**

   The query selected 16 records including all of the visits with Rosenbaum in the DrLastName field. However, note that some of the DateofService values are not in April of 2011. Because each row of the query grid is evaluated separately, all Rosenbaum records are selected regardless of criteria in any other row. To make sure that the Rosenbaum records are also in the month of April 2011 for the DateofService, you need to modify the second row of the query grid (the "or" row) to specify that criteria.

3. **Click the View button to switch to Query Design View, click the second Criteria cell in the DateofService field, then type 4/*/2011 as shown in Figure B-14**

   The criteria in one row have no effect on the criteria of other rows.

4. **Click to display the query datasheet**

   Six records are selected that meet both criteria as entered in row one *or* row two of the query grid, as shown in Figure B-15.

5. **Right-click the QuinnRosenbaumApril query tab, click Close, then click Yes to save and close the query datasheet**

QUICK TIP
The Datasheet, Design, and other view buttons are also located in the lower-right corner of the Access window.

FIGURE B-14: Query Design View with OR criteria

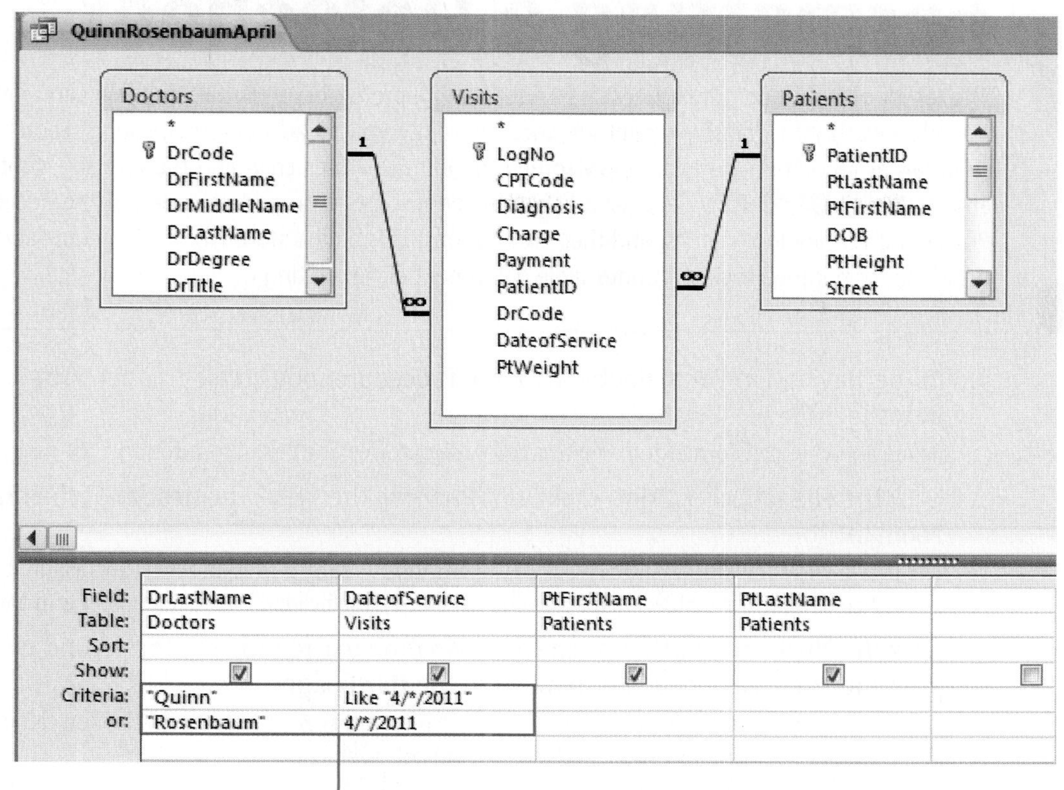

OR criteria in two rows to select both Quinn and Rosenbaum records with a DateofService in April 2011

FIGURE B-15: Final datasheet of the QuinnRosenbaumApril query

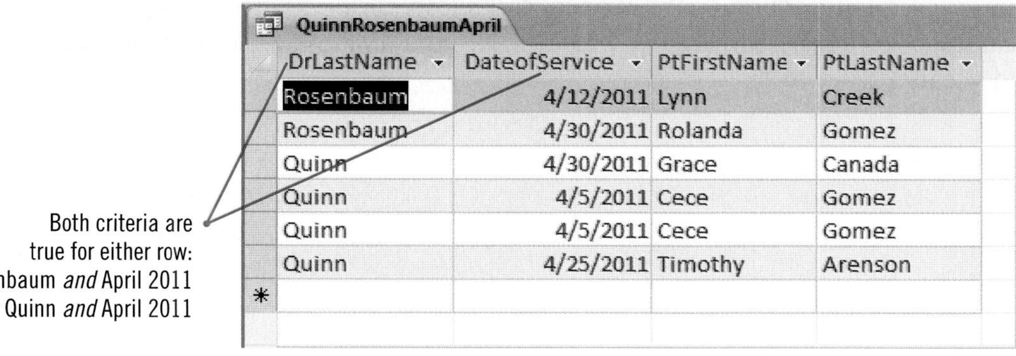

QuinnRosenbaumApril

DrLastName	DateofService	PtFirstName	PtLastName
Rosenbaum	4/12/2011	Lynn	Creek
Rosenbaum	4/30/2011	Rolanda	Gomez
Quinn	4/30/2011	Grace	Canada
Quinn	4/5/2011	Cece	Gomez
Quinn	4/5/2011	Cece	Gomez
Quinn	4/25/2011	Timothy	Arenson
*			

Both criteria are true for either row: Rosenbaum *and* April 2011 Or Quinn *and* April 2011

UNIT B

Access 2010

Formatting a Datasheet

The report object is the primary Access tool to create a professional printout, but you can print a datasheet as well. Although a datasheet printout does not allow you to add custom headers, footers, images, or subtotals as reports do, you can apply some formatting, such as changing the font size, font face, colors, and gridlines. Tony Sanchez asks you to print a list of procedure codes, also called CPT (Current Procedural Terminology) codes, and their descriptions. This data is stored in the ProcedureCodes table. You decide to format the ProcedureCodes table datasheet before printing it.

STEPS

1. **In the Navigation Pane, double-click the ProcedureCodes table to open it in Datasheet View**

   Before applying new formatting enhancements, you preview the default printout.

2. **Click the File tab, click Print, click Print Preview, then click the header of the printout to zoom in**

   The preview window displays the layout of the printout, as shown in Figure B-16. By default, the printout of a datasheet contains the object name and current date in the header. The page number is in the footer.

3. **Click the Next Page button in the navigation bar to move to the second page of the printout, then click again to move to the third page**

   The report is only two fields wide, and fits on three printed pages. In Datasheet View you can make font face, font size, font color, gridline color, and background color choices.

4. **Click the Close Print Preview button, click the Font list arrow Calibri in the Text Formatting group, click Times New Roman, click the Font Size list arrow 11, then click 14**

   With the larger font size applied, you need to resize the ProcedureDescr column to accommodate the widest entries.

5. **Use the pointer to double-click the field separator to the right of the ProcedureDescr field**

   Double-clicking the field separator widens the column as necessary to display every entry in that field, as shown in Figure B-17.

6. **Click the File tab, click Print, then click Print Preview**

   The printout is now four pages long, but with the larger font size, it is easier to read.

7. **Right-click the ProcedureCodes table tab, click Close, click Yes when prompted to save changes, click the File tab, then click Exit to close the AMP B-Riverwalk.accdb database and Access 2010**

QUICK TIP

If you need a printout of this datasheet, click the Print button on the Print Preview tab, then click OK.

FIGURE B-16: Preview of ProcedureCodes datasheet

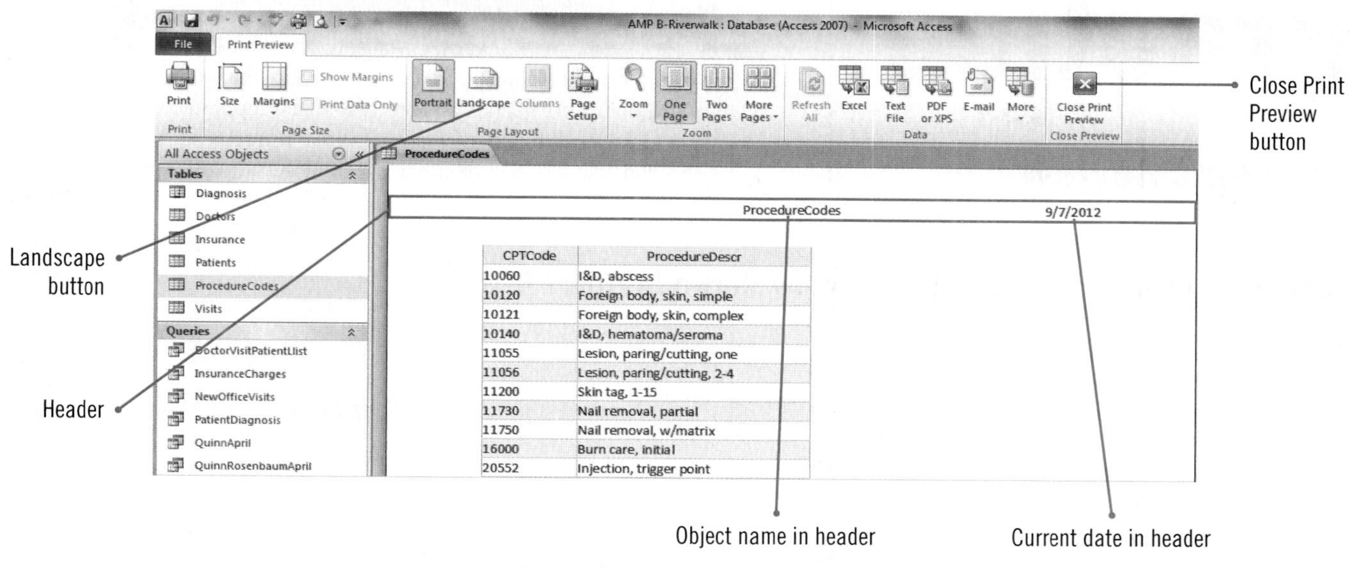

FIGURE B-17: Formatting the ProcedureCodes datasheet

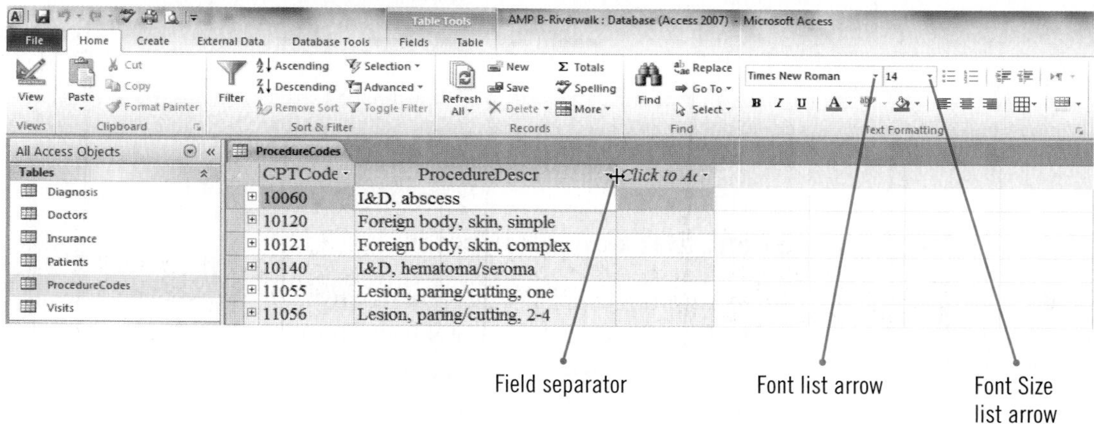

Access 2010

Practice

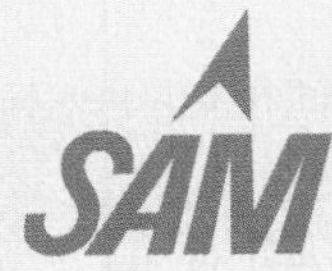

For current SAM information, including versions and content details, visit SAM Central (http://www.cengage.com/samcentral). If you have a SAM user profile, you may have access to hands-on instruction, practice, and assessment of the skills covered in this unit. Since various versions of SAM are supported throughout the life of this text, check with your instructor for the correct instructions and URL/Web site for accessing assignments.

Concepts Review

Label each element of the Access window shown in Figure B-18.

FIGURE B-18

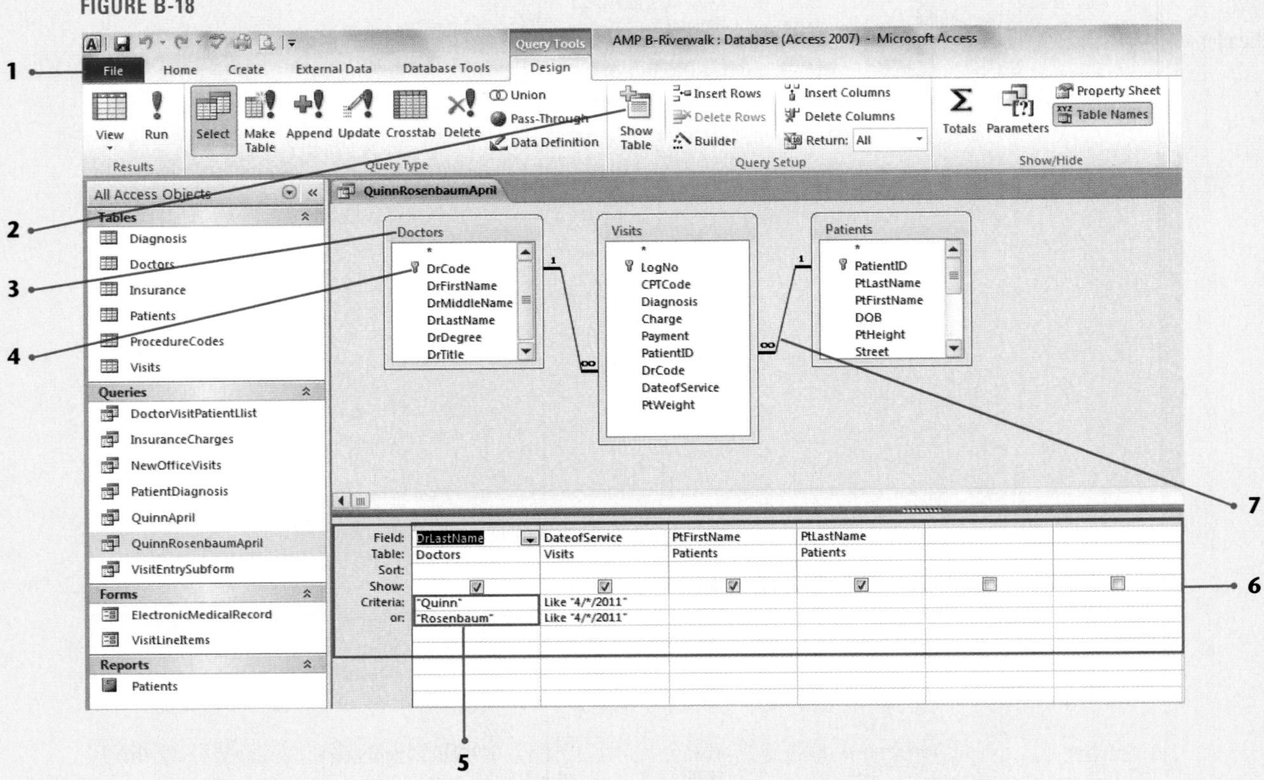

Match each term with the statement that best describes it.

8. Query grid
9. Criteria
10. Filter
11. Syntax
12. Field lists
13. Sorting
14. Wildcard
15. Is Null

a. Creates a temporary subset of records
b. Small windows that display field names
c. Rules that determine how criteria are entered
d. Limiting conditions used to restrict the number of records that are selected in a query
e. Used to search for a pattern of characters
f. Criterion that finds all records where no entry has been made in the field
g. The lower pane in Query Design View
h. Putting records in ascending or descending order based on the values of a field

Select the best answer from the list of choices.

16. AND criteria:

- **a.** Must all be true for the record to be selected.
- **b.** Determine sort orders.
- **c.** Determine fields selected for a query.
- **d.** Help set link lines between tables in a query.

17. SQL stands for which of the following?

- **a.** Standard Query Language
- **b.** Special Query Listing
- **c.** Structured Query Language
- **d.** Simple Query Listing

18. A query is sometimes called a logical view of data because:

- **a.** You can create queries with the Logical Query Wizard.
- **b.** Queries do not store data, they only display a view of data.
- **c.** Queries contain logical criteria.
- **d.** Query naming conventions are logical.

19. Which of the following describes OR criteria?

- **a.** Selecting a subset of fields and/or records to view as a datasheet from one or more tables
- **b.** Using two or more rows of the query grid to select only those records that meet given criteria
- **c.** Reorganizing the records in either ascending or descending order based on the contents of one or more fields
- **d.** Using multiple fields in the query design grid

20. Which of the following is *not* true about a query?

- **a.** A query can be used to create calculated fields.
- **b.** A query can be used to create summary statistics.
- **c.** A query can be used to enter and edit data.
- **d.** A query is the same thing as a filter.

Skills Review

1. Use the Query Wizard.

- **a.** Open the AMP B-B2.accdb database from the drive and folder where you store your Data Files, then save the database as **AMP B-Diabetes.accdb**. Enable content if prompted.
- **b.** Create a new query using the Simple Query Wizard. Select the FirstName, LastName, and City fields from the Patients table, the VisitDate field from the Visits table, and the FirstName and LastName fields from the Employees table. Choose the Detail option, and enter **PatientListing** as the name of the query.
- **c.** Open the query in Datasheet View, widen all columns to see all data, then change any record with Casti Moseman in the Employees_FirstName and Employees_LastName fields to your own name. (Note that the table name precedes the FirstName and LastName fields because the same field name is used in both the Patients and Employees tables.)

2. Work with data in a query.

- **a.** Change any occurrence of Lili Santana in the Employees_FirstName and Employees_LastName fields to your instructor's name.
- **b.** Click any value in the VisitDate field, then click the Descending button in the Sort & Filter group on the Home tab to sort the records in descending order on the VisitDate field.
- **c.** Use the Calendar Picker to choose the date of **2/28/2011** for the first record.
- **d.** Save and close the PatientListing query.

3. Use Query Design View.

- **a.** Click the Create tab, click the Query Design button, double-click Patients, double-click Medications, double-click MedDescription, and then click Close to add these three tables to Query Design View.
- **b.** Drag the split bar down between the upper and lower parts of the window, and then drag the bottom edge of the Patients table down to display all of the field names in that table.
- **c.** Add the following fields from the Patients table to the query design grid in the following order: **FirstName**, **LastName**, **TypeOfDiabetes**, and **DiagnosisDate**. Add the following field from the MedDescriptions table: **MedDescrip**. View the results in Datasheet View, observing the number of records that are selected.
- **d.** In Design View, enter criteria to display only those records with a TypeOfDiabetes value of **II** (two capital Is), then observe the number of records that are selected.
- **e.** Save the query with the name **TypeII**, and close it.

Skills Review (continued)

4. Sort and find data.

a. Open the ConsultsByEmployee query in Datasheet View to observe how the records are currently sorted (in ascending order based on the EmployeeLast field).

b. In Query Design View, choose an ascending sort order for the VisitDate field as well.

c. Display the query in Datasheet View, noting how the records have been resorted.

d. Click any value in the EmployeeLast field, then use the Find and Replace dialog box to find all occurrences of **Fonzi**, and replace them with **Washington**.

e. Save and close the ConsultsByEmployee datasheet.

5. Filter data.

a. Filter the Patients table datasheet for only those records where the City equals **Urbandale**.

b. Use the filter and sort buttons to add records to the filter where the City equals **Clive**.

c. Change the name of patient Sharon Burnett to your name, and if requested by your instructor, print the first page of the filtered Patients datasheet.

d. Save and close the Patients datasheet.

6. Apply AND criteria.

a. Copy and paste the ConsultsByEmployee query with the new query name of **2HourConsults**.

b. Add criteria to select all of the records with an Hrs value of **>=2**, then view the datasheet to make sure you've selected the correct records.

c. In Design View, add criteria to select only those records with your name in the EmployeeLast field that also have an Hrs value of >=2.

d. View the datasheet to make sure you've selected the correct records that match both criteria.

e. Save the 2HourConsults query.

7. Apply OR criteria.

a. Open the 2HourConsults query in Query Design View.

b. Add criteria to include the records with your instructor's last name as the EmployeeLast value that also have an Hrs value of >=2.

c. Save the 2HourConsults query, then switch to Datasheet View to make sure you've selected the correct records that match the new criteria.

8. Format a datasheet.

a. With the 2HourConsults query open in Datasheet View, apply an Arial Narrow font and a 14-point font size.

b. Resize all columns so that all data and field names are visible. See Figure B-19.

c. Save the 2HourConsults query.

d. If requested by your instructor, print the datasheet.

e. Close the 2HourConsults query and the AMP B-Diabetes.accdb database, then exit Access 2010.

FIGURE B-19

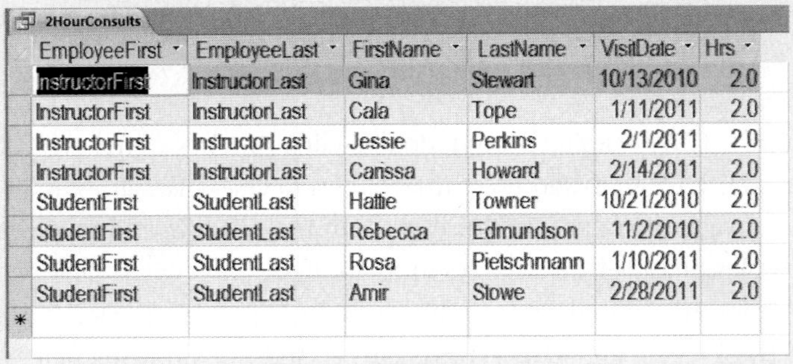

2HourConsults

EmployeeFirst	EmployeeLast	FirstName	LastName	VisitDate	Hrs
InstructorFirst	InstructorLast	Gina	Stewart	10/13/2010	2.0
InstructorFirst	InstructorLast	Cala	Tope	1/11/2011	2.0
InstructorFirst	InstructorLast	Jessie	Perkins	2/1/2011	2.0
InstructorFirst	InstructorLast	Carissa	Howard	2/14/2011	2.0
StudentFirst	StudentLast	Hattie	Towner	10/21/2010	2.0
StudentFirst	StudentLast	Rebecca	Edmundson	11/2/2010	2.0
StudentFirst	StudentLast	Rosa	Pietschmann	1/10/2011	2.0
StudentFirst	StudentLast	Amir	Stowe	2/28/2011	2.0
*					

Independent Challenge 1

You have built an Access database to track nursing assignments at a multi-location dermatology clinic. You will use queries to find specific assignment information.

- **a.** Start Access, open the AMP B-B3.accdb database from the drive and folder where you store your Data Files, then save it as **AMP B-Nurses.accdb**. Enable content if prompted.
- **b.** Open each of the five tables to review the fields and records contained in each, then close the tables. Click the Database Tools tab, then the Relationships button to see how the five tables are joined to create this relational database. This database creates a nurse schedule by linking each of the other four tables—Doctors, Nurses, Locations, and ScheduleDate—in a one-to-many relationship with the ScheduleItems table.
- **c.** Close the Relationships window. Even though you have not created this database, it's important to review the relationships so you can select the correct tables and fields needed for your queries.
- **d.** In Query Design View, build a query with all five tables. Drag the edges of the field lists to resize them and drag the title bars of the field lists so that the link lines do not overlap.
- **e.** Add the following fields to the query grid in the following order: ScheduleDate from the ScheduleDate table, LocationName from the Locations table, NurseLName from the Nurses table, and LastName from the Doctors table.
- **f.** View the datasheet, observe the number of records selected, then return to Query Design View.
- **g.** Add sort orders to sort the records in ascending order on the ScheduleDate, LocationName, and NurseLName fields.
- **h.** Add criteria to select only those records where the LastName in the Doctors table is Agri or Swabe.
- **i.** View the datasheet. Enter your own last name instead of Vasquez in the NurseLName field, widen all columns so that all data and field names are visible, and save the query with the name **Agri-Swabe** as shown in Figure B-20.
- **j.** If requested by your instructor, print the first page of the datasheet.
- **k.** Close the Agri-Swabe query and the AMP B-Nurses.accdb database, then exit Access 2010.

FIGURE B-20

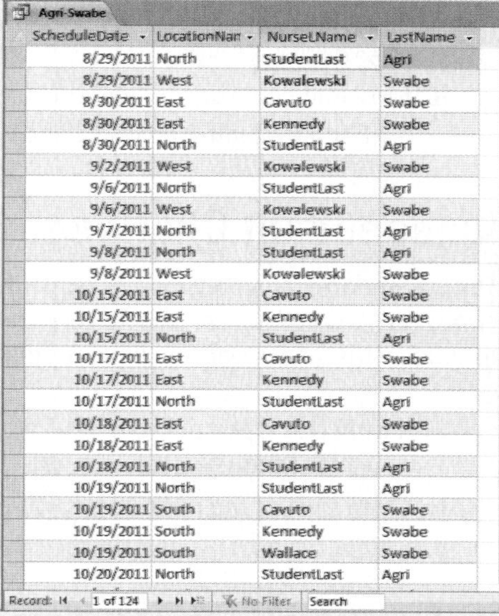

Agri-Swabe

ScheduleDate	LocationNam	NurseLName	LastName
8/29/2011	North	StudentLast	Agri
8/29/2011	West	Kowalewski	Swabe
8/30/2011	East	Cavuto	Swabe
8/30/2011	East	Kennedy	Swabe
8/30/2011	North	StudentLast	Agri
9/2/2011	West	Kowalewski	Swabe
9/6/2011	North	StudentLast	Agri
9/6/2011	West	Kowalewski	Swabe
9/7/2011	North	StudentLast	Agri
9/8/2011	North	StudentLast	Agri
9/8/2011	West	Kowalewski	Swabe
10/15/2011	East	Cavuto	Swabe
10/15/2011	East	Kennedy	Swabe
10/15/2011	North	StudentLast	Agri
10/17/2011	East	Cavuto	Swabe
10/17/2011	East	Kennedy	Swabe
10/17/2011	North	StudentLast	Agri
10/18/2011	East	Cavuto	Swabe
10/18/2011	East	Kennedy	Swabe
10/18/2011	North	StudentLast	Agri
10/19/2011	North	StudentLast	Agri
10/19/2011	South	Cavuto	Swabe
10/19/2011	South	Kennedy	Swabe
10/19/2011	South	Wallace	Swabe
10/20/2011	North	StudentLast	Agri

Record: 1 of 124 No Filter Search

Independent Challenge 2

You are working with a medical school's intern placement program. You have started an Access database to track evaluations of interns.

- **a.** Start Access, open the AMP B-B4.accdb database from the drive and folder where you store your Data Files, then save it as **AMP B-InternMgmt.accdb**. Enable content if prompted.
- **b.** Open the InternName and then the Evaluations tables. Notice that one intern is related to many evaluations as evidenced by the expand buttons to the left of the records in the InternName table.
- **c.** Close both datasheets, then using Query Design View create a query with the InternFName and InternLName fields from the InternName table, and the EvaluationDate, Prompt, Professional, Knowledgeable, and Respectful fields (in that order) from the Evaluations table.
- **d.** Sort the records in ascending order on the InternLName field, then the EvaluationDate field, and view the datasheet to make sure the sort orders are working correctly.
- **e.** In Query Design View, add criteria to select only the records for interns with the last name of **Ling** or **Walters**, then view the datasheet to make sure the criteria works as desired.

Independent Challenge 2 (continued)

Advanced Challenge Exercise

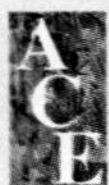

- In Query Design View, enter the following calculated field in the blank field cell to the right of the Respectful field. To create a larger space to make the entry, right-click the cell, then click Zoom. This calculation will average the four other scores. Note that each field name is surrounded by [square brackets] and the addition of the four fields is surrounded by (parentheses) before being divided by 4.
  Overall:([Prompt]+[Professional]+[Knowledgeable]+[Respectful])/4
- Display the query in Datasheet View as shown in Figure B-21.

f. Save the query using Results as the name, then change the last name of Ling to your last name. Resize the columns as needed to view all the data and field names.

g. Print the datasheet if requested by your instructor, then save and close it.

h. Close the Results query and the AMP InternMgmt-B.accdb database, then exit Access 2010.

FIGURE B-21

Results

InternFNam	InternLNam	EvaluationD	Prompt	Professional	Knowledgea	Respectful	Overall
Quan	Ling	1/7/2013	5	4	4	4	4.25
Quan	Ling	1/7/2013	5	5	4	4	4.5
Quan	Ling	1/7/2013	5	5	5	4	4.75
Quan	Ling	1/7/2013	5	5	5	5	5
Quan	Ling	1/7/2013	5	5	5	4	4.75
Quan	Ling	1/7/2013	5	5	5	5	5
Quan	Ling	1/8/2013	2	5	4	5	4
Quan	Ling	1/8/2013	5	4	5	4	4.5
Quan	Ling	1/8/2013	4	5	5	4	4.5
Quan	Ling	1/8/2013	4	5	5	4	4.5

Independent Challenge 3

You are working for an orthopedic clinic that is highly dependent on patient referrals from primary care physicians. You have created an Access database to help keep track of referrals so that you can analyze which physicians refer to your clinic and keep in touch with them regarding patient progress.

a. Start Access, open the AMP B-B5.accdb database from the drive and folder where you store your Data Files, then save it as **AMP B-Referrals.accdb**. Enable content if prompted.

b. Open each of the five tables to observe the number of fields and records in each table, then close the datasheets.

c. On the Database Tools tab, click the Relationships button to view table relationships, then close the Relationships window.

d. Create a query in Query Design View and select the ReferringDocs, Visits, and ClinicDocs tables. Select the RFirst and RLast fields from the ReferringDocs table, the DrLast field from the ClinicDocs table, and the VisitDate field from the Visits table.

e. Set an ascending sort order for the RLast, VisitDate, and DrLast fields, then view the datasheet.

f. Find an occurrence of Abbot in the RLast field and replace it with your own last name.

g. In Query Design View, add criteria to select only those records with your last name or **Caldwell** in the RLast field, each with a VisitDate greater than or equal to **1/1/2013**. (*Hint*: Use the >= operator.)

h. Save the query with the name **2013Referrals**, display it in Datasheet View as shown in Figure B-22, then print the first page of the datasheet if requested by your instructor.

i. Close the 2013Referrals datasheet and the AMP B-Referrals.accdb database, then exit Access 2010.

FIGURE B-22

2013Referrals

RFirst	RLast	DrLast	VisitDate
Mary Ann	Caldwell	Jefferson	11/6/2013
Mary Ann	Caldwell	Jefferson	12/4/2013
Mary Ann	Caldwell	Thompson	1/15/2013
Mary Ann	Caldwell	Thompson	1/18/2013
Mary Ann	Caldwell	Thompson	2/12/2013
Mary Ann	Caldwell	Thompson	2/12/2013
Mary Ann	Caldwell	Thompson	2/15/2013
Mary Ann	Caldwell	Thompson	4/29/2013
Mary Ann	Caldwell	Thompson	5/3/2013
Mary Ann	Caldwell	Thompson	5/14/2013
Mary Ann	Caldwell	Thompson	9/13/2013
Mary Ann	Caldwell	Thompson	10/4/2013
Mary Ann	Caldwell	Thompson	10/7/2013
Mary Ann	Caldwell	Thompson	10/14/2013
Mary Ann	Caldwell	Thompson	11/12/2013
Mary Ann	Caldwell	Thompson	12/2/2013
Mary Ann	Caldwell	Thompson	12/3/2013
Mary Ann	Caldwell	Thompson	12/12/2013
Mary Ann	Caldwell	Thompson	12/12/2013
Mary Ann	Caldwell	Thompson	12/12/2013
Mary Ann	Caldwell	Wambold	1/3/2013
Mary Ann	Caldwell	Wambold	1/3/2013
Mary Ann	Caldwell	Wambold	3/14/2013
Mary Ann	Caldwell	Wambold	4/25/2013
Mary Ann	Caldwell	Wambold	4/25/2013

Record: 1 of 30 No Filter Search

Real Life Independent Challenge

An Access database is an excellent tool to help record and track job opportunities. For this exercise you'll create a database from scratch that you can use to enter, edit, and query data in pursuit of a new job or career.

a. Create a new database named **AMP B-Jobs.accdb**.

b. Create a table named **Positions** with the field names, data types, and descriptions shown in Figure B-23.

FIGURE B-23: Positions table

field name	data type	description
PositionID	AutoNumber	Primary key field
Title	Text	Title of position such as Nurse, Lab Technician, or Program Manager
CareerArea	Text	Area of the career field such as Biotech, Hospital, or Pharmaceutical
AnnualSalary	Currency	Annual salary
Desirability	Number	Desirability rating of 1 = low to 5 = high to show how desirable the position is to you
EmployerID	Number	Foreign key field to the Employers table

c. Create a table named **Employers** with the field names, data types, and descriptions shown in Figure B-24.

FIGURE B-24: Employers table

field name	data type	description
EmployerID	AutoNumber	Primary key field
CompanyName	Text	Company name of the employer
EmpStreet	Text	Employer's street address
EmpCity	Text	Employer's city
EmpState	Text	Employer's state
EmpZip	Text	Employer's zip code
EmpPhone	Text	Employer's phone, including area code

d. Be sure to set EmployerID as the primary key field in the Employers table and the PositionID as the primary key field in the Positions table.

e. Link the Employers and Positions table together in a one-to-many relationship using the common EmployerID field. One employer record will be linked to many position records. Be sure to enforce referential integrity.

f. Using any valid source of potential employer data, enter five records into the Employers table.

g. Using any valid source of job information, enter at least five records into the Positions table by using the subdatasheets from within the Employers datasheet. Because one employer may have many positions, all of your Positions records may be linked to the same employer, you may have at least one position record per employer, or any other combination. (*Hint*: www.careerbuilder.com and www.monster.com are excellent online sources for job information.)

h. Build a query that selects CompanyName from the Employers table, and the Title, CareerArea, Desirability, and AnnualSalary fields from the Positions table. Sort the records in descending order based on Desirability then AnnualSalary. Save the query as **JobList**, and print it if requested by your instructor.

i. Close the JobList datasheet and the AMP B-Jobs.accdb database, then exit Access 2010.

Visual Workshop

One of the most challenging aspects of the medical profession is the vast amount of medical terminology you are required to memorize. In this exercise, query a database of medical terminology to learn the meanings of common prefixes and suffixes. Start Access, open the AMP B-B6.accdb database from the drive and folder where you store your Data Files and save it as **AMP B-MedicalTerms.accdb**. Enable content if prompted. Create a query based on the Terms table with the fields shown in Figure B-25. Criteria have been added to select only those records where the Meaning field contains the word bone or muscle. (*Hint*: Use wildcard characters in each criterion entry before and after the word bone and the word muscle to select entries with these words anywhere in the criterion entry, as in *bone* and *muscle*.) Save the query with the name **BoneAndMuscle**, then compare the results to Figure B-25, widening columns and making changes as necessary. Print the datasheet if requested by your instructor. Save and close the query, close the AMP B-MedicalTerms.accdb database, then exit Access 2010.

FIGURE B-25

BoneAndMuscle

Prefix or suffix	Meaning	Origin	Example
muscul(o)-	muscle	Latin	Musculoskeletal system
my(o)-	Of or relating to muscle	Ancient Greek μῦς, μυ- (mys, my-), muscle; mouse; m	Myoblast
myel(o)-	Of or relating to bone marrow	Ancient Greek μυελόν (myelon), marrow; bone-marr	Myeloblast
ossi-	bone	Latin	Peripheral ossifying fibroma
ost(e)-, oste(o)-	bone	Greek ὀστέον	Osteoporosis
pelv(i)-, pelv(o)-	hip bone	Latin	Pelvis
*			

UNIT C

Access 2010

Creating and Using Forms and Reports

Files You Will Need:

AMP C-C1.accdb
AMP C-C2.accdb
AMP C-C3.accdb
AMP C-C4.accdb
AMP C-C5.accdb
AMP C-C6.accdb
AMP C-C7.accdb

Although you can enter and edit data on datasheets, most database designers develop and build forms as the primary method for users to interact with a database. A **form** allows you to organize the fields on the screen in any arrangement. In addition, a form supports pictures, command buttons, and tabs that make the database easier to use and navigate. A **report** is an Access object used to create professional-looking printouts including formatting, layout, and summary options. A report can calculate subtotals, averages, counts, or other statistics for groups of records. Tony Sanchez, R.N., and office manager for Riverwalk Medical Clinic, asks you to create forms and reports to make patient electronic medical records easier to update and analyze.

OBJECTIVES

- Manage data with a form
- Use the Form Wizard
- Preview a report
- Use the Report Wizard
- Apply group and sort orders
- Add subtotals and counts
- Add and modify labels
- Back up and secure the database

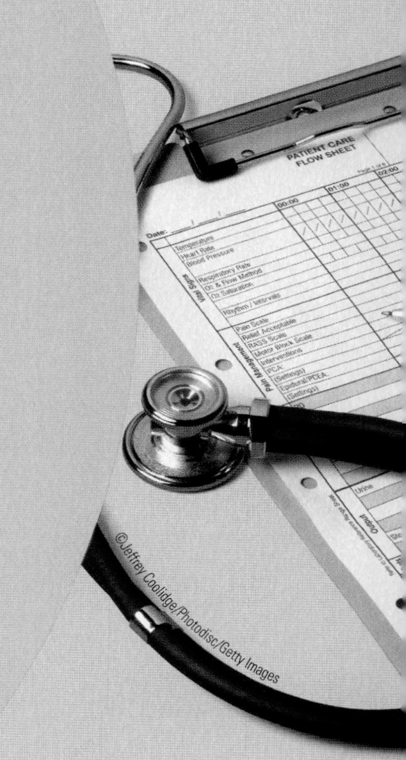

©Jeffrey Coolidge/Photodisc/Getty Images

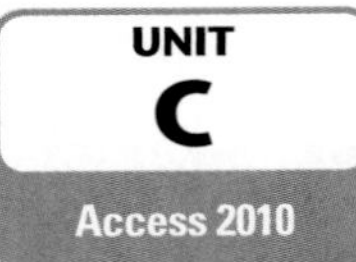

Managing Data with a Form

A **form** is an Access database object that allows you to arrange the fields of a record in any layout so you can enter, edit, and delete records. A form provides an easy-to-use data entry and navigation screen. Forms provide many productivity and security benefits for the **user**, who is primarily interested in entering, editing, and analyzing the data in the database. You work with a form previously created for the patient electronic medical record database at Riverwalk Medical Clinic to learn about the uses and benefits of forms.

STEPS

1. **Start Access, click the Open button, navigate to the drive and folder where you store your Data Files, click the AMP C-C1.accdb database file, click Open, click the File tab, click Save Database As, type AMP C-Riverwalk in the File name box, click Save, then enable content if prompted**

   Because forms are often the primary way for users to communicate with the database, they must be as easy to use and intuitive as possible.

2. **Double-click the ElectronicMedicalRecord form to open it, press [Tab] twice to move to the DOB field, click the calendar picker icon, then click 9/30/1947 as shown in Figure C-1**

   Every item on a form is called a **control**. Common controls are summarized in Table C-1 and some controls are identified in Figure C-1. Controls can be **bound**, tied to an underlying field in a table, or **unbound**, unattached to data but used to describe or clarify information. Bound controls show data from underlying records as you move from record to record. Unbound controls remain static as you move from record to record.

3. **Click the Next record button ▶ for the main form enough times to move to record 11 of 39**

   The main form navigation buttons identify which patient you are viewing. Some patients have pictures, but not all do. The subform in the lower half of the form is similar to a subdatasheet because it shows related records. In this case, the subform shows all visits for that patient. Some patients have made one, two, or three visits to the clinic.

4. **Click the Primary Diagnosis combo box list arrow for the third record in the subform, then click 305.1 on the list as shown in Figure C-2**

   Selecting 305.1 in the Primary Diagnosis combo box automatically updates the text box with Tobacco abuse, as shown in Figure C-2. This is just one of the techniques a form can employ to make data entry easy and accurate.

5. **Click the Enter New Patient command button, enter your first name in the First Name text box, press [Tab], enter your last name in the Last Name text box, then click the Print This Patient command button**

   Command buttons are common form controls that allow you to simplify and control the actions that the user can take.

6. **Click the Close command button to close the form**

   All data that you edited or entered in the form is saved in the underlying table. In this case, you updated both the Patients and Visits tables.

FIGURE C-1: **Record 1 of the Electronic Medical Record form**

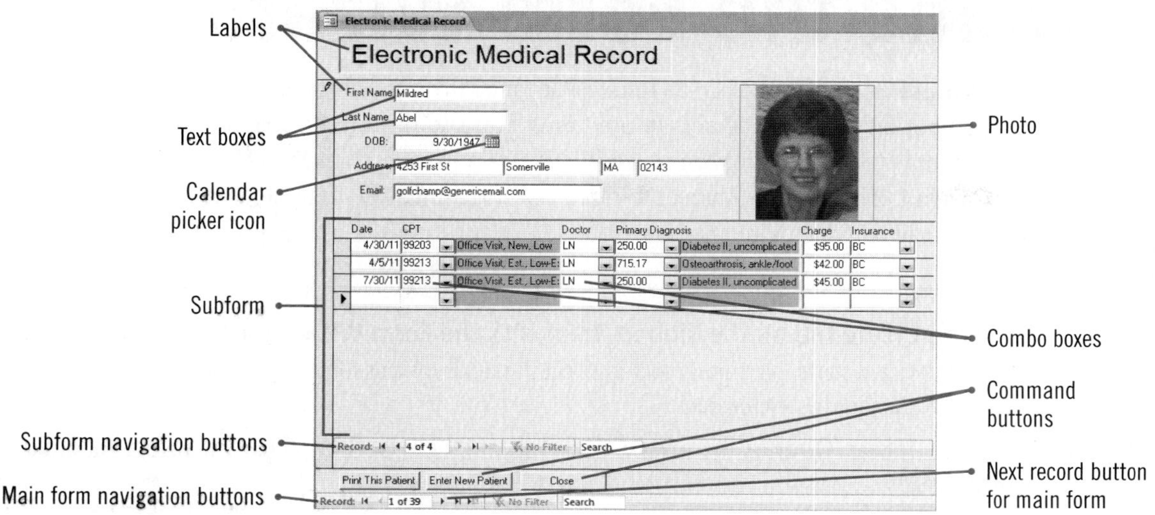

FIGURE C-2: **Record 11 of the Electronic Medical Record form**

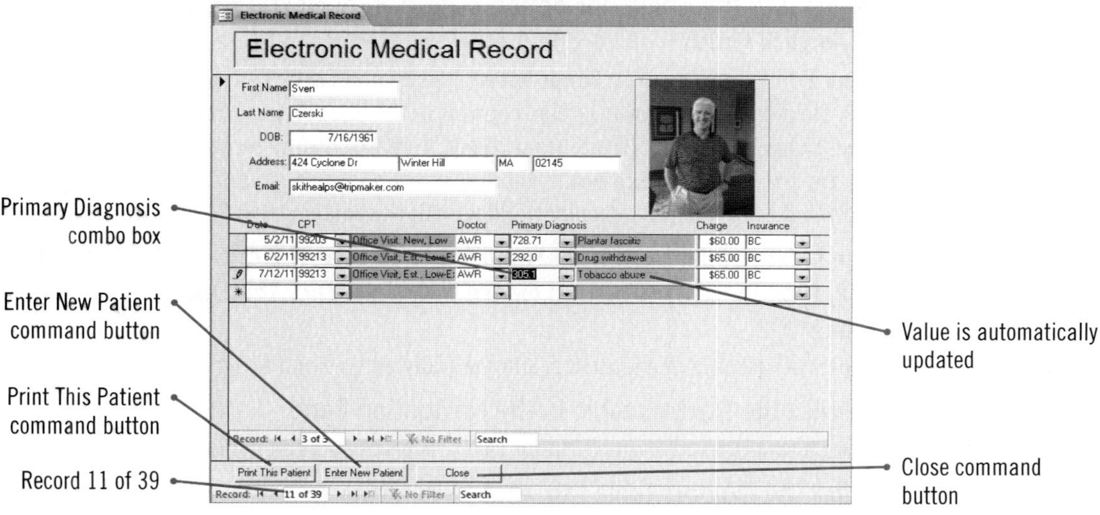

TABLE C-1: **Common form controls**

name	used to	bound	unbound
Label	Provide consistent descriptive text as you navigate from record to record; the label is the most common type of unbound control and can also be used as a hyperlink to another database object, external file, or Web page		x
Text box	Display, edit, or enter data for each record from an underlying record source; the text box is the most common type of bound control	x	
List box	Display a list of possible data entries	x	
Combo box	Display a list of possible data entries for a field, and provide a text box for an entry from the keyboard; combines the list box and text box controls		
Tab control	Create a three-dimensional aspect on a form		x
Check box	Display "yes" or "no" answers for a field; if the box is checked, it means "yes"	x	
Toggle button	Display "yes" or "no" answers for a field; if the button is pressed, it means "yes"	x	
Option button	Display a choice for a field	x	
Option group	Display and organize choices (usually presented as option buttons) for a field	x	
Line and Rectangle	Draw lines and rectangles on the form		x
Command button	Provide an easy way to initiate a command or run a macro		x

UNIT C

Access 2010

Using the Form Wizard

As the **database designer**, the person responsible for building and maintaining tables, queries, forms, and reports, you not only need to be able to use forms, you also need to be able to create forms. The **Form Wizard** prompts you for information it needs to create a form, such as the fields, layout, and title for the form. See Table C-2 for other techniques to create new forms. Tony Sanchez asks you to build a form to enter and maintain doctor information.

STEPS

1. **Click the Create tab on the Ribbon, then click the Form Wizard button in the Forms group**

   The Form Wizard starts, prompting you to select the fields for this form. You want to create a form to enter and update data in the Doctors table.

2. **Click the Tables/Queries list arrow, click Table: Doctors, then click the Select All Fields button [>>]**

   You could now select fields from other tables, if necessary, but in this case you just want to update the data in the Doctors table.

3. **Click Next, click the Columnar option button, click Next, type Doctor Entry Form as the title, then click Finish**

   The Doctor Entry Form opens in **Form View**, as shown in Figure C-3. Other form views are summarized in Table C-3. Field names are shown as label controls in the first column of the form. A **label** displays fixed text that doesn't change as you navigate from record to record. In the second column, to the right of the label controls, are text boxes. A **text box** is the most common type of control used to display field values. You enter, edit, find, sort, and filter data by working with the data in a text box control.

4. **Click the Next record button to navigate to record 2 of 6, click J in the DrMiddleName text box, type Joyce as shown in Figure C-4, right-click the Doctor Entry Form tab, then click Close**

   As you enter or edit data in a form, it is automatically entered and saved in underlying tables.

5. **Double-click the Doctors table in the Navigation Pane**

   The update to the DrMiddleName field for Dr. Carla Joyce Zimmerman is stored in the Doctors table.

6. **Right-click the Doctors table tab, then click Close**

TABLE C-2: Form creation tools

tool	icon	creates a form:
Form		with one click based on the selected table or query
Form Design		from scratch with access to advanced design changes in Form Design View
Blank Form		with no controls starting in Form Layout View
Form Wizard		by answering a series of questions provided by the Form Wizard dialog boxes
Navigation		used to navigate or move between different areas of the database
More Forms		based on Multiple Items, Datasheet, Split Form, Modal Dialog, PivotChart, or PivotTable arrangements
Split Form		where the upper half displays data the fields of one record in any arrangement, and the lower half displays data as a datasheet

FIGURE C-3: **Doctor Entry Form in Form View**

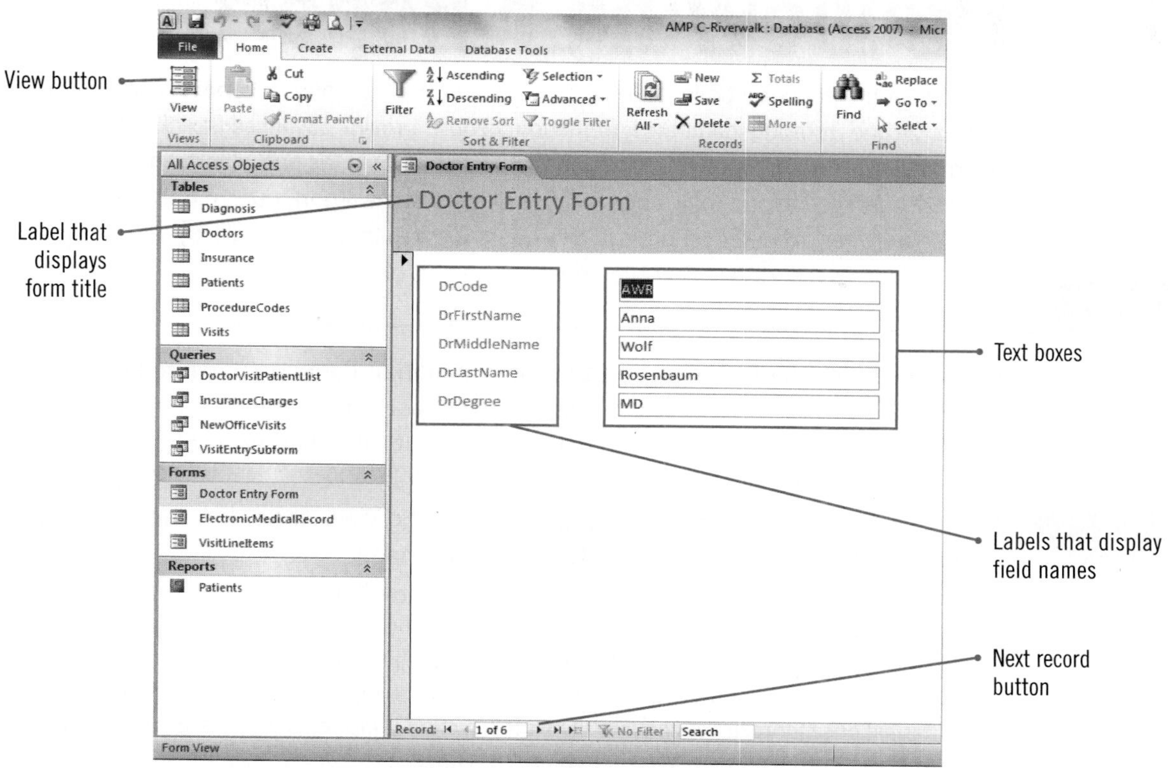

FIGURE C-4: **Editing data in a text box**

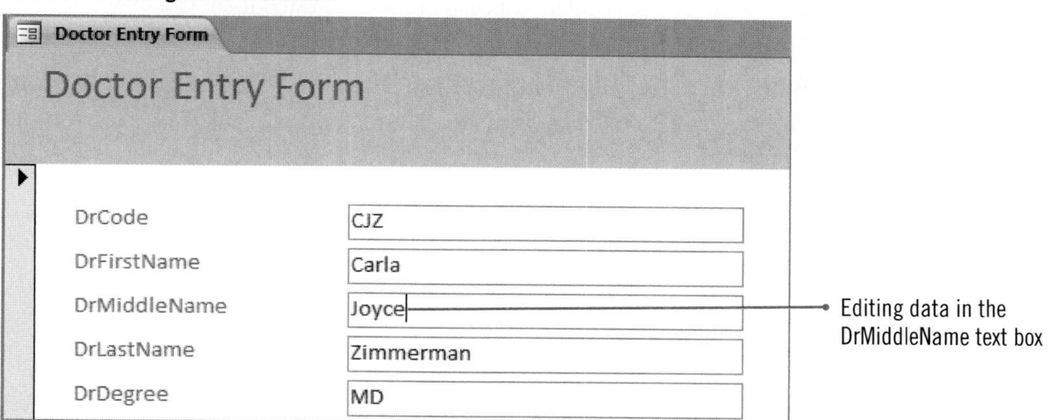

TABLE C-3: **Form views**

view	primary purpose
Form	To view, enter, edit, and delete data
Layout	To modify the size, position, or formatting of controls; shows data as you modify the form, making it the tool of choice when you want to change the appearance and usability of the form while viewing live data
Design	To modify the form header, detail, and footer section, or to access the complete range of controls and form properties; Design View does not display data

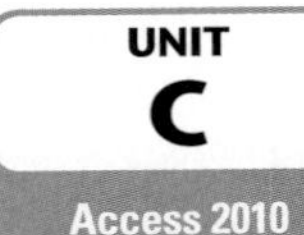

Access 2010

Previewing a Report

Although you can print a table datasheet, query datasheet, or form, a **report** object is the best choice to summarize and distribute database information. Reports provide advanced flexibility by using **sections** that determine where and how often controls in that section print in the final report. For example, controls in the Report Header section print only once at the beginning of the report, but controls in the Detail section print once for every record in the report. Table C-4 describes report sections. You and Tony Sanchez preview the Patients report to review and understand report sections.

STEPS

1. **Double-click the Patients report in the Navigation Pane as shown in Figure C-5**

   The first page of the Patients report is displayed in **Report View**, which allows you to preview the data and make some modifications to the report. Other report views are summarized in Table C-5. The first page of the Patients report contains four sections: Report Header, Page Header, Patient Header, and Detail section.

2. **Right-click the Patients report tab, click Print Preview, then click the Next Page button on the navigation bar to move to the second page**

   Print Preview shows you each page of the report as it will be printed on paper, and provides an excellent way to learn about report sections. The top of the second page of the report displays the labels in the **Page Header** section, which prints at the top of each page. The **Report Header** section is not repeated on the second and subsequent pages because it only prints at the top of the first page. The **Patient Header** section is printed once for each patient, and the **Detail** section is printed once for every record in the report. In this case, each record represents a patient visit to the clinic.

3. **Click the Last Page button on the navigation bar to move to the last page, then click the report to zoom out as shown in Figure C-6**

   By looking at the last page of the report in Print Preview, you can see the **Report Footer** section, which prints at the end of the report, as well as the **Page Footer** section, which prints at the end of each page. The Report Footer often contains calculations such as grand totals or a total count of records. The Page Footer section often contains the date and page number.

4. **Right-click the Patients report tab, then click Close to close the Patients report**

   Reports may be printed or distributed electronically via Outlook, Microsoft's e-mail program in the Microsoft Office suite.

QUICK TIP

You can also use the View buttons in the lower-right corner of a report to switch views.

TROUBLE

You may need to zoom in and out several times by clicking the report to position it where you want.

TABLE C-4: Report sections

section	where this section prints
Report Header	At the top of the first page
Page Header	At the top of every page (but below the Report Header on the first page)
Group Header	Before every group of records
Detail	Once for every record
Group Footer	After every group of records
Page Footer	At the bottom of every page
Report Footer	At the end of the report

FIGURE C-5: First page of Patients report in Report View

Patients

Report Header prints at the top of the first page

Patient Header prints once for each patient

Page Header prints at the top of each page

Detail section prints once for every record

Patient Listing

ID	Patient Name	DOB	Street	City	State	Zip
34	Abel, Mildred	9/30/1947	4253 First St	Somerville	MA	02143

Date of Service	Procedure	Diagnosis	Charge	Payment	Doctor	Weight
4/5/2011	99213	Osteoarthrosis, ankle/foot	$42.00	BC	LN	190
4/30/2011	99203	Diabetes II, uncomplicated	$95.00	BC	LN	165
7/30/2011	99213	Diabetes II, uncomplicated	$45.00	BC	LN	165

ID	Patient Name	DOB	Street	City	State	Zip
99	Arenson, Timothy	4/2/1988	2323 Garrison Dr	Somerville	MA	02141

Date of Service	Procedure	Diagnosis	Charge	Payment	Doctor	Weight
4/25/2011	99203	Gastroenteritis, noninfectious, unspec.	$75.00	BC	FPQ	190
5/24/2011	11750	COPD, NOS	$325.00	BC	FPQ	190

ID	Patient Name	DOB	Street	City	State	Zip
121	Boos, Virginia	5/9/1991	108 Sutton Dr	Boston	MA	02109

Date of Service	Procedure	Diagnosis	Charge	Payment	Doctor	Weight
5/10/2011	99202	Lyme disease	$40.00	MCD	HLN	180

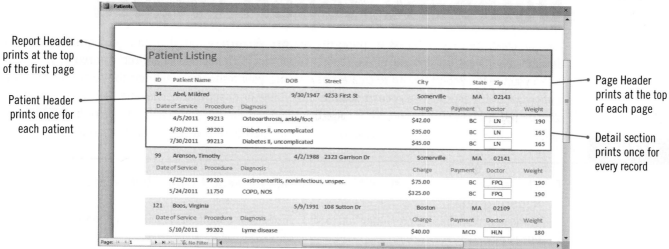

FIGURE C-6: Last page of Patients report in Print Preview

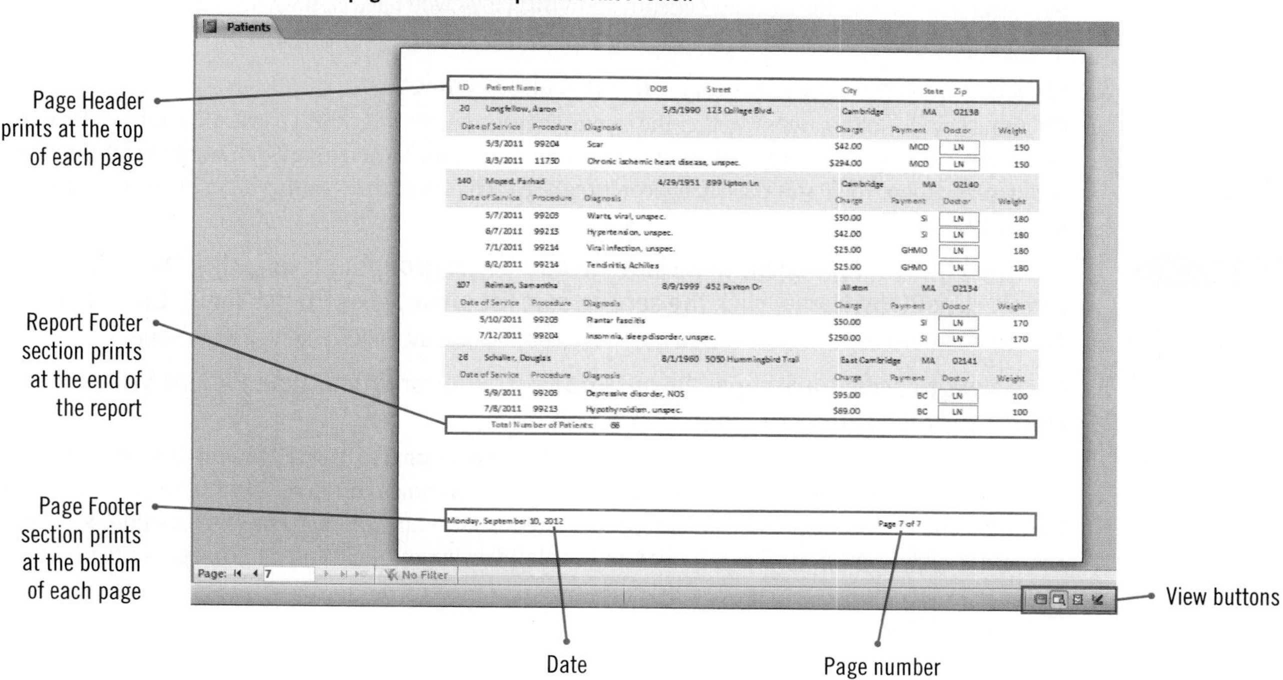

TABLE C-5: Report views

view	primary purpose
Report View	To quickly review the report without page breaks
Print Preview	To review each page of an entire report as it will appear if printed
Layout View	To modify the size, position, or formatting of controls; shows live data as you modify the report, making it the tool of choice when you want to change the appearance and positioning of controls on a report while also reviewing live data
Design View	To work with report sections or to access the complete range of controls and report properties; Design View does not display data

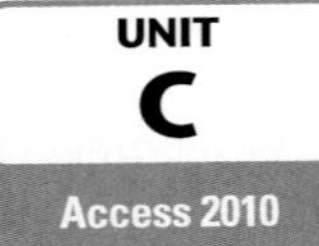

Using the Report Wizard

You can create reports in Access by using the **Report Wizard**, a tool that asks questions to guide you through the initial development of the report. Other report creation tools are summarized in Table C-6. When you use the Report Wizard to create a new report, your responses determine the record source, style, and layout of the report. The **record source** is the table or query that defines the fields and records displayed on the report. The Report Wizard also helps you sort, group, and analyze the records. Tony Sanchez asks you to use the Report Wizard to create a report to display the patients for each doctor.

STEPS

1. **Click the Create tab on the Ribbon, then click the Report Wizard button in the Reports group**

   The Report Wizard starts, prompting you to select the fields you want on the report. You can select fields from one or more tables or queries.

> **TROUBLE**
> If you select a field by mistake, click the unwanted field in the Selected Fields list, then click the Remove Field button <.

2. **Click the Tables/Queries list arrow, click Table: Doctors, double-click the DrLastName field, click the Tables/Queries list arrow, click Table: Patients, double-click PtFirstName, double-click PtLastName, click the Tables/Queries list arrow, click Table: Visits, then double-click the DateofService field**

   By selecting fields from the Doctors, Patients, and Visits tables, you have all the fields you need for the report, as shown in Figure C-7.

3. **Click Next, then click by Doctors if it is not already selected**

   Choosing "by Doctors" groups together the records for each doctor, which will create a Doctor Header section on the report. In addition to record-grouping options, the Report Wizard asks if you want to sort the records within each group. You'll sort the detail records that list each patient in ascending order by their last and then first names.

> **QUICK TIP**
> Click Back to review previous dialog boxes within a wizard.

4. **Click Next, click Next again to include no additional grouping levels, click the first sort list arrow, click PtLastName, click the second sort list arrow, click PtFirstName, then click Next**

   The last questions in the Report Wizard deal with report appearance and creating a report title.

5. **Click Next to accept a Stepped layout and Portrait orientation, type Patient Visits by Doctor for the report title, then click Finish**

   The Patient Visits by Doctor report opens in **Print Preview** in **portrait orientation** (8.5" wide by 11" tall as opposed to **landscape orientation**, 11" wide by 8.5"), as shown in Figure C-8. The records are grouped by doctor, and each patient and date of service is listed in ascending order in the Detail section. Reports are **read-only** objects, meaning that they read and display data but cannot be used to change (write to) data. As you change data using tables, queries, or forms, reports constantly display those up-to-date edits just like all of the other Access objects.

FIGURE C-7: **Selecting fields for a report using the Report Wizard**

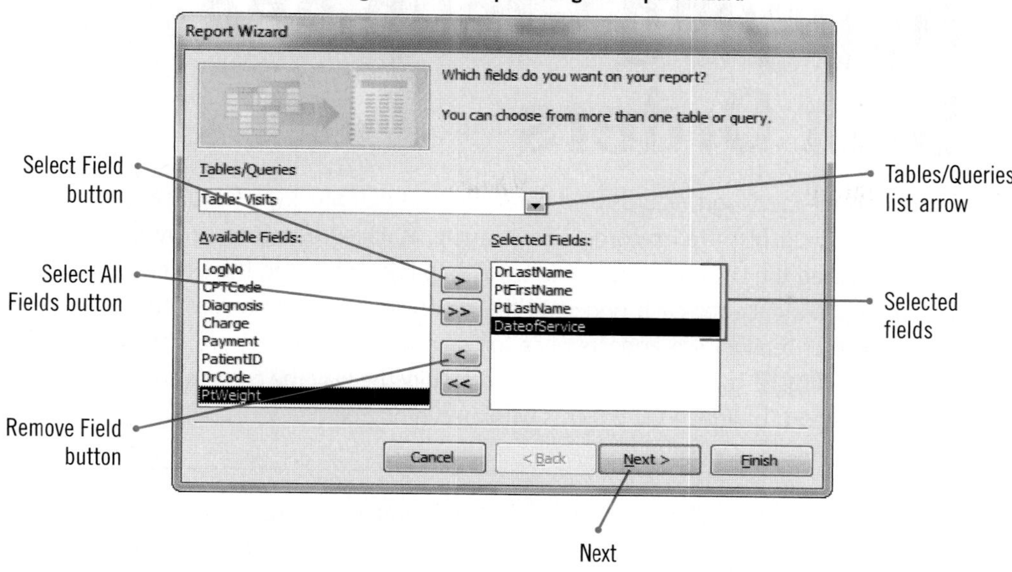

FIGURE C-8: **Patient Visits by Doctor report in Print Preview**

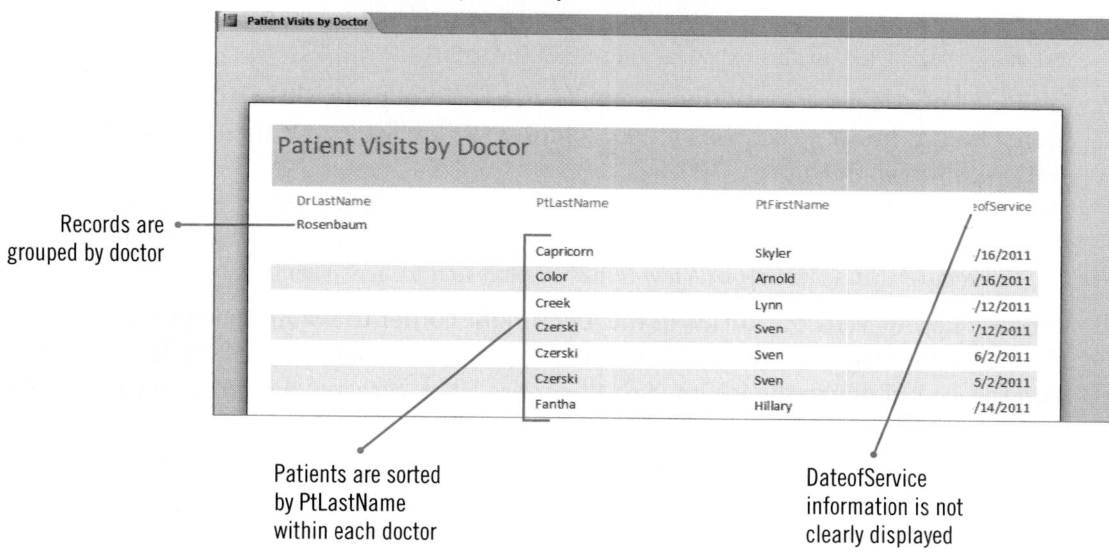

TABLE C-6: **Report creation tools**

tool	icon	creates a report:
Report		with one click based on the selected table or query
Report Design		from scratch with advanced design tools in Report Design View
Blank Report		with no controls starting in Report Layout View
Report Wizard		by answering a series of questions provided by the Report Wizard dialog boxes
Labels		to create labels by using the Label Wizard

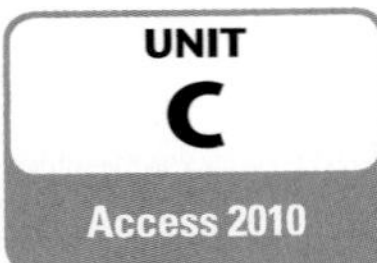

Applying Group and Sort Orders

Grouping means to sort records by a particular field *plus* provide a header and/or footer section before or after each group of sorted records. For example, if you group records by the DrCode field, the Group Header is called the DrCode Header and the Group Footer is called the DrCode Footer. The DrCode Header section appears once for each doctor in the report, immediately before the records for that doctor. The DrCode Footer section also appears once for each doctor in the report, immediately after the records for that doctor. Tony Sanchez asks you to modify the way the records are organized in the Patient Visits by Doctor report to display the patients within each doctor.

STEPS

1. **Click the Design View button in the lower-right corner of the Access window to switch to Report Design View, then click the Group & Sort button to open the Group, Sort, and Total pane as shown in Figure C-9**

   The Group, Sort, and Total pane shows you that the records are grouped by the DrCode field, then sorted by PtLastName, and then PtFirstName. A group field varies from a sort field in that a group field also provides the ability to add a Group Header or Group Footer for that field.

   You decide to change the group field from DrCode to DrLastName so that the doctors are listed alphabetically by their last name instead of their DrCode value. You also want to add a DrLastName Footer section to calculate the number of patient visits for each doctor.

TROUBLE
The More Options button becomes the Less Options button when clicked.

2. **Click the DrCode list arrow in the Group, Sort, and Total pane, click DrLastName, click the More Options button, click the without a footer section list arrow, then click with a footer section as shown in Figure C-10**

   The DrLastName Footer section is added to Report Design View. You will add a calculation to count the number of patient visits for each doctor later. For now, you decide to widen the DateofService field so that the dates are completely visible. **Layout View** is the best place to resize report controls.

3. **Click the Layout View button in the lower-right corner to switch to Report Layout View, click the DateofService label to select it, point to the left edge of the label and drag with the ↔ pointer to the left to view the entire label, click any date to select all of them, then point to the left edge of the date and drag with the ↔ pointer to the left to view the entire dates as shown in Figure C-11**

   Controls can be moved and resized using the mouse pointer symbols shown in Table C-7. The first page of the report lists Dr. Nguyen's patients first because the records are now grouped by the DrLastName field instead of the DrCode field. Dr. Nguyen's last name is first among doctors when sorting the records in ascending order by DrLastName. Previously, Dr. Rosenbaum's records were listed first because her DrCode value, AWR, was first among all doctors.

4. **Right-click the Patient Visits by Doctor report tab, click Close, then click Yes to save**

TABLE C-7: Mouse pointer symbols

symbol	when does this symbol appear?	action
↖	When you point to any unselected control on the form or report (the default mouse pointer)	Single-clicking with this mouse pointer selects a control
✥	When you point to the upper-left corner or edge of a selected control in Form or Report Design View or the middle of the control in Form or Report Layout View	Dragging with this mouse pointer moves the selected control(s)
↕, ↔, ↘, ↙	When you point to any sizing handle (except the larger one in the upper-left corner in Form or Report Design View)	Dragging with one of these mouse pointers resizes the control

FIGURE C-9: **Patient Visits by Doctor report in Design View**

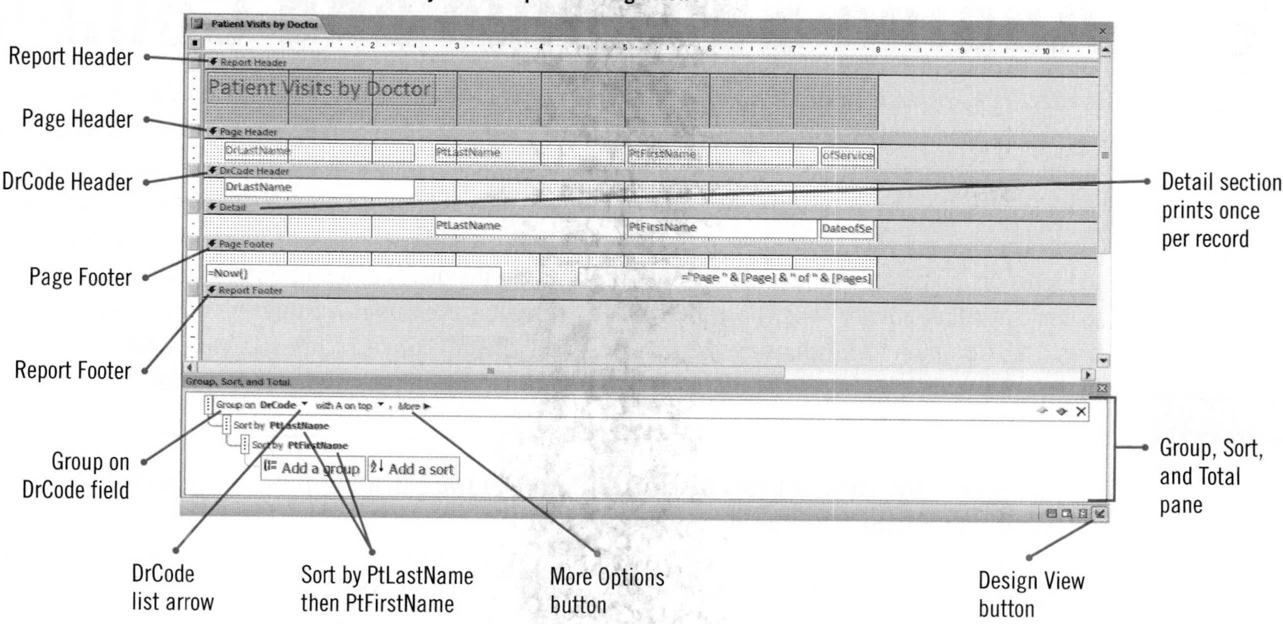

FIGURE C-10: **Modifying the grouping fields in Report Design View**

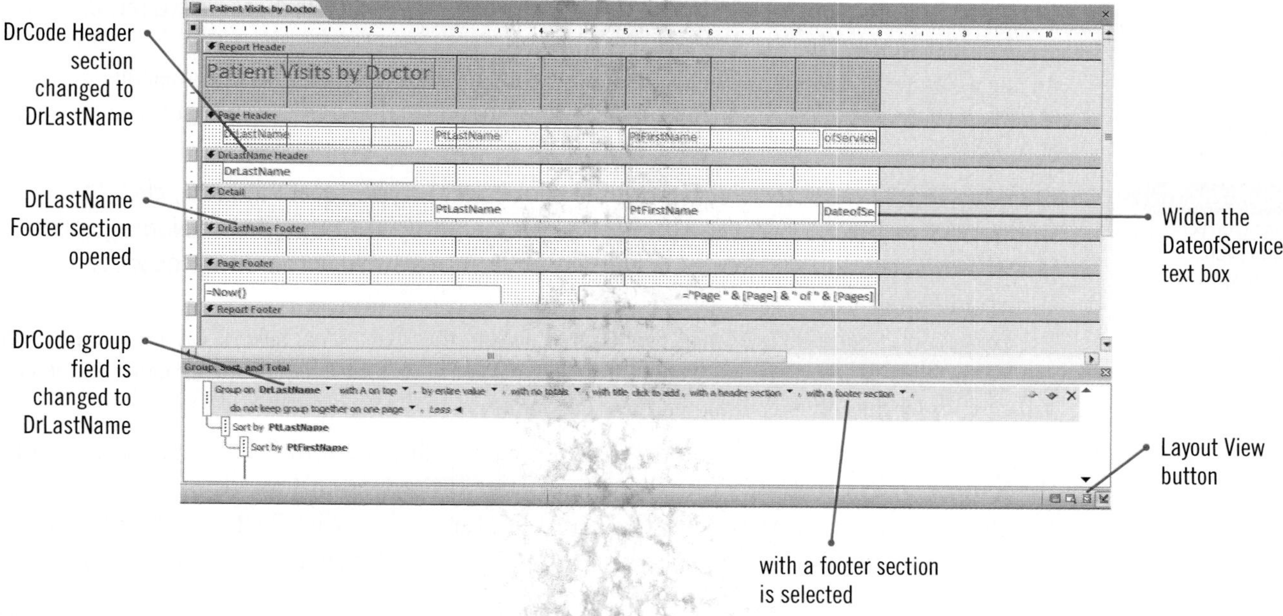

FIGURE C-11: **Resizing the DateofService controls in Report Layout View**

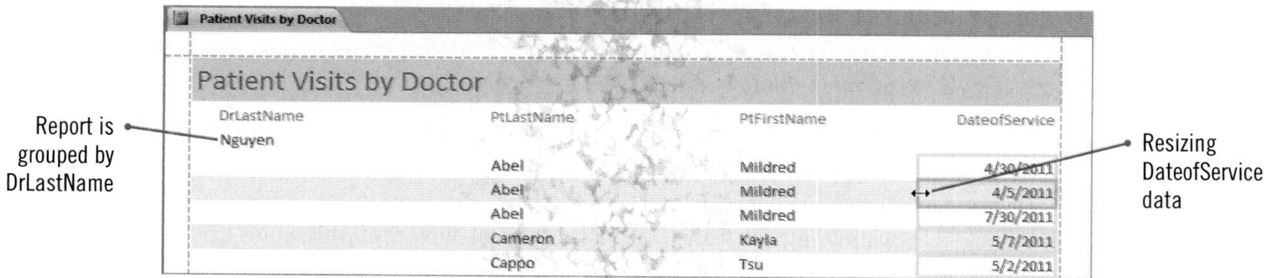

Access 2010

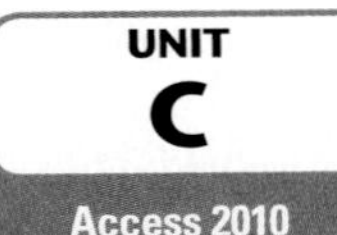

UNIT C

Access 2010

Adding Subtotals and Counts

In a report, you create a **calculation** by entering an expression into a text box in Report Design View. When a report is previewed or printed, the expression is evaluated and the resulting calculation is placed on the report. An **expression** is a combination of field names, operators (such as +, –, /, and *), and functions that result in a single value. A **function** is a built-in formula, such as Sum or Count, that helps you quickly create a calculation. Every expression starts with an equal sign (=), and when it uses a function, the arguments for the function are placed in (parentheses). **Arguments** are the pieces of information that the function needs to create the final answer. When an argument is a field name, the field name must be surrounded by [square brackets]. Common expressions are listed in Table C-8. Tony Sanchez asks you to add a calculation to the Patient Visits by Doctor report to count the total number of patients for each doctor.

STEPS

1. **Right-click the Patient Visits by Doctor report in the Navigation Pane, then click Design View on the shortcut menu**

   A logical place to add subtotals for each group is immediately after the group in the Group Footer section. You have already added the DrLastName Footer section, but need to expand it to add an expression to it.

2. **Drag the top edge of the Page Footer section down about 0.5" to create space**

   With the DrLastName Footer section open, you're ready to add a control to count the number of patient visits for each doctor. You add calculations to forms and reports by entering an expression into a text box control. Therefore, your next step is to add a new text box control to the DrLastName Footer section.

3. **Click the Text Box button in the Controls group, then click in the DrLastNameFooter section just below the PtLastName text box**

   Adding a new text box control also automatically adds a new label to its left. First, you modify the label to identify the information, then you modify the text box to contain the correct expression to sum the number of patients.

> **QUICK TIP**
> Depending on your activity in Report Design View, you may see a different number in the Text##: label.

4. **Click the Text11 label to select it, double-click Text11, type Total Patients:, click the Unbound text box to select it, click Unbound again, type =Count([PtLastName]), press [Enter], then use the ↔ pointer to widen the text box to view the entire expression as shown in Figure C-12**

   The expression =Count([PtLastName]) counts the values in the PtLastName field. Because the expression is entered in the DrLastName Footer section, it counts patient visits for each doctor. To count the number of patient visits for the entire report, insert the same expression in the Report Footer section.

5. **Drag the bottom edge of the Report Footer section down about 0.5" to create space in the Report Footer section, right-click the =Count([PtLastName]) text box, click Copy on the shortcut menu, right-click in the Report Footer section, click Paste, then press [→] enough times to position the controls in the Report Footer section directly below those in the DrLastName Footer section**

   Make one more modification to keep all of the records for each section on the same page.

6. **Double-click the DrLastName Footer section bar to open the Property Sheet, click the Format tab, click None in the Force New Page property, click the list arrow, then click After Section as shown in Figure C-13**

   This modification will create a page break after each DrLastName Footer section, which in turn will force each doctor's information to print on its own page.

7. **Switch to Print Preview, then click the Next Page button enough times to move through all pages of the report**

   There are six doctors and hence six pages in this report with Detail records. The last page of the report prints the Report Footer information, which calculates the total number of patients for the entire report, 66.

FIGURE C-12: Adding an expression to the DrLastName Footer section

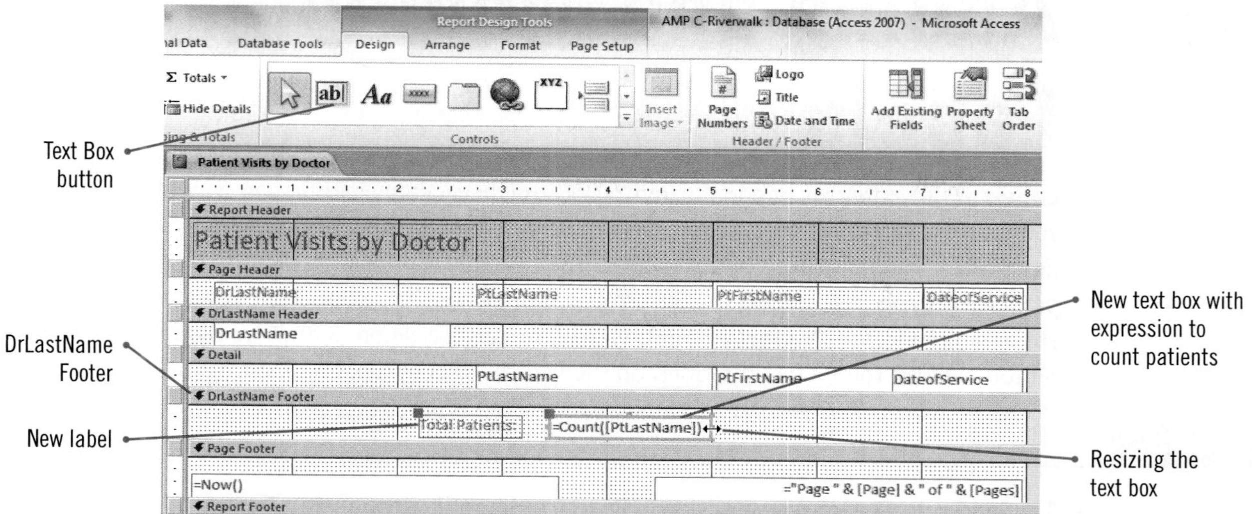

FIGURE C-13: Adding controls to the Report Footer section and changing section properties

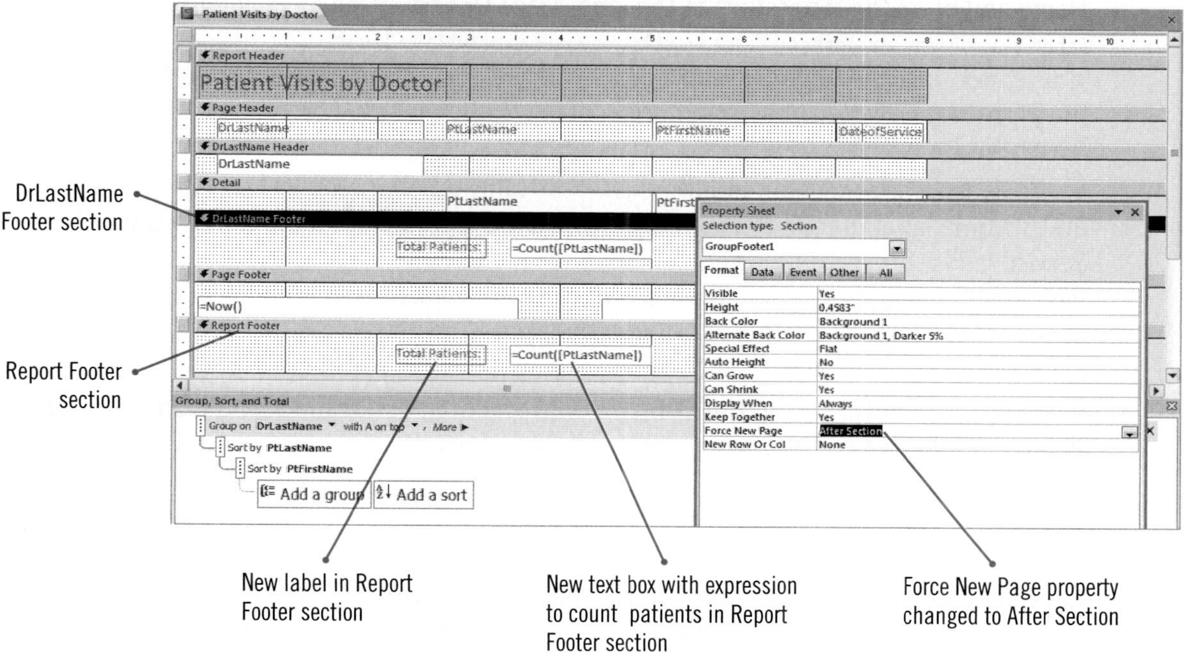

Access 2010

TABLE C-8: Sample expressions

sample expression	description
=Sum([Salary])	Uses the **Sum function** to add the values in the Salary field
=[Price] * 1.05	Multiplies the Price field by 1.05 (adds 5% to the Price field)
=[Subtotal] + [Shipping]	Adds the value of the Subtotal field to the value of the Shipping field
=Avg([Freight])	Uses the **Avg function** to display an average of the values in the Freight field
=Date()	Uses the **Date function** to display the current date in the form of mm-dd-yy
="Page " &[Page]	Displays the word Page, a space, and the result of the [Page] field, an Access field that contains the current page number
=[FirstName]& " " &[LastName]	Displays the value of the FirstName and LastName fields in one control, separated by a space
=Left([ProductNumber],2)	Uses the **Left function** to display the first two characters in the ProductNumber field

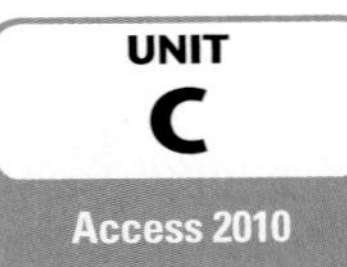

Adding and Modifying Labels

Labels are an extremely important control because they identify information on forms and reports. When you create a report with the Report Wizard, labels are automatically created and display field names to describe the data displayed by text boxes. The text that the label displays is controlled by its **Caption** property. A **property** is a characteristic of a control such as its Caption, Font Color, or Font Size. Properties are organized in the **Property Sheet**, which you can toggle on and off by clicking the Property Sheet button. You modify the labels on the Patient Visits by Doctor report to make them more professional. You also add a label with your name to the Report Header section.

STEPS

TROUBLE

Be sure to modify the labels in the Page Header section and not the text boxes in the DrLastName Header section.

1. **Switch to Design View, click the Property Sheet button in the Tools group to toggle off the Property Sheet if it is still visible, click the DrLastName label in the Page Header section, click between Dr and LastName and press the [Spacebar], then click between Last and Name and press the [Spacebar] so the label reads Dr Last Name as shown in Figure C-14**

   Labels may display any text you desire. Text boxes, such as those found in the DrLastName Header and Detail sections, must reference the precise field name as defined in Table Design View. With the first label in the Page Header section modified to include spaces between the words, you'll go ahead and modify the other three labels in the Page Header section.

2. **In the Page Header section, modify the PtLastName label to read Pt Last Name, the PtFirstName label to read Pt First Name, and the DateofService label to read Date of Service**

   With the labels in the Page Header section modified to include spaces, your report will be easier to read and more professional. You also want to add a label to the Report Header section with your name. You need to add a new label control to accomplish this.

3. **Click the Label button in the Controls group, click at about the 5" mark on the ruler in the Report Header section, type your name, then press [Enter] as shown in Figure C-15**

   With the labels in place, you decide to change their text color to black to make them more visible. You can modify each label individually, or select all of the labels at the same time to format them more productively. Table C-9 summarizes techniques for selecting multiple controls at the same time.

TROUBLE

If you make a mistake, click the Undo button on the Quick Access toolbar and try again.

4. **Click the Patient Visits by Doctor label in the Report Header section, press and hold [Shift], click the label with your name in the Report Header section, while still holding the [Shift] key, click each of the four labels in the Page Header section, release [Shift], click the Home tab, click the Font Color button list arrow, then click Automatic to apply a black font color to the six selected controls**

   You are ready to preview your changes.

5. **Switch to Print Preview as shown in Figure C-16, print the first page of the report if requested by your instructor, right-click the Patient Visits by Doctor report tab, click Close, then click Yes when prompted to save changes**

Precisely moving and resizing controls

You can move and resize controls using the mouse, but you can move controls more precisely using the keyboard. Pressing the arrow keys while holding [Ctrl] moves selected controls one **pixel** (**picture element**) at a time in the direction of the arrow. Pressing the arrow keys while holding [Shift] resizes selected controls one pixel at a time.

FIGURE C-14: Modifying labels in the Page Header section

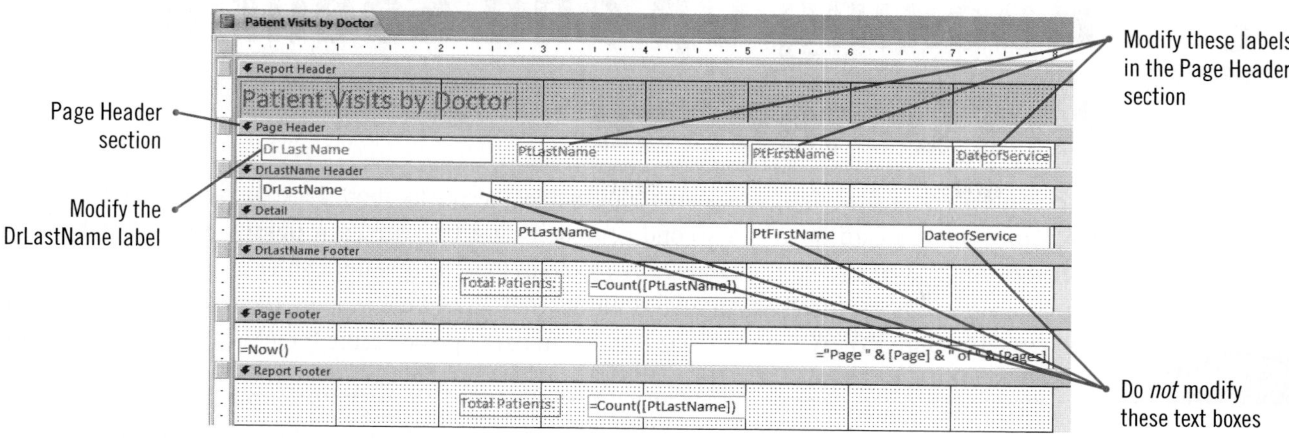

FIGURE C-15: Adding a label to the Report Header section

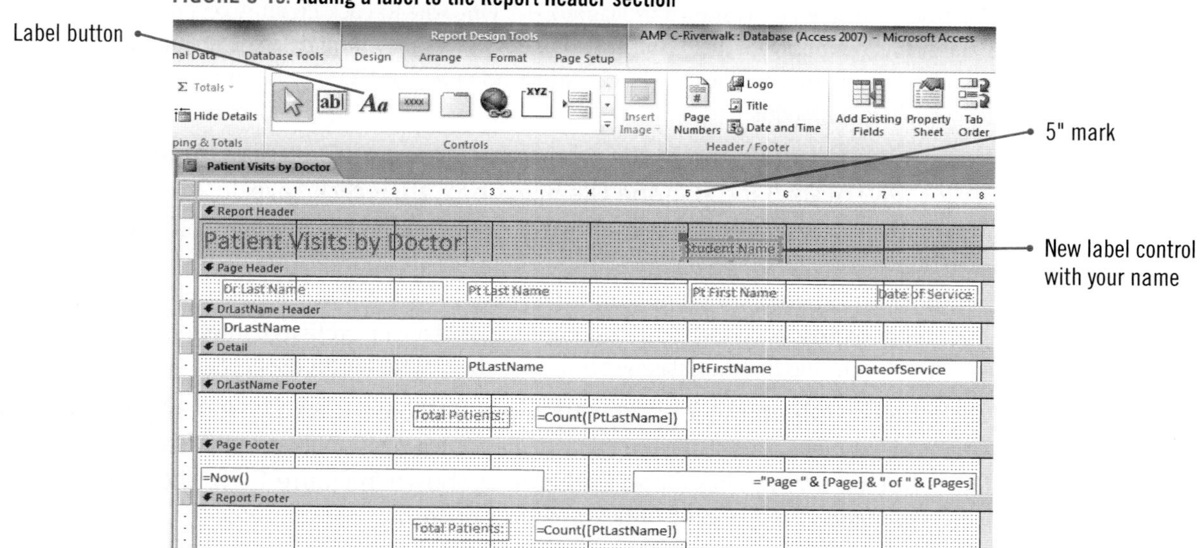

FIGURE C-16: Final Patient Visits by Doctor report in Print Preview

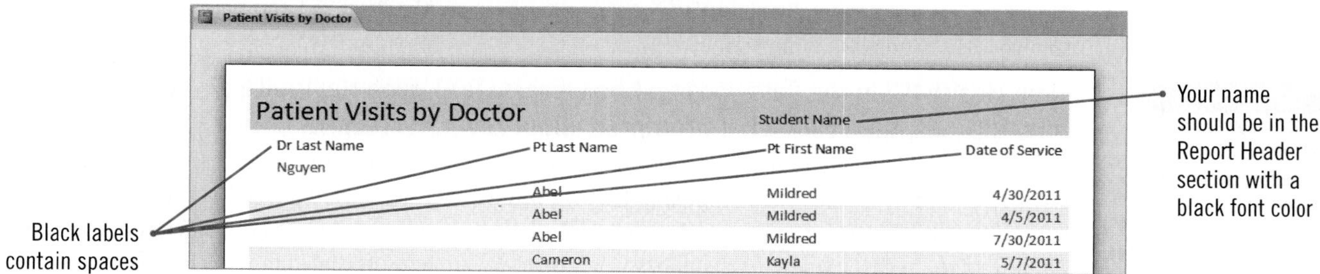

TABLE C-9: Selecting more than one control at a time in Report Design View

technique	description
Click, [Shift]+click	Click a control, then press and hold [Shift] while clicking other controls; each one is selected
Drag a selection box	Drag a selection box (an outline box you create by dragging the pointer in Report Design View); every control that is in or is touched by the edges of the box is selected
Click in the ruler	Click in either the horizontal or vertical ruler to select all controls that intersect the selection line
Drag in the ruler	Drag through either the horizontal or vertical ruler to select all controls that intersect the selection line as it is dragged through the ruler

UNIT C

Access 2010

Backing Up and Securing the Database

Backing up a database refers to making a copy of it in a secure location. Backups can be saved on an external hard drive, the hard drive of a second computer, or a Web server. A **password** is a combination of uppercase and lowercase letters, numbers, and symbols that the user must enter in order to be able to open the database. Setting a database password means that anyone who doesn't know the password cannot open the database. Tony Sanchez asks you to back up and secure the AMP C-Riverwalk database.

STEPS

1. **Click the File tab on the Ribbon, click Save Database As, then click Yes if prompted to close all open objects**

   The Save As dialog box is shown in Figure C-17. One way to back up an Access database is to use the Save Database As option. Note that **Save Database As** saves the entire database including all of its objects to a completely new database file. The **Save Object As** option saves only the current object (table, query, form, report, macro, or module).

2. **Navigate to the drive and folder where you store your Data Files, enter AMP C-Riverwalk-Backup in the File name box, then click Save**

   A copy of the AMP C-Riverwalk.accdb database is saved in the location you selected with the name AMP C-Riverwalk-Backup.accdb. Access also automatically closed the AMP C-Riverwalk.accdb database and opened AMP C-Riverwalk-Backup.accdb.

   To set a database password, you must open the database in **exclusive mode**, which means that you are the only person who has the database open, and others cannot open the file during this time.

3. **Click the File tab on the Ribbon, click Close Database, click Open, navigate to the drive and folder where you store your Data Files, click AMP C-Riverwalk-Backup.accdb, click the Open button arrow, click Open Exclusive as shown in Figure C-18, click the File tab, click Info, then click the Encrypt with Password button**

   Encryption means to make the data in the database unreadable by other software. The Set Database Password dialog box opens. If you lose or forget your password, it cannot be recovered. For security reasons, your password does not appear as you type; for each keystroke, an asterisk appears instead. Passwords are case sensitive. Therefore, you must carefully enter the same password in both the Password and Verify text boxes to make sure you haven't made a typing error.

QUICK TIP
Check to make sure the Caps Lock key is not selected before entering a password.

4. **Type Health4U! in the Password text box, press [Tab], type Health4U! in the Verify text box, click OK, then click OK if prompted about row level security**

   Passwords should be easy to remember, but not as obvious as your name, the word "password," the name of the database, or the name of your company. **Strong passwords** are longer than eight characters and use the entire keyboard including uppercase and lowercase letters, numbers, and symbols. Microsoft provides an online tool to check the strength of your password. Go to www.microsoft.com and search for password checker.

5. **Close, then reopen AMP C-Riverwalk-Backup.accdb**

   The Password Required dialog box opens.

TROUBLE
Make sure you use the exact same capitalization for the password as you did in Step 4.

6. **Type Health4U!, then click OK**

   The AMP C-Riverwalk-Backup.accdb database opens, giving you full access to all of the objects. To remove a password, you must exclusively open the database, and then go through the same steps used to set the password.

7. **Close the AMP C-Riverwalk-Backup.accdb database and exit Access 2010**

FIGURE C-17: **Save As dialog box to backup a database**

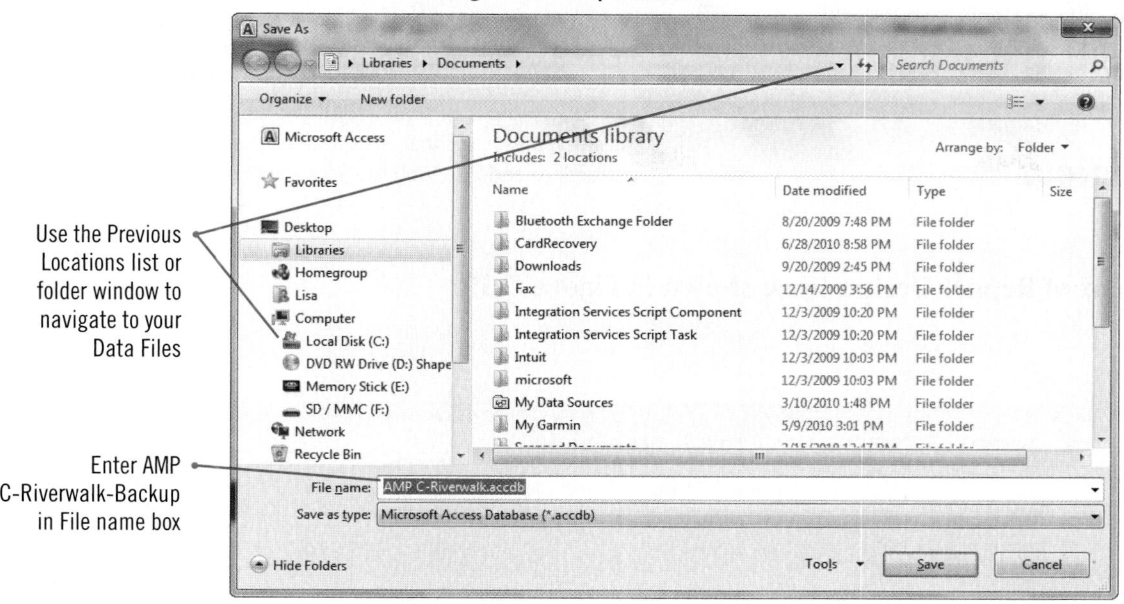

FIGURE C-18: **Opening a database in exclusive mode**

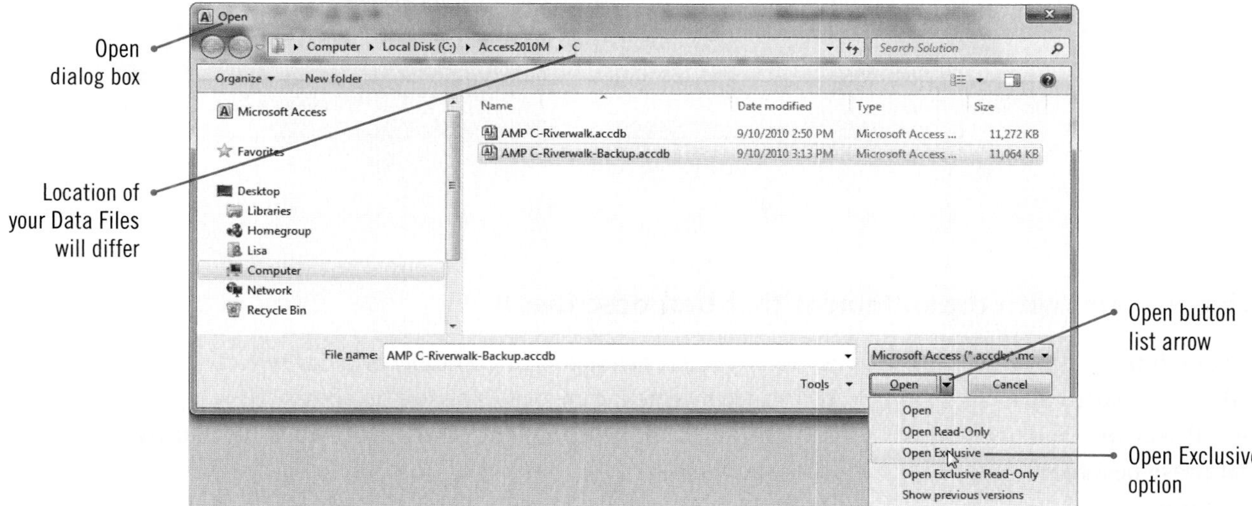

Using portable storage media

Technological advancements continue to make it easier and less expensive to store large files on portable storage devices. A few years ago, 3.5-inch disks with roughly 1 **MB** (megabyte, a million bytes) of storage capacity were common. Today, 3.5-inch disks have been replaced by a variety of inexpensive, high-capacity storage media that work with digital devices such as digital cameras, cell phones, tablet PCs, and Personal Digital Assistants (PDAs). **Secure digital (SD) cards** are quarter-sized devices that slip directly into a computer and typically store around 4 GB. **CompactFlash (CF) cards** are slightly larger, about the size of a matchbook, and store more data, around 64 **GB** (gigabyte, 64,000 MB). **USB (Universal Serial Bus) drives**, which plug into a computer's USB port, are also popular. USB drives are also called thumb drives, flash drives, and travel drives. USB devices typically store 1 GB to 10 GB of information. Larger still are **external hard drives**, sometimes as small as the size of a cell phone, that store anywhere from 20 to about 400 GB of information and connect to a computer using either a USB or FireWire port.

Practice

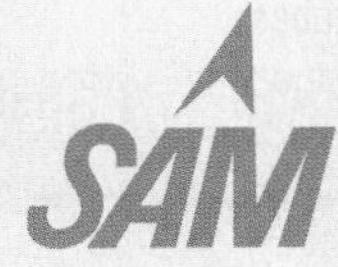

For current SAM information, including versions and content details, visit SAM Central (http://www.cengage.com/samcentral). If you have a SAM user profile, you may have access to hands-on instruction, practice, and assessment of the skills covered in this unit. Since various versions of SAM are supported throughout the life of this text, check with your instructor for the correct instructions and URL/Web site for accessing assignments.

Concepts Review

Label each element of Report Design View shown in Figure C-19.

FIGURE C-19

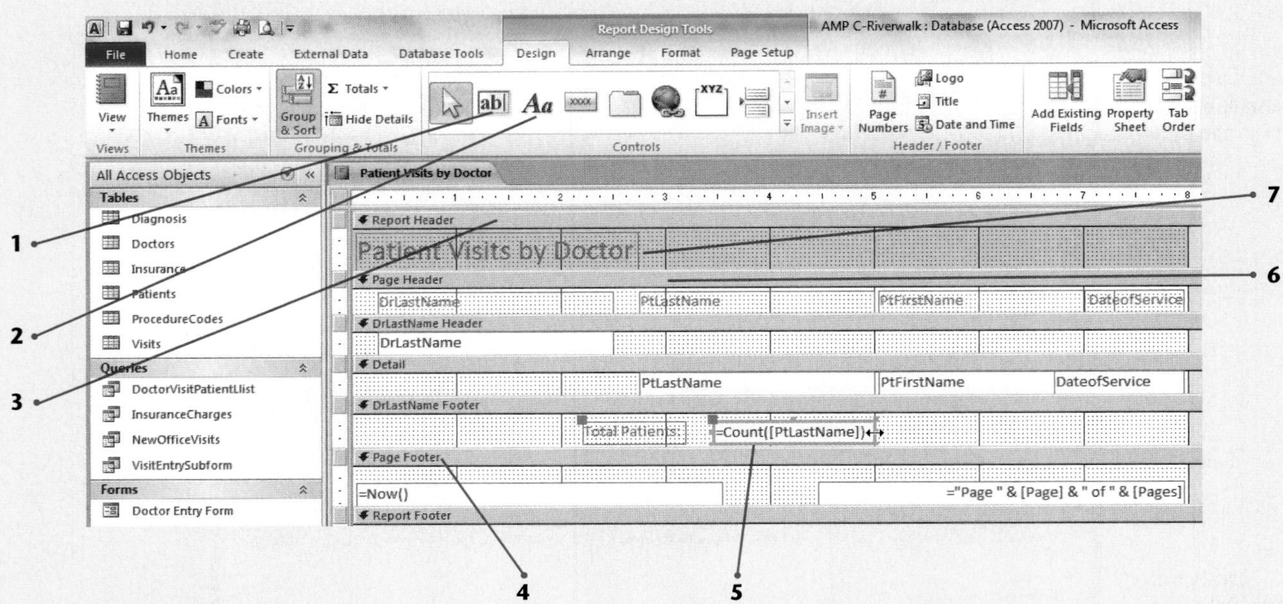

Match each term with the statement that best describes it.

8. **Expression**
9. **Calculated control**
10. **Detail section**
11. **Database designer**
12. **Grouping**
13. **Section**

- **a.** Sorting records *plus* providing a header or footer section
- **b.** Created by entering an expression in a text box
- **c.** Controls placed here print once for every record in the underlying record source
- **d.** Responsible for building and maintaining tables, queries, forms, and reports
- **e.** Determines how controls are positioned on the report
- **f.** A combination of field names, operators, and functions that results in a single value

Select the best answer from the list of choices.

14. Every element on a form is called a(n):

- **a.** Control.
- **b.** Item.
- **c.** Tool.
- **d.** Property.

15. Which of the following is *not* a valid report view?

- **a.** Print Preview
- **b.** Design View
- **c.** Layout View
- **d.** Section View

16. The most common bound control is the:

- **a.** Label.
- **b.** Combo box.
- **c.** List box.
- **d.** Text box.

17. The most common unbound control is the:

- **a.** Command button.
- **b.** Label.
- **c.** Text box.
- **d.** Combo box.

18. A title for a report would most commonly be placed in which report section?

- **a.** Report Header
- **b.** Detail
- **c.** Group Footer
- **d.** Report Footer

19. Which of the following expressions counts the number of records using the FirstName field?

- **a.** =Count([FirstName])
- **b.** =Count(FirstName)
- **c.** =Count[FirstName]
- **d.** =Count{FirstName}

20. When you enter a calculation in a text box, the first character is a(n):

- **a.** Equal sign, =
- **b.** Left square bracket, [
- **c.** Left parenthesis, (
- **d.** Asterisk, *

Skills Review

1. Manage data with a form.

- **a.** Open the AMP C-C2.accdb database from the drive and folder where you store your Data Files. Save the database as **AMP C-Diabetes.accdb**. Enable content if prompted.
- **b.** Open the EmployeeEntry form. Modify the Street Address value for the first record for Moshi Parveen from 201 SW Woodlawn Dr to **505 Foster Dr**. Modify the City from Des Moines to **Ames**, and the Zip Code from 50308 to **50010**.
- **c.** Click the New (blank) record button and create a new record using the value of **17** as the EmpNo and **your name** for the Last Name and First Name. Use fictitious but realistic data for all of the other fields to complete the record.
- **d.** Close the EmployeeEntry form.

2. Use the Form Wizard.

- **a.** Click the Create tab, then use the Form Wizard to create a form based on all of the fields in the MedDescription table. Use a Columnar layout, and type **Medicine Entry Form** to title the form.
- **b.** Navigate through the records to find MedCode 11, as shown in Figure C-20.
- **c.** Save and close the Medicine Entry Form.

FIGURE C-20

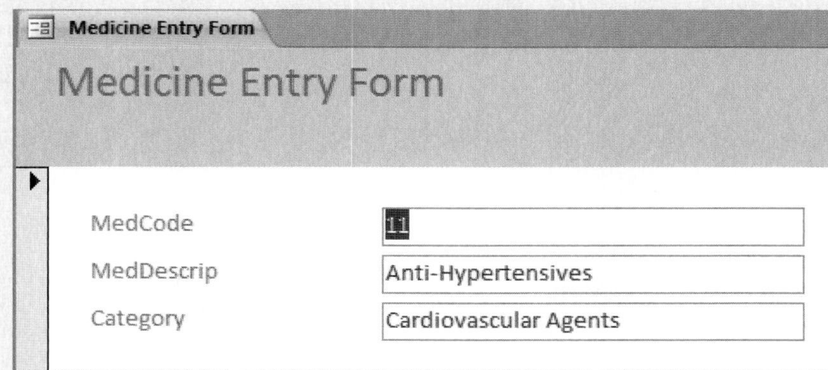

3. Preview a report.

- **a.** Open the PatientListing report in Print Preview, then move to the second (last) page of the report.
- **b.** Review both pages of the report, identifying the Report Header, Page Header, Detail, and Report Footer sections.
- **c.** Close the PatientListing report.

Access 2010

Skills Review (continued)

4. **Use the Report Wizard.**
   a. Click the Create tab, then use the Report Wizard to create a report based on the following fields in the Employees table: LastName, FirstName, and City. Group the records by City, do not add any sort orders, use a Stepped layout, and a Portrait orientation. Title the report **Employees by City**.
   b. Preview the report in Print Preview, noticing the Report Header, Page Header, City Header, Detail, and Page Footer sections.
5. **Apply group and sort orders.**
   a. Switch to Design View, and open the Group, Sort, and Total pane.
   b. Click the Add a sort button, and add LastName as a sort field under City as a group field.
   c. Click the More Options button for the City group field, then add a City Footer section.
6. **Add subtotals and counts.**
   a. Add a text box control in the City Footer section positioned under the LastName text box located in the Detail section.
   b. Modify the Text9 label to read **Count:**.
   c. Click Unbound in the text box, and enter the expression **=Count([LastName])**.
   d. Preview the report to make sure the new label and calculation in the City Footer section are working as intended.
7. **Add and modify labels.**
   a. Return to Design View, then modify the FirstName and LastName labels in the Page Header section to read **First Name** and **Last Name**. Be careful to modify the labels in the Page Header section rather than the text boxes in the Detail section.
   b. Add a new label to the Report Header section with your name.
   c. Modify all labels in the Report Header and Page Header sections to have a black font color.
   d. Preview the updated report. It should look like Figure C-21.
   e. Save and close the Employees by City report.
8. **Back up and secure the database.**
   a. Save the AMP C-Diabetes.accdb database with the name **AMP C-Diabetes-Backup.accdb** in the drive and folder where you store your Data Files.
   b. Close the AMP C-Diabetes-Backup.accdb database, reopen it in exclusive mode, and set the following password: **eat123right!**
   c. Close the AMP C-Diabetes-Backup.accdb database, and reopen it to test the password.
   d. Close the AMP C-Diabetes-Backup.accdb database and exit Access 2010.

FIGURE C-21

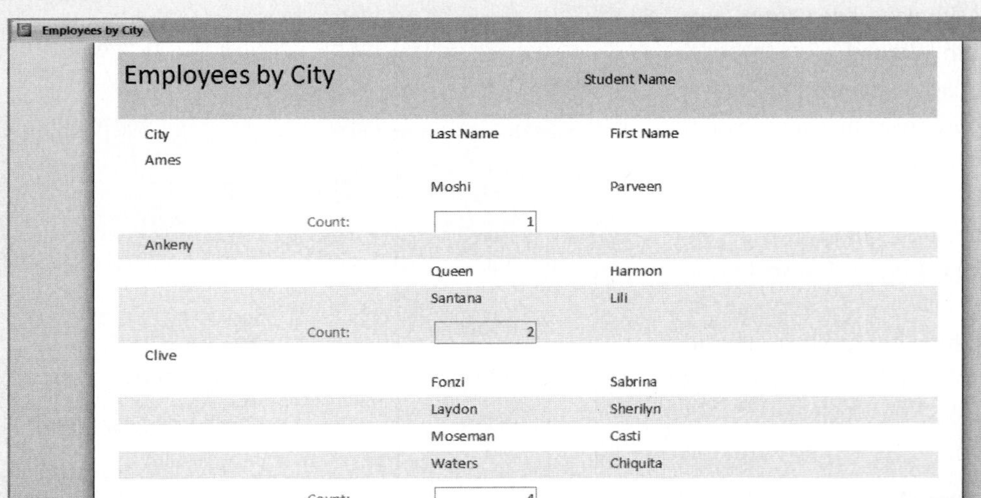

Independent Challenge 1

You have built an Access database to track nursing assignments at a multilocation dermatology clinic. You will create forms and reports to help manage and analyze the information.

- **a.** Start Access, open the AMP C-C3.accdb database from the drive and folder where you store your Data Files, then save it as **AMP C-Nurses.accdb**. Enable content if prompted.
- **b.** Open the DoctorEntry form, and add a new record using **MD** for the title and **your last name** for the Last Name field. Close the DoctorEntry form.
- **c.** Open the NurseEntry form, and add a new record using your **instructor's first and last names** in the Nurse First Name and Nurse Last Name fields. Close the NurseEntry form.
- **d.** Open the ScheduleDate form, use the FIND this date list arrow to find the 8/29/2011 date, then enter a new record for **East**, using **your name** in the Doctor column and your **instructor's name** in the Nurse column, as shown in Figure C-22.
- **e.** Close the ScheduleDate form, open the Schedule report, and print the first page if requested by your instructor. Your name and your instructor's name will be present on the schedule for 8/29/2011.
- **f.** Close the Schedule report, close the AMP C-Nurses.accdb database, and exit Access 2010.

FIGURE C-22

ScheduleDate

Work Schedule   FIND this date 8/29/2011

Date 8/29/2011 Monday 18   Add: Day Doctor Nurse   Reports: by Location by Nurse

Location	Doctor	Nurse
North	Agri	Mary Vasquez
North	Anderson	Dawn Wu
North	Fletcher	Joyce Manhattan
North	Fletcher	Lydia Hemmer
North	Northy	Michele Blago
North	Northy	Sam Fredrick
North	Northy	Tina Buck
North	Samuelson	Dana Washington
North	Samuelson	Jennifer McCully
North	Samuelson	Rebecca Rivera
South	Christenson	Ashley Jackson
South	Christenson	Shannon Kenneth
South	Market	Katie Farmer
West	Newsome	Amberley Stein
West	Newsome	Jill Kennedy
West	Newsome	Sandy Torrent
West	Newsome	Tammy Cavuto
West	Swabe	Karin Kowalewski
East	StudentLast	InstructorFirst InstructorLast

Record: 19 of 19   No Filter   Search

Independent Challenge 2

You are working with a medical school's intern placement program. You have started an Access database to track evaluations of interns and need to create a report to analyze information.

- **a.** Start Access, open the AMP C-C4.accdb database from the drive and folder where you store your Data Files, then save it as **AMP C-InternMgmt.accdb**. Enable content if prompted.
- **b.** Using the Report Wizard, create a report based on the InternFName and InternLName from the InternName table, and all of the fields except for EvalNo and InternNo from the Evaluations table.
- **c.** View the data by InternName, do not add any more grouping levels, choose EvaluationDate as the sorting field, use a Stepped layout and a Landscape orientation, and title the report **Evaluation Report**.
- **d.** Modify the labels in the Page Header section so that they match the labels shown in Figure C-23. Be careful to modify the labels in the Page Header section and not the text boxes in the InternNo Header or Detail section.

Independent Challenge 2 (continued)

e. Open the Group, Sort, and Total pane and change the InternNo group field to the InternLName field so the records are grouped by the value in the InternLName field vs. the InternNo field.

Advanced Challenge Exercise

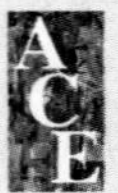

- Use Report Design View to move and resize controls so that they are all visible and fit within the 10" mark on the horizontal ruler, as shown in Figure C-23.
- In Report Design View, drag the right edge of the report to the left to fit within the 10" mark on the horizontal ruler so that the report is only 1 page wide, as shown in Figure C-23.

f. If requested by your instructor, print the first page of the report.

g. Save and close the Evaluation Report, then close the AMP C-InternMgmt.accdb database and exit Access 2010.

FIGURE C-23

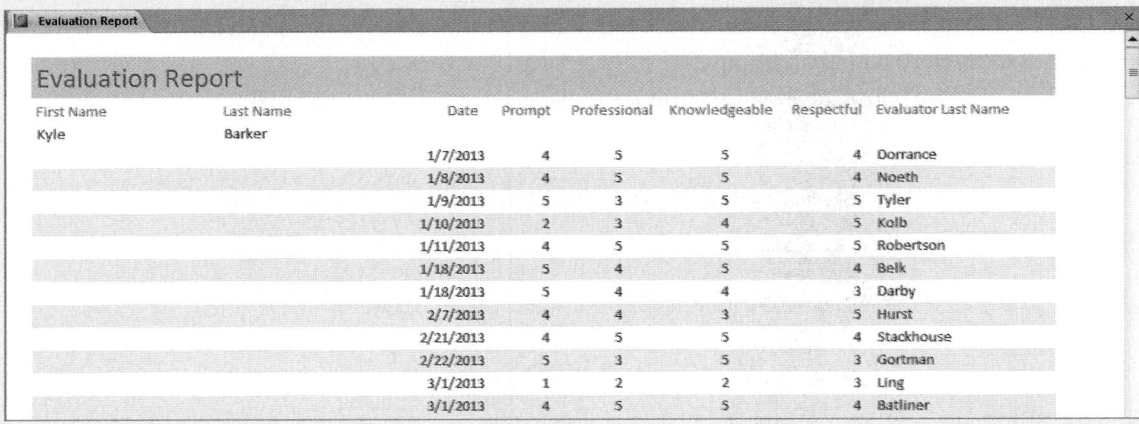

Evaluation Report

Evaluation Report

First Name	Last Name	Date	Prompt	Professional	Knowledgeable	Respectful	Evaluator Last Name
Kyle	Barker						
		1/7/2013	4	5	5	4	Dorrance
		1/8/2013	4	5	5	4	Noeth
		1/9/2013	5	3	5	5	Tyler
		1/10/2013	2	3	4	5	Kolb
		1/11/2013	4	5	5	5	Robertson
		1/18/2013	5	4	5	4	Belk
		1/18/2013	5	4	4	3	Darby
		2/7/2013	4	4	3	5	Hurst
		2/21/2013	4	5	5	4	Stackhouse
		2/22/2013	5	3	5	3	Gortman
		3/1/2013	1	2	2	3	Ling
		3/1/2013	4	5	5	4	Batliner

Independent Challenge 3

You are working for an orthopedic clinic that is highly dependent on patient referrals from primary care physicians. You have created an Access database to help keep track of referrals so that you can analyze which physicians refer to your clinic and keep in touch with them regarding patient progress. You want to analyze the data with a new report.

a. Start Access, open the AMP C-C5.accdb database from the drive and folder where you store your Data Files, then save it as **AMP C-Referrals.accdb**. Enable content if prompted.

b. Using the Report Wizard, create a new report using the RFirst and RLast fields from the ReferringDocs table and the VisitDate field from the Visits table.

c. View the data by ReferringDocs, do not add any more grouping levels, do not add any sort fields, use a Stepped layout and Portrait orientation, and title the report **Referral Report**.

d. In Report Design View, open the Group, Sort, and Total pane.

e. Change the Group field from RDocNo to RLast.

f. Open the RLast Footer section and add a text box at about the 4" mark on the horizontal ruler.

g. Delete the Text9 label in the RLast Footer section.

h. Change the Unbound text box in the RLast Footer section to **=Count([VisitDate])**.

i. Modify the labels in the Page Header section from RFirst and RLast to **Referring Dr First** and **Referring Dr Last**.

Advanced Challenge Exercise

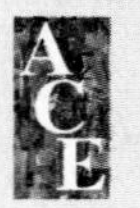

- In Report Design View, delete the VisitDate text box from the Detail section and the VisitDate label from the Page Header section.
- Drag the top edge of the RLast Footer section up so that there is no space in the Detail section.
- Preview the report, which should look like Figure C-24.

Independent Challenge 3 (continued)

j. Preview the report and print the first page if required by your instructor.
k. Save and close the Referral Report, close the AMP C-Referrals.accdb database, then exit Access 2010.

FIGURE C-24

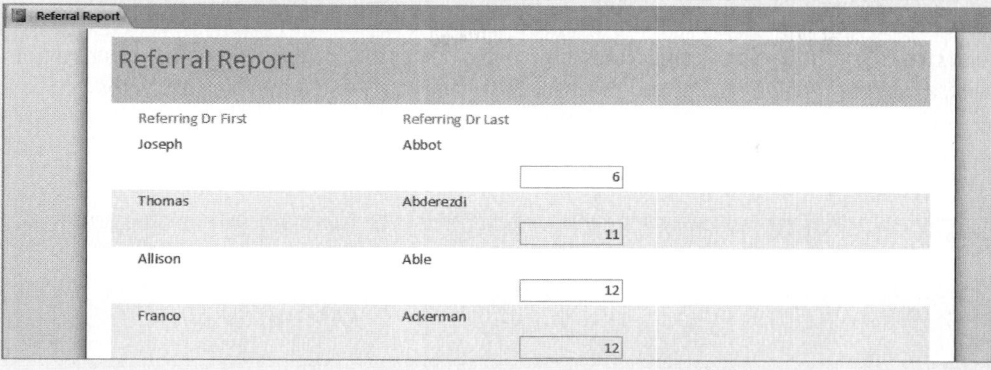

Real Life Independent Challenge

The medical profession uses a great number of abbreviations. You can use an Access database to organize and learn these abbreviations. In this exercise, you'll create a form and report to manage prescription abbreviations.

a. Start Access, open the AMP C-C6.accdb database from the drive and folder where you store your Data Files, then save it as **AMP C-Prescriptions.accdb**. Enable content if prompted.
b. Click the ScriptAbbreviations table in the Navigation Pane, click the Create tab, then click the Form button to create a new form very quickly.
c. Display the form in Form View, and enter a new record. Enter **aa** in the Abbreviation field, **ana** in the Latin field, and **of each** in the Meaning field. Save the new form with the name **ScriptAbbreviations**, then close it.
d. Click the ScriptAbbreviations table in the Navigation Pane, click the Create tab, then click the Report button.
e. Switch to Report Design View, delete all controls from the Report Footer section, open the Group, Sort, and Total pane, then click Add a sort button.
f. Choose Abbreviation as the sort field, then display the report in Print Preview, as shown in Figure C-25.
g. Close the report, saving it as ScriptAbbreviations, close the AMP C-Prescriptions.accdb database, then exit Access 2010.

FIGURE C-25

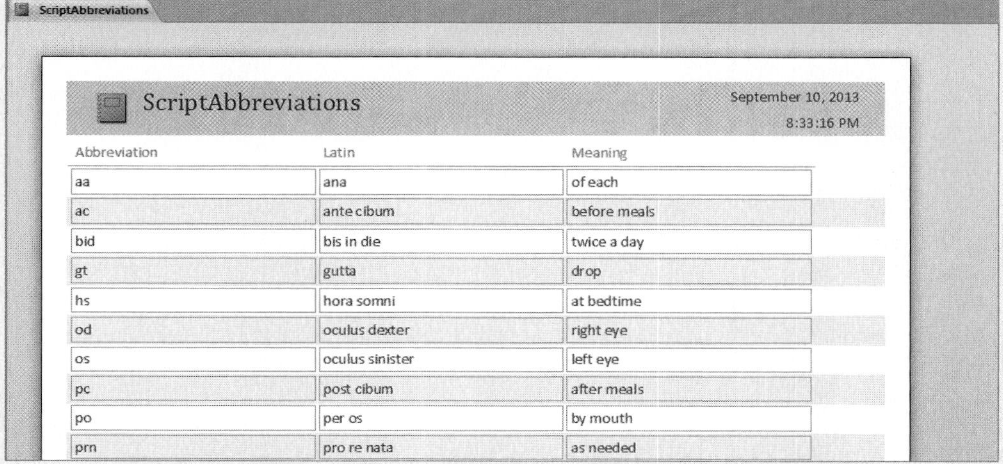

Abbreviation	Latin	Meaning
aa	ana	of each
ac	ante cibum	before meals
bid	bis in die	twice a day
gt	gutta	drop
hs	hora somni	at bedtime
od	oculus dexter	right eye
os	oculus sinister	left eye
pc	post cibum	after meals
po	per os	by mouth
prn	pro re nata	as needed

Access 2010

Visual Workshop

One of the most challenging aspects of the medical profession is the vast amount of medical terminology you are required to memorize. In this exercise, you will create a report of medical terminology. Start Access, open the AMP C-C7.accdb database from the drive and folder where you store your Data Files, and save it as **AMP C-MedicalTerms.accdb**. Enable content if prompted. Use the Report Wizard to create a report based on all of the fields in the Terms table. Do not add any grouping levels, sort the records on the Prefix or suffix field, choose a Tabular layout and a Portrait orientation, and title the report **Medical Terminology**. In Report Design View, add your name as a label to the Report Header section and change the font color to black, as shown in Figure C-26, and print the first page if requested by your instructor.

FIGURE C-26

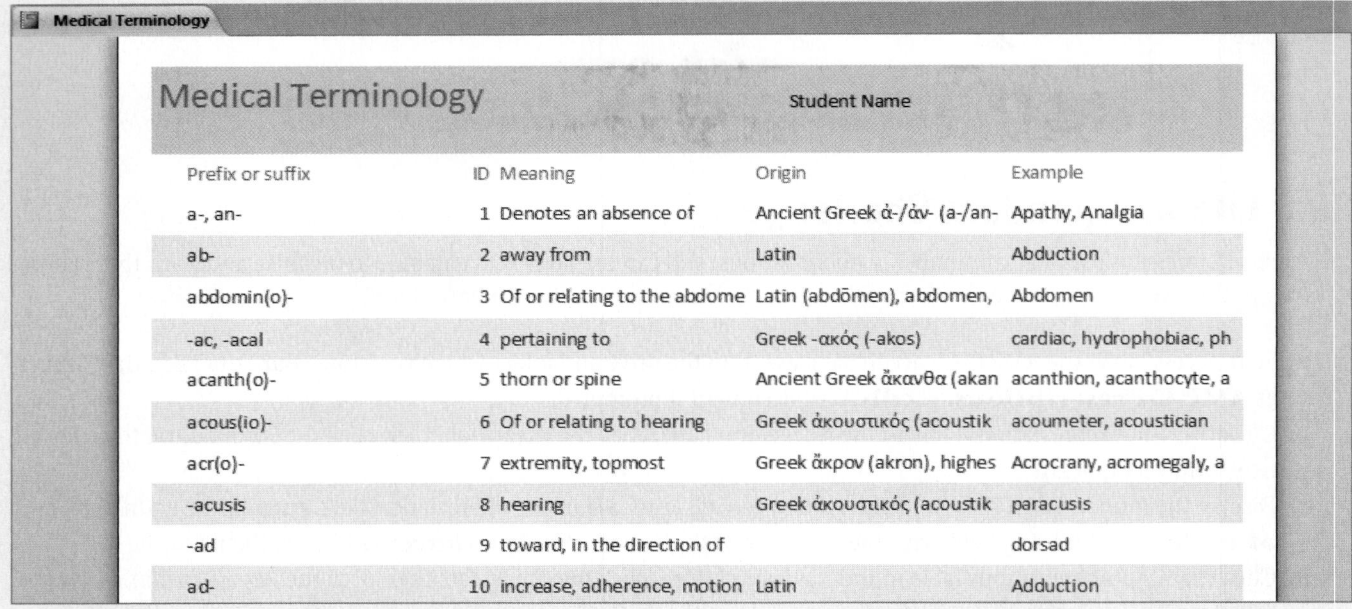

Medical Terminology

Medical Terminology Student Name

Prefix or suffix	ID	Meaning	Origin	Example
a-, an-	1	Denotes an absence of	Ancient Greek ἀ-/ἀν- (a-/an-	Apathy, Analgia
ab-	2	away from	Latin	Abduction
abdomin(o)-	3	Of or relating to the abdome	Latin (abdōmen), abdomen,	Abdomen
-ac, -acal	4	pertaining to	Greek -ακός (-akos)	cardiac, hydrophobiac, ph
acanth(o)-	5	thorn or spine	Ancient Greek ἄκανθα (akan	acanthion, acanthocyte, a
acous(io)-	6	Of or relating to hearing	Greek ἀκουστικός (acoustik	acoumeter, acoustician
acr(o)-	7	extremity, topmost	Greek ἄκρον (akron), highes	Acrocrany, acromegaly, a
-acusis	8	hearing	Greek ἀκουστικός (acoustik	paracusis
-ad	9	toward, in the direction of		dorsad
ad-	10	increase, adherence, motion	Latin	Adduction

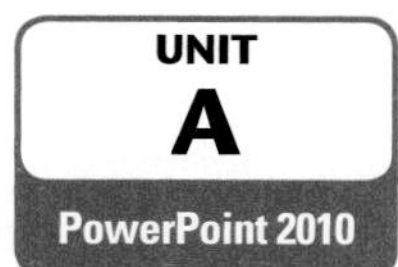

Creating a Presentation in PowerPoint 2010

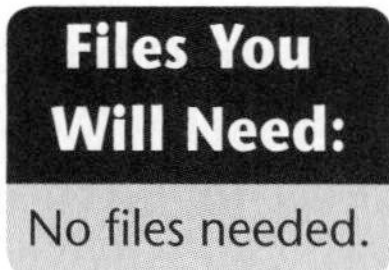

Microsoft PowerPoint 2010 is a powerful computer software program that enables you to create visually dynamic presentations. With PowerPoint, you can create individual slides and display them as a slide show on your computer, a video projector, or over the Internet. You work at the Riverwalk Medical Clinic (RMC), a large medical facility in Cambridge, MA. Part of your job at the clinic is to put together training and educational materials for the nursing training supervisor, Rebecca Haines. Rebecca has asked you to create a presentation on venomous bites and stings which she can present at the next medical staff training.

OBJECTIVES

- Define presentation software
- Plan an effective presentation
- Examine the PowerPoint window
- Enter slide text
- Add a new slide
- Apply a design theme
- Compare presentation views
- Print a PowerPoint presentation

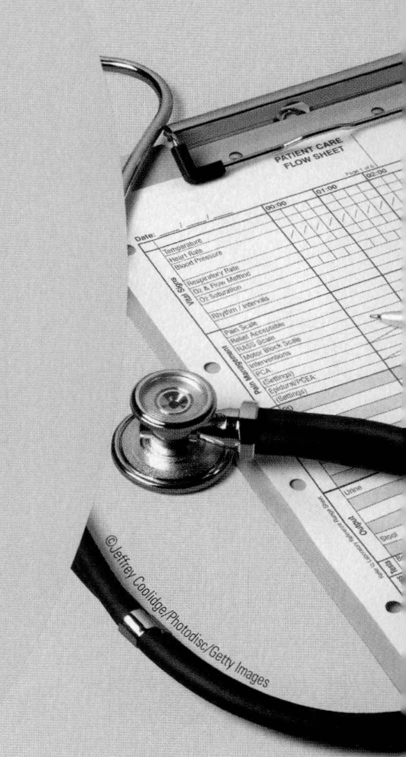

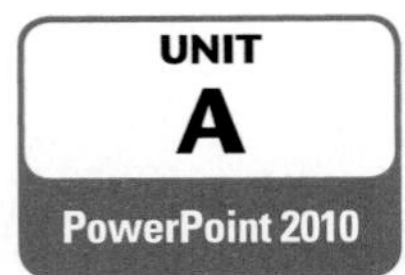

Defining Presentation Software

Presentation software is a computer program you use to organize and present information to others. Whether you are explaining a new medical procedure or moderating a meeting, presentation software can help you effectively communicate your ideas. You can use PowerPoint to create presentations, as well as speaker notes for the presenter and handouts for the audience. Table A-1 explains how your information can be presented using PowerPoint. You begin work on the venomous bite and sting presentation Rebecca will use at the next clinic training session. Because you are only somewhat familiar with PowerPoint, you get to work exploring its capabilities. Figure A-1 shows how a presentation looks printed as handouts. Figure A-2 shows how the same presentation might look printed as notes for a speaker.

DETAILS

You can easily complete the following tasks using PowerPoint:

- **Enter and edit text easily**
  Text editing and formatting commands in PowerPoint are organized by the task you are performing at the time, so you can enter, edit, and format text information simply and efficiently to produce the best results in the least amount of time.

- **Change the appearance of information**
  PowerPoint has many effects that can transform the way text, graphics, and slides appear. By exploring some of these capabilities, you discover how easy it is to change the appearance of your presentation.

- **Organize and arrange information**
  Once you start using PowerPoint, you won't have to spend much time making sure your information is correct and in the right order. With PowerPoint, you can quickly and easily rearrange and modify text, graphics, and slides in your presentation.

- **Incorporate information from other sources**
  Often, when you create presentations, you use information from a variety of sources. With PowerPoint, you can import text, photographs, numerical data, and facts from files created in programs such as Microsoft Word, Corel WordPerfect, Adobe Photoshop, Microsoft Excel, and Microsoft Access. You can also import graphic images from a variety of sources such as the Internet, other computers, a digital camera, or other graphics programs. Always be sure you have permission to use any work that you did not create yourself.

- **Present information in a variety of ways**
  With PowerPoint, you can present information using a variety of methods. For example, you can print handout pages or an outline of your presentation for audience members. You can display your presentation as an on-screen slide show using your computer, or if you are presenting to a large group, you can use a video projector and a large screen. If you want to reach an even wider audience, you can broadcast the presentation over the Internet so people anywhere in the world can use a Web browser to view your presentation.

- **Collaborate on a presentation with others**
  PowerPoint makes it easy to collaborate or share a presentation with colleagues and coworkers using the Internet. You can use your e-mail program to send a presentation as an attachment to a colleague for feedback. If you have a number of people who need to work together on a presentation, you can save the presentation to a shared workspace on the Internet so everyone in your group using a Web browser has access to the presentation.

FIGURE A-1: PowerPoint handout

8/23/2013

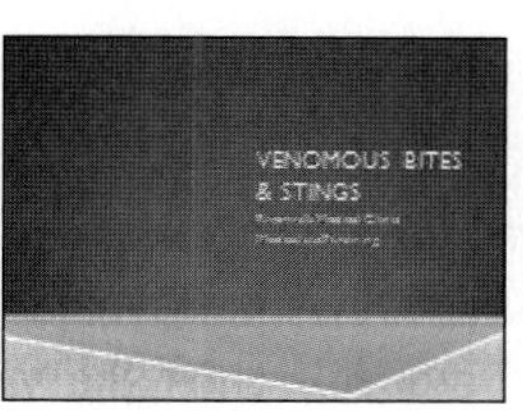

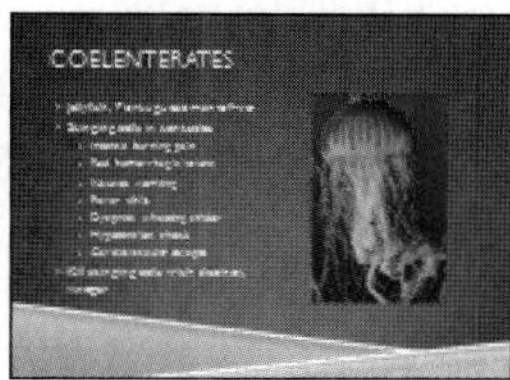

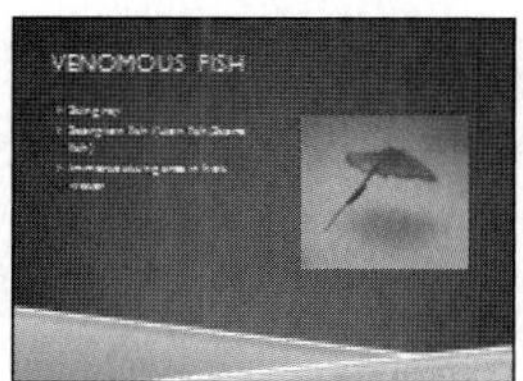

FIGURE A-2: PowerPoint notes page

8/23/2013

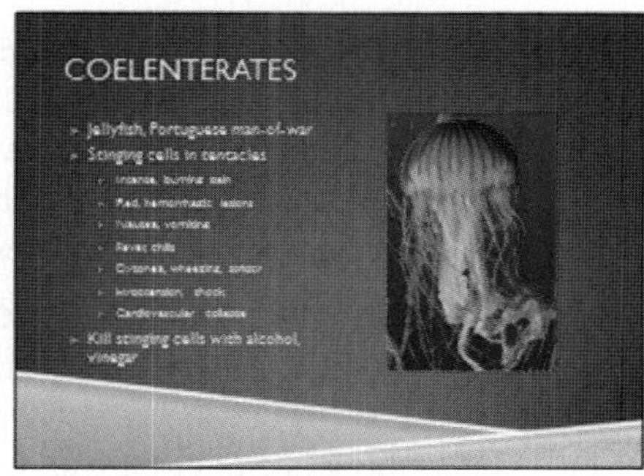

Sea urchins also venomous. Use vinegar to remove spines.

2

PowerPoint 2010

TABLE A-1: Presenting information using PowerPoint

method	description
On-screen presentations	Run a slide show from your computer or through a video projector to a large screen
Notes	Print a page with the image of a slide and notes about each slide for yourself or your audience
Audience handouts	Print handouts with one, two, three, four, six, or nine slides on a page
Broadcast a slide show	Broadcast a slide show to other viewers who watch using a Web browser
Outline pages	Print a text outline of your presentation to highlight the main points

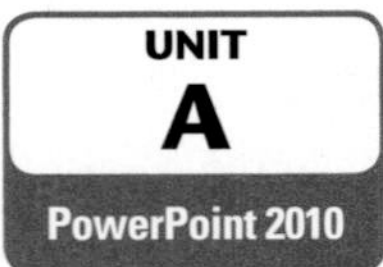

Planning an Effective Presentation

Before you create a presentation, you need to have a general idea of the information you want to communicate. PowerPoint is a powerful and flexible program that gives you the ability to start a presentation simply by entering the text of your message. If you have a specific design or theme you want to use, you can start the presentation by working on the design. In most cases you'll probably enter the text of your presentation into PowerPoint first and then tailor the design to the message and audience. When preparing your presentation, you need to keep in mind not only to whom you are giving it, but also where you are giving it. It is important to know what equipment you will need, such as a sound system, computer, or projector. Use the planning guidelines below to help plan an effective presentation. Figure A-3 illustrates a storyboard for a well-planned presentation.

DETAILS

In planning a presentation, it is important to:

- **Determine and outline the message you want to communicate**
  The more time you take developing the message and outline of your presentation, the better your presentation will be in the end. A presentation with a clear message that reads like a story and is illustrated with appropriate visual aids will have the greatest impact on your audience. Start the presentation by giving a general description of bee and spider bites. See Figure A-3.
- **Identify your audience and delivery location**
  Audience and delivery location are major factors in the type of presentation you create. For example, a presentation you develop for a staff meeting that is held in a conference room would not necessarily need to be as sophisticated or detailed as a presentation that you develop for a large audience held in an auditorium. Room lighting, natural light, screen position, and room layout all affect how the audience responds to your presentation. This presentation will be delivered in a large conference room to the clinic's medical staff.
- **Determine the type of output**
  Output choices for a presentation include black-and-white or color handouts, on-screen slide show, or an online broadcast. Consider the time demands and computer equipment availability as you decide which output types to produce. Because the presentation will be given in a large conference room to a large group and a computer and projection equipment are available, you decide that an on-screen slide show is the best output choice for the presentation.
- **Determine the design**
  Visual appeal, graphics, and presentation design all work to communicate your message. You can choose one of the professionally designed themes that come with PowerPoint, modify one of these themes, or create one of your own. You decide to choose one of PowerPoint's design themes to convey the new tour information.
- **Decide what additional materials will be useful in the presentation**
  You need to prepare not only the slides themselves but also supplementary materials, including speaker notes and handouts for the audience. You use speaker notes to help remember key details, and you pass out handouts for the audience to use as a reference during the presentation.

FIGURE A-3: Storyboard of the presentation

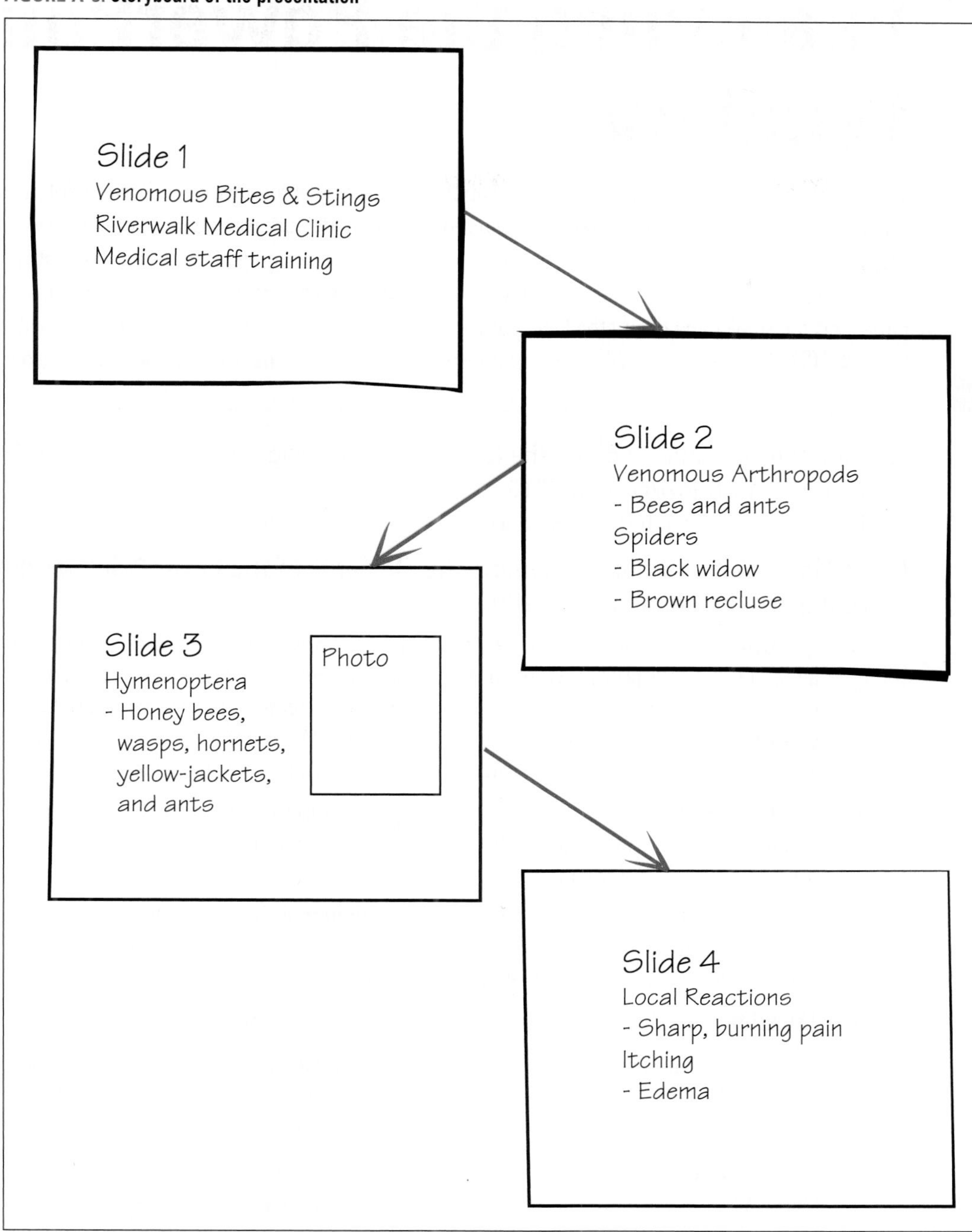
Slide 1
Venomous Bites & Stings
Riverwalk Medical Clinic
Medical staff training
Slide 2
Venomous Arthropods
- Bees and ants
Spiders
- Black widow
- Brown recluse
Slide 3
Hymenoptera
- Honey bees, wasps, hornets, yellow-jackets, and ants
Photo
Slide 4
Local Reactions
- Sharp, burning pain
Itching
- Edema

PowerPoint 2010

Understanding copyright

Intellectual property is any idea or creation of the human mind. Copyright law is a type of intellectual property law that protects works of authorship, including books, Web pages, computer games, music, artwork, and photographs. Copyright protects the expression of an idea, but not the underlying facts or concepts. In other words, the general subject matter is not protected, but how you express it *is*, such as when several people photograph the same sunset. Copyright attaches to any original work of authorship *as soon* as it is created; you do not have to register it with the Copyright Office or display the copyright symbol, ©.

Fair use is an exception to copyright and permits the public to use copyrighted material for certain purposes without obtaining prior consent from the owner. Determining whether fair use applies to a work depends on its purpose, the nature of the work, how much of the work you want to copy, and the effect on the work's value. Unauthorized use of protected work (such as downloading a photo or a song from the Web) is known as copyright infringement and can lead to legal action.

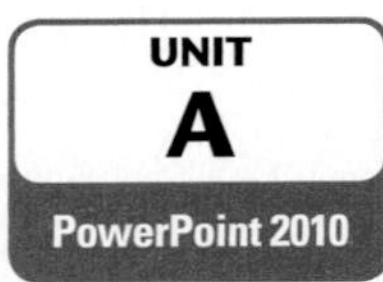

Examining the PowerPoint Window

When you first start PowerPoint, a blank slide appears in the PowerPoint window. PowerPoint has different **views** that allow you to see your presentation in different forms. By default, the PowerPoint window opens in **Normal view**, which is the primary view that you use to write, edit, and design your presentation. Normal view is divided into three areas called **panes**: the pane on the left contains the Outline and Slides tabs, the large pane is the Slide pane, and the small pane below the Slide pane is the Notes pane. You move around in each pane using the scroll bars. The PowerPoint window and the specific parts of Normal view are described below.

STEPS

TROUBLE

If you have trouble finding Microsoft PowerPoint 2010 on the All Programs menu, check with your instructor or technical support person.

1. **Click the Start button on the taskbar, click All Programs, click Microsoft Office, then click Microsoft PowerPoint 2010**

   PowerPoint starts and the PowerPoint window opens, as shown in Figure A-4.

Using Figure A-4 as a guide, examine the elements of the PowerPoint window, then find and compare the elements described below:

- The **Ribbon** is a wide (toolbar-like) band that runs across the entire PowerPoint window that organizes all of PowerPoint's primary commands. Each set of primary commands is identified by a **tab**; for example, the Home tab is selected by default, as shown in Figure A-4. Commands are further arranged into **groups** on the Ribbon based on their function. So, for example, text formatting commands such as Bold, Underline, and Italic are located on the Home tab, in the Font group.
- The **Outline tab** displays the text of your presentation in the form of an outline, without showing graphics or other visual objects. Using this tab, it is easy to move text on or among slides by dragging text to reorder the information.
- The **Slides tab** displays the slides of your presentation as small images, called **thumbnails**. You can quickly navigate through the slides in your presentation by clicking the thumbnails on this tab. You can also add, delete, or rearrange slides using this tab.
- The **Slide pane** displays the current slide in your presentation.
- The **Notes pane** is used to type text that references a slide's content. You can print these notes and refer to them when you make a presentation or print them as handouts and give them to your audience. The Notes pane is not visible to the audience when you show a slide presentation in Slide Show view.
- The **Quick Access toolbar** provides access to common commands such as Save, Undo, and Redo. The Quick Access toolbar is always visible no matter which Ribbon tab you select. This toolbar is fully customizable. Click the Customize Quick Access Toolbar button to add or remove commands.
- The **View Shortcuts** icons on the status bar allow you to switch quickly between PowerPoint views.
- The **status bar**, located at the bottom of the PowerPoint window, shows messages about what you are doing and seeing in PowerPoint, including which slide you are viewing, and the design theme applied to the presentation. In addition, the status bar displays the Zoom slider controls, the Fit slide to current window button, and information on other functionality such as signatures and permissions.
- The **Zoom slider** is in the lower-right corner of the status bar; use to zoom the slide in and out quickly.

FIGURE A-4: PowerPoint window in Normal view

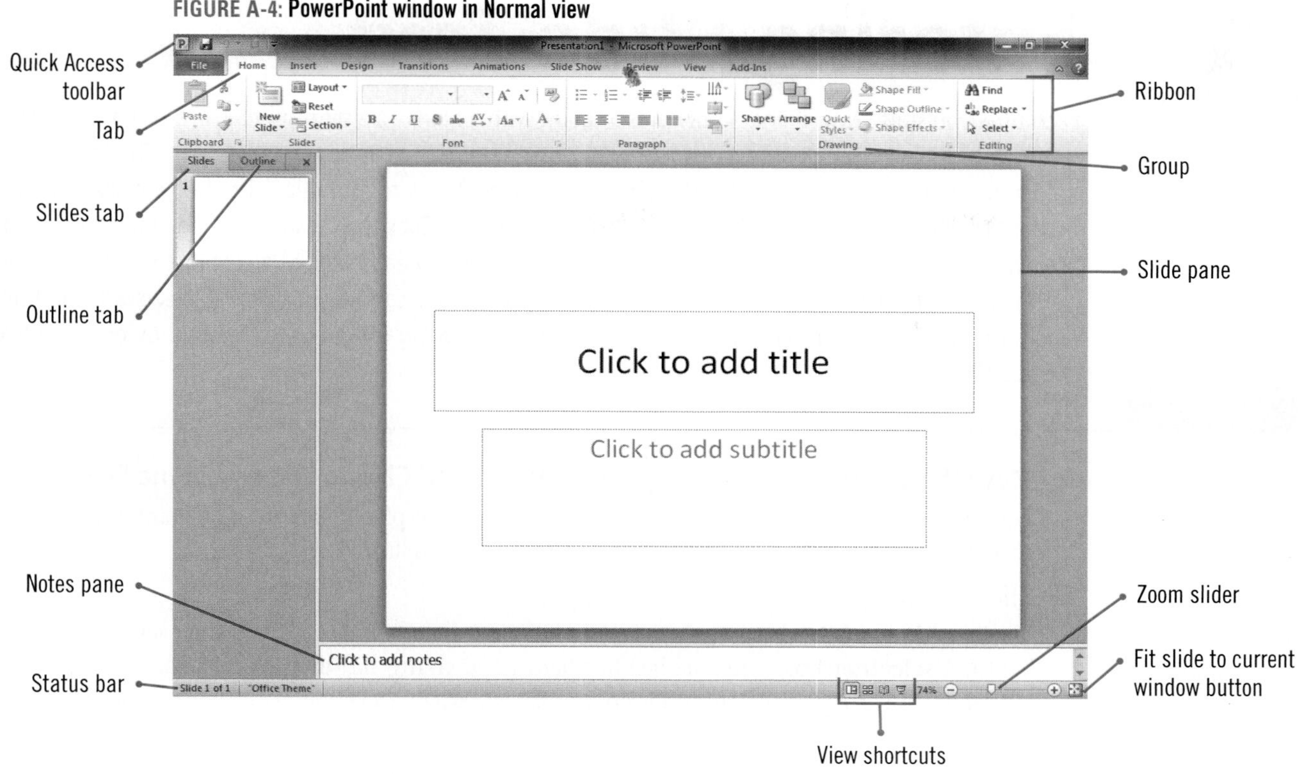

PowerPoint 2010

Viewing your presentation in grayscale or black and white

Viewing your presentation in grayscale (using shades of gray) or pure black and white is very useful when you are printing a presentation on a black-and-white printer and you want to make sure your presentation prints correctly. To see how your color presentation looks in grayscale or black and white, click the View tab, then click either the Grayscale or Black and White button in the Color/Grayscale group. Depending on which button you select, the Grayscale or the Black and White tab appears, and the Ribbon displays different settings that you can customize. If you don't like the way an individual object looks in black and white or grayscale, you can change its color. Click the object while still in Grayscale or Black and White view, then choose an option in the Change Selected Object group on the Ribbon.

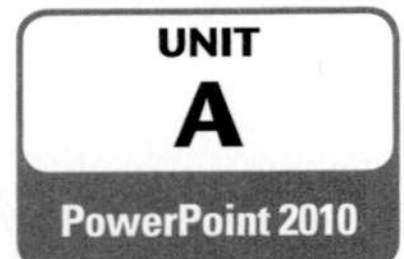

Entering Slide Text

Each time you start PowerPoint, a new presentation with a blank title slide appears in Normal view. The title slide has two **text placeholders**—boxes with dotted borders—where you enter text. The top text placeholder on the title slide is the **title placeholder**, labeled "Click to add title." The bottom text placeholder on the title slide is the **subtitle text placeholder**, labeled "Click to add subtitle." To enter text in a placeholder, click the placeholder and then type your text. After you enter text in a placeholder, the placeholder becomes a text object. An **object** is any item on a slide that can be modified. Objects are the building blocks that make up a presentation slide. Begin working on your presentation by entering text on the title slide.

STEPS

1. **Move the pointer over the title placeholder labeled Click to add title in the Slide pane**
   The pointer changes to I when you move the pointer over the placeholder. In PowerPoint, the pointer often changes shape, depending on the task you are trying to accomplish.
2. **Click the title placeholder in the Slide pane**
   The **insertion point**, a blinking vertical line, indicates where your text appears when you type in the placeholder. A **selection box** with a dashed line border and **sizing handles** appears around the placeholder, indicating that it is selected and ready to accept text. When a placeholder or object is selected, you can change its shape or size by dragging one of the sizing handles. See Figure A-5.
3. **Type Venomous Bite & Sting Symptoms and Treatment**
   PowerPoint wraps and then center-aligns the title text within the title placeholder, which is now a text object. Notice that the text also appears on the slide thumbnail on the Slides tab.

TROUBLE
If you press a wrong key, press [Backspace] to erase the character.

4. **Click the subtitle text placeholder in the Slide pane**
   The subtitle text placeholder is ready to accept text.
5. **Type System Management, then press [Enter]**
   The insertion point moves to the next line in the text object.
6. **Type Medical Staff Training, press [Enter], type Riverwalk Medical Clinic, press [Enter], then type your name**
   Notice that the AutoFit Options button appears near the text object. The AutoFit Options button on your screen indicates that PowerPoint has automatically decreased the size of all the text in the text object so that it fits inside the text object.
7. **Click the AutoFit Options button, then click Stop Fitting Text to This Placeholder on the shortcut menu**
   The text in the text object changes back to its original size and no longer fits in the text object.
8. **In the subtitle text object, position I to the right of Management, drag left to select the entire line of text, press [Backspace], then click outside the text object in a blank area of the slide**
   The System Management line of text is deleted and the AutoFit Options button closes, as shown in Figure A-6. Clicking a blank area of the slide deselects all selected objects on the slide.
9. **Click the Save button on the Quick Access toolbar to open the Save As dialog box, then save the presentation as PMP A-RMC Training in the drive and folder where you store your Data Files**
   Notice that PowerPoint automatically enters the title of the presentation as the filename in the Save As dialog box.

FIGURE A-5: **Title text placeholder ready to accept text**

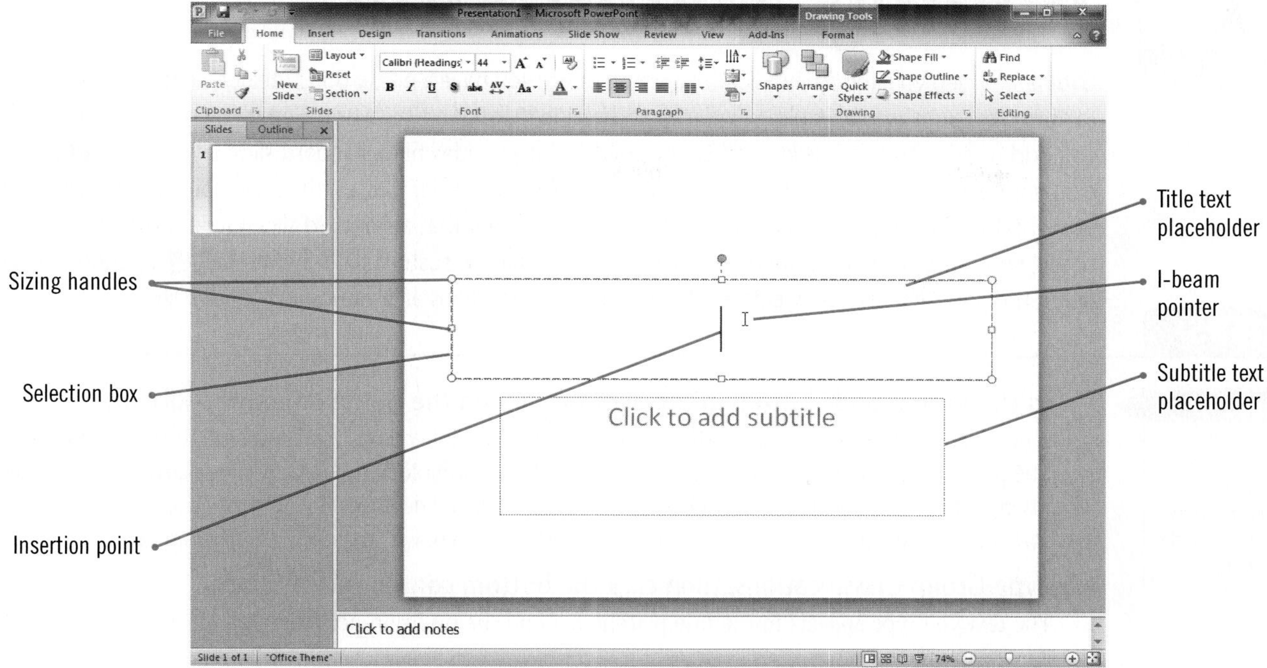

FIGURE A-6: **Text on title slide**

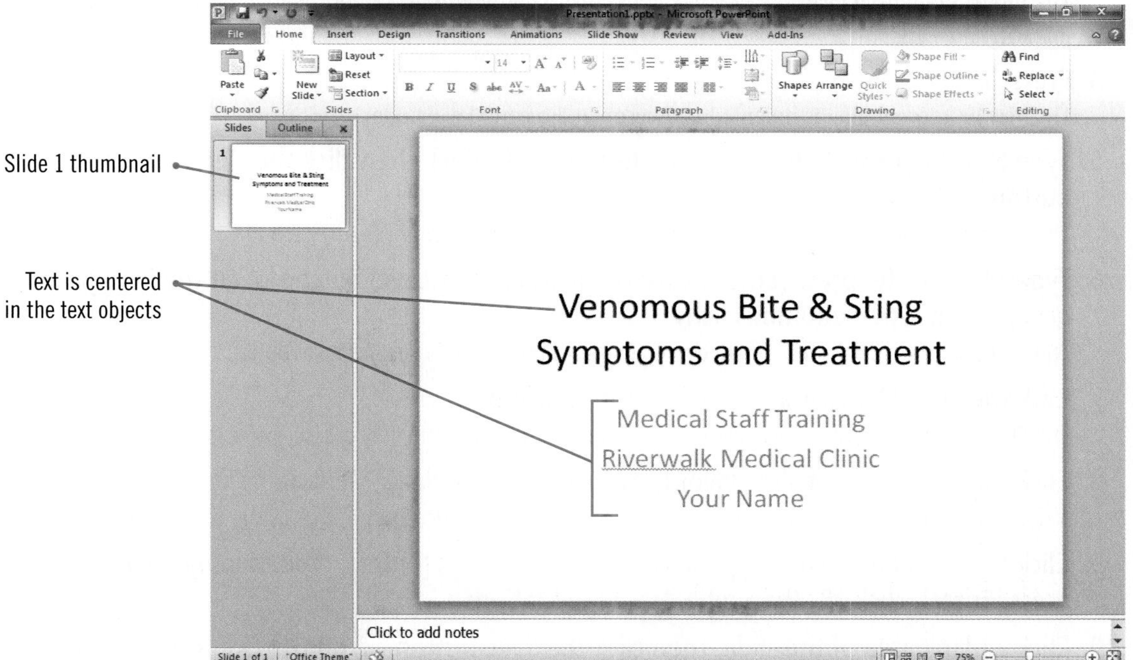

Saving fonts with your presentation

When you create a presentation, it uses the fonts that are installed on your computer. If you need to open the presentation on another computer, the fonts might look different if that computer has a different set of fonts. To preserve the look of your presentation on any computer, you can save, or embed, the fonts in your presentation. Click the File tab, then click the Options button. The PowerPoint Options dialog box opens. Click Save in the left pane, then click the Embed fonts in the file check box. Click the Embed all characters option button, then click OK to close the dialog box. Click Save on the Quick Access toolbar. Now the presentation looks the same on any computer that opens it. Using this option, however, significantly increases the size of your presentation, so only use it when necessary. You can freely embed any TrueType or OpenType font that comes with Windows. You can embed other TrueType fonts only if they have no license restrictions.

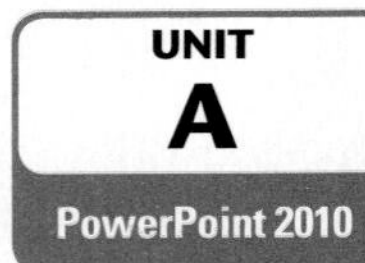

Adding a New Slide

Ordinarily when you add a new slide to a presentation, you have a pretty good idea of what you want the slide to look like. For example, you may want to add a slide that has a title over bulleted text and a picture. To help you add a slide like this quickly and easily, PowerPoint provides nine standard slide layouts. A **slide layout** contains text and object placeholders that are arranged in a specific way on the slide. You have already worked with the Title Slide layout in the previous lesson. In the event that a standard slide layout does not meet your needs, you can modify an existing slide layout or create a new, custom slide layout. To continue developing the presentation, you create a slide that defines venomous arthropods and marine life.

STEPS

QUICK TIP
You can easily change the slide layout of the current slide by clicking the Layout button in the Slides group.

1. **Click the New Slide button in the Slides group on the Home tab on the Ribbon**
   A new blank slide (now the current slide) appears as the second slide in your presentation, as shown in Figure A-7. The new slide contains a title placeholder and a content placeholder. A **content placeholder** can be used to insert text or objects such as tables, charts, or pictures. Table A-2 describes the content placeholder icons. Notice that the status bar indicates Slide 2 of 2 and that the Slides tab now contains two slide thumbnails.
2. **Type Group Classifications, then click the bottom content placeholder**
   The text you type appears in the title placeholder and the insertion point appears at the top of the bottom content placeholder.
3. **Type Arthropods, then press [Enter]**
   The insertion point appears directly below the text when you press [Enter] and a new first-level bullet automatically appears.
4. **Press [Tab]**
   The new first-level bullet is indented and becomes a second-level bullet.

QUICK TIP
You can also press [Shift][Tab] to decrease the indent level.

5. **Type Insects, press [Enter], type Spiders, press [Enter], then click the Decrease List Level button in the Paragraph group**
   The Decrease List Level button changes the second-level bullet into a first-level bullet.
6. **Type Marine Life, press [Enter], click the Increase List Level button in the Paragraph group, then type Venomous fish**
   The Increase List Level button changes the first-level bullet into a second-level bullet.
7. **Click the New Slide list arrow in the Slides group**
   The Office theme layout gallery opens. Each slide layout is identified by a descriptive name.
8. **Click the Two Content slide layout, then type Anaphylaxis Management**
   A new slide with a title text placeholder and two content placeholders appears as the third slide.
9. **Click the left placeholder, type Remove stinger, press [Enter], type Manage airway, press [Enter], click , then type Assist ventilations**
10. **Click a blank area of the slide, then click the Save button on the Quick Access toolbar**
    The Save button saves all of the changes to the file. Compare your screen with Figure A-8.

FIGURE A-7: New blank slide in Normal view

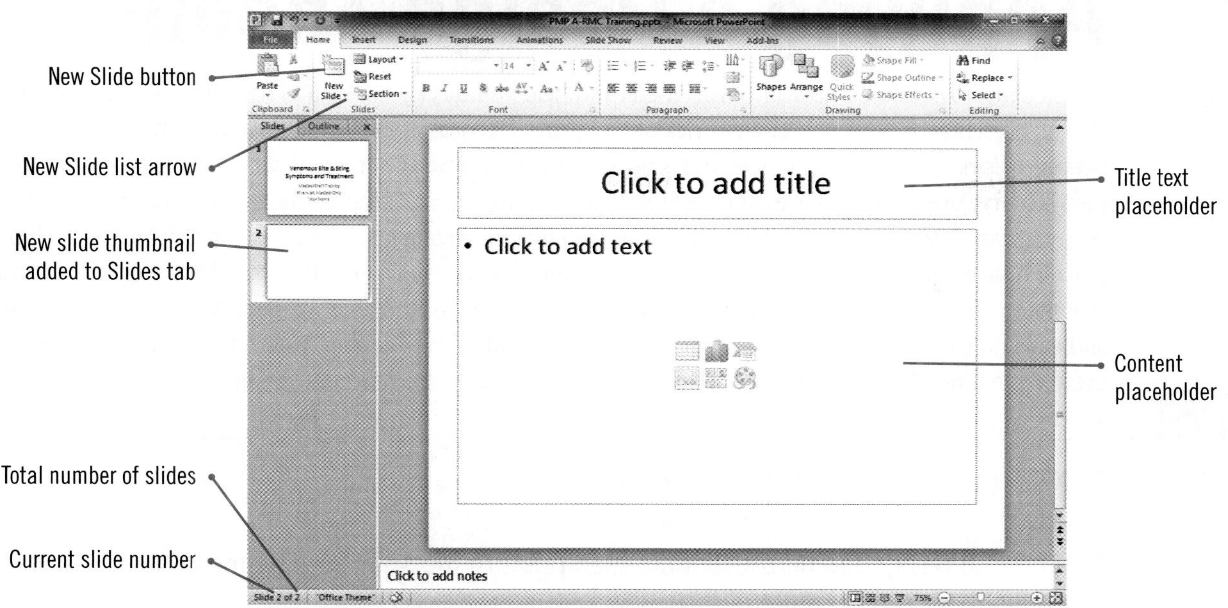

FIGURE A-8: New slide with Two Content slide layout

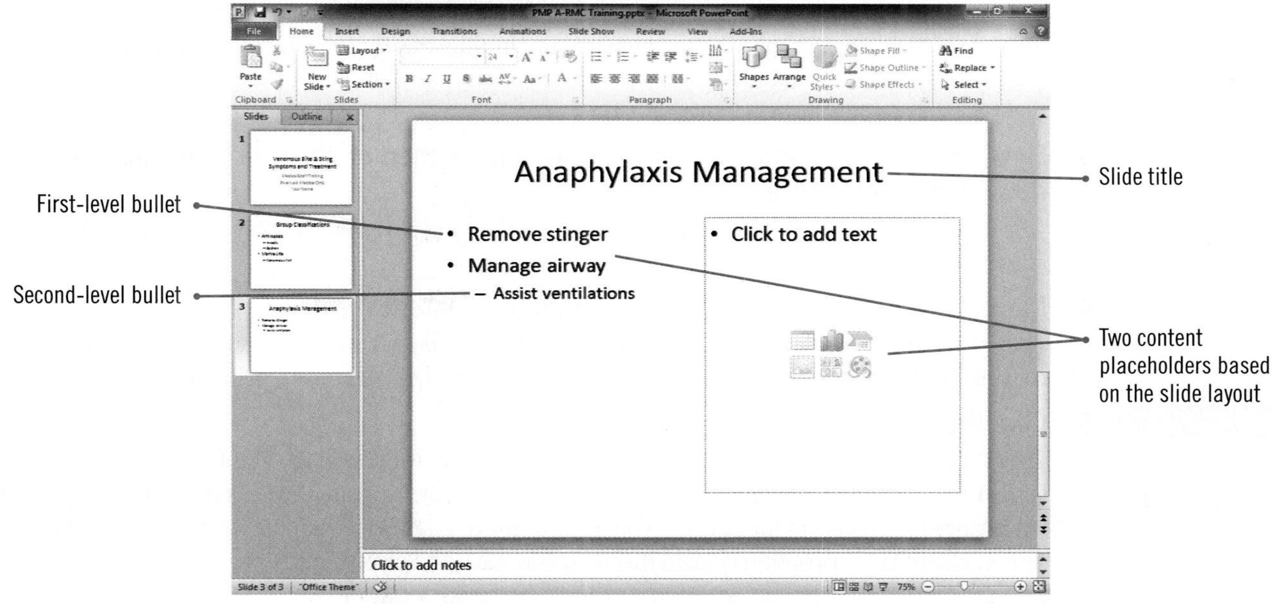

TABLE A-2: Content placeholder icons

click this icon	to insert a
	Table
	Graph chart
	SmartArt graphic
	Picture from a file
	Piece of clip art
	Video clip

PowerPoint 2010

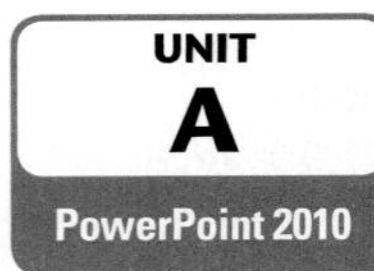

Applying a Design Theme

PowerPoint provides a number of design themes to help you quickly create a professional and contemporary looking presentation. A design **theme** includes a set of 12 coordinated colors for fill, line, and shadow, called **theme colors**; a set of fonts for titles and other text, called **theme fonts**; and a set of effects for lines and fills, called **theme effects** to create a cohesive look. In most cases, you would apply one theme to an entire presentation; you can, however, apply multiple themes to the same presentation, or even a different theme on each presentation slide. You can use a design theme as is, or you can alter individual elements of the theme as needed. Unless you need to use a specific design theme, such as a company theme or product design theme, it is faster and easier to use one of the themes supplied with PowerPoint. If you design a custom theme, you can save it to use in the future. You decide to change the default design theme in the presentation to a new one.

STEPS

1. **Click the Slide 1 thumbnail on the Slides tab**
   Slide 1, the title slide, appears in the Slide pane.
2. **Click the Design tab on the Ribbon, then point to the Adjacency theme in the Themes group as shown in Figure A-9**
   The Design tab appears and a Live Preview of the Adjacency theme is displayed on the slide. A **Live Preview** allows you to see how your changes affect the slides before actually making the change. The Live Preview lasts about 1 minute and then your slide reverts back to its original state. The first (far left) theme thumbnail identifies the current theme applied to the presentation, in this case, the default design theme called the Office Theme. Depending on your monitor resolution and screen size, you can see between five and eleven design themes visible in the Themes group.
3. **Slowly move your pointer over the other design themes, then click the Themes group down scroll arrow once**
   A Live Preview of the theme appears on the slide each time you pass your pointer over the theme thumbnails, and a ScreenTip identifies the theme names.
4. **Move over the design themes, then click the Couture theme**
   The Couture design theme is applied to all the slides in the presentation. Notice the new slide background color, graphic elements, fonts, and text color. You decide that this theme isn't right for this presentation.

QUICK TIP

One way to apply multiple themes to the same presentation is to click the Slide Sorter button on the status bar, select a slide or a group of slides, then click the theme.

5. **Click the More button in the Themes group**
   The All Themes gallery window opens. At the top of the gallery window in the This Presentation section is the current theme applied to the presentation. Notice that just the Couture theme is listed here because when you changed the theme in the last step, you replaced the default theme with the Couture theme. The Built-In section identifies all 40 of the standard themes that come with PowerPoint.
6. **Right-click the Angles theme in the Built-In section, then click Apply to Selected Slides**
   The Angles theme is applied only to Slide 1. You like the Angles theme better and decide to apply it to all slides.
7. **Right-click the Angles theme in the Themes group, then click Apply to All Slides**
   The Angles theme is applied to all three slides. Preview the next slides in the presentation to see how it looks.
8. **Click the Next Slide button at the bottom of the vertical scroll bar**
   Compare your screen to Figure A-10.
9. **Click the Previous Slide button at the bottom of the vertical scroll bar, then save your changes**

FIGURE A-9: Slide showing a different design theme

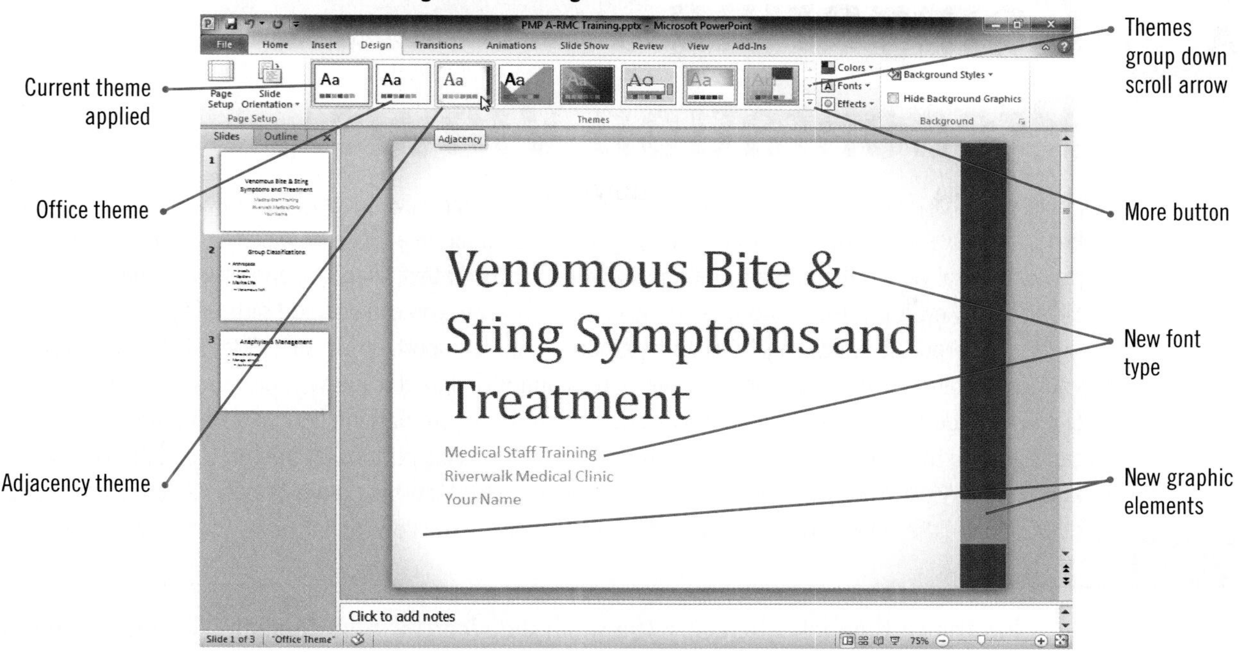

FIGURE A-10: Presentation with Angles theme applied

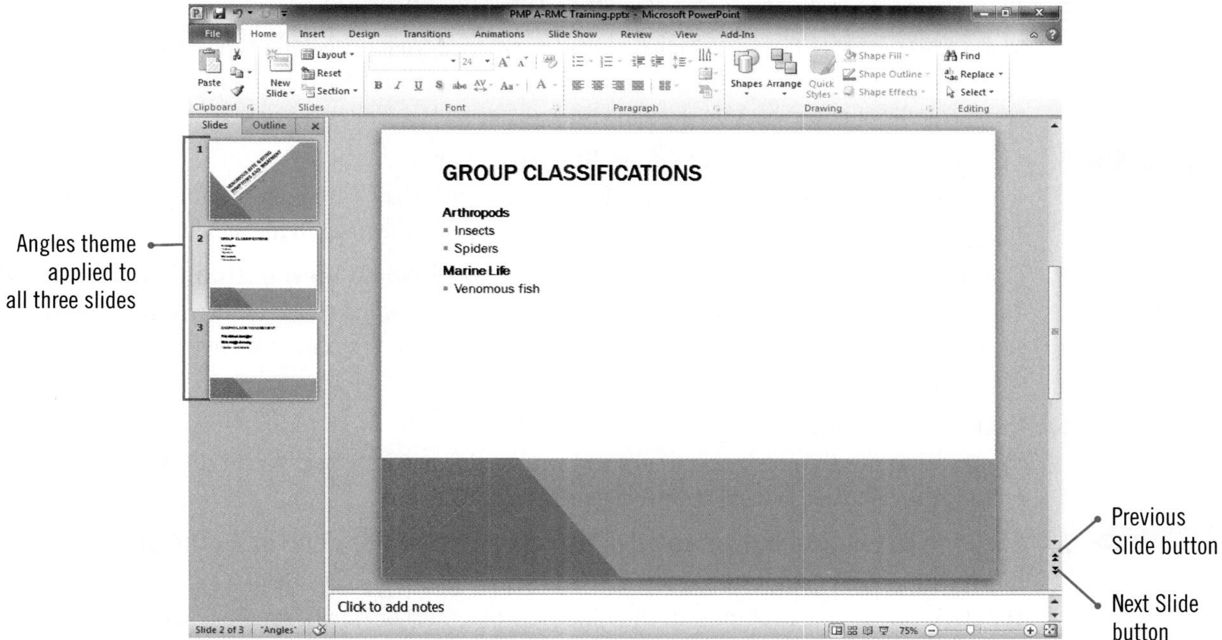

PowerPoint 2010

Customizing themes

You are not limited to using the standard themes PowerPoint provides; you can also modify a theme to create your own custom theme. For example, you might want to incorporate your school's or medical office's logo colors on the slide background of the presentation, or be able to type using fonts your company uses for brand recognition. To modify an existing theme, you can change the color theme, font theme, or the effects theme, and then save it for future use by clicking the More button in the Themes group, and then clicking Save Current Theme. You also have the ability to create a new font theme or a new color theme from scratch by clicking the Theme Fonts button or the Theme Colors button and then clicking Create New Theme Fonts or Create New Theme Colors. You work in the Create New Theme Fonts or Create New Theme Colors dialog box to define the custom theme fonts or colors.

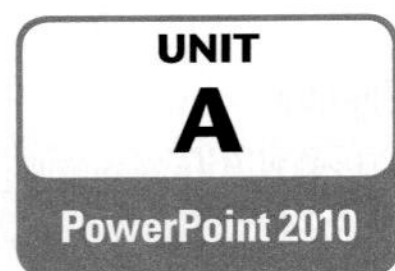

Comparing Presentation Views

PowerPoint has five primary views: Normal view, Slide Sorter view, Notes Page view, Slide Show view, and Reading view. Each PowerPoint view displays your presentation in a different way and is used for different purposes. Normal view is the primary editing view where you add text, graphics, and other elements to the slides. Slide Sorter view is primarily used to rearrange slides; however, you can also add slide effects and design themes in this view. You use Notes Page view to type notes that are important for each slide. Slide Show view displays your presentation over the whole computer screen and is designed to show your presentation to an audience. Similar to Slide Show view, Reading view is designed to view your presentation on a computer screen. To move easily among the main PowerPoint views, use the View Shortcuts buttons located on the Status bar next to the Zoom slider. Most PowerPoint views can be accessed using the View tab on the Ribbon. Table A-3 provides a brief description of the PowerPoint views. Examine each of the PowerPoint views, starting with Normal view.

STEPS

1. **Click the Outline tab, then click the small slide icon next to Slide 2 in the Outline tab**

   The text for Slide 2 is selected in the Outline tab, and Slide 2 appears in the Slide pane, as shown in Figure A-11. Notice that the status bar identifies the number of the slide you are viewing, the total number of slides in the presentation, and the name of the applied design theme.

2. **Click the Slides tab, then click the Slide 1 thumbnail**

   Slide 1 appears in the Slide pane. Thumbnails of the slides in your presentation appear again on the Slides tab. Since the Slides tab is by default narrower than the Outline tab, the Slide pane enlarges. The scroll box in the vertical scroll bar moves back up the scroll bar.

> **QUICK TIP**
> You can also switch between views using the commands in the Presentation Views group on the View tab.

3. **Click the Slide Sorter button on the status bar**

   A thumbnail of each slide in the presentation appears in the window. You can examine the flow of your slides and drag any slide or group of slides to rearrange the order of the slides in the presentation.

4. **Double-click the Slide 1 thumbnail, then click the Reading View button on the status bar**

   The first slide fills the screen as shown in Figure A-12. Use Reading view to review your presentation or to show your presentation to someone directly on your computer. The status bar controls at the bottom of the window make it easy to move between slides in this view.

5. **Click the Slide Show button on the status bar**

   The first slide fills the entire screen now without the title bar and status bar. In this view, you can practice running through your slides as they would appear in a slide show.

> **QUICK TIP**
> You can also press [Enter], [Spacebar], [Page Up], [Page Down], or the arrow keys to advance the slide show.

6. **Click the left mouse button to advance through the slides one at a time until you see a black slide, then click once more to return to Normal view**

   The black slide at the end of the slide show indicates that the slide show is finished. At the end of a slide show you automatically return to the slide and PowerPoint view you were in before you ran the slide show, in this case, Slide 1 in Normal view.

7. **Click the View tab on the Ribbon, then click the Notes Page button in the Presentation Views group**

   Notes Page view appears, showing a reduced image of the current slide above a large text placeholder. You can enter text in this placeholder and then print the notes page for your own use.

8. **Click the Normal button in the Presentation Views group**

FIGURE A-11: Normal view with the outline tab displayed

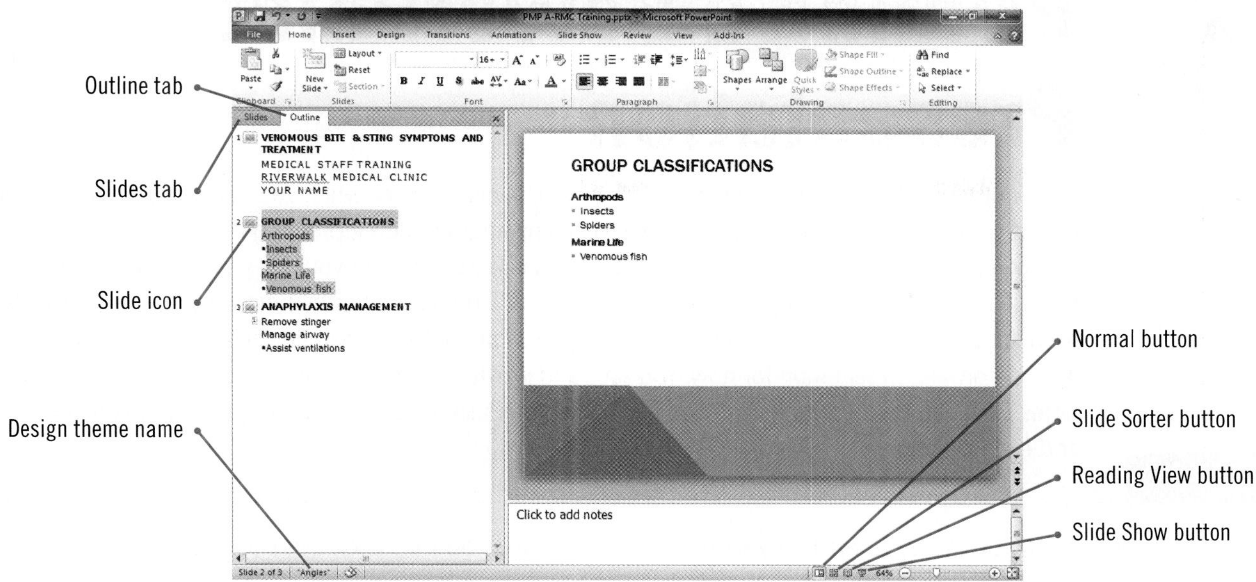

FIGURE A-12: Reading view

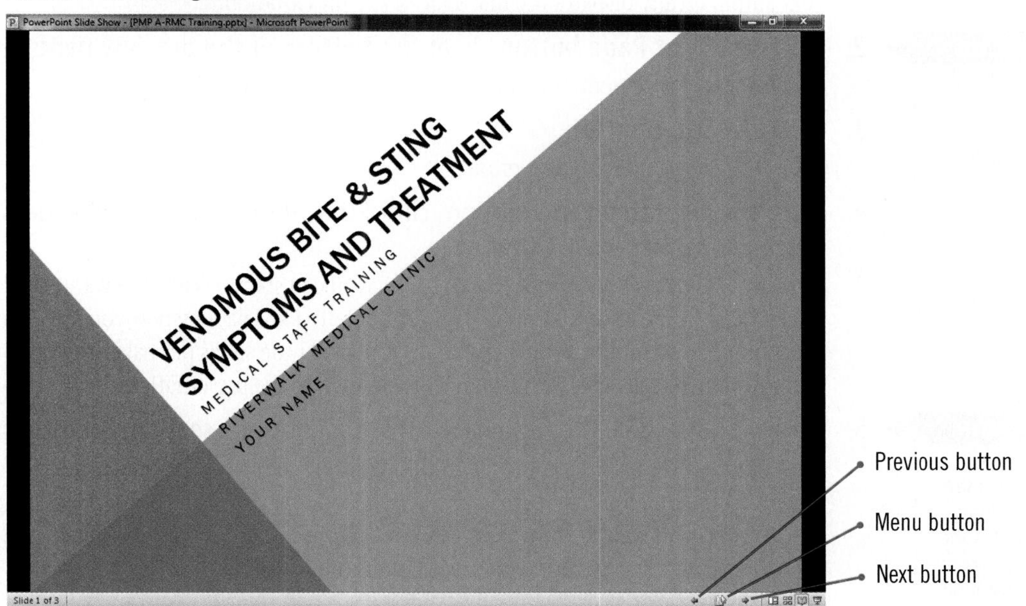

TABLE A-3: PowerPoint views

view name	button	button name	description
Normal		Normal	Displays the Outline and Slides tabs, the Slide pane, and the Notes pane at the same time; use this view to work on your presentation's content, layout, and notes concurrently
Slide Sorter		Slide Sorter	Displays thumbnails of all slides; use this view to rearrange and add special effects to your slides
Slide Show		Slide Show	Displays your presentation on the whole computer screen
Reading View		Reading View	Displays your presentation in a large window on your computer screen
Notes Page	(no View Shortcuts button)		Displays a reduced image of the current slide above a large text box where you can enter or view notes

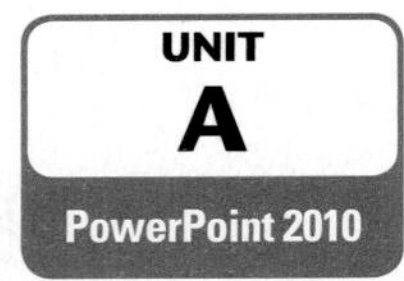

Printing a PowerPoint Presentation

You print your presentation when you want to review your work or when you have completed it and want a hard copy. Reviewing your presentation at different stages of development gives you a better perspective of the overall flow and feel of the presentation. You can also preview your presentation to see exactly how each slide looks before you print the presentation. When you are finished working on your presentation, even if it is not yet complete, you can close the presentation file and exit PowerPoint. You are done working on the presentation for now. You save and preview the presentation, then you print the slides and notes pages of the presentation so you can review them later. Before leaving for the day, you close the file and exit PowerPoint.

STEPS

1. **Click the Save button on the Quick Access toolbar, click the File tab on the Ribbon, then click Print**

   The Print window opens as shown in Figure A-13. Notice the preview pane on the right side of the window that automatically displays the first slide of the presentation.

2. **Click the Next Page button at the bottom of the preview pane, then click again**

   Each slide in the presentation appears in the preview pane.

3. **Click the Print button**

   Each slide in the presentation prints.

4. **Click the File tab on the Ribbon, click Print, then click the Full Page Slides button in the Settings section**

   The Print Layout gallery opens. In this gallery you can specify what you want to print (slides, handouts, notes pages, or outline), as well as other print options. To save paper when you are reviewing your slides, you can print in handout format, which lets you print up to nine slides per page. The options you choose in the Print window remain there until you change them or close the presentation.

5. **Click 3 Slides, click the Color button in the Settings section, then click Pure Black and White**

   PowerPoint removes the color and displays the slides as thumbnails next to blank lines as shown in Figure A-14. Using the Handouts with three slides per page printing option is a great way to print your presentation when you want to provide a way for audience members to take notes. Printing pure black-and-white prints without any gray tones can save printer toner.

6. **Click the Print button**

   The presentation prints one page showing all the slides of the presentation as thumbnails next to blank lines.

7. **Click the File tab on the Ribbon, then click Close**

   If you have made changes to your presentation, a Microsoft PowerPoint alert box opens asking if you want to save changes you have made to your presentation file.

8. **Click Save, if necessary, to close the alert box**

   Your presentation closes.

9. **Click the File tab on the Ribbon, then click Exit**

   The PowerPoint program closes, and you return to the Windows desktop.

QUICK TIP

To quickly print the presentation with the current Print options, add the Quick Print button to the Quick Access toolbar.

QUICK TIP

To print slides appropriate in size for overhead transparencies, click the Design tab, click the Page Setup button in the Page Setup group, click the Slides sized for list arrow, then click Overhead.

FIGURE A-13: Print window

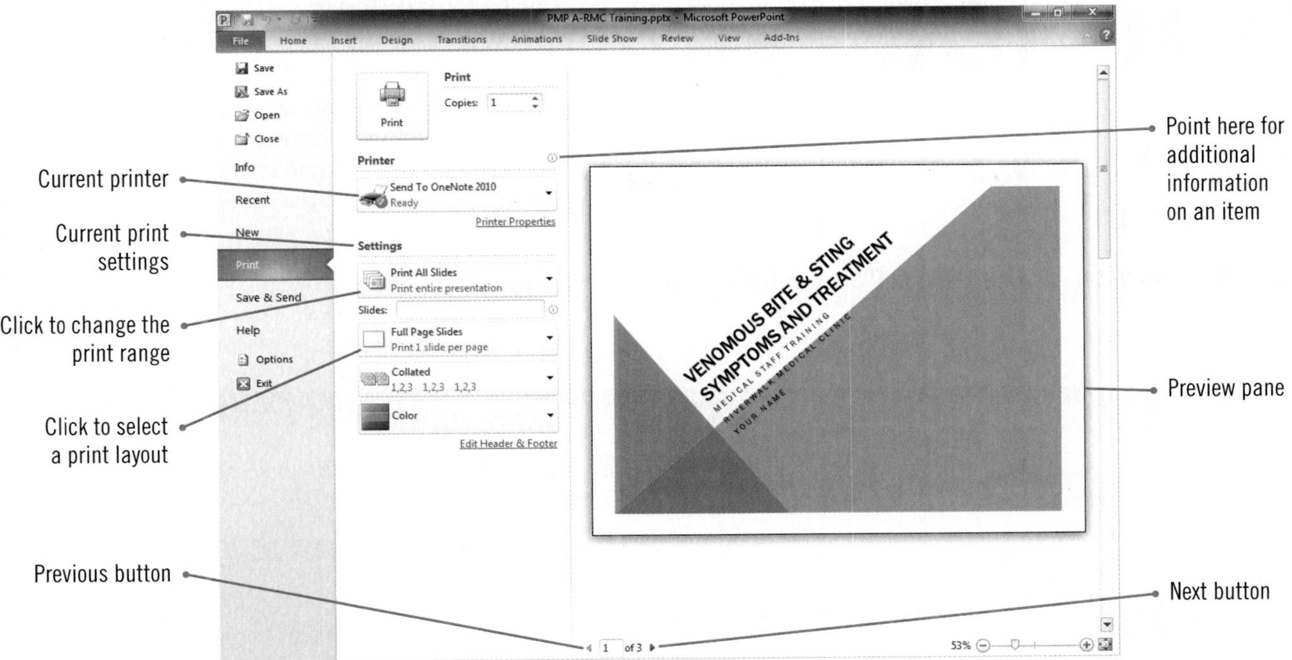

FIGURE A-14: Print window with changed settings

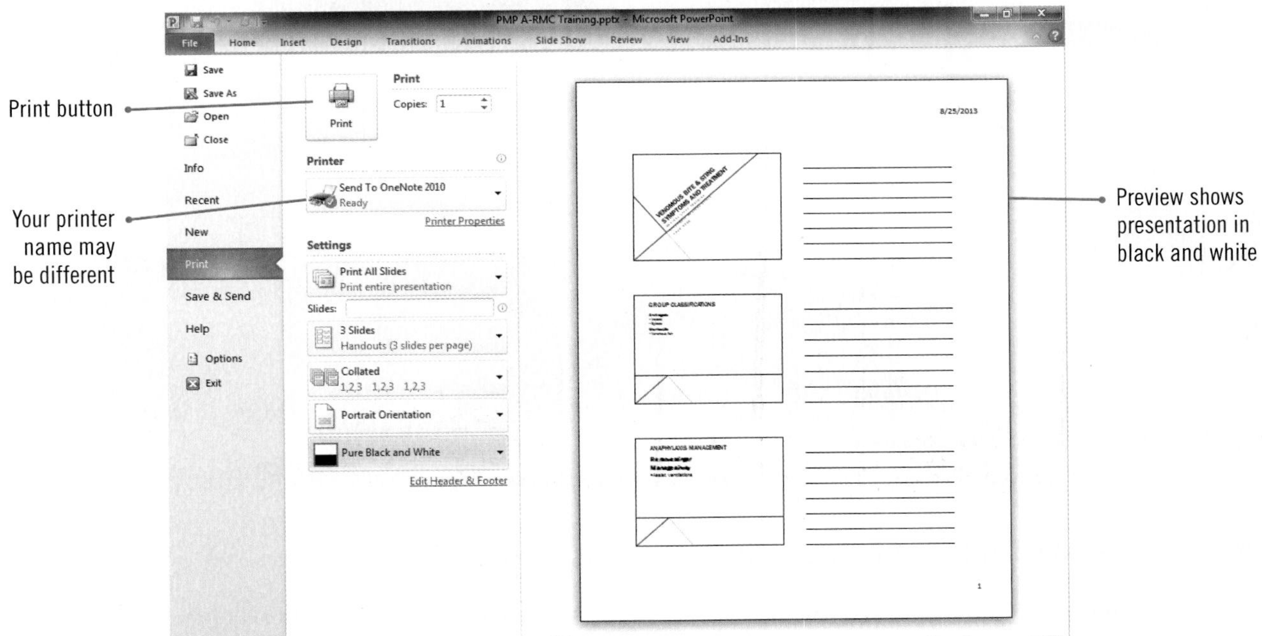

Windows Live and Microsoft Office Web Apps

All Office programs include the capability to incorporate feedback—called online collaboration—across the Internet or a company network. Using **cloud computing** (work done in a virtual environment), you can take advantage of Web programs called Microsoft Office Web Apps, which are simplified versions of the programs found in the Microsoft Office 2010 suite. Because these programs are online, they take up no computer disk space and are accessed using Windows Live SkyDrive, a free service from Microsoft. Using Windows Live SkyDrive, you and your colleagues can create and store documents in a "cloud" and make the documents available to whomever you grant access. To use Windows Live SkyDrive, you need a free Windows Live ID, which you obtain at the Windows Live Web site. You can find more information in the "Working with Windows Live and Microsoft Office Web Apps" appendix.

Practice

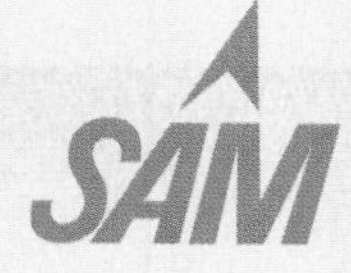

For current SAM information, including versions and content details, visit SAM Central (http://www.cengage.com/samcentral). If you have a SAM user profile, you may have access to hands-on instruction, practice, and assessment of the skills covered in this unit. Since various versions of SAM are supported throughout the life of this text, check with your instructor for the correct instructions and URL/Web site for accessing assignments.

Concepts Review

Label each element of the PowerPoint window shown in Figure A-15.

FIGURE A-15

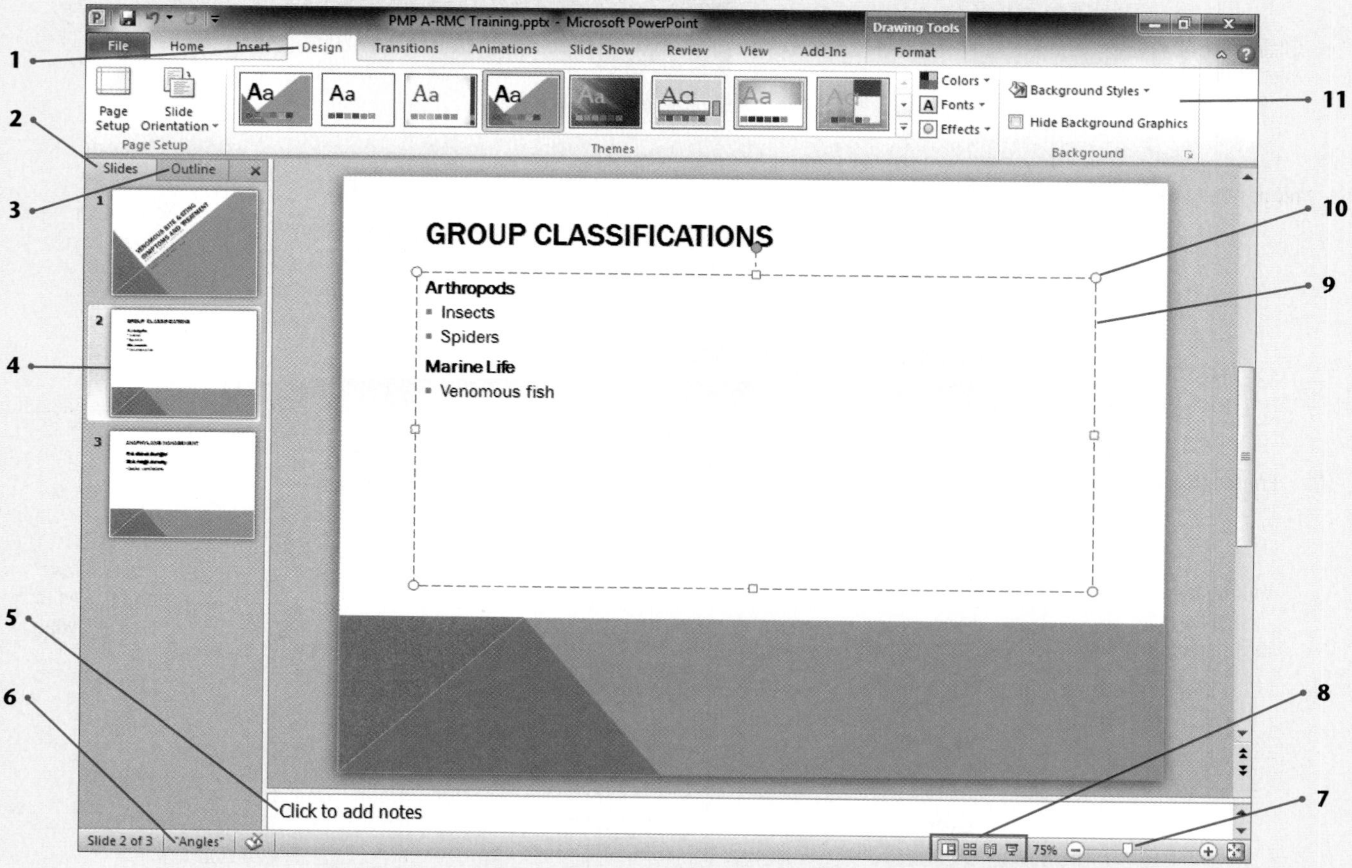

Match each term with the statement that best describes it.

12. Reading view
13. Notes pane
14. Slide Show view
15. Slide Layout
16. Ribbon
17. Zoom slider

a. A view that displays a presentation over an entire computer screen and that is used to show to an audience
b. Allows you to change the size of the slide in the window
c. A view that is used to review a presentation or to show someone a presentation directly on a computer screen
d. Arranges placeholders in a specific way on the slide
e. Used to type text that references slide content
f. Used to organize all of the commands in PowerPoint

Select the best answer from the list of choices.

18. Which statement about incorporating information is *not* correct?
- **a.** You can import text and numerical data into PowerPoint.
- **b.** You can open a PowerPoint presentation in another program to incorporate data.
- **c.** Images from Adobe Photoshop can be inserted into a presentation.
- **d.** Graphic images from a digital camera can be inserted into PowerPoint.

19. Finish the following sentence: "Copyright protects the expression of an idea,...":
- **a.** But not the underlying facts or concepts.
- **b.** Including all general subject matter.
- **c.** Only if you have it registered with the Copyright Office.
- **d.** Under the Fair Use policy.

20. Which of the following is/are located on the status bar and allows you to quickly switch between views?
- **a.** Fit slide to current window button
- **b.** Switch view button
- **c.** Zoom Slider
- **d.** View Shortcuts

21. What is the blinking vertical line that appears when you type text?
- **a.** Text handle
- **b.** Placeholder
- **c.** Text insertion line
- **d.** Insertion point

22. The view that fills the entire screen with each slide in the presentation without the title bar is called:
- **a.** Slide Show view.
- **b.** Fit to window view.
- **c.** Reading view.
- **d.** Normal view.

23. Other than the Slide pane, where else can you enter slide text?
- **a.** Reading pane
- **b.** Notes Page view
- **c.** Outline tab
- **d.** Slides tab

24. What does the slide layout do in a presentation?
- **a.** The slide layout puts all your slides in order.
- **b.** A slide layout automatically applies all the objects you can use on a slide.
- **c.** A slide layout defines how all the elements on a slide are arranged.
- **d.** The slide layout enables you to apply a template to the presentation.

25. Which of the following is not included in a design theme?
- **a.** Effects
- **b.** Pictures
- **c.** Colors
- **d.** Fonts

Skills Review

1. Examine the PowerPoint window.
- **a.** Start PowerPoint, if necessary.
- **b.** Identify as many elements of the PowerPoint window as you can without referring to the unit material.
- **c.** Be able to describe the purpose or function of each element.
- **d.** For any elements you cannot identify, refer to the unit.

2. Enter slide text.
- **a.** In the Slide pane in Normal view, enter the text **Anchorage Regional Medical Center** in the title placeholder. Refer to Figure A-16 as you complete the slide.
- **b.** In the subtitle text placeholder, enter **Nursing Internship Program**.

FIGURE A-16

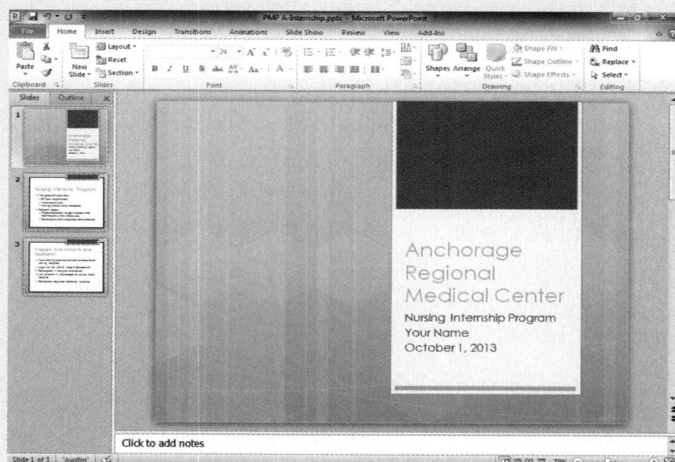

Skills Review (continued)

c. On the next line of the placeholder, enter your name.
d. On the next line of the placeholder, enter **October 1, 2013**.
e. Deselect the text object.
f. Save the presentation using the filename **PMP A-Internship** to the drive and folder where you store your Data Files.

3. **Add a new slide.**
   a. Create a new slide.
   b. Using Figure A-17, enter text on the slide.
   c. Create another new slide.
   d. Using Figure A-18, enter text on the slide.
   e. Save your changes.
4. **Apply a design theme.**
   a. Click the Design tab.
   b. Click the Themes group More button, then point to all of the themes.
   c. Locate the Grid theme, then apply it to the selected slide.
   d. Move to Slide 1.
   e. Locate the Austin theme, then apply it to Slide 1.
   f. Apply the Austin theme to all of the slides in the presentation.
   g. Use the Next Slide button to move to Slide 3, then save your changes.
5. **Compare presentation views.**
   a. Click the View tab.
   b. Click the Slide Sorter button in the Presentation Views group.
   c. Click the Notes Page button in the Presentation Views group, then click the Previous Slide button twice.
   d. Click the Reading View button in the Presentation Views group, then click the Next button on the status bar.
   e. Click the Normal button on the status bar, then click the Slide Show button.
   f. Advance the slides until a black screen appears, then click to end the presentation.
   g. Save your changes.
6. **Print a presentation.**
   a. Print all the slides as handouts, 4 Slides Horizontal, in color.
   b. Print the presentation outline.
   c. Close the file, saving your changes.
   d. Exit PowerPoint.

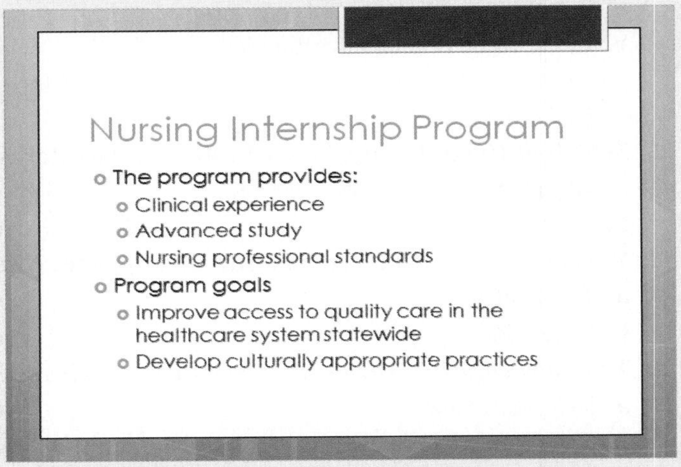

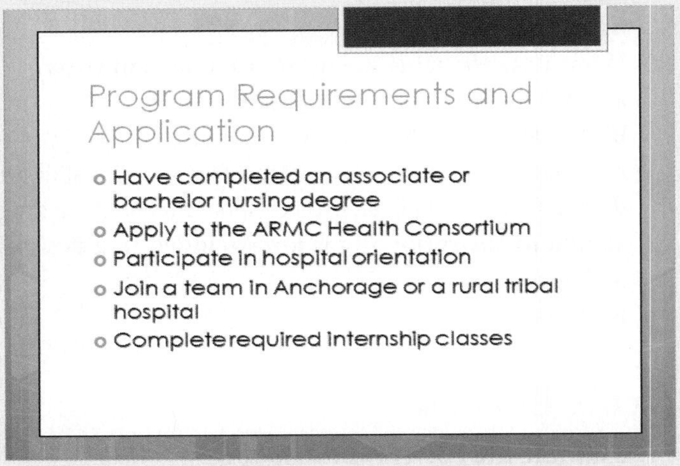

FIGURE A-17

Nursing Internship Program
The program provides:
Clinical experience
Advanced study
Nursing professional standards
Program goals
Improve access to quality care in the healthcare system statewide
Develop culturally appropriate practices

FIGURE A-18

Program Requirements and Application
Have completed an associate or bachelor nursing degree
Apply to the ARMC Health Consortium
Participate in hospital orientation
Join a team in Anchorage or a rural tribal hospital
Complete required internship classes

Independent Challenge 1

You work for the Alabama Health Education Consortium (AHEC) in Montgomery, Alabama which offers certified courses to health professionals throughout the state. One of your jobs is to develop presentations on different certified programs offered by AHEC. Your supervisor has asked you to create a presentation which describes the latest disaster preparedness and response training offered by AHEC.

a. Start PowerPoint.
b. In the title placeholder on Slide 1, type **Alabama Health Education Consortium**.
c. In the subtitle placeholder, type **Disaster Preparedness and Response**, press [Enter], type **State Certified Training**, press [Enter], then type your name.
d. Apply the Thatch design theme to the presentation.
e. Save your presentation with the filename **PMP A-AHEC** to the drive and folder where you store your Data Files.
f. Use Figures A-19 and A-20 to add two more slides to your presentation. (*Hint*: Slide 3 uses the Comparison layout.)
g. Use the commands on the View tab to switch between all of PowerPoint's views.
h. Print the presentation using handouts, 3 Slides, in black and white.
i. Save and close the file, then exit PowerPoint.

FIGURE A-19

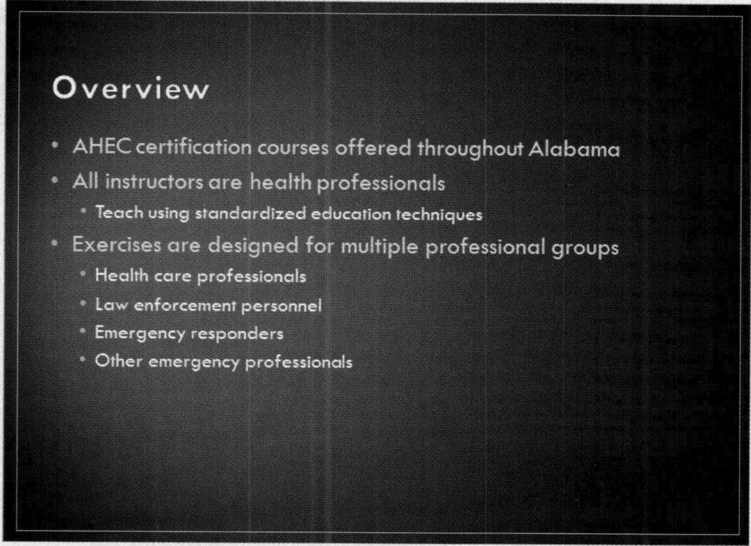

FIGURE A-20

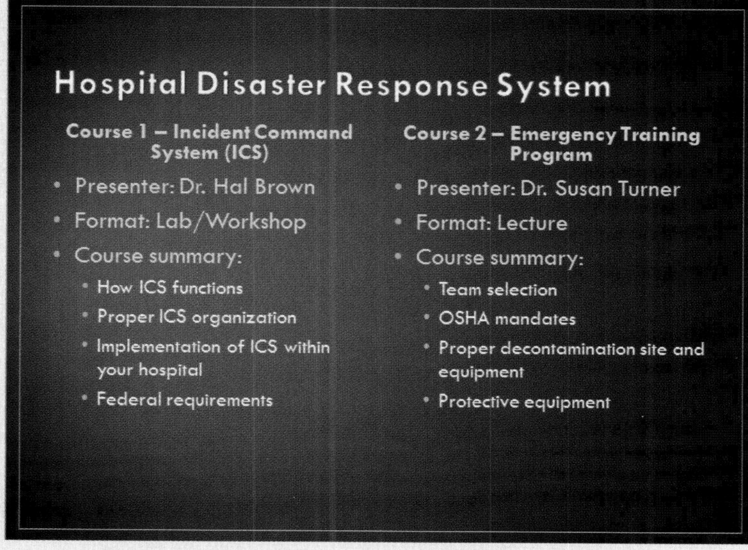

PowerPoint 2010

Independent Challenge 2

You have just been hired by Medico International, a non-profit medical organization that provides medical care and disaster relief to people stricken by disaster, conflict, and poverty around the world. You need to create a presentation which describes what Medico does and the services it offers. Assume the following: Medico follows internationally-accepted health guidelines; field staff reviews potential commitments based on need; some programs offered include community health, disaster response, HIV and AIDS care, and medical training. The presentation should have at least four slides.

a. Spend some time planning the slides of your presentation and use the Internet, if possible, to research information that will help you formulate your ideas. What is the best way to show the information provided?

b. Start PowerPoint.

c. Give the presentation an appropriate title on the title slide, and enter today's date and your name in the subtitle placeholder.

d. Add slides and enter appropriate slide text.

e. Using the Section Header layout on the last slide of the presentation, include the following information:
Medico International
USA

f. Apply a design theme. A typical slide might look like the one shown in Figure A-21.

FIGURE A-21

Advanced Challenge Exercise

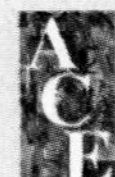

- Open the Notes Page view.
- Add notes to two slides.
- Print the Notes Page view for the presentation.

g. Switch views. Run through the slide show at least once.

h. Save your presentation with the filename **PMP A-Medico** where you store your Data Files.

i. Close the presentation and exit PowerPoint.

Independent Challenge 3

For the last three years you have worked for the Dental Surgery Center in Lincoln, Nebraska. The Dental Surgery Center is a large surgery and general practice facility with eight surgeons and doctors on staff. To better educate the public in the Lincoln area, you need to create a presentation that provides tooth care tips which can be displayed on the company Web site. You can include both child and adult tooth care tips, which might include topics such as infant tooth decay, infant teething and thumb-sucking; and permanent tooth care. Use the Internet, if possible, to research information that will help you formulate your ideas. The presentation should have at least five slides.

a. Spend some time planning the slides of your presentation. What type of information would a consumer like to read about on the company Web site?

b. Start PowerPoint.

c. Give the presentation an appropriate title on the title slide, and enter today's date and your name in the subtitle placeholder.

d. Add slides and enter appropriate slide text.

Independent Challenge 3 (continued)

e. On the last slide of the presentation, type the following information:
   Prevention tips provided by:
   - Dental Surgery Center
   - Lincoln, Nebraska
f. Apply a design theme. A typical slide might look like the one shown in Figure A-22.
g. Switch views. Run through the slide show at least once.
h. Save your presentation with the filename **PMP A-Dental** where you store your Data Files.
i. Close the presentation and exit PowerPoint.

FIGURE A-22

Primary Tooth Care for Children

- Primary teeth brushing
  - Use soft-bristled brushes
  - Brush at least 2 times per day
  - Apply small portion of toothpaste
    - Do not swallow toothpaste
    - Use a fluoride toothpaste, especially after the age of 12
  - Floss once a day

Real Life Independent Challenge

You work for the National Medical Institute (NMI), a medical education and certification company. The wound care certification course is one of the primary courses offered by NMI. Your boss and one of the clinical instructors, Dr. Nancy Phillips, wants you to create a presentation which describes the certification program for a seminar she will give next month.

a. Spend some time planning the slides of your presentation. Assume the following: the course meets National Alliance of Wound Care requirements; classes are administered by certified faculty; class topics include wound assessment and wound management. Use the Internet, if possible, to research information that will help you formulate your ideas.
b. Start PowerPoint.
c. Give the presentation an appropriate title on the title slide, then type **National Medical Institute**, your name, and today's date in the subtitle placeholder.
d. Add slides and enter appropriate slide text. You must create at least three slides. Typical slides might look like the ones shown in Figure A-23 and Figure A-24.
e. View the presentation.
f. Save your presentation with the filename **PMP A-Wound Course** where you store your Data Files.
g. Close the presentation and exit PowerPoint.

FIGURE A-23

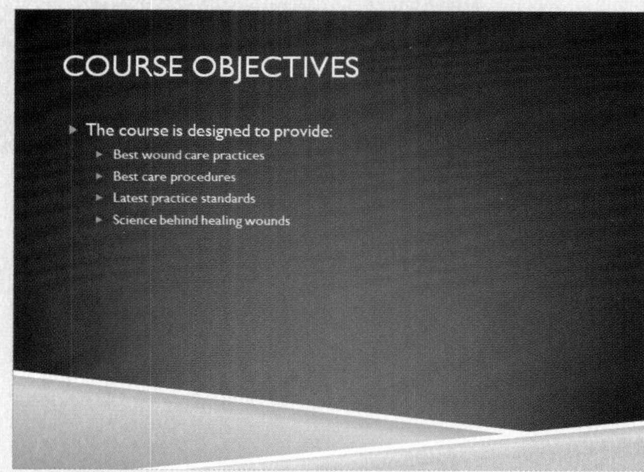

FIGURE A-24

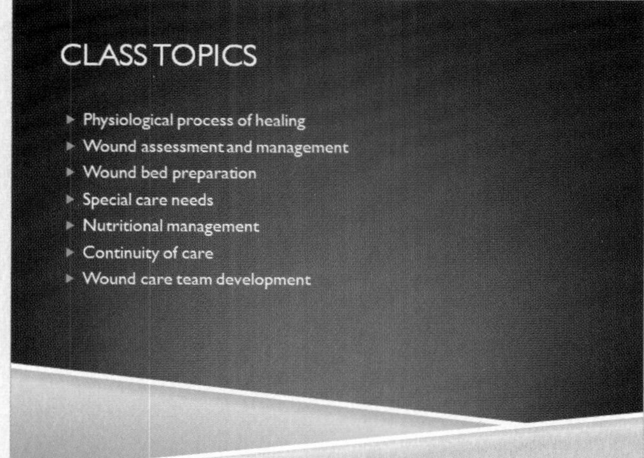

Visual Workshop

Create the presentation shown in Figures A-25 and A-26. Make sure you include your name on the title slide. Save the presentation as **PMP A-CPR** where you store your Data Files. Print the slides.

FIGURE A-25

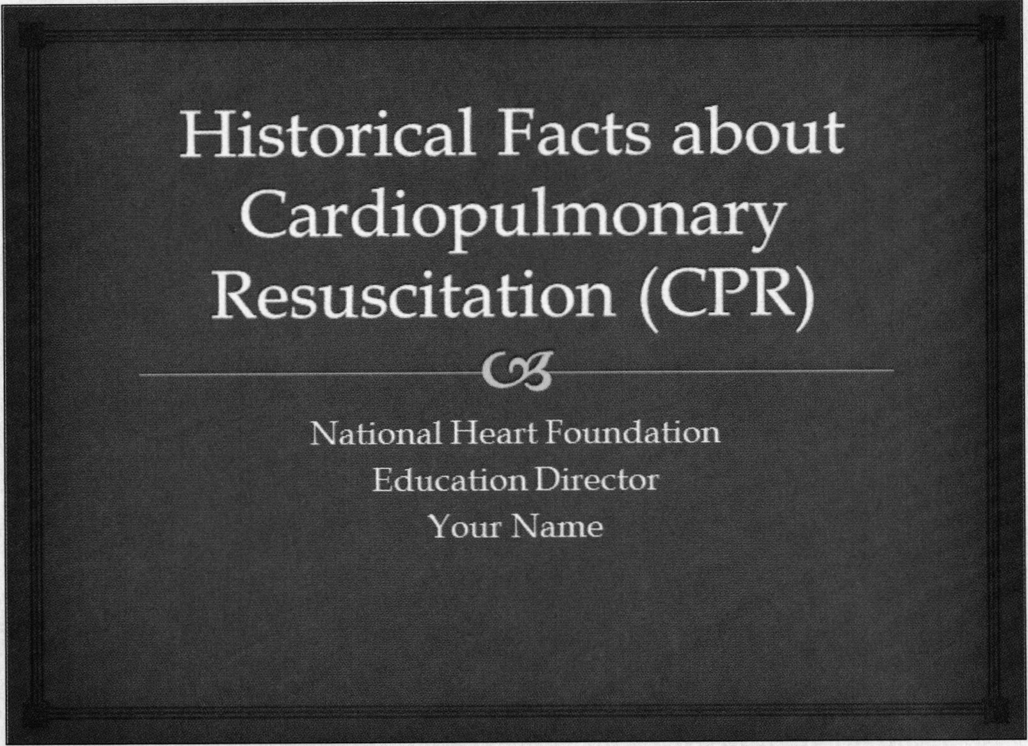

FIGURE A-26

Early History of CPR

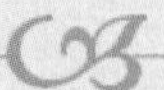

- 1740- Paris Academy of Sciences recommends mouth to mouth for drowning victims
- 1767- First organized effort to deal with unexpected death
- 1891- Dr. Friedrich Maass performed first chest compressions
- 1903- Dr. George Crile reported first external chest compressions

UNIT

B

PowerPoint 2010

Modifying a Presentation

Files You Will Need:

PMP B-1.pptx
PMP B-2.pptx
PMP B-3.pptx
PMP B-4.pptx
PMP B-5.pptx

In the previous unit you learned how to enter slide text, add a new slide, and apply a design theme. Now, you are ready to take the next step in creating professional-looking presentations by learning to format text and work with drawn objects. In this unit, you'll enter text in the Outline tab, format text, draw and modify objects, add slide footer information, and check the spelling in the presentation. You continue working on the venomous bite and sting presentation.

OBJECTIVES

- Enter text in the Outline tab
- Format text
- Convert text to SmartArt
- Insert and modify shapes
- Edit and duplicate shapes
- Align and group objects
- Add slide headers and footers
- Use proofing and language tools

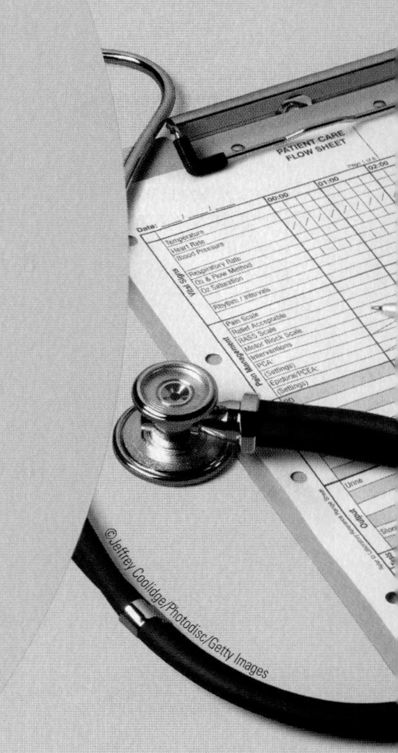

UNIT
B
PowerPoint 2010

Entering Text in the Outline Tab

You can enter presentation text by typing directly on the slide in the Slide pane, or, if you'd rather focus on the presentation text without worrying about the layout, you can enter text in the Outline tab. The outline is organized so that the headings, or slide titles, appear at the top of the outline. Beneath the title, each subpoint, or each line of bulleted text, appears as one or more indented lines under the title. Each indent in the outline creates another level of bulleted text on the slide. You switch to the Outline tab to enter text for two more slides for your presentation.

STEPS

QUICK TIP
To open a PowerPoint 97-2003 presentation in PowerPoint 2010, open the presentation, click the File tab, click the Convert button, name the presentation file in the Save As dialog box, then click Save.

1. **Start PowerPoint, open the presentation PMP B-1.pptx from the drive and folder where you store your Data Files, then save it as PMP B-RMC Training.pptx**
   A presentation with the new name appears in the PowerPoint window.
2. **Click the Slide 3 thumbnail in the Slides tab, then click the Outline tab**
   The Outline tab enlarges to display the text that is on the slides. The slide icon and the text for Slide 3 are highlighted, indicating that it is selected.
3. **On the Home tab on the Ribbon, click the New Slide list arrow in the Slides group, then click Title and Content**
   A new slide, Slide 4, with the Title and Content layout appears as the current slide below Slide 3. A blinking insertion point appears next to the new slide in the Outline tab. Text that you enter next to a slide icon becomes the title for that slide.
4. **Type Bite & Sting Deaths, press [Enter], then press [Tab]**
   When you first press [Enter] you create a new slide, but because you want to enter bulleted text on Slide 4 you press [Tab] so that the text you type is entered as bullet text on Slide 4. See Figure B-1. Notice the text you type is in all uppercase letters because that is how the font is set in the design theme.
5. **Type 50% insects, press [Enter], type 14% spiders, press [Enter], type 30% snakes, press [Enter], type 06% other, then press [Enter]**
   Each time you press [Enter], the insertion point moves down one line.
6. **Press [Shift][Tab]**
   Because you are working in the Outline tab, a new slide, Slide 5, is created when you press [Shift][Tab].
7. **Type EPI Auto-Injector, press [Ctrl][Enter], type Actions, press [Enter], press [Tab], type Dilates arways, make sure you misspell the word "arways," press [Enter], type Constricts blood vessels, press [Enter], then type Raises peripheral resistance, BP**
   Pressing [Ctrl][Enter] while the cursor is in the title text object moves the cursor into the content placeholder.

QUICK TIP
Press [Ctrl][Enter] while the cursor is in the text object to create a new slide with the same layout as the previous slide.

8. **Position the pointer on the Slide 4 icon in the Outline tab**
   The pointer changes to ✥. Slide 4, the Bite & Sting Deaths slide, is out of order.
9. **Drag the Slide 4 icon up until a horizontal indicator line appears above the Slide 3 icon, then release the mouse button**
   The fourth slide moves up and switches places with the third slide, as shown in Figure B-2.
10. **Click the Slides tab, then save your work**
    The Outline tab closes and the Slides tab is now visible in the window.

FIGURE B-1: **Outline tab showing new slide**

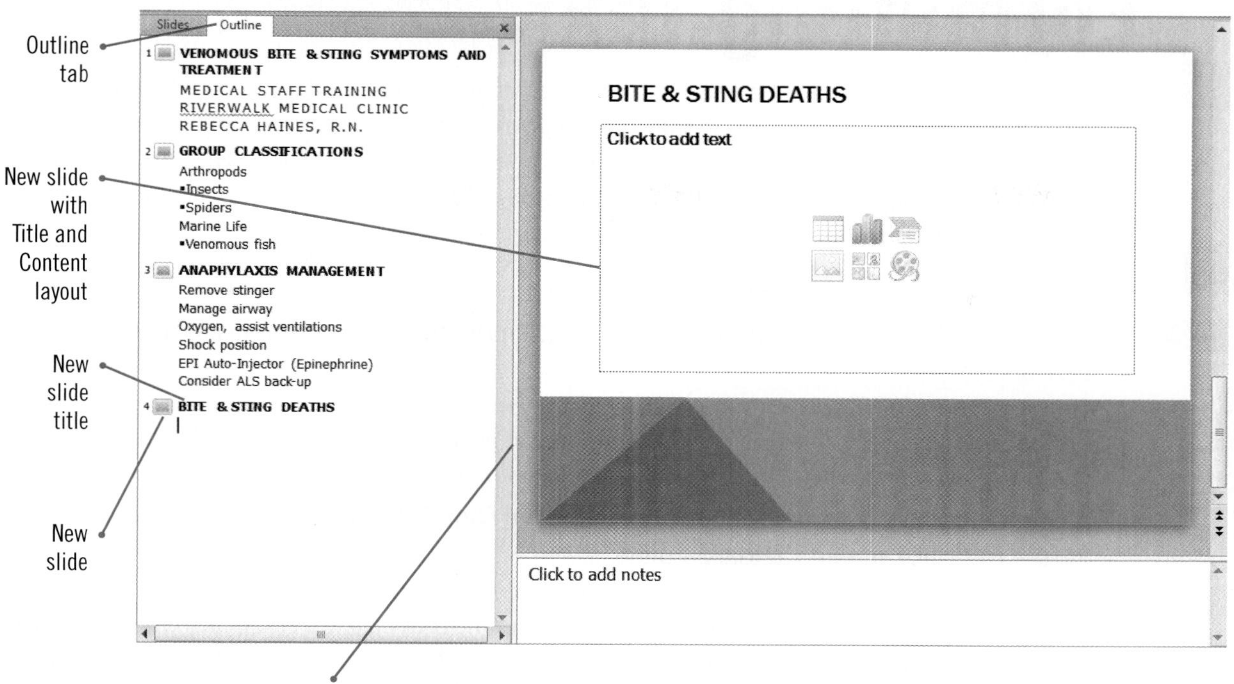

FIGURE B-2: **Outline tab showing moved slide**

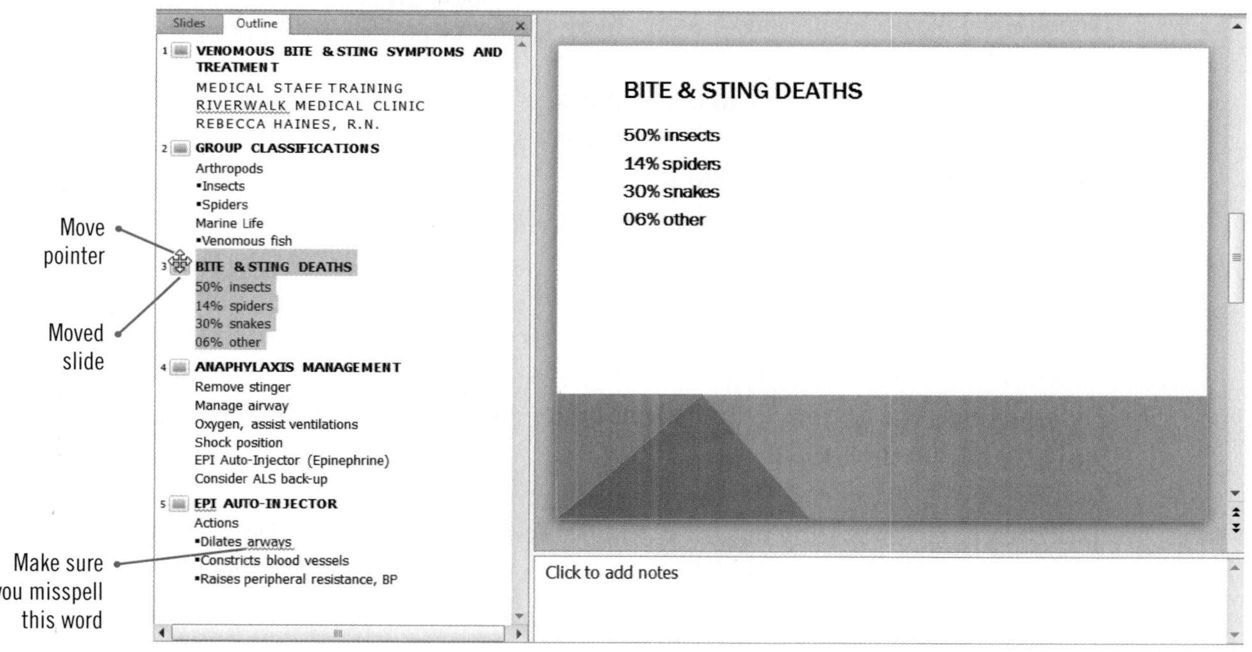

Setting permissions

In PowerPoint, you can set specific access permissions for people who review or edit your work, so you have better control over your content. For example, you may want to give a user permission to edit or change your presentation but not allow them to print it. You can also restrict a user by permitting them to view the presentation, without the ability to edit or print the presentation, or you can give the user full access or control of the presentation. To use this feature, you first need to have access to an Information Rights Management Service from Microsoft or another rights management company. Then, to set user access permissions, click the File tab, click Info, click the Protect Presentation button, point to Restrict Permission by People, then click an appropriate option.

UNIT
B
PowerPoint 2010

Formatting Text

Once you have entered and edited the text in your presentation, you can modify the way the text looks to emphasize your message. Important text should be highlighted in some way to distinguish it from other text or objects on the slide. For example, if you have two text objects on the same slide, you could draw attention to one text object by changing its color, font, or size. You decide to format the title text on Slide 1 of the presentation.

STEPS

QUICK TIP
To show or hide the Mini toolbar, click the File tab on the Ribbon, then click Options.

1. **Click the Slide 1 thumbnail in the Slides tab, then double-click Venomous in the title text object**

   The word "Venemous" is selected, and a small semitransparent Mini toolbar appears above the text. The **Mini toolbar** contains basic text-formatting commands, such as bold and italic, and appears when you select text using the mouse. This toolbar makes it quick and easy to format text, especially when the Home tab is not open.

2. **Move the pointer over the Mini toolbar, click the Font Color list arrow, then click the Purple color box under Standard Colors**

   The text changes color to purple as shown in Figure B-3. As soon as you move the pointer over the Mini toolbar, the toolbar becomes clearly visible. When you click the Font Color list arrow, the Font Color gallery appears showing the Theme Colors and Standard Colors. Notice that the Font Color button on the Mini toolbar and the Font Color button in the Font group on the Home tab change color to reflect the new color choice.

QUICK TIP
To select an unselected text object, press [Shift], click the text object, then release [Shift].

3. **Move the pointer over the title text object border until the pointer changes to, then click the border**

   The entire title text object is selected, and changes you make now affect all of the text in the text object. When the whole text object is selected, you can change its size, shape, or other attributes. Changing the color of the text helps emphasize it.

4. **Click the Font Color button in the Font group**

   All of the text in the title text object changes to the purple color.

5. **Click the Font list arrow in the Font group**

   A list of available fonts opens with Franklin Gothic Medium, the current font used in the title text object, selected at the top of the list in the Theme Fonts section.

6. **Click Algerian in the All Fonts section**

   The Algerian font replaces the original font in the title text object. Notice that as you move the pointer over the font names in the font list the text on the slide displays a Live Preview of the different font choices.

7. **Click the Underline button in the Font group, then click the Increase Font Size button in the Font group**

   All of the text now displays an underline and increases in size to 32.

8. **Click the Character Spacing button in the Font group, then click Tight**

   The spacing between the letters in the title text box decreases slightly. Compare your screen to Figure B-4.

9. **Click a blank area of the slide outside the text object to deselect it, then save your work**

FIGURE B-3: Selected word with Mini toolbar open

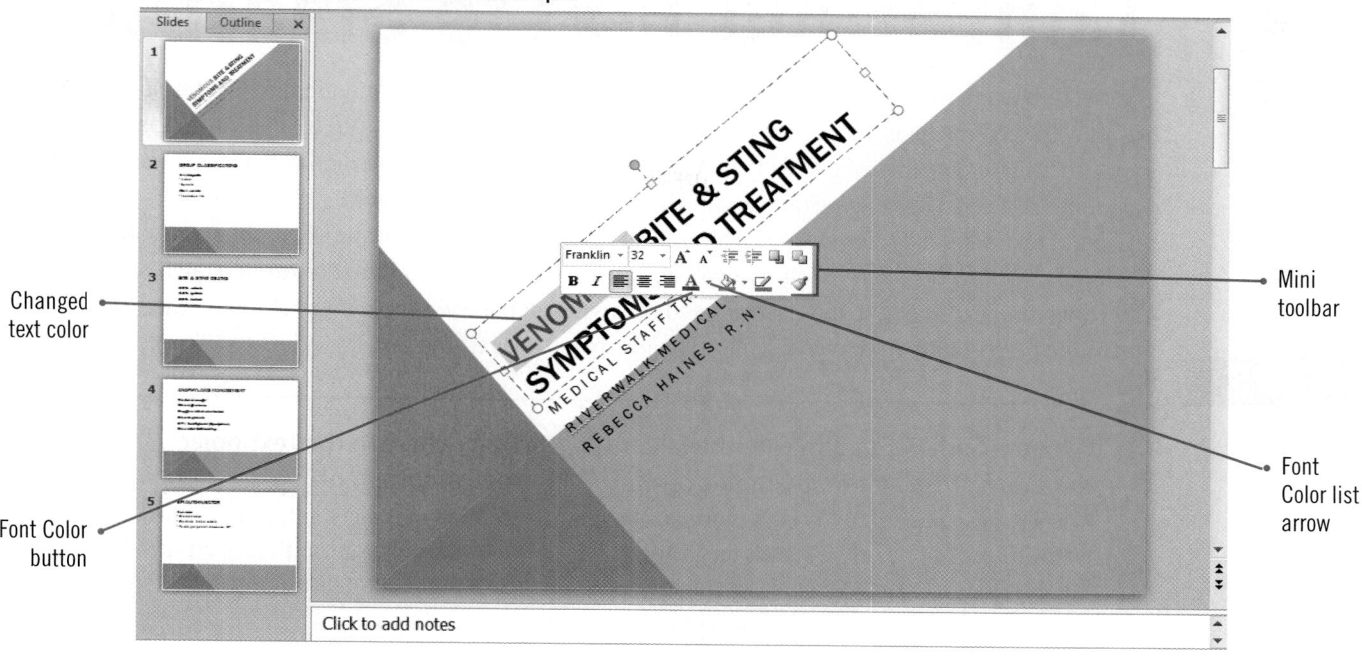

FIGURE B-4: Slide showing formatted text

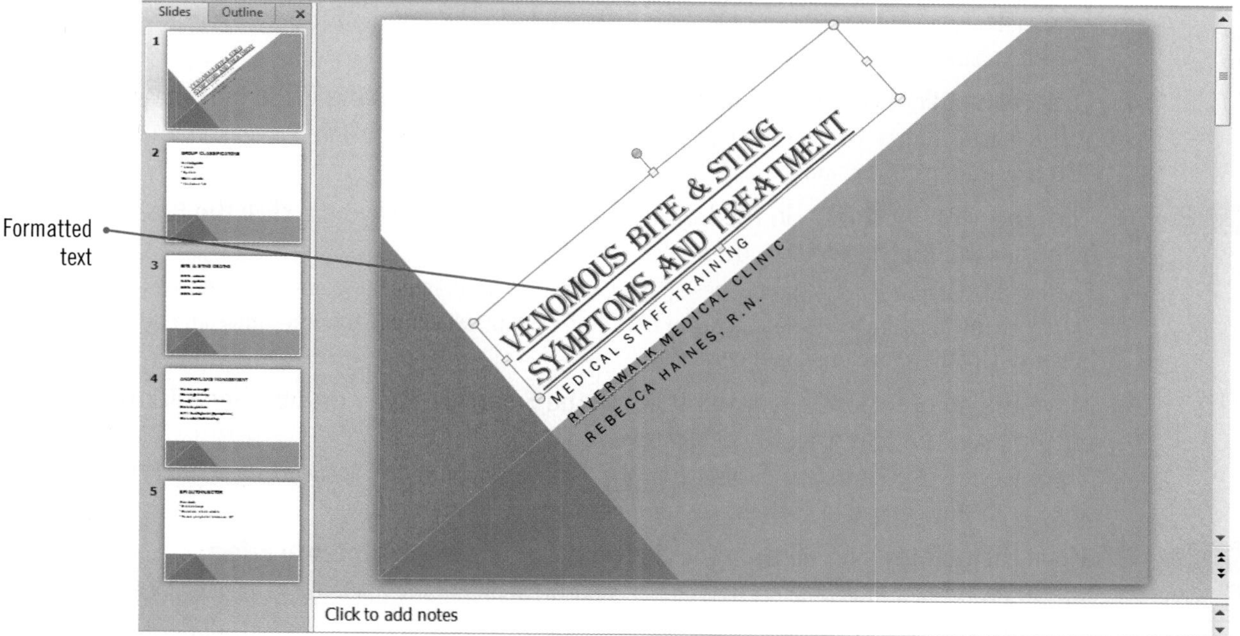

Replacing text and fonts

As you review your presentation, you may decide to replace certain text or fonts throughout the entire presentation using the Replace command. Text can be a word, phrase, or sentence. To replace specific text, click the Home tab on the Ribbon, then click the Replace button in the Editing group. In the Replace dialog box, enter the text you want to replace then enter the text you want to use as its replacement. You can also use the Replace command to replace one font for another. Simply click the Replace button list arrow in the Editing group, then click Replace Fonts to open the Replace Font dialog box.

UNIT B
PowerPoint 2010

Converting Text to SmartArt

Sometimes when you are working with text, it just doesn't capture your attention, no matter how you dress it up with color or other formatting attributes. The ability to convert text to a SmartArt graphic increases your ability to create dynamic-looking text. A **SmartArt** graphic is a professional-quality diagram that visually illustrates text. There are eight categories, or types, of SmartArt graphics that incorporate graphics to illustrate text differently. For example, you can show steps in a process or timeline, show proportional relationships, or show how parts relate to a whole. You can create a SmartArt graphic from scratch or create one by converting existing text you have entered on a slide with a few simple clicks of the mouse. You want the presentation to appear visually dynamic so you convert the text on Slide 3 to a SmartArt graphic.

STEPS

1. **Click the Slide 3 thumbnail in the Slides tab, click anywhere in the text object, then click the Convert to SmartArt Graphic button in the Paragraph group**
   A gallery of SmartArt graphic layouts opens. As with many features in PowerPoint, you can preview how your text will look prior to applying the SmartArt graphic layout by using PowerPoint's Live Preview feature. You can review each SmartArt graphic layout and see how it changes the appearance of text.
2. **Move the pointer over the SmartArt graphic layouts in the gallery**
   Notice how the text becomes part of the graphic and the color and font change each time you move the pointer over a different graphic layout. SmartArt graphic names appear as ScreenTips.
3. **Click the Pyramid List layout in the SmartArt graphics gallery**
   A SmartArt graphic appears on the slide in place of the text object, and a new SmartArt Tools Design tab opens on the Ribbon, as shown in Figure B-5. A SmartArt graphic consists of two parts: the SmartArt graphic itself and a Text pane where you type and edit text.
4. **Click each bullet point in the Text pane, then click the Text pane Close button**
   Notice that each time you select a bullet point in the Text pane, a selection box appears around the text objects in the SmartArt graphic.
5. **Click the More button in the Layouts group, click More Layouts, click the Basic Matrix layout in the Matrix section, then click OK**
   The SmartArt graphic changes to the new graphic layout. You can radically change how the SmartArt graphic looks by applying a SmartArt Style. A **SmartArt Style** is a preset combination of simple and 3-D formatting options that follows the presentation theme.
6. **Move the pointer slowly over the styles in the SmartArt Styles group, then click the More button in the SmartArt Styles group**
   A Live Preview of each style is displayed on the SmartArt graphic. The SmartArt styles are organized into sections; the top group offers suggestions for the best match for the document.
7. **Move the pointer over all the styles in the gallery, then click Intense Effect**
   Notice how the new Intense Effect style adds a bevel and top-left corner lighting to the text boxes.
8. **Click a blank area of the slide outside the SmartArt graphic object to deselect it, then save your work**
   Compare your screen to Figure B-6.

TROUBLE
If the Text pane does not open as shown in Figure B-5, click the Text Pane button in the Create Graphic group.

QUICK TIP
Text objects in the SmartArt graphic can be moved and edited like any other text object in PowerPoint.

QUICK TIP
Click the Convert button in the Reset group then click Convert to Text to revert the SmartArt graphic to a standard text object.

FIGURE B-5: Text converted to a SmartArt graphic

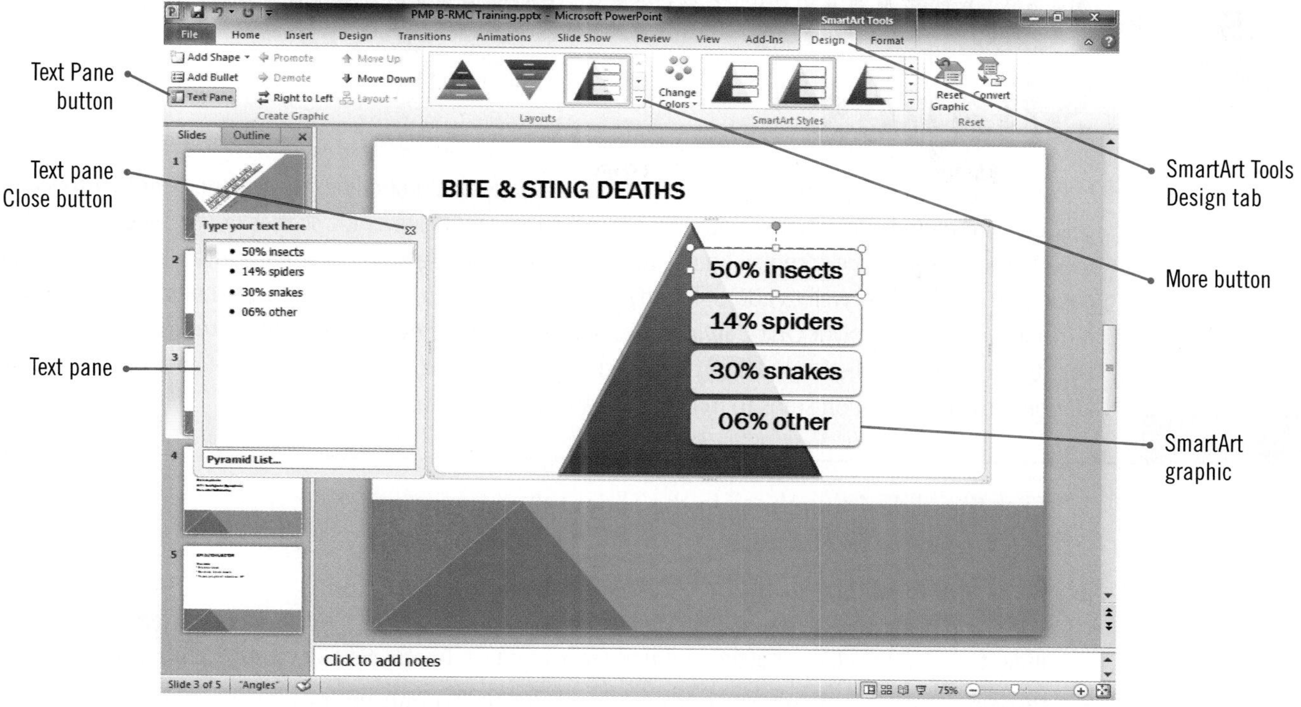

FIGURE B-6: Final SmartArt graphic

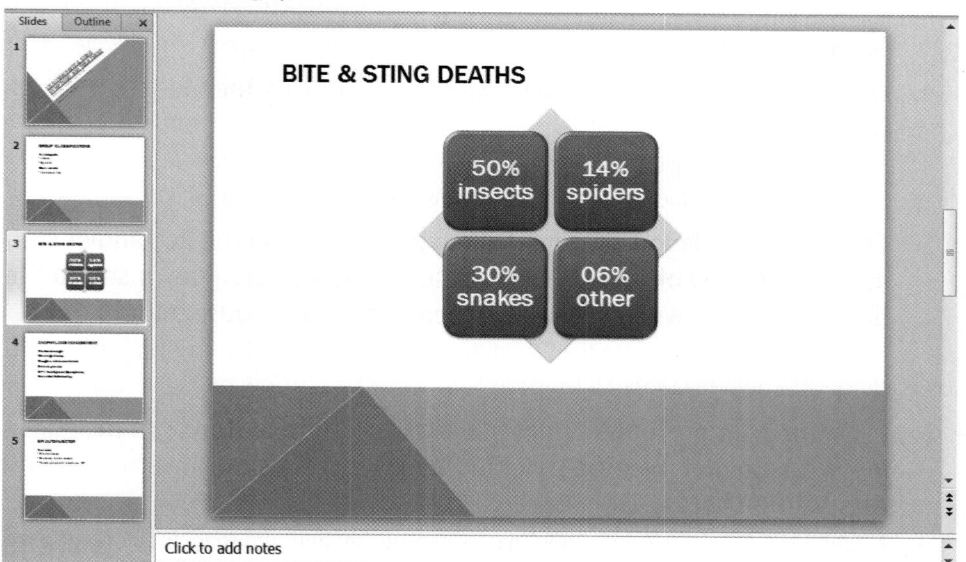

Choosing SmartArt graphics

When choosing a SmartArt graphic to use on your slide, remember that you want the SmartArt graphic to communicate the message of the text effectively; not every SmartArt graphic layout achieves that goal. You must consider the type of text you want to illustrate. For example, does the text show steps in a process, does it show a continual process, or does it show nonsequential information? The answer to this question will dictate the type of SmartArt graphic layout you should choose. Also, the amount of text you want to illustrate will have an effect on the SmartArt graphic layout you choose. Most of the time key points will be the text you use in a SmartArt graphic. Finally, some SmartArt graphic layouts are limited by the number of shapes that they can accommodate, so be sure to choose a graphic layout that can illustrate your text appropriately. Experiment with the SmartArt graphic layouts until you find the right one, and have fun in the process!

UNIT B

PowerPoint 2010

Inserting and Modifying Shapes

In PowerPoint you can insert many different types of shapes including lines, geometric figures, arrows, stars, callouts, and banners to enhance your presentation. You can create single shapes or combine several shapes together to make a more complex figure. You can modify many aspects of a shape including its fill color, line color, and line style, as well as add other effects like shadow and 3-D effects. Instead of changing individual attributes, you can apply a Quick Style to a shape. A **Quick Style** is a set of formatting options, including line style, fill color, and effects. You decide to draw some shapes on Slide 4 of your presentation that identify simple prevention steps to manage anaphylactic symptoms.

STEPS

1. **Click the Slide 4 thumbnail in the Slides tab**
   Slide 4 appears in the Slide pane.
2. **Press and hold [Shift], click the text object, then release [Shift]**
   The text object is selected. If you click a text object without pressing [Shift], a dotted selection box appears, indicating that the object is active and ready to accept text, but the text object itself is not selected.
3. **Position the pointer over the bottom-middle sizing handle, notice the pointer change to ⇕, then drag the sizing handle up until the text object looks like Figure B-7**
   The text object decreases in size. When you position the pointer over a sizing handle, it changes to ⇕. The pointer points in different directions depending over which sizing handle it is positioned. When you drag a sizing handle, the pointer changes to +, and a faint gray outline appears, representing the size of the text object.
4. **Click the Shapes button in the Drawing group or click the More button in the Drawing group**
   A gallery of shapes organized by type opens. Notice that there is a section at the top of the gallery where all of the recently used shapes are placed. ScreenTips help you identify the shapes.
5. **Click the Snip Diagonal Corner Rectangle shape in the Rectangles section, position + in the blank area of the slide below the text object, drag down and to the right to create the shape, as shown in Figure B-8, then release the mouse button**
   A rectangle shape appears on the slide, filled with the default color. To change the style of the shape, apply a Quick Style from the Shape Styles group.
6. **Click the Drawing Tools Format tab, click the More button in the Shape Styles group, move the pointer over the styles in the gallery to review the effects on the shape, then click Subtle Effect — Olive Green, Accent 4**
   A light green Quick Style with coordinated gradient fill, line, and shadow color is applied to the shape.
7. **Click the Shape Outline list arrow in the Shape Styles group, point to Weight, then move the pointer over the line weight options to review the effect on the shape**
   The outline line weight changes every time you move the pointer over a different effect.
8. **Click 2 ¼ pt, click in a blank area of the slide, then save your work**

QUICK TIP

If you press [Shift] as you drag to create a shape, the shape maintains even proportions.

TROUBLE

If your shape is not approximately the same size as the one shown in Figure B-8, drag one of the corner sizing handles to resize the object.

FIGURE B-7: **Resized text object**

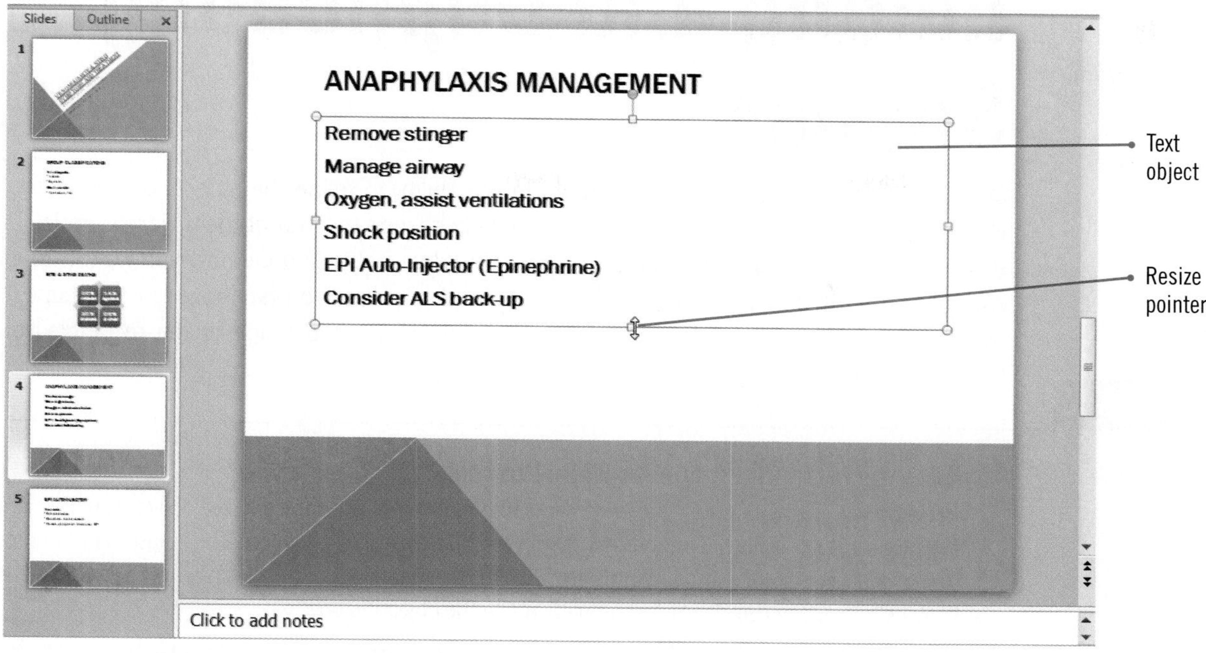

FIGURE B-8: **Slide showing Snip Diagonal Corner Rectangle shape**

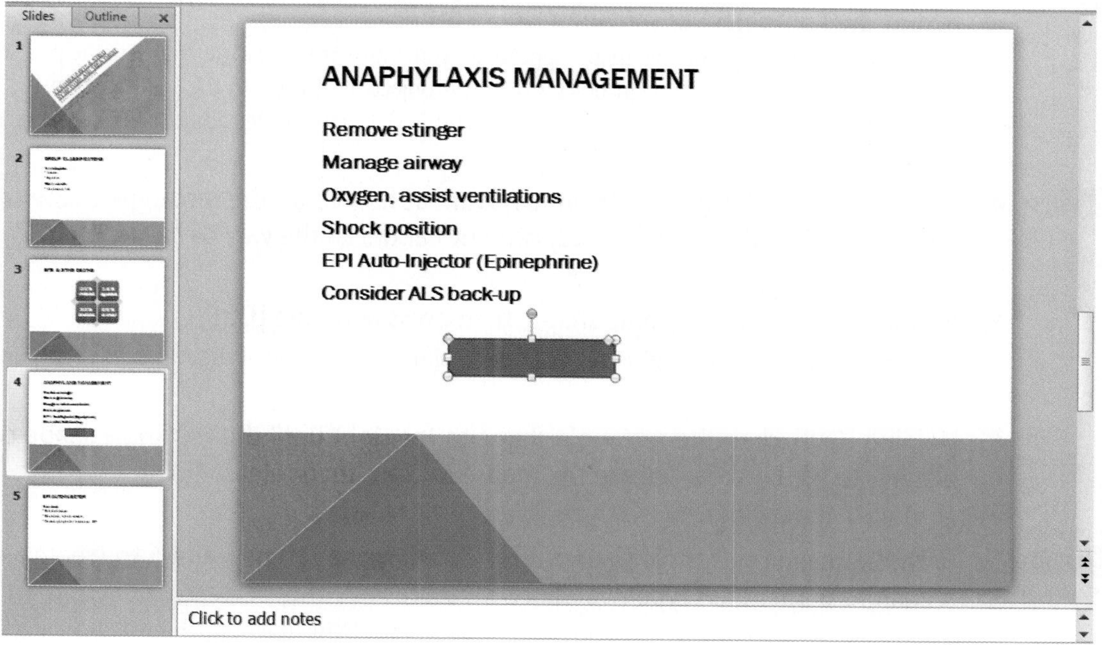

PowerPoint 2010

Changing the size and position of shapes

Usually when you resize a shape you can simply drag one of the sizing handles around the outside of the shape, but sometimes you may need to resize a shape more precisely. When you select a shape, the Drawing Tools Format tab appears on the Ribbon, offering you many different formatting options including some sizing commands located in the Size group. The Width and Height commands in the Size group allow you to change the width and height of a shape. You also have the option to open the Size and Position dialog box, which allows you to change the size of a shape, as well as the rotation, scale, and position of a shape on the slide.

UNIT
B
PowerPoint 2010

Editing and Duplicating Shapes

Once you have created a shape you still have the ability to refine the aspects of the object. PowerPoint allows you to adjust various aspects of shapes to help change the look of them. For example, if you create a shape with an arrowhead but the head of the arrow does not look quite how you want it to look, you can change it. You can also add text to most PowerPoint shapes, and you can move or copy shapes. You want three identical rectangles on Slide 4. You first change the shape of the rectangle you've already created, and then you make copies of it.

STEPS

1. **Click the rectangle shape on Slide 4 to select it**

   In addition to sizing handles, two other types of handles appear on the selected object. You use the **adjustment handle**—a small yellow diamond—to change the appearance of an object. The adjustment handle appears next to the most prominent feature of the object, like the diagonal sides of the rectangle in this case. You use the **rotate handle**—a small green circle—to manually rotate the object.

2. **Drag the left-middle sizing handle on the rectangle shape to the right approximately ¼", then release the mouse button**

3. **Position the pointer over the middle of the selected rectangle shape so that it changes to , then drag the rectangle shape so that the rectangle aligns with the left edge of the text in the text object as shown in Figure B-9**

   A semitransparent copy of the shape appears as you move the rectangle shape to help you position it. PowerPoint uses gridlines to align objects; it forces objects to "snap" to the grid. To turn the snap-to-grid feature off while dragging objects, press and hold [Alt]. Make any needed adjustments to the rectangle shape position so it looks similar to Figure B-9.

4. **Position the pointer over the right adjustment handle on the rectangle shape so that it changes to , then drag the adjustment handle all the way to the left**

   The rectangle shape appearance changes.

5. **Position over the rectangle shape, then press and hold [Ctrl]**

   The pointer changes to , indicating that PowerPoint makes a copy of the rectangle shape when you drag the mouse.

6. **Holding [Ctrl], drag the rectangle shape to the right until the rectangle shape copy is in a blank area of the slide, release the mouse button, then release [Ctrl]**

   An identical copy of the rectangle shape appears on the slide.

7. **With the second rectangle shape still selected, repeat Steps 5 and 6 to create a third rectangle shape, then type Avoidance Measures**

   A dotted line appears through the center of the shapes identifying their centerline and helping you align the shapes. The text appears in the selected rectangle shape. The text is now part of the shape, so if you move or rotate the shape, the text moves with it. Compare your screen with Figure B-10.

8. **Click the middle rectangle shape, type Medical I.D., click the left rectangle shape, type Early Treatment, then click in a blank area of the slide**

   Clicking a blank area of the slide deselects all objects that are selected.

9. **Save your work**

QUICK TIP
You can easily display or hide gridlines by clicking the Gridlines check box in the Show group on the View tab.

TROUBLE
To make precise adjustments, press and hold [Alt], then drag the adjustment handle.

QUICK TIP
All shape objects use the dotted alignment line to help you align shapes to an object's top, bottom, or side.

FIGURE B-9: Slide showing resized shape

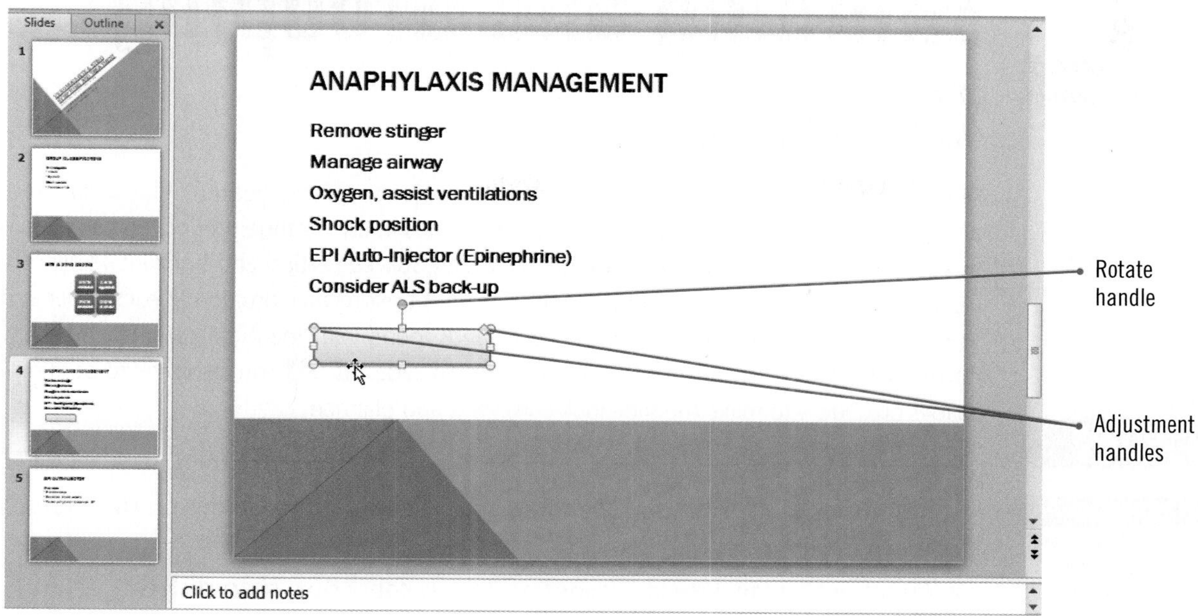

FIGURE B-10: Slide showing duplicated shapes

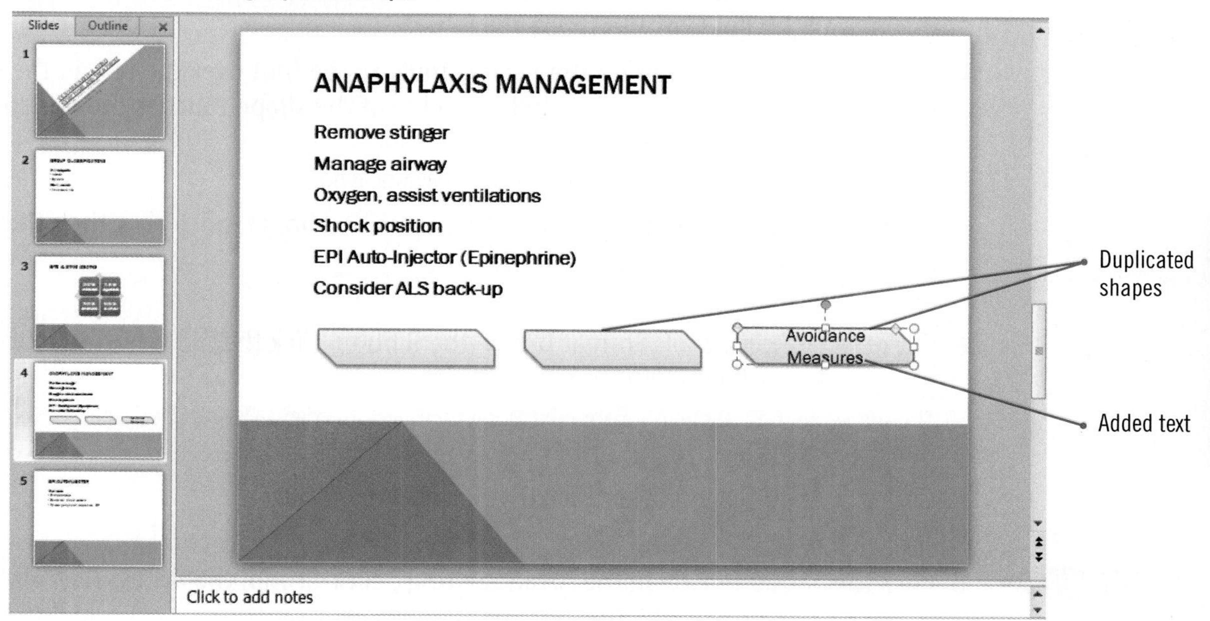

PowerPoint 2010

Stacking objects

Every object on a slide, whether it is a text object, a shape, a chart, a picture, or any other object, is stacked on the slide in the order it was created. So, for example, if you add three shapes to a slide, the first shape you create is on the bottom of the stack, and the last shape you create is on the top of the stack. Each object on a slide can be moved up or down in the stack depending on how you want the objects to look on the slide. To move an object to the front of the stack, select the object, then click the Bring Forward button in the Arrange group on the Drawing Tools Format tab. To move an object to the back of the stack, click the Send Backward button in the Arrange group on the Drawing Tools Format tab. You can also open the Selection and Visibility pane by clicking the Selection Pane button in the Arrange group to view and rearrange all of the objects on the slide.

UNIT B PowerPoint 2010

Aligning and Grouping Objects

After you are finished creating and modifying your objects, you can position them accurately on the slide to achieve the look you want. Using the Align commands in the Arrange group, you can align objects relative to each other by snapping them to a grid of evenly spaced vertical and horizontal lines. The Group command **groups** objects into one object, which secures their relative position to each other and makes it easy to edit and move them. The Distribute commands found with the Align commands evenly space objects horizontally or vertically relative to each other or the slide. You are ready to position and group the shapes on Slide 4 to make the slide look consistent and planned.

STEPS

QUICK TIP

To add a new guide to the slide, press [Ctrl], then drag an existing guide. The original guide remains in place as you move the new guide. Drag a guide off the slide to delete it.

1. **Right-click a blank area of the slide, then click Grid and Guides on the shortcut menu**
   The Grid and Guides dialog box opens.
2. **Click the Display drawing guides on screen check box, then click OK**
   The PowerPoint guides appear as dotted lines on the slide and intersect at the center of the slide. They help you position a rectangle shape.
3. **Position over the horizontal guide in a blank area of the slide, press and hold the mouse button until the pointer changes to a measurement guide, then drag the guide down until the guide position box reads 1.25**
4. **Position over the Early Treatment rectangle shape (not over the text in the shape), then drag the shape so that the bottom edge of the shape touches the horizontal guide as shown in Figure B-11**
   The rectangle shape attaches or "snaps" to the horizontal guide.
5. **With the Early Treatment shape selected, press and hold [Shift], click the other two rectangle shapes, then release [Shift]**
   All three shapes are now selected.
6. **Click the Drawing Tools Format tab on the Ribbon, click the Align button in the Arrange group, then click Align Bottom**
   The shapes are now aligned horizontally along their bottom edges. The higher shapes move down and align with the bottom shape.
7. **Click the Align button, then click Distribute Horizontally**
   The shapes are now distributed equally between themselves.

QUICK TIP

Rulers can help you align objects. To display the rulers, position the pointer in a blank area of the slide, right-click, then click Ruler on the shortcut menu.

8. **Click the Group button in the Arrange group, click Group, then press [Left Arrow] or [Right Arrow] until the Rotate handle is on or very near the vertical grid line as shown in Figure B-12**
   The objects group to form one object without losing their individual attributes. Notice that the sizing handles and rotate handle now appear on the outer edge of the grouped object, not around each individual object.
9. **Drag the horizontal guide up until the guide position box reads 0.00, click the View tab on the Ribbon, then click the Guides check box in the Show group**
   The guides are no longer displayed on the slide.
10. **Click a blank area of the slide, then save your work**

FIGURE B-11: Repositioned shape

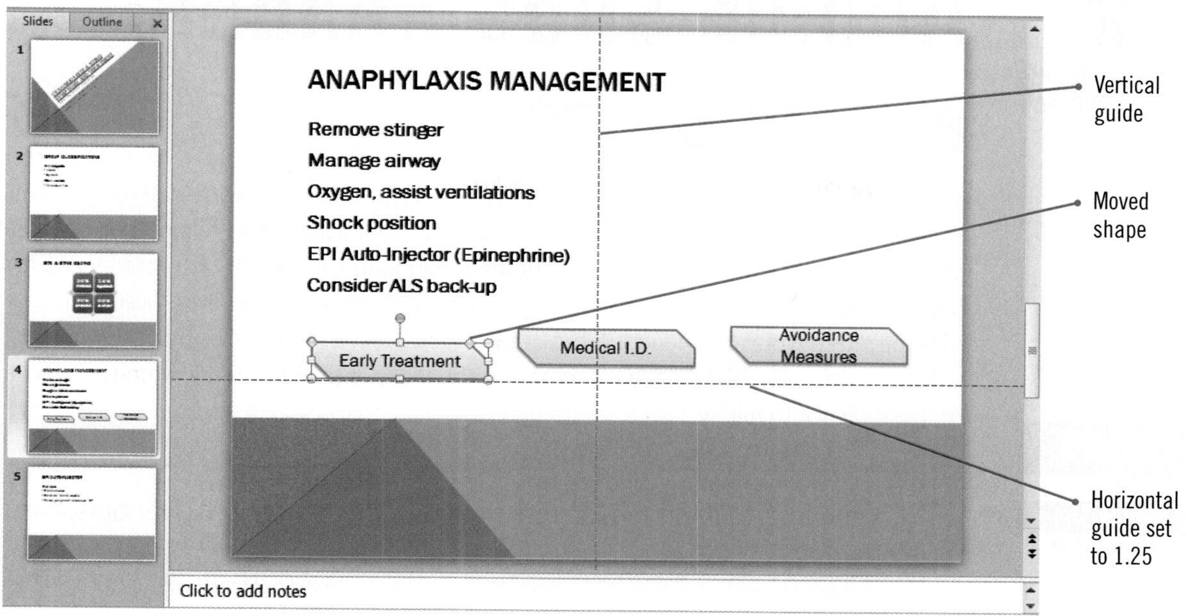

FIGURE B-12: Aligned and grouped shapes

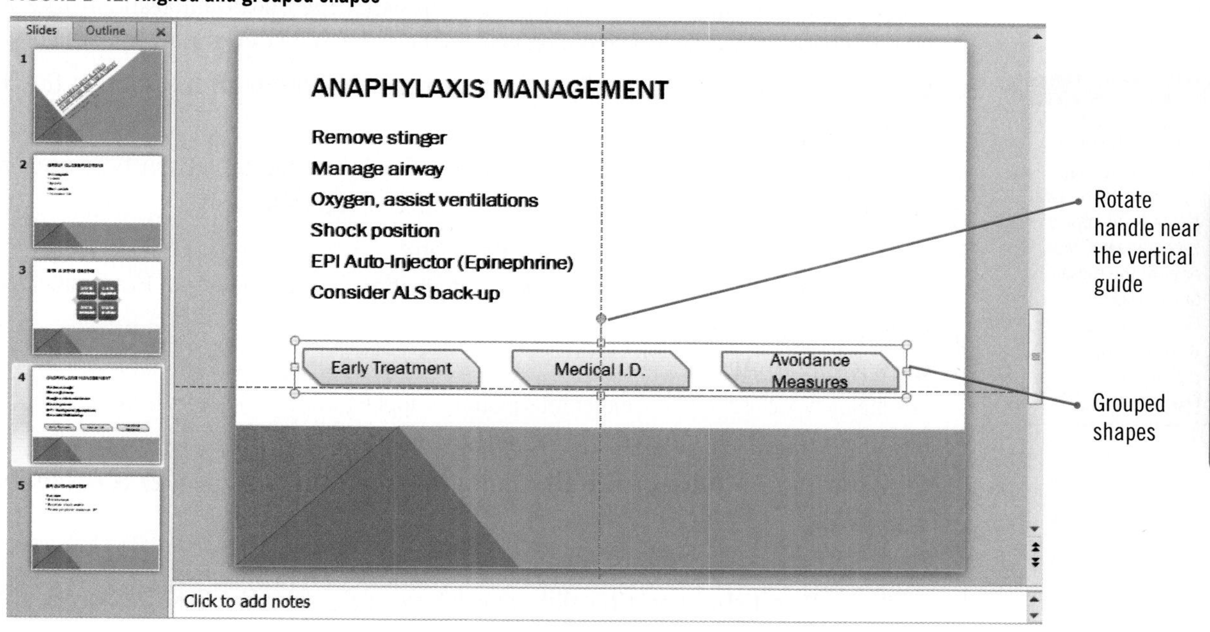

PowerPoint 2010

Distributing objects

There are two ways to **distribute** objects in PowerPoint: relative to each other and relative to the slide edge. If you choose to distribute objects relative to each other, PowerPoint evenly divides the empty space between all of the selected objects. When distributing objects in relation to the slide, PowerPoint evenly splits the empty space from slide edge to slide edge between the selected objects. To distribute objects relative to each other, click the Align button in the Arrange group on the Drawing Tools Format tab, then click Align Selected Objects. To distribute objects relative to the slide, click the Align button in the Arrange group on the Drawing Tools Format tab, then click Align to Slide.

Adding Slide Headers and Footers

Header and footer text (such as a company, school, or product name, the slide number, and the date) can give your slides a polished look and make it easier for your audience to follow your presentation. On slides, you can add text to the footer; however, notes or handouts can include both header and footer text. Footer information that you apply to the slides of your presentation is visible in the PowerPoint views and when you print the slides. Notes and handouts header and footer text is visible when you print notes pages, handouts, and the outline. You add footer text to the slides of the RMC training presentation to make it easier for the audience to follow.

STEPS

QUICK TIP
The placement of the footer text objects on the slide is dependent on the presentation theme.

1. **Click the Insert tab on the Ribbon, then click the Header & Footer button in the Text group**
   The Header and Footer dialog box opens, as shown in Figure B-13. The Header and Footer dialog box has two tabs: a Slide tab and a Notes and Handouts tab. The Slide tab is selected. There are three types of footer text, Date and time, Slide number, and Footer. The rectangles at the bottom of the Preview box identify the default position and status of the three types of footer text placeholders on the slides.
2. **Click the Date and time check box to select it**
   The date and time suboptions are now available to select. The Update automatically date and time option button is selected by default. This option updates the date and time every time you open or print the file.

QUICK TIP
If you want a specific date—such as the original date that the presentation was created—to appear every time you view or print the presentation, click the Fixed option button, then type the date in the Fixed text box.

3. **Click the Update automatically list arrow, then click the eighth option in the list**
   The time is added to the date.
4. **Click the Slide number check box, click the Footer check box, then type your name**
   The Preview box now shows that all three footer placeholders are selected.
5. **Click the Don't show on title slide check box**
   Selecting this check box prevents the footer information you entered in the Header and Footer dialog box from appearing on the title slide.
6. **Click Apply to All**
   The dialog box closes and the footer information is applied to all of the slides in your presentation except the title slide. Compare your screen to Figure B-14.
7. **Click the Slide 1 thumbnail in the Slides tab, then click the Header & Footer button in the Text group**
   The Header and Footer dialog box opens again.
8. **Click the Don't show on title slide check box to deselect it, click the Footer check box, then select the text in the Footer text box**

TROUBLE
If you click Apply to All in Step 9, click the Undo button on the Quick Access toolbar and repeat Steps 7, 8, and 9.

9. **Type RMC Medical Training Series, click Apply, then save your work**
   Only the text in the Footer text box appears on the title slide. Clicking Apply applies the footer information to just the current slide.

FIGURE B-13: **Header and Footer dialog box**

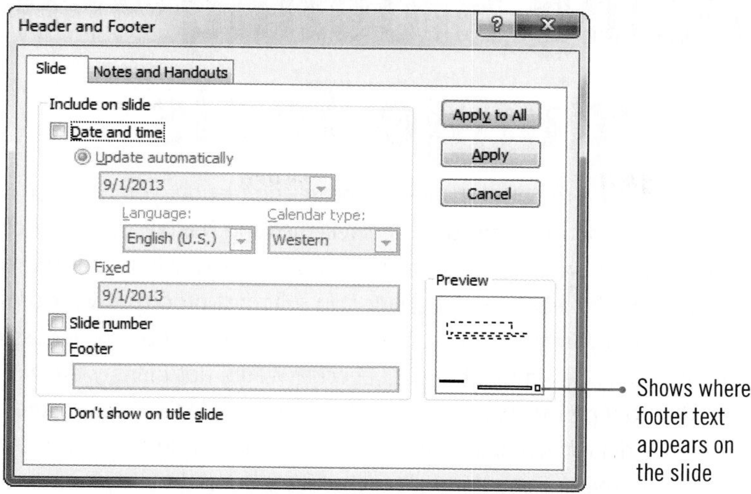

FIGURE B-14: **Slide showing footer information**

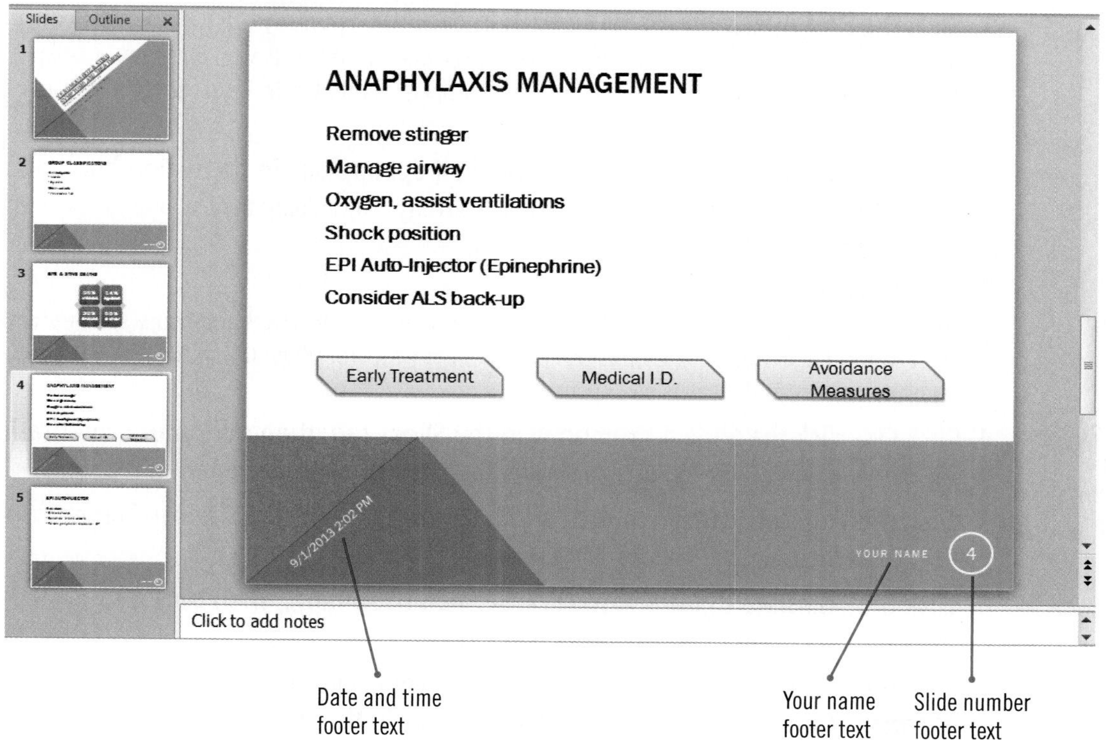

Entering and printing notes

You can add notes to your slides when there are certain facts you want to remember during a presentation or when there is information you want to hand out to your audience. Notes do not appear on the slides when you run a slide show. Use the Notes pane in Normal view or Notes Page view to enter notes for your slides. To enter text notes on a slide, click in the Notes pane, then type. If you want to insert graphics as notes, you must use Notes Page view. To open Notes Page view, click the View tab on the Ribbon, then click the Notes Page button in the Presentation Views group. You can print your notes by clicking the File tab to open Backstage view then clicking Print. Click the Full Page Slides list arrow in the Settings section (this button retains the last setting for what was printed previously so it might differ) to open the gallery, and then click Notes Pages. Once you verify your print settings, click the Print button. Notes pages can be a good handout to give your audience to use during the presentation. If you don't enter any notes in the Notes pane and print the notes pages, the slides print as thumbnails with blank lines to the right of the thumbnails to provide space to write notes.

UNIT B
PowerPoint 2010

Using Proofing and Language Tools

As your work on the presentation file nears completion, you need to review and proofread your slides thoroughly for errors. You can use the spell-checking feature in PowerPoint to check for and correct spelling errors. This feature compares the spelling of all the words in your presentation against the words contained in PowerPoint's electronic dictionary. You still must proofread your presentation for punctuation, grammar, and word-usage errors because the spell checker recognizes only misspelled and unknown words, not misused words. For example, the spell checker would not identify the word "last" as an error, even if you had intended to type the word "cast." PowerPoint also includes language tools that translate words or phrases from your default language into another language using the Microsoft Translator. You're finished working on the presentation for now, so it's a good time to check spelling. You then experiment with language translation because the final presentation might be translated into German.

STEPS

TROUBLE
If your spell checker finds another word, such as your name on Slide 1, click Ignore All in the Spelling dialog box.

1. **Click the Review tab on the Ribbon, then click the Spelling button in the Proofing group**
   PowerPoint begins to check the spelling in your presentation. When PowerPoint finds a misspelled word or a word it doesn't recognize, the Spelling dialog box opens, as shown in Figure B-15. In this case, PowerPoint identifies a word on Slide 1 and suggests a replacement word.
2. **Click Ignore All, then click Ignore All again if Epi appears in the dialog box**
   Both of these unidentified words are spelled correctly. PowerPoint then identifies the misspelled word "airway" on Slide 5 and suggests a correct spelling.
3. **Click Change**
   PowerPoint changes the misspelled word and then continues to check for errors. If PowerPoint finds any other words it does not recognize, either change or ignore them. When the spell checker finishes, the Spelling dialog box closes, and an alert box opens.

QUICK TIP
The spell checker does not check the text in inserted pictures or objects.

4. **Click OK, click the Slide 4 thumbnail in the Slides tab, then save your presentation**
   The alert box closes. Now you need to see how the language translation feature works.
5. **Click the Translate button in the Language group, then click Choose Translation Language**
   The Translation Language Options dialog box opens.
6. **Click the Translate to list arrow, click German (Germany), then click OK**
   The Translation Language Options dialog box closes.
7. **Click the Translate button in the Language group, click Mini Translator [German (Germany)], then double-click airway in the text object**
   The Microsoft Translator begins to analyze the selected text and a semitransparent Microsoft Translator box appears below the text.

QUICK TIP
To copy the translated text to a slide, click the Copy button at the bottom of the Microsoft Translator box, right-click the slide, then click a Paste option.

8. **Move the pointer over the Microsoft Translator box**
   A German translation of the text appears as shown in Figure B-16. The translation language setting remains in effect until you reset it.
9. **Click the Translate button in the Language group, then click Mini Translator [German (Germany)]**
   The Mini Translator is turned off.
10. **Submit your presentation to your instructor, then exit PowerPoint**

FIGURE B-15: Spelling dialog box

Spelling

Selected word from Suggestions list

Suggestions list

Unrecognized word

Not in Dictionary: Riverwalk

Change to: River walk

Suggestions: River walk

Resume | Ignore All | Change | Change All | Add | Suggest | Options... | AutoCorrect | Close

FIGURE B-16: Slide showing translated text

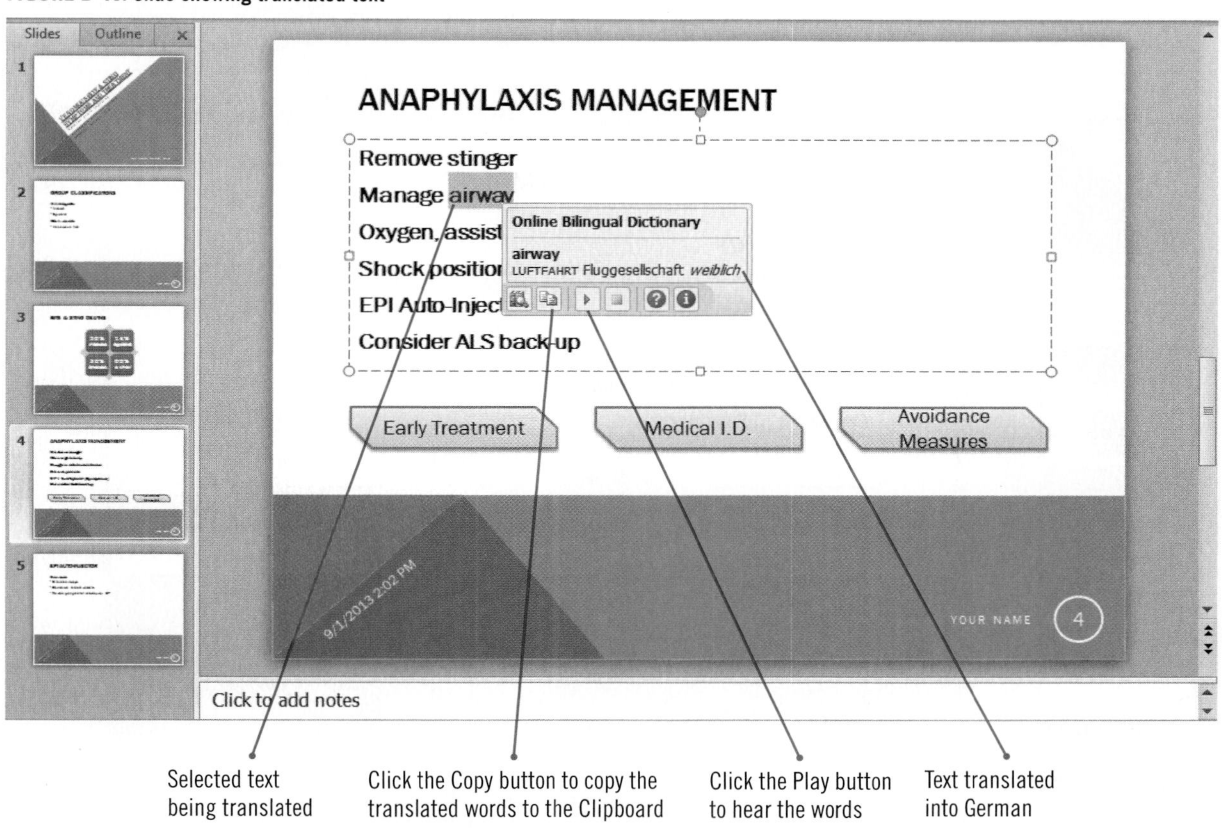

PowerPoint 2010

Checking spelling as you type

PowerPoint checks your spelling as you type. If you type a word that is not in the electronic dictionary, a wavy red line appears under it. To correct an error, right-click the misspelled word, then review the suggestions, which appear in the shortcut menu. You can select a suggestion, add the word you typed to your custom dictionary, or ignore it. To turn off automatic spell checking, click the File tab, then click Options to open the PowerPoint Options dialog box. Click the Proofing button, then click the Check spelling as you type check box to deselect it. To temporarily hide the wavy red lines, click the Hide spelling errors check box to select it. Contextual spelling in PowerPoint identifies common grammatically misused words, for example, if you type the word "their" and the correct word is "there," PowerPoint will identify the mistake and place a wavy blue line under the word. To turn contextual spelling on or off, click the Proofing button in the PowerPoint Options dialog box, then click the Use contextual spelling check box.

Practice

Concepts Review

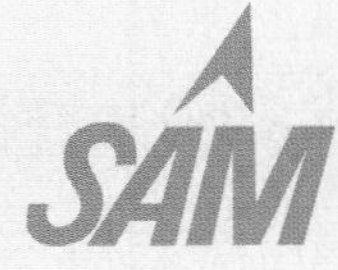

For current SAM information, including versions and content details, visit SAM Central (http://www.cengage.com/samcentral). If you have a SAM user profile, you may have access to hands-on instruction, practice, and assessment of the skills covered in this unit. Since various versions of SAM are supported throughout the life of this text, check with your instructor for the correct instructions and URL/Web site for accessing assignments.

Label each element of the PowerPoint window shown in Figure B-17.

FIGURE B-17

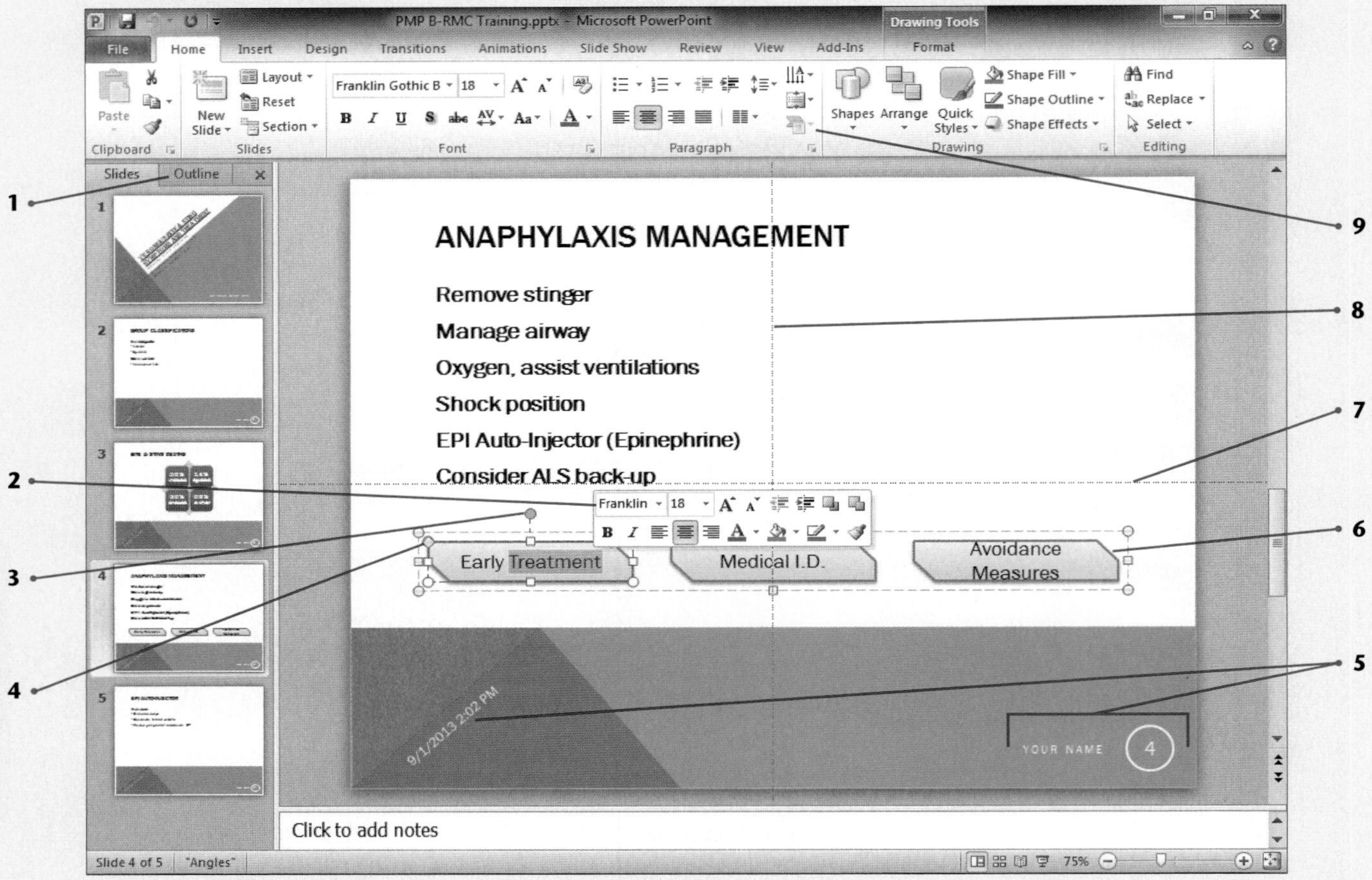

Match each term with the statement that best describes it.

10. Quick Style	**a.** Use to space objects evenly
11. Rotate handle	**b.** A diagram that visually illustrates text
12. Distribute	**c.** Use to manually turn an object
13. Mini toolbar	**d.** Combines multiple objects into one object
14. SmartArt graphic	**e.** Use to format selected text
15. Group	**f.** A preset combination of formatting options that you apply to an object

Select the best answer from the list of choices.

16. Which of the following statements is *not* true about the Outline tab?
- **a.** Each line of indented text creates a new slide title.
- **b.** You can enter text directly.
- **c.** It is organized using headings and subpoints.
- **d.** Headings are the same as slide titles.

17. What appears just above text when it is selected?
- **a.** QuickStyles
- **b.** Option button
- **c.** Mini toolbar
- **d.** AutoFit Options button

18. What does the adjustment handle do to a shape?
- **a.** Changes the appearance of a shape
- **b.** Changes the style of a shape
- **c.** Changes the size of a shape
- **d.** Changes the shape to another design

19. A professional-quality diagram that visually illustrates text best describes which of the following?
- **a.** A shape
- **b.** A SmartArt graphic
- **c.** A slide layout
- **d.** A QuickStyle object

20. Which of the following is not *true* about checking spelling in PowerPoint?
- **a.** The spell checker identifies unknown words as misspelled.
- **b.** Spelling is checked as you type.
- **c.** You can fix a misspelled word by right-clicking it and selecting a correct word.
- **d.** All misused words are automatically corrected.

21. What is *not* true about grouped objects?
- **a.** Grouped objects have one rotate handle.
- **b.** Sizing handles appear around the grouped object.
- **c.** Each object has individual sizing handles and a rotate handle.
- **d.** Grouped objects act as one object.

22. What do objects snap to when you move them?
- **a.** Slide edges
- **b.** Hidden grid
- **c.** Drawing lines
- **d.** Anchor points

Skills Review

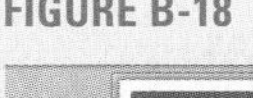

1. Enter text in the Outline tab.
- **a.** Open the presentation PMP B-2.pptx from the drive and folder where you store your Data Files, then save it as **PMP B-Code Blue**. The completed presentation is shown in Figure B-18.
- **b.** Create a new slide after Slide 2 with the Title and Content layout.
- **c.** Open the Outline tab, then type **Policy Purpose**.
- **d.** Press [Enter], press [Tab], type **Define staff response guidelines**, press [Enter], type **Outline emergency equipment**, press [Enter], then type **Code Blue for adult cardiopulmonary emergency**.
- **e.** Move Slide 3 above Slide 2.
- **f.** Switch back to the Slides tab, then save your changes.

FIGURE B-18

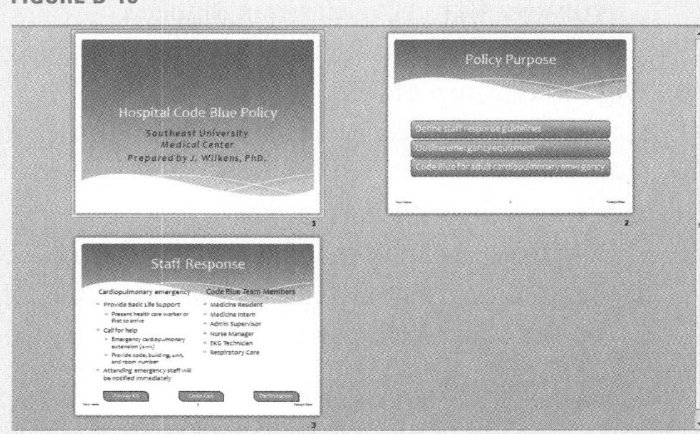

2. Format text.
- **a.** Go to Slide 1.
- **b.** Select the name **Southeast University**, then move the pointer over the Mini toolbar.
- **c.** Click the Font Color list arrow, then click Dark Blue, Text 2 under Theme Colors.

PowerPoint 2010

Skills Review (continued)

   d. Select the text object, then change all of the text to the color Dark Blue, Text 2.
   e. Click the Font Size list arrow, click 28, then click the Italic button.
   f. Click the Character Spacing button, click Loose, then save your changes.

3. Convert text to SmartArt.
   a. Click the text object on Slide 2.
   b. Click the Convert to SmartArt Graphic button, then apply the Vertical Block List graphic layout to the text object.
   c. Click the More button in the Layouts group, click More Layouts, click List in the Choose a SmartArt Graphic dialog box, then click Vertical Bullet List.
   d. Click the More button in the SmartArt Styles group, then apply the Intense Effect style to the graphic.
   e. Close the Text pane if necessary, then click outside the SmartArt graphic in an empty part of the slide.
   f. Save your changes.

4. Insert and modify shapes.
   a. Go to Slide 3, press [Shift], click both text objects, release [Shift], then drag the bottom-middle sizing handle up to decrease the size of the text objects.
   b. Click the Shapes button in the Drawing group, then insert the Round Diagonal Corner Rectangle shape from the Shapes gallery similar to the one in Figure B-19.
   c. On the Drawing Tools Format tab, click the More button in the Shape Styles group, then click Light 1 Outline, Colored Fill – Green, Accent 3.
   d. Click the Shape Effects button in the Shape Styles group, point to Shadow, then click Offset Diagonal Bottom Right.
   e. Click the Shape Outline list arrow in the Shape Styles group, then click Black, Text 1, Lighter 25%.
   f. Click a blank area of the slide, then save your changes.

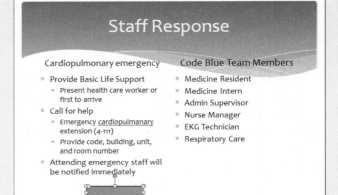

FIGURE B-19

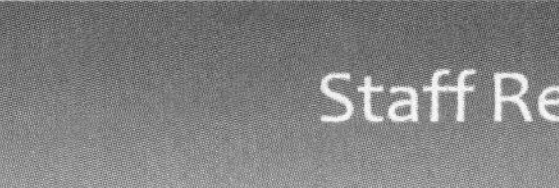
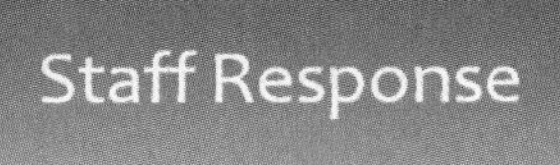

5. Edit and duplicate shapes.
   a. Select the rectangle shape, then drag the left adjustment handle all the way to the right.
   b. Drag the rectangle shape so it lines up with the text in the left text object about ½ inch from the bottom of the slide.
   c. Click the Rotate button in the Arrange group, then click Flip Horizontal.
   d. Using [Ctrl] make two copies of the rectangle shape.
   e. Type **Defibrillation** in the right rectangle shape, type **Code Cart** in the middle rectangle shape, then type **Airway Kit** in the left rectangle shape.
   f. Click a blank area of the slide, then save your changes.

6. Align and group objects.
   a. Select the right rectangle shape, press [Shift], then move it so it lines up with the right edge of the text in the right text object.
   b. Select all three rectangle shapes.
   c. Click the Drawing Tools Format tab if necessary, click the Align button, then click Align Bottom.
   d. Click the Align button in the Arrange group, then click Distribute Horizontally.
   e. Group all three rectangles together, then display the drawing guides on the screen.

Skills Review (continued)

   f. Move the horizontal guide down until 3.17 appears, then press [Up Arrow] or press [Down Arrow] until the bottom of the rectangle shapes are on or near the horizontal guide. Compare your screen to Figure B-20.
   g. Remove the drawing guides from your screen, then save your work.

FIGURE B-20

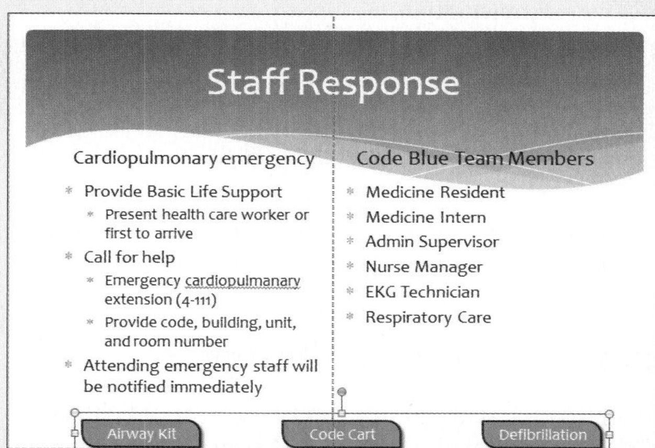

7. **Add slide headers and footers.**
   a. Open the Header and Footer dialog box.
   b. On the Slide tab, click the Date and time check box to select it, click the Fixed option button, then type today's date in the Fixed text box.
   c. Add the slide number to the footer.
   d. Type your name in the Footer text box.
   e. Apply the footer to all of the slides except the title slide.
   f. Open the Header and Footer dialog box again, then click the Notes and Handouts tab.
   g. Type today's date in the Fixed text box.
   h. Type the name of your class in the Header text box, then click the Page number check box.
   i. Type your name in the Footer text box.
   j. Apply the header and footer information to all the notes and handouts.
   k. Save your changes.
8. **Use proofing and language tools.**
   a. Check the spelling of the document, and change any misspelled words. Ignore any words that are correctly spelled but that the spell checker doesn't recognize. There is at least one misspelled word in the presentation.
   b. Move to Slide 3, then set the Mini Translator language to Russian.
   c. View the Russian translation of two or three individual words and a phrase on Slide 3.
   d. Choose one other language (or as many as you want), translate words or phrases on the slide, reset the default language to Arabic, then turn off the Mini Translator.
   e. Save your changes, submit your presentation to your instructor, close the presentation, then exit PowerPoint.

PowerPoint 2010

Independent Challenge 1

You work in the Department of Transportation Office of Emergency Services in Washington D.C. You are a trained medical first responder and you have been asked to update the department's procedures for radiological transportation accidents. You will present the information you develop at a conference later in the month. You need to continue working on the presentation you started already.

   a. Start PowerPoint, open the presentation PMP B-3.pptx from the drive and folder where you store your Data Files, and save it as **PMP B-DOT Procedures**.
   b. Use the Outline tab to enter the following as bulleted text on the Responsibilities slide:
      Size up accident scene
      Initiate response actions
      Relay information to appropriate officials
      Maintain accident scene control
   c. Apply the Technic design theme to the presentation.
   d. Change the font color of the slide title on Slide 5 to Gold, Accent 2, Lighter 40%.
   e. Change the bulleted text on Slide 4 to the Segmented Process (List) SmartArt graphic layout, then apply the Moderate Effect SmartArt Style.

Independent Challenge 1 (continued)

Advanced Challenge Exercise

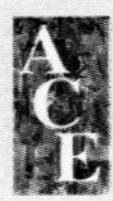

- Open the Notes Page view.
- To at least two slides, add notes that relate to the slide content that you think would be important when giving this presentation.
- Save the presentation as **PMP B-DOT Procedures ACE** to the drive and folder where you store your Data Files. When submitting the presentation to your instructor, submit the Notes Pages.

f. Check the spelling in the presentation (there is at least one spelling error), then view the presentation in Slide Show view.

g. Add your name as a footer on the notes and handouts, then save your changes.

h. Submit your presentation to your instructor, close your presentation, then exit PowerPoint.

Independent Challenge 2

You work for MedFlight Inc., an air ambulance helicopter service based in Truckee, CA. You have been asked by your boss to develop a presentation outlining the company's membership program and medical services.

a. Start PowerPoint, open the presentation PMP B-4.pptx from the drive and folder where you store your Data Files, and save it as **PMP B-MedFlight**.

b. Apply the Hardcover design theme to the presentation.

c. On Slide 3 select the three coverage shapes, then using the Align command distribute them vertically and align them to their right edges.

d. On Slide 3 select the three shapes, Family Coverage, Application Process, and MedFlight Member, then using the Align command distribute them horizontally and align them to their bottom edges.

e. Select all of the shapes, then apply Intense Effect – Black, Dark 1 from the Shape Styles group, then move the shapes down as shown in Figure B-21.

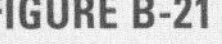
FIGURE B-21

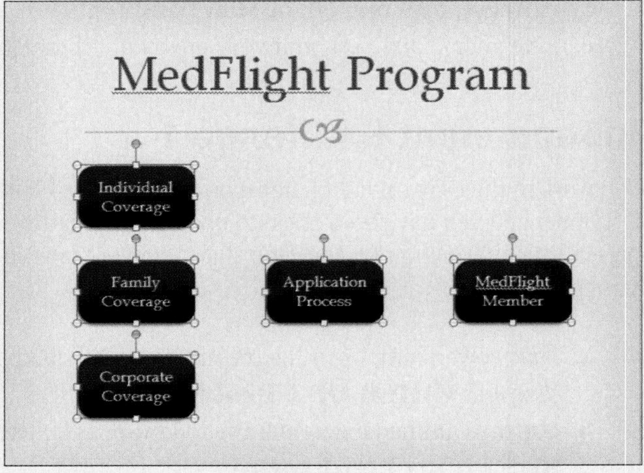

f. Using the Arrow shape from the Shapes gallery, draw a 2 ¼-pt arrow between all of the shapes. (*Hint*: Draw one arrow shape, change the line weight to 2 ¼-pt using the Shape Outline button, then duplicate the shape.)

g. Create a fifth slide to end the presentation, then type the following information in the Outline tab:

Truckee Regional Medical Center
- **Level II Trauma Center**
- **Pediatric Critical Care Unit**
- **STEMI Receiving Center**
- **Rural Cardiac Alert Program**

h. Check the spelling in the presentation, view the presentation in Slide Show view, then view the slides in Slide Sorter view.

i. Add the page number and your name as a footer on the notes and handouts, then save your changes.

j. Submit your presentation to your instructor, close your presentation, then exit PowerPoint.

Independent Challenge 3

You are an office assistant in a dental office in St. Cloud, Minnesota. The office manager has just asked you to create a presentation on fluoride that will be used in a community dental education project. Use the Internet to find information on fluoride and create your own content for the presentation.

- **a.** Start PowerPoint, create a new presentation, then apply the Flow design theme to the presentation.
- **b.** Type **Fluoride And You** as the main title on the title slide, and **Dental Wellness Center** as the subtitle.
- **c.** Save the presentation as **PMP B-Fluoride** to the drive and folder where you store your Data Files.
- **d.** Add four more slides with the following titles: Slide 2-**General Facts**; Slide 3-**What is Fluoride?**; Slide 4-**Is Fluoride Important?**; Slide 5-**Is Fluoride Safe?**.
- **e.** Enter appropriate text into the text placeholders of the slides. Use both the Slide pane and the Outline tab to enter text.
- **f.** Convert text on one slide to a SmartArt graphic, then apply the SmartArt graphic style Inset Effect.

Advanced Challenge Exercise

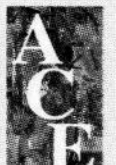

- Click the Replace list arrow in the Editing group on the Home tab, then click Replace Fonts.
- Replace the Calibri font with the Eras Medium ITC font.
- Save the presentation as **PMP B-Fluoride ACE** to the drive and folder where you store your Data Files.

- **g.** Check the spelling in the presentation, view the presentation as a slide show, then view the slides in Slide Sorter view.
- **h.** Add the slide number and your name as a footer on all the slides, then save your changes.
- **i.** Submit your presentation to your instructor, close your presentation, then exit PowerPoint.

Real Life Independent Challenge

One of your assignments this semester in your nursing course at City Junior College is to create a presentation on skin tissue damage which you will present to the class. You have chosen to create a presentation on tissue damage caused by frostbite. Most of the raw information is already on the slides; you primarily need to jazz it up by adding a theme and some text formatting.

- **a.** Start PowerPoint, open the presentation PMP B-5.pptx from drive and folder where you store your data files, and save it as **PMP B-Frostbite**.
- **b.** Add a new slide after the Frostbite Causes slide with the same layout, type **Symptoms** in the title text placeholder, then enter the following as bulleted text in the Outline tab:
  Progressive numbness
  Loss of sensitivity to touch
  Pain will fade as condition worsens
  Skin changes color, first white then white-purple
  Affected area feels "wooden"
  Ultimately death of body tissue
- **c.** Apply the Elemental design theme to the presentation.
- **d.** Select the title text object on Slide 1 (*Hint*: Press [Shift] to select the whole object.), then change the text color to Yellow.
- **e.** Change the font of the title text object to Corbel.
- **f.** Click the subtitle text object, click the AutoFit Options button, then click Stop Fitting Text to This Placeholder.
- **g.** Change the text on Slide 5 to a SmartArt graphic. Use an appropriate diagram type for a progressive list.
- **h.** Change the style of the SmartArt diagram using one of the SmartArt Styles, then view the presentation in Slide Show view.
- **i.** Add the slide number and your name as a footer on the notes and handouts, then save your changes.
- **j.** Submit your presentation to your instructor, close your presentation, then exit PowerPoint.

Visual Workshop

Create the presentation shown in Figures B-22 and B-23. Add today's date as the date on the title slide. Save the presentation as **PMP B-Flu Prevention** to the drive and folder where you store your Data Files. (*Hint*: The SmartArt style used for the SmartArt is a 3-D style.) Review your slides in Slide Show view, then add your name as a footer to the notes and handouts. Submit your presentation to your instructor, save your changes, close the presentation, then exit PowerPoint.

FIGURE B-22

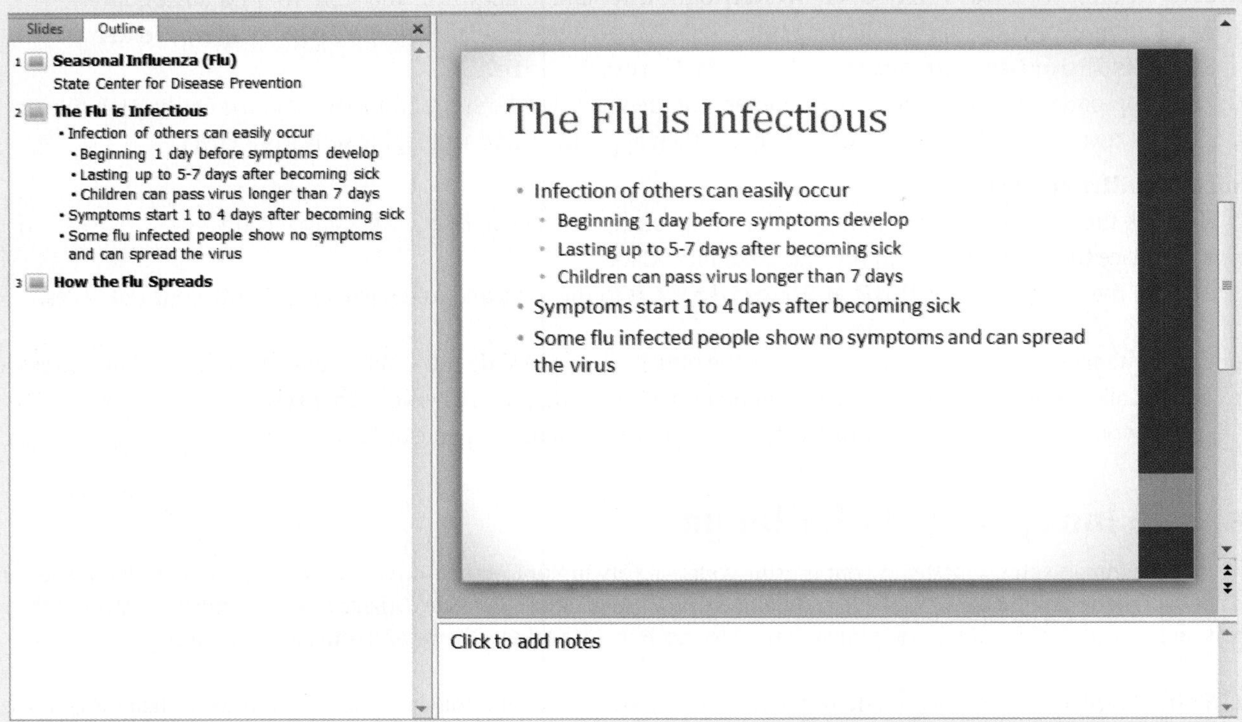

FIGURE B-23

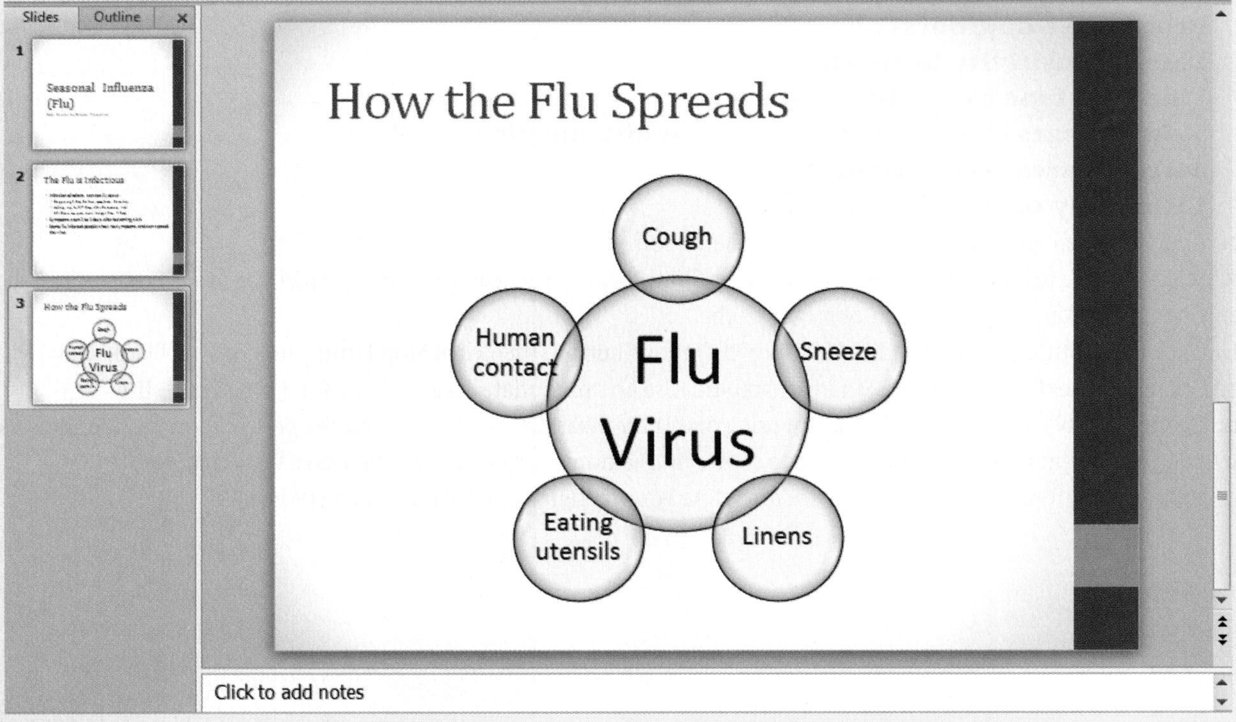

UNIT
C
PowerPoint 2010

Finalizing a Presentation

Files You Will Need:

PMP C-1.pptx
PMP C-2.docx
PMP C-3.jpg
PMP C-4.jpg
PMP C-5.pptx
PMP C-6.docx
PMP C-7.jpg
PMP C-8.pptx
PMP C-9.pptx
PMP C-10.docx
PMP C-11.jpg

A good presenter will make use of visual elements, such as tables, graphics, and photographs, in conjunction with text to help communicate the presentation message. Visual elements keep the presentation interesting, illustrate concepts, and help the audience focus on what the presenter is saying. And, though not required, having a consistent professional-looking theme throughout your presentation helps you gain and retain your audience's interest in the subject you are presenting. Once you are finished working with the text and other objects of your presentation, you are ready to apply slide show effects, which determine the way the slides, and objects on the slides, appear in Slide Show view. In this unit, you continue working on the presentation by inserting and formatting visual elements, including a table, clip art, and a photograph. Then you are ready to finalize the look of the slides and add effects to make the presentation interesting to watch.

OBJECTIVES

Insert text from Microsoft Word
Insert clip art
Insert and style a picture
Insert a table
Modify masters
Customize the background and theme
Use slide show commands
Set slide transitions and timings
Animate objects

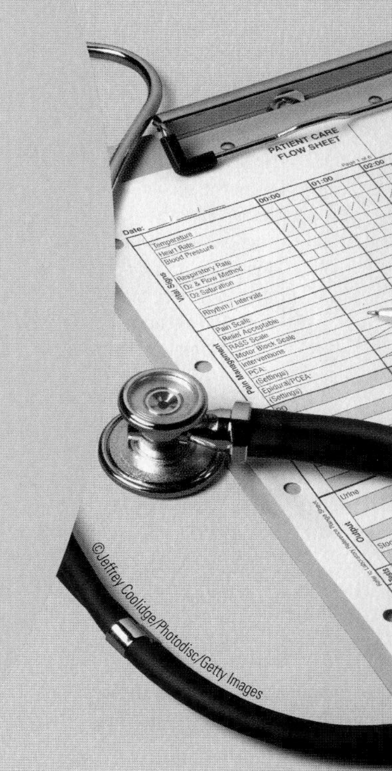

©Jeffrey Coolidge/Photodisc/Getty Images

UNIT C

PowerPoint 2010

Inserting Text from Microsoft Word

It is easy to insert documents saved in Microsoft Word format (.docx), Rich Text Format (.rtf), plain text format (.txt), and HTML format (.htm) into a PowerPoint presentation. If you have an outline saved in a document file, you can import it into PowerPoint to create a new presentation or create additional slides in an existing presentation. When you import a document into a presentation, PowerPoint creates an outline structure based on the styles in the document. For example, a Heading 1 style in the Word document becomes a slide title and a Heading 2 style becomes the first level of text in a bulleted list. If you insert a plain text format document into a presentation, PowerPoint creates an outline based on the tabs at the beginning of the document's paragraphs. Paragraphs without tabs become slide titles and paragraphs with one tab indent become first-level text in bulleted lists. You have a Microsoft Word document with information about venomous spiders that you want to insert into your presentation to create several new slides.

STEPS

1. **Start PowerPoint, open the presentation PMP C-1.pptx from the drive and folder where you store your Data Files, save it as PMP C-RMC Training, click the Outline tab, then click the Slide 4 icon in the Outline tab**

   Slide 4 appears in the Slide pane. Clicking a slide icon in the Outline tab highlights the slide text indicating the slide is selected. Before you insert an outline into a presentation, you need to determine where you want the new slides to be placed. You want the text from the Word document inserted as new slides after Slide 4.

2. **Click the New Slide list arrow in the Slides group, then click Slides from Outline**

   The Insert Outline dialog box opens.

3. **Navigate to the drive and folder where you store your Data Files, click the Word document file PMP C-2.docx, then click Insert**

   Four new slides (5, 6, 7, and 8) are added to the presentation. See Figure C-1.

4. **Read the text for the new Slide 5 in the Slide pane, then review the text on slides 6, 7, and 8 in the Outline tab**

   Information on Slide 8 refers to information that is not needed for this presentation.

5. **Click the Slides tab, then right-click the Slide 8 thumbnail in the Slides tab**

   A shortcut menu opens displaying related, or contextual, commands that are currently available.

6. **Click Delete Slide on the shortcut menu**

   Slide 8 is deleted, and the next slide down becomes the new Slide 8 and appears in the Slide pane.

7. **Click the Slide 6 thumbnail in the Slides tab, then drag it above Slide 5**

   Slide 6 and Slide 5 change places. You want the text of the inserted outline to adopt the presentation theme.

8. **Click the Reset button in the Slides group**

   Notice that the font type and formatting attributes of the slide text changes to reflect the current theme fonts for the presentation. The Reset button resets the slide placeholders to their default position, size, and text formatting based on the Angles presentation design theme.

9. **Click the Slide 6 thumbnail, press and hold [Shift], click the Slide 7 thumbnail, release [Shift], click the Reset button, then click the Save button on the Quick Access toolbar**

   Now all of the newly inserted slides have the same design theme as the rest of the presentation. Compare your screen to Figure C-2.

QUICK TIP

If your presentation has numerous slides, you can organize them into sections in the Slides tab. To create a section, click the slide in the Slides tab where you want the section to begin, click the Section button in the Slides group on the Home tab, then click Add Section.

FIGURE C-1: **Outline tab showing imported text**

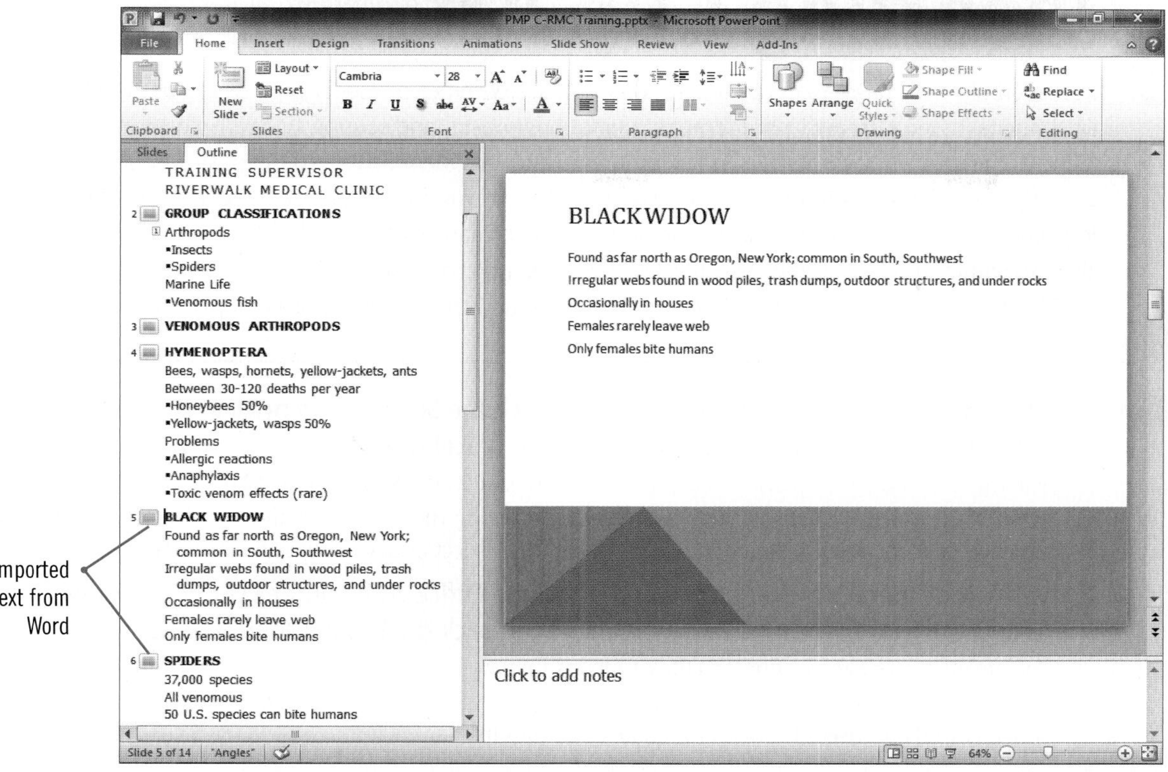

FIGURE C-2: **Slide showing correct theme fonts**

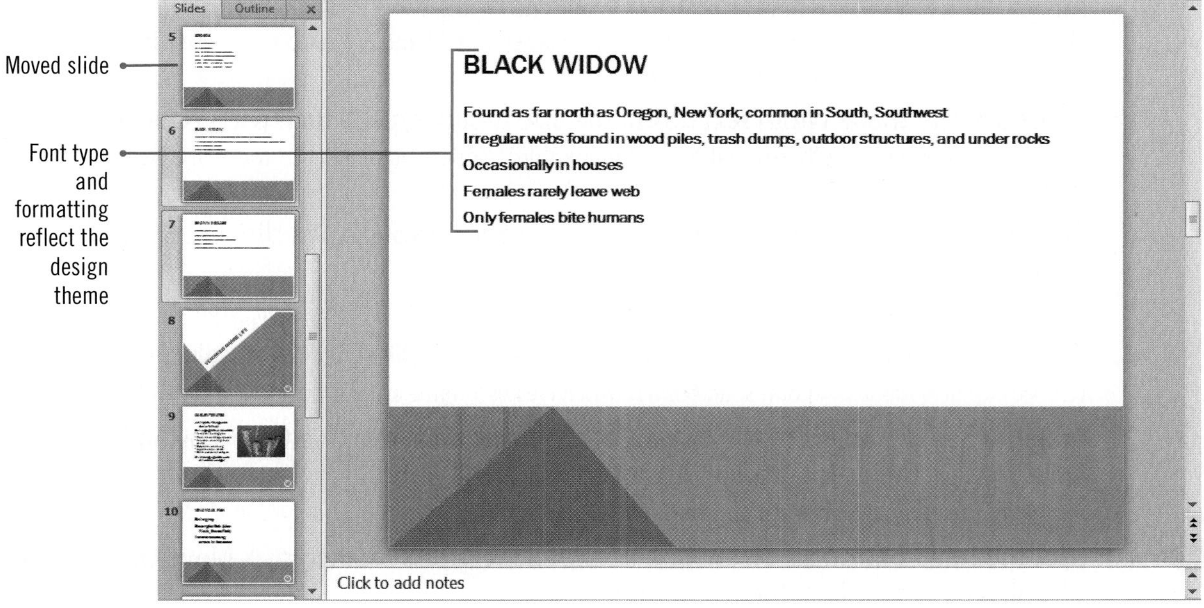

PowerPoint 2010

Inserting slides from other presentations

To insert slides from another presentation into the current presentation, click the New Slide list arrow in the Slides group, then click Reuse Slides. The Reuse Slides task pane opens on the right side of the window. Click the Browse button, click Browse File in the drop down list, locate the presentation you want to use, then click Open. Click each slide you want to place in the current presentation. The new slides automatically take on the theme of the current presentation, unless you check the Keep source formatting check box. You can also copy slides from one presentation to another. Open both presentations, change the view of each presentation to Slide Sorter view or use the Arrange All command to see both presentations, select the desired slides, then copy and paste them (or use drag and drop) into the desired presentation.

Inserting Clip Art

In PowerPoint you have access to a collection of assorted types of media clips. The types of clips include illustrations (called **clip art**), photographs, animations, videos, and sounds. Clips are stored in the Microsoft **Clip Organizer**, a separate file index program, and are identified by descriptive keywords. The Clip Organizer is organized into folders called **collections** that you can customize by adding, moving, or deleting clips. Clip art and other media clips are available from many sources, including the Microsoft Office Web site and commercially available collections that you can purchase. To enhance the presentation, you add a clip from the Clip Organizer to one of the slides, and then adjust its size and placement.

STEPS

QUICK TIP
You can insert clip art anywhere on a slide by clicking the Clip Art button in the Images group on the Insert tab.

1. **Click the up scroll arrow in the Slides tab, click the Slide 2 thumbnail in the Slides tab, then click the Clip Art icon in the Content placeholder**

   The Clip Art task pane opens. At the top of the task pane in the Search for text box, you enter a descriptive keyword to search for clips. If you want to limit or define the types of media clips for which PowerPoint searches, click the Results should be list arrow, and then select or deselect specific media types.

2. **Verify that there is a check mark in the Include Office.com content check box, select any text in the Search for text box, type bee, then click the Results should be list arrow**

   You are only interested in finding clip art images that are located in the Illustrations category. Searching in only the categories in which you are interested significantly reduces the number of media clips through which PowerPoint needs to search to produce your results.

TROUBLE
If you don't see the clip shown in Figure C-3, select another one.

3. **Click the check boxes to remove all check marks, click the Illustrations check box, click the Go button, then click the clip art thumbnail shown in Figure C-3**

   The bee clip appears in the content placeholder, and the Picture Tools Format tab is active on the Ribbon. Although you can change a clip's size by dragging a corner sizing handle, you can also **scale** it to change its size proportionally by a specific percentage or size.

4. **Select 3 in the Shape Width text box in the Size group, type 2, then press [Enter]**

   The bee clip is proportionally reduced in size by one-third. Notice the number in the Shape Height text box changes from 3 to 2.

5. **Click the Picture Border list arrow in the Picture Styles group, then click the Black, Text 1 color box in the top row**

   A black border is placed around the bee clip.

6. **Click the Picture Border list arrow, point to Weight, then click the 2 ¼ pt solid line style**

   The bee clip now has a 2 ¼-point solid border, which creates a frame around the clip.

7. **Drag the bee clip object to the bottom of the blank area, click the Color button in the Adjust group, then click Orange, Accent color 2 Dark**

   You prefer the original placement and color of the bee clip.

QUICK TIP
Click the Reset Picture button in the Adjust group to discard all the formatting changes.

8. **Click the Undo button list arrow on the Quick Access toolbar, click Move Object, click a blank area of the slide, then save your changes**

   Notice that by using the Undo button list arrow, you can undo multiple actions in one step, in this case the Recolor Picture and the Move Object commands.

9. **Click the Results should be list arrow in the Clip Art task pane, click the All media types check box, click Go, then click the task pane Close button**

   Now the next time you search for a clip, PowerPoint will search through all media types. Compare the slide on your screen to the slide shown in Figure C-4.

FIGURE C-3: Screen showing Clip Art task pane

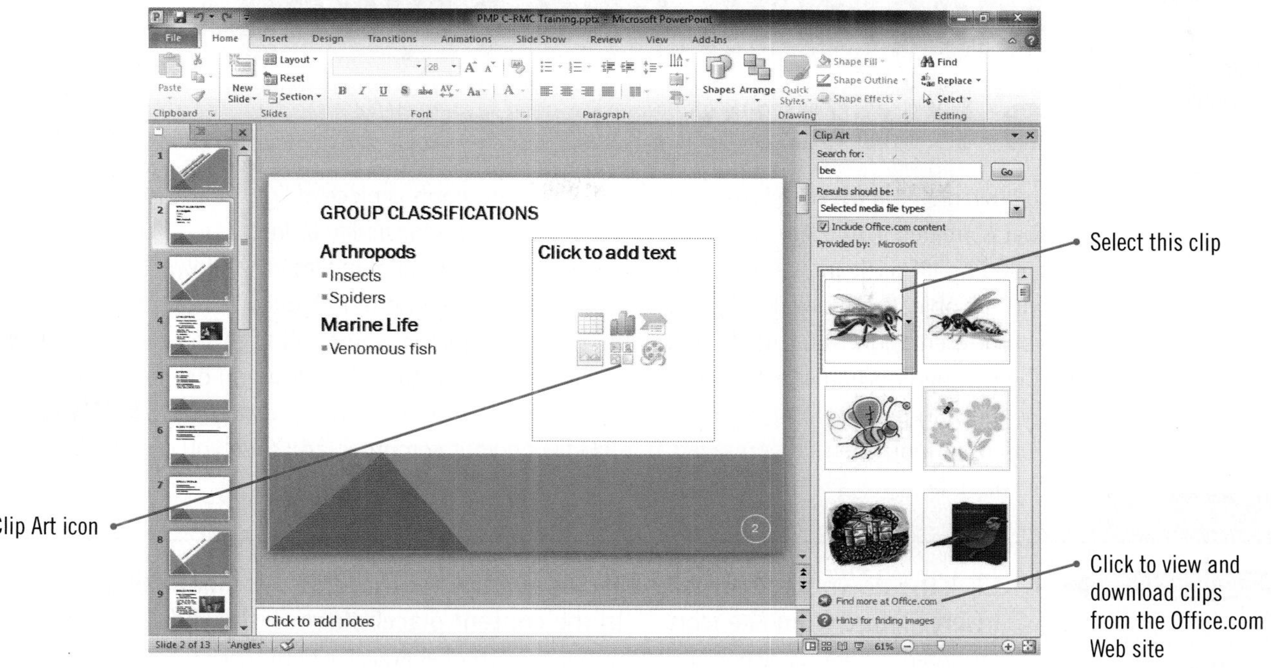

FIGURE C-4: Slide with formatted bee clip

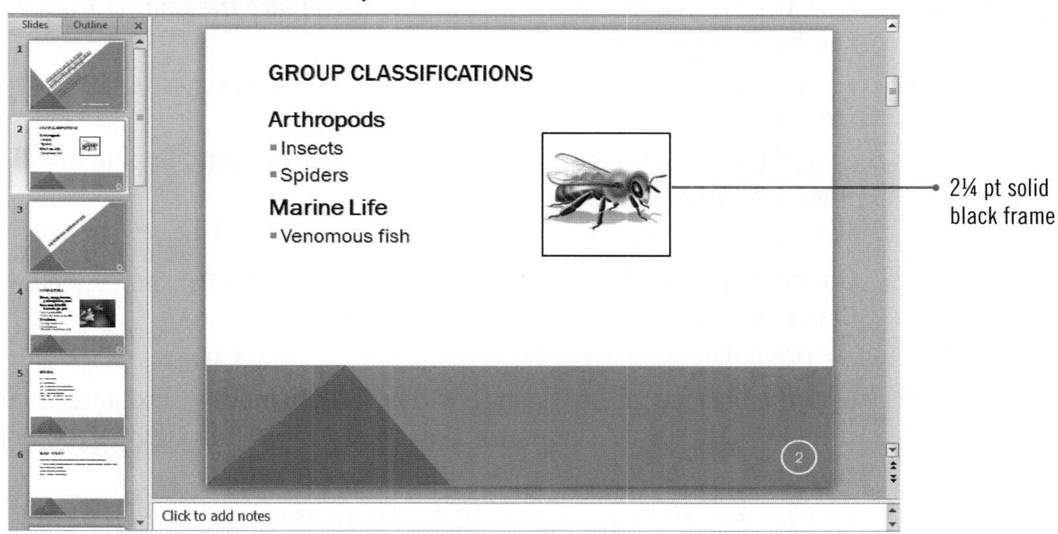

PowerPoint 2010

Sending a presentation using e-mail

You can send a copy of a presentation over the Internet to a reviewer to edit and add comments. You can use Microsoft Outlook to send your presentation. Although your e-mail program allows you to attach files, you can send a presentation using Outlook from within PowerPoint. Click the File tab, click Save & Send, click Send Using E-mail in the center pane, then click Send as Attachment. Outlook opens and automatically creates an e-mail with a copy of the presentation attached to it. You can also attach and send a PDF copy or an XPS copy of the presentation using your e-mail program. Both of these file formats preserve document formatting, enable file sharing, and can be viewed online and printed.

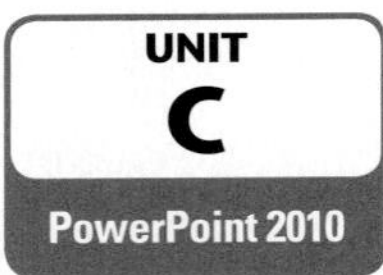
UNIT C PowerPoint 2010

Inserting and Styling a Picture

In PowerPoint, a **picture** is defined as a digital photograph, a piece of line art or clip art, or other artwork that is created in another program. PowerPoint gives you the ability to insert 14 different types of pictures including JPEG File Interchange Format and BMP Windows Bitmap files into a PowerPoint presentation. As with all objects in PowerPoint, you can format and style inserted pictures to help them fit the theme of your presentation. You can also hide a portion of the picture you don't want to be seen by **cropping** it. The cropped portion of a picture remains a part of the picture file unless you delete the cropped portion by applying picture compression settings in the Compression Settings dialog box. In this lesson you insert a picture that you saved as a JPG file on your computer, and then you crop and style it to best fit the slide.

STEPS

QUICK TIP
You can also insert a picture by clicking the Picture button in the Images group on the Insert tab.

1. **Click the down scroll arrow in the Slides tab, click the Slide 10 thumbnail, then click the Insert Picture from File icon in the content placeholder on the slide**
   The Insert Picture dialog box opens displaying the pictures available in the default Pictures library.
2. **Navigate to the drive and folder where you store your Data Files, select the picture file PMP C-3.jpg, then click Insert**
   The picture appears in the content placeholder on the slide, and the Picture Tools Format tab opens on the Ribbon. The picture would look better if you cropped some of the image from the right and left edges.

QUICK TIP
Click the Crop button list arrow to take advantage of other crop options including cropping to a shape from the Shapes gallery and cropping to a common photo size or aspect ratio.

3. **Click the Crop button in the Size group, then place the pointer over the right cropping handle of the picture**
   The pointer changes to ⊢. When the Crop button is active, cropping handles appear next to the sizing handles.
4. **Drag the right cropping handle to the left and the left cropping handle to the right, as shown in Figure C-5, then press [Esc]**
   PowerPoint has a number of picture formatting options, and you decide to experiment with some of them.
5. **On the Picture Tools Format tab, click the More button in the Picture Styles group, then click Compound Frame, Black (2nd row)**
   The picture now has a black frame.
6. **Click the Corrections button in the Adjust group, move your pointer over the thumbnails to see how the picture changes, then click Sharpen: 50% in the Sharpen and Soften section**
   The picture clarity is better.
7. **Click the Artistic Effects button in the Adjust group, move your pointer over the thumbnails to see how the picture changes, then click a blank area of the slide**
   The artistic effects are all interesting but none of them will work well for this picture. You decide to compress the picture to delete the cropped areas and make the file smaller.

QUICK TIP
If you want to apply an effect from the Artistic Effects gallery to a compressed picture, compress the picture first to maintain the best picture quality possible.

8. **Click the Compress Pictures button in the Adjust group, make sure the Use document resolution option button is checked, then click OK**
   The cropped portions of the picture are deleted and the picture is compressed.
9. **Drag the lower-right sizing handle down until the bottom of the picture touches the blue shape, drag the picture to the center of the blank area, then save your changes**
   Compare your screen to Figure C-6.

FIGURE C-5: Using the cropping pointer to crop a picture

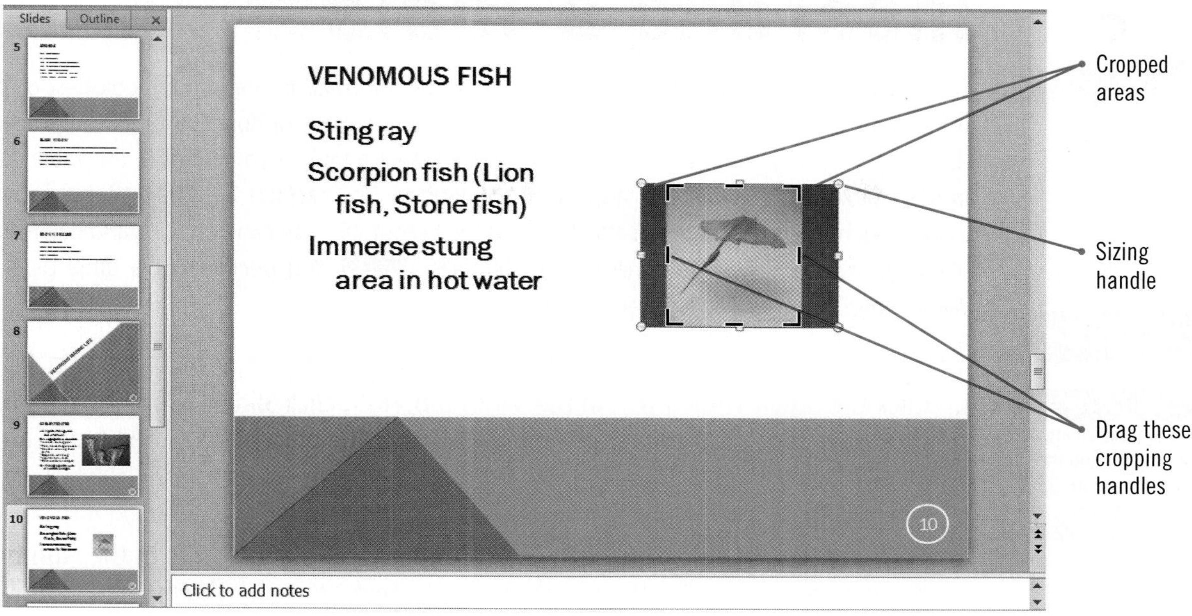

FIGURE C-6: Cropped and styled picture

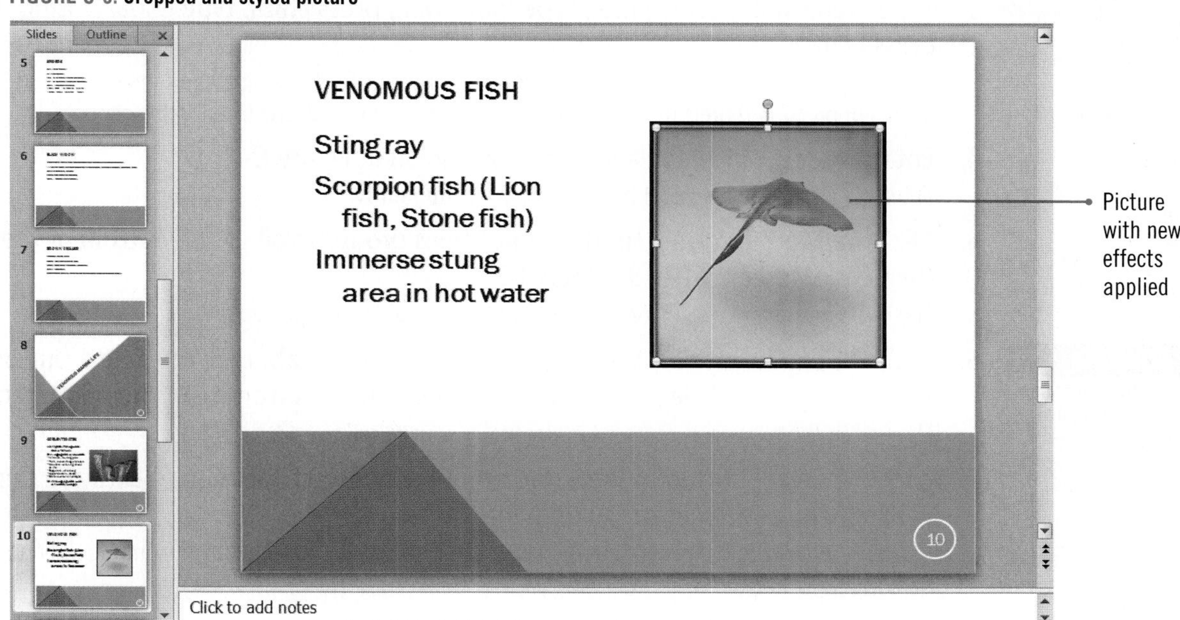

PowerPoint 2010

Things to know about picture compression

It's important to know that when you compress a picture you change the amount of detail in the picture, so it might look different than it did before the compression. Compressing a picture changes the amount of color used in the picture with no loss of quality. By default, all inserted pictures in PowerPoint are automatically compressed using the settings in the PowerPoint Options dialog box. To locate the compression settings, click the File tab, click Options, then click Advanced in the left pane. In the Image Size and Quality section, you can change picture compression settings or stop the automatic compression of pictures.

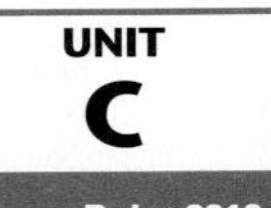

PowerPoint 2010

Inserting a Table

As you create your presentation, you may have some information that would look best organized in rows and columns. For example, if you wanted to compare treatment options for a medical procedure, a table is ideal for this type of information. Once you have created a table, two new tabs, the Table Tools Design tab and the Table Tools Layout tab, appear on the Ribbon. You can use the Design tab to apply color styles, change cell borders, and add cell effects. Using the Layout tab, you can add rows and columns to your table, adjust the size of cells, and align text in the cells. You decide that a table best describes how medications affect cardiac emergencies.

STEPS

QUICK TIP
You can also create a table by clicking the Table button in the Tables group on the Insert tab, then dragging over the table grid to create the size table you want.

1. **Click the down scroll arrow in the Slides tab, right-click Slide 13 thumbnail in the Slides tab, click New Slide on the shortcut menu, click the title placeholder, then type Cardiac Emergencies**
   A new slide with the Title and Content layout appears.
2. **Click the Insert Table icon in the content placeholder, type 3 in the Number of columns text box, click the Number of rows text box, click the up arrow until 6 appears, then click OK**
   A formatted table with three columns and six rows appears on the slide, and the Table Tools Design tab opens on the Ribbon. The table has 18 cells. The insertion point is in the first cell of the table and is ready to accept text.

QUICK TIP
Press [Tab] when the insertion point is in the last cell of a table to create a new row.

3. **Type Medication, press [Tab], type Indication, press [Tab], type Usual Dosing, then press [Tab]**
   The text you typed appears in the top three cells of the table. Pressing [Tab] moves the insertion point to the next cell; pressing [Enter] moves the insertion point to the next line in the same cell.
4. **Enter the rest of the table information shown in Figure C-7**
   The table would look better if it were formatted differently.
5. **Click the More button in the Table Styles group, scroll to the bottom of the gallery, then click Medium Style 3 – Accent 2**
   The background and text color change to reflect the table style you applied.

QUICK TIP
Change the height or width of any table cell by dragging its borders.

6. **Click the upper-left cell, click the Table Tools Layout tab, click the Select button in the Table group, click Select Row, then click the Center button in the Alignment group**
   The text in the top row is centered horizontally in each cell.
7. **Click the Select button in the Table group, click Select Table, then click the Center Vertically button in the Alignment group**
   The text in the whole table is centered vertically within each cell. The table would look better if all the rows were the same height.
8. **Click the Distribute Rows button in the Cell Size group, click the Table Tools Design tab, then click the Effects button in the Table Styles group**
   The Table Effects gallery opens.
9. **Point to Cell Bevel, click Hard Edge (3rd row in the Bevel section), click a blank area of the slide, then save the presentation**
   The 3-D effect makes the cells of the table stand out. Compare your screen with Figure C-8.

FIGURE C-7: Inserted table with data

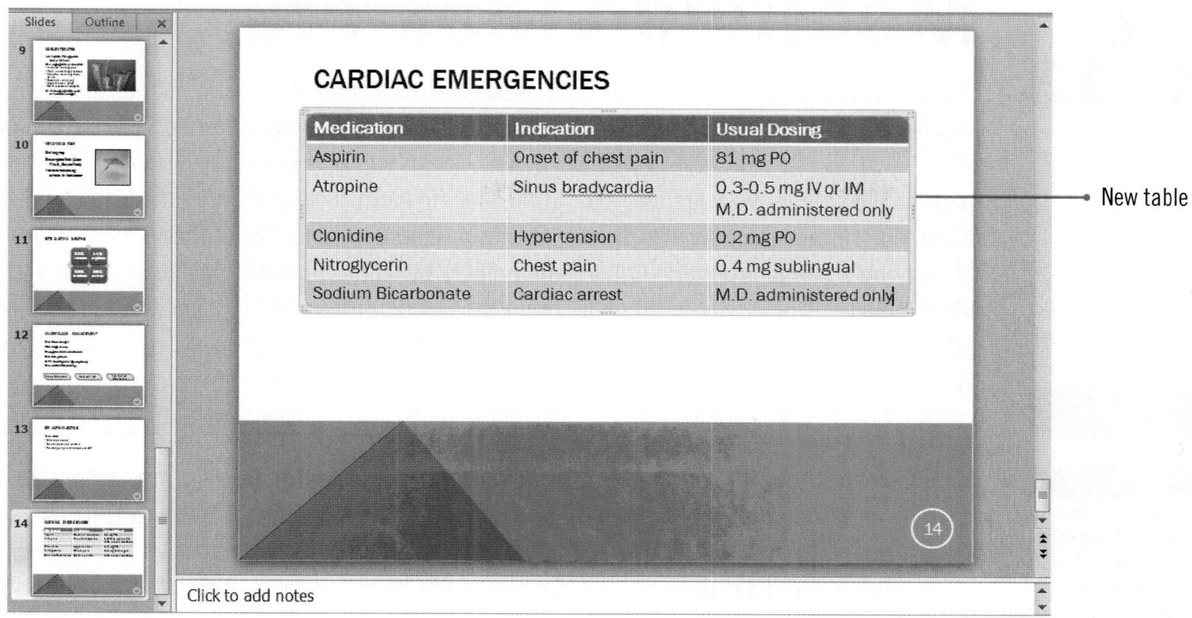

FIGURE C-8: Formatted table

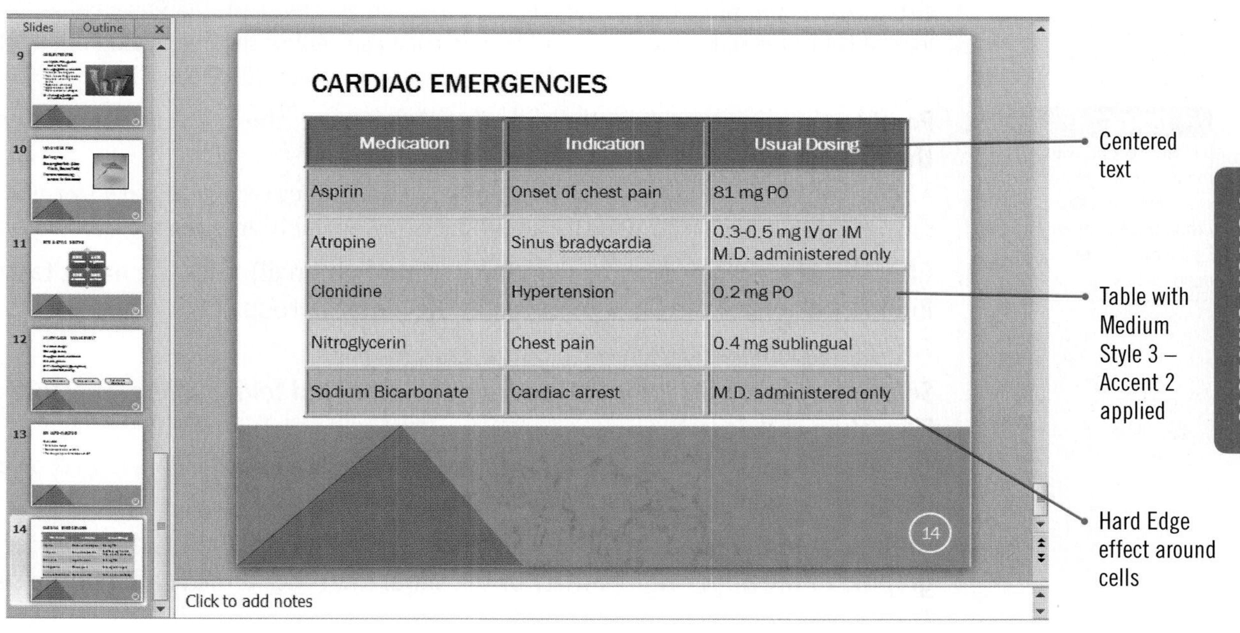

PowerPoint 2010

Drawing tables

Choose the slide where you want the table, click the Table button in the Tables group on the Insert tab, then click Draw Table. The pointer changes to ✎. Drag to define the boundaries of the table in the area of the slide where you want the table. A dotted outline appears as you draw. Next, you draw to create the rows and columns of your table. Click the Table Tools Design tab on the Ribbon, click the Draw Table button in the Draw Borders group, then draw lines for columns and rows. Be sure to draw within the boundary line of the table.

UNIT C
PowerPoint 2010

Modifying Masters

Each presentation in PowerPoint has a set of **masters** that store information about the theme and slide layouts, including the position and size of text and content placeholders, fonts, slide background, color, and effects. There are three Master views: Slide Master view, Notes Master view, and Handout Master view. Changes made in Slide Master view are reflected on the slides in Normal view; changes made in Notes Master view are reflected in Notes Page view, and changes made in Handout Master view appear when you print your presentation using a handout printing option. The primary benefit to modifying a master is that you can make universal changes to your whole presentation instead of making individual repetitive changes to each of your slides. You want to add the Riverwalk Medical Clinic company logo to every slide in your presentation, so you open your presentation and insert the logo to the slide master.

STEPS

QUICK TIP
You can press and hold [Shift] and click the Normal button on the status bar to display the slide master.

1. **Click the View tab on the Ribbon, click the Slide Master button in the Master Views group, then click the Angles Slide Master thumbnail (first thumbnail) in the slide thumbnail pane**
   A new tab, the Slide Master tab, appears next to the Home tab on the Ribbon. The Slide Master view appears with the slide master displayed in the Slide pane as shown in Figure C-9. The slide master is the theme slide master (the Angles theme in this case). Each theme comes with its own associated slide masters. Each master text placeholder on the slide master identifies the font size, style, color, and position of text placeholders on the slides in Normal view. For example, the Master title placeholder positioned at the top of the slide uses a black, 28 pt, uppercase, Franklin Gothic Medium font. Slide titles use this font style and formatting. Design elements that you place on the slide master appear on every slide in the presentation. The slide layouts located below the slide master in the slide thumbnail pane follow the information on the slide master. All changes you make to the slide master, including font changes, are reflected in all of the slide layouts.

QUICK TIP
When working with slide layouts, you can right-click the thumbnail to open a shortcut list of commands.

2. **Point to the slide layouts in the slide thumbnail pane, then click the Two Content Layout thumbnail**
   As you point to each slide layout, a ScreenTip appears identifying each slide layout by name and lists if any slides in the presentation are using the layout. Slides 2, 4, 9, and 10 are using the Two Content Layout.
3. **Click the Angles Slide Master thumbnail (first thumbnail), click the Insert tab on the Ribbon, then click the Picture button in the Images group**
   The Insert Picture dialog box opens.
4. **Select the picture file PMP C-4.jpg from the drive and folder where you store your Data Files, then click Insert**
   The Riverwalk Medical Clinic graphic logo appears on the slide master and will appear on all slides in the presentation, except the title slide and section header slides.
5. **Click 1.71" in the Shape Width text box in the Size group, type 1, press [Enter], drag the graphic to the upper-right corner of the slide, then click a blank area of the slide**
   The graphic snaps into the corner of the slide.
6. **Click the Slide Master tab on the Ribbon, then click the Preserve button in the Edit Master group**
   Preserving the selected master assures that the Angles slide master remains with this presentation even if you eventually use another master. Compare your screen to Figure C-10.
7. **Click the Normal button on the status bar, click the Insert tab on the Ribbon, then click the Header & Footer button in the Text group**
8. **Click Apply to All, click the Slide 5 thumbnail in the Slides tab, then save your changes**
   Now all of the slides in the presentation including the three slides inserted from the Word outline have slide numbers.

FIGURE C-9: Slide Master view

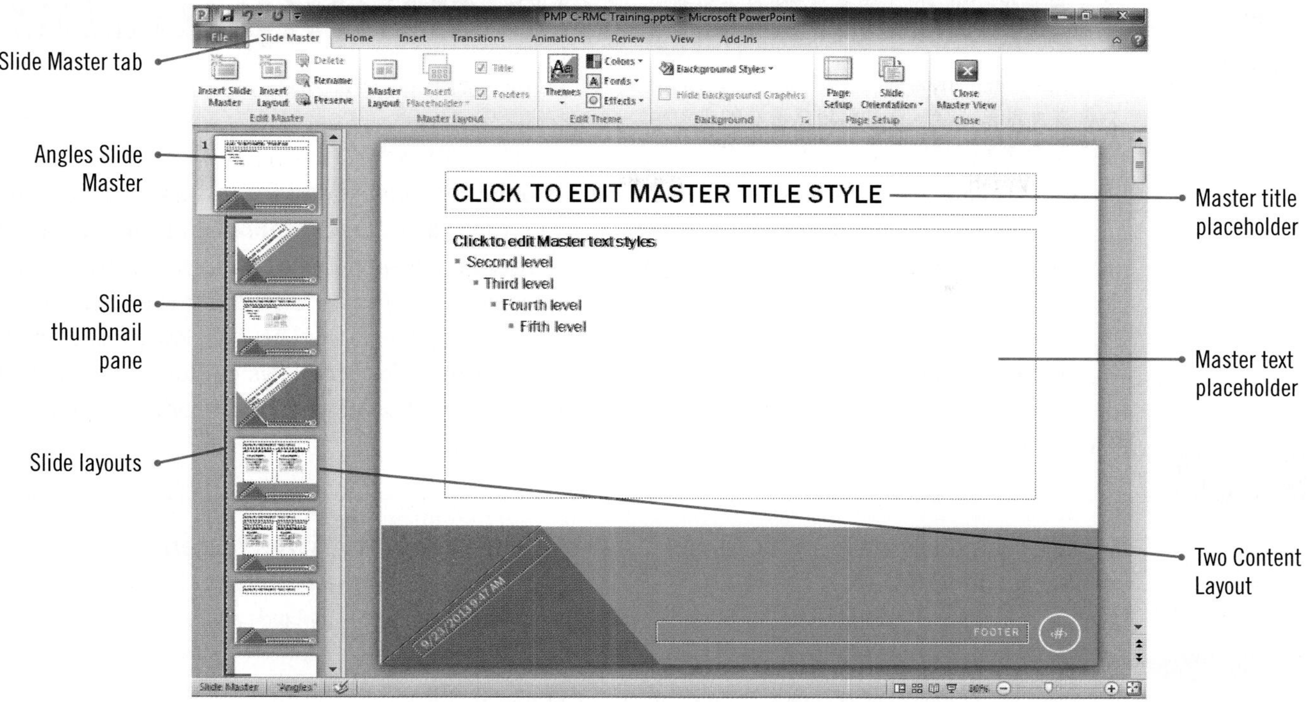

FIGURE C-10: Graphic added to slide master

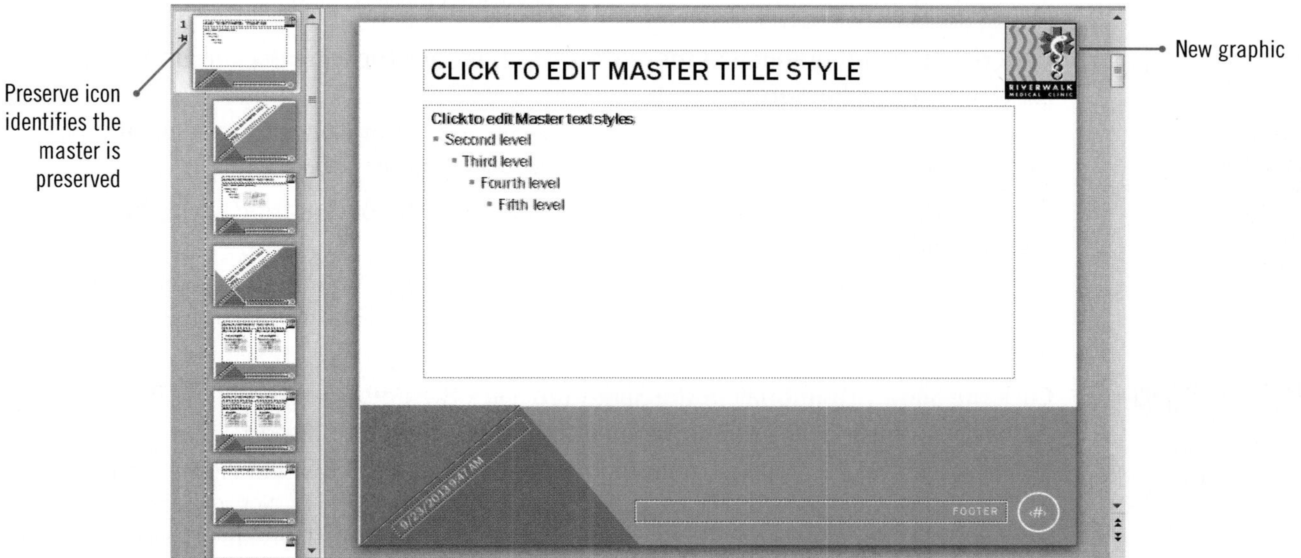

Creating custom slide layouts

As you work with PowerPoint, you may find that you need to develop a customized slide layout. For example, you may need to create presentations for a client that have slides that display four pictures with a caption underneath each picture. To make everyone's job easier, you can create a custom slide layout that includes only the placeholders that you need. To create a custom slide layout, open Slide Master view, and then click the Insert Layout button in the Edit Master group. A new slide layout appears in the slide thumbnail pane. You can choose to add several different placeholders including Content, Text, Picture, Chart, Table, SmartArt, Media, and Clip Art. Click the Insert Placeholder list arrow in the Master Layout group, click the placeholder you want to add, drag + to create the placeholder, then position the placeholder on the slide. In Slide Master view, you can add or delete placeholders in any of the slide layouts. You can rename a custom slide layout by clicking the Rename button in the Edit Master group and entering a descriptive name to better identify the layout.

PowerPoint 2010

UNIT C
PowerPoint 2010

Customizing the Background and Theme

Every slide in a PowerPoint presentation has a **background**, the area behind the text and graphics. You modify the background to enhance the slides using images and color. A **background graphic** is an object placed on the slide master. You can quickly change the background appearance by applying a background style, which is a set of color variations derived from the theme colors. Theme colors determine the colors for all slide elements in your presentation, including slide background, text and lines, shadows, fills, accents, and hyperlinks. Every PowerPoint theme has its own set of theme colors. See Table C-1 for a description of the theme colors. The presentation needs some design enhancements. You decide to modify the background of the slides by changing the theme colors and fonts.

STEPS

1. **Click the Design tab on the Ribbon, then click the Background Styles button in the Background group**
   A gallery of background styles opens. Review the different backgrounds using Live Preview.

2. **Move over each style in the gallery, then click Style 2**
   Figure C-11 shows the new background on Slide 5 of the presentation and the other slides in the Slides tab. Even though you are working in Normal view, the new background style is applied to the slide master and slide layouts. The new background style does not appear over the whole slide, which indicates there are background items on the slide master preventing you from seeing the entire slide background.

> **QUICK TIP**
> To apply a new background style to only selected slides, select the slides on the Slides tab or in Slide Sorter view, right-click the background style in the Background Styles gallery, then click Apply to Selected Slides.

3. **Click the Slide 4 thumbnail in the Slides tab, then click the Hide Background Graphics check box in the Background group**
   All of the background items (the RMC logo and colored shapes at the bottom of the slide) are hidden from view, and only the text objects, slide number, and bee photo remain visible.

4. **Click the Hide Background Graphics check box, click the Background Styles button in the Background group, then click Style 1**
   All of the background items and the white background appear again. The white background color you started with actually looks the best. Theme colors that complement the RMC logo would look better than the current theme colors.

5. **Click the Slide 1 thumbnail in the Slides tab, click the Colors button in the Themes group, move the pointer over each of the built-in themes, then click Aspect**
   The new theme colors are applied to the slide master and all of the elements in the presentation including background items, the table on Slide 14, and the SmartArt graphic on Slide 11. Notice the title text font, color, and formatting did not change; this is known as an **exception**. Exceptions are changes that you make directly to text on the slide, which do not match the theme fonts on the slide master.

> **QUICK TIP**
> To create custom theme colors, click the Colors button, then click Create New Theme Colors. You can also create custom theme fonts by clicking the Fonts button, then clicking Create New Theme Fonts.

6. **Click the down scroll arrow in the Slides tab, click the Slide 11 thumbnail, click the Effects button in the Themes group, move the pointer over each of the built-in themes, then click Elemental**
   Notice how the new theme effects change the SmartArt graphic. Like the theme colors, the new theme effects are applied to the slide master and to all of the slides in the presentation.

7. **Click the Slide 9 thumbnail in the Slides tab, click the Fonts button in the Themes group, move the pointer over each of the built-in themes, click Composite, then save your work**
   The new theme fonts are applied to the presentation. Compare your screen to Figure C-12.

FIGURE C-11: Slide with new background style applied

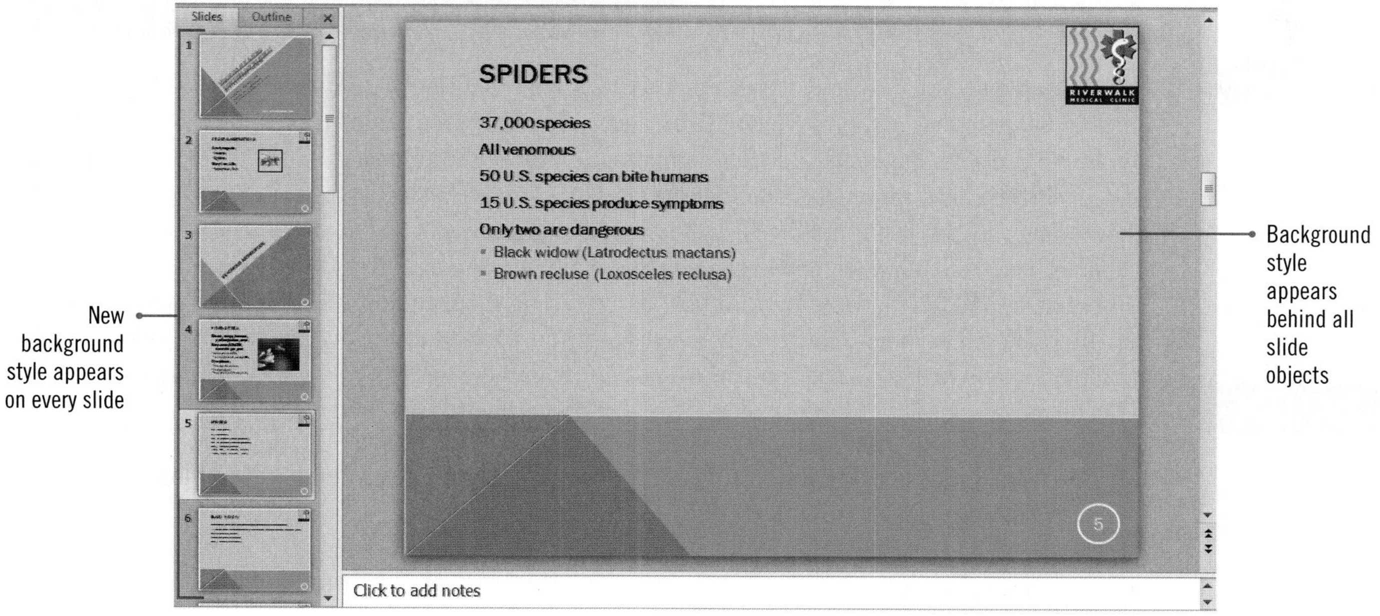

FIGURE C-12: Slide showing new theme colors and theme fonts

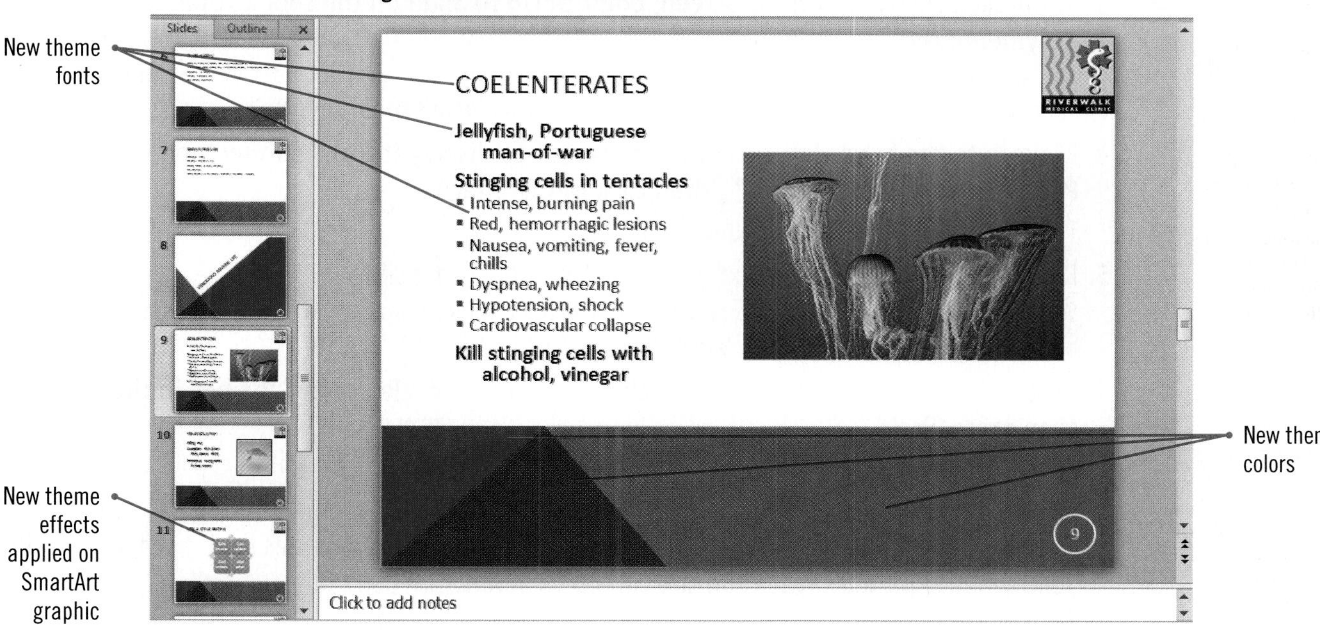

PowerPoint 2010

TABLE C-1: Theme colors

color element	description
Text/Background colors	Contrasting colors for typed characters and the slide background
Accent colors	There are six accent colors used for shapes, drawn lines, and text; the shadow color for text and objects and the fill and outline color for shapes are all accent colors; all of these colors contrast appropriately with background and text colors
Hyperlink color	Colors used for hyperlinks you insert
Followed Hyperlink color	Color used for hyperlinks after they have been clicked

UNIT C

PowerPoint 2010

Using Slide Show Commands

With PowerPoint, you can show a presentation on a computer using Slide Show view. Slide Show view is used primarily to deliver a presentation to an audience, either over the Internet using your computer or through a projector connected to your computer. As you've seen, Slide Show view fills your computer screen with the slides of the presentation, showing them one at a time. Once the presentation is in Slide Show view, you can use a number of slide show options to tailor the show to meet your needs. For example, you can draw, or **annotate**, on slides or jump to different slides in other parts of the presentation. You want to learn how to run a slide show and use the slide show options so you can be prepared to help Rebecca when she gives the presentation. You run the slide show of the presentation and practice using some of the custom slide show options.

STEPS

1. **Drag the Slides tab scroll box to the top, click the Slide 1 thumbnail in the Slides tab, then click the Slide Show button on the status bar**
   The first slide of the presentation fills the screen.
2. **Press [Spacebar]**
   Slide 2 appears on the screen. Pressing [Spacebar] or clicking the left mouse button is the easiest way to move through a slide show. See Table C-2 for other Slide Show view keyboard commands. You can also use the Slide Show shortcut menu for on-screen navigation during a slide show.

QUICK TIP
During a slide show you can also type the slide number, then press [Enter] to jump to a slide.

3. **Right-click anywhere on the screen, point to Go to Slide on the shortcut menu, then click 4 Hymenoptera**
   The slide show jumps to Slide 4. You can highlight or emphasize major points in your presentation by annotating the slide during a slide show using one of PowerPoint's annotation tools.

TROUBLE
The Slide Show toolbar buttons are semitransparent and blend in with the background color on the slide.

4. **Move to the lower-left corner of the screen to display the Slide Show toolbar, click the Pen Options menu button, then click Highlighter**
   The pointer changes to the highlighter pointer.
5. **Drag to highlight all the text with bullet points on the slide**
   While the annotation tool is visible, mouse clicks do not advance the slide show; however, you can still move to the next slide by pressing [Spacebar] or [Enter].
6. **Click on the Slide Show toolbar, click Pen, draw a circle around the bee in the picture, then press [Esc]**
   Pressing [Esc] or [Ctrl][A] while using an annotation pointer (pen pointer or highlighter pointer) switches the pointer back to . Compare your screen to Figure C-13.
7. **Click on the Slide Show toolbar, click Eraser, the pointer changes to , then click the yellow highlight annotation on the top bullet point**
   The annotation is erased.
8. **Press [Esc], click , then click Erase All Ink on Slide**
   The annotations on Slide 4 are erased. You also have the option of saving annotations you don't delete in Slide Show view when you quit the slide show. Saved annotations appear as drawn objects in Normal view.

QUICK TIP
To temporarily hide your slide during a slide show, right-click the screen, point to Screen, then click Black Screen or White Screen.

9. **Click the Slide Show menu button on the Slide Show toolbar, point to Go to Slide, then click 1 Venomous Bite & Sting Symptoms on the menu**
   Slide 1 appears.
10. **Press [Enter] to advance through the slide show, then when you see a black slide, press [Spacebar]**
   The black slide indicates the end of the slide show, and you are returned to Slide 1 in Normal view.

FIGURE C-13: Slide 4 in Slide Show view showing annotations

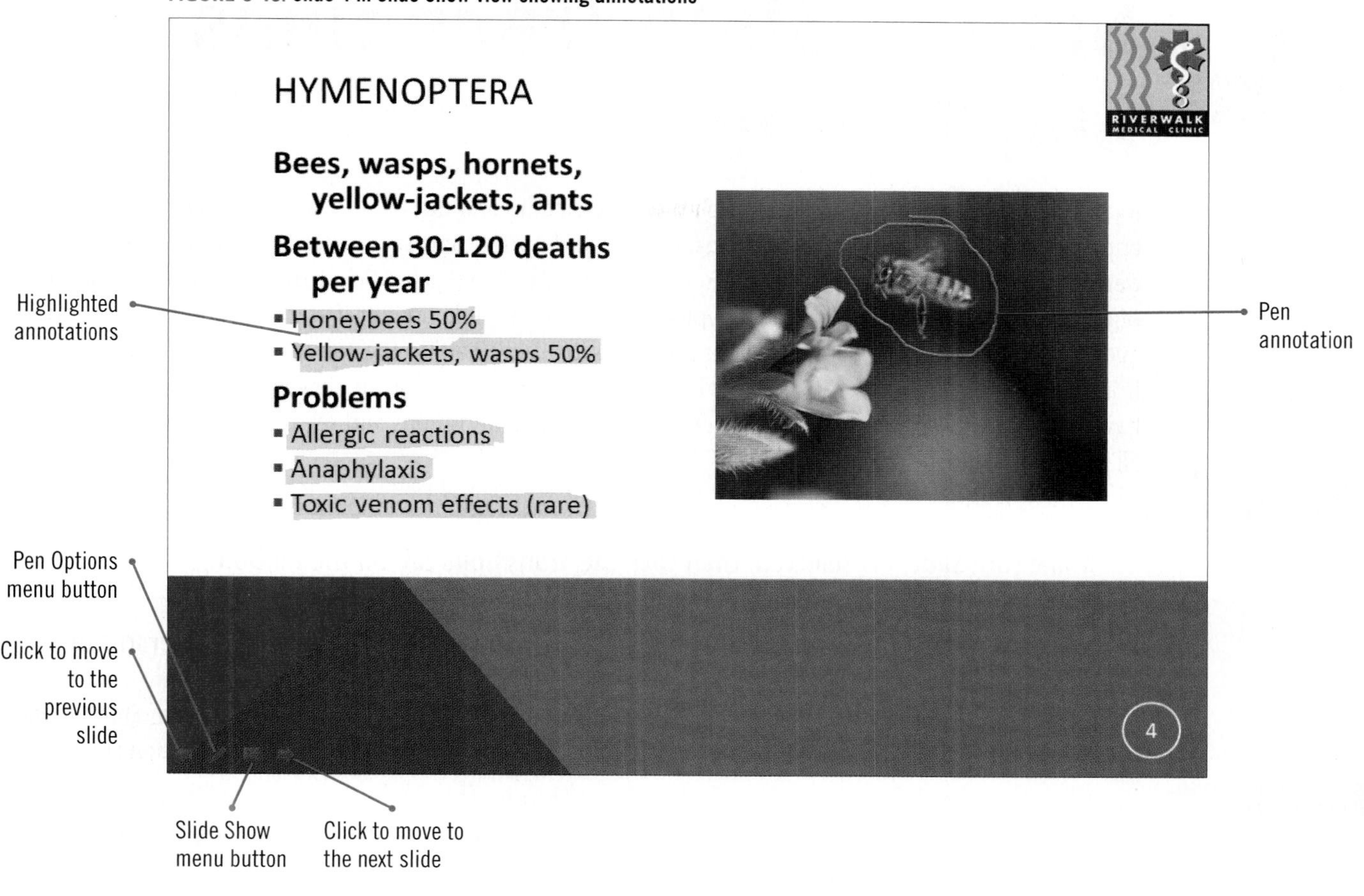

PowerPoint 2010

TABLE C-2: Basic slide show keyboard commands

keyboard commands	description
[Enter], [Spacebar], [PgDn], [N], [down arrow], or [right arrow]	Advances to the next slide
[E]	Erases the annotation drawing
[Home], [End]	Moves to the first or last slide in the slide show
[H]	Displays a hidden slide
[up arrow] or [PgUp]	Returns to the previous slide
[W]	Changes the screen to white; press again to return
[S]	Pauses the slide show; press again to continue
[B]	Changes the screen to black; press again to return
[Ctrl][M]	Shows or hides annotations on the slide
[Ctrl][A]	Changes pointer to
[Esc]	Stops the slide show

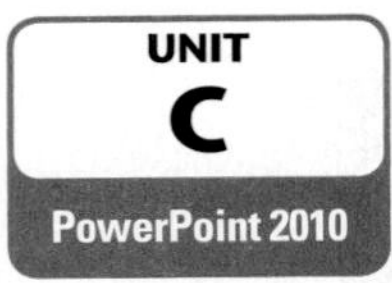

Setting Slide Transitions and Timings

In a slide show, you can specify how each slide advances in and out of view, and for how long each slide appears on the screen. **Slide transitions** are the special visual and audio effects you apply to a slide that determine how it moves on and off the screen during the slide show. **Slide timing** refers to the amount of time a slide is visible on the screen. Typically, you only set slide timings if you want the presentation to automatically progress through the slides during a slide show. Setting the correct slide timing, in this case, is important because it determines how much time your audience has to view each slide. Each slide can have a different slide timing. You decide to set slide transitions and seven-second slide timings for all the slides.

STEPS

1. **Make sure Slide 1 is selected, then click the Transitions tab on the Ribbon**

   Transitions are organized by type into three groups.

2. **Click the More button in the Transition to This Slide group, then click Glitter in the Exciting section**

   The new slide transition plays on the slide, and a transition icon appears next to the slide thumbnail in the Slides tab, as shown in Figure C-14. You can customize the slide transition by changing its direction and speed.

> **QUICK TIP**
> You can add a sound that plays with the transition from the Sound list arrow in the Timing group.

3. **Click the Effect Options button in the Transition to This Slide group, click Diamonds from Top, click the Duration down arrow in the Timing group until 2.00 appears, then click the Preview button in the Preview group**

   The Glitter slide transition now plays from the top of the slide for 2.00 seconds. You can apply this transition with the custom settings to all of the slides in the presentation.

4. **Click the Apply To All button in the Timing group, then click the Slide Sorter button on the status bar**

   All of the slides now have the customized Glitter transition applied to them as identified by the transition icons located below each slide. You also have the ability to determine how slides progress during a slide show—either manually by mouse click or automatically by slide timing.

5. **Click the On Mouse Click check box under Advance Slide in the Timing group to clear the check mark**

   This clears the option that manually advances slides during a slide show. You can set both manual and automatic slide timings within the same presentation, which is why you need to clear the manual option. Now you can set an automatic slide timing.

> **QUICK TIP**
> Click the transition icon under any slide in Slide Sorter view to see its transition play.

6. **Click the After up arrow until 00:07.00 appears in the text box, then click the Apply To All button**

   The timing between slides is 7 seconds as indicated by the time under each slide in Slide Sorter view. See Figure C-15. When you run the slide show, each slide will remain on the screen for 7 seconds. You can override a slide's timing and speed up the slide show by pressing [Spacebar], [Enter], or clicking the left mouse button.

7. **Click the Slide Show button on the status bar, then watch the slide show advance automatically**

8. **When you see the black slide at the end of the slide show, press [Spacebar], then save your changes**

   The slide show ends and returns to Slide Sorter view with Slide 1 selected.

FIGURE C-14: **Applied slide transition**

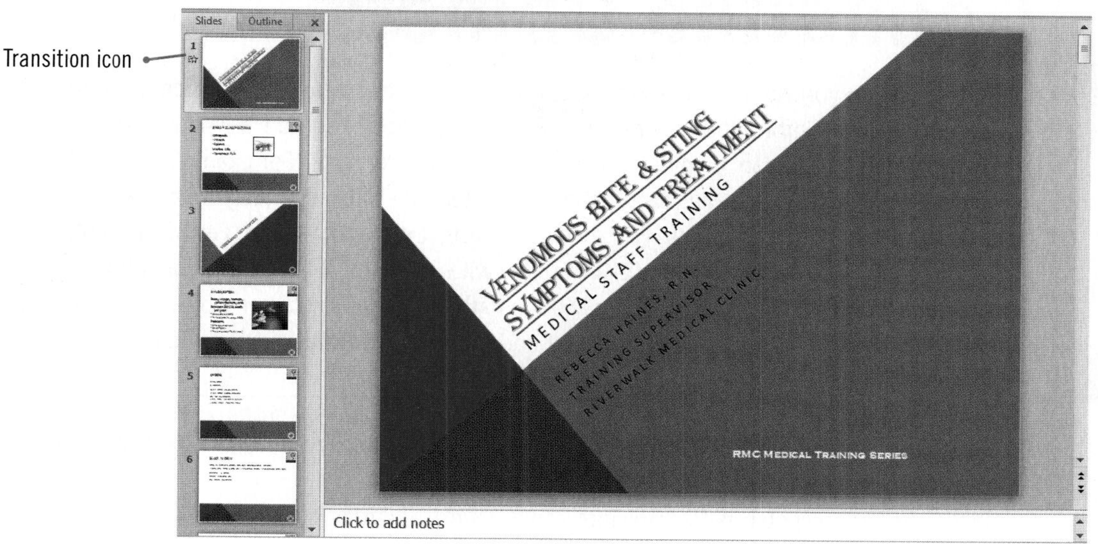

FIGURE C-15: **Slide Sorter view showing applied transition and timing**

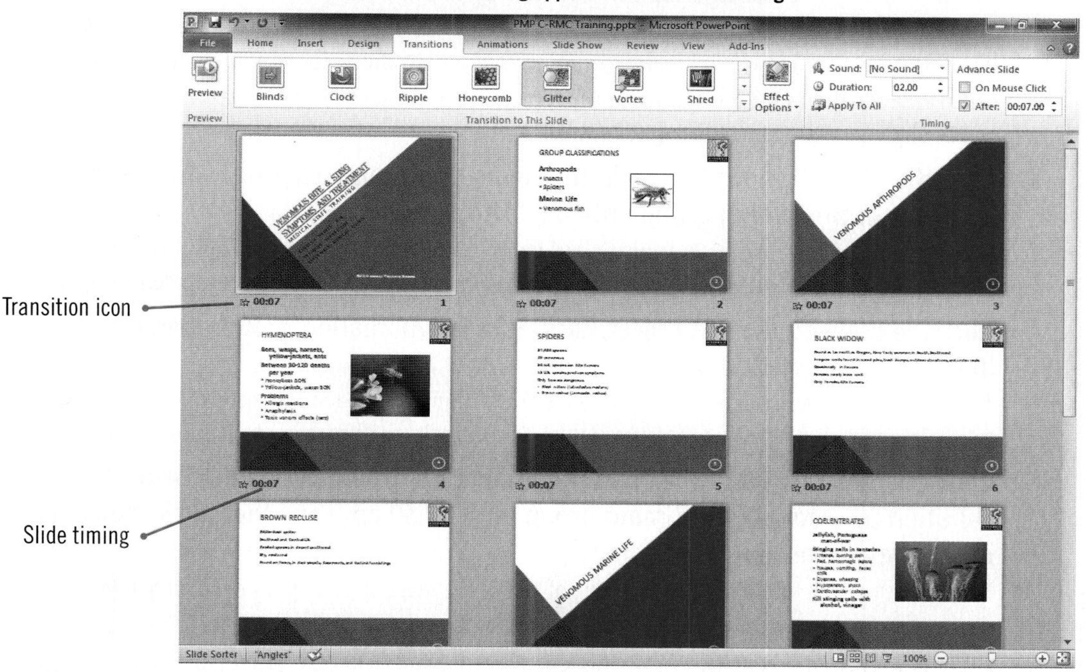

Rehearsing slide show timings

You can set different slide timings for each slide. For example, you can have the title slide appear for 20 seconds, the second slide for 1 minute, and so on. You can set timings by clicking the Rehearse Timings button in the Set Up group on the Slide Show tab. Slide Show view opens and the Recording toolbar shown in Figure C-16 opens. It contains buttons to pause between slides and to advance to the next slide. After opening the Recording toolbar, practice giving your presentation. PowerPoint keeps track of how long each slide appears and sets the timing accordingly. When you are finished rehearsing, PowerPoint displays the total recorded time for the presentation. The next time you run the slide show, you can use the timings you rehearsed.

FIGURE C-16: **Recording toolbar**

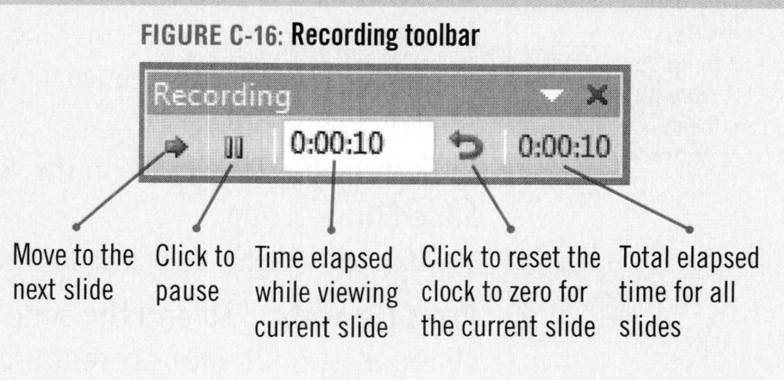

PowerPoint 2010

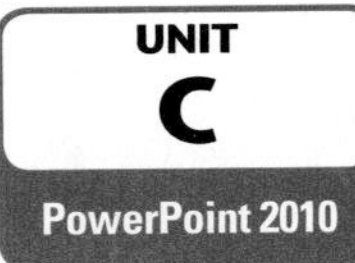

Animating Objects

Animations let you control how objects and text appear on the screen during a slide show and allow you to manage the flow of information and emphasize specific facts. You can animate text, pictures, sounds, hyperlinks, SmartArt diagrams, charts, and individual chart elements. For example, you can apply a Fade animation to bulleted text so that each paragraph enters the slide separately from the others. Animations are organized into four categories, Entrance, Emphasis, Exit, and Motion Paths. The Entrance and Exit animations cause an object to enter or exit the slide with an effect. An Emphasis animation causes an object visible on the slide to have an effect and a Motion Path animation causes an object to move on a specified path on the slide. You animate the text and graphics of several slides in the presentation.

STEPS

1. **Double-click the Slide 9 thumbnail to return to Normal view, click the Animations tab on the Ribbon, then click the jellyfish picture**

   Text as well as other objects, like a picture, can be animated during a slide show.

QUICK TIP
There are additional animation options for each animation category located at the bottom of the animations gallery.

2. **Click the More button in the Animation group, point to each of the animation options in the gallery, then click Shape in the Entrance section**

   As you point to each animation option a Live Preview of the effect plays. Animations can be serious and business-like or humorous, so be sure to choose appropriate effects for your presentation. A small numeral 1, called an animation tag 1, appears at the top corner of the picture. **Animation tags** identify the order in which objects are animated during slide show.

3. **Click the Effect Options button in the Animation group, click Box, then click the Duration up arrow in the Timing group until 04.00 appears**

   Effect options change for each animation. Changing the shape of the animation to box complements the picture, and increasing its timing gives it a more dramatic effect. Compare your screen to Figure C-17.

4. **Click the bulleted list text object, click in the Animation group, then click Grow & Turn in the Entrance section**

   The text object is animated with the Grow & Turn animation. Each line of text has an animation tag with each paragraph displaying a different number. Accordingly, each paragraph is animated separately.

5. **Click the Effect Options button in the Animation group, click All at Once, click the Duration up arrow in the Timing group until 02.50 appears, then click the Preview button in the Preview group**

   Notice that the animation tags for each line of text in the text object now have the same numeral (2), indicating that each line of text animates at the same time after the jellyfish picture.

QUICK TIP
If you want to individually animate the parts of a grouped object, then you must ungroup the objects before you animate them.

6. **Click the Slide 12 thumbnail in the Slides tab, press [Shift], click the shapes object, release [Shift], click in the Animation group, scroll down, then click Loops in the Motion Paths section**

   A motion path object appears over the shapes object and identifies the direction and shape, or path, of the animation. When needed, you can move, resize, and change the direction of the motion path. Compare your screen to Figure C-18.

7. **Click the Slide Show tab on the Ribbon, then click the From Beginning button in the Start Slide Show group**

   The slide show begins from Slide 1. The animations make the presentation more interesting to view.

8. **Press [Spacebar] to end the slide show, add your name to the slides footer, save your changes, submit your presentation to your instructor, then close the presentation**

FIGURE C-17: Slide showing animation applied to picture

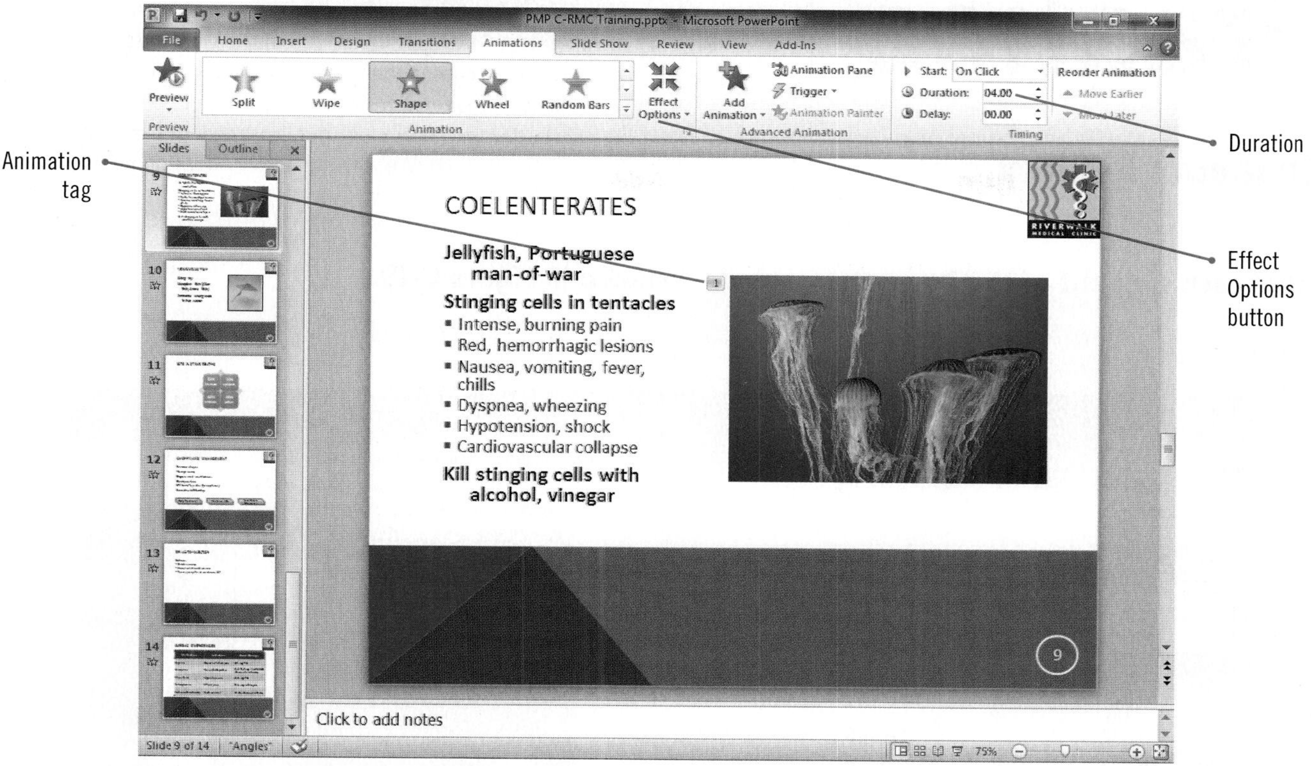

FIGURE C-18: Slide showing animated shapes object

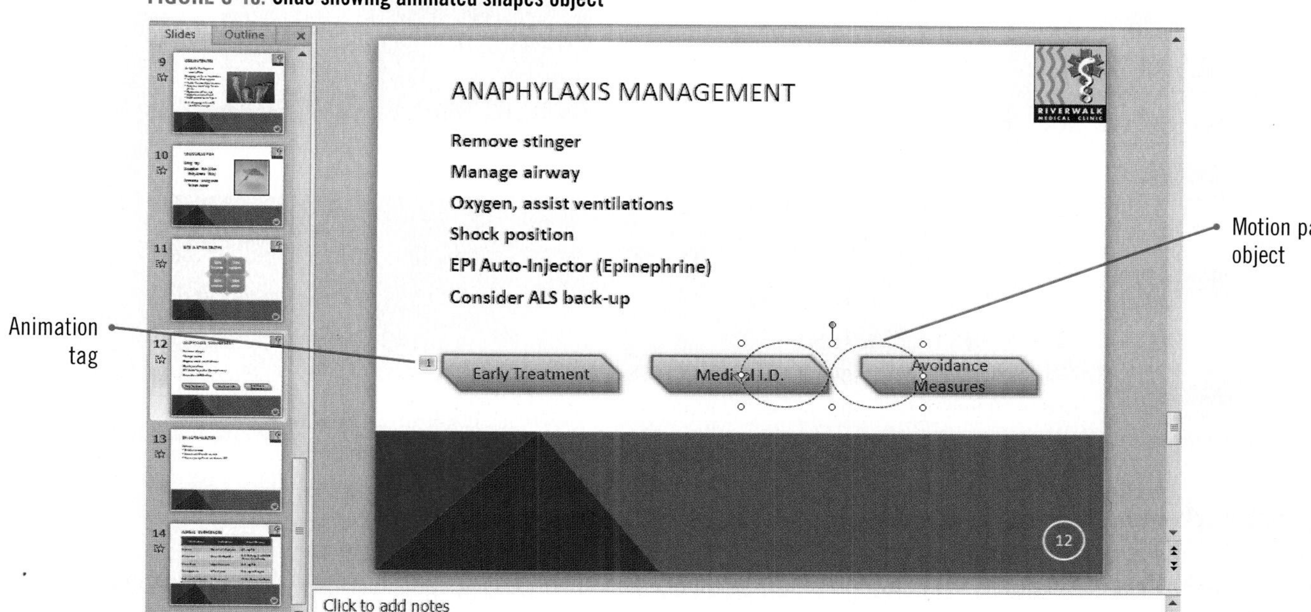

PowerPoint 2010

Saving a presentation as a video

You can save your PowerPoint presentation as a full-fidelity video, which incorporates all slide timings, transitions, animations, and narrations. The video can be distributed using a disc, the Web, or e-mail. Depending on how you want to display your video, you have three resolution settings from which to choose: Computer & HD Displays, Internet & DVD, and Portable Devices. The Large setting, Computer & HD Displays (960 × 720), is used for viewing on a computer monitor, projector, or other high definition displays. The Medium setting, Internet & DVD (640 × 480), is used for uploading to the Web or copying to a standard DVD. The Small setting, Portable Devices (320 × 240), is used on portable devices including portable media players such as Microsoft Zune. To save your presentation as a video, click the File tab, click Save & Send, click Create a Video, choose your settings, then click the Create Video button.

Practice

Concepts Review

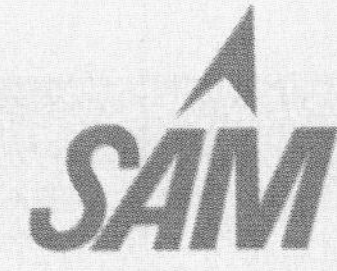

For current SAM information, including versions and content details, visit SAM Central (http://www.cengage.com/samcentral). If you have a SAM user profile, you may have access to hands-on instruction, practice, and assessment of the skills covered in this unit. Since various versions of SAM are supported throughout the life of this text, check with your instructor for the correct instructions and URL/Web site for accessing assignments.

Label each element of the PowerPoint window shown in Figure C-19.

FIGURE C-19

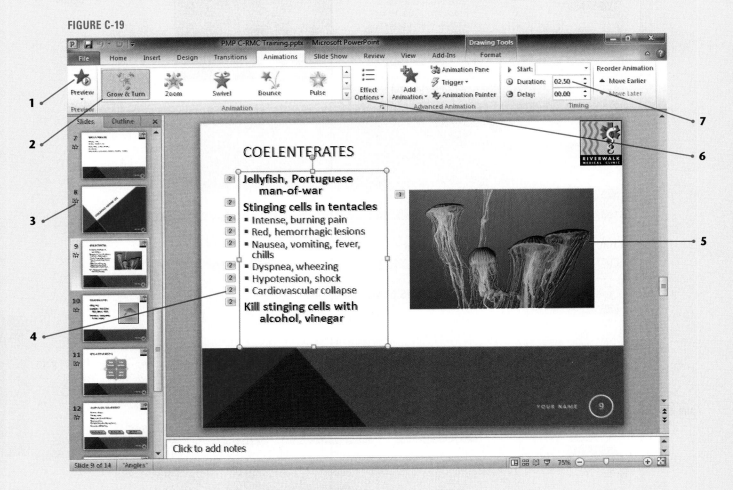

Match each term with the statement that best describes it.

8. **Animation tag**
9. **Crop**
10. **Transitions**
11. **Annotate**

a. Visual effects that determine how a slide moves in and out of view during a slide show
b. Identifies the order in which objects are animated
c. To draw on a slide during a slide show
d. Hides a portion of a picture

Select the best answer from the list of choices.

12. An object placed on the slide master defines which of the following items?

- **a.** Background graphic
- **b.** Logo
- **c.** Shape
- **d.** Master placeholder

13. According to this unit, which media type is defined as line art or art work created in another program?

- **a.** Picture
- **b.** Clip art
- **c.** Video
- **d.** Animation

14. The effect that controls how an object appears on the screen during a slide show is called a(n):

- **a.** Transition
- **b.** Animation
- **c.** Path
- **d.** Template

15. A presentation designed and formatted with background elements, colors, and other graphic elements that you can use to create a new presentation is a ______________.

- **a.** template
- **b.** theme
- **c.** video
- **d.** gallery

Skills Review

1. Insert text from Microsoft Word.

- **a.** Open the file PMP C-5.pptx from the drive and folder where you store your Data Files, then save it as **PMP C-Rescue**. You will work to create the completed presentation as shown in Figure C-20.
- **b.** Click Slide 4 in the Slides tab, then use the Slides from Outline command to insert the file PMP C-6.docx from the drive and folder where you store your Data Files.

FIGURE C-20

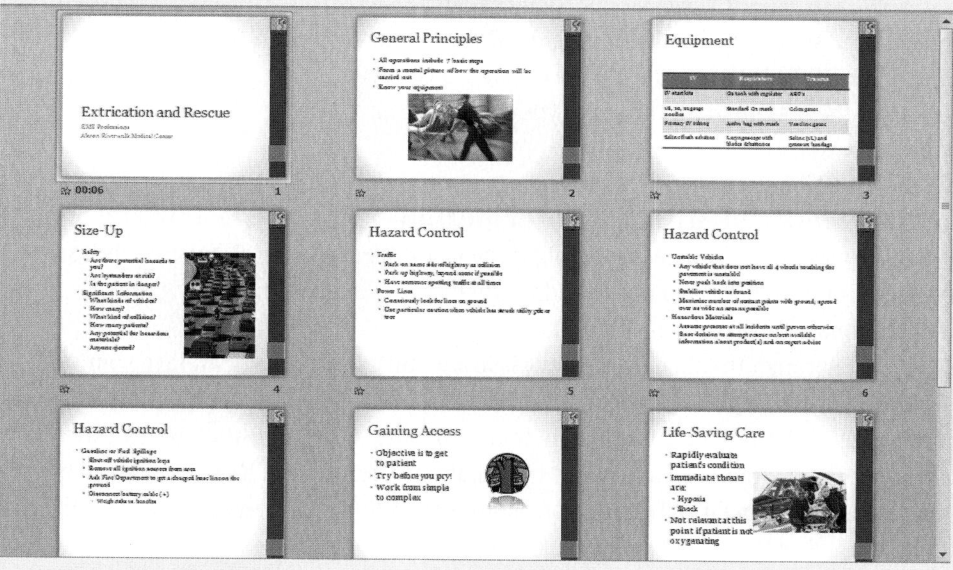

- **c.** In the Slides tab, drag Slide 7 above Slide 6.
- **d.** In the Slides tab, delete Slide 8, Hazard Control.
- **e.** Select Slides 5, 6, and 7 in the Slides tab, reset the slides to the default theme settings, then save your work.

2. Insert clip art.

- **a.** Select Slide 8, click the Clip Art icon in the content placeholder, then search for clip art using the keyword **accident**.
- **b.** Insert the clip art shown in Figure C-20, then close the Clip Art task pane.
- **c.** Click the Picture Effects button, point to Reflection, then click Tight Reflection, touching.
- **d.** Drag the clip art so its top lines up with the top of the text object, then save your changes.

Skills Review (continued)

3. **Insert and style a picture.**
   a. Select Slide 11, then insert the picture PMP C-7.jpg.
   b. Crop the rear wheel on the car from the right side of the picture, then resize the picture to fit the blank area of the slide.
   c. Drag the picture up so it lines up with the top of the text object.
   d. Click the Color button, change the picture color to Grayscale, then save your changes.
4. **Insert a table.**
   a. On Slide 3 insert a table with three columns and five rows.
   b. Enter the information shown in Table C-3, then change the table style to Medium Style 3 – Accent 3.
   c. In the Table Tools Layout tab, center the text in the top row, then distribute the table rows.
   d. Move the table to the center of the blank area of the slide, then save your changes.

TABLE C-3

IV	Respiratory	Trauma
IV start kits	O2 tank with regulator	ABD's
18, 20, 22 gauge needles	Standard O2 mask	Celox gauze
Primary IV tubing	Ambu bag with mask	Vaseline gauze
Saline flush solution	Laryngoscope with blades & batteries	Saline (1L) and pressure bandage

5. **Modify masters.**
   a. Open Slide Master view using the View tab, then click the Adjacency Slide Master thumbnail.
   b. Insert the picture PMP C-4.jpg, then resize the picture so it is 0.75" wide.
   c. Drag the picture to the upper-right corner of the slide within the design frame of the slide, then deselect the picture.
   d. Preserve the Agency master, switch to Normal view, then save your changes.
6. **Customize the background and theme.**
   a. Click the Design tab, then open the Background Styles gallery.
   b. Change the background style to Style 5, then click the Colors button.
   c. Click Concourse, click the Fonts button, scroll down, then click Civic.
   d. Check the spelling of the presentation, then save your changes.
7. **Use slide show commands.**
   a. Begin the slide show on Slide 1, then proceed to Slide 4.
   b. Use the Pen to circle the words **Significant Information**.
   c. Move to Slide 5, then use the Highlighter to highlight the words **Traffic** and **Power Lines**.
   d. Right-click the slide and go to Slide 1, move to Slide 4, then erase all ink on the slide.
   e. Move to Slide 5, then erase the ink on the slide.
   f. Press [Home], advance through the slide show, don't save any ink annotations, then save your work.
8. **Set slide transitions and timings.**
   a. Go to Slide Sorter view, click the Slide 1 thumbnail, then apply the Vortex transition to the slide.
   b. Change the effect option to From Bottom, change the duration speed to 3.00, then apply to all the slides.
   c. Change the slide timing to automatically transition slides every 6 seconds, then apply to all of the slides.
   d. Switch to Normal view, view the slide show, then save your work.
9. **Animate objects.**
   a. Go to Slide 3, click the Animations tab, then select the table.
   b. Apply the Swivel effect to the table, go to Slide 4, then apply the Float In effect to the title text object.
   c. Select the text object, click the More button in the Animation group, click More Entrance Effects, then apply an animation of your choice from the Exciting group.
   d. Edit the animations as needed, view the slide show, then save your changes.
   e. Submit your presentation to your instructor, close your presentation, and exit PowerPoint.

Independent Challenge 1

You work at the Duluth City Hospital and one of your jobs is to train emergency staff personnel. You have recently created a presentation on dealing with patients under the influence. You continue to work on the presentation by inserting objects and working with the slide background.

a. Open the file PMP C-8.pptx from the drive and folder where you store your Data Files, then save it as **PMP C-Lesson 1**.
b. Add your name as the footer on all of the slides, then apply the Median theme.
c. Create a new slide after Slide 7 with the Title and Content layout, then type **Drug Induced Emergencies** in the title text object.
d. Create a table with 3 columns and 4 rows, enter the data in Table C-4, center the top row of data, then distribute the rows of the table.
e. Insert clip art of a patient on Slide 6, then position, crop, and format as necessary. (*Hint*: Use the keyword **patient** to search for clips.)
f. Apply the Reveal transition to all the slides, then apply animations to objects on at least two slides.
g. Apply the Style 9 background style, then change the theme colors to Solstice.
h Check the spelling of the presentation, view the slide show, make any necessary changes, then save your work.
i. Submit the presentation to your instructor, then close the presentation, and exit PowerPoint.

TABLE C-4

Medication	Usual Dosing	Indication
Activated Charcoal	1 tube	Medication overdose, poisoning
Cogentin	1 to 4 mg IM	Antipsychotic drug induced symptoms
Narcan	0.4 to 2 mg IV	Narcotic overdose

Independent Challenge 2

You work for the EMS department at Children's Hospital in Bradenton, Florida. You are in the process of developing a presentation on the basic components of the EMS system used by all the EMS providers in the city. You work on completing the presentation that you will give next week at an EMS conference. You insert an outline, a picture, and then apply transitions and slide timings.

a. Start PowerPoint, open the file PMP C-9.pptx from the drive and folder where you store your Data Files, and save it as **PMP C-EMS Basic**.
b. Add your name and today's date to Slide 1 in the Subtitle text box.
c. On Slide 7, click the Clip Art icon, locate an appropriate photograph for the slide, resize the picture, then use a picture effect.
d. Apply the background Style 11 to the presentation.
e. Insert the Word document file PMP C-10.docx to create additional slides from an outline after Slide 1.
f. Select Slides 2 and 3, then reset the slides to their default settings.
g. Change the layout on Slide 5 to the Two Content slide layout, then insert an appropriate clip art for the slide.
h. Format the clip art with a 3 pt Light Yellow, Accent 4 border.
i. Add the Flip transition and an 8 second automatic slide timing to all of the slides in the presentation, then view the final slide show.

Advanced Challenge Exercise

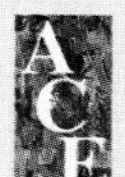

- Click the Slide Show tab, then click the Rehearse Timings button.
- Set slide timings for each slide in the presentation.
- Save new slide timings.

j. Check the spelling, save the presentation, submit the presentation to your instructor, close the file, and exit PowerPoint.

Real Life Independent Challenge

You work at the City Health Clinic in Casa Grande, Arizona, and you have been asked by your supervisor to create a presentation on poisonous snakes found in the southwest. The presentation will be used to educate students in public schools in and around Casa Grande. Your presentation should include the following topics: general facts on 2 or 3 different types of snakes, bite symptoms, and snakebite management. Use the Internet to research relevant information (*Internet connection required*). Create a presentation using your own pictures or pictures from the PowerPoint Clipart Organizer.

- **a.** Start PowerPoint, create a new blank presentation, and save it as **PMP C-Reptiles** to the drive and folder where you store your Data Files.
- **b.** Create slides to accommodate the information you find, then locate and insert the pictures you want to use.
- **c.** Animate objects on at least three slides, then format the animations as needed.
- **d.** Apply an appropriate design theme, then apply an appropriate title and your name to the title slide.
- **e.** Check the spelling, then view the final slide show and use slide show commands during the slide show.
- **f.** Add a slide number and your name as footer text to all of the slides, save your work, then submit your presentation to your instructor.
- **g.** Close the file, and exit PowerPoint.

Visual Workshop

Create a one-slide presentation that looks like Figure C-21. The slide layout shown in Figure C-21 is a specific layout designed for pictures. Insert the picture file PMP C-11.jpg to complete this presentation. Add your name as footer text to the slide, save the presentation as **PMP C-City Service** to the drive and folder where you store your Data Files, check the spelling of the presentation, then submit your presentation to your instructor.

FIGURE C-21

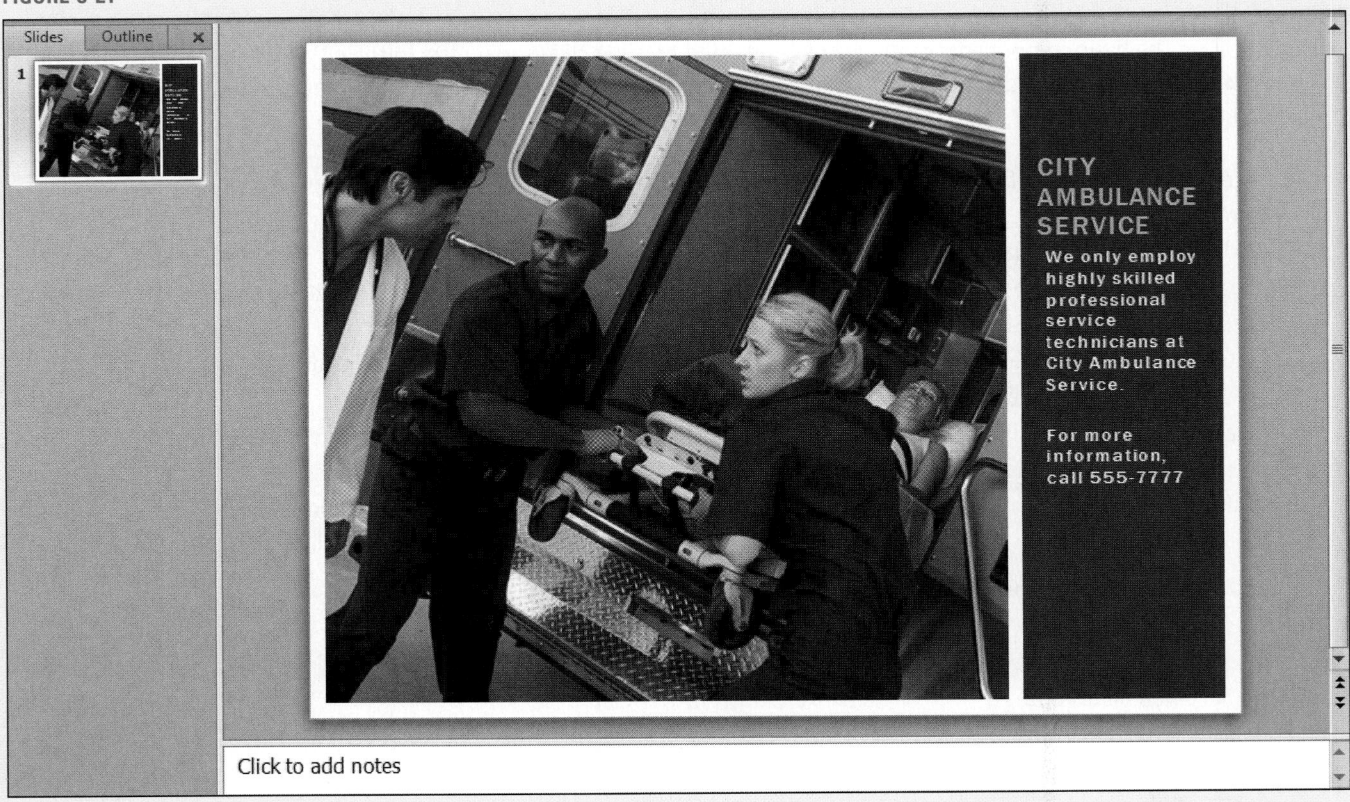

Appendix
Web Apps
Office 2010

Working with Windows Live and Office Web Apps

Files You Will Need:
WEB-1.pptx
WEB-2.xlsx

If the computer you are using has an active Internet connection, you can go to the Microsoft Windows Live Web site and access a wide variety of services and Web applications. For example, you can check your e-mail through Windows Live, network with your friends and coworkers, and use SkyDrive to store and share files. From SkyDrive, you can also use Office Web Apps to create and edit Word, PowerPoint, Excel, and OneNote files, even when you are using a computer that does not have Office 2010 installed. You work in the Vancouver branch of Quest Specialty Travel. Your supervisor, Mary Lou Jacobs, asks you to explore Windows Live and learn how she can use SkyDrive and Office Web Apps to work with her files online.

(*Note*: SkyDrive and Office Web Apps are dynamic Web pages, and might change over time, including the way they are organized and how commands are performed. The steps and figures in this appendix were accurate at the time this book was published.)

OBJECTIVES

- Explore how to work online from Windows Live
- Obtain a Windows Live ID and sign in to Windows Live
- Upload files to Windows Live
- Work with the PowerPoint Web App
- Create folders and organize files on SkyDrive
- Add people to your network and share files
- Work with the Excel Web App

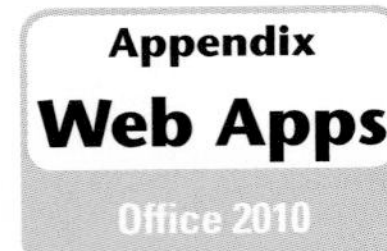

Exploring How to Work Online from Windows Live

You can use your Web browser to upload your files to Windows Live from any computer connected to the Internet. You can work on the files right in your Web browser using Office Web Apps and share your files with people in your Windows Live network. You review the concepts and services related to working online from Windows Live.

DETAILS

- **What is Windows Live?**

  Windows Live is a collection of services and Web applications that you can use to help you be more productive both personally and professionally. For example, you can use Windows Live to send and receive e-mail, to chat with friends via instant messaging, to share photos, to create a blog, and to store and edit files using SkyDrive. Table WEB-1 describes the services available on Windows Live. Windows Live is a free service that you sign up for. When you sign up, you receive a Windows Live ID, which you use to sign in to Windows Live. When you work with files on Windows Live, you are cloud computing.

- **What is Cloud Computing?**

  The term **cloud computing** refers to the process of working with files online in a Web browser. When you save files to SkyDrive on Windows Live, you are saving your files to an online location. SkyDrive is like having a personal hard drive in the cloud.

- **What is SkyDrive?**

  SkyDrive is an online storage and file sharing service. With a Windows Live account, you receive access to your own SkyDrive, which is your personal storage area on the Internet. On your SkyDrive, you are given space to store up to 25 GB of data online. Each file can be a maximum size of 50 MB. You can also use SkyDrive to access Office Web Apps, which you use to create and edit files created in Word, OneNote, PowerPoint, and Excel online in your Web browser.

- **Why use Windows Live and SkyDrive?**

  On Windows Live, you use SkyDrive to access additional storage for your files. You don't have to worry about backing up your files to a memory stick or other storage device that could be lost or damaged. Another advantage of storing your files on SkyDrive is that you can access your files from any computer that has an active Internet connection. Figure WEB-1 shows the SkyDrive Web page that appears when accessed from a Windows Live account. From SkyDrive, you can also access Office Web Apps.

- **What are Office Web Apps?**

  Office Web Apps are versions of Microsoft Word, Excel, PowerPoint, and OneNote that you can access online from your SkyDrive. An Office Web App does not include all of the features and functions included with the full Office version of its associated application. However, you can use the Office Web App from any computer that is connected to the Internet, even if Microsoft Office 2010 is not installed on that computer.

- **How do SkyDrive and Office Web Apps work together?**

  You can create a file in Office 2010 using Word, Excel, PowerPoint, or OneNote and then upload the file to your SkyDrive. You can then open the Office file saved to SkyDrive and edit it using your Web browser and the corresponding Office Web App. Figure WEB-2 shows a PowerPoint presentation open in the PowerPoint Web App. You can also use an Office Web App to create a new file, which is saved automatically to SkyDrive while you work. In addition, you can download a file created with an Office Web App and continue to work with the file in the full version of the corresponding Office application: Word, Excel, PowerPoint, or OneNote. Finally, you can create a SkyDrive network that consists of the people you want to be able to view your folders and files on your SkyDrive. You can give people permission to view and edit your files using any computer with an active Internet connection and a Web browser.

FIGURE WEB-1: **SkyDrive on Windows Live**

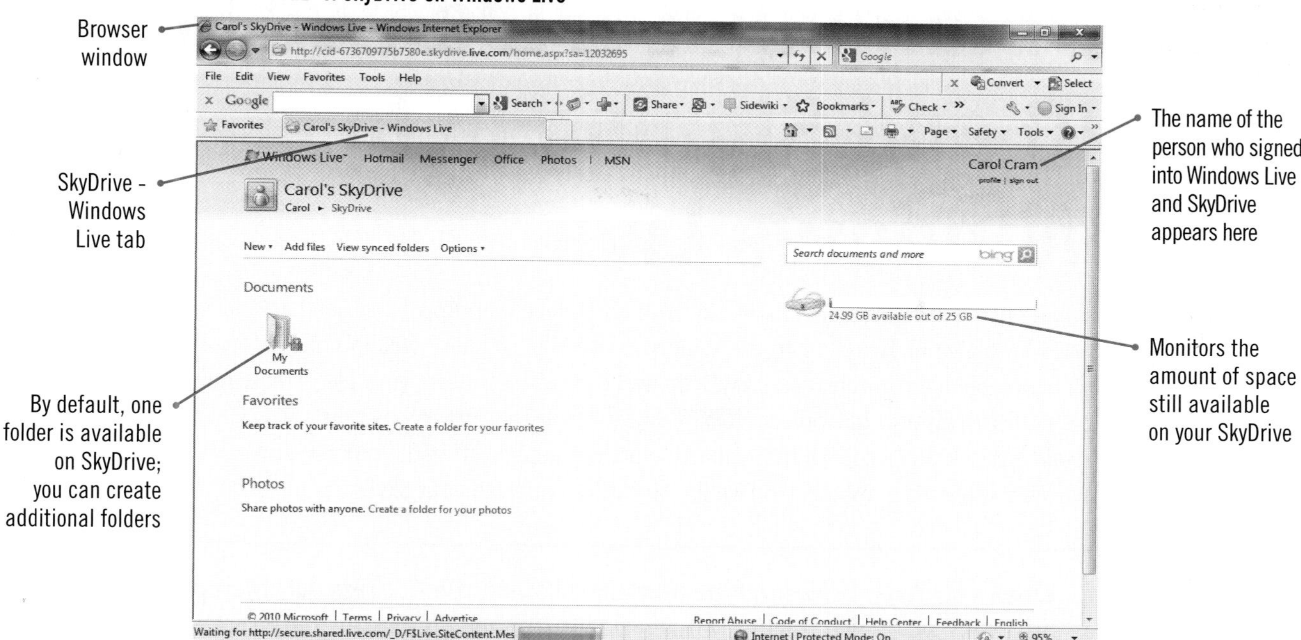
Browser window
SkyDrive - Windows Live tab
By default, one folder is available on SkyDrive; you can create additional folders
The name of the person who signed into Windows Live and SkyDrive appears here
Monitors the amount of space still available on your SkyDrive
Carol's SkyDrive
Documents
Favorites
Photos
24.99 GB available out of 25 GB

FIGURE WEB-2: **PowerPoint presentation open in the PowerPoint Web App**

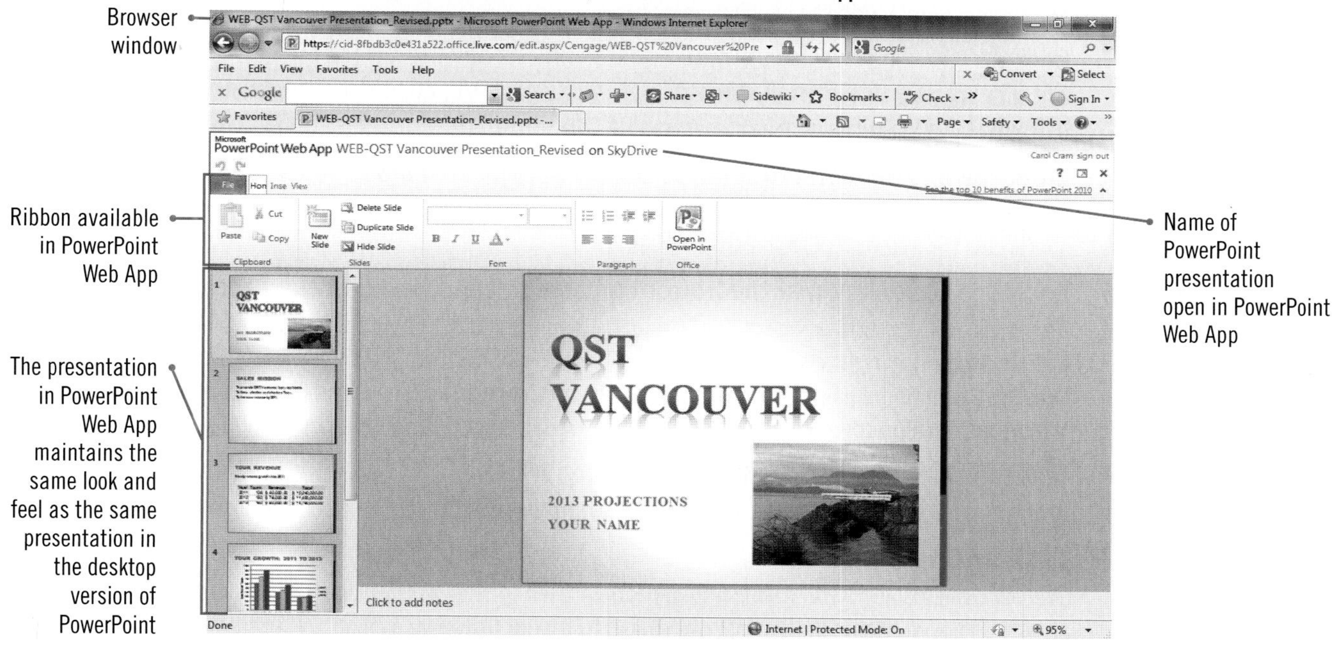
Browser window
Ribbon available in PowerPoint Web App
The presentation in PowerPoint Web App maintains the same look and feel as the same presentation in the desktop version of PowerPoint
Name of PowerPoint presentation open in PowerPoint Web App
QST VANCOUVER
2013 PROJECTIONS
YOUR NAME
Click to add notes

TABLE WEB-1: **Services available via Windows Live**

service	description
E-mail	Send and receive e-mail using a Hotmail account
Instant Messaging	Use Messenger to chat with friends, share photos, and play games
SkyDrive	Store files, work on files using Office Web Apps, and share files with people in your network
Photos	Upload and share photos with friends
People	Develop a network of friends and coworkers, then use the network to distribute information and stay in touch
Downloads	Access a variety of free programs available for download to a PC
Mobile Device	Access applications for a mobile device: text messaging, using Hotmail, networking, and sharing photos

Appendix
Web Apps
Office 2010

Obtaining a Windows Live ID and Signing In to Windows Live

To work with your files online using SkyDrive and Office Web Apps, you need a Windows Live ID. You obtain a Windows Live ID by going to the Windows Live Web site and creating a new account. Once you have a Windows Live ID, you can access SkyDrive and then use it to store your files, create new files, and share your files with friends and coworkers. Mary Lou Jacobs, your supervisor at QST Vancouver, asks you to obtain a Windows Live ID so that you can work on documents with your coworkers. You go to the Windows Live Web site, create a Windows Live ID, and then sign in to your SkyDrive.

STEPS

QUICK TIP
If you already have a Windows Live ID, go to the next lesson and sign in as directed using your account.

1. **Open your Web browser, type home.live.com in the Address bar, then press [Enter]**
   The Windows Live home page opens. From this page, you can create a Windows Live account and receive your Windows Live ID.
2. **Click the Sign up button *(Note: You may see a Sign up link instead of a button)***
   The Create your Windows Live ID page opens.
3. **Click the Or use your own e-mail address link under the Check availability button or if you are already using Hotmail, Messenger, or Xbox LIVE, click the Sign in now link in the Information statement near the top of the page**
4. **Enter the information required, as shown in Figure WEB-3**
   If you wish, you can sign up for a Windows Live e-mail address such as yourname@live.com so that you can also access the Windows Live e-mail services.

TROUBLE
The code can be difficult to read. If you receive an error message, enter the new code that appears.

5. **Enter the code shown at the bottom of your screen, then click the I accept button**
   The Windows Live home page opens. The name you entered when you signed up for your Windows Live ID appears in the top right corner of the window to indicate that you are signed in to Windows Live. From the Windows Live home page, you can access all the services and applications offered by Windows Live. See the Verifying your Windows Live ID box for information on finalizing your account set up.
6. **Point to Windows Live, as shown in Figure WEB-4**
   A list of options appears. SkyDrive is one of the options you can access directly from Windows Live.

TROUBLE
Click I accept if you are asked to review and accept the Windows Live Service Agreement and Privacy Statement.

7. **Click SkyDrive**
   The SkyDrive page opens. Your name appears in the top right corner, and the amount of space available is shown on the right side of the SkyDrive page. The amount of space available is monitored, as indicated by the gauge that fills with color as space is used. Using SkyDrive, you can add files to the existing folder and you can create new folders.
8. **Click sign out in the top right corner under your name, then exit the Web browser**
   You are signed out of your Windows Live account. You can sign in again directly from the Windows Live page in your browser or from within a file created with PowerPoint, Excel, Word, or OneNote.

FIGURE WEB-3: **Creating a Windows Live ID**

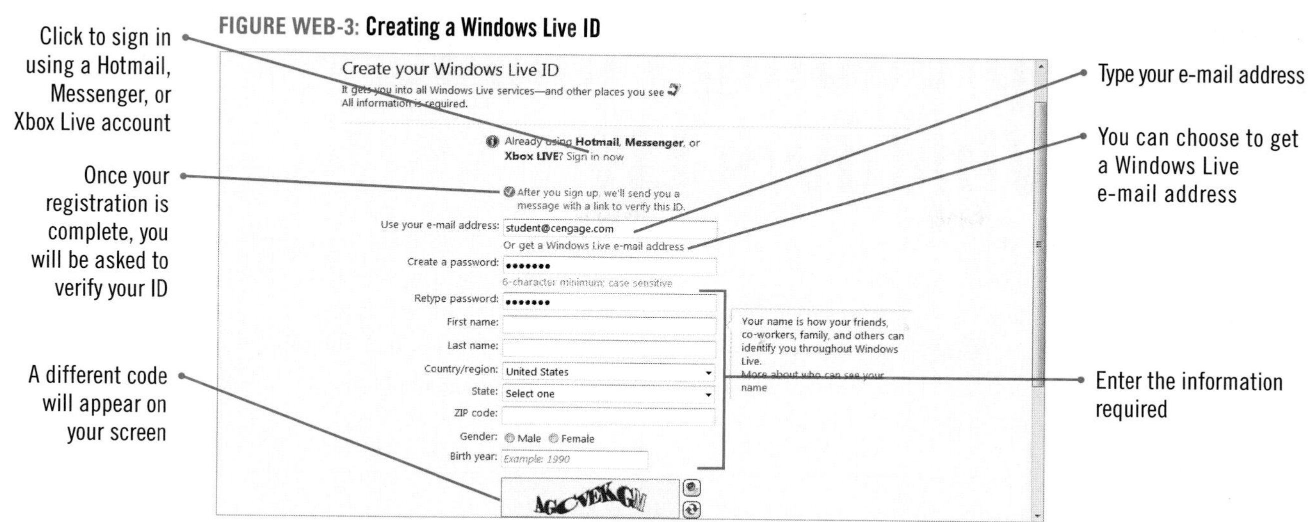

FIGURE WEB-4: **Selecting SkyDrive**

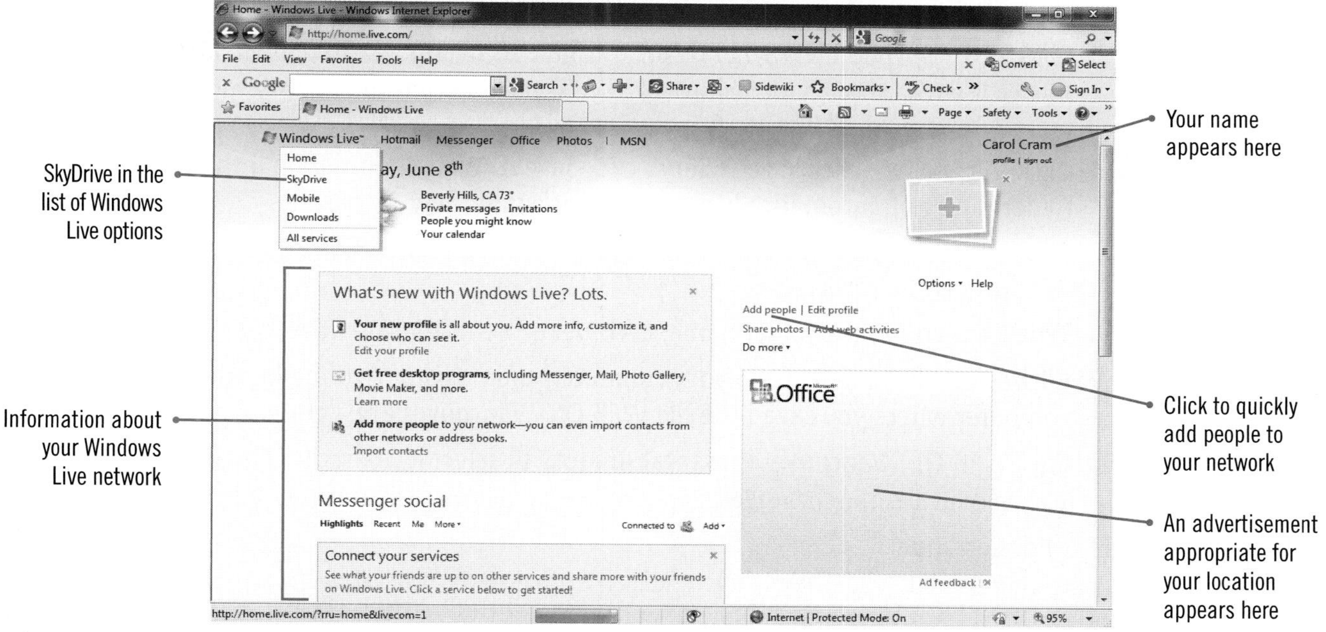

Verifying your Windows Live ID

As soon as you accept the Windows Live terms, an e-mail is sent to the e-mail address you supplied when you created your Windows Live ID. Open your e-mail program, and then open the e-mail from Microsoft with the Subject line: Confirm your e-mail address for Windows Live. Follow the simple, step-by-step instructions in the e-mail to confirm your Windows Live ID. When the confirmation is complete, you will be asked to sign in to Windows Live, using your e-mail address and password. Once signed in, you will see your Windows Live Account page.

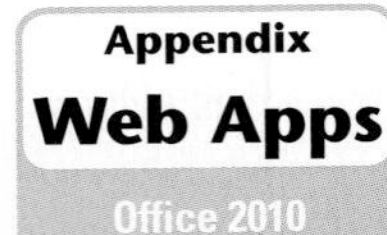

Uploading Files to Windows Live

Once you have created your Windows Live ID, you can sign in to Windows Live directly from Word, PowerPoint, Excel, or OneNote and start saving and uploading files. You upload files to your SkyDrive so you can share the files with other people, access the files from another computer, or use SkyDrive's additional storage. You open a PowerPoint presentation, access your Windows Live account from Backstage view, and save a file to SkyDrive on Windows Live. You also create a new folder called Cengage directly from Backstage view and add a file to it.

STEPS

1. **Start PowerPoint, open the file WEB-1.pptx from the drive and folder where you store your Data Files, then save the file as WEB-QST Vancouver Presentation**
2. **Click the File tab, then click Save & Send**
   The Save & Send options available in PowerPoint are listed in Backstage view, as shown in Figure WEB-5.
3. **Click Save to Web**
4. **Click Sign In, type your e-mail address, press [Tab], type your password, then click OK**
   The My Documents folder on your SkyDrive appears in the Save to Windows Live SkyDrive information area.
5. **Click Save As, wait a few seconds for the Save As dialog box to appear, then click Save**
   The file is saved to the My Documents folder on the SkyDrive that is associated with your Windows Live account. You can also create a new folder and upload files directly to SkyDrive from your hard drive.
6. **Click the File tab, click Save & Send, click Save to Web, then sign in if the My Documents folder does not automatically appear in Backstage view**
7. **Click the New Folder button in the Save to Windows Live SkyDrive pane, then sign in to Windows Live if directed**
8. **Type Cengage as the folder name, click Next, then click Add files**
9. **Click select documents from your computer, then navigate to the location on your computer where you saved the file WEB-QST Vancouver Presentation in Step 1**
10. **Click WEB-QST Vancouver Presentation.pptx to select it, then click Open**
    You can continue to add more files; however, you have no more files to upload at this time.
11. **Click Continue**
    In a few moments, the PowerPoint presentation is uploaded to your SkyDrive, as shown in Figure WEB-6. You can simply store the file on SkyDrive or you can choose to work on the presentation using the PowerPoint Web App.
12. **Click the PowerPoint icon on your taskbar to return to PowerPoint, then close the presentation and exit PowerPoint**

QUICK TIP
Skip this step if the computer you are using signs you in automatically.

FIGURE WEB-5: Save & Send options in Backstage view

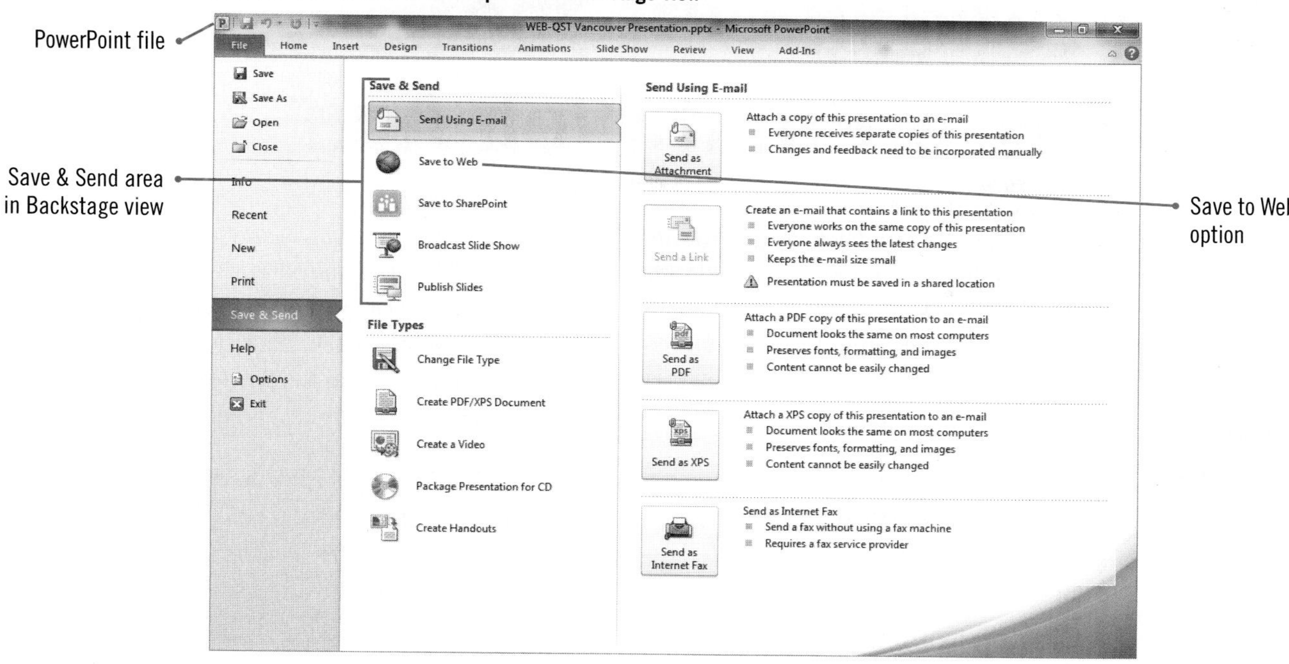

FIGURE WEB-6: File uploaded to the Cengage folder on Windows Live

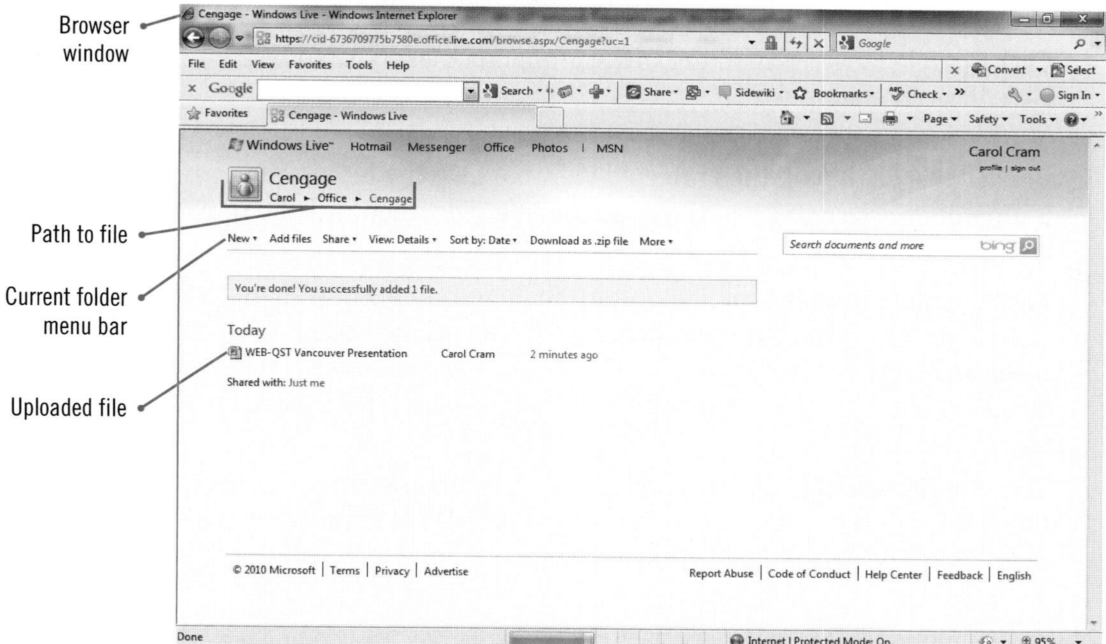

Appendix
Web Apps
Office 2010

Working with the PowerPoint Web App

Once you have uploaded a file to SkyDrive on Windows Live, you can work on it using its corresponding Office Web App. **Office Web Apps** provide you with the tools you need to view documents online and to edit them right in your browser. You do not need to have Office programs installed on the computer you use to access SkyDrive and Office Web Apps. From SkyDrive, you can also open the document directly in the full Office application (for example, PowerPoint) if the application is installed on the computer you are using. You use the PowerPoint Web App to make some edits to the PowerPoint presentation. You then open the presentation in PowerPoint and use the full version to make additional edits.

STEPS

TROUBLE
Click the browser button on the taskbar, then click the Windows Live SkyDrive window to make it the active window.

1. **Click the WEB-QST Vancouver Presentation file in the Cengage folder on SkyDrive**
   The presentation opens in your browser window. A menu is available, which includes the options you have for working with the file.
2. **Click Edit in Browser, then if a message appears related to installing the Sign-in Assistant, click the Close button to the far right of the message**
   In a few moments, the PowerPoint presentation opens in the PowerPoint Web App, as shown in Figure WEB-7. Table WEB-2 lists the commands you can perform using the PowerPoint Web App.

QUICK TIP
The changes you make to the presentation are saved automatically on SkyDrive.

3. **Enter your name where indicated on Slide 1, click Slide 3 (New Tours) in the Slides pane, then click Delete Slide in the Slides group**
   The slide is removed from the presentation. You decide to open the file in the full version of PowerPoint on your computer so you can apply WordArt to the slide title. You work with the file in the full version of PowerPoint when you want to use functions, such as WordArt, that are not available on the PowerPoint Web App.
4. **Click Open in PowerPoint in the Office group, click OK in response to the message, then click Allow if requested**
   In a few moments, the revised version of the PowerPoint slide opens in PowerPoint on your computer.
5. **Click Enable Editing on the Protected View bar near the top of your presentation window if prompted, select QST Vancouver on the title slide, then click the Drawing Tools Format tab**

QUICK TIP
Use the ScreenTips to help you find the required WordArt style.

6. **Click the More button in the WordArt Styles group to show the selection of WordArt styles, select the WordArt style Gradient Fill - Blue-Gray, Accent 4, Reflection, then click a blank area outside the slide**
   The presentation appears in PowerPoint as shown in Figure WEB-8. Next, you save the revised version of the file to SkyDrive.
7. **Click the File tab, click Save As, notice that the path in the Address bar is to the Cengage folder on your Windows Live SkyDrive, type WEB-QST Vancouver Presentation_Revised.pptx in the File name text box, then click Save**
   The file is saved to your SkyDrive.

TROUBLE
The browser opens to the Cengage folder but the file is not visible. Follow Step 8 to open the Cengage folder and refresh thelist of files in the folder.

8. **Click the browser icon on the taskbar to open your SkyDrive page, then click Office next to your name in the SkyDrive path, view a list of recent documents, then click Cengage in the list to the left of the recent documents list to open the Cengage folder**
   Two PowerPoint files now appear in the Cengage folder.
9. **Exit the Web browser and close all tabs if prompted, then exit PowerPoint**

FIGURE WEB-7: **Presentation opened in the PowerPoint Web App from Windows Live**

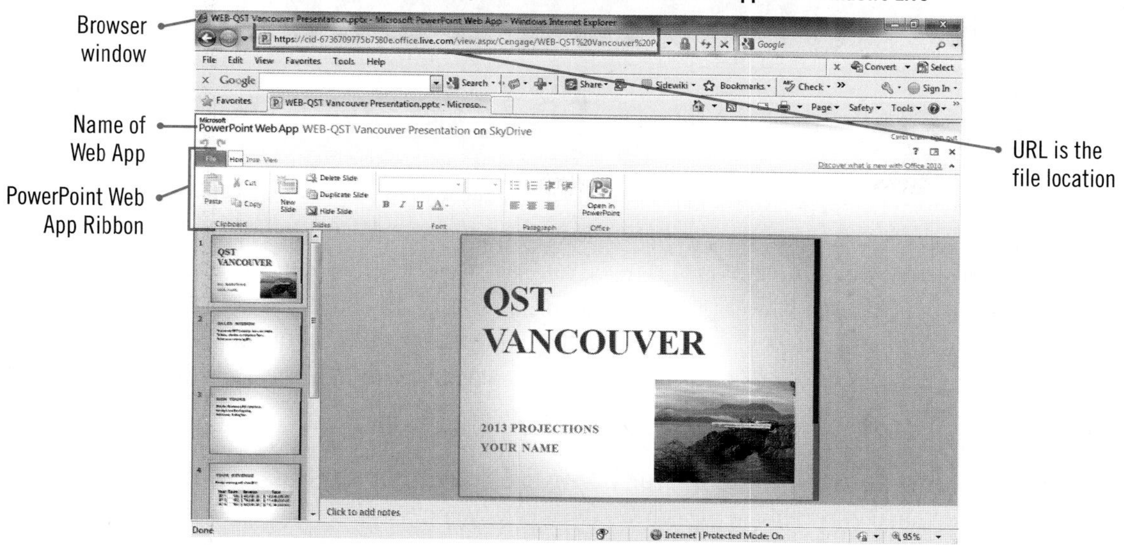

FIGURE WEB-8: **Revised PowerPoint presentation**

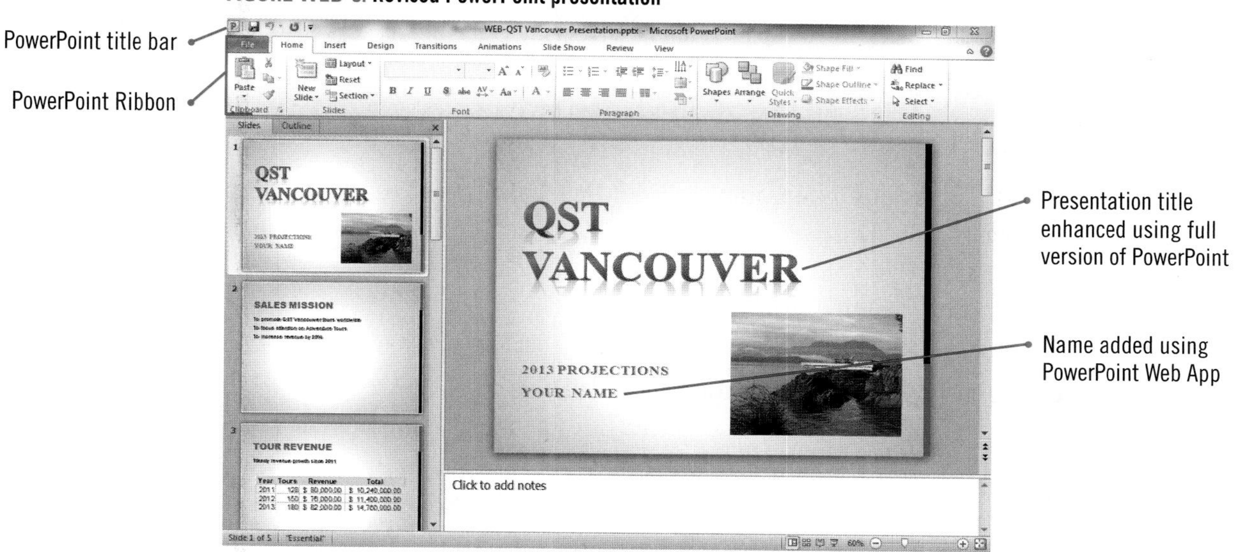

TABLE WEB-2: **Commands on the PowerPoint Web App**

tab	commands available
File	• Open in PowerPoint: select to open the file in PowerPoint on your computer • Where's the Save Button?: when you click this option, a message appears telling you that you do not need to save your presentation when you are working on it with PowerPoint Web App. The presentation is saved automatically as you work. • Print • Share • Properties • Give Feedback • Privacy • Terms of Use • Close
Home	• Clipboard group: Cut, Copy, Paste • Slides group: Add a New Slide, Delete a Slide, Duplicate a Slide, and Hide a Slide • Font group: Work with text: change the font, style, color, and size of selected text • Paragraph group: Work with paragraphs: add bullets and numbers, indent text, align text • Office group: Open the file in PowerPoint on your computer
Insert	• Insert a Picture • Insert a SmartArt diagram • Insert a link such as a link to another file on SkyDrive or to a Web page
View	• Editing view (the default) • Reading view • Slide Show view • Notes view

Appendix
Web Apps
Office 2010

Creating Folders and Organizing Files on SkyDrive

As you have learned, you can sign in to SkyDrive directly from the Office applications PowerPoint, Excel, Word, and OneNote, or you can access SkyDrive directly through your Web browser. This option is useful when you are away from the computer on which you normally work or when you are using a computer that does not have Office applications installed. You can go to SkyDrive, create and organize folders, and then create or open files to work on with Office Web Apps. You access SkyDrive from your Web browser, create a new folder called Illustrated, and delete one of the PowerPoint files from the My Documents folder.

STEPS

TROUBLE
Go to Step 3 if you are already signed in.

TROUBLE
Type your Windows Live ID (your e-mail) and password, then click Sign in if prompted to do so.

1. **Open your Web browser, type home.live.com in the Address bar, then press [Enter]**
   The Windows Live home page opens. From here, you can sign in to your Windows Live account and then access SkyDrive.
2. **Sign into Windows Live as directed**
   You are signed in to your Windows Live page. From this page, you can take advantage of the many applications available on Windows Live, including SkyDrive.
3. **Point to Windows Live, then click SkyDrive**
   SkyDrive opens.
4. **Click Cengage, then point to WEB-QST Vancouver Presentation.pptx**
   A menu of options for working with the file, including a Delete button to the far right, appears to the right of the filename.
5. **Click the Delete button ☒, then click OK**
   The file is removed from the Cengage folder on your SkyDrive. You still have a copy of the file on your computer.
6. **Point to Windows Live, then click SkyDrive**
   Your SkyDrive screen with the current selection of folders available on your SkyDrive opens, as shown in Figure WEB-9.
7. **Click New, click Folder, type Illustrated, click Next, click Office in the path under Add documents to Illustrated at the top of the window, then click View all in the list under Personal**
   You are returned to your list of folders, where you see the new Illustrated folder.
8. **Click Cengage, point to WEB-QST Vancouver Presentation_Revised.pptx, click More, click Move, then click the Illustrated folder**
9. **Click Move this file into Illustrated, as shown in Figure WEB-10**
   The file is moved to the Illustrated folder.

FIGURE WEB-9: Folders on your SkyDrive

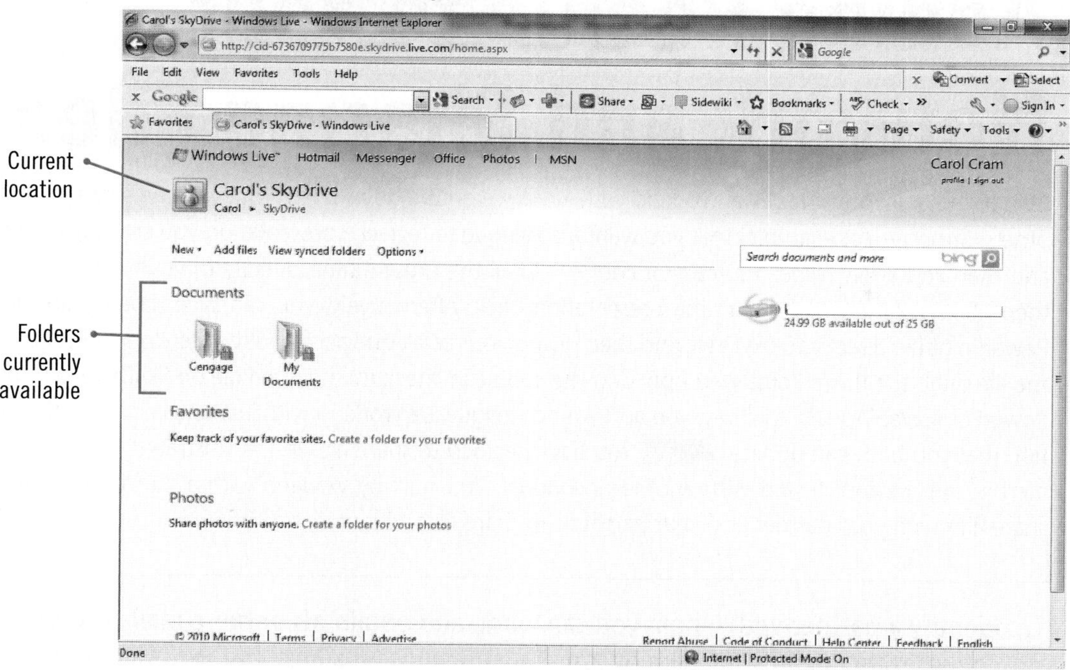

FIGURE WEB-10: Moving a file to the Illustrated folder

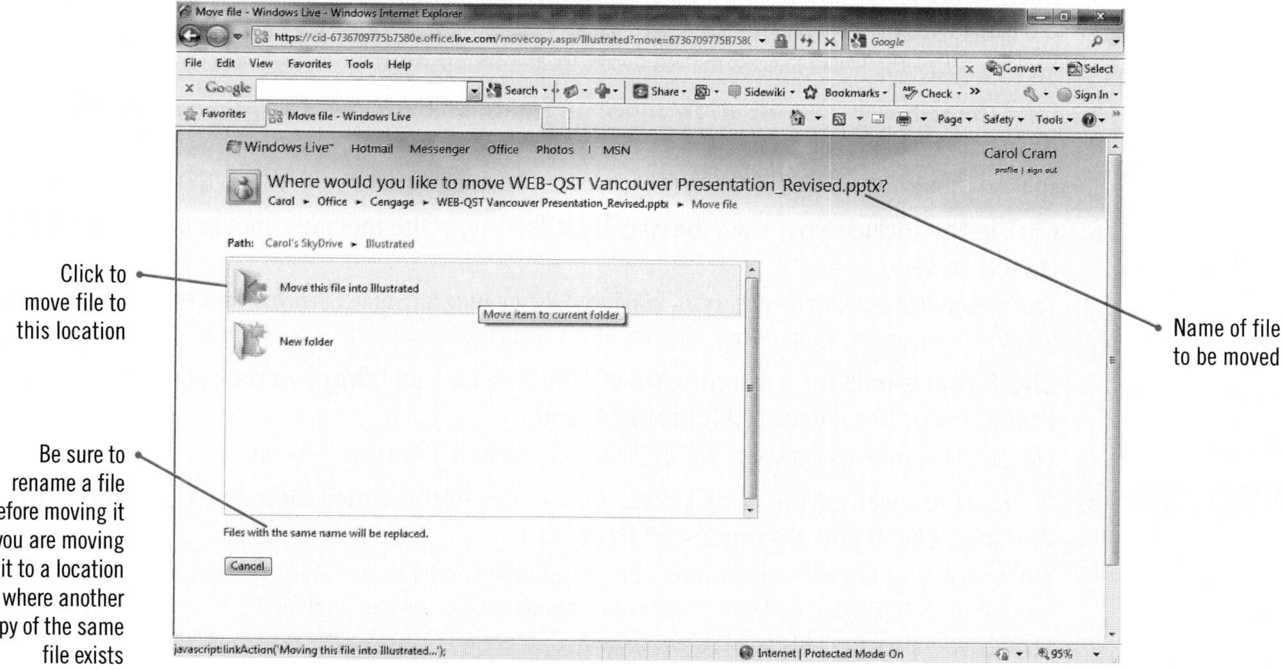

Appendix
Web Apps
Office 2010

Adding People to Your Network and Sharing Files

One of the great advantages of working with SkyDrive on Windows Live is that you can share your files with others. Suppose, for example, that you want a colleague to review a presentation you created in PowerPoint and then add a new slide. You can, of course, e-mail the presentation directly to your colleague, who can then make changes and e-mail the presentation back. Alternatively, you can save time by uploading the PowerPoint file directly to SkyDrive and then giving your colleague access to the file. Your colleague can edit the file using the PowerPoint Web App, and then you can check the updated file on SkyDrive, also using the PowerPoint Web App. In this way, you and your colleague are working with just one version of the presentation that you both can update. You have decided to share files in the Illustrated folder that you created in the previous lesson with another individual. You start by working with a partner so that you can share files with your partner and your partner can share files with you.

STEPS

TROUBLE
If you cannot find a partner, read the steps so you understand how the process works.

1. **Identify a partner with whom you can work, and obtain his or her e-mail address; you can choose someone in your class or someone on your e-mail list, but it should be someone who will be completing these steps when you are**
2. **From the Illustrated folder, click Share**
3. **Click Edit permissions**
   The Edit permissions page opens. On this page, you can select the individual with whom you would like to share the contents of the Illustrated folder.
4. **Click in the Enter a name or an e-mail address text box, type the e-mail address of your partner, then press [Tab]**
   You can define the level of access that you want to give your partner.
5. **Click the Can view files list arrow shown in Figure WEB-11, click Can add, edit details, and delete files, then click Save**
   You can choose to send a notification to each individual when you grant permission to access your files.
6. **Click in the Include your own message text box, type the message shown in Figure WEB-12, then click Send**
   Your partner will receive a message from Windows Live advising him or her that you have shared your Illustrated folder. If your partner is completing the steps at the same time, you will receive an e-mail from your partner.
7. **Check your e-mail for a message from Windows Live advising you that your partner has shared his or her Illustrated folder with you**
   The subject of the e-mail message will be "[Name] has shared documents with you."
8. **If you have received the e-mail, click View folder in the e-mail message, then sign in to Windows Live if you are requested to do so**
   You are now able to access your partner's Illustrated folder on his or her SkyDrive. You can download files in your partner's Illustrated folder to your own computer where you can work on them and then upload them again to your partner's Illustrated shared folder.
9. **Exit the browser**

TROUBLE
If you do not receive a message from Windows Live, your partner has not yet completed the steps to share the Illustrated folder.

QUICK TIP
You will know you are on your partner's SkyDrive because you will see your partner's first name at the beginning of the SkyDrive path.

FIGURE WEB-11: **Editing folder permissions**

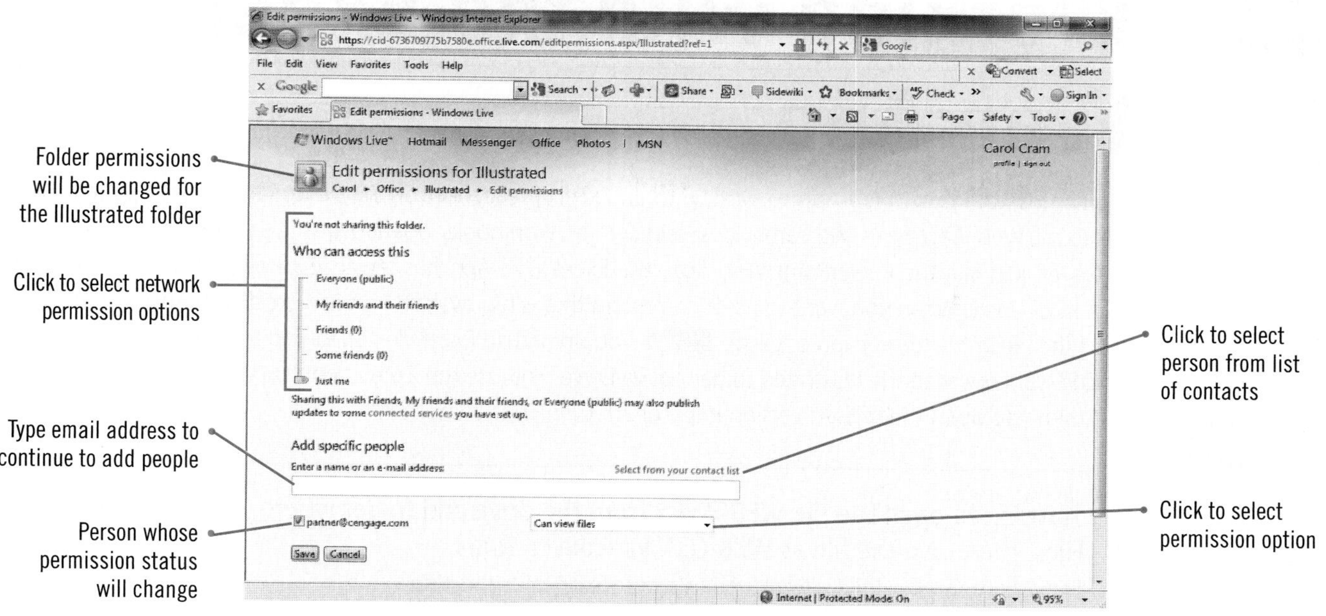

FIGURE WEB-12: **Entering a message to notify a person that file sharing permission has been granted**

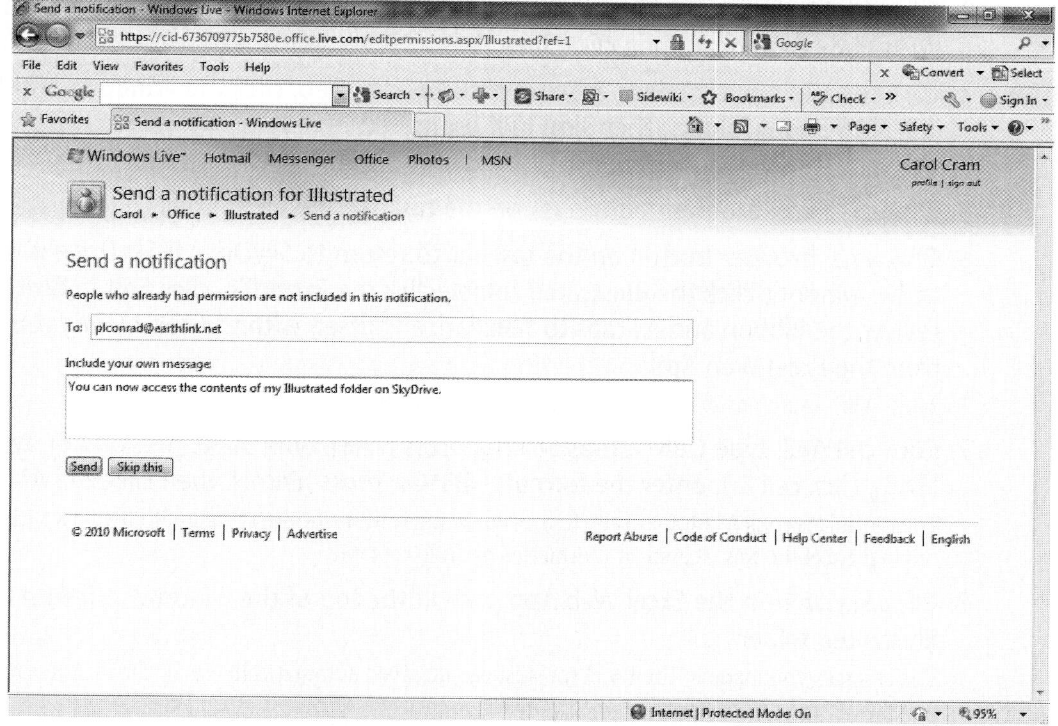

Sharing files on SkyDrive

When you share a folder with other people, the people with whom you share a folder can download the file to their computers and then make changes using the full version of the corresponding Office application. Once these changes are made, each individual can then upload the file to SkyDrive and into a folder shared with you and others. In this way, you can create a network of people with whom you share your files.

Appendix
Web Apps
Office 2010

Working with the Excel Web App

You can use the Excel Web App to work with an Excel spreadsheet on SkyDrive. Workbooks opened using the Excel Web App have the same look and feel as workbooks opened using the full version of Excel. However, just like the PowerPoint Web App, the Excel Web App has fewer features available than the full version of Excel. When you want to use a command that is not available on the Excel Web App, you need to open the file in the full version of Excel. You upload an Excel file containing a list of the tours offered by QST Vancouver to the Illustrated folder on SkyDrive. You use the Excel Web App to make some changes, and then you open the revised version in Excel 2010 on your computer.

STEPS

1. **Start Excel, open the file WEB-2.xlsx from the drive and folder where you store your Data Files, then save the file as WEB-QST Vancouver Tours**
   The data in the Excel file is formatted using the Excel table function.
2. **Click the File tab, click Save & Send, then click Save to Web**
   In a few moments, you should see three folders to which you can save spreadsheets. My Documents and Cengage are personal folder that contains files that only you can access. Illustrated is a shared folder that contains files you can share with others in your network. The Illustrated folder is shared with your partner.
3. **Click the Illustrated folder, click the Save As button, wait a few seconds for the Save As dialog box to appear, then click Save**
4. **Click the File tab, click Save & Send, click Save to Web, click the Windows Live SkyDrive link above your folders, then sign in if prompted**
   Windows Live opens to your SkyDrive.
5. **Click the Excel program button on the taskbar, then exit Excel**
6. **Click your browser button on the taskbar to return to SkyDrive if SkyDrive is not the active window, click the Illustrated folder, click the Excel file, click Edit in Browser, then review the Ribbon and its tabs to familiarize yourself with the commands you can access from the Excel Web App**
   Table WEB-3 summarizes the commands that are available.
7. **Click cell A12, type Gulf Islands Sailing, press [TAB], type 3000, press [TAB], type 10, press [TAB], click cell D3, enter the formula =B3*C3, press [Enter], then click cell A1**
   The formula is copied automatically to the remaining rows as shown in Figure WEB-13 because the data in the original Excel file was created and formatted as an Excel table.
8. **Click SkyDrive in the Excel Web App path at the top of the window to return to the Illustrated folder**
   The changes you made to the Excel spreadsheet are saved automatically on SkyDrive. You can download the file directly to your computer from SkyDrive.
9. **Point to the Excel file, click More, click Download, click Save, navigate to the location where you save the files for this book, name the file WEB-QST Vancouver Tours_Updated, click Save, then click Close in the Download complete dialog box**
   The updated version of the spreadsheet is saved on your computer and on SkyDrive.
10. **Exit the Web browser**

TROUBLE
If prompted, sign in to your Windows Live account as directed.

QUICK TIP
Alternately, you can open your Web browser and go to Windows Live to sign in to SkyDrive.

FIGURE WEB-13: **Updated table in the Excel Web App**

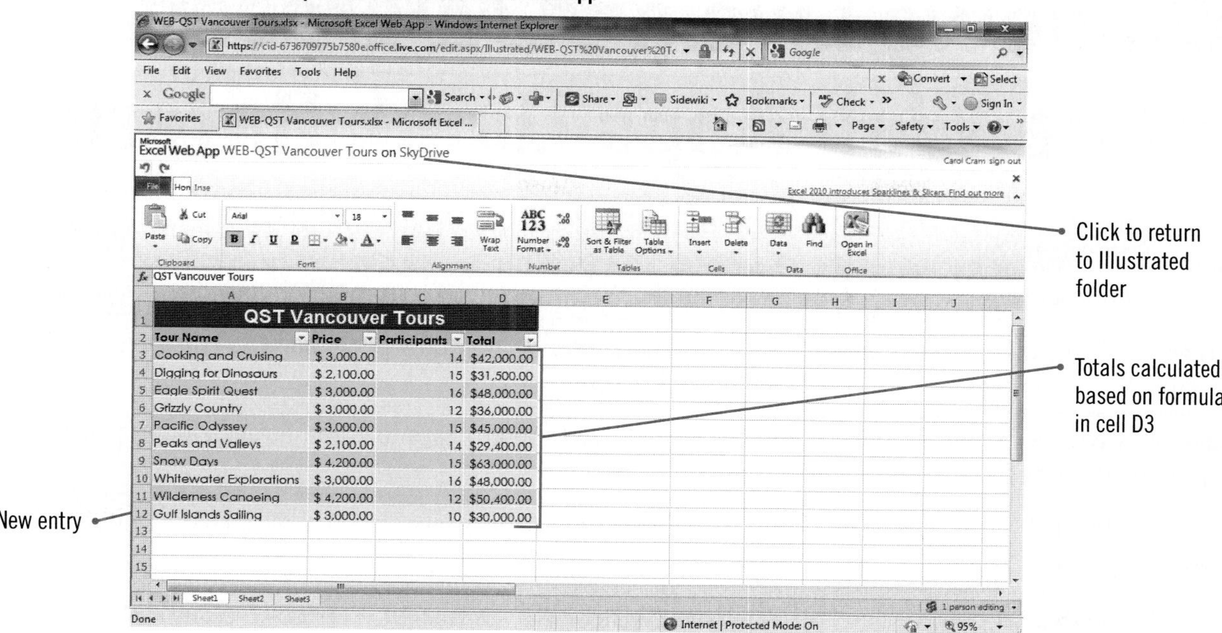

TABLE WEB-3: **Commands on the Excel Web App**

tab	commands available
File	• Open in Excel: select to open the file in Excel on your computer • Where's the Save Button?: when you click this option, a message appears telling you that you do not need to save your spreadsheet when you are working in it with Excel Web App; the spreadsheet is saved automatically as you work • Save As • Share • Download a Snapshot: a snapshot contains only the values and the formatting; you cannot modify a snapshot • Download a Copy: the file can be opened and edited in the full version of Excel • Give Feedback • Privacy Statement • Terms of Use • Close
Home	• Clipboard group: Cut, Copy, Paste • Font group: change the font, style, color, and size of selected labels and values, as well as border styles and fill colors • Alignment group: change vertical and horizontal alignment and turn on the Wrap Text feature • Number group: change the number format and increase or decrease decimal places • Tables: sort and filter data in a table and modify Table Options • Cells: insert and delete cells • Data: refresh data and find labels or values • Office: open the file in Excel on your computer
Insert	• Insert a Table • Insert a Hyperlink to a Web page

Exploring other Office Web Apps

Two other Office Web Apps are Word and OneNote. You can share files on SkyDrive directly from Word or from OneNote using the same method you used to share files from PowerPoint and Excel. After you upload a Word or OneNote file to SkyDrive, you can work with it in its corresponding Office Web App. To familiarize yourself with the commands available in an Office Web App, open the file and then review the commands on each tab on the Ribbon. If you want to perform a task that is not available in the Office Web App, open the file in the full version of the application.

In addition to working with uploaded files, you can create files from new on SkyDrive. Simply sign in to SkyDrive and open a folder. With a folder open, click New and then select the Web App you want to use to create the new file.

Windows Live and Microsoft Office Web Apps Quick Reference

To Do This	Go Here
Access Windows Live	From the Web browser, type **home.live.com**, then click Sign In
Access SkyDrive on Windows Live	From the Windows Live home page, point to Windows Live, then click SkyDrive
Save to Windows Live from Word, PowerPoint, or Excel	File tab | Save & Send | Save to Web | Select a folder | Save As
Create a New Folder from Backstage view	File tab | Save & Send | Save to Web | New Folder button
Edit a File with a Web App	From SkyDrive, click the file, then click Edit in Browser
Open a File in a desktop version of the application from a Web App: Word, Excel, PowerPoint	Click Open in [Application] in the Office group in each Office Web App
Share files on Windows Live	From SkyDrive, click the folder containing the files to share, click Share on the menu bar, click Edit permissions, enter the e-mail address of the person to share files with, click the Can view files list arrow, click Can add, edit details, and delete files, then click Save

Glossary

Absolute cell reference In a formula, a cell address that refers to a specific cell and does not change when you copy the formula; indicated by a dollar sign before the column letter and/or row number. *See also* Relative cell reference.

Accessories Simple Windows programs that perform specific tasks, such as the Calculator accessory for performing calculations.

Active The currently available document, program, or object; on the taskbar, when more than one program is open, the button for the active program appears slightly lighter.

Active cell The cell in which you are currently working.

Active window The window you are currently using; if multiple windows are open, the window with the darker title bar.

Address A sequence of drive and folder names that describes a folder's or file's location in the file hierarchy; the highest hierarchy level is on the left, with lower hierarchy levels separated by the symbol to its right.

Address bar In a window, the white area just below the title bar that shows the file hierarchy, or address of the files that appear in the file list below it; the address appears as a series of links (separated by the symbol) you can click to navigate to other locations on your computer.

Adjustment handle A small yellow diamond that changes the appearance of an object's most prominent feature.

Aero A Windows 7 viewing option that shows windows as translucent objects and features subtle animations; only available on a computer that has enough memory to support Aero and on which a Windows Aero theme has been selected.

Aero Flip 3D A Windows 7 feature that lets you preview all open folders and documents without using the taskbar and that displays open windows in a stack if you press [Ctrl][ ][Tab]; only available if using a Windows Aero theme.

Aero Peek A Windows 7 feature that lets you point to a taskbar icon representing an open program and see a thumbnail (small version) of the open file; only visible if the computer uses a Windows Aero theme.

Align To place objects' edges or centers on the same plane.

Alignment The placement of cell contents in relation to a cell's edges; for example, left-aligned, centered, or right-aligned. Also the position of text in a document relative to the margins.

Anchored When a floating graphic is associated with a paragraph so that it moves with the paragraph if the paragraph is moved; an anchor symbol appears next to the paragraph when the floating graphic is selected and formatting marks are displayed.

AND criteria Criteria placed in the same row of the query design grid. All criteria on the same row must be true for a record to appear on the resulting datasheet.

Animation tag Identifies the order an object is animated on a slide during a slide show.

Annotate A freehand drawing on the screen made by using the pen or highlighter tool. You can annotate only in Slide Show view.

Application program Any program that lets you work with files or create and edit files such as graphics, letters, financial summaries, and other useful documents, as well as view Web pages on the Internet and send and receive e-mail.

Argument Information necessary for a formula or function to calculate an answer.

Arithmetic operators In a formula, symbols that perform mathematical calculations, such as addition (+), subraction (–), multiplication (*), division(/), or exponentiation (^).

Ascending order Lists data alphabetically or sequentially (from A to Z, 0 to 9, or earliest to latest).

AutoComplete A feature that automatically suggests text to insert.

AutoCorrect A feature that automatically detects and corrects typing errors, minor spelling errors, and capitalization, and inserts certain typographical symbols as you type.

AutoFill Feature activated by dragging the fill handle; copies a cell's contents or continues a series of entries into adjacent cells.

AutoFill Options button Button that appears after using the fill handle to copy cell contents; enables you to choose to fill cells with specific elements (such as formatting) of the copied cell if desired.

AutoFit A feature that automatically adjusts the width of a column or the height of a row to accommodate its widest or tallest entry.

AutoNumber A field data type in which Access enters a sequential integer for each record added into the datasheet. Numbers cannot be reused even if the record is deleted.

Automatic page break A page break that is inserted automatically at the bottom of a page.

Avg function A built-in Access function used to calculate the average of the values in a given field.

Axis label Text in the first row and column of a worksheet that identifies data.

Back up To make a copy of a database and store it in a secure location.

Background The area behind the text and graphics on a slide.

Background graphic An object placed on the slide master.

Backstage view The set of commands related to managing files and the information about them, including opening, printing, and saving a document, creating a new document, and protecting a document before sharing it with others.

Backup A duplicate copy of a file that is stored in another location.

Backward-compatible Software feature that enables documents saved in an older version of a program to be opened in a newer version of the program.

Bibliography A list of sources that you consulted or cited while creating a document.

Bitmap graphic A graphic that is composed of a series of small dots called "pixels" and often saved with a .bmp, .png, .jpg, .tif, or .gif file extension.

Blog An informal journal that is created by an individual or a group and available to the public on the Internet; short for weblog.

Blogger The person who creates and maintains a blog.

Boilerplate text Text that appears in every version of a merged document.

Bold Formatting applied to text to make it thicker and darker.

Border A line that can be added above, below, or to the sides of a paragraph, text, or table cell; a line that divides the columns and rows of a table. Also refers to a window's edge; drag to resize the window.

Bound control A control used in either a form or report to display data from the underlying field; used to edit and enter new data in a form.

Brightness The relative lightness of a photograph.

Building block A reusable piece of formatted content or document part that is stored in a gallery.

Bullet A small graphic symbol used to identify an item in a list.

Calculation A new value that is created by entering an expression in a text box on a form or report.

Calculation operators Symbols in a formula that indicate what type of calculation to perform on the cells, ranges, or values.

Calendar Picker A pop-up calendar from which you can choose dates for a date field.

Canvas In the Paint accessory program, the area in the center of the program window that you use to create drawings.

Caption A property that specifies the text displayed by a control such as a label.

Case sensitive Describes a program's ability to differentiate between uppercase and lowercase letters; usually used to describe how an operating system evaluates passwords that users type to gain entry to user accounts.

Category axis Horizontal axis in a chart, usually containing the names of data categories; in a 2-dimensional chart, also known as the x-axis.

Cell The intersection of a column and a row in a worksheet or table.

Cell address The location of a cell, expressed by cell coordinates; for example, the cell address of the cell in column A, row 1 is A1.

Cell pointer Dark rectangle that outlines the active cell.

Cell reference A code that identifies a cell's position in a table. Each cell reference contains a letter (A, B, C, and so on) to identify its column and a number (1, 2, 3, and so on) to identify its row.

Cell styles Predesigned combinations of formats based on themes that can be applied to selected cells to enhance the look of a worksheet.

Center Alignment in which an item is centered between the margins.

Character spacing Formatting that changes the width or scale of characters, expands or condenses the amount of space between characters, raises or lowers characters relative to the line of text, and adjusts kerning (the space between standard combinations of letters).

Chart A visual representation of numerical data, usually used to illustrate trends, patterns, or relationships.

Chart sheet A separate sheet in a workbook that contains only a chart, which is linked to the workbook data.

Charts Pictorial representations of worksheet data that make it easier to see patterns, trends, and relationships; *also called* graphs.

Check box A box that turns an option on when checked or off when unchecked.

Citation A parenthetical reference in the document text that gives credit to the source for a quotation or other information used in a document.

Click To quickly press and release the left button on the pointing device; also called single-click.

Click and Type A feature that allows you to automatically apply the necessary paragraph formatting to a table, graphic, or text when you insert the item in a blank area of a document in Print Layout or Web Layout view.

Click and Type pointer A pointer used to move the insertion point and automatically apply the paragraph formatting necessary to insert text at that location in the document.

Clip A media file, such as a graphic, photograph, sound, movie, or animation, that can be inserted into a document.

Clip art A collection of graphic images that can be inserted into documents, presentations, Web pages, spreadsheets, and other Office files.

Clip Organizer A library of the clips that come with Word.

Clipboard A temporary storage area for items that are cut or copied from any Office file and are available for pasting. *See also* Office Clipboard and System Clipboard.

Close button In a Windows title bar, the rightmost button; closes the open window, program, and/or document.

Cloud computing When data, applications, and resources are stored on servers accessed over the Internet or a company's internal network rather than on users' computers.

Collections The folders in the Clip Organizer where the clip art is stored.

Color saturation The vividness and intensity of color in a photograph.

Color tone The relative warmth or coolness of the colors in a photograph.

Column break A break that forces text following the break to begin at the top of the next column.

Column heading Box that appears above each column in a worksheet; identifies the column letter, such as A, B, etc.

Column separator line The thin line that separates the field names to the left or right.

Combination chart Two charts in one, such as a column chart combined with a line chart, that together graph related but dissimilar data.

Command An instruction to perform a task, such as opening a file or emptying the Recycle Bin.

Command button A button you click to issue instructions to modify program objects.

Comment An embedded note or annotation that an author or a reviewer adds to a document; appears in a comment balloon, usually to the right of the document text.

CompactFlash (CF) card A card about the size of a matchbook that you can plug into your computer to store data.

Comparison operators In a formula, symbols that compare values for the purpose of true/false results.

Compatible The capability of different programs to work together and exchange data.

Compatibility The ability of different programs to work together and exchange data.

Complex formula A formula that uses more than one arithmetic operator.

Conditional formatting A type of cell formatting that changes based on the cell's value or the outcome of a formula.

Content control An interactive object that is embedded in a document you create from a template and that expedites your ability to customize the document with your own information.

Content placeholder A placeholder that is used to enter text or objects such as clip art, charts, or pictures.

Contextual tab Tab on the Ribbon that appears when needed to complete a specific task; for example, if you select a graphic, the Picture Tools Format tab appears.

Contrast The difference in brightness between the darkest and the lightest areas of a photograph.

Control Any element on a form or report such as a label, text box, line, or combo box. Controls can be bound, unbound, or calculated.

Copy To place a copy of an item on the Clipboard without removing it from a document. Also, to make a duplicate copy of a file, folder, or other object that you want to store in another location.

Copy and paste To move text or graphics using the Copy and Paste commands.

Criteria Entries (rules and limiting conditions) that determine which records are displayed when finding or filtering records in a datasheet or form, or when building a query.

Criteria syntax Rules by which criteria need to be entered. For example, text criteria syntax requires that the criteria are surrounded by quotation marks (" "). Date criteria are surrounded by pound signs (#).

Crop To trim away part of a graphic. The act of making a picture smaller by taking away parts of the top, bottom, and sides.

Current record The record that has the focus or is being edited.

Cut To remove an item from a document and place it on the Clipboard.

Cut and paste To move text or graphics using the Cut and Paste commands.

Data field A category of information, such as last name, first name, street address, city, or postal code.

Data marker A graphical representation of a data point in a chart, such as a bar or column

Data point Individual piece of data plotted in a chart.

Data record A complete set of related information for a person or an item, such as a person's contact information, including name, address, phone number, e-mail address, and so on.

Data series The selected range in a worksheet whose related data points Excel converts into a chart.

Data series marker A graphical representation of a data series, such as a bar or column.

Data Source In mail merge, the file with the unique data for individual people or items; the data merged with a main document to produce multiple versions.

Data type A required property for each field that defines the type of data that can be entered in each field. Valid data types include AutoNumber, Text, Number, Currency, Date/Time, and Memo.

Database designer The person responsible for building and maintaining tables, queries, forms, and reports.

Datasheet A spreadsheet-like grid that displays fields as columns and records as rows.

Datasheet View A view that lists the records of the object in a datasheet. Tables, queries, and most form objects have a Datasheet View.

Date function A built-in Access function used to display the current date on a form or report; enter the Date function as Date().

Default In a program window or dialog box, a value that is already set by the program; you can change the default to any valid value.

Delete To permanently remove an item from a document.

Descending order Lists data in reverse alphabetical or sequential order (from Z to A, 9 to 0, or latest to earliest).

Design View A view in which the structure of the object can be manipulated. Every Access object (table, query, form, report, macro, and module) has a Design View.

Desktop A shaded or picture background that appears to fill the screen after a computer starts up; usually contains icons, which are small images that represent items on your computer and allow you to interact with the computer

Desktop background The shaded area behind your desktop objects; can show colors, designs, or photographs, which you can customize.

Detail A section in a report that is printed once for every record in the report.

Details pane A pane located at the bottom of a window that displays information about the selected disk, drive, folder, or file.

Device A hardware component that is part of your computer system, such as a disk drive or a pointing device.

Dialog box A window with controls that lets you tell Windows how you want to complete a program command.

Dialog box launcher An icon available in many groups on the Ribbon that you can click to open a dialog box or task pane, offering an alternative way to choose commands. *Also called* launcher.

Distribute To evenly divide the space horizontally or vertically between objects relative to each other or the slide edges.

Document The electronic file you create using Word.

Document properties Details about a file, such as author name or the date the file was created, that are used to describe, organize, and search for files.

Document window The portion of a program window in which you create the document; displays all or part of an open document.

Documents folder The folder on your hard drive used to store most of the files you create or receive from others; might contain subfolders to organize the files into smaller groups.

Double-click To quickly press and release or click the left button on the pointing device twice.

Draft view A view that shows a document without margins, headers and footers, or graphics.

Drag To point to an object, press and hold the left button on the pointing device, move the object to a new location, and then release the left button.

Drag and drop To use a pointing device to move or copy a file or folder to a new location.

Drawing gridlines A grid of nonprinting lines that appears within the margins in Print Layout view to help you size, align, and position graphics. *See also* Gridlines.

Drive A physical location on your computer where you can store files.

Drive name A name for a drive that consists of a letter followed by a colon, such as C: for the hard disk drive.

Drop cap A large dropped initial capital letter that is often used to set off the first paragraph in a document.

Edit To make changes to a file.

Edit mode The mode in which Access assumes you are trying to edit a particular field, so keystrokes such as [Ctrl][End], [Ctrl][Home], [←], and [→] move the insertion point within the field.

Edit record symbol A pencil-like symbol that appears in the record selector box to the left of the record that is currently being edited in either a datasheet or a form.

Electronic spreadsheet A computer program used to perform calculations and analyze and present numeric data.

Embedded chart A chart displayed as an object in a worksheet.

Embedded object An object that is created in one application and inserted to another. Embedded objects remain connected to the original program file in which they were created for editing.

Encryption To make the data in the database unreadable by tools other than opening the Access database itself, which is protected by a password.

Endnote Text that provides additional information or acknowledges sources for text in a document and that appears at the end of a document.

Exception A change you make directly to text on the slide, which does not match the theme fonts on the slide master.

Exclusive mode A mode indicating that you are the only person who has the database open, and others cannot open the file during this time.

Exploding Visually pulling a slice of a pie chart away from the whole pie chart in order to add emphasis to the pie slice.

Expression A combination of values, functions, and operators that calculates to a single value. Access expressions start with an equal sign and are placed in a text box in either Form Design View or Report Design View.

External hard drive A device that plugs into a computer and stores more data than a typical USB drive, anywhere from 20 to 200 GB of information and connect to a computer using either a USB or FireWire port.

Field In a table, a field corresponds to a column of data, a specific piece or category of data such as a first name, last name, city, state, or phone number.

Field list A list of the available fields in the table or query that the field list represents.

Field name The name given to each field in a table.

Field selector The button to the left of a field in Table Design View that indicates the currently selected field. Also the thin gray bar above each field in the query grid.

File An electronic collection of stored data that has a unique name, distinguishing it from other files, such as a letter, video, or program.

File extension A three- or four-letter sequence, preceded by a period, at the end of a filename that identifies the file as a particular type of document; documents in the Rich Text Format have the file extension .rtf.

File hierarchy The tree-like structure of folders and files on your computer

File list In Windows Explorer, the right section of the window; shows the contents of the folder selected in the Navigation pane on the left.

File management the ability to organize folders and files on your computer.

File properties Details that Windows stores about a file, such as the date it was created or modified.

File tab Provides access to Backstage view and the Word Options dialog box.

Filename A unique, descriptive name for a file that identifies the file's content.

Filter In a mail merge, to pull out records that meet specific criteria and include only those records in the merge.

Filter By Form A way to filter data that allows two or more criteria to be specified at the same time.

Filter By Selection A way to filter records for an exact match.

First line indent A type of indent in which the first line of a paragraph is indented more than the subsequent lines.

Floating graphic A graphic to which text wrapping has been applied, making the graphic independent of text and able to be moved anywhere on a page.

Focus The property that indicates which field would be edited if you were to start typing.

Folder An electronic container that helps you organizes your computer files, like a cardboard folder on your desk; it can contain subfolders for organizing files into smaller groups.

Folder names A unique, descriptive name for a folder that helps identify the folder's contents.

Font The typeface or design of a set of characters (letters, numbers, symbols, and punctuation marks).

Font effect Font formatting that applies a special effect to text, such as small caps or superscript.

Font size The size of characters, measured in points (pts).

Font style Format such as bold, italic, and underlining that can be applied to change the way characters look in a worksheet or chart.

Footer Information, such as text, a page number, or a graphic, that appears at the bottom of every page in a document or a section.

Footnote Text that provides additional information or acknowledges sources for text in a document and that appears at the bottom of the page on which the note reference mark appears.

Foreign key field In a one-to-many relationship between two tables, the foreign key field is the field in the "many" table that links the table to the primary key field in the "one" table.

Form An Access object that provides an easy-to-use data entry screen that generally shows only one record at a time.

Form View View of a form object that displays data from the underlying recordset and allows you to enter and update data.

Form Wizard An Access wizard that helps you create a form.

Format The appearance of a cell and its contents, including font, font styles, font color, fill color, borders, and shading. *See also* Number format.

Format Painter A feature used to copy the format settings applied to the selected text to other text you want to format the same way.

Formatting marks Nonprinting characters that appear on screen to indicate the ends of paragraphs, tabs, and other formatting elements.

Formula A set of instructions used to perform one or more numeric calculations, such as adding, multiplying, or averaging, on values or cells.

Formula bar The area above the worksheet grid where you enter or edit data in the active cell.

Formula prefix An arithmetic symbol, such as the equal sign (=), used to start a formula.

Full Screen Reading view A view that shows only the document text on screen, making it easier to read and annotate.

Function A special, predefined formula that provides a shortcut for a commonly used or complex calculation, such as SUM (for calculating a sum) or FV (for calculating the future value of an investment).

Gadget An optional program you can display on your desktop that presents helpful or entertaining information, such as a clock, current news headlines, a calendar, a picture album, or a weather report.

Gallery A visual collection of choices you can browse through to make a selection. Often available with Live Preview.

Gigabyte (GB or G) One billion bytes (or one thousand megabytes).

Gridlines Evenly spaced horizontal and/or vertical lines used in a worksheet or chart to make it easier to read. *See also* Table gridlines or Drawing gridlines.

Group In a Microsoft program window's Ribbon, a section containing related command buttons.

Grouping A way to sort records in a particular order, as well as provide a section before and after each group of records.

Gutter Extra space left for a binding at the top, left, or inside margin of a document.

Hanging indent A type of indent in which the second and subsequent lines of a paragraph are indented more than the first.

Hard disk A built-in, high-capacity, high-speed storage medium for all the software, folders, and files on a computer.

Hard page break *See* Manual page break.

Header Information, such as text, a page number, or a graphic, that appears at the top of every page in a document or a section.

Header row The first row of a table that usually contains the column headings.

Highlighted Describes the changed appearance of an item or other object, usually a change in its color, background color, and/or border; often used for an object on which you will perform an action, such as a desktop icon.

Highlighting Transparent color that can be applied to text to call attention to it.

Home group A named group of Windows 7 computers that can share information, including libraries and printers.

Horizontal ruler A ruler that appears at the top of the document window in Print Layout, Draft, and Web Layout view.

Horizontal scroll bar *See* Scroll bar.

Hyperlink Text or a graphic that opens a file, Web page, or other item when clicked. *Also called* link.

I-beam pointer The pointer used to move the insertion point and select text.

Icon A small image, usually on the desktop, which represents items on your computer, such as the Recycle Bin; you can rearrange, add, and delete desktop icons.

Inactive window An open window you are not currently using; if multiple windows are open, the window(s) with the dimmed title bar.

Indent The space between the edge of a line of text or a paragraph and the margin.

Indent marker A marker on the horizontal ruler that shows the indent settings for the active paragraph.

Infinity symbol The symbol that indicates the "many" side of a one-to-many relationship.

Inline graphic A graphic that is part of a line of text.

Insertion point A blinking vertical line that appears when you click in the formula bar or in an active cell; indicates where new text will be inserted.

Integrate To incorporate a document and parts of a document created in one program into another program; for example, to incorporate an Excel chart into a PowerPoint slide, or an Access table into a Word document.

Interface The look and feel of a program; for example, the appearance of commands and the way they are organized in the program window.

Italic Formatting applied to text to make the characters slant to the right.

Join line The line identifying which fields establish the relationship between two related tables.

Justify Alignment in which an item is flush with both the left and right margins.

Keyboard shortcut A combination of keys or a function key that can be pressed to perform a command.

Keyword A descriptive word or phrase you enter to obtain a list of results that include that word or phrase.

Label An unbound control that displays text to describe and clarify other information on a form or report.

Labels Descriptive text or other information that identifies data in rows, columns, or charts, but is not included in calculations.

Landscape Page orientation in which the contents of a page span the length of a page rather than its width, making the page wider than it is tall.

Landscape orientation Page orientation in which the page is wider than it is tall.

Launch To open or start a program on your computer.

Launcher *See* Dialog box launcher.

Layout View An Access view that lets you make some design changes to a form or report while you are browsing the data.

Left-align Alignment in which the item is flush with the left margin.

Left function An Access function that returns a specified number of characters, starting with the left side of a value in a Text field.

Left indent A type of indent in which the left edge of a paragraph is moved in from the left margin.

Legend In a chart, information that identifies how data is represented by colors or patterns.

Library A window that shows files and folders stored in different storage locations; default libraries in Windows 7 include the Documents, Music, Pictures, and Videos libraries.

Like operator An operator used in a query to find values in a field that match the pattern you specify.

Line spacing The amount of space between lines of text.

Link Text or an image that you click to display another location, such as a Help topic, a Web site, or a device.

Link (text box) A connection between two or more text boxes so that the text flows automatically from one text box to another.

Link line The line identifying which fields establish the relationship between two related tables.

List box A box that displays a list of options from which you can choose (you may need to scroll and adjust your view to see additional options in the list).

Live Preview A feature that lets you point to a choice in a gallery or palette and see the results in the document without actually clicking the choice.

Log in To select a user account name when a computer starts up, giving access to that user's files.

Logical view The datasheet of a query is sometimes called a logical view of the data because it is not a copy of the data, but rather, a selected view of data from the underlying tables.

Log off To close all windows, programs, and documents, then display the Welcome screen.

Macro An Access object that stores a collection of keystrokes or commands such as those for printing several reports in a row or providing a toolbar when a form opens.

Mail merge To merge a main document that contains boilerplate text with a file that contains customized information for many individual items to create customized versions of the main document.

Main document In a mail merge, the document with the boilerplate text.

Major gridlines In a chart, the gridlines that represent the values at the tick marks on the value axis.

Manual page break A page break inserted to force the text following the break to begin at the top of the next page.

Margin The blank area between the edge of the text and the edge of a page.

Masters One of three views that stores information about the presentation theme, fonts, placeholders, and other background objects. The three views are Slide Master view, Handout Master view, and Notes Master view.

Maximize button On the right side of a window's title bar, the center button of three buttons; use to expand a window so that it fills the entire screen. In a maximized screen, this button turns into a Restore button.

Maximized window A window that fills the desktop.

Megabyte (MB or M) One million bytes (or one thousand kilobytes).

Menu A list of related commands.

Menu bar A horizontal bar in a window that displays menu names, or categories of related commands.

Merge To combine adjacent cells into a single larger cell. *See also* Mail merge.

Merge field A placeholder that you insert in the main document to indicate where the data from each record should be inserted when you perform a mail merge.

Merged document In a mail merge, the document that contains customized versions of the main document.

Microsoft Answers A web site that lets you search forums, Microsoft Help files, and onscreen video demonstrations.

Microsoft Graph A program that creates a chart to graphically depict numerical information when you don't have access to Microsoft Excel.

Microsoft Windows 7 An operating system.

Microsoft Word Help button A button used to access the Word Help system.

Mini toolbar A toolbar that appears faintly above text when you first select it and includes the most commonly used text and paragraph formatting commands.

Minimize button On the right side of a window's title bar, the leftmost button of three buttons; use to reduce a window so that it only appears as an icon on the taskbar.

Minimized window A window that is visible only as an icon on the taskbar.

Minor gridlines In a chart, the gridlines that represent the values between the tick marks on the value axis.

Mirror margins Margins used in documents with facing pages, where the inside and outside margins are mirror images of each other.

Mixed reference Cell reference that combines both absolute and relative cell addressing.

Mode indicator An area on the left end of the status bar that indicates the program's status. For example, when you are changing the contents of a cell, the word 'Edit' appears in the mode indicator.

Module An Access object that stores Visual Basic programming code that extends the functions of automated Access processes.

Mouse pointer A small arrow or other symbol on the screen that you move by manipulating the pointing device; also called a pointer.

Move To change the location of a file, folder, or other object by physically placing it in another location.

Multilevel list A list with a hierarchical structure; an outline.

Multiuser A characteristic that means more than one person can enter and edit data in the same Access database at the same time.

Name box Box to the left of the formula bar that shows the cell reference or name of the active cell.

Navigate To move around in your computer's folder and file hierarchy. Also, to move around in a worksheet; for example, you can use the arrow keys on the keyboard to navigate from cell to cell, or press [Page Up] or [Page Down] to move one screen at a time.

Navigate downward To move to a lower level in your computer's folder and file hierarchy.

Navigate upward To move to a higher level in your computer's folder and file hierarchy. In Word, a Windows, a pane on the left side of a window that contains links to folders and libraries on your computer; click an item in the Navigation pane to display its contents in the file list or click the or symbols to display or hide subfolders in the Navigation pane.

Navigation buttons Buttons in the lower-left corner of a datasheet or form that allow you to quickly navigate between the records in the underlying object as well as add a new record.

Navigation mode A mode in which Access assumes that you are trying to move between the fields and records of the datasheet (rather than edit a specific field's contents), so keystrokes such as [Ctrl][Home] and [Ctrl][End] move you to the first and last field of the datasheet.

Navigation pane In Windows, a pane on the left side of a window that contains links to folders and libraries on your computer; click an item in the Navigation pane to display its contents in the file list or click the or symbols to display or hide subfolders in the Navigation pane. In Word, a pane showing the headings and subheadings as entries that you can click to move directly to a specific heading anywhere in a document. The Navigation pane opens along the left side of the document window.

Negative indent A type of indent in which the left edge of a paragraph is moved to the left of the left margin.

Nested table A table inserted in a cell of another table.

Normal template The template that is loaded automatically when a new document is created in Word.

Normal view Default worksheet view that shows the worksheet without features such as headers and footers; ideal for creating and editing a worksheet, but may not be detailed enough when formatting a document.

Note reference mark A mark (such as a letter or a number) that appears next to text to indicate that additional information is offered in a footnote or endnote.

Notes Page view A presentation view that displays a reduced image of the current slide above a large text box where you can type notes.

Notes pane The area in Normal view that shows speaker notes for the current slide; also in Notes Page view, the area below the slide image that contains speaker notes.

Notification area An area on the right side of the Windows 7 taskbar that displays the current time as well as icons representing programs; displays pop-up messages when a program on your computer needs your attention.

Nudge To move a graphic a small amount in one direction using the arrow keys.

Number format A format applied to values to express numeric concepts, such as currency, date, and percentage.

Object Independent element on a worksheet (such as a chart or graphic) that is not located in a specific cell or range; can be moved and resized and displays handles when selected.

Office Clipboard A temporary storage area shared by all Office programs that can be used to cut, copy, and paste multiple items within and between Office programs. The Office Clipboard can hold up to 24 items collected from any Office program. *See also* System Clipboard.

Office Web App Versions of the Microsoft Office applications with limited functionality that are available online from Windows Live SkyDrive. Users can view documents online and then edit them in the browser using a selection of functions. Office Web Apps are available for Word, PowerPoint, Excel, and One Note.

One-to-many line The line that appears in the Relationships window and shows which field is duplicated between two tables to serve as the linking field. The one-to-many line displays a "1" next to the field that serves as the "one" side of the relationship and displays an infinity symbol next to the field that serves as the "many" side of the relationship when referential integrity is specified for the relationship. Also called the one-to-many join line.

One-to-many relationship The relationship between two tables in an Access database in which a common field links the tables together. The linking field is called the primary key field in the "one" table of the relationship and the foreign key field in the "many" table of the relationship.

Online collaboration The ability to incorporate feedback or share information across the Internet or a company network or intranet.

Open To use one of the methods for opening a document to retrieve it and display it in the document window.

Operating system A program that manages the complete operation of your computer and lets you interact with it.

Option button A small circle in a dialog box that you click to select only one of two or more related options.

OR criteria Criteria placed on different rows of the query design grid. A record will appear in the resulting datasheet if it is true for any single row.

Order of precedence Rules that determine the order in which operations are performed within a formula containing more than one arithmetic operator.

Orphan The first line of a paragraph when it appears alone at the bottom of a page.

Orphan record A record in the "many" table of a one-to-many relationship that doesn't have a matching entry in the linking field of the "one" table.

Outdent *See* Negative indent.

Outline tab The section in Normal view that displays your presentation text in the form of an outline, without graphics.

Outline view A view that shows the headings of a document organized as an outline.

Page Break Preview A worksheet view that displays a reduced view of each page in your worksheet, along with page break indicators that you can drag to include more or less information on a page.

Page Footer A section in a report that is printed at the bottom of each page.

Page Header A section in a report that prints at the top of each page.

Page Layout view Provides an accurate view of how a worksheet will look when printed, including headers and footers.

Pane A section of the PowerPoint window, such as the Slide or Notes pane.

Paragraph spacing The amount of space between paragraphs.

Password A special sequence of numbers and letters known only to selected users, that users can create to control who can access the files in their user account area; helps keep users' computer information secure.

Paste To insert items stored on the Clipboard into a document.

Paste Options button Button that appears onscreen after pasting content; enables you to choose to paste only specific elements of the copied selection, such as the formatting or values, if desired.

Path An address of a file or folder, shown as a sequence of hierarchy locations separated by a triangular arrow.

Patient Header In the sample Patients report, the Patient Header is a group section that is printed once for each patient.

Picture A digital photograph, piece of line art, or clip art that is created in another program and is inserted into PowerPoint.

Pixel (picture element) One pixel is the measurement of one picture element on the screen.

Placeholder A dashed line box where you place text or objects.

Plot area In a chart, the area inside the horizontal and vertical axes.

Point (n.) The unit of measurement for text characters and the space between paragraphs and characters; 1/72 of an inch.

Point (v.) To position the tip of the mouse pointer over an object, option, or item.

Pointer *See* Mouse pointer.

Pointing device A device that lets you interact with your computer by controlling the movement of the mouse pointer on your computer screen; examples include a mouse, trackball, touchpad, pointing stick, on-screen touch pointer, or a tablet.

Pointing device action A movement you execute with your computer's pointing device to communicate with the computer; the five pointing device actions are point, click, double-click, drag, and right-click.

Portrait Page orientation in which the contents of a page span the width of a page, so the page is taller than it is wide.

Portrait orientation A way to print or view a page that is 8.5 inches wide by 11 inches tall.

Portrait orientation Page orientation in which the page is taller than it is wide.

Power button 1) The physical button on your computer that turns your computer on. 2) The Start menu button or button on the right side of the Welcome screen that let you shut down or restart your computer. Click the button arrow to log off your user account, switch to another user, or hibernate the computer to put your computer to sleep so that your computer appears off and uses very little power.

PowerPoint Viewer A special application designed to run a PowerPoint slide show on any compatible computer that does not have PowerPoint installed.

PowerPoint window A window that contains the running PowerPoint application. The PowerPoint window includes the Ribbon, panes, and Presentation window.

Presentation software A software program used to organize and present information.

Preview pane A pane on the right side of a window that shows the actual contents of a selected file without opening a program; might not work for some types of files.

Previewing Viewing a document on screen to see exactly how it will look when printed.

Primary key field A field that contains unique information for each record. A primary key field cannot contain a null entry.

Print area The portion of a worksheet that will be printed; can be defined by selecting a range and then using the Print Area button on the Page Layout tab.

Print Layout view A view that shows a document as it will look on a printed page.

Print Preview A view of a file as it will appear when printed.

Program A set of instructions written for a computer, such as an operating system program or an application program; also called an application.

Program window The window that opens after you start a program, showing you the tools you need to use the program and any open program documents.

Properties Characteristics or settings of a file, folder, or other item, such as its size or the date it was created.

Property A characteristic that further defines a field (if field properties), control (if control properties), section (if section properties), or object (if object properties).

Property Sheet A window that displays an exhaustive list of properties for the chosen control, section, or object within the Form Design View or Report Design View.

Query An Access object that provides a spreadsheet-like view of the data, similar to that in tables. It may provide the user with a subset of fields and/or records from one or more tables. Queries are created when the user has a "question" about the data in the database.

Query design grid The bottom pane of the Query Design View window in which you specify the fields, sort order, and limiting criteria for the query.

Query Design View The window in which you develop queries by specifying the fields, sort order, and limiting criteria that determine which fields and records are displayed in the resulting datasheet.

Quick Access toolbar A small toolbar on the left side of a Microsoft application program window's title bar, containing icons that you click to quickly perform common actions, such as saving a file.

Quick Part A reusable piece of content that can be inserted into a document, including a field, document property, or a preformatted building block.

Quick Style A set of format settings that can be applied to text or an object to format it quickly and easily; Quick Styles appear in galleries. *See also* Style.

Quick Style set A group of paragraph and character styles that share common fonts, colors, and formats, and are designed to be used together in a document to give it a cohesive look.

RAM (random access memory) The storage location that is part of every computer that temporarily stores open programs and documents information while a computer is on.

Range A selection of two or more cells, such as B5:B14.

Reading view A view you use to review your presentation or present a slide show to someone on a computer monitor.

Read-only An object property that indicates whether the object can read and display data, but cannot be used to change (write to) data.

Record A row of data in a table.

Record source In a form or report, the property that determines which table or query object contains the fields and records that the form or report will display. It is the most important property of the form or report object. A bound control on a form or report has Control Source property. In this case, the Control Source property identifies the field to which the control is bound.

Recycle Bin A desktop object that stores folders and files you delete from your hard drive(s) and that enables you to restore them.

Reference operators In a formula, symbols which enable you to use ranges in calculations.

Referential integrity A set of Access rules that govern data entry and help ensure data accuracy.

Relational database software Software such as Access that is used to manage data organized in a relational database.

Relative cell reference In a formula, a cell address that refers to a cell's location in relation to the cell containing the formula and that automatically changes to reflect the new location when the formula is copied or moved; default type of referencing used in Excel worksheets. *See also* Absolute cell reference.

Removable storage Storage media that you can easily transfer from one computer to another, such as DVDs, CDs, or USB flash drives.

Report An Access object that creates a professional printout of data that may contain such enhancements as headers, footers, and calculations on groups of records.

Report Footer A section in a report that prints at the end of the report.

Report Header A section in a report that is not repeated on the second and subsequent pages because it only prints at the top of the first page.

Report View An Access view that maximizes the amount of data you can see on the screen.

Report Wizard An Access wizard that helps you create a report.

Restore Down button On the right side of a maximized window's title bar, the center of three buttons; use to reduce a window to its last non-maximized size.

Ribbon In many Microsoft application program windows, a horizontal strip near the top of the window that contains tabs (pages) of grouped command buttons that you click to interact with the program.

Right-align Alignment in which an item is flush with the right margin.

Right-click To press and release the right button on the pointing device; use to display a shortcut menu with commands you issue by left-clicking them.

Right indent A type of indent in which the right edge of a paragraph is moved in from the right margin.

Rotate handle A green circle that appears above a graphic when the graphic is selected; drag the rotate handle to rotate the graphic.

Sans serif font A font (such as Calibri) whose characters do not include serifs, which are small strokes at the ends of letters.

Save To store a file permanently on a disk or to overwrite the copy of a file that is stored on a disk with the changes made to the file.

Save As Command used to save a file for the first time or to create a new file with a different filename, leaving the original file intact.

Save command A command on the File tab or Quick Access toolbar that saves the current object.

Save Database As An Access command that saves an entire database including all of its objects to a completely new database file.

Save Object As command A command on the File tab that saves the current object with a new name.

Scale To resize a graphic so that its height to width ratio remains the same.

Screen capture A snapshot of your screen, as if you took a picture of it with a camera, which you can paste into a document.

ScreenTip A label that appears when you position the mouse over an object; identifies the name of a button or feature, briefly describes its function, conveys any keyboard shortcut for the command, and includes a link to associated help topics, if any.

Scroll To adjust your view to see portions of the program window that are not currently in a window.

Scroll arrow A button at each end of a scroll bar for adjusting your view in a window in small increments in that direction.

Scroll bar A vertical or horizontal bar that appears along the right or bottom side of a window when there is more content than can be displayed within the window, so that you can adjust your view.

Scroll box A box in a scroll bar that you can drag to display a different part of a window; indicates your relative position within a document.

Search criteria Descriptive text that helps Windows identify the program, folder, file, or Web site you want to locate.

Secondary axis In a combination chart, an additional axis that supplies the scale for one of the chart types used.

Section A portion of a document that is separated from the rest of the document by section breaks.

Section break A formatting mark inserted to divide a document into sections.

Secure digital (SD) card A small device that slips directly into a computer, and typically stores around 256 MB.

Select To change the appearance of an item by clicking, double-clicking, or dragging across it, to indicate that you want to perform an action on it.

Selection box A dashed border that appears around a text object or placeholder, indicating that it is ready to accept text.

Select pointer The mouse pointer shape that looks like a white arrow oriented toward the upper-left corner of the screen.

Serif font A font (such as Times New Roman) whose characters include serifs, which are small strokes at the ends of letters.

Shading A background color or pattern that can be applied to text, tables, or graphics.

Sheet tab scrolling buttons Allow you to navigate to additional sheet tabs when available; located to the left of the sheet tabs.

Sheet tabs Identify the sheets in a workbook and let you switch between sheets; located below the worksheet grid.

Shortcut An icon that acts as a link to a program, file, folder, or device that you use frequently.

Shortcut key *See* Keyboard shortcut.

Shortcut menu A menu of context-appropriate commands for an object that opens when you right-click that object.

Shut down To turn off your computer.

Simple Query Wizard An Access wizard that prompts you for information it needs to create a new query.

Single-click *See* Click.

Sizing handles Small series of dots at the corners and edges of an object indicating that the object is selected; drag to resize the object.

SkyDrive An online storage and file sharing service. Access to SkyDrive is through a Windows Live account. You can store up to 25 GB of data in a personal SkyDrive, with each file a maximum size of 50 MB.

Slide layout This determines how all of the elements on a slide are arranged, including text and content placeholders.

Slide pane The section of Normal view that contains the current slide.

Slide Show view A view that shows a presentation as an electronic slide show; each slide fills the screen.

Slide Sorter view A view that displays a thumbnail of all slides in the order in which they appear in your presentation; used to rearrange slides and slide transitions.

Slide timing The amount of time a slide is visible on the screen during a slide show.

Slide transition The special effect that moves one slide off the screen and the next slide on the screen during a slide show. Each slide can have its own transition effect.

Slider A shape you drag to select a setting, such as the slider on the View menu that you drag to select a view.

Slides tab The section in Normal view that displays the slides of your presentation as small thumbnails.

SmartArt graphic A diagram, list, organizational chart, or other graphic created using the SmartArt command and used to provide a visual representation of data. Eight layout categories of SmartArt graphics are available in Word: List, Picture, Process, Cycle, Hierarchy, Relationship, Matrix, and Pyramid.

SmartArt graphics Predesigned diagram types for the following types of data: List, Process, Cycle, Hierarchy, Relationship, Matrix, and Pyramid.

SmartArt Style A pre-set combination of formatting options that follows the design theme that you can apply to a SmartArt graphic.

Soft page break *See* Automatic page break.

Sort Change the order of, such as the order of files or folders in a window based on criteria such as date, file size, or alphabetical by filename.

Sort (data) To organize data, such as table rows, items in a list, or records in a mail merge, in ascending or descending order.

Sparkline A quick, simple chart located within a cell that serves as a visual indicator of data trends.

Spin box A text box with up and down arrows; you can type a setting in the text box or click the arrows to increase or decrease the setting.

Split To divide a cell into two or more cells, or to divide a table into two tables.

SQL (Structured Query Language) A language that provides a standardized way to request information from a relational database system.

Start button The round button on the left side of the Windows 7 taskbar; click it to start programs, to find and open windows that show you the contents of your computer, to get help, and to end your Windows session, and turn off your computer.

Status bar The bar at the bottom of the Word program window that shows information about the document, including the current page number, the total number of pages in a document, the document word count, and the on/off status of spelling and grammar checking, and contains the view buttons, the Zoom level button, and the Zoom slider. In Excel, the bar at the bottom of the Excel window that provides a brief description about the active command or task in progress.

Strong password A password longer than eight characters that uses a combination of uppercase and lowercase letters, numbers, and symbols.

Style A named collection of character and paragraph formats that are stored together and can be applied to text to format it quickly. *See also* Quick Style.

Subdatasheet A datasheet that is nested within another datasheet to show related records. The subdatasheet shows the records on the "many" side of a one-to-many relationship.

Subfolder A folder within another folder for organizing sets of related files into smaller groups.

Subscript A font effect in which text is formatted in a smaller font size and placed below the line of text.

Subtitle text placeholder A box on the title slide reserved for subpoint text.

Suite A group of programs that are bundled together and share a similar interface, making it easy to transfer skills and program content among them.

Sum function A mathematical function that totals values in a field.

Superscript A font effect in which text is formatted in a smaller font size and placed above the line of text.

Switch User To lock your user account and display the Welcome screen so another user can log on.

Symbol A special character that can be inserted into a document using the Symbol command.

System Clipboard A clipboard that stores only the last item cut or copied from a document. *See also* Clipboard and Office Clipboard.

Tab A part of the Ribbon or a dialog box that includes groups of buttons for related commands.

Tab leader A line that appears in front of tabbed text.

Tab (ruler) A location on the horizontal ruler that indicates where to align text. *See also* Tab stop.

Tab stop A location on the horizontal ruler that indicates where to align text.

Table A grid made up of rows and columns of cells that can contain text and graphics.

Table Design View A view of a table that provides the most options for defining fields.

Table gridlines Nonprinting blue dotted lines that show the boundaries of table cells. *See also* Gridlines.

Table style Predesigned formatting that can be applied to a range of cells or even to an entire worksheet; especially useful for those ranges with labels in the left column and top row, and totals in the bottom row or right column. *See also* Table.

Task pane A separate pane that contains sets of menus, lists, options, and hyperlinks such as the Animation task pane that are used to customize objects.

Taskbar The horizontal bar at the bottom of the Windows 7 desktop; displays the Start button, the Notification area, and icons representing programs, folders, and/or files.

Template In Word, a formatted document that contains placeholder text you can replace with new text. A file that contains the basic structure of a document including headers and footers, styles, and graphic elements. In Excel, a predesigned, formatted file that serves as the basis for a new workbook; Excel template files have the file extension .xltx.

Text annotations Labels added to a chart to draw attention to or describe a particular area.

Text box A box in which you type text, such as the Search programs and files text box on the Start menu.

Text box (document) A container that you can fill with text and graphics; created from the Insert tab in Word.

Text concatenation operators In a formula, symbols used to join strings of text in different cells.

Text effect Formatting that applies a visual effect to text, such as a shadow, glow, outline, or reflection.

Text label A text box you create using the Text Box button, where the text does not automatically wrap inside the box. Text box text does not appear in the Outline tab.

Text placeholder A box with a dotted border and text that you replace with your own text.

Theme A set of unified design elements, including theme colors, theme fonts for body text and headings, and theme effects for graphics that can be applied to a document all at once.

Theme colors The set of 12 coordinated colors that make up a PowerPoint presentation; a color scheme assigns colors for text, lines, fills, accents, hyperlinks, and background.

Theme effects The set of effects for lines and fills.

Theme fonts The set of fonts for titles and other text.

Thumbnail A small image of a slide. Thumbnails are visible on the Slides tab and in Slide Sorter view.

Tick marks Notations of a scale of measure on a chart axis.

Title The first line or heading on a slide.

Title bar The shaded top border of a window that displays the name of the window, folder, or file and the program name. Darker shading indicates the active window.

Title placeholder A box on a slide reserved for the title of a presentation or slide.

Title slide The first slide in a presentation.

Toggle button A button that turns a feature on and off.

Toolbar In an application program, a set of buttons you can click to issue program commands.

Touch pointer A pointer on the screen for performing pointing operations with a finger if touch input is available on your computer.

Translucency The transparency feature of Windows Aero that enables you to locate content by seeing through one window to the next window.

Unbound control A control that does not change from record to record and exists only to clarify or enhance the appearance of the form, using elements such as labels, lines, and clip art.

USB flash drive (also called a pen drive, flash drive, jump drive, keychain drive, or thumb drive) A removable storage device for folders and files that you plug into a USB port on your computer; makes it easy to transport folders and files to other computers.

Universal Serial Bus (USB) drive A device that plugs into a computer's USB port to store data. USB drives are also called thumb drives, flash drives, and travel drives. USB devices typically store 1 GB to 10 GB of information.

User The person primarily interested in entering, editing, and analyzing the data in the database.

User account A special area in a computer's operating system where users can store their own files.

User interface A collective term for all the ways you interact with a software program.

Value axis In a chart, the axis that contains numerical values; in a 2-dimensional chart, also known as the y-axis.

Values Numbers, formulas, and functions used in calculations.

Vertical alignment The position of text in a document relative to the top and bottom margins.

Vertical ruler A ruler that appears on the left side of the document window in Print Layout view.

Vertical scroll bar *See* Scroll bar.

View A way of displaying a document in the document window; each view provides features useful for editing and formatting different types of documents. Views include Print Layout (the default), Full Screen Reading, Web Layout, Outline, and Draft.

View buttons Buttons on the status bar that you use to change document views.

View Shortcuts The buttons at the bottom of the PowerPoint window on the status bar that you click to switch among views.

Web Layout view A view that shows a document as it will look when viewed with a Web browser.

Welcome screen An initial startup screen that displays icons for each user account on the computer.

What-if analysis A decision-making tool in which data is changed and formulas are recalculated, in order to predict various possible outcomes.

Widow The last line of a paragraph when it is carried over to the top of the following page, separate from the rest of the paragraph.

Wildcard A special character used in criteria to find, filter, and query data. The asterisk (*) stands for any group of characters. For example, the criteria I* in a State field criterion cell would find all records where the state entry was IA, ID, IL, IN, or Iowa. The question mark (?) wildcard stands for only one character.

Window A rectangular-shaped work area that displays a program or a collection of files, folders, and Windows tools.

Windows Aero *See* Aero.

Windows Explorer An accessory program that displays windows, allowing you to navigate your computer's file hierarchy and interact with your computer's contents.

Windows Live A collection of services and Web applications that people can access through a login. Windows Live services include access to e-mail and instant messaging, storage of files on SkyDrive, sharing and storage of photos, networking with people, downloading software, and interfacing with a mobile device.

Windows Remote Assistance A Windows feature that lets you connect with another computer using an Internet connection.

Windows Search The Windows feature that lets you look for files and folders on your computer storage devices; to search, type text in the Search text box in the title bar of any open window, or click the Office button and type text in the Search programs and files text box.

Workbook A collection of related worksheets contained within a single file.

Word processing box A text box you create using the Text Box button, where the text automatically wraps inside the box.

Word processing program A software program that includes tools for entering, editing, and formatting text and graphics.

Word program window The window that contains the Word program elements, including the document window, Quick Access toolbar, Ribbon, and status bar.

Word wrap A feature that automatically moves the insertion point to the next line as you type.

WordArt A drawing object that contains text formatted with special shapes, patterns, and orientations.

Works cited A list of sources that you cited while creating a document.

Worksheet A single sheet within a workbook file; also, the entire area within an electronic spreadsheet that contains a grid of columns and rows.

Worksheet window Area of the program window that displays part of the current worksheet; the worksheet window displays only a small fraction of the worksheet, which can contain a total of 1,048,576 rows and 16,384 columns.

X-axis The horizontal axis in a chart; because it often shows data categories, such as months or locations, *also called* Category axis.

XML Acronym that stands for eXtensible Markup Language, which is a language used to structure, store, and send information.

XML format New file format for Word documents beginning with Word 2007.

Y-axis The vertical axis in a chart; because it often shows numerical values, *also called* Value axis.

Z-axis The third axis in a true 3-D chart, lets you compare data points across both categories and values.

Zoom level button A button on the status bar that you use to change the zoom level of the document in the document window.

Zoom slider An adjustment on the status bar that you use to enlarge or decrease the display size of the document in the document window.

Zooming in A feature that makes a document appear bigger but shows less of it on screen at once; does not affect actual document size.

Zooming out A feature that shows more of a document on screen at once but at a reduced size; does not affect actual document size.

Index

C

D

E

F

G

H

I

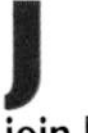

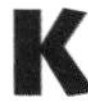

L

M

N

Q

R

S

T

U

V

W

Z